ENCYCLOPEDIA
OF THE
WORLD'S MINORITIES

ENCYCLOPEDIA
OF THE
WORLD'S MINORITIES

Volume 2
G–O

CARL SKUTSCH, EDITOR
MARTIN RYLE, CONSULTING EDITOR

ROUTLEDGE
NEW YORK AND LONDON

1-05

Published in 2005 by
Routledge
Taylor & Francis Group
270 Madison Avenue
New York, NY 10016
www.routledge-ny.com

Published in Great Britain by
Routledge
Taylor & Francis Group
2 Park Square
Milton Park, Abingdon
Oxon OX14 4RN
www.routledge.co.uk

10 9 8 7 6 5 4 3 2 1

Library of Congress Cataloging-in-Publication Data

Encyclopedia of the world's minorities / Carl Skutsch, editor; Martin Ryle, consulting editor.
     p. cm.
   Includes bibliographical references.
     ISBN 1-57958-392-X (alk. paper)
     1. Ethnic groups—Encyclopedias. 2. Minorities—Encyclopedias.
I. Skutsch, Carl.   II. Ryle, Martin (J. Martin)   III. Title.

GN495.4.E63 2005
305.8'003—dc22   2004020324

Advisory Board Members

Table of Contents

List of Entries

Aborigines

Acehnese

Achebe, Chinua (Nigerian)

Adams, Gerry (Northern Ireland Catholic)

Afar

Affirmative Action

Afghanistan

Africa: A Continent of Minorities?

African-American Nationalism and Separatism

Africans: Overview

Africans: Europe

Afrikaners

Afro-Brazilians

Afro-Caribbeans

Afro-Cubans

Afro-Latin Americans

Afrocentricity

Aga Khan (Ismaili)

Ahmadiyas

Ainu

Alawis

Albania

Albanians

Alevis

Algeria

Ali, Muhammad (African-American)

Alsatians

Altai (Altaians)

Ambedkar, Bhimrao Ramji (Dalit)

American Indian Movement (AIM)

Americo-Liberians

Amerindians: (North America)

Amerindians: (South and Central America)

Amish

Andhras

Andorra

Angola

Annobonés

Anti-Semitism

Antigua and Barbuda

Anuak

Apartheid

Arab-Americans

Arabs: North African

Arabs: Palestinians

Arafat, Yasser (Palestinian)

Arakanese

Argentina

Armenia

Armenians

Arvanites

Asians in Latin America

Assam Movement

Assamese

Assimilation

Assyrians

Australia

Austria

Autonomy

Avars

Aymara

Ayta

Azerbaijan

Azerbaijani

Bahamas

Bahrain

Bai

Bakhtyari

Baluchis

Bangladesh

Bantu

Barbados

Bariba

Bashkir

Basques

Batak

Belarus

Belarusians

Belgium

Belize

Bengalis

Benin

Berbers

Bertha

Bhindranwale, Jarnail Sant (India-Sikh)

Bhutan

Bihari

Bilin

Bilingualism

Bolivia

Bonner, Neville Thomas (Aborigine)

Thematic List of Entries

Biographies

Achebe, Chinua (Nigerian)
Adams, Gerry (Northern Ireland Catholic)
Aga Khan (Ismaili)
Ali, Muhammad (African-American)
Ambedkar, Bhimrao Ramji (Dalit)
Arafat, Yasser (Palestinian)

Bhindranwale, Jarnail Sant (India-Sikh)
Bonner, Neville Thomas (Aborigine)

Césaire, Aimé (Martiniquais)
Chavez, Cesar (Mexican-American)

Dalai Lama (Tibetan)
De Klerk, F.W. (Afrikaner)
Du Bois, W.E.B. (African-American)

Fanon, Frantz Omar (Algerian)
Farrakhan, Louis (African-American)

Gandhi, Mohandas Karamchand (India)
Garang, John (Sudanese)
Garvey, Marcus (Jamaican)
Gheorghe, Nicolae (Roma Romania)
Grant, Bernie (United Kingdom)
Guillen, Nicolas (Cuban)

Hall, Stuart (United Kingdom Afro-Caribbean)
Hamer, Fannie Lou (African-American)
Hooks, Bell (African-American)
Hume, John (Northern Ireland Catholic)

Jackson, Jesse (African-American)
James, C.L.R. (Trinidadian)
Jinnah, Muhammad Ali (Pakistani)
Jordan, Barbara (African-American)

Katari, Tupac (Aymaran)
King, Martin Luther, Jr. (African-American)

Le Pen, Jean Marie (French)
Levesque, Rene
Luthuli, Albert (South African)

Mabo, Edward (Torres Strait Islander, Australia)
Malcolm X (African-American)

Mandela, Nelson (South African)
Marcos, Subcomandante (Amerindian)
Marley, Bob (Jamaican)
Menchú, Rigoberta (Amerindian)
Morrison, Toni (African-American)
Muhammad, Elijah (African-American)

Nasser, Gamal Abdel (Egyptian)
Ngugi wa Thiong'o (Kenyan)

Ocalan, Abdullah (Kurd)

Parnell, Charles Stewart (Irish)
Peltier, Leonard (Amerindian)
Pope Shenouda III (Coptic Christian)
Prabhakaran, Vellupillai (Sri Lanka-Tamil)

Ramos-Horta, José (East Timor)
Rugova, Ibrahim (Albanian)

Saro-Wiwa, Ken (Ogoni Nigerian)
Selassie, Haile (Ethiopian)
Senghor, Leopold (Senegalese)
Silva, Benedita da (Afro-Brazilian)
Singh, Tara (Sikh)

Tiruchelvam, Neelan (Tamil-Sri Lanka)
Trimble, David (Northern Ireland)
Tutu, Desmond (South African)

Washington, Booker T. (African-American)
Wright, Richard (African-American)

Zana, Leila (Kurd)

Groups

Aborigines
Acehnese
Afar
Africans: Europe
Africans: Overview
Afrikaners
Afro-Brazilians
Afro-Caribbeans
Afro-Cubans
Afro-Latin Americans
Ahmadiyas

THEMATIC LIST OF ENTRIES

Nations

Topics

Preface

Social and political changes around the world have added an urgency to the study of minorities and minority issues. Globalization, immigration, migration, civil conflict, and ethnic tensions have brought greater public awareness to minority groups and greater academic interest to minority studies. Similarly, the international community's commitment to self-determination, cultural diversity, human differences, and the preservation of traditions has attracted the attention of the public and focused the energies of a worldwide array of scholars working in a range of subject areas.

Reflecting the interdisciplinary and international character of minority studies, the *Encyclopedia of the World's Minorities* includes the work of over 300 contributors from 40 countries specializing in areas as varied as anthropology, cultural studies, ethnography, history, international relations, linguistics, political science, and religion. These scholars work at universities and colleges as well as research centers and organizations around the globe that seek to further our understanding of minority issues and monitor the situation of minority groups. Within this community, the subject is rigorously and often contentiously argued, but the degree of interest and the intensity of debate ultimately testify to its importance. Because the study of minorities involves the difficult issues of rights, justice, equality, dignity, identity, autonomy, political liberties, and cultural freedoms, the discussions in the encyclopedia apply to many areas of public interest and student inquiry.

One of the concepts most vigorously debated by those working in minority studies is the meaning of "minority" itself. This is because the meaning does matter. In the early twentieth century, the African-American political thinker W.E.B. Du Bois declared the color line to be the defining issue of the age. From that time forward the line that demarcates a minority group, acknowledges a minority concern, or defines a minority right has had considerable consequence. The *Encyclopedia of the World's Minorities*, like minority studies itself, attempts not to finalize this definition but to present its histories and complexities.

Traditionally, a minority group has been understood to have an indigenous relationship to an area—what is called an autochthonous relationship—where it is, at a given time, numerically inferior to another group. Such a group is understood to share a cultural characteristic that one member identifies in another. This shared culture may take the form of ethnicity, race, customs, language, or religion; and it receives larger legitimacy by virtue of its long-standing presence in a region. Although this definition functions within limited contexts and is acknowledged throughout the encyclopedia, it is far from universal, because it fails to account for a surplus of historical issues and influences that we confront today.

For example, according to this orthodox definition of minority, a member of an indigenous group may enjoy a legal relationship to a nation that vastly differs from that of an immigrant, a permanent resident, or a migrant worker, all of whom may share the cultural markers of a minority group but have none of the protections. Governments that secure protections, rights, and entitlements—which may include access to employment, political processes, education, health care, the media, and the judicial system—only for recognized minorities may thereby exclude non-indigenous groups from these same privileges. The encyclopedia presents how minority studies discusses the tensions created by conferring legal privileges to indigenous minorities and withholding them from others.

Although numerical inferiority may seem a reasonable, if only intuitive, way to define minority status, it is not sufficient within minority studies. Slavery in the American South, apartheid in South Africa, and the Baathist system in Iraq—where a numerically inferior group dominated a numerically superior group—all serve to remind us that a consideration of cultural and political *non-dominance* must enter our understanding of what minority status means. Numerical superiority of one group often enforces cultural and political dominance over another group, but numbers alone do not adequately define minority or fully describe the relative influence and self-determination one group may enjoy.

In this sense, minority status has come to define a political relationship rather than an inherent or changeless attribute of a people. The discipline does not agree that minority status requires that a people share immutable characteristics that are often associated with race and ethnicity. Religion and language, for example, are not immutable identities, because they can be acquired or change, but they do figure significantly in minorities' self-identification. Recently, some scholars have argued for a definition that accounts for power and equality, in which a minority is any group that has historically been relegated to a status unequal to that of a dominant group, regardless of distinct cultural or ethnic attributes; this definition would include sexual minorities. The encyclopedia brings these issues to light, presents these arguments, and summarizes broader opinion.

The broad opinion might conclude from these debates that the most inclusive definition of a minority or minorities is preferred. Certainly there is truth in this. Nevertheless, for those attempting to create law and public policy that is responsible to an electorate, a pragmatic approach to minority issues is, however flawed, a fundamental but ever-changing reality. For example, principles such as self-determination and cultural autonomy are universally recognized (at least among democratic nations and those creating law and public policy) yet pragmatically circumscribed to prevent instability and secessionist conflicts where coexistence and integration are possible and preferred. Coexistence, intercultural communication, and civil processes are as important to minority studies as independence, difference, and diversity. Incremental progress is also a valued strategy in the discussion of minority issues. On the one hand, national laws regarding minorities are often more restrictive than international proclamations. Thus individual nations, such as the member states of the European Community, while respecting certain basic rights for all, provide substantial protections, politically and culturally, to those minority groups officially recognized by the state. On the other hand, the United Nations uses a very broad definition of minority status and rights—one that may serve groups as they argue and agitate against political facts—but the protections that this definition *guarantees* are unhappily too few. The unhappy compromise is often a reality for the world's minorities.

Organization of the Encyclopedia

Calculations and compromises are necessary in the creation of a work that covers such a large subject. The *Encyclopedia of the World's Minorities* does not contain an entry on every minority group in every nation and region of the world. It presents for the user a thorough resource on minority studies. The information here covers the vast and diverse study of the world's minorities, introducing students to the field and providing an international perspective that enables students to pursue their own interests. To give structure to the scope of such a project, a four-pronged rationale was chosen that creates an accessible architecture for readers of the encyclopedia. This strategy organizes the encyclopedia into four clearly defined entry types: *topics*, *nations*, *groups*, and *biographies*.

Of the 562 entries in the encyclopedia, 75 **Topics entries** introduce students to the broad ideas, concepts, and concerns shared by those working on minority issues. Readers will find definitions and histories of such terms as "Autonomy," "Self-determination," and "Nationalism." Entries of this kind also include organizations and institutions, such as Sinn Féin, the League of Nations, and Minority Rights Group International. These entries help to familiarize students with the language of the discipline and to understand how organizations participate in the field and are discussed within it.

Nations entries (173 in total) describe the history of minorities living within national borders and so explain the political and legal apparatus that states formally create in relation to their minority populations as well as the informal conditions experienced by those groups. In nation entries the reader will find information not only about the dominant group in a country, such as the Swedes in Sweden, but about those other groups that share in the nation-state, such as the Finnish and Saami minorities in Sweden. In this respect, the encyclopedia encourages readers to think outside of categories they commonly associate with the idea of a country—to think of a nation as an assemblage of peoples and cultures rather than as a single, monolithic entity.

Groups entries, composing the largest category with a total of 251 essays, explain the history of peoples living as minorities around the world. These entries discuss whether the group is a single-nation minority or one living in multiple nations, detailing its language, religion, and political and social conditions. Each group entry also contains up-to-date population data garnered from, among other sources such as national censuses, the 2003 *World Factbook* published by the CIA for the United States Government. Group entries are of two kinds: one covers groups who, wherever they are found, live as a minority, such as the Roma (Gypsies); the other covers groups who enjoy a dominant place in a homeland but are found elsewhere as minorities, such as the Japanese. This distinction is important to recognize because the notions of identity and cultural legitimacy are so often linked with a place of origin or with a nation that the situation of stateless peoples is often ignored. Similarly, minorities seeking greater protections have often resorted to nationalism to assert political liberties.

Biographies introduce persons who figure significantly in the history of minority communities and who, through their actions or words, have articulated the larger interests of minority peoples. A total of 62 such entries include Marcus Garvey, Mahatma Gandhi, and Ngugi wa Thiong'o. Biographical entries credit an individual's importance but also reveal how leaders of minority campaigns and struggles influence one another in vastly different parts of the world, showing that a minority group identifies not always only with itself but also with other minority groups as they look to each other for guidance.

Ultimately, an encyclopedia is a wealth of integrated information that maps an area of interest and provides as many access points to that information as possible. In creating this map, the encyclopedia aims to present fact, not opinion. Its entries describe rather than persuade, explain arguments rather than take sides, present rather than resolve areas of contention. The *Encyclopedia of the World's Minorities* contains 562 **signed scholarly essays** about nations, groups, and issues around the world that, written in clear, accessible prose, create a detailed map of a complicated terrain. Each entry includes a selection of **further readings** and **cross-references** (listed in "see also" sections at the end of each entry) to other articles for those readers who wish to explore a topic in greater depth. **Blind entries** serve to guide the reader through the work. A thorough, **analytic index** provides the reader with a critical tool for accessing the work in its entirety.

Creating an encyclopedia is never a solitary undertaking. I would like to extend my appreciation to the editorial board. Their help in formulating the final table of contents was invaluable. I would especially like to thank Martin Ryle, professor of history, emeritus, the University of Virginia, Charlottesville, Virginia. His willingness to review the final manuscript in the closing months of the project was nothing short of heroic. His guidance and commitment to the encyclopedia made its publication possible. Finally, I would like to thank the hundreds of contributors whose work here will further our understanding of the world's minorities.

Notes on Contributors

Rafis Abazov, Harriman Institute, Columbia University, New York, USA.

Jon Abbink, African Studies Centre, Leiden University, The Netherlands.

Marat Akchurin, Bethesda, Maryland, USA.

Shawn Alexander, W.E.B. Du Bois Department of Afro-American Studies, University of Massachusetts at Amherst, USA.

Agron Alibali, Boston, Massachusetts, USA.

Erik Allardt, Department of Sociology, University of Helsinki, Finland.

Mehdi Parvizi Amineh, International Institute for Asian Studies, Leiden, The Netherlands.

Guy Arnold, London, United Kingdom.

Michael Azariadis, Perth, Australia.

Tuncay Babali, Department of Political Science, University of Houston, Texas, USA.

D. Shyam Babu, Rajiv Gandhi Institute for Contemporary Studies, New Delhi, India.

Michael Banton, University of Bristol, United Kingdom.

Abdoulaye Barry, University Gaston Baerger, Saint Louis, Senegal.

Trevor Batrouney, RMIT University, Balwyn, Australia.

Florian Bieber, Nationalism Studies Program, Central European University, Budapest, Hungary.

Charles Boewe, Pittsboro, North Carolina, USA.

Nadia Joanne Britton, Department of Sociological Studies, University of Sheffield, United Kingdom.

Susan Love Brown, Department of Anthropology, Florida Atlantic University, USA.

Anne Brydon, Department of Sociology and Anthropology, Wilfrid Laurier University, Waterloo, Ontario, Canada.

Marcelo Bucheli, Department of History, Stanford University, California, USA.

Debra Buchholtz, Banbury, Oxfordshire, United Kingdom.

Jeff Burke, Religious Studies Program, Lynchburg College, Virginia, USA.

Joan Manuel Cabezas Lopez, University of Barcelona, Catalonia, Spain.

Laura M. Calkins, Vietnam Archive, Texas Tech University, USA.

Gregory R. Campbell, Department of Anthropology, University of Montana at Missoula, USA.

Tim Carmichael, African Studies Center, Michigan State University, USA.

Wendy Carter, USA.

Ellis Cashmore, School of Health, Staffordshire University, Stafford, United Kingdom.

Derek Catsam, Falls Church, Virginia, USA.

Shukai R. Chaudhari, The Nepal Indigenous Development Society, Ratnanagar Tandi, Chitwan, Nepal.

Tan Chee-Beng, Department of Anthropology, The Chinese University of Hong Kong.

James Chin, School of Administrative and Political Studies, University of Papua New Guinea.

Jamsheed Choksy, Middle Eastern Studies Program, Indiana University, USA.

T. Matthew Ciolek, Research School of Asian and Pacific Studies, Australian National University.

Andrew Clark, History Department, University of North Carolina at Wilmington, USA.

Samuel Cohen, Department of English, Lehman College, City University of New York, USA.

Robert O. Collins, Department of History, University of California at Santa Barbara, USA.

Daniele Conversi, Department of Policy Studies, University of Lincolnshire, Lincoln, United Kingdom.

Allan Cooper, Department of Political Science, Otterbein College, Ohio, USA.

Susan Crate, Department of Geography, Miami University, Oxford, Ohio, USA.

NOTES ON CONTRIBUTORS

Nigel Crawhall, South African San Institute/Indigenous Peoples of Africa Coordinating Committee, Cape Town, South Africa.

Kevin Curow, Bad Homburg, Germany.

Farhad Daftary, Institute of Ismali Studies, London, United Kindgom.

Loring Danforth, Department of Anthropology, Bates College, Maine, USA.

John Davies, Department of Economics, Acadia University, Wolfville, Nova Scotia, Canada.

Darién J. Davis, History Department, Middlebury College, Vermont, USA.

John H. Davis, New York, USA.

Fernand de Varennes, School of Law, Murdoch University, Perth, Australia.

Anne Decoret-Ahiha, Universitè Lyon II, France.

Neil Denslow, Independent Scholar, Dorset, United Kingdom.

Barbara Dilly, Department of Sociology and Anthropology, Creighton University, Nebraska, USA.

Elena Dingu-Kyrklund, Center of Research in International Migration and Ethnic Relations, Stockholm University, Sweden.

Audra Diptee, Department of History, University of Toronto, Ontario, Canada.

Aleksandra Djajic Horváth, Department of History and Civilization, European University Institute, Florence, Italy.

Ivana Djuric, Zagreb, Croatia.

Stephanie Hemelryk Donald, Murdoch University, Perth, Australia.

Yves Dorémieux, Anthropology Department, Center for Mongolian and Siberian Studies, University Paris X, France.

Haley Duschinski, Harvard University, Boston, Massachusetts, USA.

James Eder, Department of Anthropology, Arizona State University, USA.

Fadwa El Guindi, University of Southern California, USA.

Robyn Eversole, Centre for Regional and Rural Development, RMIT University, Hamilton, Victoria, Australia.

Brigit Farley, Department of History, Washington State University, Tri-Cities, USA.

Mariana Ferreira, Anthropology, University of Tennessee, USA.

Peter Finke, Max Planck Institute for Social Anthropology, Halle/Saale, Germany.

Sterling Fluharty, Department of History, University of Oklahoma, USA.

Bernard Formoso, Departement d'ethnologie, Universite Paris X–Nanterre, France.

Germán Freire, University of London, United Kingdom.

Victor Friedman, University of Chicago, Illinois, USA.

Hillel Frisch, Department of Political Studies, Bar-Ilan University, Ramat-Gan, Israel.

Steve Garner, School of Sociology, University of the West of England, Bristol, United Kingdom.

Erika H. Gilson, Princeton University, New Jersey, USA.

Benito Giordano, University of Manchester, United Kingdom.

Martí Grau, Barcelona, Spain.

Joseph Graves, Jr., Glendale, Arizona, USA.

Juan Carlos Gumucio, Department of Cultural Anthropology and Ethnography, Uppsala University, Sweden.

Annette Hamilton, Department of Anthropology, Macquarie University, Sydney, New South Wales, Australia.

Kevin David Harrison, Department of Linguistics, Swarthmore College, Pennsylvania, USA.

Maximilian Hartmuth, University of Vienna, Austria.

Ai Hattori, Alexandria, Virginia, USA.

Angela Haynes, Minority Rights Group, London, United Kingdom.

Dagmar Hellmann-Rajanayagam, Department of Economic and Social Science, University Erlangen-Nuremberg, Germany.

Arthur Helweg, Department of Anthropology, Western Michigan University, USA.

Kristin Henrard, Department of International and Constitutional Law, University of Groningen, The Netherlands.

J. Scott Hill, Richmond, Virginia, USA.

Jeremy Hodes, Kambah, Australia.

Krisadawan Hongladarom, Department of Linguistics, Faculty of Arts, Chulalongkorn University, Bangkok, Thailand.

Tian Hongliang, Department of Anthropology, The Chinese University of Hong Kong.

Michael Houf, Department of History, Texas A&M University–Kingsville, USA.

Jayne Ifekwunigwe, School of Social Sciences, University of East London, United Kingdom.

Rad Ilie, Cluj-Napoca, Romania.

Andrew Irving, London, United Kingdom.

Guillaume Jacques, Paris 7–Denis Diderot University, France.

Amjad Jaimoukha, Jordan Engineers Association, Royal Scientific Society, Amman, Jordan.

Annu Jalais, London School of Economics, United Kingdom.

Laksiri Jayasuriya, Department of Social Work, University of Western Australia.

Richard Jenkins, Migration and Ethnicity Research Center, University of Sheffield, United Kingdom.

Hou Jingrong, The Chinese University of Hong Kong.

Lars Karstedt, Universitat Hamburg, Germany.

Olga Kazmina, Moscow, Russia.

Ime Kerlee, Emory University, Georgia, USA.

Deepa Khosla, Department of Government and Politics, University of Maryland, USA.

Reinhard Klein-Arendt, Institute for African Studies, University of Cologne, Germany.

Laszlo Kocsis, Transylvania, Romania.

Charles C. Kolb, National Endowment for the Humanities, Washington, District of Columbia, USA.

Boris Koltchanov, Riga, Latvia.

Jill E. Korbin, Department of Anthropology, Case Western Reserve University, Ohio, USA.

Chima J. Korieh, Department of History, Central Michigan University, Michigan, USA.

Jørgen Kühl, Aabenraa, Denmark.

Olga Kul'bachevskya, Institute of Ethnology and Anthropology, Russian Academy of Sciences, Moscow, Russia.

P.R. Kumaraswamy, Jawaharlal Nehru University, New Delhi, India.

Yves Laberge, Département de sociologie, Institut Québécois des Hautes Etudes Internationales, Canada.

Andrea Laing-Marshall, Historical Department, Wycliffe College, Toronto, Ontario, Canada.

Laura Laubeova, Prague, Czech Republic.

Benjamin Lawrance, Department of History, Stanford University, California, USA.

Barbara Leigh, Institute for International Studies, Unviersity of Technology, Sydney, New South Wales, Australia.

Keith Leitich, Seattle, Washington, USA.

Rohini Lele, University of Pune, India.

David Leonard, Comparative Ethnic Studies, Washington State University, USA.

Hal Levine, Department of Anthropology, Victoria University of Wellington, New Zealand.

Jerome Lewis, Department of Anthropology, London School of Economics and Political Science, United Kingdom.

Wei Li, Department of Geography, Arizona State University, USA.

Yianna Liatsos, Department of Comparative Literature, Rutgers University, New Jersey, USA.

Peter Limb, Michigan State University, USA.

Pamela Lindell, Sacramento, California, USA.

Michael Lipson, Department of Political Science, Concordia University, Montreal, Quebec, Canada.

Miles Litvinoff, OneWorld International, London, United Kingdom.

Ludomir Lozny, Department of Anthropology, Hunter College, City University of New York, USA.

Leo Lucassen, Department of Social History, University of Amsterdam, The Netherlands.

Tamba M'bayo, Department of History, Michigan State University, USA.

Charles Macdonald, Campus St. Charles, Universite de Provence, Marseille, France.

Sarah Manapa, Biola University, California.

Richard R. Marcus, Department of Political Science, Yale University, Connecticut, USA.

NOTES ON CONTRIBUTORS

Alexandra Marois.

Oliver Marshall, Centre for Brazilian Studies, Oxford University, United Kingdom.

Marco Martiniello, Belgian National Fund for Scientific Research and University of Liege, Belgium.

Bruce Matthews, Faculty of Arts, Acadia University, Wolfville, Nova Scotia, Canada.

Duncan McCargo, Institute for Politics and International Studies, University of Leeds, United Kingdom.

Pamela McElwee, Department of Anthropology, Yale University, Connecticut, USA.

John McGurk, Claremorris, Mayo, Ireland.

Eugene McLaughlin, Faculty of Social Sciences, The Open University, Milton Keynes, United Kingdom.

Joanne McLean, School of Environmental & Information Sciences, Charles Sturt University, Albury, Australia.

Manuella Meyer, Brown University, Rhode Island, United States.

Jean Michaud, Paris, France.

Paul E. Michelson, Department of History, Huntington College, Indiana, USA.

Alessandro Michelucci, Florence, Italy.

Maged Mikhail, West Covina, California, USA.

Monique Milia-Marie-Luce, Trinité, Martinique.

Ruth Murbach, Département des sciences juridiques, Université du Québec à Montréal, Canada.

Rachel Newcomb, Department of Anthropology, Princeton University, New Jersey, USA.

Beatrice Nicolini, Storia e Istituzioni dell'Africa, Università Cattolica del Sacro Cuore, Milano, Italy.

Stephan Nikolov, Sofia, Bulgaria.

Donnacha Ó Beacháin, Tbilisi, Georgia.

Denise T. Ogden, Penn State University, USA.

Jonathan Okamura, Department of Ethnic Studies, University of Hawaii, USA.

Brendan O'Leary, Convenor of the Government Department, London School of Economics, United Kingdom.

Dennis Papazian, Armenian Research Center, The University of Michigan-Dearborn, USA.

Joshua Pasternak, Routledge, New York, USA.

Doug Pennoyer, School of Intercultural Studies, Biola University, California, USA.

John Edward Phillips, Faculty of Humanities, Hirosaki University, Japan.

Anne Pitsch Santiago, University of Maryland, USA.

Hugh Poulton, London, United Kingdom.

Sabiyha Robin Prince, Columbia, Maryland, USA.

Pavel Puchkov, Moscow, Russia.

Eva Rakel, Amsterdam, The Netherlands.

Riccardo Redaelli, Milano, Italy.

Javaid Rehman, Department of Law, University of Leeds, United Kingdom.

Massimo Repetti, Genova, Liguria, Italy.

Annette Richardson, University of Alberta, Edmonton, Canada.

Edward A. Riedinger, Latin American, Spanish, and Portuguese Collection, Ohio State University Libraries, USA.

Mika Roinila, Department of Geography, State University of New York at New Paltz, USA.

Elisa Roller, Brussels, Belgium.

Victor Roudometof, Department of Social and Political Sciences, University of Cyprus, Nicosia, USA.

Helena Ruotsala, School of Cultural Studies, University of Turku, Finland.

Sue Russell, Biola University, California, USA.

P. Sahadevan, School of International Studies, Jawaharlal Nehru University, New Delhi, India.

Oscar Salemink, Department of Social and Cultural Anthropology, Vrije Universiteit Amsterdam, The Netherlands.

Amandeep Sandhu, Department of Sociology, University of Victoria, British Columbia, Canada.

L. Natalie Sandomirsky, Auburndale, Massachusetts, USA.

Christopher Saunders, Department of Historical Studies, University of Cape Town, Rondebosch, South Africa.

Richard Scaglion, Department of Anthropology, University of Pittsburgh, Pennsylvania, USA.

Antonia Yétúndé Fælárìn Schleicher, National African Language Resource Center, University of Wisconsin, USA.

Ulrike Schuerkens, Paris, France.

Richard Schur, American Studies Department, The University of Kansas, USA.

Murali Shanmugavelan, Communication for Development Programme, Panos Institute, London, United Kingdom.

Marika Sherwood, Oare, Kent, United Kingdom.

Andrei Simic, Department of Anthropology, University of Southern California, USA.

Gregory M. Simon, Department of Anthropology, University of California, San Diego, USA.

Scott Simon, Department of Sociology, University of Ottawa, Ontario, Canada.

Stefaan Smis, Faculty of Law, Vrije Universiteit Brussels, Belgium.

David Norman Smith, Department of Sociology, University of Kansas, USA.

Ingmar Söhrman, Göteborg University, Sweden.

Subhash Sonnad, Department of Sociology, Western Michigan University, USA.

Ernst Spaan, Netherlands Interdisciplinary Demographic Institute, The Hague, The Netherlands.

Sabira Ståhlberg, Varna, Bulgaria.

Erin Stapleton-Corcoran, Chicago, Illinois, USA.

Sian Sullivan, SOAS, London, United Kingdom.

Ingvar Svanberg, Department of East European Studies, Uppsala University, Sweden.

Nicola Tannenbaum, Sociology/Anthropology Department, Lehigh University, Pennsylvania, USA.

George Tarkhan-Mouravi, Tibilisi, Georgia.

Wade Tarzia, Arts & Humanities Division, Naugatuck Valley Community College, Connecticut, USA.

Philip Taylor, Department of Anthropology, The Australian National University, Canberra.

Louis Tenawa, UREDS International, Yaoundé, Cameroon.

Shanthi Thambiah, Gender Studies Program, University of Malaya, Kuala Lumpur, Malaysia.

Ewa M. Thompson, Department of German and Slavic Studies, Rice University, Texas, USA.

Patrick Thornberry, Department of International Relations, Keele University, Newcastle Under Lyme, Staffordshire, United Kingdom.

Lenora Timm, Department of Linguistics, University of California, Davis, USA.

Reeta Chowdhari Tremblay, Department of Political Science, Concordia University, Montreal, Quebec, Canada.

Frances Trix, Ann Arbor, Michigan, USA.

Linda Tie Hua Tsung, Language Center, Hong Kong University of Science & Technology, China.

Greta Uehling, University of Michigan, USA.

Saskia Van Hoyweghen, Antwerpen, Belgium.

Virginie Vate, Paris, France.

Charles Verharen, Department of Philosophy, Howard University, Washington, District of Columbia, USA.

Richard Verrone, The Vietnam Archive, Texas Tech University, USA.

Eduardo J. Ruiz Vieytez, Institute of Human Rights, University of Deusto, Bilbao, Basque Country, Spain.

Iain Walker, Orléans, France.

Charles Westin, Centre for Research in International Migration and Ethnic Relations, Stockholm University, Sweden.

Wim Willems, Institute for Migration and Ethnic Studies, University of Amsterdam, The Netherlands.

Brian Williams, Department of History, University of London, United Kingdom.

Davina Woods, Clever Women Consultants, Melbourne, Victoria, Australia.

Theodore Wright, Niskayuna, New York, USA.

G

Gabon

Capsule Summary

Country Name: République du Gabon
Total Population: 1,321,560 (July 2003)
Minority Population: Fang, Sira, Nzebi, Mbete, Myene, Nemga, Seke, Kota, and Téké
Languages: French (official), spoken by about one-third of Gabonese and read by about one-fourth; Fang, 49% of the population, Sira, Nzebi, and Mbete with about 50,000 speakers each
Religion: Christian (75%); traditional religions (indigenous, animist), (23%); Muslim (2%)

The Gabonese Republic straddles the equator, bordered by Equatorial Guinea and Cameroon to the north, the Republic of the Congo (Brazzaville) to the south and east, and the Atlantic Ocean to the west. It has about 1.3 million inhabitants, half of whom live in the two main cities: Libreville, the capital, and Port-Gentil. This urban concentration may partly explain the high literacy rate. Nonetheless, the population figures reflect the effects of excess mortality due to acquired immunodeficiency syndrome (AIDS), which is high in Gabon.

Executive and legislative powers are vested in officials elected by universal suffrage. The President holds executive power and vast powers of appointment. The legislative body is bicameral. The judicial system is patterned on French law. The current constitution was approved in 1991. It provides for a multiparty system, but actually the Gabonese Democratic Party (PDG) rules. French is the official language.

Rich in natural resources, Gabon has a strong economy by African standards and one of the most prosperous of black African countries. In 2002 its GDP per-capita income was $6,500, which represents four times that of most nations of sub-Saharan Africa. Most of the country's affluence is due to mineral resources: manganese, high-grade iron ore, and uranium. Its energy resources, among the greatest in Africa, consist of hydroelectric power, oil, and natural gas. The government encourages foreign investments but controls planning and implementation.

Gabon is inhabited by more than 40 ethnic groups that speak different languages. All of them, except for groups of Pygmies who live in the forest, speak Bantu languages. The Fang, who constitute about one-half of the population, live north of the Ogooué River. Their language is the most widely spoken one. Though relative late-comers to the area, they are politically influential. The Myene group, including Mpongwe and Orungu, is small now, but was important in the history of Gabon because of its location on the northern coast. Smaller groups include Benga and Seke in the northwest. The largest groups south of the Ogooué are Sira and Nzebi; smaller groups are Téké and Kota in the east and Vili along the southernmost coast. About three-fourths of the population are Christian, mostly Roman Catholic. There are a few Muslims; others have kept traditional African religions. These are deeply ingrained and often coexist with Christianity.

History

For thousands of years Pygmies inhabited the rainforest that still covers three-fourths of Gabon. Archaeologists believe that Bantu peoples arrived in the region around 1300 BCE. Portuguese navigators first landed in the estuary of the Ogooué River in 1472. From the late 1500s, Dutch, French, Spanish, and English navigators also bartered salt and manufactured goods for hardwoods, ivory, and slaves. Coastal trade climaxed at the height of the transatlantic slave trade. Peoples from the interior sent undesirables and war captives down the waterways to the coast to await the arrival of European ships. Northwestern coastal clans, Orungu and Mpongwe, also profited from the slave trade, as did the southern Vili. Only the Fang did not take part in the slave trade. However, their often belligerent coastward migrations displaced many interior peoples. By the nineteenth century the presence of growing numbers of Fang changed the ethnic balance in Gabon.

In 1839, when the French began colonizing Gabon, attempting to halt the slave trade and protect French trading companies, their ships were often attacked by Gabon's coastal peoples angry at France's attempts to abolish the slave trade. French Admiral Louis-Edouard Bouët-Willaumez signed treaties with most Mpongwe chiefs, who agreed to end the slave trade and accept French sovereignty. After 1850, the French extended their control along the coast and sent explorers into the interior; foremost among these was Pierre Savorgnan de Brazza, who established French authority on the upper Ogooué and on the Loango coast. An enlarged Gabon was attached to the French Congo under Brazza as governor.

After his departure, the underfunded French colonial administration sold concessions to private companies, granting them trade monopolies and exclusive authority over their territories. Concessionaries ruthlessly implemented forced labor to exploit the rubber and ivory resources. They obliged people to abandon subsistence farming, and disrupted indigenous trade routes. Thousands perished.

In 1910, after the concessionary system had failed, the French created the Federation of French Equatorial Africa, composed of the present-day Republic of Congo (Brazzaville), Central African Republic, Chad, and Gabon, and instituted a two-tiered social system. A small elite enjoyed citizenship status. Most of the population was subject to the *indigénat*, a system that imposed inferior legal status accompanied by oppressive tax and labor obligations. French occupation of the Gabon interior encountered little opposition; but the *indigénat* provoked considerable resistance. Local rebellions became common. However, the embryonic Gabonese anticolonialist movement was ineffective, because the Mpongwe elite and Fang newcomers, who threatened the Mpongwe's privileged status, remained divided.

During and after World War II, relations between France and its African colonies changed rapidly and by 1960 sub-Saharan colonies, including Gabon, were granted independence. Gabon continued to favor close relations with France. Attempts by the republic's first president, Fang Léon M'ba, to institute a single-party regime provoked a rebellion by young military officers in February 1964. But M'ba, backed by French economic interests, was restored to power by French paratroopers. This intervention facilitated the rise of Omar Bongo to the presidency after M'ba's death (1967). Many Gabonese welcomed Bongo, a Téké from the southeast, hoping that his accession would end Fang-Mpongwe rule. Bongo carefully co-opted his political opponents and consolidated his personal power by means of the Gabonese Democratic Party (PDG). Ruled by autocratic presidents since independence from France in 1960, Gabon introduced a multiparty system and a new constitution in the early 1990s that allowed for a more transparent electoral process and for reforms of governmental institutions.

The rapid growth in oil exports gave Gabon one of the highest per-capita incomes in sub-Saharan Africa. During the 1980s, however, Bongo's regime faced significant political and economic challenges, due mainly to declining oil prices. Gabon had difficulty servicing its large debt and was forced to implement an austerity program, which hurt the middle classes and the poor. Unemployment rose and bureaucrats' wages were cut. The international press exposed the regime's corruption and dictatorial traits. There were strikes and protests. Major riots in Libreville and Port-Gentil led the government to declare a state of emergency and French troops intervened again. Since then, divisions in the opposition have enabled Bongo to be reelected twice. Although his government has invested in transportation and social services, the country's wealth still primarily benefits him and his clique. Most of the population remains impoverished.

L. NATALIE SANDOMIRSKY

Further Reading

Adams, Adrian, *La Terre et les Gens du Fleuve: Jalons, Balises*, [The Land and the People of the River: Milestones and Beacons], Paris: l'Harmattan, 1985

Barnes, James F., *Gabon: Beyond the Colonial Legacy*, Boulder, Colorado: Westview Press, 1992

De Saint-Paul, Marc A., *Gabon: The Development of a Nation*, New York: Routledge, 1989

Gardinier, David E., *Gabon*, Santa Barbara, California: ABC-CLIO, 1993

——, *Historical Dictionary of Gabon*, Lanham: Scarecrow Press Inc, 1994

Gaulme, Francois, *Le Gabon et Son Ombre* [Gabon and Its Shadow], Paris: Karthala, 1988

Weinstein, Brian, *Gabon: Nation-Building on the Ogooué*, Cambridge: M.I.T. Press, 1867

Yates, Douglas A., *The Rentier State in Africa, Oil Rent Dependency & Neocolonialism in the Republic of Gabon*, Lawrenceville: Africa World Press, 1996

Gagauz (Christianized Turks)

Capsule Summary

Location: southern Moldova (Moldavia), southwestern Ukraine (Bessarabia), coastal Romania, and Bulgaria (Dobruca)
Religion: Orthodox Christianity
Population: 220,000
Language: Oghuz Turkish

The Gagauz are a unique Orthodox Christian Turkish people who are concentrated, for the most part, in the southern regions of the former Soviet republic of Moldova. According to the most widely accepted theory, this small Turkic people are the descendants of Turks who entered the Byzantine controlled Balkans in the middle of the thirteenth century and converted from Islam to Orthodox Christianity. They subsequently resided in the coastal regions of what is today Romania and Bulgaria under Ottoman rule from the fourteenth century to the early eighteenth century. In the eighteenth century most of the Gagauz migrated to lands in southern Moldavia, controlled at that time by the Russian Empire, where they settled in a concentrated area. Today the Gagauz live in a semiautonomous region in southern Moldova centered on the Gagauz city of Komrat known as Gagauz Yeri (Gagauz Lands) and are undergoing subtle Russification.

Society

The ancestors of the Gagauz were Turkmen nomads from western Anatolia but, following their arrival in the Byzantine Empire in 1260, they appear to have become sedentary farmers and craftsmen. Traditionally the Gagauz have been engaged in cattle-breeding, fishing on the coasts of the Black Sea, and farming. Their conversion from Islam to Orthodox Christianity ensu-red peaceful relations with their Orthodox Romanian and Bulgarian neighbors who were also Orthodox Christians. The Gagauz culture has borrowed much from the Bulgarians, but this did not stop them from giving their allegiance to the Greek patriarch in Constantinople.

For most of their history Gagauz literature was limited to ecclesiastical works written in the Turkish language using a Greek alphabet known as Karamanli. There is, however, a rich body of folklore among the Gagauz known as *mani* or *turku* (epics), which were collected and put in written form during the Soviet period. Today, the Gagauz of Moldova intermarry with Russians (but rarely with the majority Moldovans) and approximately three-fourths of the Gagauz speak Russian.

History

There has been considerable debate concerning the origins of the Gagauz. Mikhail Cakir, a Bulgarian historian, has attempted to prove that the Gagauz are actually Turks who arrived with the Ottomans in the 1380s and subsequently converted to Christianity. Research by Paul Wittek in the 1950s, however, appears to have settled this controversy in favor of an Anatolian Seljuk origin for the Gagauz.

According to Wittek, the ancestors of the Gagauz were defeated Turkish nomads (Turkmen) who supported an unsuccessful sultan to the throne of the Turkish Seljuk Empire in 1260. Several loyal Turkish clans fled with the defeated Muslim sultan to the realm of the Christian Emperor of Byzantium seeking refuge and were settled in the plains of the Dobruca (modern Romania and Bulgaria, a coastal strip ideally suited for nomads located on the Black Sea). Here the defeated Seljuk Sultan, Kay Kavus, and his followers converted from Islam to Orthodox Christianity and est-ablished an independent border kingdom (the Despotate of Kalliakra) in vassalage to the Byzantine Emperor. The ethnonym of the Gagauz is, in fact, a rendering of the name Kay Kavus.

Among evidence to support the theory tracing the Gagauz to thirteenth century immigrations from Anatolia is that the Gagauz still use the term *Allah* (Arabic, God) for God. Ottoman records describing their conquest of the Dobruca region of Bulgaria record the Ottoman Sultan Bayazid Yildirim's astonishment at finding Turkish Christians descended from the legendary Seljuk dynasty in the Balkans, and Byzantine accounts record the migration of Kay Kavus' Turkish followers to the region.

Following the Ottoman conquest of the Dobruca region inhabited by the Gagauz (the region's name can be traced to the name of the Gagauz ruler Dobrotic) in the 1380s, the Gagauz were protected by the sultans as officially recognized Christian subjects and were included in the Orthodox *millet* (ethno-religious community) headed by the Greek patriarch in Istanbul. While the Gagauz initially flourished under the Ottomans' benign rule, their condition deteriorated as the Ottoman Empire itself underwent a period of decline in the early eighteenth century. As the Ottoman central authorities lost control over the provinces, local warlords and *janissary* (infantry) garrisons rose to prominence and oppressed the people of the Balkans. At this time the Gagauz and Bulgarians were exposed to the plundering raids of a particularly notorious chieftain, Pasvanoghlu, the *pasha* or governor of the Bulgarian city of Vidin. In response to these depredations, most of the Gagauz people and many Bulgarians migrated north of the Danube River (between the years 1750 and 1850) and into the Russian province of Bender located in southern Moldovia (Moldova), known as Bessarabia or the Bucak, seeking the czar's protection. The Russians were only too happy to settle this non-Romanian people in the Moldovian region (the Moldovians are north Romanians) to weaken Romania's claim to this disputed territory. While Bessarabia was returned to Romania after World War I, it was annexed by the Soviet Union during World War II and the Gagauz lands in the newly formed Moldovian Soviet Socialist Republic were collectivized and their language given a Cyrillic alphabet and state support.

Contemporary Issues

The collapse of the Soviet Union in 1991 led to the rise of ethnic tensions in the newly independent state of Moldova, which resulted in warfare between the republic's Russian minority (who carved out an independent republic in the Trans-Dniester region) and the Moldovan majority. To avoid a similar sort of confrontation with the Gagauz minority that was seeking cultural and political autonomy, the Moldovan authorities allowed the Gagauz to establish an autonomous zone in the areas where they formed more than 50 percent of the population in 1994. Conflict between the Gagauz (who have tended to ally themselves with the Russians in Moldova) and the Moldavans was thus avoided by a unique territorial solution that could serve as a model for ethnic disputes in other parts of post-Communist Eurasia. Today the Gagauz are an object of interest to Turks in Turkey who are reestablishing links with the "Outer Turks" (i.e., Turkic peoples of the former Soviet Union such as the Kazakhs, Uzbeks, Tatars, etc.), but the differences in religion between the Christian Gagauz and Muslim Turks still create barriers between the two Oghuz Turkish-speaking peoples.

BRIAN WILLIAMS

See also **Moldova; Russia; Turks**

Further Reading

Bruchis, M., *Nations, Nationalities, People: A Study of the Nationalities Policy of the Communist Party in Soviet Moldavia*, Boulder, Colorado: East European Monographs, 1984

Cavanaugh, C., "Conflict in Moldova: The Gagauz Factor," *Radio Free Europe/Radio Liberty*, 1, no. 32 (1992)

King, Charles, *Post-Soviet Moldova: A Borderland in Transition*, London: The Royal Institute of International Affairs, 1995

Menges, Karl, *The Turkic Language and Peoples*, Wiesbaden: Otto Hassarowiz, 1968

Peker, G., "The Process of Gagauz Autonomy: Past, Present and Future," *Eurasian Studies*, II, no. 2 (1995)

Socor, V., "Gagauz in Moldavia Demand Separate Republic," *Report on the USSR*, September 7, 1990

Williams, Brian Glyn, "Mystics, Nomads and Heretics: The Dissemination of Heterodox Islam from Central Asia to the 13th Century Romanian Dobruca," *International Journal of Turkish Studies*, 7, no. 1–2 (2001)

Wittek, Paul, "Yazijioghlu' Ali on the Christian Turks of the Dobruca," *Bulletin of the School of Oriental and African Studies*, no. 24 (1952)

Zajaczkowski, W., "On Contemporary Gagauz Literature," in *Proceedings of the Fourth International Conference on the Theoretical Problems of Asian and African Literature*, edited by M. Galik, Bratislavia: Literary Institute of the Slovak Academy of Sciences, 1983

Zajaczowski, Wlodzimierz, "Gagauz," in *Encyclopaedia of Islam*, vol G, Leiden: E.J. Brill, 1978

Gambia, The

Capsule Summary

Official Name: Republic of The Gambia
Total Population: 1,5 million (July 2003)
Majority Population: Mandinka (42%)
Minority Populations: Fulani (18%); Wolof (16%); others (24%)
Languages: English (official), Mandinka, Wolof, Fula, and other indigenous vernaculars
Religions: Muslim (90%); Christian (9%); indigenous beliefs (1%)

The Republic of the Gambia is situated on the Atlantic coast of West Africa and is centered on the Gambia River. The country is a strip of land 15 to 30 miles wide on either side of the river, and almost 300 miles long, and is Africa's smallest nonisland nation. Except for a short coastline, it is entirely surrounded by Senegal. Its peculiar shape and size are a result of territorial compromises made during the colonial period of the nineteenth century by Britain, which controlled the Gambia River, and France, which controlled the neighboring colony of Senegal.

The total population is just over 1.5 million, consisting of the majority Mandinka people and minority populations of Fulani, Wolof, Jola, Soninke, and other ethnic groups who also live in Senegal. The Gambia is one of Africa's most densely populated countries and has one of the continent's highest birth rates at 40.77 births/1,000 population (2003 estimates). The official language is English, but national languages include Wolof, which is the most widely spoken national language, Mandinka, and Fulfulde. Most Gambians are Muslim, although there are some Christians and other local religions. The capital, Banjul (called Bathurst until 1973), is located where the Gambia River flows into the Atlantic Ocean and has a population of about 75,000. The current government is a multiparty democracy with a strong military component. The economy is based primarily on peanut production and export, and the GDP per-capita income in 2002 was $1,800, making The Gambia one of the poorest countries in the world.

History

Prior to the imposition of European colonial rule in the nineteenth century, the Gambia River region was dominated by several small Muslim Mande and Wolof kingdoms. Agriculture and fishing constituted the local economy. Fulani pastoralists and Soninke merchants also lived in the kingdoms, especially those on the upper Gambia. The first Europeans to arrive in the area were the Portuguese in the 1440s, followed by the English, the French, and the Dutch. All traded with kingdoms on the river, seeking agricultural products and also slaves. The transatlantic slave trade became increasingly important in the region in the sixteenth and seventeenth centuries. The slave trade along the Gambia River was made famous by its depiction in Alex Haley's book and the television series from the 1970s, *Roots*. By the eighteenth century, the British dominated trade along the river while the French controlled trade to the north and south. The British built a fort at Bathurst at the mouth of the river on the Atlantic coast in 1816 and made The Gambia a colony of the British West African Federation. With the abolition of the slave trade in the early nineteenth century, the British encouraged the production and export of peanuts, which grew well in the local soils and climate. Peanut cultivation dominated the colonial economy of The Gambia, which was the poorest and smallest colony in British West Africa.

Several small political parties were formed in the colony in the 1950s, but because of its weak economy and small size, moves toward independence in The Gambia lagged behind other West African nations. On February 18, 1965, The Gambia became an independent country within the British Commonwealth with David Jawara, who had won a previous election, becoming Prime Minister, and his party, the People's Progressive Party, dominating Parliament. The Gambia became a republic in 1970 and Jawara, who had changed his name to Dawda Jawara and was knighted in 1966, was made president. The Gambia formed a short-lived federation of Senegambia with Senegal between 1982 and 1989 and today remains a republic under multiparty democratic rule.

The Gambian economy, as it had been during colonial rule, was based on the production and export of peanuts. Jawara faced little political opposition and remained popular among all ethnic groups in the country, owing primarily to the lack of decisive national issues. During the Sahelian droughts of the 1970s and 1980s, the Gambian environment and economy were seriously affected, especially in the middle and upper river areas. Peanut production declined, and more youths began to migrate to Banjul in search of employment. The capital became increasingly diverse ethnically with people from all over the region moving into the city. A failed military coup in 1981 led to talks of integration with Senegal, whose population contained similar ethnic groups, but the merger never occurred. In 1994, a group of military officers successfully ousted Jawara and Yaha Abdul Jammeh declared himself president. The military regime outlawed the People's Progressive Party, and after a series of postponements, permitted elections in late 1996 and early 1997. Jammeh, who had retired from the military, was elected president and his political party, the Alliance for Patriotic Reorientation and Construction, dominated the national assembly.

The Gambian economy continues to be characterized by traditional subsistence agriculture, primarily peanuts. Fisheries and tourism are also foreign exchange earners, although tourism declined precipitously with the 1994 coup. In recent years, the population of Banjul has been augmented by refugees from the civil wars in Sierra Leone and Liberia, two other English-speaking nations in a region largely French-speaking. The area along the Gambia River has always had a diverse population and the various ethnic groups often intermarry and are often barely distinguishable from one another. Islam is another unifying factor, as virtually all groups are Muslim. The small Christian population in the country has never suffered any persecution or discrimination. The Gambia has an exemplary record of toleration for minorities and has never experienced any ethnic violence or conflicts. Political parties have avoided becoming dominated by one or another ethnic group. The Gambian military, which remains a very strong presence, is fully integrated, and the current government includes people from virtually all ethnic groups in the country.

ANDREW F. CLARK

Further Reading

Curtin, Philip, *Economic Change in Precolonial Africa: Senegambia in the Era of the Slave Trade*, Madison: University of Wisconsin, 1975

Gailey, Harry, *A History of the Gambia*, New York: Praegar, 1965

———, *Historical Dictionary of the Gambia*, Lanham, Maryland: Scarecrow Press, 1987

Gray, John, *A History of the Gambia*, London: Frank Cass, 1940

Hughes, Arnold, editor, *The Gambia: Studies in Society and Politics*, Oxford: University Press, 1991

McPherson, M., and S. Radelet, editors, *Economic Recovery in the Gambia*, Washington, DC: USAID, 1995

Wright, Donald, *The World and a Very Small Place in Africa*, New York: Sharpe, 1997

Gandhi, Mohandas Karamchand (India)

Mohandas Karamchand Gandhi (called Mahatma or "great-souled" Gandhi) was an Indian nationalist, spiritual leader, and considered by many to be the father of his country. He is best known among his enduring achievements for the establishment and practice of *Satyagraha* ("holding on to the truth," or "firmness in truth" in Sanskrit) and theory and campaign of active nonviolent resistance. The term, which he first coined in South Africa, derives from *satya* ("truth"), which he believed could only be achieved through *ahimsa* ("nonharming," "nonviolence," or "love") and *brahm-acharya* ("celibacy" or a "striving towards God").

After studying in London and practicing law in India, Gandhi went to Natal, South Africa, in 1893 to protest mistreatment of Indian immigrants by whites. Gandhi's first experience of racism occurred in South Africa, where he was ejected from a Pretoria-bound train. Despite holding a first-class ticket, he was told to go to the third-class compartment because, in South Africa, Indians were only allowed on third-class compartments. Indians living in South Africa were without political rights and called "coolies," a term of derision. Galvanized by his experiences, Gandhi began campaigning for the rights of Indians in South Africa under the auspices of the Natal Indian Congress, an organization that he founded in 1904.

During his time in South Africa, Gandhi struggled for the rights of Indians in South Africa, developing the concept of *Satyagraha* as a means of political resistance. He conceived of his own life as a practice or experiment in the cultivation of *satyagraha*, a philosophical and complex study of the relationship between oppressors and the oppressed. When the Transvaal (Republic of South African) government passed a bill that required every Indian to register for fingerprinting, Gandhi mobilized the population—including Hindus, Muslims, Christians, and Parsis—in opposition to this law and succeeded in overturning it. While Gandhi struggled for more rights for Indians in South Africa, he did not advocate on behalf of the local Africans. In 1909 Gandhi authored *Hind Swaraj* ("Indian Home Rule"), a short but cogent treatise in which he outlined his critique of modernity through what he described as "a severe condemnation of modern civilization" (p. 16). Gandhi asserted that India had suffered submission not only at the hands of the British but by modern civilization and industrialization. Gandhi returned to India permanently in 1915 and initiated monumental reforms and consciousness raising over the next 40 years. Such shifts included the establishment of *ashrams* where people practiced his tenets of nonviolence and communal brotherhood across religions. Gandhi immersed himself in nonviolent resistance against the British colonial authorities through his support of myriad human rights causes. In 1919 the British government installed the repressive Rowlatt Acts, also known as the Black Acts, which gave the Indian viceroy's government powers to suppress any subversion by censoring the press and detaining political activists without trial

among other policies. In response, Gandhi organized a movement against the British government that advocated the revival of the country's political independence (*swaraj* or "self-ruling"). For this purpose, he founded the *Satyagraha ashram* in Ahmedabad. When, in 1919, a group of 10,000 unarmed Indian men, women, and children gathered at Jallianwala Bagh in Amritsar to hold a protest meeting (despite the ban on public assemblies), General Reginald Dyer, the British Military Governor of Punjab, ordered his troops to fire into the crowd, killing hundreds and wounding many more. It marked a turning point for many moderate Indians who began to ally with revolutionary movements against the British Raj. Gandhi helped mobilize the cause when he wrote the report of the Punjab Congress Inquiry Committee investigating the event. Over the next few years he initiated what would be known as the noncooperative movement against the government. In protest, he returned the Kaisar-i-Hind medal that he had received from the British for his work in South Africa and, in general, advocated the withdrawal from British institutions.

Following a six-year imprisonment for sedition as a result of a 1922 revolt at Chauri Chaura, he turned his attention to healing and preserving Indian-Muslim differences. Realizing the need for unity, Gandhi paid particular attention to the issues of Indian Muslims. When the Muslims of India rallied in opposition to the conditions imposed on Turkey in the treaty of Sevres (1920), Gandhi befriended the Muslim leaders of the *Khilafat* movement and commenced a noncooperation movement on August 1, 1920. While in prison a second time in 1924 for 21 days he conducted his first public fast in response to Hindu-Muslim riots that broke out at Kohat, a military barracks. In 1932 he commenced the so-called Epic Fast to protest British treatment of the Hindu "untouchables" (*harijans* or *dalits*), in effect a critique of the Hindu caste system. The untouchables were the lowest class in Indian society and suffered from poverty, lack of education, and a near dissolution of their human rights. Gandhi equated the practice of "untouchability," and more broadly a hierarchy of classes in the name of religion, to "a sin against humanity." He regularly broke the "nonintercourse rule" by sitting among untouchables in the villages, and he even adopted an untouchable girl into his home. By admitting such a family into his Ahmedabad Ashram in 1915, he risked alienation from his wife and many of his followers who protested his actions. In 1924 he supported a *satyagraha* movement at Vaikam (Kerala), fighting to give the untouchables the right to use a road passing a Hindu temple.

By giving the untouchables the name of *Harijans*— "children of God"—Gandhi tried to lessen the stigma against them. During 1932–33, Gandhi undertook four fasts in support of the anti-untouchablity cause. When the British tried to award a separate electorate to the untouchables in the second Roundtable Conference in London in 1931, Gandhi opposed the British scheme on the grounds that it reinforced the caste system in the Indian nation. Opposed by rising social protest led by Gandhi, the British government changed its proposal.

Gandhi lived in a *Harijan* colony in 1947 in New Delhi as a sign of his support. While many argue that Gandhi achieved a great deal for the untouchables, there are others— Bhimrao Ramji Ambedkar, the most prominent untouchable leader of India's nationalist movement, for example—who found his actions to have been driven by his belief that the status of *Dalit* people was to be raised while retaining elements of the traditional caste system.

In the later part of his life, when India was nearing independence from Britain in 1947, Gandhi worked to mend the differences between Hindus and Muslims. Although he originally opposed a two-nation theory in which Muslims and Hindus would have their own separate nations, he accepted it in later years. Through most of his life, Gandhi believed that British rule had driven a wedge among the disparate groups in India; if British were removed, Indians, Gandhi believed, would solve their communal differences.

During the formalization of the plan for India's independence, the differences between the Congress and the Muslim League reflected a larger communal split that had developed between the communities. When communal riots broke out in Calcutta and later spread to other parts of Bengal and Bihar, Gandhi went to live in East Bengal and walked barefoot from village to village, spreading his message of peace and nonviolence. In March 1947 he moved to Bihar to support the minority Muslim community in the midst of violence.

On August 15, 1947, Independence Day, Gandhi was in Calcutta fighting communal riots through fasting. At the end of August, in the wake of fresh riots in Calcutta, Gandhi embarked on a fast unto death to be only broken if the communal violence subsided. But this had no effect on the rioting. While Hindus, Muslims, and Sikhs were migrating across the border of the newly created Pakistan and India, Gandhi advised them to remain in their places of residence. On January 12, 1948, Gandhi undertook another fast to end the communal violence; but he broke the fast on January 18 when news reached him that a multireligious committee has signed an agreement to protect the Muslim minority's life and property.

The orthodox Hindu leadership accused Gandhi of unduly favoring the Muslims. One member of this group, Nathuram Godse, fired three lethal shots at Gandhi in the belief that Gandhi had weakened India by befriending Muslims. For the generations to come, Gandhi left behind the message of nonviolence in political struggle. Martin Luther King, who led the fight for the rights of African Americans in the Civil Rights movement in the United States, was inspired by Gandhi's concept of nonviolent struggle for political rights.

Biography

Mohandas Karamchand Gandhi. Born October 2, 1869, in Porbander, Kathiawar (presently in the state of Gujarat). Studied at Alfred High School in Rajkot; University of Bombay, 1887; University of London, Law, 1891. Founder Natal Indian Congress, 1894, and *Young India* and *Navajivan*, 1919, and *Harijan*, 1933. Editor, *Indian Opinion*, Natal, South Africa, 1904–1915. President, the Indian National Congress, 1924–1925. Awards: Boer War medal, 1899; Zulu War medal, 1906; Kaisar-i-Hind medal, 1915. Died in New Delhi, India, January 30, 1948.

Selected Works [M.K. Gandhi]

Hind Swaraj, 1909
Autobiography: The Story of My Experiments with Truth (two volumes), 1927–1929
Satyagraha in South Africa, 1928
From Yeravda Mandir: Ashram Observances, 1932
The Constructive Programme: Its Meaning and Place, 1941
Collected Works of Mahatma Gandhi (Volumes 1 to 100), New Delhi: Publications
Division of Government of India, 1958–1994

AMANDEEP SANDHU

See also **Ambedkar, Bhimrao Ramji (Dalit); India; Untouchables (Harijans/Dalits/Scheduled Castes)**

Further Reading

Ambedkar, B.R., *What Congress and Gandhi Have Done to Untouchables*, Bombay: Thacker, 1945
Borman, William, *Gandhi's Non-Violence*, New York: State University of New York Press, 1986
Dhawan, G.N., *The Political Philosophy of Mahatma Gandhi*, Ahmedabad: Navajivan, 1951
Fox, Richard, *Gandhian Utopia: Experiments with Culture.* Boston: Beacon Press, 1989
Nanda, B.R., *Gandhi and His Critics*, Delhi: Oxford University Press, 1985
Sharp, Gene, *Gandhi as a Political Strategist*, Boston: Porter Sargent, 1979

Garang, John (Sudanese)

John Garang de Mabior, leader of the Sudan People's Liberation Army (SPLA) and Sudan People's Liberation Movement (SPLM), is an influential political figure in the Sudan and a leading spokesperson for its minority peoples. He is a Dinka, one of the largest ethnic groups among "southerners" (also including Nuer, Anouak, Shilluk, Toposa, Moru, Lotuho, Madi, Bari, Zande, and others) who together form a persecuted African minority (34 percent) of a national population of 29.8 million (2000). These southern minorities, which are largely Christian or of traditional religions, have a history of conflict with northern Arab rulers. Arab colonization of the south became more effective in the nineteenth century, but the region remained neglected under Arab and then British colonial rule. After independence in 1956, repressive northern rule and attempts to impose Islam exacerbated the conflict, driving southern leaders such as Garang into revolt.

Garang emerged as a leader against the background of a civil war that has ravaged Sudan for much of the postcolonial period. The first phase began in 1955 when southern troops mutinied against northern domination and later formed the Anya-Nya ("snake venom") guerrilla army. In 1972 President Jaafar al-Nimeiri (military ruler, 1969–85) signed the Addis Ababa peace agreement providing limited southern autonomy, but in 1983 he unilaterally redrew provincial boundaries and imposed Islamic *shari'a* law, reigniting the war. Garang, then a Sudan army officer, was sent to quell mutiny but instead joined the rebels. After formation of the SPLA in 1983, he became commander and also leader of its political wing, the SPLM. Garang, like other southerners, viewed the imposition of *shari'a* as cultural domination and exploitation by Khartoum, excluding them from the benefits associated with southern oil and water reserves. Such shared grievances among minorities have provided Garang with a strong, if often divided, power base.

Bolstered by Ethiopian aid, Garang's SPLA achieved significant military victories, which contributed to the weakening of the Khartoum regime and the 1985 coup that overthrew Nimeiri. In 1986 Garang and northern opposition leaders signed the Koka Dam declaration for peace and democracy. The short-lived democratic government was overthrown in 1989, however, by a military fundamentalist Islamic regime, the National Islamic Front (NIF), led by Omar al-Bashir, who intensified northern domination and thus the war. The SPLA grew from an estimated 12,000 in 1986 to 50,000 in 1991 and by 1992 claimed to control 90 percent of the south. The 1991 fall of Garang's ally, Mengistu, in Ethiopia and internal splits weakened the SPLA and led to the loss of key towns, but Garang soon gained support from Uganda and the United States and by late 1996 had retaken lost territory. However, the war and associated famine had produced devastating effects: an estimated 1.5 million deaths and 3.5 million refugees by the mid-1990s.

Garang's career has been surrounded by controversies on minority and human rights issues. At various times, Khartoum has accused him of regionalism and of being a puppet of Ethiopia or the United States. Resisting pressure from secessionists, he has consistently supported a unified, secular, federal democratic state, a multicultural society tolerant of all religions, and a program of self-determination and equal development of all regions that seeks to safeguard the interests of minorities, including nonsouthern peoples such as the Nuba. Garang's emphasis on national unity has produced allies from among those supportive of Sudan's territorial integrity, such as the northern opposition with whom he formed the National Democratic Alliance (NDA), but has drawn criticism from secessionists who accuse him of failing to support southern independence.

Garang's policies should be seen in the context of regional politics, which have tended to divide along ethnic lines between pan-Sudanese and southern nationalists, reflecting long-standing minority rivalries often manipulated by Khartoum. Rivalries between minority leaders from Equatorian and Nilotic regions were pronounced in the limited-power regional Assembly of 1972–83. Some Equatorians continued to favor secession and saw Garang's SPLA as Dinka dominated. Nuer-Dinka recriminations over cattle rustling also fanned factionalism. Between 1983 and 1990, Garang was able to keep the SPLA relatively united, but in 1991 Riek Machar, a Nuer leader, split from the

GARANG, JOHN (SUDANESE)

movement and by 1993 three other factions had
emerged. Although the dissidents espoused secession
and accused Garang of autocratic leadership and Dinka
hegemonism, that several of them joined forces with
the northern army bombing civilians in the south
diminished their credibility. Garang has played an
ambiguous role in this complex political environment;
criticized by rivals for authoritarianism, he nevertheless
publicly called for unity among all oppressed minorities. In 1995 one faction reconciled with Garang, and
in 1999 Dinka-Nuer feuds were substantially healed at
the Wunlit Peace and Reconciliation Conference.

All sides in this conflict have been accused of
human rights violations. Garang has steadfastly condemned government policies of repression, forced
Arabization and Islamicization of minorities and dispossession of their lands, "ethnic cleansing," aerial
bombardment of civilians, and has charged the regime
with genocide and racism. The government has been
accused by the United Nations, the United States, the
Anti-Slavery Society, and Amnesty International of
gross violations of human rights including kidnapping
and enslavement of thousands of women and children.
Amnesty International has condemned the lack of a
fair trial for dissidents executed by the SPLA. Peter
Nyaba, an SPLM member, has criticized Garang's
authoritarianism. It is difficult to assess the extent of
Garang's personal involvement in these matters.

In the 1990s a military stalemate led to on–off peace
negotiations between Garang and Khartoum. To try to
surmount the impasse, Garang proposed in 2000 a
period of confederation with separate northern and
southern constitutions. The Machakos Protocol of 2002
saw a memorandum of understanding on cessation of
hostilities but conflict continued. Highly critical of
Khartoum's oil projects and Jonglei Canal scheme as
diverting resources from minorities, Garang has instead
supported a policy of appropriate technology. Despite
the persistence of conflict and internal divisions to
which he has partly contributed, Garang has remained
the foremost political leader and military commander
of southern Sudanese minorities for two decades. It is
unlikely that any lasting peace or resolution of minority
grievances can take place without him and the organization he has built.

Biography

John Garang de Mabior. Born June 23, 1945, in Wagkulei
village, Bor County, Jonglei Province, Sudan. Attended school
in Sudan and Magamba Senior Secondary School, Lushoto,
Tanzania. Research associate, Department of Economics and
Rural Economy, University of Dar-es-Salaam, 1969–70.
Bachelor of Science 1971, Grinnel College, Iowa. Joined
Anya-Nya liberation army of southern Sudan in 1970, adjutant
to leader General Joseph Lagu. After 1972 peace agreement,
integrated into Sudan Armed Forces as captain; adjutant Bahr
al-Ghazal Province, 1972–73; operations officer, Torit Garrison,
Equatoria, 1974. Infantry Officer Diploma, U.S. Army Infantry
School, Ft. Benning, Georgia, 1974–75. Instructor, Sudan
Military College, 1975. Commander, 105th Infantry Battalion,
Bor, 1976–77. Graduate research in agricultural economics,
Iowa State University, Ames, 1977–81; Ph.D. 1981. Economic
advisor, Sudan Army Economic Institution, Deputy-Director,
Military Research Branch, Sudan Army General Headquarters,
and lecturer, Department of Rural Economy, University of
Khartoum, 1982–83. Colonel in Sudan Army; May 1983, sent to
Bor to suppress revolt; instead took charge of SPLA. Commander
in Chief, SPLA 1983–, Chairman, SPLM 1984–, Chairperson,
National Democratic Alliance Joint Military Command,
Chairperson of SPLM Council, March 1994–. Currently lives
in liberated zones of southern Sudan.

Selected Works

"Identifying, Selecting, and Implementing Rural Development
Strategies for Socio-Economic Development in the Jonglei
Projects Area, Southern Region, Sudan," Ph.D. dissertation,
Iowa State University, 1981
John Garang Speaks, edited by Mansour Khalid, 1987; 2nd
edition, as *The Call for Democracy in Sudan*, 1992
"The Speech of the SPLM Chairman and Commander in Chief
SPLA on the 17th Anniversary of the SPLM/SPLA," 2000
(keynote address to National Democratic Alliance Second
Congress)

PETER LIMB

See also **Autonomy; Christians: Africa; Civil War,
United States; Colonialism; Ethnic Conflict; Human
Rights; Racism; Refugees; Religion vs. Ethnicity;
Secession; Self-Determination; Slavery; Sudan**

Further Reading

Deng, Francis Mading, *War of Visions: Conflict of Identities
in the Sudan*, Washington, DC: The Brookings Institution,
1995
Johnson, Douglas, "The Sudan People's Liberation Army and
the Problem of Factionalism," in *African Guerrillas*, edited
by Christopher Clapham, Oxford: Currey; Kampala,
Uganda: Fountain; and Bloomington: Indiana University
Press, 1998
Nyaba, Peter Adwok, *The Politics of Liberation in South Sudan:
An Insider's View*, Kampala, Uganda: Fountain, 1997
Verney, Peter, et al., *Sudan: Conflict and Minorities*, London:
Minority Rights Group, 1995

Garifuna

Capsule Summary

Location: Honduras, Belize, Nicaragua, and Guatemala
Total Population: 100,000–400,000
Languages: English, Spanish, Carib-Arawak, and regional dialects
Religion: African and Amerindian mix, including Gubida (possession ritual)

The Garifuna, or Garinagu, is a Caribbean ethnic group of mixed African-American ancestry who live in coastal villages from the Gulf of Honduras to the Mosquito Coast in Belize, Guatemala, and Honduras. Their numbers are uncertain and estimates range from 100,000 to 400,000.

Like the Black Seminole in Florida or the Jamaican Maroons, the Garífuna, also known as the Black Caribs, arose as a result of local adaptations to past mercantilist and colonialist policies in the Caribbean region. Their West African ancestors were settled on the Caribbean island of St. Vincent around 1635, having survived a shipwreck while being taken to America as slaves. Garífuna identity arose gradually there as the result of intermarriage with the island's Carib indian population and in peaceful coexistence with the island´s French settlers. However, tensions soon grew after 1763, when the island became a British possession, because of demands for more lands made by newly arrived settlers. In 1796, seeing themselves cornered, the Garífuna rose in revolt. They were defeated and their leader, Chief Joseph Chatoyer, was killed; 4,200 of them were subsequently forcibly relocated to the nearby island of Baliceaux. Detained in harsh conditions, many perished there. The survivors, only 2,250 individuals, were removed once again in the following year. This time they were taken to the island of Roatán, off the coast of Honduras. Many perished during the crossing and they were left with enough supplies for only three months. They survived after planting cassava plants they had taken to their new destination hidden in their clothes.

Very soon the Garífuna began to establish themselves on the mainland. In Belize, they founded towns like Dangriga, Barranco, and Punta Gorda, where they continued to live in traditional Island Carib fashion, with an economy based on cassava farming and fishing.

Women do most of the farming and are also widely known for their tradition of making cassava bread. In general, women are the center of not only the household but also Garífuna society as a whole. Descent is traced through the mother's family and women are known for their leadership and articulate speech while taking a decisive part in social matters. Traditionally, Garífuna men are often away hunting and fishing. At the same time, recent tendencies show a shift toward a wage economy and continued migration to nearby cities or the United States. Increased demands from the outside society, such as land for tourist development, have mobilized the Garífuna to defend their rights as a people. Although the basis of subsistence is mainly an adaptation to conditions prevailing in the Caribbean, the culture as a whole is a fusion of traditional West African, Amerindian, and Spanish elements.

An early instance of this fusion is Paranda music, by now an almost forgotten Garífuna genre and rhythm. With drumming styles that can be traced all the way back to St. Vincent and West Africa, it is a mix of African percussion, Cuban son, and American Blues. According to one of its remaining practitioners, songs can be about people in the village, girlfriends, or even the devastating hurricane that, in 1961, killed hundreds and destroyed much of Dangriga.

Showing the dynamism and growing assertiveness of Garífuna culture, a new musical form, punta rock, was invented in the 1970s. Adding guitars to the traditional drum rhythm, it owes much to the work of pioneer artists like Pen Cayetano, and is part of a cultural renaissance that enjoys the practical support of communities in producing new dance groups, bands, books, and articles.

Traditional rituals are related both to the recent past and to African culture. At the celebration of Arrival Day on April 12, which commemorates the arrival to Roatán Island, people approach the shore in boats and wave banana leaves as a symbol of the cassava. In the town of Dangriga, a similar festival, held on November

19th, is known as the Day of The Landing. During this holiday, the town comes alive. Dishes with fish, pork, and cassava are served and various handicrafts can be bought.

The rites of death constitute the most sacred cultural expression of the Garifuna. Based on dance, drum, and ancestor worship, various rites maintain the relation of the lineage with the recently deceased and the ancestors.

In the rite called Amuyadahani, or "Bathing the Spirit of the Dead", held some months after the funeral, the immediate family attends to the need of the spirit of the deceased who is in need of refreshment and strength. This short ceremony begins with religious songs, and then the eldest member fills a gourd with water and throws it into a dug pit, saying, "Here, this is for your bath".

The most sacred of these ceremonies is the *Dugu*, "The Feasting of the Dead." It is made to restore physical and spiritual well-being when members of the family of somebody recently deceased are troubled by nightmares and misfortune. All relatives are expected to attend, no matter how far away they live and the rites are held in the village where the lineage originated. Healing is attempted during several days of dancing and drumming and sharing of food. A priest (*buyai*) is summoned to communicate with the ancestral spirits with the help of his messengers, the *yuruhu*. The most sacred part of the Dugu is the dance of *mali*, in which the placating of the spirits of the ancestors takes place. The congregation forms behind the buyai, who faces the drummers, as they all move in a counterclockwise direction. Each mali is dedicated to an ancestral spirit. Normally, some dancers enter into a trance, signifying that the ancestors have arrived at the ceremony. At the end of the ritual, they go to the sea to collect shellfish and the favorite dishes of the ancestors. Upon return, they dress and attend a requiem mass.

The Garífuna speak a Carib-Arawak language, adding words from English, French, and Spanish. Most are bilingual, speaking English or Spanish in addition to their own language. Some also speak regional Maya dialects.

JUAN CARLOS GUMUCIO

Further Reading

Gonzalez, Nancie L., *Sojourners of the Caribbean: Ethnogenesis and Ethnohistory of the Garifuna*, University of Illinois Press, 1988

Sutherland, Anne, *The Making of Belize*, Westport, Connecticut: Bergen and Garvey, 1998

Garvey, Marcus (Jamaican)

Marcus Garvey was a leading and outspoken proponent of black nationalism in the United States in the twentieth century who founded the Universal Negro Improvement Association, an organization dedicated to promoting worldwide unity among all blacks, pride in African heritage, and the "back to Africa" movement. He gained millions of followers and was proclaimed, in his time, a redeemer and hero for the black race.

Marcus Mosiah Garvey, Jr., was born in St. Ann's Bay, Jamaica, on August 17, 1887, the youngest of 11 children. In 1906, at age 14, Garvey and his mother moved to Kingston, where he found work in a printing shop and became acquainted with the living and working conditions of the laboring class. He began to involve himself in social reform and participated in a Printers' Union strike in 1907 and published three issues of the newspaper *Garvey's Watchman* in 1909. Garvey left Jamaica in 1910 and traveled throughout Central and South America. He worked as a newspaper editor in Panama and Costa Rica. He visited the Panama Canal Zone, Ecuador, Nicaragua, Honduras, Colombia, and Venezuela and witnessed consistent discrimination against blacks in all of the countries in which he traveled.

Garvey returned to Jamaica in 1912 and appealed to Jamaica's colonial government to help improve the plight of West Indian workers in Central America.

Garvey then left for England in search of additional financial backing for his efforts and also attended Birkbeck College of the University of London. While there, he worked for and published an article in the *African Times and Oriental Review* magazine. Garvey also began to study the history of Africa and traveled throughout Europe. In 1914, Garvey returned to Jamaica and, with Amy Ashwood, organized the Universal Negro Improvement Association (UNIA) and its coordinating body, the African Communities League. The mission of the UNIA was to promote African heritage, worldwide black unity, and, in non-African countries where blacks were the minority, a back-to-Africa movement. In 1916, Garvey traveled to the United States for the first time, moved to New York City, found a job as a printer, and began publicly speaking on the streets of Harlem about his view of the black race and the problems it encountered in the United States and in the world. Garvey then embarked upon a yearlong, 38-state speaking tour of the United States. Upon returning to New York, he founded, with 13 others, the New York branch of the UNIA, and continued to make public lectures about the plight of the black race in America.

In 1917, the UNIA published its first issue of *The Negro World*, in which Garvey and the UNIA voiced it opinions. Garvey and the UNIA campaigned against lynching, Jim Crow laws, denial of black voting rights, and racial discrimination. The UNIA differentiated itself from other civil rights organizations by advocating separation between the races rather than segregation. Garvey doubted whether whites in the United States would ever agree to African Americans being treated as equals and suggested that African Americans should leave the United States and resettle in Africa. He wrote that he believed in the principle of Europe for the Europeans, Asia for the Asians, and Africa for the Africans, both at home and abroad. The UNIA and Garvey began recruit those who were willing to travel to Africa and rid the continent of white people. To this end, a military force was formed and equipped with uniforms and weapons. Garvey appealed to the new militant feelings of black Americans that followed the end of the World War I and asked that those who had been willing to fight for democracy in Europe join his army and fight for equal rights in the United States. In 1919, Garvey formed the Black Cross Navigation and Trading Company and, with $10,000,000 invested by his supporters, purchased two steamships to take black Americans to Africa. The UNIA held its first convention in New York in 1920, attended by 25,000 people, where Garvey was elected provisional president of Africa.

At its peak, the UNIA boasted over 2 million members and 1,100 branches in more than 40 countries, most of which were located in the United States. The Association had offices in such diverse places as Cuba, Panama, Costa Rica, Ecuador, Venezuela, Ghana, Sierra Leone, Liberia, Namibia, and South Africa. Garvey launched some business ventures, notably the Black Star Shipping Line, which soon encountered financial difficulty, and promoted two other business organizations—the African Communities League and the Negro Factories Corporation (incorporated in 1919). He tried to salvage his African colonization plan by sending a delegation to appeal to the League of Nations for transfer to the UNIA of the African colonies taken from Germany during World War I. His importance and influence declined substantially when he was arrested and imprisoned on charges that he had used the US mail to defraud potential investors in the Black Star Line. He entered jail in 1925 to serve a five-year term. In 1927, his half-served sentence was commuted, and he was deported to Jamaica by order of President Calvin Coolidge. The UNIA could not escape the scandal and, by 1930, ceased to exist.

In Jamaica, Garvey turned his energies to Jamaican politics, campaigning on a platform of self-government, minimum wage laws, and land and judicial reform. He was easily defeated at the polls. In 1935, Garvey left for England where, in near obscurity, he died on June 10, 1940, in a cottage in West Kensington.

Biography

Marcus Mosiah Garvey. Born in St. Ann's Bay, Jamaica, on August 17, 1887. Attended elementary public schools in Jamaica. Attended Birkbeck College, University of London, 1912–1914. Founder, Universal Negro Improvement Association (UNIA), 1914. Founder, African Communities League, 1914. Founder, Black Star Shipping Line, 1919. Founder, Negro Factories Corporation, 1919. Deported to Jamaica, 1927. Died, June 10, 1940, England.

Selected Works

The Tragedy of White Injustice, 1978
The Poetical Works of Marcus Garvey, 1983
Message to the People: The Course of African Philosophy, 1986
The Philosophy and Opinions of Marcus Garvey, Or, Africa for the Africans, edited by Amy J. Garvey, 1986
Aims and Object of Movement, 1987

RICHARD VERRONE

Further Reading

Cronon, Edward, and John Hope Franklin, *Black Moses: The Story of Marcus Garvey and the Universal Negro Improvement Association*, University of Wisconsin Press, 2nd edition, 1969

Hill, Robert A., and Barbara Bair, editors, *Marcus Garvey: Life and Lessons*, University of California Press, reprint edition, 1988

Hill, Robert A., et al., editors, *The Marcus Garvey and Universal Negro Improvement Association Papers*, University of California Press, 9 vols., 1983–1996

Davis, Lenwood G., *Marcus Garvey*, Greenwood Publishing Group, 1980

Lewis, Rupert, et al., editors, *Garvey: Africa, Europe, the Americas*, Africa World Press, 1994

Gender and Minority Status

Minority status and gender are inextricably linked and are manifest in societal relationships, histories, and narratives. Women of minority status live within a variety of restrictions and processes of socialization that differ from one culture or one ethnicity to another.

Often, minority women are subject to specific forms of control or proscription by family members and the social environment. Controls are often exercised more stringently in environments such as the Western democracies, which are considered particularly dangerous for minorities originating in other countries or in the periphery. Among many minority groups, one recurrent problem or issue that causes parents to treat daughters differently from sons is a need or a desire to keep families intact. The responsibilities required by a job, schooling, or some other professional endeavor (spending long hours away from home, commuting, being away overnight) are not easily accepted by parents of young women. Often parents fear for the honor of their daughters and fear that the whole family could be affected by too many liberties (which are often seen as Western-influenced). This attitude imposes limitations that hinder young women's professional future. Return migration, which is often planned, makes it difficult for women to develop long-term professional projects or goals, such as earning advanced degrees. Often, it is unthinkable for parents to return home and leave their daughters behind, alone, in the host country. But when a daughter returns with her parents to her country of origin, she is likely to have fewer options for practicing her profession, and fewer choices in general, so that her ambitions are constricted. All these factors may constitute problems or raise conflicts for young women who seek professional status outside the social customs or norms of their minority group. Moreover, the indigenous majority in a country or culture typically has only vague knowledge of the problems of minority women; as a result, this majority also denies minority women professional options and opportunities.

Second-Generation Minority Women

Researchers have found that the level of education of second-generation minority women or those who entered a host country before six years of age does not differ from that of autochthonous women. However, minority women tend to end their education when they reach age 20 and do not begin higher education in colleges or universities. Minority women who arrived in the country of residence at age six to nine years or older tend to have a much lower level of education. Often, their educational level is markedly low: in France, for instance, an average of 70 percent of minority girls finish school in classes for low-level pupils (compared with 40 percent of minority boys, and only 10 percent for the nation as a whole). Minority women who come from a country that has no compulsory education most often do not attend school in the host country; if they do go to school there, they typically leave at the primary level. Minority women and girls coming from Southeast Asia are an exception: they tend to have high levels of education, less that 20 percent of them follow a vocational course in school, and 20 percent of them attend institutions of higher education. Still, even Southeast Asian girls and women often take short technical courses of study, a fact that Tribalat (1995) underlined in her study of France.

Second-generation women tend to regard an occupation as a means of achieving family objectives and as a legitimate opportunity to escape from traditional ties.

These young women attend schools in host countries, try to gain access to the labor market, and commonly assume that education will increase their chances in the labor market. But migrant girls, even if they receive a good education, disappear rather soon from the occupational statistics. In their case, a gender-specific segmentation of the labor market operates: often, these women work in private households and are marginalized with respect to social security. Studies of Turkish women in Germany have found that for these women acquiring financial independence has little value, and they cannot market their own labor. Debates and discussions in Great Britain and the United States reveal that gender-based social inequality is reinforced by social inequality based on origin, and moreover that new gender inequalities arise. Immigrant women from the periphery often become domestic servants for white women—for instance in Italy, Germany, and the United States. Studies from Yugoslavia indicate that in countries where only some categories of women are socially accepted, women who fall outside those categories see emigration as a way to escape from this situation. Research on Italian women showed that women, even when they have small children, may provide an impetus for whole families to migrate.

Gender and Migration Theory

"Migration theory" has long been criticized for being blind to gender. Relatively recent researchers, inspired by feminism and feminist research, have made some efforts to redress this omission, focusing on particular aspects of women's migration. Such researchers have argued, for instance, that women migrants are triply oppressed: first, simply as women; second, as workers rather than entrepreneurs; and third, as aliens in the host country. Furthermore, women migrants may accept or be resigned to such oppression, considering it natural and normal. Also, sociological and anthropological literature on migration now offers explanations of female migration in contrast to male migration. These studies may take up women's decision-making process—even among women who migrate without dependents—in order to analyze how the decision to migrate is affected by a woman's own role as a member of a household and by the role of others in the family, such as the male head of the household. Factors influencing the decision may include, for instance, the illness of older family members or the costs of children's schooling.

Another factor that has an impact on minority female migrants is the labor market, which often has an inter-national division of labor. This division of labor channels minority women toward low-wage work, notably housework and child care in the homes of wealthier autochthonous women. Through their domestic labor, minority women allow indigenous women to participate in the higher level labor market. Of course, minority women also work in other areas, especially in traditionally female domains, such as taking care of babies in day care centers or other facilities, taking care of old people in private homes or institutions, and working as nurses in hospitals. For migrants, these areas are becoming a labor market segregated by sex. Often, migrant women cannot find jobs in their own professions, and even university graduates have to take work that is far below their educational level. In their countries of origin, these women typically had low incomes; by coming to a host country (especially to host countries in the northern hemisphere), they hope to improve their economic situation—but only rarely do they achieve professional success.

This outcome might seem to imply that migrant women would be impelled to return to their home countries. It is true that women who migrate alone frequently travel between their home country and the host country; however, these women are seldom interested in resettling at home. The home countries typically have a standard of living that is far below what women have become accustomed to in the host country; in addition, despite her difficulties in the host country, a woman can live there without many of the constraints that would otherwise be imposed by her family. In her country of origin, she would face a social reality that is no longer compatible with her preferred way of life. Even women who migrate with eventual family reunification in mind have problems in considering a possible return home. For one thing, they may have gotten used to urban life and urban amenities, which they cannot find at home. Another obstacle to returning home may be a woman's children, who often prefer to remain in the host country. Still another obstacle to returning is the loss or diminution of the migrant's pension earned in the host country.

Health

Worldwide, there is a connection between minority status and poverty. In world systems theory, most European nations are described as upper class or middle class; by contrast, most nonwhite nations are poor and are described as lower class. Most of the nonwhite nations have a long history of economic dependence on industrialized nations. The health status of minority women emerges from this related situation.

According to world systems theory, groups that suffer economic deprivation must also experience difficulties in other domains of the social structure. In many societies, distribution of income is based on color status, and minority women's lack of income causes deprivation in terms of other valuable resources and commodities, such as health care. Research has found that health status is correlated with socioeconomic status. The negative health status of minority women is based on the fact that poor women do not have enough money to pay for health care and therefore have little or no access to such care. But even middle-class minority women often live in areas where there is a lack of health services, because doctors do not want to establish a practice in a minority neighborhood.

Another problem, noted by Bayne-Smith (1995), is that many women of color are raising children without a partner. In the United States, for example, it has been estimated that 30 to 40 percent of black and Latino males have run afoul of the criminal justice system. As a result, for minority women there is only a small pool of men available for one-to-one relationships, and in turn there are a high number of out-of-wedlock births. Childbearing out of wedlock affects not only women of color but, obviously, their children as well. Bayne-Smith comments that with regard to social stratification, unwed teenage mothers and their children are usually relegated to the bottom of the hierarchy: they have poor educational and career opportunities, they have low-paying jobs, they experience longer periods of unemployment, they have unstable relationships, and their health status is low. Children of these often young mothers are of low birth weight and suffer from malnutrition and otherwise poor health during childhood. It has been shown that this problematic health issue is perpetuated in succeeding generations.

Crime

Another factor that shapes women's minority status is crime. Research indicates that women are overwhelmingly more likely than men to be victims of sexual assault, domestic violence, and theft. In Great Britain, crime surveys have found that 50 percent of violent offenses against female victims involve domestic violence, compared with only 6 percent for male victims. In the United States, it is argued, "crime" has become

a code word for "race": detention and imprisonment have increasingly replaced other systems of racial control, such as ghettoes, as a way of keeping women and men of color in their place; money to support low-income women and their children has been cut back; and money to arrest and detain marginal women has been increased.

One study found that in Los Angeles, 43 percent of girls being processed in the juvenile justice system were Latinas, 34 percent were white, and 23 percent were African-American; but only 34 percent of the Latinas and 20 percent of the African-American girls were recommended for a treatment-oriented facility rather than detention, compared with 75 percent of white girls. Not surprisingly, girls in the juvenile justice system often came from low-income homes and so were at risk already; this risk was aggravated by detention, which tends to lead to criminality in adult life, specifically drug abuse, theft, and prostitution. In fact, more than half of the women in prisons in the United States are African-American (46 percent) and Hispanic (14.2 percent). Chesnay-Lind (1997) found that more than three times as many young black women as young white women have contact with the criminal justice system. This fact is linked to harsh measures against using and selling drugs. Minority women from foreign countries often carry drugs because of threats to their families or abusive relationships with men involved in the drug trade. When arrested, they seldom have a history of involvement with the criminal justice system.

ULRIKE SCHUERKENS

See also **Equal Opportunity**

Further Reading

Anker, Richard, *Gender and Jobs: Sex Segregation of Occupations in the World*, Geneva: International Labour Office Publications, 1998

Bayne-Smith, Marcia, *Race, Gender, and Health*, Thousand Oaks, California, London, and New Delhi: Sage, 1995

Chesnay-Lind, Meda, *The Female Offender: Girls, Women, and Crime*, Thousand Oaks, California, London, and New Delhi: Sage, 1997

Hillmann, Felicitas, *Jenseits der Kontinente: Migrationsstrategien von Frauen nach Europa*, Pfaffenweiler: Centaurus, 1996

Pozetta, George E., *Ethnicity and Gender: The Immigrant Women*, New York and London: Garland, 1991

Tribalat, Michèle, *Faire France: Une enquête sur les immigrés et leurs enfants*, Paris: La Découverte, 1995

Genocide

The term *genocide* means the killing of a race, a tribe, or a religious or ethnic group. Genocide as an unfortunate phenomenon of physical extermination of a minority group has remained part and parcel of human history. However, it was only after the genocidal acts committed by the Nazis during World War II that genocide was condemned as an international crime. In 1948 the United Nations adopted the Convention on Prevention and Punishment of the Crime of Genocide, which condemns genocide and prohibits its exercise in times of war and peace. The condemnation of genocide has recently been reaffirmed by the Statute of the International Criminal Court (1998). Although genocide is now universally condemned as an international crime, there are substantial concerns about the continuing exercises of genocidal activities within contemporary societies. Many minorities and groups live under the shadow of extinction; some continue to suffer from physical destruction, partially if not completely.

Overview of the Historical Practices of Genocide

Genocide has been practiced since the beginning of human history. Many tragic instances of genocide could be recounted. These would include the horrifying massacres resulting from Assyrian warfare during the seventh and eighth centuries BCE and the Roman obliteration of the city of Carthage and all its inhabitants. Religion has been used as a weapon for generating intolerance and for the ultimate destruction and genocide of religious minorities. Within the texts of religious scriptures, various forms of genocide of religions minorities are sanctioned. The tragic wars of the medieval period and the Middle Ages, the crusades, and the *Jihads* (Islamic holy wars) translated these religious ordinances to complete and thorough use. Many of the contemporary genocidal conflicts are based around religious supremacy. The process of colonization resulted in the extermination and genocide of indigenous and colonized peoples. More recently, during the nineteenth and twentieth centuries the mechanism of genocide has been practiced on a very wide scale.

Thus, the Armenian genocide conducted by the Ottoman Turks between 1895 and 1896 resulted in the massacres of nearly 200,000 Armenians. The Turks repeated this practice of genocide of the Armenian people during World War I. The rise of nationalism and totalitarian ideologies such as Nazism and Stalinism and the upsurge of racial, religious, and linguistic extremism in the twentieth century generated the wholesale extermination of minorities. The crimes of physical extermination conducted by the Nazis against the Jewish population in Europe were of unparalleled gravity. The tragedies of the Jewish people, of their incarceration in concentration camps, and their mass executions conducted in gas chambers provides a painful legacy to human history. It is estimated that of 8.3 million Jews who remained in Germany after 1939, about 6 million were killed. Describing the processes of genocide, Leo Kuper states that the camps were established after the Nazis experimented with mobile killing squads. He writes "Organized on the model of modern industrial plants, the killing centers processed their victims for slaughter, as if on a conveyor belt they eliminated waste; they gathered in, with careful inventory, their few possessions, their clothes, gold teeth, women's hair, and they regulated the distribution of these relics. And some of the killing centers were combined with slave camps, in which the exploitation of labor was carried to the extreme of expendability, with such leading German firms as I.G. Farben and Krupp, for example, establishing branches in the vicinity of gas chambers (Kuper 1982, 7).

Terminology

As noted above, although the practice of genocide is ancient, the term itself is fairly recent. Raphael Lemkin, a Polish jurist of Jewish origin, is credited with developing the modern principles relating to genocide and indeed for having coined the term itself. In 1933, he presented his ideas based on the protection of groups in a special report to the Fifth International Conference for the Unification of Penal Law. He later elaborated his views in a celebrated work, *Axis Rule in Occupied Europe*, in which he noted that the term genocide is derived partly from the Greek word *genos*, meaning race, tribe, or nation, and partly from the Latin verb *caedere*, which denotes the act of killing. In his view, "By 'genocide' we mean destruction of a nation or of an ethnic group . . . generally speaking, genocide does not necessarily mean the immediate destruction of a nation, or except when accompanied by mass killings of all members of a nation. It is intended rather to signify a coordinated plan of different actions aiming at the destruction of essential foundations of life of national groups. . . . The objective of such a plan would be disintegration of the political and social institutions of culture, language, national feelings, religion, and the economical existence of national groups, and the destruction of personal security, liberty, health, dignity, and even lives of the individual[s] belonging to such groups. Genocide is directed against the national group as an entity, and the actions involved are directed against individuals, not in their individual capacity, but as members of the national group" (Lemkin 1944, 79).

Response to Genocide in the Aftermath of World War II

Lemkin's immediate point of concern, and indeed his primary example, was derived through the survey of Nazi oppression in Europe. While hundreds of thousands of innocent men, women, and children became victims of Nazi genocidal activity, horrors generated by these acts forced the international community to react to these atrocities. Therefore, it is not surprising that one of the major objectives of the allied war against the Nazi and their collaborators was to prevent acts of genocide and to punish those involved in such activities. Nor was it surprising that at the end of World War II, in its very first session, the United Nations General Assembly included in its agenda a resolution entitled "Resolution on the Crime of Genocide" and adopted it as Resolution 96(1) on December 11, 1946. The General Assembly was unanimous in declaring Genocide as a Crime under international law, which the civilized world condemned. The General Assembly Resolution was followed by a legal binding treaty, the Convention on the Prevention and Punishment of the Crime of Genocide. The Convention was adopted on December 11, 1948. The Convention has carried great moral significance although, as we shall see in practice, it has not deterred states or groups from conducting acts of genocide.

Features of the Genocide Convention—Including Substantial and Practical Weaknesses

After the coming into operation of the United Nations Charter (October 1945), the Genocide Convention was the first international treaty to have dealt directly with the issue of the physical protection of groups, and it still remains the primary conventional obligation in this respect. There is no mention of minorities in the treaty, the text of which is directed more at the offenders, an ordinance against offenders rather than a proclamation of the rights of groups. On the other hand, it remains clear that the dynamics of the state structure makes minorities the natural beneficiaries of the Genocide Convention and hence it is meaningful to consider the Convention as part of the charter of minority rights.

The unanimity with which the Convention was adopted and the means in which various provisions have been structured is revealing in many senses. First, the terminology of the Convention makes it clear that the substantive principles enunciated in the treaty are fully recognized, regardless of subsequent ratifications of the treaty. Second, it manifests the view that there is a legal obligation on all states to take action not only to prevent the occurrence of genocide, but also to punish those involved in committing it. The preamble of the Convention, while noting the General Assembly Resolution 96(1) of December 11, 1946, which condemns genocide as a crime under international law, calls for international cooperation to rid mankind of what it terms an "odious scourge." According to Article 1 "The contracting parties confirm that genocide whether committed in time of peace or in time of war, is a crime under international law which they undertake to prevent and to punish." The Article not only confirms the prohibition of genocide in times of war and peace but also attempts to provide for a universal jurisdiction. According to Article 2 of the Convention genocide means any of the following acts committed with intent to destroy, in whole or in part, a national, ethnic, racial, or religious group, as such:

(1) Killing members of the group;
(2) Causing serious bodily or mental harm to members of the group;
(3) Deliberately inflicting on the group conditions of life calculated to bring about its physical destruction in whole or in part;
(4) Imposing measures intended to prevent births within the group;
(5) Forcibly transferring children of the group to another group.

Genocide, according to Article 2, is not only aimed at the total destruction of a group, but also covers its partial destruction. On the other hand, it is also to be noted that none of the characteristics, that is, national, ethnic, racial, or religious, are defined. From the definition as preserved in the Convention, it would appear that whereas categories (a) to (c) can be described as classic cases of "physical genocide," and category (d) as "biological genocide," category (e) is more controversially aimed at reflecting elements of "cultural genocide," the legal validity of which is subject to debate. Indeed as the *travaux préparatoires* (the preparatory documents of the Convention) suggest, the issue of inclusion of "cultural" genocide had proved highly controversial, with several member states arguing vigorously over the risk of political interference in the domestic affairs of states. The lengthy debates conducted on the subject reflect that those in favor of retaining "cultural" genocide within the definition pointed out the imperative nature of preserving the group identity, without which it would seem meaningless to talk about the existence of groups. It was argued that there was an obvious and natural relationship between physical and cultural extermination, making it vital to protect both the physical and the cultural existence of groups. "Cultural" genocide, however, was ultimately excluded from the definition. There were fears on the part of most of the states of converting the legally binding instrument into a mere formula of political rhetoric, of providing a pretext for unnecessary intervention and establishing a grave hurdle in the state-building process on the part of the newly emerging states.

The practicality of incorporating the offence of "cultural" genocide was also brought into question: International and national tribunals would be unable to gauge the accuracy and extent of the allegations brought forth and the governments would not be in a position to adequately safeguard themselves from such charges. State practice has exposed other weaknesses within the provisions of the Genocide Convention as well as the regime of international criminal law. Wanton destruction of groups may also take the form of deportation, mass displacement, and the plantation of an alien population. There have been innumerable contemporary instances where states have employed some or all of the aforesaid means to destroy the existence of the groups. Concern over the omission of these activities has attracted the attention of many commentators. According to Drost, "[t]he five acts of genocide enumerated in Article II [of the Genocide Convention] do not cover all possible ways and means of intentionally destroying a human group as such. Deliberate destruction of human groups may well take the form of deportation or mass displacement, of internment and enslavement with forced labour, of denationalisation by systematic terrorism, torture, inhumane treatment and physical intimidation measures" (Drost, 1959, p. 124).

A further reflection of a serious gap, and closely related to the issue of "cultural genocide," is the absence of a prohibition of demographic changes that could transform the proportion of a population. Indeed, Ermacora's point is a valid one when he observes that "another form of genocide can be the demographic change in a given area. This demographic change does not fall under the acts enumerated . . . in the Convention" (Ermacora, 1983, p. 314). There has also been growing concern that modern-day developments have created newer threats to the survival of certain groups. Activities such as the use of nuclear and chemical explosions, toxic environmental pollution, acid rain, or the destruction of rain forests threaten the existence of peoples in several parts of the world. A serious flaw within the definition of genocide as provided by the Genocide Convention relates to the omission of political groups. Thus, governments have escaped retribution or punishment despite having murdered members of political opposition. The unfortunate effect is that extermination of political opponents such as the Ibos of Nigeria (1966), or communists of Indonesia (1965), or the Bengalis of East Pakistan is not regarded as genocide.

Examples of Modern Practices of Genocide

Notwithstanding the criminalization of genocide, acts of genocide have continued to take place in many parts of the world. Several genocidal conflicts have taken place in the states that have emerged from the residue of colonization. In several states of Asia, Africa, Latin America, and Europe minorities have become victims of genocidal conflicts. The minorities in the postcolonial states of Asian and Africa have suffered the most adverse consequences. Some examples would prove useful. In the modern history of South Asia, the partition of British India and the secession of East Pakistan represent tragedies of enormous magnitude. The partition of August 1947, which created the independent states of India and Pakistan also resulted in the persecution and genocide of religious minorities. It is estimated that nearly 16 million people were uprooted and more than 1 million people lost their lives. The frenzy and madness that this partition brought about took its toll on the religious minorities on either side of the frontier. Innocent Muslims, Hindus, and Sikh civilians became involved in the bloody "holy" wars. While the Muslim minorities left behind in India became an easy prey for the Hindus, equally brutal massacres took place inside the frontier of Pakistan for Hindus and Sikhs. In most instances, angry and violent mobs, infuriated at the (often widely exaggerated) stories of the killings and torture of their coreligionists and the rape, assaults, and other forms of degradation of their women, lost their senses. In a mood of vengeance they went ahead killing, in the most inhuman and brutal manner possible, anyone belonging to the opposing religion. In many parts of India and Pakistan the religious minorities became victims of a campaign of physical extermination and their harrowing stories have filled volumes.

The province of Punjab, which was vivisected in an artificial manner, had left nearly 5 million Hindus and Sikhs in (West Punjab) Pakistan and more than 5 million Muslims in India (Eastern Punjab). Not surprisingly, it became one of the worst affected areas, where nearly half a million people perished, becoming victims of the genocidal conflict. Describing the incidents that took place in Punjab during August–September 1947, Collins and Lapierre state that:

> It would be unique, a cataclysm without precedent, unforeseen in magnitude, unordered in pattern, unreasoned in savagery. For 6 terrible weeks, like the ravages of the medieval plague, a mania for murder would sweep across the face of northern India. There would be no sanctuary from its scourge, no corner free from the contagion of its virus. Half as many Indians would lose their lives in that swift splurge as Americans in four years of combat in World War II ... [t]he new nation [of Pakistan], like its neighbor was about to be engulfed by the most massive migration of human history. The violence racking the Punjab was producing its inevitable result, the result sought by the desperate men behind it on both sides of the border. From one end of the Punjab to the other, taking whatever possessions they could, by car, bicycle, train, mule, bullock, cart and on foot; a terrified people were fleeing their homes towards any promise of safety. They would produce an exchange of population, an out pouring of humanity, on a scale and intensity, never recorded before. By the time the movement reached floodtide in late September, 5 million people, enough to form, if they joined hands, a column stretching from Calcutta to New York, would be uprooted most of them in the brief span of three months. Their unprecedented exodus would create ten times the number of refugees the creation of Israel would produce in the Middle East, three or four times the number of displaced persons who had fled Eastern Europe after the War. It began, for the wretches who composed it, in a million different ways with a million different parting gestures. (1975, pp. 284–294)

There is substantial evidence to suggest that during the East Pakistan civil war (March to December 1971) large-scale violations of human rights including genocide of Hindus were conducted by the West Pakistan military forces. Commenting on the events of the civil war the International Commission of Jurist opine.

The principal features of this ruthless operation were indiscriminate killing of civilians, including women and children and the poorest and weakest members of the community, the attempt to exterminate or drive out of the country a large part of the Hindu population; the arrest, torture, and killing of Awami League activists, students, professional, and businessmen and other potential leaders among the Bengalis, the raping of women, the destruction of villages and towns; and the looting of property. All this was done on a scale difficult to comprehend. There is overwhelming evidence that Hindus were slaughtered and their houses and villages were destroyed simply because they were Hindus. The oft repeated phrase "Hindus are the enemies of the state," as a justification for the killing, does not gainsay the intent to commit genocide; rather does it confirm the intention.

Within Africa, groups such as the Tutsis and Hutus in Rwanda and Burundi, the Ibos in Nigeria, and the indigenous Africans of southern Sudan have become victims of genocide. In 1963, soon after Rwanda won its independence, there was large-scale genocide of the Tutsi minority, resulting in the massacre of approximately 20,000 Tutsi men, women, and children. In neighboring Burundi, the genocidal conflict between Tutsis and Hutus went on for several years, resulting in the massacre of hundreds of thousands. Immediately after 1962, when Burundi gained its political independence, relations began to turn sour between the minority Tutsis and majority Hutus. In 1965, with the failure of a Hutu-backed coup attempt, several thousand Hutus were massacred. This triggered a bloody genocidal conflict resulting in the massacre of thousands of Tutsis, but more significantly of at least 100,000 Hutus. This conflict between the Hutus and Tutsis in both Rwanda and Burundi has gone on and seems almost unending. In Rwanda, during 1994 the orgy of "ethnic cleansing" resurfaced with unprecedented vigor. Thus, in the weeks after the assassination of the President of Rwanda, Juvénal Habyarimana, it is estimated that between 500,000 and 1 million Tutsis became victims of genocide. The 1994 wave of genocide and ethnic cleansing has been the most tragic in the history of the region. The indigenous non-Arabized Africans of southern Sudan have also been victimized ever since the establishment of the independent state of Sudan in 1956. The Arab, relatively prosperous, and the politically and militarily dominant north has persisted with forced cultural, linguistic, and religious assimilation of the southerners and deployed starvation as mechanism to attain the liquidation and virtual extermination of hundreds of thousands of non-Arab indigenous southerners. The rigor and upsurge of religious fundamentalism, which has been characterized in many parts of the world, is typically reflected in the mood of the Khartoum government—religious, racial minorities, and political opponents becoming unfortunate victims of a policy of discrimination, persecution, physical extermination, and genocide. The consequences have been highly tragic for the minority groups of southern Sudan. According to a report produced by the United States Committee for Refugees in December 1998, as a result of the persistent repression, nearly 80 percent of the entire population of southern Sudan has been displaced, with about 2 million people having perished since 1983.

Large-scale genocide of minority groups has taken place in the Middle East and Asia. The Kurds, as a Minority Rights Group report comments, "are the fourth most numerous people in the Middle East. They constitute one of the largest races, indeed nations, in the world today to have been denied an independent State. Whatever the yardstick for national identity, the Kurds measure up to it." However, the atrocities that have been committed against the now-fragmented Kurdish people, and the inadequate international response toward the plight of the Kurds in Iran, Iraq, Turkey, and Syria, remains one of the most unfortunate stories of human history. There is evidence to suggest that the Kurds have been made victims of genocide and that they have been and continue to be persecuted and discriminated in each of the states they inhabit.

In the case of Iraq, atrocities have resulted in the extermination and displacement of hundreds of thousands of innocent men, women, and children. During the "reign of terror" perpetuated by President Saddam Hussein, the Kurds, alongside other minorities such as the Shi'ites and the Marsh Arabs, have become victims of a genocidal campaign. During the presidency of Saddam Hussein, there have been constant attacks made on Kurdish villages. The Kurds received the treatment of belonging to the fifth column during the Iran-Iraq war. In 1987, the Kurds became the victims of chemical attacks by the Iraqi forces. During the month of April, several villages in the Sulaymaniya province and in the Balisan valley were attacked by mustard gas, leaving hundreds of innocent people dead or permanently disabled. Unfortunately, as the Minority Rights Group report goes on to state, "[a]lthough news of these chemical attacks was disseminated internationally, no steps were taken to restrain Iraq. Furthermore, although a United Nations Commission investigated and confirmed the alleged use of chemical weapons by Iraq against Iran, it did not investigate allegations of their use against Iraqi Kurds, since it was not authorized to do so."

On March 17, 1988, the Iraqis used poisonous gas in Halabja, killing at least 5,000 people, with several thousand blinded, wounded, and injured, and there are reports that similar attacks continued thereafter, particularly in the immediate aftermath of the cease-fire with Iran. Some international attention in recent years has been focused on the position of the Kurds in Iraq, which may in itself be due to political reasons. The limited protection that had been provided to the Kurds in the immediate aftermath of the Gulf crisis, through the creation of "safe havens," fell far short of adequate and permanent protection for the Kurdish people. The legal basis under which the limited enforcement action was undertaken is open to question; certainly, it was difficult to accept the view that the Security Council Resolution 688, as such, was sufficient to provide such a firm legal basis. The attempts by the United States and the United Kingdom (the most recent being the bombing campaigns in January 2001) to destroy the military arsenal of Iraq and to protect the no-fly zone do not appear to have resulted in major successes. It must be accepted that the threat to the Kurds will remain as long as President Saddam's regime stays intact. Kurds are also being victimized in Turkey and Iran. The recent initiative on the part of the Turkish government to wipe out the PKK rebels, and the allegations of brutality and violations of the human rights of the Kurdish population, endorse this point.

There is also substantial evidence to support the view that genocide of religious groups has taken place in several countries. The plight of the Bahá'ís in Iran is a chilling reminder of what fundamentalist states can do to dissident religious and ideological groups. Ever since the birth of the Bahá'í faith in Iran during the nineteenth century, its followers have been subjected to discrimination, persecution, and extermination. Iranian clerics, in particular, have been strongly opposed to the existence of Bahá'ísm and have campaigned for the eradication of the Bahá'í faith. After the Iranian Revolution of 1979, the extermination of Bahá'ísm became an official governmental policy—a policy that has continued. The Bahá'ís have been persecuted and castigated as "instruments of Satan," "spies," and followers of devil and of the super powers and their agents. According to Mayer,

> The government, sometimes acting directly and at other times indirectly through allied groups, has carried out a campaign of terror against the Bahá'ís. They were fired from jobs, their property was confiscated, their homes were subject to invasion at any time by persons bent on harassment and plunder in the guise of the investigation of crimes, and they were murdered with impunity. Hundreds of Bahá'ís were arrested, imprisoned and subjected to brutal torture, and the Bahá'í leaders were executed on a variety of trumped-up charges. In addition, their shrines and houses of worship were destroyed and desecrated and all of their associations were forcibly disbanded. (Mayer 1995, p. 136)

Genocidal conflicts have also arisen in many other parts of the world. Although religious cleavages, as in the case of India, Lebanon, Northern Ireland, Cyprus, and the former Yugoslavia, have sometimes been the key element in starting such conflicts, as the situation in Pakistan illustrates, ethnic and linguistic dissonance can be equally destructive. Indeed, as the cases of Tibet, Sri Lanka, and, more recently, the former Yugoslavia and the former Soviet Union illustrate, it is quite possible that a combination of several factors can lead to such genocidal conflicts. Although atrocities have occurred in virtually every republic of the former Yugoslavia, it would appear that the Muslims in Bosnia-Herzegovina have been the prime targets of genocide, victims of Serbian aggression. Exact figures are difficult to obtain and probably are not of extreme significance; although several million have become displaced or have become refugees, uncountable numbers have perished, have been tortured or gang raped, or become victims of the systematic policies of ethnic cleansing. The insignificant role that the United Nations or individuals states have played in the actual physical protection of the minorities creates disillusionment. Critics have also questioned the usefulness of the international laws on the prohibition and punishment of the crime of genocide.

Problems of Punishment and Accountability for the Crime of Genocide

Our survey thus far has revealed the widespread nature of the crime of genocide. The important question therefore that must be addressed is the existence of any effective sanctions and punishment for those conducting this crime of genocide. There are substantial difficulties of accountability and punishment, the main problem being that genocide is most frequently conducted or condoned by governments themselves. Unless and until these governments are removed from power, it is almost impossible to apprehend and punish those who have committed genocide. It is quite possible for genocidal regimes to stay in power for a very long time (as in the case of Iraqi government led by President Saddam Hussein) and defy all laws on the prohibition of genocide. In strict doctrinal terms, international law refuses to allow forcible intervention into another state even when that state is conducting acts of genocide.

After the Cold War, some changes may have been brought about in the international legal perspective in relation to intervention to protect minority groups and to punish those conducting acts of genocide. Thus, after the large-scale violations of human rights, the ethnic cleansing and genocide of ethnic, religious, racial, and religious groups in the former Yugoslavia and Rwanda, steps were undertaken to punish those involved in genocide. The tragic events that unfolded at the end of the Cold War also highlighted the necessity of establishing an international criminal court to try and to punish criminals instigating and conducting genocide and crime against humanity. In the absence of a permanent international court, the United Nations Security Council, acting under Chapter VII of the United Nations Charter, in its Resolution 827 (1993) and Resolution 955 (1994), established the ad hoc tribunals for former Yugoslavia and Rwanda.

These Tribunals have conducted several trials and convicted several individuals for the crime of genocide. However, the aforementioned tribunals have a limited mandate. They are not established on a permanent basis, nor can they investigate crimes committed outside the territories of the former Yugoslavia and Rwanda. To be able to try and to punish all those conducting heinous crimes against humanity and genocide anywhere in the world, it is vital to have an international criminal court. It is positive to note that after decades of struggle and hesitancy, the international community has also been able to reach an agreement on the establishment of an international criminal court. In July 1998, a statute for the international criminal court was adopted in Rome. The court would be able to try individuals for acts of genocide and crimes against humanity. The statute also set up mechanisms for the apprehension, trial, and punishment for those found guilty of the offense of genocide. The statute of the court is still a considerable distance away from becoming operational, although it is anticipated that the eventual establishment of a permanent international court would be a source of deterrence for all those intending to commit genocide.

JAVAID REHMAN

See also **India; Kurds; Pakistan; Rwanda; Sikhs; Yugoslavia**

Further Reading

Collins, Larry, and Dominique Lapierre, *Freedom at Midnight*, London: Collins, 1975

Drost, Pieter, *Crimes of State*, Leiden: Sijthoff, 1959

Ermacora, Felix, "The Protection of Minorities Before the United Nations," *Recueil des Cours de l'Académie de Droit International*, 182, no. IV (1983)

Kuper, Leo, *International Action against Genocide*, London: Minority Rights Group, 1982

Kuper, Leo, *The Prevention of Genocide*, New Haven: Yale University Press, 1985

Lemkin, Raphael, *Axis Rule in Occupied Europe*, Washington: Carnegie Endowment for International Peace, 1944

McDowall, David, *The Kurds*, London: Minority Rights Group, 1991

Mayer, Ann Elizabeth, *Islam and Human Rights: Tradition and Politics*, Boulder, Colorado: Westview Press, 1995

Rehman, Javaid, *The Weakness in the International Protection of Minority Rights*, The Hague: Kluwer Law International, 2000

Thornberry, Patrick, *International Law and the Rights of Minorities*, Oxford: Clarendon Press, 1991

Whitaker, Ben, *Revised and Updated Report on the Question of the Prevention and Punishment of the Crime of Genocide*, New York: United Nations, U.N. Document E/CN.4/Sub.2/1985/6

Georgia

Capsule Summary

Location: southwestern Asia, bordering the Black Sea, between Turkey and Russia
Total Population: 4,934,413 (July 2003)
Language: Georgian; main minority languages and dialects include Abkhaz, Armenian, Azeri, Ossetian, Russian, Batsbi, Kurd, Megrel, Svan, and Laz
Religions: predominantly Orthodox Christian (83.9%), Sunni and Shiya Muslim (9.9%), Armenian-Gregorian (5.7%), Yezid (a unique dualist religion practiced by some ethnic Kurds), also Catholic, Baptist, and other smaller Christian groups

Georgia is a small country (occupying an area of approximately 27,000 square miles or about 69,929.68 square kilometers) located mainly to the south of the Greater Caucasus ridge, and to the east of the Black Sea. It borders Russia to the north, Azerbaijan to the east, and Armenia and Turkey to the south. Its capital is Tbilisi, a city with approximately 1.3 million people, located on both sides of the river Mtkvari (or Kura).

Georgia is a presidential republic, headed by a directly elected president; its parliament is made up of 150 deputies elected from party lists under a proportional system and 85 lawmakers elected from single-mandate constituencies under a majority system.

The country reestablished its sovereignty in 1991, and subsequently two of its three Soviet-time autonomies—Abkhazia and South Ossetia—unilaterally declared independence and are not currently under control of the central government in Tbilisi, although their sovereignty is not recognized by any international party. In addition to the Ajara Autonomous republic, Georgia is divided into 11 regions (*mkhare*) further subdivided into up to 70 smaller districts, or *rayons*.

Georgia is a truly multiethnic country, with many ethnicities counting it as their home. The Georgians are the biggest ethnic group living in Georgia, comprising up to 83 percent of the country's population. The Georgian language, together with Megrel (Mingrelian), Svan, and Laz, make up the Kartvelian linguistic group, and its relation with other language families of neighboring ethnicities, such as Indo-European, Semitic, North-Caucasian, and Altaic, is a subject of various scientific speculations. In a unique manner, some of the ethnic subgroups of Georgians speak

499

languages that are distinct from Georgian proper, such as Megrel and Svan, and unlike the Orthodox Christian majority, some, such as the Ajarians, belong to the Sunni Muslim faith but preserve their common ethnic identity as Georgians.

Other ethnic minorities in Georgia include the Abkhaz, mainly populating the former Autommnomous Soviet Republic of Abkhazia, with Sukhumi as the capital city. Other Abkhaz have either recently emigrated to Russia, or are the descendents of the nineteenth century *muhajirs*, who emigrated to the Ottoman Empire after the Russian conquest of the Caucasus and still live predominantly in Turkey.

The second biggest ethnic minority in Georgia is Armenians (about 6 percent), who are either descendent of Armenian groups historically living in Georgia or who come from Armenians resettled by the Russian Empire in the nineteenth century from Turkey and Iran through population exchange agreements. Armenians live predominantly in the southern province of Samtskhe-Javakheti, the city of Tbilisi, and in Abkhazia.

Azeris make another (about 6 percent) ethnic community, inhabiting predominantly eastern regions of Georgia (Marneuli, Bolnisi, and Dmanisi rayons). Ossetians make up the majority of the former Soviet South Ossetian autonomy, with the capital in Tskhinvali, although many Ossetians also live in other parts of Georgia as well as in the Russia's Autonomous Republic of North Ossetia—Alania. Other ethnic groups include Greeks (both Turkic-speaking and Greek-speaking) and Russians (including descendents of religious dissidents—Molokans and Duhobors) who resettled to southern Georgia from Russia in the nineteenth century. There are smaller numbers of Kurds, Assyrians, Batsbis (a small endemic group speaking a unique language related to Chechen), Jews (Sefardic Jews who resettled to Georgia 26 centuries ago and Ashkenazi Jews who came much later; now both groups are frequently emigrating to Israel), Ukrainians, Lezgins, Chechens, and Assyrians.

Ethnic Georgians, apart from Georgia, live in large numbers in several neighboring countries. In Turkey, traditionally there are many Muslim *Gurji* (Georgians in Turkish) and ethnically related Laz in the areas east of the Black Sea port of Trabzon, and also in big cities such as Istanbul and Ankara. There is a traditional community of both Christian and Muslim *Inghilo-*Georgians in west Azerbaijan. The majority of ethnic Georgians in Iran are the descendants of Georgians deported in the early seventeenth century by Shah Abbas to the areas around the ancient capital Isfahan.

There is an increasing number of Georgians in Russia, where in addition to traditional diaspora there was significant inflow of the new economic emigration, counting more than half a million. There are also growing Georgian communities in the United States and in Western Europe (France, Germany, and the Netherlands), where the first wave of Georgian emigration arrived after the Soviet takeover of Georgia in 1921.

History

Georgia derives its unique cultural and political tradition from early ancient times. Beginning with the early Georgian states of Egrisi (or Colchis to the ancient Greeks), Georgia was a battlefield for the continuous rivalry of Eastern and Western powers, such as Persia and the Roman Empire, Byzantium, Arabs, Turks, Mongols, and finally the Russians who succeeded in annexing Georgia in 1801.

Christianity was adopted in Georgia in 334 CE , under King Mirian III of Kartli-Iberia; the Georgian alphabet was created then for translating holy texts. The first Georgian inscriptions appeared in Jerusalem in the fifth century, followed soon after by the first known literary text, the *Martyrdom of St. Shushanik.* The best known literary text in Georgian—*The Knight in Panther's Skin* by Shota Rustaveli—was created under the queen of the united Georgian kingdom at the peak of its strength in the beginning of the thirteenth century.

In the aftermath of the October revolution of 1917 in Russia, the Georgian Democratic Republic briefly acquired independence under Social-Democratic (Menshevik) rule until February 25, 1921, when the Red Army occupied Tbilisi and established the Georgian Soviet Socialist Republic. For 70 years Georgia was ruled from Moscow, but then in 1991, with dissolution of the Soviet Union, once again declared independence and elected president Zviad Gamsakhurdia.

The first years of independence appeared to be extremely hard for the Georgian people. Nationalist rhetoric and haphazard policies of President Gamsakhurdia led to interethnic tensions, secessionist conflict in South Ossetia, public dissatisfaction, and in the beginning of 1992, his ousting. Successors formed military council to rule the country but failed to avoid disorder and economic crisis. This was followed by the secessionist conflict in Abkhazia and the civil war. Several hundred thousand refugees from the conflict regions further aggravated the political and economic crisis.

Eduard Shevardnadze, who was invited to Georgia by the victorious Military Council in 1992, gradually took control into his own hands and from 1995—when he was elected to be the president of the country—succeeded in achieving political stabilization and economic growth, which was disrupted, however, during the Asian economic crisis of 1997–1998. Since that time Georgian political and economic reform has been hindered in its development by poor governance, overwhelming corruption, and unresolved conflicts in Abkhazia and South Ossetia.

In November 2003, after the opposition groups led by young Mikhail Saakashvili, the leader of the National Movement, were able to channel the general dissatisfaction of the population with failing economic conditions and the rigged parliamentary elections, mass protest led to Shevardnadze's resignation and the peaceful change of power dubbed the "revolution of roses." On January 4, 2004, Saakashvili got elected by a landslide majority of vote to become the new president of Georgia.

Georgian Society

Georgia's economy, strongly entangled with the Soviet economic system, used to be centered on production of tea and wine and on strong mining (manganese, arsenic, and mineral water) and industry. Rich natural resources and excellent sea resorts provided Georgia with relative economic prosperity in Soviet times. With independence, Georgia lost the markets for its production and the necessary cheap energy such as electric power. Civil wars and general disorder followed and undue privatization schemes caused total disruption of the country's economy, a catastrophic fall in its GDP, huge foreign dept that equals almost half of the GDP, and the impoverishment of the population. According to official (and the World Bank's) estimates, currently approximately 52 percent of the population lives below the poverty line, and the per-capita GDP is about US$3200. In 2003, the International Monetary Fund suspended its programs in Georgia due to the slowdown of reform.

Since 2001 the Georgian economy has restarted its growth, strongly boosted by big-scale investment projects. A highly symbolic event on May 23, 2003, was the launching of the construction of the Georgian stretch of the giant Baku-Tbilisi-Ceyhan oil pipeline, to be followed shortly afterward by the Baku-Erzurum gas pipeline. Their completion in two to three years will help Georgia to escape its dependence on Russian energy supplies—often used as political leverage. Currently all international assistance programs are also resuming operation.

While Shevardnadze's peaceful resignation and Saakashvili's election as Georgia's president brought in strong Western support and opened many new opportunities, there are many challenges ahead. Parliamentary elections are to be held anew on March 28, 2004, and may lead to the complete dominance of the ruling block—the National Movement and the United Democrats. Still, notwithstanding increasing American and European assistance, it will be very difficult to fulfill many promises given to the population, including quick economic improvement and full uprooting of corruption, withdrawal of Russia's military bases, and particularly reestablishment of Georgia's territorial integrity. At the same time, Georgia's firm orientation toward integration with European structures and NATO caused an adverse reaction from Russia, which uses its influence with the secessionist autonomies to create additional troubles for the still weak Georgian state.

In another development, on October 14, 2002, President Shevardnadze and Catholicos-Patriarch of the Georgian Orthodox Church, Ilia II, signed a Constitutional Agreement between the State and the Georgian Orthodox Church. Nonetheless, religious life in the country is far from harmonious. Although most believers in Georgia belong to the Orthodox Church, violence by extremist groups of orthodox zealots toward confessional minorities such as Evangelical Baptists, Jehovahís Witnesses, and Pentecostals marred the tradition of religious tolerance and caused outcry from human rights and religious freedom watchdogs from all over the world.

Georgian national culture strongly values and respects women, and a rude or indiscreet attitude toward women is strongly condemned. Women are believed to have the prevailing right to custody of children in the case of divorce. There is no explicit division of labor by gender, and there is hardly any profession without women involved. Still, top-level political or business careers are less accessible for a woman, and one can find only a few in the government or in the parliament. Males more often dominate both public and family life, while most housework is the responsibility of women. The situation is gradually changing, and traditional stereotypes of gender-defined social roles are losing authority.

Behavioral stereotypes are changing in many areas. With the "revolution of roses" and the younger generation of politicians coming forward, there is an amazing increase in the readiness for civil participation, in optimism, self-confidence, pro-democracy, and pro-Western orientation of the population. If this trend is not reversed, democracy will mature in Georgia, not so much through formal transformation and structural change as much as through liberation of the human mind.

GEORGE TARKHAN-MOURAVI

Further Reading

Allen, W.E.D., *A History of the Georgian People from the Beginning down to the Russian Conquest in the 19th Century*, London: Kegan Paul, 1932; New York: Barnes & Noble, 1971

Charachidzé, Géorges, *Le Système Religieux de la Géorgie Païenne*, Paris: Maspero, 1969

Gerber, Jürgen, *Georgien: Nationale Opposition und kommunistische Herrschaft seit 1956* (Bundesinstitut für ostwissenschaftliche und internationale Studien, Köln, Band 32), Baden-Baden: Nomos, 1997

Jones, Stephen F. (alias C.J. Peters), "The Georgian Orthodox Church," in *Eastern Christianity and Politics in the Twentieth Century*, edited by Pedro Ramet, Durham: Duke University Press, 1988

Lang, David M., *The Georgians* (Ancient Peoples and Places, 51), London: Thomas and Hudson, 1966

Nodia, Ghia, *Political Turmoil in Georgia and the Ethnic Policies of Zviad Gamsakhurdia*, in *Contested Borders in the Caucasus*, edited by Bruno Coppiters, Brussels: VUB University Press, 1996

Rayfield, Donald, *The Literature of Georgia: A History* (Caucasus World Series), London: Routledge-Curzon, 2000

Salia, Kalistrat, *History of the Georgian Nation* (Trans. Katharine Vivian), Paris: Acadmie Franaise, 2nd edition, 1983

Sumbadze, N., and G. Tarkhan-Mouravi, *Political Change and Public Opinion in Georgia: 2002–2003*, Tbilisi: IPS, 2004

Suny, Ronald G., *The Making of the Georgian Nation*, Bloomington: Indiana University Press, 1988 and 1994; London: Tauris, 1991

Tamarati, M., *L'Èglise Géorgienne des Origines Jusqau nos Jours*, Rome, 1910

Toumanoff, Cyril, *Studies in Christian Caucasus History*, Georgetown: Georgetown University Press, 1963

Germans

Capsule Summary

Location: northern Europe, western Europe, central Europe, eastern Europe, and Asia; emigrant communities in North and Latin America, Oceania, and Africa

Total Population: a majority in Germany, 75 million; a minority outside Germany, approximately 2.4–3.0 million in 27 different European and Asian states (Denmark, Belgium, France, Italy, Poland, Czech Republic, Slovak Republic, Hungary, Slovenia, Croatia, Bosnia-Hercegovina, Yugoslavia, Belarus, Ukraine, Estonia, Latvia, Lithuania, Russian Federation, Kazakhstan, Kyrgyzstan, Turkmenistan, Uzbekistan, Tajikistan, Moldova, Georgia, Azerbajdzhan, Armenia). Unknown numbers in other parts of the world, but estimated at 10–12 million with German ancestry. A total of 3.3–4.4 million in 17 countries outside Europe and Asia are German-speaking (Argentina, Australia, Belize, Brazil, Canada, Chile, Columbia, Ecuador, Israel, Mexico, Namibia, Paraguay, Peru, South Africa, Uruguay, United States, and Venezuela)

Languages: German; several German minorities are bilingual or predominantly speakers of majority languages, for example, Russian, Hungarian, and Polish. Austrians also speak German, but are no longer considered to be ethnic Germans. German-speaking Swiss nationals are not considered to be German.

Religions: Catholic, Lutheran, Baptist, Mennonite, other

The Germans are an ethnic group living predominantly in the nation-state Germany in central Europe, where they form the majority population of 91.1 percent. Germans also live as national minorities in western, northern, central, and eastern Europe as well as Asia. Germany recognizes ethnic Germans in Denmark and 23 eastern European and Asian states as German minorities, to whom it obligates itself with support. Further, Germans are living in Belgium, France (Alsace and Lorraine), and Italy (South Tyrol and 11 so-called language islands). These German minorities are, however, not officially recognized as kin-minorities by Germany, although nongovernment organizations in Germany affiliate themselves with these and other German-speaking communities in and outside Europe.

The majority population of Austria (population, 8,136,000; Austrians, 99 percent) is also German-speaking. The same applies to the German-speakers in Switzerland (total population, 7,268,000; German-speakers, 65 percent). Historically, the Austrians have been mostly included as Germans. However, after 1945 a distinct and separate Austrian ethnicity has developed, although major parts of Austria's population still might consider themselves as Germans. Some German minorities are historically affiliated to the Austrian culture and dialect. Thus, some minorities actually do identify themselves with two kin-states, Germany and Austria. In Russia, some German groups identify with Switzerland, describing themselves as Russian Swiss-Germans. The German South Tyrolese are affiliated with Austria, although some extremist groups advocate a pan-German concept of ethnicity.

The German language is of Indo-European origin and belongs to the west-Germanic group along with Dutch, Frisian, and English. Although its standard norm is in common and used by all German minority communities in teaching and media, a variety of dialects are used on a day-to-day basis. However, assimilation is progressive, and in most German minorities in central and eastern Europe, German is turning into a symbolic language, replaced by majority dialects and languages. Exceptions are the Germans in South Tyrol and Romania. Ethnic revival among the Germans in eastern Europe and the post-Soviet states include a linguistic revival as well, which is supported by language courses and improved teaching facilities. However, language courses in the former Soviet Union are often used to gain language skills sufficient to apply for migration permits with Germany's authorities.

German-speaking individuals and communities with a gross number of 3.3–4.4 million people live in other parts of the world. Although, in many cases, they do form German-speaking communities and consider themselves as at least hyphenated Germans, these groups are not normally considered minorities. These German-speaking individuals and groups have been formed due to migration over centuries, especially in the 1800s and 1900s. In some cases, however, religious German-speaking minorities have moved as communities from state to state, finally arriving at their present-day location. This is, for instance, the case for German-speaking Mennonite, Baptist, and Hutterian communities in the Americas; some of them originally migrated from central Europe to Russia, eventually around 1900 migrating further to North and South America.

History

Germans became ethnic minorities due to two processes: migration and border revisions. With the German eastward expansion in the late Middle Ages

(Ostsiedlung), Germans migrated into east central Europe, settling in the Baltics, Prussia, and parts of present-day Poland. Around 1200, German settlers arrived in Transylvania. Later, German groups migrated and settled along the river Danube. In the Middle Ages, Germans traders and merchants settled in Russian cities. From the 1760s, Russia invited German (and other) settlers to migrate to Russia, eventually creating so-called German colonies along the river Volga, the Ukraine, and later even the Caucasus, the Urals, and Siberia. Germans also settled in the Alpine area and in other regions that, for 1,000 years, were parts of the German-Roman Empire. German culture also gained influence in neighboring states.

Border revisions took place on several occasions in modern history. After World War I, Germans became minorities with the dissolution of Austria-Hungary and the German Empire. This led to the creation of new German minorities in most central European states: Poland, Czechoslovakia, Hungary, Yugoslavia, Ukraine, and parts of Romania. In some cases, German groups became new minorities within states, which traditionally have had German minority groups (for instance, Ukraine and Romania). The Treaty of St. Germain/Paris provided that South Tyrol should become incorporated into Italy, including the majority population of Germans. In three cases, German minorities emerged due to the outcome of plebiscites according to the Versailles Peace Treaty of 1919: In the region of Schleswig two plebiscites conducted in February and March 1920 led to the partition of the area, incorporating a German minority in Denmark. In Upper Silesia, a plebiscite in 1921 led to the partition of the region, creating minorities on both sides of the new borderline. Finally, a registration of intention took place in the hitherto German districts of Eupen and Malmedy, which were incorporated into Belgium after 1918. Only a few Germans voted for returning the area to Germany. A small German-Austrian minority was created in Hungary due to a plebiscite on the Austrian-Hungarian border in the Burgenland in 1921. Alsace and Lorraine (Elsass-Lothringen) were disputed between France and Germany for centuries. In 1871, the area was incorporated into the new German Empire. In 1919 it was reunited with France, but with the German occupation of France, Alsace-Lorraine was ceded to Germany. After 1945, when the region was retroceded to France, Germany declined any official recognition of a German minority in France.

During the Nazi era, several border revisions took place in central Europe, incorporating Austria, Slovenia, the Sudetenland, and eventually the Czech lands and Poland into Germany. From the late 1930s, German minorities were resettled in the course of population transfers from their traditional homelands in the Baltic states, Russia, Italy, and the Balkans and within the borders of Nazi Greater Germany. In former parts of Poland, ethnic Germans were resettled in areas from where the previous Polish and Jewish population was deported, and, in the case of the Jews, became subject to genocide. The ethnic Germans were elements in Nazi politics aiming at a Germanification of central and eastern Europe. Following the defeat of Germany in May 1945, large population transfers, deportations, and expulsions took place, eventually forcing 12–14 million ethnic Germans to migrate west. Some 200,000 Germans from Hungary, Yugoslavia, Romania, and Poland were deported as forced labor to the Soviet Union, the last deportees returning in 1952. In 1941 and in the following years, Stalin's Soviet Union deported most ethnic Germans (so-called Soviet Germans) beyond the Urals where they were placed in fenced special settlements and in Gulags, and eventually resettling them in central Asia and Siberia. Rehabilitation eventually was granted in several stages from 1955 through the 1990s.

After 1945, the status of German minorities in western Europe was changed. West Germany no longer acted as a kin-state for ethnic or linguistic German minorities in Belgium, France, and Italy. Austria became a kin-state of the Germans in South Tyrol, and autonomous structures with regional self-government eventually were established in South Tyrol. The situation of the German-speaking population in Belgium was determined by the federalization of the Belgian state. A German-language region was established in 1963 in the Eupen-Malmedy region. The German-speaking community in Belgium has its center in Eupen. Only the Germans in Denmark differed from this general trend of disengagement. West Germany, and its state of Schleswig-Holstein, took up an active part as a kin-state for this group. The rights of the Germans in Denmark were finally guaranteed with the Copenhagen Declaration of March 1955.

Migrations

After 1945, a constant flow of ethnic German migrations took place, eventually bringing several hundreds of thousands of Germans to primarily West Germany, whereas only a relatively small number of ethnic Germans went to East Germany. From 1987, the Soviet Union under Gorbachev allowed almost free emigration of ethnic Germans and other ethnic/religious groups. With the dissolution of the communist regimes in central Europe, massive migration movements manifested themselves from especially Poland and Romania, effectively draining the German minorities. Between 1950 and 2000, more than 4.1 million ethnic Germans migrated to Germany—more than 3 million migrating from 1980 to 2000. Almost 1.5 million ethnic Germans came from Poland. Some 2 million, or almost half of all emigrants, came from the former Soviet Union, 430,000 from Romania, more than 100,000 from former Czechoslovakia, about 20,000 from Hungary, and some 90,000 from former Yugoslavia. In spite of these massive migration waves, considerable German minorities still exist in most of these countries. Thus, migration probably will continue in the future, especially from the post-Soviet states with some 100,000 migrants annually. However, it is estimated that in recent years more than two-thirds of these post-Soviet Germans enter Germany because of family ties to ethnic Germans, not because of their own ethnicity. The motives for emigration were multifarious. Up to the 1980s, discrimination, stigmatization, and fear of assimilation were key motives. Later, the search for welfare and the good life in Germany became more important. Ongoing nationality conflicts, crime, social, economic, or ecological disasters in the former Soviet Union must also be considered as important motives for the perpetual migrations.

German Minorities

Germans are living as national or linguistic minorities in 27 European and Asian states. In Poland, up to 800,000 ethnic Germans might still be found. The largest concentrations live in Upper Silesia. Some 40,000 live in former East Prussia (Masuria) and Gdansk, whereas the remainder are scattered. Some 300,000 are enlisted members of the main cultural association of the German minorities. Polish Germans are represented in the state parliament, Sejm, and at the regional and local level as well. The German associations in the Czech Republic estimate the number of ethnic Germans in the country today to be around 100,000 persons. In the last census of 1991, only some 49,000 identified as Germans. In Slovakia, the association of Carpathian Germans estimate that the German minority included some 10,000–15,000 individuals. However, only 6,000 identified themselves as Germans in the last census of 1991.

According to official estimates adopted by the German minority itself, some 200,000–220,000 ethnic Germans are still living in Hungary. This figure has been used for decades and has not changed due to an extremely limited emigration, assimilation, increasing, or decreasing birth rates. A sincere estimate might put the number around 100,000 Germans, essentially all of them fully integrated into Hungarian society and with no wish to leave the country. Today, only some 80,000 ethnic Germans can be found in Romania, down from 359,000 in the 1977 census and shrinking from 119,500 identifying as Germans in the 1992 census. The Germans have traditionally settled in distinct areas with separate ethnic German identities. Today, some 25,000 Germans are living in Transylvania, 30,000 in the Banat region, 10,000 in Sathmar, 2,000 in Bukovina, and finally 10,000 in the rest of Romania. Some of the Germans in especially the Banat affiliate themselves with Austria as their kin-state. An unknown number of Germans are still living in Slovenia. The figure might be estimated at a total of about 1,000–2,000. Most of them are living on the Austrian border and in Maribor; some 100 Germans live in western Slovenia. The Slovenian Germans, however, mostly identify with Austria as a kin-state, reducing Germany's importance as a kin-state to a rather insignificant size. The number of Germans still living in Croatia is estimated to be about 5,000–7,000 individuals, mostly in eastern Slavonia around Osijek, and in the capital of Zagreb. In Yugoslavia, in the region of Voivodina, some 4,000 ethnic Germans are living concentrated in, and in the surroundings of, Novi Sad and Subotica.

Bosnia and Herzegovina

In the states of the former Soviet Union, it is estimated that up to 1.1–1.2 million ethnic Germans are still living in communities scattered all over Eurasia. The activist organizations of the former Soviet Germans especially in the Russian Federation, however, do claim far larger numbers and talk about at least 2 million ethnic Germans remaining in a unspecified number of communities. The largest communities are to be found in the Russian Federation, where approximately 800,000 were living in the late 1990s. Some German population concentrations can be found in western Siberia. Here, two German national districts (*rayony*) were established in 1991 and 1992 in Halbstadt in the Altai Region and in Asowo in the Omsk district. Further concentrations can be found in the regions Novosibirsk

and Tomsk. Other concentrations of German population are located in several parts of Russia, including the region of Leningrad. It is estimated that at least 5,000 ethnic Germans from other parts of the former Soviet Union have settled in the Kaliningrad region on the Baltic Sea, which up to 1945 was a part of Germany's East Prussia. A limited number of ethnic Germans are living near the interwar autonomous German Volga Republic, which was founded as an autonomous workers' commune in 1918, later became a republic, and finally was dissolved after the banishment and deportation of the Volga Germans in 1914 to the Trans-Urals. The recreation of the Volga Republic has high priority among the Russian Germans, but this ambition, in spite of promises and announcements by former Russian president Boris Yeltsin, does not seem to have any realistic chance of implementation. The Russian government instead has created a national-cultural nonterritorial autonomy for the Russian Germans. In January 1998, the "Federal National-Cultural Autonomy of the Russian Germans" was officially registered by the authorities of the Russian Federation as the representative nonterritorial autonomous body of the Russian Germans.

In the Central Asian republic of Kazakhstan, there are currently some 240,000 ethnic Germans, especially in the northern parts of the country in strongholds of the Russian populations. Many of the Kazakh Germans wish to migrate to Germany or to migrate to the autonomous German districts in Russian Siberia. In the Ukraine some 40,000 ethnic Germans are living; many have resettled to the regions of Odessa and Trans-Carpathia. In Kyrgyzstan less than 20,000 ethnic Germans are still living, down from some 100,000 in 1989. Due to a strong emigration movement from this republic, it will not be long before the German minority is dissolved. In Tajikistan only some 2,000 ethnic Germans are left, and emigration still takes place. In Turkmenistan some 3,500 ethnic Germans identified themselves as such in the last census in 1996, but due to ongoing emigration the actual number has shrunk even more. According to official data available in Uzbekistan, some 20,000 ethnic Germans make up the German minority in this country. Most of these Germans want to migrate to Germany.

Only a small German minority is found in Belarus, where some 3,000–4,000 ethnic Germans are living, scattered all over the country. In Armenia, only a few Germans are left; in Azerbajdzhan some 1,000 Germans are living still, but have mostly assimilated themselves to the more heavily populated Russian community in this country. In Georgia, some 2,000 Germans are remaining. In Moldova, the German minority numbers about 7,500 individuals, most of them unable to speak German at all. In the Baltic states, a total of 14,000–16,000 ethnic Germans can be found: In Estonia, some 2,000 are living, mostly Russian German immigrants, and only 15 percent of them hold an Estonian passport. In Latvia, the German minority today numbers about 4,000 people, half of them Russian German immigrants, and some 900 so-called Baltic Germans who speak Latvian are Latvian citizens and have integrated and adapted to Latvian society. The largest German minority in the Baltic region lives in Lithuania. Here, a total of 8,000 ethnic Germans are living, fully integrated in the Lithuanian society and mostly Lithuanian citizens as well. It must be noted that in the case of the former Soviet Union, these figures only apply to the estimated ethnic German population in each state mentioned. This does not imply that there is only one German ethnic minority in each of these countries. The actual number of German minorities is much higher.

German communities are also found in northern and western Europe: In Denmark, in the southern part of the peninsula of Jutland, a German minority that numbers 12,000–20,000 people has been living since the Danish-German border in this area was determined based on a plebiscite in 1920. They form an organized minority with own organizations, institutions, and educational facilities funded by both Denmark and Germany. In a European context, both states have described the minority regulations in the Danish-German border region with national minorities on both sides as a model case. In Belgium, German-speaking inhabitants live in the Eupen, Malmedy, and St. Vith districts bordering Germany, in the area around the city of Montzen/Welkenraedt, and in the district of Arlon bordering Luxembourg. In the so-called German-language community of eastern Belgium, some 69,000 German-speakers live. Here, German is an official language. Another 20,000–25,000 German-speakers live in the two other areas. German is the third official language of Belgium, next to Dutch and French.

In France, German dialect-speakers live in Alsace and Lorraine. Their ethnic affiliation is unclear; France recognizes no German minority, and Germany does not recognize any of the indigenous German-speakers in France as a German kin-minority. Exact numbers are unknown, but it is estimated that up to half of the 400,000 inhabitants of Lorraine are familiar with the German dialect Frankish spoken there, whereas up to

60 percent of the 1,625,000 inhabitants of Alsace have skills in the region's dialect Alsatian (Elsaesserdeutsch). Thus, some 1.1–1.2 million persons might speak German. However, it is unclear whether all of these consider themselves as ethnic Germans as well—probably not. A rather small militant group claims a German ethnicity. In Italy, in the autonomous province of South Tyrol, some 287,000 ethnic Germans make up a majority of 63 percent of the region's 460,000 inhabitants. The German population predominantly affiliates itself with Austria. Austria took up a guardian role for the South Tyrolese after 1945. Further, a few thousand Germans are scattered over at least 11 linguistic German islands in northern Italy between the Italian-French and the Italian-Austrian-Slovene border. Some of these minor groups are linguistically related to the Swiss canton of Wallis, others to Bavarian dialects.

Present Day Status

After the upheavals of 1989–1991, West Germany's (and, from 1990, Germany's) foreign policy aimed at guaranteeing and safeguarding the rights of the German minorities in eastern Europe and Asia. This eventually led to a number of bilateral state treaties between Germany and the Soviet Union/post-Soviet States, Poland, Hungary, Czechoslovakia (eventually the Czech Republic and the Slovak Republic), and Romania, regulating the status and situation of the German minorities. The internationalization of minority issues within the framework of the Council of Europe and the Organization for Security and Cooperation in Europe, and the development of international legal instruments, was another important trend in this respect. Germany's main objective is to enable the ethnic Germans to stay in their traditional countries of settlement, and, consequently, limit the number of people migrating to Germany. Germany provided funding and support for education, media, culture, health, small businesses, and local government for German minorities. Finally, Germany supports the development of democratic structures among the German minorities.

Germans in Other Parts of the World

Germans, German-speaking people, or people of German ancestry can also be found in other parts of the world. Although no specific and reliable number is known, it is estimated by the pan-German VDA-Verein für Deutsche Kulturbeziehungen im Ausland that 14–15 million Germans live worldwide outside of Germany, Austria, and Switzerland. If the ethnic

Germans in Asia and Europe are subtracted, some 10–12 million Germans or descendants of Germans or hyphenated Germans remain. Most of them live in the Americas, followed by Africa and Oceania. However, while these Germans often do form communities, they do have the characteristics of most minority populations. They have mostly assimilated voluntarily, although German communities can still be found, and strong interests in the homeland or land of the ancestors is still strong, influencing the individual's identity as well. Their origin and history, however, does not legitimize a nondifferentiated description. Although they all speak German or German dialects and cherish German traditions, they do not conform to any perceived single genre or definition of "Germanness." Some communities are German-speaking, but identify themselves primarily as religious communities rather than national minorities.

Germans left central Europe over several centuries, starting in the 1600s and 1700s, but especially in the course of the mass migrations in the 1800s and early 1900s. After World War II several hundred thousand Germans emigrated as well. Thus, the point of emigration and the circumstances are different. Many left for religious reasons, others looking for a brighter future, others because of political interest. A fourth group wanted to leave their previous identity behind, looking for a stock in the new homelands as mainstream citizens of the United States, Canada, or Australia. After World War II, many Nazi's escaped to South America, joining preexisting German communities. Thus, several million ethnic Germans migrated over the last 200 years. For instance, in the period 1820–1930 some 5.9 million Germans migrated to the United States, mostly settling and eventually assimilating in the cities of New York, Chicago, and Milwaukee, others in rural areas in the Midwest, Northeast, and New England. In 1996, 523,000 persons born in Germany lived in the United States.

In1989, up to 4.4 million German-speakers lived in 17 states outside Europe and Asia. The largest numbers of German-speaking people are found in the United States (1.6 million spoke German at home in 1980), Brazil (estimates range from 500,000 to 1.5 million),

Canada (in 1986, some 439,000 were German native-speakers, whereas 113,000 spoke German at home), and Argentina (about 300,000). Medium-size groups of German-speakers lived in Paraguay (125,000 in 1985), Australia (in 1986, about 110,000 spoke German at home), Israel (in 1978, about 96,000 Jews from Germany and Austria), and Mexico (50,000–60,000). Small groups are found in South Africa (41,000 in 1986), Chile (20,000–35,000), Venezuela (25,000), Namibia (20,000), Columbia (10,000–12,000 in 1988), Uruguay (8,000–9,000 in 1979), Peru (4,500), Belize (3,300), and Ecuador (3,000).

JØRGEN KÜHL

See also **Argentina; Armenia; Australia; Austria; Azerbaijan; Belarus; Belgium; Belize; Bosnia and Herzegovina; Brazil; Canada; Chile; Colombia; Croatia; Czech Republic; Denmark; Ecuador; Estonia; Europeans; France; Georgia; Germany; Hungary; Israel; Kazakhstan; Kyrgyzstan; Latvia; Lithuania; Mexico; Moldova; Namibia; Paraguay; Peru; Poland; Russia; Slovakia; Slovenia; South Africa; Tajikistan; Turkmenistan; Tyrolese German-speakers; Ukraine; Uruguay; Uzbekistan; Venezuela; Yugoslavia**

Further Reading

Bade, Klaus J., editor, *Deutsche im Ausland—Fremde in Deutschland: Migration in Geschichte und Gegenwart*, München: Beck, 1992

Born, Joachim, and Sylvia Dickgiesser, *Deutschsprachige Minderheiten: Ein Überblick über den Stand der Forschung für 27 Länder*, Mannheim: Institut für deutsche Sprache im Auftrag des Auswärtigen Amtes, 1989

Brunner, Georg, *Nationality Problems and Minority Conflicts in Eastern Europe*, Gütersloh: Bertelsmann Foundation Publishers, 1996

Hinderling, Robert, and Ludwig M. Eichinger, editors, *Handbuch der mitteleuropäischen Sprachminderheiten*, Tübingen: Gunter Narr, 1996

Kühl, Jørgen, *Tyskere i Øst*, Aarhus: Aarhus University Press, 1997

Runblom, Harald, editor, *Migrants and the Homeland: Images, Symbols, and Realities*, Uppsala Multiethnic Papers, 44, Uppsala, 2000

Wolff, Stefan, editor, *German Minorities in Europe: Ethnic Identity and National Belonging*, Oxford: Berghahn, 2000

Germany

Capsule Summary

Country Name: Federal Republic of Germany
Location: central Europe, bordering the Baltic Sea and the North Sea, between the Netherlands and Poland, south of Denmark
Total Population: 82,398,326 (2003)
Language: German (minority languages: Danish, Sorbian, Frisian, and Romanes)
Religions: Roman Catholic; Lutheran
Minority Populations: Danes, Sorbs, Frisians, Roma, and Sinti (Gypsy)
Other Ethnic Communities: Poles, Turks, Kurds, and many others

Germany is a federal republic in central Europe that shares borders with Denmark in the north, the Netherlands, Belgium, Luxembourg, and France in the west, Switzerland and Austria in the south, and Poland, and the Czech Republic in the east. The earliest origins of the modern state go back to around 800, when the western parts of present-day Germany, together with France and other areas, were part of Charlemagne's Franconian Empire. After the dissolution, Germany became an empire, but with hundreds of separate entities. The German empire was dissolved after the Napoleonic Wars; the German Emperor became Emperor of Austria, but cooperation still took place within the *Deutscher Bund*. In the mid-1850s, a process of empire building took place under the leadership of Prussia, fighting wars against Denmark in 1864, and Austria in 1866, eventually leading to the creation of the second German Empire following the German-French war of 1870–71. With the incorporation of the previously Danish lands of Schleswig and Holstein after the war of 1864, a Danish-speaking community of 175,000–200,000 became a minority in Prussia/Germany. Germany became one of the major European forces.

In 1914, Germany was involved in World War I, and members of national minorities had to serve in the armies. After the defeat in 1918, the German Empire was dissolved, and a German republic was established. In 1920, two plebiscites in Schleswig determined the new Danish-German border, reuniting most of the Danish minority with Denmark, leaving a small Danish minority behind. Minority rights were granted in the so-called Weimar Constitution. In 1933, Adolf Hitler seized power and installed a totalitarian dictatorship with repression and persecution of minorities. Germany was involved in World War II from 1939 to 1945, and committed genocide against Jews, Roma (gypsies), and several other ethnic groups.

After the defeat in May 1945, Germany was subdivided in four occupation zones, eventually developing into two German states: West and East Germany, the latter a communist system under Soviet dominance. In West Germany, a democratic system formed the basis of society, guaranteeing equal rights and nondiscrimination. However, no minority protection article was included in the constitution of 1949. The boundary between the two Germanys was eventually closed by East Germany when erecting the Berlin Wall in August 1961, effectively interrupting contacts between the Sorbs and minorities in western Europe. In November 1989, the border regime was dissolved. In October 1990, Germany was unified as a federal republic, and Berlin once again became the capital.

Within its borders, Germany recognizes four different minority groups, Danes, Frisians, Sorbs, and Roma/Sinti, which all together make up 230,000–240,000 persons, or less than 0.3 percent of the total population and ten times smaller than the Turkish community in Germany. In their traditional regions, however, the minorities make up larger shares of the population.

In the northernmost German federal state of Schleswig-Holstein, some 50,000 persons (or 0.06 percent of Germany's population) are affiliated with the Danish national minority. The Danish minority are scattered across the traditional region of Schleswig in the northern part of the state. Its relative share of the population of the state of Schleswig-Holstein is 1.8 percent. In the region of South Schleswig it is 8–10 percent. In some villages, up to a third of the local population belongs to the Danish minority. In the city of Flensburg, about 20 percent of the population is affiliated with the minority. The Danish minority is organized in a functional autonomy with own schools, media, libraries, organizations, and institutions. Some 6,000 pupils attend the Danish private schools. The main cultural organization counts about 15,000 members, including some 600 National Frisians. The minority even has its own political party, SSW (South Schleswig Voters Association), which in 2001 held some 160 seats in local councils and had three members of the state parliament, *Landtag*. In the last state elections in 2000, the SSW received 60,000 votes, up 22,000 from the previous elections in 1996, gaining one seat in the *Landtag*. Dialogue with the federal government in Berlin is secured through a liaison committee, which was established in 1965. Funding for the Danish minority is provided by Denmark and Germany. The Danish minority is accepted by the majority, widely integrated, and no tension based on national differences is found.

There are two Frisian communities in Germany as well. They are related to and cooperate with the Frisian ethnic group in the Netherlands, numbering some 450,000 people. The smaller Frisian community in Germany lives in the Saterland, in the state of Niedersachsen, and consists of 1,000–2,000 people (0.001–0.002 percent). The larger group of North Frisians lives in the northern part of Schleswig-Holstein, on the North Sea shore and islands in an area where parts of the Danish minority also live. The North Frisians count for a total of 50,000–60,000 people (0.06–0.07 percent), but only 10,000 (0.01 percent) are actually native speakers, and another 20,000 do understand one of the nine Frisian dialects. The 10,000 native speakers must be subdivided into so-called National Frisians, identifying themselves as a national minority and possessing their own ethnicity, and the regionalist North Frisians with a German national identity but a distinct Frisian subidentity. The latter group does not consider itself a national minority, but is a regional community with objective features identical with those of the National Frisians. Because of the lack of subjective ethnicity, they are not a national minority. The German government, however, includes both National and Regional Frisians in the system of minority protective measures, and defines them as an entity with the German term *Volksgruppe* or ethnic group. The National Frisians cooperate with the Danish minority in the field of culture, schools, and politics. One of the three SSW members of the *Landtag* is a National Frisian. Germany provides some limited funding for cultural activities. A special liaison committee with the state legislature *Landtag* deals with issues concerning the Frisian community.

The Sorbs live in the German federal states of Saxony and Brandenburg in former East Germany. Today, they number a total of 60,000 persons (0.07 percent), two-thirds of them in Upper Lusatia in Saxony, one-third living in Lower Lusatia in Brandenburg. In some municipalities, 90 percent of the local population is Sorbian. On average, their relative share is 10 percent, in the cities less than 2 percent. In the Sorbian regions, official signs are bilingual, which dates back to East Germany. Sorbian is taught in more than 70 public schools with about 5,000 pupils. The Sorbs have organized themselves within an association of Lusatian Sorbs with 5,800 members. Germany provides funding for the Sorbs.

Those gypsies holding German citizenship are subdivided into the groups of Roma and Sinti. Together they number up to 70,000 individuals (0.085 percent), mostly living in the state capitals and the metropolitan areas in the western parts of Germany. The German Gypsies became subject to persecution and Nazi genocide during 1933–1945. They still experience discrimination by other groups and individuals, although the Sinti and Roma are widely integrated into German society. They have established their own organizations representing their interests toward the authorities. Germany funds the main office of the Central Council of the German Sinti and Roma in Heidelberg. The minority language Romanes is not taught in public schools except in some special projects, and the Gypsies themselves are against language training in public schools. The stand of the German Gypsies is far more difficult than the other minorities, because many members of the group face stigmatization.

Germany does not recognize any other ethnic group as national minorities protected under international law. This also applies to the Polish ethnic group, which up to the late 1950s actually had been recognized as a national minority. In the 1970s, 1980s, and 1990s, the Polish ethnic group grew due to immigration from Poland. Thus, this ethnic community today only to a very limited extent includes members of the former recognized national minority. No other ethnic communities are recognized as minorities.

The legal status of the minorities has been different, depending on the group concerned. The Danish minority had a stronger stand because of support from its kin-state, Denmark, whereas none of the other groups can rely on a kin-state. In September 1949, the Schleswig-Holstein state government notified the rights of the Danish minority in the so-called Kiel Declaration, emphasizing the individual's free und unrestricted choice of national affiliation, and establishing a contact committee concerning the interest of the Danish group. This committee existed from 1950 to 1958. The state constitution included recognition of the Danish minority as well. Although the Kiel Declaration provides that the regulations should also be valid for the Frisian group, this never became fact. In 1953, the federal election law exempted parties of national minorities from the 5 percent minimum share in federal elections. In March 1955, the West German government guaranteed the rights of the Danish minority with the Bonn Declaration, which was notified unilaterally, but based on negotiations with Denmark and parallel with a similar unilateral declaration by the Danish government, the Copenhagen Declaration concerning the German minority in Denmark. Shortly after, the political party SSW was exempted from the 5 percent voting barrier in state elections, and the Kiel Declaration was abolished. The revised state constitution of 1990 emphasizes that the authorities in Schleswig-Holstein protect the minorities and ethnic groups. The Danish and Frisian communities are protected and supported by the state. The Sorbs were included in the constitution of East Germany, and special provisions concerning the Sorbs were included in the German Unification Treaty of 1990, guaranteeing the rights of the group. The state constitutions of Brandenburg and Saxony include recognition and legal guarantees for the Sorbs. The Roma and Sinti enjoy no explicit protection. However, the state constitutions of Mecklenburg-Vorpommern and Sachsen-Anhalt, both in former East Germany, do provide certain guarantees for ethnic minorities in general, which should include the Gypsy communities as well. In the 1990s, Germany extended its minority policy by ratifying the Council of Europe's instruments on minority protection: the Charter on Regional or Minority Languages of 1992, and the Framework Convention for the Protection of National Minorities of 1995. All four traditional national minorities and their languages were included in the ratification. There is no significant difference between the German average population and the communities of Danes, Sorbs, and Frisians concerning education and social status. The situation of the Roma/Sinti is somewhat different because of traditional discrimination, exposed social positions, and widespread illiteracy especially among older members of the group.

Interminority Cooperation

The national minorities in Germany have traditionally had contacts with each other, and have also periodically cooperated closely with each other. Following the incorporation of Schleswig-Holstein in Prussia in 1867, the Danes during the German Empire, 1871–1918, cooperated in political terms with especially the Polish minority. In the interwar period, cooperation took place between the Danes, Frisians, Poles, Sorbs, and Lithuanians in Germany. They also cooperated in the early period of the European Nationality Congresses of the interwar years. They even created an association of national minorities in Germany that was dissolved in 1939. The Polish minority's property was confiscated, and the organization was dissolved by the Nazis in February 1940. The Polish minority never gained its previous strength after World War II. Although an office in the Ministry of the Interior in West Germany in the 1950s was responsible for contacts with both the Polish and Danish national minorities, the Polish community lost its significance as a minority around the 1960s, and the Poles in the Ruhr area were assimilated. Present-day Polish communities consist mostly of Polish immigrants who arrived in West Germany during communism in Poland and also after 1989. Still, Polish is used widely in Catholic congregations in the Ruhr area.

The Danish minority in West Germany and the Sorbian in East Germany had some contacts in the 1950s, but these stopped because of the Cold War and growing tension around 1960. After the Berlin Wall was demolished in November 1989, contacts were reestablished. Following German unification in 1990, the four traditional minorities have initiated a closer cooperation. In 1992, they advocated a special article in the revised German constitution guaranteeing the rights of all four minorities. The conservative majority in the constitutional committee, however, declined this proposal. Eventually, the four minorities decided to move ahead in their cooperation, addressing issues of joint interest, such as the wish for a liaison officer for national minorities with the German government or parliament. All national minorities in Germany also cooperate within the framework of the pan-European Federal Union of European Nationalities, which originally was created in 1949.

In January 2002, Germany and 11 other European Union countries introduced the Euro, the common European currency. As of 2002, the GDP per-capita income was US$26, 200.

JØRGEN KÜHL

See also **Denmark; Frisians; Germans; Poland; Sorbs**

Further Reading

Berdichevsky, Normann, "The German-Danish Border: A Successful Resolution of an Age Old Conflict or its Redifinition?" *Boundary & Territory Briefing*, vol. 2, no. 7, Durham: International Boundaries Research Unit, 1999

Born, Robert, Uwe Danker, and Jørgen Kühl, editors, *Nationale mindretal i det dansk-tyske grænseland 1933–1945*, Aabenraa: Institut for grænseregionsforskning 2001

CBSS Working Group on Assistance to Democratic Institutions: Round Table on "The Rights of Minorities in the Baltic Sea Region" (Moscow, March 30–31, 2000), Stockholm, 2000

Hahn, Hans Henning, and Peter Kunze, editors, *Nationale Minderheiten und staatliche Minderheitenpolitik in Deutschland im 19: Jahrhundert*, Berlin, 1999

Holander, Reimer Kay, and Thomas Steensen, editors, *Friesen und Sorben: Beiträge zu einer Tagung über zwei Minderheiten in Deutschland in Sankelmark*, Bredstedt: Nordfriisk Instituut, 1991

Kühl, Jørgen, *The Federal Union of European Nationalities. An Outline History 1949–1999*, Aabenraa: Danish Institute of Border Region Studies, 2000

Kühl, Jørgen, *The »Schleswig Experience«: The National Minorities in the Danish-German Border Area*, Aabenraa: Danish Institute of Border Region Studies, 1998

Minderheiten im deutsch-dänischen Grenzbereich, Kiel: Landeszentrale für politische Bildung Schleswig-Holstein, 1993

Schmalz-Jacobsen, Cornelia, and Georg Hansen, editors, *Ethnische Minderheiten in der Bundesrepublik Deutschland: ein Lexikon*, München: Beck, 1995

Scholze Dietrich, editor, *Die Sorben in Deutschland: Sieben Kapitel Kulturgeschichte*, Bautzen: Lusatia Verlag, 1993

Tägil, Sven, editor, *Ethnicity and Nation Building in the Nordic World*, London: Hurst, 1995

Gheorghe, Nicolae (Roma, Romania)

Nicolae Gheorghe is a Roma activist, scholar, and author of numerous articles and studies related to Roma and the present situation of the Roma in central and eastern Europe. In the 1970s and 1980s, he pursued informal contacts with Roma leaders and scholars in eastern and western Europe. This led him to broadcast on Radio Free Europe (under the pseudonym Alexandru Danciu) a critique of the Roma policies of the communist regime in Romania.

Following the overthrow of the communist regime in 1989, he served for several months as a councilor for Roma affairs to the Romanian government's Council for National Minorities. In 1992, he founded the Romanian Roma Ethnic Federation. He also served on the board of the European Roma Rights Center in Budapest, and as a member of the Project on Ethnic Relations (PER) Council for Ethnic Accord in Romania. In 1993, he was a cofounder and the executive director of the Roma Center for Social Intervention and Studies (Romanii CRISS) in Bucuresti, a position he held until 1999. He was vice-president of the International Romani Union and lobbied for Roma rights at the United Nations, the Council of Europe, and the Organization for Security and Cooperation in Europe (OSCE), where he was instrumental in getting these issues included in the OSCE's 1990 Copenhagen Document. In 1999, he became director of the Contact Point for Roma and Sinti Issues at the OSCE's Office for Democratic Institutions and Human Rights (ODIHR) in Warsaw, Poland.

Gheorghe has prepared reports for or consulted as an expert for projects of the European Commission, the Council of Europe, PER, OSCE, UNICEF, and the Commission on Security and Cooperation in Europe of the US Congress. He is the coauthor of a 1997 policy paper on *The Roma in the Twenty-First Century*, which forcefully outlined the consequences for the Roma of the collapse of communism in central and eastern Europe as well as the challenges, opportunities, and implications of the new era for the Roma. Noting that the Roma were among the last in Europe to adopt ethnonationalism and the related effort to promote ethnic mobilization and carve out their own political space, the paper discusses their struggle to overcome tradition, fragmentation, and previous indifference to politics; the dangers facing the Roma in the new Europe; Romani options; issues of territoriality, discrimination, separation, and assimilation; relations with international organizations and nongovernmental organizations; and legal and political strategies. The paper provided essential clarification of two essential questions—what do the Roma want, and how much are they prepared to fight for it—along with a discussion of some of the underlying assumptions of Roma political dialogue.

Much of this was crystallized in the creation of an OSCE *Action Plan on Roma and Sinti Issues*, prepared in 2003 by Gheorghe and others. The Action Plan reflected a sense of an increasing gap between Roma activism and what was happening on the ground. The Plan calls for a more pragmatic focus, concentrating efforts on issues where international organizations can actually make a difference while moving away from approaches based on emotional appeals and overly ambitious wish lists. At the same time, continued efforts would be made to affirm and protect Roma rights in the fluid situation that has prevailed since 1989, particularly those related to education and immigration as Europe's internal borders open.

Biography

Nicolae Gheorghe. Born November 12, 1946, in Romania. Educated at the University of Bucuresti, 1968–1972, in Sociology. Researcher and Senior Researcher, Center (later Institute) for Sociology of the Romanian Academy, Bucuresti, 1972–1999. Governmental councilor for Roma affairs, Council for National Minorities, 1990. Cofounder and executive director, Roma Center for Social Intervention and Studies (Romanii CRISS), Bucuresti, 1993–1999. Director of the Contact Point for Roma and Sinti Issues at the Organization for Security and Cooperation in Europe (OSCE) Office for Democratic Institutions and Human Rights (ODIHR), Warsaw, Poland, 1999–present. Awards: Human Rights Prize of the French National Consultative Commission of Human Rights, 1992; Bruno Kreisky Award for Human Rights, 1993; European Union/USA Prize for Democracy, 1998.

Selected Works [Nicolae Gheorghe]

"Dealing with Multiculturality: Minority, Ethnic, National and Human Rights," *OSCE ODIHR Bulletin*, 1994/1995 (with Thomas Acton)
Roma/Gypsies: A European Minority, 1995 (with J.-P. Liegeois)
The Roma in the Twenty-First Century: A Policy Paper, 1997 (with Andrzej Mirga)
"The Social Construction of Romani Identity," in *Gypsy Politics and Traveller Identity*, edited by Thomas Acton, 1997
"Policy Making on Roma in Central and Eastern Europe Countries: Inventory, Challenges, Commitments, Good Practice, and Weakness," *International Expert Symposium on Roma Questions*, 2000 (with others)
Action Plan on Improving the Situation of Roma and Sinti Within the OSCE Area, 2003 (with others)
OSCE Supplementary Human Dimension Meeting on Roma and Sinti Report, 2003 (with others)

PAUL E. MICHELSON

See also **Roma (Gypsies)**

Globalization and Minority Cultures

Terms

The terms *global, global village, globalize, globalism,* and *globalization* increasingly became part of the normal conversation of sociologists during the 1990s. *Globalization* has to do with all aspects of society and culture that have been globalized. In other words, *globalization* refers to the growth of a global culture.

Those who are detractors from globalization see it as Western imperialism and a form of global assimilation. Some of globalization's greatest detractors come from the countries of Asia.

For those who support globalization it is an opportunity to integrate the best aspects of all of the cultures on earth and to create a more respectful and tolerant human society.

Globalization caused by a variety of social and cultural developments including, but not exclusively, those economically based. Globalization is thus more than merely the sociology of international relations. It is also more than a meeting of nation-states as a unified form of industrial society. It is also more than simply the consequence of economic globalization. Globalization is about the world as a system of societies, each society physically occupying its own territorial area and constituting a unified and distinct entity but as an element within a system is also linked to all other societies. The links are between the economic, belief, and political systems of society as a whole.

Globalization is seen as distinct from modern patterns of imperialism because, instead of assimilation through colonization, globalization supports the ideal of integration and respect for diversity. It is upon the principles of respect, democracy, and due process that a global culture can be built.

Minority cultures are the cultures of minority groups that live within a larger society. As politicians and social scientists use the term, a minority is necessarily subordinate to the dominant group within a society. That a group is subordinate is more important in defining a minority than that a group may be small in number. The term *minority group* is applied to social groups that are oppressed or stigmatized because of racial, ethnic, biological, or other characteristics. Singled out because of their physical or cultural characteristics from the rest of society, minority groups are afforded differential and unequal treatment and are thus objectives of collective discrimination. In sociological talk, a minority must be a distinct social group. The role of minority groups varies from society to society, depending on the structure of the social system and the relative power of the minority group. A minority group is typically poorer and politically less powerful than the dominant group.

History

Despite the use of the term "new global economy," the international economic integration of the 1990s is not unprecedented. During the half-century before World War I there was a large cross-border flow of goods, capital, and people, which ended abruptly with World War I, after which the world moved into a period of fierce trade protectionism and tight restrictions on capital movement. The volume of world trade fell sharply. International capital flows virtually dried up in the interwar period as governments imposed capital controls to try to insulate their economies from the impact of a global slump.

Falling transport costs drove nineteenth-century globalization. Transport costs and trade barriers fell faster; international capital flows as a share of national output were far larger; and cross-border migration was far greater. One element of this globalization was increasing international trade. The trade boom was partly due to more liberal government policies, with Britain being the first big country to open its markets. Falling transport costs, however, provided an even bigger boost to trade than government policy. Thanks to cheaper transport and lower tariffs, prices across the world converged. Trade was an important part of globalization, but migration had a far bigger impact. Money too flowed across the world as never before. As cheap American and Ukrainian grain imports threatened farmers' jobs in the late 1870s, continental Europe closed its agricultural markets. The United States closed its markets too. Finally, globalization went into reverse as World War I and the Great Depression pushed governments further toward austerity.

Economics

For those who focus purely on economics, globalism or globalization in the most general sense refers to the process in which goods and services, including capital, move more freely within and among nations. Economic liberalization began in the 1980s. It achieved global proportions after the fall of communism in 1991. The World Trade Organization (WTO) replaced GATT in 1995. Trade flourished and signaled the rebirth of the global capital market. World markets became free from all state constraints and capital moved across borders. Multinational corporations moved from country to country depending on tax legislation and the expense of labor. There has been a growing integration of national economies. This has changed the way the world works. National economies are steadily becoming more integrated as cross-border flows of trade, investment, and financial capital increase.

The major items traded in the globalized market are information and capital. Capital is money, and manufactured material or equipment, which contributes to productive work. Technological change allows capital to move almost instantaneously. Changes in monetary policies, as well as in what is traded and the importance of capital, have created a global market distinctively different from previous eras.

Critics of globalization predict that increased competition from low-wage developing countries will destroy jobs and push down wages in rich economies. For decades there have been the two options of an economy. The "command economy" is the now mainly archaic state-directed socialist system and the other is the "market economy" of world capitalism. Detractors from globalization and the command economy have suggested the "community economy," which serves the human and ecological community, as its focus.

In theory, free trade should push prices together as competition forces high-cost producers to lower their prices. However, the financial markets are not yet truly integrated either. While product and capital markets have become more integrated, labor markets have not. In a labor market human effort is a commodity that is bought and sold under terms that, in law, are deemed to constitute a contract. Mobility of workers between jobs is often sluggish or nonexistent. Due to factors such as discrimination, labeling, racism, and sexism, economic explanations of the labor-market process must be replaced by sociological analysis.

Tens of millions of people currently work outside their home countries. However, language, cultural barriers, and incompatible educational and professional qualifications all combine to keep labor markets national. People with higher qualifications, more experience, and wider or multiple skills are offered jobs before those who have less to offer. Such considerations, however, are made without consideration of why the individual may have less to offer or of whom has the greatest need for paid employment. If labor markets are to become more globalized, there must be greater identification of the cultural, institutional, and structural factors that help determine people's allocations to one or another labor market. Imperfections of labor market processes, the reward systems operating in the different markets, and the nature of power relationships in the market must be considered if globalization is to be a reality for labor markets.

Sweatshops that employ people as virtual slave laborers are tolerated as part of the new world trade. Public services such as hospitals and schools that minority groups are most dependent on are constantly attacked as inconsistent with the needs of capital and the market. Schools and hospitals have their government funding devolved to mimic private enterprises. Doctors and teachers are required to take on the skills of the business manager, with a market in which people are no longer students or patients but customers. The services become more like a business and less like a service, with income and output taking on more meaning than learning outcomes or patient well-being.

By allowing more efficient use of world resources, globalization should boost average incomes. A boost to average income logically means that government would have less of a need to redistribute income through fiscal and social policies. Social policies are a key factor in patterns of consumption as a measure of economic and hence social inequality. The need to access resources has been a motivator in the past for

social movement; a more efficient use of world resources may therefore lead to a more stable population that depends on adequate funding, leadership, and organization. Today, more economies than ever before have opened their borders to trade and investment. Not only developed countries, but also developing countries in Asia and Latin America, have embraced market-friendly reforms. This has led to the displacement of large numbers of people from their homes in Asia, Africa, and Latin America to the West as either refugees or labor migrants.

The Spread of Democracy

The growth of a global economy has accompanied the decline of the nation-state. Territorial boundaries are becoming difficult to maintain and laws and regulations difficult to enforce. The style of political and economic decision making presents an obstacle to civic input but sees an increase in interaction between the state and the most powerful multinational corporate leaders.

The United States of America has emerged as the only world superpower. This has allowed the United States tremendous influence in setting the terms for global trade. The style of globalism pushed by the United States has favored the free movement and protection of capital while being, at best, indifferent and, at worst, hostile to more place-dependent labor. It is the dual relationship of mobile capital and fixed, unorganized, and unprotected labor that has created the conditions for capital to dominate. It is the United States that has consistently been the most extreme on liberalizing capital and protecting it as it moves across boundaries, and the most neglectful of labor and fragile markets. Protecting labor expresses itself not only in strong unions and workers' benefits but also in a strong social security system. The United States has purposefully moved toward weaker labor unions and a feeble social security system.

Representative democracy is widely accepted across eastern Europe to Africa. However, globalization and representative democracy as an element of globalization are not without detractors or resistance. A network of intellectuals in Asia launched a debate that questioned representative democracy as a universal form of governance. They have questioned the International Monetary Fund, which has demanded protection of capital, and encouraged or tolerated the suppression of labor and the environment in powerless countries. Capital is actively directed to markets with low wages, where workers are sometimes abused and labor organizations suppressed. Strongly linked with the questioning of such Western-dominated organizations as the International Monetary Fund is the connection between representative democracy and the defining of human rights. Malaysian intellectual Chandra Muzaffar, in his 1996 book *Human Wrongs*, denigrated human rights as an advanced form of Western imperialism. Many Asian intellectuals have come out in favor of a discussion on the right to food, housing, basic sanitation, and the preservation of one's own identity and culture.

Eastern intellectuals see Western globalism as not only attempting to suppress labor, but also seeking to suppress social welfare systems and support for public expenditures that do not directly benefit the expansion of capital. The social welfare system and other public services such as schools are supported through taxes, and taxes reduce short-term benefits to capital. Although proponents of Western-style globalism purport to support democracy, it is only in a role subservient to capital. They believe that Western globalism has not just transformed the flow of capital—it has transformed the role of government and the meaning of citizenship. The transformed role of government is not to protect citizens or public services such as hospitals and schools but to protect and facilitate the flow of capital. The talk is all about free markets but not about free citizens.

Globalization must lead to a closer association between East and West. There must be a greater recognition of the dependence of one on the other and vice versa. For those who see globalization as dominance by the West, then globalization must be replaced by a global "convivencia," as suggested by Malaysian politician and intellectual Anwar Ibraham. A global convivencia would see a more harmonious and enriching experience of living together among people of diverse religions and cultures.

Globalization has developed as a variety of global systems supported by representative democracy and freer economic interaction between countries has grown. Some of the worldwide arrangements are military systems, patterns of consumption, and consumerism, sports, tourism, and cosmopolitanism. All of them are represented in some way by media, such as television news programs, magazines, Web sites, and advertising.

Global military systems such as the United Nation's Peace Keeping Forces have been deployed in areas of the world where the tendency to look for military solutions to political problems and conflicts has grown. Most of the deployment has been in areas of the world still deemed, by organizations such as the United Nations, as developing. Factors, which may lead to military intervention from a global force, include gross violations of human rights.

The patterns of consumption and consumerism depict a global economic system of massive consumption at the top and massive misery at the bottom. It is a system that is doing damage to the environment. Consuming a grossly disproportionate share of the world's resources, the West suffocates in its own affluence while even within wealthy nations more and more people are abandoned to poverty. The United States America has 6 percent of the world's population however it consumes 35 percent of the earth's resources

The Olympic games is the most prominent example of global sports however there are team and individual sports such as football, of varying codes and tennis. Some sports have become apart of the worldwide tourism industry, which organizes tours so that people may include watching their favor sport while on vacation. Also as a part of the tourism trade we have cities all over the world vying to be the most cosmopolitan and thus the most desirable city to visit if not live in.

Communication, Information Technology, and Multimedia

Enthusiastic free marketers have promoted economic activity across borders and cultures by digitalizing and transmitting computer programs, which can be produced and sold almost everywhere. The supporters of globalization predict that such commercial activity allows for the growing populations of the developing world to participate in the world economy and to find a prosperous future.

Plunging communication costs have driven globalization. The process that is transforming the world into the proverbial "global village", rapidly shrinking distances, compressing space and time, is globalization via the latest forms of communication, information and multimedia technology. Multimedia technology is technology that combines text, still or moving images, and sounds that provide more information than can be obtained from the text alone. To be able to use multimedia technology an individual must be able to access a computer with electricity and a telecommunications line connecting it to the Internet. The Internet is a set of linked computers worldwide that use telephone and satellite communications. The Internet is unregulated and governments and universities pay for the international transmissions. The Internet rose from a military need to have a system that was too widespread to be crippled by bombing. If an individual can afford a computer, the correct programs, and telephone contact, then they have the ability to communicate worldwide and this is being used by many minority groups who have registered themselves as interactive E-mail list or E-groups to communicate events and discuss issues ranging from political strategies to family linkups. As yet, the world economy is still far from being genuinely integrated; thus technology will continue to strengthen globalization but only for those who can access it.

In a global multimedia world, cultures have rights to faithful and respectful representation. Media reports on events show the culture or cultures of a country. Advertisements of products include images, views, backgrounds, and cultures of different racial, ethnic, and religious groups. Media are a cultural conveyor and the roles that people from different cultural groups play in shaping the end products must be considered. In the visual world of television and mass publications it is often more profitable to recycle old images, thus continuing stereotypes, than it is to represent minorities as they truly are. Dominance of the Western view of the world is perpetuated via global news programs such as CNN and the BBC World Service.

Contemporary Thought

Detractors see globalization as eroding non-Western local traditions and cultural practices. True, it has eliminated industries such as local film and television, which promote indigenous and local cultures. However, globalization is not, as a process, exclusively in the control of Western political and economic powers. Southeast Asia has competitive and advanced economies.

More important, however, than the economic impact of globalization is that it involves a new consciousness of the world as a single place. Globalization is a growing awareness at a global level that the world is a continuously constructed environment. It is a social process. In the process of globalization the limits of geography on social and cultural arrangements fade. Just as an individual's identity as a member of a particular local social group is constructed, an individual's identity as a member of a global society can also be seen as constructed.

Earth is a planet on which the same fashion accessory is manufactured and sold across every continent. One can send and receive electronic mail from the middle of a forest or the top of a mountain, eat a brand name food product in Melbourne, Australia, as well as Moscow in Russia, and pay for all this by using a credit card linked to a bank account in Manhattan, New York; therefore, the world is globalized. It can only be globalized for all, however, if all have the resources to purchase the goods and services available.

DAVINA B. WOODS

Further Reading

Handy, Charles, *The Hungry Spirit—Beyond Capitalism: A Quest for Purpose in the Modern World*, London: Hutchinson, 1997

ICHRITI, editor, *Human Rights and Economic Globalisation: Directions for the WTO*, Sweden: Global Foundation, November 1999 (ISBN 9197373907)

Marshall, Gordon, editor, *Oxford Dictionary of Sociology*, New York: Oxford University Press, 1998

Powell, John A., and S.P. Udayakumar, *The Impacts of Globalisation on Racial and Ethnic Minorities*, PRRAC May/June 2000: *Poverty & Race*, vol. 9, no. 3

Sinclair, Ian, editor, *Collins Dictionary Computing*, Glasgow: Harper Collins Publishers, 3rd edition, 2000

Wallis, Jim, *The Soul Of Politics: A Practical And Prophetic Vision For Change*, London: Fount, an imprint of Harper-Collins, 1994

Grant, Bernie (United Kingdom)

Bernard Alexander Montgomery Grant, better known as Bernie Grant, was born in 1944 in Georgetown, British Guiana (today Guyana), to school teacher-parents who named him after two World War II generals. He went on to become a member of the British Parliament (MP), popular and well-loved among the black community in Britain, but unpopular and even feared among the wider population for his maverick disposition and causes. He was the well-known and most controversial of the four ethnic minority MPs who made history in 1987 as they entered the House of Commons, which had not had a representative from a nonwhite ethnic minority community for half a century. Grant inspired the Parliamentary Black Caucus, cofounded with his fellow first black parliamentarians.

After attending St. Stanislaus College, a Jesuit-run secondary school, he worked as an analyst in the bauxite plants in Guyana. He then migrated with his family to England in 1963, where he attended Tottenham Technical College in North London, and later embarked on the study of engineering at Heriot Watt University in Edinburgh. He grew disillusioned when he found that work experience placements in South Africa offered as an element of his coursework were available only to white students.

Grant drew to politics when, during the university vacation in 1970, he worked for the Post Office at the International Telephone Exchange in Kings Cross, London. A strike began that year and Grant emerged as one of his branch's chief organizers. He remained as the exchange representative for the telephonists working within the Workers Revolutionary Party, thus building a lifelong commitment to trade union politics. He subsequently worked as a British Railways clerk, a National Union of Public Employees area officer, and as a partisan of the Black Trade Unionists Solidarity Movement. In 1978 he became a full-time trade union official. His union activities followed in the footsteps of his uncle, who had been president of the Guyana Teachers' Union and the Guyana TUC.

Grant also became actively involved in the political fight against racism during the 1970s, working with the left-wing Anti-Nazi League (ANL) to challenge the activities of the right-wing National Front in his workplace at a time of their growing popularity throughout the United Kingdom.

He became a full-time official for the National Union of Public employees (NUPE), joined the Labour Party, and, in 1978, became the local Labour councillor for the borough of Haringey, North London, where he lived, rising to then become Leader of Haringey Council. His election as leader coincided with a period of intense conflict between Margaret Thatcher's radical conservative government (elected for a third term in the 1987 general elections) and several Labour-run local authorities, one of which was Haringey. The tab-loid press criticized him for his anti-establishment views, and the Haringey Council under his leadership was the focus of a stream of negative stories.

Such negative press was fueled by Grant's highly visible support for controversial projects, especially those on behalf of disadvantaged communities and individuals. He openly supported the campaign for black sections in the Labour Party that demanded more black representation and the adoption of a "black agenda" against the wishes of the party leadership.

He was regarded as a menace by the Labour leadership under Neil Kinnock, due to his previous involvement with the Trotskyite left and to his continued association with the black sections campaign. Grant had a reputation for being antipolice and felt that black people were targeted unfairly by policing policies. He became nationally known in 1985 by an ill-judged remark about the violent riots on the Broadwater Farm housing estate in Tottenham that led to the brutal murder of policeman Keith Blakelock. It was reported that he stated that the police had been given "a bloody good hiding." He later stated regularly but unconvincingly that he had been misquoted and in fact had said that the people thought that the police had got a bloody good hiding. Whatever the truth, the remark turned him into a hate figure for the tabloid press, who vilified him.

His support for black sections in parliament led him to contest the parliamentary seat for the north London constituency of Tottenham as the black sections campaign argued that certain Parliamentary seats with significant black populations should be occupied by black candidates. He stood for selection against Norman Atkinson, who had held the seat for 20 years. Despite opposition by the Labour Party establishment, in 1987 Grant was elected as a Member of Parliament for Tottenham.

He entered Parliament dressed in African robes, and his career entered a new, more internationally oriented phase. His sympathies were pro-Arab; he honed an awareness of international issues as a result of family ties in Ghana and Guyana and was interested in both Africa and the Caribbean, embracing pan-African causes. His friendship with Dominican Labour Party activist, later Member of Parliament, and finally Prime Minster, Roosevelt Douglas, led to his association with Colonel Gadafy in Libya and opposition to the sanctions that had been imposed on the African state as a penalty for perceived sponsorship of international terrorism.

Grant identified with and allied himself with the left wing of the Labour Party and forged alliances among the radical and antiracist left. He became leader of the Socialist Campaign Group of MPs in the House of Commons. As a member of the group Grant stood for the deputy leadership of the Labour Party, with Ken Livingston standing as Leader, after the death of John Smith in 1992 to provide a left-wing alternative to the favorite and future leader Tony Blair (prime minister since 1997).

Grant was committed to the Caribbean economy, the regeneration of inner cities, and reduction in unemployment. He worked with the unemployed, the black community, and the left, but defended the UK monarchy. After the 1985 Broadwater Farm riots, he campaigned for the release of Winston Silcott, the black youth who had been convicted of the murder of P.C. Blakelock and whose conviction was eventually quashed. He called on Metropolitan Police Commissioner Sir Paul Condon to take early retirement after a damning report into the inquiry into the 1993 murder of black teenager Stephen Lawrence.

Although a staunch advocate for local causes, Grant gravitated toward internationalist interests, serving on the National Executive of the Anti-Apartheid Movement in Britain, and maintaining a long-standing friendship with Nelson Mandela, whom he supported throughout his imprisonment and subsequent release. He maintained a keen interest in Central America, Ireland, and Cyprus and was heavily involved in the campaign for reparations for slavery to Africa and the Caribbean and those who were the descendants of slaves.

The year 1993 marked a turning point in his relationship with the British government. He helped diffuse a potentially explosive situation following the death, at the hands of the police, of a Jamaican migrant, Joy Gardner, who police were trying to deport from the United Kingdom. Grant began to keep a lower profile—in part due to his ill health and in part due to his new relationship with the Labour Party leadership that co-opted him as an advisor on race. He became a pragmatic politician, and the mainstream UK press began to alter its depiction of him from that of a "firebrand" to that of a "statesman."

His last intervention in the House of Commons was on November 11, 1999, when he sought an apology for the part that Britain had played in slavery. He campaigned for a permanent memorial in London to the "unknown slave" in Trafalgar Square alongside Nelson's column as an acknowledgment of the contribution of the millions of slaves by whose labor the wealth of Britain was made. His wife, Sharon Grant, was on the short list to succeed him as Labour candidate for Tottenham, but was beaten by David Lammy, who won the by-election in 2000.

Biography

Bernard Alexander Montgomery Grant. Born February 17, 1944, in British Guiana, now Guyana. Elected to the Haringey borough council, north London, 1977; elected Member of Parliament (MP) for Tottenham, 1987. Organized the Parliamentary Black Caucus, 1987–89; organized various African-centered organizations and movements, including the African Reparations Movement and the Global Trade Centre to link local businesses with partners in Africa and the Caribbean (1990s). Chair of the Standing Conference Against Racism in Europe (SCORE); member of the Committee of Eminent Persons on Reparations for Africa; and chair of the African Reparations Movement (UK). Married Sharon Lawrence (1998); awarded Honorary Doctorate by Pace University, New York, in May 1993, for his work for equal rights. Died April 8, 2000.

ANGELA HAYNES

See also **United Kingdom**

Greece

Capsule Summary

Location: southeastern Europe
Total Population: approximately 10 million (98% ethnic Greeks)
Language: Greek
Religion: Eastern Orthodox (97.6%), Roman Catholic (0.4%), Protestant (0.1%), Muslim (1.3%), and other (0.4%)

Greece covers an area of 131,957 square kilometers (about 51,000 square miles) and approximately 98 percent of its inhabitants are ethnic Greeks (that is, Graecophone Eastern Orthodox Christians). No official information exists with regard to the breakdown of different ethnic groups. Greece is a parliamentary republic with a per-capita gross national product of around US$7,500. As with the other Balkan states, Greece was part of the Ottoman Empire, but over the last two centuries it has been thoroughly Westernized and became a European Union member in 1980.

History

The formation of the modern Greek state in 1832 led to calls for its territorial expansion into Ottoman lands. The Greek state was eventually successful and by 1920 had doubled its territory and population. The ultimate Greek dream was the conquest of Constantinople and Anatolia, both with large Greek Orthodox populations. However, the attempt to conquer Anatolia failed, and by 1923 the Greek and Turkish states agreed to a population exchange that practically terminated the Greek presence on Anatolia. More than 1 million refugees resettled in the territory of modern Greece. After 1923, issues of modernization and development became dominant in Greek politics. The country's commitment to the West and its attempts at modernization were rewarded in 1980 when Greece joined the European Union.

Despite post-World War II modernization, Greece continues to struggle with its neighbors about issues of minorities and self-determination. The most well-known case is the long-standing dispute with Turkey concerning the status of Cyprus. In the 1990s, Greece entered into an international dispute with the Yugoslav Republic of Macedonia over the use of the word "Macedonia" in the state's official name. Greeks consider the legacy of the ancient Macedonians to be part of their national heritage and were opposed to letting another nation lay claim to the name and the legacy. Moreover, many Greeks were fearful of resurgent Macedonian irredentism and of talk about Macedonian minorities. Although the rift between the two sides remains, Greek-Macedonian relations improved significantly after 1995.

National Integration

Officially Greece is a homogeneous country without any ethnic divisions, with the exception of small groups of Protestants and Catholics, and the Muslims of Western Thrace. Although this "official" description is not far from the truth, it is important to note that this is the outcome of consistent and largely successful efforts at national integration. Until the mid-twentieth century, the population of Greece included groups of Romanian-speaking Vlachs, Albanians, Slavic-speaking Macedonians or Macedonian Slavs, Turks, Bulgarians, Pomaks, and Roma.

The (Greek-speaking and Romanian-speaking) Vlachs used to be pastoral nomads living scattered throughout the Balkans. Because of their commercial prominence and economic interests they were overwhelmingly in support of nineteenth century Greek nationalist efforts in Epirus and Macedonia. For example, rich Vlach merchants are responsible for numerous endowments throughout Greece. In due course of time and with the expansion of the educational system and urbanization, the Vlachs were assimilated into the broader Greek society and are virtually indistinguishable from other Greeks today.

Because the Vlachs and the Roma used to be nomads, no reliable statistics exist. In the post-1945 period, there are only informal (and, for the most part, unreliable) estimates with regard to their size. This is because Vlachs (or their descendents) would strongly object to their classification as an "ethnic group" (since such a classification would imply that they are not Greeks). With respect to Roma, this is a stigmatized category, subject to prejudice and discrimination, and therefore labeling is an obstacle to accurate counts.

Many Orthodox Albanians lived in Greece since the period of the Ottoman rule. They participated in the Greek revolution and considered themselves part of the emerging Greek nation. A minority of Muslim Albanians (no more than 30,000) came into existence after World War I, when the Greek state assumed control of the region of Thesprotia (or Chamouria) in Epirus. There were several contested issues with regard to the treatment of this group during the interwar period. During World War II, while Greece was under the control of the Axis forces, this group aligned itself with the occupiers. Subsequently, it was attacked by Greek right-wing guerrilla forces that set their villages on fire, forcing them to flee into Albania.

In the post-1923 period, thousands of Turkish-speaking Greek Orthodox Christians and Pontic Greeks fled to Greece. Despite this apparent heterogeneity, the population was thoroughly homogenized over the next 60 years. Today, the overwhelming majority of the aforementioned groups consider themselves to be 100 percent Greek. Preservation of their own cultural specificity remains strong among the Anatolian refugees and Pontic Greeks, two groups that maintain viable subcultures of their own.

The key determinant for national integration has been loyalty to the state. The post-1923 Greek refugees were forced to flee Turkey because of their Greek heritage and this meant that their loyalty to the state was unquestioned. For just two groups (Turks and Slavic Macedonians), loyalty to the state was questionable, leading to thorny minority issues.

Minorities in Modern Greece

The first group includes the Muslim (Pomak, Roma, and Turkish) population of western Thrace. This population was excluded from the Greek-Turkish exchange of population on the basis of a reciprocal agreement that also allowed the Greeks of Istanbul to stay in their city.

According to the Lausanne Treaty (1923), this group was considered a religious minority, a claim maintained by the Greek state to this day. Practically, this meant the preservation of the religious authority of the *Mufti* (professional jurist who interprets Muslim law) as the supreme arbiter in all communal manners. During the post-1950 period, modernization slowly encroached upon this population, transforming the initially religious community into a secular ethnic group. The lack of adequate secular education resulted in two internal trends. The Bulgarian-speaking Pomaks were (and continue to be) gradually acculturated into the Turkish group, and the Muslim Turks, who desired to be educated in their own tongue, found it necessary to go to Turkey. The Greek state employed an obscure rule to deprive most of this latter group of their Greek citizenship, effectively barring them from returning to their villages.

The serious flaws of this policy were compounded by the desire of the Turkish republic to act as a benefactor for the minority. Subsequently, for the last 30 years, this group has been caught in the maelstrom of the Greek-Turkish confrontation. Many Greeks consider the minority's claims to have full recognition under the law a prelude to a separatist or autonomist political movement. During the 1990s, the Greek government responded to loud protests by Muslim deputies, which led to a gradual improvement of the minority's conditions.

The second group is that of the Macedonian Slavs or Macedonians. Greek attitudes toward this group have been shaped by the broader Greek-Macedonian dispute. During the interwar period, there were from 200,000 to 400,000 Slavs in northwestern Greek Macedonia who were subjected to an acculturation campaign while also coming into conflict with the Greek Orthodox refugees who settled into the region.

Already partially aware of their cultural differences, the Slavic Macedonians' alienation from the Greek nation-state further increased during World War II. Most of them supported the Greek communist party in exchange for a promise of regional autonomy. However, the Greek communists were defeated in the Greek Civil War (1944–49), and many of the Slavic Macedonians fled to the People's Republic of Macedonia. As with the other guerilla fighters who fled to eastern Europe, the right-wing Greek governments of the 1950s confiscated their property and barred their return to Greece. Post-World War II immigration to Australia and Canada further reduced the numerical strength of this group. In the 1990s a small, vocal Macedonian human rights movement developed in northern Greece, but its electoral support remains marginal (around 7,000 votes).

VICTOR ROUDOMETOF

See also **Greeks**

Further Reading

Augustinos, Gerasimos, "Hellenism and the Modern Greeks," in *Eastern European Nationalism in the Twentieth Century*, edited by Peter F. Sugar, Lanham, Maryland: American University Press, 1995

Danforth, Loring M., *The Macedonian Conflict: Ethnic Nationalism in a Transnational World*, Princeton, New Jersey: Princeton University Press, 1995

Karakasidou, Anastasia N., *Fields of Wheat, Hills of Blood: Passages to Nationhood in Greek Macedonia, 1870–1990*, Chicago: University of Chicago Press, 1997

Mavrogordatos, George Th., *Stillborn Republic: Social Coalitions and Party Strategies in Greece, 1922–1936*, Berkeley: University of California Press, 1983

McNeill, William Hardy, *The Metamorphosis of Greece since World War II*, Chicago: University of Chicago Press; and Oxford: Blackwell, 1978

Mouzelis, Nicos P., *Modern Greece: Facets of Underdevelopment*, New York: Holmes and Meier; and London: Macmillan, 1978

Roudometof, Victor, *Collective Memory, National Identity and Ethnic Conflict: Greece, Bulgaria and the Macedonian Question*, Westport, Connecticut: Praeger, 2002

Roudometof, Victor, *Nationalism, Globalization, and Orthodoxy: The Social Origins of Ethnic Conflict in the Balkans*, Westport, Connecticut: Greenwood Press, 2001

Roudometof, Victor, editor, *The Macedonian Question: Culture, Historiography, Politics*, Boulder, Colorado: East European Monographs, 2000

Tsikelidis, Constantinos, and Dimitris Christopoulos, editors, *To Meionotiko Phenomeno stin Ellada: Mia Symvoli ton Koinonikon Epistimon* (The Minority Issue in Greece: A Contribution from the Social Sciences), Athens: Kritiki, 1997

Greeks

Capsule Summary

Location: southeastern Europe, Australia, United States, Canada, and Germany
Total Population: approximately 4 million
Language: Greek
Religion: Eastern Orthodox

The Greeks of southeastern Europe live predominately in Greece. However, Greeks also live in 140 countries around the globe. Therefore, it is necessary to differentiate between two groups of Greeks: the communities of diaspora Greeks, located mostly in Western Europe, Canada, Australia, and the United States, and the small minority groups of Greeks living in Turkey, Albania, the former Soviet Union, and Bulgaria. These groups are the remnants of the Greek Orthodox population previously dispersed throughout the eastern Mediterranean in the premodern period (for details, see the entry "Greece" in this volume).

History of Immigration

The Greeks dispersed throughout the eastern Mediterranean during the Ottoman period, but after Greek independence in 1832, they were slowly concentrated into the lands of the modern Greek state. The Greek-Turkish exchange of population in 1923 was a turning point for this process. However, while Greeks from the former Ottoman lands gradually found their way into Greece, there were also immigration waves from modern Greece into North America, western Europe, and Australia. Consequently, a considerable percentage of Greeks continue to live outside the Greek state. The total number of diaspora Greeks is probably somewhere between 3 and 5 million, and half of this population resides in the United States, Australia, and Canada.

During the 1870–1925 period, approximately 800,000 Greeks immigrated to the United States. It is difficult to determine the precise figures, because many of them entered as Ottoman subjects and not as Greek citizens. This population settled mainly in the Northeast and the Midwest, and most observers agree that the total number of Greek Americans today is somewhere between 1 and 3 million. During the post-World War II period, further immigration waves were directed toward Germany, Australia, and Canada. In sharp contrast to the Greek Americans, these are more recent immigrants, many of whom want to return to their original birthplaces, maintain close ties to their homeland, and tend to intermarry. Conversely, Greek Americans are mostly second- or third-generation ethnic Greeks who do not contemplate returning to Greece and who tend to marry outside their ethnic group.

Most of the Greek Americans live in New York City, New Jersey, Boston, Chicago, Columbus, Ohio, and other metropolitan areas. There are several prominent Greek Americans in modern US public life, including George Stephanopoulos (former aid to President Bill Clinton, and ABC news journalist), Michael Dukakis (former United States presidential candidate), and George Tenet (current head of the Central Intelligence Agency, CIA).

Greeks in the Balkans

Approximately 300,000 Greeks live in Turkey, Albania, and Bulgaria. Additionally, there are about 350,000 Greeks who used to live in the former Soviet Union, many of whom immigrated to Greece in the 1990s. Of these groups, the most important and numerous is the Greeks of southern Albania (or Northern Epirus). The Greeks and Albanians have repeatedly failed to reach an agreement, even with regard to the size of the Greek population. The Albanians contest the figure of 250,000 reported by the Greeks and insist that the real figure is considerably lower.

This population was made part of the Albanian state in 1920, after the international community agreed on a final demarcation line between the Greek and Albanian states. The Greek minority lived on an ill-defined strip of land that was included in the territory of Albania. This territory became known as "Northern Epirus" and was the subject of a bitter dispute between Greece and Albania for most of the twentieth century. The Greek army briefly occupied the territory in 1940 during World War II. Greece maintained a formal state of war with Albania until 1987, when Greece recognized Albanian territorial integrity, and the only remaining dispute concerns the rights of the Greek minority.

During the interwar period, the Albanian state persecuted the Greek minority and denied them of their own educational apparatus. During the post-World War II period, the communist regime ruthlessly suppressed all forms of religious expression, including Greek Orthodoxy. The minority's revival began with the collapse of the communist regime in the 1990s, during which the minority question became a point of contention between the Greek and Albanian states. However, the Greek minority has been successful in gaining minimum recognition by the Albanian state. Many of the ethnic Greeks in Albania have immigrated to Greece in search of better opportunities. It is debatable whether the immigrants would be willing to return to their homes, and many have speculated that, with time, the majority of Albanian Greeks will end up in Greece.

Of the other two groups, the Greek population in Bulgaria is estimated to be approximately 18,000. To this figure, one should add approximately 60,000 Greek-speaking Vlachs, who were pastoral nomads and settled in the urban areas in the 1960s and 1970s. The Greek state is currently encouraging their immigration, whereas the Bulgarian state has consistently denied their existence as a separate group, let alone as ethnic Greeks.

The last group, the Greeks of Turkey, is estimated at around 5,000, living mainly in Istanbul. This small group comprises the remains of the Greek Orthodox population of the city, estimated to be around 300,000 in the 1920s. The minority's numbers were greatly reduced as a result of the Turkish policy of ethnic homogenization in the 1920s. More pressure and harassment followed the eruption of the Greek Cypriot nationalist movement in the 1950s. The movement aimed at the unification of Cyprus with Greece at the expense of the Turkish Cypriot group. This was the context for a series of riots as well as state persecution against the Greek minority that forced the majority of the Istanbul Greeks to seek shelter in Greece. A long-standing dispute still exists with regard to the property of Greeks who fled to Greece in the 1950s, whose property was confiscated by the Turkish state without compensation.

VICTOR ROUDOMETOF

See also **Greece**

Further Reading

Alexandris, A., *The Greeks of Istanbul and Greek-Turkish Relations*, Athens: Center for Asia Minor Studies, 1983

Constas, Dimitri C., and Athanassios G. Platias, editors, *Diasporas in World Politics: The Greeks in Comparative Perspective*, London: Macmillan, 1993

Danforth, Loring M., *The Macedonian Conflict: Ethnic Nationalism in a Transnational World*, Princeton, New Jersey: Princeton University Press, 1995

Dodos, Demosthenes Ch., *Eklogike geographia ton meionoteton* (Electoral Geography of Minorities), Athens: Exantas, 1994

Hasiotis, Ioannis, editor, *Oi Ellines tis Rossias and kai tis Sovietikis Enosis* (The Greeks of Russia and the USSR), Thessaloniki, Greece: University Studio Press, 1998

Journal of the Hellenic Diaspora (1974–)

Moskos, Charles C., Jr., *Greek Americans: Struggle and Success*, Englewood Cliffs, New Jersey: Prentice Hall, 1980; 2nd edition, New Brunswick, New Jersey: Transaction Books, 1989

Psomiades, Harry J., and Alice Scourby, editors, *The Greek American Community in Transition*, New York: Pella, 1982

Roudometof, Victor, "Transnationalism and Globalization: The Greek Orthodox Diaspora Between Orthodox Universalism and Transnational Nationalism," *Diaspora*, 9, no. 3 (2000)

Grenada

Capsule Summary

Location: Grenada, the most southern of the Windward Islands, is situated approximately 100 miles (161 km) north of the Venezuelan coast in the eastern section of the Caribbean Sea. With the inclusion of the southern Grenadines in the northeast, the island covers a total land area of 133 square miles (345 square kilometers). Grenada is about 21 miles (34 km) long from north to south and 12 miles (18 km) wide from east to west. The capital is St. George.

Total Population: 89,258 (July 2003 estimate)
Language: English (official language), and French-African patois
Religion: Roman Catholic (majority), Anglican, Methodist, and Seventh-Day Adventist

Grenada, also known as the "isle of spice," is one of the smaller islands located in the Lesser Antilles region of the Caribbean. Originally inhabited by Arawak, and later Carib Indians, the island was first sighted by Christopher Columbus in 1498. The Caribs controlled the island until 1650. At that time, the French governor of Martinique bought the island from a French company and created a settlement at St. George's. In 1672, the island became a colony of France, until 1762 marked British control over it. Similar to the fate of precolonial native populations in Latin America and the Caribbean, Caribs were forced to work for the colonial enterprise. Those who refused were subjected to the customary barbarities that included whipping, cutting off of body parts, rape, and killing. While runaways were hunted down by authority figures, those who submitted died of exhaustion and ill treatment from their overseers. Illness, such as influenza, decimated the remainder of the population. Given the quick demise of the "expendable" workforce, the colonial administration decided to import slaves from Africa. As a result, most of the current population in Grenada is black. At the same time, there is a minority consisting of mulattoes and other groups. For example, there is a small minority of East Indians, who are descendants of indentured laborers brought to replace the freed slaves, whites, who are descendants of French and British settlers, and more recently, immigrants from North America and Europe.

Grenada, like other Caribbean islands, is a culturally rich and diverse nation due to its historic formation. At the same time, its political economy is of great importance to those who are interested in the sociocultural fabric of the nation and the Caribbean region in general. In 1833, the black slaves were freed. Despite this policy measure, Great Britain still maintained tight control over the island. Among important historical junctures, the general election of August 1967 marks one of the most important tides in Grenada. Specifically, the Grenada United Labor Party (GULP) defeated the Grenada National Party (GNP) and took control over the state under the leadership of Eric M. Gairy. Hence, under Gairy, Grenada became an independent nation on February 7, 1974. As prime minister, Gairy did not enjoy much popularity. He ruled by decree by personally controlling the legislature and most of the economy. In response, opposition mounted and culminated in a coalition called the New Jewel Movement (NJM). As Gairy was abroad on March 13, 1979, the NJM orchestrated a diplomatic and bloodless coup that created a People's Revolutionary Government (PRG) under the dynamic leadership of Maurice Bishop. After this

historic juncture, the most dramatic turn in Grenada's history occurred on October 1983: a US military invasion.

The official public justification for this intervention offered by the Reagan administration was the need to protect US citizens on the island (including students in a local medical school). This explanation was further legitimated by a request for decisive action by conservative governments in the Caribbean region (including the Seaga team in Jamaica). Unofficially, many observers claim that the real motivation behind the invasion was Grenada's radical leftist position toward domestic and more specifically international affairs. Many argue that the PRG's foreign affairs policy aroused and aggravated US fears of communist encroachment. The party's alignment with Cuba and its declaration of solidarity with revolutionary movements throughout the Third World entailed the forging of close ties with the Soviet Union and with the east European community.

Struggles within the government finally climaxed in the autumn of 1983. In early October, a group of Stalinist radicals, under Bernard and Phyllis Coard, seized power from Bishop and executed him. Given the chaotic climate created by this political power vacuum, the Reagan administration decided to invade. Hence, on October 25th, a contingent of US troops landed on Grenada, overcame modest resistance efforts, and quickly garnered control of the island.

With the offset of turbulent events, and US invasion, one of the state's biggest obstacles was political legitimacy. Despite the political turmoil, the United States facilitated elections on December 1984, and a moderate formation known as the National Party, headed by Herbert A. Blaize, was able to win. Given Grenada's distance (among other factors), the country ceased to be a main priority to US interests. Hence, five years and $110 million in aid after invasion, the United States slowly withdrew from the island. After US military rule, the country has endured a slow transition toward a market economy. Per-capita GDP is $5,000 (2002 estimate). Export earnings have declined because of the crop diseases and falling world prices (for nutmeg, bananas, and cocoa). At the same time, unemployment and the number of people below the poverty line have continued to increase. Thus, Grenadians are left to realize their own political, socioeconomic, and cultural projects.

MANUELLA MEYER

See also **Afro-Caribbeans**

Further Reading

Brizan, George, *Grenada: Island of Conflict From Amerindians to People's Revolution 1498–1979.* London: Zed Books Ltd., 1984

O'Shaughnessy, Hugh, *Grenada: Revolution, Invasion and Aftermath. London: Sphere Books Limited, 1984*

Smith, Courtney, "The Grenadian Revolution in Retrospect," in *Modern Caribbean Politics,* edited by Anthony Payne and Paul Sutton, Baltimore and London: The Johns Hopkins University Press, 1993

Guatemala

Capsule Summary

Country Name: Republic of Guatemala
Location: central America
Total Population: 13.9 million
Languages: Spanish, Amerindian dialects
Religions: Roman Catholic, Protestant, and traditional Maya

The Republic of Guatemala (República de Guatemala) in Central America is bordered by Mexico to the west and north, Belize to the northeast, Honduras to the east, and El Salvador to the southeast. The Pacific Ocean marks its southern extent, while a short coastline in the northeast opens upon the Caribbean Sea. It has an area of 42,042 square miles (108,889 square kilometers). There are three distinct regions: the sparsely populated Northern Plain; the mountainous Guatemalan Highlands or interior uplands, the area in which most Guatemalans reside; and the fertile Pacific Coast Lowlands. The coastal regions are tropical while the highlands have a temperate climate.

In 1523 the Spanish explorer Pedro de Alvarado invaded Guatemala; the Audiencia de Guatemala was established in 1570 and independence was attained in 1821, and Guatemala was a part of the United Provinces of Central America beginning in 1823. Thereafter, a variety of military and civilian governments ruled and the 36-year guerilla war ending in 1996 reestablished peace. However, there were more than 100,000 casualties (mostly Amerindians) and the displacement of more than 1 million Guatemalans.

Guatemala's population numbers about 13,909,384 (July 2003 estimate); approximately 55 percent are mestizo (mixed Indian and Spanish extraction) and descendants of indigenous Maya peoples. The mestizos are also called *ladino*, a term commonly used in Central America. Ladino defines individuals who are Spanish-speakers and follow Spanish-American lifestyles in terms of clothing, housing, and food consumption. In addition, the term covers those Indians who have adopted Spanish-American culture. Hence, the term is indicative of cultural rather than biological traits because indigenous peoples are often categorized as ladino for social or political reasons. The dominance of an Amerindian culture within the Guatemalan Highlands distinguishes Guatemala from its Central American neighbors. Approximately 43 percent of the population is Amerindian; Europeans, blacks, and Asians account for the remainder. The annual demographic growth rate is 2.7 percent. During the latter half of the twentieth century, the civil conflicts in rural areas occupied by Amerindians led to the mass migration of refugees into neighboring Mexico, Belize, and the United States.

Based upon cultural traits, Guatemala's population is divided into two main ethnic groups: ladinos and Amerindians. The ladinos are the more commercially and politically influential group and make up most of the urban population. A majority of the blacks are the Garinagu (formerly known as the Black Carib) who inhabit the Caribbean lowlands. The Northern Plains are home to Yucateco Maya, while the Guatemalan Highlands are inhabited by Kekchi Maya, Ixil, Uspantec, Pokonchi, Pokoman, Quiche, Cachiquel, and Jacalteca. The Mam, Agualatec, Tzuntuhil, and Quiche live in the Pacific lowlands.

Spanish is the official language of Guatemala but is not universally understood among the Amerindians. There are 24 indigenous languages, principally Quiche (Q'eqchi or Kiche), Cakchiquel (Kaqchikel), Kekchi

(Kiche), Mam, Garífuna, and Xinca. Maya dialects are still spoken, especially in rural areas. The largest Amerindian groups are the Mam, who reside in the western departments of Guatemala; the Quiché, who occupy areas to the north and west of Lake Atitlán; the Cakchiquel, who extend from the eastern shores of Lake Atitlán to Guatemala City; and the Kekchi, who are concentrated in the sierras to the north and west of Lake Izabal. Many of the Amerindians also speak Spanish.

Demographic estimates for these Amerindian groups are unreliable, especially since the era of civil strife and migration. However, the censuses conducted by the Summer Institute of Linguistics during the 1990s provide the most reliable data. There are 56 languages spoken in Guatemala, of which 53 are living languages and three are extinct; the principle languages and numbers of speakers are:

Achí: 82,300–87,300
Aguateca: 18,000
Cachiquel: 518,300 (divided into eight regional groups)
Chortí: 31,500
Chuj: 41,600
Garífuna: 16,700
Ixil: 69,000
Jacalteco: 88,700
Kanjobal: 143,500
Kekchí: 400,000
Mam: 490,000–510,000 (divided into five regional groups)
Mopá Maya: 2,600
Pokoman: 239,000
Polomchí: 85,000–90,000
Quiché: 702,500 (divided into six regional groups)
Sacapulteco: 37,000
Suipacapense: 6,000
Tacaneco: 1,200
Tzutujil: 83,800
Uspanteco: 3,000

There were 100 Chicomultec speakers in 1982, 12 Itzá speakers in 1986, and fewer than 20 Xinca speakers in 1990. These are now considered extinct languages. Contrasting census data from 1980 suggests that there were then 540,000 Quichean speakers, 196,000 Pokomam speakers, and 335,000 speakers of the Mamean languages. The latter is divisible into Mam, Ixil, and Aguateca. In 1980 there were about 35,000 Chortí speakers who are linguistically and culturally related to the Chol and Chontal of Mexico; the

data suggest a decline in this population due to migration to Mexico. The Peace Accords signed in December 1996 provide for the translation of some official documents and voting materials into several indigenous languages.

The capital, Guatemala City, is the region's major metropolitan center, with 700,000 inhabitants (2.5 million in the metropolitan area); six other cities have populations in excess of 20,000, among these are Escuintla, Mazatenango, Puerto Barrios, Quetzaltenango, and Retalhuleu. Most of Guatemala's population is rural, although urbanization is accelerating rapidly.

The predominant religion in Guatemala is Roman Catholicism (59 percent), but Roman Catholicism among Amerindians is heavily infused with beliefs of pre-Hispanic origin. Probably the most significant Roman Catholic shrine in Central America is the Black Christ of Esquipulas (which is named for the dark wood from which it was carved) located in eastern Guatemala. Protestant religions account for about 40 percent, and traditional Maya religions for 1 percent.

CHARLES C. KOLB

Further Reading

Dávila, Amílcar, and Oswaldo Salazar, *Historia moderna de la etnicidad en Guatemala*, Guatemala: Universidad Rafael Landívar, 4 vols., 1996–1998

Dombrowski, John, et al., *Area Handbook for Guatemala*, Washington, DC: US Government Printing Office, 1970

Dow, James W., editor, *Encyclopedia of World Culture, Volume VIII: Middle America and the Caribbean*, Boston: G.K. Hall & Co., 1995

Ember, Melvin, and Carol Ember, editors, *Countries and Their Cultures*, New York: Macmillan Reference, under the auspices of the Human Relations Area Files (Yale University), 2001

Guatemala, in *The CIA World Factbook 2002*. http://www.odci.gov/cia/publications/factbook.af.html

Jackson, Robert H., *Race, Caste and Status: Indians in Colonial Spanish America*, Albuquerque: University of New Mexico Press, 1999

Languages of Guatemala, *Ethnologue* [Summer Institute of Linguistics], 1999. http://www.ethnologue.com/show_country.asp?name =Guatemala

Lima Soto, Ricardo, *Estudio de la Realidad de Guatemala: Aspecto Cultural*, Guatemala: Universidad Rafael Landívar, 1994

Minority Rights Group, *No Longer Invisible: Afro-Latin Americans Today*, London: Minority Rights Group, 1995

Vogt, Evon Z., editor, *Handbook of Middle American Indians, Volume 7: Ethnology*, 2 parts, Robert Wauchope (general editor), Austin: University of Texas Press, 1969

Guillén, Nicolás

Born on July 10, 1902, seven days after the formation of the Cuban republic, Nicolás Guillén was probably the most popular Cuban poet of this century. His father, Nicolás Guillén Urra, was very active in politics in his hometown of Camaguey. The family owned a printing shop, and at a very early age Nicolás learned the skills of the profession. The young Guillén began writing poetry at age 14. In 1919, he published his first poems in the newspaper *Camaguey Gráfico*. According to Guillén, he was influenced by the modernist Rubén Dario, but he was an important part of the movement known as the *vanguardia* along with the poets César Vallejo, Octavio Paz, Pablo Neruda, and Vicente Huidobro, among others.

In 1922, Guillén organized his first major book of poetry, *Cerebro y Corazón*, which was not edited and published until 1964. During the years 1927–1930, Guillén published verses in the journals *Revista de Avance* and *Otro*. He was also an important contributor to the column "Ideales de Una Raza" of the conservative *Diario de la Marina*, edited at the time by Gustavo E. Urrutia. Guillén published articles critical of Cuban race relations and poems, which celebrated African-Cuban culture and African-American culture hemispherically defined. Many of the poems published for this column eventually became part of the corpus of work of the literary movement known as *Negrismo*.

Negrismo celebrated the mulatto nature of Cuban national identity while unveiling the contribution of Africans and Spanish to Cuban history. While the celebration of African-Cuban culture was central to Negrismo, the movement was more reconciliatory and accommodating than confrontational than its French Caribbean counterpart, *negritude*, for example. Indeed, Guillén was intent on showing the union of a Cuban race through the joining of Spain with Africa. He did this best in his poetry. He revolutionized Cuban poetry by including popular elements such as the *son*, a popular African-Cuban dance rhythm, which originally had little prestige.

Guillén gained widespread acclaim with his publications in the 1930s. *Motivos de son* (1930), *Songoro cosongos*, untitled "Poemas Mulatos" (1931), and *West Indies Ltd.* (1934) in which he celebrated African-Cuban culture while denouncing racism and exclusion of blacks throughout the region. In 1937, he published *Cantos para soldados y sones para turistas*, the same year in which he attended the antifascist conference of writers in Madrid. His political activities would intensify thereafter. Guillén was a member of the Communist Party although he had earlier been jailed for his leftist activities. Guillén, who had been an avid supporter of the republican cause in the Spanish Civil War, eventually produced his *Poema en cuatro angustias y una esperanza* (1937) about his experience in Spain.

After an unsuccessful bid for the mayorship of his home province of Camaguey, Guillén began to deepen his international contacts and commitments. In the 1940s, his writings continued to underscore his leftist leanings while emphasizing his commitment to world justice. During this period he traveled throughout Latin America including Haiti, Venezuela, Peru, Brazil, and Argentina.

On his return to Cuba, Guillén once again made an unsuccessful attempt for political office, this time as a senatorial candidate for the Communist Party in the Province of La Habana in 1948. In 1949, he traveled to New York as a member of the Cuban delegation at the Cultural and Scientific Conference for World Peace, and in Paris he participated in the World Congress of Peace Advocates.

In the early 1950s, Guillén found himself at odds with the dictatorship of Fulgencio Batista (1952–1959). Thus, from 1953–1959 Guillén lived most of his life in exile, traveling to South America and Europe. Two years after receiving the Lenin Peace Prize (1954), Guillén published his book of elegies, *La paloma de vuelo popular: Elegías*. In this work, Guillén illustrates his acute awareness of injustice, including in the United States. In addition to dedicating poems to major world figures, Guillén composed "Elegía a Emmett Till" to a slain young African-American teenager in the midst of racial conflict.

With the triumph of the revolution in 1959, the government of Cuba named Guillén the nation's poet laureate. In 1961, the Cuban government appointed him to the National Education Council and named him president of the Cuban Union of Writers and Artists (UNEAC). He later traveled to Brazil as cultural advisor to the Ministry of External Affairs to assist in the creation of the VI Bienal of São Paulo, one of the most important cultural events of Latin America. Fidel Castro's presidential decree of 1962 made him an extraordinary ambassador and plenipotentiary minister of the Foreign Service. In 1964, Guillén published *Tengo*, which is regarded as a tribute to the gains of the revolution. This was followed by *El Gran Zoo* (1967), *La rueda dentada* (1972) and *El diario que a diario* (1972), and *Sol de domingo* (1982).

Nicolás Guillén died in Havana at the age of 87 on July 16, 1989. Guillén's poetry and work continues to be celebrated by Cubans in and outside of Cuba. Without a doubt, he was one of Cuba's most important poets of the twentieth century.

Biography

Born in Camaguey, Cuba, July 10, 1902. Poet. Co-editor of literary section of *Las Dos Repúblicas* in Camaguey; contributor to various literary reviews in Camaguey. Contributing poet to "Ideales de una raza," a column in *Diaro de la Marina*, Havana. Member of the Negrista movement of the 1930s, and editor of two Cuban newspapers, *Información* and *El Loco*. Recipient of Lenin International Peace Prize, 1954. Cuban poet laureate, 1960. Died in Havana, Cuba, July 16, 1989.

Selected Works

Motivos del Son, 1930
Sóngoro Cosongo: poemas mulattos, 1931
West Indies, Ltd., 1934
Cantos para soldados y sones para turistas, 1937, 1952
España: Poema en cuatro angustias y una esperanza, 1937
El son entero; suma poética, 1929–1946, 1947
Elegía a Jaques Romain en el cielo de Haití, 1948
Versos Negos, 1950
Elegía a Jesús Menéndez, 1951
Elegía cubana, 1952
Los mejores versos por Nicolás Guillén, 1961
Poesías, 1962
Tengo, 1964
Poemas para el Che, 1968
Diario que a diario, 1972
Cuba: Amor y Revolución, 1972
Obra Poética, 1920–1972, 1972–1973; 2nd edition, 1974

DARIÉN J. DAVIS

Further Reading

Ellis, Keith, *Cuba's Nicolás Guillén: Poetry and Ideology*, Toronto: University of Toronto Press, 1983
Smart, Ian I., *Nicolás Guillén: Popular Poet of the Caribbean*, 1990
Williams, Luis, *Self and Society in the Poetry of Nicolás Guillén*, Baltimore: John Hopkins University Press, 1982

Guinea

Capsule Summary

Country Name: Republic of Guinea
Location: West Africa; bordered by Sierra Leone, Liberia, Côte d'Ivoire, Mali, Senegal, and Guinea-Bissau
Total Population: 9,030,220 (2003)
Languages: French (official) and 30 indigenous languages and dialects including Pulaar, Malinke, and Susu
Religion: Muslims (85%), Christians (5%), and African traditional religions (10%)

The Republic of Guinea, officially known as République de Guinée, is located on the Atlantic coast of West Africa and covers an area of approximately 246,00 square kilometers (95,000 square miles). It is sometimes called Guinea-Conakry or Guinée française (French Guinea), a reminder of its history as a French colony. Guinea shares borders with Sierra Leone, Liberia, Côte d'Ivoire, Mali, Senegal, and Guinea-Bissau. The population comprises a diverse mix of ethnic groups among which the Fula (Fulani, Fulbe, Peul) are the largest. Other groups include the Susu (Soussou), Malinke (Mandigo, Mandinka), Baga, Jahanka (Diakhanke), Kpelle, Kuranko (Koranko), Mano, and Landoma. There are about 30 languages and dialects spoken in Guinea. Islam is the predominant religion and Muslims comprise about 85 percent of the population. A Christian minority accounts for about 5 percent of the population. The remaining 10 percent are believers in traditional African religions.

Guinea has an elected government headed by President Lansana Conté, who first came to power in 1984 after a military coup d'état. The people directly elect the president to a five-year term of office, and he appoints a cabinet to assist him in the administration of the government.

The precolonial history of Guinea indicates that this region was the home of hunters and gatherers about 30,000 years ago. Groups like the Baga, Coniagui, and Nalo were already settled along the Atlantic coast in the BCE era. Larger groups such as the Susu and Malinke arrived around the ninth century, at a time the Empire of Ghana wielded power over parts of northern Guinea. Muslim Fula immigrants, in search of pasture for their cattle, began to settle in the Futa Djallon area in central Guinea by the thirteenth century. In the aftermath of an Islamic jihad (holy war) in the late 1820s, Futa Djallon became a Muslim confederacy under the leadership of Karamoka Alfa Bari who assumed the title of *Almamy* (head of the Muslim community). He ruled with the help of the most prominent Fula Muslim lineages in Futa Djallon. Although non-Muslims were allowed to convert to Islam, divisions between Muslims and non-Muslims intensified when Islam became the dominant religion in the region. Many groups including the Koranko and Susu were forced to migrate and resettle in the northern part of present-day Sierra Leone. Through conquest and treaties signed with some of the indigenous chiefs, the French brought parts of Guinea under their control during the second half of the nineteenth century. The borders of modern Guinea were demarcated in the 1880s, and by the 1890s it was an autonomous French colony. The great-grandson of Almamy Alfa Bari, Alfa Yaya, resisted French colonialism toward the end of the century. So did another leader, Almamy Samory Toure, a Malinke, who attempted to rally other African leaders to fight against French domination. Samory's resistance, however, crumbled in the face of superior French firearms, and he was captured and exiled in 1899. Divisiveness among various indigenous leaders also undermined Guinean efforts to put up a unified resistance against the French.

French colonial rule in Guinea lasted approximately 65 years. During this period, traditional chiefs could only exercise administrative authority under the supervision of the French colonial administration. Cash-crop plantations were developed to grow coffee, palm oil, groundnuts, and bananas for exportation to France. Guinea's rich bauxite, iron ore, gold, and diamond deposits sustained French interest in that country. Between 1902 and 1914, the French built a railway linking Conakry (capital) and Kankan to facilitate trade and the movement of troops.

Guinea gained independence on October 2, 1958. This followed a rejection of a proposal by General Charles de Gaulle inviting Guinea to join a community of French African states. An overwhelming majority of Guineans voted against joining the French community in a referendum held on September 28, 1958. Ahmed Sékou Touré, a Malinke who traced his lineage to Samori Toure and founder of Guinea's first trade union, became the country's most vocal critique of French colonialism. His leadership qualities made him a popular choice for the country's leadership.

In postindependent Guinea, Touré adopted revolutionary socialist policies, which led to a complete pullout by the French from Guinea. He then relied on aid from the Soviet Union, thereby arousing U.S. concerns about the spread of communism in Guinea and other parts of Africa. Touré depended on a network of clients built around his minority Malinke group, which gave rise to interethnic tensions between the Malinke and the larger Fula and Susu groups. Touré silenced his opponents, especially the Fula, by confining them to prison camps. He died suddenly in March 1984. Colonel Lansana Conté, a Susu, masterminded the 1984 coup d'état and became Guinea's new leader. Dissatisfaction with Conté's government has increased over the years and the government has foiled several coup attempts.

Guinea's Muslim population is predominantly indigenous unlike those in neighboring Mali and Mauritania who claim an Arab or Berber descent. Many Guinean Muslims who conscientiously practice the religion also continue to adhere to traditional African religions and beliefs. The political dominant Susu (11 percent of the population) regard the Fula (40 percent) and the Malinke as its biggest rivals in the country's politics. In spite of their numerical strength, the Fula have never been unable to gain political dominance in postcolonial Guinea. Since 1991 the civil wars in neighboring Liberia and Sierra Leone have disrupted life in Guinea and strained that country's economy. More than 700,000 refugees from Liberia, Sierra Leone, and Guinea-Bissau have sought refugee in Guinea since the early 1990s. The Guinean government spends a considerable amount of money on defense, claiming that Guinean dissidents are helping rebels from Liberia and Sierra Leone to destabilize the country and overthrow President Conté's government. The GDP per capita as of 2002 was US$2,100.

TAMBA E. M'BAYO

Further Reading

Adamolekun, Ladipo, *Sekou Touré's Guinea*, Methuen: London, 1976

Binns, Margaret, *Guinea*, Santa Barbara, California, and Oxford, England: Clio Press, 1996

Nelson, Harold, Margarita Dobert, James McLaughlin, Barbara Marvin, and Donald P. Whitaker, *Area Handbook for Guinea*, Washington, DC: US Government Printing Office, 1975

O'Toole, Thomas, *Historical Dictionary of Guinea (Republic of Guinea/Conakry)*, Metuchen, New Jersey, and London: 1987

Guinea-Bissau

Capsule Summary

Name: Republic of Guinea-Bissau (Républica da Guiné-Bissau)
Location: West Africa, on the Atlantic coast
Population: 1,360,827 (2003)
Languages: Crioulo; African languages
Religions: traditional beliefs (65%); Islam (about 30%); Christian minorities
Groups: Balanta, Fulani, Maninka, Mandyak, and Papel are the major ethnic groups

Guinea-Bissau is a low-lying coastal region of swamps, rivers, and mangrove-covered wetlands. Only 10,800 square miles (about 27,971.87 square kilometers) are arable, over a total area of 13,948 square miles (about 36,125.15 square kilometers). Water covers the remainder. Guinea-Bissau is one of the world's poorest countries. The GNP per capita is one of the lowest in the world (US$700, as of 2002). The HDI index (Human Development Indicator) is 0.089 and places Guinea-Bissau at 169 among 174 countries.

The region was a tributary realm of the Mali Empire when the Portuguese first made contact. They arrived on the coast in the 1440s and soon the area became an important slave trade center. Portugal controlled just the coastal area, as in other parts of its empire. Actual control of the interior was not established until 1915. However, pockets of resistance held out until as late as 1936, when the Bijago minority finally gave up their armed struggle.

The African Party for the Independence of Guinea and Cape Verde (PAIGC), a political Marxist organization, was founded in 1956. Soon afterward it resorted to guerrilla warfare. The Balanta Brassa constituted the bulk of the guerrilla forces. The Fulani leaders instead collaborated with the colonial administration and became allies of the Portuguese army.

Independence was gained in September 1974. The monopoly over foreign trade imposed by the one-party socialist government damaged the trade of the Diola minority and, in general, the traditional economy. In 1980 President Cabral was overthrown in a coup by Prime Minister Bernardo Vieira. Steps were gradually taken to introduce a multiparty democracy and economic liberalization. In May 1999, rebels deposed Vieira. Kumba Yalá was elected President in January 2000.

There are approximately 30 different ethnic groups. It seems that the main groups had established themselves there by the twelfth century. Each ethnic group originally had a territory (known as *chao*), but conquest—first by the Malinke and then by the Fulani—pushed the movement of the Balanta southwards, and the war and postwar migrations have tended to muddle the settlement pattern.

The Balanta are the largest and most widely spread group. They represent about 30 percent of the population. They are divided into the subgroups Balanta Brassa, Balanta Manés, Balanta de Naga, Balanta de Mansoa, Balanta de Fora, Cunante, and Balanta Bravos. The main subgroup, Balanta Brassa, resides in the urban centers on the coast. The Balanta society revolves around the family in which patrilineal system, household, age group, and gender are major categories.

The Fulani (Fula) are about 20 percent of the population. There are several distinct subgroups such as Fulas do Bòe, Fula Forros, and Futa Fula in Guinea-Bissau. The largest one, Fulakunda or Fula Preto

(214,200), is scattered throughout the northeastern, south-central, and southeastern regions. The Fulani who intermarried with the Mandingo during their fifteenth century southward migration became known as Fula Preto ("black" Futa). Their society is patrilineal (the line of descent is traced through the father, and inheritance is passed down through the males), Muslim, and hierarchical.

The Mandyak (or Manjaco, Manjak, Kanyop) number 125,000 in Guinea-Bissau. Closely related to Papel, they live in the North.

The Maninka or Mandinka represent 9.9 percent of the population. They are a subgroup of the Mande. The Maninka society is patrilineal, Muslim, and hierarchical, with a division between free-born (noble), slaves, and artisans. Bards (griots) are responsible for handing down the oral literature in Maninka language that is regarded as one of the finest in the world.

The Biafada (or Beafada) (25,000) are a subgroup of the Tenda. They are located in the central southern region near Nalu and extend over the border into Guinea. Among the Biafada, about 70 percent are Sunni Muslims.

The Papel (or Pepel) (80,000) live on the northern coastal region. They were among the first people to have established trading relations with the Portuguese.

The Diola migrated to Guinea-Bissau from the east. Diola are a Sunni Muslim and widely scattered people that have had extensive contacts with other groups through commerce. This has contributed to the great diffusion of Dyola (Jula), their language.

Other important groups are the Mankanya (30,000), belonging to the Manjaku-Papel group; the Kunante, located in the north-central region; the Ejamat or Felupes (17,000) and the Bijagos (16,000), who live on an island offshore. Some smaller groups are the Bram, the Boencas, the Nalu, the Jarancas, and the Torancas.

All these groups speak African vernacular languages that, in turn, are divided into dialects. All African languages spoken in Guinea-Bissau derive from the Niger-Congo family, of the Atlantic-Congo language group. Portuguese is the official language, but Crioulo, a mixture of Portuguese and African elements, is more commonly spoken. There is also a Crioulo *lebi* ("light"), based on Portuguese, a Crioulo *fundu* based on an African idiom, and a dialect version (*Cacheu-Ziguinchor Creole*) spoken by 55,000 people in Senegal, with some Pidgin French vocabulary.

MASSIMO REPETTI

See also **Fulani**

Further Reading

Bigman, Laura, *History and Hunger in West Africa*, Westport, Connecticut: Greenwood Pub Group, 1993

Gaillard, Gerald, editor, *Migrations Anciennes et Peuplement Actuel des Cotes Guineennes*, Paris: L'Harmattan, 2000

Galli, Rosemary E., "The Political Economy of Guinea-Bissau," *Africa*, 59, no. 3 (1989)

Galli, Rosemary E., and Jocelyn Jones, *Guinea-Bissau: Politics, Economics and Society*, London and New York: Frances Pinter and Columbia University Press, 1987

Henry, Christine, *Les Îles où Dansent les Enfants Défunts*, Paris: CNRS Editons, 1994

Lobban, Richard, and Peter Karibe Mendy, *Historical Dictionary of the Republic of Guinea-Bissau*, Lanham: Scarecrow Press, 1996

Pélissier, René, *Naissance de la Guinée: Portugais et Africains en Sénégambie (1841–1936)*, Orgeval: Pélissier, 1989

Rodney, Walter, *A History of Upper Guinea Coast, 1545 to 1800*, Oxford: Clarendon Press, 1970

Schaffer, Frederic Charles, *Democracy in Translation: Understanding Politics in an Unfamiliar Culture*, Ithaca: Cornell University Press, 1998

Gujaratis

Location: Gujarat State, India
Total Population: approximately 50 million worldwide
Language: Gujarati
Religion: mostly Hindu

Gujaratis are the predominant ethnic group of Gujarat, a state situated in the monsoon area along the Arabian Sea on the western coast of India. Gujarat consists of three very distinct geographic areas. The Saurashtra region coincides with the Kathiawar Peninsula, an expanse of low hills and plateaus that juts into the Arabian Sea. Mainland Gujarat, home to the highly industrialized cities of Surat and Ahmedabad, lies to the east of this peninsula, beyond the Gulf of Cambay. The Kuchch region, a vast expanse of tidal mud flats and salt marshes, lies to the north of the peninsula, across the Gulf of Kuchch. The state population is approximately 50 million, of whom 90 percent speak Gujarati or one of its regional dialects. Several million Gujaratis live outside of the state, in neighboring Indian regions or in diasporic communities worldwide. Ninety percent of the people of Gujarat are Hindu by religion, and Muslims and Jains make up significant minorities.

Gujarati History

As evidenced by carved rock edicts in the Girnar Hills of Saurashtra, Gujarat formed part of the Buddhist Emperor Ashoka's Maurya Empire for several centuries before the turn of the millennium. Successive dynasties that rose to power in western India between the fifth and ninth centuries CE ruled the region as "Gurjar Bhoomi," "Gurjara Desh," "Gurjar Mandal," and by the tenth century, "Gujarat"—the abode of the Gurjar people. Muslim rulers conquered Gujarat in the thirteenth century, and the land was ruled by independent sultans and vassals of Mughal emperors for 450 years. The Marathas conquered Gujarat in the mid-eighteenth century.

The British East India Company gained control of Gujarat in 1818, administering most of the region through local princely rulers who paid tribute to the British during the colonial era. By the end of the nineteenth century, the British Raj directly governed other portions of Gujarati territory as administrative districts through the Bombay Presidency. Gujarati by birth, Mohandas K. Gandhi, the father of the India freedom struggle, established his *ashram* at Kocharab in Ahmedabad in 1915. Local leaders joined his nonviolent movement, which gradually came to national prominence through the birth of the Congress Party. Following independence in 1947, all Gujarati-speaking areas were absorbed into the emerging Indian nation. In 1956, Suarashtra and Kuchch joined mainland Gujarat as part of the composite State of Bombay. Gujarati leaders, however, issued demands for a separate linguistic state, and Gujarat was formed through the Bombay Reorganization Act of 1960.

Since 1946, central planners have been developing strategies for harnessing the potential power of Gujarat's Narmada River to alleviate the severe drought and irrigation problems of the state. Formally approved in 1979, the controversial Sardar Sarovar Project is currently the largest river valley project in western India. Proponents of the dam project claim that the harnessing of this river power will enable Gujarat to sustain its economic growth through strategic utilization of the untapped potential of Narmada runoff. Critics, however, argue that this large-scale scheme will overexploit the available resources to the benefit of the wealthy classes of society. They also point to the human cost of such a massive project, highlighting the hundreds of thousands of people whose land will be submerged or severely altered by the creation of the reservoir in Gujarat, Maharashtra, and Madhya Pradesh.

Gujarat suffered a devastating earthquake on January 26, 2001. The earthquake, which measured 6.9 on the Richter scale, occurred in a relatively resource-poor section of Kuchch that had suffered from two consecutive years of severe drought in 1999 and 2000. The World Bank estimates that more than 20 thousand people were killed and more than 167 thousand injured by the quake. Nearly 1 million homes were damaged or destroyed, and much of the social infrastructure—schools, medical clinics, water supply systems, and telecommunications—was extensively damaged or ruined. The international community has committed to providing assistance to the massive ongoing reconstruction effort in the state.

Gujarati Society

The social categories of caste and class are intricately intertwined in Gujarati society. The *Brahmins*, identified as wealthy landholders who occupy the uppermost tier in the caste hierarchy, constitute 4 percent of the total population. Other high-caste communities include *banias* (traditionally traders), *rajputs* (traditionally warriors), and other smaller occupational groups. *Patidars*, a community of wealthy peasants and entrepreneurs comprising about 12 percent of the population, occupy the middle strata of the caste hierarchy. The most significant lower caste group is the *kolis*, a large sector of poor peasants comprising nearly a quarter of the population. Scheduled Castes such as *dheds* (road sweepers) and *bhangis* (cleaners) exist outside of the caste hierarchy. Muslim Gujaratis, also considered external to the caste system, typically work as poor peasants or agricultural laborers.

Tribal peoples known collectively as *adivasis* constitute 14 percent of the total population of Gujarat. Most tribal groups, including Bhils, Dhodiyas, Gaits, and Chaudharis, occupy the hilly eastern belt of the mainland portion of the state. Although these tribal groups, particularly the Bhils, speak languages closely akin to Gujarati, they are quite different from the Gujarati people in terms of religious affiliation, structures of kinship, ritual practice, and economic division of labor. Officially recognized by the state government as Scheduled Tribes, these communities are eligible to receive special benefits and to compete for reserved seats in legislature and schools. Upper-caste Gujarati students organized violent riots in protest of the state policy of college reservations for Scheduled Tribes, Scheduled Castes, and Backward Classes in 1985.

Trade plays an important role in Gujarati society, and the *bania* castes of traders comprise a significantly higher proportion of the population here than elsewhere in India. The motivation for education among this community is quite high, and the literacy rate among *bania* males approaches 100 percent. Gujarati business people, particularly those from the industrialized mainland areas, have traveled to Bombay, to other cities in South Asia, and throughout the world in search of economic opportunity. The Gujarati communities established in former British colonies during the nineteenth century have increased as new migrants join their friends and family members overseas. Substantial Gujarati populations can be found in the United Kingdom, North America (Canada and United States), East Africa (Uganda, Kenya), South Africa (South Africa, Malawi, Tanzania, Zambia, and Zimbabwe), Fiji, Singapore, and New Zealand.

HALEY DUSCHINSKI

Further Reading

Baxi, Upendra, "Reflections on the Reservations Crisis in Gujarat," in *Mirrors of Violence: Communities, Riots, and Survivors in South Asia*, edited by Veena Das, Delhi: Oxford University Press, 1990

Breman, Jan, *Beyond Patronage and Exploitation: Changing Agrarian Relations in South Gujarat*, Delhi: Oxford University Press, 1994

Fisher, William, editor, *Toward Sustainable Development? Struggling Over India's Narmada River*, New York: M.E. Sharpe, 1995

Hardiman, David, "Adivasi Assertion in South Gujarat: The Devi Movement of 1922–3," in *Subaltern Studies III*, edited by Ranajit Guha, Delhi: Oxford University Press, 1984

Gurage

Capsule Summary

Location: southwestern area of Shewa (Shoa) region, in central Ethiopia
Total Population: nearly 2 million
Language: three related languages (Siliti, Kistane-Soddo, and West Gurage) of the south Ethiopian branch of the southern Semitic family
Religions: Ethiopian Orthodox Church; Sunni Muslims; animism

Gurage or Gerawege people designate themselves according to the names of the 14 "tribal" divisions in the Gurage cluster. The territorial divisions, each comprising several politically independent clan chiefdoms, are further distinguishable on the basis of the language (or dialect) spoken by each tribal unit: Silti, Urbarag, Aklil, Innekor, Chaha, Ennemor, Ezha, Gyeto, Mwahär, Zway, Gura, Maskan, Soddo, and Walani-Woriro. The Gurage languages (*Guraginä*) are an isolated conglomeration of Semitic-speaking ethnosystems surrounded by Cushitic languages. The linguistic distinction between "eastern" (Siliti, Kistane-Soddo) and "western" Gurage-speaking groups derives in part from Ethiopian chronicles relating to the formation of a political confederation among some western Gurage tribus in about the mid-nineteenth century, which came to be known as *Yä säbat bet Gurage* ("The Seven Gurage Houses"): Chaha, Ennemor, Ezha, Walani-Woriro, Gyeto, Mwahär, and Aklil. The Silti subgroup of the eastern Gurage lands is predominantly Sunni Muslim (nearby 95 percent of its population), as are the Walani, Ulbarag, Innekor, and Gogot groups. Soddo, Muher, Masqan, and Zeway are Christian (observing the Coptic calendar of religious events), and the rest of the groups believe in the traditional animistic Gurage religion.

The earliest mention of the name "Gerawege" seems to appear in the *Ethiopian Chronicle* relating to the being of the Ethiopian king, Amda Syon I

(1312–1342). Amda Syon is claimed to have dispatched an army, under the leadership of one Azmach Sabhat, and settled in Soddo (northern Gurage country). It is believed that, at that time, the region was inhabited by Muslim Sidamo. The military mission was intended to establish a Christian colony in the area from which to extend Amhara political hegemony further in southwest Ethiopia. Some Gurage groups claim founding ancestors from among the followers of Sabhat's army. A few groups of Gurage trace their origins to Harar.

Powerful Gurage clan chiefs and warriors had made several attempts to create a centralized state. Most notable was Azmach Sebeate, who at the end of the sixteenth century put down Oromo incursions into Gurage territory and declared himself king of Gurageland.

Throughout Gurage history, tribes and clans paid tribute annually to successive reigns of Ethiopians kings in gold, figurines, hides, and cattle, thereby retaining some political independence. Despite this payment of tribute, however, incursions from the neighboring peoples never ceased altogether, and there was no letup in the continual raiding of Gurage for slaves until the extension of the Ethiopian Empire government rule over all Gurage communities, finally, in 1889.

It is possible that the name Gurage was given by the Amhara—Ethiopia's dominant people group—to all the languages spoken by the people on their southern periphery. In Amharic, Gurage means "area of the Gura." Gura is another name for Harage, the traditional name for the area around the present-day city of Harar.

In Gurage traditional religion, *Yagzär* (the supreme god, the creator of the world) has no cult as do lesser deities, the most important of which are the cults of *Waq* (the male Sky god), of *Dämwamwit* (the female deity), and of *Bozhä* (the Thunder god), who have the responsibility of regulating the daily conduct of Gurage and affording ritual protection against theft and the destruction of property by arson.

"It's the language and the culture—we definitely have our own culture," says a Silti county official. Ninety-eight percent of the county's 130,000 citizens are Silti. One important Silti custom is their marriage ritual. When a young man is interested in marrying a woman, one of his friends will go to her parents and offer them money for their daughter. If they accept, he'll return and tell the groom to prepare for the wedding. Bride and groom will not see each other until the wedding day. After the agreement or engagement, the groom and the bride will be invited to feast with their families.

The general elevation of the Gurage country seldom rises above 2,000 meters, and the soil is generally poorer that in other regions of the Shoa plateau. Dense settlement and horticultural practices combine with natural geological erosion to decrease the amount of arable land. The Gurage traditionally depended on the enset plant (known locally as "false banana") rather than grain for their staple food and used the hoe rather than the plow. Others crops are barley, peas, and flax in the highlands; coffee and tobacco in the temperate zones; and maize, millet, and peppers in the lower altitude zone. Cattle, fat-tailed sheep, and fowl are the principal domestic animals kept for food.

Since the 1970s, Gurage language was recognized as a written idiom. The possibility of alphabetization in their own language allows the Gurage people to maintain an important record for their survival as a nation. But during the Marxist revolutionary period, forced governmental rural politics highly affected the traditional structure of the Gurage lands. The Ethiopian Constitution of 1994 may be able to create room to maneuver for Gurage aspirations of a differentiated ethnic system. On the other hand, substantial numbers, perhaps 15 to 20 percent of all Gurage, live in urban centers, particularly Addis Ababa, where they work at a range of manual tasks typically avoided by the Amhara and the Tigray. This forced urbanization (normally, fleeing from the famines) erodes the cultural ethnic heritage of the Gurage society.

JOAN MANUEL CABEZAS LÓPEZ

Further Reading

Marcus, Harold G., *A History of Ethiopia*, Los Angeles: University of California Press, 1995

Pankhurst, Richard, *The Ethiopians: A History*, Oxford, Massachusetts: Blackwell, 2001

Shack, William A., *The Central Ethiopians: Amhara, Tigriña and Related Peoples*, London: International African Institute, 1974

Shack, William A., *Gods and Heroes: Oral Traditions of the Gurage of Ethiopia*, Oxford: Clarendon Press, 1974

Gurma

Capsule Summary

Location: mostly in the east of Burkina Faso; also in the north of Benin and Togo, and areas of southwestern Niger
Total Population: approximately 800,000
Language: Gurmanchema
Religion: Traditional religion (animistic); some Muslim and Christian

The Gurma (also named Gurmanche or Biguliman-ceba) are an ethnic group living in the same-named region of Gurma, in Burkina Faso, and also in adjacent areas of Benin, Togo, and Niger. There are more than 600,000 Gurma who live in the core area of their ethnic distribution. Their language, Gurmanchema, belongs to the Oti-Volta subfamily of the Gur or Voltaic language group. The Gurmanchema language has three main dialects: Northern, Southern, and Central, but each of these main dialect clusters consists of multiple small speech patterns. Central Gurmanchema is the prestige dialect and is used for writing. Some Gurma use Zarma or Fulfulde languages. Gurma religion is mostly based in traditional systems of beliefs, predominantly structured in an animistic cosmology that affords sacred values to the objects of the natural environment. Some Gurma became Christian and Muslim, but they adopted these religions only formally because the ancestral animistic system of beliefs is still deeply embedded into the soul of the Gurma people.

It is widely believed that the Gurma migrated from present-day northeastern Ghana. Many Gurma dynasties sprang from different ethnics groups, especially Temba and Yowa. Indeed, the Temba ethnic group is deeply influenced by the political culture from Fada N'Gurma Kingdom, the biggest Gurma state formation, which was less centralized than other polities developed in the area. The Yendabri's reign (1709–1736) drove the Gurma culture to its summit. Yendabri moved the Gurma capital to Fada N'Gurma (the real core of the Gurma nation). Through its rule, the Gurma occupied the Liptako region, situated in the northern border of their territory, and founded the frontier city of Doala, which became a strategic base. In the eighteenth century, the multiple dynastic tensions disturbed the Gurma societies, but despite this, there were several periods of peaceful rule (for example, between 1761 and 1791) that provided a stable cultural atmosphere. The Gurma polities were organized in independent kingdoms that, in spite of this, recognized the ritual supremacy of the *bado* (chief) of Nungu (the other name of Fada N'Gurma city). The Gurma people fiercely fought against the Liptako and Yagha Fula warriors that invaded the Gurma space in the beginning of the nineteenth century. When French colonialist troops arrived in 1897, the Gurma people definitively lost their northern territories

The Gurma live in wooded savanna that becomes much drier and grassier to the north. Their housing consists of round mud-brick units arranged in circular compounds that are surrounded by woven straw fences. Within their compounds, the Gurma depend on cultivation and harvesting during the wet season, herding of animals during the dry. While the men work the fields, the women remain at the village to tend to the children, prepare the meals, and repair and build the family housing units. The *wuro* ("village") is the center of Gurma societies. It reflects on its grounds the traditional social representations, and constitutes the ceremonial space, the economic core of the community, and the place of the primary socialization in the Gurma culture. Women are traditionally concerned with work at home, while men normally are engaged in harvesting and milking from the age of 15. Making clothing is also a masculine activity. An ancient Gurma traditional activity is the geomancy, a kind of divination by means of figures or lines, formed by little dots or points, originally on the earth and afterward on paper. Neighboring peoples are aware of this Gurma skill that is an outcome of their animist beliefs and its inherents systems, transmitted from generation to generation.

The Usman Dan Fodio's islamic Jihad (1804), which had wide political effects on all West African peoples, led to the political supremacy of the Muslim Fula groups over the Gurma communities, who resisted bravely between 1810 and 1817. Finally, the Gurma people fell back to the south. Some migrations of Gurma advanced during the nineteenth century toward the northern areas of Togo and Benin, founding small but powerful kingdoms and attracting additional waves of Gurma to these countries. As a whole, though, in the nineteenth century, the Gurma world edged southward due to deep and strong political tensions.

As an outcome of the multiple ethnic contacts established in the Gurma territories, different subgroups arose, for example, the Folmongani. They live predominantly in swamp areas that, in ancient times, were favored by the *razzias*: during 1810–1850, for example, the Hausa peoples attacked this frontier area of the Gurma. This region, then, was the place from which emerged the Folmongani ethnic group, a fusion between Gurma and Fula that can be dated to the eighteenth century, approximately.

The Gurma political culture and language is close to the Mossi people, the demographically dominant ethnic group of contemporary Burkina Faso. In fact, the single ethnic link between Mossi and Gurma people consists in sharing a common mythical ancestor known as Gbewa. In spite of the obvious religious, linguistic, and sociological similarities, Gurma societies are clearly differentiated. Indeed, Gurma belongs to a specific historical branch, probably derived from an ancient fusion with Dagomba and Bariba autochton societies. This may explain the origin of the Gurma political structure. The Gurma kingdoms were decentralized, especially in comparison with the Mossi ones. The reason can be found in the basic role of the kinship relations in Gurma society, and its territorial impact, that is, a space centered in the village communities interwoven by clan bonds. A lasting image of the Gurma people is their unmistakable village formations. Throughout the years, the Gurma have worked to create a very distinctive, circular setup for their housing, encompassed by straw fences. This type of construction sets them apart from many neighbor groups and reflects the solid identity of the Gurma people.

JOAN MANUEL CABEZAS LÓPEZ

Further Reading

Brasseur, Georges, and Georges Le Moal, *Ethno-Demographical Maps of Western Africa (3–4)*, Dakar: Institut Fondamental de l'Afrique Noire, 1963

Izard, Michel, *Peoples and Kingdoms of the Niger Inner Delta and the Volta Bowl (12th to 16th centuries)*, in *General History of Africa (IV)*, D.T. Niane (Director), Madrid: Unesco, 1985

Madiega, Y.G., *Contribution to the Precolonial History of Gurma (Burkina-Faso)*, Wiesbaden: Franz Steiner Verlag, 1982

Guyana

Capsule Summary

Location: north coast of South America
Total Population: 702,100 (July 2003)
Language: English, Amerindian dialects, Creole, Hindi, and Urdu
Religion: Christian (50%); Hindu (35%); Muslim (10%); other (5%)
Governance: parliamentary democracy

Guyana was first colonized by the Dutch East India Company in the seventeenth century. The coastal strip was reclaimed with slave labor for use as coffee, cotton, and sugar plantations. This narrow fertile area below sea level, and protected by an elaborate system of dykes, is now home to 90 percent of Guyana's population.

The Dutch divided up the territory into three colonies: Essequibo (West), 1616; Berbice (East), 1627; and Demerara (Central), 1752. The British took over the territory ceded by the Dutch in the Convention of London, 1814, and established British Guiana in 1831. The colony's principal product was sugar, and the labor force consisted of enslaved Africans.

When slavery was abolished in 1838, planters brought in indentured laborers. These came mainly from India, but also Madeira, the Azores, Africa, and China. By 1917, more than 350,000 such workers had come to British Guiana. However, by the end of the nineteenth century, the largest groups were Afro-Guyanese, Indo-Guyanese, and lighter-skinned people born from relationships between African women and

European men, and their descendants. In the Guyanese context they are referred to as "mixed,"

However, who exactly has minority status in Guyana is a moot point. The number of Indo-Guyanese exceeded that of Afro-Guyanese for the first time only in the post-World War II period, and the former now make up the largest group within the country's population. At the time of the last census (1997) the country's ethnic composition was as follows: Indian, 47.35 percent; African, 32.7 percent; mixed, 12.2 percent; Amerindian, 6.3 percent; Portuguese, 0.26 percent; Chinese, 0.18 percent; others, 1 percent. However, in terms of religion, around 50 percent are Christians, 35 percent Hindus, and 10 percent Muslims (the two latter groups concentrated within the Indo-Guyanese communities). So when looked at from the perspective of religious affiliation, those of Indian origin do not constitute a majority.

Yet if minority status has to do with exclusion from decision making, then the Amerindians must claim that title. When the Dutch arrived, there were around 700,000 in 19 tribes inhabiting the coastal area. Numbers have dropped drastically (to around 45,300, according to the 1997 Census) and most retreated into the interior. The number of tribes is down to nine and only in the 1990s did Amerindians become seriously involved in the country's political life and governance.

Although there are now few European and Chinese-descended Guyanese, they tend to be higher up the social scale as a legacy of their access to business ownership, most of which was due to nineteenth colonial policies aimed at keeping Africans and Indians as plantation labor and facilitating other groups' social mobility. Typical of these were restrictions on communal land ownership and monopolies on licenses granted for particular activities. Many Portuguese and Chinese left the country for North America in the 1970s and early 80s, when economic conditions worsened.

Views about power relations and ethnicity in Guyanese society are split. The popular idea is one in which ethnic conflict has divided the Indian from the African since the arrival of the former in the 1830s. They latter lowered the wages that emancipated Africans could ask for on the plantations. Evidence of this conflict is usually drawn from the elections leading up to independence (May 26, 1966), that is, in the 1957–64 period. There was, indeed, politically motivated hostility: The multiethnic nationalist party that had swept Prime Minister Cheddi Jagan to power in 1953 later split into two. Each faction ended up representing one of the two major ethnic groups. The People's Progressive

Party (PPP) was led by Jagan, a US-trained dentist, appealing mainly to Indian voters, the majority of whom lived outside the urban areas; and the People's National Congress (PNC), led by Forbes Burnham, a British-trained lawyer, whose constituency was primarily black and mixed urban-based voters. The first-past-the-post election system exaggerated the majority enjoyed by Jagan's party, but his election victories in 1957, 1961, and 1964 were convincing.

In 1962–63 there were a series of riots and strikes aimed at destabilizing Jagan's administration. These were later revealed to have been promoted and funded by the Central Intelligence Agency, intent on removing Jagan (whom the US intelligence community perceived as a communist) from office. With the assistance of the British, who altered the electoral system to one of proportional representation to nullify the PPP's majority, this objective was attained.

Burnham, who took power in 1964, had been identified by the British and Americans as more friendly to the West. Yet he rigged subsequent elections and mismanaged the economy to the point where the International Monetary Fund refused further loans in the 1970s. During the period of PNC rule (1964–1992), Afro-Guyanese received the lion's share of government sponsorship, primarily in the form of the redistribution of land and state employment (a particularly important stake in a country with minimal welfare provision). This alienated most Indians.

An alternative reading of ethnic conflict put forward is one in which the principal dividing line in colonial British Guiana was between Europeans and the rest. Since class and color coincided almost exactly, the differences in life chances between Indians and Africans were less important than those between all the "nonwhite" groups and the Europeans. In fact, the historical record shows that there was very little fighting between Indians and Africans, and occasional union solidarity. Postwar strife was inspired by, if not carried out by, foreign powers, and the violence of the 1960s, when 976 died, was never repeated. The rioting after the 1992, 1997, and 2001 elections was minimal, and relatively peaceful coexistence rather than tension has been the norm, particularly since the restoration of parliamentary democracy in 1992.

Burnham died in 1985, and his successors acceded to local and international demands for fair elections. In 1992, Jagan became President and the PPP governed in a coalition with "Civic," a nonsectarian party aimed at restoring democracy to Guyana. Its leader, Sam Hinds, has been prime minister since 1992. Violence flared up around elections in 1992 and 1997, as the now-opposition PNC called for resistance to what it called a "corrupt Indian government." Jagan died in 1997, and his wife Janet (also a deputy since 1953 and former cabinet minister) took over the reigns. She handed on to current President, Bharrat Jagdeo, in 1999. The 2001 elections returned the PPP/Civic coalition to power.

Moreover, on a day-today basis, the family and personal links between Guyanese from different ethnic backgrounds by far outweigh the tension that is supposed to exist. Strong and representative trade unions, high electoral turnouts, and a slowly improving economy since the early 1990s testify to a willingness to make up for lost time in terms of normal democratic functioning.

STEVE GARNER

See also **Afro-Latin Americans; Amerindians: South and Central America**

Further Reading

Baber, C., and H.B. Jaffrey, *Guyana: Politics, Economics and Society*, London: Frances Pinter, 1986

Jagan. C., *The West on Trial*, New York: International Press, 1976

Moore, B., *Cultural Power, Resistance and Pluralism: Colonial Guyana 1838–1900*, Montreal: McGill University Press, 1995

Peake, L., and A. Trotz, "Work, Family and Organising: An Overview of the Contemporary Economic, Social and Political Roles of Women in Guyana," *Social and Economic Studies*, 50, no. 2 (2001)

Premdas, R., *Ethnic Conflict and Development: The Case of Guyana*, Aldershot: UNRISD/Avebury, 1995

Rodney, W., *A History of the Guyanese Working People*, Baltimore: Johns Hopkins University Press, 1981

Williams, B., *Stains on my Name, War in my Veins: Guyana and the Politics of Cultural Struggle*, Durham: Duke University Press, 1991

Gypsies, *See* **Roma (Gypsies)**

Haiti

Capsule Summary

Country Name: Haiti
Location: Caribbean
Total Population: 7,100,000 (2004)
Ethnic Populations: black, mulatto, Arab
Languages: Haitian Creole, French, Langaj
Religions: Voodoo, Roman Catholic, Protestant

Haiti occupies the western third of the island of Hispaniola, with the eastern portion comprising the Dominican Republic. To the east of Hispaniola lies Puerto Rico; to the west, Cuba. Haiti has a tropical climate, and its size approximates that of Maryland. Haiti has over a third more population than that state, and its inhabitants are densely settled over the small plains and valleys of an otherwise very mountainous terrain. A fifth of the land is arable. The GDP per capita as of 2002 was $1,400.

The social conditions of Haiti are directly related to the historical conditions of its development. In the eighteenth century it was a rich sugar-producing French colony. The labor for the highly profitable sugar cultivation came from an intense importation of hundreds of thousands of African slaves. The resulting population produced a tiny minority of wealthy, white French landowners at the top of Haitian society, a small minority of mixed blood mulattos, and a vast, enslaved black population. Today the country is impoverished, and its Creole languages are part of an isolated minority

in the Western Hemisphere. However, as a once wealthy colony it was an important province in the French Empire, which then extended from Quebec in the north, across the Great Lakes, down the Mississippi valley to New Orleans, and through various islands in the Caribbean.

The repression, violence, and divisions of colonial slavery have scarred and fractured Haitian society, so that today it is the poorest country in the Western Hemisphere. Slave rebellions occurred throughout the colonial period. The French Revolution of 1789 inspired a movement in Haiti that resulted in its independence by 1804. The principal social consequence of independence was the slaughter and replacement of the tiny white minority by the small mulatto minority, which remained in power until well into the middle of the twentieth century. At that time black military and political leaders began to dominate and have continued in power to this day.

Well over 95 percent of the population of Haiti is black, with about five percent, or a few hundred thousand people, being mulatto. There is only a very small white population and a tiny number of "Arab," or Middle Eastern, merchants active in urban commerce. Authoritarian civilian and military rule, repression, violence, and instability continue to mark Haitian society as they have throughout its history.

French is little spoken anymore in Haiti. It is used now as the second language of several hundred thousand, mostly mulatto, speakers. The principal language of most inhabitants is Haitian Creole French, known in that language as *Kreyòl Ayisyen*. This language also appears outside Haiti among several hundred thousand Haitian economic and political refugees in the United States, Canada, and the Dominican Republic.

Kreyòl Ayisyen has the basic syntax and grammar of French, but its vocabulary mixes much of French with various western African languages, such as Wolof, Fon, Mandingo, and Ewe. Different dialects of Kreyòl Ayisyen are found in the various geographic regions of Haiti. The principal dialects, based mainly on different manners of pronunciation, are Fablas, Plateau Haitian Creole, and Faublas-Pressoir. The dialect spoken in Port-au-Prince, the capital, is considered the standard form of the language. The spelling of Kreyòl Ayisyen is quite different from French, primarily because Kreyòl Ayisyen tries to reflect the different manner of speaking the language. It especially contrasts with standard French in, for example, the greater use of the letter *K* in many words.

Another one of the most widely known cultural phenomena of Haiti, Voodoo, is also of western African origin. Considered both a religion and a form of black magic, Voodoo is respected and feared by much of the Haitian population. However, the official dominant religion of Haiti is Roman Catholicism. The central function of Voodoo is to protect people from sickness, misfortune, and evil forces. In its form as black magic, Voodoo tries to enact misfortunes against others. It is in this manifestation that it is so widely feared. Although the religion recognizes a supreme god, Bondye, the dynamic of its supernatural forces concentrates on the animist manifestations of elements of nature and on the spirits of the dead. Through male and female priests, the religion negotiates with the supernatural forces. It has its own ritual language, known as *Langaj*. Services are conducted outdoors beneath an overhead covering, with all present participating. Spirit possession often plays a key role in ceremonies.

Because the vast majority of Haitian society was enslaved, the country's people did not own property or wealth—they were actually the property of others. Haiti, therefore, could never develop a market economy. It never had a substantial part of its population owning the means to consume and produce, and thereby establish, the dynamics of markets and middle-class stability.

In the modern world, which is rapidly witnessing the globalization and integration of markets from the Western Hemisphere to Europe and Asia, Haiti is a tragic anomaly. It is massively impoverished, unstable, and violent. It stands out in tragic anarchy, unable to build a stable, participatory economy and government.

EDWARD A. RIEDINGER

See also **Slavery**

Further Reading

Chamber, Frances, compiler, *Haiti*, World Bibliographical Series, 39, Oxford, England: Clio, revised and expanded edition, 1994

Desmangles, Leslie Gérald, *Voudoo and Roman Catholicism in Haiti*, Chapel Hill: University of North Carolina Press, 1992

Dunham, Katherine, *Island Possessed*, Chicago: University of Chicago Press, 1994

Galembo, Phyllis, *Vodou: Vision and Voices of Haiti*, Berkeley, California: Ten Speed Press, 1998

Haitian Creole-English-French Dictionary, 2 vols., Bloomington: Indiana University, Creole Institute, 1981

Lawless, Robert, *Haiti: A Research Handbook*, New York: Garland, 1990

Lefebvre, Claire, *Creole Genesis and the Acquisition of Grammar: The Case of Haitian Creole*, Cambridge, England: Cambridge University Press, 1998

Metz, Helen Chapin, editor, *Dominican Republic and Haiti: Country Studies*, Area Handbook Series, Washington, D.C.: Federal Research Division, Library of Congress, 2001

Targète, Jean, *Advanced Grammar of Haitian Creole*, Port-au-Prince: Atlier Fardin, 2nd edition, 1979

Hakka Chinese

Capsule Summary

Location: Fujian, Jiangxi, Guangdong, Sichuan, and Hainan Provinces; Taiwan, Southeast Asia, North America, Europe
Total Population: 55 million
Language: Hakka
Religions: *San jiao* or "three doctrines" (Buddhism, Taoism, Confucianism), Christianity

"Hakka" is the Cantonese pronunciation of the Mandarin word *ke jia*, which means "guest families." The term has been used in Fujian since the Qing dynasty to distinguish northern migrants from natives. More precisely, it applies to a Han dialect group whose ancestors allegedly migrated southward more than one thousand years ago to settle at the junction of Jiangxi, Fujian, and Guangdong Provinces. From there, several generations of landless peasants moved to Taiwan, where henceforth Hakka constituted the second Chinese ethnic group. During the late nineteenth and early twentieth centuries, hundreds of thousands fled poverty by migrating to Southeast Asia and western countries.

Hakka is an intermediate idiom between the Cantonese and Mandarin dialects. An apt illustration of this position between southern and northern languages is its tonal system: Cantonese has nine tones, Hakka has six, and Mandarin has four. Linguists theorize that Hakka took shape in northwestern Guangdong Province. The number of its speakers is about 2.5 percent of the total population of the People's Republic of China (32 million), and people of Hakka origin count for 25 percent of the Taiwan population (5 million). Moreover, about 18 million are scattered overseas, mainly in Thailand, Malaysia, Indonesia, Singapore, and Canada (for instance, Adrienne Clarkson, a governor-general of Canada, has Hakka ancestors).

Most Hakka claim a central or northern origin. Some historians agree with this contention, though recent studies bring to the fore the important contribution of Guangdong and Fujian natives to the formation of this people. Different theories have been published concerning the origins of the Hakka. Some scholars believe they are the descendants of the Yue, a proto-historic tribe located south of the Yellow River, whereas for others they originate from northern China,

but either are non-Han, or, on the contrary, are considered as the most authentic Han. The studies that claim a northern origin (notably that of Lo Hsiang Lin, 1933) are based on the interpretation of genealogical records. These documents make reference to successive migratory waves, starting during the Eastern Jin dynasty (317–420), and whose seats were Shanxi, Henan, and Hebei. However, only the last stages of the migration, from Sichuan to Guangdong and corresponding to the beginning of the Qing dynasty (1644–1911), are well documented.

Those who argue for the southern origin of the Hakka take into account recent archaeological findings at the border of Guangdong, Fujian, and Jiangxi Provinces. Evidence of a highly developed civilization that existed in this area before the Jin dynasty and its Chinese acculturation between the sixth and tenth centuries (because of a long administration of the south by northern bureaucrats) supports the hypothesis that Hakka culture was not imposed by conquerors but is the result of a long and complex process of interaction between northern court officials and natives.

The mountainous area of Meixian, northwest of Guangdong Province, was historically the main stronghold of the Hakka culture. The lack of sustainable lands in the region led many families to emigrate. The earliest destination, from the sixteenth century on, was Taiwan. But during the nineteenth century, North America and Southeast Asia became attractive as destinations. At that time, the Hakka were also involved in the Taiping revolt, the failure of which strengthened their migration overseas. In Southeast Asia, the major political event in Hakka history was the constitution of the Lan Fang Republic. In 1777, Guangdong Hakka briefly established an independent state in western Kalimantan. In 1884, the Dutch attacked the republic. After four years of fighting, the Guangdong Hakka were defeated and fled to Sumatra. From there they moved to Malaysia and Singapore, where they contributed significantly to the establishment of the state of Singapore.

Both in mainland China and overseas, Hakka are the most active among the Chinese groups to promote their ethnic identity. Because of the popular myth that presents them as the primitive or "authentic" Han people, they have kept in-depth clan genealogies, which they sometimes use to claim a "pure" or aristocratic pedigree. The fact that some prominent figures of recent Chinese history were Hakka, including the Soong sisters (who married Sun Yatsen and Chiang Kaishek), Deng Xiaoping, and Lee Tenghui (former president of the Republic of China), strengthens their pride. Haunted by the question of origin, which remains controversial, the Hakka intelligentsia has created and supports different research institutes (the Hakkalogy Center in Shanghai, the Hakka Research Society in Shenzhen, and the Hakka Museums in mainland China and abroad), which study the group's origins. They also use newer technologies of communication, such as the Internet, to develop transnational networks with the goal of promoting Hakka culture and identity. In 1995, the Hakka Global Network was created. It has hundreds of subscribers from over sixteen countries.

BERNARD FORMOSO

See also **Taiwan**

Further Reading

Constable, Nicole, *Guest People: Hakka Identity in China and Abroad*, Seattle: University of Washington Press, 1996

Leong, Sow-Theng, *Migration and Ethnicity in Chinese History: Hakkas, Pengmin, and Their Neighbors*, Stanford, California: Stanford University Press, 1997

Oxfeld, Ellen, *Blood, Sweat, and Mahjong: Family and Enterprise in an Overseas Chinese Community*, Ithaca, New York: Cornell University Press, 1993

Hall, Stuart (United Kingdom Afro-Caribbean)

Respected scholar and cultural theorist, Stuart Hall has been described as among the foremost black British intellectual figures of the twentieth century. A lifelong socialist and a key founder of the New Left movement, Hall's contributions to the field of cultural studies in England have identified him as a crucial figure in writings on postcolonial culture, race, class, and identity.

Born in Kingston, Jamaica, in 1932, from an Afro-Caribbean background, Hall spent his childhood and teen years in Jamaica but lived most of his academic career in England, where he emigrated with his mother in 1951. He came from a lower-middle-class Jamaican colonial family, in a country where gradations of color and class were not only linked but also extremely significant (Rojek 2003, 49). A Rhodes scholar at Merton College, Oxford, Hall experienced the racial tensions of that environment in the 1950s as an Afro-Caribbean among white English fellows. During the 1950s Hall edited, along with Charles Taylor, Raphael Samuel, and Gabriel Pearson, the New Left's socialist publication *Universities and Left Review*. In 1959, this journal merged with social historian E.P. Thompson's *New Reasoner* and became the *New Left Review*, which aimed to reestablish socialism within British political life.

Pursuing the works and theories of Thompson, Raymond Williams, and Richard Hoggart on British popular culture, the young Hall was invited in 1964 to join the new Centre for Contemporary Cultural Studies (CCCS) at the University of Birmingham. Together, they forged what was to become a genuine critical discipline, that of cultural studies. Hall's particular interests lie not only in the reproduction of culture in media studies (literature, film, etc.), but also in the connections between racism, imperialism, and cultural discourse, especially as it pertained to the mixed ethnicities of those living in Great Britain.

Although difficult to define, the field of cultural studies can be seen as an interdisciplinary approach that analyzes texts, messages, signs, cultural icons, representations, films, television programs, and news in order to understand premises, stereotypes, attitudes, symbolic meanings, and hidden ideologies—in other words, the shaping of culture and its social reproduction in various discourses. Here, culture is to be taken as mass culture, popular culture, counterculture, or culture at the margins, be it mainstream culture or within subcultures. Borrowing from sociology, media studies, ethnicity, Marxism, and later feminism, scholars in cultural studies seek to explain how power shapes culture and therefore can institutionalize a hegemonic culture. Another aim is to observe how cultural identities are produced, especially in postcolonial contexts. This theoretical framework, when linked with an understanding of how some dominant forces marginalize others, inevitably brings together issues related to class, race and gender. Hall himself viewed the field as "constructed by a number of different methodologies and theoretical positions, all of them in contention" (During 1999, 99).

Hall's reflections on the absence of representations of blacks on British Broadcasting Corporation (BBC) television were among the earliest influential critiques within media studies, during at time when scholars began to question the social construction of a national identity in England. In a November 1971 BBC-televised debate, Hall noted the problems with the manner in which black immigrants (West Indians, Asians, and Africans) were portrayed and described in the mass media. Three years later, in an essay entitled "Black Men, White Media," he analyzed how the creation (or construction) of media images functions as a politically powerful tool primarily because "by dealing with real-life problems and situations in fictional terms, it creates images without appearing to do so" (Hall 1974). His analysis further purported that when emotions and associations are attached to these images (as invariably happens), they can trigger more explosive situations in "real" life. In this and other critiques, he revealed the subtle and not so subtle, often hidden or invisible attitudes and links between the broadcasting media and power, in which power is defined politically, economically, culturally, and symbolically.

Hall's contributions also merged with intellectual work on migrations, the diaspora, marginality, multiculturalism, "whiteness" and "blackness," ethnic conflicts, and institutional racism. His ideas echo those of other postmodern thinkers such as Jacques Derrida in the belief that the constitution of the self (or subject) is irrevocably related to that which is both within that self and without, that is, what is outside or "other than" the subject. In some of his writing, he reflects upon what it might mean to be both black and British. Such a process of identity formation must take into account the various experiences and belief systems that merge in multiethnic societies. As he stated,

> It will be hard for adult West Indians or Pakistanis to accept the fact that their children and grand-children will be progressively "at-home" in a different country, as it will be for white people to accept that the presence . . . of second and third generation black people will irreversibly alter their culture and social patterns. (Mercer 2000, 236)

From the days of Thatcherism in the 1980s, Hall has always been an aggressive critic of the British government and of conservatism in general, despite the fact that he has never been a Labour Party member. As an important emerging critic of the New Right, he has argued for the cultural practices of marginal groups. Hall's writings became extremely influential in the United States and earned him credit within the field of cultural studies and related disciplines such as feminism and African-American studies. Since the 1970s Hall has published countless articles and edited numerous books on cultural studies, postcolonial studies, and media theory. Most of his writings are disseminated in journals and various collective publications.

Biography

Stuart Hall. Born 2 February 1932 in Kingston, Jamaica. Schooling in Jamaica College, Kingston. Left Jamaica in 1951 for Bristol, England; studied at Merton College, Oxford, as a Rhodes scholar, from 1951; earned master's degree in 1954. Taught as a supply teacher in various high schools around Brixton, England (1957–59). Editor of the *New Left Review,* 1959–61. Lecturer in film and television studies at Chelsea College, University of London, 1961–64. Research fellow at the University of Birmingham, 1964. Member and assistant-director (1964–79), and director (1974–79) of the University of Birmingham's Centre for Contemporary Cultural Studies. Professor of sociology at the Open University (United Kingdom), 1979–97; currently emeritus professor of sociology, the Open University. Chair of the boards of Autograph: The Association of Black Photographers and InIVA: The Institute of International Visual Arts. Member, the Runnymede Trust's Commission on the Future of Multi-Ethnic Britain, which produced the Parekh Report, 1998–2000). Awarded the Life-time Achievement Award for Contribution to Education (2003), from Windrush Foundation Awards, an organization that celebrates the contribution of Caribbean people in Britain. Resides in England.

Selected Works

"Black Men, White Media," 1974 "Cultural Studies and Its Theoretical Legacies," in During, *The Cultural Studies Reader,* 1966; 2nd edition, 1999

"New Ethnicities," ICA Documents 7, 1988; reproduced in Morley and Chen, *Stuart Hall: Critical Dialogues in Cultural Studies,* 1996

"What Is This 'Black' in Black Popular Culture?" in Morley and Chen, *Stuart Hall: Critical Dialogues in Cultural Studies*, 1996

"The Formation of a Diasporic Intellectual. Interview with Kuan-Hsing Chen," in Morley and Chen, *Stuart Hall: Critical Dialogues in Cultural Studies*, 1996

Questions of Cultural Identity (with Paul Du Gay), 1996

Cultural Representations and Signifying Practices, 1997

YVES LABERGE

See also **Afro-Caribbeans; Critical Race Theory; Diaspora; Globalization and Minority Cultures; Race**

Further Reading

During, Simon, editor, *The Cultural Studies Reader*, London: Routledge, 1993; 2nd edition, 1999

Gilroy, Paul, Lawrence Goldberg, and Angela McRobbie, *Without Guarantees: In Honour of Stuart Hall,* London: Verso, 2000

[Hall, Stuart], "Revealed: How U.K. Media Fuelled Race Prejudice," *Chronicle World* [an unsigned e-review with some quotations from Stuart Hall's hard-to-find article titled "Black Men, White Media," first published in *Savacou: Journal of Caribbean Artists Movement*, 9/10 (1974)]. http://www.thechronicle.demon.co.uk/tomsite/8_6_1rev.htm

Long, Elizabeth, editor, *From Sociology to Cultural Studies: New Perspectives*, Oxford: Blackwell, 1997

Mercer, Kobena, "A Sociography of Diaspora," in *Without Guarantees: In Honour of Stuart Hall*, edited by Paul Gilroy, Lawrence Goldberg, and Angela McRobbie, London: Verso, 2000

Miller, Toby, editor, *A Companion to Cultural Studies*, Oxford: Blackwell, 2001

Rojek, Chris, *Stuart Hall*, London: Polity, 2003

Hamer, Fannie Lou (African-American)

Fannie Lou Hamer was one of the most eloquent speakers for the civil rights movement in the United States in the 1960s and 1970s. She worked for political, social, and economic equality for herself and all minorities, especially African Americans. Hamer fought to integrate the national Democratic Party and became one of its first black delegates to a presidential convention.

Hamer was born on a plantation in 1918 in Montgomery County, in the Mississippi hill country, the last child in a family of 20 children. Her parents, Jim and Lou Ella Townsend, children of slaves, were sharecroppers who fed their whole family on $1.25 a day. They moved to Sunflower County, Mississippi, when Hamer was 2 years old. Hamer began working in the fields at age 6, when the plantation owner promised her goods from the commissary store. She contracted polio as a child, and since there was no vaccine at the time, she was left with a limp. Because of the dire economic circumstances in which the family lived, Hamer received only about 6 years of formal education. She dropped out of school in the sixth grade, but she continued her education through Bible study with the Stranger's Home Baptist Church.

In 1944, Fannie married Perry "Pap" Hamer. They moved to the Marlow plantation in Ruleville, Mississippi, and became sharecroppers. She found that, as a black worker, she was frequently treated as less than human. Perhaps the most acute example of this was the fact that Hamer was denied the basic right of having her own children because a white doctor sterilized her without her permission. Hamer, however, did adopt four daughters. The experience underscored the lack of control she felt she had over her own life as a black American. During the 1960s, she became interested in the civil rights movement and became involved in voter registration when members of the Student Nonviolent Coordinating Committee (SNCC) and the Southern Christian Leadership Conference (SCLC) came to Mississippi. In 1962, Hamer attended a SNCC meeting for the first time. She volunteered when they asked for individuals to try to register to vote. At that time, the threat of organized white racist violence, combined with strict and biased literacy requirements, made voting impossible for most Mississippi blacks. The first time Hamer tried to register, on August 31, 1962, she failed, not knowing the answer to an obscure question about the Mississippi constitution. On her second try, she failed the test again. But, in 1963, on her third attempt, she finally passed the test. Hamer was fired from the Marlow plantation for attempting to register to vote.

In order to assist other African-Americans in registering to vote, Hamer became a field secretary for SNCC and traveled across the South. On June 9, 1963, during one of the trips to South Carolina, the bus in which she and other SNCC workers were riding was stopped in Winona, Mississippi. When some of the workers went into the "white only" waiting room, the whole group was arrested. While in custody, Hamer and other workers were beaten unmercifully. Hamer suffered serious injuries that bothered her throughout the rest of her life. SNCC lawyers bailed her and the others out of jail and filed suit against the Winona police. All the whites who were charged were found not guilty. This injustice made Hamer more determined to fight for equal rights in Mississippi. She saw voting as fundamental to bringing about change in America. With the help of SNCC, Hamer filed a lawsuit (*Hamer v. Campbell*) in 1966 in an attempt to block elections in some Mississippi communities where black voters had not had the opportunity to register to vote.

Unable to attend a local precinct meeting of the Democratic Party, SNCC formed the Mississippi Freedom Democratic Party (MFDP). In the 1964 Mississippi primary, the MFDP got more votes than the regular Democratic Party; yet, at the convention in Atlantic City, the national party would not seat the MFDP's delegates, one of whom was Hamer. She spoke to the Credentials Committee during the convention about the injustices of the all-white Democratic delegation. A compromise was made in which two seats would be given to the MFDP. The Democratic Party had an all-white delegation again.

Hamer continued to work for better conditions for Mississippi minorities by organizing grassroots anti-poverty projects. She became a sought-after national speaker and worked to unite the black and white factions of the Mississippi Democratic Party. In 1965, *Mississippi* magazine named her one of six "Women of Influence" in the state. In 1968, she helped create a food cooperative, the Pig Bank, to help the poor obtain more meat in their diet. In 1969, she founded the Freedom Farm Cooperative in which 5,000 people were able to grow their own food and own 680 acres of land. In 1971, she helped found the National Women's Political Caucus. Also in 1970, she filed a lawsuit, *Hamer v. Sunflower County*, challenging the Mississippi county to properly desegregate schools. During the last ten years of her life, she continued her work on school desegregation, along with work on such issues as child day care and low-income housing. Hamer died in Mississippi on March 14, 1977, of complications resulting from cancer, hypertension, and diabetes. Her headstone bears words for which she will be most remembered: "I'm sick and tired of being sick and tired."

Biography

Fannie Lou Townsend Hamer. Born 6 October 1917 in Montgomery County, Mississippi. Attended local public schools until the sixth grade at the age of 12. Attended Stranger's Home Baptist Church Bible study. Active civil rights worker, 1964–77. Joined the Southern Christian Leadership Conference (SCLC) and the Student Nonviolent Coordinating Committee, 1962; joined the Mississippi Freedom Democratic Party (MFDP), 1964; keynote speaker for the MFDP at the 1964 Democratic Party national convention in Atlantic City. Cofounder, The Pig Bank, 1968; founder, the Freedom Farm Cooperative, 1969; cofounder, the National Women's Political Caucus, 1971. Elected to the National Women's Hall of Fame, 1993. Died in Mound Bayou, Mississippi, 14 March 1977.

RICHARD VERRONE

See also **Racism**

Further Reading

Crawford, Vicki L., Jacqueline Anne Rouse, and Barbara Woods, editors, *Women in the Civil Rights Movement: Trailblazers and Torchbearers, 1941–1965,* Bloomington: Indiana University Press, 1993
Lerner, Gerda, *Black Women in White America: A Documentary History*, New York: Vintage, 1972
Meier, August, editor, *Black Protest in the Sixties: Articles from the* New York Times, Princeton, New Jersey: Markus Wiener, 1991
Mills, Kay, *This Little Light of Mine: The Life of Fannie Lou Hamer*, New York: Plume, 1994
Rubel, David, *Fannie Lou Hamer: From Sharecropping to Politics*, Needham, Massachusetts: Silver Burdett Press, 1990

Hani

Capsule Summary

Location: Yunnan Province in the People's Republic of China, Vietnam, Myanmar, Thailand, Laos
Total Population: 2.2 million
Language: Hani
Religion: animist

The Hani are an ethnic group inhabiting the borders of southwestern China and northern Indochina. About 80 percent of them live in the southern part of Yunnan Province, in the People's Republic of China, with most settled in the Ailao Range (Red River) and the others established in the Mekong Basin (Simao Prefecture). Although southwestern China is their original home, some have migrated southward: during the seventeenth or eighteenth centuries into Vietnam (Lai Chau, Lao Cai), where they number approximately 15,000; in the middle of the nineteenth century into the Shan States of Burma, where more than 250,000 live today; and at the turn of the twentieth century into the northern mountains of Laos and Thailand (where they number respectively 70,000 and 50,000).

The Hani belong to the Tibeto-Burman branch of the Sino-Tibetan language group, and they are closely related to the Lahu and Lisu. Because of wide geographic scattering, the degree of cultural variability is high within this population, and its language divides into many dialects. There are two main idioms —Akha and Hani—and within them many subdialects, such as Jeu-G'oe, A-Jao, U-Lo, A-Kho, or Bu-Ko dialects for Akha, and Xalo, Goxo, or Yi-Choe for Hani. In Myanmar, Thailand, and Laos, Akha is the only subgroup represented. The Hani have no traditional script, although a romanization created by missionaries is used by some Christian Akha in Myanmar, and the communist government elaborated another romanized script in the 1950s for those living in China.

According to Chinese historians, the Hani are one of the few indigenous peoples of Yunnan. Administrative reports dating back to the Tang (618–907) make reference to He Man ("He Barbarians"), the supposed ancestors of those who were called Heni or Hani under the Yuan dynasty (1271–1368). From the seventh century onward, they inhabited the Ailao Range. By that point, they had already earned the admiration of Chinese chroniclers for the spectacular terraced paddy fields they built on the slopes of steep mountains. These irrigated structures remain among the famous terraced fields in the world. During the Ming dynasty (1368–1644) the Hani were ruled through the *tusi* system of indirect administration. Authority for the smallest territorial units was delegated to natives, who were usually notables belonging to esteemed lineages. Court officials replaced these chieftains under the Qing (1644–1911).

After the Opium War (1855), the Qing encouraged highlanders of southern Yunnan, including the Hani, to grow a great deal of opium. Because of the heavy taxations on this product, the Hani rebelled several times against the imperial administration or were involved in larger uprisings (such as the Taiping and Hui revolts). The ensuing crackdown by the Chinese urged a number of them to flee southward during the second half of the nineteenth century and the first decades of the twentieth century. Taking refuge into the mountainous area bordering China, Burma, Laos, and Thailand, they continued to cultivate opium poppies. After 1949, the Hani of China gained the status of "nationality" (*minzu*) from the communist government, along with the accompanying minority rights (equality, regional autonomy, freedom to develop a language).

The Akha of Myanmar, Laos, and Thailand face continuing difficulties in obtaining citizenship, land ownership, and agricultural opportunities. Moreover, in Thailand, their traditional system of slash-and-burn (swiddening) cultivation has been threatened since the middle of the 1980s by a governmental ban on logging.

The Hani/Akha is an ethnic group characterized by its lineage, with local communities spread over a vast area involving five countries. A common and rich heritage of myths and rituals gives them a strong sense of unity. Whatever the country they are currently located in, they remember the migration route their forefathers followed. They share a genealogical chart that enables them to name all their ancestors on the male line back to the "origin." Another factor of unity is the concept of Akha or Hani *zang* (a term which, depending on the context, means "way," "religion," or "customs"). *Zang* is a set of idioms in which Hani/Akha ethnoreligious identity is expressed. It includes ceremonies, knowledge, and techniques related to agriculture, animal husbandry, hunting, and traditional medicine. The Hani make a clear demarcation between themselves and outsiders (through endogamy), and between humans and jungle spirits (through the gates found at the entrance of each village), as a means of maintaining this order of things.

BERNARD FORMOSO

See also **Migrations**

Further Reading

Bernatzik, Hugo, *Akha and Miao: Problems of Applied Ethnography in Farther India*, New Haven, Connecticut: Human Relation Area Files, 1970

Lewis, Paul, *Ethnographic Notes on the Akha of Burma*, 4 vol., New Haven, Connecticut: Human Relations Area Files, 1968–70

McKinnon, John, and Wanat Bhruksasri, *Highlanders of Thailand*, New York: Oxford University Press, 1986

Haräri (Adäré)

Capsule Summary

Location: Ethiopia (Harär, Addis Ababa), Canada (Toronto), various Arabian Gulf states, Europe, the United States
Total Population: reliable statistics not available
Language: Haräri
Religion: Islam

The Haräri are a Muslim people, also known as Adäré by some of their neighbors, who hail historically from the eastern Ethiopian city of Harär, in northeast Africa. The town remains the group's homeland and a centerpiece of Haräri ethnic identity, but members are today scattered around the globe, clustering in a few major cities. Although reliable population figures are unavailable, there are about 10,000 Haräri in Harär, and probably about 4,000–5,000 in Addis Ababa (Ethiopia) and Toronto each; smaller numbers live in various Arabian Gulf states, Europe, and the United States.

Oral traditions attribute the founding of Harär town and the genesis of the Haräri ethnic group to about 1,000 years ago, when Shaykh Abadir immigrated from Arabia and effected the union of nine villages in the area. Since then Harär has served as a major center of Islamic learning in the Horn of Africa, attracting students from far and wide. It has also been a major trade center in the regional economy.

In the early 1500s, Harär was the headquarters for Islamic forces during a series of religious wars with Christian Ethiopia. Led by Imam Ahmad ibn Ibrahim al-Grañ (the Left-Handed), an army of combined Haräri, Somali, and other Muslims penetrated deeply into Ethiopia before Imam Ahmad was killed and the movement disintegrated. In its wake, a wall was built around Harär, either to protect it from further sackings by Christian armies or to provide protection from growing numbers of Oromo immigrants in the region.

From then until the nineteenth century, the Haräri occupied the top tier of a stratified ethnic hierarchy in and around the city. Over the 1800s, the power of Harär's leaders and of its economy weakened, culminating in the city's 1875 occupation by Egyptian forces. Accounts of the ensuing period vary, but generally it seems to have been a good one for the Haräri, whose local preeminence was reestablished. Because of crises at home, the Egyptians withdrew in 1885.

Only 2 years later the town was again conquered, this time by Christian Ethiopians. Though there were tensions between the new rulers and the Muslim Haräri indigenes, substantive political change came only in 1935 when fascist Italian forces took the town as part of a larger assault upon Ethiopia. Favoring Muslims over others, the Italians inaugurated a period that is generally remembered as prosperous for the Haräri. After the Italians were expelled from the country in 1941, Ethiopian rule was restored.

Resenting renewed restrictions, the Haräri founded a political organization seeking either greater local autonomy or independence. In 1947–48 the movement was brutally crushed by Ethiopian authorities, a violent episode that marked the end of "traditional" Harär as

547

it was hitherto known. Until then, the vast majority of Haräri were born, grew up, and died in Harär, even though individuals may have traveled elsewhere for trade, religious pilgrimages, or other purposes. Only after 1948, however, did large numbers of Haräri begin to emigrate permanently from the city, an exodus that continues to this day.

The Haräri are Sunni Muslims, adhering primarily to the Shafi'i school of legal interpretation and observing all major Islamic holidays. Harär is also home to a rich culture surrounding Muslim saints, who are honored on special occasions throughout the year. One Arabic name for the town, attesting to the prominence of this culture, is *madinat al-awliya*, or City of the Saints.

Haräri identity has historically been distinctly urban. In the Haräri language the urban center of Harär is referred to as *gé* (the city); the people are *gé 'usu* (the people of the city); they speak *gé sinan* (the language of the city); and their culture and way of life are *gé 'ada* (the customs of the city). Most probably, these appellations constituted one means by which the small number of urban Haräri distinguished themselves, cognitively at least, from their much more populous agricultural and pastoral neighbors, the Oromo and Somalis.

In the face of these larger groups and, since 1887, a variety of Christian Ethiopian immigrants, certain social institutions have served to maintain both social stability and a distinct Haräri ethnolinguistic identity. They include *ahli*, or family networks; *afocha*, which are ostensibly funerary associations but actually assist in a wide variety of activities; and *mariññat*, or friendship groups between males or females of similar ages. Membership and participation in each of these groups ensure that individuals interact with a broad cross section of Haräri society on a regular basis, learn about the town's history and culture, keep abreast of local events and news, and are subject to social pressures to conform to ideals of proper behavior.

The Haräri language has long been central to all of these activities. Without knowledge of the language, one could not participate in *ahli*, *afocha*, and *mariññat* activities, which are necessary to "being Haräri." Therefore, throughout history individuals who did not speak the language could not be considered Haräri. In recent decades, however, with increasing numbers of Haräri being born and raised abroad, this scenario has changed. Nowadays, those born elsewhere to Haräri parents are also considered Haräri. Whether they learn the language while growing up or not, they are accepted as Haräri when they visit the homeland or Haräri gatherings anywhere. Also, continuing a historical but small-scale trend, other peoples who convert to Islam, learn the language, and are accepted into the three main social institutions can "become" Haräri.

After the Ethiopian military dictatorship was overthrown in 1991, the new coalition government established a political system based upon ethnicity. Within it, all ethnicities were to be free to develop and use their own languages as they saw fit. In Harär, a power-sharing arrangement has been reached in which the Haräri exercise primary authority in and around the city, while Oromo administer surrounding rural areas. In their sphere, the Haräri have embarked upon the ambitious task of standardizing a writing system and employing their language in administration and education. One result is a burgeoning number of Haräri-language publications that may well assist Haräri throughout the world in teaching the language to their children and thereby help to ensure a global sense of Haräri identity, despite the fact that the group is a minority wherever its members are found.

TIM CARMICHAEL

See also **Egypt; Ethiopia; Muslims in Africa; Somalis**

Further Reading

Burton, Richard F., *First Footsteps in East Africa or, An Exploration of Harar*, 2 vols. in 1, edited by Isabel Burton, New York: Dover, 1987 (reprint of 1856 edition)

Carmichael, Tim, "Political Culture in Ethiopia's Provincial Administration: Haile Sellassie, Blata Ayele Gebre and the (Hareri) Kulub Movement of 1948," in *Personality and Political Culture in Modern Africa*, edited by Mel Page et al., Boston: Boston University African Studies Center, 1998

Gibb, Camilla C.T., "Sharing the Faith: Religion and Ethnicity in the City of Harar," *Horn of Africa*, 16, nos. 1–4 (1998)

Waldron, Sidney R., "A Farewell to Bab Haji: City Symbolism and Harari Identity, 1887–1977," in *Working Papers on Society and History in Imperial Ethiopia: The Southern Periphery from the 1880s to 1974*, edited by D. Donham and W. James, Cambridge: African Studies Center, 1979

———, "Harar: The Muslim City in Ethiopia," in *Proceedings of the Fifth International Conference on Ethiopian Studies*, edited by Robert L. Hess, Chicago: University of Illinois at Chicago Circle, 1979

Harijans, *See* Untouchables (Harijans/dalits/scheduled Castes)

Hausa

Capsule Summary

Location: West Africa, especially northern Nigeria, southern Niger, and neighboring countries
Total Population: 25–40 million
Language: Hausa
Religion: Muslim

The Hausa are the largest ethnolinguistic group in Nigeria. They (and the slightly smaller Yoruba and Ibo) are thus not usually counted among "minority groups" in Nigeria. In Niger the 5 million Hausa speakers are the clear majority of a much smaller population. There is also a Hausa diaspora in West Africa and beyond, where the Hausa exist as distinct and significant minorities.

The Hausa are primarily a linguistic group with several different original ethnic origins. They are united in having adopted the Hausa language at various different points in time, although a few groups descended from Hausa speakers who now speak other languages also claim to be ethnically Hausa. The Hausa language is the largest language of the Chadic branch of the Afro-Asiatic (or Hamito-Semitic) language family. It is arguably the largest language in Africa, after Arabic, and is widely spoken as a second language throughout much of Africa. Hausa has been written in a modified form of the Arabic alphabet since at least the seventeenth century. A Romanized form was adopted as the official language of the northern Nigerian colonial administration in the twentieth century. Arabic script Hausa is the only language besides English that appears on Nigerian paper money.

This widespread use of Hausa as a lingua franca and the resulting widespread native bilingualism, in addition to the primary importance of language in determining Hausa identity, have made it difficult to draw ethnic boundaries between the Hausa and other ethnic groups, especially in the immediate south of Hausaland proper, where many smaller linguistic groups have long used Hausa as a lingua franca. The Hausa have expanded largely through assimilating such ethnic groups, a process that continues today, especially among groups converting to Islam, since Islam has also become a major aspect of Hausa identity.

The origins of the Hausa language are obscure. Its early spread was not documented, although it shows important influence from languages in the northeast of its present distribution, especially Kanuri and to a lesser extent Tuareg. The Hausa organized a group of kingdoms between the larger Songhai and Bornu empires at some point during the Middle Ages. Most of these small kingdoms were united with adjacent areas by the Sokoto Caliphate, a nineteenth-century empire ruled by a Fulani elite who gradually assimilated Hausa civilization, becoming Hausa of Fulani origin. Most of the Sokoto Caliphate was conquered by the British at the beginning of the twentieth century, and it formed the core of the protectorate of northern Nigeria.

The Hausa diaspora has spread mostly through trade, including the internal African slave trade. As slaves were imported to meet the labor demands of the expanding economy of central Hausaland, free Hausa found themselves unable to compete and emigrated to outlying areas to practice skilled crafts and engage in commerce. Most major cities from Jenne to Jedda have their Hausa quarters, where Hausa reside under the authority of their own leaders and use their own language among themselves. It is this Hausa diaspora that is most correctly characterized as a minority group and that has spread the Hausa language and culture (including Islam) in West Africa.

The most important Hausa minority groups are those in central and southern Nigeria, as well as those in Ghana, Sudan, and elsewhere. Even a simple discussion of the complexities of ethnic, religious, and other political conflict in Nigeria is far beyond the scope of this short essay, but it should be noted that the Hausa minority in central Nigeria (the so-called "middle belt" in the south of the former northern Nigeria) has often been the focus of resentment by small indigenous groups in the area, who consider the Hausa to be settlers. These groups, in turn, are not often distinguished from Hausa by southern Nigerians, who tend to complain about a generalized "northern domination," since the majority of Nigeria's population resides in the former northern region, where Hausa was the official language. Thus the question of alleged "Hausa domination" in Nigeria depends first on defining who is Hausa, not an easy task. The system of strong regions, including the north, was broken up in the late 1960s by General Yakubu Gowon, a member of a northern minority (Angas) and the first member of any minority group to become Nigerian head of state.

The Hausa community in Ghana is centuries old and flourished during the nineteenth century as a result of the trade in kola nuts from the Asante kingdom. The widespread use of Hausa-speaking northern Nigerian minorities in the colonial military and police augmented their numbers, and Hausa is today a widely spoken lingua franca in northern and southern Ghana alike.

Hausa speakers in the Sudan number approximately half a million. Most migrated to the Sudan along the pilgrim trail to Mecca. They live mainly in the area around Khartoum and the confluence of the Blue and White Niles, where they work as urban laborers, and on the Gezira cotton-growing scheme. They play important roles in the labor movement and constitute one of the most important minority groups in the Muslim north of the country.

JOHN EDWARD PHILLIPS

See also **Diaspora; Fulani; Tuareg**

Further Reading

Adamu, Mahdi, *The Hausa Factor in West African History,* Zaria: Ahmadu Bello University Press, 1978

Coles, Catherine, Beverly Mack, and Neil Skinner, editors, *Hausa Women in the Twentieth Century,* Madison: University of Wisconsin Press, 1991

James, Ibrahim, editor, *The Settler Phenomenon in the Middle Belt and the Problem of National Integration in Nigeria,* Jos, Nigeria: Midland Press, n.d.

Lovejoy, Paul, *Caravans of Kola,* Zaria, Nigeria: Ahmadu Bello University Press, 1980

Philips, John Edward, *Spurious Arabic: Hausa in Colonial Nigeria,* Madison: University of Wisconsin African Studies Center, 2000

Works, John A. Jr., *Pilgrims in a Strange Land: Hausa Communities in Chad,* New York: Columbia University Press, 1976

Yahaya, Ibrahim Yaro, *Hausa a Rubuce: Tarihi Rubuce-rubuce cikin Hausa,* Zaria, Nigeria: Ahmadu Bello University Press

Hawaiians (Indigenous)

Capsule Summary

Location: Hawaii (United States); northeastern Pacific
Total Population: 250,000
Languages: Hawaiian, English
Religions: indigenous beliefs, Christianity

The indigenous Hawaiians, who call themselves *Kanaka Maoli*, are of Polynesian heritage. They migrated from the Marquesas Islands in the first century BCE. Their language, which has no official recognition, belongs to the Austronesian family and is thus related to the ones spoken by other Polynesian peoples, such as New Zealand's Maoris and those living in French Polynesia.

The Hawaiian archipelago, lying in the northeastern Pacific, consists of eight islands and several atolls. Of all the 50 states of the United States, Hawaii plays a very peculiar role. Not only is this the only island state, but in terms of geography and culture it belongs to another continent, Oceania.

Hawaiian society developed in total isolation for many centuries. This society was divided into three different classes and was ruled by a king. Religion was tightly linked to social and political life. In early 1700 the archipelago was inhabited by some 1 million people. The first European reaching the islands was Captain James Cook (1778), and the impact of his arrival was devastating, resulting in cultural uprooting and infectious diseases affecting thousands of islanders. One century later, in 1890, only some 40,000 Hawaiians remained. The Calvinist missionaries from New England, which had arrived in 1820, destroyed indigenous religion and replaced it with Christianity. During the same decades, Russia and Great Britain unsuccessfully tried to colonize the archipelago, which had been unified by King Kamehameha in earlier decades. The United States president declared he was going to bring the islands into the United States sphere of influence. In the meantime, a massive migration of Asians and North Americans was encouraged. In 1877 United States minister Pierce declared that the islands were "a US colony, politically and economically." Discontent grew among the indigenous population with these threats to their their independence.

In 1891 Lydia Liliuokalani ascended to the throne. Intending to protect the rights the local population was going to lose, she passed a new constitution establishing a constitutional monarchy and denied the vote to foreigners. United States landowners founded a so-called "provisional government" backed by Washington. On January 17, 1893, the royal palace in Honolulu was surrounded by armed representatives of the provisional government and the federal army. The queen was forced to surrender.

Just a few months later, newly elected president Grover Cleveland openly condemned the coup and tried to restore the Hawaiian monarchy. However, his mandate expired before he could wear down the resistance of the lobbies advocating United States expansion in the Pacific. During those decades, in fact, the United States already had many colonies in the Pacific, including Guam, Samoa, and the Philippines.

In 1896 the indigenous language was banned, and 2 years later Hawaii was officially annexed by the United States. The first United States government was established in 1900. In 1921 the American Congress allotted 200,000 acres of the poorest agricultural lands to native Hawaiians. Apparently conceived for farm and residential use, the lands were located in inaccessible areas and undeveloped. The land issue became central to indigenous claims.

On September 7, 1941, the Japanese attack of Pearl Harbor, a United States base near Honolulu, marked the beginning of the war between Japan and the United States.

The early postwar years were marked by Americanization and tourism, which both had devastating effects on indigenous culture and lifestyle. On June 27, 1959, a referendum was held, but the population was only given two choices: Hawaii could either stay a colony or become the fiftieth United States state. Most of the people voted in favor of the latter. The islands were removed from the United Nations list of non-self-governing territories without achieving independence.

Indigenous activism grew in the 1970s, resulting in many native organizations and initiatives claiming different degrees of autonomy or even independence. Many natives, strongly condemning tourist exploitation of indigenous culture, started rediscovering their native beliefs and dances. Land claims were also laid with renewed vigor.

Beginning in the early 1980s, the sovereignty issue was raised in many international forums, especially in the United Nations, where Hawaiian leaders such as Kawaipuna Paekekui Prejean and Mililani Trask have played a central role. Mililani Trask, along with her sister Haunani-Kay, is the founder of Ka Lahui Hawaii, one of the most important organizations advocating native sovereignty. It is organized as a government in exile, with a constitution, elected representatives, and a master plan for the future. Ka Lahui claims inclusion in United States policy on recognized native nations. However, no treaty was ever signed between it and the United States, so the Kanaka Maoli have never enjoyed the separate legal status that was granted to the other indigenous nations living in the United States (Indians, Inuit, and Aleut).

On January 17, 1993, the centenary of the United States invasion, 15,000 people marched in Honolulu supporting native Hawaiian sovereignty. In the summer of the same year, the legal aspects of indigenous claims were dealt with by the Kanaka Maoli Peoples' International Tribunal, which was convened by many leading indigenous scholars and activists.

Some months later, President Clinton signed the Apology Bill, admitting United States involvement in the coup d'état overthrowing the monarchy in 1883. Although this bill did not aim at changing the political status of Hawaii, it did fuel indigenous claims. Some of these campaigns aim for autonomy and a "nation within nation" status, similar to that enjoyed by Native Americans, while others work for the restoration of an independent monarchy.

ALESSANDRO MICHELUCCI

See also **Indigenous Peoples**

Further Reading

Ball, Roger, *Last among Equals: Hawaiian Statehood and American Politics*, Honolulu: University of Hawaii Press, 1984

Hasager, Ulla, and Jonathan Friedman, editors, *Hawai'i: Return to Nationhood*, Copenhagen: IWGIA, 1994

Kent, Noel, *Hawai'i: Islands under the Influence*, New York: Monthly Review Press, 1983

Notarangelo, Cristina, *Gli indigeni hawaiani*, Milan: Xenia, 2000

Parker, Linda, *Native American Estate: The Struggle over Indian and Hawaiian Lands*, Honolulu: University of Hawaii Press, 1989

Trask, Haunani-Kay, *From a Native Daughter: Colonialism and Sovereignty in Hawai'i*, Honolulu: University of Hawaii Press, 1999

Hindus

Capsule Summary

Location: India; also spread around the world
Total Population: 1 billion
Language: Hindi
Religion: Hindu

The Hindus are representatives of an ancient civilization established in India in approximately the fifth century BCE. Hindus speak Hindi, a language that is derived from the ancient Sanskrit. Over centuries, Hindus and the Hindu belief have spread to every part of the world. At present there are estimated to be over 1 billion Hindus around the world. An overwhelming majority of Hindus reside in India and Nepal. In India, the Hindus constitute over 85 percent of the total population, and in Nepal they represent 85 percent of population. As minorities within South Asia, Hindus can be found in several other countries, including Pakistan, Bangladesh, Sri Lanka, and Bhutan. There is also a small proportion of Hindus in Afghanistan and Iran. Outside of South Asia, Hindu religious minorities can be found in Africa and the Caribbean; after World War II, there was also a notable Hindu immigration to northern Europe (primarily the United Kingdom) and North America (Canada and the United States).

An analysis of Hindus from a minority rights perspective presents an interesting proposition. Hindu minorities (as numerically inferior groups in states outside of India and Nepal) suffer from various forms of discrimination, but Hinduism as a religion is based on rigid hierarchies within which lower castes or outcastes suffer at the hands of upper-caste Hindus.

The Dalits (Scheduled Castes)

Hindu society, with its rigid caste system, results in discrimination for those at the bottom of the social ladder. This discrimination is particularly evident in the case of the outcasts, also known as *Dalits*. The *Dalits* are also referred to as the "untouchables," the Harijans, and, in strict legal and constitutional terms, they are known as members of the scheduled castes. *Dalit* literally means "the oppressed," a term appropriately applied to millions of human beings who are social and cultural outcastes and live below the poverty line. The roots of oppressing the *Dalits* can be found in the Hindu caste system. The philosophy of the caste system is contained in the *Manusmriti*, a sacred Hindu text dating from the second century BCE. In historical terms, the "untouchables" were forbidden from joining the religious and social life of the community and were confined to menial polluting tasks such as animal slaughter, leather-working, and sweeping excrement from the villages. According to some sources, they were required to strike a piece of wood before entering a town or village as a warning for the people to avoid them. The introduction of Islam in the twelfth and thirteenth centuries CE led to widespread conversions by many low-caste and untouchable groups, and by the mid-nineteenth century about one-quarter of the population had converted to Islam.

In strictly legal and constitutional terms, the untouchable caste has not only been abolished by the Indian constitution (1950), but there are also criminal penalties attached to continuing with this discrimination. The constitution also aims to provide for affirmative action policies for the scheduled castes. However, despite these efforts, in practice the *Dalits* suffer from large-scale discrimination. Economic exploitation combined with social prejudices continues to place the scheduled castes at the bottom of the social ladder. They are excluded from some temples and other religious institutions and from taking advantage of many public services, such as education and health care. The *Dalit* women in particular suffer from the most acute form of discrimination. Their participation in such key areas as health, education, regular employment, and housing policies is minimal. At the beginning of the new millennium the change in social attitudes toward the *Dalits* is not very apparent, as they continue to be oppressed and marginalized.

Historical and Social Position of Hindu Minorities within South Asia

The Hindu population of Pakistan constitutes a minority of about 1.27 million, or 1.2 percent of the total population. An overwhelming majority of the Hindus, roughly 1.22 million (96 percent of the total Hindu population in Pakistan), live in the rural areas of Sindh. The Hindus of Pakistan have endured persistent campaigns of physical and cultural extermination. The Partition of India in August 1947 resulted in genocidal campaigns against religious minorities, and the Hindus in Pakistan suffered greatly. In addition to the genocide, several million Hindus were forced to become refugees. Hindus of Pakistan were victimized and condemned during the Seventeen Days' Indo-Pakistan War of 1965, and many were made to suffer confiscation of their properties and assets under the Enemy Property Ordinance (1965). The worst fears of the Hindu minority, of genocide and physical extermination, did become part of the unfortunate reality that accompanied the Pakistani civil war of 1971. The Hindus of East Pakistan became a primary target of the ruthless campaign of the West Pakistan military, which exterminated more than a million people and created 10 million refugees.

The tiny minority of Hindus that remains in Pakistan continues to find itself vulnerable to exploitation and abuse. The constitutional amendments, such as separate electorates and antiblasphemy laws, that were introduced by General Zia-ul-Haq, have adversely affected the position of the Hindu minority. More significantly, the rise in religious extremism within South Asia, with periods of tense political relations between India and Pakistan, has led to greater violence and physical attacks on Hindus. Thus the Hindus of Pakistan frequently suffer from outbursts of anti-Hindu sentiments, which are forms of backlash generated by violations of the rights of Muslims in India. In the *Babri Masjid* incident (December 1992), the anger at the demolition of the mosque in Ahodhya (India) was vented against the Hindus and their property in Pakistan.

Members of the Hindu minority in Pakistan fear persistent harassment at the hands of religious extremists and complain that there is little official protection accorded to them. Hindu activists argue that secret files are kept on them and their integrity is always in question. They are not allowed into the armed forces, the judiciary, or responsible positions in the Civil Service. These allegations are substantiated by the negligible Hindu presence in the higher echelons of administration, bureaucracy, and armed forces. Discrimination and prejudice against the Hindus are reinforced by the religious orthodoxy, within educational institutions, and by the state-controlled media. As a consequence of the oppression and discrimination, the last two decades have seen a steady exodus of Hindus from Pakistan. This exodus, however, has left behind a community that is most vulnerable and in urgent need of socioeconomic protection.

While Pakistan has almost denuded itself of its Hindu population, the Hindus form the largest minority group in Bangladesh (formerly East Pakistan). Prior to the partition of India (1947) and the creation of Pakistan, the Hindus formed a significant proportion of the population of Bengal. Immediately after the creation of Pakistan, many Hindu families migrated to the urban pockets of West Bengal in Calcutta. As already noted, in the genocidal conflicts of 1947 and 1971 many of the Hindu minorities of East Pakistan were targeted. Since the emergence of an independent Bangladesh, constitutional guarantees have been provided to religious minorities through various constitutional mechanisms. But despite provisions of equality and nondiscrimination, the Hindu minority of Bangladesh suffers from covert and overt discrimination. They point to the continuation of discriminatory legislation such as the Vested Property (Administration) Act of 1974. Through the discriminatory application of this act the properties and businesses of many Hindus that were taken away during the 1965 war with India have been retained by the state of Bangladesh. The Hindu minority is particularly concerned at state attempts to impose *Sharia* (Islamic) Law through the Eighth Amendment to the Constitution.

The political conflict within Sri Lanka involves the Hindu minority, the Tamils, and the majority Buddhist Sinhalese. A section of the Tamil population (the so-called Up Country Tamils), who are descendants of the Indian Tamils, migrated to Sri Lanka during the eighteenth and nineteenth centuries. They have particularly serious grievances against the state of Sri Lanka, which is governed by the majority Sinhalese.

At the time of independence of Sri Lanka, these Up Country Tamils were deprived of their political rights through the Sri Lankan Citizenship Acts of 1948–49. Agreements with the Indian government providing for repatriation or awarding Sri Lankan citizenship were not fully respected. This position has not changed, despite a decision in 1988 to grant all stateless persons citizenship except those who had opted to return to India. From the figures currently available, well over 300,000 Up Country Tamils remain stateless and claim discrimination at the hands of the majority Sinhalese.

Hindu Minorities outside South Asia

Outside South Asia, Hindu minorities can be found in Europe, North America, the Caribbean islands, and a number of commonwealth countries in Africa. Whereas the presence of Hindus in African countries and the Caribbean islands can be traced from British colonial times, immigration to Europe and North America is of more recent origins. A significant minority of South Asians who came as immigrants to the United Kingdom are Hindus. There are, at present, nearly 350,000 Hindus within the United Kingdom, a majority of them residing in big industrialized cities. At the time of their arrival in the 1950s and 1960s the Hindus, in common with migrants from other parts of the commonwealth, had limited educational and economic opportunities. Many of them had to accept employment as unskilled manual laborers.

Although socioeconomic and educational problems persist, the Hindus of the United Kingdom have made progress. They have had notable successes as the result of their hard work, and on the whole they represent a thriving community. There are some problems: lack of access to child-care facilities, lack of employment options, language difficulties, and claims of discrimination in immigration policies adopted by the British government.

The immigration of South Asian Hindus to North America is a recent phenomenon, only significantly evident in the last quarter of the twentieth century. During this period, Hindus migrated to the United States from all areas of India. At the end of the year 2000, there were approximately 800,000 Hindu migrants in the United States (0.4 percent of the population). The largest numbers are from northern India, and are most concentrated in New York, California, Illinois, New Jersey, and Texas. Unlike in the United Kingdom, existing immigration restrictions have encouraged educated and English-speaking Hindus to settle to the United States. But although there is a notable proportion of Hindus in economically stable vocations, there are nevertheless claims of discrimination in terms of employment and education. The Hindu minority also fear that the assimilationist policies pursued by the United States are likely to lead to a loss of cultural and religious identity.

JAVAID REHMAN

See also **India; Muslims in South Asia; Tamils; Untouchables (Harijans/Dalits/Scheduled Castes)**

Further Reading

Berreman, Gerald D., *Hindus of the Himalayas,* Berkeley: University of California Press, 1963

Flood, Gavin, *An Introduction to Hinduism,* Cambridge: Cambridge University Press, 1996

Joshi, Barbra, editor, *Untouchable! Voices of the Dalit Liberation Movement,* London: Minority Rights Group, 1986

Lipner, Julius J., *Hindus: Their Religious Belief and Practices,* London: Routledge, 1998

Mascarenhas, Anthony, *The Rape of Bangladesh,* Delhi: Vikas, 1971

Rehman, Javaid, and Nikhil Roy, "South-Asia," in *World Directory of Minorities*, edited by Miles Litvinoff, Patrick Thornberry, et al., London: Minority Rights Group, 1997 Zelliot, Eleanor, *From Untouchable to Dalit: Essays on Ambedkar Movement,* New Delhi: Monohar, 1992

Hmong

Capsule Summary

Location: southern China in Kweichow, Hunan, Szechuan, Kwangsi, and Yunan Provinces; the northern highlands of Laos, Thailand, Vietnam, and Burma; the United States, Canada, France, French Guiana, Australia, and Argentina
Total Population: 12 million
Language: Hmong
Religion: animism and Christianity

Migration is a prominent theme in Hmong history. Although the Hmong probably originated in central Siberia, they are now spread throughout southeast China, mainland Southeast Asia, the United States, and a few other Western countries. Hmong all over the world consider China as their ancestral homeland, and 5 million Hmong, the largest population, still live in China.

The Hmong migrated to the areas where they now live as a result of Han Chinese suppression. The most common Chinese terms for the Hmong are *Miao* and *Meo,* which are pejoratives connoting a supposed animal-like quality of the Hmong language. The word *Hmong,* on the other hand, is an ethnonym meaning "free people."

As a result of continued persecution by the Chinese, a series of epidemics, and depleted farmlands, approximately half a million Hmong began to migrate from China to the highland border areas of Laos, Thailand, Vietnam, and Burma in the late eighteenth and early nineteenth centuries. In these areas they have maintained a subsistence economy based on swidden (slash-and-burn) cultivation of rice and the growing of opium as a medicinal and cash crop.

The Hmong are divided into dialectically distinct subgroups whose names were reportedly ascribed by the Chinese according to a distinguishing feature of their clothing, culture, or geographic location. The largest of these groups represented in the United States are the White Hmong and the Green Hmong.

The principal structures of Hmong social organization are the nuclear family and the patrilineal clan. There are a finite number of clans; in Laos, for example, there are 25, and in Thailand 14. In the Hmong naming system, the clan name precedes the personal name. The Hmong customarily practice polygyny, wherein one man can have more than one wife, and the levirate, in which a man marries his deceased's brother's wife and assumes economic responsibility for her and her children.

Customary Hmong religion is based on the belief that spirits exist in the unseen realm, where they can affect the lives of humans. Divinations and animal sacrifice are two primary means of interpreting the wishes of spirits and appeasing them when they are disrupting human life. Shamans are the only people in Hmong society who can directly interact with the spirit realm. They do so by entering a trance. Because some illnesses are believed to be caused when a spirit captures a human soul, shamans are thought of as healers as well as religious specialists.

The Hmong in Laos became involved in the country's political struggles in 1945, when they aided the French during the Japanese invasion. The Hmong fought for the Royal Lao government after the French withdrew their forces in 1954. Beginning in 1962, Hmong men were recruited by the United States Central Intelligence Agency as soldiers of the "Secret War" in Laos. When the United States withdrew its troops from Laos in 1975, the Pathet Lao began a program of genocide against the Hmong, and 150,000 Hmong fled Laos to Thailand, where they were placed into refugee camps.

The refugee camps were overcrowded and temporary. Rather than risk their lives by repatriating to Laos, many Hmong opted to apply for refugee status in the United States and allied countries, including Canada, Australia, Argentina, and France (including French Guiana). Refugees could only be resettled if they were sponsored by a host. In the United States, this role was most often filled by Christian organizations as an incentive for conversion. The United States hosted approximately 80,000 Hmong refugees, more than any of the allied countries. Most arrived in the 1970s and 1980s.

The United States government adopted a policy of resettlement in diverse areas of the country to accelerate the process of cultural assimilation. However, many Hmong relocated to areas of the country where they had family or friends. Large Hmong communities were thereby established in areas of California, Wisconsin, and Minneapolis. These large communities often developed Mutual Aid Associations. Nonetheless, urban resettlement proved extremely difficult in the majority of cases, since most Hmong were previously rural subsistence farmers who lacked urban skills.

The extreme hardships faced by Hmong refugees in the United States have arguably been greater for adult men than for women and children. Hmong society is customarily patriarchal. However, upon resettlement in the United States, many Hmong men were unable to secure employment because they lacked training in language and job skills. Women, on the other hand, found that their embroidery (called *paj ndau*, or "flower cloth") appealed to American consumers. Children were more adaptable than adults and able to learn the language and culture more rapidly. Thus men suddenly found themselves in a virtual role reversal from soldiers and heads of households to dependents.

This situation may have contributed to a unique culture-bound syndrome called Sudden Unexpected Nocturnal Death Syndrome (SUNDS), whereby men died in their sleep without prior indications of illness. The phenomenon was largely limited to male Hmong refugees. The Centers for Disease Control concluded that SUNDS was the result of a cardiac abnormality that predisposed some individuals to lethal arrhythmias. However, some scholars have argued that the stress of culture change triggered the arrhythmias. In support of this argument, the incidence of SUNDS has virtually ceased since the 1990s.

Several thousand Hmong remained in refugee camps in northern Thailand. In 1995, the Thai government began to close the refugee camps, and thousands of Hmong began to be forcibly repatriated to Laos. Despite reports that Hmong leaders have disappeared in Laos, and other possible mistreatments of the Hmong, the vast majority of refugees had been repatriated by the year 2000.

PAMELA LINDELL

See also **Laos; Miao (Hmong); Thailand**

Further Reading

Bliatout, Bruce Thowpaou, *Hmong Sudden Unexpected Nocturnal Death Syndrome: A Cultural Study*, Portland, Oregon: Sparkle Publishing Enterprises, 1983

Chan, Sucheng, *Hmong Means Free: Life in Laos and America*, Philadelphia: Temple University Press, 1994

Donnelly, Nancy D., *Changing Lives of Refugee Hmong Women*, Seattle: University of Washington Press, 1994

Fadiman, Anne, *The Spirit Catches You and You Fall Down: A Hmong Child, Her American Doctors, and the Collision of Two Cultures*, New York: Farrar, Straus and Giroux, 1997

Hamilton-Merritt, Jane, *Tragic Mountains: The Hmong, the Americans, and the Secret Wars for Laos, 1942–1992*, Bloomington: Indiana University Press, 1993

Hendricks, Glen L., Bruce T. Downing, and Amos S. Deinard, editors, *The Hmong in Transition*, New York: Center for Migration Studies, 1986

Long, Lynellyn D., *Ban Vinai: The Refugee Camp*, New York: Columbia University Press, 1993

Quincy, Keith, *Hmong, History of a People*, Cheney: Eastern Washington University Press, 1995

Homosexuality and Minority Status

It is a commonplace of contemporary politics that if homosexuals are counted as a "legitimate" minority, then they deserve rights, and if not, then they do not. The rights in question are of two types: rights against private-sector discrimination in housing, employment, and public accommodations and rights against discrimination by the government.

But what constitutes a legitimate minority is less than clear from the discourses of the political scene itself. It is valuable to consider how equality and privileges are discussed, for example. There are those (often on the political Right) who take race, understood narrowly as a biological or genetic characteristic, as the standard for minority status and hold that a legitimate minority is any group defined by an immutable characteristic, one over which an individual has no control and for which the individual is not responsible. They then move on to claim both that white people, as defined by an immutable, genetic characteristic, are a legitimate minority and that initiatives such as affirmative action programs that burden whites by protecting other groups are therefore violations of minority rights to equal protection of the law.

One may say that these kinds of arguments are correct here to the limited extent that the "minority" in "legitimate minority" is not a statistical notion. Numerical status is often equated with minority status, but here it is defined by norms, not numbers. In the United States, the expression found in job advertisements encouraging "women and other minorities to apply" shows that the statistical definition of minority—as less than 50 percent—is not a necessary condition for the correct application of the term when it is used to invoke rights. Women are considered—by all accepted international standards—a minority properly protected, even though women, like whites, may constitute a statistical majority in a given country.

But just as minority status does not turn on numbers, neither does it turn on immutable characteristics. In considered moral opinions, immutability is neither a necessary nor a sufficient condition for right-invoking minority standing. To better understand this we should consider cases.

On the one hand, immutable characteristics are not necessary conditions for a group having minority status in a morally relevant sense. Among star cases of minorities that have properly invoked equality protections are religious minorities, even though one's religion is a matter of choice. A person's religious values are morally meaningful in one's life—fit subjects for making sacrifices of one's interests—only if they are a matter of choice, not compulsion. And the law treats the physically challenged as a protected minority even when the challenge in question is the result of actions for which the disabled individual is personally responsible, as in a negligently caused car accident or a botched suicide.

On the other hand, immutability is not a sufficient condition for invoking moral minority status. Sometimes drawing moral distinctions with respect to nonchosen properties is morally acceptable, even morally to be expected. For example, "grandfathering provisions" are not, on their own, considered unjust. A law with a grandfathering provision blocks future access to a privilege but allows those currently with the privilege to maintain it (say, a vendor's license or a past land use in the face of newly restrictive zoning). If grandfather exceptions do not front for some illegitimate goal (for example, perpetuating racial oppression in post-Reconstruction era America), then they are not felt to be substantially unjust, even though they create closed classes of people with privileges to which others, sometimes as a matter of when they were born, can have no access no matter what they do, and so ruled the American Supreme Court in 1975 in *City of New Orleans v. Dukes.* Or again, a law that lowers the inheritance tax rate will disadvantage a person whose parents have already died compared with people whose parents have not yet died. Still, this disadvantage is not an inequitable treatment, even though its falling on that individual is not a consequence of anything that he or she has done.

If a law disadvantaging members of a group marked by an immutable characteristic has some legitimate public purpose, then it does not violate equality and may employ immutable characteristics in its design. Affirmative action programs favoring women and blacks, then, are not automatically violations of any rights of whites and males. But if statistics and immutability do not determine what counts as a minority for the purposes of rights, what does? The account that best captures America's considered experience in this matter—but one that pertains to a great many other countries—is that a minority is a group that has historically been treated inequitably, and an inequitable treatment of a group is one that holds members of the group in morally lesser regard, either as less than fully human or as worth less than other groups, regardless of their actions. Individuals may be held in lower regard, even contempt, because of some action they perform—say, lying, thieving, murdering—which both permits and warrants censure and punishment. But individuals may not legitimately be held in lower regard because of some status they have, some membership in a group independent of any action that puts them in the group.

A minority, then, is a group whose members are held to have a degraded status independently of anything they do. And so, at least in the case of America, constitutional law and civil rights legislation have considered blacks, ethnic groups, women, illegitimate children, legal aliens, religious groups, and the disabled as minorities. An immutable characteristic invokes minority standing only if in addition it is culturally viewed as a degraded status, as has historically been the case for blacks, but not the blue-eyed.

On this understanding of minority status, homosexuals too should be added to the list of groups considered legitimate minorities and given strong equal protection rights. An examination of history and culture, especially jokes, invective, stereotypes, health policy, military policy, and symbolic legislation (like unenforced sodomy laws), indicates that homosexuals are held in morally lesser regard independently of what they do. To take but one example: current United States military policy, despite its claims to the contrary, discriminates purely on the basis of the despised status of homosexuals rather than on the basis of any actions that these individuals perform—something not done in all countries. For, on the one hand, a person caught performing homosexual acts can still be retained by the armed forces if he claims simply to have been drunk or skylarking rather than performing the acts because he is a homosexual. On the other hand, a person will be thrown out of the armed forces if he claims or is thought to have a homosexual identity, even if he has never performed a homosexual sexual act. So in the United States army's eyes, homosexual acts are neither necessary nor sufficient conditions for treating homosexuals less well than others, indeed for throwing them out of the very institution by which the nation has traditionally taken the measure of full civic personhood.

Whether homosexuals are or are not in their "nature" objectively like a highly distinctive ethnic group, that is how society views and threatens them: as a despised ethnic group and not as a pack of criminals. When actions *are* ascribed to homosexuals as grounds for discrimination, the actions are mere stand-ins for presumed degenerate status, just as accusations of Jews being messiahs and killers of babies are morally retrofitted to the group to justify treatments of the group motivated by considerations that have nothing to do with individuals' actions. When homosexual men are put down as "cocksuckers," it is the same cultural gesture as when Catholics are put down as "mackerel-eaters"—the attributed action merely echoes degenerate status. We know this because there are lots of people who suck cock and eat mackerel who yet are not subject to invective for doing so.

It is society's classification and treatment of homosexuals, not homosexuals' "nature," that is relevant to whether they are deserving of rights on a par with blacks, or other recognized minorities. Studies about homosexual twins, fetal hormones, hypothalamus sizes, and genetic markers, though they grab headlines, are morally irrelevant to whether homosexuals should be treated as a legitimate minority deserving strong rights to equal protection of the law.

In its May 1996 decision, *Romer v. Evans,* the United States Supreme Court took a big step in the direction of adopting this model of minority status as applied to homosexuals. The Court struck down, as a violation of the equal protection clause of the United States constitution, a Colorado state constitutional provision—Amendment 2—that barred homosexuals from getting civil rights protections through any means but further state constitutional amendment. Nowhere in the Court's opinion were the actions of homosexuals or acts of "homosexual sodomy" the focus of analysis. And Amendment 2 was as clear an example as one could find of a classification that burdened a group based solely on its perceived status rather than on any actions of its members. The Court exclusively focused on society's classification and treatment of homosexuals. It held that laws motivated by animus against some group cannot stand. Thus the Court found society's treatment of homosexuals to be irrational, even given the Court's own broad past understanding of what counts as rational. Implicit in the case, as the three-judge dissent warily noted, was the view that homosexuals have historically been held in lesser moral regard independently of what they do and so are deserving of the same strong protections as women, blacks, and historically persecuted religious groups.

RICHARD MOHR

See also **Sexuality**

Further Reading

Halley, Janet E., "The Politics of the Closet: Towards Equal Protection for Gay, Lesbian, and Bisexual Identity," *UCLA Law Review,* 36 (1989)

Koppelman, Andrew, *Antidiscrimination Law and Social Equality,* New Haven: Yale University Press, 1996

LeVay, Simon, *Queer Science,* Cambridge, Massachusetts: MIT Press, 1996

Mohr, Richard D., *A More Perfect Union: Why Straight America Must Stand Up for Gay Rights,* Boston: Beacon Press, 1994

Honduras

Capsule Summary

Country Name: Republic of Honduras
Location: Central America
Total Population: 6,669,789 (2003)
Ethnic Populations: *mestizo* (mixed Amerindian and European), (90%); Amerindian (7%); black (2%); white (1%)
Languages: Spanish, Amerindian dialects
Religions: Roman Catholic (97%); Protestant minority

The Republic of Honduras (República de Honduras) is located in Central America, between Guatemala and El Salvador to the west and Nicaragua to the south and east. The Caribbean Sea borders its northern coast, the Pacific Ocean borders its narrow coast to the south, Guatemala is to the west, El Salvador is to the southwest, and Nicaragua is situated along the entire southeastern frontier. Honduras has an area of 43,270 square miles (112,100 square kilometers), including the offshore Caribbean department of the Bay Islands, and overall is about the size of the state of Tennessee. Geographically, Honduras comprises four distinct regions: Caribbean coastal region, northeast plain, mountainous central interior, and Pacific coastal lowlands. The general terrain is mountainous, and the climate is tropical to subtropical, depending on the elevation. The Caribbean region and adjacent plain are known for banana plantations. The term *Banana Republic* was first used in the 1890s to refer to the country after the United Fruit Company established its agribusiness in Honduras. The northwestern lowlands and the western and southern highlands constitute the most densely populated parts of the country.

Christopher Columbus explored the Cabo de Honduras area in 1502, and Honduras remained a Spanish possession until independence in 1821. During the 1980s, Honduras was a haven for anti-Sandinista Contras fighting the Marxist Nicaraguan government and an ally to Salvadoran government forces fighting against leftist guerrillas. Two and one-half decades of mostly military rule ended in 1982 when a freely elected civilian government came to power. President Ricardo (Joest) Maduro has been in office since January 2002. Several political parties exist, including the Christian Democratic Party (PDC), the Democratic Unification Party (PUD), the Liberal Party (PL), the National Innovation and Unity Party-Social Democratic Party (PINU-SD), and the National Party of Honduras (PN).

Honduras's population numbers about 6,669,789 (2003); approximately 90 percent is *mestizo* (mixed Indian and Spanish extraction), also called *ladino*, a term more commonly used in Central America. *Ladino* defines individuals who are Spanish speakers and follow Spanish-American lifestyles in terms of clothing, housing, and food consumption. In addition, the term covers those Indians who have adopted Spanish-American culture. It is indicative of cultural rather than biological traits, since indigenous peoples are often categorized as ladino for social or political reasons. Approximately 7 percent of the population is Amerindian, and another 2 percent black, with the remainder of European origin and of Arab, African, or Asian ancestry. The annual demographic growth rate is estimated at 2.6 percent.

Amerindian groups, including the Miskito (Muskita or Mosquito), Pech, and Tawaka, inhabited the Mosquito region of northeastern Honduras at least since Spanish contact. The Lenca, the largest indigenous group (numbering about 50,000), live in the west and in the southwestern interior but have been acculturated and no longer speak their native language and have adopted ladino lifestyles. Several hundred Chortí (lowland Maya) formerly lived in western Honduras, but during the seventeenth and eighteenth centuries they migrated to the northeast coastal area and were practically extinct by 1920. The Chorotega migrated south from Mexico during the pre-Hispanic era and settled in the department of Choluteca. The Chorotega, like the Chortí, also speak Spanish, but they have retained distinct sociocultural and religious ways of life. Maya speakers continue to live in the western departments of Copán and Ocotepeque, the former a center of pre-Hispanic Maya society. Several hundred Pipíl live primarily in the isolated northeast coastal region (departments of Gracias a Dios and parts of Yoro and Olancho). Approximately 300 Hicaque (also called Tol) inhabit isolated mountainous rain forests.

The Lesser Antilles were the scene of Arawak and Carib conflict and eventually miscegenation immediately prior to Spanish contact. These people became known as Red Carib or Yellow Carib, but as African slaves were introduced into the Caribbean by Europeans, the descendants of these Amerindians, blacks, and African maroons became known as the "Black Carib." During the early 1800s the "Black Carib" settled in Caribbean coastal villages. This population descended primarily from freed black slaves and native Carib from the island of Saint Vincent. They arrived in Honduras following the deportation of approximately 5,000 from Saint Vincent in 1797 by the British. Initially resettling in the Honduran Islas de la Bahía, most later migrated to the mainland coast of northern Honduras. The Carib are also referred to culturally (and incorrectly) as Garífuna in Belize and Guatemala; that term refers to the language rather than the society. Black Carib language was a Carib-based Creole now replaced by Garífuna, and their culture is similar to that of the Garífuna speakers of Belize and Guatemala. Since 1980, the Black Carib have been known as the Garinagu, and they are regionally fragmented in Honduras, Belize, and Nicaragua.

The Miskito (Muskita or Mosquito), a racially mixed group with Amerindian, African, and British ethnic backgrounds, number about 10,000. They live along the northern coasts of Honduras and Nicaragua and are affiliated with large Miskito communities located in eastern Nicaragua. When the Nicaraguan Miskito population near the Río Coco was uprooted by the Nicaraguan government for security reasons in the early 1980s, many Nicaraguan Miskito migrated to Honduras. The Miskito and Garinagu (the former Black Carib) have similar racial origins, but the former are regarded as indigenous people, whereas the Garinagu are considered to be black because they retain more African cultural elements in their folklore, music, and religion. Both have been economically self-sufficient through subsistence agriculture and fishing, but many males have become wage laborers in other regions. The Creole-speaking inhabitants of the Islas de la Bahía are black or mixed white-black descendants of English-speaking whites and of blacks who came from Belize and the Cayman Islands during the mid-nineteenth century. A Honduran association for indigenous people, the Confederación de Pueblos Autóctones de Honduras, estimated the number of Garinagu living in Honduras in 1988 at 250,000 with an additional 80,000 English-speaking blacks, but the Honduran government estimated 200,000 in 2003.

Arab immigrants from the Middle East (especially Palestine and Lebanon) came to the Caribbean coast during the early part of the twentieth century. Because they held passports issued by the Ottoman Empire, they came to be called *turcos ("Turks") by Hondurans.* The Arab community retains distinctive cultural traditions and initially prospered as merchants and later as manufacturers and businesspeople, but these distinctions have blurred.

The capital is Tegucigalpa, which has 850,000 inhabitants; the city of San Pedro Sula has a population of 500,000. The metropolitan area of each city has populations of more than 1 million. Like the capital, San Pedro Sula is a significant industrial and commercial center, and there are four other urban centers with populations over 20,000, among them La Cieba, El Progresso, and Puerto Cortés. These urban centers are chiefly ladino with Amerindians residing in rural areas.

Spanish is the predominant language, although some English is spoken along the northern coast and on the Caribbean Bay Islands. Indigenous Amerindian dialects and the Garífuna dialect also are spoken. Hondurans are predominantly Roman Catholic (about 85 percent), but Protestant proselytization has resulted in significant numbers of converts among the ladinos in larger cities.

Honduras is among the poorest countries in the Western Hemisphere, with a 2002 GDP per capita income of only $2,500. In 1993 just over half its population (53 percent) lived below the poverty line. The Honduran economy remains highly dependent on the status of the United States economy, its major trading partner, which takes in 69.5 percent of all exports. Chief industries include sugar, coffee, textiles, clothing, and wood products.

CHARLES C. KOLB

See also **Amerindians (South and Central America); Garífuna**

Further Reading

Blutstein, Howard I., et al., *Area Handbook for Honduras*, Washington, D.C.: U.S. Government Printing Office, 1971

Caballero Zeitún, Elsa Lily, *Crisis y política social en Centroamérica*, Tegucigalpa: Universidad Nacional Autónoma de Honduras, 1990

Coelho, Ruy Galvão de Andrade, *Los negroes caribes de Honduras*, Tegucigalpa: Editorial Guaymuras, 1981

Dow, James W., editor, *Encyclopedia of World Culture, Volume VIII: Middle America and the Caribbean*, Boston: G.K. Hall, 1995

Ember, Melvin, and Carol Ember, editors, *Countries and Their Cultures*, New York: Macmillan Reference, under the auspices of the Human Relations Area Files (Yale University), 2001

Jackson, Robert H., *Race, Caste and Status: Indians in Colonial Spanish America*, Albuquerque: University of New Mexico Press, 1999

Minority Rights Group, *No Longer Invisible: Afro-Latin Americans Today*, London: Minority Rights Group, 1995

Rivas, Ramón, *Pueblos indíginas y garífuna en Honduras*, Tegucigalpa: Editorial Guaymuras, 1993

Hong Kong Chinese

Capsule Summary

Location: southern China at the mouth of the Pearl River, including Hong Kong Island, Kowloon, and New Territories
Total Population: 6.6 million: Chinese (98%), European, (1.5%)
Languages: Cantonese, English
Religions: Buddhist/Daoist (90%); Christian, Muslim, Sikh, Hindu, and Jewish (10%)

Hong Kong covers a land area of 424 square miles (1,098 square kilometers) and comprises a highly indented peninsula and a number of offshore islands, of which the largest are Lan Tao and Hong Kong Island. Both the mainland and the islands are highly mountainous. With the exception of the area around Yuen Long in the northwest, there are no extensive plains. The mountainous terrain and the indented coastline once impeded communication, development, and population growth. Now Hong Kong is populated by several Chinese ethnicities, including Han, Hakka, Hoklo, Chiu Chau, and Fukinese, to name but a few. Before the 1949 revolution, and after European settlement, most of these settlers came from the bordering province of Guangdong looking for the better standard of living offered in the colony. After the revolution, mainlanders came from all over and intermingled with the populace. Hong Kong Chinese are not a true ethnic minority. Under the rule of the People's Republic of China, however, because of differing attitudes and philosophy they can be considered a political and economic minority. The per capita GDP was $27,200 as of 2002.

The early inhabitants of Hong Kong traveled from the southern province of Guangdong and began a life-style similar to what they had on the mainland, of a culture based on fishing. The first contact with Europeans came in 1557 across the Pearl River Delta in Macao and continued steadily through the development of the Canton trade in the 1750s. There was hardly any population on Hong Kong until it was colonized by Great Britain.

After the British victory in the First Opium War (1839–42), China and England signed the Treaty of Nanjing in 1842 and ratified it in 1843. The treaty stipulated that China would open its ports to foreign trade, permit foreign consular jurisdiction over foreign nationals (extraterritoriality), and officially cede the island of Hong Kong in perpetuity to Great Britain. In the 1860 Convention of Beijing, which ended the Second Opium War (1858–60), Britain received further concessions from the Qing dynasty. As part of the concessions, the Qing then ceded the southern part of the Kowloon Peninsula (south of Boundary Street) and Stonecutters Island to Britain, also in perpetuity. Settlement in the colony centered around what was known as the city of Victoria, which occupied the narrow northern coastal strip on the western part of Hong Kong Island, and in Kowloon, where settlement first took place on the west coast. To complete the territory that is now Hong Kong, the United Kingdom capitalized on China's defeat by Japan in the Sino-Japanese War (1894–95). Britain received the New Territories, which became a buffer zone between Hong Kong and the expanding spheres of influence of other European countries during the "Scramble for Concessions." Under the Convention of 1898, Britain leased the New Territories, which constituted 92 percent of the total land mass of Hong Kong, for 99 years.

In the prewar years, the population of Hong Kong was basically transient, with the inhabitants seeking employment but not setting up permanent homes. Of the population of Hong Kong prior to 1949, only a small minority considered it their permanent home. This minority included the British and upper-class Chinese commercial elite of Hong Kong, who for generations had lived in the colony. Also included were those people whose ancestral home was located in the villages and towns of the New Territories. These people, having been born in British territories, were potential British subjects and, as a result, were entitled to substantially the same privileges as British subjects residing in the United Kingdom, including the right of abode in the mother country. However, for the vast majority of the inhabitants of the colony, both European and Chinese, Hong Kong was simply a place of abode for conducting business, carrying on a trade, plying a craft, and making a living. They had what might be called a "sojourner mentality." While living in Hong Kong, they maintained close contact with their "permanent home." Europeans working in Hong Kong generally sent their children back to the old country for education; they themselves would also go home temporarily on furlough. Upon the conclusion of their career in Hong Kong, most likely they would pull up stakes and return home permanently.

Most of the Chinese population of Hong Kong hailed from the adjacent province of Guangdong, and within that province from localities with easy access to Hong Kong via the established communications links (railroad and steamship service). Therefore, they were within easy reach of "home" and could spend a weekend at home and return to work in Hong Kong early the next week. Many of them went home to celebrate the Chinese New Year and the occasions of the Spring Festival (Ching-ming) and Double Ninth (Chung-chiu) to pay respects to the memory of the departed ancestors. Single men went home to look for brides to marry. Like their European counterparts, many of these Chinese sojourners also preferred to spend their retirement in their ancestral home.

The problem for Hong Kong at mid-century was that with the communist seizure of power in China, a situation of perpetual crisis prevailed on the mainland as one revolutionary movement after another was launched from the years 1950 to 1976. Those Chinese who came to Hong Kong previously, or as then current refugees (almost 1.5 million in 1949 alone), found themselves permanently and involuntarily settled in the colony. Once in Hong Kong, most residents from the mainland could no longer feel at home in their ancestral villages and were discouraged from traveling into the People's Republic of China, which also discouraged traditional religious practices. Most Hong Kong residents might still return for a short visit, but it was no longer feasible to return home to retire. In order to make the transition upon arrival in Hong Kong, therefore, the Chinese looked for ways of organizing themselves. The two most basic principles were those of shared kinship and shared district of origin. Moving in with or near to relations was an obvious way to use kinship ties to acclimate oneself in a strange city. The other principle, a shared district of origin, was more than a geographic consideration; it related to a subculture of language and custom. For example, the North Point district of Hong Kong Island is often referred to as "Little Shanghai." As time passed, however, regional groups blended more and more and began to develop a common "Hong Kong culture."

Even up through the end of World War II, Hong Kong had never determined what citizenship meant. The decision of who belonged, and who did not, was not made until the postwar era. The British colonial government not only had to classify those expatriates from home and from other nations, but also had to designate status for the Chinese residents. Hong Kong Chinese were therefore defined and separated into two categories, British Chinese, and Chinese residents. A British Chinese resident was defined as a Hong Kong Chinese person who acquired British nationality within the meaning of the British Nationality Act of 1948 and therefore had the right of settling in the United Kingdom. A Chinese resident was an immigrant who was wholly or partly of Chinese descent and had at any time been ordinarily resident in Hong Kong for a continuous period of not less than 7 years and was so registered in compliance with the laws of Hong Kong. Hong Kong Chinese, then, could not settle in the United Kingdom, but they still had to have some type of legal document that allowed for travel and proved residency.

To implement this idea, an identification card system was introduced, and the Hong Kong "belonger" status that it defined was created. This new system relegated the old distinction between British and Chinese nationality to the background. Although the distinction continued to be made, it paled in significance when compared to the overriding issue of whether a Hong Kong resident was a "belonger" or a "nonbelonger." The sole purpose of the identity cards was to validate the status of the cardholder as a legitimate, permanent resident of Hong Kong. Each cardholder was assigned a card number. This number became an integral part of each person's identity, comparable to his or her age, sex, or national origin, and playing a role for Hong Kong residents similar to that of the Social Security number for citizens of the United States. Belonger status is still a working definition of residency in Hong Kong under China's one-country–two-systems rule over Hong Kong.

What makes Hong Kong and its population distinctive is the manner in which it was transformed from a colonial backwater into a force in the international marketplace of trade, industry, and finance. Eventually, Hong Kong became, economically, one of the "Four Little Dragons" of East Asia, and it quickly emerged as one of the most dynamic economies of Asia. The success story of Hong Kong is mostly to be credited to its people; it is their indomitable spirit in the face of adversity, their ingenuity and capacity for hard work, which transformed Hong Kong in a few decades from the sleepy "treaty port" of the 1940s to a powerhouse of Asia.

Business is now the main culture in Hong Kong, and has been for the past 50 years. Many have claimed that in Hong Kong an enterprising entrepreneur can form a business in the morning, open an office or factory in the afternoon, and by evening be turning a profit. Hong Kong Chinese believed so strongly in the opportunities presented that by the 1980s Hong Kong had become Asia's leading financial center (third in the world after New York and London); Asia's largest gold-trading center; the world's largest exporter of garments, toys, and plastic products; the world's largest exporter in volume of watches, clocks, and radios; 18th among the world's trading nations; 20th among the world's exporters of domestic manufactures; the world's largest container port, surpassing Rotterdam and New York; the world's biggest single air cargo terminal; the country with the highest living standard in Asia, outside of Japan; the country with the world's largest public housing program; and the world's third largest diamond-trading center after New York and Antwerp.

Although Hong Kong society mainly revolves around business and making business contacts through social and service organizations, it remains one of the few places where many of the traditional Chinese festivals are still observed. Because of its communist ideology, today not even mainland China preserves many of these festivals, even though they began there. Most Chinese festivals have their origins in myths, gods, ghosts, heroes, and seasons based on the Chinese lunar calendar, and they can be traced back thousands of years. They also serve as occasions for family reunions. The four largest are the Lunar New Year, the Ching Ming Festival, the Dragon Boat Festival, and the Chung Yeung Festival. The Lunar New Year, also referred to as the Chinese New Year or Spring Festival, is the largest and is the one festival celebrated almost universally by Chinese worldwide. The Ching Ming Festival places a premium on family ties, ancestor worship, and filial piety; this is the day to remember, pay respects to, and sweep the graves of one's deceased ancestors. The Dragon Boat Festival is celebrated in honor of patriot and poet Qu Yuan. It falls on the fifth day of the fifth lunar month and is marked by eating rice dumplings and participating in dragon boat races. Today, it is often used to remind people of their patriotism and duties to their country. The Chung Yeung Festival is an annual family remembrance day, when offerings are made before the family shrines of deceased ancestors, capped by a family dinner. In the New Territories, where traditions could be rigidly enforced, the men from big family clans would dedicate several days to visiting the graves of all their founding ancestors, cleaning gravestones, making offerings, and kneeling together to pay their respects.

MICHAEL HOUF

See also **Hakka Chinese**

Further Reading

Endacott, G.B., *Fragrant Harbor,* Hong Kong: Oxford University Press, 1968

Osgood, Cornelius, *The Chinese: A Study of a Hong Kong Community,* Phoenix: University of Arizona Press, 1975

Szczepanik, Edward, *The Economic Growth of Hong Kong,* London: Oxford University Press, 1958

Welsh, Frank, *A Borrowed Place: The History of Hong Kong,* New York: Kodansha International, 1993

Hooks, Bell (African-American)

Born Gloria Jean Watkins in 1952 in Hopkinsville, Kentucky, bell hooks is an American scholar whose work examines the varied perceptions of black women and the development of feminist identities. She represents a critical voice in dialogue concerning identity, privilege, and society. Self-described as a dissident and feminist thinker, she is best known for her willingness to engage the often overlooked "storehouses" of privilege—race, gender (sex and sexual orientation), and class—in an effort to deconstruct conventional society. She has critiqued the persistent tendency of tradition to "otherize" anyone who deviates from the white, male, heterosexual norm. This tendency has allowed her to embrace a more complex and accurate account of identity, while providing a feminist philosophy that is forward-looking, inclusive, and altogether liberating in nature.

Early in her career, hooks adopted her nom de plume from that of her outspoken great-grandmother, Bell Hooks, to honor female legacies; she preferred to spell it in lowercase letters as a statement against the ego of the author. Hooks grew up in a segregated community of the American South. At age 19, she began writing what would become her first full-length book, *Ain't I a Woman: Black Women and Feminism* (1981), which *Publishers' Weekly* ranked in 1992 among the 20 most important women's books of the last 20 years. She studied English literature at Stanford University (B.A., 1973), the University of Wisconsin (M.A., 1976), and the University of California, Santa Cruz (Ph.D., 1983). Hooks taught English and ethnic studies at the University of Southern California from the mid-1970s, African and Afro-American studies at Yale University during the 1980s, women's studies at Oberlin College until 1994, and English at the City College of New York from 1994.

Always passionate and intent on calling on individuals to recognize and change the negative repercussions of what she terms the "white supremist capitalist patriarchy" that structures this society, hooks nonetheless found time to pursue a formal academic inquiry in English, writing her dissertation on the works of Toni Morrison. In her writing, hooks challenges unitary conceptions of identity through her explorations of the intricate workings of race, sex, and class. Her contribution to popular culture has been to offer a challenge to conventional ways of thinking. One issue upon which she has had a profound impact is feminism. Hooks is a black feminist committed to the critical consciousness of her community and has been instrumental in providing a detailed examination of the feminist movement and its relationship to the concerns of black women. Amidst a mainstream culture that tends to view identity as prototypically white and male, hooks delivers a positive and affirming message of what it means to be a woman of color. She is candid and personal in her critique of conventional culture, identifying repressive tendencies and offering pragmatic solutions. Her voice has been and is "critical" in the ongoing dialogue concerning identity, privilege, and society. She urges an end to the degradation and exploitation of black women, arguing that this is an integral step in alleviating white supremacy. She believes that the feminist movement that has emerged conducts dialogues in a distinctively "white" fashion. Hooks's main concern is with black women, and her analysis of black women's current situation in the social hierarchy necessarily deals with race and class, as well as gender.

Hooks has also made considerable progress in conceptualizing discrimination as often occurring at intersections of privilege. Her most pronounced assessment of disadvantage has come at the intersection of race and gender. The notion of teacher instruction is also an essential tenet of her philosophical worldview. For hooks, teaching is much more than simply sharing information or facts; it is a process of intellectual and spiritual growth, and it is a process carried out in community. She approaches the classroom as a "location of possibility" and freedom, believing that this location is best realized through open dialogue and a commitment to growth of the mind and spirit. In her later books, hooks critiques popular culture. Her book *Outlaw Culture* (1994) and her 1997 film *Cultural Criticism and Transformation* are dedicated solely to hooks's desire to nurture in her readers a "critical eye."

In the 1980s hooks established a support group for black women called the Sisters of the Yam, which she later used as the title of a book, published in 1993, celebrating black sisterhood. Since *Ain't I a Woman*, hooks has written dozens of other books and articles that address everything from slavery to movies to trends and ideals in education. Her more important writings include *Feminist Theory from Margin to Center* (1984), *Talking Back: Thinking Feminist, Thinking Black* (1989), *Black Looks: Race and Representation* (1992), and *Killing Rage: Ending Racism* (1995). She published her memoirs, *Bone Black: Memories of Girlhood*, in 1996. In the twenty-first century, as an intellectual and a scholar, hooks continues to challenge mainstream society's perceptions of its milieu and is a strong voice of critical consciousness and awareness of oneself and society.

Biography

Bell hooks. Born 25 September 1952 in Hopkinsville, Kentucky, as Gloria Jean Watkins. Studied at public schools in Hopkinsville; Stanford University, B.A., 1973; University of Wisconsin, M.A., 1976; University of California, Santa Cruz, Ph.D., 1983. Assistant professor, Yale University; professor, Oberlin College; professor of English, City College of New York, 1994 to present.

Selected Works

Ain't I a Woman: Black Women and Feminism, 1981
Feminist Theory: From Margin to Center, 1984
Talking Back: Thinking Feminist, Thinking Black, 1989
Yearning: Race, Class, and Cultural Politics, 1990
Black Looks: Race and Representation, 1992
Sisters of the Yam: Black Women and Self-Recovery, 1993
A Woman's Mourning Song, 1993
Teaching to Transgress: Education as the Practice of Freedom, 1994
Outlaw Culture: Resisting Representation, 1994
Art on My Mind: Visual Politics, 1995
Killing Rage: Ending Racism, 1995
Bone Black: Memories of Girlhood, 1996

Wounds of Passion: The Writing Life, 1997
Remembered Rapture: The Write at Work, 1999
Feminism Is for Everybody, 2000
Where We Stand: Class Matters, 2000
Salvation: Black People and Love, 2001

RICHARD VERRONE

See also **African-American Nationalism and Separatism; Morrison, Toni (African-American)**

Further Reading

Coen, Deborah, "The Back Page: bell hooks's Outlaw Culture," *Perspective* (February 1995)

Fox, Tom, "Literacy and Activism: A Response to bell hooks," *Journal of Advanced Composition,* 14, no. 2 (Fall 1994)

Jones, Lisa, "Rebel without a Pause," *Village Voice Literary Supplement* (October 1992)

Middleton, Joyce Irene, "bell hooks on Literacy and Teaching: A Response," *Journal of Advanced Composition,* 14, no. 2 (Fall 1994)

Montmarquet, James A., and William H. Hardy, *Reflections: An Anthology of African American Philosophy,* Belmont, California: Wadsworth Thompson Learning, 2000

Olson, Gary, and Elizabeth Hirsh, "Feminist Praxis and the Politics of Literacy: A Conversation with bell hooks," in *Women Writing Culture,* edited by Gary Olson and Elizabeth Hirsh, Albany: State University of New York Press, 1995

Quashie, Kevin E., R. Joyce Lausch, and Keith D. Miller, *New Bones: Contemporary Black Writers in America,* Upper Saddle River, New Jersey: Prentice Hall, 2001

Shohat, Ella, *Talking Visions: Multicultural Feminism in Transnational Age,* New York: New Museum of Contemporary Art, and Cambridge, Massachusetts: MIT Press, 1998

Staples, Clifford, "White Male Ways of Knowing," *PostModern Culture* (Winter 1992)

Thomson, Clive, "Culture, Identity, and the Dialogic: bell hooks and Gayatri Chakravorty Spivak," in *Dialogism and Cultural Criticism,* edited by Clive Thomson and Hans Raj Dua, London: Mestengo, 1995

Horta, José Ramos, *See* **Ramos-horta, José (East Timor)**

Hui

Capsule Summary

Location: northern and northwestern People's Republic of China (Ningxia, Gansu, Xinjiang, Hebei, Henan, and Qinghai Provinces)

Total Population: 8.6 million

Language: Han

Religion: Islam

The label *hui* applies to a "nationality" (*minzu*) of the People's Republic of China whose sizeable population ranks third behind the Han and the Zhuang. The Hui nationality comprises all the Muslims of China except the Ouigurs. These Mohammedan Chinese are also known as Hwei, Panghse, or Panthay. Although they can be found in most of the cities throughout the country, they mainly inhabit the Ningxia Hui Autonomous Region, as well as Gansu, Qinghai, Xinjiang, Henan, Hebei, and Shandong Provinces. Moreover, half a million live in Yunnan, and there are scattered settlements of Hui in Laos, Thailand, and Burma (the Wa States and the Kengtung area). They have no distinctive language and speak mandarin or local dialects. Their costume is mostly the same as that of the Han. The difference is mainly in the headdress: some Hui men wear small, rimless, round hats, and the great majority of women, in accordance with strict adherence to the Muslim faith, wear kerchiefs on their head.

The term *Hui* is an abbreviation for *Huihui,* which is first mentioned in the chronicles of the Northern Song dynasty (960–1127), which referred to the Ouigurs of Anxi (Xinjiang). During the early thirteenth century, when the Mongolian troops of Genghis Khan were undertaking their western expeditions, Muslims from Middle Asia, Persia, or Arabia either were forced to move or voluntarily migrated into China. Some of them were enrolled as scouts and soldiers, whereas others became craftsmen, tradesmen, and scholars. Initially, because of their religious beliefs, which were identical to those of the people of Xinjiang, they were identified as those Xinjiang residents, and called Hui.

But at the time of the Yuan dynasty (1271–1368), the Ouigur, more localized and difficult to control, were distinguished from the Hui. The Han progressively enlarged the latter category to comprise not only the people who moved during the westward invasion but also older waves of Muslim immigrants. The Hui thus defined had fewer rights than Mongolians but more than the defeated Han. Considered loyal servants, they were encouraged to settle in the margins of the empire, as well as along vital communication lines such as the Silk Road, to pacify and protect these strategic areas. They formed communities of peasant-soldiers maintaining combat readiness to defend the borders.

In these conditions, a Hui elite emerged that promoted its economic interests and the Islamic religion as its main distinctive features. It was during the Ming dynasty (1368–1644) that the Hui began to emerge as an ethnic group. At that time, their distribution and economic status underwent a major change. Their concentration in Gansu and Shanxi Provinces increased, and a majority of them submitted themselves to the Ming court and turned toward agriculture. The early years of the Qing dynasty saw the emergence of a new religious aristocracy of imams among the Hui of Gansu, as a result of intensified land concentration. These imams enjoyed a series of feudalistic privileges. However, in other parts of the empire their situation was less favorable. Thus, in Yunnan, competition between Han and Hui over mining concessions caused a Muslim rebellion that lasted 20 years (1855–73), coinciding with other uprisings, such as the Taiping and the Miao, which blossomed as the authority of the Manchu declined. For a time, the Hui succeeded in establishing their own state with Dali as its capital, but finally it fell to the Han in 1873, provoking the migration of thousands of Chinese Muslims into the neighboring countries of Burma and Laos.

After 1949, the Chinese government applied its nationalities policy to the northwestern provinces by creating a Hui autonomous region and several autonomous prefectures or counties in the areas where Muslims were dominant. However, the Cultural Revolution (1966–76) and the ban it imposed on religious activities were felt as a serious threat to Hui identity, and people turned to various forms of silent resistance. In the early 1980s, after the easing of restrictions on cults, mosques were quickly rebuilt or repaired. In Ningxia, the Hui autonomous region, 1,400 mosques had already been restored in 1984, and the figure was over 2000 in 2001. Today, the Qurban Festival (10th of the 12th month of the Muslim calendar) and the Lesser Bairam (fast-breaking day, closing *Ramadan*) are major events for this nationality and give the Hui a special occasion to strengthen their unity. Although the Chinese government keeps a close watch over the activities of the Hui mosques to restrain the spread of Muslim fundamentalism, this control is more relaxed than that placed on the Ouigurs in Xinjiang. The level of social and economic integration of the Hui is relatively high. Heirs of a long tradition of caravan trade in Yunnan and the northwest, they have a reputation as efficient businessmen, and some of them occupy prominent positions as managers of large trade companies in Hong Kong, Shenzhen, Shanghai, Canton, Beijing, and Kunming.

BERNARD FORMOSO

See also **China**

Further Reading

Gladney, Dru C., *Muslim Chinese: Ethnic Nationalism in the People's Republic*, Cambridge, Massachusetts, Harvard University Press, 1991

Hill, Ann Maxwell, "The Yunnanese: Overland Chinese in Northern Thailand," in *Highlanders of Thailand*, edited by J. McKinnon and Wanat Bhruksasri, Singapore: Oxford University Press, 1986

Ma Yin, *China's Minority Nationalities*, Beijing: Foreign Languages Press, 1994

Human and Minority Rights Organizations

In the development of international human rights law, human and minority rights organizations have played a prominent role. The establishment of the modern human rights regime is associated with the establishment of the United Nations Organization in 1945. The United Nations (UN), which is an intergovernmental organization, does not have as its primary focus the issue of human rights. However, a number of the organs of the UN, in particular the Economic and Social Council (ECOSOC), the Commission on Human Rights, and the Sub-Commission on the Prevention of Discrimination and Protection of Minorities, have been engaged in human rights activities. In addition to the UN, there are other intergovernmental organizations, such as the International Labor Organization (ILO), that make a significant contribution to human rights. The ILO, which was founded in 1919, has been promoting international labor standards, as well as asserting the rights of groups such as indigenous peoples.

Although the work of intergovernmental organizations is of enormous value, more significant to the human rights movement has been the role played by nongovernmental organizations (NGOs). Presently there are several thousand international and national NGOs dedicated to protecting individual and collective rights. These NGOs have helped in setting human and minority rights standards and in providing information to intergovernmental bodies and to the world at large on human rights violations. NGOs have also acted as important pressure groups, as key actors at the national level in raising mass awareness among people, and as arbiters in conflicts between states and minority groups. Several NGOs have been involved in litigation at the national and international level to protect the rights of individuals and minorities.

NGOs have historically been prominent in projecting humanitarian concerns. The initial attempts to promote human rights issues were conducted by NGOs such as Anti-Slavery International and Save the Children International Unicon (SCIU). Anti-Slavery International is the world's oldest human rights organization, dating back to 1787. Initially formulated as a voluntary society, it was at the forefront of movements to abolish the slave trade in the United Kingdom and elsewhere. Similarly, SCIU was the inspiring force behind the first declaration of the rights of the child (1924), the precursor to the International Convention on the Rights of the Child (1989). In the modern phase, human rights NGOs have been active in not only setting international standards, but also in monitoring their progress and implementation. Human rights organizations campaigned for protecting the rights of the victims of World War II and for establishing institutions that would prevent the recurrence of global warfare. The intervention of several international human rights organizations was instrumental in the incorporation of references of human rights within the Charter of the United Nations (1945). The Charter also recognizes the role of the NGOs in Article 71.

ECOSOC recognizes that NGOs should have the opportunity to express their views and that they possess special experience or technical knowledge of value to the council's work. According to ECOSOC Resolution 1996/31, in order to attain a consultative status, an organization must be concerned with issues within the competence of the ECOSOC and its subsidiary bodies. The procedure to obtain a consultative status for NGOs is set out in the UN Web site at http://www.un.org./. The role and provisions for the NGOs within the ECOSOC are elaborated through ECOSOC Resolution 1296(XLIV) of May 1968. According to Resolution 1296, NGOs are classified into three categories. Category I represents those organizations most concerned with the activities of ECOSOC. They are also presumed to make "marked and sustained contribution in achieving the objectives of the UN," "are closely involved with the economic and social lives of the peoples of the area they represent," and have a membership "which is broadly representative of major segments of the population in a large number of countries." Members of these NGOs have wide-ranging powers to attend and participate in public meetings of the ECOSOC and its subsidiary organs. Category I includes organizations such as Green Peace International, International Save the Children Alliance, and Medicins sans Frontieres (International).

Category II consists of those organizations that have a special competence in specific areas and are concerned only with a few fields of ECOSOC activity. These NGOs are known and respected internationally for their work in the special areas where they seek consultative status, although they have a "general international concern" with human rights and are "not restricted to the interests of a particular group of persons, a single nationality or the situation in a single State or restricted group of States." Although NGOs in this category have less power and influence than those in Category I, there are nevertheless important transmitters of information to ECOSOC bodies. Category II includes organizations such as Amnesty International, Human Rights Watch, International Committee of the Red Cross, and International Commission of Jurists.

Category III consists of those organizations that do not have a broad competence in human rights issues but can make "occasional and useful contributions" to the work of the council or its subsidiary organs. These NGOs are included in the list termed the "Roster." Category III organizations include Minority Rights Group International (MRG), International Movement against All forms of Discrimination and Racism (IMADR), Art 19—International Center against Censorship, International Federation for the Protection of the Rights of Ethnic, Religious and Other Minorities, and Survival International Limited.

As at February 2001, there are nearly 2,000 NGOs with a consultative status with the UN. Although these NGOs make useful contributions to the work of ECOSOC, the UN imposes certain limitations on them. Thus, the ECOSOC is the only organ of the UN that is authorized to consult NGOs, and no similar provisions have been made for other significant bodies of the UN, such as the General Assembly or the Security Council. Even within the ECOSOC, Article 71 makes reference to "consultation" with NGOs as opposed to "participation" or "co-operation" with the council, thus placing NGOs in a subservient role.

NGOs have played a notable role in setting standards for human rights and minority rights. They have been influential in the drafting of various international treaties, in particular the Convention on the Rights of the Child (1989), the African Charter of Human and People's Rights (1981), the European Convention for the Prevention of Inhuman or Degrading Treatment or Punishment (1987), and the Statute for the International Criminal Court (1998). A number of NGOs have also taken the lead in formulating standards on minority and indigenous rights. The role played by organizations such as the Minority Rights Group and Survival International in drafting international instruments such as the United Nations Declaration on the Rights of Persons Belonging to National or Ethnic, Religious or Linguistic Minorities (1992) and the UN Draft Declaration on the

Rights of Indigenous Peoples (1995) needs to be commended. A more significant contribution of the NGOs has been as providers of information and as human rights monitors. Having established their credentials as valuable partners in the protection of human and minority rights, the NGOs frequently liaise with various human rights bodies.

NGOs provide useful information to the Human Rights Commission in its consideration of the ECOSOC Resolution 1503 procedure for identifying "particular situations which appear to reveal a consistent pattern of gross and reliably attested violations of human rights." The information on violation of rights is also used by various UN working groups, country rapporteurs appointed by the UN, and special rapporteurs investigating specific violations. Annual and periodic reports produced by such organizations as Amnesty International, Human Rights Watch, and the Minority Rights Group could thus provide substantial information on breaches of human and group rights. NGO representatives often have significant insight into the problem confronting a certain group or individuals, and members of UN bodies such as the Human Rights Committee and the Committee on the Elimination of All forms of Discrimination are often able to benefit from the experiences and information provided by the NGO representatives. The members of the UN working groups on minorities and indigenous peoples have benefited enormously from the contributions and interventions made by minority and indigenous NGOs. Since most of the human rights treaties have only made provisions for receiving reports from governments of state parties, the monitoring bodies have substantial difficulties in obtaining a complete and truthful picture to form a critical view of the situation. The informal though highly significant role of the NGOs in providing this information and in some cases producing alternative reports allows the treaty-based body to critically analyze the human and minority rights situation prevalent in a state.

International NGOs also prepare reports on violations in particular states around the world. Some of these organizations are more focused on specific issues. For example, the Minority Rights Group has a special interest in the position of minority groups. Article 19 focuses in issues of censorship and freedom of expression. NGOs distribute their reports, provide the information in them to the media, and use this information to engage in lobbying or other forms of advocacy before national executive officials or legislatures and international organizations. Human and minority rights organizations thus frequently raise awareness about human rights (or group rights) violations. They ask the governments to account for these violations. Unhindered by the restrictions and restraints that prevent other states or intergovernmental bodies to act, they frequently bring to light glaring violations of human rights. In a number of instances NGO publicity through demonstrations and protests and more subtly through their letter-writing campaigns has led to the release of political prisoners and reforms in governmental policies. In addition to acting as agencies of information and campaigning against human rights violators, NGOs have also conducted substantial practical work at domestic levels. Some NGOs initiate or (as amici curiae) join in litigation before national or international tribunals. In the recent Pinochet litigation before the House of Lords (the highest court of appeal in the United Kingdom), Amnesty International made amicus curaie interventions. Amnesty International and other human rights organizations have been involved in making representations before the European Court of Human Rights and the Inter-American Court of Human Rights. These amicus curiae interventions are particularly valuable in rectifying an imbalance when an individual with limited resources is complaining against the activities of a powerful and resourceful state. These interventions can also be useful to the parties and the courts in ascertaining a legal position. Thus in several cases the European Court of Human Rights (the judicial organ in charge of administering the European Convention on Human Rights) has referred to submissions made by human rights organizations.

Not all NGO work is based on confronting states or criticizing them for violations of human rights. NGOs have also engaged in the constructive work of drafting and preparing legislation. They have set up important conferences in which members of the governments are invited to discuss and consider human and minority rights issues alongside academics and human rights activists.

JAVAID REHMAN

See also **Equal Opportunity; Human Rights; United Nations and Minorities; United Nations Declaration on Minorities; United Nations Working Group on Indigenous Populations; United Nations Working Group on Minorities**

Further Reading

Cassese, Anthony, "How Could Non-Governmental Organizations use U.N. Bodies More Effectively?" *Universal Human Rights*, 1 (1979)

Cohen, Cynthia, "The Role of Non-Governmental Organizations in the Drafting of the Convention on the Rights of the Child," *Human Rights Quarterly*, 12 (1990)

Shelton, Diana, "The Participation of Nongovernmental Organizations in International Judicial Proceedings," *American Journal of International Law*, 88 (1994)

Shestack, Jerome J., "Sisyphus Endures: The International Human Rights NGOs," *New York Law School Law Review*, 24 (1978)

Stiener, Henry, and Alston Philip, *International Human Rights in Context: Law, Politics and Morals*, Oxford: Clarendon, 2000

Van Boven, Theo, "The Role of Non-Governmental Organizations in International Human Rights Standard-Setting: A Prerequisite for Democracy," *California Western International Law Journal*, 20 (1989–1990)

———, "The Role of Non-Governmental Organizations in the Promotion and Protection of Human Rights," in *Hong Kong Bill of Rights: A Comparative Approach*, edited by Johnnes Chan and Yash Ghai, Singapore: Butterworths, 1993

Human Rights

Human rights as a philosophical concept had its roots in an obscure publication from 1537 titled *Historia Diplomática Rerum Batavia-rum,* but its spirit was already present in some of Saint Paul's epistles. The political, juridical concept of human rights as scholars regard it today first appeared in the eighteenth century during the Age of Enlightenment. Incidentally, the famous sentence "All men are created equally free and independent" was not part of the 1776 *Declaration of Independence* and was not initially present as such in the first U.S. constitution from 1787, although it was present in the beginning of *The Virginia Declaration of Rights*, published on June 12, 1776, by George Mason. This fundamental declaration insisting on the importance of equal rights was only included in an amended version of the constitution in 1789. That same year, just a month after the French Revolution, the French National Assembly reunited in Versailles agreed on a *Déclaration des Droits de l'Homme et du citoyen* (Declaration of the Rights of Man and Citizen) on August 24, 1789. The text's 17 articles, espousing specific philosophical and political rights based upon Enlightenment ideals of individualism and the separation of powers, began with the exhortation "Men are born, and remain, free and equal in rights."

Only 2 years later, in 1791, a French journalist and playwright who called herself Olympe de Gouges (born Marie Gouze, 1748–93) wrote and published the first modern pamphlet for a minority, that is, the women among the French citizenry. An important early feminist, she claimed rights for "mothers, daughters, sisters." The 17 articles of her *Déclaration des droits de la femme et de la citoyenne* (Declaration of the Rights of Woman and the Female Citizen, 1791) represented the first declaration of truly universal human rights. This was followed by *Social Contract*, proposing marriage based on gender equality.

In 1793 the *Declaration of the Rights of Man and of the Citizen* was amended to specify for the first time that the concept of freedom also applies to persons of African descent. In the next century, the renewed constitution of 1848 included statements on civil and social rights, providing for the rights of workers to reunite and the necessity of free public instruction for children. In 1924 the League of Nations adopted the *Declaration of the Rights of the Child* (also known as the *Declaration of Geneva*), marking the beginning of the international child rights movement. It affirmed that "the child must be given the means needed for its normal development, both materially and spiritually" and stated that "the hungry child should be fed."

Following the atrocities of two World Wars, a number of human rights documents appeared in the United States and Europe. The General Assembly of the World Medical Association, as part of the Geneva Conference in 1948, adopted a declaration of physicians' dedication to the humanitarian goals of medicine, which represented a potent statement on the heels of Nazi Germany's commission of medical crimes. This *Declaration of Geneva* was designed as a Hippocratic Oath for modernity.

Also in 1948, the United Nations Organization (UNO) agreed upon and authored the *Universal Declaration of Human Rights,* an overarching set of standards by which governments, organizations, and individuals would monitor behavior and ensure equal rights. Partly inspired by the French *Déclaration* from 1789 and its updated versions, this text was followed in 1950 by the *European Convention for the Protection of Human Rights and Fundamental Freedoms.* Since then the General Assembly of the United Nations has initiated the United Nations Centre for Human Rights in Geneva, with its Commission on Human Rights (53 members), which still acts as a policy-making body. It includes the Sub-Commission on Prevention of Discrimination and Protection of Minorities, made of 26 experts, which protects racial, religious, and linguistic minorities.

In less than half a century, many similar institutions and related courts and on human rights have emerged: The Council of Europe instituted on November 1, 1998, its European Court of Human Rights to hear human rights complaints from the European Council member states. The Inter-American Commission on Human Rights (IACHR), as part of the Organization of American States, was established in 1959 and supervises an Inter-American Court of Human Rights. The Inter-American Court, an autonomous judicial institution based in San José, Costa Rica, promotes and secures basic rights and freedoms in the Americas.

Contemporary Concerns and Issues

Contemporary issues and new contexts continuously challenge the ideals of human rights throughout the world stage. Diaspora, migrations, ethnic conflicts, wars, and racism can endanger populations in various ways. Through the years, some geographical or ethnic groups have written their own charters or declarations on human rights that outline their specific political priorities and philosophical commitments.

The *African Charter on Human and Peoples' Rights* (the Banjul Charter) was adopted in June 1981 by members of the Organization of African Unity in Banjul, Gambia; it entered into force October 1986. At the Second Ordinary Session of the Assembly of the Union, Maputo, in July 2003, the charter was amended to include considerations for the rights of African women, stating that the African charter "enshrines the

principle of non-discrimination on the grounds of race, ethnic group, colour, sex, language, religion, political or any other opinion, national and social origin, fortune, birth or other status." The charter led some 15 African countries to ratify another protocol establishing the principles of the first African Human Rights Court on January 25, 2004. Member states include Algeria, Burkina Faso, Burundi, Côte d'Ivoire, Gambia, Lesotho, Libya, Mali, Mauritius, Rwanda, Senegal, South Africa, Togo, Uganda, and Comoros. One remaining challenge is to see how many other African countries will sign and respect these crucial reforms.

Another example of a state-initiated human rights document is the *Arab Charter on Human Rights,* adopted in Cairo by the Council of the League of Arab States on September 15, 1994. As a possible challenge to other minorities and to Israel, the *Arab Charter* stated in its first article "racism, Zionism, occupation and foreign domination pose a challenge to human dignity and constitute a fundamental obstacle to the realization of the basic rights of peoples." However, Article 37 of the charter also includes a clear mention about minorities, stipulating "minorities shall not be deprived of their right to enjoy their culture or to follow the teachings of their religions." Some specific adjustments to the Arab charter on key issues such as torture, deportation, and the possibility of revoking citizenship were suggested lately, but one question still remains. In March 2004, the *Jordan Times* wrote "one of the problems facing these modest amendments is that no Arab state has yet ratified the 1994 charter" (Bos, "Arab Leaders to Discuss Rights amid Persecution," 2004).

In just a few decades, governments and civil society have forged quite a few dynamic organisms dedicated to promote human rights. Among others, an independent NGO, Amnesty International (AI), was founded in 1961 by British lawyer Peter Benenson. In 1962, Amnesty International had groups either established or in formation in Argentina, Australia, Belguim, Canada, Ethiopia, Ghana, Greece, India, Ireland, Israel, Jamaica, Malaya, Mexico, Myanmar (Burma), the Netherlands, New Zealand, Nigeria, Norway, the Republic of the Congo, Sri Lanka, Sweden, Switzerland, the United States, and West Germany.

Amnesty International works to prevent torture, terrorism, disappearances, and extrajudicial executions, among other global issues. It assists political asylum seekers and in general raises awareness of human rights abuses around the world. In 1977 AI won the Nobel Peace Prize for its efforts defending human rights. Today, it includes more than a million members and activists in over 140 countries. A similar NGO, Human Rights Watch based in New York City, was created in 1978 as Helsinki Watch to support minorities, endangered populations, refugees, and victims of injustice through the world. Although these organizations have no court systems or police force, they influence public opinion through inquiries, reports, publicity campaigns, and advocacy in the media. Ironically, these two organizations denounce and condemn the unfair practices of countries that signed the *Universal Declaration of the Rights of Man and Citizen* in 1948.

The multiplication of charters and organizations dedicated to human rights could create unpredicted, perverse effects. Some critics claim that specific, local charters might undermine the grounds and legitimacy of the broader, global, universal declarations. In other words, if certain nations are prompted to propose their own charters elucidating their specific vision of human rights, would this mean that the original declarations were incomplete or have become obsolete? Other critics suggest, however, that contemporary charters address specific concerns (both global and local) that arise within a context that has shifted from their historical antecedents.

YVES LABERGE

See also **Diaspora; Equal Opportunity; Ethnic Conflict; Human and Minority Rights Organizations; League of Nations and Minorities; Migrations; United Nations and Minorities**

Further Reading

Arab Charter on Human Rights, adopted by the League of Arab States, reprinted in *Human Rights Law Journal*, 18 (1997)(taken from the Human Rights Library, University of Minnesota). http://www1.umn.edu/humanrts/instree/arabhr-charter.html

Bell, Daniel A., *East Meets West: Human Rights and Democracy in East Asia*, Princeton: Princeton University Press, 2000

Blance, Olivier, *Marie-Olympe de Gouges: une humaniste à la fin du XVIIIè siècle*, Paris: Éditions René Viénet, 2003

Bos, Stefan J., "Arab Leaders to Discuss Rights amid Persecution," *Insight on the News*, March 18, 2004. http://www.insightmag.com/news/2004/03/30/World/Arab-Leaders.To.Discuss.Rights.Amid.Persecution-636080.shtml

Déclaration des Droits de l'Homme et du citoyen (Declaration of the Rights of Man and Citizen), from August 24, 1789. (Full text. English translation). http://www.derechos.net/doc/tratados/eng/79.html

Déclaration des droits de la femme et de la citoyenne, written by de Gouges, Olympe, in 1791. (Full original text. In French). http://www.cidem.org/cidem/themes/egalite_hommes_femmes/ega_infos/textes_de_ref/ega_t007.html

Declaration of the Rights of Woman (translated from the "*Déclaration des droits de la femme et de la citoyenne*"), written by de Gouges, Olympe, in 1791. (Full text. English translation). http://www.library.csi.cuny.edu/dept/americanstudies/lavender/decwom2.html

The United Nations, "Acting Rights Chief Welcomes Entry into Force of Protocol Establishing African Human Rights Court," Communiqué, January 26, 2004. http://www.unog.ch/news2/documents/newsen/hc04005e.htm

Universal Declaration of Human Rights. Adopted and proclaimed by General Assembly Resolution 217 A (III), December 10, 1948

Hume, John (Northern Ireland Catholic)

John Hume was born in the city of Derry (or Londonderry) in Northern Ireland, the oldest child of a Catholic family in the city's Bogside District. His family belonged to the first generation of Northern Irish Catholics to have access to free public education, which his family recognized as a potential escape from the city's too-familiar cycle of poverty and unemployment. He initially set out to join the priesthood, but after 3 years of theological study, Hume decided instead to pursue a teaching career.

Beginning in 1964, he taught at Derry schools, and he helped found the Derry Credit Union, the first of its kind in Northern Ireland. In 1964, he also helped establish the Derry Housing Association to relieve the city's housing shortage. Eager for more economic and political reform, and frustrated by the apparent unwillingness of the Protestant-dominated Northern Irish Parliament at Stormont in Belfast to address increasing calls from the Catholic minority for these changes, Hume became active in local civil rights activities. Following violence at a civil rights march in Derry on October 5, 1968, he was elected to the Derry Citizens' Action Committee as vice chairman.

Inspired by the example of the Reverend Martin Luther King, Jr., Hume advocated nonviolent protest, even when confronted with violence, an occurrence that became common beginning in 1968, when the Catholic civil rights struggle began to gather significant momentum. While trying to defuse a confrontation between demonstrators and the British Army in 1968, Hume was repeatedly knocked down with a fire hose and finally arrested for "obstructing Her Majesty's forces." He refused to pay the small £20 fine on principle and appealed all the way to the House of Lords, which overturned his conviction.

Hume next successfully ran for a seat in Northern Ireland's Parliament in 1969, defeating a more radical Catholic nationalist candidate. His triumph led to the formation in 1970 of the Social Democratic and Labor Party (SDLP). An early victory for the party, which renounced IRA (and Protestant paramilitary) violence, came in 1971, when the British government created the Northern Ireland Housing Executive, a nonsectarian housing authority that took responsibility for public housing out of the hands of local Protestant authorities.

Housing reform, however, seemed a relatively minor improvement in the face of growing violence, which led directly to the dissolution of the Northern Irish Parliament and direct rule by England in 1972. Still, Hume remained convinced that Northern Ireland's problems could be solved peacefully and democratically. When England and Ireland joined the European Economic Community in 1973, Hume saw it as a model of cooperation among people with occasionally conflicting agendas. When representatives from the English and Irish governments, along with members of several Northern Irish political parties, began a series of meetings at Sunningdale in 1973, Hume was a member of the power-sharing executive. Although Sunningdale's plans for reform ended with province-wide threats of Protestant strikes, the meetings laid the blueprint for all subsequent efforts for peace and reform. They also convinced Hume that there could be no progress in Northern Ireland without international pressure. He looked increasingly to the United States with its large population of Irish Americans for support of peace and reform.

Under Hume's leadership (which became official in 1979), the SDLP evolved from a socialist party to a reformist one, with a largely middle-class constituency. Hume also began to seek money from Irish-American and European economic agencies to improve housing and economic conditions in his native Derry. The relationships he formed bore fruit over the next three decades. In 1983, Hume was elected to the House of Commons at Westminster.

Hume had been fearful when the British government negotiated a secret ceasefire with the IRA in the aftermath of the failure of Sunningdale. He thought that a ceasefire might accelerate the popularity of Sinn Féin, the IRA's political wing, to the detriment of the SDLP. The party had always been unswerving in its opposition to the Catholic paramilitary organization. Hume himself, when forging ties with Irish Americans through the 1970s and 1980s, urged an end to Irish-American financial assistance to the IRA. Yet in 1987 he agreed to a series of meetings with Sinn Féin leader Gerry Adams arranged by a Belfast cleric, Father Alec Reid. The two men met several more times in secret over the next 5 years before the news became public in 1993, amidst considerable criticism for both men. Undaunted, Hume tried to use the ensuing publicity as leverage to pressure the governments in Dublin and London to enter into talks with all of Northern Ireland's political parties, Sinn Féin having been excluded from previous multiparty talks in 1973–74 and 1984–85. He also returned to the United States for another round of meetings with congressional members. As this point, Hume had become so familiar around the Capitol building that he was dubbed "the 101st Senator." He found an ally in President Bill Clinton, who in 1995 became the first United States president to visit Belfast and Derry, adding considerable clout to Hume's own vision of the peace process.

Whereas a United States president of Irish descent was a likely ally, David Trimble, the newly elected leader of the Ulster Unionist Party (UUP), was highly unlikely. Trimble had a well-earned reputation as a Protestant hard-liner who surprised nearly everyone when he agreed to meet not only with Hume, but also with political leaders from Ireland, to see if peace could be had. Following nearly 3 years of often-contentious negotiations, a committee chaired by former United States senator George J. Mitchell, and led chiefly by Hume and Trimble, was able to hammer out the Good Friday, or Belfast, Agreement of April 1998. Trimble gave his consent to the large package of reforms over the vocal protests of many in his own party, though he was ultimately able to win popular party support for the agreement. For their efforts at bringing the hope of peace to Northern Ireland where so many others had failed, Hume and Trimble shared the 1998 Nobel Peace Prize.

In November 2003, elections for the Northern Irish Assembly saw losses for Hume's SDLP and surprising gains for Sinn Féin. Hume served in the assembly from 1998 –to 2001 and continues to hold seats in the European and English Parliaments. Regardless of his subsequent political fortunes, he has earned a central place in Northern Ireland's history.

Biography

John Hume. Born 18 January 1937 in Derry, County Derry, Northern Ireland. Educated at St. Columb's College, Derry, and the National University of Ireland, from which he graduated with a B.A. in French and History. Further studied at St. Malo, Brittany, and at the Institut Catholique in Paris. Master's degree from St. Patrick's College, Maynooth, Ireland, in 1964. Founder and director, Derry Credit Union, 1964–present. Founder, Derry Housing Association, 1964. Independent Northern Irish member of Parliament for Foyle, 1969. Cofounder, Social Democratic Labor Party (SDLP), 1970. Member of Northern Ireland Assembly, 1973. Minister for commerce of Northern Ireland, 1974. Northern Ireland Convention, 1975. Special adviser to European community commissioner, consumer affairs, 1977–79. Member of English Parliament for Derry, 1979–present. Leader, SDLP, 1979. Member of English Parliament for Foyle, 1983–present. Member, New Ireland Forum, 1983–84. Member, Northern Ireland Forum 1996–98. Served in New Northern Ireland Assembly, 1998–2001. Awards: Nobel Peace Prize, 1998.

Selected Works

A New Ireland: Politics, Peace, and Reconciliation, 1996

JOHN H. DAVIS

See also **Adams, Gerry (Northern Ireland Catholic); Irish Republican Army; Northern Ireland; Sinn Fein; Trimble, David (Northern Ireland)**

Further Reading

Hennessey, Thomas, *The Northern Ireland Peace Process: Ending the Troubles,* London: Gill & Macmillan, 2000
Hume, John, *A New Ireland: Politics, Peace, and Reconciliation,* Boulder: Roberts Rinehart, 1996
Murray, Gerard, *John Hume and the SDLP: Impact and Survival in Northern Ireland,* Dublin: Irish Academic Press, 1998
Routledge, Paul, *John Hume: A Biography,* London: Harper-Collins, 1997
White, Barry, *John Hume: Statesman of the Troubles,* Belfast: Blackstaff Press, 1984

Hungarians

Capsule Summary

Location: Carpathian basin, Central Europe, between Slovakia and Romania
Total Population: 10,045,407 (in Hungary, 2003); 93,437 elsewhere
Language: Hungarian
Religions: Roman Catholic (67%); Calvinist (20%); Lutheran (5%); other (7%)

There are few peoples better acquainted with the history of minorities in Europe than the Hungarians. Situated exactly 1,000 miles (1609 kilometers) from Paris and Moscow, they have endured the lot of a small people in a central place: invasion, conquest, occupation, and shifting frontiers. Geography decreed that Hungarian history would be inextricably linked with that of the non-Hungarian minorities who shared the crown lands of St. Stephen over the centuries. When World War I shattered the Habsburg monarchy, moreover, some 3 million Hungarians became minorities overnight in the construction of the new Europe, a fate they shared with many of their neighbors, including Croats, Romanians, Slovaks, and Serbs.

History

Most historians agree that the Hungarians, a people akin to Finns and Turks, came to the Carpathian basin around the year 896 under the leadership of the Árpád dynasty. Mindful of the need for accommodation with powerful neighbors, Árpád's grandson Vajk accepted Christianity in 1000 and became Stephen I, the first Apostolic King of Hungary. The next two centuries proved eventful for Stephen's successors. They witnessed periodic uprisings among their subjects and endured an invasion by the Mongols in 1241. Subsequently, however, they enjoyed a period of continuous prosperity and expansion. Medieval Hungary attracted a wide variety of settlers and traders, many of whom eventually assimilated, so that by the year

1500, according to the historian C.A. Macartney, some four-fifths of the population identified itself as Hungarian. Although non-Hungarians continued to live in the "crown lands"—notably Croats, who enjoyed a privileged status there after 1102—Hungarian rulers presided over an increasingly united state by the sixteenth century.

Like its neighbors to the south, Hungary eventually fell victim to the Ottoman Turkish juggernaut in 1526. Once established in their Buda headquarters, the Ottomans ruled the Hungarian heartland directly, administering the province of Transylvania as an autonomous region. Meanwhile, their regional rivals, the Habsburg monarchy, took control of the westernmost part of Hungary. The brunt of the Ottomans' assault and occupation fell on the Great Plain, the area with the greatest concentration of Hungarian population. Frontier areas such as Transylvania, home to mostly non-Hungarians, suffered comparatively less. Reeling from their losses, the remaining Hungarians could not know then that five centuries would pass before they again predominated in the crown lands.

Hungarians and Habsburgs, 1683–1790

The defeat of the Ottomans at Vienna in 1683 paved the way for significant changes in Hungary, beginning with a Habsburg takeover of all the historic lands. The new rulers received a rude welcome from the Transylvanian prince Ferenc II Rakosi and his followers, who staged a determined and bloody uprising. Upon conclusion of the 1708 Peace of Szatmar, Austria fortified its position, destroying Hungarian fortresses and repopulating lands devastated by decades of occupation and revolt. Slovaks and Bohemian Jews soon joined longtime Croat and Romanian residents as well as Serbs and Gypsies who had settled in Hungary during the Ottoman occupation. They gave the area a markedly multinational character, collectively outnumbering the Hungarians in their own lands.

The reign of Empress Maria-Theresa helped reconcile Hungarians to Habsburg rule. The empress assiduously cultivated Hungarians, placing herself under the protection of St. Stephen's Crown, consulting Hungarian leaders on regional matters, and appointing Hungarian clergy to Hungarian ecclesiastical positions.

But her successor, Joseph II, abruptly terminated this idyll. In his quest for an efficient administration in his sprawling, multilingual empire, the emperor made German the official language of the empire and decreed its use in all state functions. This decision

outraged Hungarians. Emperor Joseph thus became the unwitting catalyst for a Hungarian revival.

National Revival, 1790–1849

The death of Joseph II, followed by the upheavals of the French Revolution and the Napoleonic invasion, temporarily blunted Hungarian indignation. Once order was restored in the Habsburg possessions in 1815, the delayed national awakening recommenced, drawing strength from similar movements elsewhere. The revival focused on the primacy of Hungarian language despite a strong non-Hungarian minority contingent constituting over 50 percent of the population. The Hungarian Diet took a fateful step in designating Hungarian as the official language in 1840.

The Hungarian Bid for Independence and Its Aftermath, 1848–67

As mid-century approached, the authors of the Hungarian revival mostly agreed on language and culture issues, but differed on how to navigate the road to liberal reform. When a mob sacked the French monarchy in February 1848, signaling the beginning of revolutionary ferment in Europe, the Kossuth faction seized the moment. On March 15, they proclaimed a liberal Hungarian state, united with Austria solely in the person of the emperor and including a two-house parliament, expansion of the franchise, and guarantees of legal equality for all citizens. Besieged by revolts elsewhere, Emperor Ferdinand had no choice but to approve it.

Reaction among the non-Hungarian minorities soon complicated relations between the new Hungary and Austria. Its founders advanced frankly nationalist as well as liberal objectives in declaring Hungarian the language of the land and ending Transylvania's autonomous existence. Loath to embrace Hungarian leadership, language, and culture at the expense of their own, the non-Hungarians prepared countermeasures. Slovak representatives demanded autonomy for themselves, while Serbs in the Vojvodina staged a brief uprising against Hungarian rule there. Meanwhile, the Croats elected Josip Jelacic as leader of their parliament, the *Sabor*. A soldier by training, Jelacic dramatized his opposition to the new Hungary by volunteering to oppose it by force of arms.

Faced with active opposition, Hungarian leaders transformed their legal revolution into open rebellion, recruiting such military talents as the Polish general

Joseph Bem to lead their army. In early 1849, Jelacic and the Austrians forced a retreat to Debrecen, where Kossuth proclaimed Hungarian independence in the *Nagytemplom*, the city's majestic Calvinist church. The Habsburg forces ultimately prevailed, with timely assistance from the imperial Russian army. The new Austrian emperor, 18-year-old Francis Joseph, had appealed to Czar Nicholas I, who hastened to help the younger ruler annihilate the rebellion in August 1849.

Francis Joseph took a series of symbolic and substantive measures to reassert Austrian authority in Hungary. The "Arad 13," those identified as the masterminds of the revolt, were arrested and executed. Meanwhile, construction began on a huge fortress on Buda's Gellert Hill. Then a warning against further challenges to Habsburg rule, the *Citadella*, as the fortress is known, stands today as evidence of a dispiriting interval in Hungarian history.

At first, it was decided that the entire empire—even the Romanians and Croats, who had assisted the Habsburgs in derailing the Hungarians—should be administered directly from Vienna. A centralized Austria, it was reasoned, would be a strong Austria. The Hungarians were defeated but unbowed. Eventually, events abroad favored them. In 1859, the monarchy's Italian possessions staged a successful breakaway, in part because of the threat of unrest in Hungary. In 1866, when war over German unification loomed, Prussian chancellor Otto von Bismarck openly raised the possibility of machinations in Hungary that would force Austria to fight on two fronts.

Emperor Francis Joseph thus faced a key choice in 1866: accommodate his Hungarian subjects or risk further assaults on the empire. He opted for the former in an arrangement with Hungary that resurrected the Hungary of March 1848. The Compromise of 1867(*Ausgleich*) divided the empire into two parts, joined in the person of the emperor and common ministries of finance, foreign policy, and national defense. Hungary would become master of its domestic policy, commanding equal billing in the state's title, henceforth Austria-Hungary.

The Last Years of Hungary and Habsburgs, 1867–1914

Dualist Hungary combined great assets with one serious weakness. Advantages negotiated in the 1867 compromise, along with the rapid construction of railways, made the country prosperous. A suitable capital took form in the union of Buda and Pest in 1873. But Hungarians'

relations with the non-Hungarian minorities, a key to domestic peace, were a continuous source of discord.

Initial postcompromise sentiment, codified in the Nationalities Law of 1868, looked promising. The law stressed the political unity of Hungary and designated Hungarian as the official language, yet it allowed for the use of other languages under certain circumstances. The Romanians and Croats, disillusioned with the Austrian leadership, were receptive. However, these modest concessions eventually inflamed Hungarian public opinion, which demanded changes. Thus in 1879, Hungarian became the language of instruction in all state schools, the law fortified by a regime of surveillance for schools in non-Hungarian areas. Non-Hungarian cultural and educational societies, such as the Slovak *Matica Slovenska*, were suppressed. There followed legislation mandating the Magyarization (the process of institutionalizing the ways and customs of the Magyar, or Hungarian, majority) of place names and numerous provocative legislative projects, such as making Hungarian the language of command in the Austro-Hungarian army.

By the dawn of the twentieth century, the campaign had achieved some success. One minority—assimilated Hungarian Jews—prospered, helping the Hungarians to exceed 50 percent of the population in the Hungarian lands, according to the 1910 census. For the most part, however, Magyarization alienated more non-Hungarians than it assimilated, spurring the creation of political movements that would eventually inflict substantial harm on Hungary. Magyarization in Slovakia moved Czech professor Thomas Masaryk to bring Czech and Slovak youth together by 1914. Romanians attracted international attention with an 1892 memorandum detailing the effects of Magyarization on Romanian residents of Transylvania. Despite their relatively privileged status in Hungary, Croats found common cause with Serbs in protesting aspects of the dualist regime. It can certainly be posited, moreover, that Hungary's policy toward the non-Hungarians exacerbated Austrian reaction to events in Serbia after 1903. Francis Joseph could not mitigate Hungary's policy toward his south Slavic subjects, so he was obliged to strike hard at dynamic Serbia, which was becoming a magnet for them and a danger to the integrity of his cherished empire.

"Mutilated Hungary" and Hungarians, 1914–1944

The emperor's determination to punish Serbia for the June 1914 murder of Archduke Franz Ferdinand plunged Austria and Hungary into World War I. Although Hungarians witnessed little fighting in their lands, they endured episodes of chaos and upheaval in the sudden collapse of the Habsburg monarchy and a brief communist revolution in Budapest. Moreover, they had ended the war on the losing side and therefore faced an uncertain future when the peacemakers gathered at Versailles. Like the other combatants, they placed great faith in United States president Woodrow Wilson, who promised a judicious settlement based on the principle of national self-determination.

The makers of the Hungarian part of the Versailles settlements, the Treaty of Trianon, granted one long-standing Hungarian wish in creating a unitary, independent Hungary. In so doing, however, they exacted a fearsome price. Making selective use of self-determination, the peacemakers signaled early that they would reward friends, punish foes, and defend against Bolshevik Russia. Hungary's treatment of its minorities, its flirtation with communism, and its war affiliation virtually guaranteed the transfer of Hungarian territories to British and French allies in the new Europe. Thus Czechoslovakia, whose founders had united in protest against Magyarization, acquired a portion of northern Hungary and Ruthenia. Having joined the Allies on the promise of Transylvania, Romanian leaders hastened to collect their prize, whose residents included 2 million Hungarians. The new Serb-Croat-Slovene (Yugoslav) state, meanwhile, acquired historic Croatian lands and a portion of southern Hungary (Vojvodina), with a Hungarian population numbering around 500,000. When the peace negotiations finally concluded, independent Hungary had lost two-thirds of its historic territories and over 3 million citizens.

The fate of the new Hungarian minorities varied according to the political character of their new countries. In Czechoslovakia, the Hungarians had political representation and Hungarian schools, whereas in Romania and Yugoslavia, they suffered disenfranchisement and repression from the beginning. But interwar Hungarian leaders made no such fine distinctions: immediate return of all lost territories became the motivating force of national politics.

Hungarians Under Soviet rule, 1945–1989

The end of World War II found Hungary devastated by physical destruction and loss of life—some 400,000 had perished, including most of the country's Jews. Once again, it found itself on the losing side, suffering the reimposition of Trianon borders in the 1947 Peace of Paris.

Like its neighbors, postwar Hungary became part of the Soviet Union's sphere of influence in Europe. In the last years of Stalin's rule in the Soviet Union, there was no public discussion of Hungarians outside Hungary, since such talk constituted evidence of narrow "bourgeois" nationalism. After 1953, however, the fate of the Hungarian minorities periodically resurfaced to complicate Hungary's relations with its eastern bloc neighbors. When the reformist government of Imre Nagy challenged Soviet authority in October 1956, for example, the Romanian leadership was among the loudest advocates of armed intervention, since the uprising promised to inflame the Transylvanian Hungarians. In the era of Nikita Khrushchev, Hungary enjoyed the highest standard of living in the eastern bloc. By contrast, Hungarians in Romania experienced a purposeful reduction of educational and cultural opportunities as the Romanian leadership followed an avowedly "Romanian" path. The phenomenon of "parallelization," in which Romanian educational institutions were established in order to drain support from those built for Hungarians, is typical of this period. In the 1960s and 1970s, the Kadar government made several attempts to gain some leverage with Romania and Czechoslovakia on behalf of the Hungarian minorities, but these efforts were mostly fruitless.

Hungary and Hungarians since 1989

Since the fall of communism in 1989, Hungarian leaders have focused on tasks that will allow them to rejoin Europe, such as establishing a market economy and applying for membership in NATO and the European Union. In the realm of practical politics, the fate of the Hungarian minorities has proved peripheral, though it remains alive in the national consciousness. In 1990, then Prime Minister Joseph Antall declared himself the leader of "15 million Hungarians." The 80th anniversary of the Trianon Treaty in 2000 occasioned much rhetoric bemoaning the fate of lost territories. It remains possible, given the present political and economic conditions in Central Europe, that the Hungarian minorities will reemerge as a hot issue. Hungarians in Yugoslavia escaped Slobodan Milosevic's warmongering in the early 1990s, but their prospects remain uncertain in a mostly Serbian state. The Hungarian government also must contemplate European Union demands that it seal its borders with impoverished neighbors to prevent a flood of immigrants into member nations. That could prove troublesome, since it could restrict Hungarians' contact with their relatives in Slovakia, Ukraine, Romania, and Yugoslavia. At present, it seems clear only that minority issues will remain a constant in the political and cultural life of Hungarians, wherever they reside.

BRIGIT FARLEY

See also **Croats; Hungary; Romania; Serbs**

Further Reading

Crampton, Ben, and Richard Crampton, *Atlas of Eastern Europe in the Twentieth Century*, London: Routledge, 1996

Jelavich, Charles, and Barbara Jelavich, *The Habsburg Monarchy: Toward a Multinational Empire or National States?* New York: Rinehart and Company, 1959

Kiraly, Bela, editor, *War and Society in East Central Europe, vol. VI. Essays on World War I: Total War and Peacemaking, a Case Study on Trianon,* New York: Columbia University Press, 1982

Macartney, Carlile Aylmer, *Hungary and Her Successors: The Treaty of Trianon and Its Consequences,* London: Oxford, 1965

May, Arthur J., *The Habsburg Monarchy, 1867—1914,* New York: Norton and Co., 1968

Sugar, Peter F., editor, *A History of Hungary,* Bloomington: Indiana University Press, 1990

Hungary

Capsule Summary

Country Name: Republic of Hungary
Location: east-central Europe
Total Population: 10,045,407 (July 2003)
Ethnic Populations: 400,000–500,000 Roma (Gypsies), 150,000 Germans, 110,000 Slovaks, 80,000 Jews, 80,000 Croats, 25,000 Romanians
Language: Hungarian
Religion: Catholicism (68%), Protestant (25%), other (7%)

The Republic of Hungary is a parliamentary democracy in Central Europe, northwest of Romania. Its border countries are Austria, Croatia, Romania, Serbia and Montenegro, Slovakia, Slovenia, and Ukraine; its capital is Budapest. Because of the history of the region, Hungary's concern for minority issues tends to be outward-looking rather than inward-looking. During the twentieth century, Hungary lost significant numbers of its ethnic minorities and also large numbers of Magyars (ethnic Hungarians). Following World War I, the dissolution of the Austria-Hungarian empire was formalized in the Treaty of Trianon (1920), which resulted in the loss of approximately one-third of the former territory of the Hungarian portion, as well as about one-quarter of the Magyar population. During World War II, Hungary regained large portions of its former territory at the price of allying itself with Nazi Germany, though these territories and their Magyar populations were again lost at the end of the war. More significant in the long term was the decline of the Jewish population from a prewar high of around 800,000 to a mere 80,000, most of those lost being killed in concentration camps following the German takeover of Hungary in 1944. Significant numbers of Roma (Gypsies) also perished in concentration camps, though the exact number is uncertain. Following the war, the ethnic German population in Hungary also declined by around half as the results of forceful expulsions and an official policy of anti-German discrimination. Similarly, the Slovak population declined drastically after World War II when the governments of Czechoslovakia and Hungary agreed to exchange, by force, more than 70,000 Slovaks living in Hungary for a like number of Magyars living in southern Slovakia.

Despite the violence of this history, Hungary is fortunate to be one of the most homogeneous states in Eastern Europe. This homogeneity tends to make minority issues within the country less contentious. As a result of the Treaty of Trianon and the events of World War II, Hungary lost most of its minority population and at the same time found a significant population of Magyars living outside Hungarian borders. The Hungarian government, dating back to the latter part of communist rule, has been deeply concerned with the treatment of Magyar minorities in neighboring states. This has worked to the advantage of the minorities inside Hungary, since the government has sought to make its minority policies a model for the region. Since 1945 there have been various claims by Romanian, Serbian, and Slovak nationalists that national minorities in Hungary faced persecution and forcible

Magyarization, but many of these claims have been made by nationalists outside of Hungary as a counter to Hungarian claims of more apparent discrimination against Magyar minorities within those states.

Certainly since the late 1970s, successive Hungarian governments have sought to guarantee significant cultural and linguistic rights to minorities within their country. The official line has stressed bilingualism and biculturalism rather than autonomy, and it has advanced this approach as a model for its neighbors to emulate. The current Hungarian constitution (effective since August 1949) enshrines the right of minorities to their own culture, religion, and language. Additionally, various laws also provide for the right of minorities to instruction in their native tongue, the use of ethnic names, and the use of their native tongue in legal proceedings.

Despite the relatively clean record on minority rights of the Hungarian government, particularly since the transition to democracy, Hungary is often criticized for the condition of the Roma population inside the country. According to a 2000 European Union report, gross inequalities exist between the living standards, education, and employment levels of the Roma and the rest of the population, and a deep, underlying prejudice against the Roma continues to pervade the society. The government, however, received good marks in the European Union report for its efforts to overcome the effects of decades of discrimination against the Roma minority. Similarly, most observers agree that there is widespread anti-Semitism within the population. Prominent politicians, such as Jozsef Torgyan of the nationalist and populist Independent Smallholders Party, and Istvan Csurka of the Hungarian Life and Justice Party, have drawn controversy with anti-Roma and anti-Semitic comments. Both politicians have nonetheless enjoyed some level of support from voters, particularly Torgyan, who served as the minister of agriculture from 1998 until early 2001 under the FIDESZ government of Viktor Orban.

Speaking in 1990, President Arpad Göncz set the tone for Hungarian foreign relations, and at the same time set off a major controversy, when he declared that part of his job was to "ensure the observance of the human and civil rights" of Magyar minorities outside of Hungary. Although this may have raised the specter of revanchism among Hungary's neighbors, the Hungarian governments since 1990 have renounced any desires to revise the current borders and have concentrated on diplomatic pressure as a means to improve the lot of Magyars abroad, primarily through European organs such as the Organization for Security and Cooperation in Europe (OSCE). In recent years, Hungary has encouraged the European Union to consider a state's record of minority rights as part of its criteria for expansion into Eastern Europe. In addition, Hungary has held bilateral talks with Romania, Slovakia, and Serbia. There are significant Magyar minorities in these states, and they have in recent years suffered some discrimination based upon their ethnic origin. In March 1995, Hungary and Slovakia signed a basic treaty in which they agreed to defend the rights of their respective minorities to cultural and linguistic freedom. After years of debate and negotiation, Hungary and Romania signed a similar treaty in 1996.

Under the current government of the Young Democrats (FIDESZ), the prime minister, Viktor Orban, has continued the general theme of concern for Magyar minorities abroad, and in a speech in late 2000, inspired by the potential of European Union expansion, he called for a cultural reunification of Magyars across political borders. Again, this may frighten Hungary's neighbors, but the statement is in accordance with Hungarian policies, which encourage foreign governments to support the cultural activities of national minorities within Hungary's borders.

With a market economy and a GDP per capita of $13,300 as of 2002, Hungary's economic growth appears to be a continuing trend. It joined NATO in 1999, and the nation expected to be admitted to the European Union in May 2004.

KEVIN CUROW

See also **Hungarians; Roma (Gypsies); Romania; Serbs; Slovakia**

Further Reading

Barany, Zoltan, and Aurel Braun, editors, *Dilemmas of Transition: The Hungarian Experience,* New York: Rowman and Littlefield, 1999

Bugajski, Janusz, *Ethnic Politics in Eastern Europe: A Guide to Nationality Policies, Organizations and Parties,* New York: M.E. Sharpe, 1994

East, Roger, and Jolyon Pontin, *Revolution and Change in Central and Eastern Europe,* London: Pinter Publishers, revised edition, 1997

Greskovits, Bela, *The Political Economy of Protest and Patience,* Budapest: Central European University Press, 1998

Held, Joseph, editor, *Populism in Eastern Europe: Racism, Nationalism and Society,* Boulder: East European Monographs, 1996

Karsai, Laszlo, "The Radical Right in Hungary," in *The Radical Right in Central and Eastern Europe since 1989,* edited by Sabrina P. Ramet, University Park: Pennsylvania State University Press, 1999

I

Iceland

Capsule Summary

Country Name: Republic of Iceland
Location: North Atlantic, part of the Nordic Region
Total Population: 280,798 (July 2003)
Ethnic Population: Homogeneous mixture of descendants of Norse and Celts (94%), population of foreign origin (6%)
Languages: Icelandic, English, Nordic languages, German (widely spoken)
Religions: Evangelical Lutheran (87.1%), other Protestant (4.1%), Roman Catholic (1.7%), other (7.1%) (2002)

The Republic of Iceland is Europe's second largest island, located in the central North Atlantic. It is an independent nation-state ruled by a parliamentary democracy and culturally is one of the Nordic countries. As of July 1, 2003, there were 280,798 Icelanders, over 60 percent of whom live in the capital city of Reykjavík and surrounding municipalities located in the island's southwest. The remaining population occupies farms, villages, and towns spread mainly around the coast. Nearly all Icelanders descend from the Norse and Gaels who settled the country during the ninth and tenth centuries. While in pre-modern times some women, both in and out of wedlock, had children fathered by foreigners (typically Danes, or fishers from Britain, France, Spain, or, rarely, Greenland), Iceland's comparative isolation until the nineteenth century ensured endogamy. The language, Icelandic, is derived from Old Norse with some Gaelic loanwords. Maintaining its purity is a significant aspect of nationalism, linking with the very active literary culture dating back to the twelfth century. Almost all Icelanders are literate. After a peaceful political struggle that began in the 1830s, Iceland gained full independence from Denmark in 1944. The nation's economy is based on fishing and fish processing, with manufacturing and tourism providing additional foreign export earnings. Since the 1980s, the country's cultural diversity has changed dramatically and Icelanders now negotiate multiculturalism's realities.

History

When Icelanders accepted Christianity in 1000 CE, an action based more on pragmatic than religious considerations, they gained the reading and writing skills which have proved essential for defining group identity up to present times. According to the twelfth century *Book of Settlements,* Ingólfur Árnason was Iceland's first settler, arriving near present-day Reykjavík around 870 CE. An indeterminate but small number of Irish anchorites had arrived earlier, but evidence of their fate is scant. Other settlers followed Ingólfur, and by 930 had claimed all arable land. The island's center is an uninhabitable mix of glaciers, moors, basaltic deserts, mountains, and dormant volcanoes. However, the coastal regions were suitable, with some adaptation to the local environment, for continuing the Norse pattern of animal husbandry and fodder cultivation. Written sources and recent genetic evidence indicate that over 50 percent of female settlers and about 20 percent of males were Gaelic, spouses and slaves brought by Norse farmers from Viking settlements in Britain.

The Icelandic sagas, a diverse body of literature blending fiction and history, dramatize the events during settlement as well as the Commonwealth era that lasted from the Alpingi's establishment in 930 until Iceland yielded to Norwegian control between 1262 and 1264. The Alpingi was an annual general assembly or parliament with a constitutional law code and judicial system for settling disputes. Icelandic society took a form unique in Europe at this time: it was stratified yet stateless, lacking any institutional means for enforcing legal rulings. Chieftains relied upon armed kinsmen and supporters to implement them, hence the centrality of the blood feud to the sagas. A worsening climate, crop failures, and destructive hostilities between a few powerful families during the thirteenth century brought this period to an end.

In 1380 when Norway entered into union with Denmark, Iceland came under the authority of the Danish crown. This rule was initially weak, and the Lutheran Reformation's end in 1550 marked a turn toward direct control. To block contact with English and Hansa merchants, the crown imposed a trade monopoly between 1602 and 1787. In 1662 Iceland accepted Danish absolutism, and the first census (1703) was one instrument of increased state authority. Few Danes lived on the island; colonial rule collaborated with those few Icelandic families that owned most property and controlled the lives of tenants, landless laborers, and servants. People subsisted mostly on sheep farming and growing fodder, although limited inshore fishing from open rowing boats supplemented the economy. Except during the late summer harvest and early summer migrations of laborers, farm households remained geographically, economically, and socially isolated.

Independence

By 1801 environmental deterioration, the unequal exchange of goods, and stratified social order resulted in severe poverty for many of the country's 47,240 people. Land reforms and capital investment in the fisheries came slowly, and between 1870 and 1914 about 12,000 people emigrated, mostly to prairie Canada. A nationalist movement took hold during the 1830s and slowly politicized the population through appeals to a romantic vision of the saga period and the uniqueness of Iceland's language, nature, and history. Jón Sigurðsson (1811–1879) led the movement from Copenhagen, and his birth date of June 17 is Iceland's national day.

The abundant fishing grounds surrounding the island provided the basis for the country's increasing prosperity and independence. Iceland gained Home Rule in 1904, sovereignty in union with Denmark in 1918, and full independence in 1944. Since World War II, Iceland has often experienced full employment and one of the world's highest standards of living. Between 1994 and 1999, Iceland was one of the strongest performers amongst OECD countries, thereby attracting foreign workers to the country. In 2002 the per capita GDP was US$30,200.

Icelandic Society

Understanding Iceland requires awareness of just how small, homogeneous, and interconnected the society is, and how quickly change happens. Historical isolation has been offset by rapid modernization and increased wealth in the post-war period. Many work and study abroad, and when returning home their broadened horizons influence social change. Icelanders take pride in being up-to-date technologically and culturally, and attentiveness to international ideas has generally balanced nationalist insularity during the late twentieth century. A strong women's movement since the 1970s has fought for equal rights.

Rise of Multiculturalism

Icelanders are aware of their small size and international obscurity, but an uncompromising sense of national identity provides a source of strength. Negatively, nationalism at times prompts xenophobia and racism that inhibit change to a pluralist image of the nation. Many do not consider the cultural diversity of foreign nationals, and tend to lump all foreigners into one group.

Institutionally, foreigners divide into three main groups: refugees, asylum seekers, and immigrants. The first have come at the state's invitation, with assistance from the Red Cross, from refugee camps rather than directly from their countries of origin. The first such groups since the 1956 Hungarian resettlement came from Vietnam in the late 1980s; more recently families from former Yugoslavia have arrived. Refugees are given such aid as housing, jobs, and free language training, and are assigned volunteer mentor families. About 350 people are in this category.

Only one individual, from Myanmar, has successfully applied for and received asylum, while others have failed to gain such status. Whereas refugee groups are screened by international agencies, Icelandic officials who lack special training and expertise assess individual asylum seekers, a situation which has allowed prejudice and ignorance to go unchecked. Asylum seekers are not given any aid.

Immigrants include those who marry Icelanders, those who come for temporary or long-term work, permanent relocation, or to be near their families. As of December 2000, 8,572 individuals with foreign citizenship resided in Iceland. Once an individual takes Icelandic citizenship they no longer count as foreigners, making it impossible to distinguish between native and naturalized citizens. For ten years, the number of foreigners remained steady at about 5,000 until 1998, when the number sharply rose. The largest group of foreign nationals is from Poland (1,429), over 80 percent of whom live outside Reykjavík and work in fishing plants and aluminum smelters. Between 60 and 80 percent of other foreigners live in the capital city area. In descending order, they come from: Denmark (969), United States (586), former Yugoslavia (555), former Soviet Union (520), Germany (463), Philippines (457), Thailand (429), Great Britain (388), Norway (318), Sweden (313), and other (2,145). Ethnic neighborhood

enclaves do not exist although Asian groups have formed tight social networks for mutual aid.

Adequate language training is critical for the successful integration of foreigners into Icelandic society. At present, educators, social service workers, and activists are developing curriculum and policies to combat racism and encourage multiculturalism.

ANNE BRYDON

Further Reading

Björnsson, Sigurjón, and Wolfgang Edelstein, *Explorations in Social Inequality: Stratification Dynamics in Social and Individual Development in Iceland*, Berlin: Max-Planck-Institut, 1977

Brydon, Anne, "Icelanders," in *Encyclopedia of Canada's Peoples*, edited by Robert Paul Magocsi, Toronto: Multicultural History Society of Ontario and University of Toronto Press, 1999

Hálfdanarson, Guðmundur, *Historical Dictionary of Iceland*, Lanham, Maryland and London: Scarecrow Press, 1997

Hastrup, Kirsten, *A Place Apart: An Anthropological Study of the Icelandic World*, Oxford: Clarendon Press, 1998

Hjálmarsson, Jón R., *History of Iceland*, Reykjavík: Iceland Review, 1993

Kristmundsdóttir, Sigriður Dúna, *Doing and Becoming: Women's Movement and Women's Personhood in Iceland 1870–1990*, Reykjavík: University of Iceland Press, 1997

Nordal, Jóhannes, and Valdimar Kristinsson, editors, *Iceland: The Republic*, Reykjavík: Central Bank of Iceland, 1996

Pálsson, Gísli, and E. Paul Durrenberger, editors, *Images of Contemporary Iceland: Everyday Lives and Global Contexts*, Iowa City: University of Iowa Press, 1996

Igorot

Capsule Summary

Location: Northern Luzon, Philippines
Total Population (of Cordillera languages speakers): 1 million (1.3% of total population)
Languages: Various, most bilingual with Ilokano
Religions: Non-Christian and Christian

The generic name *Igorot* comes from the Spanish *Ygolotes*, later becoming *Igorrotes*, meaning mountaineers. The name applied to non-Christian indigenous upland groups of the Cordillera of Northern Luzon and

had a derogatory connotation implying backwardness and cultural inferiority. By the end of the twentieth century the name *Igorot* has gained wider acceptance among the Cordillera peoples themselves and for some has become a source of pride, designating an identity distinct from Filipino.

There are more than ten languages and dialects spoken by the Igorot people, with many bilingual speakers in Ilokano. Major ethno-linguistic groups are the Kankanay (230,000), Ifugao (112,000), Ibaloi (88,000) Kalinga (87,000), Bontok (43,000), Itneg (20,000),

Kallahan (20,000), Isneg (10,000), Ilongot (6,000), I-wak (3,000), plus many scattered Negrito (Agta and Dumagat) groups.

The mountainous habitat of the Igorot covers the Gran Cordillera Central of Northern Luzon, a great chain of mountains that rises abruptly from the northern tip of the island to altitudes of 2,500 meters (8,202 feet), reaching a peak (Mount Pulog) of 3,200 meters (10,499 feet). It stretches from the north to the south over a distance of 300 kilometers (186 miles) and 100 kilometers (62 miles) from west to east.

Although Cordillera peoples share common traits, such as bilaterally reckoned kinship, belief in spirits, prestige feasting, and head-hunting expeditions, each group (even each local community) has its own distinct cultural identity and used to be politically autonomous. There is no overall political organization at the level of Cordillera region, but peace-pacts (bodong) were institutions linking several groups within a sub-region on the basis of a mutual agreement at a time when head-hunting was prevalent.

Anthropologists group the mountain peoples under four regional headings: North, Central, South, and Southeast. The central groups (Ifugaos, Bontoks, and southern Kalingas) at the headwaters of the Abra, Chico, and Magat river systems have developed the most sophisticated techniques of terracing and irrigation of wet rice. The Ifugaos in particular are known for their skills in terracing agriculture, their legal system, and complex polytheistic religion. They live in small hamlets forming at higher level agricultural districts. Kinship is cognatic with exogamous bilateral kindreds extending to third degree of collaterality. The society is ranked according to wealth and prestige with slaves at the bottom. Disputes not settled by negotiation lead to protracted feuds. Warfare between communities was conducted through head-hunting expeditions. The Ifugao polytheistic religion is characterized by a vast number of spirits and deities invoked during ceremonies involving up to 15 priests chanting simultaneously.

The neighboring Bontoks were noted for their compact villages and ward system, consisting of a council house, a men's clubhouse, and a ritual center. Society is ranked by age and wealth, with a hereditary aristocracy. Kankanai-speaking people in and around Sagada likewise live in compact settlements divided in wards, and have a stratified society with an aristocracy based on wealth.

The southern groups, Ibaloi and southern Kankanai, lack the village ward system of the central groups but there is a marked social differentiation between the rich and the poor.

Kalinga, Itneg (Tinggian, Tinguian), Apayao, and Gaddang form the northern groups. Among the Kalinga, settlement patterns vary from small hamlet to "towns," and rice-terracing becomes less extensive as one goes north. Kalingas are divided in endogamous geographic regions and positions of authority were held by renowned warriors who were men of prestige and wealth. At the beginning of the twentieth century they started developing trading partnerships and intraregional arbitration with the institution of peace-pacts. Society is stratified according to wealth. The Itneg people had large settlements and their society was marked by stratification based on wealth and prestige, as did the Apayao and Gaddang societies.

The Ilongot people live in the hills southeast of the Cordillera and as such are more distantly related to other Igorot people from which they are culturally distinct. They practice shifting agriculture, have a basically equalitarian society and engaged well into the second half of the twentieth century in active head-hunting expeditions.

Despite repeated attempts over three centuries to conquer them, the Spaniards were never able to dominate the peoples of the mountains, politically or culturally. During those centuries, a separate identity was emerging among the mountain people.

The United States took effective control of the region in 1902. The Americans used Christianization and education in an attempt to westernize the un-Hispanized Igorots while maintaining a strong military presence. They also appropriated the Igorots' gold fields, particularly in Benguet, whose mining companies were founded by American soldiers-turned-gold prospectors.

Recognizing that a difference existed between upland and lowland peoples, Washington officially established the Mountain Province for the Igorots by the Philippine Commission Act No. 1876 on August 18, 1912. The province consisted of seven sub-provinces: Amburayan, Apayao, Benguet, Bontoc, Ifugao, Kalinga, and Lepanto.

In 1966 the Mountain Province was partitioned into four separate provinces: Benguet, Ifugao, Kalinga-Apayao, and a truncated Mountain Province. During the administration of President Cory Aquino the Igorots remain divided among four provinces and two regions.

In 1990 Congress passed a law creating a Cordillera Autonomous Region, but in a referendum held in five provinces (Abra, Benguet, Mountain, Kalinga-Apayao, and Ifugao) autonomy failed. In 1991 the Supreme Court voided the Cordillera Autonomous Region which was replaced by the Cordillera Administrative Region divided into six provinces: Apayao, Abra, Benguet, Ifugao, Kalinga, and Mountain Province.

Mining companies and hydroelectric projects, like the Chico River Dam project during the Marcos era, have been fought against by various organizations, like the Cordillera Peoples' Liberation Army, the Cordillera Bodong ("peace-pact") Association, the Cordillera Broad Coalition, the Cordillera Peoples' Alliance, and the more radical Cordillera Peoples' Democratic Front.

Today, the Igorot people still face an uncertain future as their way of life is changing—their land getting smaller and their forests disappearing.

CHARLES MACDONALD

See also **Philippines**

Further Reading

Barton, R.F., *Ifugao Law*, Berkeley: University of California Press, 1919
————, *The Religion of the Ifugaos*, Menasha, Wisconsin: American Anthropological Association, 1946
Dozier, E.P., *The Kalinga Of Northern Luzon, Philippines*, New York: Holt, Rinehart and Winston, 1967
Jenks, A.E., *The Bontoc Igorot*, Vol. 1, Manila: Philippine Islands Ethnological Survey Publication, 1905
Keesing, F.M., *The Ethnohistory of Northern Luzon*, Stanford: Stanford University Press, 1962
Rosaldo, R., *Ilongot Headhunting 1883–1974: A Study in Society and History*, Stanford: Stanford University Press, 1980
Scott, W.H., *The Discovery of the Igorots: Spanish Contacts with the Pagans of Northern Luzon*, Quezon City: New Day Publishers, 1974

Immigrant Workers in Arab States

In addition to the traditional migratory movements of nomadic groups such as the Bedouins on the Arabian Peninsula, the Arab world has witnessed large-scale labor migration and refugee movements. Although population movements have been part of the history of the Arab states, large-scale labor migration to the developing oil-rich states of the Arabian Peninsula and Libya greatly increased as a result of the rapid economic development after the oil price boom of 1973. This phenomenon was reinforced by slow economic growth in neighboring Arab countries and the Arab-Israeli conflict. Currently the presence of immigrant labor in the Arab oil producing countries has become a vital and politically volatile issue. The oil-rich Arab states have become highly dependent on foreigners for the running of their economies. Despite more efforts to reduce the political, economic, and socio-cultural impact of immigrants, this dependency is likely to continue in the foreseeable future.

History of Labor Immigration

For centuries migrations have taken place in West Asia and North Africa. This concerns not only nomadic groups in search of new pastures for their herds, but also merchants and pilgrims visiting the holy places of Islam, such as Mecca or Medina in Saudi Arabia and Kairouan in Tunisia. Due to the open borders, these population movements were relatively unrestricted. In the Arab Gulf states, Persians (next to Arab immigrants) found a livelihood in fishing and pearl diving. In addition, ever since trading links were established between the ancient civilizations of Dilmun (now Bahrain), Harappa, and Mohenjo Daro on the Indian subcontinent (2500 BCE), Indian traders have been present in the Arab Gulf. Many of them live in Oman and the United Arab Emirates (UAE), among which such groups as the Bani (Hindus) and Shiite Muslim Khojahs from Gujarat in India, or Baluchis and Pathans from Baluchistan and Sind in Pakistan.

After the discovery and exploitation of oil reserves in the 1930s, several thousand British and American engineers and managerial staff were recruited for work in the oil fields in the Gulf. Laborers from neighboring Arab states such as Oman and Yemen's were hired into lower-skilled jobs. After the establishment of the Anglo-Persian Oil Company (1908) and the start of oil production in the region, the number of labor migrants from the Indian subcontinent increased, but their numbers were relatively small (10,000 a year) until the oil boom of the 1970s.

Labor migration up to the 1970s remained rather limited, however, due to slow economic growth and small differentials in remuneration between the oil-producing and non oil-producing states in the region. In the three decades after 1945, most labor migrants in the oil-producing states of the Gulf originated from neighboring states. Initially most migrants in the oil industry came from the southern Gulf (Qatar, Oman, and Muscat) and worked in Kuwait, Bahrain, and Saudi Arabia, where oil production had been well underway since the 1930s. Later there was a constant flux of immigrants from Lebanon, Jordan, Egypt, Iraq, north Yemen, and Sudan, most of which found employment in the oil industry, construction, and the service sector, particularly education. Much of this migration was circulatory—many labor migrants were single males, coming without dependants, and often returning to their native countries after some years.

Labor migration from Sudan and Somalia to Saudi Arabia, the Gulf states, and Libya started around 1970. In the following decades, their numbers increased gradually, and in 1985 their numbers were estimated at about 50,000 Somalis and between 350,000 and 500,000 Sudanese. The fact that many high-skilled workers were among these labor migrants lead to a "brain-drain" situation in Sudan and Somalia and a substituting flow from Ethiopia. For instance the flow of Sudanese migrants in the period represented almost two-thirds of the higher educated workforce of Sudan. In general the volume of migrants from Sub-Saharan countries directed to the Arabian Peninsula is rather insignificant, but some countries, such as Nigeria, have discovered the Middle East as potential market for labor export. Nigeria has sent a few thousand middle and high-skilled workers to the Gulf states since the late 1980s. Most of them work in the service sector, especially in health.

However, the largest migratory movements in the period up to 1973 were provoked by the Arab-Israeli conflict. After the formation of the state of Israel in 1948, an exodus of Palestinian refugees took place. Many Palestinians moved to Kuwait and Saudi Arabia. The demand for skilled labor was high in these countries—a demand that Palestinians could satisfy. After the Arab-Israeli armed conflicts of 1967 and 1973, almost a million Egyptians were displaced from the Suez-Sinai region, tens of thousands of whom moved to the Gulf states. This generally con-

cerned whole families. Labor migration from Egypt was fostered even more by the liberal labor export policy adopted by the Anwar Sadat government in 1973. In 1970 about 800,000 foreign workers were in the oil-producing countries of the Gulf. At that time 85 percent of this immigrant labor originated from neighboring Arab countries, such as Egypt, Jordan, Yemens, and Oman, in addition to a significant Palestinian population.

The Oil Boom

The oil boom of the early 1970s marked a clear watershed in that the volume and composition of the migrant populations changed significantly. The inflated oil prices in 1973 led to greatly increased capital reserves, and subsequently prompted an accelerated pace of development in the oil-producing Gulf countries. The Gulf states lacked any modern infrastructure, industry, or services, and with the newly amassed capital from oil exports the Gulf governments first aimed at a rapid buildup of the infrastructure and industrial sector. Once in place, economic diversification was pursued in a bid to diminish the dependence on oil exports alone. As the labor and skills to realize this were not available locally, the government turned to labor importation. The indigenous labor forces of the oil-producing Arab states were small and characterized by relatively low levels of education, low female labor force participation rates, and a preference for work in government services and the armed forces. As a result, the demand for immigrant labor for the construction and service sectors grew enormously—between 1975 and 1985 the total number of migrants in the Gulf states grew from 2 million to 5.5 million. As much as 88 percent of these migrants workers resided in Saudi Arabia, Kuwait, and the United Arab Emirates.

The exploitation of the large oil reserves in Libya since the 1960s has led to a high gross domestic product (GDP), and formed the pillar of the country's socialist development strategy under Colonel Ghaddafi's government. Both the oil sector and other heavy industries have been rapidly built up. Just as in the Arab Gulf, this expeditious development of the infrastructure and industry could not have been realized without the importation of foreign workers. Both highly trained workers from Europe as well as lower-skilled migrants from neighboring countries (e.g., Egypt, Tunisia, Chad), Turkey and more recently Asia (e.g., Pakistanis, Indians, Koreans, Chinese, Filipinos) have been imported as contract laborers.

In addition Libya has been a country of refuge for many Palestinians.

Shift from Arab to Asian Labor

From that point on, a shift in the recruitment of labor took place—the number of immigrant workers of Arab origin decreased in favor of South and Southeast Asian workers. Between 1970 and 1980, the number of Asians in the Middle East and North Africa (Libya) region grew from a mere 2,000 in 1970 to about 520,000 in 1979. In the Arab Gulf region, Arabs accounted for 77 percent of the total immigrant workforce in 1970, and decreased to 57 percent in 1980 and 35 percent in 1990. The reasons for this shift were mainly economic and political—Asians are cheaper, more tractable, less prone for permanent settlement, and less demanding of state benefits. Moreover, they were considered less of a threat to the political stability in comparison to Arab immigrants (Palestinians, Shiite militants), who could make more demands on the basis of Arab and Islamic solidarity and sentiment. Moreover, the racial differences make it easier to control irregular immigration.

First, there was a growing awareness on the part of the indigenous populations and governments of the Gulf Cooperation Council (GCC, composed of Saudi Arabia, Kuwait, Bahrain, Qatar, the United Arab Emirates, and the Sultanate of Oman) that the uncontrolled influx of immigrants could have disruptive effects on their society and culture. The immigrants could pose a political threat to the autocratic governments due to their numbers and because of their religious or political convictions and demands. The politicized Palestinians in Kuwait, for instance, were of concern as they made demands for equal rights and social amenities. The government of Bahrain, in territorial dispute with Iran over small islands in the Persian Gulf, distrusts the Shiite population of Iranian origin in their country and fears the spread of fundamentalist Islam.

Second, the recruitment of Asian labor was motivated by the fact that they were often better trained and generally cheaper than Arabs. Arab immigrants, more often accompanied by their families, made greater demands on the social amenities such as health services and education. Asian migrants were recruited individually on the basis of temporary contracts, and thus could make fewer such demands. Moreover, the large supply of South and Southeast Asian labor and the competition between labor exporting countries pushed down the price of Asian labor and made it possible for labor importing countries to roll down recruitment costs to the agencies in sending countries and to the migrants themselves.

Third, Arab states such as Jordan, North Yemen, and Oman experienced labor shortages themselves, partly due to labor emigration, which had a detrimental effect on their economies. Already in 1975 Jordan and Yemen had lost around a quarter of their labor forces. In North Yemen the age-old irrigation systems fell into disrepair as a result of labor export and negatively affected agricultural production.

Next to an absolute increase, the composition of the immigrant populations changed—next to the shift from Arab to Asian labor, there was a gradual shift from unskilled to skilled labor and more women. For example, the number of Pakistanis in the Gulf increased from around 40,000 in 1976 to 120,000 three years later. The yearly outflow of Bangladeshis and Indians increased from 5,500 and 4,200 in 1976 to 24,000 and 236,000 in 1979, respectively. The total stock of Pakistani immigrants in the Middle East has been estimated at 200,000 in 1976 and 1.25 million in 1979, while the number of Indians grew from 165,000 to half a million in this same period.

After 1980 the number of women in the migrant flows increased significantly. Due to the acquired oil wealth and changing consumption patterns of the indigenous populations, more households in the oil-producing states could afford to have female domestic servants (such as housekeepers, nannies, and drivers). Within Arab society there is a long tradition of having domestic servants. No longer the privilege of the elite families, middle class and lower class families can afford hiring female domestic servants, adding to their status. To a limited extent this has also made it possible for indigenous women to join the local labor forces, particularly in the medical sector, education, and retail trade. In addition to the Gulf states, foreign domestic servants can be found in all Middle Eastern countries, including Gaza and the West Bank. However, the longstanding labor exporting countries in South Asia, India, Pakistan, and Bangladesh were less prone to satisfy this demand due to growing concerns over the migration of (Muslim) women and their unprotected status within receiving countries. In the Gulf states there are no labor laws specific for domestic servants, so that living and working conditions of this category of workers depend in large part on the goodwill of their employers. Numerous reports have pointed to the vulnerability, isolation, abuse, and often difficult working conditions of these women. Despite this, countries such as Sri Lanka, the

Philippines, and Indonesia, which were relative late-comers on the Middle East labor market, were quick to fill this niche and actively promoted the export of female workers, which could help alleviate poverty and bring in hardly needed foreign exchange earnings.

From South Asian to Southeast Asian Labor

Up to the late 1970s, the south Asian continent furnished migrant labor, but in the following decades this region met with more competition from labor exporting countries in Southeast and East Asia. The Philippines, Thailand, Indonesia, South Korea, and China became significant players on the Middle Eastern labor market.

The trend toward Southeast Asian labor resulted from more active labor export policy by the Southeast and East Asian countries, combined with the more restrictive policies in the Gulf countries, based on economic motives and fears of being dominated by immigrant populations. As the Indian and Pakistani populations, having a long tradition of movement to the Gulf, were more prone to settle permanently in the recipient societies and reunite their families, the Arab labor importing countries opted for a policy aimed at achieving a strictly controlled and more transient migrant labor force. Southeast and East Asian labor migrants were generally contracted on a temporary basis for specific construction projects, whereby the single male foreign workers are recruited and accommodated by the contracted firm. Once the project is finalized, the workforce is repatriated.

After the oil price slump of 1985, the number of labor migrants in West Asia decreased from around 800,000 to about 650,000, but after 1987 the demand for foreign workers increased again. Moreover, the demand had changed from unskilled labor for construction to unskilled labor in the service sector (especially female domestic servants) and semi-skilled labor for maintenance jobs and service occupations. Domestic servants are mainly recruited from the Philippines, Sri Lanka, and Indonesia—countries that promote this type of workers despite growing concerns about their vulnerability and protection. Due to the decreased demand for less-skilled male workers, the share of Pakistan and India in the migration flow decreased in favor of Southeast Asian countries.

The Gulf Conflict, 1990 to 1991

Prior to the Gulf War (1990–1991), there were between 5 and 6 million foreign workers in the countries of the Gulf, which formed 70 percent of the total labor force of these countries. Within a year after the invasion of Kuwait by Iraq, a refugee flow of between 4 and 5 million people developed. These consisted of almost a million unassisted refugees who fled via Jordan and Syria immediately after the invasion (mainly Egyptians), those who were repatriated by their governments in 1990 and a final wave of Shiites and Kurds who fled to Turkey and Iran after the liberation of Kuwait and the ensuing repression by Saddam Hussein in Iraq. Just before the outbreak of the Gulf conflict, there were an estimated 600,000 South and Southeast Asian labor migrants in Kuwait and Iraq. Under threat of the hostilities, between August and December 1990, a half a million Asians were repatriated to their home countries. In addition, during the aftermath of the Gulf War, over a million Iraqis fled to the Islamic Republic of Iran, of which about 600,000 were still there in 1996.

Even leaving aside the costs of repatriation, this meant a considerable blow to the economies of migrant-sending countries as remittance income was forgone. The loss of remittance income was largest for countries such as Bangladesh and Sri Lanka, which are very dependent on remittances for foreign exchange. The loss for Sri Lanka after 1989 was estimated at 356 million dollars, or 33 percent of the total worldwide remittance income for Sri Lanka. The World Bank estimated the loss for Bangladesh at between US$100–160 million (20 percent of total remittances). However, after the Gulf War many migrant workers managed to return to the Gulf States, and because migrants sent remittances through national bank accounts instead of risky foreign accounts much remittance income was recovered eventually.

After the Gulf War the labor markets in the Gulf recovered rapidly, despite a more restrictive policy toward immigrants. Kuwait and Saudi Arabia's reluctance to allow Palestinian, Yemeni, and Sudanese workers back into the country, due to their countries' backing of Iraq during the war, meant renewed employment opportunities for Asian migrant workers. As many as 800,000 Yemeni's were forcibly repatriated from Saudi Arabia in 1991. Subsequently, the migration from South and Southeast Asia increased until the mid-1990s, after which a decline set in, particularly for India, Pakistan, and Bangladesh. The total number of labor migrants from the main Asian countries reached 1 million in 1990 and 2 million in 1994. At that time the large majority (90 percent) of South and Southeast Asian labor migrants was destined for the Middle East.

The oil-producing Arab countries continue to rely on foreigners for the maintenance of their economies, but their numbers and position fluctuate and are related to the performance of the economy, in particular the fluctuating oil prices. The share of foreigners in the population of the Gulf States and Libya has declined somewhat between 1990 and 2000. However, the percentages of foreigners in the local workforces remain exceptionally high compared to other countries. The United Nations Economic and Social Commission for Western Asia (UNESCWA) estimated the share of foreigners in the workforce at 51 percent in Bahrain, 70 percent in Oman, and a high 92 percent in Qatar for 1990. The proportions for Saudi Arabia, Kuwait, and the UAE were between 80 and 90 percent.

Policies of Labor-Importing Arab States

The GCC countries and Libya are governed by centralist, autocratic regimes. The policies pertaining to labor migration and immigration in the labor importing Arab countries have evolved from relatively lenient to more restrictive policy regimes. Presently the GCC countries have stricter immigration laws than for instance in Europe or North America. In order to minimize their dependency on migrant labor and to minimize the (social and economic) costs of the presence of immigrants, the national policies are geared toward the creation of a tractable, transient, foreign labor force, by way of hiring single workers on a temporary basis with strict regulations as to repatriation. To avoid over-reliance on a few labor-supplying countries, a diversification of sources of labor is pursued. Currently the GCC countries have introduced laws that stipulate that preference is given to nationals, instead of foreigners— a policy that has been coined an "Arabization or indigenization policy."

The Gulf States have adopted strict admission policies, including the use of linked entry visa and residence permits tied to work permits, the fees for which have increased over the years. Domestic travel, changing employment, and the activities of workers unions are restricted. The internal labor market is highly segmented with little possibilities for upward social mobility. Family migration and family reunification is restricted as much as possible. Illegal immigration is countered by stepped up border controls, harsh penalties, and deportations for illegal migrants and those who overstay the limits of their visas. In addition employers harboring illegal workers are subject to stiff fines, possible business closure, or jail sentences.

Naturalization is generally not permitted. Only Kuwait and the UAE have strict regulations. However, those granted citizenship, mainly Arabs, enjoy less political rights compared to the native population. Rights to asylum and family reunification are not granted to migrant workers. Those seeking employment need a sponsor (*kafeel*), and once employed, migrant workers cannot change jobs without permission from their employer and the authorities. Once a migrant worker loses one's job, the residence permit is automatically terminated. In the Gulf states there are no labor laws specific for domestic servants, so that living and working conditions of this category of workers depend in large part on the goodwill of their employers.

Libya has formulated an explicit population policy which promotes female labor force participation and social welfare, but which discourages rural-urban migration and immigration. The policy towards immigrants is highly subject to political conditions as is exemplified by the forced expulsion of thousands of Egyptians and Tunisians during the late 1980s, when political relations between Libya and these countries deteriorated.

Clandestine Migration and Regularization Campaigns

Despite more strict control and monitoring by governments, clandestine migrants can be found in all Arab states. Some of these migrants enter the country illegally by way of human trafficking organizations while others overstay their visas. In Saudi Arabia a considerable number of migrants enter the country as pilgrims, but after having visited the holy places of Islam (Mecca, Medina), stay on in the country in search of employment.

The large number of illegal migrants within their borders has become a matter of concern for the Arab governments. However, it creates a dilemma as their economies still have a shortage of workers. Therefore, many states have turned to regularization campaigns in which migrants can report themselves to the authorities and apply for residence and work permits. Alternatively, states announce amnesty that permits clandestine migrants to report and leave the country without any penalty. Amnesty campaigns in Bahrain, for instance, permitted tens of thousands of foreigners to leave in 1995, 1997, and 2000 without paying fines or being arrested. Similar campaigns have taken place in the UAE in 1996 and in Saudi Arabia in 1997.

Social Integration

The political and social rights of immigrants in the Arab states are generally restricted. The non-western immigrant populations have an inferior social and legal status *vis á vis* the national population, reflected in an absence of political rights, lower wage levels, inferior housing conditions, and restricted access to welfare state benefits. Expatriate ownership rights to land, real estate, or businesses are exceedingly constrained. Foreigners can only enter into joint ventures with a local commercial agent. Labor unions are generally not allowed, and for some groups (such as domestic servants) labor legislation is lacking.

As a result of the restrictive and segregation policies, the relations between the national and immigrant populations in the Arab states remain distant. Due to the often large differences in culture, language, and status, interaction between the groups is generally limited and instrumental in nature. Moreover, migrants are often spatially segregated from the national population, restricting interaction to the workplace—immigrant women generally work within Arab homes as domestic servants and enjoy limited freedom of action, while men often work in isolated company compounds, making long working hours with few possibilities for recreation. Hierarchy and inequality also characterizes the inter-ethnic relations in the enclave-type projects, as exemplified by differentials in wages and facilities provided. In many cases the high-level managerial positions are filled by Europeans, Americans, or nationals, while the middle-level positions are held by Arab immigrants (e.g., Palestinians and Egyptians) or more highly educated Asians (particularly Indians and Pakistanis). Lowest on the scale are the unskilled foreign workers from countries such as Sri Lanka, Bangladesh, Afghanistan, Thailand, Indonesia, and the Philippines. Those that work in cities often live in separate quarters, consisting of shared lodging and apartment blocs, in stark contrast to the often wealthy dwellings of nationals. Scarcity, high prices, and ethnic segregation characterize the housing situation. The different immigrant groups and nationalities tend to live in separate areas, examples of which are the Iranian quarter (Bastakia) in Dubai or the shantytown Jarnia Fur in Abu Dhabi. Where possible, foreign workers have managed to develop social organizations, such as sport clubs and similar associations, but immigrants are less organized in comparison to their counterparts in Europe or the United States.

The system of differentials in wages, working conditions, and civil rights, together with the differences in language, culture, and religion between the native and foreign populations, have lead to inter-ethnic tensions, rivalry, and xenophobic tendencies. While nationals have showed a preference for the hiring of Muslims, the expatriate populations of the Gulf states consist of an array of ethnic groups of different religious denominations, varying from Buddhist Singhalese from Sri Lanka, Hindus and Sikhs from India, and Catholics from the Philippines, among others. Especially in the case of domestic servants, fears over their adverse influence on local children's upbringing have been voiced in the local media. Ignorance of local customs and the often harsh penalties for criminal offenses under Islamic law (*Sharia*), such as public floggings or amputations, also lead to friction between the native and foreign populations.

In conclusion the Arab oil-producing states have become multiethnic welfare states. However, their societies are highly stratified along lines of nationality and ethnicity, with an unequal division of political rights and welfare benefits. To a certain extent, ethnic segregation is a continuation of the social stratification that existed in traditional Arab society. This was not only based on tribal affiliation, but also on clear-cut social divisions between the ruling royal families, the merchants, and subordinate groups (such as artisans, fishermen, and domestic servants). With the onset of large scale labor importation the governments of the GCC states and Libya have put in place a system of laws and regulations that attempts to restrict immigrants to their working role as much as possible, but which minimizes the chances for integration and political involvement in local society.

In general the socio-economic position of the migrant workers is insecure and is contingent on the prevailing political and economic conditions, the latter of which mainly hinge on fluctuating oil prices and exports. In the past, political conflicts and economic recession have translated into less favorable working conditions for and dismissal of migrant workers. In the long run the governments aim at reducing the dependency on migrant labor, by way of the indigenization of the labor force, whereby local workers get preference over immigrants. It can be doubted whether this goal can be achieved within the near future.

ERNST SPAAN

See also **Bahrain; Oman; Qatar; Saudi Arabia; United Arab Emirates; Yemen**

Further Reading

Abella, Manolo, "International migration in the Middle East: Patterns and implications for sending countries," in *International Migration: Regional Processes and Responses*, edited by Miroslav Macura and David Coleman, New York and Geneva: UN Economic Commission for Europe (UNECE), UNFPA, Economic Studies, no. 7 (1994)

Amjad, Rashid, *To the Gulf and Back: Studies on the Economic Impact of Asian Labour Migration,* New Delhi: ILO/UNDP, 1989

Arnold, Fred, and Nasra Shah, *Asian Labor Migration: Pipeline to the Middle East*, Boulder, Colorado: Westview Press, 1986

Birks, John, and Clive A. Sinclair, *International Migration and Development in the Arab Region*, Geneva: ILO, 1980

Eelens, Frank, Toon Schampers, and Johan D. Speckmann, *Labour Migration to the Middle East: From Sri Lanka to the Gulf*, London and New York: Kegan Paul International, 1992

Gunatilleke, Godfrey, *Migration of Asian Workers to the Arab World*, Tokio: United Nations Press, 1986

Massey, Douglas, Joaquin Arango, Graeme Hugo, A. Kouaouci, Adela Pelegrino, and John E. Taylor, *Worlds in Motion: Understanding International Migration at the End of the Millennium*, Oxford: Clarendon Press, 1998

Seccombe, Ian J., "International Migration in the Middle East: Historical Trends, Contemporary Patterns and Consequences," in *International Migration Today*, edited by Reginald T. Appleyard, Paris: UNESCO, 1988

Segal, Aaron, *An Atlas of International Migration*, London, Melbourne, Munich: Hans Zell Publishers, 1993

UN-ESCWA, "Arab labour migration in Western Asia," in *Population Distribution and Migration: Proceedings of the United Nations Expert Group Meeting on Population Distribution and Migration*, Santa Cruz, Bolivia (January 1993)

Van Hear, Nicholas, "Mass flight in the Middle East: Involuntary migration and the Gulf conflict, 1990–1991," in *Geography and Refugees: Patterns and Processes of Change*, edited by Robin Black and Vaughn Robinson, London and New York: Bellhaven Press, 1993

Immigration

Immigration is a subfield of migration studies, a field that focuses on the movement of living organisms into or out of a region. The emphasis in this article, however, is on human populations and specifically the entry of people into a new land. In actuality there is a great deal of overlap in the study of migration, immigration, and emigration, and there is not a clear line demarcation between them.

Immigrants and the immigration processes are constantly impacting the sending, receiving, and other connected communities. Among other things immigrants are often mediators or cultural brokers who influence a host culture to introduce new or discard current practices. Wherever there is a significant influx of people, change is most likely to occur. Immigrants make significant contributions to cultural change, economies, diffusion of ideas, and development of innovations especially for both the receiving and sending immigrant communities. More specifically immigrants have been responsible for major changes in language patterns, ethnic composition, and economic systems. In fact over the past 500 years, immigrants have been responsible for reshaping the human face of the earth. Here, however, the focus will be limited to the historical process of human immigration, followed by methodological and theoretical considerations for understanding immigration.

Origins of Migration

The movement of populations has been occurring since the dawn of human existence. Some groups have practiced hunting and gathering; that is, wandering to collect roots and berries, as well as spotting herds of wild animals from which food could be obtained. Those practicing transhumance in hilly or mountainous regions took their herds to high elevations for the summer and down to lower elevations in the winter. Nomadic people wandered continually finding fresh pastures for their flocks. Usually the routes were prescribed and tribes had rights to certain land plots and trails at certain times of the year, thus, no area was overgrazed. Ideally, areas are always left with sufficient vegetation so the plants can quickly replenish. The concerns of immigration studies, however, are not the influx of nomads or people practicing transhumance.

591

The concern of immigration is when people enter an area or community for *permanent* settlement. The entry may be voluntary or forced; it may be from one continent to another or rural to urban or urban to rural. It may be caused by economic opportunities or lack there of.

For the world as a whole, seven prominent migration streams have developed. They are: (1) from all points of Europe to North America, (2) from Latin countries of Europe to Middle and South America, (3) from Great Britain to Africa and Australia, (4) from Africa to America, (5) from China and India Abroad (partly inter-continental and partly intra-continental), (6) the westward movement in the United States, and (7) the eastward movement in Russia. Prior to the end of World War II, the main currents of migration were out of densely settled regions in Europe and Asia into North and South America and Oceania. Major shifts since 1950 include the net flow of people back into Europe and a net flow out of many Latin American countries.

There are two major types of immigration to deal with: forced immigration and voluntary immigration. Both types of population movements have been present from the beginnings of human history. Starting around the time of Christopher Columbus in the fifteenth century, forced immigration became a way of acquiring human capital, or human inputs to gain capital, which brought about forced immigration—more aptly described as *slavery*.

History of Immigration: Forced and Voluntary

Immigration was encouraged due to two major forces shaping European economic activity in the late 1400s: mercantilism, which measured wealth by the amount of gold acquired; and capitalism, which instilled in adherents the quest to continually maximize and minimize loss. One result of these philosophies was the commercialization of agriculture, which stimulated the implementation of plantation economies that required large gangs of cheap labor. But the materials needed to feed the mother country's industry also needed cheap labor, creating a combination that encouraged colonialization.

It is no wonder that Columbus and subsequent explorers, adventurers, and settlers in America saw the native Americans as a source of cheap labor. Columbus captured some Indians and took them back to Europe to provide free labor for plantation economies, thus helping start the process of forced immigration.

Native Americans were soon considered poor workers as they seemed prone to running away and unsuitable for plantation work in the eyes of the host society. However, people of African origin were considered hard workers and more reliable; thus began the African slave trade whereby primarily British and Dutch sea captains enslaved and transported captive Africans to the Americas as slave labor for the plantation economies—a practice that extended to other continents as well.

As lines of trade and global communications became established and more efficient, spices, metals, ivory, seamen, settlers, merchants, and slaves traversed these routes. It was the mercantile/capitalistic philosophy that resulted in the largest forced immigration in history, whereby 10 million slaves entered the Americas from Africa. The impact of this immigration can be seen today as the Caribbean, southern United States, Mexico, and Brazil have large populations descended from these people of African origins.

When the abolitionists were able to sway votes in the British Parliament, laws made it impossible for British sea captains to transport slaves. But plantation owners in the Pacific (such as Fiji and Mauritius, as well as the Caribbean) were clamoring for cheap labor. The outcome was the creation of what Hugh Tinker termed a "new system of slavery," that is, a system of indenture. It was under this system that an individual could sell oneself into servitude for a period of time. Some subscribers were voluntary, others were not. Involuntary and state-induced European immigrants to North America and other colonies included redemptioners (indentured servants), convicts, and demobilized soldiers. For the English, it was a means of getting rid of troublesome people, such as the poor, political dissenters, the Irish, idlers, vagrants, the dispossessed, Scottish crofters, and children. In fact, decedents of indentured children comprise 11 percent of Canada's current population.

A more massive scale of indentured labor came from India and China in the seventeenth and eighteenth centuries, however. It was a time of abuse where many were denied rights and faced exploitation after signing contracts; others found themselves captured or drugged and on a ship the next morning far from the sight of land. Under the new system, contractual agreements were generally breached, giving way to an inherent power imbalance between the contractor and the contractee—a not-so surprising outcome considering that the product of exchange was human capital.

All immigrants were or are not slaves—indentured or forced. The Puritans who settled earlier in the

United States provide a clear example of immigration not limited to the poor, as many of the early American settlers were in the middle or upper economic brackets. Many moved on a voluntary basis. These voluntary movements were primarily British moving from Britain to Canada, New Zealand, and Australia, where they dominated the economic and political life of these counties at the expense of the indigenous population. Britishers were prominent also in the immigration stream to the United States, South Africa, and what used to be known as Rhodesia and is now Zimbabwe and Zambia. Also during the time of the British occupancies, the Portuguese settled in Angola, Brazil, Mozambique, and a few smaller regions, while the French settled in large parts of Indochina and North Africa. Some, like the Dutch in South Africa and French Algeria identified strongly with their new abode. This new identification was shown by their self-designations or what they called themselves. The Dutch in South Africa referred to themselves as *Afrikaans* while the French in Algeria called themselves *pied-noirs*.

Mercantilism and the capitalistic ideology to maximize profits not only increased the commercialization of agriculture, but also resulted in the need for gang labor in other fields, such as cutting timber, working in mines, and building docks, railroads, and roads. However, the growth of the nascent mass industries in the United States along with the collapse of feudalism and serfdom in Europe were followed by the Great Atlantic Migration, wherein during the period from 1870 to 1914, over 35 million Europeans were transplanted to the United States. Some estimate that over a third returned to their native land from the United States, but no records were kept of people leaving the United States.

These turn-of-the-century immigrants were the human capital that labored in U.S. industries, harvesting forests, extracting ore and coal, as well as preparing land for agriculture. United States industrial might was built upon the backs of these immigrants. It was from the same sources that many chose Canada and Australia as their final destination. The preferred immigrants for North America were Western Europeans; however, the need for labor outweighed the pressure to restrict certain immigrants, thus Eastern Europeans entered on the east coast and Asians on the west coast.

Immigration in the Twentieth Century and Beyond

After World War I immigration virtually ceased to the major recipient countries, namely Australia, Canada, and the United States. Not until the 1960s did Canada open its borders to people with needed skills, as did Australia. The Civil Rights movement had pricked the conscience of the American public, and the national origins criteria of U.S. immigration laws was evaluated as unjustly discriminatory to people of certain countries. In 1965 President Lyndon B. Johnson signed into law the legislation that eliminated the national origins criteria and favored those with skills and education needed by the United States. The result was that the United States began to receive much of the best talent the world had to offer. In some cases, such as medical care in the inner cities and rural areas, the field would have collapsed if immigrant doctors trained outside the United States had not been allowed to enter the country. U.S. research labs and centers of education remain to this day dominated by foreign-born students and educators—talent that is building not only the economy but also intellectual and skilled professional communities within the United States. In the twenty-first century some countries are trying to recruit their expatriates back, but without much success.

Immigrants are a powerful force in both the sending and receiving societies. There are many who have invested heavily in their land of origin and their adopted abodes, and they generally represent a political and economic force to contend with. There are several reasons for this. First, it is generally the most daring and aggressive who leave their natal society for a new abode. Second, the immigrant is generally more entrepreneurial because one has a tendency to see opportunities and choices that the local inhabitants are likely to miss. Third, the immigrant is likely to have international contacts that allow one access to many more kinds of information and opportunities. Fourth, immigrants of this nature generally have sufficient financial means to contribute to the political and economic life in the receiving country; governments and politicians like and even depend upon that outside investment. Of course the immigrant quickly realizes the power one holds and may wisely make demands, such as being granted duel citizenship, receiving tax breaks, and so on.

Charles Keely coined the terms "new immigrant" and "new immigration" to signify the distinctive attributes of the post-1968 influx in America. Although the new immigrants may not be the majority of those entering the United States today, they have increased in prominence and numbers over the past 35 years. The vast majority originates from East Asia and South Asia. They are well-educated professionals in medicine, engineering, and science. They are fluent in written and spoken English and have attended a university modeled after the British or North American systems. As a result they are strangers in a not-so-strange land. In other words they are newly arrived in America but are familiar with the country, people, culture, and politics through their studies. Globalization and an increasingly international technological environment play no small role in this as well.

In the case of those immigrants from South Asia, they completed their higher education in a British or British-oriented college or university where English was the medium of instruction. Some were guided by American professors who taught in India under the Fulbright Hays, Ford Foundation, American Institute of Indian Studies, or other research or exchange programs. Consequently their language and educational experiences provided them with the skills that enabled them to excel in the United States.

These immigrants provide a sharp contrast to those who entered the United States at the turn of the century during America's industrialization. Those immigrants were generally a non-English-speaking people, many of peasant origin, who provided unskilled labor for American industries in manufacturing, the clothing industry, and other business enterprises. Jews sewed and marketed clothes for a pittance in New York; Chinese provided sweat and blood to build railroads; Irish, Polish, Italians, Estonians, and Latvians fed materials to machines; Germans and Scandinavians cleared land and developed farms.

Not only are the late twentieth and twenty-first century immigrants and their situations in America different from those of the past, but also the communications revolution has enabled many of them to continue to participate in Indian society while living in the United States. Unlike the migrants who left Europe at the turn of the century, realizing that they might not return, the sojourners of today are not forced to make the decision of permanent settlement. They can fly home within days and give instructions over the telephone to workers, friends, and relatives in their land of origin—in essence, they can participate in one society while residing in another.

The Immigration Act of 1965 (PL 89–236) strongly contributed to the radical change in the composition of America's immigration stream. (The so-called Hart-Cellar Act abolished the national-origin quotas that had been in place in the United States since 1882, such that immigrants were to be admitted by their skills and professions rather than by their nationality.) Even those supporting the legislation could not have guessed that Europeans would no longer dominate the immigration flow, as had been the case since North America was settled by European explorers. With the implementation of the 1965 legislation in 1968, the gates of immigration opened to a highly educated and professionally oriented people. A vast number were Asians who were professionally and technically trained, often with astute business acumen; they were a far cry from the Eastern European peasants who dominated the influx at the beginning of the twentieth century.

Assimilation and Identity

Traditionally migration studies concentrated on four broad topics: (1) causes of population shifts, (2) social-psychological concerns of immigrant adaptation, (3) social problems caused by immigration, and (4) the nature and dynamics of migrant groups and individual social networks. The vast majority of these studies used a diachronic model that only considered the dyadic interaction between host and immigrant societies. This is especially true when examining questions concerning identity.

Until the implementation and later improvement of steamships, coming to America was a hazardous and trying experience for the poor. Loss of life was high and the conditions so bad that the vast majority of those people who made the voyage swore they would never do it again under any circumstance. As a result immigrants quickly developed the ideology of leaving the homeland behind and America as the "Promised Land." Public schools were designed to indoctrinate immigrants, especially their children, to be American and assimilate to an American identity.

Between 1880 and 1930, one-fourth to one-third of the U.S. immigrant population returned, but the ideology of assimilation continued. Thus it is not surprising that those studying immigrants and immigration fell in line behind Robert E. Park and the Chicago School, interpreting immigrant behavior along assimilation lines. Park, along with other urban sociologists (Louis Wirth, Ernest Burgess, and Robert McKenzie), developed what became known as the "human ecology" model in their work that combined empirical studies with ethnicity. In this framework minority and immigrant communities accommodate to the wider or host society. The flow of influence is primarily one-way; that is the wider or hegemonic society influences the immigrant group. In some cases such as Britain and India, there was some influence between the sending and receiving societies but it was usually indirect and outside the individual immigrant's sphere of interaction.

After World War II, a communications revolution exploded. Within two decades people traveled around the globe in a matter of hours and communicated with family and friends in remote Asian villages in a matter of minutes. Migration researchers recognized and developed a conceptual framework where there is a continual three-way interactional process between the sending, receiving, and migrant communities. Such studies argued that three social arenas must be considered to comprehend the behavior of expatriates: (1) the sending community, (2) the migrant group, and (3) the receiving society. Here a three-way diachronic process is taking place; in other words, sociologists began to consider how the phenomena that shape immigration behavior (language, culture, etc.) change and develop over a period of time that is within historical contexts.

In the 1980s and 1990s concepts such as *globalization*, *transnationalism*, and *world system* reflected the realization of the increasing influence various and distant places had on each other. Most recently one of the most helpful models for understanding and interpreting the complex, changing, and varied situation is field theory where the investigator determines his or her field of enquiry and then identifies the forces or force fields involved. These force fields can, of course, influence each other. Their relationships can be interactional, or in rare cases one-way. A force field can be anything from a community to history to physical surroundings.

Of course one's theoretical approach depends on the goals one has in doing the research, but the field theory approach has become more common among scholars in organizing their research methods. It is clear from the above that the study of immigrants and immigration is a rapidly changing field and generalizations developed a decade ago may no longer be applicable. With the influence of globalization and transnationalism impacting on the world scene, immigration is a rapidly changing and dynamic field that needs to be continually monitored and adapted.

ARTHUR W. HELWEG

See also **Assimilation; Bilingualism; Colonialism; Globalization and Minority Cultures; Integration; Migrations**

Further Reading

Bean, Frank D., Georges Vernez, and Charles B. Keely, *Opening and Closing the Doors: Evaluating Immigration Reform and Control*, Santa Monica, California: Rand Corp.; Washington, DC: Urban Institute; Lanham, Maryland: Distributed by University Press of America, ©1989

Helweg, Arthur, and Usha Helweg, *An Iimmigrant Success Story: East Indians in America*, Philadelphia: University of Pennsylvania Press, 1990

Keely, Charles B., *U.S. Immigration: A Policy Analysis*, New York: Population Council, ©1979

Park, Robert E., and Ernest W. Burgess, *Introduction to the Science of Sociology, Including the Original Index to Basic Sociological Concepts*, Chicago, University of Chicago Press, 1969

Park, Robert E., *Race and Culture*, Glencoe, Illinois: Free Press, 1950

Tinker, Hugh, *A New System of Slavery: The Export of Indian Labour Overseas 1830–1920*, London: Hansib, 1993

Tomasi, Silvano, and Charles B. Keely, *Whom Have We Welcomed?: The Adequacy and Quality of United States Immigration Data for Policy Analysis and Evaluation*, Staten Island, New York: Center for Migration Studies, ©1975

Imperialism

The impact of imperialism upon peoples through the ages has been enormous. It has led to the movement of peoples and ethnic cleansing, the breakup of homogeneous groups, and the imposition of dominant cultures upon conquered people or minorities. The European-based empires of recent times have left an indelible mark upon our present world.

The policies of imperial powers through the ages have varied between the oppressive to the relatively benevolent, but the objective has been the same—the subjection of one people by another in order to enhance the influence and power of the dominant group. Heavy oppression inevitably breeds revolt. Liberal policies may prolong the rule of the imperial power, but in the end such liberalism ensures the collapse of imperial rule since it allows the growth of nationalism and demands for self-determination. Imperialism in modern times was largely about controlling less advanced, weaker peoples or nations for economic gain. The second industrial revolution, which occurred at the end of the nineteenth century, meant that the main industrialized nations sought avidly for new sources of raw materials and these were to be found, or so it was assumed, in new colonial acquisitions. Hence the speed of the Scramble for Africa, the last major area left to be colonized. Competition among the big powers was for resources, and these they hoped to find in newly colonized territories. In its turn the Scramble encouraged a new European militarism, and conflict, or potential conflict, loomed in Africa as the partition proceeded: the French fought wars in West Africa; the Italians in Libya and Ethiopia; the British in Egypt, Sudan, and Southern Africa. Between 1880 and 1914, for example, Britain added 3.25 million square miles of territory and 46 million people to its empire; France added 4 million square miles and 50 million people; Germany 1 million square miles and 15 million people. These huge additions to the European empires of that time were motivated by considerations of economic advantage and the balance of power. The British imperialist Sir Frederick D. Lugard said that "the scramble for Africa... was due to the growing commercial rivalry, which brought home to civilized nations the vital necessity of securing the only remaining fields for industrial enterprise and expansion." Despite rhetoric about a "civilizing mission," the main European powers colonized Africa for their own advantage. For example, France justified seizing Tunisia in 1882 as compensation for the fact that the British had taken Cyprus in 1878. Subsequently colonies were subject to authoritarian rule assisted by the imposition of the language, culture, and religion of the administering power. In French colonies officials ruled directly. In British colonies a system of indirect rule was established through loyal chiefs (whom the British appointed in place of hereditary chiefs) or emirs and native authorities. The practice of ruling through native authorities and keeping old tribal structures intact encouraged the continuation of multiethnic societies rather than preparing the people to come together in single, post-independence nations. These methods of rule were especially effective in Africa. In Asia, where whole nations with ancient civilizations were colonized, different methods were sometimes employed.

A primary principle of imperialism was always "divide and rule." What this meant in practice was playing one group off against another, promoting the interests of particular minorities in the hope of making these instruments of imperial control. In the latter stages of their rule in India, the British played off the Muslims against the Hindus and in retrospect must take at least some responsibility for the division of the subcontinent into India and Pakistan at independence. Divide and rule was a fluid yet constant process in many colonies, depending upon the ethnic divisions that existed. Imperial concern with ethnicity (preserving the differences between tribes) was part of the process that delayed the emergence of any sense of unity and nationalism.

The British in particular promoted what they regarded as the martial or warlike tribes, enrolling them in their colonial armies to maintain law and order. Emphasis upon tribe and tribal or ethnic differences was a method of retarding moves towards national solidarity against the imperial power. This approach was taken to its logical extreme in South Africa where the Afrikaners (descendants of the earlier Dutch imperialists) in the post-1948 apartheid era subdivided the African majority into ten tribal groups and allotted each group its own homeland, subsequently offering the homelands an independence that the international community refused to recognize.

In many cases, especially in Africa, the creation of colonies also required the establishment of political boundaries where none had previously existed. Such boundaries rarely coincided with former areas of tribal jurisdiction; instead they split formerly cohesive groups that then found themselves divided by new boundaries that separated colonies belonging to different imperial powers. The resultant problems were twofold. First, a group that had been split by these new boundaries might find that it was a minority in both the territories to which it had been consigned, whereas previously it had been a single regional power in its own right. Second, such people would disregard or evade the boundaries that colonialism had created and have continued to do so in the post-imperial age. In many respects, as a direct result of the colonial carve-up of Africa, the continent has some of the most fluid and least-regarded borders in the world. As a result of European imperialism, Africa, which was divided into territories whose frontiers respected neither ethnic nor cultural affinities, emerged into the independence era facing a wide range of minority problems.

During the latter days of empire, different ethnic groups united in their determination to achieve independence from their imperial masters. Such unity, however, was often fragile; this was especially the case where such groups had been artificially brought together within a single colony for reasons of imperial convenience as, for example, in the huge British colony of Nigeria. Once independence had been achieved, as Frantz Fanon aptly observed, " . . . Nationalism, that magnificent song that made the people rise against their oppressors, stops short, falters, and dies away on the day that independence is proclaimed." The unity of divergent groups, each of which was a minority within a colonial structure, was in danger of evaporating once independence had been achieved.

The pressures that brought an end to the European empires after 1945 released forces that gave rise to what were often internecine struggles between the groups that had temporarily coalesced to fight for national independence. As the imperial powers bowed out so different ethnic groups (both major and minor ones) felt the need to reassert their tribal or group identities in order to stake a claim for a proper place in the successor state. In the case of India such claims led to the division of the subcontinent into India and Pakistan. In the case of Nigeria, ethnic antagonisms culminated in the civil war from 1967 to 1970. In other cases, often years after the departure of the imperial authority, ethnic rivalries led to civil wars (as in Chad, Sudan, and Sri Lanka); and, though the newly emerging nations of the post-1945 era turned to nationalism as the answer to imperialism, they later discovered that ethnic nationalisms within their inherited boundaries could be as destructive, as formerly they had been a means of unity.

A study of British techniques in its Indian Empire reveals a constant concern with class and caste, for the British would never have been able to hold India as long as they did without pursuing a policy of divide and rule. This indeed allowed them to control the subcontinent for two centuries. The divisions were many: Hindu and Muslim; areas of direct rule as opposed to the princely states of which there were 560; differentiation between warlike or warrior peoples—the Sikhs, for example; and the clerk or petty tradesman class— the Babu. After 1858 following the successful British defeat of the Indian Mutiny (the first nationalist revolt), emphasis upon British racial superiority became a weapon of imperial government. The subsequent aloofness maintained by the British in India was in fact an acknowledgement of their need to maintain an apartness that emphasized their superiority over an inferior people. At the same time, this aloofness from Indian culture suggested the existence of a total gulf in understanding—the British were never going to be able to impose a genuine white western civilization upon India. Furthermore, this aloofness in its turn was superimposed on the Indian caste system that had survived from one of the world's earliest empires. A key, perhaps, to the eventual failure of all empires has been the urge to create a centralized system of government. In British India this included a uniform application of laws, the use of the English language, and the creation of a unified government/commercial infrastructure. Such developments broke down some of the racial, linguistic, and religious barriers that existed in India's polyglot society and helped to promote the nationalism whose eventual demand was "India for the Indians." The British India Government Act of 1935, which in London was seen as a progressive step forward, was rejected by the Indian Congress Party, the Princes, and the All India Muslim League, each seeing the act as divisive and aimed at prolonging British rule. According to Congress the Act "is designed to facilitate and perpetuate the domination and exploitation of the people of India and is imposed on the country to the accompaniment of widespread repression and the suppression of civil liberties." Imperial actions, even when apparently well–meaning, led to anti-imperial nationalism.

In the Far East at the end of the nineteenth century there followed in quick succession the Sino-Japanese War, the Spanish-American War, and the Russo-Japanese War with the result that both the United States and Japan emerged as formidable new imperial powers. The nineteenth and twentieth centuries witnessed the emergence of a particularly arrogant form of white racism against which the backlash became formidable in the last decades of the twentieth century. White minorities left indelible and bitter legacies in the colonies where they settled, and the presence of white tribes in the successor states continued to be the focus of longstanding resentments, as in Zimbabwe, for example, over the troubled years between 1999 and 2001. White racism had a profound impact in India, Indochina, Algeria, Kenya, South Africa, Angola, Mozambique, and elsewhere in the European empires. It was inevitable that this should be so since in every case a minority of whites imposed their will upon the indigenous majorities that were black or brown or yellow. Moreover, in settler colonies such as Algeria or Kenya the economic interests of the settlers always came first while the interests of the indigenous peoples were subordinated to settler needs. In British Kenya at the beginning of the twentieth century the Masai were systematically moved from their grazing lands to accommodate the incoming white farmers. Indeed whenever white settlement took place in Africa, African land was alienated for white use and, to add insult to injury, legislation subsequently forced the dispossessed Africans to act as labor on the land which they had lost to the white settlers. In the circumstances independence struggles, as in Kenya or Rhodesia, were focused upon grievances to do with loss of land.

There have always been powerful arguments against imperialism. J.A. Hobson in *Imperialism: A Study* (1902) argued that empire cost more than it gave to the imperial power although it suited a minority of financial interest groups. In another analysis of imperialism, V.I. Lenin, *Imperialism, the Highest Stage of Capitalism* (1917), argued that only the overthrow of capitalism would bring an end to imperialism. Both books had a major impact upon imperial and anti-imperial thinking during the twentieth century. Theories in defense of imperialism have been many: the search for prestige, the fear of rivals, the internal need for a strong external policy, the need for *lebensraum,* a sense of mission—spreading a superior civilization, strategy, and most important of all the belief that

empires made the imperial power both richer and stronger. In the post-imperial age that emerged in the aftermath of World War II, the newly independent former colonies had to learn to cope with the results of these imperial drives.

GUY ARNOLD

Further Reading

Brockway, Fenner, *The Colonial Revolution*, London: Hart-Davis, MacGibbon, 1973

Fanon, Frantz, *The Wretched of the Earth*, London: MacGibbon Kee, 1965

Hobson, J.A., *Imperialism: A Study*, London: George Allen & Unwin (first published 1902), 1954

Lenin, V.I., *Imperialism: The Highest Stage of Capitalism* (1917)

Mason, Philip, *Patterns of Dominance*, London: published for the Institute of Race Relations, Oxford University Press, 1970

Morel, E.D., *The Black Man's Burden*, New York and London: Modern Reader Paperbacks (first published 1920), 1969

Pakenham, Thomas, *The Scramble for Africa*, London: Weidenfeld and Nicolson, 1992

Robinson, Ronald, John Gallacher, with Alice Denny. *Africa and the Victorians: The Official Mind of Imperialism*, London: Macmillan, 1961

Segal, Ronald, *The Race War*, London: Jonathan Cape, 1966

Strachey, John, *The End of Empire*, London and Southampton: The Camelot Press, 1959

Woolf, Leonard, *Empire and Commerce in Africa: A Study in Economic Imperialism,* London: George Allen and Unwin (first published 1920), 1968

India

Capsule Summary

Country Name: Republic of India

Location: South Asian subcontinent, bordered on the north by China, Bhutan, and Nepal; on the west by Pakistan; and on the east by Burma and Bangladesh

Total Population: 1,049,700,118 (July 2003)

Ethnic Populations: Indo-Aryan (72%), Dravidian (25%), Mongoloid and other (3%) (2000)

Languages: Hindi (official), English (official), Bengali, Gujarati, Kashmiri, Malayalam, Marathi, Oriya, Punjabi, Tamil, Telugu, Urdu, Kanada, Assamese, Sanskrit, and Sindhi (1652 dialects)

Religions: Hindu (82.6%), Islam (11.3%), Christian (2.3%), Sikh (3%), Buddhist (0.71%), and Jains (0.48%)

India is probably the most ethnically diverse country in the world. It is also the second most populous country in the world. In fact in the year 2000 India became the second country to have a population of a billion people—one out of every seven humans live in India. Its culture stems from one of the oldest civilizations known to man—the Indus Valley Civilization. India is the dominant country of the South Asian subcontinent.

Before gaining independence from British rule in 1947, India included Pakistan, Bangladesh, and Burma. In spite of the divisions, India is still a country of religious, linguistic, social, ethnic, and racial diversity that is greater than Europe.

When India gained her independence from the British in 1947, debates ensued as to whether a national unity could be maintained amidst such diversity. So far the country has survived, but not without its tensions.

History

The history of India falls into five periods: prehistory, Vedic and classical age, kingdoms, British imperialism, and nationalism. When the Aryans started invading the Indus Valley around 1500 BCE they found a sophisticated civilization in decline. The inhabitants had sophisticated urban settlements laid out in a grid pattern, established political structures, and an agrarian economy that produced barley, wheat, and other crops. There were storage facilities and public works. There was craft specialization, a cultural unity, a common language, and colonization. There were coins and artifacts from all over the world, which indicated that the Indus Valley Civilization was a center of international trade, the tentacles of which reached out to the remote regions of the known world.

The origins of the indigenous population are unknown. Archeological fines go back to 5000 BCE where there was animal domestication, stone tools, and pottery. Around 3500 BCE, settlements began to spread out. The invaders were people with linguistic affinities to Iran and Europe and came to occupy northwestern and north-central India. Those that added to India's ethnic mix included Persians, Scythians, Arabs, Mongols, Turks, Afghans, and Europeans.

The Indus Valley Civilization began its decline around 1750 BCE, which resulted in the Vedic age beginning around 1500 BCE with the immigration of tribes of Indo-European origins, also known as Indo-Aryans.

According to Vedic and Sanskrit hymns, the Indo-Aryans were semi-nomadic pastoralists. They first settled in what is now Rajasthan, and later in the Doab, or plain, between the Ganges and Yamuna Rivers. Gradually shifting to agriculture, they formed villages and evolved into tribal societies led by a *raja* (warrior chief) who protected the tribe. The chief was assisted by Brahmin families, who among other things composed Vedic hymns. In return for being protected, tribes paid a tribute. However, the rule of the *raja* was not unchecked. There was a *sabha* (tribal assembly) that checked his authority. The economy was a mixture of pastoralism and agriculture, with cattle being the main source of wealth. This is reflected in the language as *gotra* (cowpen) describes endogamous kinship systems and *gavishitri* (the search for cows) means war. It was a time of conflicts between tribes and with local groups.

Vedic religion centered around personified forces in nature and abstract divinities. Offerings were made through *Agni* (the god of fire), who came to dominate large and domestic sacrifices—a situation which lasts to the present day. The rituals of ancient time have similarities with the rituals of today—brahaman priests were mediators between god and man and the chanting of hymns had magical significance. The performing of rituals propitiated gods to confer prosperity and valor on kings. Those outside this region were people of mixed race and considered inferior. This is probably why in north India today light skin is considered more beautiful, and people in north India feel superior because of their Aryan ancestry.

The shift from tribal to territorial identity was manifest when geographical regions were named after the tribes that occupied them. Territorial kingship also became more permanent, taxing replaced tributes, and the army became a regular part of the administrative system. Royal power was symbolized in more elaborate rituals, the king was deemed the owner of the land, the king became associated with divinity, and the role of the priest was to sustain those beliefs through rituals.

The agrarian economy expanded and with it so did urbanization. But the most important development was the emergence of a *varna* order (or caste hierarchy). The initial distinction between *Arya* (Aryan) and *Dasa* (non-Aryan) in northern India was based on skin color. The priests, warriors, and people constituted the divisions within the Aryan tribe, which evolved from lineages to caste groups with the Aryans becoming the twice-born castes. The outsiders were less important economically and broadly classed under the rubric of *shudras*, who were expected to serve the higher castes.

Ritual status became important and the stratafication and the varna became the mechanism for integrating new groups as *jatis* (or sub-castes) into the overall scheme. Ideas of purity and pollution as a basis for ranking came in which resulted in a fifth category—the untouchables. Contrary to stereotypes, mobility did take place and mixed castes did emerge, but the varna framework remained in tact.

Doubts emerged concerning the efficacy of Vedic religious beliefs and practices. Some opted out of the society and their teachings were incorporated in the *Aranyakas* and *Upanishads* as esoteric texts. The relationship of one's soul with the *Brahma* (universal soul) was raised, which lead to the doctrine of *Karma* (right action). There was a continuous interaction between Aryan and non-Aryan as acculturation and assimilation took place—called "Aryanization" and "Sanskritization." It was also the setting for the epics *Mahabharata, Ramayana,* and *Bhagavad-gita.*

In north India the Vedic age was followed by the rise of republics, monarchies, and confederacies. It was during this time that the northwest became isolated and moved away from Brahmanical tradition, aided by the Persian (530 BCE) and the Greek armies under Alexander of Macedon (327 BCE) who followed the traditional invasion route into South Asia. It was also the period in which Siddharta Gaiutama (564–483 BCE), the founder of Buddhism, lived, as did the founder of Jainism.

The rise of Chandragupta Maurya to power (321 BCE), ably advised by his Brahman prime minister Kautilya, marked the beginning of the Mauryan dynasty. The most famous Maurya was Asoka (also spelled Ashoka). His predecessor had extended the empire down to Mysore, and in his only conquest, Asoka took Kalinga (Orissa). The fighting and destruction was so intense that Asoka felt great remorse. As a result he forsook war and turned to Buddhism and issued a *Dhamma*, or set of edicts that inculcated social responsibility, ensured human dignity, and encouraged socioreligious harmony. He emphasized the paternal role of the king by building roads, rest houses, and healing centers to help his subjects. Asoka's pillars and other artifacts still dot the South Asian subcontinent.

Around 200 BCE, the Mauryan Empire went into decline. Indo-Greeks invaded the northwest into Punjab, later to be replaced by Scythians Tribal republics occupied areas and power in the South was decentralized. Although political units became dispersed and authority fragmented, there was an underlying unity that emerged through internal and external trade and the rise in importance of a mercantile community. Buddhism split between Hinayana (Lesser Vehicle) and Mahayana (Greater Vehicle), and Vedic Brahmanism evolved the concept of the trinity—Brahma (the creator), Vishnu (the preserver), and Shiva (the destroyer). The monotheistic concept of God became manifest in Shiva or Vishnu and all other deities became *avatara* (forms of the deity). Thus developed the absorbing trait of Hinduism and its basis for power on the subcontinent.

Instead of competing with other religious communities, Hindus adopted them as avatars in the Hindu pantheon. It was also during this period that *The Mahabharata, Ramayana,* and *Bhagavad-gita* were turned into religious works.

The classical age of Indian history began with the accession of Chandragupta I (320–335 CE) who founded the Gupta Dynasty, the power of which centered in the middle Ganges Valley. It was a time when Brahmans were favored and land grants to them and temples were a regular feature. After the Guptas, North India was divided into four kingdoms; further divisions followed and South Asia was never again united under self-rule until 1947. Regional kingdoms and distinctive regional cultures developed (650–1250 CE). The general pattern was for local rulers to assert their independence, and fully fledged monarchies emerged. Contact with the outside world was minimized because of the constant internal strife.

During this time the Rajputs of Rajasthan were a major force in medieval Indian society and politics. Their origins are not known, but it is thought that they came from abroad. In either case they acquired lunar and solar connections and kshatriya status. Orissa evolved as principalities integrated into a loosely structured political system. The Deccan, although a regional entity, was an area of continual conflict. Tamil Nadu had a maritime trade and was generally more stable, especially under the Cholas. Also irrigation and agricultural production increased with land grants to temples for that purpose. Kerala set down the cultural foundations in the eighth century with caste as the determining factor in socio-political organization, dominated by a Brahmin landowning group and an aristocratic landowning class that later became the Nayar caste. They developed a special marriage relationship with the brahmins and a system of matrilineal descent.

Although regionalism dominated during this period, Brahmanistic puranic cults and ideas spread as Brahmin priestly landowners and their ideas interacted with the local population so that local ideas spread and brahmanic concepts were modified to be part of the local culture. It was also during this period that agriculture expanded, as did internal and external trade. Gujarat and South India especially had extensive contact with Chinese, Arab, and Jewish traders. Merchants formed guilds and Sanskrit became the official language, although in some areas the local language took precedence, which lead to their breakaway and the language diversity on the subcontinent.

Muslim influence became strong with the founding of the Delhi Sultanate (1206–1526). Qutb un Aibak is traditionally regarded as its founder, but it really started when his slave took power in 1211 and made Delhi the capital. The Sultanate was initially dominated by a corps of Turkish slaves who provided the military leadership, governors, and officers of the court. The Turkish slaves faced competition from free immigrants who sought asylum from the Moghol devastation of central Asia and eastern Iran, as well as the Indo-Muslim element. With Khaliji's revolution the tradition of slave status with being qualified for military and administrative office was broken and an indigenous Muslim aristocracy rose up. The Moghols became a threat and regularly invaded through the Punjab. At times the Delhi empire was a Moghol protectorate. However, Hindu rulers remained in the south and Muslim rule entered Gujarat but not Rajesthan. Even in the North the Muslims were a minority, and government control over the rural Hindu aristocracy was tenuous at best.

The Mughal Empire (1526–1707 CE) came when Babur defeated the Lodhi ruler Ibrahim and obtained control of Delhi and Agra. Humayun, Akbar, Jahingar Shah Jahan, and Aurangzeb followed and had varying success in establishing administrative control over their empire, but none were ever able to break the Brahmin controls over the rural people. The final factor in the fall of the Mughals was Auragzeb's not being able to resist muslim pressure for lands, resources, and in general favored treatment that resulted in few being loyal to the ruler. Decentralization developed and increased with Hindu merchants and peasant leaders being pitted against Muslim revenue farmers and nobles—a tactic the British developed in their famous "Divide and Rule Policies."

It was during this Mughal period that Sikhism, India's youngest religion, was founded. They were a peaceful community that as a result of persecution became a militant soldier-saint brotherhood termed the *Khalsa*.

In 1701 the English East India Company based near Calcutta and their trade quickly rivaled that of the Dutch and French. Bengal became dependent on European trade, while in the south, European trade began to be transformed into political power. The British soon eliminated their French and Dutch rivals. Factional conflicts between Indian rulers brought an expansion of power. English troops would protect a ruler in return for a tribute. However, land revenues became an unbearable burden on the peasants as military costs and quest for profits heightened.

Responses to British insurgency came on many fronts. Raja Rammohan Roy (1770–1830) founded the Brahmo Samaj (1825) movement. It was a new reform Hindu faith that borrowed western Deism and Indian monotheism from Christianity. The new faith opposed idol worship, brahminism, and barbaric customs, such as widow-burning. Other movements included the Arya Samaj and Singh Subbha movements. Debating societies for social action developed and reform in Hinduism and Islam took place. There were few conversions to Christianity, but Christian influence was fiercely countered by reform and change in both Hinduism and Islam.

Because of taxes, Christian influence, and other factors, the Indian Army mutinied in 1857 which almost eliminated the British presence in India. The result was that the East India Company was abolished and the British Crown took over direct administration of the Indian Empire.

The British rule of India (1858–1947) went through five phases. The first lasted until 1870; it was a period of optimism, with the British seeing themselves on a civilizing mission. The second period lasted till the turn of the century and was characterized by doubting the benefits of British rule; India was experiencing poverty and social unrest. The third phase isolated and repressed social descent and lasted until 1919. The fourth phase was one of contradiction—liberal rhetoric with the fact of economic, intellectual, and territorial expansion. The fifth phase was concerned with the means and manner of relinquishing rule so that India would have a parliamentary system that would satisfy separate interests and communities.

To the British the Indians were barbarians and were perceived as in an early stage of human evolution. Initially the British ruled through local institutions, but developed their own bureaucracy using the westernized Indian educated in British oriented schools—the westernized Indians also becoming the teachers and political leaders.

Muslims were varied during this period. In Bengal they were disadvantaged, while in upper India the old elite sought to maintain their culture. They established a college in Aligarh which along with other educational institutions were focal points for modern interpretations of Islam with the goal of making compatible with the modern world. But the educated elite Indian and Muslims remained separate socially and in national identity.

The Congress Party wanted to represent all of India, but Muslims feared Hindu domination. Muslims were also educated in English and incorporated in the Raj. The British played on existing social, religious and economic divisions to maintain their rule; thus at the time of the granting of independence in 1947, the Congress Party faced the problem of uniting a country divided along religious, caste, race, territory, language, and rural/urban lines.

Due to British rule, three social categories were added to South Asian culture: the Western Educated Indian, the Martial Races, and the non-resident Indian (NRI), also known as the Overseas Indian or the Indian Diaspora. Western Educated Indians occupied political positions, were prominent in international trade and technological development, and dominated the bureaucracy as the Brahmins have traditionally done in the past. They were in essence the mediators between indigenous India and the West and its influence. They made up the civil service and kept continuity at the time of independence.

Certain groups like the Sikhs and the Gurkhas were known for their fighting ability and loyalty to the Crown. They were classified as martial races and given preferences in enlisting in the armed forces and special privileges accordingly. When India obtained independence in 1947, Britain maintained their right to have their Gurkha Regiment, and it was the Gurkhas that lead the invasion force onto the Falkland Islands during the Falklands War. Concerning the Overseas Indians, they developed by filling the need for cheap labor when slavery was abolished. Generally they served under an indenture system where they contracted in India to serve on a plantation or other work for so many years at an agreed wage. Abuses were more common than not, and the system was outlawed in 1920.

Emigration, although initially for cheap plantation labor, expanded business and bureaucratic/administrative dominance, as was the case in East Africa, farming business, and later well-trained professionals in Britain and North America.

Contemporary India

The results of this long historical process is a country of great diversity. Concerning race, scientific classification has been tenuous at best, but the people of India are classified according to social races; that is groups that are assumed to have a biological basis but are arbitrarily defined culturally. Broadly speaking, the people of north-central and north-western India tend to have affinities with Europe, those of northeastern India Tibetans and Burmese. Many tribal groups of the Chota Nagpur Plateau and northeastern peninsula have affinities with the Mon of Southeast Asia. The people of South India are characterized as having African or Negroid origins. It must be kept in mind that these racial classifications do not negate the fact that there is considered an overall homogeneity among India's vast population. Its is represented in the loose use of the term "Indian," "East Indian," or "Hindu," which evokes a picture of individuals with brown skin pigmentation, full black hair, and dark brown eyes. In fact a closer look shows regional differentiation seems to be a stronger influence on physical traits than racial origins.

The most important cultural determinant is religion. There are seven major religious communities—Hindu, Muslim, Christian, Buddhist, Sikh, Jain and Parsie—as well as numerous subgroups and sects. Religion in India is more than a private belief. It is usually determinate of behavior and social position; in fact the political map of South Asia is determined by religion. The country of Pakistan was established to give the Muslims their own state. It caused one of the most massive and bloodiest dislocations of humanity known to man. Hindus had to leave what was to be Pakistan and Muslims left what was to be India for Pakistan—both sides killing members off the other in the process.

For the Muslims that staid in India, they are perceived of as disadvantaged in spite of government affirmative action policies establishing quotas and institutions designed to help Muslims to advance socially and economically.

The ongoing conflict in Kashmer is a situation of a Muslim population that was ruled by a Hindu. At the time of independence, the prince opted for India, but Pakistan claimed it. There have been two Indo-Pakistan Wars fought over the region. The United Nations (UN) has recommended that a plebiscite be held, but India maintains that this is an internal matter. Interestingly enough, the people of Kashmir want to be an independent country.

The Indian state of Haryana was created out of the state of Punjab so the Sikhs would have a numerical majority in Punjab and the Hindus dominating in Haryana. Both are secular states. Some Sikhs hoped to create a Sikh state of Khalistan out of the geographical Punjab—a butterfly shaped region that bridges India and Pakistan. It was a very strong movement, especially after Mrs. Gandhi ordered the Indian Army to occupy the Golden Temple, the sacred center for the Sikhs. It caused a strong sense of alienation among this community that had been one of the most innovative, and made remarkable contributions to India as a whole. Sikhs, like the Muslims and some other minority groups, stereotype the Hindus as discriminating against them. On the other hand Hindus feel that Muslims and other minorities have been given preferential treatment at their expense. The Bharata Janta Party has risen to prominence on a platform of Hindu nationalism.

India's caste system is a society based on inequality. The basis has to do with the concept of ritual purity. Those who are closest to God are considered pure and are Brahmans or the twice-born castes—the actual specifics may vary from place to place, but the general structure pervades all of South Asia. The untouchables, or scheduled castes and tribes, are about 24 percent of the population. The scheduled castes are relegated to doing menial and dirty work, such as sweeping and cleaning filth (e.g., sewage). The caste system is outlawed by the Constitution of India and there are university positions and other affirmative action policies to uplift the untouchables, or scheduled castes, but progress has been extremely slow. Jagjivan Ram (1908–1985), an untouchable and prominent politician, was a Member of Parliament, a government minister holding numerous and varied portfolios. He worked to gain equality for untouchables. He was often held up as an example of an untouchable who gained political prominence. In actuality the untouchables are a depressed community regardless of their religious affiliation. Even in Christian and Muslim communities, untouchables are segregated from the wider society. In spite of Gandhi's labeling them *Harijans* (or "Children of God"), and the positive discrimination applied to them in the Indian Constitution, South Asia's untouchables constitute the world's largest group of economically underprivileged and ritually discriminated human groups.

Related to the scheduled castes are the scheduled tribe, who are also identified by India's constitution for affirmative programs. Also termed *Adivasi* (or original inhabitants), these communities have remained peripheral in Indian society with their distinctive life styles.

Second only to religious identity, which embraces a variety of allegiances, castes, and other groups, are large group identities which relate to geographical location. The geographical regional environments and cultures cross religious and political boundaries. One of the striking features of modern South Asia, including India, is the increasing formulation of regional identities. However, India's expanding cities draw their populations from a host of different regions, but 75 percent of the population still live in the countryside with their stable regional patterns.

North India of the Upper Gangetic Plain, especially the region between the Ganges and Yamuna Rivers, is the cultural heartland of India. It contains Delhi (the historic capital), some of the holiest centers of Hinduism, and splendid architectural structures of the past. The villages have been settled there for a long time and have remained physically and socially isolated. Caste rules apply with Jat and Rajput (warriors and land owners) who acknowledge the ritual superiority of the Brahmins and the need for their services, as well as the outcaste position of the Chamars (leather workers).

Northern India is the one region where Hindi is spoken as the natural language, but the area remains cosmopolitan as people of a variety of castes and races continue to enter the area, causing its rapid growth.

The Eastern Plains region has Bengal as its center. The intensive rice cultivation practiced is the main source of food for one-fourth of South Asia's population that resides there. Even though Bengal is divided politically between India and Bangladesh, the shared language and culture is tenaciously held onto. The region contains one of the highest population densities in the world, which worries its neighbors because it is expanding out.

The Northeast Frontier is the hill region that divides South Asia from Southeast Asia and contains fiercely preserved tribal identities. They range from the formerly head-hunting Nagas to the Mizos, who gained recognition resulting from a long guerilla campaign, to smaller tribes who maintain a completely separate identity. The region is threatened both culturally and physically as population pressures force emigration from Bengal to the surrounding hills. This has resulted social unrest and guerilla activity in the region.

The Himalayan Border Region is the sparsely settled region of the heterogeneous tribes on the southern side of the Himalayan range. Like the Northeast Frontier they were incorporated in British India's defense policy. Some in Pakistan are Islamized Tibetan speakers but almost all maintain allegiance to the Lamanistic Buddhism of their parent Tibetan culture. Since the establishment of Gurkha kingdom of western Nepal in the eighteenth century, there has been an expansion of the Nepali language and Hindu culture associated with it.

In the Northwest Region, the cultural region of Punjab is located on the invasion route into India. As a result the Muslim influence is much stronger and caste hierarchy less pronounced, but still untouchables, like the Chamars, do the sweeping and other polluting work. They are also relegated to settlements outside the village. The rich wheat-growing plains make this one of the most prosperous and productive areas of South Asia. No matter what community, one characteristic of Punjabi culture is confidence.

Western India looks out to the Arabian Sea, the center of which is Gujarat, and its industrial center of the Cotton Industry Ahmadabad. The area has many natural harbors, and Gujaratis are known for their skills in business. Not only are there numerous business castes, but also prosperous religious minorities inhabit the region, namely Jain, Parsis, and such Muslim sects as Ismalis, Bohras, and Memons. Bombay is India's foremost port, the center of India's film industry, and the capital of Maharastra—a Marathi-speaking state and the greatest area of Indo-Aryan speech. Maharastra is also famous for its traditional learning for Brahmins. Goa, being part of the Portuguese empire, resulted in the continued existence of Catholicism.

The Tribal Belt is a north-south cultural divide from Gujarat to Orissa. There are fifty different tribes, each generally speaking a member of the Indo-Aryan, Drividian or Munda family. Generally the major tribes maintain their distinctive traditions in spite of pressures to conform to the norms of Hindu society.

South Indians individually and collectively have a powerful sense of a separate regional identity within the country. Maintaining their Dravadian languages is the most proudly maintained symbol, a symbol associated with other cultural patterns such as behavioral patterns, looser clothes, spicy food and fewer restrictions on women. Caste and marriage patterns differ.

The Christian community in Kerala was founded by the Apostle Thomas but Hindu traditions, such as the caste system remain strong.

Depending on how one counts there are 16 different language communities in India and 1650 different dialects. The Indian constitution stipulated that in 1950, Hindi would replace English as the national language. As the time for the changeover to take place, there was so much social unrest in the country that the provision was ignored.

Language is important to any ethnic community because it not only communicates their cultural values and beliefs, but it symbolizes the survival and tie to the most ancient foundations of the ethnic community.

There primarily two language groups in India, Indo-Aryan and Dravidian. The Indo-Aryan dominant in both historical influence and geographical spread. Although there are similarities in structure and vocabulary to languages in Europe, they have become distinctive due to years of isolation.

During Muslim rule, Persian words were incorporated by the Muslim elite. As British rule spread, English became the lingua franca. But the Hindi of India and Urdu of Pakistan are virtually the same in everyday speech, the main difference being that Urdu uses the Persian script and Hindi the Davnagri script. The Indo-Aryan has extended far beyond its homeland and is used by Gypsies, Mauritius and Fiji with older versions in Sri Lanka.

The Dravidian languages are in the south and thought to have remote ties to Asian languages. Tamil is probably the oldest of the Dravidian languages dating back to the first century CE. The Dravidian languages have played a strong role in the development of South Indian identity. Other language groups are in border areas and less significant.

Soon after India obtained independence, many scholars, politicians and people debated whether India could maintain a unity from such diversity. Ethnic conflict and tensions remain and manifest themselves in violence. However, up until now, the union of the country has been maintained.

India's modern economy includes industries and a multitude of support services as well as traditional village farming, modern agriculture, and handicrafts. The economy has grown at a rate of 6 percent since 1990, reducing poverty by about 10 percentage points. The GDP per capita income in 2002 was approximately $2,600.

ARTHUR HELWEG

See also **Bangladesh; Bhindranwale, Jarnail Sant (India-Sikh); Buddhists; Diaspora: Indian; Hindus; Gandhi, Mohandas Karamchand (India); Pakistan; South Asian–Americans (India, Pakistan, Bangladesh); Untouchables (Harijans/Dalits/Scheduled Castes)**

Further Reading

Roland, J., and L. Breton, *Atlas of the Languages and Ethnic Communities of South Asia*, Walnut Creek, London, New Delhi: AltaMira Press, 1977

Mandelbaum, David G., *Society in India: Change and Continuity,* Berkeley: University of California Press, 1970

Mehta, Ved, *Portrait of India*, New York: Farrer, Straus and Girox, 1970

Schackle, Christopher, *South Asian Languages: A Handbook*, London: 1985

———, "Ethnography," "Peoples," *The Cambridge Encyclopedia of India, Pakistan, Bangladesh, Sri Lanka*, Cambridge, Robinson, Francis, editor, New York, Port Chester, Melbourne, Sydney: Cambridge University Press, 1989.

Schackle, Christopher, "Languages," "Culture," in *The Cambridge Encyclopedia of India, Pakistan, Bangladesh, Sri Lanka*, edited by Francis Robinson, Cambridge; New York; Port Chester; Melbourne; Sydney: Cambridge University Press, 1989

Schwartzberg, Joseph E., *A Historical Atlas of South Asia*, Chicago and London: The University of Chicago Press, 1978

Spate, O.H.K., and A.T.A. Learmonth, *India and Pakistan*, 3rd edition, London: Methuen & Co. Ltd., 1967

Tharoor, Shashi, *India: From Midnight to Millennium*, New York: Arcade Publishing, 1997

Tinker, Hugh, *South Asia: A Short History*, New York, Washington, London: Fredrick A. Praeger, 1966

———, *The Banyan Tree: Overseas Emigrants from India, Pakistan, and Bangladesh*, Oxford, New York, Delhi, Karachi: Oxford University Press, 1977

Wolpert, Stanley, *Roots of Confrontation in South Asia. Afghanistan, Pakistan, India & the Superpowers*, New York, Oxford: Oxford University Press, 1982

———, *India*, Berkeley, Los Angeles, Oxford: The University of California Press

Indigenous Peoples

Capsule Summary

Location: Worldwide, in more than 70 countries
Total Population: At least 300 million
Languages: More than 5,000 peoples speak at least 3,000 different languages and dialects

An estimated 300 million individuals of approximately 5,000 different peoples inhabit more than 70 countries in different parts of the globe, from the Artic to the South Pacific. More than 150 million indigenous people of various ethnic backgrounds and religious orientations are concentrated in India and China, including Buddhists, Hindus, and Muslims. While there is enormous cultural and linguistic diversity in these regions, Tibetan and Mongolian nomadic herders of eastern China share similar problems with isolated tribal peoples in southern India, known as the Scheduled Castes and Tribes, largely due to resettlement policies and the struggle for access to water and land resources. In fact the term indigenous or aboriginal is usually applied to peoples who were living on their lands before the arrival of foreign settlers. From this perspective, indigenous peoples are the descendants of those who inhabited a country or a geographical region at the time of the arrival of colonizers.

Among them are the Navajo, Maya, Guarani, Mapuche, and other Amerindians of North and South America; the Innu, Crees, and Aleutians of the circumpolar region; the Sami of northern Europe; the Nanai and Taiga of northern Russia and Siberia; the !Kung, Bakgatla, and Fulani of Africa; the Ilongot of the Philippines; the Arrernte and other Aborigines and Torres Strait Islanders of Australia; and the Maori of New Zealand. In several countries, such as Bolivia, Peru, Ecuador, and Guatemala, the majority of the population is indigenous. The Americas are the home to some 50 million indigenous people. In a few regions, however, such as Brazil and the United States, less than two percent of the residents are native to the area—between 90 and 95 percent of these countries' original inhabitants were decimated during the colonial period. Surprisingly about 50 indigenous groups still live in isolation in Central Brazil; that is, without systematic contact with the broader Brazilian society.

The definition of indigenous peoples advanced by the United Nations (UN) and adopted by various international organizations today transcends territoriality and relies on ethnic and cultural identity and political power:

Indigenous communities, peoples and nations are those which, having a historical continuity with pre-invasion and pre-colonial societies that developed on their territories, consider themselves distinct from other sectors of the societies now prevailing in those territories, or parts of them. They form at present non-dominant sectors of society and are determined to preserve, develop, and transmit to future generations their ancestral territories and their ethnic identity, as the basis of their continued

605

existence as peoples, in accordance with their own cultural patterns, social institutions, and legal systems. (United Nations, para. 369).

Who is Indigenous? Territory, Politics, and Identity

The problem of who is indigenous and who is not, however, remains largely controversial. Defining how the term indigenous applies to African, European, and Asian peoples is not as clear-cut as it is to Amerindians, Canadian First Nations, and Australian Aborigines. In New Zealand, "brown faces" are distinguished from Europeans, or "whites." In the Americas, "Indians" are those of non-European ancestry and non-African descent. This is not to say that the question of "who is an Indian" has been resolved in these regions—in the United States, for instance, Indianess has been defined biologically since the Dawes Act (also known as the General Allotment Act) of 1887 was enacted. One-quarter was the minimum fraction of blood allowing federally recognized Indians to claim possession of land allotments, when their own ancestral territories were opened to American citizens for homesteading. Following the U.S. Indian Reorganization Act of 1934, blood quantum requirements were relegated to the tribal level, and today standards vary from one-quarter (among the Pima of Arizona, for instance) to open enrollment, which requires tracing descent from an Indian ancestor, however remote (the case of the Cherokee Tribe of Oklahoma). Nearly 300 native peoples in the United States are currently seeking federal recognition as American Indians and question blood as a measure of indigenous identity. In Brazil, while Indianess is a matter of self-definition, various groups struggle to obtain official identification because of their mixed European and/or African and Amerindian ancestry. The purity of bloodlines, and consequently individuals' appearances, still function in most cases as the defining criteria.

Characterizing indigenous peoples in Africa, Asia, and Europe involves further considerations into the realm of power relations. Sure the Bantu-speaking Zulu of South Africa are indigenous compared to the Afrikaners, who descend from Dutch immigrants. But because Bantu peoples, who number over 60 million individuals in eastern Africa, have become politically dominant and economically affluent in countries such as Kenya, where the Bantu-speaking Kikuyu overthrew the British colonial government in 1963, they do not figure as "indigenous" in international computations. San communities of the

Kalahari Desert of Botswana and Namibia, in turn, whose small bands of hunter-gatherers number approximately 50,000 individuals, are considered indigenous. Similar concerns can be raised about the status of indigenous peoples of Europe and Asia.

It is also important to point out the relevance of using the term indigenous "peoples" rather than populations according to international law. In general, population refers to a group of individuals, which may be of relevance for the domestic law of a particular state. Peoples, however, have the right to self-determination, that is, the right to manage local and internal affairs, including economic, social, and cultural matters. This right is one of the basic principles of international law, and the consequences of the acceptance of the character of "peoples" are far reaching (Hans-Joachim Heintze 1993).

Indigenous peoples all over the world see themselves as the legitimate claimants to their ancestral territories and natural resources, and consider control over local economy, social planning, land use, and taxation essential to their existence. Thus the emphasis these communities place today in fighting for greater degrees of autonomy and self-rule. Nationwide protests by Ecuador's indigenous people, for instance, ended in February 2001 with the signing of a pact between the country's president and the Indians, who demanded a system of subsidized prices to help fight the poverty and marginalization of millions of Ecuadoreans. As the representative of the Confederation of Indigenous Nationalities of Ecuador (Conaie) put it:

> Ecuador's indigenous movement once again demonstrated that it was alive and well, and was thinking in national terms, with a united vision.... The Indian peoples constitute a social and ethical force, which is the basis of our history, the imagery and artistic forms of which impregnate the cultural practices of broad sectors of the Ecuadorean nation, and are a decisive factor in the preservation of the identity and future of Ecuador (Kinto Lucas, (February 7, 2001).

History

The Decade (1994–2003) has been dedicated to indigenous peoples worldwide. An objective of the Decade, according to the UN, "is the promotion and protection of the rights of indigenous people and their empowerment to make choices which enable them to retain their cultural identity while participating in political, economic and social life, with full respect for their cultural values, traditions and forms of social organization"

(United Nations, No. 9). Indigenous peoples have insisted on retaining distinct identities and cultural heritages especially since the emergence of new nations in the wave of decolonization following World War II. Policies of assimilation aimed at fully integrating indigenous peoples into mainstream, dominant societies—through extensive use of boarding schools, confinement on reservations, and forced labor, for instance—have proven to be not only unsuccessful, but also disastrous. This is the case, for instance, of Jesuit and Franciscan schools for Indian children created throughout North and South America in the sixteenth, seventeenth, and eighteenth centuries to annihilate "Indian culture." Some of the world's worst violations of human rights have been perpetrated against indigenous people, according to Amnesty International and Human Rights Watch, including the genocide of entire communities, assassination of prominent leaders, torture of women and children, slavery, illegal detainment, and ill-treatment in captivity.

Today indigenous peoples are often among the poorest, worst housed, and least paid and suffer from the highest prevalence rates of degenerative diseases, such as diabetes, heart disease, cancer, and hypertension. It is important to point out that biologic and genetic characteristics of indigenous peoples, including those of African, Hispanic, Amerindian, and Asian heritage, do *not* explain health disparities experienced by these populations. Recent studies show that these differences are the result of social inequality and environmental stress (U.S. Department of Health 2000). In 1992 the UN launched 1993 as the International Year of the World's Indigenous People precisely because of this catastrophic situation.

One aim of the International Year is to provide help to indigenous people and communities in areas such as health, education, development, and the environment. The emphasis must be on practical action in the form of concrete projects benefiting indigenous people. An important element of these programs should be the participation of indigenous people in their planning, implementation, and evaluation (Boutros Boutros-Ghali 1994).

The situation of indigenous people was first brought into center stage as a subject for public awareness and debate in 1953 after the International Labor Organization (ILO) published a study on indigenous people. In 1957 the ILO adopted the first international legal instruments specifically created to protect the rights of peoples whose ways of life and existence were threatened by dominating societies (Indigenous and Tribal Populations Convention, No. 107). In 1970 the UN's Subcomission on the Protection of Minorities recommended that a detailed study be made of discrimination against indigenous peoples. The first "Draft Declaration on the Rights of Indigenous Peoples" materialized in 1994, and its opening statements affirm, among other things, that:

1. "indigenous peoples are equal in dignity and rights to all other peoples, while recognizing the right of all peoples to be different, to consider themselves different, and to be respected as such";
2. "all peoples contribute to the diversity and richness of civilizations and cultures, which constitute the common heritage of humankind";
3. all doctrines, policies and practices based on or advocating superiority of peoples or individuals on the basis of national origin, racial, religious, ethnic or cultural differences are racist, scientifically false, legally invalid, morally condemnable and socially unjust";
4. "indigenous peoples have been deprived of their human rights and fundamental freedoms, resulting, *inter alia*, in their colonization and dispossession of their lands, territories and resources, thus preventing them from exercising, in particular, their right to development in accordance with their own needs and interests";
5. there is "urgent need to respect and promote the inherent rights and characteristics of indigenous peoples, especially their rights to their lands, territories and resources, which derive from their political, economic and social structures and from their cultures, spiritual traditions, histories and philosophies";
6. "control by indigenous peoples over developments affecting them and their lands, territories and resources will enable them to maintain and strengthen their institutions, cultures and traditions, and to promote their development in accordance with their aspirations and needs"; and
7. "respect for indigenous knowledge, cultures and traditional practices contributes to sustainable and equitable development and proper management of the environment"

(Draft Declaration 1994).

Contributions of Indigenous Peoples to Humanity

It is widely accepted, as stated in the Declaration above, that indigenous peoples have contributed extensively to the diversity and richness of humankind with their astronomical, mathematical, geographical, linguistic, historical, botanical, medical, sociological, anthropological, and many other knowledges. Before Spanish *conquistadors* arrived in Latin America in the early 1500s, Maya, Aztec, and Inca peoples had developed magnificent civilizations in the region. The Maya empire, whose period of greatest development was situated around 250 CE and continued to flourish for over 600 years in Central America on the Yucatan Peninsula, made great achievements in astronomy and mathematics, including the development of an accurate yearly calendar based on 365 solar days and an advanced form of writing. Today Mayan-speaking peoples make up about 45 percent of the population of Guatemala and Belize, and most of them live in poverty. The Incas of southern America, in turn, who controlled a vast territory from northern Ecuador to southern Argentina until the Spanish invasion in 1532, are perhaps best known for their elaborate engineering works and architecture, and for their *quipus*—record-keeping devices based on a complex system of knots tied on different colored strings. Quechua, the official language of the *Tawantinsuyu* or Inca Empire, is spoken today by some 8 million speakers, most of whom inhabit the Andes Mountains of Peru, Bolivia, and Ecuador.

An estimated 75 percent of the world's plant-based pharmaceuticals (including aspirin, digitalis, and quinine) derive from medicinal plants used secularly by native peoples. Many of the world's staple foods—such as corn, potatoes, lentils, peas, sugar cane, garlic, squash, and tomatoes—were first cultivated by indigenous peoples. It is also clearly understood that many indigenous peoples live in greater harmony with the natural environment than do inhabitants of industrialized and consumer societies. Biopiracy, or the misuse and misappropriation of indigenous knowledges and genetic material, is now considered a new form of colonialism. Intellectual and biologic property rights were hotly debated by indigenous leaders from different parts of the world at the 7th International Conference on Ethnobiology, held in Georgia, United States, in October 2000. Rigoberta Menchú, the Guatemalan Nobel Prize winner of 1992, situates the issue very clearly:

The recognition of the ethnic and cultural diversity of this world is an essential element in the progress of humankind. It is urgent that the economic, social, political, and cultural rights of indigenous people become the point of departure for recognizing and respecting important values, such as the concept we possess of the world and our relationship with nature (Rigoberta Menchú 1994).

MARIANA FERREIRA

Further Reading

Boutros-Ghali, Boutros, Secretary General of the UN, "Foreword," in *Voices of Indigenous Peoples: Native People Address the United Nations*, Santa Fe, New Mexico: Clear Light Publications, 1994

Burger, J., editor, *Gaia Atlas of Indigenous Peoples*, London: Gaia Books, 1990

De Villiers, Bertus, editor, *The Rights of Indigenous People: A Quest for Coexistence*, Pretoria: HSRC Publishers, 1997

Draft Declaration on the Rights of Indigenous Peoples, E/CN.4/SUB.2/1994/2/Add.1 (1994)

Greaves, Tom, editor, *Intellectual Property Rights for Indigenous Peoples: A Sourcebook*, Oklahoma City, Oklahoma: Society for Applied Anthropology, 1994

Heintze, Hans-Joachim, "The Protection of Indigenous Peoples under the ILO Convention," in *Amazonia and Siberia: Legal Aspects of the Preservation of the Environment and Development in the Last Open Spaces*, London: Graham & Trotman, 1993

Human Rights Watch, *Human Rights Watch World Report 2001*, New York: Human Rights Watch, 2000. http://www.hrw.org/reports98/publctns.htm

Lucas, Kinto, "Ecuador: Nationwide Protests End with Triumph by Indians," in *Inter Press Service*, (2001)

Maybury-Lewis, David, *Indigenous Peoples, Ethnic Groups, and the State*, Cultural Survival Studies in Ethnicity and Change series, Boston: Allyn and Bacon, 1997

Menchú, Rigoberta, "Preface," in *Voices of Indigenous Peoples: Native People Address the United Nations*, Santa Fe, New Mexico: Clear Light Publications, 1994

United Nations Economic and Social Council's Sub-Commission on the Prevention of Discrimination and Protection of Minorities Working Group on Indigenous Populations, E/CN.4/Sub.2/1983/21/Add.8 (para.369)

United Nations High Commissioner for Human Rights, *The Rights of Indigenous Peoples*, Fact Sheet No. 9, Rev. 1, http://www.unhchr.ch/html/menu5/2/fs9.htm

U.S. Department of Health and Human Services, *Healthy People 2010*, Conference Edition, Vol. 1, Washington DC (2000)

Indonesia

Capsule Summary

Country Name: Republic of Indonesia

Location: Southeastern Asia, archipelago between the Indian Ocean and the Pacific Ocean

Total Population: 234,893,453 (July 2003)

Languages: Bahasa Indonesia (official, modified form of Malay), English, Dutch, local dialects (the most widely spoken of which is Javanese)

Religions: Muslim (88%), Protestant (5%), Roman Catholic (3%), Hindu (2%), Buddhist (1%), other (1%) (1998)

Indonesia is the world's third largest democracy, the world's largest archipelago, the world's fourth most populous, and the world's most ethnically diverse country. It has experienced the vagaries of colonization and dictatorship cloaked in democracy along with peace and alternating flare-ups of ethnic tensions throughout its modern history.

The Republic of Indonesia is a country of nearly 250 million people. It has 13,670 islands that compose 1,948,700 square kilometers (752,400 square miles) from the Pacific Ocean to the Indian Ocean. Its dimensions are 1,100 miles from north to south and 3,200 miles from east to west. Although nearly 7,000 of the islands are uninhabited, Indonesia's four main islands contain the majority of the population. Sumatra, Borneo, Java, the Celebes, and Kalimantan are part of the Greater Sundra Islands in the west; and Bali, the Moluccas, Timor, and Irian Jaya (Papua) in the east are known as the Lesser Sundra Islands.

Indonesia lies in the midst of two major trade routes; consequently, it enjoys a wide variety of ethnic groups in its population makeup. The national motto is "*Bhinneka tunggal ika*" or "Unity in Diversity." The indigenous peoples of Indonesia were the Veddoid of Sri Lanka, the African Negritoid, the Melanesians, the Papuan, and the Australoid. Subsequent migrations brought Caucasian peoples. Today Indonesia has over 300 ethnic groups and 365 languages with more than 300 dialects. The main ethnic groups in present day Indonesia are the Proto Malays and the Deutero-Malays who inhabit various areas of the country.

Indonesia's minority peoples reside in isolated areas of the interior, but their wide-ranging cultures sustain them. In the populous western islands, such as Java and Bali, the inland peoples have retained their ancient social traditions. The coastal peoples are ethnically heterogeneous, especially in Sumatra, southern Celebes, and the Makares. Cultural differences are very widespread in the eastern islands of Indonesia. The Moluccas has a complex culture. The people of Ambon live along the coast, whereas the Alfurs live inland in the mountainous interior. The native Papuans living in Irian Jaya (Papua) have their own cultures; the isolated interior groups use different languages and have histories that differ from their countrymen.

The Chinese account for 6 million people—some 2 percent of the population. Some Chinese have lived in Indonesia for centuries and use the national language and Indonesia surnames. These nearly assimilated, Indonesian-born, largely Christianized Chinese are known as *peranakans*. Forcible assimilation of the *totiks*, foreign-born Chinese loyal to their own cultural traditions, means oppression for this minority group within a minority group. There is occupational diversity among the Chinese in Indonesia but the majority engages in the retail sector throughout the county, especially in Java and Sumatra. The majority of the Chinese shopkeepers are independent, barely sustaining their livelihood, and are completely dependent on their suppliers. The Chinese inhabitants of Kalimantan farm and fish, while the Chinese on Riau Island mine for a living.

Language is neither a major nor a divisive issue in Indonesia. Children in schools are taught in their local dialect initially and by the third school year are taught in *Bahasa*, a modified Malay dialect that has become the national language. However, over 300 languages are spoken throughout Indonesia. These are subdivided according to their geographic location. The two main language groups are Austronesian, which has 16 language groups and is spoken by people of Malay-Polynesian extraction. On Sumatra some 15 language groups are subdivided into numerous dialects. The island of Java uses Javanese, Madures, and Sundanese to communicate. In the Celebes the small numbers of people in the interior have retained eight different languages. The eastern islands have their own languages.

The diverse religious heritage has been and continues to be a strong cultural factor in Indonesia. Five of the major world religions are tolerated in Indonesia under the *Pancasila* policy: Islam, Buddhism, Hinduism, Christianity, and tribal religions live side by side. Islam, which has 88 percent of the population as adherents, was introduced piecemeal by traders from the twelfth century onward. Its followers live in western Java, western Sumatra, the province of Aceh, the southeast of Kalimantan, and in some Lesser Sundra Islands. Traditional Orthodox Islam, which resists both colonial and republican rule, is practiced in some areas, but in other areas it has been diluted by adaptation of aspects of Hinduism and Buddhism that had entered the archipelago centuries earlier. This mixing of faiths has caused some friction between the traditionalist Muslims and the modernist Muslims who are more secular. The traditionalists believe that modernists undermine the authority of the religious leaders. Pagan beliefs are still practiced, especially in the interiors of Sumatra, Kalimantan, Celebes, and Irian Jaya. The majority of Hindu followers live in Bali. Confucian and Buddhism are practiced by the *totik* Chinese. Catholic Christianity is practiced by 3 percent of the population; the Portuguese brought in Roman Catholicism in the sixteenth century. In the seventeenth century the Dutch brought in Calvinist Protestantism, which has 5 percent of the population as followers. Pockets of Indonesian Christians are found throughout the country. Hindus compose 2 percent of the population. Native practices and beliefs have been adapted to all of these religions making them unique.

Indonesian history provides the basis for some of the present day minority/majority conflicts. History has recorded that after the seventh century CE the ancestors of the Indonesians experienced waves of hostilities and periods of peace for centuries. One king after another found reasons to capture, conquer, and settle new territories. Consequently, Hindu and Moslem empires rose and fell prior to white contact. The first whites to settle on the archipelago were the Portuguese, who were removed in 1565; they were allowed to remain on Timor. Spanish and English traders arrived. The Dutch landed in 1596 and, realizing the riches they could extract from the archipelago, established the Dutch East India Company (VOC) in 1602 with a capital investment of 6.5 million florins. It was administered from the Netherlands by seventeen directors. The Dutch East India Company's capital city was at Djakarta, which was renamed Batavia. The minority Dutch, in their zeal for trade, had frequent conflict with the majority native rulers; exploitation of natives was

one concern. The Dutch East India Company went bankrupt and was dissolved in 1799. The area was named the Batavian Republic under Dutch control from 1795 to 1806. The British controlled the archipelago from 1811 to 1816; spheres of influence were finally defined by an 1824 treaty. In 1851 a more liberal administration was initiated, but Indonesian natives had no share in any governance over their affairs. A thirty-year war against the people of Aceh resulted in a Dutch victory that won them dominance over the entire archipelago. However, the *Partai Nasional Indonesia,* a self-government movement, was founded by Achmed Sukarno (1901–1970) in 1927. Mohammed Hattan, who founded the Perhimpuan Indonesia party, also advocated independence. They were exiled by the Dutch government that also denied the People's Council petition for self-government.

World War II intervened. Japan, desperately in need of raw materials and heavily dependent on Indonesian exports to continue their war in the Far East, occupied Indonesia from 1942 to 1945. The Dutch had fully expected to return and control the archipelago after Japan's surrender. However, on August 17, 1945, Sukarno declared independence from the Netherlands by establishing the Republic of Indonesia. Independence was reluctantly granted by the Dutch in 1949 after a fiercely fought war; many Dutch and Chinese left the country. This gave the Indonesians a chance to build their country according to their own ideals. Sukarno became the first president and united Indonesians by legally enacting the humanitarian state policy of *Pancasila,* a unifying secular policy based on nationalism, internationalism, democracy, social justice, and belief in one God. Since Sukarno did not want religions involved in politics, *agama* became the term for official state religious tolerance. Deviation from *Pancasila* was deemed treasonous. Non-religious people were thought to be atheists or communists, considered traitors, and killed.

Sukarno, who had ties with communist countries and later turned to non-alignment, was overthrown by the pro American General Suharto in a military coup on September 30, 1965. He was especially biased against the militant Muslims who had no desire to adhere to *Pancasila.* Suharto kept tight control by playing one Muslim group off against another and by stifling any thought of opposition.

The United Nations recognized Irian Barat as a part of Indonesia in 1969. Portuguese East Timor was incorporated into Indonesia in 1975. The Mass

Organization Law of 1985 was passed to quell the actions of the radical Muslim groups who believed the government should be more Muslim oriented. In 1987 violent opposition by Muslims created tensions; they were the majority but felt as if they were a threatened minority. Regional divisions emerged in predominantly Muslim Aceh regarding Javanese economic and political supremacy.

Independent-minded East Timor finally erupted when extreme violence broke out in 1991. East Timor had gained independence from Portugal in 1975 after much fighting from separatists. The political situation wavered from peace to factional fighting and major strikes. In 1976 the Indonesia military invaded and controlled the island thereafter. In 1981 a United Nations (UN) sponsored resolution allowing the Timorese to decide their political fate was rejected by Suharto. Guerilla forces resisted government military maneuvers, but they could not win against the numerically superior Indonesian army forces and government oppression. Pro Indonesia militants were killed ruthlessly. More than 200,000 people in East Timor died during the 23-year independence struggle. Independence came at great cost.

The three decades of Suharto's strong-arm tactics eventually alienated the people; moreover, his government had become corrupt. The unpopular leader was forced to resign in 1998. His political intrigues with Moslems, who felt used, conversely turned them into extremists. The power vacuum after his departure had severe implications on the archipelago. Suharto's pro Muslim vice president Dr. Bacharuddin J. Habibie became president but he was unpopular. Habibie displaced the long serving Christians of Suharto's cabinet, as well as the Christians in influential sectors, with Muslims. This caused great economic hardships; it deprived the minority Christians of their livelihood. Under Habibie, opportunism and corruption increased significantly. The fragile legal system, elite rivalries, over-population, and economic morass seriously threatened the archipelago; Habibie was given little choice but to resign. He was succeeded by Abdurrahman Wahid who had appointed Sukarno's daughter Megawati Sukarnoputrim as his vice president. However, the volatile situation escalated.

Political problems became economic problems that led to ethic conflict. A powder keg seemed to explode with the result of the elections in Poso, Sulawesie on December 13, 1998. Election results changed the formation of the electoral district's administrative structure when Muslims won the majority of the vote and the Christians had dropped to 39 percent of the vote, rather than the 59 percent they had enjoyed in previous election results. Their grave economic losses led to ethnic tensions. Violence ensued between the majority Muslim and minority Christians due to political upheavals that led to economic instability that in turn led to social dissent. Each group felt threatened and believed they were being marginalized. The consequent ethnic conflict resulted in unspeakable atrocities from both sides. Muslims were roused to frenzy over a minor injury to a youth and took revenge. They besieged a Christian neighborhood, which led to retaliation of 300 Muslims deaths, known as the "Kilo Nine massacre." People on both sides were slaughtered; homes and businesses were burned. To date over 10,000 people have been killed over this conflict.

The Chinese have also suffered as a minority. Usually if there are economic tensions the Chinese are held accountable, especially by the Muslims. After Sukarno's declaration of independence in 1945, most Chinese were deemed Dutch sympathizers and anti-Indonesian capitalists. Many Chinese left the country; those who remained bore the brunt of discontent. The Chinese became targets throughout the archipelago. The Suharto government was responsible for mass killing of Chinese in 1965 and froze diplomatic ties with China. Thousands of Chinese were forced from their homes in Aceh in 1966, and from West Kalimantan in 1967. Suharto's policy in 1967 was to outlaw Chinese elements of Indonesian society. With the "Basic Policy for the Solution of the Chinese Problem," Suharto banned the Chinese language schools and Chinese public rituals and made Chinese newspapers targets for government censure. They were restricted from particular careers, could not be part of the civil service, and had to carry identity cards—unlike the majority who did not face these restrictions. The Chinese were and are treated as second class citizens.

The Suharto government frequently whipped up anti-Chinese agitation to deflect attention from other factors, such as overpopulation, scarce resource allocations, and uncertain economy. On February 9, 1998, for example, Chinese homes were burned, stores were looted, businesses were destroyed, and churches were burned, especially in Flores and Ende. Riots accounted for over 1,000 deaths in Solo and Jakarta in May 1998. Extremist Muslims, the press, and the military fomented these events. The government also played an important role by holding the Chinese responsible for the national financial crisis when the rupiah lost 85 percent of its value. State "dirty trick" campaigns focused on increasing the hostility against the Chinese. Opposition leaders also flame the conflict. The leader of *Muhamadiyah*, a Muslim organization of 29 million members, focused on anti-Chinese rhetoric in his newspaper.

The Congress of Indigenous Peoples was held in March 1999. Representatives listed their grievances and advocated reform. The abolition of some restrictive and discriminatory laws was deemed imperative. The Congress was to meet again in five years.

In 1999 the minority Christians and the majority Muslims clashed in Ambon and the Moluccas. The focus in this conflict was on social dislocation. The transmigrants that appeared in the 1990s displaced the poor locals, threatening their scant livelihoods. At this time a resolution to the problem is unlikely. Tensions rose in May 1999 when the traditional torch ceremony honoring Pattimura, a Christian who had fought the Netherlands' colonial policy, was changed from an honorary Muslim carrying the torch to a Christian holding that honor. This antagonized the Muslim community and led to a wave of 4,500 Muslim Jihad (holy war) warriors moving to the Moluccan Islands to defend their faith. Political involvement occurred when the predominantly Muslim province of North Maluku (Maluku Utara) separated from the old Maluku province in September 1999. An organized pattern of deadly violence had emerged that sparked a civil war between Muslims and Christians; this quickly spread throughout Molucca. Thousands of people lost their homes and Christian churches were burned. More than 7,000 people were killed and 700,000 Moluccans became refugees.

Muslim extremists seemingly wished to destroy Indonesia's political, economic, and civil integrity during the political power vacuum. Some 80,000 Muslims from Yemen, Saudi Arabia, and Afghanistan came from Java to join their fellow Muslims in their struggle against the minority Christians. The Laskar Jihad, or "Holy War Warriors," were based in Java. They fought alongside the disciplined, unified fundamentalist Islamic militia founded in 2000 by Jafar Umar Thalib, an Indonesian cleric whose focus revolved around Muslim well-being. He ordered 5,000 troops to the Moluccan Islands to squelch an alleged Christian-based separatist movement. They classified Christians in the Moluccans as the most dangerous category of non-Muslims—*kafir harbi*—providing the anti-American Laskar Jihad religious reasons to kill Christians. Military hardliners enthusiastically supported Thalib, whose aim evolved into destabilizing the government of President Wahid. Thalib considered Wahid anti-Islamic for oppressing Muslims and protecting Christians. Modern weapons, support from Islamic security forces, and $9,000,000 of embezzled military funding supported Thalib, whose troops were trained by sympathetic officers of the Indonesian National Military—*Tentara Nasional Indonesia* (TNI). This put Christian militias on the defensive; conversions were forced and genital mutilation was enforced. The ultimate goal was with Islamic sharia law as a form of government. The struggle escalated because the government failed to aid the displaced people.

In response the military established a mobile reserve known as the Joint Battalion, or *Yon Gab–Batalyon Gabungan*, which could move wherever their services were required. Often confronted by the Muslim militia, the *Yon Gab* gained a pro Christian bias. The *Yon Gab* also committed atrocities and ultimately was replaced in 2001 by the army's special forces known as *Kopassus*. Indonesia was polarized between Christians and Muslims by late 2001.

An election was held and on July 23, 2001, Megawati Sukarnoputri, the popular daughter of revered President Sukarno, became Indonesia's fifth president. She became politically involved in 1987 with the Indonesian Democratic Party. Reelected in 1993, she was removed in 1996 by Suharto whose strict policies she opposed; this brought her respect from her countrymen. Sukarnoputri then established the Indonesia Democratic Party of Struggle. Her party won the election in 1999 and she ran for the presidency only to be thwarted by Muslim factions that did not want a female leader; they supported her rival, the blind and ailing Abdurraman Wahid. Sukarnoputri was appointed as vice president and Wahid turned the administration over to her. The Indonesian people have since transferred onto her their admiration for her revered father Sukarno. The people are tired of the continuous political and economic instability. To stem some of the problems, Sukarnoputri imposed a civil emergency. When the peace deals that had been made were breached, the fighting decreased somewhat throughout the archipelago but still continues. It will be difficult for her to govern during the unstable times of Indonesia's resurgent democracy, but she has made some headway.

The *Pancasila* ideology of the Republic of Indonesia was the unifying factor that unfortunately has not been as successful as Sukarno would have liked simply because it was not democratic and largely unenforceable. It forced people to do things they did not like nor want and gave them no alternatives. In addition, favoritism, geographic variances that cause economic discrepancies, religious practices that were deemed illegal, the restricting of lives of citizens, the respecting of only some traditions, and the corrupt government and dishonest military partial to the majority group do not indicate democratic ideals. Ethnic rivalry that threatens Indonesia will likely not disappear. As a result its economy continues to suffer due to the secessionist movements and the low level of security in the region. The Per Capita Gross Domestic Product in 2002 was US$3,100.

ANNETTE RICHARDSON

See also **Indonesians**

Further Reading

Aragon, L.V., *Fields of the Lord: Animism, Christian Minorities and State Development*. Honolulu, Hawaii: University of Hawaii Press, 2000

Boxer, C.R., *The Dutch Seaborne Empire: 1600–1800*, London: Hutchinson, 1977

Brooks, Karen, "The Rustle of Ghosts: Bung Karno in the New Order," *Indonesia*, 60 (October 1995)

Coppel, Charles A., *Indonesian Chinese in Crisis*, Kuala Lampur: Oxford University Press, 1983

Elson, Robert E., *Suharto: A Political Biography*, Cambridge: Cambridge University Press, 2001

Fisher, Frederick, *Indonesia*, Milwaukee, Wisconsin: Gareth Stevens Publishing, 2000

Hanifah Abu. *Tales of a Revolution*. Sydney, Australia: Angus and Robertson, 1972

"Indonesia: The War in Aceh," New York: Human Rights Watch, 2001

Labrousse, Pierre, "The Second Life of Bung Karno: Analysis of the Myth (1978–1981)," *Indonesia*, 57, (April 1993)

Legge, John D., *Sukarno: A Political Biography*, Sydney: Allen & Unwin, 1985

McBeth, John, and Oren Murphy, "Bloodbath," *Far Eastern Economic Review*, July 6, 2000

McLeod, Ross H., *Indonesia Assessment 1994: Finance as a Key Sector in Indonesia's Development*, Canberra and Singapore: Australian National University; Institute of Southeast Asian Studies, 1995

Palmier, Leslie, *Understanding Indonesia*, Aldershot, United Kingdom: Gower, 1985

Ricklefs, M.C., *A History of Modern Indonesia Since c.1300*, 2nd edition, Stanford, California: Stanford University Press, 1993

Schama, Simon, *The Embarrassment of Riches: An Interpretation of Dutch Culture in the Golden Age*. London: Fontana Press, 1988

Silk, Mark, "Religion in the News," *Wars of Religion*, 3, no. 1 (Spring 2000)

Indonesians

Capsule Summary

Location: Southeast Asia, between the Indian Ocean and the Pacific Ocean

Total Population: 234,893,453 (July 2003)

Languages: Bahasa Indonesia (official, modified form of Malay), English, Dutch, and a number of local dialects (most widely spoken of which is Javanese)

Religions: Mainly Muslims, but also Protestants, Roman Catholics, Hindus, Buddhists, and others

Indonesians are the people of Indonesia, which is located in Southeast Asia between the Indian Ocean and the Pacific Ocean. The country is the largest archipelago in the world with 17,000 islands, among which 6,000 are inhabited. The most important feature can be pointed out as the nation's multiethnicity. There coexist diverse ethnic groups, several religions, and numerous spoken languages. During the seventeenth through the first half of the twentieth centuries, Indonesia was colonized by Europeans and the Japanese until it finally gained independence in 1949. While the nation has made tremendous economic and social development since then, it continues to face political difficulties, including the ones that involve ethnic tensions.

Multiethnic Society

Indonesians are composed of many ethnic groups. Javanese is the largest group among them (45 percent), followed by Sundanese (14 percent), Madurese (7.5 percent), and coastal Malays (7.5 percent). Still other 26 percent consist of numerous minority groups suggesting the ethnic diversity of Indonesia.

Approximately 88 percent of Indonesians are Muslims, although they are ethnically diverse. Religious minorities are: Protestants (5 percent), Roman Catholics (3 percent), Hindus (2 percent), Buddhists (1 percent), and others such as indigenous beliefs (1 percent).

The official language of Indonesia is Bahasa Indonesia, which is a modified form of Malay, but there are 669 other languages and dialects spoken. Languages with 1 million or more speakers in estimated numerical order are: Javanese (70 million), Sundanese (25 million), Malay (10 million), Madurese (9 million), Minangkabau (7.5 million), Balinese (3 million), Bugisnese (2.5 million), Acehnese (2.2 million), Toba Batak (2 million), Banjarese (1.8 million), Makassarese (1.5 million), Sasak (1.5 million), Lampung (1.5 million), Dairi Batak (1.2 million), and Rejang (1 million).

It is often regarded that Bahasa Indonesia is the primary cultural feature of the twentieth century history of the nation. For centuries Malay was spoken as a lingua franca among many peoples of the archipelago. In 1928 during Indonesia's earlier struggle for independence, nationalists used the term Bahasa Indonesia and it became a symbol of national unity. Today Bahasa Indonesia is not only the language used at the government, schools, and media, but also for most Indonesians it is the primary or secondary spoken language.

History

Early in the Christian period, societies in the archipelago were largely influenced by the Indian civilization brought into by Indian merchants and Buddhist and Hindu monks. By the eighth and ninth centuries, kingdoms with close Indian connections arose in Sumatra and Java. Thrived in Sumatra was a Buddhist kingdom, Sri Vijaya, which became the dominant power during the seventh to thirteenth centuries until a Hindu kingdom of Majapahit replaced the historical significance in the thirteenth century. Islamic influence gradually penetrated in Indonesia starting the next century, and by the end of the sixteenth century Islam was more prevalent than Buddhism or Hindu. Indonesia at this time was already a hearth of multiple cultures where Muslim, Buddhist, Hindu, and indigenous values peacefully coexisted.

From the sixteenth to the mid-twentieth centuries was the era of European intrusions. The first to arrive was the Portuguese (1511), and the Dutch (1596) and the British (1600) followed. Their national interest was a profitable trade in spices and other products from Indonesia. The Netherlands ousted Portugal by 1610 allowing them to retain only eastern Timor and defeated Britain in a series of Anglo-Dutch conflicts (1610–23).

The Netherlands established the Dutch United East India Company (VOC), which dominated in spice trades until its bankruptcy in 1799. The Dutch government then took over the lucrative business and eventually held control in politics and military affairs in Indonesia by the early twentieth century. Many locals were exploited in their rich natural resources and soon found themselves in poverty and overpopulation. Further the colonizer curved out the geographical territories of today's Indonesia.

Independence movement began in the early twentieth century when nationalists arouse seeking national unity. The Indonesian Communist Party (PKI) was formed in 1920, and the Indonesian Nationalist Party (PNI) in 1927 under the leadership of Sukarno (1901–70).

In 1942 Japan drove out the Dutch and occupied Indonesia returning some levels of opportunities for political and military participation to the islanders in exchange of natural resources necessary to pursue its war effort. Two days after Japan's surrender to the Allies, Skarno and Mohammad Hatta (1902–80), another nationalist leader, proclaimed independence on August 17, 1945 (now a national holiday). Indonesia formally became independent from the Netherlands on December 27, 1949, following the National Revolution (1945–1949) against the Dutch. Skarno was elected president and Hatta became a premier.

Skarno led parliamentary democracy during the early 1950s and later replaced it with a policy called Guided Democracy from 1959 to 1965. Although he was able to unite diverse peoples and regions under his government and in one language, his regime was characterized by injustice and corruption and came to an end with a coup d'état led by General Suharto on September 30, 1965. Thousands of Communists were executed, and as many as 750,000 people altogether may have died during the revolt that lasted for three months.

Suharto's centralized regime was tightly guarded by the Armed Forces of the Republic of Indonesia (ABRI). Suharto banned the PKI, restored close relationship with western nations and Japan (who provided large packages of economic assistance), reentered the United Nations in 1966, and actively participated in founding the Association of Southeast Asian Nations (ASEAN) in 1967. Domestically he developed the standard of living of a majority of the population, and in the 1970s and 1980s the number of the poor decreased. He was reelected as president many times (1968, 1973, 1978, 1983, 1988, 1993, and 1998) and often considered as a source of the nation's order and stable development. Yet his regime received continuing international criticism, especially in the early 1990s, due to human rights violations concerning New Guinea (Irian Jaya) and East Timor. At home in 1997 government corruption (which became increasingly apparent) and economic upheaval led Suharto to step down in May 1998. In October 1999 Abdurrahman Wahid became the first democratically elected president and Megawati Sukarnoputri, the daughter of Sukarno, became a vice president.

Indonesians continue to deal with perplexing issues centered on multiethnicity today. While former Portuguese colony East Timor successfully proclaimed independence after a provincial referendum on August 30, 1999 (although its independence status is not yet formally established), the question of autonomy or independence in such regions as Aceh and Irian Jaya is recently rising more than ever and has gained international attention as well.

AI HATTORI

See also **Indonesia**

Further Reading

Baker, Richard W., editor, *Indonesia: The Challenge of Change*, New York: St. Martin's Press, 1999

Emmerson, Donald K., editor, *Indonesia beyond Suharto: Polity Economy Society Tansition*, Armonk, New York and London: M.E. Sharpe, 1999

Hitchcock, Michael, and Victor T. King, editors, *Images of Malay-Indonesian Identity*, Kuala Lumpur, New York, and Oxford: Oxford University Press, 1997

Just, Peter, *Dou Donggo Justice: Conflict and Morality in an Indonesian Society*, Lanha, Maryland and Oxford: Rowman & Littlefield, 2001

Kipp, Rita Smith, *Dissociated Identities: Ethnicity, Religion, and Class in an Indonesian Society*, Ann Arbor: University of Michigan Press, 1993

Lev, Daniel S., and Ruth McVey, editors, *Making Indonesia*, Ithaca, New York: Southeast Asia Program, Cornell University, 1999

Manning, Chris, and Peter Van Diermen, editors, *Indonesia in Transition: Social Aspects of Reformasi and Crisis*, London and New York: Zen Books, 2000

Schiller, Jim, and Barbara Martin-Schiller, editors, *Imagining Indonesia: Cultural Politics and Political Culture*, Athens, Ohio: Ohio University Center for International Studies, 1997

Tanter, Richard, Mark Selden, and Stephen R. Shalom, *Bitter Flowers, Sweet Flowers: East Timor, Indonesia, and the World Community*, Lanham, Maryland: Rowman & Littlefield, 2001

Watson, C.W., *Of Self and Nation: Autobiography and the Representation of Modern Indonesia*, Honolulu: University of Hawaii Press, 2000

Integration

The word *integration* derives from the Latin *integrare*, which means "to renew" or "to make a whole." Integration thus means the action of entering a part into a whole. Across a range of disciplines, such as economy or law, many different meanings can be found. In sociology the notion also has an ambiguous meaning. In general a part or a group inserts into a whole (a greater social collectivity) but to different degrees and in a different manner according to the fields. For the American sociologist Talcott Parsons integration is one of the functions of a social system, maintaining the coordination of its different fractions. In psychology integration is expressed by the sum of interactions of members, which provoke a feeling of identification with the group and its values. A difficulty emerges from linking these integrations because each actor may belong to several differing groups. In political science integration denotes the degree of cohesion of the whole that is being measured. Examples might be the socialization of children, the integration of migrants, or a new nation; it may be a consensus of opinions or the participation of citizens in the life of the collectivity.

Integration functions differently for different processes, for example, the integration of an economic migrant or the integration of a disabled person. We speak of somebody who is socially integrated and either successfully or poorly integrated. A pupil must integrate into a classroom culture, a laborer into a factory environment, a tenant into a house community. In each of these instances, the classroom, the factory, and the housing community represent larger host cultures. An individual is considered as being capable or incapable of integrating in varying degrees, something that both the individual and the group/culture may have different ways of measuring and evaluating.

There is a problem or process of integration when different ethnic groups meet. Problems of integration may even emerge or erupt in highly diversified societies although they are ethnically homogenous. Ruling groups are often invested in the integration of their particular society and require or ask poorly integrated groups to conform to the majority culture and norms. It is insufficient for individual actors or groups to desire integration alone; the success of the process is affected by a range of societal factors and pressures that can either inhibit or enhance a subject's integration.

Several societal subsystems that favor integration exist, for instance, institutions such as schools or common law. In other subsystems despite the political intention to integrate, segregation is favored; for example, in situations of housing where prosperous groups move into segregated districts, or in the labor market where particular jobs are destined to different classes or groups of people.

Theories of Integration

A general theory of integration ought to include two topics: (1) an explication of the choice of assimilative actions from given dispositions and conditions, and (2) an explanation of the creation of assimilative dispositions and conditions. The attempt to ascertain general rules of integration is based on two assumptions. First, that it is possible to find typical phases for migrants based on fixed sequences of adaptation, and second, that a given situation of culture change can be predicted. Three models of integration theory exist: the economic-ecological sequence, the generation sequence, and race-relations-cycles.

Economic-Ecological Sequence Model

Economic-ecological sequence models explain and rely on a temporal succession of phases through which migrants pass before complete integration in the host society. The simplest models suggest, for instance, the first phase of a resettlement as finding a job and living accommodations; a second phase of reestablishment as a successful adaptation in a satisfactory job, family

reunion, and an acceptable social network in the host society, and a third phase as the creation of an identification within the host-system.

Other models integrate demands and reactions of people from the host-society: In a first phase a demand for laborers exists in industry attracting potential workers who then enter at the lowest ranks or class of the society. Their introduction might spur discrimination, racism, and xenophobia among the upper or higher status classes or groups. In a second phase during periods of economic crises, social conflicts can potentially occur, followed by public campaigns that aim to cease or slow immigration, as migrant workers represent an economic threat to majority communities. In a third phase during an economic upturn, these campaigns more commonly cease or do not exist, and migrants already present integrate gradually (and often silently). During a fourth phase, xenophobic tendencies reappear when migrants challenge the hierarchy by trying to attain higher status positions or other economic or social advantages. In economic-ecological sequence models, economic conditions are the organizing factors that allow for the possibility of integration in the host-society.

British sociologists John Rex and Robert Moore have developed the following model for migrants of color that they explicated in a study conducted in Birmingham, England: In a first phase the immigrant is cut off from contacts with one's society of origin and has not yet integrated in the social system of the host society. One's relation with the host society is limited to job and related contacts. In a second phase the immigrant creates primary group relations with other migrants from the same ethnic group; one reproduces some of the native habits and can thus "live in the colony." In a third phase the immigrant is integrated as a legal citizen and begins to foster other contractual relations to other groups of the host society, without leaving one's ethnic colony. Finally a form of incorporation is attained. The importance of the ethnic group is thus relinquished for what is often a struggle to maintain work, lifestyle, and other aspects of membership in the host culture.

Generation Sequence Model

In the 1920s and 1930s models of assimilation based on generation cycles were developed in the United States. According to these models the immigrants of the first generation assume or assimilate only those actions of the native population that are necessary for the satisfaction of their basic needs. They form homogeneous ethnic groups with an extended system of ethnic institutions. All of their informal social relations are limited to the appropriate ethnic unit or culture. On the other hand the subjectivity of the immigrant is protected against the consequences of cultural shock (e.g., reactions of anomy, anxiety, or suicide). The second generation then experiences the cultural conflict: on the one hand they are still socialized in the cultural traditions of their parents (the first generation); on the other hand, they harbor aspirations and abilities that emerged in relation to their role in the host society. In the third generation the culture of origin is relinquished as these descendants of migrants improve their status and standing in the culture of the host society, even if some remnants of their ethnic culture persist.

This three-generation model of assimilation has been critiqued by some sociologists who argue not only that successive generations will not necessarily desire the same things from the host culture (primarily greater degrees of assimilation), but also that the host society is often characterized by a closed status system that does not permit social mobility among third-generation migrants. In 1963 Nathan Glazer and Daniel Moynihan developed a three-phase model that considered such factors. The first phase of Glazer and Moynihan's assimilation cycle is characterized by the creation of ethnic associations among the first generation—these can be related to space, profession, and status—marking the beginning of linguistic and cultural integration. In the second phase of the cycle a transformation of the ethnic group occurs in which individuals and the group act as representatives of the larger ethnicity in political conflicts. In this way ethnic identification is again compatible with cultural and structural assimilation, because an arena for dealing with confrontation has emerged. In the third phase a gradual disappearance of ethnic groups in a system differentiated by class, race, and religion takes place. Ethnic membership becomes a private rather than a public matter.

Race-Relations-Cycles

Sociological proponents of the models of race-relations-cycles claim to describe complete enumerations of phases of integration lived by ethnic groups. The "human ecology" model from Robert E. Park, who established the Chicago School of Sociology, is the best known of this type. Using empirical research Park described assimilation as a chain of typical patterns of interaction among ethnic groups. He identified general categories of relations of interaction: *contact*, *competition*, *accommodation*, and *assimilation*. In his analyses of human communities he viewed these processes as progressive and irreversible, borrowing on a biological or ecological model in which society functions like an organism. Factors such as regulations and restrictions placed on immigrants and other racial barriers might slow down and even halt the process of integration, but according to Park the process would not change direction or reverse.

In a race-relations-cycle model the *contact* phase is a direct consequence of migration and is characterized by exploratory contacts. An individual seeking satisfaction in work and life becomes aware of and engages in competition with others for both jobs and housing. In this second *competition* phase, conflicts emerge when the immigrant does not restrict oneself to resources offered by the native population. Discrimination may occur. As a result of these experiences the individual either adapts to the situation or else rescinds certain claims. Reciprocal relations are constructed that involve a retreat from professional aspirations for the powerless group, particular social spaces, and the acceptance of lower class positions. In the *accommodation* phase specific ethnic job markets as well as spatial segregation are created; these become self-evident and legitimate structures in the mind of the migrant. *Assimilation*, as a fourth phase, occurs as the ethnic group begins to lose particular characteristics, behaviors, and other signifiers as ethnic differentiation slowly disappears.

Robert Park and Ernest Burgess first defined *social distance* as the tendency to approach or withdraw from a racial group. Emory Bogardus conceptualized a scale that could measure social distance empirically and applied his research to long-term studies of Chinese, Japanese, and Philippine immigrants. His Bogardus Ethnic (or Social) Distance Scale, developed in the 1920s, asks people how willing they would be to interact with various racial and ethnic groups in specified social situations. Bogardus's seven-phase model of race relations emphasizes reactions that occur within the host society (1929/1930). At first the immigrant is considered with curiosity; one may be perceived as odd or outside the norm. Next the immigrant's difficult situation is recognized by members of the host group. The immigrant's economic utility in reproduction and willingness to take low-status jobs (i.e., in the factory) is recognized. According to Bogardus, because of the given job possibilities, chain migration begins among the outcast group. He calls this phase "economic welcome." Next, as a reaction to growing migrations, industrial and social antagonisms (prejudice and xenophobic tendencies) erupt in reaction to fears of competition in certain fields. A particular case of antagonism is the resistance to mixed neighborhoods. These developments contribute to the creation of immigration legislation that attempts to place restrictions (work and residence) upon immigrants. Political campaigns against migrants are organized to assure the political, economic, or social hegemony of the host country. Such immigration policies are often recognized as discriminating and a slowing down of original conflicts is introduced. Bogardus finally asserts that this model functions cyclically, eventually presenting the second generation with similar difficulties.

Critics of the various race-relations-cycle models argued that the suggested sequences are neither general, nor progressive, nor irreversible. These sequences can end in a permanent conflict or a subordination of a group. According to Hartmut Esser (1980) the main weakness of these theories is that the models reveal a mechanical integration and do not show that these are in reality consequences of complex unique processes. Esser stresses that the statement about the final assimilation of migrants signifies that authors of these theories share an ideology of equal opportunity that suggests a complete incorporation of ethnic groups in the core culture of the host society, whereas assimilation is most often a process of attributing the lowest status group of a society to migrants.

Theories of Assimilation

Beside cycle models, theoretical approaches are used to analyze the multiple appearances of integration factors. One of these approaches is Ronald Taft's, who underlines that each analysis of the integration process must evaluate processes of re-socialization and change among reference groups and identity (1966). According to Taft, a theory of assimilation should be a particular case of a more general theory of attitude change. It would thus be applicable to many situations that show similar processes of change. Taft suggests, for instance, religious or political conversions, marriage, and other important events of the life cycle.

Taft discussed five facets of integration conditions: (1) cultural knowledge and capacity, (2) social interaction including social acceptance, (3) interpersonal contacts and membership identification, (4) social and emotional identification, and (5) conformity to group norms related to values, habits, and the outward appearance. Furthermore, he distinguished several complementary aspects: (1) the motivation of the individual who seeks to attain certain conditions, (2) a set of behaviors manifesting the effort to attain a situation, and (3) the perception of and actual completion of the social situation. The conditions of final integration are summarized by Taft in three aspects: First, positive and negative attitudes toward assimilation are examined among the immigrant, one's ethnic group, and the host system. Second, the manner of the envisaged assimilation is decisive. Taft presumes that an orientation develops that is favorable to integration. Social distance to the immigrant group, their visibility (i.e., through evident skin color, clothing, etc.), and the process of admission into the host society play key roles. Finally, factors such as intelligence, adaptability, tolerance, and one's motivation toward integration are important.

The significance of Taft's approach lies in his considering the integration process as mutually influenced by actions, experience, and learning; direction, range, and the intensity of an individual's process of integration depends upon subjective characteristics and environment.

Arnold Rose's theory of the acceptance of migrants relies on concrete, analyzable factors, namely the openness and accessibility of "passing through" the host system. In this context Rose considers how laws, political practices of immigration, attitudes and distance of the population of the host society, and the existence of programs such as language courses and aid for the new immigrant function. The second condition for acceptance is the relationship of the immigrants to their context of origin, such as relatives who must be considered as "costs" of efforts to settle definitely in the host country. The third condition is the importance of the cultural resemblance between systems of emigration and immigration. Factors such as religion, language, national character, and difference between countryside and urban area are here evoked. Similar to Richard Thurnwald, whose theories revolved around transformative processes of cultural change, Rose developed his approach by taking account of the motivations of migrants that induce opportunities and barriers to integration as characteristics of each system of integration.

A model that is equally oriented to factors such as the individual and one's environment is that of Jercy Zubrzycki, who analyzed the integration of Polish immigrants in Great Britain (1956). He distinguished three different links between immigrants and host society: *conflict*, *accommodation*, and *assimilation*. He defined two factors necessary for an adjustment: (1) already existing dispositions to adaptation and integration on the side of immigrants, and (2) attitudes of members of the host society for whom integration is desired or not undesired. According to Zubrzycki, motivation is of particular importance among the dispositions of adaptation. Motivation is defined by the conditions of migration—voluntary and economic migrants are more easily motivated to attempt integration than displaced persons or persons who migrate for social reasons. Characteristics of host societies, such as its level of social mobility and accessibility, cultural similarity to the immigrant's country of origin, and so forth, influence motivation. Moreover, the capacity to accept different roles and an orientation in the direction of the future favor the adaptation of immigrants. Related to characteristics of the host society are cultural similarities in language, religion, historical tradition, political and emotional proximities between the immigrant and host social systems, absence of xenophobic tendencies, and immigration politics (which favor integration).

From these aforementioned theories it becomes evident that intentions, capacities, opportunities, and barriers relating to persons and environments permit (or oppose) a process of integration. According to these approaches, no single factor is attributed an overall influence, and there exists no irreversible sequence of integration.

Conclusion

Clearly integration can function as a stabilizing or destabilizing force within modern, complex societies. The variables described in theories of integration help locate and apply institutional solutions for the problems of integration. Because migration is generally voluntary, migrants seek jobs and money in sectors that are not attractive to the native population or that require tasks that the native population is not willing to assume. These possibilities permit an optimal use of the migrants' capacities without creating conflicts (i.e., there exists little if any competition for this type of work in the host society). In these situations conflicts are minor and based on personal criteria so that protest movements are not likely. Moreover, ethnic solidarity among the native population creates a situation where societal conflicts are rare. Migration and integration thus allow societal structures to appear stable. A condition of the pursuit of this situation is the maintenance of neither a complete assimilation nor an ethnic stratification that would resemble a caste. Immigration of successive groups will thus lead to mobility of its members, which does not exclude individual mobility but differs according to groups.

ULRIKE SCHUERKENS

See also **Equal Opportunity, Ethnic Conflict, Melting Pot vs. Ethnic Stew, Migrations, Multiculturalism, Multiethnic State, Population Shifts, Racism**

Further Reading

Bogardus, Emeroy S., "A Race Relations Cycle," *American Journal of Sociology*, 35, (1929/1930)

Dewitte, Philippe, editor, *Immigration etIintégration: L'état des Savoirs*, Paris: Ed. de la Découverte, 1999

Eisenstadt, Shmuel N., *The Absorption of Immigrants, a Comparative Study Based Mainly on the Jewish Community in Palestine and the State of Israel*, London: Routledge & Kegan Paul, 1954

Esser, Hartmut, *Aspekte der Wanderungssoziologie, Assimilation und Integration von Wanderern, Ethnischen Gruppen und Minderheiten: Eine Handlungstheoretische Analyse*, Darmstadt, Neuwied: Luchterhand, 1980

Glazer, Nathan, "The Integration of American Immigrants," in *Law and Contemporary Problems*, 21 (1956)

Glazer, Nathan, and Daniel P. Moynihan, *Beyond the Melting Pot: The Negroes, Puerto Ricans, Jews, Italians and Irish of New York City*, Cambridge, Massachusetts, London: M.I.T. Press, 1963

Gordon, Milton M., "Toward a General Theory of Racial and Ethnic Group Relations," in *Ethnicity, Theory and Experience*, edited by Nathan Glazer and Daniel Moynihan, Cambridge, Massachusetts, London: Harvard University Press, 1975

Levine, Donald N., "Integration. I. Cultural Integration," in *International Encyclopedia of the Social Sciences*, Vol. 7, New York, Toronto: MacMillan, 1968

Lockwood, David, "Social Integration and System Integration", in *Explorations in Social Change*, edited by George K. Zollschan and Walter Hirsch, London: Routledge & K. Paul, 1964

Park, Robert E., *Race and Culture*, Glencoe, Illinois: Free Press, 1950

Rex, John, and Robert Moore, *Race, Community and Conflict: A Study of Sparkbrook*, London: Oxford University Press, 1967

Taft, Ronald, *From Stranger to Citizen: A survey of Studies of Immigrant Assimilation in Western Australia*, London: Tavistock Publishing, 1966

Weinberg, Abraham A., "Acculturation and Integration of Migrants," in *International Social Science Bulletin*, 5 (1953)

Zubrzycki, Jercy, *Polish Immigrants in Britain: A Study of Adjustment*, The Hague: M. Nijhoff, 1956

International Conventions

Minority rights, like other human rights, require legal protection. The laws can be enacted only by the governments of sovereign states, not by international organizations. The function of the latter is to help the representatives of states to agree on common principles and to promise one another that they will give effect to these. This they do by entering into treaties. If two states make a treaty to regulate the boundary between their territories, each party to the agreement will watch to see that the other party fulfills its promises. When there are over 150 parties to an international human rights treaty, some of them being micro-states with small populations, it is impracticable for each of them to check up on every one of the others. So United Nations (UN) human rights treaties provide for the states parties to elect a treaty-monitoring body to do this work for them.

The process of treaty-making has often started with states agreeing, at meetings under the auspices of the UN, upon principles which have then been embodied in a declaration. The best known of these is the Universal Declaration of Human Rights (1948). The next step has been to translate the declaration into legal language (in treaty form), such that states, by ratifying it, can promise one another that they will observe its provisions. Some proposals for conventions have been discussed first in the Sub-Commission on the Promotion and Protection of Human Rights (*q.v.*), and then have moved through a sequence of bodies until, widespread agreement having been achieved, they have been submitted to the UN General Assembly; first in the form of a declaration, and then, if sufficient support has been forthcoming, as a covenant or convention.

Early in 1960 both the Sub-Commission and the Commission on Human Rights noted with deep concern that during the previous year there had been a series of attacks on Jewish burial grounds and places of worship in several European countries, but particularly in what was then the Federal Republic of Germany. The Sub-Commission described them as manifestations of anti-Semitism. The General Assembly, which was also concerned about racial discrimination in non-self-governing territories, con-

demned "all manifestations and practices of racial, religious and national hatred." About the same time, since some African delegations were calling for a convention against racial discrimination, the Assembly considered the possibility of a convention against both racial and religious discrimination. It later decided in favor of a declaration against racial discrimination, which might later be followed by a convention, and in favor of a separate declaration on religious discrimination. Thus it was that the Sub-Commission prepared the first draft of what came to be the UN Declaration on the Elimination of All Forms of Racial Discrimination (1963), later supplemented or superseded by the International Convention on the Elimination of All Forms of Racial Discrimination (1965). Neither of these texts makes specific mention of anti-Semitism.

The adoption of a separate convention was not the most logical course because it had been agreed in 1961 that the International Covenant on Civil and Political Rights (which was nearly ready) would provide in Article 26 that:

All persons are equal before the law and are entitled without any discrimination to the equal protection of the law. In this respect the law shall prohibit and discrimination and guarantee to all persons equal and effective protection against discrimination on any ground such as race, colour, sex, language, religion, political or other opinion, national or social origin, property, birth or other status.

It would have been possible to extend the scope of such provisions in the Covenant by adopting additional protocols to amplify the protections against the various forms of discrimination (like racial discrimination), but delegations wanted to expedite action against what were called the racist regimes in southern Africa and thought a separate convention the best instrument for this.

The International Convention on the Elimination of All Forms of Racial Discrimination nowhere uses the word "minority," but it is one of the most important legal instruments for protecting minority rights. In its first article it defines racial discrimination, for the purposes of the Convention, as:

Any distinction, exclusion or preference based on race, colour, descent, or national or ethnic origin which has the purpose or effect of nullifying or impairing the recognition, enjoyment or exercise, on an equal footing, of human rights and fundamental freedoms in the political, economic, social, cultural or any other field of public life.

Articles 2 through 7 lay down the obligations of states' parties to the Convention. Articles 8 through 16 establish the arrangements for monitoring fulfillment of the obligations for the regulation of inter-state disputes, the consideration of individual complaints, and the application to non-self-governing territories. Articles 17 through 25 include the customary final clauses covering signature, ratification, denunciation, reservations, and so forth.

The Convention introduced a new procedure for implementation of its provisions. States parties undertook to submit reports on what they had done to fulfill their obligations, have these reports examined by a committee of 18 independent experts (whom they themselves elected), which then reported to the General Assembly. Sovereign states had never before subjected themselves to such a discipline. One commentator (Buergenthal 1977, 118) believed that the states expected the Committee would be no more than a timid depository of their self-serving reports, and that they were unprepared when they found (in the space of a very few years) that the Committee's reports could be a serious embarrassment.

Although the Convention states that the Committee's reports shall be "based on the examination of the reports and information received from the States Parties," it has found ways of reporting on the implementation of the Convention in states whose reports are seriously overdue and of reporting—if necessary to the Security Council—on situations in which it believes that action is required in order to prevent racial discrimination. The Committee normally meets annually for two three-week sessions.

At the end of the year 2000, 156 states were parties to the Convention. This figure may be compared with that of 189 UN member states. Thirty states had made a declaration permitting the Committee to receive and consider complaints from individuals or groups within their jurisdiction who claimed that their states had failed to provide them with the promised protections. Seventeen opinions on such complaints had been adopted. In 2000 the Committee reported on its consideration of reports from 24 states, evaluating the effectiveness of measures for the protection from racial or ethnic discrimination of a great variety of minorities. In the same year it issued opinions on three complaints (brought against Denmark, Australia, and the Slovak Republic). It also conducted a thematic discussion on the question of discrimination against Roma minorities (primarily in Europe), and adopted General Recommendation XXVII, which includes 46 recommendations to states about measures to be taken to protect the rights of Roma in the fields of personal security, education, living conditions, media, and participation in public life.

The rights of members of minorities to be free from racial discrimination in the field of employment are also protected by conventions adopted by the International Labour Organization (ILO), notably Convention 111 on Employment and Occupation. ILO Convention 169 concerning Indigenous and Tribal Peoples in Independent Territories (discussed in another entry) is also to be noted.

MICHAEL BANTON

See also **Sub-Commission: Promotion and Protection of Human Rights; United Nations and Minorities**

Further Reading

Banton, Michael, *International Action Against Racial Discrimination*, Oxford: Clarendon Press, 1996

———, *Combating Racial Discrimination: The UN and Member States*, London: Minority Rights International, 2000

Buergenthal, Thomas, "Implementing the UN Racial Convention," *Texas International Law Journal*, 12 (1977)

International Indian Treaty Council (IITC)

The International Indian Treaty Council (IITC) originated in the United States, where it still has its main base. It brings together indigenous peoples from across the Americas and the Pacific to address issues of local and global concern. Most of the issues it deals with have to do with the sovereignty and self-determination of indigenous peoples, or the recognition and protection of their rights, traditional cultures, and sacred lands. The IITC supports grassroots efforts to those ends by offering training, legal advice, and technical assistance. In Spanish it is the *Consejo Internacional de Tratados Indios* (CITI), a name that often appears in print. The American Indian Movement (AIM) formed the IITC in 1974 to serve as its diplomatic arm. It attained international stature in 1977. That is when the United Nations (UN) recognized it as a non-governmental organization (NGO) with consultative status to the Economic and Social Council (ECOSOC). It was the first organization of its kind so recognized by the UN. Since its inception the IITC has used a wide range of local, national, and international channels to promote and defend the rights and sovereignty of indigenous peoples. It has also worked within the UN to set an international standard for indigenous rights. A lot of work remains, but the IITC's path-breaking efforts so far have benefited peoples around the world.

Background

The rights and sovereignty of indigenous peoples have been under attack since Europeans first set foot on their lands. After World War II, the U.S. government set up the Indian Claims Commission to resolve land claims that had arisen out of the treaties it made with Indian peoples and then broke. The Claims Commission did not rule on the legality of the land transfers; it only offered to pay the Indians for the lands they had lost. By settling the claims in this way, it cleared title to vast tracts of land. While this satisfied non-Indian (mainly corporate) interests, it ignored the Indians' inherent treaty rights as recognized under U.S. and international law. The government also renewed its assault on Indian community life and cultures with

added vigor. This led to two policies designed to erase their cultural distinctiveness and speed their absorption into mainstream society. Social scientists refer to this process as forced assimilation. One of the policies was relocation, and the other was termination. Relocation often moved Indians from their reservation homes to distant cities. It uprooted them culturally as well as physically. Termination withdrew the federal recognition of certain Indian peoples. As a result their reservations ceased to exist and the government no longer met its treaty obligations to them. This deprived them of many of the resources upon which they depended and left them destitute.

By the time the Civil Rights Movement got under way in the 1960s, Indians were angry and ready to act. Soon the Red Power Movement took shape, with AIM at its forefront. A series of events in the early 1970s got intense media coverage. One was the Trail of Broken Treaties caravan, which traveled to Washington DC in 1972 to deliver a 20-Point Indian Manifesto to the president. It ended with the occupation of the Bureau of Indian Affairs building. Another unfolded the next year on the Lakota (Sioux) reservations of South Dakota. It resulted in a violent 71-day stand-off between AIM and heavily armed federal agents at Wounded Knee. Less spectacular forms of direct action also took place during this period. While the media coverage raised public awareness, it did little to help restore Indian lands and treaty rights.

AIM convened a conference on the Standing Rock Reservation in South Dakota in 1974. Its purpose was to explore what Indians could do about their treaty rights and lands. Over 5000 representatives from 97 indigenous nations attended the week-long gathering. It was to become the inaugural meeting of the IITC. After days of discussion and guidance from spiritual leaders and elders, the group decided to take its case to the UN. They produced The Declaration of Continuing Independence. This document created the IITC and defined its diplomatic role. Since a large number of those present were Lakotas (Sioux), the declaration highlighted matters of particular concern to them. One was the burning issue of the Black Hills. The United States had taken these sacred lands from the Lakotas in 1877 in violation of a treaty they had signed at Fort Laramie in 1868. The declaration also recognized the Provisional Government of the Independent Oglala Nation, which traditional leaders had set up under the provisions of that same treaty. These two themes, treaty rights and sovereignty, have shaped the work of the IITC.

The IITC set up office on the UN Plaza in New York under the leadership of Jimmie Durham, a Cherokee activist. It also petitioned the UN for recognition as an NGO with consultative status to ECOSOC. While waiting for the UN's decision, it got ready to enter the international arena. Its strategy included making important contacts, sending people to international conferences, and sponsoring a seminar on international law for Indian leaders. With the problem of discrimination against indigenous peoples being a relatively new UN concern, the IITC could not have timed its request better. The UN granted it NGO status in 1977. This paved the way for other indigenous organizations to petition for the same. By 1981 the World Council of Indigenous Peoples (WCIP) and the Indian Law Resource Center had joined the IITC. Many others soon followed, including some that had originally relied on the IITC.

International Standard Setting

The IITC has played a leading role in the UN's efforts to set an international standard for indigenous rights. Such a standard would clarify and thus strengthen the standing of indigenous peoples under international law. Powerful nation states have made the task very difficult. One of the ways in which they have done so is by rejecting all language that implies that the indigenous peoples within their national borders are sovereign. The matter of sovereignty is central to the whole exercise in the eyes of the indigenous organizations involved. They see the rather cumbersome phrase "indigenous peoples" as of strategic importance in setting such a standard. That phrase has also been the main barrier to its achievement. International law guarantees all "peoples" the right of self-determination. The word "peoples," therefore, clearly implies what American Indians call sovereignty. That is its appeal for the indigenous organizations. That is also the threat that it poses to nation states like the United States and Canada. The IITC remains strongly committed to the use of the term "indigenous peoples."

The IITC used its new NGO status to get Indians included in an international conference held at the UN headquarters in Geneva. The Sub-Committee on Discrimination, Apartheid, and Colonialism of the Special NGO UN Committee on Human Rights (UNCHR) orga-

nized the 1977 event. More than 100 Indians from across the Americas were among the 60 indigenous nations in attendance. The conference produced several important outcomes. One was the Draft Declaration of Principles for the Defense of the Indigenous Nations and Peoples of the Western Hemisphere. This document contained a concise but clear statement of indigenous rights. Another was a recommendation that the UN hold a conference on the relationship between land and indigenous rights. In 1981 the NGO Sub-Committee on Racism organized an International NGO Conference on Indigenous Peoples and the Land. It invited five indigenous organizations to solicit and submit written statements and to send delegations. The IITC was one of them.

The IITC had a direct hand in another major outcome of the 1977 NGO conference. That was the creation of the Working Group on Indigenous Populations (WGIP) in 1982. The WGIP operates under the UNCHR Sub-Commission on the Prevention of Discrimination and Protection of Minorities. A key part of its original mandate was to draft a Declaration on the Rights of Indigenous Peoples. It was to submit it to the UN General Assembly by 1992—a deadline it did not meet. Both the WGIP and its parent subcommission adopted the Draft Declaration long ago, but as of February 2004 the UN General Assembly had yet to approve it. The IITC continues to work toward its adoption by that body.

Rights and Sovereignty

The IITC still carries the concerns of indigenous peoples to the international community and fights hard for their rights and sovereignty. However, it now offers training and support based on its years of experience on the front line. This could have an even greater long-term impact than many of its other activities. By sharing its expertise in this way, the IITC enables indigenous peoples to take effective action at the local and national levels on their own. It also prepares them to act in the international arena. This broadens the scope of action possible and promotes linkages among groups. In doing so it strengthens the overall position of indigenous peoples. The IITC continues to work closely with grassroots organizations to address specific rights violations. Most of those have to do with a combination of environmental and cultural or human rights issues. Underlying them all are questions pertaining to sovereignty and self-determination.

The environmental purview of the IITC is broad and still expanding. It ranges from environmental protection and sustainable development to treaty and land rights. One of the first issues it took to the UN stemmed from the broken 1868 Fort Laramie Treaty previously mentioned. Since that time it has dealt with many instances of wrongfully taken lands, denied sovereignty, and genocide. It has also repeatedly addressed the adverse impact of resource extraction, military activity, and the dumping of toxic wastes on the lands of indigenous peoples. Activists now describe these kinds of violations as environmental racism. Evidence compiled by the IITC shows how such activities have damaged the health, soils, food resources, and waters of many indigenous peoples. In 1981, for example, it reported on the high rate of certain kinds of cancer found among American Indians who live near uranium mines and processing facilities to the International Conference on Indigenous Peoples and the Land. In other contexts it has presented similar findings with regard to the peoples who live near nuclear test sites in the Pacific.

The IITC also addresses abuses to the cultural rights of indigenous peoples. These include violations of their sacred sites, religious freedom, and intellectual property rights. The IITC has supported many grassroots efforts aimed at protecting sacred lands from desecration and environmental damage. The Medicine Lakes Highlands in northern California and Bear Butte in South Dakota are two high-profile examples. Both have suffered environmental degradation due commercial development in the past, and remain under threat in the present. Tourism is an issue in both cases. The physical remains of indigenous peoples are another concern. A group called American Indians Against Grave Desecration is one of the IITC's projects. It seeks the return for reburial of all Indian remains and associated sacred objects now held at institutions around the world.

Scholars refer to this as repatriation. The IITC also supported the Yaquis in their complaint over the appropriation and objectification of some of their sacred paraphernalia by non-Indian others. It argued that sacred paraphernalia, along with folklore and traditional practices, are intellectual property. As such they warrant the same legal protection as industrial patents.

The IITC also advocates on behalf of individuals and groups who have had their more widely recognized human rights violated—Leonard Peltier is a well-known example. The IITC began campaigning for his release from prison during its earliest days. It has since gone to the defense of other indigenous peoples unlawfully detained. In addition it has intervened on behalf of the many incarcerated Indians denied the right to engage in traditional religious practices. These and countless other examples not cited illustrate what the IITC has accomplished and how very much remains to be achieved in the fight for the rights and recognition of indigenous peoples.

DEBRA BUCHHOLTZ

See also **Peltier, Leonard (Amerindian); American Indian Movement (AIM); Indigenous Peoples; United Nations Declaration on Minorities; United Nations Working Group on Indigenous Populations**

Further Reading

Deloria, Vine, Jr., *Behind the Trail of Broken Treaties: An Indian Declaration of Independence*, Austin: University of Texas Press, 1974; 2nd edition, 1985

International Indian Treaty Council Home Page, <http://www.treatycouncil.org> (Jan. 7, 2004)

Ortiz, Roxanne Dunbar, *The Indians of America: Human Rights and Self-Determination*, London: Zed Books, and Haarlem; Netherlands: de Kruipscheen, 1984

Internet and Minorities

Those groups who are (or recently were) systematically marginalized and disadvantaged in relations with the rest of their society can find in the Internet a valuable ally. However, the effective use of the Internet to ameliorate the situation, or simply to communicate the truth about their lives, is far from being a routine matter.

The New Medium

For a long time since its inception in 1969 the Internet was regarded as largely an experimental resource. However, its formal status dramatically changed in a single day in September 1998 when the U.S. Congress published the complete and intricate "Starr Report" on the Clinton-Lewinsky affair. This publication took place online and ahead of its subsequent releases by more traditional means of newspapers, radio, television, and books. The legislators' unprecedented decision to bypass the well-established media in favor of the World Wide Web (WWW) meant that the Internet had finally came of age and officially became the fifth branch of mass communication.

In early 2001 the Internet provided a planetary forum for nearly 410 million people. The forum comprised over 100 million host machines, mainly in North America, Europe, and the Pacific Rim of East Asia, but also present in large numbers in other parts of the globe. The Internauts have contributed to and drawn upon the services of over 25 million web sites serving more than 1.5 billion web pages. They also used about 200,000 mailing lists, 37,000 chat-rooms, 30,000 Usenet newsgroups, and tens of thousands of Internet channels with music, video, radio, audio books, and TV (Zakon 2000, Nua 2000, Topica 2000).

The Internet is a remarkable phenomenon. The system is both global and local in its reach. It is fairly simple and fairly inexpensive to use from almost anywhere and anytime. It supports several activities: (1) transactions with remote computerized systems, (2) interpersonal and group communication, (3) publishing, and (4) finding, storage, and redistribution of digital information. Because of its format such information is readily searchable, indexable, and reusable.

On the Internet the English language is dominant due to its affinity with simple, fast-transmitting ASCII encoding scheme. The Internet is a rich space filled with originals, copies, and fragmentary remnants of all the previous months and years of communication and informational efforts of its users. However, it commingles and blurs the distinctions in traditional media between good and bad taste, hype and fact, and opinion and analysis. The Internet supports both overt and public activities (via identifiable computer addresses and plaintext documents) as well as activities which are covert, anonymous, or private. The latter scenario is enabled by a plethora of "hosted" web sites and mailing-lists, generic web-mail, chat-rooms, encrypted documents, as well as anonymized dial-up, web-surfing and e-mail online privacy services.

This all means that the Internet is a brand new environment—one that imposes new rules of conduct and new relationships among its users. For those who are intimate with its logic, the Internet can provide a remarkably level playing field. Most of the customary face-to-face expressions of power and status are not immediately apparent in cyberspace, and are difficult to communicate there effectively. Moreover, since all interactions are remote and mediated by a machine, the cyberspace favors a style which is civil yet decidedly speedy, clipped, and informal. "On the Internet", according to a popular saying, "no one knows you're a dog" (or an underdog). Unless you volunteer details about yourself (and this information is readily verifiable), no one online knows who you really are. Thus, all e-publishing and communicating parties are initially an "important somebody" (and at the same time a "likely nobody") until they are proven otherwise by their accumulating electronic reputations. This means that while in "real life" not all people would treat each other as equals, on the Internet the sheer logic of navigational circumstances and chance encounters inclines them to do so. The Internet fosters a culture of equality of opportunity. This trend is further promoted by the non-hierarchical and thus essentially democratic, if not anarchic, organization of cyberspace. Its hosts, sites, devices, and servers operate side-by-side, whether as colleagues and peers, or as ruthless competitors.

The Electronic Agora

The Internet is an immensely competitive environment. Here everyday millions of participants vie with each other for attracting (and keeping) the largest possible slice of e-traffic, and thus the largest possible share of Internauts' eyes and minds. The size of the online audience is always a strictly limited commodity. There are only a few hours a day a person can spend online, while every e-mail message sent or received and each networked document created or visited uses-up a portion of that limited time. The competition is real and the stakes are high. Once gained, the online readership is directly convertible into cash, strategic alliances with other sites, social prestige, and political power. In that sense the struggle for audience on the Internet is very much like the struggle for ratings observable in the world of radio and TV stations. The online competition is fierce, for 20 percent of all of today's web-traffic is captured by the 10 most popular sites, 40 percent by the top 100, 60 percent by the top 1,000, and 80 percent by the top 10,000 sites. The remaining tens of millions of servers share the leftover 20 percent of the traffic (Kahle, 2001).

The size of an Internet site's audience is, ultimately, a function of that resource's hard-earned reputation. This remains so despite numerous promotional campaigns conducted on and off the Internet. Such reputation forms a self-fulfilling prophecy. It can be measured in terms of numbers of electronic bookmarks or hyperlinks leading to it, volume of hourly or daily traffic, frequency of word-of-mouth recommendations, and friendly off-line references.

Networked resources enjoy trust (as well as regular and much prized repeat visits) if the offered content is: unique and detailed; fresh; fully referenced (i.e., attributable to a named and contactable source); factually correct; presented in the language of the target audience (and, if possible, in English or other international languages); expressed in a simple, succinct, and understated manner; and easily correctable (i.e., any factual and/or typing errors, if reported by readers, are speedily corrected, and readers' input is duly acknowledged). Online reputations are also made (or lost) by the resources' usability. Networked resources attract increased numbers of readers if they have: an easy to remember (and record down) electronic address; simple, compact, interoperable, and user-friendly architecture and format; quick response times; and easily indexable by major search engines (e.g., www.google. com, www.altavista.com) and catalogued by authoritative resource directories. See, for example: "University of Minnesota Human Rights Library" (www1.umn.edu/humanrts); "WWW Virtual Library on Migration and Ethnic Relations" (www.ercomer.org/wwwvl); "Virtual Library of Internet Resources on National and Ethnic Minorities in Central and Eastern Europe and the Former Soviet Union" (lgi.osi.hu/ethnic/weblibrary); "Indigenous Studies WWW Virtual Library" (www.cwis.org/wwwvl/indig-vl.html); or "The International Clearing House for Endangered Languages" (www.tooyoo.l.u-tokyo.ac.jp/ichel.html).

In other words networked initiatives whose content and architecture are merely transplanted from other contexts (like book publishing or TV broadcasting) alienate their audiences. Similarly, those who operate with little or no thought for Internauts' actual expectations and for the rules of "netiquette" inevitably lose users' interest and goodwill (Nielsen, 1995–2001).

This means that a well-prepared, imaginative, and dedicated professional or a small team, with an inexpensive but skillfully managed site or a mailing list, can attain online visibility and following far greater than that achieved by bloated sites established by many hundreds of amply resourced and staffed but Internet-illiterate organizations. This point is clearly made by such electronic initiatives as: "Bytes For All" (about making the Internet generally accessible, especially in South Asia, www.bytesforall.org); "The Information Exchange for Korean-American Scholars" (a resource to inform and empower the "high-tech coolies," www.skas.org); "Tibet Information Network" (reports on the situation of Tibetans in China, Nepal, and India, www.tibet-info.net); "Independent Information Centre Glasnost - Caucasus" (about ethnic conflicts in the North Caucasus, www.glasnostonline.org); and "The Fourth World Documentation Project" (archives of documents related to pre-industrial societies, www.cwis.org/fwdp.html).

The Contest for Online Minds

Members of a minority (as well as its supporters and allies)—whether in the home country or abroad—can use the Internet to: (1) intensively liaise and network amongst themselves and with other friendly groups, (2) document their culture, language, history, and achievements, and (3) inform and educate the neutral sections of public opinion about their plight and grievances. Such networked information (like all Internet's information) is available both locally and globally. Here digital involvements (unlike the traditional media) are remarkably productive and cost-effective. If an online document or message is able to adequately inform say 1 to 2 people, it has a potential –(in principle at least) to reach and inform virtually the entire networked world.

Of course all such publishing and liaising activities can be (and frequently are) countered and neutralized by those within their society (as well as outside of it) who are interested in maintaining the inequitable status quo. Their motives may vary.

Some of these adversaries might propagate interests of their own minority group. Others might be in the employment of a state that is keen to quash challenges to its ideology. Still others might be hired by businesses seeking to silence opposition to their intended high-impact ventures (e.g., urban redevelopment, toxic waste dumps, forest logging, or hydroelectric schemes). This often leads to a situation where one or both sides could be tempted to use unethical methods of infiltration, info-pollution, and paralysis of the other side's mailing lists and Usenet newsgroups. Virulent propaganda, hate mail, denial of history, and disinformation campaigns is certainly common on the Internet. Also, as in other areas of life, individuals as well as governmental agencies might resort to criminal activities as well. Indeed the online world is awash with daily news of sabotage, "hacktivism," denial-of-service attacks, deliberate infection with computer viruses, and other forms of information warfare

(Goldberg, 2001). This is illustrated by a spate of 1999 and 2000 electronic attacks on the Falun Gong religious movement's web sites and e-mail addresses in the United States, Australia, and the United Kingdom, with at least one hacking attempt that appeared traceable to the Chinese Public Security Ministry in Beijing. It is also illustrated by the alleged involvement of Burma's military junta in targeting the "Happy 99" e-mail virus at its overseas opponents active on the Internet(Strobel, 2000).

All these electronic activities, whether legal or nefarious, are invariably monitored and commented upon by a wide range of self-appointed online arbiters. Research sites tend to comment (e.g., via scholarly e-mail lists, such as those catalogued in Kovacs, 1999) on the truthfulness and accuracy of the electronic publications. At the same time international human rights watchdogs and NGOs that deliver humanitarian aid or work on resolution of ethnic tensions are likely to pay attention to the procedural fairness of relationships, on and off the Internet, in the areas of their concern. In consequence, sooner or later, woe is to a server which errs deliberately or whose management sabotages the networked world. Indeed on the Internet it takes months and years before a good name is earned, yet it can take a mere few hours to lose it entirely.

Naturally all these unprecedented opportunities (as well as dangers) become a reality for all types of minorities only if they can secure at least minimal access to the Internet. Such access, however, presupposes not only the presence of an adequate technological infrastructure, but also (above all) the absence of oppressive political controls and eviscerating regulations. To cite a computer expert with first-hand knowledge of life under a dictatorship, "the problem of the Internet in [my homeland] has never been technical or economic. As in any country, it's 70 percent political" (reported in Symmes,

1998:188). Thus it is not an accident that totalitarian states cannot tolerate the unfettered use of modern communications. There the citizens' access to the Internet is either rationed, monitored and censored, or disabled altogether. Biannual statistics on the size of the Internet in various countries (e.g., "Internet Domain Survey," www.isc.org/ds) if juxtaposed with data on the countries' human rights record (e.g., "Human Rights Watch," www.hrw.org) make very instructive reading indeed.

T. Matthew Ciolek

See also **Equal Opportunity; Ethnic Conflict; Globalization and Minority Cultures; Human and Minority Rights Organizations; Languages, Disappearing; Multiculturalism**

Further Reading

Goldberg, Ivan, Information Warfare, also known as I-War, IW, C4I, or Cyberwar, Institute for the Advanced Study of Information Warfare (IASIW), 2001: www.psycom.net/iwar. 1.html

Kahle, Brewster, Personal Communication, January 6, 2001, brewster@alexa.com, Unpublished results of a systematic survey, 2001: www.alexaresearch.com

Kovacs, Diane K., and The Directory Team, editors, The Directory of Scholarly and Professional E-Conferences, 1999: n2h2.com/KOVACS

Nielsen, Jakob, The Alertbox: Current Issues in Web Usability, 1995–2001: www.useit.com/alertbox

Nua, Internet, How Many Online? 2000: www.nua.ie/surveys/how_many_online/index.html

Rinaldi, Arlene H., The Net: User Guidelines and Netiquette, 1998: www.fau.edu/netiquette/netiquette.html

Strobel, Warren P. "A glimpse of cyberwarfare: Governments ready information-age tricks to use against their adversaries," *US NewsWorld Report*, 13 (March 2000): www.usnews.com/usnews/issue/000313/cyberwar.htm

Symmes, Patrick, "Che is Dead", *Wired*, 6, no.2 (1998)

Topica, Inc., Liszt, The Mailing List Directory, 2000: www.liszt.com (The site also publishes extensive catalogues of current Usenet newsgroups and IRC channels.)

Zakon, Robert H., Hobbes' Internet Timeline, v5.2, 2000: info.isoc.org/guest/zakon/Internet/History/HIT.html

Inuit

Capsule Summary

Location: Throughout the Arctic, including East Greenland, Canada, Alaska, and Chukotka
Total Population: 150,000
Language: Varies with region
Religion: Varies

Approximately 150,000 Inuit live in a variety of Arctic environments across a vast and sparsely populated geographical area stretching some 3,200 miles from east Greenland across the north of Canada to the coasts of Alaska and Chukotka. Inuit cultures represent some of the most extraordinary human-environment adaptations to be found on Earth. Traditionally Inuit have subsisted from hunting marine and terrestrial mammals and fishing. Today hunting and fishing remain vital activities for the economies of many Inuit communities, but commercial fishing, oil-related business, financial enterprise, and other activities such as sheep farming (in south Greenland) are increasingly important.

The word Inuit means "the people" (singular, *inuk* or "person") and is applied generally across the Arctic to refer to Eskimo-speaking peoples. However, this common usage obscures the diversity of Inuit groups, who are known as Kalaallit, Inughuit, and Iit in west, northwest, and east Greenland; Inuit and Inuvialuit in Canada; Iñupiaq, Yup'ik, and Alutiiq in Alaska; and Yup'ik in Siberia. "Inuit" as a more general term of reference was adopted by the Inuit Circumpolar Conference—(an NGO representing the rights and interests of all Inuit in 1977) in preference to the term "Eskimo."

Origins and History

Archaeological, linguistic, cultural, and physical anthropological evidence suggests that Inuit have their origins in Siberia and possibly in Central Asia. Using artifacts found at ancient Siberian sites in the Lake Baikal region, dating back some 12,000 to 25,000 years, archaeologists have constructed a picture of a wide-ranging, semi-nomadic culture that survived by hunting large animals, such as reindeer, woolly rhinoceros, musk-ox, and mammoth. Most likely some groups moved progressively northwards to the coasts of

northeast Asia. There is evidence of similar hunting cultures living on the shores of the Bering Sea at least 18,000 years ago. These people, who are now regarded as the Paleo-Eskimo ancestors of the present-day Inuit, entered the New World by crossing Beringia, an intercontinental land bridge connecting Siberia to Alaska.

The peopling of Arctic North America was a gradual process rather than a large-scale migration from Asia, beginning with the exploration of new hunting grounds instead of a search for new land to settle. Initially the Paleo-Arctic hunters probably maintained a home base on the Siberian side of Beringia, with some occasional forays over to the Alaskan side in search of game. The animals these people depended on for food gradually moved eastwards from northeastern Asia as a result of major climatic changes during the last ice age and the immediate postglacial period. Several waves of Paleo-Arctic peoples did the same and began to range far and wide in search of game in Alaska, eventually moving into Canada and across the tundra and northern shores of the North American Arctic.

The ancestors of present-day Alaska Natives can be traced to two distinct migrations that occurred between 5,000 to 10,000 years ago. The first migration was of inland Na-Dene speaking groups, which includes the Athapaskan peoples of Alaska, northern Canada, British Columbia, and California. The second migration, around 7,000 years ago, was that of Eskimo-Aleut speaking groups. These arrived in North America with a maritime-focused culture and mode of subsistence. Around 4,000 years ago, the Aleut and Eskimo groups diverged and developed similar, yet distinctive, ways of life. This is a crucial date in the chronology of Arctic peoples because from this time archaeologists and anthropologists have been able to trace (with fair accuracy) the social, economic, and technological development of the many Inuit groups of Alaska, Canada, and Greenland.

Society

Traditionally the Inuit depended primarily on seals, whales, and other sea mammals, caribou, and fish. Seals provided the staple food throughout the year for both humans and dogs; sealskins were used to make clothing and shelter; and other parts of the seal provided materials for making boats, fishing lines, harpoon lines, and, crucially, oil for heating and light. Social organization was built around the immediate kin group, and social obligations to help one's kin and to share meat and fish were key cultural principles. Groups were on the whole small in number (based around nuclear families) and largely nomadic. In summer families traveled over hunting and fishing grounds and lived in skin tents, and in winter families tended to group together and live in semi-permanent settlements. Winter houses were semi-subterranean and made of stone and sod, with a frame of driftwood, whalebone, or caribou antler. During long winter journeys, some Canadian Inuit groups built shelters from blocks of snow—the common misconception is that these shelters were called igloos, when in fact *iglu* is the Inuit word for "house").

Summer transportation was by *qajaq* or *umiaq*, or by foot across the tundra; in winter the dogsled was more or less known by all Inuit groups. Traditional clothing for men and women consisted of watertight boots, trousers, and a parka, all made mainly from sealskin or caribou fur. Traditional Inuit religious beliefs were animistic. Inuit lived in an aware world where everything in the universe had a spirit that could affect the lives and fortunes of humans. Much of daily life was spent not only trying to procure food, but also ensuring that taboos and rituals were observed to avoid harming the spirits of animals. The shaman was a prominent figure in all Inuit communities—someone who had the knowledge and power to influence and control the spirits that were all-pervasive throughout the natural world. A wealth of Inuit myths have been collected from all over the Arctic by missionaries, travelers, and anthropologists; and these deal with the daily concerns of the Inuit—the preparation for a successful hunt, the appeasement of animal spirits, and the intricate relations between humans, animals, and the environment.

The Inuit Today: Social Change and Self-Determination

Today the Inuit fall within the following geographical and cultural groupings: the Greenland Inuit (living on the west, northwest, and east coasts of the country); the Canadian Inuit (living in Labrador, Quebec, Nunavut, and the Northwest Territories); the Alaskan Inuit, who are divided into Iñupiaq, Yup'ik, and Alutiiq/Sugpiaq peoples (living in the northern, western, and

southwestern parts of the state); and the Siberian Yup'ik of Chukotka in northeastern Siberia. In this section, the discussion of each of these groups focuses on recent experiences of rapid social and economic change and movements for self-determination and self-government.

Greenland Inuit

In Greenland the Inuit population comprises three distinct cultural and linguistic groups: (1) the majority Kalaallit, who inhabit the west coast from Nanortalik district in the south to Upernavik district in the north; (2) Inughuit (popularly known as the Polar Eskimos and famous for being the world's most northerly indigenous inhabitants) in the north around Avanersuaq/Thule; and (3) Iit on the east coast. Since Home Rule was introduced in Greenland in 1979, the country has been known officially as Kalaallit Nunaat ("the Greenlanders' Land"), although both "Inuit" and "Greenlanders" are used as more generic and interchangeable terms to refer to the indigenous population.

The coastal areas of Greenland have been inhabited by Inuit groups for about 4,500 years. The first Paleo-Eskimo migrants arrived in the far north of the island between 2500 and 2000 BCE. European settlement in Greenland can be traced to circa 985 CE. Norse settlements existed there for almost 500 years as farmers keeping cattle, sheep, and goats, and as marine mammal hunters. The Icelandic sagas record that the Norse communities in Greenland knew of, and most likely came into contact with, a people they called *skraelings*. In the sixteenth and seventeenth centuries, the Greenland Inuit experienced contact with European whalers and explorers, and Danish colonization dates from 1721.

For over 200 years, the Danes followed an isolationist policy towards Greenland and the indigenous Inuit. The Danes controlled trade and Greenland was effectively a closed country. After World War II, however, Denmark ended its isolationist policy and emphasis was placed on social welfare and infrastructural change as part of a process of modernization of both the country and Inuit society. Commercial fishing was placed at the center of policies of economic development, and people were moved from small hunting settlements and resettled in larger towns on the west coast.

By the late 1960s and early 1970s Greenlandic Inuit society had been transformed from one based primarily on small-scale subsistence hunting and fishing to a modern, export-oriented economy. The majority of the Inuit population were now living in the fast-growing west coast towns, and this demographic transition brought its own problems. Life in the settlements had been characterized by and organized around kinship. Movement to the towns led to the disruption of kin-based groups and individuals experienced alienation, social and economic marginality, and discrimination, made worse by ethnic tensions and increasing numbers of Danes who were living in Greenland because of the need for construction workers, teachers, doctors, and administrators.

One direct result of these social changes and upheavals was the emergence of Inuit political parties and a heightened sense of Inuit identity. Greenlandic politicians and political activists began to campaign for Home Rule in the early 1970s. Greenlanders thus became the first population of Inuit origin to have achieved a degree of self-government by 1979. Although Greenland remains a part of the Kingdom of Denmark, the Home Rule Authorities have embarked on an ambitious policy of nation-building. Fishing is vital to the economy of the country as a whole, and many small communities still depend on marine mammal hunting; but in the future Greenland is likely to develop its rich minerals and hydrocarbons.

Canadian Inuit

Canadian Inuit live across the entire length of the Canadian North, from the Mackenzie Delta region close to the border with Alaska to Baffin Island and further south in Quebec and Labrador. The Inuit of the Mackenzie Delta region prefer to call themselves "Inuvialuit" while Inuit is used as a term of reference and address elsewhere in the Canadian North (although the Inuit of Nunavut and the Inuit of Labrador are distinguished as "Nunavummiut" and "Sikumiut," respectively). Until the middle of the twentieth century, many Inuit groups in Canada still retained a semi-nomadic lifestyle based around the hunting of seals and caribou.

The Hudson's Bay Company dominated Canada's fur trade from the time it received its charter in 1670 right up to the early twentieth century. During this period the Canadian Inuit became dependent on Hudson's Bay Company trading posts. In the twentieth century, their lives were also affected by the expansion of other forms of economic development, such as mining and the exploitation of hydrocarbons. Following World War II there was an expansion of mining activity, and together with the development of hydroelectric projects this reinforced a southern Canadian vision of the Far North as a vast storehouse of natural resources, of which the development and exploitation was regarded as necessary for the future of the Canadian nation.

The effects of social and economic development on Canadian Inuit have been considerable. Government resettlement policies only exacerbated the erosion of the Inuit subsistence hunting culture, and the Inuit have been drawn into a position of greater dependency on Canadian government and institutions. The presence in small Inuit settlements of large numbers of southern Canadians who went North to work as administrators, trade managers, teachers, and construction workers caused considerable resentment among Inuit, and ethnic conflict between the two groups was common. Since the 1950s the prevailing Canadian government attitude was one of incorporating the Inuit into the mainstream economic, social, and cultural life of Canada. According to the popular imagination as well as in official legislation, the Inuit were believed to be living on the edge of starvation in a barren, inhospitable wilderness. Through education and training, the indigenous inhabitants of the Arctic were to become modern Canadians, able to improve their lifestyle options and take their place in the new period of economic development on the Canadian Arctic frontier.

In response to social change and large-scale economic development, the Canadian Inuit have attempted to achieve a degree of self-determination in recent decades. In 1971 the Inuit Tapirisat of Canada (ITC) was founded in Ottawa as a voice for Inuit throughout Canada's North. In 1984 the Inuvialuit Final Agreement gave 35,000 square miles of the Northwest Territories to the Inuvialuit, together with financial compensation and other rights to resources in return for their surrendering further territorial claims. In 1975 the Inuit of northern Quebec signed a land claims agreement against the backdrop of controversy surrounding hydroelectric development in James Bay. In 1992 the Tungavik Federation of Nunavut and the Government of Canada signed an agreement that addressed Inuit land claims and harvested rights, and committed the federal government to establishing Nunavut ("our land") in the Canadian Eastern Arctic. Nunavut was inaugurated on April 1, 1999, and comprises some 200 million hectares of northern Canada. The majority population of Nunavut is approximately 80 percent Inuit, and the government is effectively Inuit-led. However, the settlement did not create a new ethnic Inuit state, but public government within the limits defined by the Canadian constitution. Nonetheless, Nunavut has given the Inuit of the eastern Arctic a greater degree of autonomy and self-government than any other Aboriginal group in Canada.

Alaskan Inuit

In Alaska the Iñupiat (singular *Iñupiaq*) inhabit the Arctic tundra plains of the North Slope, the boreal forests of the northwest, and the coastal lowlands of the Bering Sea. The other major group, the Yup'ik, live along the coasts and rivers of southwest Alaska. In the south, around Cook Inlet, the Kenai Pensinsula, Kodiak Island, and the Alaska Peninsula, live the Alutiiq and Sugpiaq-speaking peoples who have been traditionally referred to in the literature as Pacific Eskimos.

Prior to European contact, coastal Iñupiat groups specialized in hunting the bowhead whale, walrus, seals, and polar bears, and the social and cultural life of inland groups revolved around caribou hunting. Today whaling and the hunting of other marine mammals remains a strong part of their culture and economic life. Whaling meant that a distinctive and more socially stratified society emerged on the North Slope. Social status has traditionally been determined by the skill and knowledge of the hunter and the hunter's ability to catch an abundance of game and thus share out meat throughout the community. In complete contrast to the Iñupiat of the North Slope, the Yup'ik peoples of southwest Alaska inhabit a subarctic landscape. The Yup'ik are seal, beluga whale, and walrus hunters. The Yup'ik are renowned for their complex ceremonial life. For example, elaborate masks carved from wood, or made from sealskin, and depicting animal spirits and mythical figures are worn at community feasts and dances to celebrate the memory of the ancestors.

The European discovery of Alaska is credited to Vitus Bering, a Danish explorer on a Russian expedition in 1741. When Bering's expedition returned home with sea otter furs, the subsequent course of Alaska's economic development based on the exploitation of its natural resources was set. Alaska was prominent in both the Russian and British fur trades, and over a period of 140 years fur seals, sea otters, and some species of fur-bearing land mammal were exploited to near extinction. Beginning in 1847 American whalers from New England hunted the bowhead whale in the waters of Bering Strait, thus seriously affecting the viability of the indigenous Iñupiat hunt. From the 1880s gold mining formed the basis for the expansion of the Alaskan economy and its subsequent settlement by non-indigenous peoples, and the agenda for Alaska's late-twentieth/early twenty-first century economic development was set with the discovery of vast reserves of oil and gas at Prudhoe Bay on the North Slope in 1968.

The integration of Alaskan Inuit cultures into mainstream American social, cultural, and economic life has followed a pattern similar to the experiences of Inuit groups living elsewhere in the Arctic. The encounter with whalers, traders, missionaries, and administrators has meant disease, exploitation, rapid social and cultural change, and economic and social dependency. Whalers and traders had already partly disrupted the indigenous spiritual belief system by the time the first Presbyterian missionaries arrived on the North Slope at the end of the nineteenth century. Catholic missionaries, however, who arrived in the Yup'ik area of southwest Alaska at the same time, found that the Native people had been more resistant to the influence of outside religious beliefs and practices, especially those of the Russian Orthodox Church, and traditional spiritual beliefs still provided the foundation of much daily life. In both the Iñupiat and Yup'ik areas, missionaries soon established boarding schools and assumed responsibility for religious and secular education until federal schools were established in the first half of the twentieth century. Until the mid-1970s the education system in rural Alaska's Native communities was assimilationist in aim. Native children were to be educated as citizens of the United States and many had to leave their home villages for a high school education. In 1975 a revision in the administration of education established regional schools districts and village high schools, and although this went some way to empowering communities with regard to education, the education curriculum remained the same. Native schoolchildren learned the same subjects as children elsewhere in the United States. Today, although schools in rural Alaska are effectively under local control, they remain institutions that are not really part of the social and cultural fabric of Native communities.

During the twentieth century there were improvements in health care and the Alaskan Inuit population steadily increased; more hunters and trappers moved to larger villages from smaller, remote settlements; customary subsistence activities declined; and alternative employment opportunities became available both in the villages and in other parts of Alaska. Although hunting and trapping remain an important and integral part of the Alaskan Inuit village economies, many people now find permanent and seasonal employment in commercial fishing, the oil industry, and in urban centers such as Anchorage and Fairbanks.

The discovery of oil at Prudhoe Bay on Alaska's North Slope together with fears of other large-scale, industrial development resulted in the established of the Alaska Federation of Natives (AFN) in 1967. The AFN lobbied the U.S. Congress for the appropriate settlement of land claims for Alaska Natives, and in 1971 the U.S. Congress passed the Alaska Native Land Claims Settlement Act (ANCSA). ANCSA did not recognize a Native claim to the whole of the state of Alaska, but it did establish twelve regional Native corporations, giving them effective control over one-ninth of the state. ANCSA extinguished Native claims to the rest of Alaska and 962.5 million dollars was given in compensation. In effect ANCSA made Alaska's Native people shareholders in corporate-owned land.

Siberian Yup'ik

The Siberian Yup'ik (plural *Yupiit*) speak one of four Yup'ik dialects (the others, mainland Yup'ik, Pacific Yup'ik, and Nunivak Yup'ik, are spoken in Alaska), but it is a dialect perhaps linguistically more closely related to the language spoken by the Chukchi of Siberia. The Siberian Yup'ik communities are thinly scattered along the isolated coasts of Chukotka in northwestern Siberia, and the entire population numbers around 2,000 people. The Siberian Yup'ik economy has traditionally revolved around the hunting of bowhead and grey whales, seals, walrus, caribou, and polar bears. Like other Inuit groups, their social organization, culture, spiritual beliefs, religious practices, and mythology have been inextricably linked to the animals they depend on for survival.

Contact between Siberian Yup'ik and Europeans first occurred in the tenth century, but it was only in the eighteenth century that regular, extensive, and prolonged contact began to take place with Russians. Siberian Yup'ik communities experienced wave after wave of epidemics, such as smallpox, mumps, influenza, and chicken pox, which seriously affected the demographic composition of northeastern Siberia. The Yup'ik, however, suffered the extreme impact of Soviet economic policies during the twentieth century. The Soviets established the Committee of the North in 1928 and Yup'ik economic life was collectivized through the organization of boat crews into seasonal hunting co-operatives. Following the end of World War II, many Yup'ik villages were closed by the Soviet authorities and the inhabitants were resettled in Chukchi villages. This set in motion a process that is continuing today of social and cultural integration with the Chukchi population. At this time Soviet collectives hunting dominated whale and walrus hunting along the coast of Chukotka, almost decimating stocks, and this monopolization of a vital economic activity for the indigenous population made it extremely difficult for Yup'ik boat crews to land whales or walrus and thus undermined the subsistence culture.

In the 1950s and 1960s what was left of traditional Yup'ik culture and livelihoods was marginalized even further as a process of resettlement reduced the number of Siberian Yup'ik villages from 50 to 12. Major social, economic, and infrastructural changes swept across the region—roads, pipelines, nuclear power plants, and military installations had a massive impact on the human and physical environment. During the Cold War the Soviets were also nervous about the proximity of the United States to Siberia, as well as the Yup'ik population on Big Diomede Island and the village of Naukan who were related to the Alaskan Yup'ik on the other side of the Soviet-American border. To prevent contact and possible U.S.-inspired espionage between the Siberian and Alaskan Yup'ik communities, the Soviets removed the people from Big Diomede and Naukan.

Through the institutions of Russian society, such as government and education, attempts were made to bring the Yup'ik into the mainstream of Russian social, cultural, and economic life. Yup'ik children, like children from other indigenous communities, were sent to village schools or to boarding schools because of a policy of Russification. They were expected to go through entirely the same education system as Russian children in urban areas, such as Moscow, Leningrad, and Kiev, and to learn a totally new view of the world that was quite different from the cultural upbringing they had so far experienced. Yup'ik children became dependent on the state and in many cases also lost the ability to speak their own language. Yup'ik hunters and fishers were also deprived of their traditional livelihoods and many soon had no other choice but to enter the wage economy, mostly by becoming laborers in menial jobs, either in the villages or in Soviet construction projects or by working in collective fox farms.

Despite the tremendous changes that have transformed much of their traditional life, the Siberian Yup'ik have maintained a distinctive ethnic identity within Russia. In many ways this identity has strengthened since the collapse of the Soviet Union in 1991.

They have formed organizations concerned with cultural survival and self-determination, which are themselves members of the Russian Association of the Peoples of the North (RAIPON). The island of Big Diomede and the village of Naukan were resettled by Siberian Yup'ik in 1992, and throughout the 1990s economic, cultural, and political links have been established with Eskimos in Alaska. Collectivization is no longer the means by which economic life is organized, and the Siberian Yup'ik are free to resume traditional hunting once more. However, this is also a matter of economic and cultural survival because the collapse of the Soviet Union and the subsequent economic crisis affecting the Russian Federation has made the links between Siberian Yup'ik villages and the rest of Russia increasingly tenuous. Marine mammal hunting has once again become vital to the Yup'ik coastal communities of the Russian Far East. However, because knowledge and skills surrounding whaling had mostly disappeared in the small Siberian Yup'ik communities, in the mid-1990s the Siberians appealed to Alaskan whalers for assistance in obtaining appropriate whaling technology and training in how to go whaling once more. Alaska's North Slope Borough set up a project with the American-Russia Center of the University of Alaska-Anchorage, which aimed to help Siberian Yup'ik document local knowledge about marine mammals and teach local hunters to relearn long-forgotten hunting skills.

Indigenous Knowledge, the Arctic Environment, and Sustainability

Today, like other Arctic peoples, the Inuit face threats to their cultures, livelihoods, and homelands from environmental problems, for example, transboundary pollution and climate change, large-scale industrial activity, rapid social and cultural change, and other exogenous forces such as the activities of animal-rights groups and environmental movements that are campaigning against traditional Inuit hunting activities (i.e., sealing and whaling). Despite the overwhelming social and economic changes that have occurred in the Arctic over the last 50 years or so, many Inuit communities from east Greenland to the Bering Sea coast of Siberia continue to rely on the harvesting of terrestrial and marine resources for subsistence purposes. Inuit say that no individual has the right to claim that they own the animals. Access to resources is based on communal rights, and hunting is guided by community regulations, which are often unwritten. The sharing of the catch from the hunt remains at the very heart of the hunting culture.

In Greenland, Canada, and Alaska, Inuit groups have begun to outline and put into practice their own environmental strategies and policies to safeguard the future of Inuit resource use and to ensure a workable participatory approach among indigenous peoples, scientists, and policy-makers to the sustainable management and development of resources. From an Inuit perspective, threats to wildlife and the environment do not come from hunting, but from climate change and from airborne and seaborne pollutants that enter the Arctic from industrial areas far to the south of traditional Inuit homelands. Threats also come from the impact of nonrenewable resource extraction within the Arctic, such as oil and gas development and mining. In recent decades the Inuit have set themselves the challenge to counteract such threats and to devise strategies for environmental protection and sustainable development.

The Inuit argue that adequate systems of environmental management and the most appropriate forms of sustainability are only possible if they incorporate local knowledge and Inuit cultural values. In this way the Inuit have claimed the right for international recognition as resource conservationists. The success of this approach has been possible in part by the work of the Inuit Circumpolar Conference (ICC), a pan-Arctic indigenous peoples' organization that represents the rights of Inuit in Greenland, Canada, Alaska, and Siberia. Since its formation, the ICC has sought to establish its own Arctic policies based on indigenous knowledge about the environment that reflects Inuit concerns about future development together with ethical and practical guidelines for human activity in the Arctic.

MARK NUTTALL

See also **Canada; Russia; Self-Determination; Siberian Indigenous Peoples**

Editor's Note

This entry was excerpted from the *Encyclopedia of the Arctic*, edited by Mark Nuttall, 3 volumes, New York: Routledge, 2003.

Further Reading

Caulfield, Richard, *Greenlanders, Whales and Whaling: Sustainability and Self-Determination in the Arctic*, Hanover: University Press of New England, 1997

Chance, Norman, *The Iñupiat and Arctic Alaska*, New York: Holt, Rinehart and Nicolson, 1990

Dahl, Jens, *Saqqaq: An Inuit Hunting Community in the Modern World*, Toronto: University of Toronto Press, 2000

Damas, David, *Handbook of North American Indians, Volume 5, Arctic*, Washington, DC: Smithsonian Institution, 1984

Dorais, Louis-Jacques, *Quaqtaq: Modernity and Identity in an Inuit Community*, Toronto: University of Toronto Press, 1997

Fienup-Riordan, Ann, *Eskimo Essays: Yup'ik Lives and How We See Them*, New Brunswick, New Jersey: Rutgers University Press, 1990

Nuttall, Mark, *Arctic Homeland: Kinship, Community and Development in Northwest Greenland*, Toronto: University of Toronto Press, 1992

Wenzel, George, *Animal Rights, Human Rights: Ecology, Economy and Ideology in the Canadian Arctic*, Toronto: University of Toronto Press, 1991

Iran

Capsule Summary

Country Name: Jomhuri-ye Eslami-ye Iran, or Islamic Republic of Iran

Location: Middle East, between Iraq and Pakistan

Total Population: 68,278,826 (July 2003)

Majority Population: Persians (51%)

Minority Populations: Azeri (24%), Gilaki and Mazandarani (8%), Kurd (7%), Arab (3%), Lur (2%), Baloch (2%), Turkmen (2%), other (1%)

Official Language: Farsi (New Persian)

Other Important Languages: Azeri, Gilani, Mazandarani, Kurdish, Arabic, Luri, Balochi, English, French

Religions: Shi'a Muslim (89%), Sunni Muslim (10%), Zoroastrian, Jewish, Christian, and Baha'i (1%)

General

The Jomhuri-ye Eslami-ye Iran, or Islamic Republic of Iran (formerly known as Iran and as Persia), is a nation-state located in southwest Asia. It shares international borders with Iraq and Turkey to the west; Afghanistan and Pakistan to the east; and Azerbaijan, Armenia, and Turkmenistan to the north. The Caspian Sea forms Iran's northern coastline. The Persian Gulf and the Gulf of Oman form the country's southern coastline. The country is largely a plateau, 636,300 square miles in size, plus several small islands in the Persian Gulf. The capital city, Tehran, is located in the northcentral region, just south of the Elburz mountain range. Per capita Gross Domestic Product (GDP) in 2002 was US$6,800 (U.S. Dollars 1 = Iranian Rials 1,750–5,700 official variable exchange rate; U.S. Dollars 1 = Iranian Rials 7,850–8,000 market exchange rate). Major exports include petroleum and natural gas products (75.2 percent) and carpets (11 percent).

A new constitution, adopted after a revolution in 1979, replaced an autocratic monarchy of *Shahs* with a theocratic Islamic Republic based on Muslim law (or *Shari'a*). The supreme religio-political national authority (or *Faqi*) is elected for life by an assembly of Shi'ite Muslim religious jurists (or *Mujtahids*) based on knowledge of theology and law. An Islamic constitution endorses universal suffrage, with the age of voting established at 16 years or older. Executive, legislative, and judicial branches of government also exist. The executive branch of government is headed by a President elected by voters to a 4-year term in office. The President appoints a Cabinet of Ministers with approval of the legislature and chairs the National Security Council. The legislative branch of government consists of a Consultative Assembly (or *Majles*), comprising 270 Members or national representatives. Election of these Members to 4-year terms is supervised by a Council of Guardians. This Council of Guardians (comprising six members appointed by the Faqi and six members appointed jointly by the High Council of the Judiciary and the Majles) also determines the constitutionality of all laws. Divergences between the Majles and the Council of Guardians are mediated by a Committee to Determine the Expediency of the Islamic Order. Recognized minority communities (such as the Jews, Christians, and Zoroastrians or Mazdeans) have token representation in the Majles. Local government consists of: Governors-General for provinces, Governors for counties, and Mayors for cities—all appointed by the Minister of the Interior. City administration also involves Councilmen elected locally. Village-level administration centers upon a Village Master and a Council of Elders. The judicial branch of government is headed by a Chief Justice. Additionally there are a Supreme Judicial Council and a system of lower Courts and Tribunals. Members of the judiciary are required to be Shi'ite Muslim religious jurists. Individual and civic rights, plus commercial, civil, and criminal codes—including a system of retribution or *qisas*—are based on Islamic law. Public enforcement of law is overseen by Revolutionary Guards (or *Pasdaran-e Inqilab*) under the Ministry of the Interior.

History and Society

The first well-documented human habitation dates to the Middle Paleolithic period around 100,000 BCE. The socioeconomic organization of those people involved small groups of hunter-gathers. Between 10,000 and 6,000 BCE, in the Late or Upper Paleolithic and the Early Neolithic periods, domestication of plants and animals led to permanent settlements, as at the site of Jarmo. One set of settlements coalesced into a kingdom, known as Elam, in the southwest. Little is known about the Elamites themselves, though images of warriors on glazed tile reliefs from the later Achaemenid period are believed to represent them. During much of the Old Elamite period, which began around 2200 BCE, the territory was divided into city-states, such as Susa and Anshan. During the first half of the second millennium BCE, authority came to be centered in a high-king (or *sukkal-mah*), who ruled over the monarchs of individual cities. During the Middle Elamite kingdom (ca. 1450–1100 BCE), battles between the Elamites and Mesopotamians were a constant aspect of life. In the late twelfth century BCE, Babylonian invaders demolished the Middle Elamite kingdom and enslaved thousands of Elamites. The centuries that followed are known as the Neo-Elamite period (from around 1100–550 BCE). Cities continued as civic and commercial centers, but on a smaller scale. Another cultural complex was centered around Luristan in western Iran, and flourished from 1000 to 650 BCE during the Iron Age. This culture is credited with having created a distinctive copper-bronze technology using the lost wax and sheet metal-work processes. Because they created many objects relating to horses, an equestrian or semi-nomadic culture has been postulated.

None of the indigenous peoples referred to this region as "Iran." That term would come to be used only after 1500 BCE with the migration of Iranians onto the plateau from Central Asia. These immigrants gave their name to the land itself—Iran. The Iranians brought with them worship of Ahura Mazda (the faith now called Zoroastrianism or Mazdaism). One tribe, the Persians, referred to southwestern Iran as Parsa—from which the modern provincial term Fars and the name of the Iranian language Farsi or New Persian are derived. Another tribe, the Medes, settled in the west and northwest of the plateau, and so that region came to be known as Media. Their kingdom, under a hereditary monarchy, lasted from approximately 673 to 550 BCE. The two principal Median cities were their capital, Ecbatana (adjacent to the modern city of Hamadan), and Tepe Nush-i Jan. Social class in Median society was indicated by colored clothing—especially, white for priest and purple for warriors. The rights and obligations of women and children fell within the domain of the household of each adult, free-born male. In 550 BCE a Persian nobleman named Cyrus II, whose maternal lineage linked him to the Median rulers, founded the Achaemenian dynasty (550–331 BCE). At its zenith, under Darius I and Xerxes I, that regime ruled a multinational empire stretching from Egypt to the Indus river valley. Each ethnic and religious group within the empire was granted official permission and funds to pursue their mores and beliefs so long as they recognized the ruling dynasty's authority. Jews, who had been enslaved by the Babylonians since 587 BCE, were freed and permitted to rebuild the Temple in Jerusalem. Major cities of the Achaemenian era included Persepolis, Pasargadae, and Susa. Relations with the Greeks took a turn for the worse towards the end of Darius I's reign. Eventually, Achaemenian power ended with the Greco-Macedonian conquest under Alexander in 331 BCE.

During a power struggle after Alexander's demise, his general Seleucus I gained control of Iran and established a dynasty. The Seleucids ruled Iran from 312 to 141 BCE. Migration of Greeks on to the Iranian plateau took place. They built Hellenistic cities (such as Seleucia on the Tigris river), intermarried with Iranians, and introduced Greek customs, dress, and language to Iran. A variety of religious cults flourished during the Seleucid era—merging Zoroastrian and Greek devotionalism. But, during the late third century BCE, a nomadic Iranian tribe called the Parni migrated into northeastern Iran. The Parni were famous for their horsemanship. They took over the province of Parthia (present-day Khurasan) from the Seleucids by 238 BCE. The first Parthian capital city was Nisa (now located in the Central Asia Republic of Turkmenistan). Once the

Parthians reached western Iran, they moved their capital to Ctesiphon (near present-day Baghdad, now the capital of Iraq). Repeated military clashes took place between the Parthians and the Romans along a common border in Mesopotamia. Reasons for this dynasty's downfall lay, however, in internal socioeconomic issues. A few specimens of Parthian literature have survived; so have commercial contracts. In 224 CE a Persian nobleman named Ardashir I ousted the Parthian regime and founded the Sasanian dynasty, which was also based at the city of Ctesiphon. Sasanian Iran adopted Zoroastrianism as the religion of state. Zoroastrians formed the major confessional group, with Jews and Christians regarded as officially protected minorities. Members of the latter two communities paid a poll tax (or *gazidag*) to the state. A social class system that had existed for several centuries was institutionalized. Under that system the king of kings and royal family stood at the apex, followed by princely families and magi. Next came members of the nobility, followed by free men, women, and scribes, then merchants, artisans, farmers, herdsmen, and finally slaves. Political and social upheavals included invasions by Turkish tribes from the east. At its height the Sasanian kingdom encompassed modern-day Iran, Iraq, Azerbaijan, Armenia, the United Arab Emirates, northern Arabia, Afghanistan, and parts of Turkmenistan.

Sasanian rule ended with the Arab invasion of Iran in the early to middle seventh century CE. Arrival of Arab troops and tribesfolk brought a new religion—Islam, and a new language—Arabic. Between the eighth and thirteenth centuries, Iran was ruled first by the Arab Umayyad dynasty (661–750 CE) and then by the Arabo-Persian 'Abbasid dynasty (750–1258 CE) as part of the Muslim caliphate. During that time conversion of the Iranian population first to Sunni Islam and gradually to Shi'i Islam occurred. Zoroastrians became a minority like Jews and Christians—living as a protected (or *dhimmi*) community and paying a poll tax (or *jizya*). Gradual disintegration of 'Abbasid rule witnessed the rise of indigenous principalities—most important of which were the Samanids (892–1005 CE) and Buyids (924–1055 CE)—whose princes served as patrons for the revival of Iranian culture and the Persian language culminating in a national epic titled the Book of Kings (or *Shahnama*) by the poet Ferdowsi (d. circa 1020 CE). Large-scale Turkification of Iranian society commenced in the tenth century CE with the arrival of the Ghaznavids (924–1055 CE), then the Qarakhanids (eleventh century CE), and finally the Seljuks (1037–1194 CE), who followed the Sunni form

of Islam. Muslim religious education benefited greatly from the spread of theological colleges (or *madrasas*) staffed by religious scholars (or *Ulama—Mollahs*) at cities like Nishapur. The Seljuk period also witnessed rebellions by Isma'ili or sevener Shi'ites who became renowned to Europeans as the Assassins. Major tumult of medieval Iranian society occurred with the Mongol conquests in the thirteenth century CE. Ilkhanid rule over Iranian society between 1256 and 1335 CE was followed rapidly by the advent of Timur (Temur) or Tamerlane who established the Timurid dynasty (1370–1507 CE). Partially as a response to the socioeconomic turmoil, Sufism or mystical forms of Islam became popular.

Iran was reunified politically by the Safawids, an Irano-Turkish dynasty that arose from a Sufi order (or *tariqa*). Ithna-Ashari (or twelver Shi'ism) was established as the official religion. The Safawid period witnessed extensive urbanization at cities such as Esfahan. It was also the time of unsuccessful military confrontations with the Ottoman Turks, who were Sunnis. On the other hand cordial relations were established with the Mogul rulers, also Sunni Muslims, of India. In 1622 CE the British East India Company seized the island of Hormuz and used it to control the flow of maritime trade through the Persian Gulf. The British forced concessions from the Safawids, including unencumbered trade within Iran, settlement of disputes according to English common law, and the right to bear and use arms. European customs, clothing fashions, commercial guilds, banking, and art became popular. The British dealt mainly with Christian mercantile communities within Iran. To a certain extent the Jews of Iran profited from this trade. Parsis from India also functioned as intermediary merchants. The Zoroastrians of Iran, however, did not profit from those economic developments—barely surviving persecution by the Shi'ite majority. As trade surplus shifted in favor of the Europeans, the Iranian economy gradually collapsed. Riots occurred as the currency (termed *denars*) experienced rapid devaluation and food shortages arose. Decentralization of authority also took place, resulting in tribal groups becoming more powerful. Eventually a Ghilzai tribal prince named Mahmud led an invasion from Afghanistan and controlled Iran between 1722 and 1729 CE. The Ghilzai Afghans were ousted by a Qizilbash Irano-Turkman tribe named the Afsharids whose political authority lasted from 1736 to 1796 CE. An Iranian tribe from the Zagros mountains called the Zand also ruled (1750–1794 CE) certain southern and central provinces.

The Zand and Afsharid regimes were overthrown by another Qizilbash Turkman tribal leader, Aqa Mohammed Khan, who established the Qajar dynasty (1779–1921 CE). The second ruler, Fath 'Ali Shah, subsidized by revenue from trade with the British, fought and lost battles to the Russians, surrendering the Caucasus to them by treaties in 1813 and 1828 CE. As unpaid debts owed to England and Russia increased, the British took over policy-making for the Iranian imperial bank while the Russians drilled Iranian troops into a Cossack-style army to protect the Qajar shahs from a population that felt exploited by foreigners and abandoned by their increasingly Europeanized elite classes. Mass protests began against the monarchy, uniting merchants, clergy, political moderates, reformers, pan-Islamists, urban inhabitants, landlords, and farmers. That opposition culminated in the Constitutional Revolution (1905–1911 CE). A Majles was established. Laws guaranteeing freedom of the press and mass education were passed. The Majles also refused to accept new financial loans from the colonial powers. The Russians and British, sensing the rise of local power among Iranians, negotiated the Anglo-Russian Treaty of 1907, dividing Iran into spheres of influence: Russian control extended from Baghdad to Yazd, and then to Merv; and British control extended from Bandar Abbas to Kerman, and on to Herat. The treaty did leave a central, neutral zone to the Iranians. Iranian revolutionaries attempted to assassinate the reigning Qajar shah, Mohammed 'Ali, but failed. That ruler retaliated with the help of a Cossack troop brigade—the Majles was closed, its leaders were captured and killed. A second national assembly was set up, under much restricted terms with its members elected by only the elites of Iranian society. The shah and new parliament did realize, however, that the economy had to be reformed without Anglo-Russian influence. The Russians objected and moved troops toward Tehran. In December 1911 CE, the Qajars dissolved the second assembly and accepted Russian demands. This marked the end of the Constitutional Revolution which had brought women into the political arena, and led to the formation of women's groups and the publication of newspapers by women. Oil had been discovered in Iran in 1908 CE under a concession granted to a British company. In 1914 the British government took control of southwestern Iran where that oil had been found. As a result Iranian nationalists supported Germany during World War I. Iranian contact with Germany led to Russian troops invading northern Iran, Turkish troops invading western Iran,

and British troops invading from the southeast. The strife led to famine between 1918 and 1919 CE. By 1921 much of southern Iran was directly held by the British, and northern Iran was directly controlled by the Bolsheviks.

Then the British supported a military coup that brought an Iranian colonel named Reza Khan to power as Prime Minister. Reza Khan took the family name Pahlavi and in the spring of 1926 CE had a special Constituent Assembly declare him the shah of a new Pahlavi dynasty. Educational and judicial reforms under Reza Shah attempted to reduce the influence of Shi'i religious authorities and lay the basis for a modern state. A "uniform dress law" was passed decreeing that indigenous clothing for men and women had to be replaced by western styles. Women were no longer required to wear the veil. Iranian noble titles were abolished with the exception of shah; all other persons were addressed as Mr., Mrs., Miss, Master, and so forth. Civil marriage was established. The law of divorce was modified to grant women legal standing and rights akin with those in western countries at that time. Women were encouraged to seek education and enter the work force at all levels. New Persian was imposed as the language of the country over regional dialects. When Nazi Germany attacked the Soviet Union in June 1941, Iran declared political neutrality. In retaliation Soviet forces invaded Iran from the northwest while the British army entered both via Iraq and along the coast of the Persian Gulf. Iran was divided between the Soviets and the English, in terms of administrative and military control, along an east-west line that ran near Tehran. Reza Shah realized that the Allies would not deal with him anymore, so he abdicated in favor of his son Shapur Mohammed, who took the throne name Mohammed Reza Shah Pahlavi.

The new shah, Mohammed Reza, had only nominal authority over Iran until the end of World War II when the country gained independence. Several political parties began to merge, including the Tudeh, "Masses," party in Azerbaijan, and other provinces. The Majles began to function again together with a Senate (half of whose members were appointed by the Shah and the remainder were elected). During the mid to late 1940s CE American, British, and Soviet companies had begun to export oil from Iran while paying the Iranians only nominal concessions. The issue of Iranian control and pricing of oil eventually resulted in political confrontation between Mohammad RezaShah Pahlavi, who was viewed as favoring the West, and Dr. Mohammad Mosaddeq, who led the National Front Party which sought Iranian control of the oil wealth. In March 1951 the Majles passed a bill to nationalize the Anglo-Iranian Oil Company and the Senate approved that bill. Then members of the Majles elected Mosaddeq as Prime Minister. The Pahlavi shah tried and failed to dismiss Mosaddeq. In August that shah flew to exile in Rome. An Anglo-American coup d'état swiftly reinstalled the shah in power. By 1961 the monarchy was firmly in charge. He dissolved the twentieth parliament that year, then enacted the Land Reform Law distributing state and Shi'ite clerical lands to farmers. A campaign to eliminate illiteracy also was begun. The White Revolution was initiated in 1963 to modernize Iran's economy and society. By 1972 the percentage of owner-occupied farmland had risen to 78 percent. Per capita income rose from the equivalent of US$176 in 1960 to the equivalent of US$2,500 by 1978. The Jewish, Christian, and especially Zoroastrian minorities prospered as the ruling dynasty hearkened to Iran's pre-Islamic past as a time of national glory.

Once again a gradual transfer of economic control from Iranians to foreigners built up local resentment. At the same time, the Pahlavi dynasty alienated Shi'i leaders by stripping the latter's privileges. Opposition to the regime began to be suppressed and opponents driven into exile, or arrested and tortured, and some times killed. One such individual forced into exile, first to Turkey in 1964 and then to Iraq in 1965 for denouncing the land reforms, was Ayatollah "sign of god" Ruhollah Khomeini. In January 1978 theological students at Qum (where that ayatollah had taught) protested repression of the Shi'ite majority—riots broke out and spread to Esfahan, Shiraz, Tabriz, and Mashhad. In September 1978 government troops fired on demonstrators at Tehran killing many individuals, including Shi'ite clerics and their students, communists, merchants from the bazaar whose business had steadily declined, and western-educated intellectuals who wished to replace monarchy with democracy. By November the uprising had spread and the shah and his generals were using martial law to suppress the crowds. All the while, Khomeini had been denouncing the Pahlavis, protesting the plight of the clergy and common folk, and stating that Iran should be a Muslim rather than a western-style nation. Recordings of his speeches (smuggled across the Iran-Iraq border) were increasing in circulation despite attempts by the secret police (SAVAK) to halt the spread of such literature. By November 1978 Khomeini had moved to Paris where he met with other Iranian dissidents. In December 1978 the United States government advised the ruling family to leave Iran for their personal safety—they did so in January 1979. Ayatollah Khomeini returned to Tehran and established a Revolutionary Council to run the country. Thus began a government by the Shi'i religious leaders, a theocracy that continues to the present. Committees of mollahs tried and executed the elites of the precious regime. Many Iranians fled to the west to escape those repressions—giving rise to large expatriate Iranian communities in the United States (especially in the Los Angeles, California, area) and England. Relations with the United States deteriorated amidst charges of espionage, resulting in American embassy staffers being held hostage by militant students in Tehran. Only in the late 1990s CE, as the religious fundamentalism of Iranian politicians moderated, did diplomatic relations with western countries begin to normalize.

The population of Iran is approximately 68,278,826 (in 2003), with an annual average rate of population growth of 1.08 percent. The infant mortality rate is 44.17 deaths/1,000 live births. Life expectancy of women is approximately 70 years; that of men is 68 years. Partly as a result of a war between Iran and Iraq in the 1980s, 86 percent of the population is under 46 years of age. Overall adult literacy is 79.4 percent, with 85.6 percent of adult men literate and 73 percent of adult women literate.

JAMSHEED CHOKSY

See also **Iranians; Muslims: Shi'a in Sunni Countries; Parsis; Zoroastrians**

Further Reading

Adamec, Ludwig, editor, *Historical Gazetteer of Iran,* Graz: Akademische Druck-u. Verlagsanstalt, 1976–1988

Barthold, Wilhelm, *An Historical Geography of Iran,* translated by S. Soucek, Princeton, New Jersey: Princeton University Press, 1984

Bill, James A., *The Eagle and the Lion: The Tragedy of American-Iranian Relations*, New Haven, Connecticut: Yale University Press, 1988

Cambridge History of Iran, 7 vols., Cambridge: Cambridge University Press, 1968–1991

Encyclopaedia Iranica, New York: Bibliotheca Persica, 1985–

Farman-Farmaian, Sattereh, and Dona Munker, *Daughter of Persia: A Woman's Journey from Her Father's Harem Through the Islamic Revolution*, New York: Bantam, 1992

Frye, Richard N., *The Golden Age of Persia*, London: Weidenfeld and Nicolson, reprinted 1988

———, *The History of Ancient Iran*, Munich: C.H. Beck, 1984

Gnoli, Gherardo, *The Idea of Iran: An Essay on Its Origins*, Rome: Istituto Italiano per il Medio ed Estremo Oriente, 1989

Khomeini, Ruhollah, *Islam and Revolution: Writings and Declarations of Imam Khomeini*, translated by H. Algar, Berkeley: Mizan Press, 1981

Momen, Moojan, *An Introduction to Shi'i Islam*, New Haven: Yale University Press, 1985

Mottahedeh, Roy P., *The Mantle of the Prophet: Religion and Politics in Iran*, New York: Simon and Schuster, 1985

Wilber, Donald N., *Iran Past and Present: From Monarchy to Islamic Republic*, 9th edition, Princeton, New Jersey: Princeton University Press, 1981

Yavari-d'Hellencourt, Nouchine, editor, *Les Femmes en Iran: Pressions Sociales et Strategies Identitaires*, Paris: L'Harmttan, 1998

Iranians

Capsule Summary

General name: Iranians

Specific names: Persians, Tajiks, Pashtons and Pakhtons (Pathans), Kurds, Balochis, Ossets, Parsis, Gilanis, Mazandaranis, Luris, and others

Locations: Major communities in Iran, Afghanistan, Tajikistan, and Pakistan; minority communities in Iraq, Turkey, Central Asia, United States, India, and Canada

Total Population: 68,278,826 in Iran, 16 million in Afghanistan and Pakistan, 5 million Kurds throughout the Middle East, 2 million in Tajikistan, 500,000 Ossets in Caucasia, 250,000 in the United States, 76,400 in India

Major Language: Farsi (New Persian)

Other Important Languages: Balochi, Gilani, Kurdish, Luri, Mazandarani, Ossetic, Pakhto and Pashto, Tajiki

Religions: Shi'a Muslim (89%), Sunni Muslim (10%), Zoroastrian, Jewish, Christian, and Baha'i (1%)

General

Broadly the term "Iranians" encompasses all speakers of the Iranian branch of the Indo-European language family. In contemporary times the population includes most inhabitants of Iran, Afghanistan, and Tajikistan; large groups in the western provinces of Pakistan, northern Iraq, and northeastern Turkey; smaller groups in Syria, the Caucasus, and the Pamirs; plus diaspora groups in India, Europe, and North America—approximately 68.1 million individuals. The range of languages spoken by Iranians include Farsi (or New Persian), Tajiki, Pakhto and Pashto, Kurdish, Balochi, Ossetic, and several regional and tribal dialects of the Iranian plateau. Specifically in a geopolitical sense the designation now refers to the citizens of the nation of Iran.

History

The ancestors of Iranian language speakers probably separated from the Indo-Iranian-speaking Indo-European tribal peoples in Central Eurasia during the late third millennium or early second millennium BCE. Iranian tribal migrations during the second and first millennia BCE spread those people across Central Asia, onto the Iranian plateau, and into Afghanistan, Baluchistan, and the northwestern mountainous regions of the Indian subcontinent (now the North West Frontier province of Pakistan). In Iran those people formed a series of states with a distinctive culture—the Median, Achaemenian, Parthian (or Arsacid), and Sasanian kingdoms between the seventh century BCE and the seventh century CE. Iranian languages and cultures proved resilient despite the Arab conquest of the eighth century CE and the Turkish invasions of the tenth through the thirteenth centuries CE. Iranians did, however, undergo major religious changes—from Zoroastrianism to Sunni Islam, and eventually to Shi'i Islam between the eighth and the seventeenth centuries CE.

Society

Ethnically, in the nation of Iran, Iranians now consist of a majority Persian population (51 percent of the overall population) who speak, read, and write in Farsi. Important minority ethnic groups include the Gilanis and Mazandaranis (8 percent of the overall population) of the Caspian littoral, who are literate not only in Farsi but also in their own Iranian-language dialects of Gilani and Mazandarani. The Kurds (7 percent of the overall population), whose community is scattered between Iran, Iraq, and Turkey and whose aspirations for a separate state uniting those communities geopolitically have been quashed violently, continue to use Kurdish (which is another Iranian language). The descendents of Arab settlers (3 percent of the overall population) and Turkish settlers (the Azerbaijanis,

24 percent of the overall population) have retained the Arabic language and the Azeri Turkish language, respectively, but most are bilingual and use New Persian whenever necessary. Smaller Iranian tribes such as the Luris (2 percent of the overall population) based in the central Zagros mountains, the Balochis (2 percent of the overall population) based in the southeastern desert and mountains, and the Bakhtiyaris, Qashqa'i, and others (together 3 percent of the overall population) also retain their own dialects, clothing, and customs while using Farsi for cross-communal interaction. English and French mores and languages, legacies of European influences in pre-modern and modern times, are influential in middle-class and upper-class families. Approximately 58 percent of all those Iranians are urbanized. Tribal migrations have been curtailed during the past century with settlement of nomadic groups periodically enforced by the state. The Shi'ite version of Islam is the major sociopolitical and devotional influence in modern Iran (93 percent of the overall population), with a major theological center at Qum. Sunni Muslims (6 percent of the overall population), Christians (0.3 percent of the overall population), Jews (0.05 percent of the overall population), and Zoroastrians or Mazdeans (0.05 percent of the overall population) are recognized as official religious minorities, with legal rights albeit secondary to followers of Shi'ism and occasionally the targets for persecution. Bahais (0.6 percent of the overall population), on the other hand, are regarded as heretics by Shi'ites and have been subjected to discrimination. Present-day emigration, both officially and as refugees, of Bahais and other religious minorities to Western countries and other Middle Eastern nations is a legacy of the theocratic stance of the current regime in Iran.

In Afghanistan, where Pashto was adopted as the official language in 1936 CE, and in Pakistan, there are approximately 10 million Pakhto and Pashto speakers, 5 million Farsi speakers, and 1 million Balochi speakers. Afghan society experienced tribal warfare, revolt against monarchy, invasion by the Soviets and battles with the Russians, communism, and Islamic fundamentalism during the last half of the twentieth century CE. Societal strife and resulting famine led to massive population relocations, especially eastward into Pakistan. In Tajikistan there are approximately 2 million Persian (Dari) speakers. The Kurdish-speaking population in the Middle East is about 5 million. Ossets number around 0.5 million in Central Asia.

Migrations to India in the tenth century CE produced the Parsis, who gradually adopted the Gujarati language as part of their assimilation into Indian culture but some of whom still speak Persian. Immigration of Kurds to escape political repression produced communities in Europe and North America from the mid-twentieth century onward. After the Iranian revolution from 1978 to 1979 CE, middle-class and upper-class Iranians began relocating to the United States—forming a community now numbering approximately 250,000 with the largest concentration in Los Angeles, California. Smaller communities have settled in France and England. In those new settings the traditional mores of Iranian society have begun to experience considerable cultural stress as marked by ongoing decline in indigenous language use and familial practices among the children of immigrants.

JAMSHEED CHOKSY

See also **Iran; Muslims: Shi'a in Sunni Countries; Parsis; Zoroastrians**

Further Reading

Amighi, Janet K., *The Zoroastrians of Iran: Conversion, Assimilation, or Persistence*, New York: AMS Press, 1990

Barth, Fredrik, *Nomads of South-Persia: The Basseri Tribe of the Khamseh Confederacy*, New York: Humanities Press, 1964

Beck, Lois, *The Qashqa'i of Iran*, New Haven, Connecticut: Yale University Press, 1986

Bozorgmehr, Mehdi, editor, *Iranians in America*, Iranian Studies, 31, no. 1 (1998)

Choksy, Jamsheed K., *Conflict and Cooperation: Zoroastrian Subalterns and Muslim Elites in Medieval Iranian Society*, New York: Columbia University Press, 1997

"Ethnography," in *Encyclopaedia Iranica*, vol. 9, edited by E. Yarshater, New York: Bibliotheca Persica Press, 1999

"Festivals," in *Encyclopaedia Iranica*, vol. 9, edited by E. Yarshater, New York: Bibliotheca Persica Press, 1999

Friedl, Erika, *Women of Deh Koh: Lives in an Iranian Village*, Washington, DC: Smithsonian Institution Press, 1989

Kelley, Ron, Jonathan Friedlander, and Anita Colby, editors, *Irangeles: Iranians in America*, Berkeley: University of California Press, 1993

Momen, Moojan, *A Short Introduction to the Baha'i Faith*, New York: Oneworld, 1997

Momeni, Jamshid A., editor, *The Population of Iran: A Selection of Readings*, Honolulu: East-West Center, 1977

Moreen, Vera B., *Iranian Jewry's Hour of Peril and Heroism*, New York: American Academy for Jewish Research, 1987

Nashat, Guity, editor, *Women and Revolution in Iran*, Boulder, Colorado: Westview Press, 1983

Schmitt, Rüdiger, editor, *Compendium Linguarum Iranicarum*, Wiesbaden: Ludwig Reichert Verlag, 1989

Tapper, Richard, *Frontier Nomads of Iran: A Political and Social History of the Shahsevan*, New York: Cambridge University Press, 1977

———, editor, *The Conflict of Tribe and State in Iran and Afghanistan*, New York: St. Martin's Press, 1983

Iraq

Capsule Summary

Country Name: Al Jumhuriyah al Iraqiyah, or Republic of Iraq
Location: Middle East, bordering the Persian Gulf, between Iran and Kuwait
Total Population: 24,683,313 (July 2003)
Languages: Arabic (official), Kurdish (Official in Kurdish regions), some English, Turkish, Turkoman, Syriac, Assyrian, and Armenian
Religions: Muslims (97%, [Shi'a 60%–65%, Sunni 32%–37%]), Christians, Yazidi, Mandaean, and Baha'I (3%)

The Republic of Iraq (in Arabic Al-'Iraq, or Al-Jumhuriyah al-'Iraqiyah) is a nation with an area of 435,052 square kilometers (167,975 square miles) and is about twice the size of the state of Idaho. Iraq is bordered on the north by Turkey, on the east by Iran, on the west by Syria and Jordan, and on the south by Saudi Arabia and Kuwait. There are four regions that have a role in the nation's demographic characteristics: (1) a sparsely populated Upper Plain (dry grasslands north of Samarra), (2) a Lower Plain (the area from the city of Samarra to the Persian [Arabian] Gulf), which is an area of major habitation, (3) the North-eastern Mountains (Kurdistan, occupied by Kurds and other tribes), and (4) thinly populated Desert (the southern and western areas of Iraq that form part of the Syrian Desert). Iraq comprises three cultural areas: (1) Kurdish in the north centered around Mosul, (2) Sunni Islamic Arabs in the center around Baghdad, and (3) Shi'ia Arabs in the south centered on Basra.

Called Mesopotamia ("Land Between the Rivers") since classical times, the region's extensive alluvial plains along the Tigris and Euphrates rivers gave rise to early civilizations. The region became known as Iraq in the seventh century ce. Formerly part of the Ottoman Empire, Iraq was occupied by Britain during the course of World War I. In 1920, it was declared a League of Nations mandate under British administration. Modern Iraq was created after World War I and gained its independence in 1932. Today (in 2004) Iraq has 18 governorates of which three are Kurdish. Approximately 25 percent of the Iraqi population is rural.

The first official census in 1947 estimated 4,816,185 inhabitants; by 1986 the population grew to 16,175,000; and five years later was 19,026,000. Although data are not absolutely reliable since 1990, a recent demographic estimate is 24,683,313 (July 2003). Arabs comprise 75 to 80 percent of Iraq's population, with Kurds as the second largest ethnic group accounting for 15 percent of the national population. Baghdad, the capital, has a mostly Arab population of 2,969,000 (2000), and there are three cities with populations over 200,000: Basra (located on the Persian Gulf with 370,000 inhabitants), Kirku (in Kurdistan with 209,000), and Mosul (also in Kurdistan with 295,000).

There are significant Kurdish minorities in Iraq, Iran, Turkey, and Syria forming a large population (16 million, 2000) that inhabits a wide arc from eastern Turkey and northwestern Syria through Soviet Azerbaijan and Iraq to northwest Iran. Iraqi Kurds (3,100,000, 2003) speak a form of Persian Farsi, live in northern and northeastern Iraq, and are mostly Sunni Muslim. During the Iran-Iraq War (1980–1988) at least 300,000 Kurds were deported from hundreds of villages, effectively depopulating one-third of Iraqi Kurdistan.

The Assyrians are Aramaic speakers and number about 1.5 million, living primarily as merchants or farmers in major cities and rural areas of northeastern Iraq. In general they are Christians and affiliated with one of four churches: Chaldean (Uniate), Nestorian, Jacobite (Syrian Orthodox), and the Syrian Catholic. Another 100,000 live in the United States.

Yazidis are linked to the extreme Shi'a (Ghulat) sects and worldwide number 300,000 persons—the main group of 150,000 live in northwest Iraq. They are farmers and herdsmen who live in small and isolated groups, are of Kurdish stock, and are distinguished by a syncretism of religious elements of paganism, Zoroastrianism, Christianity, and Islam.

Turkmen, who speak a Turkish dialect (Turkoman), are village dwellers who number about 10,000 (2000); they live in northeast Iraq between Kurdish and Arab regions and near the city of Irbil. In Iraq they number more than 50,000 during the last half century, but were assimilated rapidly into the general population. Worldwide there are about 6.0 million Turkmen, the majority residing in northern Iran, Central Asia, and Afghanistan.

About 5,000 Aramaic-speaking Chaldean Christians (mostly Catholic, formerly called Nestorians) live in northern Iraq near Mosul. Culturally they are divided into two groups: Turco-Persian and Indian. An additional 150,000 Chaldeans currently live in the United States (primarily near Detroit, Michigan), and about 30,000 Syriac Iraqis live in the United States (2000).

The Mandaeans are a small religious sect in Ahwaz, Iran, and southern Iraq, who maintain beliefs resembling that of Gnosticism and Parsis. Also known as Christians of St. John, Sabians, or Subbi, they number a few thousand in Iraq; about 90,000 live mainly in the United States, Europe, and Australia.

Since the 1970s labor shortages resulted in an influx of foreigners (particularly Egyptians), whose numbers once exceeded 2 million (1990).

About 200,000 Iranians living in the south and east were deported to Iran in 1980 and 1981. In 1990 there were approximately 20,000 Christians and 5,000 Jews in Iraq; a recent report (January 2004) suggests that only 25 Jews remain. Persian-speaking Lurs live near the Iranian border, as do a small number of Armenians.

Arabs established the slave trade in the ninth century, which lasted a millennium, bringing Africans across the Indian Ocean from present-day Kenya, Tanzania, Sudan, Ethiopia, and elsewhere in East Africa to Iraq, Iran, Kuwait, Turkey, and other parts of the Middle East. Iraqis of African descent are largely concentrated in Basra.

The two major sects of Islam are represented more equally in Iraq than in any other Middle Eastern nation. A majority of Arab Iraqi Muslims are members of the Shi'ite sect (60 percent) and the Sunni population composed of both Arabs and Kurds (32 percent); 3 percent of Iraq's citizens are Christians, Jews, Bahais, Mandaeans, Yezidis, and others. Ethnically and linguistically, the

Shi'ites are Arabs with a small number of Turkmen, while the Sunnites include Arabs, Turks, Turkmen, and Kurds. Other religions include Christians (3.5 percent), Yazidis (1.4 percent), Mandaeans, Jews, and Baha'i (together, less than 1 percent). Chaldeans are affiliated with the Roman Catholic church. Found throughout the country are Jacobites and Nestorian Assyrians affiliated with the Eastern Orthodox church.

The economy in Iraq is dominated by its oil sector, which provides approximately 95 percent of its foreign exchange earnings. The Per Capita Gross Domestic Product was estimated at US$2,400 in 2002.

CHARLES C. KOLB

See also **Iran; Muslims: Shi'a in Sunni Countries; Muslims: Sunni in Shi'a Countries**

Further Reading

Andrews, F. Davis, editor, *The Lost People of the Middle East*, Salisbury, North Carolina: Documentary Publications, 1982

Basri, Carole, *The Jews of Iraq*, Jerusalem: Institute of the World Jewish Congress, 2002

Ember, Melvin, and Carol Ember, editors, *Countries and Their Cultures*, New York: Macmillan Reference, under the auspices of the Human Relations Area Files (Yale University), 2001

Gunter, Michael, *The Kurdish Predicament in Iraq*, New York: St. Martin's Press, 1999

Inati, Shams, *Iraq: Its History, People, and Politics*, Amherst, New York: Humanity Books, 2003

"Iraq," in *The CIA World Factbook 2003* http://www.odci.gov/cia/publications/factbook.af.html, 2003

Morony, Michael, *Iraq After the Muslim Conquest*, Princeton, New Jersey: Princeton University Press, 1984

Nyrop, Richard F., editor, *Iraq: A Country Study*, 3rd edition, Washington, DC: U.S. Government Printing Office, 1979

Ireland

Capsule Summary

Country Name: Republic of Ireland

Location: Western Europe, occupying five-sixths of the island of Ireland in the North Atlantic Ocean, west of Great Britain

Population: 3,924,140 (July 2003)

Languages: English (majority), Irish (Gaelic) spoken mainly in areas located along the western seaboard

Religions: Roman Catholic (91.6%), Church of Ireland (2.5%), other (5.9%) (1998)

Ireland lies in the Atlantic Ocean to the west of Britain and to the extreme northwest of the continent of Europe. Its strategic location shares major air and sea routes between North America and northern Europe.

Over 40 percent of Ireland's population resides within 97 kilometers (60 miles) of its capital, Dublin.

Ireland's name is derived from the Old Irish *Eriu* or in Modern Irish *Eire*, but in Latin Ireland is often *Hibernia* and *Scotia*, the latter applied exclusively to Scotland. The varying name of the state is a reflection of its twentieth century history. In the Proclamation of 1916 at the Easter Rising, the word *Poblacht*, anglicized "The Republic," was used; though the first Dail (Parliament) of 1919 did not define the state as such, the Declaration of Independence refers to The Republic. Between 1919 and 1921 Dail documents translate *Poblacht* as *saorstat* (the state). In the violent political split following the Anglo-Irish Treaty of 1922, which in turn was followed by the Irish Civil War (1922–1923), the country was named "The Irish Free State," which between 1922 and 1937 gave Ireland the same constitutional status as Canada, Australia, New Zealand, and South Africa. Opponents of the Treaty reverted to the Irish word used in the 1916 Proclamation, *Poblacht* (The Republic). After 1932 there was much pressure on de Valera to declare a formal Republic as a sovereign independent state, as proclaimed in 1916. But in a new constitution in 1937, The Irish Free State was superseded by *Eire*, and critics north and south refused to apply the name to one section of a partitioned Ireland. Although this name continues to be used on postal communications, it is now used derisively to refer to the southern Irish state by both unionists and nationalists. After World War II an inter-party government passed the Republic of Ireland Act in 1948 to describe the state as The Republic of Ireland.

In pre-famine Ireland the population was 8.2 million. It was reduced to 6.5 million by 1851 from death and emigration; by 1911 it fell to 4.4 million. By 1926 the Free State population was just short of 3.0 million; by 1961 it was 2.8 million. Northern Ireland, the partitioned Six Counties of Ulster, had a steady increase of population—from 1.25 million in 1926 to 1.4 million in 1956. The new economic policies, the subsequent and comparative prosperity, and the decline in emigration saw a rise in The Republic's population to 3.5 million in 1986 and to 3,924,140 in 2003.

Catholicism is the majority religion on the island of Ireland, but nowadays many Catholics differ from their church's teachings on such matters as divorce, abortion, cohabitation, pre-marital sex, contraception, individual confession, and the like. According to British statistics more than 5,300 women from The Republic had abortions in Britain in 1999. The general power of the Catholic Church in Ireland has waned in recent years as witnessed by the decline in the numbers of vocations to priesthood and religious orders, the decline in mass-going, and the number of schools now under lay control that were formerly run by the religious orders of Sisters and Brothers. Although formerly huge numbers of Irish clergy went abroad on missionary work, there is now a remarkable turn-around in that many parishes do not have their own Catholic priests. The 1991 census reveals the following figures of the denominations in The Republic: Catholic, 3,228,327; Church of Ireland, 82,840; Presbyterian, 13,199; Methodist, 5,037; Jewish, 1,581; Other, 45,080; No Religion, 66,270; and Not Stated, 83,375.

In Northern Ireland the same census revealed: Catholic, 605,639; Presbyterian, 336,891; Church of Ireland, 279,280; Methodist, 59,517; Brethren, 12,446; Baptist, 19,484; Congregationalist, 8,176; Unitarian, 3,213; Other, 79,129; and Not Stated, 114,827. The greater variety of evangelical protestant sects in the North compared to the South is noticeable and likewise the preponderance of Presbyterians over the Church of Ireland in the North can be seen as a legacy from the seventeenth century Scottish plantations. In The Republic the Quakers are a small historic minority, but whose humanitarian work during the Irish Famine of the late 1840s is still gratefully recalled.

English is the spoken and written language of the majority of the inhabitants of Ireland. English with Norman French first came into Ireland with the Anglo-Norman invasion of the twelfth century. But its use began to decline with the Gaelicization of large sections of the new settler communities in a revival of the Irish language, the original language of the Celtic peoples of Ireland. But English was maintained in the Pale (the area of Anglicization comprising about a 30-mile radius of Dublin) and in the towns. However, from the 1550s with the onslaught of colonization from England under the Tudor monarchs, the use of English became more widespread, helped by government policy including the penal laws that ensured that native Irish speakers came to look upon their language and culture as marks of conquest, failure, and backwardness. The Act of Union of 1801 enhanced the prestige of English, and the national schools used English as the medium of instruction. Famine and emigration in the middle of the nineteenth century greatly reduced the number of Irish speakers so that today the English language is the principal vernacular, and the dialect known as "Hiberno-English" is characterized by conservatism in language structure; archaic, obsolescent, and quaint English vocabulary; and the adoption of Irish sounds in the pronunciation of English. Interaction and cultural exchanges have naturally influenced every aspect of Irish history and society.

The Gaeltacht is the collective name for those areas of Ireland where the Irish language is spoken. In 1922 Irish was still the main means of communication in parts of Cork, Kerry, Galway, Mayo, Donegal, and Tyrone, with smaller pockets of Irish speakers in Louth, Kilkenny, and Clare. The Dublin government has given preferential treatment, including grants for Irish-speaking children, employment schemes, and Irish now has its own radio and television stations. The status of Irish as an official language since 1922 has helped to modernize what was an ancient tongue— mainly orally transmitted yet having a rich, classical, and for the most part a scribal literature. *Caighdean Oifigiuil* (or Official Standard) is now employed by all writers in a regularized spelling and grammar, and in modern times the Department of Education provides technical terms for Irish speakers. From 1893 the Irish language organization, the Gaelic League, aimed to revive Irish as a spoken and literary language, and its paper *An Claidhemh Soluis* sponsored the publication of verse and prose to heighten public awareness of Gaelic culture. League members took a prominent part in the 1916 rising in Dublin and in the subsequent growth of the Sinn Fein Party and the Irish Republican Army. The League was banned in 1919, but today it is generally known by its Irish name, *Conradh na Gaeilge*, and is still active in the promotion of the Irish language and literature.

The history of Ireland and of Anglo-Irish relations over 800 years is complex in itself and complicated by varying interpretations. Until the middle of the twelfth century Ireland's links were more with Scotland and Wales than with England, but there was a short-lived Viking kingdom of Dublin and of York. After the Anglo-Norman and Cymru invasion of the twelfth century, England's relations with Ireland became an uneasy mixture of colony and Gaelic and feudal lordships. Yet in the rhetoric of colonialism there was the theory of "two nations"—one dominant over the other. Despite the Gaelic revival in the late fourteenth and early fifteenth centuries, feudal-type lordships became the norm in what England called "the lordship of Ireland." Henry VIII changed this status to "the kingdom of Ireland" in 1541. But under Elizabeth I revolutionary changes led to what eventually and inexorably became a re-conquest of Ireland and a renewal of colonial government in which the Old English

colonists (mainly Catholic) were gradually displaced from administrative and legal positions by the New English products of the Protestant Reformation. The arrival of New English colonists (first in the Munster Plantation after 1588, and then after the defeat of O'Neill and O'Donnell in the Ulster Plantation, and eventually in Leinster in the aftermath of Oliver Cromwell's conquest and land settlements) legitimized their positions by a racist mentality whose roots can be ultimately traced back to the writings of Giraldus Cambrensis in the first invasion of Ireland. But the puritan revolution of 1650 led to the demise of the Catholic Old English who still in their theories held to the concept that Ireland was an equal though separate kingdom under the British Crown. The Restoration of the Monarchy with Charles II in 1660 did little for the economic or political power of the Old English erstwhile ruling class. They did, however, still persist into the eighteenth century in supporting the Stuarts in abortive efforts. The late eighteenth century saw the emergence of Protestant patriotism committed to the defense of a separate Irish constitution and for a brief period "Grattan's Parliament" would indicate that they were now a kingdom and not a colony. But the American and French Revolutions showed the way for successful republican government. Yet in the insurrection of 1798, "the Year of the French" Irish republicanism ended in defeat and victory for the British Crown forces. In 1800 by the Act of Union, a United Kingdom of Britain and Ireland was born— in theory equal partners, but in practice it left in Ireland an ascendancy of Protestant landlords, excluding the Catholic middle classes from power at every level. The history of the early nineteenth century is dominated by the movement for Catholic Emancipation (1829), the Great Famine (1845–1847), and the rise of Irish constitutional nationalism seen in the Home Rule attempts and its more violent manifestation in the Fenian Movement. To unionists north and south, Home Rule meant "Rome Rule" because any future Irish parliament unlike Grattan's totally Protestant one would have a ready-made Catholic majority. With the Republican rising in 1916, Home Rule became discredited, and the cause of independence and separatism from England helped the rise of a new Sinn Fein party dedicated to that cause. The ups and downs of Ireland's political future and constitutional status from the Rising in 1916 to the formal declaration of a Republic in 1949 may be seen in the various names for the Irish State at the beginning of this entry.

Today Ireland's newly created wealth and phenomenal economic growth with a surplus in the treasury, full employment, and comparatively low inflation has, however, created many social and other problems that only the prescient could have envisaged. For example, the treatment of asylum seekers has given rise to concerns over civil rights and the latent racism in Irish society. The country's per capita GDP is 10 percent above that of the four big European economies, and in 2002 was approximately $29,300. Drugs (especially in the cities) are now commonplace, and the consumption of alcohol has reached epidemic proportions, while a new car-owning class has caused traffic chaos and a terrible cost in the number of youth killed driving high performance vehicles. It may also be several years before the government's initiatives in health, transport, and education will make any meaningful improvement. Unprecedented levels and rates of change in Ireland have created many challenges for the next generation, especially in retaining the best of its traditional values while embracing the new.

JOHN MCGURK

See also **Catholics in Northern Ireland; Irish Republican Army; Northern Ireland; Travelers (Irish Nomads)**

Further Reading

Chambers Dictionary of World History, 1994

Connolly, S.J., editor, *The Oxford Companion to Irish History*, 1998

Coogan, Tim Pat, *Wherever Green is Worn*, 1999

Elliott, M., *Catholics of Ulster*, New York: Basic Books, 2001

Keogh, Dermot, *Twentieth Century Ireland: Nation and State*, Dublin: Gill & Macmillan, 1994

Lee, J.J., *Ireland 1912–1985*, Cambridge: Cambridge University Press, 1989

Irish Republican Army

The Irish Republican Army (IRA) is a paramilitary group dedicated to the unification of Northern Ireland with the Republic of Ireland. Their official name is the Provisional Irish Republican Army, or Provisional IRA, often referred to as "Provos." This is to distinguish them from the "official" IRA (OIRA). In 1969 following the outbreak of violence in Northern Ireland, the OIRA stuck to socialist politics, while the Provos advocated armed resistance to the Protestant majority population and to subsequent British rule in Northern Ireland. Both groups still favored the unification of Northern Ireland with the Republic of Ireland. The roots of the IRA reach back to the nineteenth century secret society, the Fenians, a nationalist group active in Ireland, England, the United States, and Canada. They were mostly unsuccessful in their efforts at winning widespread support for an armed uprising, and by the late nineteenth century their remnant formed a successor group, the Irish Republican Brotherhood (IRB). In 1922 after the six Ulster counties that would eventually comprise Northern Ireland had been separated from the now-independent Republic of Ireland by the terms of the Anglo-Irish Treaty, IRB members who fought against the Treaty became more and more frequently referred to as the IRA. Between the slow, though often violent, settling into peace in the 1920s until the advent of the Northern Irish "Troubles" in 1969, the IRA existed as a mostly marginal group. Although they were responsible for periodic episodes of violence, they did not occupy anything close to the major role in Irish and British history that they played between 1969 and the Good Friday Agreement of April 1998. Since that time they have more or less renounced violence, letting the group's political wing, Sinn Fein (Irish for "we ourselves"), play an increasingly important role in both Northern Irish and Irish politics.

History

The history of nationalism in Ireland is difficult to trace with precision, as are the origins of an awareness on the part of the Irish people as a distinct and separate ethnic group. Evidence of each exists as far back as the historical record, yet historians differ as to the nature and degree of these feelings. For the purposes of the history of the IRA, it is easier to trace a line beginning with the failed rebellion of 1798 to the "Troubles" that began in 1969, although the earlier movement, as well as those that come between it and the IRA, were each distinctive. The goals of the 1798 uprising were aimed at gaining Catholic emancipation and parliamentary reform. The movement consisted of Catholics and Protestants and took in the Defenders (a mostly secret paramilitary group) and the United Irishmen (a mostly bourgeois) Protestant club devoted to radical politics.

Following the devastating effects of the Irish potato famine, or Great Famine (1845–1850), more militant forms of Irish nationalism gathered greater force. The 1850s saw the emergence of Fenianism, a nationalist group advocating armed rebellion and abstention from mainstream politics. Following an unsuccessful uprising in 1867, many Fenians renounced violence and prepared for a political solution to the problem of Irish independence, usually referred to as "Home Rule." They were succeeded in the same year by the IRB.

In 1913 IRB members helped to form the Irish National Volunteers, a militia group offering armed resistance to the Ulster Volunteers, a Protestant paramilitary group that had been organized earlier in the year to "protect" Ulster's majority Protestant population. Many Irish Volunteers then went off to fight for England in World War I. Those who refused stayed behind and joined with IRB supreme council members and the much smaller Irish Citizens Army to lead the 1916 Easter Rising in which a coup d'etat was attempted in Dublin. Hopes for additional weapons were spoiled when the German steamer *Aud* was intercepted by the British navy, and an anticipated taking up of arms in the provinces outside Dublin failed to materialize. This left approximately 1,200 men trying to wrest Ireland from English control by first seizing the General Post Office on the morning following Easter, April 24th. Some historians have argued that the swift response of the British was far too brutal—it included executing the 16 surviving organizers and putting Dublin under essentially martial law, which had the unintended effect of radicalizing the populace. Others have claimed that the attempted uprising made a successful rebellion seem possible.

In any event the Rising decimated the ranks of the Irish Volunteers. The events of the Rising, along with fears that England would resort to conscription in Ireland, inspired greater support. After the end of the war, what was now known as the IRA continued to exist, although they lacked effective, centralized leadership. The group as a whole strongly protested the partitioning of Northern Ireland under the terms of the Anglo-Irish Treaty in 1922. A civil war broke out, with the IRA now being called the Irregulars to note that they had broken with the provisional government established by one of their former leaders Michael Collins. After a year of fighting, IRA leader Frank Aiken called for a ceasefire in 1923. With no real military options, politics was the only remaining avenue to unification with Northern Ireland, but this was complicated by the decision of the Sinn Fein party to sever its association with them in 1925. Attempts to form a new IRA-affiliated party failed in 1929 and 1931. A socialist left wing broke from the IRA in 1934. Irish Prime Minister Eamon de Valera, another former Volunteer, outlawed the IRA in 1936.

Early in 1939 the IRA engineered a series of unsuccessful bombings in England and was otherwise inactive and politically irrelevant. In the years following the end of World War II, the group both re-established its affiliation with Sinn Fein and re-dedicated itself to an armed effort to unify Ireland. The latter campaign lacked popular support. In the 1950s the group was at odds with itself once again as certain members embraced socialism, believing that leftist politics was a more effective tool with which to curry the support of the public. While dormant as an actual fighting force, the remaining members throughout The Republic and Northern Ireland maintained their belief in the necessity of armed struggle to reunite Ireland.

With the outbreak of violence in Northern Ireland in 1969, the IRA splintered. Civil rights protests by Northern Irish Catholics, designed to peacefully agitate for greater political and economic privileges, were repeatedly broken up by violent mobs of Protestants, which led to violent Catholic riots. At that year's Army Convention, the majority that favored a military solution to partition and abstention from politics broke away to form the Provos. The remaining members took the modified name of the OIRA.

Beginning in 1969, the Provos' reorganization into an active paramilitary operation was swift and, to the degree that lives were lost and violence became common, successful. For years the group had, ironically enough, used British military manuals to create and maintain its hierarchies and chains of command. In an effort to gain popular support and to keep peaceable Catholics from giving up members, they appealed to the long history of struggle against British rule in Ireland, to Ulster's long history as a center of rebellion, and to the nationalist republican tradition that stretched from the Defenders and United Irishmen of the late eighteenth century to the Volunteers and IRB, who were so instrumental in securing independence for the rest of Ireland. Of course more violent methods were also used to keep potential informants silent.

The IRA received an unintended boost in membership with the tragic events of "Bloody Sunday," January 30, 1972. The Northern Irish police force, the Royal Ulster Constabulary (RUC), failed to disperse a peaceful civil rights demonstration. An elite British parachute unit had been standing by, and descended on the remaining crowd with a hail of gunfire based on their belief that they were facing an IRA-sponsored insurrection. The army killed 13 unarmed people, none of them IRA members. The incident also won the IRA a larger measure of support among both Northern Irish Catholics and Irish Americans. The latter became key suppliers of money and weapons, especially Armalite rifles, that kept the self-appointed "people's army," a group of mostly working class Northern Irish Catholics, well armed and financially stable.

With the British army a regular presence in Northern Ireland, intelligence, military, and police forces tried to root out IRA leaders and members, especially when IRA-planted bombs began exploding in England in 1974. By the mid-1970s, the IRA were regarded as a criminal terrorist group. The Provos realized that in spite of numerous bombings and shootings the British army was in Northern Ireland to stay. The IRA also fought virtual open warfare through the 1970s with Protestant paramilitary groups in the poorer sections of the cities of Derry and Belfast. Having failed at the initial goal of pushing out British forces by destabilizing civic order, the group prepared for a long war with its "enemies"—the army, the RUC, and rival Protestant groups.

By the 1980s many high-ranking members began to tire of the endless rounds of violence. While the IRA and its cause were internationally known, no political gain had resulted. Support among the Catholic population, never as widespread as British authorities and Northern Irish Protestants had feared, was generally low. In the early 1980s, Sinn Fein resurfaced as the group's political arm. IRA leaders such as Gerry Adams and Martin McGuiness spoke of achieving the group's goals through a combination of "Armalite and the ballot box." England's Conservative government, elected in 1979, still regarded the IRA as criminal, not political, terrorists. Hunger strikes at the Long Kesh prison (known as the Maze) saw IRA prisoners demanding the rights of political prisoners. Ten men died and the international attention created by the strikes won a bit of sympathy for the IRA's cause, though not enough for the British army to cease its efforts to bring the group to heel.

Only in the 1990s did the pace of violence done by the IRA and Protestant paramilitary groups begin to slow through a combination of exhaustion on the part of the people most affected by the violence, increased economic prosperity, and increased international pressure from Ireland, Great Britain, and the United States (following the election of Bill Clinton in 1992). Sinn Fein also began to make inroads as a genuine political force in Catholic areas, though its influence still considerably lagged that of the Social Democratic and Labor Party (SDLP), which held the support of most Catholics. Gerry Adams emerged as a charismatic and controversial leader who worked ceaselessly to cultivate the image of Sinn Fein as a legitimate political party with more on its agenda than support for unification and the IRA. By 1995 talks began among Irish, British, Northern Irish, and American politicians to try once again to bring peace to the region, previous efforts having failed in 1973 and 1985. The IRA began to entertain the possibility of letting its weapons caches be destroyed. Sporadic violence remained an issue as ceasefires came and went in 1994 and 1997. The Good Friday (or Belfast) Agreement, signed on April 10, 1998, called for a power-sharing executive with vastly increased Catholic participation in Northern Ireland's government. It also led to electoral reform, anti-discrimination laws, job-creation plans, and the comprehensive reorganization of the RUC, thought for decades to be guilty of anti-Catholic bias and collusion with Protestant paramilitaries. These steps fell far short of Sinn Fein's and the IRA's wish for a united Ireland, but they were huge steps forward. In the years since the Good Friday Agreement, Sinn Fein has seen its influence grow in proportion to the waning influence of the IRA. Other Catholic paramilitary groups have been formed, but none has the reach or influence that the Provos enjoyed. It remains to be seen whether Northern Ireland can remain both a stable and open society with no role to play for the IRA.

JOHN H. DAVIS

See also **Catholics in Northern Ireland; Ireland; Sinn Fein**

Further Reading

Bell, J. Bowyer, *The Irish Troubles: A Generation of Violence 1967–1992*, New York: St. Martin's Press, 1993

————, *The Secret Army: The IRA*, Somerset, New Jersey: Transaction Publishers, 3rd revised edition, 1997

Conroy, John, *Belfast Diary: War as a Way of Life*, Boston: Beacon Press, 1995

Coogan, Tim Pat, *The IRA: A History*, Boulder, Colorado: Roberts Rinehart, reprint edition, 1994

Elliott, Marianne, *Catholics of Ulster: A History*, New York: Basic Books, 2001

English, Richard, *Armed Struggle: The History of the IRA*, Oxford, New York: Oxford University Press, 2003

Moloney, Ed, *A Secret History of the IRA*, New York: W.W. Norton & Company, 2002

Mulholland, Marc, *The Longest War: Northern Ireland's Troubled History*, Oxford: Oxford University Press, 2002

O'Malley, Padraig, *Uncivil Wars: Ireland Today*, Dublin: Blackwater Press, 1999

Ismailis

Capsule Summary

Location: Asia, Africa, the Middle East, Europe, and North America
Total Population: Several million
Languages: Many, including Persian, Arabic, and Indic languages
Religion: Shi'a Islam

The Ismailis are an important religious community belonging to the Shi'a branch of Islam. Numbering several million, the Ismailis are today scattered as religious minorities in more than 25 countries of Asia, Africa, the Middle East, Europe, and North America. The Ismailis belong to a diversity of ethnic groups and speak a variety of languages, including Persian, Arabic, and Indic languages.

The Ismailis have had a long and complex history dating back to the eighth century, when they first appeared as an independent Shi'i Muslim community. By the middle of the ninth century the Ismailis had organized a dynamic, revolutionary movement, designated as the *da'wa* (or mission), against the established order under the 'Abbasid caliphs who acted as spokesmen of Sunni Islam. More specifically the primary religio-political objective of the Ismaili movement was to install the Ismaili *imam* (or the spiritual leader) to a new caliphate in rivalry with the 'Abbasid caliphate centered at Baghdad. It was the belief of the Ismailis as Shi'i Muslims that their imam belonging to the Prophet Muhammad's family was the sole authoritative source for interpreting and explaining the message of Islam to the faithful. The message of the Ismaili movement was disseminated by a network of *da'is* (or religio-political) missionaries in many regions of the Muslim world, from North Africa to Central Asia and the Indian subcontinent, receiving much popular support among different social strata.

The early success of the Ismaili mission culminated in 909 CE in the foundation of an Ismaili state, known as the Fatimid caliphate, in North Africa. The Ismaili imam now ruled over an important state that soon evolved into a major empire stretching from North Africa to Egypt and Arabia, as well as Syria and Palestine, also including the island of Sicily. During the Fatimid period of their history (909–1171 CE) the Ismailis practiced their faith openly within the boundaries of the Fatimid state, whereas elsewhere they continued to be persecuted by many other Muslim dynasties. The Fatimid period indeed represented the "golden age" of Ismailism when Ismaili thought and literature also attained their summit. The recovery of Ismaili literature in the twentieth century, which initiated the modern scholarship in Ismaili studies, attests to the richness and diversity of the literary and intellectual traditions of the Ismailis.

From early on the Ismailis had developed a distinctive system of religious thought based on a fundamental distinction between the exoteric (*zahir*) and esoteric (*batin*) aspects of the sacred scriptures and the commandments and prohibitions of religion. The main components of this system were comprised essentially of a cyclical view of the religious history of mankind and a cosmological doctrine. These doctrines were fully elaborated in Fatimid times by numerous learned *da'is* who were at the same time the scholars and authors of their community. A number of Ismaili *da'is* operating in Iran and Central Asia also amalgamated their theology with Neoplatonism and other philosophical traditions giving rise to the distinctively Ismaili intellectual tradition of "philosophical theology." Ismaili law was also codified in the Fatimid period mainly due to the efforts of Qadi al-Nu'man (d. 974), the foremost Fatimid jurist. At the same time, the Ismailis founded a number of institutions of learning as well as major libraries in their capital city of Cairo, which itself was founded by the Fatimids in 969. In Egypt the Fatimids patronized intellectual activities in general and Cairo grew into a major center of Islamic scholarship, sciences, and art, in addition to playing a prominent role in international commerce. Indeed by the end of the eleventh century the Ismailis had made important contributions to Islamic thought and culture.

The Ismailis experienced a major schism in 1094 revolving around a succession dispute. As a result the Ismaili community and da'wa were permanently subdivided into the rival Musta'li and Nizari factions, named after the two sons of the Fatimid Ismaili caliph-imam al-Mustansir (1036–1094) who had claimed their father's heritage. Al-Musta'li and the later successors to the Fatimid caliphate were recognized as imams by the (Musta'li) Ismailis of Egypt, Yaman, Gujarat in western India, and a portion of those in Syria. On the other hand the rights of Nizar, the original heir-designate to the Fatimid throne and the Ismaili imamate who had been set aside by a powerful vizier through military force, were recognized by the (Nizari) Ismailis of Iran and a majority in Syria. Later the Ismailis of Central Asia as well as Sind and other regions of the Indian subcontinent also joined the Nizari faction of Ismailism.

The Musta'li Ismailis themselves split into a number of major and minor groupings. From the time of the downfall of the Fatimid dynasty in 1171, the Musta'li Ismailis were represented solely by the Tayyibi branch, which found its stronghold in Yaman. The Tayyibi Musta'li Ismailis, who have not had any manifest imam since the 1130s and in his absence have been led by da'is with absolute authority, retained many of the traditions of the Ismailis of the Fatimid period. They have also preserved a good portion of the Ismaili literature of that period. By the end of the sixteenth century, the Tayyibi Ismailis themselves were subdivided into Daudi and Sulaymani factions over the issue of the rightful successor to the office of the da'i. By that time the Tayyibis of India, known locally as Bohras and belonging mainly to the Daudi branch, had outnumbered their Sulaymani co-religionists in Yaman. Subsequently, the Daudi Bohras were further subdivided in India because of periodic challenges to the authority of their da'i.

In 1785 the headquarters of the Daudis of India was established in Surat, then under British control. Since 1817 the office of the da'i of the Daudi Bohras has been handed down on a hereditary basis in the progeny of Shaykh Jiwanji Awrangabadi, and the community has experienced incessant strife resulting from opposition to the authority of the da'i. Under Tahir Sayf al-Din (1915–1965), the fifty-first da'i, the Daudi Bohras were polarized between his traditionally minded supporters and a number of reform groups campaigning for secular education and individual rights, as well as the democratization of the institutions of the community. The present da'i, Sayyidna Muhammad Burhan al-Din, succeeded his father as the fifty-second in the series in 1965.

Centuries of persecution and forced conversion to Sunni Islam in India took their toll on the Bohra population there. By the 1990s the Daudi Bohra population of the world was estimated at around 900,000, more than half of whom lived in Gujarat while the largest single Bohra community is situated in Bombay where the da'i has established the headquarters of his central administration. Other urban centers of Daudi Bohras in India are located in Doha, Udaipur, Ujjain, Surat, Ahmadabad, and Sidhpur. Outside of India, the largest Daudi Bohra communities are found in Pakistan and East Africa, to where Bohras had emigrated from the early decades of the nineteenth century. A small Sulaymani Tayyibi Ismaili community, numbering around 100,000, still exists in Yaman. The Sulaymani leadership has remained hereditary in the Makrami family of Yaman who established their headquarters in Najran, annexed in 1934 to Saudi Arabia. The present da'i of the Sulaymanis, the forty-ninth in the series, al-Sharafi al-Husayn al-Makrami, succeeded to office in 1976.

By contrast to the Tayyibi Ismailis, the Nizari Ismailis acquired political prominence. By the mid-1090s they had in fact possessed a state of their own centered at the mountain fortress of Alamut in northern Iran. The original founder of this state as well as the independent Nizari da'wa was Hasan Sabbah (d. 1124) who designed a revolutionary strategy, based on the seizure of numerous fortresses, against the Saljuq Turks whose alien rule was detested by the Iranians. Hasan Sabbah did not succeed in defeating the Saljuqs, and the latter did not manage to uproot the Nizari Ismailis despite their superior military power. The Nizari state, with its territories scattered in Iran and

Syria, survived for some 166 years until it collapsed under the onslaught of the Mongol hordes in 1256. Despite their preoccupation with their survival in an extremely hostile milieu, the Nizaris of the Alamut period (1090–1256) maintained a literary tradition and elaborated their teachings in response to changed circumstances.

In Syria where the Nizaris held a network of fortresses, they reached the peak of their power and glory under Rashid al-Din Sinan (d. 1193), their most renowned leader. The Nizari Ismailis of Syria had extended military and diplomatic encounters with the Crusaders who made them famous in medieval Europe as the Assassins, the followers of a mysterious Old Man of the Mountain. The Crusaders and their occidental historians were also responsible for fabricating and disseminating a number of fanciful tales about the secret practices of the Nizari Ismailis—legends which attained their most popular rendition in the account of Marco Polo (d. 1324), the Venetian traveler to the Orient.

The Nizari Ismailis survived the Mongol debacle. However, in the first centuries following the destruction of their state and fortresses in Iran, the community remained disorganized and without access to their imams who had gone into hiding. Many of the Iranian Ismailis who had escaped from the Mongol massacres found refuge in Central Asia, Afghanistan, and India, where Nizari Ismaili communities already existed. The scattered Nizari communities now developed independently under their local leaderships; many also adopted Sufi and other external guises to protect themselves against further persecution.

By the middle of the fifteenth century the Nizari Ismaili imams emerged in central Iran and initiated a revival in the literary and missionary activities of the community. These activities proved particularly successful in Central Asia and the Indian subcontinent, where large numbers of Hindus were converted in Sind, Gujarat, and other regions. The Indian Nizaris became locally known as Khojas, and they developed a unique literary genre in the form of devotional hymns known as *ginans*. In the 1840s the forty-sixth Nizari imam, Hasan Ali Shah (1817–1881), who had been given the honorific title of Aga Khan (q.v.) by the Qajar monarch of Iran, emigrated to India and initiated the modern period in the history of the community. Meanwhile an important Nizari Ismaili (Khoja) community was established in East Africa by the emigrants from Gujarat and other regions of India. Since the 1970s, however, most of the East African Khojas as well as

Bohras have been obliged to emigrate to the West owing to anti-Asian policies of certain African regimes. By and large the Nizari Khojas have retained their traditional communal organization, which includes officers called *mukhi* acting as the social and religious head of any local Khoja community (or *jama'at*) and his assistant called *kamadia*. Every Khoja community of a certain size has its own *mukhi* and *kamadia* with clear duties, including the collection of religious dues and presiding over religious ceremonies in the *jama'at-khana* (or congregation house) where the Khojas gather for religious as well as social and cultural purposes. By the twentieth century the Nizari Ismaili communities outside of the Indian subcontinent, too, were organized in a similar manner.

The last two Nizari imams, Sultan Muhammad Shah, Aga Khan III (1885–1957) and Prince Karim Aga Khan IV, the forty-ninth and current imam who succeeded to his position in 1957 on the death of his grandfather, have adopted numerous modernization policies, especially in the areas of education, social welfare, and female emancipation, also developing new administrative organizations for their followers. The present Nizari Ismaili imam has developed a multitude of programs and institutions of his own for the socio-economic and educational benefits of his community as well as the non-Ismaili populations of certain countries in Africa and Asia. To that end he has created a complex institutional network generally referred to as the Aga Khan Development Network (AKDN). Modern Nizari Ismailis, a progressive and educated Muslim minority, do not engage in proselytization activities, but the community has religious functionaries designated as teacher (*mu'allim*) and preacher (*waez*) who perform the vital tasks of providing religious education for members of the community and delivering sermons on special occasions. Today the Nizari Ismailis, representing a diversity of ethnic and cultural backgrounds and numbering several million, live in India, Pakistan, Tajikistan, China, Afghanistan, Iran, Syria, and numerous countries of Africa and Europe, as well as in Canada and the United States.

FARHAD DAFTARY

See also **Aga Khan (Ismaili); Muslims: Shi'a in Sunni Countries**

Further Reading

Barrucand, Marianne, editor, *L'Egypte Fatimide, Son Art et Son Histoire*, Paris: Presses de l'Université de Paris-Sorbonne, 1999

Corbin, Henry, *Cyclical Time and Ismaili Gnosis*, London: K. Paul International in association with Islamic Publications, 1983

Daftary, Farhad, *A Short History of the Ismailis: Traditions of a Muslim Community*, Edinburgh: Edinburgh University Press, 1998

———, *The Assassin Legends: Myths of the Isma'ilis*, London: I.B. Tauris, 1994

———, *The Isma'ilis: Their History and Doctrines*, Cambridge, Massachusetts: Cambridge University Press, 1990

Halm, Heinz, *The Fatimids and their Traditions of Learning*, London: I.B. Tauris in association with The Institute of Ismaili Studies, 1997

Hodgson, Marshall G.S., *The Order of Assassins: The Struggle of the Early Nizari Isma'ilis against the Islamic World*, The Hague: Mouton, 1955

Nanji, Azim, *The Nizari Isma'ili Tradition in the Indo-Pakistan Subcontinent*, Delmar, New York: Caravan Books, 1978

Israel

Capsule Summary

Country Name: Medinat Yisra'el, or State of Israel
Location: Middle East, along the Mediterranean coast between Egypt and Lebanon
Total Population: 6,116,533 (July 2002)
Languages: Hebrew, Arabic
Religions: Jewish (80.1%), Muslim (14.6%, mostly Sunni Muslim), Christian (2.1%), other (3.2%) (1996)

Israel's non-Jewish population is broadly classified as Arabs, Bedouins, and Druze. The Arabs are further subdivided into Muslim and Christian Arabs. Greek Catholics and Greek Orthodox constitute more than 70 percent of the Christian community; there are Roman Catholics, Maronites, Armenians, Protestants, and Anglicans. For functional reasons the minorities are divided between those who do compulsory military service (such as Bedouins, Druze, Circassians, and Christian Arabs) and the Muslim Arabs who do not.

The establishment of Israel in truncated Palestine in 1948 was accompanied by political, social, and psychological hardships for the Arabs as the majority transformed into a minority overnight. The Arab population of Palestine lost its majority status, involuntarily acquired the citizenship of Israel, and suddenly became an ethnic, national, linguistic, religious, and cultural minority in a pre-dominantly Jewish state. For a variety of reasons and compulsions, the political and economic leadership of the Arabs fled Palestine leaving behind the Arab population strongly attached to the land politically and culturally leaderless.

Palestinians who did not leave the mandated Palestine when the state of Israel was established constitute significant portion of Israel's minority population. They are commonly known as Israeli Arabs. In 1948 the Arabs numbered about 150,000; presently the figure stands at 880,000 and constitute around 20 percent of Israel's population. Most of the Arabs lived in six "mixed cities" with a Jewish majority: namely, Jerusalem, Tel Aviv-Jaffa, Ramle, Lydda, Haifa, and Acre; and two Arabs towns (Nazareth and Shefar Am). Besides there are 27,000 Bedouins in encampments in the Negev and Galilee.

There is a small minority of Circassians living primarily in Kafr Kama and Rihaniyya villages in the Galilee. The Druze Arabic-speaking offshoot of Ismailiyya sect constitutes around 9 percent of the non-Jewish population, most of whom living in the villages in the Western Galilee and Mount Carmel. In 1967 the Druze villages on the Golan Heights came under Israeli control and most of the 15,000 Golan Druze have refused Israeli citizenship.

Since the first Knesset election in 1949, the Arabs have been exercising their voting rights, and their voting percentage is high and comparable to the Jewish sector. Under the proportional representation electoral system, a united Arab list can send up to 18 seats in the Knesset.

Generally Arab votes went to Jewish parties including the religious parties, while the Labor party cornered the lion's share. The Labor Party, which ruled Israel until 1977, usually floated a minority list to secure the Arab votes. Normally securing four to five seats, this list was a hasty electoral arrangement, which remained local, factional, and centered around regional notables and never evolved into a full-fledged political group or party. Dwindling popularity of the list compelled the Labor Party to abandon this practice and place Arab members in realistic slots in the regular Labor list itself.

For long Arab effects to form an independent non-Zionist political party that would struggle for Arab demands and grievances remained unfulfilled. In 1965 an Arab list called *al-Ard* (The Land) was disqualified as an anti-state and subversive move. Until the formation of Arab Democratic Party in 1988, the Communist party remained the only anti-Zionist option for the Arab voters. In 1996 the Islamic Movement, which was active in the local politics, decided to fight the Knesset elections and fielded a joint list with the Arab Democratic Party.

The Arab community made significant progress since the Labor Party came to power in 1992, and for much of its tenure the Rabin-Peres government depended upon the support of the five Arab MKs in pursing its peace policies towards the Palestinians as well as for its political survival. In return for this support, Rabin abolished the much-hated office of the Arab Adviser and increased budget allotments to the Arab sector, but the Arab parties are yet to become *kosher* to be a coalition partner. In March 2001 Salah Tarif became the first non-Jewish person to become a member of an Israeli cabinet.

Legally Israeli Arabs enjoy full citizenship and equality of status, but in practice there are inbuilt discriminations between Israel's Jewish and Arab populations. In the economic arena, the Arab community suffers from confiscation and expropriation of lands, budgetary discrimination, exclusion of Arab settlement from preferential treatment meted out to the Jewish communities, absence of incentives for Arab agriculture, and non-recognition of Arab settlements. The Arab community also lacks institutions such as the Jewish Agency, which subsidizes a number of infrastructural developments in the Jewish sector.

Legitimate differences over language, religion, culture, ethnicity, school curriculum, and prolonged neglect of the community segregate the Arab minority from the Jewish majority. Issues such as the Kafr Kassem massacre in 1956 and the expropriation of Arab lands have further contributed to sense of alienation among the Arab public. Demanding equality with the Jewish population, they consider themselves as part of the Palestinian nation but citizens of the State of Israel.

The activities of the Arab community were regarded as concerns of Israel's security system, and most of the areas inhabited by the Arabs were placed under Military government whereby the movements of the Arabs from within and outside the Arab areas were greatly restricted. This arrangement continued until its abolishment on December 1, 1966. Due to the ongoing Israel's conflict with the Arab countries, Israeli Arabs are exempted from the compulsory military service. Bedouins do voluntary service while military service has gradually been made compulsory for the Druze and Circassians.

Identifying with the Palestinians across the June 1967 borders, the Israeli Arabs have supported negotiations with the PLO and the creation of an independent Palestinian state in the occupied territories. In identifying with the political agenda of the PLO, the Israeli Arabs have generally avoided endorsing or participating in terror campaigns against Israel. Even the first Palestinian *intifada* of 1987 did not induce Israeli Arabs from indulging in violent activities. The same is not true of the *al-Aqsa intifada* in 2000 when Israeli Arabs resorted to violent protest over the events in the occupied territories and Israeli responses.

Religious courts, which enjoy communal jurisdiction, govern issues concerning personal status, and while ecclesiastical courts deal with the Christian communities the *Sharia* courts govern the Muslims. The application of the communal law has been reformed with provisions for challenging the verdicts of religious courts in the Supreme Courts.

Israel's economy grew rapidly in the early 1990s, and growth was strong at 7.2 percent in 2000. However, an increase of tensions in the Israeli-Palestinian conflict; problems in the technology sector, construction, and tourism; and growing inflation led to small declines in GDP in 2001 and 2002. In 2002 Per Capita GDP was estimated at US$19,500.

P.R. KUMARASWAMY

See also **Circassians; Druze**

Further Reading

Jiryis, Sabri, *The Arabs in Israel*, New York: Monthly Review Press, 1976

Kumaraswamy, P.R., *Political Legitimacy of the Minorities: Israeli Arabs and the 1996 Knesset Elections, The Emirates Occasional Papers*, no.20, Abu Dhabi: ECSSR, 1998

Landau, Jacob, *The Arab Minority in Israel, 1967–1991: A Political Aspects*, Oxford: Clarendon Press, 1993

———, *The Arabs in Israel: A Political Study*, London: Oxford University Press, 1969

Rekhees, Elie, editor, *Arab Politics in Israel at a Crossroads*, Tel Aviv: Moshe Dayan Center for Middle Eastern and African Studies, 1996

Stendel, Ori, *The Arabs in Israel*, Brighton: Sussex Academic Press, 1996

Italians

Capsule Summary

Location: Southern Europe, bordering the Mediterranean Sea
Total population: 58 million
Language: Italian (official), German (parts of Trentino-Alto Adige region are predominantly German speaking), French (French-speaking minority in Valle d'Aosta region), Slovene (Slovene-speaking minority in the Trieste-Gorizia area), Catalan (in the northwest part of the island of Sardinia)
Religion: Roman Catholic (mainly)

The Italians are an ethnic group living in the Republic of Italy, which has a population of approximately 58 million. In addition, according to estimates by the Italian Ministry for Foreign Affairs, there are a further 4 million Italians (or those of Italian decent) living outside the Italian Republic. In terms of language, Italian is by the far the most dominant language spoken, but German and French as well as Slovene and Catalan are also spoken within the territory of the Italian Republic.

History

According to the Austrian statesman Metternich, for over a thousand years, from the fall of Rome until the middle of the nineteenth century, Italy remained merely "a geographical expression." Compared with other European nation-states, such as France, Spain, and Britain, Italy was unified much later and indeed not until 1861. Before unification, Italy was divided politically into four main spheres of control: (1) the possessions and dependencies of the Austrian Empire, (2) the Papal States in the center of the peninsula, (3) the Kingdom of Piemonte and Sardinia in the north-west, and (4) the Kingdom of Naples and Sicily in the south. Furthermore, there were a number of small territories that maintained a degree of independence among the main rival powers. Consequently, strong local and regional identities have historically been very strong in Italy and are still very much a part of contemporary Italy. Indeed when the Italian State was proclaimed in 1861, linguistic variation was so pronounced that less than 10 percent of all Italians were able to speak the national language. Although a standard Italian language based on the dialect of educated Florentines had developed, very few people spoke it and so it remained an artificial second language to the majority of the population. Moreover, there was a plethora of local dialects spoken in different places, some of which are still spoken today.

The intellectual movement of the *Risorgimento* (or Resurgence) accompanied the creation of the Italian national-state. This consisted of philosophers, soldiers, and state figures such as Mazzini, Garibaldi, and Cavour. The main impetus for the unification of Italy came from the Piemontese monarchists who understood that regional differentiation was the principal obstacle to the process of unification. In fact *"Fatta l'Italia, dobbiamo fare gli italiani"* ("Having made Italy, we must now make Italians") was their slogan. During the first half of the nineteenth century, therefore, Italy was geographically and politically situated between two of the main powers in Europe at that time, the French and the Austrians. At the Congress of Vienna in 1814 and 1815 (following the defeat of Napoleon) the restoration of Italy was strictly defined and controlled by the Austrian Empire, which gained control of the Lombardy and Veneto regions of Italy. The only Italian state that remained relatively independent of Austria was the Kingdom of Piemonte. Thus Piemonte, especially due to its proximity to France, became an important buffer between the two powers—a factor which would become key in successive years.

Between 1848 and 1849 there were revolutionary conspiracies and insurrections in Italy, as well as France, Spain, and Germany. In Italy, Piemonte declared war twice on the Austrian Empire and was defeated on both occasions. Nevertheless, the revolutions from 1848 to 1849 did mark a turning point for Piemonte; it maintained its own constitution granted by Austria in 1848, and from then on its political development diverged markedly from the rest of Italy. Shortly afterward, a parliament was established in Piemonte, albeit one that had limited power, although it soon began to exercise authority and facilitate political change. In 1854 Cavour became Prime Minister of Piemonte. He instigated far-reaching economic and financial reforms as well as skillfully negotiating the interests of the Kingdom abroad. The increased power of Piemonte combined with the success of its economic and political reforms ensured that the political climate and balance of power within Italy was altered.

In 1859, ten years after the initial uprisings, Piemonte fought a successful war against the Austrians. Cavour had conspired with Napoleon III of France in order to gain French support for the war. Piemonte gained Lombardy and Tuscany from the Austrians in 1860 and Nice and Savoy were ceded to the French. In the South of Italy, Garibaldi, whose popular nationalism had attracted volunteers to fight for the nationalist cause, annexed the Kingdom of Naples and Sicily. This effectively united Southern Italy with the Northern state of Piemonte when Garibaldi finally handed over these possessions to King Victor Emmanuel II of Piemonte. In March 1861 Victor Emmanuel II was declared King of a unified Italy, after the Papal states fell to the Piemontese army. However, it was not until after 1870, following the withdrawal of French troops from Rome and the occupation by the Italian army, that the city finally became the capital of Italy. Italian unification was not without its problems but the process managed to create a liberated Italian state, which was free from exploitation from dominant imperial powers.

During the period after Unification, Italy underwent further political, social, and economic changes as the nascent Italian national-state began its process of modernization. The problem remained that the newly formed national-state did not generate a great deal of commitment from the majority of Italian society. The challenges to the liberal Italian state intensified during the first two decades of the twentieth century with the growth of different political forces such as Socialism, political Catholicism, Nationalism, and Fascism. All of these political movements posed serious threats to the legitimacy of the Italian government. However, it was not until 1922 when Benito Mussolini came to power that the parliamentary system was abandoned in favor of a dictatorial, Fascist state within the space of only two years.

The Fascist period under Mussolini proved to be a difficult one for Italy mainly because of its alliance in 1943 with Germany during World War II, which was a fatal decision for Italian Fascism. Mussolini's popularity declined drastically in the face of food shortages, Allied aerial bombings, industrial action mainly in the North of Italy, and rural discontentment. His government subsequently fell and a period of intense political turmoil ensued, which culminated in the signing of an armistice between Italy and the Allies, which effectively ended Italy's connection with Hitler's Germany. However, this did not mark the end of the conflict, which actually intensified, especially in the North of Italy as the German forces tried to maintain their control over Italian territory. Eventually, the Germans surrendered in 1945 in the face of the Italian Resistance forces and the Allies.

The Italian Republic

The events after the surrender of the Germans and the Allied victory are particularly important in the context of the ushering in of a new democratic era in Italy with the birth of the Italian Republic in 1948. This period was one in which Italy suffered immensely. However, from this hiatus came some of the motivations for the drive towards democracy and socio-economic growth in Italy. These were the need to instill political stability after the demise of Fascism; the need to improve the socially and economically impoverished nature of the country in the aftermath of the ravages of war; and ultimately to maintain the integrity of the Italian national-state, which was still only 80 years old.

In 1946 the first free general elections in over two decades were held in Italy. Voters were asked to perform a double duty: (1) to decide by referendum between the Monarchy and a Republic, and (2) to elect their representatives to the Constituent Assembly, whose principal task was that of developing the Constitution for the Italian Republic. The Monarchy was defeated in the referendum, which was a crucial event in the shaping of the Italian Republic. The Constituent Assembly also drew up the Italian Constitution, which became the basis for the democratic, economic, and social development of post-war Italy.

Since 1948 Italy has undergone a range of economic and social transformations and has become one of the most developed industrialized countries of the world. Indeed it is a member of the G8 club of advanced nations. Yet in spite of these transformations, Italy still remains a country of marked social, economic, and regional contrasts. The most significant, enduring, and persistent division in Italy is between the relatively prosperous North, in which most social strata enjoy a reasonable standard of living, and the relatively poorer South, which remains beset by sharp income inequalities, high levels of both underemployment and unemployment, relatively poor public service provision, and relatively high levels of crime and social disorder. Furthermore, superimposed on this North-South dualism there are smaller scale, localized divisions that exist (in some cases that have existed for many years) in terms of wealth, dialect, culture, and level of development. Moreover, new divisions are being replaced or modified with others. For example, increased material wealth has reduced levels of absolute poverty, but consumerist values have affected the coherence and structure of family and community life. The influence of education, media, and television have ensured very high levels of literacy and public services, but social disorder, crime, and secularization have changed the structure of Italian society. Increased employment opportunities have improved living standards but have brought new problems. For example, Italy is now a country of immigration rather than emigration, which has created new challenges.

BENITO GIORDANO

Further Reading

Duggan C., *A Concise History of Italy*, Cambridge: Cambridge University Press, 1994

Gundle, S., S. Parker, editors, *The New Italian Republic: From the Fall of the Berlin Wall to Berlusconi*, London: Routledge, 1996

Hine, D., *Governing Italy: The Politics of Bargained Pluralism*, Oxford: Monument Press, 1993

Putnam, R.D., *Making Democracy Work: Civic Traditions in Modern Italy*, Princeton, New Jersey: Princeton University Press, 1993

Riall, L., *The Italian Risorgimento: State, Society and National Unification*, London: Routledge, 1994

Ivory Coast, *See* Côte D'ivoire

J

Jackson, Jesse L. (African-American)

Jesse Louis Jackson has been recognized as a leading American social and political figure in the movement for justice and democracy. An author and activist, orator, politician, and spiritual leader, he is known around the world for his work in human rights and economic justice, and he was the first black man to make a serious bid for the U.S. presidency.

Jackson was born on October 18, 1941, in Greenville, South Carolina. His mother was a successful hairdresser, and his stepfather, a postal employee, adopted him in 1957. Jackson attended the public schools in Greenville and eventually graduated tenth in his high school class. His academic and athletic background earned him a football scholarship at the University of Illinois in Chicago, where he enrolled in 1959. After several semesters, he transferred to the predominantly black Agricultural and Technical (A&T) College of North Carolina (Greensboro), where he received a B.A. in sociology in 1964. He moved to Chicago in 1966, did postgraduate work at the Chicago Theological Seminary, and was ordained a Baptist minister in 1968. While at A&T he was elected student body president and became a civil rights leader in his senior year, actively encouraging the sit-ins, demonstrations, and boycotts. Jackson joined the civil rights movement full time in 1965 when he became a young organizer in the Southern Christian Leadership Conference (SCLC) as an assistant to Dr. Martin Luther King, Jr. He went on to direct the SCLC's Operation Breadbasket, the economic arm of the SCLC, and served as the organization's national director from 1967 to 1971. On April 4, 1968, with Jackson nearby, King was assassinated while standing on the balcony of his hotel room. Jackson's appearance on national television the next day with his bloodied turtleneck vaulted him into national prominence. Jackson's ego, stirring oratory, and charismatic presence caused the media to anoint him, and not Ralph Abernathy, as King's successor. In 1971, however, Jackson was suspended from the SCLC after its leaders claimed that he was using the organization to further his personal agenda. That same year, after his suspension from the SCLC, Jackson founded Operation PUSH (People United to Save Humanity), an organization of economic empowerment aimed at expanding educational and economic opportunities for disadvantaged and minority communities. He traveled the country and spoke out against racism, militarism, and the class divisions in America, and he became a household name throughout the nation with his slogan "I Am Somebody." In 1976, Jackson created PUSH-Excel, a program aimed at motivating children and teens to succeed.

Jackson's support in the African-American community allowed him to influence both local and national elections. He was involved in the election victory of the first African-American mayor of Chicago, Harold Washington, in 1983. Washington's victory was attributed in part to Jackson's ability to convince over 100,000 African Americans, many of them youths, to register to vote. Jackson's debut on the international scene occurred when President Jimmy Carter approved his visit to South Africa, where he attracted huge crowds at his rallies as he denounced apartheid. After growing increasingly disenchanted with the existing political scene, Jackson decided that he would campaign against Walter Mondale and Gary Hart in the 1984 Democratic presidential primaries. His campaign centered on a platform of social programs for the poor and the disabled, alleviation of taxes for the poor, increased voting rights, effective affirmative action initiatives for the hiring of women and minorities, and improved civil rights for African Americans, poor whites, immigrants, homosexuals, Native Americans, and women. He also called for increased aid to African nations and more consideration of the rights of Arabs. Jackson received 3.5 million votes, and possibly 2 million of those voters were newly registered. After the 1984 election, Jackson devoted his time between working for Operation PUSH in Chicago and his new National Rainbow Coalition in Washington, DC, formed in 1986 and designed to be a force for reform within the Democratic party. It also provided Jackson with a platform from which to mount his 1988 presidential bid. Jackson's campaign received a much broader base of support than in 1984 and finished second to Massachusetts governor Michael Dukakis. His 1988 candidacy attracted 7 million votes, with his campaign workers registering 2 million new voters. In 1990, Jackson was named one of two "shadow senators" to Congress from Washington, DC, to press for the district's statehood.

A hallmark of Jackson's work has been his commitment to youth. He has visited thousands of high schools, colleges, and universities, encouraging excellence and urging young people to reject drugs. He has worked with unions to organize workers and has successfully mediated labor disputes. Jackson has received many honors for his work in human rights and social justice. In 1991, the U.S. Postal Service put his likeness on a postal cancellation. He is only the second living person to receive such an honor. He received the prestigious NAACP Spingarn Award and has been awarded more than 40 honorary degrees. For 10 years, Jackson has been on the Gallup list of 10 men in the world most respected by Americans. Jackson has played a role in such international struggles as the anti-apartheid movement, the liberation of Namibia and Angola, and self-determination movements in Latin America. In his capacity as international diplomat for human rights, Jackson secured the release of captured Navy Lt. Robert Goodman from Syria in 1984, as well as the release of 48 Cuban and Cuban-American prisoners in 1987. He was the first American to bring hostages out of Kuwait and Iraq in 1990.

Jackson received his master of divinity degree from the Chicago Theological Seminary on June 3, 2000. He had been only three courses short of earning his degree when he left the school to work with a minister more than three decades earlier. On August 9, 2000, President William J. Clinton awarded a Presidential Medal of Freedom, the highest civilian honor, to Jackson. Jackson is married and has five children, including a son, Jesse Jackson, Jr., who is a Democratic congressman from Illinois. In January 2001, in response to tabloid reports, Jackson issued a statement admitting that he fathered a daughter, born in 1999, with a former staff member of his Rainbow Coalition, Dr. Karin L. Stanford.

Biography

Jesse Louis Jackson. Born 8 October 1941 in Greenville, South Carolina. Studied at public schools in Greenville; University of Illinois; North Carolina Agricultural and Technical State University, B.A.,1964; Chicago Theological Seminary until 1965. Founder, People United to Save Humanity (PUSH), 1971, and the National Rainbow Coalition, 1984; Founder, Rainbow/PUSH Coalition, 1996; Recipient, NAACP Spingarn Award; Awarded the Presidential Medal of Freedom, 2000; Master of Divinity, Chicago Theological Seminary, 2000.

Selected Works

Straight from the Heart, 1987
Keep Hope Alive, 1989
Afraid of the Dark: What Whites and Blacks Need to Know About Each Other, 2000
It's about the Money: The Fourth Movement of the Freedom Symphony: How to Build Wealth, Get Access to Capital, and Achieve Your Financial Dreams, 2000

RICHARD VERRONE

See also **African-Americans**

Further Reading

Barker, Lucius Jefferson, *Our Time Has Come: A Delegate's Diary of Jesse Jackson's 1984 Presidential Campaign*, Urbana: University of Illinois Press, 1988
Barker, Lucius J., and Ronald W. Walters, editors, *Jesse Jackson's 1984 Presidential Campaign: Challenge and Change in American Politics*, Urbana: University of Illinois Press, 1989
Broh, C. Anthony, *A Horse of a Different Color: Television's Treatment of Jesse Jackson's 1984 Presidential Campaign*, Washington, DC: Joint Center for Political Studies, 1987
Frady, Marshall, *Jesse: The Life and Pilgrimage of Jesse Jackson*, New York: Random House, 1996
Hertzke, Allen D., *Echoes of Discontent: Jesse Jackson, Pat Robertson, and the Resurgence of Populism*, Washington, D.C.: CQ Press, 1993
Morris, Lorenzo, *The Social and Political Implications of the 1984 Jesse Jackson Presidential Campaign*, New York: Praeger Publishers, 1990
Simon, Charnan, *Jesse Jackson: I Am Somebody*, Danbury, Connecticut: Children's Press, 1997
Stanford, Karin L., *Beyond the Boundaries: Reverend Jesse Jackson in International Affairs*, Albany, New York: State University of New York Press, 1997
Wilkinson, Brenda, *Jesse Jackson*, Englewood Cliffs, New Jersey: Silver Burdett Press, 1990

Jains

Capsule Summary

Locations: Mostly in India.
Total Population: Approximately 6 to 7 million.
Languages: Prakrit, Ardhamagadhi, Hindi, Gujarati, Marathi, Kannada, and other Indian languages.
Religion: Jainism.

Jains are followers and practitioners of Jainism, or the Jaina religion. The names *Jaina* and *Jainism* are based on the term *Jina* meaning *spiritual victor, conqueror*, or *liberator*. There are different versions about the origin of Jain religion. The popular version is that Vardhamana Mahavira, a prince from the state of Bihar in northern India who was Jainism's most prominent preacher is generally considered to be the organizer of the Jain religion. This would place it in the sixth century BCE. Another version forwarded in the Jain literature, however, is that Mahavira is only the twenty-fourth Jina or Tirthankara (ford makers, or religious preceptors). According to this version, there were 23 other Tirthankaras before him, starting with Rishabha, thus indicating Jainism to be a very old religion extending back from 2500 BCE. The religion originated in India and predates. However, it is not as widespread as Buddhism, especially outside India. Jainism, like Buddhism, can be characterized as a protest movement against the caste system and some of the religious rituals and customs practiced by Hindus. Jainism, like Buddhism, is an independent religion and not one of the Hindu sects in spite of some commonalities between them and recent claims that Jainism is a part of Hinduism. The Jains probably started migrating toward western India by 300 BCE. Many of the kings and emperors in western and southern India were Jains or Jain sympathizers. While the Jains constitute significantly less than one percent of the population, their contributions to Indian life in general, and art, architecture, literature, economy, politics, and philosophy in particular, have been significant and out of proportion to their population. However, because of the small size of their population, there is comparatively very little study of the religion in spite of the existence of a large number of old manuscripts.

Jain Communities

There are approximately 6 to 7 million Jains in India according to many estimates. The number given in the 1991 census was 3.35 million members. The census figures are expected to be unreliable because many Jains prefer not to identify themselves as such in the census. There is concern that the number of Jains will be dwindling in the years to come. The Jains migrated from northern India to the western and southern parts of India along the trade routes as early as the fourth century BCE to avoid a forthcoming famine. Many of them stayed in the areas where they migrated and did not return. The migration from the north continued off and on. Thus, the Jain population is more widespread in the western and southern parts of India even though it originated in the north. Among the Indian states with a large population of Jains are Maharashtra, Rajasthan, Gujarat, Madhya Paradesh, and Karnatka. However, they are not even a plurality of the population in any of the states in India. In some states, there are less than 100 Jains. The Jains have also migrated to other parts of the world; there are approximately 75,000 Jains residing in those areas. The three countries outside India with the largest Jain migration are South Africa, the United States, and the United Kingdom. Based on the precepts of ahimsa, or nonviolence, the Jains have traditionally shunned occupations such as farming that might involve violence to other life forms, although there are a few exceptions. Many Jains are gainfully employed in commerce. They are also actively engaged in industry, professional, and white collar work as lawyers, educators, accountants, and medical personnel, and the majority of the Jains live in urban areas.

As a small minority surrounded by Hindus, the Jains have been acculturated to many of the Hindu social customs and practices for 2,500 years, and this has resulted in many commonalities between the two groups. Jain wedding ceremonies, for example, borrow many practices from the surrounding Hindus, but they retain their unique character. In some cases, Hindu priests with knowledge of the Jain rituals and procedures have conducted the marriage ceremony if a Jain preacher is not available. Marriages among Jains and Hindus are not uncommon. In such cases, the majority of the marriages include a Jain male choosing a bride from another religion rather than the other way around. The assumption is that the children will adhere to the father's religion. Jains do not have preachers. The Jains, however, have two levels of practitioners: the laity and the ascetics consisting of monks and nuns. Those of the Digambara sect believe that the ascetic capacities of women are limited. In the Svetambara sect, women are considered to be legitimate aspirants for salvation and are allowed to follow the ascetic life as *sadwhis* (nuns) and aim toward liberation and salvation. However, in the nonreligious realm the rights of women in both sects are recognized. Traditionally, Jaina women have exerted a great deal of control in the household affairs.

The major festivals of Jainism observe the five major stages in the life of Mahavira: conception, birth, renunciation, enlightenment, and voluntary death. After he felt that the mission of his life had been accomplished, Mahavira voluntarily fasted until he died of starvation. In a few rare cases, the Jains are allowed to fast until death, not because of desperation, sorrow, or grief, but if they feel that they have had a good life, that their life's work is done, and that they are ready for such a sacrifice.

Religious Principles and Practices

Religion plays a crucial role in the lives of all Jains. The actual customs and practices vary from region to region, as they are affected by the culture surrounding them. There are five important principles or guidelines that Jains follow: ahimsa or nonviolence in thought, communication, and action is foremost, along with speaking the truth, nonattachment or detachment from worldly goods, abstention from misappropriations, and sexual control. These apply to men and women, and the standards for the monks and nuns are more austere. Jainism has a continuous monastic tradition. *Puja*, or worship of eight substances, is another obligation of all Jains. Again, right faith, right knowledge, and right conduct are identified as the three jewels of Jainism. Jain cosmology is the most extensive of all religions, and the descriptions of daily rituals and practices are the most detailed of any religion. Many Jain monks and nuns wear facemasks to avoid harming even the smallest living beings. Similarly, their diet often excludes milk, because consumption of milk might deny the calf of the use of the mother's milk. It does not, however, mean that Jains have not engaged in wars in the past. Jain kings were engaged in warfare because it was necessary for the survival of their subjects. Jainologists have given many different religious explanations for such apparent contradictions.

Jains believe that every living thing has an immortal soul, and they believe in reincarnation. The ultimate goal of life is to complete detachment of karma to achieve nirvana, or the joining of other immortal souls that are in a static state. Renunciation of everything is one of the important activities for a Jain on the path to a better rebirth. The world is seen as eternal but revolving in different cycles. The Jain religion is divided into two major sects. The Digambara, or sky-clad (nude), monks do not wear any clothes (public places are recent exceptions), indicating an extreme form of renunciation and non-attachment to everything, including clothing. The Svetambara monks and nuns wear white clothes. Both sects are further subdivided into many sects. The Jains have not emphasized proselytization to recruit converts to their faith, although they will accept newcomers who believe in the faith and practice it. The Jains have faithfully adopted the practice of preaching their religion to the masses in their local language. One of the latent functions of this practice has been the proliferation of Jain literature in different languages and significant contributions of Jains to the local literature, although the early Jain literature was in Prakrit and Ardhamagadhi languages, both of which are variations from classical Sanskrit. The Jains do not believe in a single supreme deity. A few of the Hindu deities have been adopted by some Jains, and they have crept into the rituals such as worship and festivals. These deities, however, are not given prominence and they are secondary to the Tirthankaras, who are highly revered.

Jaina Contributions

This small community of Jains has made significant contributions to Indian culture. In addition to the major contributions to different languages in the country, the Jaina mountain and cave temples in Gujarat, Rajasthan, and Maharashtra states provide very good examples of the distinctive Jaina architecture. Jains also built some wooden temples. Jaina stupas or *stambhas* (towers or pillars) are usually very elaborate, with carvings and unique architectural characteristics. A 58-foot (17.68-meter) statue of Gomateshwara in Karnataka is more than a thousand years old. Jain paintings have established many traditions in India. The Jains can be considered an exemplary Indian minority. There is very little crime and violence in the Jaina communities. The Jains have accumulated wealth and income far beyond their proportion in the population. They have traditionally engaged in philanthropic activities that include donations to temples, schools, and hospitals, and they are known for their philanthropic contributions. This small community has produced a large number of entrepreneurs as well. In addition to the economic sphere, Jainism affected the Indian political scene during the Indian freedom movement. The concept and practice of ahimsa was borrowed, modified, and extended to the political field as a strategic tool by M.K. Gandhi. The practice of nonviolence has since been borrowed by many other minorities around the world in their empowerment movements. Jains are also highly tolerant of other faiths because one of their important doctrines is the relative nature of truth and the emphasis on many sides of reality. Jains have much to offer.

SUBHASH SONNAD

See also **Buddhists; India; Gandhi, Mohandas Karamchand (India)**

Further Reading

Carrithers, Michael, and Caroline Humprey, editors, *The Assembly of Listeners: Jains in Society*, Cambridge: Cambridge University Press, 1991

Cort, John E., editor, *Open Boundaries: Jain Communities and Cultures in Indian History*, Albany: State University of New York, 1998

Dundas, Paul, *The Jains*, London: Routledge, 1992

Sangave, Vilas A., *Jaina Community: A Social Survey*, Bombay: Popular Prakashan, 1980

Jamaica

Capsule Summary

Country Name: Jamaica

Location: Caribbean

Total Population: 2,750,000 (2004)

Ethnic Populations: Black, mulatto, East Indian, black–East Indian, white, Chinese

Languages: Jamaican Creole (also Jamaican Patois, Patwa, or Jamaican) English

Religions: Anglican, Baptist, Brethren, Church of God, Jehovah's Witness, Methodist, Moravian, Pentecostal, Rastafarian, Roman Catholic, Seventh-Day Adventist, Spiritist, United Church

Slightly smaller than the state of Connecticut, Jamaica is an island in the central Caribbean Sea, south of Cuba. Mostly mountainous and bordered by a narrow coastal plain, the island rises in its interior to more than 7,000 feet (2,134 meters). The higher altitudes have a temperate climate, whereas the coastal areas are tropical. The population is settled mostly in towns along the coast and more sparsely in the foothills and mountain valleys. The level coastal area provides the best agricultural land, but there is also agricultural activity in the interior.

On his second voyage to the New World (1494), Christopher Columbus landed on Jamaica, initially establishing the island as a Spanish colony. This settlement decimated the native population. None of these populations have survived so that Jamaica has no minority indigenous population. The Spanish character of Jamaica has also disappeared because of English conquest and occupation of the island during the mid-seventeenth century.

English settlement intensified the agricultural development of Jamaica, concentrating primarily on the cultivation of sugar. This crop was grown on large plantations for export. The labor requirements for the

activity were intense and were satisfied through the massive importation of black slaves from Africa, thereby establishing an essential characteristic of the Jamaican population with consequences that survive to the present: a small, wealthy white population dominating a mass of poor blacks. During the eighteenth century, two small minorities that entered the Jamaican population were Jews and Scotsmen, the former engaging in commercial and trade activities in the cities and the latter in engineering and professional duties.

The nineteenth century witnessed changes in the mosaic of socioeconomic and ethnic minorities in Jamaica that persist to the present. Sugar plantations declined over the first half of the century as slavery was abolished and international markets dwindled. A class of peasant and smallholder farmers, however, maintained itself. Agriculture in general revived toward the end of the century as banana cultivation began, and timely shipping gave this crop regular markets in the United States and Europe. To work on the banana plantations, however, East Indian and even Chinese immigrants were contracted.

Today three-fourths of the population is black and only a few percent white. About one-sixth is mulatto, a mixture of black and white. Just over three percent of the population are of East Indian and Afro–East Indian descent, and a smaller percentage have an East Asian heritage.

The most salient cultural heritage of Jamaica is black, or African. Whereas in Jamaica this population is the majority, in the rest of the world outside Africa it is a minority. This Jamaican population has played a significant role from the twentieth century in raising the cultural consciousness of black African minorities around the world.

During the early twentieth century, a Jamaican intellectual, Marcus Garvey, began a movement that promoted pride in African culture, asserting black dignity. He founded the Universal Negro Improvement Association. Through this organization and his writings, he pioneered his ideas of "black power" and a "back to Africa" movement. Garveyism projected itself throughout the Caribbean, the United States, and Great Britain, provoking considerable unease and hostility in the latter countries.

Some of his followers in Jamaica added a religious dimension to his ideas. Garvey had preached that salvation for blacks would come with the rise of a black prince out of Africa. In 1930, Ras Tafari, meaning Prince Tafari, became emperor of Ethiopia as Haile Selassie. His ascension initiated a "Rastifarian" movement in Jamaica that assumed a spiritual and messianic character similar to a religion.

In imitation of Ethiopian warriors, Rastifarians wove their hair into long braids, referred to as dreadlocks or the "Rasta" style. Many used ganja, the drug cannabis or marijuana, which they considered a holy herb. Police pursuit of Rastifarians provoked growing support of them because it seemed that pride in African heritage and power were being suppressed. Rastifarianism achieved growing influence in Jamaica.

The Rastifarian cultural style and a form of music, reggae, that emerged around it established a global identify and following of pride in African heritage. Reggae merged with the rebellious character of Rastifarianism. The music brought together Afro-Caribbean rhythms, U.S. jazz, and international rock, receiving international projection after the 1970s from the Jamaican composer and singer Bob Marley.

Jamaica has been described as the "loudest" island in the Caribbean because, through its development of Garveyism, the Rastifarian movement, and reggae, it gave a worldwide voice to the black African cultural heritage.

Reggae songs also advanced the native language of the island, Jamaican Creole. This language developed as a combination of standard English mixed with African and other languages. Known also as Jamaican Patois or Patwa, it is spoken by the vast majority of Jamaicans. Most of them use both official, standard English and Patwa.

Average life expectancy for Jamaicans is relatively high, at just over 75 years. Although the infant mortality rate is high, the death rate has declined due to improved public sanitation and health. Nonetheless, Jamaica has a minority of over one percent infected with the virus for AIDS. Per capita income is less than $4,000 per year, considerably lower than other nations in the Caribbean, such as the British Virgin Islands, the Netherlands Antilles, Puerto Rico, or Martinique. The Gross Domestic Product (GDP, 2002) is $3,800 per capita. Population increase is low because the Jamaican economy cannot produce a sufficient number of adequate-paying jobs for its inhabitants. Many emigrate therefore primarily to the United States, Canada, or Great Britain. Jamaica received independence from the latter country in 1962 and has since been a member of the British Commonwealth of Nations. The economic prospects for Jamaica are uneven because the country depends primarily on tourism and exports of bauxite (for aluminum), which has highly fluctuating international market values.

EDWARD A. RIEDINGER

See also **Afro-Caribbeans; Creole**

Further Reading

Bakan, Abigail B., *Ideology and Class Conflict in Jamaica: The Politics of Rebellion*, Montreal: McGill-Queen's University Press, 1990

Edmonds, Ennis B., *Rastafari: From Outcasts to Culture Bearers*, Oxford, England: Oxford University Press, 2003

Edwards, Bryan, "Observations on…the Maroon Negroes of the Island of Jamaica," in *Maroon Societies: Rebel Slave Communities in the Americas*, edited by Richard Price, Baltimore: Johns Hopkins Press, 3rd edition, 1996

Ingram, Kenneth E., *Jamaica*, Vol. 45, *World Bibliographical Series*, Oxford, England: Clio, revised edition, 1997

Lalla, Barbara, *Defining Jamaican Fiction: Marronage and the Discourse of Survival*, Tuscaloosa: University of Alabama Press, 1996

———, *Language in Exile: Three Hundred Years of Jamaican Creole*, Tuscaloosa: University of Alabama Press, 1990

Mason, Peter, *Jamaica: A Guide to the People, Politics and Culture*, London: Latin America Bureau, 2000

Meditz, Sandra W., and Dennis M. Hanratty, *Islands of the Commonwealth Caribbean*, in Area Handbook Series, Washington, D.C.: Federal Research Division, Library of Congress, 1989

Moneith, Kathleen E.A., and Glen Richards, editors, *Jamaica in Slavery and Freedom: History, Heritage and Culture*, Kingston, Jamaica: University of the West Indies Press, 2002

Patrick, Peter, *Urban Jamaican Creole*, Amsterdam: J. Benjamins Pub, 1999

Salewicz, Chris, and Adrian Boot, *Reggae Explosion: The Story of Jamaican Music*, New York: Harry N. Abrams, 2001

Sherlock, Philip, and Hazel Bennett, *The Story of the Jamaican People*, Kingston, Jamaica: Ian Randle Publishers, 1998

James, C.L.R. (Trinidadian)

Cyril Lionel Robert James, popularly known as CLR, was born in 1901 in Arouca, Trinidad, in what was then a part of the colonial British West Indies. His early schooling was at Queen's Royal College, which was modeled after a British Public School, in a pedagogical tradition and with a curriculum that he later said was designed to make him into a member of the British middle class. The ethos of his early training emphasized Victorian values of class at the expense of the racial realities that dominated the social world of colonial Trinidad. At school, he excelled in history, literature, and the game of cricket, a sport that the British had exported to the colonies. It is these pursuits that would inform his political activities throughout his long career as a writer and political activist until his death in 1989.

His early activism in Trinidad included the publication of two journals, *Trinidad* and *The Beacon* that promoted West Indian literature and became an important rallying point for an early intelligentsia's assault on colonialism and imperialism and their claims for a West Indian nation. In the early 1930s, James had begun a lifelong association with Marxism and was for many years a Trotskyite. He migrated to England in 1932 and became deeply involved in the radical politics of the time. He helped found the Revolutionary Socialist League by 1936, edited the League's newspaper, was a delegate to the Fourth International in 1938, and developed a reputation as a labor activist and a popular speaker on labor and colonial matters. During these years, he also reported on cricket for the *Manchester Guardian* and the *Glasgow Herald* and established his reputation as prolific writer. Apart from the short stories published before he left Trinidad, between 1936 and 1939 he also wrote a novel, a play in which he acted with the famous Afro-American singer/actor/political activist Paul Robeson, a history of the Third International, a general history of black revolt, an account of the Haitian Revolution, and published a translation, from the French, of a book on Stalin.

His work on the Haitian revolution, *The Black Jacobins*, became one of the cornerstones of the emerging modern historiography of the Caribbean. Eric Williams, the author of another celebrated work, *Capitalism and Slavery*, is on record as acknowledging that it is in James's study that the thesis of *Capitalism and Slavery* is first stated clearly, concisely, and, to the best of his knowledge, in English. The work, according to James, was conceived not so much as a contribution to Caribbean historiography but as a manifesto for the African revolution against colonialism and imperialism and for African independence. James had also been deeply involved in the Pan-African movement and, together with fellow Trinidadian and boyhood friend, George Padmore, had been instrumental in the establishment of the International African Service Bureau. This Bureau was responsible for the massive campaign of public education on Colonial matters and the organization of the political campaign in the United Kingdom that supported movements for independence in a number of African territories. James counted among his friends and associates a number of Africans, many of whom would later become not only leaders in the fight for independence but hold leadership positions in the post-independence state. Among them would be Kwame Nkrumah, who would later become the first Prime Minister and first President of the independent Gold Coast, renamed Ghana. James would publish *Nkrumah and the Ghana Revolution* in 1977, a history of the movement to Independence in Ghana and his understanding of the problems of ex-colonial societies as they dealt with the problems of independence.

James spent the years between 1938 and 1953 in the United States, during which time he developed theories on Marxism and contemporary society, lectured and published extensively on the role of Afro-Americans in revolutionary struggle, and was active speaking and writing for sharecroppers in southeast Missouri. Originally a member of the Socialist Workers Party, he left the Workers Party and with other collaborators formed the Johnson-Forest Tendency. He eventually left the Trotskyite Movement in 1950. Apart from writing for the *New International*, James also published *Notes on Dialectics* and *State Capitalism and World Revolution*. James eventually conflicted with the authorities due to the anticommunist McCarthyism of the time; he was interned on Ellis Island as an undesirable alien and then expelled from the United States. James used his sojourn on Ellis Island to complete his study of Herman Melville's *Moby Dick*, which was eventually published as *Mariners, Renegades and Castaways*.

On his expulsion to England in 1953, James returned to cricket journalism for the *Manchester Guardian* as well as the production of his usual torrent of political theory and commentary on world revolutionary struggles expounded in public lectures, pamphlets, and articles. During this stint in England, James also turned his attention to the Caribbean and, in particular, the movement for an Anglo-Caribbean Federation as a prelude to eventual political independence. He returned to Trinidad on the invitation of some of his old political colleagues and became the secretary of the West Indian Federal Labour Party. He also took on the role of editor for *The Nation*. This paper was the organ of the ruling party, the People's National Movement (PNM), headed by Eric Williams, the Chief Minister of the twin island colony of Trinidad and Tobago. Between 1958 and 1962, James engaged in a relentless campaign of public political education through his writings in *The Nation* and through public lectures. He was a proponent of West Indian nationalism and an effective campaigner for the purging of Caribbean cricket of its stultifying inheritance of colonial attitudes of racial and color discrimination. His most enduring contribution to the political education of the society was his series of lectures characteristically called "Every Cook Can Govern," the title of an earlier publication and later republished as *Modern Politics*, which outlined the history of democracy and his Marxist-influenced understanding of the next stage of human political development—socialism or barbarism.

This collaboration between James and the nationalist movement led by Eric Williams, his erstwhile political protégé, did not last very long because James's understanding of party organization and strategy for anti-imperial struggle, honed by years of radical Marxist politics, soon ran counter to the dominant tendencies and personalities of the PNM. His clear ideological difference as expressed in his public lectures, his principled and uncompromising stand on the American occupation of military bases in Trinidad, began to make James persona non grata in official circles. The collapse of the Federation and Trinidad's move to independence hastened his break with the nationalist party. James was forced out of the party and eventually headed back to England in 1962 and published *Party Politics in the West Indies*, a scathing and penetrating critique of the historical roots and structural limitations of political organizations and political personality in the Caribbean. The following year, 1963, the classic *Beyond a Boundary* was published. Part autobiography, part history of cricket, this further established James's reputation as one of the twentieth century's major public intellectuals with an international stature.

James returned to Trinidad in 1965 to cover an international cricket series for an English newspaper. Suspected of being engaged in subversive activities, he was placed under house arrest by the Eric Williams government now in its third year of independence. James later started a political party, the Workers and Farmers Party, and contested the 1966 general elections with embarrassingly devastating electoral results. On his defeat he returned to England and, between 1968 and 1980, he visited the United States and continued his characteristic prolific program of public lectures and publishing of political pamphlets and temporary associations with some universities, in particular the University of the District of Colombia and its university prison program. In England, his association with *Race Today* was marked by a series of articles he wrote attempting to throw light on the enduring problematic issues of race and class in the struggle for human liberation. In the late 1980s, and after the collapse of the Soviet Union, he was rediscovered by a new generation of radical political activists and postmodernists who appreciated James's early grappling with politics and cultural theory and a Caribbean intelligentsia constructing an intellectual lineage.

He died in Brixton, London in 1989, and his remains were taken to Trinidad where the funeral arrangements were handled by the Oilfield Workers Trade Union with the support of the state now governed by a different political party who, in 1986, had awarded him the Trinity Cross, the nation's highest honor.

Biography

C.L.R. James. Born 1901 in Arouca, Trinidad. Highest level of formal education was secondary school. Attended Queen's Royal College in Trinidad. In 1986, was awarded the Trinity Cross, the highest national honor of Trinidad and Tobago. Died in London, England, in 1989.

Selected Works

Beyond a Boundary, 1963
Black Jacobins: Toussaint L'Ouverture and the San Domingo Revolution, 1963
Mariners, Renegades and Castaways: The Story of Herman Melville and the World We Live In, 1985
Minty Alley, 1971
Nkrumah and the Ghana Revolution, 1977

AUDRA DIPTEE

See also **Haiti**

Further Reading

Grimshaw, Anna, editor, *The C.L.R. James Reader*, Oxford, England, and Cambridge, Massachusetts: Blackwell, 1992
Grimshaw, Anna, editor, *Special delivery: The letters of C.L.R. James to Constance Webb, 1939–1948,* Oxford; Cambridge, Massachusetts: Blackwell, 1996
Ragoonath, Bishnu, *Tribute to a Scholar: Appreciating C.L.R. James*, Kingston, Jamaica: Consortium Graduate School of Social Sciences, 1990

Japan

Capsule Summary

Country Name: Japan
Location: East Asia, between the North Pacific Ocean and the Sea of Japan, east of the Korean Peninsula
Total Population: 127,214,499 (July 2003)
Language: Japanese
Religions: Shinto, Buddhism, Christianity

Japan is a country of islands that lies off the eastern coast of the Asian continent. Four main islands of Hokkaido, Honshu (the mainland), Shikoku, and Kyushu stretch out in a 3,800-kilometer-long (2,361-mile-long) narrow arc from north to south. Honshu is the largest island, accounting for more than 60 percent of the total land area. The Japanese archipelago also consists of about 3,000 smaller islands. The total area of the country is 377,819 square kilometers (131,749 square miles), which is slightly smaller than California.

The capital of Japan is Tokyo, and other major cities include Yokohama, Osaka, Nagoya, Sapporo, Kobe, Kyoto, and Fukuoka. Total Japanese population is 127.4 million (2002) at its current growth rate of 0.11 percent. Approximately 80 million inhabitants of the urban population are concentrated on the Pacific side of Honshu and in northern Kyushu.

The people speak Japanese and believe in Shinto, Buddhism, or Christianity (0.7 percent of the population). Whereas Japan's racial composition is often considered homogeneous both inside and outside the country, some minorities continue to exist despite the government's assimilation policies. Those groups include the Ainu, the Burakumin, the Okinawans, ethnic Koreans, and foreign residents.

Government

Japan is a constitutional monarchy with a parliamentary government. Its constitution was established on May 3, 1947, while the nation was occupied by the United States. The prime minister heads the government with the Diet consisting of the House of Representatives and the House of Councillors. Main political parties include Liberal Democratic Party (LDP), Democratic Party of Japan (DPJ), New Clean Government Party (or *Komei-to*), Japan Communist Party (JCP), and Social Democratic Party (SDP). The Emperor, who held sovereignty from the Meiji Restoration (1868) to the pre–World War II era, is now defined as a symbol of the nation.

Economy

Modern Japan is highly industrialized and its free market economy is the second largest in the world. Economic reconstruction after the end of World War II, especially from the 1960s to the 1980s, achieved one of the highest economic growth rates in the world's modern history. However, its bubble economy collapsed in the early 1990s and significantly slowed the Japanese economy, from which the nation still suffers today. Japan's GDP in 2002 was $3.55 trillion with –0.3 percent real growth rate. Per capita GDP counted $28,000 the same year.

Religions

Two principal religions in Japan are Shinto, which is the only indigenous religion of Japan, and Buddhism, which was imported from China in 538 CE. After the Meiji Restoration (1868), and particularly during World War II, Shinto was promoted as a state religion and played a greater political role. The religion no longer holds such privileges under the current constitution. Buddhism had significant influence upon social, political, intellectual, and cultural life for the following centuries. Japanese Buddhism belongs to the Mahayana (Greater Vehicle) school and preaches salvation in paradise for the mass population. Shinto and Buddhism have became intertwined over years and coexist in social and culture life today in terms of faith and practice.

Christianity was brought to Japan in 1549. It was forbidden during the Tokugawa period in the 1600s but was reintroduced in the late 1800s. It is estimated that there are about 1.4 million Christians in Japan today.

Historical Background

Traditional Japanese legend states that Japan was founded in 600 BCE by the Emperor Jinmu who was a direct descendant of the sun goddess. Surrounded by the ocean, the only countries that feudal Japan had contact with were China and Korea for the centuries to come. The very first contact with the West occurred in 1542, when a Portuguese ship made its way to Japan by accident. During the next century, Japan's shogunate feared that the incoming Westerners, mainly traders and missionaries, would result in a military conquest by European powers and therefore placed tight restrictions on foreigners. Eventually, it allowed only Dutch and Chinese merchants at Nagasaki and excluded all others. This isolation policy lasted for 200 years until 1854, when Commodore Matthew Perry of the U.S. Navy forced Japan to reopen its ports.

Japan's rapid Westernization resulted in the Meiji Restoration (1868)—resignation of the shogunate, restoration of the imperial status, abolition of the feudal system, and establishment of a Western legal and political system. Newly born modern Japan achieved international recognition when it defeated China (1884–85) and then Russia (1904–1905). From the end of the Sino-Japanese War to 1910, Japan annexed the Pescadores Islands, Taiwan, southern Sakhalin, and Korea.

Japan continued to gain higher status at the international level through World War I, in which it fought on the side of the Allies. In the tide of Western militarization, Japanese military leaders became increasingly influential during the 1920s and especially the 1930s. Japan invaded Manchuria and founded Manchukuo, a puppet state of Japan, in 1931, and then mainland China in 1937. Japan entered World War II in 1941, when it attacked Pearl Harbor, Hawaii.

Japan declared its surrender in 1945 after the atomic bombings of Hiroshima and Nagasaki. At the end of the war, it returned all overseas possessions including Manchuria, Taiwan, and Korea. Japan was occupied by the Allies, mainly the United States led by General Douglas MacArthur. Although the return of Japanese sovereignty in 1952 and the reversion of Okinawa in 1972 officially ended U.S. control over Japan, 75 percent of Okinawa's land remains reserved for the U.S. military, and a number of territorial and social problems persist today.

Minorities in Japan

Japan has been traditionally unaccustomed to ethnic and other differences, mainly due to its geographical location, which has created a collective identity. Additionally, Japan's feudal history and modern wartime abuse on other Asian populations cultivated a soil for discrimination against minorities. Historically, groups of people identified as different were often considered polluted and received social discrimination. While the degree and forms of discrimination have changed over time and vary from group to group, those prejudiced include the Ainu, the first inhabitants of Japan's northernmost Hokkaido, the ethnically Japanese Burakumin, the Okinawans, the largest minority group in Japan with a population of 1.3 million in the Ryukyu Islands, ethnic Koreans, and some foreigners. Koreans and other foreign residents such as Chinese are often descendants of those forcibly brought to Japan for unskilled labor during occupation of Taiwan (1895–1945) and Korea (1905–1945).

There is no measurement to estimate how many minorities live in Japan today because minorities generally do not receive official recognition in the political effort to assimilate their ideologies and lifestyles to those of the rest of the population. The general assimilation policy, or *doka seisaku* in Japanese, originally used for colonized peoples, helped improve in some areas such as health and public. The 1965 Law on Special Measures for Dowa Projects toward the Burakumin is often considered to have successfully improved the living conditions of the people. However, a large portion of the minorities still feel socially and culturally segregated and view the effort toward assimilation, which overlooks their ethnic identities, to be the root of discrimination.

AI HATTORI

See also **Buddhists; Japanese-Americans**

Further Reading

Denoon, Donald, and Gavan McCormack, editors, *Multicultural Japan: Palaeolithic to Post-Modern*, Cambridge, and New York: Cambridge University Press, 1996

De Vos, George A., and William O. Wetherall, *Japan's Minorities: Burakumin, Koreans, Ainu and Okinawans*, London: Minority Rights Group, 1983

Dower, John W., *Embracing Defeat: Japan in the Wake of World War II*, New York: W.W. Norton & Company, 2000

Gordon, Andrew, *The Modern History of Japan: From Tokugawa Times to the Present*, New York: Oxford University Press, 2003

Henshall, Kenneth G., *A History of Japan: From Stone Age to Superpower*, New York: Palgrave Macmillan, 1997

Ikeno, Osamu, and Roger J. Davis. editors, *The Japanese Mind: Understanding Contemporary Culture*, Boston: Charles E Tuttle Co., 2002

Jansen, Marius B., *The Making of Modern Japan*, Belknap Press, 2002

McClain, James L., *Japan: A Modern History*, New York: W.W. Norton & Company, 2002

Weiner, Michael, editor, *Japan's Minorities: The Illusions of Homogeneity*, New York: Routledge, 1997

Japanese-Americans

Capsule Summary

Location: United States, mostly in western states
Total Population: Approximately 1 million
Language: Predominantly English as first language
Religion: Predominantly Christian

Japanese Americans are an ethnic minority that numbers about 1 million and constitutes approximately 0.4 percent of the U.S. population with about two-thirds of them in California and Hawaii. They have been present in significant numbers in the United States since the late nineteenth century when labor migration began. Compared to other nonwhite minorities in the United States, Japanese Americans have attained relatively high socioeconomic and political statuses but are still subject to various forms of racial discrimination.

Japanese immigration to the United States and Hawaii in substantial numbers began in 1885 with the arrival of the first shipload of predominantly young men who had been recruited to work on the sugar plantations in Hawaii. Eventually nearly 220,000 Japanese immigrated to Hawaii and another 250,000 to the continental United States, primarily from the southwestern prefectures of Japan before their entry was banned by the 1924 U.S. Immigration Act. Before this large-scale migration, there were some Japanese in the United States such as government officials, businessmen, and students. The Wakamatsu colonists (named after their home city), who arrived in 1869 to develop an agricultural community in northern California, are often referred to as the first Japanese immigrants in America.

Japanese immigrants on the west coast of the United States were initially employed in agricultural labor, mining, railroads, and salmon canneries, whereas in Hawaii they worked on the sugar and pineapple plantations. Prior to World War II, Japanese immigrants became shopkeepers, domestic servants, skilled and semiskilled workers, truck farmers, gardeners, and laundry and nursery operators. The arrival of tens of thousands of picture brides beginning in 1908 resulted in greater family and community life and the cultural reproduction of Japanese customs and traditions in America.

Japanese immigrants encountered substantial racism and discrimination as they sought to participate in the larger society. In the early 1900s, they were demonized as the "yellow peril" threatening Americans and their way of life. The California legislature passed a resolution that called for the termination of Japanese immigration on the grounds that they could not assimilate for racial reasons. This agitation contributed to the so-called Gentlemen's Agreement between the United States and Japan in 1908 that limited immigration only to those who had close relatives in the United States. In California, the Alien Land Law of 1913, targeting Japanese farmers, prohibited aliens from buying land, leasing it for more than three years, and passing on land to their children. In 1922, the U.S. Supreme Court affirmed in *Ozawa v. United States* that Japanese were ineligible to become American citizens through naturalization, and this racist prohibition remained in effect until 1952. California and other western states banned intermarriage between Japanese Americans and whites until the late 1940s. Thus, although Japanese Americans were harshly criticized for being "unassimilable," legal barriers were established to prevent their assimilation into society.

The internment of more than 110,000 Japanese Americans in U.S. concentration camps during World War II is the most significant and tragic event in their history. The U.S. government maintained that military necessity justified such "relocation" because of rumors of Japanese American sabotage spread after the bombing of Pearl Harbor on December 7, 1941, but there was no documented incident of sabotage by a Japanese American during the war. Racism was the primary reason for the incarceration of Japanese Americans since German Americans and Italian Americans, who together totaled about 1 million, including 200,000 aliens, were not subject to such mass evacuation even though the United States was at war with Germany and Italy.

On February 19, 1942, President Franklin D. Roosevelt issued Executive Order 9066 that authorized the Secretary of War and military commanders to exclude "any or all persons" (not specifically Japanese) from designated areas in California, Oregon, Washington, and Arizona. Despite two-thirds of them being U.S. citizens, Japanese Americans in those areas were forcibly sent to ten concentration camps in isolated areas of California, Arizona, Utah, Wyoming, Colorado, Idaho, and Arkansas where they spent the war in crude barracks surrounded by barbed wire fences and armed guards. Deprived of their freedom and constitutional rights of due process and equal protection, Japanese Americans had to sell their homes, farms, businesses, and property at bargain rates, and their financial losses have been estimated at $400 million in 1945 dollars. In the camps, many Japanese Americans protested their unjust treatment by organizing strikes and demonstrations, refusing to be drafted into the U.S. Army until their rights were restored, and renouncing their citizenship.

After a redress movement was initiated by the Japanese American community in the 1970s, the U.S. Congress passed the Civil Liberties Act in 1988 that provided $20,000 in reparations to each living survivor of the camps and an admission that their "basic civil liberties" had been violated due to "racial prejudice." The more than 80,000 remaining internees in the early 1990s also received a formal letter of apology from President George Bush.

Japanese Americans have been referred to as the most socioeconomically assimilated nonwhite minority in the United States because of their relatively high socioeconomic status. Compared to whites, Japanese Americans have considerably higher median family income, occupational status, and educational attainment in terms of college completion. Thus, since the mid-1960s, Japanese Americans have been falsely stereotyped as a model minority that has succeeded on their own because of their hard work, perseverance, family sacrifice, and devotion to education. Another employment problem encountered by Japanese Americans is the discriminatory glass ceiling that restricts their promotion into upper-level corporate management and executive positions despite their occupational and educational qualifications.

One reason for the comparatively high socioeconomic status of Japanese Americans is because, unlike other Asian American minorities, they do not have a majority immigrant population. Only about one-third of Japanese Americans are foreign born because Japanese do not immigrate in large numbers to the United States. About 40 percent of Japanese Americans live in California and are followed by those in Hawaii, New York, and Washington. Despite their relatively small population, they wield some degree of political strength, particularly in Hawaii where they compose about 20 percent of the population. Japanese Americans represent the state in both the U.S. Senate (Daniel K. Inouye) and U.S. House of Representatives (Patsy T. Mink) and constitute the largest group of state legislators.

JONATHAN OKAMURA

See also **Japan**

Further Reading

Fujita, S.S. and D. O'Brien, *Japanese American Ethnicity: The Persistence of Community*, Seattle: University of Washington Press, 1991

Glenn, E.N., *Issei, Nisei, War Bride: Three Generations of Japanese American Women in Domestic Service*, Philadelphia: Temple University Press, 1986

Ichioka, Y., *The Issei: The World of the First Generation Japanese Immigrants, 1885–1924*, New York: Free Press, 1988

Kotani, R.M., *The Japanese in Hawaii: A Century of Struggle*, Honolulu: Hawaii Hochi Ltd., 1985

Takahashi, J., *Nisei/Sansei: Shifting Japanese American Identities and Politics*, Philadelphia: Temple University Press, 1997

Tamura, E.H., *Americanization, Acculturation, and Ethnic Identity: The Nisei Generation in Hawaii*, Urbana and Chicago: University of Illinois Press, 1994

Jews *See* **Diaspora: Jewish**

Jingpo *See* **Kachin (Jingpo)**

Jinnah, Muhammad Ali (Pakistani)

Mohammad Ali Jinnah, called *Quad-i Azam* (Great Leader) in Pakistan, was born on December 25, 1876 (a date still subject to controversy) to a family of an Ismaili merchant of Karachi. He received his primary education at home; from 1887 to 1892 he was sent first to the Sindh Madrasat al-Islam High School and later to Christian Missionary Society High School in Karachi. In 1893, his father sent him to London to acquire some business experience; however, once there, Jinnah decided to study law, joining Lincoln's Inn, a legal institution that prepared students for the bar. In 1896, he became the youngest Indian to be called to the bar as a barrister.

Before his departure from India in 1892, his father had arranged a traditional marriage between the 16-year-old Jinnah and a distant younger relative, who died soon after his departure. During his period in England, his mother also died. Back in India in 1896, the worsening of his family's economic conditions obliged him to find a permanent job, becoming within few years an influential lawyer in Bombay. In 1918, he married Rattanbai "Ruttie" Petit, the young daughter of an extremely wealthy Parsee (the small but influent Zoroastrian minority of India) businessman. She gave him a daughter, Dina, before dying after a long illness in 1929.

Ruttie's end was a severe blow for Jinnah, whose own health deteriorated during the 1930s, though his frequent illnesses were carefully hidden from the public eye. After the creation of Pakistan, the state for the Muslims of India, in 1947, his poor health collapsed: Jinnah spent his last months fighting illness and died on September 11, 1948 in Karachi.

Jinnah began his long political career in 1896 when he joined the Indian National Congress, the party founded in 1885, which—at the time—was asking London to grant India the status of a dominion. In 1906, he attended the Calcutta session of the National Congress as a secretary of the president of Congress. Thanks to his legal experience, in 1910 Jinnah was elected to the Indian Imperial Legislative Council. During this period, admiration for the British system and the idea of the unity between the Hindu majority and the Muslim minority in the Indian subcontinent were the main elements of his political thought.

In 1913, he joined also the All India Muslim League, a movement founded in 1906 for the protection of the interests and rights of the Indian Muslims. In Jinnah's view, both the Indian National Congress and the Muslim League should elaborate a common political agenda vis-à-vis the British government. It was through his efforts that the two parties held common meetings in Bombay, signing the so-called Lucknow Pact, a scheme of constitutional reform containing guarantees for the rights of the Muslim minority and for the creation of separate Hindu and Muslim electorates in India—the only suitable option, for Jinnah, which would guarantee visible representation for his minority. For this reason, the Maratha leader Gopal Krishna Gokhale spoke of Jinnah as the "Ambassador of Hindu-Muslim unity".

In 1919, Jinnah resigned by his seat at the Legislative council as a reaction to the radicalization in the political lines both of the Indian movements and the British government, keeping himself aloof from any active political life. Although at the end of the 1920s he was elected to the new central Assembly and was selected as one of the Indian delegates to participate in the so-called Round Table Conferences in London (1930–1932) to discuss the political and institutional reform of British dominance in India, he did not represent a leading political figure of the Indian political arena. From 1930 to 1935, he remained in London, practicing at the Privy Council bar.

He returned to India only in 1935, after the promulgation of the Government of India Act. At the time, he was still thinking in terms of Hindu-Muslim cooperation in India, but the worsening of the interreligious relations over the entire subcontinent and the overwhelming victory of the National Congress at the 1937 elections forced him to reconsider his position.

In 1936, he became the President of the Parliamentary Board of the Muslim League. Within a few years, Jinnah had completely reorganized this movement, traditionally weakened by personal rivalries and loose central coordination. With the outbreak of World War II in 1939, members of the Indian National Congress resigned by their posts in the provincial governments. Jinnah, on the contrary, opted for some form of collaboration on the war efforts with the British, a move which strengthened his organization and favored the participation of the Muslim League in the government of several provinces.

On March 22–23, 1940, in Lahore, the League adopted the final resolution for the creation of a separate state for the Indian Muslims, named Pakistan, after the end of British rule. After the war, though it was tenaciously fought by the Mahatma Mohandas Gandhi (1869–1948) and the other Hindu leaders, the idea of the Partition of India into two different states became the only viable option. Hindus and Muslims were divided by interethnic and interreligious violence, which neither the English nor the Indian political leaders were able to prevent. In 1947, the British government decided to give India total independence, which was declared on August 15, 1947; on the same day, Pakistan emerged as an independent state. Jinnah became its first Governor-General and President of the Constituent Assembly, trying to forge a secular and liberal state, linked to the West and adopting the Western concepts of democracy and liberalism.

Biography

Muhammad Ali Jinnah, also called *Quad-i Azam* (Great Leader). Born December 25, 1876 in Karachi, India (now Pakistan). Studied at home in Bombay (until 1887); Sindh Madrasat al-Islam High School, Karachi; Christian Missionary Society High School, Karachi; Lincoln's Inn, London, 1893-96. Called to the bar, London, 1895. Lawyer in Bombay, from 1896 on. Joined the Indian National Congress, 1906; member of the Indian Imperial Legislative Council, 1910-1919; joined the All-India Muslim

League, 1913; member of the Round Table Conferences, London, 1930-32; practicing before the Privy Council Bar, London, 1930-35; President of the Parliamentary Board of the Muslim League, India, 1936; Governor-General and President of the Constituent Assembly of the new state of Pakistan, Karachi, August 15, 1947. Died in Karachi, Pakistan, September 11, 1948.

REDAELLI RICCARDO

See also **India; Pakistan**

Further Reading

Afzal, M. Rafique, editor, *Speeches and Statements of the Quaid-i-Azam Mohammad Ali Jinnah, 1911–36 and 1947–48,* Lahore, 1966

Ahmad, Jamil-ud-din, editor, *Speeches and Writings of Mr. Jinnah,* Lahore: Muhammed Ashraf, 1976

Ahmed, S. Akbar, *Jinnah, Pakistan and Islamic Identity. The search for Saladin,* London and New York: Routledge, 1997

Jalal, Ayesha, *The Sole Spokeman: Jinnah, the Muslim League and the Demand of Pakistan,* Cambridge: Cambridge University Press, 1985

Majumdar, S.K., *Jinnah and Gandhi: Their Role in India's Quest for Freedom,* Calcutta, India: Firma K.L. Mukhopadhyay

Mujtahid, Sharif al-, *Quad-i-Azam Jinnah: Studies in Interpretation,* Karachi: Quad-i-Azam Academy, 1981

Wolpert, Stanley, *Jinnah of Pakistan,* New York: Oxford University Press, 1984

Jordan

Capsule Summary

Total Population: 5,460,265 (July 2003)

Minority Populations: Circassians 2–3 percent, Chechens less than 1 percent, Armenians less than 1 percent, and Kurds

Languages: Arabic, Circassian, Chechen, and Armenian.

Religions: Sunni Islam 94 percent, Christianity 5 percent, Shi'ites, Druze, and Baha'is are found in small numbers.

Jordan is located in the Middle East, surrounded by Israel and the Palestine Authority to the west, Syria to the north, Iraq to the east, and Saudi Arabia to the east and south. It has a population of 5.4 million (52.3 percent males). The rate of population growth was 2.5 percent in 1997. Jordan is a constitutional hereditary monarchy with a government formed and headed by a prime minister chosen by the king. There is a bicameral parliament elected every four years. According to the Jordanian Constitution, there are no ethnic minorities, and all citizens have the same duties and enjoy the same rights. Accordingly, census statistics concerning religious, ethnic, and political minorities, and especially the number of Jordanians of Palestinian origin, are not released, although data is available. This reflects the sensitivity of the social and political balance, where publication of figures possibly indicating numerical supremacy of the nondominant group, namely the Palestinians, would tilt the scales against the dominant one. Some 'ethnic minorities,' like the Circassians and Chechens, generally refuse to be so classified, claiming a significant share in the establishment of the modern state, and refusing to be branded with a tag that would marginalize them and possibly lead to a compromise of their relatively dominant positions. In the case of ethnic minorities of the same religion as the dominant group, feelings of otherness are reduced both ways. Arabs make up the majority of population. There is a significant nonethnic and non-religious divide among the Arab populace, namely between Eastern Jordanians and those of Palestinian origin, but which is vigorously denied officially. Ethnic minorities include the Circassians and Abkhaz-Abaza (2–3 percent) who form a group with an influence that far exceeds their relative number, the Chechens and Ingush (less than 1 percent), who basically form one ethnic and linguistic group, Armenians (less than 1 percent), Kurds, Turkomans, Gypsies, Assyrians, Baha'is, and Dagestanis. After the 1992–93 Abkhaz-Georgian war, the Abaza identity was accentuated, but no separate institutions have emerged. The Circassians and Chechen-Ingush are guaranteed a quota of three deputies in the 80-seat Lower House, and two senators in the Upper House. It is conventional to appoint a minister from them. Religious minorities include Arab Christians (5 percent), Armenians, Baha'is, Druze, and Shi'ites. Christians have a quota of 9 seats in parliament. Apart from the Circassians-Abaza-Chechens, no other ethnic groups are allotted political quotas. The small Armenian community is not politically active, being both an ethnic and religious minority. Many of its members emigrated back to Armenia and the West in the 1990s. Arabic is the official language. Other languages include Circassian, which is taught at one school run by the Circassian Charity Association, Chechen, and Armenian. GDP per capita is $4,300 (2002).

History

Jordan was conquered by the Muslim Umayyads from Byzantium in 630 CE. When the Abbasids moved their capital to Baghdad, the area witnessed a decline throughout the Ottoman period. Until the establishment of Hashemite rule in 1921, the population consisted of Bedouins, peasants, and town-dwellers. The Christians, who are mainly of Arab descent, had age-old settlements in Salt, Ajlun, Madaba, Karak, and Husson. The Circassians started to settle in Jordan in 1878 following the end of the Russian-Circassian war and their expulsion from the Caucasus. They reestablished Amman, which later became the capital, and were concentrated in surrounding villages and in Jerash. They succeeded in establishing a rudimentary administrative system and a gendarmerie, which made their settlements quite attractive to other people who started to flock to them in large numbers. Soon these became substantial social and commercial centers. At the beginning of the twentieth century, groups of Chechen immigrants from the Caucasus were settled in Sweileh, Zarqa, Sukhneh, and the Azraq Oasis.

Society

Jordanian society is basically tribal in nature, and most sections of society are conservative in their social attitudes. Religion has a moderating effect. The concept of familial honor is paramount, and redemption of family name at times reaches extremes as when suspected female adulterers are murdered by their close kin. Two laws work in parallel: civil law and the unwritten tribal code, which is regulated by special elected councils. Although many of its tenets are outmoded, it has a role to play in keeping the peace as mischief-makers would think twice before committing a tort. The Circassians and Chechens are ethnically related and have some common customs and traditions, but their languages, though kindred, are mutually unintelligible. They are perceived as one group by outsiders and, in fact, form a joint tribal council to manage tribal affairs and resolve disputes with other sections of society. There are a significant number of landlords among the Circassians in Amman, but their relative importance is diminishing with time. In 1948, an influx of Palestinian refugees settled in Jordan following the establishment of the State of Israel. There was another wave of Palestinian refugees following the 1967 Arab-Israeli War. In 1970, the clash between Jordanian army units and the Palestinian militias resulted in the expulsion of the Palestine Liberation Organization (PLO) and the polarization of the populace. A considerable political effort has been expended in maintaining *social cohesion* or stopping tensions from erupting into open conflict. Jordanians of Palestinian origin complain of discriminatory exclusion from positions in the public sector and government (significantly also in the security forces), whereas aboriginal Jordanians retort that the private sector is in Palestinian hands, with corresponding employment restrictions on non-Palestinians. The authorities are sensitive to the concept of the alternative homeland, that is, establishment of a Palestinian state in Jordan and possible transfer and settlement of hundreds of thousands of Palestinians from the West Bank and Gaza Strip. This division and perceived threat of marginalization of Eastern Jordanians poses a potential threat to stability in Jordan as long as the Israeli-Palestinian issue remains unresolved and the status of the Jordanian Palestinians remains unclear. Jordan provides a vivid example of a society in which differences within the dominant ethnic group stemming from political considerations are more acute than those between this group and other religious and ethnic minorities.

AMJAD JAIMOUKHA

See also **Armenians; Chechens; Circassians; Kurds**

Further Reading

Patai, Raphael, *The Kingdom of Jordan*, Princeton, New Jersey: Princeton University Press, 1958

Peake, Frederick, *A History of Jordan and Its Tribes*, Coral Gables, Florida: University of Miami Press, 1958

Satloff, Robert B., *Troubles on the East Bank: Challenges to the Domestic Stability of Jordan*, New York: Praeger, 1986

Weightman, G.H., "Minorities: The Circassians," *Middle East Forum*, 37, no. (1961)

Jordan, Barbara (African-American)

Barbara Jordan was born in Houston, Texas on February 21, 1936, to a black Baptist minister, Benjamin Jordan, and a domestic worker, Arlyne Jordan. She attended Roberson Elementary and Phyllis Wheatley High School. While at Wheatley, she was a member of the Honor Society and excelled in debating. She graduated in 1952 in the upper five percent of her class. She wanted to study political science at the University of Texas-Austin but was discouraged because the school was still segregated. She attended Texas Southern University and pledged Delta Sigma Theta Sorority. At TSU, she was a national champion debater, defeating her opponents from schools such as Yale and Brown and tying those from Harvard. After graduating magna cum laude from TSU in 1956 with a double major in political science and history, she expressed an interest in attending Harvard University School of Law, but she opted to go to Boston University where she received her law degree in 1959. Ultimately, she was the recipient of honorary doctorate degrees from 25 colleges and universities including Texas Southern University, Tuskegee Institute, Princeton University, and Harvard University. Jordan taught political science at Tuskegee Institute in Alabama for 1 year before returning to Houston in 1960. She then worked as Administrative Assistant to the County Judge of Harris County, the first black woman to hold that position. In 1960, she also worked for the campaign to nominate John F. Kennedy as the Democratic Party's presidential candidate. In 1966, Jordan became the first black woman to win a seat in the Texas Senate and the first black elected to the state Senate since 1883. She authored the state's first successful minimum wage bill and pushed for civil rights legislation. In 1972, she was elected President *Pro Tempore* of the Senate, and, in the tradition of the Senate, served June 10, 1972, as governor for a day—the first black woman governor in the history of the United States. Her brief record in the Texas State Senate is viewed with respect. On March 21, 1967, she became the first black elected official to preside over that body; was the first black state senator to chair a major committee, Labor and Management Relations; and the first freshman senator ever named to the Texas Legislative Council.

In 1972, Jordan was elected to the U.S. House of Representatives and became the first Black Texan in the U.S. Congress. As a member of the House, she maintained the reputation of a skilled politician and of a forceful and dynamic individual. She served as a member of the House Judiciary Committee, the House committee on Government Operations, and the Steering and Policy Committee of the Democratic Caucus. While on the Judiciary Committee, she earned national attention for her eloquent speech in favor of impeaching President Richard M. Nixon during the Watergate affair and for the statement she made at the 1974 impeachment hearing of President Nixon. In casting a "yes" vote, Jordan stated, "My faith in the Constitution is whole, it is complete, it is total." Having become a national celebrity, Jordan was chosen as a keynote speaker for the Democratic National Convention in 1976, and again in 1992. She was the first black selected to keynote a major political convention. During the 1992 Democratic Convention, Jordan once again earned praise for her powerful keynote address against racism and intolerance among both whites and blacks. President Jimmy Carter considered her for attorney general and United Nations Ambassador, but she chose to remain in Congress. Both as a state senator and as a U.S. Congressman, Jordan sponsored bills that championed the cause of poor, black, and disadvantaged people. One of the most important bills as senator was the Workman's Compensation Act, which increased the maximum benefits paid to injured workers. As a congresswoman, she sponsored legislation to broaden the Voting Rights Act of 1965 to cover Mexican Americans in Texas and other southwestern states and to extend its authority to those states where minorities had been denied the right to vote or had had their rights restricted by unfair registration practices, such as literacy tests.

In December 1977, Jordan chose not to seek reelection. She left the House to teach public policy at the Lyndon B. Johnson School of Public Affairs at the University of Texas at Austin for 16 years. In 1987, she was an eloquent voice against Supreme Court nominee Robert Bork. In 1991, Jordan was appointed as Special Counsel for Ethics by Governor Ann Richards. In 1994, she served as Chairwoman of the United States Commission on Immigration Reform with the Clinton Administration and was a major influence in shaping recent reforms in the nation's immigration laws. In 1994, President William Clinton awarded her the Presidential Medal of Freedom, the highest award to a civilian in the country. Her many awards include the Nelson Mandela Award for Health and Human Rights, the 77th NAACP Spingarn Award, the Eleanor

Roosevelt Val-Kill Medal. Jordan died of complications from pneumonia on January 17, 1996.

Biography

Barbara Charline Jordan. Born February 21, 1936, in Houston, Texas. Studied at public schools in Houston; Texas Southern University, Houston, Texas, B.A., 1956; Boston University, Boston, Massachusetts, LL.D., 1959. Was a professor of Political Science, Tuskegee Institute, Tuskegee, Alabama, 1959–60; Administrative Assistant to County Judge of Harris County, Texas, 1960–66; Senator, State of Texas, 1966-72; Representative for the Eighteenth Congressional District, State of Texas, United States House of Representatives, 1972–79; keynote speaker at Democratic National Convention, 1976; Professor of Public Policy, Lyndon Baines Johnson School of Public Affairs, University of Texas at Austin, 1979–95, and from 1982 holder of its Lyndon B. Johnson Centennial Chair in National Policy. Was named Counselor to Texas Governor Ann Richards, 1991; was appointed by President Clinton to Chair the U.S. Commission on Immigration Reform, 1993. Honors include selection as 1976 *Time* Woman of the Year, best living orator; being named one of 25 most influential women in America; Nelson Mandela Award for Health and Human Rights, Eleanor Roosevelt Val-Kill Medal, 77th NAACP Spingarn Medal, 1992, and the Medal of Freedom, 1994. Died in Austin, Texas, January 17, 1996.

Selected Works

Barbara Jordan: A Self-Portrait, New York, 1979

RICHARD VERRONE

See also **African-American Nationalism and Separatism**

Further Reading

Blue, Rose, et al, *Barbara Jordan: Politician*, Chicago: Chelsea House Publishers, 1992

Holmes, Barbara Ann, *A Private Woman in Public Spaces: Barbara Jordan's Speeches on Ethics, Public Religion, and Law*, Harrisburg, Pennsylvania: Trinity Press International, 2000

Jeffrey, Laura S., *Barbara Jordan: Congresswoman, Lawyer, Educator*, Berkeley Heights, New Jersey: Enslow Publishers, Inc., 1997

Johnson, Linda Carlson, *Barbara Jordan, Congresswoman*, The Library of Famous Women Series, Woodbridge, Connecticut: Blackbirch Press, 1990

McNair, Joseph D., *Barbara Jordan: African American Politician*, Chicago: Child's World, 2000

Mendelsohn, James, *Barbara Jordan: Getting Things Done*, Breckenridge, Colorado: Twenty First Century Books, 2001

Patrick-Wexler, Diane, *Barbara Jordan*, Austin, Texas: Raintree/Steck Vaughn, 1995

Rhodes, Lisa Renee, *Barbara Jordan: Voice of Democracy*, New York: Franklin, Watts, Inc., 1998

Rogers, Mary Beth, *Barbara Jordan: American Hero*, New York: Bantam Doubleday Dell Publishers, 2000

Teutsch, Austin, *Barbara Jordan: The Biography*, edited by Harry Preston, Golden Touch Press, 1997

K

Kabards

Capsule Summary

Location: Central North Caucasus, mainly in the Kabardino-Balkarian and Karachai-Cherkess Republics of the Russian Federation
Total Population: Approximately 1 million, including diaspora in Turkey and the Middle East
Religions: Sunni Islam (98%), Orthodox Christian (2%)

Ethnically, the Kabards (Kabardians) form one of the main tribal divisions of the Circassians. Presently, they occupy the middle and northern regions of the Kabardino-Balkarian Republic (12,500 square kilometers, or 4,826.25 square miles; 1 million people) making up about 60 percent of the population; they form the majority of the Cherkess population of 100,000 in the Karachai-Cherkess Republic (14,100 square kilometers, or 5,444 square miles; 500,000 people); and they are found in a few villages in Adigea and the Krasnodar and Stavropol regions. A Christian community in Mozdok in North Ossetia speaks a dialect of Kabardian. About 700,000 Kabardians reside in the Caucasus, forming almost three-quarters of the Circassian population and almost 0.5 percent of the total population in Russia. Kabardian communities are also scattered in the Middle East, especially in Turkey, Syria, and Jordan. This diaspora formed as a result of the Russian-Circassian war of the nineteenth century and subsequent mass expulsion.

Kabardian and Beslanay form the eastern branch of Circassian. Kabardian is an official and literary language in both Kabardino-Balkaria and Karachai-Cherkessia, where it is referred to as Cherkess. Cyrillic orthography has replaced Latin since 1937. The Kabardian language in Kabardino-Balkaria is divided into four subdialects named after the main rivers in the republic. Some authorities divide the language into Greater and Lesser Kabardian, the dialects spoken in Kabarda to the west and east of the Terek, respectively. Kuban Kabardian is spoken in a few villages in Adigea. The status of Kabardian has been improving slowly since the collapse of the Soviet Union in 1991, and the language is not thought to be under threat of extinction.

History

The earliest recorded instance of any differentiation of Kabardian from the rest of the Circassian nation was in *The Book of Administration of the Empire*, written in the tenth century by Emperor Constantine VII, Porphyrogenitus. According to this text, the Zikhis, or Western Circassians, occupied the eastern Black Sea littoral, and the Kasakhs, or modern-day Kabardians, lived in the hinterland. In the early thirteenth century, some Kabardians left their original homeland in the Kuban region and occupied the Crimea in 1237 CE. At the beginning of the fifteenth century, the Crimean Kabardians resettled in the middle of the North Caucasus, a move made possible only after the demise of the Golden Horde. The establishment of

Little and Great Kabarda dates back to the middle of the thirteenth century.

Prince Inal Tighwen established a strong empire in the fifteenth century, uniting all Circassians and Abkhazians. However, after his demise Kabarda was riven into rival principalities. Civil war ensued, and Prince Idar emerged as the sole potentate. During this chaotic period, the Beslanay swarmed off. The Kabardians established a strong state in the sixteenth and seventeenth centuries with Chantchir as its capital.

The feudal princes of Kabarda dominated the North Caucasus up to the start of the eighteenth century, reducing the Ossetes and the Turkic remnants of the Kipchaks to vassalage. All powers with vested interests in the area, namely Russia and the Ottoman Port, sought to court and bestow honors on its princes. In 1561 Tsar Ivan the Terrible married Princess Maria, Temriuk's daughter, to cement the so-called "union" between Russia and Kabarda. During this period, the influential aristocratic family of Cherkasskys was formed, mainly of Kabardian princes who had served in the Russian court.

In 1736 a war broke out between Russia and the Ottoman Empire, and in the 1739 Treaty of Belgrade, the independence of Kabarda was formally guaranteed. In 1771 the Kabardians protested against the imperial administration and the construction of the Caucasian Military Line. The Russians defeated the Kabardians in 1771 in their first open battle. In 1779 Empress Catherine II ordered the pacification of Kabarda. In 1810 the Russians conducted a campaign of terror, causing the Kabardians to petition for peace. Some Kabardians, dubbed *Hejeret* (immigrant Circassians), moved west to the land between the upper Kuban and Zelenchuk Rivers to continue the struggle. By 1816 Kabarda was on its knees after four decades of open conflict in which the number of Kabardians had fallen from 350,000 before the war to a mere 50,000.

In 1822 Yarmolov moved against the Kabardians and imposed harsh punishments on the population. The Caucasian Military Line was pushed further into Kabardian territory, and many massacres were committed against the populace, which had been ravaged by the plague for nearly 14 years. The intensity of conflict subsided in 1825.

Many Kabardians were forced to leave their native lands during the exodus years of 1862 to 1864. During the tsarist years, Kabarda was subsumed under the Stavropol Province. Cossack and Slav settlers found a new home in the northeastern parts of Kabarda. In September 1921 the Kabardian Autonomous Oblast (AO) was formed, and in January 1922 the Balkar Okrug was attached to the Kabardian AO, forming the Kabardino-Balkarian AO. In 1922 the Karachai-Cherkess AO was established. In December 1936 the status of Kabardino-Balkaria was elevated to an autonomous republic within the Russian Soviet Socialist Republic. After World War II, the Kura region in northeast Kabarda was severed and joined to North Ossetia. In 1991 Kabardino-Balkaria and Karachai-Cherkessia became constituent republics of the Russian Federation with no right of secession.

The Kabardino-Balkar parliament is made up of two chambers, the Council of the Republic, and the Council of Representatives. Of the 160 seats, the Kabardians occupy 120, the Balkars 11, and the Russians 29. The Kabardian nationalists are mainly represented by the Adige Xase, which is a member of the International Circassian Association. The national movement gained great momentum in the early 1990s, but nationalists' influence has been diminishing since the mid-1990s. Their principal demand is that historical Kabarda be restored as a first step toward the reestablishment of Greater Circassia, with a concomitant repatriation of the diaspora. President Vladimir Kokov, a Kabardian, won the 1997 elections, putting more pressure on the already beleaguered nationalists, and was poised to win the 2001 elections since the Duma allowed third and fourth terms for regional leaders. The Kabardians, who maintain a dominant position in the republic, and the Balkars have been at loggerheads since the latter were rehabilitated after their banishment. Some Cossacks also aspire to secession. In the Karachai-Cherkess Republic, the Karachai are the dominant group, with the Cherkess and Abaza trying to reestablish a separate political entity. A small chance of open conflict exists, which could involve other kindred people in the North Caucasus. Although members of the diaspora enjoy the right to return to their ancestral lands, the authorities actively discourage this because of Russian, Balkar, and Karachai fears of increased Circassian dominance, and the native Kabardians' fear of competition.

Society

The Kabardians are part of the wider Circassian society, having almost the same traditions and customs. The Kabardian feudal system was very elaborate and the *Xabze*, or code of conduct, was highly developed. Despite feudalism, there was enough social cohesion to allow the formation of a huge empire in the fifteenth century, a strong state in the sixteenth and seventeenth centuries, and enough clout to dominate the central northern Caucasus until the middle of the eighteenth century. The caste system was undone by 1864. Kabardian society is at present in turmoil as a result of the worsening economic situation.

The Kabardian pantheon consisted of some three score deities that regulated the cosmos. Pagan and animistic beliefs, some of which are enshrined in the Nart legends, are still prevalent. Soviet propaganda and isolation have resulted in a superficial knowledge and practice of Islam. The Kabardians of Mozdok are nominal Orthodox Christians, but culturally they are almost indistinguishable from their Muslim kin.

AMJAD JAIMOUKHA

See also **Circassians; Karachai**

Further Reading

Istoriya Kabardino-Balkarskoi ASSR c drevneishikh vremen do nashikh dnei (History of the Kabardino-Balkarian ASSR from Ancient Times to the Present), 2 volumes, Moscow, 1967

Jaimoukha, Amjad, *The Circassians: A Handbook,* Richmond, Surrey: Curzon Press; New York: Palgrave, 2001

Smirnov, N.A., editor, *Istoriya Kabardi s drevneishikh vremen do nashikh dnei (History of Kabarda from Ancient Times to the Present)*, Moscow, 1957

Studenetskaya, E., "Zhizn i kultura kabardinskogo naroda" ("The Life and Culture of the Kabardian People"), in *Collection of Articles on the History of Kabarda*, Nalchik, issue 3, 1955

Kachin (Jingpo)

Capsule Summary

Location: Dehong prefecture, Yunnan, Southwest of China, and Myanmar
Total Population: 119,209 in China; approximately 300,000 in Myanmar
Languages: Major languages: Jingpo, Zaiwa
Religion: No mainstream religion

The Kachin people, approximately 300,000, live in the Northern Hills of Burma (Myanmar) in the headwaters of the Irrawaddy. They spread over the border in to the Dehong Dai-Jingpo autonomous prefecture in Yunnan, where they are known as hill people or as Jinghpaw or Jingpo—this being the name of the dialect they speak. The Kachin form part of a population living in an area of approximately 50,000 square miles (129,500 square kilometres). Most of this population are Shan (also known as Dai) people who inhabit the valleys and cultivate rice using the paddy system. Unlike the Kachin, the Dai people are Buddhist. There are 119,209 Jingpo living on the Chinese side of the border.

The Jingpo people have been officially recognized as one of 55 ethnic minorities by the government of the People's Republic of China (PRC).

The Kachin live in hills ranging from 1,000 to 2,595 meters (3,280 to 8,414 feet) above sea level.

The area has a warm and damp climate, and the hills are vegetated with rich tropical forests and mountains, subtropical forests, and evergreen forests. The Kachin have for six centuries cultivated upland rice in this region using slash-and-burn techniques and rotational cropping. Traditionally, the rotation of these crops takes 8 to 12 years.

The Kachin live in isolated communities of village clusters, which are broken down into villages and again into individual households. Each community may comprise up to 12 individual villages, which in turn may be made up of between 2 and 40 households. Traditionally, the ownership of the land used by the village cluster was vested in a particular lineage, which was represented in the form of the chief, or *Shanguang*. Tenancy rights then belonged to other lineages represented by each village headman. This serf-type system then filtered down to other families who worked in the fields and those who worked within the headman's household. In China this system was dismantled by 1958, with the traditional owners being installed as government officials. The power to make decisions within the community were then devolved upon village councils.

Members of these village clusters may speak up to six dialects of up to four languages, which may not be mutually intelligible. The total number of distinguishable dialects spoken in the Kachin hills is enormous. Linguists usually distinguish five separate languages (other than Dai), with numerous subbranches. These five major groups are Zaiwa and Jinghpaw (or Jingpo), which belong to the Tibetan-Burmese subbranch of the Chinese-Tibetan language family, within which most dialects are mutually intelligible; Maru, within which most dialects are mutually unintelligible; Nung, with several distinct dialects that are mutually unintelligible; and Lisu, in which several regional dialects use Burmese grammar.

The Kachin/Jingpo written language is a Latin-based script that was developed by American missionaries in the nineteenth century. During the 1950s, the Chinese government created a Pinyin script for use by a branch of the Jingpo people who speak Zaiwa.

Traditional people believe that "all things on earth have spirits." They worship almost all natural things, such as forests, trees, animals, mountains, and rivers, and they believe the spirits of their ancestors reside in large trees and forests. For this reason, the Kachin/Jingpo keep the forests holy and have rigid rules governing how they can be used. For example, in designated "holy forests" no trees or shrubs can be destroyed. Permission must be sought from the village elder for tree felling in designated "landscape forests." According to custom, breaking these rules will bring sickness or disaster to the village.

The Kachin practice a hierarchical intermarriage system, that is, intermarriage between the Shanguan families and commoners. The family retains a system of inheritance by the youngest son while the elder sets up a separate family. After marriage, the youngest son remains to support his parents and inherit most of the family property. Women have a low status in Kachin society.

According to local legends and historical records, the ancestors of the Kachin were originally from the southern part of the Xikang-Tibetan plateau. They gradually migrated south to the northwestern part of Yunnan, west of the Nujiang River. They were referred to as Xunchuanman and were mainly engaged in hunting. The Xunchuanman were divided into two large tribal groups, the Chashan and Lima, during the Yuan Dynasty (1271–1368). The Yuan imperial court set up a provincial administrative office in Yunnan. The Chasha and Lima were controlled by hereditary nobles, or *Shanguang*. The Kachin were divided into three classes: The highest class was the *Shanguan*, followed by the commoners, and slaves were the lowest rank; all were decided by birth, not by property. In China the *Shanguang* system remained in place until the 1950s.

The traditional system gave the *Shanguang* control not only over the villages and the people therein, but also over vast tracts of forests. Together with the elders of the community, the heads of villages, and the leaders of religious affairs, the *Shanguang* decided which tract of forestland could be slashed and burnt for cultivation each year and how the lands would be allocated to each household. In China this system was phased out in 1958, when vast tracts of virgin forests were taken over by the state and other small forest areas near villages and farmlands were shifted to the community. Additionally, the religious traditions, which included the holding of land resources sacred, have broken down in recent years in China, particularly during the Cultural Revolution in the 1960s and 1970s.

These pressures—which have caused widespread deforestation—together with an increasing population, have resulted in the traditional rotational times for cropping being reduced, with resulting lower yields. Access to economic development through education continues to be poor, and today the incidence of poverty among the Kachin/Jingpo is high. They obtain little education and pursue mainly a subsistence lifestyle. This situation is not dissimilar from that of many hill tribes in parts of India and Southeast Asia.

LINDA TSUNG

See also **China; Myanmar**

Further Reading

Leach, E.R., *Political Systems of Highland Burma*, London: The Athlone Press, 1977

Ren, Z, and T. Clem, Sustainability Issues and Socio-economic Change in the Jingpo Communities of China, *International Journal of Social Economics*, 26, nos. 1–3 (1999)

Kadazan-Dasun

Capsule Summary

Location: Sabah, Malaysia
Total Population: Approximately 600,000
Language: Kadazandusun
Religions: Mostly Christian, with some Muslim

The term Kadazan-Dasun, or Kadazandusun, refers to several ethnic groups who speak similar languages belonging to the Dusunic language family. These communities share a common history, as well as linguistic and cultural features. The Kadazandusun collectively make up the largest indigenous group in Sabah, representing 25–30 percent of the population in Sabah and approximately 3 percent of the population in Malaysia. The groups that make up the Kadazandusun community are located on the west coast of Sabah and in the central and northern interior areas. The interior groups generally refer to themselves as Dusun, whereas the coastal groups refer to themselves as Kadazan. Other Kadazandusun groups refer to themselves by tribal names such as Lotud, Tatana, Kimaragan, Kuijau, and Gana. The majority of Kadazandusun are Christians, although many are Muslim and some still follow their traditional beliefs.

Until the turn of the eighteenth century and the coming of the British Chartered Company to North Borneo, the majority of the Kadazandusun, like other indigenous people in the interior, had little contact with anyone outside their own community. Head-hunting, which was a central feature of Kadazandusun life, kept people isolated in their longhouse communities. The family was the main production unit, each one planting hill or wet rice. The basic political unit was the village, with the village headman as the leader, who was guided by traditional law. The traditional Kadazandusun belief system focused on the rice-planting and harvesting cycles. A *Bobohizan*, or priestess, performed the rituals necessary to promote a good harvest.

The first major change to the Kadazandusun community was the arrival of the British Chartered Company in Sabah in 1978. The British Chartered Company allowed indigenous communities to continue their traditional lifestyles. They formalized the position of village headman and made the headman responsible for implementing the policies of the Company. Perhaps the greatest impact of Company policies was the cessation of head-hunting and the ending of feuds. This opened much of the Kadazandusun area to trade and provided other economic opportunities. Another change to the Kadazandusun community at this time was the introduction of Christianity. In 1887 the first Catholic mission was established in Penampang. The mission began an English-medium school and developed a writing system for Kadazandusun.

The second major change to have an impact on the Kadazandusun community was the incorporation of Sabah into the Federation of Malaysian States in 1963. The federal government implemented three policies that had a tremendous influence on the Kadazandusun communities and the future of the Kadazandusun language. The first was the implementation of a national language policy, which made Bahasa Malaysia the sole national language of Malaysia. The second was the implementation of the National Education Policy, which sought to provide equal access to education to all Malaysians. A further goal of the Education Policy act was to help implement the National Language Policy by making Bahasa Malaysia the medium of instruction for all government and government-supported schools. The third set of policies that affected the Kadazandusun communities were the New Economic Policies, which sought to eradicate poverty and bring economic development to all Malaysians.

The effect of all three policies was a greater spread of Bahasa Malaysia and the loss of Kadazandusun. In many villages, especially along the coastal regions, people began to work in government offices or private business that used Bahasa Malaysia or English as the medium of communication. Parents increasingly used Bahasa Malaysia or English with their children in the home in order to help them succeed in school. Community leaders became concerned over what they perceived as a decline in the use of the Kadazandusun language and the loss of the Kadazandusun identity.

When Sabah joined the Federation of Malaysia, it was initially governed by a Kadazandusun-based party from 1963 to 1967. However, from 1963 to 1985, the state government was controlled by ethnic Malays, who encouraged immigration of Muslim peoples from the Philippines and Indonesia to increase the Muslim influence and continue Muslim dominance in the state government. In 1985 a new political party, the Parti Bersatu Sabah (PBS), dominated by Catholic Kadazandusuns, swept the state elections. With this election victory, the Kadazandusun were able to implement policies that improved their status and that brought a revived interest in Kadazandusun identity. However, the election of a non-Muslim government increased tensions between the state of Sabah and the Malay-Muslim-dominated federal government. When the PBS pulled out of the national coalition in 1990, these tensions increased, and the federal government began to withdraw development monies from the state. In 1994 the PBS lost power to a National Front coalition backed by the federal government, which promised a new Sabah through increased development monies (Khan 1995). Despite the desire for greater political autonomy, the Kadazandusun community was not able to gain enough political strength to gain victory over the National Front, which was supported by the majority Chinese and Muslim populations.

Despite the loss of political power, the Kadazandusun community sought to unite itself and promote its identity and language. The issue of standardization arose when the Minister of Education stated that the federal government would consider including the Kadazandusun language as part of the curriculum in the Sabah education system. In 1995 an agreement was made between the Kadazan Dusun Cultural Association and the United Sabah Dusun Association to call the Dusun and Kadazan languages Kadazandusun. They also agreed to develop and promote the standardization of a single Kadazandusun language so that it could be taught in the schools. Today, the Kadazandusun language is taught in 147 primary schools and is an elective at the University of Malaysia in Sabah.

Two organizations have been formed to preserve the language and culture of the Kadazandusun community and to promote Kadazandusun identity. The Koisaan Cultural Development Institute (KDI) seeks to gather information on the traditional culture of the Kadazandusun and record it so that it will not be lost. The Kadazandusun Language Foundation was established in 1996 to develop materials and promote their use in the Kadazandusun community.

Despite these efforts, it is uncertain whether members of the Kadazandusun community are willing to support the maintenance of their identity at the expense of benefits that are gained from the federal government. Like many minority communities around the world, the Kadazandusun must find a balance between participation in the Malaysian nation and preservation of their Kadazandusun identity.

SUE RUSSELL

See also **Malaysia**

Further Reading

Kadazan Dusun Cultural Association, <www.rombituon.com/kdca> Kadazandusun Language Foundation, <www.infosabah.com.my/klf> Khan, Mizan, Kadazans in Malaysia, 1995, <www.bsos.emd. edu/cidcm/mar/malkad.htm>

Lasimbang, Rita, Carolyn Miller, and Francis Otigil, "Language Competence and Use among Coastal Kadazan Children: A Survey Report," in *Maintenance and Loss of Minority Languages*, edited by Willem Fase, Koen Jaspert, and Sjaak Kroon, Philadelphia: John Benjamins, 1992

Williams, Thomas Rhys, *A Borneo Childhood,* New York: Holt, Rinehart and Winston, 1969

Williams, Thomas Rhys, *The Dusun,*. New York: Holt, Rinehart and Winston, 1965.

Kalmyk

Capsule Summary

Location: Southern European Russia, mostly in the territory of Kalmykia
Total Population: 165,800 (1989)
Language: Kalmyk
Religion: Buddhist

The Kalmyks are a Mongol people living in southern European Russia. Their homeland, Kalmykia, south of the Volga River and west of the Caspian Sea, is a region of plains and dry steppes north of the Caucasus range. The Kalmyks, who constitute the only Buddhist nation on European territory, are the descendents of Western Mongolian tribes that left their Central Asian homeland in the seventeenth century and settled in the steppe lands of the lower Volga River.

The vast majority of Kalmyks in Russia live in the Kalmyk Republic, one of 21 ethnically defined autonomous republics within the Russian Federation. By 1989 the Kalmyk Republic had about 320,000 inhabitants, of which 45 percent were Kalmyks, 39 percent were ethnic Russians, and the remaining 16 percent were other peoples from the region (Dargins, Chechens, Kazakhs, Avars, Kumyks), Germans, Ukrainians, and Belarusians. The large Slav population is mostly concentrated in the cities, especially in the capital of the Kalmyk Republic, Elista, which has a population of approximately 95,000. Kalmykia covers a land area of 76,100 square kilometers (29,382 square miles), which is about the size of South Carolina or the Czech Republic and has a stretch of approximately 100 kilometers (39 square miles) of Caspian Sea coastline.

Their language, Kalmyk, is a Western Mongol language related to the Mongolian spoken in Mongolia. Only a small proportion of ethnic Kalmyks nowadays know how to speak, read, and write in Kalmyk, whereas virtually all know Russian. The Kalmyks are adherents to Lamaism, the Tibetan branch of Buddhism, which distinguishes them as one of the three Buddhist peoples of the Russian Federation (the others being the Buriat and Tuvan). Lamaism, which was brought to the region by missionary monks from Mongolia, was first adopted by the Kalmyks in the eighteenth century.

The migration of the Kalmyks to the Volga was the last wave of expansion of Central Asian nomads into the West. The Kalmyks were Western Mongol tribes heading for the steppe region near the Caspian Sea during the first decades of the seventeenth century. There, in this Southwestern-European Buddhist colony surrounded by the Muslim and Turkic peoples of the steppes, they founded Buddhist monasteries, maintained relations with distant Tibet, and used the vertically written Western Mongolian script. An independent *khanate* was established on lands newly acquired by the expanding Russian Empire. The *khans* ruling this confederation of tribes were directly appointed by the Dalai Lama in Tibet. A treaty of allegiance to the Russian Tsar was signed whereby the Kalmyk Khanate recognized the Russian tsar's superior authority but was granted relative autonomy in internal affairs.

In the second half of the eighteenth century, the privileges of the Kalmyks were circumcised step by step, thereby increasing the willingness to return to their original homeland. In 1771 more than 100,000 Kalmyks chose to leave eastward for China because of increasing oppression by Russia. A minority stayed behind and accepted nominal Russian rule while enjoying certain degrees of self-government in return for undertaking military service. The Kalmyk Khanate was dissolved, and its territory was incorporated into the neighboring Astrakhan Province. By 1897, more than a century later, the Kalmyks still constituted a share of more than 95 percent of the population of the sparsely populated region, compared with only 45 percent in 1989. After the Bolshevik coup in October 1917, a Kalmyk congress voted for secession from Russia and declared Kalmykia independent. In 1920 the region was eventually occupied by the Red Army. Many Buddhist temples, monasteries, and religious cult objects were systematically destroyed in the following decades. The Kalmyks were given their own national-territorial entity in the form of an autonomous district on Russian territory in 1920, which was later upgraded into the Kalmyk Autonomous Soviet Socialist Republic (Kalmyk ASSR), with its own constitution.

When the Germans invaded the region in 1942, many anticommunist Kalmyks joined them. After the German withdrawal following the defeat of Stalingrad, the Red Army returned in 1943, which proved to have devastating consequences for the Kalmyks. The whole population was collectively accused of treason; Stalin ordered their deportation to Asian areas of the Soviet Union, which resulted in the death of a large number of the Kalmyk people. In 1956 the Kalmyks were officially rehabilitated at the 20th Congress of the Communist Party of the Soviet Union (CPSU), after Stalin's death. Their return to Kalmyk lands was permitted, and those who survived deportation and exile returned to their homeland north of the Caucasus. The Kalmyk ASSR, which had been abolished in 1943, was restored to its former status. The Gorbachev reforms of the 1980s and following the collapse of the Soviet Union then fueled a Kalmyk religious and nationalist revival.

In 1990 the Kalmyk ASSR, one of the least-developed regions of both the Soviet Union and Russia, proclaimed its sovereignty and later changed its name into The Republic of Kalmykia—Khalmg Tangch. In 1993 Kirsan Ilyumzhinov, a young Kalmyk millionaire, won the Republic's presidential elections, a post created in 1991, with some 65 percent of the vote. Ilyumzhinov knew how to exploit his ethnic Kalmyk origin and his image as a succesful businessman to gain public support. His vision was one of a modern, capitalist future for Kalmykia; he spoke of a "second Kuwait" and had no scruples about promising the electorate a wealthy and prosperous future. Although these promises were not fulfilled, Ilyumzhinov's policy of national cultural renewal and conservation to counteract the process of Russification during the

Soviet decades has largely been successful. The low percentage of Kalmyks who actually speak their ethnic language justified the introduction of the language bill signed into law in 1999 in order to strengthen the use and preservation of the Kalmyk language. With a share of about two-thirds, the Kalmyks are overrepresented in the Republic's parliament. Buddhist teachers have been sent in from abroad to help with the religious revival. The fourteenth Dalai Lama, who has even been offered permanent residence in Kalmykia by President Ilyumzhinov, visited the Republic in 1991 and 1992.

Unlike various other regions of Russia, serious plans about secession from Russia were never spun in Kalmykia, which certainly stems from an awareness of the backwardness of the Republic, its lack of its own means of subsistence, and its consequent dependence on subsidies from the central government. Unlike other regions, Kalmykia was also spared interethnic conflicts.

MAXIMILIAN HARTMUTH

See also **Mongols; Russia**

Further Reading

Halkovic, Stephen A., *The Mongols of the West*, Bloomington, Indiana: Research Institute for Inner Asian Studies, Indiana University, 1985

Khodarkovsky, Michael, *Where Two Worlds Met: The Russian State and the Kalmyk Nomads, 1600–1771*, Ithaca, New York: Cornell University Press, 1992

Pohl, J. Otto, *Ethnic Cleansing in the USSR, 1937–1949*, Contributions to the Study of World History No. 65, Westport, Connecticut: Greenwood Press, 1999

Smith, Graham, editor, *The Nationalities Question in the Soviet Union*, London: Longman, 1990

Kannadigas

Capsule Summary

Location: South Western India, mostly in the State of Karnataka
Total Population: Approximately 53 million
Language: Kannada
Religions: The majority are Hindus; others include Muslims, Christians, Jains, and Sikhs

The Kannadigas constitute a group of people whose mother tongue is the Kannada language, or those who reside in the Karnataka area, or those who feel that they partake of the Kannada culture. Karnataka is one of the 28 states in India, and Kannada is one of the 18 official languages. Kannada is the official language of the state of Karnataka. Linguistically, it is one of the Dravidian family of languages. Dravidians are considered to be one of the groups of original inhabitants of India. Kannada has borrowed a large portion of its vocabulary from Sanskrit during the last millennium and has also been affected by the Marathi and Telagu languages from the neighboring states. During the British rule of India, Kannadigas were distributed over 22 different administrative units in three different states and in other princely states. After India gained independence, the state was officially created in 1956 as part of a national reorganization of states, and the different areas were unified and named Mysore State. In 1973, it was renamed Karnataka State, which more accurately reflected its past heritage. The capital is Bangalore. Karnataka has a population of approximately 53 million. In addition, a small minority of Kannadigas reside in different states in India or in other countries. Karnataka is located in the southwestern part of India flanked by the Arabian Sea in parts of the west, with other Indian states surrounding it.

History

The date of the origin of the Kannada language is a matter of debate. Many different terms were used in the past to denote the language, and sometimes the area as well. Although some have claimed that the origins of the language go back to BCE, the oldest references found so far go back to the fourth century CE. The language seems to have matured as an independent language with its own literature around the ninth century CE. At least ten major languages or dialects are spoken in this area. A large number of kings and emperors have ruled over the Karnataka area. With records starting from the sixth century onward, a number of dynasties and rulers were based in this area. The area has expanded and contracted with each succeeding victory or defeat in the wars with bordering states. Trade from this area was probably established in the first century BCE.

Historically, Karnataka has contributed to the Indian culture on many fronts. For example, Karnataka is generally considered to be the place of origin of the sixteenth century Carnatic music, or south Indian style of music, elaborated by Purandaradas, although it later took roots, developed, flourished, and was adopted in the neighboring states of Karnataka. Among the other well-known contributions is Gol Gumbaz, a giant, round whispering gallery and an imposing 58-foot statue constructed by the Muslims and Jains, respectively.

Similarly, the Bhakti (Devotional) cult movement in Karnataka, named Das Koota (group of worshipers), was popularized by Purandaradas and Kanakadas and spread to other areas. The Virsaiva movement led by Basava, which originated in Karnataka in the twelfth century, was similar to the earlier efforts by Jain and Buddhist religions to reform the Hindu ritualism and caste system. The Virsaiva movement also unequivocally propagated gender equality.

Current Social Facts and Facets

Population growth in Karnataka was 17 percent in the decade of 1991–2001. Poverty rates and literacy rates are close to the Indian average. The majority of the population is literate, and the literacy rates for rural areas are uniformly lower than those in urban areas. The literacy rates for women, the lower castes, and the tribal groups are lower than the average. Karnataka has a proportionately greater number of professional schools and universities compared with most other states. The sex ratio, or the number of women per 1,000 males, was 964 according to the 2001 census, which is slightly higher than the national average. As in other parts of India, the unemployment and underemployment rates are high, and workers often blame this on foreign companies as well as migrants from other states. Kannadigas have always been very accommodating of other groups with different religions or languages. Although some Kannadigas have migrated to other parts of the world, their rate of migration is low compared with some other states and ethnic groups from India. They are widely dispersed in these countries, and many activities are arranged to keep them connected with one another.

Occupations and Economic Development

Traditionally, a majority of Kannadigas were engaged in agriculture and lived in rural areas. Women form a significant part of the agricultural labor force. Migration to the urban and suburban areas in the state increased rapidly in the 1950s and has continued unabated since then. Still, a large majority of the population lives in rural areas, and a majority of the population is still engaged in agriculture. Similarly, a large proportion of the scheduled castes (a list published by the Government of India) and tribes still depend on farm labor and forest resources. Mining, deforestation, and the building of a number of dams has had a negative impact on the agricultural industry and the environment, and the state has witnessed protest movements in the form of meetings and strikes.

The state produces wood carvings and metalwork of some renown, but it is not a highly industrialized state, except for a well-known software industry and the production of electronic goods. Bangalore is often described as the "Silicon Valley" of India or Southeast Asia. A number of industries from the United States, for example, have established local branches or offices in Bangalore. The software industry is becoming more sophisticated and trying to reach more countries. Hence, the presence and number of multinational companies in Karnataka is increasing significantly, reflecting the current situation in the software sector.

Religion

In Karnataka State, Hindus form a large majority of the population, followed by Muslims. None of the other religious groups, such as Christians, Jains, Buddhists, Sikhs, or other religious groups, exceeds two percent of the population. In spite of their small numbers, the minorities have historically played a significant role in the culture of the Kannadigas. For example, a number of Jain holy shrines have been built in Karnataka, and the one in Shravan Belgola is often considered the second-most important shrine for the Jains in India. Similarly, a number of popular churches have been built in southern Karnataka. As is true of India in general, religion and caste play a major role in Kannada society. The efforts of the founders of the aforementioned Virsaiva movement were not immune to the caste system. Ironically, the followers are now considered as another one of the Hindu castes and are called Lingayats or Virsaivas. Currently, a plurality of Kannadigas belong to the Lingayat group. The scheduled castes and tribes jointly constitute about a fifth of the population. The scheduled groups receive preferential treatment in government services, representation in the legislature, and admission to professional schools. The Hindu religion is made up of many different castes, and the forms of worship vary considerably, as the Hindu religion is not structured. However, religious festivals, celebrations, and fairs are common to all groups and are celebrated often. Hindus in this area worship male as well as female deities in multiple forms and names.

Language, Literature, and the Arts

By all accounts, Kannada is a hard language to learn for most because it is Dravidian in origin. There is, however, extensive literature in the Kannada language, as the works of a number of authors have been translated from different languages. The quality and contribution of the Kannada language is gradually being recognized because of the seven national literary awards presented to Kannada authors. More awards have been won here than by any other state in India, some of which are significantly larger. Occasionally, a few Kannadigas have started writing in English. Kannadigas have also contributed to the Indian drama, especially in the form of Yaksgana plays. This is a native form of dramatic representation of the epics and other significant events in Indian history. In addition, Yaksgana can also be seen as a contribution to the folk music.

Problems and Issues

As a minority group, Kannadigas are distinguished from other Indian groups by their language. Kannadigas, as a minority group in India, have not been subject to genocide, atrocities, or large-scale violence; however, they feel they are discriminated against, either directly or indirectly. Until the early part of the last century, the Kannadigas residing in the north of Karnataka felt that they did not have a chance to learn their own language properly, as 16 of the 17 princely states in the area had imposed the Marathi language on their citizens. Because the Kannadigas are a small minority, they have minimal political leverage. Like many other groups and states, the Kannadigas feel that they are being neglected or discriminated against by the central government in the areas of transportation, irrigation, water distribution, generation of electricity, border disputes, and Hindi hegemony on radio programs. For example, of the 21 rivers that flow through Karnataka, many of them originate in the state. Although some other states have been allowed to build dams and control the water in that state, the Kannadigas feel that they have been discriminated against in this regard. Often, Kannadigas are also discriminated against when seeking jobs in other states.

In addition, issues exist for Kannadigas who are a minority within Karnataka State. Women, for example, get lower wages than men, their literacy rate is low, and they have a lower status in society compared with men. There is a widespread prevalence of the dowry system, or bride price, which is demeaning to women and also makes them a major financial burden on the family. That is one of the reasons why families prefer male children and try to avoid having female children.

Another issue is the inequality among the lower castes, tribal people, and other backward groups compared with the higher-caste groups in the state. The income, unemployment rates, and educational levels of these backward groups are significantly lower than in other groups in the society, in spite of the fact that Karnataka has, in many cases, a quota of 50 percent or more for educational admission, government jobs, and seats on the legislature and in other village administrative units. The reservation or quota process is intended to be an affirmative action process for the scheduled castes, tribes, and other backward classes and castes. However, many from the upper classes and castes are not satisfied with this type of arrangement. Currently, there is a preference among the middle and upper classes in Karnataka to enroll their children in schools where English is the medium of instruction. Because the poor cannot afford such schools, this practice is likely to create a gap among those educated in such schools and others who attend schools with poor resources. These issues are applicable to most groups and states throughout India and are not limited to the Kannadigas. But each state and community has a responsibility to address these problems, and the resolution of these problems has been a slow process.

SUBHASH SONNAD

See also **India**

Further Reading

Ishwaran, Hiremallur, *Ligayata, Jain, Mattu Brahmana Dharmagalu: Mathgaa Ondu Toulanika Adhyayana*, volumes 1–3, Benguluru, India: Priyadarsini Prakashana, 1997

Sheshgirirao, L.S, G.R. Channabasappa, and R.N. Chandrashekhar, editors, *Kannada, Kannadiga, and Karnataka,* Benguluru, India: Kannada Pustaka Pradhikara, 2nd revised edition, 1996

Venkatesa, Mallepuram Ji, *Samba Krti Samputa: Kamnadu-Karnata*, volumes 1–4, Benguluru, India: Karnataka Sarkara, Kannada Pustaka Pradhikara, 1999

Karachai

Capsule Summary

Location: North Caucasus region of Europe, mostly in the Karachai-Cherkess Republic in the Russian Federation
Total Population: Approximately 200,000, including diaspora
Language: Karachai
Religion: Sunni Muslim

The Karachai are a Turkic group living in the North Caucasus region, mainly in the Karachai-Cherkess Republic (14,100 square kilometers, or 5,500 square miles). They constitute 33 percent of the population, the rest being Cherkess, Abazin, Nogai, and Russian. The Karachai, who use the self-designation *Karachaila*, live mainly in the southeast in the Karachai and Little Karachai regions, with the center at Karachaevsk, a small town of 30,000 inhabitants. They are ethnically of the same stock as the Balkars in the neighboring Kabardino-Balkaria, and both groups speak essentially the same language, which belongs to the Kipchak division of the Uralo-Altaic language family. A common Karachai-Balkar literary language based on Cyrillic orthography was devised in the Soviet period. A Karachai diaspora is located in Turkey near Amasya, Bilecik, and Eskişehi, and a few thousand remnants of the deported people are located in Central Asia.

The Karachai are descendants of the Kuban-Bulgar and Kipchak tribes. Turkic elements are thought to have intermingled with the Alans to form the modern Karachai people. During the Mongol invasion of the thirteenth century CE, the Karachai found refuge in the Caucasus Mountains. Russia annexed the Karachai territory in 1828, but the Karachai resisted occupation for more than 30 years, eventually succumbing to Russian superiority. Many Karachai found refuge in Ottoman lands. In 1920 the Bolsheviks set up the Mountain Autonomous Soviet Republic in the North Caucasus, which included the lands of the Karachai, but 2 years later this fell apart, and a separate Karachai-Cherkess region was established. Instead of uniting the ethnically and linguistically related Karachai and Balkar, on the one hand, and the Kabardians and Cherkess-Abaza, on the other, the Soviets opted to sow the seeds of conflict by attaching the Karachai to the

Cherkess-Abazas and the Balkars to the Kabardians. This Machiavellian move is the cause of the social and political upheavals that have been wracking both the Karachai-Cherkess and Kabardino-Balkar Republics since the collapse of the Soviet Union. In 1926 Karachai-Cherkessia was divided in two, each people having its own separate region. A decade later, they were merged yet again. Moscow deported the Karachai, about 80,000 at the time, to Central Asia 8 years later over alleged collaboration with the Germans, and a considerable chunk of their territory was given to Georgia. The Karachai-Cherkess Oblast was restored in 1957, when most of the Karachai were allowed to return home. After the collapse of the Soviet Union, Karachai-Cherkessia was upgraded to a republic in the Russian Federation. In July 1992, nationalists demanded restoration of Karachai autonomy.

The Karachai, on one hand, and the Cherkess and Abaza, on the other, are locked in a power struggle, with each group trying to amass as many political and economic advantages as possible. Both ethnic groups claim to be the indigenous people, although some modern Karachai historians are now claiming that the Circassians are medieval immigrants from Kurdistan, among other far-fetched claims. Vladimir Khubiev, a Karachai, had been running the republic since 1983 before he was soundly defeated in the 1999 presidential elections. His successor, Vladimir Semenov, an ex-army general, had to contend with vociferous Cherkess and Abaza protests against alleged vote rigging and intimidation. Since 1995 the Cherkess, Abaza, and some Slavs have been demanding the reestablishment of the Cherkess Oblast and its incorporation into the Stavropol region. Less than 2 years into his term, reports were afloat that erstwhile supporters of Semenov were demanding his resignation on the grounds of reneging on his election promises. There are still nationalist demands to unite the Karachai and Balkar into one republic and repatriate the communities in Central Asia while paying them restitution. Although open conflict is unlikely, it is still a possibility. In such a case, kindred people from other nearby republics would inevitably be sucked into the vortex of violence. This would pit the Adiga-Abkhaz-Abaza group against the Turkic Karachai-Balkars. Barring a massive return of the Cherkess and Abaza diasporas from Turkey and the Middle East, the Karachai are expected to maintain their political supremacy and even attain a numerical majority in the near future, given the high birth rate of the Karachai and the tendency of Russians to move back to Russia proper in response to the mounting ethnic tension in the North Caucasus.

Each family is led by a family council, which consists of the men of the oldest generation and the eldest woman. The senior woman plays a significant role in maintaining the family pride and honor, as hospitality is important to Karachai social relations. From an early age, the children assist their parents with household responsibilities. Boys help their fathers tend to the livestock and often live in camps with the older men. Girls help their mothers with the housework and learn how to embroider. The Karachai originally lived in pine houses made with sliding shutters. Today, their houses are built with large glass windows, wooden floors, and iron roofs. The homes usually have two stories, and most have porches. Karachai cuisine is based mainly on meat and milk products. The traditional economy of the Karachai is based on agriculture, hunting, animal husbandry, especially sheep breeding, and some handicrafts. In exchange for cattle products, the Karachai obtain fabrics, crockery, salt, and other amenities. Crafts include felt decoration and gold stitching and weaving. Tourism in Teberda and other resorts is potentially lucrative, but there is a need for substantial investment in this sector. Music and song play a central role in festivities. Although the Karachai are Sunni Muslims, with a mosque in every village, a considerable corpus of pagan beliefs and ceremonies, including sacrificial rites, are infused with Muslim traditions, as is the case with other North Caucasian peoples. Remnants of the ancient pantheon are still invoked. There is a belief in evil spirits and magic, and there are also traces of shamanism. The Spiritual Board of the Muslims of the Karachai-Cherkess Republic was set up in 1990, and a separate board at odds with the local authorities was established in 1991.

AMJAD JAIMOUKHA

See also **Balkars**

Further Reading

The Displaced Peoples of the Caucasus in Soviet Times, Richmond: Curzon Press, forthcoming.

Grannes, Alf, "The Soviet Deportation in 1943 of the Karachays: A Turkic Muslim People of North Caucasus," *Journal of Institute of Muslim Minority Affairs,* 12, no. 1 (1991)

Miziyev, I.M., *The History of the Karachai-Balkarian People from the Ancient Times to Joining Russia,* translated from Russian by P.B. Ivanov, Nalchik: Mingi-Tau (Elbrus), 1994, no. 1 (Jan./Feb.); Moscow, 1997

Traho, Ramazan, "Literature on the Chechen-Ingush and Karachai-Balkars," in *Caucasian Review,* 5, 1957

Tütüncü, Mehmet, editor, *The Turkic Peoples of the Caucasus,* Richmond: Curzon Press, forthcoming

Karakalpaks

Capsule Summary

Location: Western Central Asia, in the Southern Aral Sea Basin, mostly in the Karakalpakstan Autonomous Republic of Uzbekistan. Small groups also in other parts of Uzbekistan, Turkmenistan, Kazakhstan, and Afghanistan (variant spellings include Kara Kalpak, Qara Qalpaq, Qaraqalpaq, Qoraqalpog)

Total Population: Approximately 500,000

Language: Karakalpak

Religion: Muslim

The Karakalpak are a Turkic people living in an autonomous state that carries their name, Karakalpakstan, located in the western region of Uzbekistan. Their homeland stretches over 61,000 square miles (157,990 square kilometers) and consists of settlements south of the Aral Sea, along the River Amu Darya, and vast, largely uninhabited deserts on either side of the river—the Ust Yurt Plateau in the west, and the Kyzyl Kum Desert in the east. This territory comprises 37 percent of the total area of Uzbekistan, although the Karakalpak make up only 2 percent of the total population. In their own state, the Karakalpak are a minority today: There are slightly more Uzbeks and almost as many Kazakhs.

The Karakalpak appear to be a typical eastern Kipchak Turkic mix including some Mongol elements. Like several other Central Asian Turkic groups, they have a complex genealogy and their origin is obscure. This is further complicated in the Karakalpak case because they were identified by a descriptive term, the "Black Hats," which they eventually assumed as their "ethnic" name. Even today, in practically all of the Turkic languages, the name *kara kalpak* means "black hat," as the head covering (*kalpak*) resembled a hood. Yet *kara* ("black") has several meanings, and within the nomadic steppe culture of the Turks, their name suggests a slightly inferior social status. Historically, they appear to leave their nomadic roaming more readily than other groups to settle the land and work the soil. This was a lifestyle the nomadic society considered to be for the "common" (*kara*) folk, not for the aristocracy, the galloping conquering horsemen.

Russian sources mention Black Hats in the twelfth century in alliance with Russia against the Kipchaks; Black Hats are also mentioned in Arab sources. However, the first reliable information about them as an identifiable tribal entity with its own distinct language dates from the sixteenth century. The seventeenth and eighteenth centuries find them moving southward, ever closer to their present homeland, and eventually settling first along the Syr Darya River and the Aral Sea, and then emigrating still further south toward the Amu Darya River. Although they, too, at times were part of different Central Asian tribal confederations, they apparently preferred a sedentary life. They were subjected to constant raids by neighboring tribes and were forced to pay tribute to Kazakh overlords in grain in the early eighteenth century. They even sought out protection from the Russians, who, according to some sources, accepted them as subjects in 1743. In 1811 they came under the control of the Khanate of Khiva, although not too happily, as there were several uprisings. In 1873, with the expanding Russian presence in the region, Russian protection was again sought, and the Karakalpaks on one side of the Amu Darya came under direct Russian control while the others remained in the Khanate of Khiva. After the Russian Revolution in 1917, some of the Karakalpaks were incorporated into the Turkestan Autonomous Soviet Socialist Republic (ASSR), while the others in the Khanate of Khiva became part of the newly created Khorezm People's Soviet Republic.

The creation of Karakalpak as a nation began only in the 1920s during the Soviet era. In 1925 the Karakalpak Autonomous Republic within Kazakhstan was created, which in 1932 was declared an Autonomous Soviet Republic. Then in 1936 the country was made a part of Uzbekistan, and in 1991, following Uzbekistan's declaration of independence, it became an autonomous republic within Uzbekistan.

It has been said that because they lack a distinct historical tradition, the Karakalpaks have little nationalistic sentiment and are new to the concept of ethnic nationalism. The rich oral tradition with which they identify is shared by many of the other Turkic tribes: Epics dealing with heroic deeds, hardships endured in the hands of unjust overlords, and life in exile are all identical to those of other Turkic peoples, some living at great distances. In spite of years of Soviet control, they are, like most of the Central Asian Turks, Sunni Muslims. Their primary loyalty, however, is to family and tribal clans—family groups with a common male ancestor—as they still identify with a tribal federation of two major lines consisting of 15 and 14 tribes each.

The main identifying trait of the Karakalpak people is the unique Karakalpak language, which survived in spite of being in close proximity to the more prestigious, related Turkic languages. Karakalpak belongs to the Kipchak group of Turkic. It can be considered a "southern" variant of Kazakh, having retained the basic characteristics of Kazakh but also of older forms, and includes more Persian borrowings. The language is taught in schools and also as a second language to the non-Karakalpak population. The Karakalpak language had no written literary tradition before the Soviet era. Educated Karakalpak read and wrote in an eastern Turkic *lingua franca* using the Arabic script. An alphabet for the Karakalpak language based on the Arabic script was introduced in 1925, and a switch to the Cyrillic alphabet was mandated in 1940. The Karakalpaks are now committed to changing once more to a Latin-based alphabet.

Over most of the last two centuries, the Karakalpaks have been associated with a territory bearing their name. Today, they find themselves heir to a major ecological disaster area with environmental devastation of enormous proportions. Before Sovietization, their predominantly nomadic lifestyle did not tax the water sources of this essentially desert environment. There were settlements along the Amu Darya, pastures for grazing sheep, and fishing in the Aral Sea. Farming with irrigation from waters diverted from the rivers for this purpose had always provided the essentials, but beginning in the late 1950s, the Soviets made the decision to switch to cotton as the only crop and to divert water on a massive scale to increase cotton yields. More settlers were brought in, putting further demands on the scarce water resources. Eventually, the rivers ceased replenishing the Aral Sea, which until 1960 was the fourth-largest lake in the world. By 1993, it had lost 60 percent of its volume, with the shoreline receding up to 60 miles (96.5 kilometers)

in some places. The greatly increased salinity killed off fish, and winds blowing salt dust from the exposed bed of the Aral Sea mixed with residues of chemical fertilizers and pesticides are now creating severe health conditions among the people. Infant mortality and nose and throat cancer rates are among the highest in the world. The environmental changes have affected the climate by increasing temperatures and shortening the growing season. A severe drought in the fall of 2000 further worsened conditions among the Karakalpak, and Uzbek leaders had to seek help from the United Nations.

The near future seems rather bleak for the Karakalpak, who are isolated, without direct links to the world at large, and living in a distant hinterland of Uzbekistan. Even though the largest oil and gas deposits in Uzbekistan are in the Karakalpak region, any development is far off into the future. Yet throughout the ages, the Karakalpaks have been a patient people and have survived adversity and oppression, mostly by moving on, an option that does not exist today. These might be their most trying times.

ERIKA H. GILSON

See also **Afghanistan; Kazakstan; Turkmenistan; Uzbekistan**

Further Reading

Benningsen, Alexandre, and S. Enders Wimbush, *Muslims of the Soviet Empire,* London: C. Hurst & Co., 1985

Ellis, W.S., "A Soviet Sea Lies Dying," *National Geographic,* 177, no. 2 (1990)

Hanks, Reuel R., "A Separate Space? Karakalpak Nationalism and Devolution in Post-Soviet Uzbekistan," *Europe–Asia Studies,* July (2000)

Muminov, I.M., et al., *Istoriia Karakalpakskoi ASSR,* Tashkent, 1974

Olson, James S., editor, *An Ethnohistorical Dictionary of the Russian and Soviet Empires,* Westport, Connecticut: Greenwood Press, 1994

Togan, A. Zeki Velidi, *Bugünkü Türkili Türkistan ve YakinTarihi* (*Turkistan Today and Her Recent History*), 1947; 2nd edition, Istanbul: Enderun Kitabevi, 1981

Yilmaz, Salih, "Karakalpak Türkleri ve Bugünkü Karakalpakistan," ("The Karakalpak Turks and Karakalpakistan Today"), *Türk Dünyasi Özel Sayisi,* 16 (1997)

Karen

Capsule Summary

Location: Borderland between Burma and Thailand, including part of the Irrawaddy, Sittang, and Salween deltas, as well as the Sittang and Tenasserim ranges
Total Population: 5 million
Language: Karenic branch, Sino-Tibetan family
Religions: Buddhist, animist, Christian

Karen is the English pronunciation of the term *kayin* that the Burmese applied for centuries to a number of populations speaking related languages and living in the mountainous area separating Burma and Siam. The Siamese equivalent to *kayin* is *kariang*. The Thai also use the generic term *yang*. Depending on their language and geographic distribution, the people thus designated prefer to call themselves Sgaw (Kanyaw), Pwo, Pa-O, and Kayah for the major groups, and Paku, Bwe, Geba, Padaung (the famous "long-necked" people), Gek'o, and Yinbaw for the minor ones. According to linguists, the Karen tonal languages form a separate branch of the Sino-Tibetan stock, besides having a wide range of Tibeto-Burman idioms. The Karenic languages, most of them mutually unintelligible, are in turn divided into several local dialects. Pwo and Pa-O form one linguistic subgroup, whereas the Sgaw, Yinbaw, and Padaung form another. Although the Karenic languages have no traditional script, an American Baptist missionary, Jonathan Wade, created a writing system in 1832 by adapting Burmese letters to Sgaw Karen. It was later adjusted to Pwo Karen, and many Christian books, including the Bible, were translated into these two languages. The script was also used in 1843 to launch a Sgaw newspaper, *Sah Muh Taw* (*The Morning Star*), which was the first native newspaper published in Southeast Asia. However, use of the script is limited to Baptist Karen, with the Buddhists (who represent 70 percent of the total population) and animists (about eight percent) ignoring it. A majority of hill-dwelling Karen are still monolingual. Those who live on the plains, in valleys, and in towns are able to speak either Thai or Burmese.

The only demographic statement recorded on the Karen population is in the 1931 census of Burma, which recorded a total of 1.34 million. The Sgaw Karen were evaluated at 500,000 and the Pwo at 473,000, whereas the Pa-O and Kayah were 223,000 and 32,000 respectively. In 1969 the global figure for Thailand was 300,000, chiefly Sgaw and Pwo. With an estimated population of 400,000 in 2000, Karen were the main and most scattered hill tribe of the Thai kingdom, with settlements distributed in eight of the ten provinces bordering Burma. In this latter country, the Karen numbered about 4 million, or ten percent of the national population. The overseas Karen, who are scattered throughout Southeast Asia and in Western countries, number about half a million.

The Karen live in the mountainous borderland of eastern Burma and western Thailand, from Taunggyi in the Shan states southward, through Tenasserim, as far as the Kra Isthmus. According to the federation system of the Union of Burma, this region partly corresponds to the Kayah and Karen States. There are also Karen in the Irrawaddy and Salween valleys near the old Mon capital of Pegu, and in the lowlands of the Irrawaddy delta around Rangoon. In Thailand, the Karen live mostly in the north and western areas along the Burmese border (the Mae Hong Son, Chiang Mai, Kanchanaburi, Tak, Petchaburi provinces). In the two countries, their main economic activity is paddy cultivation—wet-rice agriculture for those dwelling in the plains and valleys, and slash-and-burn agriculture for the majority living in forested hills. The latter have, as subsidiary activities for trading purposes, the gathering of stick-lac, honey, beeswax, cardamom, and ivory. The harvesting of opium poppies or the sale of drugs is not part of Karen activities. On the other hand, the leaders of the Karen rebellion in Burma were involved in illegal logging of teak and other precious woods to finance their guerrilla activities. Although the traditions of the Karen may vary significantly from one group to another, and even from valley to valley inside the same group, all Karen reckon kinship bilaterally, divorce is quite uncommon, and polygamy is not allowed. Before the creation of a Karen state, there was no indigenous political authority beyond the village level. The leadership pattern was basically two-headed, with a headman and religious leaders.

However, in many cases the headman himself could be the religious leader of the community. Except for a few Christian fundamentalist communities, proselytism is not practiced. It is not infrequent to visit villages where animists, Buddhists, and Christians coexist, the members of each cult community taking part in festivals organized by the others.

History

Very little attention has been given to the Karen in the Thai or Burmese chronicles, although they have lived for centuries under the nominal authority of these kingdoms. It is possible that they were among the earliest of the present hill tribes to move into Burma, but their place of origin and roads of migration remain unknown. There are no traces of an ancient presence in China. Old inscriptions describing the *kariang* suggest that they have been in central Burma since the thirteenth century, and they are mentioned occasionally in Burmese royal orders from the end of the sixteenth century onward. But the most reliable historical records concerning them are ones left by British officials and American missionaries. Before the British colonization, it seems that Karen speakers did not share a common identity. At that time, the Burmese and Thai sources depicted the Kayin/Kariang alternatively as "wild" forest people and "cattle of the hills" (in reference to the *razzia* for slaves organized in their villages). As "frontier people" living on the margin of two expansionist and competing states, they were concurrently used as scouts and backup troops by the Thai and the Burmese in their military campaigns against each other. Consequently, they were considered unreliable people by both sides.

According to Anders Jørgensen (1998), the situation of the Karen changed drastically in the seventeenth and eighteenth centuries. During this period, Burma evolved from a bipolar political space, with the Burmese of Pagan challenging the Mon of Pegu, into a country with a unique political center situated in the north, while in Siam there was a gradual weakening of the kingdom, resulting in diminished control of the marginal areas. The Karen took advantage of this situation to sift into the plains of lower Burma and to infiltrate the valleys of northern Siam occupied by the Lawa. This move brought them into closer contact with the central power than before and also into a competing position with the lowlanders for wet-rice cropping. Messianic movements and uprisings among the Karen were the result of the interethnic tensions thus created.

The first Karen rebellion occurred in lower Burma in 1740 and restored the old Mon kingdom for a few years. Later on, during the First Anglo-Burmese War (1824–1826), when the British invaded Arakan and Tenasserim, the Karen seized the opportunity to rebel against the Burmese and provided the British with scouts. In the early stage, the Karen took control of a large part of the Irrawaddy delta, but were later beaten back by the Burmese, and many of their villages were destroyed. However, the harshness of the crackdown did not discourage them, and ten years later, in 1837, a "prophet," named Min Laung proclaimed the independence of the Yunzalin Valley, near Pegu, by raising a force of 10,000 Karen. After several attempts, the Burmese finally defeated him by mobilizing a large army.

The Burmese–Karen antagonism reached its apex when, during the Second Burmese War of 1852, Karen scouts led the British into Rangoon to seize the Shwedagon Pagoda, the supreme symbol of the Buddhist kingdom. When the colonial troops retreated, large numbers of Karen fled to British-controlled territory to avoid bloody reprisals. This event definitely sealed the close cooperation the British and the majority of Karen entertained throughout the colonial period. Baptist missions and British officialdom then nurtured the Karen, in a way reminiscent of the relationship between the Indians and Jesuits in seventeenth-century Paraguay.

The Rise of Karen Nationalism

The Burmese–Karen antagonism aside, many factors contributed to this close cooperation. First, the Sgaw, Pwo, and other Karen groups were receptive to Christian missionary action. This receptiveness was favored by certain themes in their mythology, most notably the prophecy of the imminent return of a lost sacred book, which the converts identified as the Bible. The earliest missionaries (French, Italian, and Portuguese Catholics) visited Tenasserim in 1795, but massive conversions started under the British rule of Lower Burma and were mainly the case under American Baptist missionaries. Although the converts never represented more than 25 percent of the total Karen population, they were cherished by the colonial authorities, received a western education in the missionary schools, and were consequently given preference when applying for positions in the colonial system. There gradually arose a Christian Karen elite of teachers, doctors, clergy, and lower-grade officials.

The British also knew that the Karen could be useful in watching over the long border with Siam, which was not properly demarcated until 1890. At the same time, the Siamese employed the Karen for the same purpose, both parties confirming them in the status of frontier people. Last, teak was one of the main reasons the British had invaded Burma. As noted by Jonathan Falla, "the Karen lived in the teak forests, and the Karen were the expert elephant drivers, without whom teak extraction would have been very difficult."

The confrontation with the Burmese, combined with their Christian acculturation, gave rise during the nineteenth century to Karen self-consciousness among the westernized elite, and later on to nationalist aspirations. Thus, in 1881 a Karen National Association was founded by Sir San Crombie Po, a doctor who published in 1928 *Burma and the Karens*, a plea for the creation of an autonomous Karen state. Willing to shed this turbulent colony, but also to preserve their economic interests, the British supported the idea at the end of World War II. A Karen Central Organization unifying the Buddhist and Christian Karen around common goals was formed in 1945, which became the Karen National Union (KNU) in 1947. Its leaders were negotiating a peaceful transition to relative autonomy with Aung San when, unfortunately, the latter was assassinated.

The day after the Union of Burma was declared in January 1948, the KNU proclaimed Karen independence. This was the beginning of a rebellion that continues to this day. For a while, the Karen, supervised by ex-British army officers, held large areas of the country. They even attempted to capture Rangoon, but failed. In 1954, although they were already on the defensive, they created a Karen state, named Kawthoolei ("Flowerland"), consisting of poor hill tracts around the Salween River. The Karen National Liberation Army (KNLA), a military force of 4,000 to 7,000 soldiers under the command of a Seventh Day Adventist general named Bo Mya, was constituted in the 1960s to defend this territory. However, the defections caused by internal factionalism, and the success of the Four Cuts policy instituted by Ne Win, the leader of the 1962 military coup, progressively eroded the movement. The Ne Win policy was to cut the Karen off from their own people; to cut off access to the outside world; to cut the KNLA supply lines; and to cut off their heads. Because of the systematic implementation of this strategy for more than 30 years, the KNLA lost ground year after year, and in February of 1995, the KNLA was finally driven away from its headquarters in Manerplaw. This offensive was the fact of a dissident Karen organization (the Democratic Kayin Buddhist Organization, or DKBA), supported by the State Law and Order Restoration Council (SLORC) military junta. The rout forced 10,000 civilians and 4,000 fighters to seek refuge inside Thai territory. This came to swell the number of Karen who had fled previous attacks and were grouped into refugee camps. At the end of the 1990s, about 100,000 Karen were living in these camps.

Since the fall of Manerplaw, the KNLA have split into small guerrilla units to carry out hit-and-run attacks on the Burmese. However, it has lost the implicit support of the Thai government it had benefited from for decades. Several reasons explain this shift in Thai policy. First, the Thai authorities used to employ the Karen as a buffer force against the Burmese army, but they were no longer able to play this role. Second, the kingdom must cope with the 100,000 or so refugees and with important inflows of illegal workers who cross into the country from Burma. The traffic of cheap drugs from this neighbor is also intensifying. Consequently, Thailand logically wants to strengthen its control of the frontier. Moreover, the Thai authorities have interpreted as a betrayal the hijacking of a bus and the hostage-taking of hundreds of patients and staff at a Ratchaburi hospital in January 2000. This action and the seizure of the Myanmar Embassy in October 1999 were attributed to a small group of Christian fundamentalists, the God's Army, who had broken away from the KNU. Perpetuating a long tradition of millenarist movements within the Karen group of populations, the God's Army was headed by 12-year-old twins who were supposed to possess miraculous powers.

Messianism also flourishes among the Karen Buddhists. For instance, in the Thai province of Kanchanaburi, because of the construction of a dam that flooded a large area the Pwo Karen had been occupying for centuries, this group revitalized in 1989 a messianic ritual centered on the cult of the White Elephant, an Earth God and symbol of the fecundity of nature in the Buddhist world. As another example, near Pa-An, the capital of the Karen state of Burma, a Buddhist "saint," named Thamanya Hsayadaw, a Pa-O Karen, created an "ideal city" in the 1990s whose 15,000 inhabitants, mainly Pa-O, were entertained through the redistribution of sizeable donations made to the saint. For his adepts, Thamanya Hsayadaw is a living Buddha. The Burmese government relies on his charisma and on that of other Buddhist saints to negotiate cease-fires with the minorities to whom they belong. Thus, another Karen magic monk, Myan Gyi Ngu Hsayadaw, played a key role in the 1990s in cutting down the KNU rebellion. He created the Democratic Karen Buddhist Association, whose army seized the KNLA headquarters in 1995. In response to his precious help, the Burmese junta has given partial administrative autonomy to the site he occupies with his followers.

The Karen as Guardians of Nature

To avoid amalgam, few among the Karen of Thailand come down publicly in favour of the KNLA or the other rebel groups struggling for an independent state in Burma, and most of them have condemned the desperate actions of the God's Army. In fact, integration into the Thai Nation is the objective pursued by the majority. Even the Christian leaders are concerned that they not stand apart from Thai society. In the 1970s the Karen Baptist Church (KBC) became affiliated with the Church of Christ in Thailand, whose leadership is ethnically Thai and Chinese. Furthermore, the KBC no longer sponsors schools of its own but provides guesthouses so young Karen can attend Thai schools.

Nevertheless, a social and economic integration respectful toward Karen cultural differences is not easy to realize in the present Thai context. Like other hill tribes, the Karen are considered lower-grade citizens. Moreover, as time has passed, the Karen in general have been marginalized from the Siamese economy, and following the national ban on logging imposed in the 1980s, their slash-and-burn agriculture has become more and more controversial in the Thai view. Having no ownership titles for the hill paddy fields they exploit, they have no land rights to assert and are either moved out or becoming illegal squatters on increasing portions of forest converted into wildlife sanctuaries.

Prejudice toward the Karen as destroying forests is all the more questionable, since traditionally the Pwo, Sgaw, or Pa-O placed great emphasis on the management of natural resources. Their customs included many rules about how and when to extract goods, or how to prevent the forest from being overexploited. In recent years, to promote this knowledge, as well as to develop a positive image of their community, certain Karen leaders have joined a larger movement of activists coming from various parts of Thai society. This movement synthesizes the Buddhist notions of harmony and respect for life with Western environmentalist idioms to counter the consequences of the rapid capitalist transformation of the country and its social, environmental, and cultural effects. One of the strategies developed by the Karen from this perspective has been to invite Thai Buddhist monks to "ordain" trees. In these ceremonies, a number of trees are draped with a monk's robe and are appointed as guardians of a given area. This area becomes a sacred place which, in theory, is unlikely to be violated by logging.

BERNARD FORMOSO

See also **Buddhists; Myanman; Thailand**

Further Reading

Falla, Jonathan, *True Love and Bartholomew: Rebels on the Burmese Border*, Cambridge: Cambridge University Press, 1991

Hamilton, J.W., *Pwo Karen: at the Edge of Mountain and Plain*, Saint Paul, Minnesota: West Publications, 1976

Jørgensen, Anders B., "Karen Natural Resources Management and Relations to State Polity," in *Facets of Power and its Limitations: Political Culture in Southeast Asia*, edited by Ing-Britt Trankell and Laura Summers, Uppsala: Uppsala Studies in Cultural Anthropology 24, 1998

Keyes, Charles F., editor, *Ethnic Adaptation and Identity: The Karen on the Thai Frontier with Burma*, Philadelphia: Institute for the Study of Human Issues, 1979

Keyes, Charles F., *The Golden Peninsula: Culture and Adaptation in Mainland Southeast Asia*, New York: Macmillan, 1976

Lebar, Franck, Gerald Hickey, and John Musgrave, "Karen," in *Ethnic Groups of Mainland Southeast Asia*, New Haven: HRAF Press, 1964

Marshall, Harry I., *The Karen Peoples of Burma: A Study in Anthropology and Ethnography*, Columbus: Ohio University Press, 1922

Renard, R.D., *Kariang: History of Karen–T'ai Relations from the Beginnings to 1923*, University Microfilms International, 1980

Stern, Theodore, "Ariya and the Golden Book: A Millenarian Buddhist Sect among the Karen," *Journal of Asian Studies*, 27, no. 2

Winter, R.P., *The Karens of Burma: Thailand's Other Refugees*, Washington, DC: United States Committee for Refugees, 1987

Kashmiris

Capsule Summary

Location: Himalayan Ranges, Indian subcontinent
Total Population: 8.5 million
Language: Kashmiri
Religions: Muslim, some Hindu

Kashmiris are the indigenous people of Kashmir Valley, an ethnically distinct region located in the northern area of the Indian subcontinent in the vicinity of the Karakoram and western Himalayan mountain ranges. The region is bounded to the northeast by the Uighur Autonomous Region of Sinkiang (China), to the east by the Tibet Autonomous Region (China), to the south and southwest by Punjab and Himachal Pradesh (India), and to the west by the Northwest Frontier Provinces (Pakistan). The region comprises mostly mountainous terrain rising in tiers from the plains in the south to high-altitude valleys ringed by lofty mountain peaks. The largest of these valleys is Kashmir Valley in the Pir Panjal mountain range, traversed by the Jhelum River and its tributaries.

Kashmir has been the subject of intense dispute between the neighboring countries of India and Pakistan since the Partition in 1947. India administers the southern and southeastern portions of the region as the State of Jammu and Kashmir, while Pakistan administers the northern and western portions as Azad (Free) Kashmir and the districts of Gilgit and Baltistan of the Northern Areas. Kashmiris speak the Kashmiri language, which contains many diverse elements from Dardic, Persian, Sanskrit, and Punjabi. Kashmiris are predominantly Muslim, with a small but significant Hindu community.

History

Because of its isolated location in the high Himalayas, Kashmir developed an independent historical tradition. The earliest known text of Kashmir is the *Nilamata Purana*, which recounts sacred legends regarding the origins of the valley. Kalhana's *Rajatarangini*, a chronicle of dynastic history written in the middle of the twelfth century, contains extremely valuable information on the social and political conditions of the region during ancient times. Buddhism flourished in the region for many centuries, especially under the patronage of Emperor Ashoka around 250 BCE. Hinduism slowly gained influence, such that both religions were prominent by the period of Lalitaditya's expansive rule in the eighth century CE. Islam entered the region in the fourteenth century, first through Muslim saints and *rishis*, and then through Muslim rulerships. This was a period of mass conversion in Kashmir. The Mughal period began with Akbar's conquest of the Kashmir Valley in 1586 and ended with the death of Aurungzeb in 1707. During this time, Moghul emperors, including Jahangir, Shah Jehan, and Zafar Khan, built pavilions and gardens throughout the Kashmir Valley, especially in the city of Srinagar. Kashmir was ruled by the Afghans (1756–1819), the Sikhs (1819–1846), and the Dogras (1846–1947). Maharaja Gulab Singh founded the princely state of Jammu and Kashmir, which included the Kashmir Valley, Jammu, Ladakh, Gilgit, Hunza, and Nagar, in 1846. It was the largest princely state in India before the partition of the subcontinent in August 1947.

In 1947 Maharaja Hari Singh, the princely ruler of Jammu and Kashmir, hesitated to accede to either India or Pakistan. As Pathan tribesmen began invading the state from the Northwest Frontier area, the Maharaja, in need of protection, quickly acceded to India, and the Indian army responded to the invasions. The ensuing war between India and Pakistan lasted until a United Nations cease-fire came into effect on January 1, 1949. A modified version of this cease-fire line serves as the Line of Control. India and Pakistan have disputed the territory of Kashmir since that time.

The Indian state of Jammu and Kashmir consists of the three separate regions of Jammu, the Kashmir Valley, and Ladakh, each characterized by different patterns of ethnicity, language, and religion. Sheikh Abdullah, who led the "Quit Kashmir" movement against Dogra rulership, was the most prominent and popular leader in the state until his death in 1982. Pakistan administers Azad Kashmir, not as a province or agency, but as an independent government that maintains economic and administrative links with Pakistan. It also administers Gilgit and Baltistan as parts of the territory known as the Northern Areas. In addition to these divisions, China has in recent years claimed control of the northeast sector of Ladakh along the international boundary. The continual conflicts and clashes over the territory of the region have created hardships and suffering for the Kashmiri people. There has been intense civil unrest in the Kashmir Valley since 1989, with many different militant groups fighting for independence or union with Pakistan.

Society and Culture

Kashmir, with its many valleys, is widely known for its lush agricultural landscape, including apple orchards, rice paddies, vegetable gardens, and saffron fields. The main crop is rice, with other agricultural products such as apples, pears, apricots, almonds, walnuts, peaches, and cherries growing in abundance. The valley is also rich in forests, with mulberry trees providing the mainstay of the silk industry. The tourism industry has historically been another important part of the region's economy.

Kashmiris are known worldwide for their unique artistry, handiwork, and craftsmanship. The Kashmiri shawl industry, which flourished during the Mughal period, continues in contemporary times through the production of fine *pashminas* (cashmeres), *jamowars*, and intricate embroideries. The Kashmiri carpet industry, introduced into the region through Sultan Zain-ul-Abidin in the fifteenth century, features handwoven wool carpets, some with a silken sheen. Smaller products include the *namda*, a felt rug made from beaten wool and then embroidered, and the *gabba*, a covering produced through the blending of separate pieces of colorful wool.

Kashmiris share a core cultural ethos known as *kashmiriyat*, which is founded on the syncretic cultural and religious traditions of the region. Most Kashmiris are Sunni Muslims, with a sprinkling of Shiites. Their version of Islam has been highly influenced by the Sufi mystic traditions of the region, with prominent saints including Sheikh Noor-ud-Din Rishi (Nund Rishi),

Lalleshwari (Lal Ded), and Shah Hamadan. Kashmiri Hindus, who in the twentieth century comprised approximately one-tenth of the population of the Kashmir Valley, are all members of the Brahmin caste. These Hindus, known as Kashmiri Pandits, practice the worship of Shiva and Shakti. Kashmiri Muslims and Hindus have traditionally revered the same local saints and worshiped at the same local shrines. The vast majority of Kashmiri Pandits left the Kashmir Valley at the height of the militancy in 1989.

There is a large Kashmiri diaspora worldwide, with large communities in Britain, Europe, the Gulf States, and North America. Kashmiris from Azad Kashmir (the Mirpur and Kotli districts) relocated to Britain in the 1950s, especially to the towns of Bradford, Birmingham, Manchester, Leeds, and Luton, on account of the availability of unskilled work. Kashmiris from the Kashmir Valley have relocated to Saudi Arabia as professionals and temporary workers.

HALEY DUSCHINSKI

See also **India; Pakistan**

Further Reading

Balraj Puri, "*Kashmiriyat*: The Vitality of Kashmiri Identity," *Contemporary South Asia*, 4, no. 1 (1995)

Butalia, Urvashi, editor, *Speaking Peace: Women's Voices from Kashmir,* London and New York: Zed Books, 2002

Ganguly, Sumit, *The Crisis in Kashmir: Portents of War, Hopes of Peace*, Washington, DC: Woodrow Wilson Press; Cambridge: Cambridge University Press, 1999

Lawrence, Walter, *The Valley of Kashmir,* London: H. Frowde, 1895

Madan, T.N., *Family and Kinship: A Study of the Pandits of Rural Kashmir*, Delhi: Oxford University Press, 1990

Rai, Mridu, *Hindu Rulers, Muslim Subjects: Islam, Rights, and the History of Kashmir*, Princeton: Princeton University Press, 2004

Schofield, Victoria, *Kashmir in Conflict: India, Pakistan, and the Unending War,* London, New York: I.B. Tauris, 2000; 2nd edition, 2003

Varsheny, Ashutosh, "India, Pakistan, and Kashmir: Antinomies of Nationalism," *Asia Survey,* 31, no. 1 (1991)

Zutshi, Chitralekha, *Islam and Political Culture in Kashmir,* Oxford: Oxford University Press, 2004

Katari, Tupac (Aymaran)

The uprising led by Tupac Katari in 1780 in Upper Peru against the Spanish viceroyalty, although short-lived, sent shock waves throughout South American colonial society. The historic memory of that struggle and of Katari's personal fate carries great significance in the contemporary social and political mobilization among the indigenous populations of Bolivia.

The future leader was born in 1750 as Julián Apaza, in the Aymara village of Sicasica in the highlands of Upper Peru. In the second half of the eighteenth century, the Spanish-American colonial possessions, and not the least in the Andine region, underwent increasingly severe social tensions and conflicts. The harsh living conditions of the native population, with forced labor, involuntary displacements, and heavy taxes, together with unchecked racial discrimination, led to repeated instances of Indian and popular rebellions during this period. The tax increase of 1778 caused a new wave of protests in the region, as was the case with the *Comuneros* uprising of Nueva Granada (Colombia).

Apaza began as a salesman of coca and wine and traveled extensively. During the 1770s, he established regular contacts with people engaged in the growing Indian movement, among them José Gabriel Condorcanqui, known later as Tupac Amaru, the leader of the great uprising around Cusco, in Peru. Apaza was married to Bartolina Sisa, who later was also to play a prominent role in the resistance movement.

The uprising began in Upper Peru in September 1780, in part connected to developments in Peru and Cusco and in part as a result of local circumstances. As an expression of that fact, Julián Apaza took the name of Tupac Katari, in honor of Tupac "Amaru" (*serpent* in Quechua) and Tomás "Katari" (*serpent* in Aymara). The latter was the *curaca* of Chayanta, Potosí, and had recently acted as the leader of an uprising protesting the new fiscal policies decided by the authorities. Katari's messianic revolutionary plan was aimed at the restoration of an Indian nation based on communitarian principles.

After a period of indecisive operations, events took a new turn when, in March 1781, a Spanish force carried out repressive operations, killing hundreds of Indians considered "dangerous" in villages not far from La Paz. Katari arrived with his guerrilla troops and, after giving battle at Ventillas, the Spanish retreated to La Paz.

The next step was to besiege that town with his army of 40,000 Quechua and Aymara men and women armed with slings, lances, and maces. Chuquiago, or La Paz, was by then a town of some 30,000 inhabitants, and its encirclement lasted more than 3 months. During this period, the Spanish forces suffered severe casualties, and when captured, they were sometimes subjected to humiliations, such as being forced to chew coca leaves. Among the many women who took an active part in the siege was Gregoria Apaza, Katari's younger sister. Katari's wife, Bartolina Sisa, also had her own troop command in the "human wall" surrounding La Paz, called the "Virreina."

In May, the uprising in Peru was defeated, and Tupac Amaru was executed in Cusco. In the beginning of July, the siege of La Paz was lifted with the arrival of Spanish reinforcements from Charcas, and soon after, Bartolina was taken prisoner by the Spanish. However, the siege was soon renewed, even though it was apparent by then that the attackers lacked the heavy armament needed to take the city by assault. Katari made several attempts to rescue his captured wife; at the same time, a dam was built above the city to cause a flood that would undermine the walls surrounding it. This plan failed as well, and new reinforcements caused the Indians to retreat from El Alto, on the plateau above La Paz, from where their operations had been conducted.

As had been the case in the uprising of Tupac Amaru, there was considerable dissension among the forces surrounding Katari. Finally, while rallying fresh troops to continue the fight in the vicinity of Lake Titicaca, he was betrayed by one of his own and captured. After a summary trial, he was sentenced to death and, on November 15, 1781, executed in the plaza of the village of Peñas, some 60 kilometers (37 miles) from La Paz. As with Tupac Amaru 6 months earlier, Katari's execution was brutal. The defeated leader was beaten, mutilated, and finally, still alive, tethered to four horses, drawn, and quartered. Then, to further terrorize the native population, various parts of his body were sent to different localities to be exhibited. Soon afterward in La Paz, Bartolina Sisa was also executed. In 1783, their 10-year-old son was apprehended and never heard from again. With that final act of merciless hatred, this chapter in the history of the region ended. In spite of the great forces initially mobilized, the effort had failed, mainly because of insufficient military power and the instability of social alliances and allegiances within Indian society. Nevertheless, its considerable repercussions were felt 40 years later at the very beginnings of the republic and continue until today.

After the emergence in the 1960s of the *Katarista* movement among Aymara university students in La Paz, two tendencies developed. One, Movimiento Indio Tupaj Katari (MITKA), emphasized the ethnic aspect, and the other, Movimiento Revolucionario Tupaj Katari (MRTK), insisted on the class factor in the revolutionary struggle. This was an early expression of the complex scenario in which the name of Tupac Katari is still invoked in Bolivia today, as it is by many of those involved in the cause for social justice and indigenous political participation.

J. Carlos Gumucio Castellon

See also **Bolivia; Peru**

Further Reading

Costa de la Torre, Arturo, *Episodios historicos de la rebelion indigena de 1781*, La Paz: Camarlinghi, 1974

Del Valle de Siles, M. Eugenia, *Testimonios del cerco de La Paz: El campo contra la ciudad*, La Paz: Ultima Hora, 1980

Grondin, Marcelo, *Tupac Katari y la rebelion campesina de 1781–1783*, Oruro: INDICEP, 1975

Guzman, Augusto, *Tupaj Katari*, Mexico: Fondo de Cultura Economica, 1944

Monje Ortiz, Zacarias, *Sucasuca Mallcu*, La Paz: Universo, 1942

Valencia Vega, Alipio, *1908—Julian Tupaj Katari: Caudillo de la liberacion india: Ensayo de interpretacion*, Buenos Aires: 1950

Kayapó

Capsule Summary

Location: Brazil, near the upper Xingú River
Total Population: 4,000
Languages: Gê, Kayapó
Religions: Tribal

The Kayapó belong to the Northwestern branch of the Ge family of South American Indian peoples. The Southern Kayapó lived in northern Matto Grosso and were described by the middle of the eighteenth century as people with "no fixed dwellings, but [who] wander continously, living on game and wild fruits." When more closely contacted in 1902, they numbered 2,500. Fifty years later, they had been reduced to some 10 individuals.

Further north, in the region of the Upper Xingú River, an affluent of the Amazon, some 4,000 Kayapó (or *Mebêngokrê,* as they call themselves) live in several villages today, of which Gorotire is the largest. They occupy a designated Indian reserve that covers about 100,000 square kilometers (38,610 square miles).

The area is made up mostly of tropical rainforest with a few open grasslands in the eastern part. As in other South American tropical societies, the traditional economy is based on semisedentary subsistence farming, with gardens of manioc, corn, and sweet potatoes. The exploitation of wild resources through gathering, hunting, and fishing is another important means of obtaining a food and protein supply; fishing is sometimes done by using bundles of a vine, *timbo*, which is beaten with sticks so that it releases a substance that causes the fish to float to the surface.

The Kayapó are well-known for their body painting, with intricate geometric designs, headdresses, and lip plugs. Worn at all times, body painting is used as ornamentation and is also related to ritual, status, and social behavior. Thus, black motifs represent normal, everyday conditions, whereas red motifs symbolize periods of restrictive taboos. Lip plugs are falling into disuse for cultural as well as practical reasons.

Traditionally, a Kayapó village was arranged in a large ring around a plaza, with the men's house in the center. The only social center for the women was at one end of the plaza, where the community oven was placed. According to tradition, in the early days of the twentieth century, many lived in one big ancestral village, Pyka-to-ti, "The Beautiful Village." Because of the increase in deaths caused by then-unknown diseases, the village was abandoned by 1920. A more recent change was that villages were constructed not in circles, but with the houses along Western-style streets.

Traditionally, the Kayapó share with other Ge peoples a complex social organization in which villages are divided into dual groupings, clans, and associations according to age, sex, and occupation. Participation in almost all aspects of life—naming, games, ceremonies, and marriage—is governed by the individual's relationships and associations. Chiefs are held in very high regard because of their prestige. They might have some privileges, such as a house of their own, but no real power.

Commemoration ceremonies among the Kayapó center around the belief in the centrality of human existence, something they share with other South American native cultures. They situate themselves at the center of the universe, within the village, surrounded by the forest, and halfway between heaven and the lower world.

Ceremonies relate to all aspects of life, in initiations such as name giving, or commemoration, as in the corn festival that is repeated during the entire growing period. Agriculture is a common mythical theme. The Kayapó believe that agriculture was a gift that was originally given to their ancestors from Nhak-pok-ti, the daughter of the rain. Another myth explains how, long ago, an opossum taught the Kayapó to eat corn.

The major deities are the sun and the moon. Circles are one of the Kayapó's key symbols The course of the sun and moon are understood to be circular, and most of the Kayapo's dances and rituals are performed in circular configurations.

The Kayapó's myths are similar to other Ge-speaking tribes, with each group having its own variations of a particular story. Ceremonies, in which specialized roles are "owned" by different lineage groups, or *nekrêx*, are an integral part of Kayapó life. Some kind of ceremony is almost always being prepared or enacted that involves elaborate body adornment, songs, and dances. However, the diminishing numbers of Kayapó, their dispersal, and a reduction in knowledge have considerably diminished the frequency of ceremonies.

The Kayapó are careful in their relations with various kinds of spirits. As a precaution, to ensure personal safety from these beings, women who go into the garden smoke continually so that the spirits who haunt the gardens will not follow them home. Returning from hunting expeditions, the hunters sing on the way back to the village to ensure that the souls of the animals they have killed remain in the forest. Multiple deaths in one household mean that the house is contaminated by the spirits of the dead. The house is considered unsafe, and the family will abandon it. The same applies to whole villages, as was the case with Pyka-to-ti.

Healers, called *metema-ri*, and shamans cure sickness and defend against spirit attack. They have a vast knowledge of the proper use of medicinal plants and magical techniques to obtain health or have a successful hunt. The various skills related to healing are learned by young men before they marry.

Of course, nothing in the traditional health system affords adequate protection against diseases that come from the outside world. An epidemic of measles that struck the village of Kokrajmoro, 20 years after the initial contact, killed 34 percent of an uninoculated population within 2 weeks. The mortality was such that nobody was left who could tend the crops.

At the same time, with revenues from timber and gold mining, the Kayapó have bought airplanes and hired pilots to police their territory against foreign encroachment. Radio and video equipment and recorders are used in the fight to maintain social and territorial integrity and to document the traditional rituals. Among their great achievements is the successful opposition, in 1989, to the projected building by the government of a series of hydroelectric dams on the Xingú River. Only time will tell whether these social and technological transformations will merely transform Kayapó culture or make it disappear.

JUAN CARLOS GUMUCIO

See also **Brazil; Indigenous Peoples**

Further Reading

Stout, Mickey, and Ruth Thomson, "Modalidade em Kayapó," *Série Lingüística*, 3, 1974 (in Portuguese)

Kazaks

Capsule Summary

Location: Kazakstan, Russia, Xinjiang in China, Uzbekistan, Mongolia, Turkey
Total Population: Approximately 11 million
Languages: Kazak, Russian
Religion: Sunni Muslim

The Kazaks (Qazaqs, Kazakhs) are the largest ethnic group in the Republic of Kazakstan, an independent country since December 1991. Roughly 7 million Kazaks live in contemporary Kazakstan, thus constituting 40 percent of the population there. The Chinese Kazaks (1.1 million) are concentrated to the northwestern parts of Xinjiang. Minor enclaves are probably still to be found in the provinces of Gansu and Qinghai. Large groups are also living in Mongolia (150,000), Kyrghyzstan (40,000), Uzbekistan (1,100,000), Turkmenistan (90,000), and Russia (700,000). Since the independence of Kazakstan, many Kazaks have left Russia, Mongolia, and China and resettled in the new country.

A significant diaspora of Kazak refugees is living in Turkey (5,000); these are of Chinese origin and immigrated during the 1950s. The Kazak diaspora in Europe (Germany, France, and Sweden) and the United States is insignificant and, with few exceptions, consists of Kazaks who have emigrated as guest workers from Turkey. The remaining Kazaks in northern Iran are refugees from Kazakstan who left their native country in the early 1930s. Some Iranian Kazaks are recent refugees from Afghanistan. Official contacts between Iranian Kazak communities and Kazakstani authorities have been established since the 1990s, and the government has permitted their repatriation.

The Kazak language belongs to the Turkic branch of the Altaic languages and is related to other Central Asian Turkic languages. It is written using a Cyrillic alphabet. In China, a modified Arabic script has been used for the Kazak language since 1980. Because of the long Russian political and cultural dominance over the Kazak territory, a large number of the Kazaks, especially among the well-educated and the urban elite, prefer Russian over the native Kazak language.

This will change in the near future, however, since the official language policy in independent Kazakstan favors the Kazak language over Russian. The Kazaks are a nation within Kazakstan and a recognized ethnic minority population in China, Russia, Uzbekistan, and Mongolia.

History

The steppe has always been populated by nomads who have been united into tribal federations. The silk routes passed through the area, thus functioning as a connecting link between the Mediterranean and East Asia. In the southern part, commercial centers such as Otrar and Taraz were founded; however, they were destroyed by the Mongols in the thirteenth century. Many states and empires competed during the late Middle Ages for control over the steppe. Toward the end of that period, in the late fifteenth and early sixteenth centuries, the nomadic tribes of the steppe were united in a political confederation known as Kazak Orda. The contemporary Kazaks emerged from this federation as a consolidated ethnic group. During the sixteenth century, the Kazak nomads enlarged their territory on the Central Asian steppes. Although they were united under Qasim Khan and partly during the reign of his successor, Tahir Khan, they soon split into smaller nomadic tribal federations. The nomadic groups were politically unified into three large, territorially based tribal federations known as the Larger, Middle, and Lesser Zhüz. The Larger Zhüz lived mainly in the east and southeastern part of Kazakstan as well as in the Ili Valley. The Lesser Zhüz were found mainly in western Kazakstan in the southwest, and the Middle Zhüz lived in between, in what today constitutes central Kazakstan as well as in northern Xinjiang and southwestern Mongolia. This division into three Zhüz is still kept and comprises an important dimension in contemporary Kazak identity.

The Kazak Zhüz are subdivided in patrilateral lineages, which remain a significant cultural factor in their social life. The exogamous lineages not only provide a chart for identifying individuals according to their heritage, but they also establish the rules for much social behavior. A correct understanding of the force of lineages is vital when interpreting contemporary Kazak society.

Kazak history is intertwined with Russian expansion. Since the mid-seventeenth century,, the Kazaks developed into a buffer between the two expanding empires of Russia and China. As a result of the expansion of the Dzungar Mongols in the eighteenth century, Kazak tribes began to seek the protection of the Russian czar in the 1730s and 1740s. However, many Kazaks migrated eastward after the Manchu troops finally defeated the Dzungar Mongols in 1758 and became vassals under Imperial China. In the 1820s a new system of administration was introduced in Kazak territory by the Russian regime. In 1822 the territory of the Middle Zhüz was divided into Russian administrative units, and Russian military jurisdiction was introduced. The same process was carried out in 1824 for the Lesser Zhüz. These changes in czarist policy led to revolts among the Kazaks, but the czarist authorities continued their colonial policy toward the nomads. New taxation methods were introduced, and from the 1830s onward, the Kazaks were no longer allowed to cultivate land. In 1847 the Larger Zhüz finally lost its independence. After the abolition of serfdom in Russia in 1861, Russian peasants started to move eastward to settle and cultivate land on the Kazak plain. An 1895 czarist Russian commission reserved land for new settlers in areas that had been mainly used by the Kazak nomads. During the so-called Stolypin agrarian reform between 1906 and 1912, when 19 million hectares of land on the Kazak plain were set aside for farming, a new mass settlement of Russian peasants took place.

The Soviet Era

In 1916 the czarist government decided that Kazaks, who traditionally had been exempted from military service, should be drafted into labor units. This led to a widespread revolt on the steppe and in the Ferghana Valley. As a punishment, the Russian government decided to drive the nomads who participated in the revolt from their lands. Many of them fled to China. During the February Revolution of 1917 under the leadership of Alikhan Bukeikhan, the Kazaks formed a semi-independent state called Alash Orda, whose autonomy came to an end in 1920 when the Bolsheviks finally integrated the Kazak steppe under their control.

In the Soviet Union, the Kazaks became recognized as one of its nations. The Kazak steppe territory was incorporated as an autonomous Soviet socialist republic in the summer of 1920 as part of Russia. However, Kazakstan became a union republic with its contemporary borders in December 1936 and received the official name of the Kazak Soviet Socialist Republic.

The Kazaks have paid a high price for have being part of the Russian and Soviet Empires. The history of the Kazaks is a history of suffering and persecution. They were forced into sedentarization by the czarist Russian army, the political persecutions in connection with the revolutionary events had stroked them hard, the civil war left many dead, and during Stalin in the 1930s they were almost annihilated. The collectivization program in Soviet Central Asia and Kazakstan in the late 1920s led to conflict and great difficulties for the nomads. The Kazaks were forced to settle, and many nomadic families saw their herds starving on pastures that could no longer sustain them. Thousands of Kazaks fled to Xinjiang in China and to Afghanistan. Almost half of the Kazak population died during this period. The final disintegration of the traditional Kazak culture came in connection with the so-called Virgin Soil Scheme in the 1950s, when many farmers moved into Kazak territory. In addition to this, a system of contamination of their environment was created by the Soviet military complex.

During the 1970s and 1980s, the Kazaks developed a high degree of ethnic pride, and the rate of assimilation seemed low. The former capital of Alma-Ata grew to a large city with many prestigious government and official buildings. The urban areas became highly influenced by Russians, who also demographically dominated northern parts of the republic.

From National Uprising to Independence

On December 16, 1986, an outbreak of nationalistic tumults occurred in Alma Ata. Then-President Mihkail Gorbachov, in striving to change the political structure of the Soviet Union, removed the Kazak Dinmukhammad Kunaev, who had been in power since 1964, from his post as first general party secretary of Kazakstan. Kunaev was replaced by a Russian national who was sent to clean up the corruption and economic mismanagement that marked Kunaev's regime. The riots, later described as peaceful demonstrations, ended with mass arrests and severe police brutalities, with many maltreated and a few killed. The Alma Ata events were officially reported to have resulted in 1,700 injuries and about 8,500 arrests.

With the dissolution of the Soviet Union in the fall of 1991, Kazakstan unexpectedly became an independent country. Like other former Soviet republics, contemporary Kazakstan has had to define and redefine its national identity while at the same time going through a process of transition to a market economy and a structural transformation of the administrative and political framework.

During the Soviet era, only a few traditional Muslim manners, such as the circumcision of boys and funeral customs, were followed by the Kazaks. However, most Kazaks still identify themselves as Muslims, although until recently Islam had a very low profile in the Republic. Changes have now taken place, and religion has become more visible in the society. The Muslims of Kazakstan are under the jurisdiction of the Spiritual Directorate of Kazakstan, which was created in 1990. This reorganization was officially supported by president Nursultan Nazarbaev and may be seen as part of the creation of a state-controlled Islamic organization. Many new mosques were built throughout the country during the last decade. In 1996 a new mosque named after the old Communist Party leader, Dinmukhamad Kunaev, was opened in the city of Turkistan, an odd case of religious and nationalistic fusion not uncommon in contemporary Kazakstan. More significant, however, is the revival of the Yasavi Sufi movement within Kazakstan. The founder of the Yasaviyya, Ahmad Yasavi, was buried in the mid-twelfth century in Kazakstan. In the new nation building, Yasavi has become an important national symbol for contemporary Kazakstan.

Social and Ecological Problems

During the years of independence, the socioeconomic situation has become bad in many parts of Kazakstan. Non-Kazaks are discriminated against, and certain stratas are excluded from important areas of society. Although many investments have been made by foreign companies and trade agreements have been signed with many countries. Kazakstan is an increasing poor country. Many people are now living under severe economic and social conditions.

The most serious problem, however, is the growing threat to the environment and the ecological catastrophe that Kazakstan is facing. The ecological situation makes Kazakstan one of the most polluted countries in the world. This is a question of both pure destruction of the environment and the consequences of the nuclear tests that have been carried out in the Semey (Semipalatinsk) area of Kazakstan since 1949 and, up to 1963, the atmospheric testing of nuclear weapons that took place. There has also been significant leakage of radioactivity in conjunction with underground testing. In spite of the fact that the Soviet authorities were aware of the risks involved, the local population was not properly informed. It was only in the 1980s that people in the area first began to realize that the tests had led to genetic damage and a reduction in the effectiveness of human immune systems. The nuclear test program was closed down after independence.

Other environmental questions involve the Aral Sea, the Caspian Sea, and Lake Balkhash, all of which are victims of far-reaching ecological damage. The salination of enormous areas of western Kazakstan has made the area uninhabitable. The drinking water is heavily contaminated and nearly unfit for human consumption. The health situation has deteriorated drastically. There are reasons to expect environmental refugees from Kazakstan when the situation becomes acute.

During the 1980s, the Kazaks of China underwent rapid social changes. Chinese authorities supported the development of minority cultures with schooling, the publication of books and newspapers, and acceptance of the operatation of religious institutions. The economic changes in China allowed the Kazaks to continue with pastoralism and dairy production. However, the last few years have been marked by increasing political persecution against minorities in China, especially in Xinjiang, where most of the Kazaks are living. Because of the deprived economic conditions of the country, contemporary Mongolian Kazaks are living under very bad economic and social circumstances. No recent data are available on the situation for the Kazaks in Russia and Uzbekistan.

INGVAR SVANBERG

See also **China; Kazakstan; Mongolia; Russia; Turkey; Uzbekistan**

Further Reading

Akiner, Shirin, *The Formation of Kazakh Identity: From Tribe to Nation State*, London: Royal Institute of International Affairs, 1995

Benson, Linda, and Ingvar Svanberg, *China's Last Nomads: The History and Culture of China's Kazaks*, New York: M.E. Sharpe, 1998

Holm-Hansen, Jørn, *Territorial and Ethnic-Cultural Self-Government in Nation-Building Kazakhstan*, Oslo: Norsk institutt for by- och regionforskning, 1997

Olcott, Martha Brill, *The Kazakhs*, Stanford, CA: Hoovard University Press, 1987

Svanberg, Ingvar, editor, *Contemporary Kazaks: Cultural and Social Perspectives*, Richmond: Curzon, 1999

Svanberg, Ingvar, Kazak Refugees in Turkey: A Study of Cultural Persistence and Social Change, Uppsala: Almqvist & Wiksell International, 1989

Kazakstan

Capsule Summary

Location: Central Asia
Total Population: 16,763,795 (July 2003 estimate)
Minority Populations: Russians, Ukrainans, Uzbeks, Uygurs, Germans, Tatars, and numerous other groups
Languages: Kazak (state language), Russian (language of interethnic communication)
Religions: Muslim (mostly Sunni), Christian (mostly Orthodox)

Kazakstan is one of the former Soviet republics in Central Asia that gained its independence in 1991. Its territory is 2,717,000 square kilometers (1,049,034 square miles), within the Commonwealth of Independent States second only to the Russian Federation. Kazakstan borders on Russia to the north, the People's Republic of China to the east, and Kyrgyzstan, Uzbekistan, and Turkmenistan to the south. In the southwest it has access to the Caspian Sea. The population is estimated at 16 million. The majority of these are Kazaks (50–55 percent) and Russians (30–35 percent). Other groups include the Germans, Ukrainians, Uygurs, Uzbeks, Tatars, and numerous others. The name of the state derives from the dominant ethnic group, the Kazaks.

History

Kazakstan is dominated by vast steppes and semideserts with few oases and by mountain ranges primarily along the southern and eastern borders. For almost 3,000 years, it has been inhabited primarily by pastoral nomads who migrated seasonally in search of pastures, often over long distances. The earliest of these nomadic tribes were Iranian speakers such as the Scythians and the Sarmatians. Since the fifth and sixth centuries, these groups were gradually replaced by Turkic-speaking groups who immigrated in succeeding waves from the east.

The final ethnic transformation of this region was a result of the expansion of the Mongol empire during the fourteenth century. Most of the soldiers in the Mongolian army were, in fact, Turkic speakers who mixed with earlier tribes that had already settled in Central Asia. One of the outcomes of this fission of earlier and later arrivals was the Kazaks. They first appear as a group in the fifteenth century as part of the Uzbek confederation, and later established an independent Khanate. This was, however, only short-lived, and for most of their history Kazaks were divided into three distinct hordes who often warred with each other.

This made them an easy target for annexation by the Russian tsar in the eighteenth and nineteenth centuries. Soon, Kazak nomads suffered from an influx of European settlers who regarded the extensive steppe territories as nonutilized land. Hundreds of thousands of Kazaks fled to China in search of new pastures. New waves of immigrants and widespread uprisings among Kazaks and other Central Asians during World War I resulted in severe famines as their herds perished.

The civil war following the October Revolution again took a heavy toll in the steppes, which was only to be followed by the greatest tragedy in Kazak history: their forced collectivization in the late 1920s. Within 3 years, from 1929 to 1932, almost 90 percent of their herds perished and 1.5 million (or 40 percent of the total Kazak population) died of hunger. In later years, however, the Kazaks adapted to the Soviet state and were provided with their own republic, the Kazak Soviet Socialist Republic, in 1936. Similar to other republics, most of the formal leadership was by ethnic Kazaks, although they had only limited power toward the ultimate decision makers in Moscow.

Kazakstan since Independence

Kazakstan declared its independence on December 16, 1991, as the last of all the former Soviet republics. Since then, it has been ruled by President Nursultan Nazarbayaev, who has prevented the formation of any serious opposition to his regime. Kazakstan is officially a presidential democracy. In recent years, international observers have increasingly criticized the government for corruption and irregularities during elections.

Traditionally, the Kazaks were pastoral nomads. Since their annexation by the Russian Empire, their economic situation has severely declined because European peasants have appropriated much of the most fertile land. The socialist transformation further harmed the livestock sector. In the 1950s, Khrushchev started the Virgin Land campaign, during which large tracks of pasture land were again turned into wheat fields. On the other hand, Kazakstan was the only Central Asian republic that experienced a notable degree of industrialization. Much of that was devoted to the exploitation of the country's abundant mineral resources and resulted in severe ecological damage. Degradation of the soil caused by the excessive use of pesticides and by nuclear tests near the city of Semipalatinsk in the northeastern part of the country further contributed to Kazakstan becoming one of the worst ecological disasters in the world.

The dissolution of the socialist economy left Kazakstan in a state of despair. With some reluctance, Western advice for rapid privatization was finally implemented. The results, especially in the rural areas, were devastating. Widespread unemployment, the depletion of the livestock herds, and extremely unfortunate terms of trades were some of the reasons. Production declined dramatically in all sectors of the economy. The years since 2000 have seen a gradual recovery, which has primarily been fueled by revenues from the oilfields in the western part of the republic. The GDP per capita exceeds $7,000 per annum ($7,200, 2002 estimate).

Kazakstan has always been a kind of miniature version of the Soviet Union, with over 140 ethnic groups officially residing here. Since the 1930s, Kazaks have been a minority in their own republic because of the loss of life during collectivization and the steady influx of European settlers. During World War II, Kazakstan also became one of the prime destinations for deported peoples such as the Germans or Crimean Tatars. In 1989, when the last Soviet census was taken, Kazaks constituted a relative majority again, with 42 percent. Only in 1999 did they become the absolute majority. Russians made up 36 percent of the population in 1989, but since then this figure has declined to less than 30 percent because of the out-migration to Russia. A similar trend is observable for the Ukrainians and Germans, who once each numbered close to 1 million. The majority of Germans by now have migrated to Germany; however, European immigrants still form a majority in the northern provinces, which many Russian nationalists claim as their legitimate territory.

Other minorities include the Uzbeks (400,000), Tatars (300,000), and Uygurs (200,000), all of whom are Turkic-speaking Muslims, as are the Kazaks themselves. The Uzbeks are an old, established population in the southern part of the country, whereas the Tatars and Uygurs migrated from Russia and China, respectively, during the nineteenth and twentieth centuries.

Smaller minorities include the Koreans, who were one of the deported peoples, as were the Chechens, the Meskhetian Turks, and other Caucasian groups. One very unique minority can be seen—the so-called "Repatriants," or descendants of the Kazaks who have left for China, Mongolia, and other places since the eighteenth century. To counter the unfavorable ethnic composition, they were invited to come "home" by Nazarbayev shortly after independence. Approximately 200,000 of them followed this call, but they faced great difficulties integrating into society.

Kazakstan faces a unique problem among the post-Soviet states. Its ethnic composition and its long border with Russia (where Europeans form the majority on both sides) pose serious obstacles for a primarily ethnically defined national identity. On the other hand, cultural differences among the various groups are more pronounced than, for example, in neighboring Uzbekistan. The answer to this seemed to be a clear-cut distinction between a Kazak (ethnic) and a Kazakhstaniy (national) identity. Some allegations, such as the religious suppression of non-Muslims, are certainly exaggerated, but there exists the potential for conflict. Ethnic relations are characterized by competition and the Kazakization of key economic and political positions. Many members of minority groups complain about the need to learn Kazak, which has become the new state language, although many Kazaks speak it only poorly themselves. So far, the interethnic tensions have not translated into violent conflicts, and according to opinion polls, none of the groups expects those to happen in the near future.

PETER FINKE

See also **Germans; Kazaks; Russians; Tatars; Uygurs, Uzbeks**

Further Reading

Bremmer, Ian, "Nazarbaev and the North: Statebuilding and Ethnic Relations in Kazakhstan," *Ethnic and Racial Studies*, 17 (1994)

Capisani, Giampaolo, *The Handbook of Central Asia: A Comprehensive Survey of the New Republics*, London: Tauris, 2000

Olcott, Martha Brill, *The Kazakhs*, Stanford, California: Stanford University Press, 1987; 2nd edition, 1995

Schatz, Edward, "Framing Strategies and Non-Conflict in Multi-Ethnic Kazakhstan," *Nationalism and Ethnic Politics*, 6 (2000)

Svanberg, Ingvar, editor, *Contemporary Kazaks: Cultural and Social Perspectives*, Richmond, United Kingdom: Curzon, 1999

Kenya

Capsule Summary

Location: East African coast bounded by Somalia, Ethiopia, Sudan, Uganda, and Tanzania
Total Population: 31,639,091 (July 2003 estimate)
Languages: Swahili, English, numerous indigenous languages.
Religions: Protestant (38%), Roman Catholic (28%), indigenous beliefs (26%), Muslim (7%), other (1%)

Situated on the East Coast of Africa and bisected by the equator, Kenya covers some 580,000 square kilometers (223,938 square miles) and has a population of some 31.6 million (2003 estimate). The two most widely used languages are Kiswahili and English. The system of government is presidential, and the per capita GDP is $1,100 (2002 estimate).

Historically, Kenya has acted as a meeting point for population movements so that its people are a mixture of Bantu, Nilotic, Nilo-Hamitic, and Cushitic tribes, and these groups are based on linguistic and cultural similarities. The three main language groups are the Bantu, Nilotic, and Cushitic; The Bantu are found in Central and Western Kenya, the Nilotic in the West and Northwest, and the Cushitic in the Northeast. Altogether, some 70 tribal groups are distinguished by their linguistic and cultural differences. From at least the ninth century, what developed into the coastal Islamic culture has been strongly influenced by Persian and Arab influences from across the Indian Ocean; the result is the widespread use of the Swahili language, which is now the *lingua franca* of Kenya and has replaced English as the country's official language. The boundaries of modern Kenya—that is, colonial Kenya—shifted several times during the colonial period, and in the process upset or altered the ethnic groups that were included within the country.

Britain proclaimed Kenya to be a Protectorate in 1895. Boundary adjustments in 1902 led to the westward shift of the country so as to include the former eastern province of Uganda (also by then a British colony) on the borders of Lake Victoria. In 1924 Jubaland in the northeast was transferred to Italian Somalia. In 1926 another boundary extension led to the incorporation of northern Turkana into Kenya. The effect of such border adjustments was that it made the people of the affected regions feel they had an affinity with similar peoples across these borders as well as those inside Kenya. In recent times, during and after the colonial era, non-African minorities have included Asians and Europeans, and an Arab minority was present in the region long before colonial times. These minorities have represented only a tiny percentage of the whole population, although the influence they have wielded has been out of proportion with their numbers. The opening up of Kenya to white settlement at the beginning of the twentieth century and the alienation of the "White Highlands" for this purpose represent the most important impacts of colonialism. This led to significant conflict, especially with the Kikuyu, who claimed that the alienated land was traditionally theirs. Land was always at the center of African protests against colonialism, and the Kikuyu determination to retake control of their land eventually led to the Mau Mau rebellion of 1952–1959, which hastened the progress to independence. This was eventually achieved in 1963 under the nationalist leader Jomo Kenyatta, a Kikuyu, who ruled Kenya until his death in 1978. He was succeeded by Daniel arap Moi, a Kalenjin, who remained head of state through to the new millennium.

Although social communal and land use habits remain strong, according to tribal traditions, they were weakened substantially during the colonial era, partly as the result of white settlement in the White Highlands and partly as the result of rapid urbanization, which has continued at an even faster pace in the years since independence. Nonetheless, the great majority of people remain agriculturalists or pastoralists. At the same time, an increasing number of people from different tribal or communal backgrounds mingle in the country's rapidly growing urban centers. Urban life has had the effect of eroding tribal differences, although most urban dwellers retain important links with their rural communities. Most groups live in traditional tribal territories and regard these as their own, but modern conditions are inevitably creating increasingly complex relationships between groups and breaking down older tribal barriers.

During the colonial years, and especially toward the end, the Kikuyu and Luo emerged as the strongest advocates of Kenyan nationalism; after independence, these two groups came to dominate the political scene, with the result that one of the principal strengths of Moi's claim to leadership has been the fact that he represented the country's smaller ethnic groups who resented Kikuyu and Luo domination. Ninety percent of the population is made up of 11 ethnic groups: These are the Bantu speakers (Kikuyu, Embu, Kamba, Meru, Gusii, Luhya, and Nyika) and the Nilotic speakers (Luo, Masai, Kalenjin, and Turkana). The possibility of tribal division and conflict has been a major political concern for Kenya's rulers since independence.

The three non-African minorities—the Europeans, Indians, and Arabs—have played a significant role in the development of modern Kenya. The majority of the Europeans came from Britain; others came from South Africa, continental Europe, and the United States. Their principal activities have been as farmers, businessmen, civil servants (the colonial administration), and missionaries. They retained their Western culture and the English language, and Christianity may be seen as their principal legacy to the country. The Indian minority, introduced into Kenya at the beginning of the nineteenth century by the British, are found in the urban centers and are mainly occupied in business and commerce. They have retained a remarkable cohesiveness as an ethnic group. Their main languages are Hindustani, Punjabi, and Gujarati, and they adhere to either the Hindu or Muslim religions. The Arabs came to the Kenya (Swahili) Coast long before either the Europeans or Asians, perhaps as early as 900 CE, and brought their religion of Islam with them. Some Arabs are the descendants of these first Arab traders. More Arab migrants were to come in the sixteenth century following the arrival of the Portuguese on the coast.

A total of 75 languages are spoken in Kenya, and Swahili became the official language in 1974, replacing English, the language of the former colonial power. Most of the population hold traditional African beliefs, although there are a significant number of African Christians. The main Christian churches are represented in the country, and the Europeans are predominantly Christian. The Arabs are Muslim, whereas the Indians are either Muslim or Hindu.

GUY ARNOLD

See also **Africa: A Continent of Minorities?**

Further Reading

Arnold, Guy, *Kenyatta and the Politics of Kenya,* London, J.M. Dent & Sons, 1974

Gregory, R.G., *India and East Africa: A History of Race Relations within the British Empire, 1890–1939,* Oxford: Oxford University Press, 1972

Kenyatta, J., *Facing Mount Kenya,* London: Heinemann, 1979

Mangat, J.S.A., A *History of the Asians in East Africa, c. 1886–1945,* Oxford: Clarendon Press, 1969

Ojany, F.F., and R.B. Ogendo, *Kenya: A Study in Physical and Human Geography,* London: Longman, 1973

Report of the East African Royal Commission, 1953–1955, Cmd 9475, London: HMSO, 1955

Khakass

Capsule Summary

Location: Republics of Khakasia and Tuva in Russia, China
Total Population: 90,000
Languages: Khakas, Russian
Religions: Russian Orthodox, native religion

The ethnic label Khakas (Khakass; self-designation *xakas*) is a unifying identity created in the 1920s for various related Turkic-speaking groups. The vast majority of the Khakas live within Khakasia, a republic within the Russian Federation located in West Siberia, on the left bank of the Yenisei River. Because of immigration, the Russians are the majority of the population in Khakasia. The Khakas are mainly a rural people, and many Khakas live under poor conditions as farmers in their traditional villages.

Other Khakas are found in the Krasnoyarsk Territory. Furthermore, some 2,000 Khakas live in the neighboring republic of Tuva. A small group of Khakas speakers was reported from the Wujiazi village in the Fuyun district of Heilongjiang province in China. They are said to originate from a group of Turks settled there after deportation from the Altai area by the Qing Emperor Qianlong in 1761.

The Khakas People

The Khakas constitute a conglomerate of various Turkic tribes that are believed to be descendants of the so-called Yenisei Kirghiz, as mentioned in Tang dynasty annals dating from the ninth century. During the seventeenth century, Turkic tribes inhabited the Sayan Mountains and the Minusinsk Depression, the same area where most of the Khakas still live. Some of these tribes have long traditions as cattle breeders, whereas others were hunters and fishermen. Until the beginning of the twentieth century, these Turkic tribes were divided into several territorial administrative units, once created by the Mongols. They were known as Beltir, Kacha, Koybal, Kyzyl, Shor, and Sagai, all of whom speak their own dialects. The Russians categorized them all under the umbrella denomination Abakan Tatars or Minusinsk Tatars.

In 1923 local intellectuals developed the self-designation Khakas, with the aim of create a common ethnonym for these tribal groups. Gradually, it became adopted and accepted by the population.

History

The territory of Khakasia was under the Mongols in the thirteenth to fourteenth centuries. During the next three centuries, it was ruled by local khans, who were vassals to various Mongol rulers. Khakasia was joined to Russia under Peter I in 1707. Numerous Russian settlers moved in to mine copper in the eighteenth century. Around the gold mines of Minusinsk, an industrial center has developed since the 1820s. Following the construction of the Trans-Siberian Railway in the 1890s, the Khakas became a minority in the area. They were influenced by the Russian impact, and at the end of the nineteenth century, they converted to Russian Orthodox Christianity.

In 1923 a Khakas national district was established, which attained the status of a region in 1925. It was then leveled to an autonomous province, first within the West Siberian Territory in 1930 and later within the Krasnoyarsk Territory in 1934.

The Bolshevik regime and industrialization brought changes to the region. Mixed marriages between Khakas and Russians became rather common, and the importance of the Russian language was constantly highlighted.

With the breakup of the Soviet Union, the old administrative system also became obsolete. Khakasia attained the status of a republic in 1991.

The present population is less than 600,000, although only about 80,000 of them are Khakas. In 1926 the ethnic Khakas made up half of the population in the region, but today they represent merely 11 percent. The urbanization is 70 percent. Because of massive immigration, the Russians represent more than 80 percent of the republic's population. Abakan, the capital, has a population of about 170,000, of which only five percent are Khakas. They are mainly rural people and live in villages engaged in farming, hunting, or livestock breeding.

The republic produces timber, coal, iron ore, aluminium, gold, molybdenum, and tungsten. However, Khakasia is still greatly underdeveloped. Despite its rich natural resources, economic activity is low in Khakasia, although jade from local deposits is exported to Hong Kong.

Cultural and Language Revival

The Khakas speak a Siberian or North Turkic language related to Chulym, Karagass, and Altay. A few glosses were recorded by the Swede Johan Peter Falck in the 1770s. The first real description of one of the dialects was published by the Finn Mathias Alexander Castrén in 1857.

Khakas was not developed as a literary language until the Soviet regime. In 1924 a Cyrillic alphabet and a written language based on the Kacha dialect were introduced. A few textbooks for schools and some translations from Russian were published. A local newspaper began to publish in 1927. In 1929 the written language switched to the Latin alphabet. However, in 1939 a second Cyrillic alphabet, somewhat different from the first, was reintroduced. Since 1953 the Sagai dialect has also been of importance in the creation of the literary language.

Long before the new written language could be consolidated, Khakas was influenced by the Russian language. Today, the Khakas written language has been improved on the basis of the Sagai dialect. According to recent information, there are two newspapers in Khakas and also a TV program for 2 hours daily.

The education of children in the Khakas language began in 1926. According to the 1989 census, the Khakas language was the mother tongue of nearly 77 percent of the Khakas. About 67 percent of them were also fluent in Russian. In the mid-1990s only seven percent of children were taught in the Khakas language and 50 percent of children learned it as a school subject. Despite positive changes in the attitude toward the mother tongue and an increase of the number of schools and schoolchildren learning the Khakas language, the future for the language is still not secure. It is regarded as an endangered language by many scholars.

Although the literary language is heavily influenced by Russian borrowings, the local Khakas of all ages in the villages still speak and understand their native tongue. The Russian language has not spread to the villages, and the elderly hardly speak it at all. The aforementioned Khakas dialect from Heilongjiang in China is almost extinct. Only a handful of people are still fluent in their native idiom.

As a minority within their own republic, the Khakas have had limited opportunities to develop and revive their ethnic culture. Leaders of the republic are more concerned with economic and political issues. Native politicians are in the minority and lack the political strength to work for ethnic issues. However, there is an increasing interest in the native language and culture among contemporary Khakas. Another expression of this national self-esteem is the religious change taking part among them. Before being converted to Orthodox Christianity, the Khakas followed an indigenous religion. Nowadays, a shamanistic revival is occurring, as the people have never really abandoned those practices. At the same time, foreign missionary activities have increased. The Khakas' ethnic music, with its special male "throat singing," has attracted interest worldwide.

INGVAR SVANBERG

See also **Siberian Indigenous Peoples**

Further Reading

Akiner, Shirin, *Islamic Peoples of the Soviet Union,* London: KPI 1986 (with an Appendix on the non-Muslim Turkic peoples of the Soviet Union)

Emsheimer, Ernst, "On the Ergology and Symbolism of a Shaman Drum of the Khakass," *Imago Musicae,* 5 (1988)

Potapov, Leonid, "The Khakasy," in *The Peoples of Siberia,* edited by Maxim G. Levin and Leonid Potapov, Chicago: Chicago University Press, 1964

Svanberg, Ingvar, "Turkic Ethnobotany and Ethnozoology as Recorded by Johan Peter Falck," *Svenska Linnésällskapets Årsskrift 1986–1987* (1987)

Khmer

Location: Cambodia, Vietnam, Thailand, Europe, North America, Australia
Total Population: 11 million
Language: Khmer
Religion: Theravada Buddhism

The Khmer are the majority ethic group living in the nation of Cambodia and are to be found as a minority group in neighboring Vietnam and Thailand as well as many other countries to which they have relocated in recent years.

Orientation

Most Khmer live in Cambodia in the lowlands surrounding the Mekong River and around the great lake Tonle Sap, the lifeblood of the country. The majority practice agriculture, with wet rice being the main crop, supplemented by the production of palm sugar, fruit, and vegetables; livestock rearing; fishing; aquaculture; and work in cottage and service industries. Many Khmer live and work in urban centers, especially the capital, Phnom Penh, which is the country's largest administrative, service, and industrial processing center and is dwarfed by neighboring Bangkok and Ho Chi Minh City. The country is poor and is rapidly being brought into the global manufacturing and trade economy.

The language of the Khmer, also called Khmer or Cambodian, belongs to the Mon Khmer family of languages, which extends very widely throughout mainland Southeast Asia; it accounts for the greatest number of speakers in this family. The Khmer language is influenced in content and form by loans from Sanskrit, and its script is derived from this source. Khmer is also influenced by Pali, the original language of the Buddhist scriptures. Many Khmer, particularly those living in Southern Vietnam, also speak Vietnamese; those in or adjacent to Thailand speak Thai; and knowledge of French and English is quite common—all legacies of the colonial, postcolonial, and diaspora influences to which the Khmer have been exposed.

The principal religion of the Khmer is Theravada Buddhism, a faith widespread in Southeast Asia. Distinctive, beautifully decorated Buddhist temples comprise the social and cultural core of Khmer communities wherever they are living. Many Khmer men take orders for a period of their life and during that time reside, study, and perform religious rituals in the temple, venturing out only to gather alms or officiate at rites. The temples also function as a school, cemetery, and venue for important community festivals and ceremonies such as New Year; the anniversaries of the birth, enlightenment, and death of Buddha; and annual monastic retreats. To a large extent, Buddhism's precepts form an underlying moral code by which Khmer people live. Alongside Buddhism runs a strong current of popular belief in nature spirits and the souls of ancestors, local protector spirits, and historical figures accorded posthumous efficacy. These are interwoven with Hindu or Brahman rites and beliefs. Buddhist iconography, such as Buddha statues, and the monks themselves are commonly considered to have magical powers.

History

Historically the Khmer have occupied something of an economic and cultural crossroads between the major civilizations of Asia. The first major state in the vicinity was the kingdom of Funan, whose influence extended over present day Vietnam and Cambodia. Funan was annexed by Chenla in the mid sixth century, and is widely considered the first Khmer state. The Khmer state known as Kambudja developed a sophisticated hydraulic network forming the basis for wet-rice agriculture. It was well-known to Chinese traders and was involved in important economic and cultural exchanges, with India in particular. The most important and famous phase of this period was the Angkor Period from 802 to 1432. At that time, the political center of the state was the monumental and ceremonial complex of Angkor Wat, a site whose sacred architecture was intimately associated with the rituals of kingship and dynastic succession.

The period succeeding Angkor was one of dynastic decline, political weakening, and predations by rival powers, but the eventual eclipse of Angkor was also associated with fundamental realignments of power in maritime Southeast Asia in the middle of the second millennium of the Modern Era. The center of Khmer power shifted to closer to the coast, on the Mekong River, taking advantage of the rise in regional commerce. It was at this time that Hindu religious influences were supplanted by Therevada Buddhism, then spreading throughout much of mainland Southeast Asia. The Khmer state, however, was to find itself squeezed mercilessly by its two expanding neighbors, Vietnam and Thailand. The Cambodian polity was successively invaded and annexed by these two powers, losing western provinces to Thailand and the entire lower Mekong Delta to Vietnam in the eighteenth century. At this point, substantial numbers of Khmer in these annexed regions, formerly identifying with the Khmer king, found themselves as minority subjects and targets of assimilation.

When France colonized Indochina, it took over Cambodia, stopped the expansionism of the Thais and Vietnamese, and successfully negotiated the return of the provinces taken by Thailand. However, it consolidated the borders and made the part of Cambodia annexed by the Vietnamese into a French colony. In the latter region, called Cochinchina, the Khmer were a minority, subject to political, economic, and cultural policies that favoured the French, ethnic Vietnamese, and Chinese. This region was given over to rice exports, and many Khmer became tenants and laborers working to produce rice for export on other people's land. Meanwhile, in Cambodia, French colonization did little to promote the economic development of the Khmer people. The institution of kingship, an ethnic Khmer preserve, was maintained and the traditional elite and patronage relationships of rural society were substantially undisturbed. On the other hand, the French political presence gave a great fillip to the ethnic Vietnamese residents of the protectorate, who were favored as administrators, and the economic orientation of the French colonialism greatly boosted the opportunities for the Chinese entrepreneurial minority. Both groups poured into Cambodia, thus fueling ethnic tensions. The frustrations of the ethnic Khmer elite formed the impetus for an ethnonationalist movement of revolt against the French.

Khmer nationalism was not initially subject to the deadly internal disputes that rent the Vietnamese nationalist movement. Formal independence was secured from France in 1954, and Prince Norodom Sihanouk abdicated the throne in 1955 to become prime minister, the most influential figure in independent Cambodia. Up to 90 percent of the population was ethnic Khmer, occupying a range of social positions from aristocrats, government officials, Buddhist monks, and military officials to artisans, laborers, and farmers. Until 1970, the divisive wars raging in Vietnam did not heavily influence Cambodia, but fighting eventually spilled over, and the polarization of politics led to a coup against Sihanouk in 1970. From this time on, the state became increasingly identified with ethnic Khmer identity, and the ethnic Vietnamese became targets of ethnic-based violence and political attacks. This fed on older grievances relating to the loss of territory in the eighteenth century, resentments fanned during the French period, as well as the threatening presence of Vietnamese troops on Khmer soil. Under the United States-backed Lon Nol regime, many thousands of Cambodia's ethnic Vietnamese were killed and forced into repatriation, a precursor of the ethnocidal terror of the succeeding Khmer Rouge regime.

The Khmer Rouge initially emerged under the sponsorship of the Vietnamese-dominated Indochinese Communist party, which, in the postindependence era, inherited many of the ambitions over Indochina nurtured by the French. However, when the Khmer Rouge came to power in 1975, part of a wave of communist victories in Indochina, they proved to be extremely hostile to the ethnic Vietnamese and to all other non-Khmer groups. Their vision for the state they renamed as Kampuchea was of a classless, economically self-sufficient, and ethnically pure Khmer nation. To this effect, they emptied the cities, considered receptacles of impure and foreign culture, attacked the intelligentsia and Buddhist religious hierarchy, forced people to work collectively in the rice paddies, and launched genocidal attacks against non-ethnic Khmer groups such as the Chinee, the Cham, and the Vietnamese. Although only reigning for a short period, from 1975 to 1979, until displaced by a rapid Vietnamese invasion, the impact of the Khmer Rouge on Cambodian society proved extremely destructive. The task of reconstructing cultural and religious traditions destroyed in the process, not to mention reuniting unraveled families, healing shattered minds and bodies, treating those who continue to be maimed on a daily basis by land mines, and restoring a battered economy continues to this day.

The Vietnamese occupied most of the country for a decade but were not able to eliminate the Khmer Rouge. Their presence, in fact, gave Khmer Rouge leaders a pretext to stir up hostilities against Vietnamese expansionism. The conflict, which simmered throughout the 1980s, spewed forth an appalling toll of casualties, most of whom were innocent victims of exploding mines. The Vietnamese-dominated period is also associated with the arrival of a new wave of carpetbaggers and further high-minded attempts to reform Khmer culture into a Vietnamized socialist mold. Peace and normalization came in the early 1990s with the Vietnamese withdrawal, the formation of the United Nations Transitional Authority, and the holding of internationally supervised elections. Cambodia has embarked on a nominally democratic but politically factionalized and unstable path since that time. Economically, it has entered into the ranks of dollar-spending countries, and its economy has grown fairly rapidly. On the down side, there have been occasional outbursts of deadly ethnic violence directed against the Vietnamese, a failure to fully reign in and bring the Khmer Rouge to justice, and justified concerns about the impact on Cambodian society, culture, and the environment of political corruption and the burgeoning market economy.

The Khmer as a Minority

At various points in recent Cambodian history, Khmer nationalists have raised pressures in the ethnonationalist consciousness by describing themselves as a minority in their own country. This is not and never came close to being the case, although it was considered compelling enough to obtain a degree of popular support for the stigmatization and persecution of the Vietnamese in Cambodia.

The biggest Khmer minority is to be found in the southern provinces of Vietnam, in the region formerly annexed by the Vietnamese court in the eighteenth century. Numbering anywhere between 700,000 and 2 million, they refer to themselves as the Khmer Krom, the Southern Khmer. This appellation is not accepted by the Vietnamese authorities, who consider it as expressing ambitions for reunification with Cambodia. Officially, they are described as "Vietnamese people of Khmer origin." Over the centuries, many have been assimilated into an ethnic Vietnamese identity, losing their language, religion, and identity as Khmer. Although possessing citizenship and benefiting from an educational aid scheme, the Khmer in Vietnam are extremely poor, living chiefly by agriculture on relatively inaccessible and inferior lands. Landlessness, unemployment, and low levels of education are extremely common problems. They are stigmatized in the wider society and often considered as foreigners rather than as indigenous people. The Khmer tend to live separately from the Vietnamese and, as in Cambodia, Buddhist temples comprise the cultural center of Khmer communities. Undoubtedly, this has helped them preserve their unique culture. But this isolation spells a loss of competence in the dominant political, cultural, and economic structures of their region. Many are not fully fluent in Vietnamese, the language of business and administration, and yet are also illiterate in their mother tongue, Khmer. Many Khmer living in southern Vietnam consider themselves a misrepresented, colonized people yet fear that to espouse such sentiments publicly would bring down serious retribution on their heads.

The Khmer who left the country in the 1970s and 1980s live dispersed throughout North America, Europe, and Australasia. Many passed through a liminal period of living in refugee camps on the Thai border and then spent years adjusting to their new country's language, culture, and economic system. The transition from a kin-based agrarian country to an urbanized industrial, consumerist environment was not easy. The Khmer community continues to experience problems such as a language barrier for the older generation and a generation gap. One of the signs of their increasing stability, however, is the construction of Buddhist temples and the observance of religious ceremonies. Buddhism provides not only the religious underpinning of existence, but for those who are a minority, it also provides a social focus and serves as an important symbol of their ethnic identity. Other aspects of traditional culture, such as New Year's celebrations, weddings, and performances of theatre, music, and dance have been revived in the Khmer people's new lands.

PHILIP TAYLOR

See also **Australia; Cambodia; Thailand; Vietnam**

Further Reading

Chandler, David, *A History of Cambodia*, Colorado: Westview Press, 1992

Ebihara, May, Carol A. Mortland, and Judy Ledgerwood, editors, *Cambodian Culture since 1975: Homeland and Exile*, Ithaca: Cornell University Press, 1994

International Centre for Ethnic Studies, *Minorities in Cambodia*, London: Minority Rights Group International, 1995

Kiernan, Ben, *The Pol Pot Regime: Race, Power and Genocide in Cambodia under the Khmer Rouge, 1975–79*, New Haven and London: Yale University Press, 1995

Mabbett, Ian, and David Chandler, *The Khmers*, Oxford: Blackwell, 1995

Martin, Marie Alexandrine, *Cambodia: A Shattered Society*, Berkeley: University of California Press, 1994

Martin Luther King, Jr. (African American)

Martin Luther King, Jr., was one of the most important figures of the twentieth century. King was born in Atlanta, Georgia, as the son and grandson of Baptist ministers. He would follow in their footsteps. King blended this religious background with a strong belief in the social gospel in his career as a crusader for civil rights, workers' rights, nonviolent activism, and anti-imperialism. King was probably the central figure in the American civil rights movement, and he inspired people across the globe to act on behalf of their rights.

King first came to prominence during the Montgomery Bus Boycott. King's emergence owed as much to the fortune of circumstances as to his own considerable gifts, which had become apparent in his stint as pastor of Montgomery's Dexter Avenue Baptist Church, where he had begun working while finishing his Ph.D. work at Boston University in 1954. The local leadership of the emerging boycott, which began after the arrest of Rosa Parks for violating that city's Jim Crow segregation statutes on a local bus, chose King to lead the newly created Montgomery Improvement Association, at least in part because he was not beholden to any of the factions within Montgomery's black community. The boycott lasted for 381 days, and King rose to national prominence as a result of his eloquent and unyielding leadership of the boycott.

After the end of the boycott in December 1956, King realized the need for a new civil rights organization based in the black church that could continue the spirit of militant nonviolence that had characterized the Montgomery movement. In January 1957, a group of black Southern ministers met in King's hometown of Atlanta to discuss plans for attacking segregation in the future. From this meeting emerged what would become known as the Southern Christian Leadership Conference (SCLC). The ministers named King the organization's first president. Within a few weeks, King's picture graced the cover of *Time* magazine, and he was widely recognized as the most prominent black leader in America. The 1958 publication of *Stride toward Freedom*, King's account of the Montgomery campaign, served to solidify King's public image.

In the years from 1957 to 1960, King revealed his wide-ranging interests and showed how he envisioned injustice and the struggle against it as a concern not only of the American South, but also of the United States and the world as a whole. During this time, he traveled to newly liberated Ghana to meet with that country's revolutionary hero and newly elected President Kwame Nkrumeh; he visited India and met with Prime Minister Jawaharlal Nehru as well as with many of the followers of Mohandas Gandhi, whose nonviolent teachings and practices had made a huge impression on the young minister. On the home front, King and other civil rights leaders met with Vice President Richard Nixon, President Dwight Eisenhower, and Democratic Presidential candidate Senator John Kennedy in hopes of enlisting their support for the civil rights causes King championed. In most cases, their response was tepid. It was clear to King and others that it would take concerted action on the part of activists to cause politicians at the highest level to respond to the plight of black Americans, especially in the South.

Something of a turning point occurred in October 1960 in the waning days of the tightly contested Presidential campaign. King, who had returned to Atlanta to share copastorate duties with his father at the Ebenezer Baptist Church, and more importantly, to allow him to devote more time and presence to the SCLC and the emerging freedom struggle. While leading a sit-in demonstration at Rich's department store in Atlanta, King was arrested and sentenced to 4 months of hard labor for violating the terms of a 1956 conviction on dubious charges of driving with expired plates and without a valid Georgia driver's license. In the aftermath of the conviction, John Kennedy called Coretta Scott King and expressed his concern for her and her husband's well-being. Attorney General Robert Kennedy then interceded with the Georgia authorities to orchestrate King's release. At the same time, Vice President Nixon, the Republican Presidential candidate, had done nothing. This did not escape the notice of the black community. King never formally endorsed Kennedy, but he did make several public pronouncements that the Democratic campaign used in its favor. Furthermore, King's father, "Daddy King," a lifelong Republican, famously announced after the Kennedy intercession, "I've got all my votes," referring to the influence he and other black social and religious leaders had on black voters, "and I've got a suitcase, and I'm going to take them up there and dump them in his lap." Kennedy won the election by the slimmest of margins, and most historians acknowledge the significance of the African-American vote in the 1960 campaign.

It was during this time that the civil rights movement had undergone something of a transformation. Although King was involved in sit-in campaigns such as the one at the Rich's department store, the sit-in movement derived its impetus not from King and the SCLC, but rather from a student movement that had emerged in the wake of a series of sit-ins in Nashville, Tennessee, and, most notably, Greensboro, North Carolina. These sit-ins had led to the organization of the Student Nonviolent Coordinating Committee (SNCC). The SNCC was dedicated to direct action against segregation in the South, and its rise provided a direct challenge to King's leadership and preeminence in the movement. Many students saw King's approach as too cautious and as anachronistic. These students believed that a more aggressive approach to integration was necessary. To his credit, King was quick to adjust to this new order. Whatever the criticisms of King, it is evident that he was far more concerned with justice being served than with his necessarily being at the forefront of such change. Nonetheless, King's natural abilities, his talents as a speaker, his national profile, and the esteem in which he was held meant that he would continue to be at the forefront of the civil rights movement even as that movement expanded and created other leaders and organizations. Furthermore, King adroitly balanced his leadership of grassroots movements with his stature as a national leader.

1960 and 1961 saw students engage in high-profile sit-ins across the South. It also saw the Freedom Rides, which traveled through the South to test court-ordered integration of buses and facilities. After violence in

Alabama caused the Congress of Racial Equality (CORE) to halt the Freedom Rides, members of the SNCC stepped into the breach, filling jails at Mississippi's notorious Parchman Farms prison. King supported the student movement even when that movement criticized him for allegedly being above the fray. However, King's experiences leading the Albany Movement in 1961 revealed some of the limitations of direct-action protests in the absence of either a larger plan of action or a local police force willing to engage in violence that in turn drew national attention. The Albany Campaign was intended to integrate that city's public facilities. However, conflicts between the SNCC, SCLC, and National Association for the Advancement of Colored People (NAACP), as well as the lack of a clear objective, proved to be nearly insurmountable barriers. Eventually, the various groups worked together to form the Albany Movement. Like the Freedom Riders, the Albany Movement saw as one of its chief objectives a desire to test segregation ordinances in the city's bus stations. Following the public challenges of the Freedom Riders, the Interstate Commerce Commission backed the 1960 Supreme Court ruling that that segregation in bus and train stations was illegal, and their mandate went into effect on November 1, 1961. As the Movement expanded to include other facilities in Albany, it became clear that Police Chief Laurie Pritchett was not about to allow his police force to engage in the kind of violence that had garnered national attention for the Freedom Riders in Anniston and Montgomery. Instead, his forces arrested hundreds of participants but did so without brutality and without fanfare. In December 1961, local leaders called on Martin Luther King, Jr., in hopes that his presence would galvanize support and garner national attention. Twice in 1961 and 1962 King was arrested, but in the end the Albany Movement was ineffective at ending Jim Crow in the town, and it went down as one of the few monumental failures of King's tenure as a civil rights leader.

By 1963, however, King found the appropriate stage on which to regain his status as the premier leader of the African-American freedom struggle. Birmingham, Alabama, was known as the most intransigent city in America when it came to civil rights. King called it "probably the most thoroughly segregated city in the United States." Beginning in March, King would be at the forefront of "Project C" (for "Challenge"), along with local leaders such as Minister Fred Shuttlesworth, which would comprehensively confront Jim Crow in the city. At the heart of the challenge would be a boycott of the city's white businesses. The city's volatile police commissioner, Bull Connor, dealt with protesters brutally, often unleashing police dogs and fire hoses on protesters. The images of men, women, and children being attacked by dogs and swept off their feet by high-powered hoses captured national attention. The SCLC effectively managed to gain maximum exposure for the campaign . In April, while King was in jail for leading the protests, he responded to eight clergymen who had publicly challenged his role in Birmingham. King responded with a 6,500-word letter that he crafted in jail in the margins of the *Birmingham News* and on scrap paper. His "Letter from a Birmingham Jail" would prove to be one of the most forceful, powerful, and influential documents in American history. Events in Birmingham, as well as in the rest of the South, led President Kennedy finally to put himself behind civil rights with a proposed comprehensive civil rights legislation.

In many ways, 1963 marked the pinnacle of King's career. In addition to the Birmingham Campaign, King gave his most famous speech in August of that year when hundreds of thousands of civil rights supporters attended the March on Washington. King's "I Have a Dream" speech marked the emotional and rhetorical pinnacle of an event intended to focus attention on the freedom movement and the proposed civil rights legislation. Although King began speaking from a prepared text, his most famous and powerful words came when he extemporized, "I have a dream. It is a dream deeply rooted in the American dream that one day this nation will rise up and live out the true meaning of its creed—we hold these truths to be self-evident, that all men are created equal." The speech remains one of the most quoted in American history and tends to encapsulate for many King's nonviolent ethos. The speech and the Birmingham Campaign led *Time* magazine to name King its 1963 "Man of the Year." In July of the next year, Congress passed the Civil Rights Act of 1964, the most comprehensive bill of its kind in American history and arguably the most important piece of legislation in the history of Congress. On December 10, King received the Nobel Peace Prize in Oslo, Norway, at 35, the youngest ever to do so.

Despite these successes, King had to deal with harassment and invasions of his privacy from the FBI, whose director, J. Edgar Hoover, believed King and his civil rights organizations to be subversive. Although Hoover's smear campaign was largely ineffective at ruining King's reputation, it did have the effect of making King's difficult work more challenging.

Only in recent years has it become clear just how extensively the FBI had attempted to undermine the status of the most important black leader of his generation.

King spent much of the first half of 1965 mobilizing a highly visible voting rights campaign in Selma, Alabama. During the direct-action challenges of the Freedom Rides, the Kennedy Administration had entreated King and other leaders to focus on voting rights as the best way for African Americans to attain civil rights. However, many activists resented having the Kennedys tell them where they ought to focus their energies and believed that the Kennedy emphasis on voting rights was merely an attempt to delay further action on the daily segregation most blacks faced in the South. However, with the passage of the Civil Rights Act, most activists realized the importance of political power for African Americans. This was especially evident in the wake of the violence during Freedom Summer in Mississippi in 1954 and also in the failed attempt to get the Mississippi Freedom Democratic Party seated in place of the all-white Democratic Party delegates from Mississippi at the 1964 Democratic Convention. Thus, by 1965 King and others were full force behind drawing attention to voting rights that would also lead to a comprehensive Voting Rights Act.

King focused his energies on Selma, Alabama, where he helped to orchestrate demonstrations beginning early in 1965. Events came to a head on March 7, when police acting at the behest of Governor George Wallace attacked marchers crossing the Edmund Pettus Bridge on a march from Selma to Montgomery. The police used tear gas and clubs to stop the marchers. King was in Atlanta when this attack occurred. However, he quickly returned to Selma, which had become yet another flash point of national and international attention as the result of the police brutality on March 7, to continue with the thousands of black and white activists who had joined the Selma campaign. President Lyndon Johnson responded as well by proposing the legislation that he would sign into law on August 6, 1965. On March 25, under the protection of court orders, the activists successfully marched from Selma to Montgomery, where King addressed them from the capitol steps.

The Selma Campaign proved to be the last event devoted solely to the question of black civil rights in the South. He had entered a phase of his life in which he would risk his status as the most admired black spokesman among white Americans by opposing the Vietnam War, challenging racial conditions in the North in cities such as Chicago, where he initiated a campaign for equality in 1966, and engaging in class-based coalitions including a Poor People's Campaign that kicked off in 1967. He discovered that tactics that had proved successful in attacking segregation in the South were not so successful in the North. King also found that many blacks, particularly those trapped in northern urban ghettoes, were disinclined to support the kind of nonviolent rhetoric and action that had characterized King's successful career. Instead, many African Americans came to embrace such fiery leaders as Malcolm X, who believed blacks should assert their rights "by any means necessary," and advocates of Black Power. As King's focus shifted from the South to the North, he often found himself on the defensive against such revolutionary challenges.

Nonetheless, the last years of King's life are instructive. They reveal King's evolution from a regional figure interested in black civil rights to a national leader aware of linkages of issues of race, class, imperialism, and power. In many ways, the last years of King's life allow for a more radical reading of his career—one that is more complex than those who might want to sanitize his legacy would prefer. King died from an assassin's bullet on the balcony of the Lorraine Motel in Memphis the evening of April 4, 1968. He was there to lend support to a city sanitation workers' strike. The previous evening he had delivered a prescient speech in which he told listeners, "I may not get there with you. But I want you to know tonight that we, as a people, will get to the promised land."

In 1986 Congress passed, over President Reagan's opposition, a National Martin Luther King, Jr., holiday. Several states, including New Hampshire and Arizona, refused to sanction the new holiday for many years, although both do today. Other states, such as Virginia, juxtapose the King holiday with a celebration of Confederate General Robert E. Lee's birthday. These exceptions reveal America's contested racial terrain even while reconfirming King's preeminence in the pantheon of great American leaders.

Capsule Biography

Martin Luther King, Jr. Born Michael King, Jr., 15 January 1929 in Atlanta, Georgia. Studied at public schools in Atlanta; left Booker T. Washington High School without graduating, having skipped grades 9 and 12 to attend Morehouse College, Atlanta, Georgia; B.A., 1944; Crozer Theological Seminary, Chester, Pennsylvania, B.A., 1951; Boston University, Ph.D., 1955. Received 20 Honorary Doctorates from 1957 to 1967. Was ordained a Baptist minister in 1948. Held the pastorate at Dexter Avenue Baptist Church, Montgomery, Alabama, 1954–59 and was copastor, with Martin Luther King, Sr., of Ebenezer Baptist

Church, Atlanta, Georgia, 1960–1968. President, Montgomery Improvement Association, 1955–56. Founder and president, Southern Christian Leadership Conference (SCLC), 1957–68. Vice president, National Baptist Convention, 1958–61. Served as president of the National Sunday School and Baptist Teaching Union Conference of the National Baptist Convention. Awards (King won hundreds of awards over the course of his career. The following is a small sampling.): Listed in *Who's Who in America*, 1957; Spingarn Medal, 1957; Russwarm Award—National Newspaper Publishers, 1957; Second Annual Achievement—The Guardian Association of the Police Department of New York, 1958; Aims Field-Wolf Award for *Stride toward* Freedom; *Time* magazine Man of the Year, 1963; named *American of the Decade*—Laundry, Dry Cleaning, and Die Workers International Union, 1963; John Dewey Award—United Federation of Teachers, 1964; John F. Kennedy Award—Catholic Interracial Council of Chicago, 1964; Nobel Peace Prize, 1964 (at 35 the youngest ever to receive the award); Marcus Garvey Prize for Human Rights, Jamaican Government, 1968 (posthumous); Rosa L. Parks Award, SCLC, 1968 (posthumous).

Selected Works

Stride toward Freedom: The Montgomery Story, 1958

Strength to Love, 1963

Where Do We Go from Here: Chaos or Community? 1967

Trumpet of Conscience, 1968

The Words of Martin Luther King, Jr., selected by Coretta Scott King, 1983

A Testament of Hope: The Essential Writings of Martin Luther King, Jr., edited by James Melvin Washington, 1986

The Papers of Martin Luther King, Jr., Vol. 1: Called to Serve, January, 1929–June, 1951, edited by Clayborne Carson, Ralph Luker, and Penny A. Russell, 1992

The Papers of Martin Luther King, Jr., Vol. 2: Rediscovering Precious Values, July, 1951–November, 1955, edited by Clayborne Carson, Ralph Luker, Penny A. Russell, and Peter Holloran, 1994

The Papers of Martin Luther King, Jr., Vol. 3: Birth of a New Age, December, 1955–December, 1956, edited by Clayborne Carson, Stewart Burns, Susan Carson, Peter Holloran, and Dana Powell, 1997

Autobiography of Martin Luther King, Jr., edited by Clayborne Carson, 1998

A Knock at Midnight: Inspiration from the Great Sermons of Reverend Martin Luther King, Jr., edited by Clayborne Carson and Peter Holloran, 1998

The Papers of Martin Luther King, Jr., Vol. 4: Symbol of the Movement, January, 1957–December, 1958, edited by Clayborne Carson, Susan Carson, Adrienne Clay, Virginia Shadron, and Kieren Taylor, 2000

A Call to Conscience: The Landmark Speeches of Dr. Martin Luther King, Jr., edited by Clayborne Carson and Peter Holloran, 2001

DEREK CATSAM

See also **African Americans**

Further Reading

Branch, Taylor, *Parting the Waters: America in the King Years, 1954–1963*, New York: Simon & Schuster, 1988

Branch, Taylor, *Pillar of Fire: America in the King Years, 1963–1965*, New York: Simon & Schuster, 1998

Colaiaco, James A., *Martin Luther King Jr.: Apostle of Militant Nonviolence*, New York: St. Martin's Press, 1988

Dyson, Michael Eric, *I May Not Get There with You: The True Martin Luther King, Jr.*, New York: Touchstone, 2000

Fairclough, Adam, *To Redeem the Soul of America: The Southern Christian Leadership Conference and Martin Luther King, Jr.*, Athens: University of Georgia Press, 1987

Garrow, David J., *Bearing the Cross: Martin Luther King, Jr., and the Southern Christian Leadership Conference*, New York: Random House, 1986

Harding, Vincent, *Martin Luther King, the Inconvenient Hero*, Maryknoll, New York: Orbis Books, 1996

Lewis, David Levering, *King: A Critical Biography*, New York: Praeger, 1970

Lincoln, C. Eric, editor, *Martin Luther King, Jr.: A Profile*, New York: Hill & Wang, 1970

Lischer, Richard, *The Preacher King: Martin Luther King, Jr., and the Word That Moved America*, New York: Oxford University Press, 1995

Oates, Stephen B., *Let the Trumpet Sound: The Life of Martin Luther King, Jr.*, New York: Harper & Row, 1982

Komi

Capsule Summary

Location: Northeast area of the European part of the Russia Federation

Total Population: Aproximately 500,000

Languages: Komi-Permiak, Komi-Zyrian

Religion: Orthodox Christian

The Komi are an ethnic group living in the northern areas of Russia, in the septentrional Ural Mountains. Two groups are called Komi in Russia, the Komi proper, or Zyrian Komi, of the Komi Republic and the Permyak Komi of the Komi-Permian Autonomous District. The distinction in dialects or national groups was made official in 1923, and the two dialectal forms were established with different writing standards. In any case, total official disregard has led to the sad reality of a literary language with no literature, as shown in the case of the Komi-Permyak. In the Komi Republic, there has been a kinder attitude toward the language, but the republic is increasingly being colonized by Russian migrants.

The Zyrian Komis live in the Komi Republic (whose capital is Syktyvkar) and in neighboring areas (the Kola Peninsula, the Nenets Autonomous District of the Archangelsk Province, and throughout Siberia). In 1989 there were 291,500 Komis in the Republic and 336,400 in total (76.1 percent of whom spoke the language). However, massive immigration of Russians to the Komi territory has reduced them to a minority: In 1926 they numbered 85 percent, and in 1989 just 23 percent. In industrial centers such as Vorkuta, they constitute one percent of the population. The Komi Republic is the first Finno-Ugrian area of Russia where the local language was instituted as the official language in parallel with Russian, although it is not clear whether this will properly enforce the language. The Permyak Komis live in the Komi-Permian Autonomous District (whose capital is Kudymkar) of the Perm Province and in this region. The Permyak Komis include also the Yazva Komis or Krasnovishersk Permyaks, who live in the northwestern part of the Perm Province. In 1989 there were 95,400 Permyak-Komis in the Autonomous District and 152,000 in all of Russia.

The ethnic name *Komi* is the self-designation of both the Komi-Zyrians and the Komi-Permyaks. This name is clearly linked with the name of their old homeland, *Kommu*. In the eighth century, the ethnic ancestors of the Komi-Permyak remained in the territory of the Kama basin, and the other group of Komi (Zyrians) moved northward. The languages of these groups was the same and registered few dialect differences.

Both Komi communities progressively came into contact with neighboring peoples, mainly the Veps, Karelinas, Mansi, Nenets, and Russians. Mansi ethnic groups raided Komi settlements, but the Komi people, in turn, had a deep cultural and economic influence on the Mansi. In contrast, Komi relations with the Nenets since the thirteenth century were intensively economic, and the Komi adopted reindeer cattle. However, their strongest contact was with the Russians. Indeed, this contact started in the ninth century, when merchants from the state of Novgorod arrived in the Komi area, but became more relevant in the fourteenth century, during a time of violent Christianization of the native Komi groups. Ending with the traditional Komi religion system, based in autochthon cults centered in shamanistic practices and in an animistic background (one shared with other peoples of northern Russia and Siberia), Russian rulers tried unsuccessfully to incorporate the Komi social communities into their national system. But the Komi peoples strongly resisted these attempts and admirably remained a differentiated ethnic body through the absorption of external cultural elements (e.g., many language borrowings), which were perfectly incorporated into the ethnic Komi structure and reinforced their whole ethnic system.

When the Komi-Permian National District was formed in 1925, the native population of the upper reaches of the Kama River—who made up the main ethnic body in the region—acquired the official name Permian Komi so as not to be confused with the Zyrian Komi or with the whole body of populations of the Near-Kama (called Permyaks according to the toponym). By the end of the fifteenth century, the area of Upper Kama had become a part of Russia. Moscow strengthened its hold over the region by violent Christianization of the natives. However, time and again, the land fell prey to plundering raids of the Siberian and Tatar Khans.

During the reign of Ivan IV (Ivan The Terrible) in the middle of the sixteenth century, settling and development of the Kama area was improved by Russia, which constituted a process of internal colonization: The territory of the state was expanded, administrative institutions were set up in the area, and firm economic bonds were established. Russian colonization was accompanied by fierce exploitation of the local population, and the imposition of external rule with offspring, such as the administrative partition of the Komis in the second decade of the seventeenth century. This territorial process of forced division generated two separates languages (Permian and Zyrian), but the two peoples have continued to reach out to one another by maintaining tight cooperation in different ways. The Komis frequently rebelled against the Russian landlords and rulers, for example, in the so-called Caravan Mutiny of 1861, which spread throughout the Komi districts. Under the Great Russian Rule, an important effort to eradicate the ethnic culture of the Komi people was then achieved.

An agreement on self-determination was signed in 1996 between the Russian Federation and the Komi

Republic. This agreement gave the Komi government the opportunity to further develop the Republic. The Komi have started to recover from the severe environmental damage caused by oil spills and fires. The recognition of the Komi national movement within the political framework of the Komi Republic has benefited the Komi people's efforts to maintain and develop their own national identity. Komi representatives continue to participate effectively in the United Nations Working Group on Indigenous Populations, as well as the inter-sessional Working Group, to develop a Declaration on the Rights of Indigenous Peoples. The local language is now used widely in the mass media, but two difficulties facing the Komi nation are a lack of political stability in the Russian Federation and the centralist tendencies of their government.

JOAN MANUEL CABEZAS LÓPEZ

See also **Russia**

Further Reading

Kublitsi, Gennadi, *Traditions and Customs of the USSR Peoples*, Moscow, Novosti, 1989

Tsypanov, E.A., *The Komi Language*, Syktyvkar: Syktyvkar State University, 1992

Turubanov, Afanasi. N., *The History of the Republic of Komi from Ancient Times to Nowadays,* Syktyvkar: Institute of Language, Literature and History, 1999

Korea, North and South

Capsule Summary

Country Name: Democratic People's Republic of Korea (North Korea) and Republic of Korea (South Korea)

Location: The Korean Peninsula extends southward from the Asian mainland. The peninsula is divided along the 38th parallel, with North Korea occupying 55 percent of the land. To the north of the Korean eninsula, the Yalu and Tumen Rivers form a natural boundary with the People's Republic of Korea and Russia. To the east, Korea is bordered by the Sea of Japan (East Sea), and the Yellow Sea to the west and southwest. The Korean Peninsula stretches 1,000 kilometers (620 miles) north to south and is around 216 kilometers (134 miles) wide at its narrowest point

Total Population: Democratic People's Republic of Korea (North Korea), 22,466,481 (July 2003 estimate); Republic of Korea (South Korea), 48,289,037 (July 2003 estimate)

Language: Korean

Religions: In North Korea, religion has officially been banned by the Korean Worker's Party, but nonfunctioning Buddhist temples and Christian churches do exist; in South Korea: Buddhism, Christianity, Confucianism, shamanism

The Korean Peninsula covers approximately 85,000 square miles (220,150 square kilometres) and is located on the southeastern tip of the Asian mainland. Korea is bordered by seas to the east, south, and southwest and by the Yalu and Tumen Rivers to the north, providing a natural demarcation with the People's Republic of China and the Russian Federation. Per capita GDP in North Korea is $1,000 (2002 estimate), whereas per capita GDP in South Korea is $19,600 (2002 estimate).

Despite the presence of the various migrations of nomadic tribes to the Korean Peninsula during the Neolithic and Bronze Ages, it was not until the formation of the Koguryo Kingdom (57 BCE–661 CE) on the northern half of the peninsula in the first century BCE that it can be said there were the beginnings of a Korean state. But it was not until the rise of the Paikche (18 BCE–661 CE) and Silla Kingdoms (37 BCE–935 CE) on the southern half of the Korean Peninsula and the ensuing Three Kingdoms Period (57 BCE–935 CE) that a unified Korean state came into being. Warfare among the Koguryo, Paikche, and Silla Kingdoms eventually led the Silla to form an alliance with the Tang Dynasty of China, enabling Silla to defeat their rival Paikche in 668 CE and unify the Korean Peninsula into a nation-state. Following the Three Kingdoms Period (57 BCE–661 CE), Korea was unified under a series of dynastic monarchies—the Unified Silla (676–935 CE), the Koryo, (918–1392 CE) and the Yi (1392–1910 CE)—until 1910, when Japan annexed Korea and Korea became a Japanese colony.

The nation-state that emerged out of the conflict among the Three Kingdoms was the Unified Silla (676–917 CE). During the Unified Silla monarchy, rule was consolidated; authority rested with the monarchy, and a centralized bureaucracy was created. As such, this became one of the greatest eras of cultural development in the history of Korea. The Unified Silla survived for over 200 years, but by the beginning of the ninth century, rival warlords had weakened the Silla to the point that the last Silla king offered his kingdom to the Koguryo, thus beginning the Koryo Dynasty (918–1392 CE). Stability was restored under the Koryo Dynasty until the middle of the thirteenth century, when Mongols invaded and laid waste to the Korean Peninsula. The Koryo monarchy was eventually restored in 1259 and lasted until Yi Song-gye, a former commanding general of the Koryo army, staged a military coup and established the Yi Dynasty (1392–1910). It was during the reign of King Sejong (1418–1450) that Korea's northern boundaries were formalized, and where they remain to this day.

Following the fall of the Yi Dynasty in 1910, Japan annexed Korea and inaugurated a 35-year period of social and economic change throughout the Korean Peninsula. Japan's occupation and administration of the Korean Peninsula had a long-lasting and profound effect on Korea. Japan, eager to exploit the natural resources as well as the human power available on the Korean Peninsula, developed the Korean economy through the construction of heavy industry and the modernization of agriculture. Nonetheless, Korea suffered tremendously at the hands of the Japanese as Korea's resources were allocated to support Japan's war effort. Korea gained independence on August 14, 1945, following Japan's surrender, ending World War II. The surrender of Japan on August 14, 1945, brought Japanese rule to an end on the Korean Peninsula and a period of instability, as the division of Korea emerged when the Soviets and Americans established separate governing structures. Escalating tensions eventually led to the Korean War (1950–1953) and the formation of the Democratic People's Republic of Korea (also known as North Korea) and the Republic of Korea (also known as South Korea).

The Korean War (1950–1953) had its origins in the political endgame of World War II. At the end of World War II, the victorious allies (the United States, the Soviet Union, France, and England) decided to temporarily divide and occupy Korea, which had been formally occupied by Japan. The Soviet Union occupied the North while the United States occupied the South. As the Cold War between the West and the Soviet Union intensified, both South Korea and North Korea established their own governments, claiming sovereignty over the entirety of the Korean Peninsula. These rival animosities eventually led to periodic military confrontations and then to war on June 25, 1950, when North Korean troops poured over the 38th parallel. Following 3 years of fighting, a stalemate ensued, with fighting settling around the 38th parallel. Eventually, on July 27, 1953, the Democratic People's Republic of Korea and the United States signed an armistice agreement, thus formalizing the division of the Korean Peninsula. The ramifications of the Korean War are still felt today. Geographically and politically, the Korean Peninsula is still divided along the 38th parallel—a consequence of 50years of struggle for peace and reconciliation.

Minorities in South Korea

South Korean culture is relatively homogenous compared with the majority of countries in the world. There is a very small Chinese minority (approximately 20,000) in South Korea, but the overall population is overwhelmingly made up of Koreans. However, regional tensions have been a part of Korea's history, dating back as far as the Three Kingdoms period. These tensions have centered mainly on the YoungNam, a group rooted in the Kyongsang provinces in the southeastern region, and the HoNam, a group that calls the southwestern province of Cholla home. People were thus identified by the region in which they were born. There had been some migration by HoSamese workers in search of better economic opportunities. However, under President Chung-hee Park in the 1960s, the YoungNam benefited from the success of industrialization, whereas the HoNamese were marginalized. YoungNamese dominance continued throughout the next three decades. Honamese resistance was met with crushing punishment by the YoungNam authorities, including the revolt in May 1980 in Kwangju, where more than 2,000 protesters were allegedly killed. In 1993 President-Elect Young Sam Kim included efforts to invest in the Cholla region as part of his democratic reforms. However, scandal, civil disobedience, and the Southeast Asian financial crisis led to the election, in 1997, of Kim Dae Jung from the Cholla region. Under Kim, the political and economic discrimination against the HoNamese has declined. Although significant numbers of HoNamese call for autonomy, the primary concern of most HoNamese is the desire for equal opportunities and a fair share of public funds and political power.

Minorities in North Korea

North Korea has no distinct minorities, but religion (Buddhism, Confucianism, Christianity, and Chondogyo

[Religion of the Heavenly Way]) has been officially suppressed. The country has a very small number of Chinese and ethnic Japanese.

KEITH LEITICH

See also **Koreans**

Further Reading

Adams, Edward B., *Korea's Golden Age: Cultural Spirit in Silla in Kyongju,* Seoul: Seoul International Publishing House, revised edition, 1991

Eckert, Carter J., Ki-baik Lee, Young Ick Lew, Michael Robinson, and Edward W. Wagner, *Korea Old and New: A History,* Seoul: Ilchokak Publishers, 1990

Lee, Pyong-do, "Three Kingdoms and Their Civilization," *Korea Journal*, 4, no. 7, (1964)

Leitich, Keith A., "The Korean Peninsula: A Fifty-Year Struggle for Peace and Reconciliation," in *History behind the Headlines*, Farmington Hills, Michigan: Gale Group, 2000

Lone, Stewart, and Gavan McCormack, *Korea since 1850*, New York: St. Martin's Press, 1993

Oberdorfer, Don, *The Two Koreas: A Contemporary History*, Reading, Massachusetts: Addison-Wesley, 1997

Yang, Sung Chul, *The North and South Political Systems: A Comparative Analysis,* Boulder, Colorado: Westview Press, 1994

Koreans

Capsule Summary

Location: Korean Peninsula, with sizable expatriate communities in Central Asia and North America
Total Population: The Democratic People's Republic of Korea (North Korea) 21 million; the Republic of Korea (South Korea) 46.9 million
Language: Korean
Religions: In North Korea, religion has officially been banned by the Korean Worker's Party, but nonfunctioning Buddhist temples do exist; in South Korea, Buddhism, Christianity, Confucianism, shamanism

Koreans are an ethnic group living on the Korean Peninsula, comprising modern-day North and South Korea. In addition, there are large expatriate Korean communities in the former Soviet republics of Kazakhstan and Uzbekistan as well as in the United States. The Korean language belongs to the Altaic family of languages and is related to Finnish, Hungarian, and Turkish. Most Koreans are either Buddhist or Christian, but Confucianism and shamanism are also practiced. Koreans were unified under a series of dynastic monarchies—the Three Kingdoms (57 BCE–668 CE), the Unified Silla (676–935 CE), the Koryo, (918–1392 CE) and the Yi (1392–1910)—until 1910, when Japan annexed Korea. Koreans gained their independence following Japan's surrender ending World War II but have been separated both geographically and politically as a result of the Korean War. The Koreans are an amalgamation of the peoples that migrated to the Korean Peninsula beginning in the Bronze Age. Successive migrations between 3,000 and 2,500 BCE saw the arrival of the Puyo, the Ye, and the Maek from the Eurasian steppe, intermingling with the indigenous comb pottery culture. With the downfall of the Shang Dynasty in neighboring China in 1,200 BCE, the Tung-i from southern Manchuria and eastern coast of China began migrating southward onto the Korean Peninsula. The intermingling between the successive migrations of people led to the people who would become Koreans. Ancient Chinese historians described the inhabitants of the Korean Peninsula as being clannish, having an aesthetic blend and a volatile character. Koreans, as a people, came into existence during the Three Kingdoms Period (57 BCE–668 CE), when the inhabitants of the Koguryo, Paekche, and Silla kingdoms were characterized as a common race sharing a common spoken language. By the time of the Unified Silla (669 –917 CE), Koreans had developed into a recognizable people

Early Korean society was organized around the clan, with several clans forming a tribe. Early Koreans practiced sustenance-based agriculture, cultivating barley, millet, corn, maize, and rice as well as domesticating animals. The Three Kingdoms Period saw the emergence of a Korean society distinct from that of the neighboring Shang Chinese society. By the time of the Unified Silla, Korean society had become unified and strengthened under successive Silla rulers. Following

KOREANS

the Hideyoshi invasion and the subsequent invasion by
the Manchus in the sixteenth century, the Yi Dynasty
established a strict policy of excluding foreigners, thus
isolating Korean society for a period of over 300 years.
Then, in the nineteenth century, Koreans came in contact with the outside world, when first the Japanese and
then the Americans and British extracted concessions
and the establishment of legations through diplomatic
negotiations meant to open Korea to foreign trade and
investment. Ordinary Korean citizens, by and large,
remained isolated from foreign influence and retained
their traditional way of life. It was the onset of World
War II that brought both hardship and misery for
Koreans as the Japanese mobilized young men and boys
into the military and heavy industry in Manchukuo,
while young Korean women and girls were made to
serve as prostitutes for the Japanese army. As a consequence, many Koreans began emigrating to Manchuria
and the Russian Far East in an attempt to escape the
Japanese and begin a new life. Yet for those Koreans
who settled in the Russian Far East, life would be
worse as Stalin ordered the deportation of all Koreans
living in Far East. Inexplicably, after centuries of isolation, attempted assimilation, mobilization, and war,
Koreans remained homogeneous. Free of many of the
constraints imposed by their Northern neighbors,
South Korean society flourished in the years following
the Korean War.

Koreans in the Russian Far East suffered one of the
greatest tragedies of World War II. Stalin, fearing
Koreans would ally with the Japanese, engineered the
mass deportation of Koreans from the Russian Maritime
Province to Central Asia. Koreans were rounded up and
loaded into freight cars and transported to the Central
Asian republics of Kazakhstan, Kyrgyzstan, and
Uzbekistan. During the long period of deportation,
many Koreans, in particular children and the elderly,
died of malnutrition and disease. Scurvy, typhoid, diph-
theria, dysentery, measles, and scarlet fever each took
the lives of many of the families as they were forced to
live in unsanitary conditions aboard the trains and had
little or no food for most of the sojourn to Central Asia.
The survivors endured great hardship as they found
themselves having to adapt to an unfamiliar environment. Upon their arrival, Koreans had no place to live
other than what they could build, so many families were
forced to live in warehouses, barns, mosques, and converted prisons while they built homes for themselves.
Following World War II, Koreans remained in the Central Asian republics and began integrating into the local

society, where they soon began to thrive as merchants
and traders. To this day, large Korean communities can
still be found in Kazakhstan and Uzbekistan.

Following the Korean War (1950–1953), Koreans
suffered a devastating psychological trauma when the
Korean Peninsula was divided politically into the Communist North and the capitalist South. The war and
subsequent division of the Korean Peninsula had far-
reaching effects on Koreans as families and civil society
were divided along the 38th parallel. North Koreans
became isolated from their South Korean counterparts,
as the North Korean state restricted contacts between
the South and controlled almost every aspect of life.
North Koreans became subject to intensive and pervasive state indoctrination. Even though North Koreans
had 11 years of free and compulsory education, access
to free comprehensive health care, and free housing,
foreign travel was prohibited and travel within North
Korea was restricted and monitored. Information was
strictly controlled by the state, and surveillance was
used to ferret out all dissent. As a consequence, ordinary North Koreans became isolated from their South
Korean counterparts, and North Korean society has
developed in seclusion for the past 50 years.

KEITH LEITICH

See also **Buddhists; Korea**

Further Reading

Chang, Yunshik, "Women in a Confucian Society: The Case of
    Chosun Dynasty Korea (1392–1910)," *Asian and Pacific
    Quarterly of Cultural and Social Affairs*, 14, no. 2 (1982)
Dredge, C. Paul, "Korean Funerals: Ritual as Process," in *Religion
    and Ritual in Korean Society*, edited by Laurel Kendall and
    Griffin Dix, Berkeley: University of California Press, 1987
Eckert, Carter J., Ki-baik Lee, Young Ick Lew, Michael Robinson,
    and Edward W. Wagner, *Korea Old and New: A History*,
    Seoul: Ilchokak Publishers, 1990
Gelb, Michael, "An Early Soviet Ethnic Deportation: The Far
    Eastern Koreans," *The Russian Review*, 54, no. 3 (1995)
Huttenbach, Henry E., "The Soviet Koreans," *Central Asian
    Survey*, 12, no. 1
Macdonald, Donald Stone, *The Koreans: Contemporary Politics
    and Society*, Boulder, Colorado: Westview Press, 1988
Nahm, Andrew, *Korea: Tradition and Transformation, A History
    of the Korean People*, Seoul and Elizabeth, New Jersey, 1988
Oka, Natsuko, *Deportation of Koreans from the Russian Far
    East to Central Asia. Migration in Central Asia: Its History
    and Current Problems*, JCAS Symposium Series 9, Osaka,
    Japan: The Japan Center for Area Studies, National Museum
    of Ethnology, 2000
Yi, Hong-jik, "Early History of Korean Society," *Korea Journal*,
    4, no. 7 (1964)

KOSOVO, *See* Yugoslavia

Kurds

Capsule Summary

Location: Eastern Turkey, Northern Iraq, Western Iran, Northern Syria, Armenia, Azerbaijan
Population: Approximately 25 to 26 million
Languages: Kurmanji, Sorani, Pahlawani
Religions: Majority, Sunni Islam; minority, Shiite Islam, Alevi Islam, Yazidi, and Yarsani (angel worship)

The Kurds, a diverse ethnic group divided between Turkey, Iraq, Iran, Syria, and the former Soviet republics of Azerbaijan and Armenia, are the largest nation in the world without a state of their own. Whereas the surrounding Arab, Turkish, and Persian populations emerged in the twentieth century with national states in which to express their identities and culture, the Kurdish lands were divided among the neighboring states. In the mid-1990s, approximately 14 million Kurds resided in Turkey, out of a total population of approximately 60 million; Iran was home to approximately 7 million Kurds, out of a total population of 61 million; Iraq had a Kurdish population of 4.5 million, out of total population of 20 million; Syria had a population of 1.3 million, out of approximately 12 million, and the former Soviet Union was home to less than a million.

Society

The Kurds today are divided not only among several states but among themselves. There are, for example, two main Kurdish languages (which are as close as French and Italian), namely Kurmanji, which is spoken in Turkey and northern Iraq, and Pahlawani (often known as Zaza), which is spoken in Turkey and Iran, as well as regional dialects such as Laki, Sorani (south Kurmanji), and Gurani. The Kurds are also divided on a religious basis. Although most Kurds adhere to the Sunni form of Islam, many Kurds in Iran are Shiites, while some Kurds in Turkey are Alevis, adhering to an unorthodox syncretistic form of Islam. There are also small minorities of Kurds known as Yazidis (found mainly in the former Soviet Union) and Yarsanis (found in southern Iraq and Iran), who believe in reincarnation and worship pre-Islamic avatars or angels, such as *Malak Tawus,* the Peacock Angel.

Traditionally, the Kurds have had a patriarchal society based on seminomadic sheep and goat herding and farming in the rugged mountains of eastern Anatolia and western Iran. The inaccessible nature of the isolated Kurdish villages, which are separated by mountains, has prevented any wider sense of unity based on a shared sense of Kurdishness. As a result, Kurdish society has been organized on a tribal basis, and even today most Kurds have greater loyalty to their regional tribal affiliation than any wider identification with the term Kurd.

History

The Kurds are an ancient Indo-European people, ethnically related to the Persians, who first appeared in ancient Assyrian sources and the Old Testament as the Kardu. They were known throughout history as a proud, untamed people who refused to be subdued by the neighboring states. The Greek general Xenephon, who marched through the territory of the Kurds in the fourth century BCE, for example, mentioned that the Kurds were a stubborn people who did not pay homage to the Persian King of Kings at a time when the Persian rulers ruled an empire in Asia extending from the Indus River to Greece. During the Medieval period, the lands of the Kurds, located in the Zagros Mountains in western Persia and the high mountains of eastern Anatolia, were overrun by waves of Turkic tribes emigrating from Central Asia. In this period, the powerful Turkic-Islamic dynasties of the Middle East, such as the Seljuk Dynasty of Persia (1055–1196), granted the

Kurds considerable autonomy, largely due to their inability to subdue the warlike Kurdish tribes.

Although the Kurds traditionally worshipped the ancient Indo-European gods of Persia, they gradually came under the influence of Sunni Islam from the eleventh to the thirteenth centuries. One of the greatest figures in the Medieval Islamic world, Saladin, the conqueror of crusader-held Jerusalem and Egypt and a chivalrous opponent of Richard the Lion Heart, was himself a Kurd.

For the most part, however, the Kurds were not involved in the formation of states or empires in the Middle East and tended to live as herders or farmers in the remote mountainous frontier zones between the states of Syria, Persia, and Anatolia. Their homeland became the scene of 200 years of warfare between the Sunni Muslim Ottoman Empire and the Shiite Muslim Safavid state of Iran/Persia starting in the 1500s. On most occasions, the Kurds sided with the Ottoman sultans in their struggle with the Persians, largely as a response to the Persian shahs' policy of engaging in a scorched-earth policy in the frontier zones between the two states to prevent the invading Ottoman armies from living off the land. Since the lands being destroyed in this process were largely Kurdish, and their inhabitants were Sunni Muslims, the Kurds supported the Ottomans in return for a certain amount of autonomy.

The power bases of the traditionally autonomous Kurdish chieftains were, however, attacked by centralizing Ottoman sultans in the nineteenth century, and this initiated a long period of conflict in which Ottoman and later Republican Turkish authorities attempted to gain control over this traditionally ungovernable people. At this time, the Ottomans controlled three-fourths of Kurdistan, including Kurdish lands in what is today northern Iraq, northern Syria, and Turkey, while the Qajar Dynasty of Persia and the Russians exerted control over the Kurds of Iran and the southern Caucasus.

With the collapse of the Ottoman Empire during World War II, the Kurds came to the attention of the victorious Entente powers. As part of his Fourteen-Point policy calling for the creation of separate states for all peoples of the Ottoman Empire, American President Woodrow Wilson contemplated granting the Kurds independence, and in fact a clause in the Treaty of Sevres of 1920 had stipulations for an independent Kurdish state. Whereas the Arabs and Turks had urban elites that had, under the influence of the West, articulated national movements, the largely tribal, rural Kurds lacked the nationalist intelligentsia necessary to create a nationalist program for their people.

Divided into mutually suspicious tribes headed by traditional chieftains and religious sheikhs, the Kurds were unable to unite on the basis of any shared, but latent, sense of ethnicity at this crucial juncture in their history.

For this reason and others related to the interests of the Western powers, the Kurds of the former Ottoman Empire found themselves divided between the newly established Republic of Turkey and the British Mandate protectorate of Iraq, the latter being an artificial construct that included lands dominated by Arabs in the south and Kurds in the north. The Kurds of both these states rebelled against attempts by the authorities to control them in the 1920s, but these rebellions, which were still religious or tribal in nature, were brutally crushed by the Turkish army and British air force.

Contemporary Issues

Far from recognizing the Kurds' ethnic identity, the Republic of Turkey launched a military and political campaign to suppress the culture of the Kurds (who were officially labeled "Mountain Turks") in an effort to create a homogeneous Turkish nation state with no centrifugal ethnic threats to Kemal Ataturk's secular-nationalist regime. After the suppression of a Kurdish uprising in the Dersim region of eastern Anatolia, in which thousands of Kurds lost their lives (1937–1938), the Kurds of Turkey acquiesced to 50 years of state-enforced Turkification that saw their language banned from the public arena and their efforts at gaining a political voice suppressed by mass arrests.

The Kurds fared slightly better in Iran, largely as a result of the fact that their culture, which was considered to be Iranic, was not suppressed by the Iranian government. The Iranian Kurds, however, made one brief attempt to gain independence in the aftermath of the Soviet invasion of northwest Iran during World War II. With the Soviets exerting loose control over much of the area inhabited by Kurds in western Iran, a Kurdish urban intelligentsia established a short-lived Kurdish republic centered on the city of Mahabad (northwestern Iran), known as the Mahabad Republic. This Soviet protectorate was, however, easily suppressed by the Iranians one year after its founding in 1946, and its president was executed.

The Kurds' next attempt to gain autonomy occurred in Iraq in 1970. After simmering tension between the Baghdad regime and the Kurds of this country, who inhabited the northern regions around the oil-producing cities of Mosul and Kirkuk, the Ba'ath Party leader

Saddam Hussein at long last granted the Kurds an autonomous zone in an Iraq that was officially recognized as consisting of two distinct peoples, the Kurds and Arabs. The promises of autonomy and increased political clout for the Kurds never materialized, however, and the Iraqi Kurds turned to warfare against the Iraqi regime in 1974 to forcefully create an autonomous zone in northern Iraq. When the Kurdish fighters, known as *peshmergas,* switched from guerrilla tactics to frontal warfare in 1975, however, they were crushed by the regular Iraqi army.

Following this defeat, the Iraqi Kurds commenced over a decade of low-intensity guerrilla warfare against the Baghdad regime. This rebellion was led by two Kurdish guerrilla movements known as the KDP (Kurdish Democratic Party) and the PUK (Patriotic Union of Kurdistan). Far from showing a united front, however, the Kurds of these two parties often engaged in bitter infighting among themselves, which often surpassed their struggle against the Baghdad regime in its brutality.

It should be noted that, during this period, Iran supported the struggle of the Kurds in Iraq as a policy designed to weaken its Arab neighbor. When war broke out between Iran and Iraq in 1980, the Iraqi Kurds rose in rebellion with the support of the Iranians. Iraqi leader Hussein subsequently made world headlines in 1988 when he suppressed the Kurds by using poison gas on such villages as Halabja, where 5,000 Kurdish civilians were killed. This was the first use of gas against civilian populations since it was outlawed following World War I and resulted in international condemnation of the Baghdad regime.

The Kurds of Iraq again made headlines in the West following Iraq's 1990 invasion of Kuwait. During the Allied campaign against Hussein, the Kurds were encouraged to revolt by Western leaders, who held out the promise of autonomy in return for Kurdish military support. Immediately following the conclusion of the Gulf War, however, Hussein turned his army loose on the rebellious Kurdish regions, and more than 1.2 million Kurds fled to Iran while another half million fled to the Turkish border. The television broadcasts of this episode impelled Britain and the United States to come to the assistance of their Kurdish proxies, and an Allied-patrolled protectorate was established north of the 36th parallel in Iraq as a no-fly zone for Iraqi aircraft.

As this struggle was taking place in Iraqi Kurdistan, there was a similar radicalization of the much larger Kurdish population of Turkey, which had become impoverished because the lack of government investment in the economy and infrastructure of the Kurdish east. In 1984 Turkey faced its greatest internal challenge ever, with the founding of a party known as the PKK (Kurdish Workers Party) by Marxist Kurdish leader Abduallah Ocalan (known to his followers as Apo). The Turkish authorities responded to the minor ambushes launched by this guerrilla movement by destroying hundreds of Kurdish villages in the eastern areas of Turkey, making as many as 3 million Turkish Kurds homeless in the process. This drove thousands into the arms of the PKK militants, who waged a bloody guerrilla war with Turkish troops that left tens of thousands dead before the rebellion gradually ended in 1999. With the arrest of Kurdish leader Abdullah Ocalan in 1999, an informal truce was declared between the PKK and the Turkish army, but this remained one of the most volatile areas in the Middle East. Millions of Kurds were forced from their homes in southeastern Turkey to live as second-class citizens in shantytowns around the major cities of Turkey. The Kurds' political rights in Turkey still continue to be ignored by the mass of Turkish society, who consider the PKK to be terrorists as a result of their bloody campaign for independence.

BRIAN WILLIAMS

See also **Armenia; Azerbaijan; Iran; Iraq; Syria; Turkey, Syria**

Further Reading

Amnesty International, *Turkey: A Policy of Denial,* London: EUR, 1995.

Chaliand, Gerard, editor, *A People without a Country: The Kurds and Kurdistan,* New York: Olive Branch Press, 1993

Eagleton, William, *An Introduction to Kurdish Carpets and Other Weavings,* New York: Interlink, 1996

Ghareeb, E., *The Kurdish Question in Iraq,* Syracuse: Syracuse University Press, 1981,

Hassanpour, A., *Nationalism and Language in Kurdistan, 1918–1985,* San Francisco: Mellen University Press, 1986,

Imset, I., *The PKK: A Report on Separatist Violence in Turkey, 1973–92.* Ankara: Turkish Daily News Publications, 1992

Izadly, Mehrad, *The Kurds: A Concise Handbook,* Washington DC: Taylor and Francis, 1992

Laizer, S., *Martyrs, Traitors and Patriots: Kurdistan after the Gulf War,* London: Zed, 1996

McDowell, David, *A Modern History of the Kurds,* London: IB Tauris, 1996

Middle East Watch, *Genocide in Iraq: The Anfal Campaign against the Kurds,* London: 1993

Rugman, J., and R. Hutchings, *Ataturk's Children: Turkey and the Kurds,* New York: Cassell, 1996

von Bruinessen, Martin, *Agha, Shaikh and State: On the Social and Political Organization of Kurdistan,* London: Zed, 1992

Kyrgyz

Capsule Summary

Location: Kyrgyzstan, Uzbekistan, Kazakstan, Tajikistan, Xinjiang in China, Afghanistan, Turkey
Total Population: Over 3 million
Language: Kyrgyz
Religion: Sunni Islam

With the breakup of the Soviet Union in 1991, the former Kirghiz Soviet Socialist Republic became an independent state. This mountainous republic, dominated by Tian Shan, borders to China to the east, Tajikistan to the south, Uzbekistan to the west, and Kazakstan to the north. After a decade of state building, shaky democratization, and economic transition Kyrgyzstan has become a nation among others. The ethnic Kyrgyz (self-designation, *qïrgïz*) are a majority in their own republic, comprising 55 percent of its population of 5 million inhabitants (2003 estimate). Other ethnic groups include the Russians, Uzbeks, Ukrainians, Germans, Tajiks, Uighurs, Dungans, and Koreans.

Over 600,000 Kyrgyz in the world are living outside Kyrgyzstan. During the Communist era, the Kyrgyz had a very small out-migration to other areas of the Soviet Union. Now the biggest group can be found in Uzbekistan (370,000). According to recent sources, 42,000 Kyrgyz live in Russia, 55,000 in Tajikistan, 11,000 in Kazakstan, and 2,000 in Turkmenistan.

In the Chinese province of Xinjiang, the Kyrgyz live mostly within the Kizilsu Autonomous area and in the Ili valley. The Chinese Kyrgyz total over 150,000. They live a rather traditional way of life as herdsmen in mountainous areas. There is also a Kyrgyz group of 1,600 in northern Afghanistan, who immigrated there in the late nineteenth century. Another group of 2,000 Kyrgyz refugees, who left Pamir in the 1930s, moved from Afghanistan to northern Kashmir in 1978 and eventually settled in the Van area of eastern Turkey in 1982. Thus, about 4,000 Kyrgyz in total live in Turkey, including families who immigrated there in 1953. An insignificant number of Kyrgyz live in Germany, Sweden, and the United States.

The history of the Kyrgyz people is complex and intertwined with the fate of various tribal federations in Central Asia. By the sixth century, Turkic tribes united to establish the Western Turkic Khanate, with its capital of Suyab in the Chui Valley. In the tenth to twelfth centuries, the Kara-Khanid Khanate was formed and later destroyed by the Mongol Empire. The latter having split, the Chagatai Khanate included the lands of contemporary Kyrgyzstan.

During the late seventeenth century, the Kyrgyz were conquered by the Oirat Mongols. Many Kyrgyz fled from Tian Shan to other mountain areas in Central Asia. When the Qing Dynasty defeated the Oirat federation in 1758, the Kyrgyz were able to return to their former pastures in Tian Shan, where they were organized under local rulers. In the early nineteenth century, the Kyrgyz were conquered by the Kokand Khanate. The Russians finally defeated Kokand in 1876, and the Kyrgyz area was incorporated into the Russian Government of Turkestan. The Kyrgyz were known as Kara-Kirghiz in czarist Russia.

When Russian settlers began to move in, some Kyrgyz migrated to Pamir and Afghanistan. Kyrgyz nomads took part in the Central Asian uprising against the czarist rule in 1916, and many fled to China.

In 1918 the Kyrgyz territory was included in the Turkestan Autonomous Soviet Socialist Republic. In 1924 the Kyrgyz area became autonomous within the Russian Federation and a full Soviet Socialist Republic (SSR) in 1936. The Soviet regime brought changes to the nomadic Kyrgyz culture. The nomads were forced to settle and forced into the collectivization system. Workers from other areas of the Union of Soviet Socialist Republics (USSR) moved in and changed the demographic situation. Urban populations became Russified in the 1960s–1980s because of administrative policy, while the rural Kyrgyz kept their language and the traditional culture. Religious institutions were discriminated against. Despite the industrialization of some areas, most of Kirghiz SSR remained rather underdeveloped through the Soviet era.

Independence (1991) brought changes to Kyrgyzstan. A new national consciousness developed within the state. The capital of Frunze changed its name to Bishkek. A cultural awakening and rewriting of history took place. Following the September 11, 2001, attacks on the United States, the Kyrgyz leadership agreed to allow a North Atlantic Treaty Organization (NATO) force within Kyrgyzstan.

However, the country still suffers from economic problems with increasing impoverishment. Ethnic unrest, with clashes between Kyrgyz and Uzbeks, took place in the Osh area in 1990, and frictions are still prevalent in the area. Ethnic conflicts have been rather uncommon, although out-migration of non-Kyrgyz has been high since the independence. Many Russians feel themselves discriminated against and have left the country since the independence. In 2000 the authorities tried to stem the exodus of skilled Russians by making Russian an official language. At the same time, the Kyrgyz are moving in from other areas, especially Tajikistan. About 8,000 ethnic Kyrgyz returned to Kyrgyzstan in 1993–2002. The Kyrgyz are nowadays recognized as ethnic minority populations in Kazakstan, Uzbekistan, Tajikistan, and China. In Uzbekistan, more than 40 schools use Kyrgyz as the language of instruction, with similar schools in Tajikistan as well.

The Kyrgyz in China live under rather poor conditions in underdeveloped parts of Xinjiang. Chinese authorities have promoted the Kyrgyz culture since the early 1980s. There are Kyrgyz schools and other institutions, and books and magazines in Kyrgyz are published. Some ethnic unrest was reported among the Kyrgyz of Xinjiang during the 1990s.

The Kyrgyz language belongs to the Turkic branch of the Altaic languages and is related to other Central Asian Turkic languages. It can be divided into northern and southern dialects. The written Kyrgyz language is based on the northern dialects. Kyrgyz was developed as a written language during the Soviet regime. A modified Arabic script was adopted in 1924. In 1928 it was replaced by the Unified Turkic Latin alphabet. Since 1940 it has been written with a modified Cyrillic script. In China, the Arabic script has been used for the Kyrgyz language since 1980.

The urban Kyrgyz of Kyrgyzstan are mostly bilingual. Kyrgyz is the new state language by law and is now promoted in all sectors of the society.

Among the Turkic nomads of Central Asia, the more remote Kyrgyz became Muslims rather late, and most did not convert until the late seventeenth century. They are by tradition Sunni Muslims of the Hanafi school. A few traditional Sufi orders have been active among the Kyrgyz. The impact of Islam has increased since independence. Mosques are built, and religious holidays are celebrated. A Kyrgyz translation of the Koran was published in 1991. About 1,500 Kyrgyz per year attend the hajj in Saudi Arabia. However, their folk religion has continued to play an important role until today.

INGVAR SVANBERG

See also **Afghanistan; China; Kazakstan; Kyrgyzstan; Tajikistan; Turkey; Uzbekistan**

Further Reading

Akiner, Shirin, *Islamic Peoples of the Soviet Union,* London: KPI, 1986

Crisp, Simon, "Kirgiz," in *The Nationalities Question in the Soviet Union*, edited by Graham Smith, London: Longman, 1990

Hatto, Arthur Thomas, *The Memorable Feast in the Honour of Köketai Chan: The Kirghiz Epic Poem*, Oxford: Oxford University Press, 1977

Imart, Guy, *From "Roots" to "Great Expectations": Kirghizia and Kazakstan between the Devil and the Deep-Green Sea*, Bloomington: Indiana University Press, 1990

Imart, Guy, *Le Kirghiz (Turk d'Asie Centrale Soviéthique): Description d'une langue de littérisation récente 1–2*, Aix-en Province, France: Publications de l'Université de Provence, 1981

Micallef, Roberta, and Ingvar Svanberg, "Turkic Central Asia," in *Islam Outside the Arab World*, edited by David Westerlund and Ingvar Svanberg, Richmond: Curzon, 1999

Shahrani, M. Nazif, *The Kirghiz and Wakhi of Afghanistan: Adaptation to Closed Frontiers and War*, Seattle: University of Washington Press, 2002

Kyrgyzstan

Capsule Summary

Location: Former Soviet Central Asia, bordering on southern Kazakhstan, eastern Uzbekistan, northern Tajikistan, and the Chinese Republic of Xinjiang to the east

Total Population: 4,892,808 (July 2003 estimate)

Main Ethnic Groups: Kyrgyz (60%), Russians/Slavs (20%), Uzbeks (13%), Germans (0.5%), Uighurs (1%)

Languages: Kyrgyz, Russian, Uzbek, Tajik, Uighur

Religions: Mainly Sunni Muslim; Russians are generally Christian Orthodox. Thanks to the liberal policy of the government on religious matters, several other Christian churches are now active in the Kyrgyz Republic

Kyrgyzstan (Republic of Kyrgyz or Kyrgyz Republic, the official name since 1993) is a former Soviet Republic of 198,500 square kilometers (766,409 square miles) located at the core of Central Asia. Its per capita GDP is $2,900 (2002 estimate). Its territory, bordering on southern Kazakhstan, eastern Uzbekistan, northern Tajikistan, and the Chinese Republic of Xinjiang to the east, is characterized by impressive mountain ranges: the Pamir-Alai range, which dominates the southwest of the country, and the Tian Shan mountains in the North. These mountains have also played a role in the ethnic and political division of the country, creating a physical barrier that divides the Kyrgyz territory in two main niches.

Kyrgyzstan has been an independent presidential republic since August 1991, and its political system is dominated by the president of the Republic (Askar Akaev since 1990); the Parliament (called *Zhogorku Kenesh*—Supreme Council) has two chambers. According to the latest estimates, the total population of the Republic is approximately 4.5 million. Although the word *Kyrgyzstan* means "land of the Kyrgyz," until the end of the 1980s, Kyrgyz were only a minority inside the Republic. At present, because of their high birth rate and the migration of Russians and Slavs after 1991, the Kyrgyz account for around 60 percent of the total population. Among the other ethnic groups, the most prevalent are the Russians (18 percent), concentrated in the urban areas; the Uzbeks (13 percent), living in the south of the Republic and whose tense relations with the Kyrgyz are a primary security concern for the Republic; the Uighurs (40,000–50,000);

and the ethnic Germans of the Volga in Central Asia, who were deported by Stalin (2.4 percent).

As was the case in the other Soviet Central Asian republics, the Kyrgyz economy also suffered greatly from the collapse of the Soviet Union. This was reflected in the decline of the GDP from U.S.$11.9 billion in 1990 to U.S.$7.0 billion in 1997 (in parity of purchasing power). However, the adoption of market-led reforms and foreign investments is contributing to the economic recovery of the country.

The origins of the Kyrgyz and their arrival in the region now called Kyrgyzstan is still the subject of controversy. Under Mongol dominance, only during the fifteenth century were some Kyrgyz tribes (a mixture of Mongol and Turkic groups) able to gain greater autonomy. Organized into nomadic, pastoral tribal groups and lineages of descent without a strong centralized political center, the Kyrgyz maintained a traditional lifestyle during the following centuries that remained largely unaffected by the loose control foreign powers tried to impose on their region.

The Russians considered the Kyrgyz, whom they named the Kara-Kyrgyz, a group of Kazaks (whom the Russians erroneously called Kyrgyz); for decades, this misleading ethnic classification hampered the recognition of the Kyrgyz as one of the main nationalities within the Union of Soviet Socialista Republics (USSR). After the Soviet revolution in 1921, the territory of the Kyrgyz became part of the new Turkestan Autonomous Soviet Socialist Republic within the Soviet Russian Federation. In 1924, 1925, and 1927 several administrative changes led to the creation of a Kiro-Kazakh Autonomous Republic still within the Russian Federation, including the territory of both Kazakhs and Kyrgyz (whose land became an autonomous region, named the Kara-Kyrgyz Oblast). Finally, in 1936 Moscow created the Soviet Socialist Republic of Kyrgyzstan, separated from both Russia and Kazakhstan, with Frunze—now renamed Bishkek—as its capital.

A common problem for all the Central Asian Soviet Republics was that Stalin's frontier policy had created artificial borders that segmented all the main ethnic groups, exacerbating their historical tensions and antagonism, and creating a number of ethnic and cultural minorities inside each republic. Interethnic disputes were always latent during the Soviet period and were to emerge following the 1991 independence.

For the Kyrgyz Republic, the largest minority group is represented by the Uzbeks, mainly settled in the portion of the Ferghana Valley allotted to Kyrgyzstan (in the districts of Osh and Jalalabad). The traditional cultural and economic differences between these two groups—and their historical animosity—erupted dramatically in 1990, when a dispute over land and water degenerated into violent clashes with hundreds of casualties. With the collapse of the USSR, the situation worsened: On the one hand, Uzbeks feared being discriminated against politically and linguistically, and on the other, the Kyrgyz complained against the perceived better economic positions of the Uzbeks (who were predominant in the fields of agriculture, trade, and handcrafts) and were suspicious about Uzbek irredentism.

Notwithstanding President Akaev's relatively liberal and moderate policy, the Uzbeks felt deprived of their culture and language, and as a consequence, secessionist movements and the idea of a reunification of all Uzbeks within a "Greater Uzbekistan" gained support amongst ethnic Uzbeks. The nationalist policy adopted by the autocratic leader of Uzbekistan, Islam Karimov, also contributed in the radicalization of mutual interethnic hostility.

The situation of the ethnic Russians, Slavs, and Germans is somewhat different. Concentrated in the urban areas, they represent the technical and administrative cadres who are still essential for the management of the country. It was therefore a priority for Kyrgyzstan to avoid a mass migration of these ethnic groups. Akaev's attempts to create a friendly interethnic atmosphere were nevertheless challenged by the increasing Kyrgyz nationalism, some ambiguous decisions about the status of the Russian language, political representation, and the worsening of the economic situation that characterized the 1990s. The result was a limited migration of Russians and Slavs toward their republics, which, in some cases, affected the Kyrgyz industrial system and contributed to increasing consensus for political movements such as the *Semirechie Cossacks*. In particular, many Germans—mainly descendants of the Germans deported from the western part of the Soviet Union after the Nazi invasion of 1941—left the country. The German government consented to the migration of those of proven German descent, giving in the meantime some degree of financial support to those who did not move from Kyrgyzstan.

Although the Uighurs are only a small community, the freedom of association they enjoyed after 1991 provoked political tensions with China (7 million Uighurs are settled in the Chinese Autonomous Republic of Xinjiang). The Peking government considers Uighur nationalism as a major threat to its internal stability, and reacted harshly against the cultural and political agenda of the Uighur associations of Kyrgyzstan. To prevent any political crisis with China, since 1996 Bishkek has decided to reduce the visibility of the Uighur profile and Uighur activism.

RICCARDO REDAELLI

See also **Germans; Kyrgyz; Russians; Uygurs; Uzbeks**

Further Reading

Anderson, John, *Kyrgyzstan—Central Asia's Island of Democracy?* Amsterdam: Harvood Academic Publishers, 1999

Gleason, Gregory, *The New Central Asian States*, Boulder, Colorado: Westview Press, 1997

Howell, John, "Coping with Transition: Insights from Kyrgyzstan," *Third World Quarterly*, 17, no. 1 (1996)

Olcott, Martha Brill, *Central Asia's New States: Independence, Foreign Policy, and Regional Security*, Washington, DC: United States Institute of Peace Press, 1996

Smith, Dianne L., *Opening Pandora's Box: Ethnicity and Central Asian Militaries*, Carlisle Barracks, Pennsylvania: Strategic Studies Institute, 1998

L

Languages, Disappearing

Language is not only an important vehicle for communication, but for many minority groups in the world, language is also the primary marker of cultural and social identity. Language often defines who belongs to the minority group. It is also the means through which cultural knowledge and values are transmitted to future generations. The approximately 6,000 to 10,000 languages that are spoken around the world reflect unique cultures and ways of life. When languages disappear, the cultural knowledge and social identity of these unique minority groups also disappear.

Throughout history languages have disappeared as civilizations have flourished and waned. When languages are no longer spoken, the cause is often broader cultural and social change. However, in recent times languages have disappeared at an alarming rate. Some estimate that approximately 20–50 percent of the world's languages are moribund, that is, with children no longer learning them as their mother tongue. Others predict that in the next century, 90 percent of the world's languages will be moribund. Although researchers do not agree on the rate of disappearance, there is a consensus on how languages disappear and the reasons why they disappear.

Generally, languages do not suddenly disappear. It is possible that a natural catastrophe or war wipes out an entire minority group. However, in most cases languages disappear over one or more generations in a process called "language shift." Language shift often begins when minority groups face increasing contact with the institutions of the more powerful nation-state in which they are located. The first generation of contact may learn the language of these institutions in order to gain the benefits they have to offer. They may choose to teach their children the language of the nation-state so that they are able to participate in the educational systems. The mother tongue of these children shifts from the minority language to the majority language. These children may or may not have the proficiency to transmit the minority language to their children. Although in most cases it takes several generations before language shift is complete, it is possible for a language to disappear within three generations once the process of language shift has started.

There are several reasons why languages disappear, and why they are disappearing at a rapid rate today. One of the reasons for the disappearance of minority languages is that economic and social change impacts the demographic composition of the traditional areas inhabited by minority peoples. These changes often are introduced through colonization, nationalization, and globalization. There are several examples in both North and South America where depopulation occurred through conquest and colonization. Disease, warfare, slavery, and resettlement disrupted traditional social networks and brought contact with speakers of other languages. Intermarriage with people from other groups also occurred because of greater contact and loss of marriageable partners. Generally, when communities and marriages have speakers of the majority and minority languages, it is the majority language that is spoken, and the minority language is not transmitted to the next generation.

A change in the economic base through the pressures of globalization also contributes to demographic changes leading to language shift. Economic changes are often associated with a large number of speakers out of the minority group's area emigrating to pursue economic opportunities. These opportunities often require the knowledge of a majority language. Participation in the institutions of the nation-state also requires the knowledge of the majority language. Many nation-states develop language policies that favor a national language to promote solidarity and loyalty to the nation-state. National institutions introduced into minority communities use and promote the language of the nation-state. Parents often deliberately teach their children the majority language so that they can participate in these opportunities, which leads to language shift.

Contact with the dominant group not only introduces new resources and new languages into a community, but also introduces new values and identities. In some cases where languages have disappeared, people in minority communities have reevaluated their traditions and values when comparing them to those of the majority culture. Often language shift reflects a shift in the personal goals of groups and individuals. People may learn the language of the majority because they desire to be associated with a more prestigious group or to change their identity. For example, they may begin to associate the minority language with negative traits, such as backwardness and ignorance, and the majority language with positive traits, such as progressiveness and education. People use language to identify themselves with the more prestigious group. People may also adopt the values of the majority culture, such as formal education and economic rewards. They may choose to abandon the values of the minority culture, including the language associated with them, to obtain these rewards.

Although there has been an increase in the disappearance of languages, there is also an increase in concern over their disappearance. Some linguists and scholars have turned their attention to preserving and maintaining minority languages. One of the first steps is identifying moribund and endangered languages. In 1996, a clearinghouse for endangered languages was created to identify languages that needed to be given priority for linguistic research. Especially in cases where the language is already moribund, there is a need for linguistic description before the language disappears entirely.

In some minority communities there are efforts to promote the use of the minority language in school. For some language communities, this means that they actually have to reintroduce children to their own minority languages. For this to occur, linguists and people in the community work together to produce materials in the minority language. Children must be given the opportunity to learn, listen to, and speak their minority language.

SUE RUSSELL

See also **Equal Opportunity; Globalization and Minority Cultures**

Further Reading

Brenzinger, Matthias, editor, *Language Death,* New York: Mouton de Gruyter, 1992

Crystal, David, *Language Death*, Cambridge University Press, 2000

Dorian, Nancy C., editor, *Investigating Obsolescence*, Cambridge: Cambridge University Press, 1989

Fishman, Joshua A., *Reversing Language Shift*, Clevedon, England: Multilingual Matters, 1991

Robins, Robert H., and Eugenius M. Uhlenbeck, editors, *Endangered Languages*, Oxford and New York: Berg, 1991

Lao-Tai

Capsule Summary

Location: northeast Thailand
Total Population: 20 million
Language: Isan
Religion: Buddhist

Lao-Tai is an ethnic label that refers to the Lao inhabiting the Khorat Plateau on the right bank of the Mekong River, northeast of Thailand. Because of this location and the desire to put forward their Thai citizenship rather than their Lao cultural affiliation, they call themselves and are usually called *Isan* (a Lao word derived from the Pâli *isara,* which means "northeast"). Although the Isan have long been culturally and politically dominated by the Siamese of the Central Plain, they are not, numerically speaking, a minority in Thailand. On the contrary, with a population estimated at 20 million, they are the main ethnic component of the nation, before other Tai groups such as the Siamese and Khon Muang. The great majority of factory or construction workers and service employees of Bangkok are Lao-Tai temporary migrants. It is also noteworthy that the number of Lao in Thailand is more than seven times the number of those living in Laos. Isan is a Lao dialect permeated with Siamese loan words, whose proportion may vary significantly from one place to another. It is written according to the Thai script.

Since at least the fourteenth century, the bulk of the Khorat Plateau inhabitants have been of Lao origin. The fact that there is no geographic hurdle between the region and the left bank of the Mekong, but mountainous barriers in the south and the west, explains why this area has been for so long colonized by the Lao. From the conquest by Fa Ngum in 1353–54 up to the late seventeenth century, the plateau was part of the Lao kingdom of Lan Xang. Following the division of Lan Xang into three new kingdoms, Luang Prabang, Vientiane, and Champassak, the northeast of the present Thailand was alternately controlled by Vientiane and Champassak up to 1778. At that time Taksin, the founder of the new Siamese kingdom of Bangkok-Thonburi, subjected the local nobility to his rule. In 1804 Chao Anu was recognized as a vassal king of

Vientiane by the Siamese. But he rebelled in 1827, and his armies invaded the Khorat Plateau. Finally the Siamese defeated the Lao and occupied Vientiane. To weaken their opponents on a long-term basis, they destroyed all buildings in the city and removed all the population from the Vientiane Plain to resettlement in Siam. Throughout the decades that followed the Chao Anu revolt, the Siamese systematically reorganized the administration of their Isan provinces to provide a better defense of their northeastern frontier against French attack and to prevent new rebellions. During this period, the Lao demographic imbalance between the right and left banks of the Mekong took its present form, as the Siamese implemented a massive resettlement of Lao populations across the river to the Khorat Plateau. The Treaty of 1907 between Siam and France, which instituted the Mekong as the international border, marked the final annexation of the Plateau to Siam.

The northeast region is an arid, overpopulated, and remote area, and the Lao-Tai farmers are among the poorest peasants in the country. As a consequence, they share a long tradition of unrest and dissidence. In the 1960s, armed clashes between Thai troops and revolting peasants frequently occurred, and the region became a communist stronghold. Alarmed by this development, the Thai government launched an ambitious program of accelerated rural development that was mainly financed with United States aid. The overt purpose of this policy was not to improve the living conditions of the poor, but rather to prevent the immediate emergence of a strong revolutionary movement in this strategic part of the country. This program and other historical factors converged to calm the insurgency, although the problem of regional underdevelopment remained unsolved. This problem is still manifest, and for want of income the Lao-Tai peasantry forms the bulk of temporary migrants moving to other regions of Thailand or abroad.

Because 40 percent of the rice-growing farms of Thailand are concentrated into the northeast, this region may be considered the rural heart of the country. Lao-Tai peasants do not only form the masses of the kingdom's petty farmers. They are also the champions of Theravada Buddhism at the national level. Lao-Tai men make up more than 50 percent of the Buddhist clerical staff in Thailand and 60 percent of the Bangkok monks, and in 1997, about 45 percent of the Buddhist temples of the country were located in the northeast. The fact that in Thailand the career of monk is one of the main means of social advancement for poor and uneducated males explains this figure, while poverty and the wish for material improvement explains why 70 percent of the construction workers, 60 percent of the industry laborers, and 80 percent of Thai sex workers come from the northeastern or northern parts of the country.

By actively contributing to the development of Thailand's economy and Buddhism, the Isan are discreetly promoting their own idioms and traditions. After centuries of Siamese domination, their demographic dynamism allows them to resist cultural assimilation into Siamese ways. For instance, the Lao-Tai dialect has been recently codified through the publication of several dictionaries; after decades of stigmatization, the most typical Isan dishes are now appreciated

by the Bangkok middle class, and various Lao customs, such as *mo lam* singing, a nontheatrical vocal genre, and the *Bang fai* (Rocket festival), have become very popular in modern Thailand. However, the lack of effort on the part of the government to improve their economic situation does not facilitate the integration of the Lao-Tai into the nation-state, and most of them are affected by a split identity, as they are torn between Laos and Thailand, between cultural affinities and political allegiance.

BERNARD FORMOSO

See also **Thailand**

Further Reading

Keyes, Charles F., *Thailand: Buddhist Kingdom as Modern Nation-State*, Boulder, Colorado: Westview Press, 1987
Klausner, William, *Reflections on Thai Culture,* Bangkok: Siam Society, 1983
Luther, Hans, *Peasants and State in Contemporary Thailand*, Hamburg: Institute für Asienkunde 98, 1978
Wyatt, David, *Thailand, a Short History*, London: Yale University Press, 1984

Lao-Theung

Capsule Summary

Location: Lao People's Democratic Republic (Laos); similar ethnic groups spread throughout northern Indochina in Thailand, Burma, Vietnam, and China
Total Population: 1–1.5 million within Laos
Languages: various languages from the Mon-Khmer language family (Austroasiatic)
Religions: animist; Buddhist and Christian minorities

Lao-Theung, or "upland Lao," is the title given by the Lao People's Democratic Republic (LPDR, or more commonly known as Laos) to a conglomeration of distinct ethnic groups, most of which live in areas 300—1,000 meters in altitude and speak a language in the Austroasiatic language family. Lao-Theung is one of three classifications for ethnic groups in Laos: the others are Lao-Lum, for the lowland-dwelling and Tai-Lao-speaking peoples; and Lao-Sung, for groups at higher altitudes who speak Tibeto-Burmese or

Hmong-Mien languages. Groups within the Lao-Lum category constitute around 60 percent of the country's population, while Lao-Theung and Lao-Sung make up around 25–30 percent and 10–15 percent, respectively. Despite the simplified use of three main ethnic categories, Laos is a highly diverse country; more than 200 distinct ethnic groups have been identified so far by some anthropologists.

The Lao-Theung can be considered the "indigenous" people of Laos, since they likely inhabited the area long before Tai-Lao speakers migrated northward. Lao-Theung are currently found in almost every province of the country, from the far mountainous north to the southern Boloven Plateau. In the north, the Lao-Theung are represented mainly by the Khmu and Lamet ethnic groups, and in the south are found an assortment of other Mon-Khmer speakers in more than 25 separate, self-identifying groups, including such people as the Suay, Makong, Taoy, Taliang, Katu, Lawae, Alak, and Ngae.

It has often been said that Laos is less a nation than a loose assortment of ethnic groups, none constituting an outright majority. It is believed that lowland Tai-Lao-speaking migrants displaced tribal groups into the uplands beginning a thousand years ago. When Western contact with the area began several centuries ago, the Lao had established a number of principalities and kingdoms, with political and economical domination over the tribal midland and upland dwellers. These groups were collectively referred to as *Kha*, which is generally taken to be a derogatory term meaning slave.

French colonial rule began in the latter half of the nineteenth century, and it strengthened the role of lowland Lao in administration of the country, despite the fact that in many areas the Lao speakers were the minority. In the early 1900s, occasional groups of minorities engaged in several small-scale armed rebellions against the French and Lao administrators, with little success. After independence from France was negotiated in 1953, many of the same unpopular practices toward minorities and use of the derogatory word *Kha* continued under the new Royal Lao Government (RLG).

The threefold classification of ethnic groups into Lao-Lum, Lao–Theung, and Lao-Sung to replace the term *Kha* first emerged in the 1950s and was popularized by the communist revolutionary forces, the Pathet Lao. The Pathet Lao actively encouraged ethnic minorities to join their side and oppose what they called the inattention and outright disdain toward minorities by the RLG. The Pathet Lao were successful in recruiting a number of ethnic minorities, particularly in the south, into their liberation forces.

Since the establishment of the communist-led LPDR in 1975, official attention has been paid to ethnic minorities to ensure continuing national unity, and there is a ban on ethnic discrimination enshrined in the new constitution. However, although the government may pay lip service to the minority groups, more often assimilation, rather than ethnic preservation, is encouraged. There is also a somewhat paternalistic emphasis on economic and social development, because minorities are often seen as uneducated and unknowledgeable. For example, the government has encouraged upland minorities to relocate to lowland areas, since their highland agriculture is blamed for much of the deforestation in Laos. In addition, there are significant plans for hydropower development in the uplands, particularly the damming of several tributaries of the Mekong River, which will flood areas many Lao-Theung groups consider their homelands.

It has been estimated that there are at least 37 distinct ethnic groups classified as Lao-Theung, although depending on the definition of "ethnic group," this number can be much higher. The largest group in terms of population is the Khmu, with over 400,000 people. The smallest groups, such as the Numbri and Salang, number only a handful of families. Little is known about most of the Lao-Theung groups; ethnographic research has been difficult the latter half of this century because of war and the secretive communist government, and so only the broadest of generalizations can be made.

Most Lao-Theung groups reside in relatively limited geographic areas within the country. Additionally, many of the ethnic groups called Lao-Theung are not exclusively found in Laos and spill across borders into neighboring countries. All the Lao-Theung speak some language in the Mon-Khmer language family, but whereas some of the languages are mutually intelligible, such as Khmu and Lamet, others are not. None of the Lao-Theung are said to have a written script.

The Lao-Theung, as upland dwellers, have primarily made their living through swidden (slash-and-burn), or rotational, agriculture. Within this system, forestlands are cleared and fields planted; after harvesting, they are then abandoned to fallow for a number of years to restore soil fertility before the cycle is repeated. Some Lao-Theung groups primarily plant glutinous, or sticky, rice in their swiddens, but some groups plant crops such as corn, cassava, and beans. Wild tubers and other gathered forest products such as bamboo shoots are also important in many of their diets.

Agricultural practices among the Lao-Theung are often linked with deeply held spiritual beliefs. For example, in Katu agriculture there are taboos on certain months of cultivation and on days fields are burned. Most Lao-Theung are animists and pay particular attention to the world of spirits, who may cause illness or misfortune if ignored. There is also considerable reverence paid to ancestral spirits, who form an important aspect of household religious and family rituals. Many of these beliefs continue today, despite the intrusion of lowland Lao customs into highland areas.

PAMELA MCELWEE

See also **Laos**

Further Reading

Chamberlain, James, Charles Alton, and Arthur Crisfield, *Indigenous Peoples Profile. Lao People's Democratic Republic (Part One)*, Vientiane, Laos: CARE International for the World Bank, 1996

Chazee, Laurent, *The Peoples of Laos: Rural and Ethnic Diversities*, Bangkok: White Lotus, 1999

Evans, Grant, *The Politics of Ritual and Remembrance: Laos Since 1975*, Chiang Mai, Thailand: Silkworm Books, 1998

Evans, Grant, editor, *Laos: Culture and Society*, Chiang Mai, Thailand: Silkworm Books, 1999

Gunn, Gregory, "Sambrau (The White Python): The *Kha* (Lao Theung) Revolt of 1936—9," *Sojourn*, 3, no. 2 (1988)

Ireson, Carol, and Randy Ireson, "Ethnicity and Development in Laos," *Asian Survey*, 31 (1991)

Oveson, Jan, "All Lao? Minorities in The Lao People's Democratic Republic," in *Legislating Modernity among the Marginalized: Southeast Asian Government Programs for Developing Minority Ethnic Groups*, edited by Chris Duncan, in press

Trankell, Ing-Britt, "'The Minor Part of the Nation': Politics of Ethnicity in Laos," in *Facets of Power and Its Limitations: Political Culture in Southeast Asia*, edited by Ing-Britt Trankell and Laura Summers, Uppsala: Uppsala Studies in Cultural Anthropology, 1998

Laos

Capsule Summary

Country Name: Lao People's Democratic Republic (LPDR, or Laos)
Location: southeastern Asia, northeast of Thailand, west of Vietnam
Total Population: 5,921,545 (2003)
Ethnic Population: Lao-Lum (lowland); Lao-Theung (upland); Lao-Sung (highland), including the Hmong (Meo) and the Yao (Mien); ethnic Vietnamese/Chinese
Languages: Lao (official), French, English, various ethnic languages
Religions: Buddhist, animist, various Christian denominations

Laos, now the Lao People's Democratic Republic (LPDR, or Laos) is a landlocked Southeast Asian country that borders Vietnam, Thailand, China, Cambodia, and Burma and has a population of approximately 5.5 million. It has an area of 236,000 square kilometers (92, 040 square miles, slightly larger than Utah), 6,000 square kilometers (2,340 square miles) of which is water, and has a terrain of mostly rugged mountains interrupted by some plains and plateaus located throughout the country. The largest and most notorious plain is the Plain of Jars, located in Xiangkhoang Province. Only about four percent of the total land area is arable. The Mekong River flows along much of the country's western border with Burma and Thailand. The capitol of Laos, Vientiane, is located on the bank of the Mekong along the Lao-Thai border. The climate in Laos is marked by two distinct seasons: the rainy (May to November) and the dry (December to April).

Laos was inhabited five or more millennia ago by Austroasiatic peoples. From the first century CE, princely fiefdoms associated with the bronze and pottery culture of Ban Chiang developed in the middle Mekong River valley, as did other kingdoms reflective of the Cham and Mon peoples. By the eighth century, the Mon *mandala* was under Khmer domination. The Mongol intervention in the region by the thirteenth century produced local dynastic struggles for power that led to the founding of the Kingdom of Lan Xang ("Million Elephants"). The reign of the first king of Lan Xang, Fa Ngum (r. 1354–73), marked the beginning of recorded Lao history. From the fourteenth to twentieth centuries, Laos and its small confederation of communities in Lan Xang were dominated by neighbors and other nations such as Burma, Siam, the Khmer kingdom, Vietnam, Japan, and France. Since World War II, Laos has been a pawn in the larger Cold War struggle between the Soviet Union and the United States. Each side sought domination of the country as an ally in the more public war in Vietnam, and each politically, financially, and militarily backed various individuals from powerful Lao families throughout the years to try to gain this control. Two international Geneva conferences (in 1954 and 1961–62) and three coalition governments failed to establish any sort of stable and acceptable government. A communist insurgency orchestrated by the Pathet Lao (Lao Nation) and dominated by North Vietnam finally overthrew foreign domination. Aided by the withdrawal of Western forces in 1973 (most notably the United States, which maintained a large political and covert military presence in Laos during the Second Indochinese War) and the subsequent collapse of South Vietnam and Cambodia, the Neo Lao Hak Xat (Lao Patriotic Front) established the LPDR on December 2, 1975, thus ending seven centuries of monarchial rule. Today Laos remains one of the few remaining official communist states in the world.

Laos is one of the world's poorest countries. Its 2002 estimated gross domestic product (GDP) hovered around $10 billion annually, with a real growth rate of 5.7 percent and a GDP per capita amount of $1,800. Subsistence agriculture accounts for 53 percent of the GDP and provides for 80 percent of employment, and industry (22 percent), particularly hydroelectric production, and services (27 percent) account for the remainder of the GDP. Forty-six percent of the population lives below the poverty line, and in 2002 the inflation rate was 10 percent. Laos has no railroads, a rudimentary road system, and limited external and internal communications (although Internet access was available in Vientiane in 2000). Electricity is only available in a few urban areas.

The population of Laos is ethically diverse. Before the two Indochinese Wars, sources commonly identified more than 60 different ethnic groups, but the 1985 census only listed 47 minority groups. A detailed formal study of all of the minority groups in Laos has never been undertaken. The same 1985 census did distinguish three general ethnic group classifications reflecting common origin and language grouping: the Lao-Lum (lowland, 68 percent), the Lao-Theung (upland, 22 percent), and the Lao-Sung (highland, 9 percent. There is also a small (1 percent) number of ethnic Vietnamese, Thai, Cambodian, Burmese, Indian, Chinese, and French residing in Laos. The majority of Lao (the Lao-Lum) practice Buddhism (proposed in an October 1999 constitutional amendment to be named as the official state religion), and the mountain-dwelling minority groups practice varying forms of animism, or ancestor/spirit worship. Since the 1970s and the establishment of the LPDR, the Lao government, in an increasing effort to modernize the country, has officially discouraged the practice of spirit (*phi*) worship in the rural villages. Despite this, many villages continue to practice *phi* worship and hold annual ceremonies that aim to secure the continuing good fortune of the village and its inhabitants and reaffirm the importance of the village as a cohesive social unit.

The largest minority peoples in the Lao-Lum group are the Lao and Phu Thai; the largest in the Lao-Theung group are the Kammu, Katang, Makong, and Suai; and the largest in the Lao-Sung group are the Hmong and Akha. The Hmong make up more than two-thirds of the Lao-Sung. Hmong entered northwestern Vietnam from China prior to 1800 to escape persecution and pacification campaigns, and early settlements in northeastern Laos were reported around the turn of the nineteenth century. The Hmong adopted slash-and-burn farming methods in the mountains out of necessity because the lowland basins were already settled by other minority groups. During the Second Indochinese War, the United States armed, trained, and directed the Hmong as a fighting force against the Pathet Lao. By the end of the civil war in 1975, and despite valiant fighting, the Hmong had suffered many casualties, had many villages uprooted and destroyed, and were subsequently tracked down and persecuted by the LPDR government. In the face of the Lao government's campaign against them, many Hmong escaped to the West, notably to the United States, and set up communities where they live today.

RICHARD VERRONE

See also **Hmong; Lao-Theung**

Further Reading

Castle, Timothy N., *At War in the Shadow of Vietnam: U.S. Military Aid to the Royal Lao Government, 1955–1975,* New York: Columbia University Press, 1993

Chan, Sucheng, *Hmong Means Free: Life in Laos and America,* Philadelphia: Temple University Press, 1994

Cordell, Helen, *Laos,* vol. 133, World Bibliography Series, Oxford: Clio Press, 1991

Dommen, Arthur J., *Conflict in Laos: The Politics of Neutralization,* New York: Praeger, revised edition, 1971

Hall, D.G.E., *A History of Southeast Asia,* New York: St. Martin's, 4th edition, 1981

Hamilton-Merritt, Jane, *Tragic Mountains: The Hmong, the Americans, and the Secret Wars for Laos, 1942–1992,* South Bend: Indiana University Press, 1993

Langer, Paul F., *The Soviet Union, China, and the Pathet Lao: Analysis and Chronology,* Santa Monica, California: Rand Corporation, 1972

Langer, Paul F., and Joseph J. Zasloff, *North Vietnam and the Pathet Lao: Partners in the Struggle for Laos,* Cambridge: Harvard University Press, 1970

LeBar, Frank M., et al., *Ethnic Groups of Mainland Southeast Asia,* New Haven, Connecticut: Human Relations Area Files Press, 1964

Savada, Andrea M., editor, *Laos: A Country Study,* Washington, D.C.: The American University, 3rd edition, 1994

Stuart-Fox, Martin, *Historical Dictionary of Laos,* Lanham, Maryland: Scarecrow Press, 2001

———, *A History of Laos,* Cambridge: Cambridge University Press, 1997

Latin Americans

Capsule Summary

Location: the Caribbean, Central America, North America, South America
Total Population: 500–520 million
Languages: Spanish, Portuguese
Religions: all religions represented, but population predominantly Roman Catholic

Latin American is a general term used to collectively define a large group of people from 19 independent republics of the New World, including the 18 countries whose national language is Spanish, and Brazil, where Portuguese is spoken. Some also include people from the independent nation of Haiti, where French and Creole are spoken, as well as other Caribbean and South American nations. Mexicans, Latin Americans (from Central or South America), and Cubans are just a few subgroups among those with Latin American ancestry.

Latin Americans have always been a diverse group. The differences are illustrated by the various terms used to describe them, including *Hispanic, Latino,* and *Spanish,* and the use of the country name to aid in identification, such as *Cubano, Brazilian,* or *Colombian.* Latin American countries also have many indigenous groups, such as the Mayans of Guatemala and Southern Mexico

The Mayan, Aztecs, and Incan empires were among the first to occupy Latin America. Beginning in the early 1500s, the Spanish conquistadores took over much of the land, completely changing its political and social structure. To develop a sufficient labor supply, the Spanish turned to slavery. Initially the native Indian population was chosen as slaves, but they often escaped to the countryside. In addition, the Indian people were not accustomed to the strenuous nature of the work and often refused to work. Consequently, black Africans were imported to replace the Indians as slaves. By the late eighteenth century there were over 2.4 million African slaves working in the Caribbean and South America. In order to communicate, slaves learned Spanish or Portuguese. Slavery lasted into the nineteenth century. It was often abolished when Latin American colonies won their independence from Spain and Portugal. Venezuela was the first to declare independence in 1821, followed by Chile (1823), Mexico (1829), Peru (1854), Puerto Rico (1873), Cuba (1880), and Brazil (1888).

The Spanish were heavily influenced by the Romans in the development of their political system. This influence is seen in many Latin American countries. For example, the legal and judicial system in most of Latin America comes from the Napoleonic Code. Instead of juries, judges make the final decisions on cases brought to the courts. Most towns in Latin America have a town square or plaza. In the plaza one will find the main Catholic church and government buildings, the most predominate of which is the municipal or state center. Christianity is also a Roman remnant carried by Spaniards to Latin America.

Latin Americans are dispersed throughout the world, but they primarily live in North America (Mexico and the United States), the Caribbean (Cuba, Dominican Republic, and Puerto Rico), Central America (Costa Rica, El Salvador; Guatemala, Honduras, Nicaragua, and Panama), and South America (Argentina, Bolivia, Brazil, Chile, Colombia, Ecuador, Paraguay, Peru, Uruguay, and Venezuela). Latin Americans draw from a variety of races to identify themselves. The vast majority are some form of mestizo, a mixture of European and indigenous people, or mulatto, a mixture of European- and African-descended people.

In the nineteenth century, large groups of Chinese and Japanese emigrated to South America and the Caribbean to work in various industries, including agriculture and railroads. In the early twentieth century, other migrants added to the mix of Latin Americans' racial and ethnic identity, including Lebanese, Armenians, and Palestinians who fled war, and European Jews fleeing the Nazis during World War II. In recent years, indigenous populations in places like the rain forests of the Amazon and Mexico have formed social movements to preserve their cultural and economic rights. In addition, African descendants residing in Latin American countries (such as Brazil, Colombia, Ecuador, the Dominican Republic, and Puerto Rico) have revived their African heritage. Thus the racial and ethnic identity of Latin Americans is as diverse as the people. As a result of this diversity, racial tensions persist. Discrimination is heavier for those with darker skin tones and for those that have more pronounced facial features, as is typical of black and indigenous peoples.

Although Latin Americans come from all faiths, they are predominantly Christian, with Roman Catholicism being the major religion. In addition, some Latin Americans are Protestant, Pentecostal, Evangelical, Muslim, Jewish, and Afro-Latin American. For Latin Americans, religion plays a significant role in everyday activities. Wherever they reside, they carry the traditions of their culture of origin, such as the *quinceanera,* which marks a young girl's passage into womanhood, and the celebration of all major Catholic festivals. During Christmas, putting up the home nativity scene, or *nacimiento*, is an important part of almost every family's holiday celebration. Foods vary widely by region, including many fish and meat dishes like tamales, empanadas, arroz con pollo, and tacos.

Latin Americans are in general collectivists. In a highly individualistic culture, society allows for and expects individual initiative. The members in these cultures have perceived freedom and are supposed to look after personal self-interests. In contrast, a highly collectivist culture places more emphasis on group goals. Members in collectivist cultures are expected to watch after the interests of their in-group and to hold only the opinions and beliefs permitted by their group. In exchange, the group offers stability and protection. As a result of the collectivist emphasis, the family unit is very prominent in Latin American culture. The family unit extends beyond the immediate family to include grandparents, uncles, aunts, and cousins. Families often gather together to celebrate holidays, birthdays, baptisms, first communions, graduations, and weddings. The emphasis on the family is called *familismo*. Children in Latin American families are often taught the importance of honor, good manners, and respect for authority and the elderly. In most Latin American families, the father is the head of the family and the mother is in charge of the household. In general, Latin American cultures tend to be male oriented (*machismo*) and based on strong authoritarian leaders. This system was influenced by the strict hierarchical organization of the Catholic Church.

Over the course of the last 20 years, Latin America has rejected authoritarian rulers and has adopted constitutional, democratic governments as the norm. Unfortunately, Latin American history is one of oppression and repression, of de facto governments and other governments that mask as democracies but in reality are dictatorships. This history makes change slow. Human rights issues are of major concern in Latin American countries. Seven Latin American countries are on the United States State Department's list of countries with persistent violations of human rights: Colombia, Ecuador, Guatemala, Perú, the Dominican Republic, Venezuela, and Cuba.

Political repression takes the form of summary executions, disappearances, torture, and arbitrary detentions. These violations occur almost daily in some Latin American countries, resulting in massive exile and displacement of populations. Many of those guilty of committing human rights violations go unpunished. Much of the day-to-day existence for many Latin Americans is one of poverty and repression from the military and governments that have not altered their ways. According to Amnesty International, there are more documented killings of both men and women human rights defenders in Latin America and the Caribbean than in any other region of the world. Defenders of human rights have faced threats and intimidation, and some have been forced to flee their homes, sometimes their country. Often defenders of human rights issues become victims of unfounded slander campaigns designed to discredit their work. In addition, Latin Americans throughout Latin America and the Caribbean suffer many violations of internationally recognized worker rights, including child labor and employment discrimination. These rights are violated with impunity, causing immeasurable damage. Corruption and political instability remain roadblocks to reducing poverty and improving the economies of Latin American countries. In addition, the strength of the drug trade in many Latin American countries inhibits the government's power to end human rights abuses.

To help improve the economic and social environments, many emerging democratic governments have created truth commissions to address past periods of human rights violations and to consolidate democracy. There are more than 20 truth commissions in existence, many in Latin American countries such as Argentina, Chile, El Salvador, Peru, and Guatemala. These commissions also serve as a tool to educate future generations to help ensure that human rights violations are not repeated. The healing process from past abuses can take decades. For example, Argentines continue to heal from the brutal military dictatorship that ruled their country from the mid-1960s to the early 1980s. In Guatemala, political violence continues as the country recovers from the civil war that ended in 1996.

In 2003, to further support reform, the International Criminal Court (ICC) was formed. The ICC oversees the prosecution of individuals accused of genocide, crimes against humanity, and war crimes. Several Latin American countries have ratified the ICC treaty, including Ecuador, Panama, Brazil, Uruguay, Honduras, and Colombia. As other countries join, the ICC will become a major disciplinary body.

Another serious problem for Latin Americans is poverty. It is estimated that 44 percent of Latin America's inhabitants are poor. The slums in urban areas of Latin America are growing, and about 48 percent of rural Latin Americans live in extreme poverty. For a majority of Latin American working people, income levels have declined for two decades because of the region's foreign debt crisis, which erupted in Mexico in 1982 and spread to the rest of Latin America. According to one estimate, 70 million Latin Americans live on less than $5 a day, and 40 percent live on less than $2 a day. In Guatemala, Honduras, and Bolivia, over 70 percent of the population live in poverty.

There is also racial inequality among Latin Americans. Whites hold most of the prominent positions, with mestizos and mulattos being among the poor. The indigenous people are the poorest of the poor. Latin Americans have been historically disadvantaged in the global economy. Because much of the exports are from products with widely fluctuating prices, Latin American countries have difficulty gaining economic stability. They also have income disparity. In 2003, the richest 10 percent of Latin Americans owned 40 percent of the total income, while the poorest 30 percent earned less than 8 percent. Although many Latin American countries have opened their borders to improve their economies, the outcome has been greater gaps between the rich and poor. In many Latin American countries, education remains a privilege for the wealthy, since the poor rarely complete high school. To improve the lot of Latin Americans, there needs to be an improvement in the educational, economic, and political institutions and infrastructures.

On a positive note, many Latin American countries, such as Chile and Mexico, are focusing on reducing poverty, improving education, and making other social improvements. Brazil, Chile, and Mexico are the most economically progressive. Even before the Free Trade Area of the Americas process was launched in 1994, many Latin American countries were working to improve their economies. Several, including Argentina and Venezuela, have political instability, which creates barriers to growth. Brazil and Mexico combined account for nearly two-thirds of Latin America's GDP. In addition, during the 1980s and 1990s, many Latin American countries turned to privatization of traditionally public companies, which has opened the door to foreign investment. In the 1990s foreign investment for privatization represented 36 percent of all foreign direct investment in Latin American countries. Benefits of privatization include improved efficiency and productivity. However, the debt crisis of the 1980s brought inflation rates above 30 percent for three out of four countries in Latin America. Although it is unclear whether the reforms were directly responsible, by the end of 1996, only one country had an annual inflation rate over 30 percent. Despite the benefits of privatization, failures have fed resentment of privatization efforts because corruption has ensured an unequal distribution of monies.

In the present-day United States, Latin Americans are a major influence. Statistics released in 2002 show that a total of 20 million of the world's 150 million migrants were born in a Latin American or Caribbean country. Seventy percent of that 20 million settled in the United States, which has long been a major destination for Latin Americans. The United States's Hispanic population grew much faster than the population as a whole, increasing from 35.3 million on April 1, 2000, to 38.8 million on July 1, 2002. This makes the Latin American community the nation's largest minority. Whereas the rate of growth in the United States as a whole was 2.5 percent, the Hispanic population grew 9.8 percent between Census Day, April 1, 2000, and July 1, 2002. The results show that about 53 percent of the recent growth among Latin Americans can be attributed to net international migration, while natural increases, the difference between births and deaths, accounted for the remaining 47 percent. About 80 percent of the Latino population in the United States comes from Mexico, Cuba, and Puerto Rico.

Hispanic American buying power is about $580 billion. By 2008 their buying power is expected to reach almost $1 trillion. The states with the greatest concentration of Hispanic buying power include California, Texas, Florida, New York, Illinois, New Jersey, Arizona, Colorado, Georgia, and New Mexico. Latin American immigrants come to the United States for many reasons: to flee from political strife, to join family already living in the United States, or to have more promising economic opportunities.

DENISE T. OGDEN

See also **Afro-Brazilians; Afro-Caribbeans; Afro-Cubans; Afro-Latin Americans; Amerindians; Antigua and Barbuda; Argentina; Asians in Latin America; Bahamas; Barbados; Belize; Bolivia; Brazil; Canada; Chile; Colombia; Colonialism; Costa Rica; Cuba; Dominican Republic; Ecuador; El Salvador; Grenada; Guatemala; Haiti; Honduras; Jamaica; Mexico; Nicaragua; Panama; Paraguay; Peru; Portugal; Puerto Rican-Americans; Saint Kitts and Nevis; Saint Lucia; Uruguay; Venezuela**

Further Reading

Cleary, Edward L., *Crisis and Change: The Church in Latin America Today*, Maryknoll, New York: Orbis Books, 1985

Cleary, Edward L., and Hannah Stewart-Gambino, editors, *Conflict and Competition: The Latin American Church in a Changing Environment*, Boulder, Colorado: Lynne Rienner, 1992

Collier, Simon, *From Cortes to Castro: An Introduction to the History of Latin America, 1492–1973*, New York: Macmillan, 1974

Crow, John A., *The Epic of Latin America,* Berkeley: University of California Press, 4th edition, 1946

Diamond, Larry, Juan J. Linz, and Seymour Martin Lipset, editors, *Democracy in Developing Countries,* Boulder, Colorado: Lynne Rienner, 1989

Gilbert, Alan, *Latin America,* New York: Routledge, 1990

Henríquez, Ureña Pedro, *A Concise History of Latin American Culture*, translated by Gilbert Chase, New York: Praeger, 1966

Herring, Hubert, *A History of Latin America,* New York: Alfred A. Knopf, 1965

Klien, Herbert S., *African Slavery in Latin America and the Caribbean,* New York: Oxford University Press, 1986

Lockhart, James, and Stuart Schwartz, *Early Latin America: A History of Colonial Spanish America and Brazil,* Cambridge and New York: Cambridge University Press, 1983

Madariaga, Salvador de, *The Rise of the Spanish American Empire*, New York: The Macmillan Company, 1947

Needler, Martin C., *An Introduction to Latin American Politics: The Structure of Conflict,* Englewood Cliffs, New Jersey: Prentice Hall, 2nd edition, 1983

Shorris, Earl, *Latinos,* New York: W.W. Norton, 1992

Skidmore, Thomas E., and Peter H. Smith, *Modern Latin America,* New York: Oxford University Press, 3rd edition, 1992

Wade, Peter, *Race and Ethnicity in Latin America,* London: Pluto, 1997

Latvia

Capsule Summary

Country Name: Latvia
Location: eastern coast of the Baltic Sea
Total Population: 2,348,784 (2003)
Ethnic Populations: Russians, Belarusians, Ukrainians, Poles, Lithuanians, Jews, Roma, others
Languages: Latvian (state language), Russian (widely spoken; main minority language)
Religions: Evangelic Lutheran, Roman Catholic, Russian Orthodox, Russian Old-Believers

Latvia is a country on the eastern cost of the Baltic Sea in Europe. It is a parliamentary republic. More than 42 percent of Latvia's residents belong to minority groups, and about 40 percent of the population is Russian-speaking. Latvian is the only state language. Most Latvians belong to Evangelic Lutheran or Roman Catholic churches, while most Russians, Belarusians, and Ukrainians attend Russian Orthodox or Old-Believers' churches. The GDP per capita as of 2002 was $8,900.

Latvia had traditionally been ethnically heterogeneous. In 1914, about 40 percent of its population of 2.6 million was ethnically non-Latvian. The minority presence was especially strong in major cities. The devastation of World War I had forced many residents, mostly urban, to flee, thus plunging the country's population down to 1.6 million and considerably changing its ethnic composition. By 1935 the population had grown to almost 2 million, while the share of non-Latvians remained relatively high, at 24 percent, including 206,000 Russians (10.59 percent), 93,000 Jews (4.79 percent), 62,000 Germans (3.19 percent), and 49,000 Poles (2.51 percent).

Latvia's independence was first declared on November 18, 1918. Following the armed struggle for independence, Latvia developed as a parliamentary democracy between 1920 and 1934. Policies implemented during that period demonstrated a high degree of tolerance and accommodation of minority interests.

Citizenship legislation stipulated territorial but not ethnic criteria, thus granting Latvian citizenship to practically all residents. Minority cultural and political organizations, as well as a press, have developed. Minorities were represented in the parliament and took part in several governmental coalitions. Education law allowed for a wide network of minority schools to be established with state and local governments providing financing and facilities. By 1934, alongside 1,500 Latvian schools (i.e., schools with Latvian language of instruction), the state financed 236 Russian schools, 100 Jewish schools, and 88 German schools, as well as schools for Polish, Lithuanian, Estonian, and Belarusian minorities .

The coup d'état in May 1934 led to the establishment of an authoritarian regime, which curtailed minority rights. In the cultural domain, authorities advocated assimilation for minorities, closing most of their schools. The New Law on People's Education introduced the policy that any child with at least one ethnically Latvian parent had to study in a Latvian language school.

World War II brought new devastation to the country, as executions, deportations, and exile affected much of the population. The German population, whose presence in the country had greatly influenced the course of Latvia's history since the thirteenth century, practically ceased to exist. The Molotov-Riebentrop Pact of August 1939 brought Latvia into the Soviet sphere of interests, and Nazi Germany urged the Baltic Germans to leave. The Jewish minority had made a considerable contribution to the development of Latvia since the sixteenth century. However, most of Latvia's Jews perished in the Holocaust. Only about 1,000 Jews survived the Nazi occupation.

In 1940, the Soviet Union illegally annexed Latvia. All Latvia's communities suffered from repression in the wake of this act, including local Russian and Jewish minorities, whose elite were persecuted.

During the Soviet era, Latvia's population grew, largely because of migration from other parts of the Soviet Union; by 1989 the percentage of non-Latvians was 48 percent. However, the development of minority cultures during the Soviet era was severely restricted, since the state maintained strict control over all spheres of life and ruthlessly eliminated all forms of self-organization, including cultural and minority advocate groups.

The rapid growth of the non-Latvian population caused ethnic Latvians to fear that they would become a minority in the country. This trend was reversed, however, after the restoration of Latvia's independence in August 1991, and from 1990 onward the proportion of ethnically non-Latvians has been in continual decline because of emigration and negative natural increase. In 2003, ethnic Russians constituted 29.6 percent of the total population, ethnic Belarusians 4.1 percent, Ukrainians 2.7 percent, Poles 2.5 percent, Lithuanians 1.4 percent, and others 2 percent.

A unique aspect of Latvia's situation is that a large proportion of its minorities do not have any citizenship. In October 1991, the Latvian parliament restored the prewar citizenry, thus depriving citizenship rights to one-third of its own voters. Radical Latvian politicians called for the exportation of noncitizens. Only in April 1995 was a separate law adopted that legalized their continued residence in Latvia. Since 1995, only a small fraction of noncitizens (about 5 percent) have been naturalized.

Latvia's legislation limits the rights and opportunities of noncitizens in political, economic, and social spheres. The overall effect of these measures (combined with language legislation; see following text) on minorities is higher rates of unemployment and underrepresentation in decision-making bodies and state bureaucracies.

Latvia has a Latvian-speaking majority (around 60 percent) and a Russian-speaking minority (around 40 percent). Other minority languages, although also present in Latvia, are not so widespread. Only 5 percent of the population employs a language other than Latvian or Russian in the home. Language legislation imposes the Latvian language and curtails the usage of all other languages, including minority languages, in education, electronic media, state and private employment, and other areas. Since 1991, education in Russian has been eliminated in the state universities, and by 2004 secondary education in minority languages was eliminated.

The fall of communism allowed for the development of various cultural, religious, and political nongovernmental organizations in Latvia. Thus far, they have failed to acquire mass membership and cannot claim to represent entire minority populations. Since the late 1980s, a number of non-Russian minority schools and classes have been established, catering to the Belarusian, Jewish, Polish, Estonian, Lithuanian, Roma, and Ukrainian populations. However, less then 1 percent of all pupils are enrolled in these schools.

BORIS KOLTCHANOV

See also **Belarusians; Lithuanians; Poles; Roma (Gypsies); Russians; Ukrainians**

Further Reading

Antane, Aina, and Boris Tsilevich, "Nation-Building and Ethnic Integration in Latvia," in *Nation-Building and Ethnic Integration in Bipolar Post-Soviet Societies: The Cases of Latvia and Kazakhstan*, edited by Pal Kolsto, Boulder, Colorado: Westview, 1999Dribins, Leo, editor, *National and Ethnic Groups in Latvia*, Riga: Ministry of Justice of the Republic of Latvia, National Affairs Section, 1996

Kamenska, Anhelita, *The State Language in Latvia: Achievements, Problems and Prospects*, Riga: Latvian Center for Human Rights and Ethnic Studies, 1995

Lieven, Anatol, *The Baltic Revolution: Estonia, Latvia, Lithuania and the Path to Independence*, New Haven, Connecticut: Yale University Press, 1994

Misiunas, Romuald J., and Rein Taagepera, *The Baltic States: Years of Dependence, 1940–1980*, London: Hurst, 1983

Mitrofanov, Miroslav, "Language in a Multicultural Community: The Case of Daugavpils," in *Managing Diversity in Plural Societies: Minorities, Migration and Nation-Building in Post-Communist Europe*, Nepean, Ontario: Forum Eastern Europe, 1998,

Pettai, Vello, "Emerging Ethnic Democracy in Estonia and Latvia," in *Managing Diversity in Plural Societies: Minorities, Migration and Nation-Building in Post-Communist Europe*, Nepean, Ontario: Forum Eastern Europe, 1998,

Tsilevich, Boris, "Judicial, Legislative and Educational Approaches to Overcome Discrimination in the Baltic Countries," in *The New Yalta: Commemorating the 50th Anniversary of the Declaration of Human Rights in RBEC Region*, New York: Regional Bureau for Europe and CIS of the UNDP, 1998

Le Pen, Jean Marie (French)

On April 22, 2002, the day after the first round of the presidential election in France, the name of Jean Marie Le Pen was mentioned in newspapers around the world. Jean Marie Le Pen was voted through to the second round of elections, with 16.8 percent of the cast votes, against 19.8 percent for Jacques Chirac, his future adversary. Le Pen's strong showing was unusual, given his political views, which are to the far right of the political spectrum. However, his presence in the second round of voting served as a reminder that Jean Marie Le Pen and his party, the Front National (FN), have been active players in French politics for more than 20 years.

Although 2002 did not represent the first time that Le Pen had stood in a presidential election, it was the first time he had received such a significant portion of the vote. In 1981 he was unable to procure the 500 signatures he needed to present himself as a candidate. He has stood for election three other times. In 1974, he obtained 0.7 percent of the cast votes. In 1988, he received 14.4 percent, and in 1995, 15.2 percent.

Thus, 2002 was not the first time Le Pen had been prominent on the national scene. He first appeared on the political stage in the 1950s as the secretary general for the 1965 presidential campaign of the far-right candidate Jean-Louis Tixier-Vignancour. Le Pen is recognized for his public speaking skills; less positively, he is known for making racist remarks regarding some prominent French politicians, Jewish people, and some historical events.

The creation of the FN presented Le Pen with a platform from which to present his ideas about France and the world. He has always acted as leader of the party, although he faced dissent from Bruno Mégret, who left the party in 1998 to form the National Republican Movement (MNR), which hoped to present a more modernized version of far-right politics. The FN primarily focuses on four general themes: exaltation of the French national identity; defense of traditional values; the threat of Europe and France losing their national identity to a greater European identity; and resistance to immigration.

The issue of immigration enabled Le Pen to gain significant media coverage and increase the number of his supporters. According to Le Pen, immigration is a danger for France, especially immigration from North Africa. He proposes returning all immigrants to their native countries. Le Pen particularly stigmatizes Algerian immigrants. According to Le Pen, immigrants are responsible of the persistence of unemployment in

France, as well as for increases in overall drug addiction, delinquency, and prostitution. When Le Pen presented his ideas in an uncertain and anxious social and economic atmosphere, his ideas were received with a notable degree of support. This allowed the FN to gain a more secure place in the French political landscape, as did a change in the ballot system. The FN is represented in different elected positions, including mayor and communal counsillor, in towns including Dreux, Orange, and Vitrolles. It has formed alliances with other right-leaning parties so as to obtain some key executive positions.

The year 2004 was potentially a crucial year for Le Pen (then age 76), as he campaigned for the presidency in regional elections in the region of Provence-Alpes-Côte-d'Azur. Given his age, it may be that he hoped for a final, definitive victory or accomplishment to mark his political career.

Biography

Jean Marie Le Pen. Born 20 June 1928 in *la Trinité-sur-Mer*, department of *Morbihan*. Studied at Assas University. Graduated in social politics and law. President of the association *la Corpo* of the students of Assas, 1949–51. Served as a legionary in the War of Indo-China, 1953. Deputy of Paris, January 1956. Enlisted in a battalion of parachutists in the war of Algeria, secretary-general of the National Front of Combatants. Deputy of Paris, 1958. Founder of the Society of Studies and Public Relations (SERP), a phonographic publishing house, 1963. Founder of the Front National (FN), 1972. Communal councillor of the 20th district of Paris, 1983. Deputy of Paris and president of the FN at the National Assembly 1986–88. Regional councillor of Île-de-France 1986–92. European deputy, 1984; reelected in 1989, 1994, 1999. Regional councillor of Provence-Alpes-Côte-d'Azur, 1992; reelected in 1998. Forced to resign in April 2000 following a sentence for "violence on persona trustee of the public authority." Living in Saint-Cloud, department of Hauts-de-Seine.

MONIQUE MILIA-MARIE-LUCE

See also **France; French**

Further Reading

Camus, Jean-Yves, *Le Front National: Histoire et analyses*, Paris: O. Laurens, 1996; 2nd édition augmentée, 1997.
Milza, Pierre, *Les fascismes,* édition du Seuil, 1985
Souchard, Maryse, Stéphane Wahnich, Isabelle Cuminal, and Virginie Wathier, *Le Pen, les mots: Analyse d'un discours d'extrême-droite*, Paris: édition La Découverte, 1997

League of Nations and Minorities

After World War I, the Austro-Hungarian Empire was dismantled, and new boundaries were drawn to promote the self-determination of peoples. President Woodrow Wilson had said that the Allies were guaranteeing the peace settlement and should not be expected "to leave elements of disturbance unremoved, which we believe would disturb the peace of the world." It was therefore proposed that the Covenant of the League of Nations should include provisions for the protection of minorities. Precedents in international law had existed for such protection, such as a treaty in 1815 concerning the reunion of Belgium with the Netherlands and the treaty concluding the Crimean War. When the Covenant was under discussion, several states were anxious that the League should have no power to supervise the way they treated their minorities, so it was proposed that new states, as a condition for their admission to the League, should be required to treat racial or national minorities the same as the majority. In the end these proposals failed and the protection of minorities was left to specific agreements, which came to be known as the Minorities Treaties. The humanitarian stipulations that President Wilson originally intended to be universal were, for political reasons, finally imposed on only a small number of states.

The first group of treaties included those imposed on the defeated states of Austria, Hungary, Bulgaria, and Turkey. The second included either new states created out of the dissolution of the Ottoman Empire or states whose boundaries were altered to achieve self-determination, including Czechoslovakia, Greece, Poland, Romania, and Yugoslavia. Third, special provisions regarding minorities were included in the regimes established for the Åland Islands, Danzig, the Memel Territory, and Upper Silesia. General provision was made in each treaty to ensure the protection of "common rights," namely, the acquisition of nationality based on habitual residence or parental birthplace, the right to life and liberty, the free exercise of religious belief, and equal admission to public employment, commerce, or profession. Only nationals were to enjoy civil and political rights. Minorities were to have an equal right to control their own schools and use their language. The treaties established two basic principles: the principle of equality or nondiscrimination, and the principle that persons belonging to minorities could exercise certain special rights by acting in combination. The Minorities Treaties promised that the enjoyment of these rights would be supervised by the League of Nations, but only states concerned for persons outside their frontiers who shared the same ethnic origin as their own nationals were motivated to invoke the supervisory procedures. In the 1930s opinion was moving in favor of a universal antidiscrimination provision, but the system lapsed with the dissolution of the League in 1946.

The principles discussed in the League were subsequently developed in the United Nations. They also affected the conception of what sort of group was to be considered a minority. It is important that readers in the twenty-first century are not misled on this point. When, in 1948, some delegations to the United Nations wanted the Universal Declaration on Human Rights to include positive measures for the protection of minorities, they did not have in mind the sorts of groups that have been called minorities in the United Statues. They thought of national minorities of the kind with which the League had been concerned. This is one reason why some states have maintained that there are no minorities within their boundaries.

MICHAEL BANTON

See also **Self-Determination; United Nations and Minorities**

Further Reading

Fawcett, James, *The International Protection of Minorities*, London: Minority Rights Group, 1979

Hannum, Hurst, *Autonomy, Sovereignty, and Self-Determination: The Accommodation of Conflicting Rights*, Philadelphia: University of Pennsylvania Press, 1990

McKean, Warwick, *Equality and Discrimination under International Law*, Oxford: Clarendon, 1983

Lebanese

Capsule Summary

Location: United States, Latin America, Europe, Middle East, Canada, Australia, New Zealand
Total Population: 1,785,000 in Lebanon; 690,000 worldwide
Languages: Arabic (official state language of Lebanon), French, English, Armenian
Religions: Maronite Catholicism, Islam (both Sunni and Shiite), Greek Orthodox, Melkite Catholicism, Druse

Three major waves of emigration from Lebanon in the nineteenth and twentieth centuries produced substantial and continuing Lebanese minorities throughout the world. The first extended from around 1880 to the end of World War I, the second from the end of World War II to the 1970s, and the third during and after the 1975–90 war in Lebanon. Over the two centuries, emigration from Lebanon has been caused by various combinations of political, economic, and social factors.

In the first great migration wave, an estimated 120,000 had left Lebanon by 1900, seeking economic opportunities in countries of mass migration. Although the goal for most was the United States, many ended up in Brazil, Argentina, and other Latin American countries. By 1896 emigration from Lebanon was running at 5,500 a year. In 1900–1914 some 225,000 "Syrians" or "Turks" (the designations for Lebanese in the United States and Latin America, respectively) had emigrated. It is estimated that during this first wave some 350,000 Lebanese left, two thirds to the United States and most of the rest to Latin America. Much smaller numbers were to be found in Canada, Australia, and

New Zealand. The first wave of emigrants were predominantly young, single males from a Christian background. They typically started as peddlers or hawkers as a first step along the pathway of economic and social mobility, which brought with it eventual assimilation to the host society.

The second wave after World War II consisted primarily of economic migration in family groups, with peaks coinciding with conflicts in the Middle East such as the 1967 Arab-Israeli War. There was also a movement of young men from Lebanon for study and/or employment in the more developed economies of Europe and elsewhere in the Middle East. This labor migration led either to permanent settlement abroad or return to Lebanon.

During the civil war period, some 990,000 Lebanese, or 40 percent of the population, sought refuge, either temporarily or permanently, from political conflict in Lebanon. Of these, some 300,000 returned to Lebanon. One-half of the remainder went elsewhere in the Middle East, and the other half emigrated to Europe, North and South America, Africa, and Australia. These emigrants were of diverse economic status and multisectarian, and they migrated in family groups.

Lebanese as Minorities

Lebanese exist as minority populations in the Middle East, the United States, Latin America, Australia, West Africa, Europe, and the Caribbean. The Arab countries and other countries of the Middle East have been an important destination, especially during times of political upheaval. Those who left Lebanon often returned to their home country. Given its proximity to Lebanon, Cyprus has been an important staging post for those fleeing from Lebanon before their return or emigration elsewhere. While the earliest emigration in the region was for trading opportunities in Egypt, in later years the oil-rich Gulf states and Saudi Arabia were major destinations.

North America includes the United States, which contains the largest Lebanese minority in the world, and Canada, with a much smaller Lebanese population. Since the latter part of the nineteenth century, tales of wealth to be amassed in "Amrika" and especially in "Nayurk" ensured a massive emigration to the United States. The imposition of a quota system in 1924 slowed the inflow, and many who intended to settle in the United States found their way to Canada, Mexico,

the Caribbean Islands, and South America. An estimated 2 million Americans are of Lebanese descent. The early Lebanese immigrants and their descendants have all but completely assimilated, whereas the latest wave have maintained a close connection to their former homeland. The Lebanese community in the United States is sufficiently large to have established places of worship for all the sects, with some churches being founded as early as the 1890s. The Lebanese also established educational, cultural, and charitable organizations in the early twentieth century, but sectarian divisions meant that a single national secular organization to represent the Lebanese was not established until 1967.

By 1917 all immigrants to the United States were required to be literate and free of diseases and disabilities. This forced some to seek admission to other countries, such as Brazil, Argentina, and other Latin American countries. The Lebanese minorities in Argentina and Brazil are the largest in the world after that of the United States. Other substantial minorities are to be found in Mexico, Uruguay, Venezuela, Bolivia, Chile, Guinea, Colombia, Ecuador, Costa Rica, the Dominican Republic, and Haiti. First-wave settlers were peddlers and small shopkeepers, whereas later generations became involved in a great variety of industries. Over the years Lebanese moved from rural areas to major towns and cities. For example, some 70 percent of Lebanese in Brazil live in Sao Paulo.

The settlement of Lebanese in Australia and New Zealand largely followed the pattern found in the United States. It is marked by three waves of settlement, economic and social mobility over the generations, and the almost complete assimilation of first- and second-wave families. Third-wave immigrants and their families are retaining more of their Lebanese culture than did the families of earlier immigrants. The Lebanese-born and their descendants number some 250,000. The Lebanese in Australia are heavily concentrated in the larger cities, with Sydney being home to some 75 percent of Australia's Lebanese. Lebanese churches, mosques, and other cultural and welfare organizations have been established in the larger centers. West Africa includes eleven coastal countries from Senegal to Nigeria and three countries in the interior: Mali, Burkina Faso, and Niger. In these colonial and postcolonial states, Lebanese often took the role of "middle men" in the economy, trading such diverse goods as rubber, diamonds, coffee, cocoa, and retail goods. Traders and storekeepers spread far and wide across

West Africa. By 1950 Lebanese had moved from villages to towns and into a wider range of industries. The adaptation of Lebanese to these societies was based largely on ethnic differentiation, with the Lebanese tending to form ethnic enclaves rather than becoming assimilated into the host society. However, over time, those living and working in West Africa came to see themselves as "Afro-Libanais" rather than as Lebanese.

Lebanese minorities are to be found in many countries of Europe, including France, Denmark, Germany, Britain, the Netherlands, and Austria. Young Lebanese immigrated to Europe to gain professional education and occupations or to find a place of refuge in times of war and civil disturbance. France has been the major destination, given its traditional language and cultural ties with Lebanon. France has the largest Lebanese minority in Europe, numbering some 100,000 permanent residents, students, and visitors. Although they have been living and working there for many years, many Lebanese have not opted for permanent settlement in France.

All Caribbean islands have Lebanese people, whose adaptation has involved different degrees of assimilation or ethnic differentiation, depending on attitudes of the host society and government. For example, in Trinidad the Lebanese have remained fairly distinct, tending to marry within the ethnic group, whereas in Jamaica they have often married outside the ethnic group and have become involved in a wide variety of occupations. In these societies Lebanese have often occupied an intermediary economic and social position between indigenous people and European elites.

Lebanese communities reflect different and often conflicting attitudes toward the host society. For example, communities can be divided into "old" and "new" Lebanese. The "old" migrants, who immigrated before the 1975–90 war in Lebanon, have accumulated cultural capital in the host society and are proud of their economic and social achievements, which they feel are being threatened by the new arrivals. This group established a range of community organizations, such as churches, mosques, schools, and other cultural and social bodies. The "new" migrants, who emigrated during and after the war in Lebanon, have been confronted with settlement difficulties, including unemployment, vilification, and cultural conflicts among the young. Following the two Gulf Wars and September 11, 2001, many are critical of what they see as negative stereotypes of Lebanese and Arabs in the media and of their treatment by government bodies.

Two distinct patterns may be found in the adaptation of Lebanese to the host societies in which they live: assimilation or cultural differentiation. In mass migration societies, the early Lebanese immigrants typically experienced a cultural loss as the process of assimilation accelerated with every generation. In countries such as Argentina, where government policy was strongly assimilationist, the process was widespread and thorough. Assimilation often involved the changing or adaptation of Lebanese names to Anglo-Saxon or Latin ones. It was to be found also in the loss of the Arabic language and less adherence to eastern churches such as Maronite, Melkite, or Orthodox.

The second pattern, in which the Lebanese formed ethnic enclaves, is to be found in those states where Lebanese were not accepted as equals by the incumbent European elites, such as the French in the Ivory Coast or the Spanish in Brazil. In these societies their intermediary economic status was converted into an intermediary social status. In West Africa, in particular, most Lebanese would return to Lebanon when the time came for retirement.

In almost every country where they settled and worked, Lebanese suffered from various degrees of racial discrimination. In the early part of the century, the occupation of peddling was heavily criticized as nonproductive and parasitical. This merged with racial criticism of the "Turk" or "Syrian" (as the Lebanese were then known) among politicians and in the popular press, and a number of states (Australia in 1901, Canada in 1908, and the United States in 1924) enacted legislation to prohibit or severely limit the entry of this group, among others. During the same period there were anti-Lebanese riots (Sierra Leone, 1919) and deportations (Côte d'Ivoire, 1928–38) in West African states. A second form of discrimination was the denial of citizenship. However, over time, both forms of discrimination gave way in the face of efforts by the Lebanese to gain equal treatment with other groups. In some societies, Lebanese were resented for their economic success.

Emigration inevitably raises the question of identity. In some societies of mass migration, most Lebanese embarked on the pathway of becoming full citizens and members of the host society. For these people, the term *Lebanese background* refers to their family's past rather than to their current status. In other cases, people choose to adopt a hybrid identity: "Lebanese-Australian" or "Afro-Libanais." Then there are others who continue to identify themselves simply as "Lebanese."

Family, village, and religion are important as identifiers for Lebanese. In some countries and even internationally, there are conventions of villages and towns, families and religions. In this way Lebanese can see themselves as members of transnational bodies linked by the latest in communications technology. Thus globalization is making an impact on the social relations of Lebanese and their identities.

TREVOR BATROUNEY

See also **Assimilation; Muslims: Shi'a in Sunni Countries**

Further Reading

Aboud, Brian, "The Arab Diaspora: Immigration History and the Narratives of Presence, Australia, Canada and the USA," in *Arab-Australians Today: Citizenship and Belonging,* edited by Ghassan Hage, Carlton South, Victoria, Australia: Melbourne University Press, 2002

Batrouney, Andrew, and Trevor Batrouney, *The Lebanese in Australia,* Melbourne: AE Press, 1985

Batrouney, Trevor, "Lebanese-Australians: Return Visits to Lebanon and Issues of Identity," paper presented at conference *Lebanese Presence in the World,* Beirut, Lebanon: Centre for Migration Studies, Lebanese American University, June 28–29, 2001

Humphrey, Michael, *ISLAM, Multiculturalism and Transnationalism: From the Lebanese Diaspora,* London: Centre for Lebanese Studies and I.B. Tauris, 1998

———, "Lebanese Identities between Cities, Nations and Trans-Nations," paper presented at conference *Lebanese Presence in the World,* Beirut, Lebanon: Centre for Migration Studies, Lebanese American University, June 28–29, 2001

Issawi, Charles, "The Historical Background of Lebanese Emigration: 1800–1914," in *The Lebanese in the World: A Century of Migration,* edited by Albert Hourani and Nadim Shehadie, London: Centre for Lebanese Studies and I.B. Tauris, 1992

Klich, Ignacio, "*Criollos* and Arabic Speakers in Argentina: An Uneasy *Pas de Deux,* 1888–1914," in *The Lebanese in the World: A Century of Migration,* edited by Albert Hourani and Nadim Shehadie, London: Centre for Lebanese Studies and I.B. Tauris, 1992

Knowlton, Clark, "The Social and Spatial Mobility of the Syrian and Lebanese Community in Sao Paulo, Brazil," in *The Lebanese in the World: A Century of Migration,* edited by Albert Hourani and Nadim Shehadie, London: Centre for Lebanese Studies and I.B. Tauris, 1992

Labaki, Boutros, "Lebanese Emigration during the War (1975–1989)," in *The Lebanese in the World: A Century of Migration,* edited by Albert Hourani and Nadim Shehadie, London: Centre for Lebanese Studies and I.B. Tauris, 1992

Leichtman, Mara, "Reexamining the Transmigrant: The Afro-Libanais of Senegal," paper presented at conference *Lebanese Presence in the World,* Beirut, Lebanon: Centre for Migration Studies, Lebanese American University, June 28–29, 2001

Naff, Alixa, *Becoming American: The Early Arab Immigrant Experience,* Carbondale: Southern Illinois University Press, 1985

Nicholls, David, "Lebanese of the Antilles: Haiti, Dominican Republic, Jamaica and Trinidad," in *The Lebanese in the World: A Century of Migration,* edited by Albert Hourani and Nadim Shehadie, London: Centre for Lebanese Studies and I.B. Tauris, 1992

Tabar, Paul, *Lebanese Migrants in Australia and New Zealand: An Annotated Bibliography,* Lebanon: Lebanese Emigration Research Center, Notre Dame University Press, 2004

Lesotho

Capsule Summary

Country Name: Lesotho
Location: southern Africa, an enclave surrounded by the territory of South Africa
Total Population: 1,861,959 (2003)
Languages: Sesotho, English
Religions: Christian, indigenous beliefs

This tiny country of 30,000 square kilometers (11,700 square miles) is situated in southern Africa and is an enclave entirely surrounded by its neighbor, South Africa. The official languages are Sesotho and English. The country is a constitutional monarchy whose king, Letsie III, is head of state. The Basotho make up the majority of the population (85 percent), and the remainder, except for a handful of expatriates (mainly Europeans or South Africans working in business or economic assistance programs), are subgroups of the Zulus. Lesotho is a poor, underdeveloped country with a per capita GDP of US$2,700 (2002).

The first groups of the Basotho, a Bantu people, settled in what is now Lesotho during the sixteenth century. Their modern history begins in the nineteenth century with the great disturbances, "wars of calamity," or the *mfecane* that arose out of Shaka Zulu's quest for power and dominance over all the Zulu and related peoples in the region centered around modern Natal. Many of the Basotho, who were closely related to the Zulus of southern Africa, were turned into refugees by the *mfecane* and, to escape the embrace of Shaka Zulu, they moved into the rugged mountain territory of Lesotho. Their different groups were welded together by Moshoeshoe, one of the outstanding African leaders of the nineteenth century, who led them into the mountain fastnesses of Lesotho to create the Basotho Nation. By the middle of the nineteenth century, however, the small ethnically cohesive Basotho Nation found itself caught up in a wider conflict that developed between the British imperialists then establishing their control over Natal from the Cape and the Boers (Afrikaners) busy creating the new republic of the Orange Free State for themselves. Although, at first, he was able to keep the advancing Boers at bay, Moshoeshoe realized that he was not strong enough to do so indefinitely, and in 1868 he persuaded Britain to declare a protectorate over Basutoland, the state he had created. However, initially, to avoid expense, Britain handed over control of Basutoland to Cape Colony; this was an unsatisfactory arrangement, and after a war between the Basotho and the Cape (colonial) authorities, Britain resumed direct control in 1884. Basutoland was to remain a British protectorate until independence in 1966. An important proviso, agreed to by Britain and the Basotho, was that no white settlement should be permitted in the territory. The country remained a monarchy through colonial times and into the independence era, and the present king (2001), Letsie III, is a direct descendant of Moshoeshoe (the Great).

Under the Act of Union of 1910, whereby Britain united the four territories of southern Africa to form the Dominion or Union of South Africa, it also made provision for Basutoland to be incorporated into South Africa should the people agree to such an arrangement. Throughout the years 1910–66 the people of Basutoland were unwavering in their opposition to becoming part of their neighbor, South Africa. Even so, in real terms the Basotho represent a minority within the territory of South Africa that surrounds their tiny country.

Lesotho became independent in 1966, and the political life of the country thereafter often took the form of a power struggle between the prime minister, on the one hand, and the king and his supporters on the other, with the king determined to be more than just a constitutional monarch. Lesotho's postindependence politics were greatly complicated by the role played by South Africa. From 1966 (independence) to 1994 (the end of apartheid), South Africa, whose territory entirely surrounds Lesotho, used its economic and (sometimes) military strength to threaten and intervene in the affairs of its small neighbor, with the result that much of the country's energies were taken up in the first 30 years of its independent existence defying or holding at bay South African pressures.

The economy of Lesotho is heavily dependent upon that of South Africa. Up to a quarter of adult males migrate to South Africa at any one time on a temporary basis to work in the mines or on the land, while Lesotho's own land is overfarmed and unable to support the needs of the population. There are few other resources except a vast hydroelectric power potential, and most of that—the Oxbow Scheme—has been mortgaged to South Africa. The annual revenues from its membership in the South African Customs Union, remittances from migrant workers, and international aid are the three main sources of national income.

Lesotho's strength lies in the homogeneity of its people: 85 percent are Basotho, and they have a proud, close tradition of ethnic solidarity; the Zulus, the minority group, are closely related to the Basotho. The Sotho are a conglomerate of tribes that belong to the Southern Sotho linguistic stock. They unite in their loyalty to the royal house of Moshoeshoe. The core group are the Kwene, composed of the Molileli, Monaheng, Hlakwana, Kxwakxwa, and Fokeng. This core group considers itself superior to two other groups that have been absorbed into Lesotho's homogeneous society. These are the Nguni (Ngoni), which include the Phetla, Polane, and Phuti; and another Nguni group, which includes the Mahlape (from Natal) and the Themba (Cape or South Nguni). The Nguni are offshoots of the Zulus.

Over 80 percent of the population is Christian: there are 100,000 Anglicans, over 700,000 Roman Catholics, and slightly over 200,000 members of the Lesotho Evangelical Church, while about another 100,000 belong to various African independent churches.

GUY ARNOLD

See also **Bantu; South Africa**

Further Reading

Ashton, H., *The Basuto*, London and New York: Oxford University Press, 1952; 2nd edition, 1967

Hailey, Lord, *South Africa and the High Commission Territories*, London: Oxford University Press, 1965

Halpern, Jack, *South Africa's Hostages: Bechuanaland, Basutoland and Swaziland,* Harmondsworth, Penguin Books, 1965

Sanders, Peter, *Moshoeshoe, Chief of the Sotho*, London: Heinemann, 1976

Spence, J. E., *Lesotho: The Politics of Dependence*, London: Oxford University Press for the Institute of Race Relations, 1967

Lévesque, René (Canadian)

René Lévesque was the cofounder of the Parti Québécois (PQ) and the premier of Quebec for two terms between 1976 and 1985. Parti Québécois is a political party that advocates national independance for Quebec. Lévesque was the hope for many generations of francophones who wanted to gain more respect from English-Canadians. He helped to forge a new national identity for those who considered themselves French-Canadians until the 1970s and, afterwards, as "Québécois." This identity shift meant they no longer regarded themselves as a francophone minority within an English-speaking Canada, but rather as a part of a French nation named Quebec. For Lévesque, Quebec was not just a founding province of Canada; it was a nation in itself, distinct for linguistic reasons and strong enough to become an independent country.

Raised in the Gaspé peninsula, Lévesque was already well known when he entered politics in 1960 because he had hosted a very popular weekly show, *Point de mire* (1956–59), dedicated to current affairs and international relations, on the French language television network, Radio-Canada. Every week, Lévesque appeared as a communicator who could explain international conflicts and foreign crises using only a boardwalk, a map, and a chalk. He began working at 19 as a freelance reporter for several radio stations. In 1943, he was hired as war correspondent in Europe for the U.S. Army. After his political career (1960–85), he returned to television for a few months, until his death in 1987.

Fluent in English as well as French, Lévesque often said that he felt at home in London. Although he was fascinated by the United States, he confessed in 1969 that he felt bored when he traveled in English Canada, but he never felt hostile toward English-Canadians. He often repeated that he did not identify with the Canadian identity and that he never felt the sentiment to be a Canadian. Despite these personal opinions, he believed that Quebec ought to be French-speaking by definition, showing a francophone image and multicultural identity with respect to natives and English-speaking citizens.

> The Party pushes for better English teaching, but on the other hand, collectively, community-wise in Quebec, the basic official language and the language of promotion should be French. (Lévesque, quoted in Michel Lévesque, editor, *René Lévesque: textes et entretiens*, 1991 [1975], p. 141)

As a politician, Lévesque maintained two careers. From 1960 to 1970, he was a dynamic deputy and a dominant figure. This was the era of the "*Révolution tranquille*" (a peaceful, quiet revolution), a decade of prosperity that succeeded the conservative politics of Prime Minister Maurice Duplessis (1890–1959), a populist politician and premier of Quebec who was reelected many times between 1944 and 1959. From 1960 to 1966, Lévesque spearheaded the nationalization of hydroelectricity in Quebec, when all the independent power companies were bought by the Quebec government, giving the state the control of energy on its own territory.

It is during this period of fast changes and reforms (1960–68) that Lévesque understood the capacity for Quebec to become an independent country, as did many much poorer African colonies that became autonomous after World War II. But he always believed that the independence of Quebec had to be accomplished democratically; this was one of the ideas behind his founding of Parti Québécois in 1968. Thus with PQ began Lévesque's second political career.

As one of the guests representing the Quebec government, Lévesque happened to be just a few meters behind Général Charles De Gaulle in July 1967, when the president of France created a commotion by saying, "Vive le Québec libre!" at Montreal's city hall. This unexpected declaration meant that France would approve an independent and autonomous Quebec. Many English-Canadians, including Canada's prime minister Lester B. Pearson, were shocked and asked for an explanation, but Lévesque remained silent about this incident.

In 1966, Lévesque was reelected for the third time as deputy but left the Liberal Party in 1967 to become an independent deputy. After founding Parti Québécois, he ran for election twice, in 1970 and 1973, but failed. Between 1970 and 1975, he worked as reporter and published political essays.

In a 1975 interview, Lévesque explained the identity shift that occurred in Quebec during the 1960s:

> What we had before were people who called themselves French Canadians, but French Canadians were just another minority. Now the French people are becoming conscious that they themselves are really a national majority and that they better get themselves an institutional framework to replace what broke down 20 years ago. (Lévesque, quoted in Michel Lévesque, editor, *René Lévesque: textes et entretiens*, 1991 [1975], p. 142)

On November 15, 1976, Lévesque was elected as the 27th premier of Quebec, and he promoted many reforms. First, all political parties in Quebec were forced by a new law to indicate publicly the list of persons and companies who financed them, with the amount they gave. In any case, the donation limit was $3,000; this way, no one could buy an election. Even in 2004, Canada's federal government has not yet achieved such transparency, but the law stills applies in Quebec for provincial campaigns. Second, he created a "no fault" policy in a nationalized automobile insurance system. But the most important law was the Bill 101 on language rights, which was created to stop the tendency to anglicize a francophone Quebec, isolated in an anglophone country (and continent). Before that, in 1975, airplane controllers in Quebec were forced to talk to each other on the waves in English for security reasons, even if they were francophones. Many people could not be hired in various positions if they did not speak English. Even if they were a majority in Quebec, francophones had to learn the "minority" language to find a job. In addition, before 1976, many commercial signs in Montreal were written only in English. Bill 101, therefore, came as a relief for many French-speaking Québécois but was perceived

as controversial for the dominant anglophone minority and economic leaders, who were challenged by this reversed situation. Before he was elected premier of Quebec, Lévesque also made clear what he wanted concerning immigration in the province of Quebec. He felt that legislation ought to be written to terminate the dominance of the English language.

On May 20, 1980, Lévesque's government asked the 6 million people of Quebec to vote in a historical referendum: 59 percent of the voters said "No" to Lévesque's project of an autonomous, independent Quebec. He conceded defeat because he was a democrat who respected the people's decision. Nonetheless, Lévesque was reelected in 1981 for a second term, with even more votes than in the previous election, probably because people were satisfied by his government (a rare situation in Quebec).

In 1982, the Canadian federal government imposed a new Canadian constitution on the province of Quebec that could not guarantee Quebec's previous laws and linguistic power. Lévesque could not accept a reduction of his province's political power and refused to sign. All nine English-speaking provinces secretly agreed to sign this constitution without Quebec's approval. As a consequence, still in 2004, Quebec is ruled by a constitution that none of its provincial premiers have signed or approved. Furthermore, all political parties in Quebec have always rejected it.

Lévesque retired in 1985 and published his memoirs the next year. He died at 65, on November 1, 1987. Just one year after his death, Montreal and Quebec City named boulevards in his honor. Lévesque had a potent influence on many politicians, including Jacques Parizeau and Lucien Bouchard, who both succeeded him. Chief Billy Diamond, one of the fathers of the Cree nation in Quebec, stated that Lévesque had "done more than anyone else to improve our relations [between natives and nonnatives]" (Billy Diamond, quoted in Luc Chartrand, "Mon meilleur premier ministre," *L'Actualité*, 25, no. 12 (August 2000), p. 20).

Biography

René Lévesque. Born 24 August 1922 in New Carlisle, Canada (Quebec). Son of an attorney. Studied at public schools, Classical College, and later at the Collège Saint-Charles Garnier, in Quebec City. Began a B.A. in law (unfinished) in 1941, Université Laval (Quebec City). Foreign correspondent for the U.S. Office of War Information in London, 1943–45; also freelance film critic for various independent newspapers, 1946–51. Reporter for Radio-Canada, 1951–60. Cofounder of the Parti Québéco (PQ), 1968; president, 1968–85.

Provincial deputy (Laurier County), 1960–67; independent provincial deputy, 1967–70; deputy for the PQ (Taillon County), 1976–85. Minister in the Liberal Cabinet, 1960–66. Premier of Quebec, 1976–1985. Reelected as premier in 1981. Retired from politics 3 October 3 1985. Awards: Prix Olivar-Asselin (1957) for TV show *Point de mire*. Named "*Grand Officier de la Légion d'honne*" and received the *Médaille de la ville de Paris* [Medal of the City of Paris], November 1977. Received an *Honoraris Causa* doctorate from La Sorbonne, 1980. Died in Montreal, Canada (Quebec), 1 November 1987.

Selected Works

Attendez que je me rappelle, 1986; as *Memoirs*, translated by Philip Stratford, 1986

Aux Quatre Vents (unreleased radio play), 1999

Option Québec, 1968; 2nd edition, 1997; as *An Option for Quebec*, 1968

YVES LABERGE

See also **Canada; Québécois**

Further Reading

Bélanger, Yves, et Michel Lévesque, editors, *René Lévesque: l'homme, la nation, la démocratie*, Sillery, Québec: Presses de l'Université du Québec, 1992

Chartrand, Luc, "Mon meilleur premier ministre," *L'Actualité*, 25, no. 12 (August 2000)

"Le Fleur-de-Lys dans l'œil du coq," Le Québec et la France. http://www.er.uqam.ca/nobel/m153660/france.htm

Lévesque, Michel, editor, *René Lévesque: textes et entretiens, 1960–1987*, Sillery, Québec: Presses de l'Université du Québec, 1991

Migneault, Hugues, *Le Choix d'un peuple* 1985, documentary

Perrault, Pierre, *Un pays sans bon sens*, 1970 [1968], documentary

Todd Hénaut, Dorothy, "A Song for Quebec," in the television series *Canada True North*, PBS, 1988

Liberation Tigers of Tamil Eelam (LTTE), *See* Tamil Tigers

Liberia

Capsule Summary

Country Name: Liberia
Location: West Africa; bordered by Sierra Leone, Republic of Guinea, Côte d'Ivoire, and the Atlantic Ocean
Total Population: 2.8 million
Languages: English (official) and about 34 indigenous languages and dialects; Bassa, Gola, Kpelle, Kru, and Vai widely spoken
Religions: Christianity, Islam, African traditional religions

The republic of Liberia is located on the western bulge of West Africa along the Atlantic coast and covers an area of about 111,370 square kilometers (42,988 square miles). Sierra Leone and Guinea border it to the north, Côte d'Ivoire to the east, and the Atlantic coast to the south and west. Liberia has a population of 2.8 million (1999 UN estimate), comprising 16 principal indigenous groups (95 percent) and Americo-Liberians (5 percent), descendants of the original settlers mostly found in Monrovia (capital) and other coastal cities. The main ethnic groups are the Bassa, Gio, Gola, Kpelle, Krahn, Kru, Mandingo, and Vai.

The bulk of Liberia's Christians (30 percent) are Americo-Liberians belonging to different denominations. Muslims form a small minority of which the Mandingo is the largest group. The outbreak of the Liberian civil war in December 1989 caused massive displacements of the population, forcing thousands to seek refuge in neighboring Sierra Leone, Guinea, Côte d'Ivoire, and other West African countries. Liberia is Africa's oldest republic, and it survived the colonial period without losing its independence. The president of Liberia is elected by popular votes to a 6-year term, and he appoints a cabinet to assist him in carrying out the functions of government. The country's GDP per capita is $240 (1998).

The history of modern Liberia begins with the repatriation of liberated black slaves from the United States, who first landed on Providence Island near Monrovia in 1822. Various indigenous groups related to the Kissi, Bassa, Krahn, and Vai had already inhabited the area historically known as the Grain Coast long before the settlers arrived. The Vai, for example, probably settled in this part of West Africa as early as the fourteenth century following the collapse of the Empire of Mali, which forced some groups to migrate toward the coast. Around the sixteenth century waves of the Manes' invasions also forced groups like the Kru and Grebo to head toward the coastal areas. The arrival of the Portuguese around the mid-fifteenth century brought these groups into the European-African trading network that paved the way for the Transatlantic Slave Trade.

Liberia has its roots in the concern over the issue of slavery, which intensified in the aftermath of the American War of Independence. The decision to send free blacks back to their ancestral land was supported by the United States government, which looked to the American Colonization Society (ACS, established in 1816) to implement the scheme. Under the auspices of the ACS, the first group of settlers arrived on the Liberian coast in 1822. Tropical diseases like malaria took a heavy toll on the early settlers.

Liberia became an independent republic on July 26, 1847, after the settlers severed ties with the ACS. However, it was not until the 1860s that the United States government formally recognized Liberia as a sovereign state. Throughout the nineteenth century Liberia struggled to maintain its independence as its Americo-Liberian leaders struggled against British and French attempts to colonize that country. In addition, the Americo-Liberian minority faced stout opposition from indigenous groups, who contested their political dominance. Despite these internal and external threats, Liberia remained Africa's only independent black republic before 1957.

With a total population of about 2.8 million, Liberian society comprises 16 ethnic groups, an Americo-Liberian community, and some foreign residents. Though the minority Americo-Liberians accounts for only about 2.5 percent of the total population, they provide much of the country's political and social leadership. Americo-Liberians are concentrated in Monrovia and other cities along the coast, such as Buchanan, Greenville, Harper, and Robertsport. They speak English and a Creole form called "Liberian English," which is an informal *lingua franca* in Liberia. The bulk of Liberia's Christians are Americo-Liberians belonging to various churches, including the Anglican, Baptist, Lutheran, Methodist, and Roman Catholic.

The largest among Liberia's 16 ethnic groups are the Bassa, Gio, Gola, Kpelle, Krahn, Kru, Mandingo, and Vai, who live throughout the interior and along the southern coast. Most practice traditional African religions, but the Mandingo are predominantly Muslims. Among some of these groups traditional secret societies like the Poro (male) and Sande (female) continue to play important social functions to help prepare their youth for adult life.

Foreign residents in Liberia include Americans, Asians, Europeans, and Africans from neighboring countries. They serve in various capacities and play important roles in the country's economy. Indian and Lebanese businesspeople, for example, are found throughout Liberia, mostly engaged in import/export commercial activities. Liberia's most valuable agricultural export is rubber, and its largest export commodity is iron ore. Before the Liberian civil war, multinational companies like Firestone Plantations Company and Goodyear invested huge sums of money in the country to grow rubber for exportation. The declining world demand for iron ore and rubber during the 1970s adversely affected the Liberian economy.

Until 1980 the Americo-Liberian True Whig Party had dominated Liberian politics for almost a century. Opposition to Americo-Liberian dominance culminated in riots over a proposed increase in the price of rice in 1979. In 1980, President William R. Tolbert was overthrown and killed in a bloody coup led by Master Sergeant (later General) Samuel K. Doe, a Krahn. The constitution was suspended, and prominent members of the previous Americo-Liberian–dominated government were publicly executed. A new constitution was drawn up and approved by a popular referendum in 1984. A significant element of the new constitution was that it eliminated property qualifications for voters. With Liberia's economy worsening and President Doe becoming increasingly repressive, many Liberians began to express doubt about their country's future. The Liberian civil war began in 1989 when rebels led by Charles Taylor, a former government official of Americo-Liberian descent, launched his forces, the National Patriotic Front of Liberia (NPFL), against Doe's government. Doe was captured and brutally murdered by a rebel faction in September 1990. Seven years of fighting left thousands of Liberians dead and much of the country in ruins. Hordes of Liberians sought refuge in neighboring countries. Charles Taylor was declared winner of the 1997 presidential elections after gaining 75 percent of the votes.

Taylor came under increasing attack from neighboring nations at the end of the 1990s because he was suspected of assisting the rebel forces in Sierra Leone. In the meantime, Liberian rebel forces were agitating—with, according to Taylor, the support of other countries. As the Liberian government forces battled the rebel groups, international pressures on Taylor to step down increased. Thousands suffered displacement and starvation. In 2003 Taylor stepped down and went into exile in Nigeria. His former vice president, Moses Blah, acted as Liberia's interim leader.

TAMBA M'BAYO

See also **Americo-Liberians; Slavery; West Africa**

Further Reading

Beyan, Amos, *The American Colonization Society and the Creation of the Liberian State: A Historical Perspective, 1822–1900,* Lanham, Maryland, and London: University Press of America, 1991

Dunn, D. Elwood, *Liberia,* Santa Barbara, California, and Oxford: Clio Press, 1995

Dunn, D. Elwood, and Svend E. Holsoe, *Historical Dictionary of Liberia,* Metuchen, New Jersey, and London: Scarecrow Press, 1985

Sawyer, Amos, *The Emergence of Autocracy in Liberia: Tragedy and Challenge,* San Francisco: Institute for Contemporary Studies, 1992

Shick, Tom, *Behold the Promised Land: A History of Afro-American Settler Society in Nineteenth-Century Liberia,* Baltimore, Madison, and London: Johns Hopkins University Press, 1980

Sisay, Hassan, *Big Powers and Small Nations: A Case Study of United States-Liberian Relations,* Lanham, Maryland: University Press of America, 1985

Staudenraus, P.J., *The American Colonization Movement, 1816–1865,* New York: Columbia University Press, 1961

Liechtenstein

Capsule Summary

Country Name: Liechtenstein
Location: Europe, between Austria and Switzerland
Total Population: 33,145 (2003)
Ethnic Populations: Turkish, Italian
Language: German (official), Alemannic dialect
Religions: Roman Catholic 76.2 percent, Protestant 7 percent, unknown 10.6 percent, other 6.2 percent(June 2002)

Liechtenstein is a 160-square-kilometer (62-square-mile) state with a population of 33,145 people that lies between Austria and Switzerland bordering the Rhine River. The fourth smallest country in Europe, its population is approximately one-third foreigners, mainly Germans, Austrians, and Swiss. It comprises 11 communities (or communes): Balzers, Eschen, Gamprin, Mauren, Planken, Ruggell, Schaan, Schellenberg, Triesen, Triesenberg, and Vaduz.

Liechtenstein has a majority population of nearly 90 percent Alemanni, with the remainder of the population comprised of Turks and Italians. People from Valais, a Swiss canton, settled in Triesenberg around 1400 and are known as the Walsers. The official language is German, but the Alemannic dialect is spoken except in Triesenberg, which has its own variation.

Roman Catholicism is the main religion observed, but Protestantism and other religions are also practiced.

The area encompassing present-day Liechtenstein has been inhabited since at least 3000BCE. Celts, Romans, and a Germanic ethnic group called the Alemanni settled the area around 500; their descendants form the majority of the present-day population. Charlemagne governed the area until 814. Thereafter it was deemed two separate fiefs: Schellenberg and Vaduz. In 1396 it became a fief of the Holy Roman Empire (HRE). To retain a seat in the HRE's Imperial Diet, Liechtenstein became an imperial principality through the amalgamation, on January 23, of Schellenberg and Vaduz as decreed by Emperor Karl VI. A Viennese prince, Johann-Adam Liechtenstein, gained Schellenberg in 1699 and Vaduz in 1712. Although he never resided there, he gave his name to the state.

During the Napoleonic era, Liechtenstein was part of the Confederation of the Rhine, but it gained independence in 1806. Thereafter it was part of the German Confederation, which dissolved in 1866. A customs union with Austria-Hungary in 1852 ended in 1918 after the demise of the Austrian-Hungarian Empire. Liechtenstein then tied itself to Switzerland.

The October 1921 constitution allowed for a hereditary constitutional monarchy ruled by the head of the House of Liechtenstein, who serves as head of state. The current reigning prince is Hans Adam, the son of Francis Joseph II, who was the first prince to live in Vaduz and who reigned from 1938 until 1984. Hans Adam has served as regent since 1984. He is reportedly worth $2 billion. He has threatened to leave if he is not granted more power. In a referendum on March 16, 2003, Hans Adam gained almost dictatorial powers when over two-thirds of the resident 17,000 voters (including women, who were only enfranchised in 1984) supported his demands. The constitution was revised and he became an absolute monarch. In August 2003 Hans Adam announced that his son Alois would take over in 2004.

Ethnic groups residing in Liechtenstein include the Alemannic (86 percent of the population), Italian, Turkish, and other (14 percent). Liechtenstein's small size and landlocked geography require a unique dependency on neighbors. Despite its size and limited natural resources, however, the country maintains a standard of living on a par with its European neighbors. Foreign affairs are entrusted to the Swiss, whose currency is the legal tender. Francis Joseph slowly transformed Liechtenstein into an industrialized country, and it has become a financial center that is a tax haven for over 5,000 companies. Industries include electronics, metal manufacturing, ceramics, pharmaceuticals, food products, precision instruments, tourism, and optical instruments. It has one of the highest standards of living in Europe, with a per capita GDP of $25,000 (1999).

ANNETTE RICHARDSON

See also **Germans; Germany; Switzerland**

Further Reading

Gurney, Gene, *Kingdoms of Europe*, New York: Crown, 1982

Meier, Regula, *Liechtenstein*, Santa Barbara, California: Clio Press, 1993

Raton, Pierre, *Liechtenstein: History and Institutions of the Principality*, Vaduz: Liechtenstein Verlag, 1970

Lithuania

Capsule Summary

Country Name: *Lietuvos Respublika* (Republic of Lithuania)
Location: northeastern Europe
Total Population: 3,592,561
Language: Lithuanian
Religions: Roman Catholic, Russian Orthodox Lutheran, Jewish, Muslim, Evangelical Christian, Baptist, others

Lithuania is located in northeastern Europe; it borders Latvia in the north, Belarus in the south and southeast, Poland in the southwest, and the Russian Federation (Kaliningrad Oblast) in the west. Sweden is across the Baltic Sea in the northwest. The country has a land area of 65,300 square kilometers (25,174 square miles), and it is the largest of the three former Soviet Baltic states.

The population of Lithuania is estimated at 3,592,561. It is predominantly urban, with around 67.8 percent of the people living in cities and towns. The country's capital city, Vilnius (Wilno in Polish), is home to 553,329 people (2001), or 16 percent of the population. Lithuania has a negative population growth rate of –0.29 percent, and it is estimated that the population could decline to 3,220,000 by 2020. Lithuania has a relatively high population density, standing at around 53.5 people per square kilometer (138 people per square mile).

Lithuania is a unitary republic, and its form of government is presidential democracy. The government is the legal successor of the independent government that existed from 1918, when it gained independence from the Russian Empire (Russia then acquired Livonia from Rzecz Pospolita, the Polish-Lithuanian Union), until 1940, when it was annexed by the Soviet Union. The country was the first Soviet Republic to declare its independence from the USSR in March 1990, but the Soviet Union did not recognize its independence until September 1991. In October 1992 the country adopted its new constitution. The *Seimas* (Parliament) is a unicameral 141-member national legislative body. The president is the head of state and is elected by popular vote for a 5-year term with a maximum of two terms. The president nominates the prime minister, who must be approved by the *Seimas*. Since independence a number of political parties, ranging from radical nationalist groups to Christian Democrats, have appeared in the country. According to the constitution, 70 seats are allocated to political organizations that have gained 5 percent or more of the total votes. Despite some tensions between the Lithuanians and ethnic minorities and the emergence of several extreme right organizations, there have never been militant conflicts or confrontations during the post-Soviet era.

Lithuania is a multiethnic country. Ethnic Lithuanians, who are ethnically and linguistically close to the Latvians, make up 80.6 percent of the country's population (2003). Ethnic Russians make up the largest minority of around 8.7 percent of the population, while ethnic Poles make up 7 percent, Belarusians 1.6 percent, and various other groups together the remaining 2 percent of the population. The current ethnic structure was formed after World War II, when the Soviet government encouraged migration from various parts of the Soviet Union. However, unlike neighboring Estonia or Latvia, Lithuania experienced smaller-scale emigration of Russians and other nationalities from the USSR. As a result, throughout the Soviet era the proportion of the Lithuanians in the republic remained roughly the same, at around 79–80 percent. After independence in 1991, around 60,000 residents opted to leave the country.

The Lithuanian language was made an official language of the country in 1988. According to the 1989 census, only around 37.9 percent of ethnic Lithuanians said that they could speak Russian, although the Soviet government promoted the advantage of Russian as a lingua franca in education, the mass media, and everyday life. Unlike in Estonia and Latvia, language policy was not a central issue in political debates because the Law on Citizenship, adopted in 1989, granted citizenship to all people who lived in Lithuania, without the restrictions seen in Estonia or Latvia. Russian and Polish are still widely used in the country, although the younger generation prefers to learn English or German.

In the 1990s Lithuania, like neighboring Poland, saw a growing interest in religion, viewed as part of its strengthening national identity. The majority of ethnic Lithuanians (90 percent) and Poles are of Roman Catholic background, and most of the Russians belong to the Russian Orthodox Church. The newly established Christian Democratic Party won 15 seats in the 1996 parliamentary elections. However, religion does not play an important role in the average Lithuanian's political life, despite the growth of religious practice and the influence of the churches, especially the Catholic Church. There are also many other small religious communities whose religious practice is generally tolerated.

Lithuanians experienced major economic changes after 1991 as they attempted to reform an economy that largely relied on agriculture and manufacturing. These reforms were based on three main mechanisms: rapid mass-privatization, price liberalization, and currency reforms. The Lithuanian government privatized most of the enterprises in the industrial and agricultural sectors between 1991 and 1993. Lithuania introduced its currency in two stages: first came the *talonas* in May 1992, and then the *Litas* in June 1993. The exchange rate of the Lithuanian *Litas* was pegged to the United States dollar from May 1994.

Lithuania's GDP per capita is among highest in the former Soviet countries (in purchasing power parity), at around US$8,400 (2002 estimate). Despite macroeconomic stability and success in structural changes, the economic changes led to a steep economic recession, with economic output declining by around 50 percent between 1991 and 1994, although it recovered in the late 1990s. The unemployment rate remains at over 10 percent of the labor force (1999 CIA estimate), affecting mainly industrial workers, rural people, and women with children, but there is no strong evidence that poverty is correlated with any particular ethnic groups. According to World Development Indicators, there is growing economic disparity among the Lithuanian population, as the wealthiest 20 percent of the population controls 40.3 percent of the wealth, while the poorest 20 percent of the population controls only 7.8 percent (1996). In 1998 the UNDP's Human Development Index (HDI) put Lithuania in 52nd place, behind Croatia, Trinidad and Tobago, and Dominica, but ahead of the Seychelles, Grenada, and Mexico.

RAFIS ABAZOV

See also **Lithuanians**

Further Reading

Petersen, Roger, *Resistance and Rebellion: Lessons from Eastern Europe (Studies in Rationality and Social Change)*, Cambridge and New York: Cambridge University Press, 2001

Popovski, Vesna, *National Minorities and Citizenship Rights in Lithuania, 1988–93 (Studies in Russia and East Europe),* New York: St. Martin's, 2000

Senn, Alfred, *Gorbachev's Failure in Lithuania,* New York: St. Martin's, 1997

Smith, Graham, editor, *The Baltic States: The National Self-Determination of Estonia, Latvia, and Lithuania,* Basingstoke, Hampshire, Palgrave, 1996 Stanley, Valdys, and Judith Sedaitis, *Lithuania: The Rebel Nation,* Boulder, Colorado: Westview Press, 1996

Lithuanians

Capsule Summary

Location: east-central Europe, mostly in the territory of Lithuania and Poland
Total Population: 3,592,561 (2003)
Language: Lithuanian
Religions: Roman Catholic (primarily), Lutheran, Russian Orthodox Church, Protestant, evangelical Baptist

The Lithuanians are an ethnic group living in the eastern part of central Europe. There are approximately 3.5 million Lithuanians, most of them (around 80 percent) living in the republic of Lithuania. Approximately 500,000 Lithuanians live in various regions in Belorussia, Poland, Canada, the United States, and Australia. The Lithuanian language is one of the most archaic in Europe and belongs to the Indo-European language family. It is linguistically different from the Slavic languages spoken by other neighboring ethnic groups (Belarusian, Russian, etc.), and it is written in Latin, not Cyrillic. The majority of Lithuanians adhere to Roman Catholicism.

The ancestors of Lithuanians could be traced to the east of the Baltic Sea as early as 2000 BCE. Gradually, various Lithuanian tribes were consolidated into a federation under pagan king Mindaugas in the early thirteenth century. Mindaugas accepted Christianity (Catholicism) in 1251 and established a powerful state between Poland and the Muscovite Kingdom, and he successfully fought the Teutonic Knights, who invaded from Germany. In the early fourteenth century the Grand Duchy of Lithuania acquired most of the Belarusian territory, establishing Vilnius (Wilno in Polish) as the capital. During this era the Belarusian nobility retained their privileges and their Eastern Orthodox Christian identity, and their language was used in the state administration. In 1386, Grand Duke Jogaila married Polish queen Jadwiga and was crowned as Wladyslaw II Jagiello, becoming king of Poland.

In the middle of the sixteenth century, under the pressure from Russia, Lithuania formed the Polish-Lithuanian Commonwealth with the powerful Polish Kingdom, the *Rzech Pospolita*. In the new confederation the Polish language became the official language of the state and the Lithuanian nobility increasingly adopted Polish culture, customs, and language. It was the Lithuanian peasants who preserved the traditional Lithuanian culture, folk songs or *dainos*, and language. However, by the beginning of the seventeenth century the power of the *Rzech Pospolita* was gradually eroded by internal feuds, and in 1629 it lost most of the territory of Lithuania to Sweden. In the eighteenth century, following the rise of Russia, Austria, and Prussia as the major European powers, the Polish-Lithuanian confederation was divided, and most of the Lithuanian territory was acquired by Russia. The Russian Empire brought some positive changes, ending the political feuds and instability, but the Lithuanian minority's cultural and political freedoms were suppressed. In response, Lithuanian nationalists revolted in 1812, in 1831, and in 1863; at the end of the nineteenth century they tried to organize opposition around the Lithuanian-language magazines *Austra* and *Varpas*. Some restrictions on Lithuanian language and education were relaxed after the first Russian Revolution of 1905–7, but the demands to establish Lithuanian self-governance were rejected.

After the collapse of the Russian Empire in 1917, the Lithuanian nationalists declared the independence of Lithuania and the establishment of an independent provisional government. Meanwhile, the pro-Bolshevik groups founded the Belarusian-Lithuanian Soviet Socialist Republic. After the turmoils of the Russian civil war and Polish-Russian conflict in 1920, Lithuania emerged as an independent republic with Kaunas as the capital. A significant part of the republic, including the historic capital Vilnius (Wilno), was lost to Poland.

In March 1939 Nazi Germany annexed the Lithuanian seaport Klaipeda (Memel) and in September 1939 attacked Poland, starting the World War II. Under a special treaty with the Soviet Union, Germany allowed the Soviet government to acquire most of the territory of Lithuania, including the Lithuanian territories under Polish control. In 1940 the Soviet government installed a pro-Soviet regime and transferred most of the Lithuanian territory around Vilnius, which previously was under Polish control, to Lithuanian jurisdiction. Lithuania was declared the Lithuanian Soviet Socialist Republic (never recognized by the major Western powers). However, in 1941 Nazi Germany invaded the Soviet Union and occupied Lithuania, establishing a pro-Nazi regime. The occupation had a devastating effect on the Lithuanian society, as many ethnic minorities, particularly Jews (one of the largest ethnic groups in the country), were executed or purged in the Nazi death camps.

In 1944 the Soviet Union reestablished its control over Lithuania. As in other Soviet Union republics, considerable part of the Lithuanian political opposition and intelligentsia ended in Siberian labor camps, and major freedoms were suppressed. Under Soviet rule the Lithuanians experienced major changes, such as modernization, industrialization, and urbanization. A significant number of people, mainly Russians, migrated from various parts of the Union of Soviet Socialist Republics (USSR) to Lithuania during the post–World War II era. Most of the immigrants settled in the large cities and towns of Lithuania, and they were mainly employed in the rapidly growing industrial sector. Nevertheless, Lithuania remained one of the least Russified republics in the former USSR.

In 1988 Lithuania's reform-minded intelligentsia founded the *Sajudis*, the Lithuanian National Movement. The movement gained wide support and pushed for the declaration of the Lithuanian language as the official language of the state. In February 1990, the *Sajudis* won the first contested parliamentary elections. In March 1990 the Parliament declared restoration of independence, but the Soviet Union did not recognize its independence until September 1991.

At first the *Sajudis'* nationalist policy provoked some fears among the ethnic minorities because it promoted the Lithuanian language, a Lithuanian national identity, and a cultural renaissance. Between 1989 and 1991 more than 16,800 people, mainly of Slavic origin, emigrated from Lithuania, although almost 11,700 people, mainly Lithuanians from other parts of the USSR, moved in. Despite initial uncertainty, there were no mass political uprisings or interethnic conflicts after independence, and the migration gradually stabilized at an annual average rate of 0.14 migrants per 1,000 population (2003 estimate).

One of the important features of the post-Soviet development in Lithuania is the significant role of the Lithuanian overseas diaspora in the political life of the republic. One of the indicators of this influence is the election of Valdas Adamkus, an American of Lithuanian origin, as the president of Lithuania in 1998.

The ethnic structure of the country was formed after World War II and did not change much after 1991 because all ethnic groups were equally hit by the economic recession and high unemployment. Ethnic Lithuanians make up 80.6 percent of the country's population (2003 estimate). Ethnic Russians make up the largest minority, at around 8.7 percent of the population, and ethnic Poles make up 7 percent, Belarusians 1.6 percent, and various other groups together the remaining 2 percent of the population. Lithuania's relations with the ethnic minorities, including Russians, have been less troublesome than those of Estonia and Latvia because the new citizenship law (1989) declared that all residents, regardless of ethnic origin, were eligible to apply for naturalization. By 1993 almost 90 percent of nonethnic Lithuanian residents had been granted citizenship. However, the ethnic minorities need to learn Lithuanian language to have access to public services. Although most of the ethnic Lithuanians are Roman Catholics, and most of the Russians and Belarusians belong to the Russian Orthodox Church, throughout the 1990s there were no conflicts related to religion affiliation.

RAFIS ABAZOV

See also **Diaspora; Lithuania; Russia**

Further Reading

Eidintas, A., and Vytautas Zalys, *Lithuania in European Politics: The Years of the First Republic, 1918–1940,* New York: St. Martin's, 1998

Misiunas, R., and Rein Taagepera, *The Baltic States: Years of Dependence,* London: C. Hurst, 1983

Petersen, Roger, *Resistance and Rebellion: Lessons from Eastern Europe (Studies in Rationality and Social Change),* Cambridge and New York: Cambridge University Press, 2001

Popovski, Vesna, *National Minorities and Citizenship Rights in Lithuania, 1988–93 (Studies in Russia and East Europe),* New York: St. Martin's, 2000

Saulius, Suziedelis, *Historical Dictionary of Lithuanian,* Lanham, Maryland: Scarecrow Press, 1997

Senn, A., *Lithuania Awakening,* Berkeley: University of California Press, 1990

Smith, Graham, et al., editors, *Nation-Building in the Post-Soviet Borderlands: The Politics of National Identities,* Cambridge, United Kingdom, and New York: Cambridge University Press, 1998

Stanley, Valdys, and Judith Sedaitis, *Lithuania: The Rebel Nation,* Boulder, Colorado: Westview Press, 1996

Lurs

Capsule Summary

Location: southwestern Iran (Luristan, Bakhtaran, and Kohki-luyeh) and adjacent zones of Iraq; southwestern zone of Irani Azerbaijan
Total Population: 5 million
Language: Lur
Religion: Shi'a Muslim

The Lur language belongs to the Iranian family of Indo-European languages. It is closely related to other idioms of the region, especially to the Kurdish branch of languages. Moreover, several scholars include the Lurs in a larger Kurdish group of people that is culturally and linguistically related. The traditional economy and social structure of both Lurs and Kurds have several points of similarity, and they live under the same ecological constrictions of the Zagros hills and other high mountainous regions.

Since the Lur men regularly have contacts outside their own communities, they are generally bilingual. The women, however, usually only speak Lur. The Lur language is also spoken by neighboring ethnic communities: Bakhtiari, Mamasani, Bovir-Ahmadi, and Kuhgiluyeh. The language has two main dialects: Lur Buzurg, which is spoken by the Bakhtiari, the Kuhgiluyeh, and the Mamasani, who are thought to be a group of the same great branch as the Lurs; and Lur Kuchik, spoken by other different Lurs groups. The main Lur community is divided into two main groups: the Pish-e Kuhi ("above the hills"), predominantly sedentary peasants, and the Posht-e Kuhi ("on the top of the hills"), a nomadic people that live in the northwestern areas of Luristan. The Mamasani Lurs live around the city of Fars and are also mainly nomads. These different Lur communities are subdivided into more than 60 tribal groups.

The tribal structure of Lur society was an important mechanism that guaranteed their survival as an independent people. Lur tribal political units are called *il*. Each *il* consists of several distinct groups that the Lurs call *oulad*. Each of these *oulad* is made up of several families that have a common ancestor. The *oulad* itself is divided into small villages of three to eight "tent households." The tent household includes a husband, wife, and children, along with their flock of sheep or goats. Each Lur tribe is led by a hereditary chief (*khan*), who is normally recruited by one of the *oulad*. A yearly tax on grains and animals provides financial support for the *khan*. For all practical purpuses, the Lur tribes are politically independent and can maintain relations of cooperation or opposition with other Lur communities or with the neighboring ethnic groups that occupy the same natural landscape.

Lurs are Shi'a Muslims. However, many Lurs belong to the Ahl-e Haqq sect (the "People of the Truth"), which is also known by other Shi'a as the Ali Ilahi. The Ahl-e Haqq Muslim sect offers the Lurs a formal way to adopt Islam without renouncing their pre-Islamic beliefs. An example of how the Ahl-e Haqq sect bridges the divide between Islam and pre-Islam indigenous religion is the shrines dedicated to holy men that are scattered throughout the region. These shrines are believed to possess healing powers, and each year there are important pilgrimages that constitute social rituals of community cohesion.

The city of Khorramabad is an important political and economic center, and Borujerd is also a center of activities. About half of the Lurs are shepherds, traveling as nomads 6 to 8 months out of the year. From October to April, they live in low-lying pastures, and in the hot, dry season they go to the mountains looking for fresh food for their animals. The Lurs that prefer farming activities are settled in permanent villages and raise principally wheat and barley.

Prior to 1900 the majority of Lurs were pastoral nomads. During the 1920s and 1930s, the Iranian government of Reza Shah undertook several coercive campaigns to settle the nomadic Lurs. Following the abdication of Reza Shah in 1941, many of the recently settled tribes reverted to nomadism. Afterward, in the 1960s, Mohammad Reza Shah's government tried with some success, through various economic development programs, to encourage the remaining nomadic Lurs to settle. These ethnocide politics destroyed an important part of the traditional society that was the original basis for the Lur culture. Most Lurs are now settled in sedentary communities not only in the traditional Lur villages and hamlets, but also in the main Irani cities.

This process of forced urbanization threatens their status as a differentiated and well-integrated cultural system. If this trend persists, it will end in their final assimilation into the Persian modern identity, especially because the majority of Lurs live in villages and towns of former Luristan or have migrated to great cities, increasing the acculturation process.

JOAN MANUEL CABEZAS LÓPEZ

See also **Azerbaijan; Iran; Iraq; Kurds**

Further Reading

Abrahamian, Ervand, *Iran between Two Revolutions,* Princeton: Princeton University Press, 1982
Amirsadeghi, Hossein, *Twentieth Century Iran,* London: Heinemann, 1977
Planhol, Xavier de, *Minorités en Islam,* Paris: Flammarion, 1997

Luthuli, Albert (South African)

Albert John Mvumbi Luthuli was a distinguished South African political leader and prominent opponent of white minority rule. Zulu chief, teacher, president of the African National Congress (ANC), and first African to be awarded the Nobel Peace Prize, he was a major South African political figure of the 1950s and early 1960s. Luthuli was a leading spokesperson for South Africa's oppressed majority but also a firm defender of the rights of minority peoples.

The first part of Luthuli's life was spent in educational pursuits. He qualified as a teacher and later taught at Adams College, near Durban. His work as a teacher and his brief period as officeholder in the Natal African Teachers' Association in the 1920s and early 1930s sensitized him to the needs of Africans who suffered from low wages and poor working and living conditions. Elected chief of Umvoti Mission Reserve (1936–52), he developed a close understanding of the daily humiliations, disenfranchisement, and economic exploitation of the black majority by the ruling white minority. Luthuli's education and status as a chief propelled him into the black elite, but, like other members of this elite, he lived in a racist society in which opportunities for black advancement increasingly were blocked under segregationist and then apartheid policies that drove many into politics.

Luthuli joined the Natal ANC in 1945 and was elected to the purely advisory Natives' Representative Council in 1946. He opposed the more conservative Natal ANC leader A.W.G. Champion and defeated him as Natal ANC president in 1951. Champion had done little to actively oppose apartheid and had resisted ANC unity with Indian South Africans, who formed a substantial minority, especially around Durban. He also did little to quell the African–Indian riots that erupted in 1949. In contrast, Luthuli led vigorous united actions against apartheid by the ANC, the South African Indian Congress, and the Natal Indian Congress, notably the 1952 defiance campaign. By then a popular leader, he was forced to give up his chieftaincy in 1952 when he refused a government directive to resign from the ANC. Luthuli's response was memorable: "Who will deny that 30 years of my life have been spent knocking in vain, patiently, moderately and modestly at a closed and barred door?" (Luthuli, *The Road to Freedom Is via the Cross,* 1970, 7–8).

This defiance in support of the rights of the oppressed majority projected Luthuli to national prominence, and in December 1952 he was elected ANC national president, a position he held until his death. He frequently was persecuted by apartheid officials and at one time was physically attacked by Afrikaners. After 1952, he suffered almost continual banning and house arrest and was arraigned, together with other antiapartheid leaders, on charges of high treason in 1956, only being released in 1957. In this crucial period of resistance, Luthuli found ways, despite state harassment, to continue to provide inspired leadership to all those fighting apartheid, such as by holding political meetings in his home and having his speeches read in absentia.

Issues of religion, majority and minority rights, and nonviolence were prominent in Luthuli's career. He was strongly influenced by the Christian, liberal traditions common among the educated strata of Africans. A lay preacher in the Methodist church, he frequently used Christian metaphors in his political speeches. He advocated Gandhian nonviolent passive resistance, and in his personal testament of faith, *The Road to Freedom Is Via the Cross,* he called on all South Africans to actively oppose the apartheid minority government in nonviolent struggle. Luthuli condemned racist state policies and supported a multiracial, multicultural society. He believed in the eventual emergence of a nonracial society and that whites eventually could be won away from supporting apartheid. This commitment proved especially important in his home province of Natal, where his strong support for ANC unity with the Indian congresses helped overcome ethnic tensions.

Luthuli, however, did not neglect his own culture. Concerned that African culture not be dominated completely by Westernization, he had earlier formed the Zulu Language and Cultural Society. However, throughout his career he not only worked to protect this culture but also sought to reconcile Zulu, Christian, and other influences in South African society, and his cultural and religious tolerance helped him to cement political unity.

African nationalist ideas prevailing in the post-1940 ANC influenced Luthuli's ideas and work. His moderation, consistent advocacy of black rights, and elevated status as ANC leader made him an important force for unity in the ANC. His position as a chief in a rural area also allowed him to serve as a bridge between urban radicals and moderate rural peoples.

Luthuli also was a source of unity between the ANC and African labor. He attacked the way in which most African workers were forced by state legislation and racial prejudice to remain unskilled, and he encouraged the interlocking membership of the ANC and trade unions. He was fond of stating, "The ANC was the shield and the unions the spear." While wary of radicals, he remained tolerant of different political tendencies in the Congress Alliance led by the ANC. There was some ambiguity in his attitude to the seminal Freedom Charter, which was adopted (in his absence) at the Congress of the People in 1955 and which embraced some radical economic goals as well as the unity of the African majority and minority peoples against apartheid. However, once the ANC adopted the charter, Luthuli became a strong supporter.

In the early 1960s, Luthuli's pacifism did not prevent him from acknowledging that the move by other ANC leaders, such as Nelson Mandela, to resort to armed struggle had taken place only when all peaceful avenues had been closed off by the minority regime. Luthuli's legacy endured in the ANC's strong commitment to a multiracial democratic society based upon majority rule but also tolerant of minorities, goals eventually embodied in the policies of the country's first majority rule government in 1994 and the remarkably progressive 1997 constitution.

Biography

Albert John Mvumbi Luthuli (also spelled Lutuli). Born 1898 near Bulawayo, Zimbabwe. Educated in Natal at Groutville mission school, Ohlange Institute, Edendale Methodist school (teaching there for 2 years) and Adam's College, Amanzimtoti, where he taught until 1935. Secretary (1928) and president (1933), Natal African Teachers' Association. Chief of Umvoti Mission Reserve, Groutville, 1936–52 (dismissed by government). Church-sponsored lecture tour of United States, 1948. Joined ANC, 1945. Elected to Natives' Representative Council, 1946–51. President of Natal ANC, 1951; president of ANC, 1952–67 (reelected 1955, 1958). Served with banning orders, 1952–54, 1954–56, 1959–67. Defendant in Treason trial, 1956; released, 1957. Detained for 5 months in 1960 for burning pass. Awards: Nobel Peace Prize, 1960 (received 1961: first African to receive this honor); elected rector of University of Glasgow, 1962. Died in Groutville, 21 July 1967, allegedly hit by train.

Selected Works

Our Chief Speaks, 1952
Freedom Is the Apex: Chief A. Lutuli Speaks to White South Africans, 1959

"The Effect of White Minority Rule on Non-Whites," in *South Africa: The Road Ahead,* compiled by Hildegarde Spottiswoode, 1960

Let My People Go: An Autobiography, 1962

The Road to Freedom Is via the Cross, 1970

Luthuli: Speeches of Chief Albert John Luthuli, compiled by E.S. Reddy, 1991

PETER LIMB

See also **Afrikaners; Apartheid; Christians: Africa; Gandhi, Mohandas Karamchand (Indian); Mandela, Nelson (South African); Racism; Religion vs. Ethnicity; South Africa**

Further Reading

Benson, Mary, *Chief Albert Lutuli of South Africa,* London: Oxford University Press, 1963

Callan, Edward, *Albert John Luthuli and the South African Race Conflict,* Kalamazoo: Western Michigan University Press, 1962; revised edition, 1965

"Chief Albert John Mvumbi Luthuli, Isitwalandwe, 1898–1967," *Sechaba,* 1, no. 8 (1967)

Gordimer, Nadine, "Chief Luthuli," *Atlantic Monthly,* 203, no. 4 (1959); reprint, in *The Essential Gesture: Writing, Politics, and Places,* by Gordimer, edited by Stephen Clingman, New York: Knopf, and London: Jonathan Cape, 1988

Graybill, Lyn S., *Religion and Resistance Politics in South Africa,* Westport, Connecticut: Praeger, 1995

Legum, Colin, "Lutuli, Albert John Mvumbi," in *Dictionary of African Biography,* edited by L.H. Ofosu-Appiah, vol. 3, New York and Algonac, Michigan: Reference, 1995

Luthuli, Albert John, *The Road to Freedom Is via the Cross,* London: African National Congress, 1970

Luxembourg

Capsule Summary

Country Name: Grand Duchy of Luxembourg
Location: Western Europe, landlocked between Belgium, Germany, and France
Total Population: 454,157 (July 2003)
Languages: Luxembourgish (national language), German (administrative language), French (administrative language)
Religions: Roman Catholic, Protestant, Jewish, Muslim

Luxembourg is officially known as the Grand Duchy of Luxembourg, the only Grand Duchy in the world. The country area is 2,586 square kilometers (998 square miles—smaller than Rhode Island). The capital, Luxembourg City, is located in the southern part of the country. There are two geographic regions in Luxembourg: the mountainous northern part and the rolling plateau (Bon Pays) in the south. The highest point is Buurgplaatz (559 meters/1,834 feet), in the Ardennes Plateau. Luxembourg has a moderate climate with mild winters and cool summers, a mean annual temperature of 10°C (50°F), and a yearly rainfall of about 815 millimeters (about 32 inches).

The name of the national culture is Luxembourg. It derives from the name of the medieval dynasty of rulers. The population consists of Celtic-base ethnic groups (with French and German blend), Portuguese, Italians, Slavs, and other Europeans. The citizens of Luxembourg follow their own culture, best exemplified by their language—Letzeburgesch (Luxembourgisch), which is neither German nor French. French and German are also used in official publications and in schools. June 23 is the national holiday. The national flag consists of three equal horizontal bands of red (top), white, and light blue.

The region of Luxembourg was a part of the Roman Empire and later the Frankish kingdom and Charlemagne's empire. In 1060 it came under the rule of Count Conrad, founder of the house of Luxembourg. For the next four centuries, Spain and Austria alternately dominated the country. In 1815, the Congress of Vienna established Luxembourg as a Grand Duchy, and in 1839 it was recognized as a sovereign state. The Grand Duchy joined the League of Nations in 1920. In 1945, it became a member of the United Nations and in 1948 joined the Benelux Economic Union. Since 1949 Luxembourg has been a member of the North Atlantic Treaty Organization and, since 1958, the European Union.

Luxembourg is one of the world's most industrialized countries. The gross domestic product is composed of 1 percent agriculture, 30 percent industry, and

69 percent services. Per capita GDP was U.S. $48,900 in 2002. The monetary unit of Luxembourg is the euro. Ores and minerals, chemicals, machinery and electrical equipment, nonprecious metals, clothing accessories, and foodstuffs are chief imports. Exports are mainly iron and steel manufactures, textiles, chemicals, machinery and transportation equipment, and cut diamonds. Germany, France, the United Kingdom, and the United States are the principal trading partners. Other export partners include Germany, France, Belgium, the United Kingdom, Italy, Spain, and the Netherlands.

Luxembourg is a constitutional hereditary monarchy. The grand duke has the constitutional right to organize the government, which consists of a prime minister and at least three other ministers. The legislative power is vested in a unicameral chamber of deputies composed of 60 members elected every 5 years. The major political parties are the Action Committee for Democracy and Justice, the Christian Social People's Party, the Democratic Party, the Green Party, the Luxembourg Socialist Workers' Party, and the Marxist and Reformed Communist Party. The country is divided into 12 cantons, each of which is subdivided into communes. Luxembourg maintains a small (900) army of volunteers; other armed forces include the Grand Ducal Police. Education is compulsory for all children between the ages of 6 and 15, and illiteracy is almost nonexistent. The University Center of Luxembourg (1969) is situated in Luxembourg City, and the country also has several schools of music and technology.

LUDOMIR LOZNY

Further Reading

Calmes, Christian, *The Making of a Nation from 1815 to the Present Day: Contemporary History of Luxembourg*, Luxembourg City: Imprimerie Saint-Paul, 1989

Newcomer, J., *The Grand Duchy of Luxemburg: The Evolution of Nationhood, 963 A.D. to 1983*, Lanham, Maryland: University Press of America, 1984

Nissen, Jasper, "Luxemburg," in Enzyklopädie der Pferderassen, 3 Bde, Bd. 1, Deutschalnd, Belgien, Niederlande: Franckh-Kosmos Verlag, 1997

Trausch, Gilbert, *Le Luxembourg sous l'Ancien Regime*, Luxembourg City: Editions Bourg-Bourger, 1977

M

Mabo, Edward (Torres Strait Islander, Australia)

The name Edward Mabo will forever be linked to native title and land rights in Australia, as it was Mabo (1936–1992), a Torres Strait Islander, who successfully challenged the Queensland government and established beyond doubt that he did in fact own his traditional family land on Murray (Mer) Island, in the Torres Strait. This victory overturned two centuries of accepted legal tradition that Australia had been *terra nullis* (empty land) when the British arrived in 1788. It is now recognized that indigenous land ownership existed in Australia before European settlement and that, in some cases, it was not subsequently extinguished.

An activist, visionary, and patriot, Mabo was a tireless and tenacious campaigner for upholding the rights of Torres Strait Islanders. A leader in the large and diverse Townsville Torres Strait Islander community, he was one of the first to call for self-rule for Torres Strait communities. Mabo was a man of enormous energy and vision, coupled with passionate and unwavering opinions that, while putting many off, enabled him to single-mindedly challenge the existing status quo and relentlessly pursue his ten-year struggle for justice against the Queensland government.

Born Koiki Sambo on June 29 1936, at Murray Island, to Robert Zezou Sambo and Annie Mabo, his mother died shortly afterwards. He was then adopted, in accordance with Torres Strait Islander custom, by his uncle, Benny Mabo. His formal education was limited to primary school, where he was strongly influenced by his white school teacher, Robert Miles, with whom he lived for two years and through whom he gained proficiency in English, his third language. From 1953–57 he worked in the fishing industry on various trochus luggers operating out of Murray Island. In 1957 he moved to mainland Queensland, working in a variety of laboring jobs, including as a railway fettler, deck hand, and cane cutter.

In 1959, Mabo married Bonita Nehow, whom he had met in Innisfail while cutting sugar cane, and they settled in Townsville and raised a family. It was here that he immersed himself in black community politics. As president of the Council for the Rights of Indigenous People, he was instrumental in establishing Australia's first indigenous community school, the Townsville Aboriginal and Islander Health Service and a legal aid service. He became involved in the trade union movement as a representative and spokesman for Torres Strait Islanders on the Townsville-Mount Isa rail reconstruction project in 1960, and in 1967, he initiated, with trade union support, a seminar in Townsville, known as *We are Australians—What is to Follow the Referendum?*, that involved over 300 people.

In 1973, he was refused permission by the Murray Island Council to return to home to see his dying father. This incident galvanized Mabo into what would become a lifetime of activism on behalf of his land, his people, and his right to return to his beloved homeland.

In the mid 1970s Mabo was further shocked to discover that his family holdings on Murray Island were, along with all the outer Torres Strait Islands, actually owned by the Queensland government. He resolved to win his land back, determined that no one could take it away from him.

In 1982, Mabo, along with four other Murray Islanders, commenced court action to gain legal title to their family land, *Mabo and others v. the State of Queensland*. In 1985, the Queensland government retaliated through the *Queensland Coast Islands Declaratory Act*, intending to defeat Mabo's claim by extinguishing retrospectively any native title that may have existed on his land, through passing responsibility for all coastal islands to their nearest authority. However in 1988, this Act was invalidated by the Supreme Court on the grounds that it was contrary to the *Commonwealth Racial Discrimination Act*, 1975.

In 1991, the High Court of Australia heard the case, ruling on June 3 1992, in favor of Mabo, (*Mabo v State of Queensland (No 2) (1992)*) overturning the principle of *terra nullis*, and for the first time recognizing that a form of native title still existed in Australia. Tragically, Mabo did not live to celebrate the victory, dying of cancer five months earlier. On June 4 1995, the day after his tombstone in Townsville was unveiled in a traditional ceremony, his grave was desecrated by vandals in a racist attack. Subsequently his remains were relocated to Murray Island, where he was laid to rest in a traditional ceremony on September 18, 1995.

Capsule Biography

Edward (Eddie) Mabo. Born on June 29, 1936 on Murray (Mer) Island, Torres Strait. Education. Primary School, Murray Island. Diploma of Teaching, James Cook University, 1981–84 (Not completed). Employment. Fisherman, Murray Island, 1953–57. Laborer, Townsville Harbor Board, 1962–67. Secretary, Aboriginal and Torres Strait Islander Advancement League, Townsville, 1962–69. Gardener, James Cook University, Townsville, 1967–75. President of the Council for the Rights of Indigenous People, Townsville, 1970 Director and Principal, Black Community School, Townsville, 1973–85. Member, Aboriginal Arts Council, 1974–78. Member, National Aboriginal Education Committee, 1975–78. President, Yumba Meta Housing Association, Townsville, 1975–80. Member, Australian Institute of Aboriginal Studies Education Advisory Committee, 1978–9. Assistant Vocational Officer, Aboriginal Employment and Training Branch, Commonwealth Employ-

ment Service, Townsville, 1978–81. Field Officer, Aboriginal Legal Service, Townsville, 1985–6. Director, ABIS Community Cooperative Society Ltd, Townsville, 1986–7. Assistant Director, Aboriginal Arts, Moonba Festival, Melbourne, 1987. Community Liaison Officer, 5th Festival of Pacific Arts, Townsville, 1987–88. Vice-Chairman, Magani Malu Kes, Townsville, 1987–88. Awards: Member, Aboriginal Arts Board of the Australia Council. Member, National Education Committee, mid 1980s. Chairman, Torres Strait Border Action Committee. Posthumously awarded the Human Rights Medal, Australian Human Rights Commission, 1992. Named Australian of the Year by the *Australian* Newspaper, 1993. Died in Brisbane, January 21, 1992. Funeral held on February 1, 1992, Belgian Gardens Cemetery, Townsville. Reburied on September 18, 1995, Murray Island, Torres Strait, Australia

Selected Works

"Perspectives from Torres Strait," *The Torres Strait Border Issue: Consolidation, Conflict or Compromise*, edited by James Griffin, 1979

"Land Rights in Torres Strait," in *Black Australians: Prospects for Change*, edited by Erik Olbrei, 1982

"Music of the Torres Strait," *Black Voices*, 1, no. 1, (1984)

"Murray Island," in *Workshop on Traditional Knowledge of the Marine Environment in Northern Australia*, edited by F. Gray and L. Zann, 1985

Edward Koiki Mabo: His Life and Struggle for Land Rights, with Noel Loos, 1996

JEREMY HODES

See also **Australia; Torres Strait Islanders**

Further Reading

Atwood, Bain, and Andrew Markus, *The Struggle for Aboriginal Land Rights: A Documentary History*, Sydney: Allen & Unwin, 1999

Bartlett, Richard, *The Mabo Decision, and the Full Text of the Decision in Mabo and Others v State of Queensland*, Sydney: Butterworths, 1993

Cunningham, Adrian, *Guide to the Papers of Edward Koiki Mabo in the National Library of Australia*, Canberra: National Library of Australia, 1995

Sanders, William G., editor, *Mabo and Native Title: Origins and Institutional Implications*, Canberra: Australian National University, 1994

Sharp, Nonie, *No Ordinary Judgment: Mabo, the Murray Islanders' Land Case*, Canberra: Aboriginal Studies Press, 1996

Stephenson, M., and Suri Ratnapala, *Mabo, a Judicial Revolution: The Aboriginal Land Rights Decision and Its Impact on Australian Law*, Brisbane: University of Queensland Press, 1993

Macedonia

Capsule Summary

Country Name: The Former Yugoslav Republic of Macedonia (FYROM)

Location: Southwestern part of Balkan Peninsula (Southeastern Europe), bordering on Greece, Albania, Bulgaria, and rump Yugoslavia)

Total Population: 2,063,122 (July 2003)

Languages: Macedonian (70%), Albanian (21%), Turkish (3%), Serbo-Croatian (3%), other (3%)

Religions: Macedonian Orthodox (67%), Muslim (30%), other (3%)

The Republic of Macedonia (the Former Yugoslav Republic of Macedonia) is a parliamentary democracy whose borders are defined primarily by a series of mountain ranges separating it from Bulgaria, Greece, Albania, and FR Yugoslavia (Kosovo and Serbia). Its area is 9,925 square miles (15,973 sq.km). Macedonian is a Slavic language, most closely related to Bulgarian and Serbian.

History

The territory of the Republic of Macedonia has always been ethnically mixed and the population multilingual. From the end of the fourteenth century until the outbreak of the First Balkan War in 1912, it was part of the Ottoman Empire. In the Treaty of Bucharest, which ended the Second Balkan War in 1913, most of what is now the Republic of Macedonia was assigned to Serbia and subsequently became part of Yugoslavia. During World War II, most of the territory was annexed by Bulgaria and the westernmost region was part of an Albanian puppet state. Macedonia was declared a Peoples (later Socialist) Republic on August 2, 1944, with Macedonian as its official language, and it subsequently became a part of socialist Yugoslavia. The current border was finalized in 1948. As a result of the Yugoslav Wars of Succession, which began on June 26 1991, the Republic held a referendum for independence on September 8 1991 and adopted an independent constitution on November 17, 1991 (slightly amended on January 6, 1992).

Under the Ottomans, Turkish was the dominant urban language and Greek dominated the Church.

During the nineteenth century, Bulgarian, Serbian, and Greek propaganda competed for the loyalty of the Christian peasant majority, and a separate, modern Macedonian national consciousness also emerged. Between the two World Wars, Serbian was the only language of education available outside of religious institutions. During World War II, schooling was in either Bulgarian or Albanian, depending on who controlled the territory. While Macedonia was part of the SFR Yugoslavia, Serbo-Croatian was the language of the army, a compulsory subject in all schools, and the language of communication at the federal and inter-republic levels. Thus, while Macedonian was the official majority language at the republic level, it was a minority language in Yugoslavia. Within Macedonia, Albanian and Turkish had official minority status and were supported by public elementary and secondary schools as well as language and literature departments at the University of Skopje and separate tracks at the School of Education. These two languages were also used for publicly funded radio, television, theaters, and tri-weekly newspapers, as well as other activities. During the 1980s, some of this support was curtailed or eliminated, but tiny amounts of support for Romani and Vlah began. After independence, public funding for Albanian and Turkish was increased, and such support for Romani and Vlah was greatly expanded. At the same time, political changes made private print and non-print media possible. The rise of multiparty politics resulted in the politicization of ethnicity, and there are currently Macedonian, Albanian, Turkish, Serbian, and Romani political parties as well as multiethnic parties. Many local NGOs and most cultural organizations are also defined along ethnic lines.

In SFR Yugoslavia, the terms *nationality* and *ethnic group* (this latter only for Roms and Vlahs) had replaced *minority* by 1974. The 1991 Macedonian constitution used only *nationality*. Albanian leaders have objected to the use of the term *minority* in reference to Macedonia's Albanians, arguing that their numbers are too large to be referred to by a term that implies "small."

Ethnic, Linguistic, and Religious Structure

The following 1994 census figures cite *declared ethnicity*; *declared mother tongue*; and *declared religious affiliation* (in this order): Macedonian (1,295,964), Macedonian (1,332,983), Orthodox (1,283,689); Albanian (441,104), Albanian (431,363), Muslim (581,203); Turkish (78,019), Turkish (64,665), Christian (28,400); Romani (43,707), Romani (35,120), Catholic (7,405); Muslim (15,418), Serbian (33,315), Protestant (1,215); Serbian (40228), Vlah (7036), and Other (33122). Ethnic populations included Macedonian 64.2 percent, Albanian 25.2 percent, Turkish 3.8 percent, Roma 2.7 percent, Serb 1.8 percent, and other 2.3 percent in 1994. Others included Croats, Bosnians, Bulgarians, Egyptians, Montenegrins, and Greeks.

A portion of the Albanians and Turks of the municipality of Debar boycotted the 1994 census, objecting that they would not be fairly counted. The figures for declared ethnicity include estimates for this population, whereas the figures for mother tongue and religion do not, hence the discrepancies in the totals. The majority of those declaring Macedonian, Vlah, Serbian, Bulgarian, and Montenegrin ethnicity are Orthodox Christians, most of those declaring Albanian, Turkish, Romani, Bosniac, Egyptian, and Muslim ethnicity profess Islam. The majority of those declaring themselves Catholic, Protestant, or Christian (without further sectarian specification) declared Macedonian ethnicity. Most other Catholics are ethnic Croats and Albanians. The majority of Egyptians (a non-Romani speaking group of Romani origin) declared Albanian as their mother tongue and most of the rest declared Macedonian. Most of those declaring Muslim ethnicity speak Macedonian or some variant of the former Serbo-Croatian. The category Vlah includes both Aromanian and Megleno-Romanian (two closely related Romance languages that are related to Romanian). There are no absolute one-to-one correspondences among the three categories of ethnicity, language, and religion. Thus, for example, a few people declaring Muslim ethnicity declared a Christian religious affiliation, and 20 declared themselves to be atheists.

There have been Jews in Macedonia since pre-Christian times, but on the eve of World War II, most Macedonian Jews spoke Judezmo, a language related to Spanish and brought to the Balkans by Jews expelled from Spain in 1492. On 11 March 1943, the Nazis and their collaborators deported 7,200 of the 7,400 Jews living in what became the Republic to the Treblinka death camp. Most survivors went to Israel, and today there are about 150 Jews in Macedonia.

Legal Status of Minority Languages and Religions

The preamble of the Macedonian constitution contains the following phrase:

"...Macedonia is established as a national state of the Macedonian people, in which full equality as citizens and permanent co-existence with the Macedonian people is provided for Albanians, Turks, Vlahs, Roms and other nationalities living in the Republic of Macedonia..."

The proposed amended preamble makes no reference to nations or nationalities but only to "citizens of the Republic of Macedonia." Article 7 of the Constitution establishes Macedonian as the official language of the Republic and specifies that in units of local self-government with a majority or "considerable number" belonging to a nationality (*i.e.*, ethnic minority), their language is also official. Article 35 of the 1994 Census Law provided for the census to be conducted in Albanian, Turkish, Romani, Vlah, and Serbian in addition to Macedonian. Article 88 of the 1996 Law on Local Self-Government defined *considerable number* as 20 percent. The proposed amended constitutional Article 7 begins like the old one but adds that "[a]ny other language spoken by at least 20 percent of the population is also an official language" followed by specifications concerning usage and concluding: "With respect to languages spoken by less than 20 percent of the population of a unit of local self-government, the local authorities shall decide on their use in public bodies."

Albanian is the only minority language spoken by more than 20 percent of the population. Article 19 of the Constitution guarantees religious freedom but also names the Macedonian Orthodox Church "and other religious communities and groups." The proposed amended Article 19 specifies separation of state and religious institutions (in addition to guaranteeing religious freedom) and names "[t]he Macedonian Orthodox Church, the Islamic Religious Community in Macedonia, the Catholic Church, and other religious communities and groups."

Higher education has become a focus of dispute among other conflicts among Macedonians and Albanians. In 1995 a group of Albanians opened an Albanian-language university in the suburbs of

Tetovo, and it was declared illegal by the Macedonian government, who accused the University of being a separatist political project rather than an educational institution. In an attempt to resolve the issue, the international community has sponsored the founding of Southeast European University in Tetovo, where the languages of instruction will be Albanian, English, and Macedonian. SEEU is scheduled to open in October 2001, but faculty and students of Tetovo University are opposed to the project. Another dispute has involved Macedonian-speaking Muslim parents in western Macedonia demanding Turkish (in the Debar region) or Albanian (in the Kichevo region) elementary schools for their children. Human rights advocates argue that parents have the right to chose their children's schooling, while the Macedonian government argues that it is not required to provide schooling in a language that is not the children's mother tongue.

At the time of independence in November 1991, Macedonia was the least developed of the Yugoslav republics, and suffered from the lack of infrastructure and various UN sanctions on Yugoslavia, the new republic's largest market. Macedonia's commitments to economic reform and free trade—which were on the increase—were subsequently undermined by ethnic Albanian insurgencies in 2001. One-third of the workforce (estimated 1.1 million) is unemployed, and the per capita GDP in 2002 was US$5,100. Moreover, money laundering is a problem on a local level due to organized crime activities.

VICTOR FRIEDMAN

See also **Macedonians; Yugoslavs (Southern Slavs)**

Further Reading

Borden, Anthony, and Ibrahim Mehmeti, editors, *Reporting Macedonia: The New Accommodation*, London: Institute for War & Peace Reporting, 1998

Fraenkel, Eran, "Urban Muslim Identity in Macedonia: The Interplay of Ottomanism and Multilingual Nationalism," in *Language Contact, Language Conflict*, edited by Eran Fraenkel and Christina Kramer, New York: Peter Lang, 1993

Friedman, Victor A., "Observing the Observers: Language, Ethnicity, and Power in the 1994 Macedonian Census and Beyond," in *Toward Comprehensive Peace in Southeastern Europe: Conflict Prevention in the South Balkans*, edited by Barnett Rubin, New York: Council on Foreign Relations/Twentieth Century Fund, 1996

Friedman, Victor A., "The Romani Language in the Republic of Macedonia: Status, Usage, and Sociolinguistic Perspectives," *Acta Linguistica Hungarica*, 46, no. 3–4 (1999)

Kolonomos, Zhamila, editor, *Sefardski oglaski: Studii i sek«avanja za Evreite od Makedonija* (Sepharddic Echoes: Studies and Memories of the Jews of Macedonia), Skopje: Gurga, 1995

Kramer, Christina, and Brian Cook, editors, *Guard the Word Well Bound: Proceedings of the Third North American-Macedonian Conference on Macedonian Studies* (Indiana Slavic Studies 10), Bloomington, Indiana: Slavica, 1999

Tanaskovic, Darko, "The Planning of Turkish as a Minority Language in Yugoslavia," in *Language Planning in Yugoslavia*, edited by Ranko Bugarski and Celia Hawkesworth, Columbus, Ohio: Slavica, 1992

Wilkinson, H.R., *Maps and Politics: A Review of the Ethnographic Cartography of Macedonia*, Liverpool: University of Liverpool, 1951

Winnifrith, T.J., *The Vlachs: History of a Balkan People*, London: Duckworth, 1987

Macedonians

Capsule Summary

Location: Southwestern part of Balkan Peninsula (Southeastern Europe, mainly in the Republic of Macedonia and neighbor states, republics of former Yugoslavia, and émigrés in Canada, Australia, United States and Western Europe)

Total Population: approximately 1.6–2 million

Language: Macedonian

Religion: Eastern Orthodox Christian, with few Muslims

The Macedonians are an ethnic group in the Southwestern Balkans, forming the main population of the Republic of Macedonia (about 65–67 percent). Currently they number approximately 1.6 million in the Republic of Macedonia itself, claiming more than a million settled in other countries (about 500,000–550,000 in neighbor ones, and about 500 thousand overseas). Separate Macedonian identity was almost never mentioned before the end of nineteenth century either by locals, or by foreign travelers or diplomats. It was first appreciated internationally among Communist circles in the 1930s and was included as a sixth main nation within the frames of the post-World War II Yugoslavia. The Macedonian language belongs to the Southern Slavic subfamily of the Slavic language group. It was formed relatively late—about the end of nineteenth century, to reach its literary form completely only after the World War II in the Federal Yugoslav Republic of Macedonia—and is based on the West-central dialects Veles, Prilep, and Bitola. Together with soft consonants *lj*, *nj* (љ, њ) that exist also in Serbian and Croatian, specific for its phonetical system are middle-palatal consonants ѓ and ќ, sound dental *dz* (ѕ), and sonant *r*. Stress is expiratory and fixed, falling always on the third syllable from the end. Grammatical construction is analytical, names are never inflected, and the article, which exists in three forms, is put in the end of the words. Macedonian orthography is phonetical, and its official alphabet is Cyrillic.

History

Only a few authors, mainly in Skopje, trace their ethnicity's background to the Ancient Macedonians related to the Ancient Greeks, Thracians, and Ilyrians and famous for the rule and conquests of Philip II and especially his son, Alexander Macedonian The Great (fifth–fourth centuries BCE). These lands were later under the domination of the Roman and Byzantine Empires, the Old Bulgarian and Old Serbian Kingdoms, and, between 1389 and 1912, the Ottoman Empire. Christianity in its Eastern Orthodox rite was introduced here in the ninth century CE by two of the seven immediate disciples of Saints Cyril and Methodius, St. Kliment from Ohrid and St. Naum. Kliment and Naum also introduced the Slavonic Cyrillic alphabet. Settled here in the fifth through seventh centuries CE, Slavic tribes including Berzites, Rinhynes, Sagudates, Stroumyans, etc., and Bulgarians under Kouber (670–675), contributed together with Albanians, Vlachs (Aromanians), Gypsies, and others, along with ever changing circumstances and influences, for a mixed and competing devotion from the population. Separate Slavo-Macedonian identity was almost unknown until the last decades of the nineteenth century, when even within a single family one could identify as a Greek, while another as a Bulgarian, and so on. Macedonian identity was enforced also by the fact that these people remained under Turkish rule decades longer than their neighbors. The significant number who placed too much hope in help from Queen Sofia against the Turks were further alienated by the Bulgarian absorption with internal problems.

It was only after Balkan Wars in 1913 that Macedonia was partitioned between Serbia, Greece, and Bulgaria, and each of the states aimed at unconditional imposition of its nationhood over the local population. In the Aegean (Greek) part, the so-called *Slavophones* were never recognized as a distinct ethnicity; in addition, Greeks from Asia Minor were resettled here while most of the indigenous Slavophone population was forced to depart for Bulgaria and Yugoslavia, leaving their property. Separate Macedonian ethnicity acquired its first formal international recognition among Communist (Komintern) circles in the 1930s and was included as a sixth main nation within the frames of the post-World War II Yugoslavia. After Bulgarian troops came into Macedonia in 1941 as Nazi Germany's allies, communist authorities in Skopje did a lot after the war to equate the terms *Bugarin* (Bulgarian) and *Bugaroman* (Bulgarophile, Bulgarofan) with the Fascist occupier. This excused the new authorities for murdering, imprisoning, and exiling hundreds of *Bugaromans-fascists*. Simultaneously, on the Bulgarian side of the border, following instructions from Moscow, their counterparts were hastily preparing the transfer of Pirin Macedonia to Skopje/Belgrade authority. Later it was secretly planned for Bulgaria itself to be included in Yugoslavia as a seventh republic. These moves were halted only after disapproval by the United States and democratic Europe who did not tolerate any border changes, but also because of the quarrel between Stalin and Tito that emerged in 1948 and led to an "exclusion" of Yugoslavia from the communist movement. Further, Moscow used Macedonian issue as one of the tools for imposing tighter control over Bulgaria and as a pressure device in the complicated game with Belgrade and the defiant Yugoslav leader, Marshall Tito.

There is still great controversy among scholars about the character of Macedonian ethnicity and language—from attempts to find proofs for their early existence, even using loosely and skewed interpretation of evidence, to complete denial of their authenticity. Surely, earlier standardization of the Serbian and Bulgarian literature on the basis of relatively too distant, local acedonian dialects (for the Serbian, Northwestern ones, for Bulgarian, Eastern) left a huge linguistic space which naturally resisted such a negligence toward locally spoken dialects. Some local authors, who strived to make their writings more understandable for their immediate fellow citizens by using regional tongues—such as Joakim Krcovski, Kiril Pejcinovic, Jordan Hadzi Konstantinov-Dzinot, Dimitar and Konstantin

Miladinov Brothers, and others—believed they are contributing to shaping the Bulgarian national consciousness against Hellenization and to a creation of a common Macedo-Bulgarian literary language. The struggle for the emancipation of the Bulgarian Church from the Greek Patriarchate led to the development of two distinctive groups among local patriotic intelligentsia: the first, called Unitarian, advocated a single *Bulgarian* literary language but considered local specificities to a greater degree, while the second was separatists (Macedonists) who advocated a completely different Macedonian literary language. Separatism continue to rise after 1878 when Macedonia, still often referred to as Lower Bulgaria, remained under Ottoman Turkish domination while neighbor Bulgaria itself achieved a degree of autonomy under the Berlin Treaty. In 1888, Ġorġi Pulevski founded in Sofia the Slavo-Macedonian Literary Society, which was soon banned but later reestablished as Young Macedonian Literary Society. The Society published a journal *Loza* (Grapevine) and aimed at "raising one of the Macedonian dialects to the level of literary language for all Macedonians." Curiously, among founding members was Andrej Ljapcev from the town of Stip in Vardar Macedonia, future Prime Minister of Bulgaria. 1893 saw the founding of both the Student Society Vardar in Belgrade and the Macedonian Central Revolutionary Organization, known later as VMRO. In 1902 Dimitrija Cupovski, Krste Misirkov, and more than a dozen other young intellectuals founded in St. Petersburg the Slavo-Macedonian Scientific-Literary Society. The next year, 1903, saw the tragic glory of the ruthlessly defeated Ilinden uprising; at the end of the year Kr. Misirkov published in Sofia the most resolute ideological manifesto of the separatist Macedonists—*Za Makedonckite Raboti* (On the Macedonian Affairs). Among the other, it was there recommended that for a basis of the literary language to be adopted the Prilep-Bitola dialect, which is equally distant from both Serbian and Bulgarian. This book's circulation was almost completely destroyed by the Bulgarian authorities. As an illustration of all haziness of the issue, by the end of his life Misirkov refuted his own earlier positions, and accepted the Bulgarian version. It was only when a Macedonian Republic was established within the Yugoslav Federation under Marshall Tito, that the standard literary language was accepted and fixed, around 1945–50. Attempts to impose this language and identity in Pirin Macedonia (Bulgaria) during 1945–48, however, were met with defiance from the local population, for whom the Prilep-Bitola dialect was relatively alien. Adding to the problem was Serbization, adopted in order to escape further from Bulgarian influence, and the attempts to impose the language were ceased after the Stalin-Tito row.

Society

The population of Macedonia was among the first Christianized Slav peoples, when in the ninth century, the Bulgarian kingdom under Boris Michael I adopted Christianity. Traditional Macedonian society had many common features with most adjacent South Balkan peoples, especially the Christian ones: Bulgarians, Greeks, and Serbs. In rural areas, until the 1920s-1930s, many patriarchal customs associated with the large family—such as common use of the land and cattle, brides being introduced to the family while female members usually quitting it upon marriage, and living under the undisputed authority of the eldest male—were preserved. Relatively mild climate in the valleys permitted advancement of agriculture, in particular early grown fruits and vegetables (strawberries, cherries, tomatoes, etc.), rice, wheat, high quality oriental tobacco, and excellent grapes. Mountainous pastures allowed livestock—most particularly sheep—to be raised for the production of wool, milk, white and yellow cheese, and meat. In towns and cities like Bitola, Prilep, Tetovo, Struga, Ohrid, and Skopje, handicrafts were developed such as tailoring, furdressing, millinery, shoemaking, cooperage, smithy, carpentry, and so on. Guilds elaborated and adhered to strict codes for the right of entry into a craft, professional ethics, etc. Artists and architects, mostly self-styled, were building churches, bridges, public edifices, painting icons, and creating typical wood-carving altars of exclusive beauty; the Debar school of carving masters was famous far beyond. Around lakes like Ohrid, Prespa, and Dojran, people found their livelihood in fishing. A natural major city of the whole region then was Salonika (Greek Thessaloniki, Macedonian/Bulgarian *Solun*); with a large and for that time, heavily mixed population of Macedo/Bulgarians, Greeks, Jews, Armenians, Turks, and many others, it was cosmopolitan and evoked mutual tolerance and respect toward the confession, customs, and specificity of others.

Pauperization, together with violence by the oppressor, ignited both resistance and mass emigration—beginning with Bulgaria, considered to be the closest "abroad," and overseas, as well as migration from the rural to urban areas. These processes essentially destroyed the traditional society. While beyond the borders those who identify themselves as Macedonians (and in Greece as Slavs too) still face harassment and denial, in the Republic of Macedonia an issue of a mounting concern is the ever growing share of Albanians among the population. Albanians, who demonstrate an extremely high birth rate, are considered to be between 1/4 and 1/3 from the Republic of Macedonia (exact population data are not available because of their refusal to participate in the censuses, as well as because of the uncontrolled lingering of a number of Kosovars with their relatives in Macedonia). Even now no viable political majority in Macedonia is possible without one or more of the Albanian parties, which insist on proclaiming Albanians as the second "state-forming" element—that is, to transform the state into "Albano-Macedonian." Albanians form their own "enclaves" in Western Macedonia, influential in the towns of Tetovo, Gostivar, Struga, as well as over some districts of Skopje, where Macedonians feel uneasy. Together with the fragile, uncertain stability, more and more "Albanian only" neighborhood and possibly an independent Kosovo may lead to some unwanted changes in the small republic and even threaten its existence, saying nothing about further complications and hostilities all over the Balkan peninsula.

STEPHAN E. NIKOLOV

See also **Macedonia**

Further Reading

Danforth, Loring M., *The Macedonian Conflict: Ethnic Nationalism,* Princeton, NJ: Princeton University Press: 1995

Friedman, Victor A., "The Modern Macedonian Standard Language and Its Relation to Modern Macedonian Identity," in *The Macedonian Question: Culture, Historiography, Politics,* edited by Victor Roudometof, Boulder: East European Monographs No. DLIII, 2000

Karakasidou, Anastasia, *Fields of Wheat, Hills of Blood: Passages of Nationhood in Greek Macedonia, 1879–1990,* Chicago: University of Chicago Press, 1997

Poulton, Hugh, *Who Are the Macedonians?*, London: Hurst and Co: 1994; Bloomington, Indiana: Indiana University Press: 1995

Roudometof, Victor, editor, *The Macedonian Question: Culture, Historiography, Politics*, Boulder: East European Monographs No. DLIII, 2000

Shashko, Philip. "The Emergence of the Macedonian Nation: Images and Interpretations in the American and British Reference Works 1945–1991," in *Studies in Macedonian Language, Literature, and Culture,* edited by B Stolz, Ann Arbor, MI: Michigan Slavic Publications, 1991

Madagascar

Capsule Summary

Country Name: Republic of Madagascar
Location: Southern Africa, island in the Indian Ocean, east of Mozambique
Total Population: 16,979,744 (July 2003)
Languages: Malagasy (official), French (official), and Comorian
Religion: Catholic (21%), Protestant (20%), Muslim (7%), indigenous beliefs (52%)

Madagascar is an island country in the western Indian Ocean. It broke away from the continent of Africa about 170 million years ago. The population is a mixture of Indo-Malay and Bantu (African) heritage. In the first century CE, people escaping what is now Indonesia sailed west in search of a new home, inhabiting Madagascar. Immigrants from Africa are believed to have started coming around the eighth century CE. Over the millennium there has been significant inter-marriage leading to the creation of 18 ethnic groups each with their own dialects of the Malagasy language (*Merina, Betsileo, Betsimisiraka, Sakalava, Bara, Antandroy, Antaifasy, Antaimoro, Antaisaka, Antanosy, Mahafaly, Mahoa, Antambahoaka, Bezanozano, Sihanaka, Tsimihety, Antankarana,* and *Tanala*). Each of these groups is some combination of Indo-Malay and Bantu origins; however the *Merina* of the central plateau tend to have more dominant Asian physical features while people of the *cotier* ethnic groups of the lowlands tend to have more dominant African physical features.

The history of Madagascar's political systems is inextricably woven to its relationship with foreign powers. In the sixteenth century, the central plateau was dominated by loose feudal structures uniting localized *fokonolona* (village councils). Over time, this transformed into a system of hilltop monarchies. One king, Andrianampoinimerina (1787–1810), began establishing control over the other Imerina monarchies and the majority of the central and southern parts of the country. His successor, Radama I, concluded an agreement in 1817 that abolished the slave trade. In return, he received British military and financial assistance. With this new strength, Radama I and Radama II were able to extend *Merina* control over most of the island.

In the late nineteenth century, the French attempted to rule Madagascar indirectly through the established *Merina* monarchy. They ran into a willful Queen Ranavalona III. In 1896, France deposed the queen and installed Governor Joseph Simon Galliéni. Yet even as the French established a colonial government in Antananarivo, provincial officers relied heavily on established *Merina* patronage systems. Consequently, *Merina* upheld French rule in exchange for a position of privilege. While the Malagasy population was subject to a separate set of land use laws than the resident French population, the *Merina* were allowed to grow their own crops for their own benefit under land-use laws closer to those that governed the French. Over time, the French continued to exert greater force over the Malagasy in terms of social control, societal restructuring, and land-use rights. The *Merina* were not only exempted from much of this, but in fact were often officers charged with carrying out these French-led initiatives.

In 1947, Madagascar saw one of the largest and most violent uprisings against colonialism in the world, eventually costing an estimated 100,000 lives. In many regions this uprising was as much against *Merina* sub-colonialism as French colonialism. By the time the Malagasy Republic gained full independence on June 26, 1960, the *Merina* were well-advantaged with greater access to markets, education, and resources than any other ethnic group.

At the time of independence there was a great fear that appointing a *Merina* leader would lead to further civil unrest. The French thus looked for someone that was not *Merina* but would maintain the established system of power to the benefit of French access to natural resources and *Merina* control of industry and the greater political sphere. They found such a man in Philibert Tsirinana. Though President Tsirinana was of *Tsimihety* origins, he came to power with significant French and *Merina* support. While initially he found some success, by 1969 his policies had let to financial ruin and many Malagasy began to decry the persistent reliance on French trade and dominance of *Merina* in the political, economic, and social spheres. In what many Malagasy view as the "real" independence of Madagascar, a coup ousted Tsirinana from office in May 1972.

In June 1975 the military directorate put Admiral Didier Ratsiraka in power. Ratsiraka removed his uniform in favor of a scientific socialist platform, but his rule retained its autocratic tenor. He moved much of the power base out of the capital in order to draw support from his home *Betsimisiraka* and other *cotier* regions. In 1991 the government was crippled by an eight-month, 80,000-strong, civil servants strike in Antananarivo. The freeze in government activities, banking, and private sector development led to an economic crisis in the capital. The people of Antananarivo turned their attentions to supporting Zafy Albert and his *Hery Velona* (living forces) coalition of opposition parties. Under significant pressure, President Ratsiraka signed the Panorama Convention on October 31, 1991, paving the way for the country's first democratic elections, held on November 25, 1992. Zafy Albert soundly defeated Didier Ratsiraka and took the office of the presidency in January 1993.

Zafy Albert centralized his own power, moving the country more towards an unitary system. As Ratsiraka never successfully overturned multi-sectoral *Merina* privilege, the urban base meant an increased role for *Merina* forces in the central government once again. Zafy Albert's presidency was marred by significant charges of corruption, and he was impeached in 1997. New elections were held and Ratsiraka won back the presidency, taking office in January 1998.

The strongest divide in Malagasy political and social life today remains between the *Merina* and the *cotier*. *Merina* exceptionalism is well-characterized in the myth of *Ibonia* ("He of the clear and captivating glance") which tells the story of how a "Trouble Child" of divine birth conquers all other great leaders, making them his servants. *Merina* maintain control of the capital, the majority of the country's economy, the education system, and the nexus of power. The enmity towards the *Merina* was evidenced in 1995 when political opponents to *Merina* exceptionalism burned down the *Rova* (the Queens Palace) in Antananarivo. A hierarchical system within *Merina* society still exists and those who come from a royal heritage retain a certain privilege.

Outside the Central Highlands, *Merina* are often viewed with disdain.

The *Merina-cotier* divide is evidenced in the country's economy. Madagascar has a per capita Gross Domestic Product (GDP) of $800 (2002). Although opportunities for many *Merina* in Antananarivo are growing, most Malagasy continue to live beyond the pale of socioeconomic growth.

RICHARD MARCUS

Further Reading

Allen, Philip M., *Madagascar: Conflicts of Authority in the Great Island*, Boulder, Colorado: Westview Press, 1995

Covell, Maureen Ann, *Historical Dictionary of Madagascar*, Lanham, Maryland: Scarecrow Press, 1995

Covell, Maureen Ann, *Madagascar: Politics, Economics, and Society,* London and New York: F. Pinter, 1987

Ellis, Stephen, *The Rising of the Red Shawls: A Revolt in Madagascar, 1895–1899*, Cambridge and New York: Cambridge University Press, 1985

Feeley-Harnik, Gillian, *A Green Estate: Restoring Independence in Madagascar,* Washington, DC: Smithsonian Institution Press, 1991

Goodman, Steven M., and Bruce D. Patterson, editors, *Natural Change and Human Impact in Madagascar*, Washington, DC: Smithsonian Institution Press, 1997

Grimes, Barbara F., *Ethnologue: Languages of the World*, Dallas, Texas: SIL International, 13th edition, 1996. http://www.sil.org/ethnologue/countries/Mada.html

Kottak, Conrad Phillip, *The Past in the Present: History, Ecology, and Cultural Variation in Highland Madagascar*, Ann Arbor: University of Michigan Press, 1980

Larson, Pier Martin, *History and Memory in the Age of Enslavement: Becoming Merina in Highland Madagascar, 1770–1822*, Portsmouth, New Hampshire: Heinemann; Oxford: James Currey; Cape Town: David Philip, 2000

Minten, Bart, and Manfred Zeller, editors, *Beyond Market Liberalization: Welfare, Income Generation and Environmental Sustainability in Rural Madagascar,* Aldershot: Ashgate, 2000

Tronchon, Jacques, *L'Insurrection Malgache de 1947: Essai d'Interprétation*, Paris: Karthala, 1986

Maharashtrians

Capsule Summary

Location: Northern part of peninsular India
Total population: Approximately 80 million
Language: Marathi
Religion: Predominantly Hindu

Maharashtra is the third most populous state in India, which has a federal constitution. More than 80 percent of Maharashtrians are Hindus. Of the remaining, the followers of Islam and Buddhism form the largest groups. Three-fourths of the Maharashtrians speak Marathi, a language of the Indo-European family which evolved from Sanskrit. It has a history of about 1000 years. The majority of the Maharashtrians belong to the Australoid-European race. The State of Maharashtra came into existence in 1960 when the Indian provinces were reorganized on the basis of language.

Maharashtra occupies 9.36 percent (3,07,690 sq. km.) of the total area of India. Geographically three distinct regions can be identified: the narrow coastal strip adjoining the Arabian Sea, the Sahyadri ranges parallel to it, and the large eastern plateau. Culturally five regions are identified: Kokan, Deccan, Khandesh, Marathwada and Vidarbh. Maharashtra is considered a relatively advanced and better-industrialized state of India.

History

Archaeological investigations have revealed that there was human habitation in this area more than 150,000 years ago. Historical evidence is available from about eighth century BCE when parts of Maharashtra were under the rule of Maurya dynasty. Maharashtra or parts of it were ruled by different dynasties till the thirteenth century CE, prominent among them being the Satvahans, the Vakatakas and the Yadavas. During the rule of the Yadavas the pioneer saints, Dnyaneshwar and Namdev started the Bhakti (devotional) movement. This Bhakti cult has made a deep impression on the culture of the Maharashtrians.

Meanwhile the Muslims had already established their empire at Delhi in the North. Eventually they penetrated to the South and ruled in different parts including Maharashtra, at different times. Some of the Maratha feudal lords, Bhosales being prominent among them, resented the domination of the alien Muslim rulers and rebelled against them. Under Shivaji (1630–1680), their most capable leader, they created their independent kingdom. Since then Maharashtrians have idolized Shivaji who is the most venerated and adored personality in Maharashtra. Inspired by the example of Shivaji, the Peshwas who were Prime Ministers of the Bhosale dynasty established their hegemony in several parts of India. Finally, they were overpowered by the British East India Company at the beginning of the nineteenth century. In 1858, India came under the rule of the British Crown. Until the beginning of the British rule, the socioeconomic structure of India remained feudal.

The Colonial Period

The British established a unified legal and administrative machinery, built modern means of transport and communication and initiated the institutions of modern western education. The newly educated generation of Indians became increasingly aware of the exploitative nature of British rule. Political awakening slowly took place and soon the struggle for independence began under the aegis of Indian National Congress. In its first phase the struggle was led by Lokmanya Tilak (1856–1920) who was a Maharashtrian. After his death, the leadership was taken over by Mahatma Gandhi (1869–1948). The people of Maharashtra participated actively in this struggle for freedom. In 1947 India attained its independence and ceased to be a British colony.

Post-Independence Period

Maharashtra was the first state to initiate suitable legislation investing local self-governing institutions with substantial financial and administrative powers.

The Congress Party, the heir to the Indian National Congress, has been the ruling party in Maharashtra for most of the post-independence period. Like the whole of the Indian society, Maharashtrian society is also a caste-ridden society. It is divided into a hierarchy of caste groups. The castes have taken the form of pressure groups in the democratic politics in India. The Congress Party has its base mainly in the Maratha caste, which is the numerically largest landowning class in Maharashtra. The other two major parties (Bharatiya Janata Party and the ShivSena) have their support among the so-called upper castes like Brahmans and the middle

level castes. There are many other smaller parties like the Janata Dal, the Socialists, the Communists and so on. Mention must be made of the Republican Party which represents depressed castes, formerly known as untouchables. These castes along with various tribes are making their mark in the politics of Maharashtra. There is also a party called Shetkari Sanghatana that represents peasants. Industrial workers traditionally had their loyalties mainly with the Communist and Socialist parties. But in recent times these parties have lost their following among the workers to an appreciable extent.

Maharashtrian Society

About 60 percent of the population reside in rural areas and about the same proportion of the working population depend on agriculture. Apart from cereals, the important cash crops are sugarcane and cotton. The state has a large area under horticulture. Only a few cities are industrialized, Mumbai (Bombay) being the leading among them. Mumbai is a natural port and, with a population of around 12 million, among the world's largest metropolises. The foremost industries are chemicals, food products, rubber, plastic, petroleum, and spare parts for vehicles.

Maharashtra is known for its cooperative movement, conspicuous in which are the 115 cooperative sugar factories. In 1999, the GDP of Maharashtra (2.14 trillion rupees or US$47.5 billion) was 15 percent of India's total GDP.

Despite the rigidity of caste, reformist movements with a liberating potential have existed since the eleventh century in the form of the Mahanubhav cult and the Bhakti movement. The colonial period saw still more loosening of the caste taboos. Mahatma Jotirav Phule (1827–1890), founder of the Satyashodhak movement, made a forceful attack on the domination of Brahmans and opened schools for women and untouchables who had been deprived of education for ages. Later Dr. Bhimrav Ambedkar (1891–1956), himself a member of a depressed caste, fought dedicatedly for the rights of depressed castes. He is held in high esteem not only by the depressed classes but also by all the people in the country. Though the ideas of purity/pollution related to caste are on the decline, the traditional place of a caste in the caste hierarchy and its contemporary socioeconomic status still coincide to a large extent. Depressed castes and tribes together constitute about 20 percent of the total population. Independent India adopted the policy of protective discrimination towards them. However they have a long way to go before their socioeconomic status is raised to a satisfactory level. Caste-based violence is not unknown, although its extent is small. Relations between Hindus and Muslims are on the whole harmonious, although riots do take place sporadically.

There were agitations by peasants and tribals during the 1970s, and the feminist movement has been growing since that time. Groups working against superstitious beliefs and for the protection of environment are making sustained efforts.

The people of Maharashtra are believed to be hard working, honest and straightforward. Their warlike qualities are acknowledged by all. These characteristics of the Marathi people may have been shaped by their habitat. The land is not fertile, rain is uncertain and rivers are dry except during the monsoon season.

The households of the Marathi people are male dominated. However, women from Maharashtra are believed to enjoy a better status in comparison with those in several other states of India. Contrary to the common belief, the joint family is not a norm, though the kinship ties are strong.

The level of education in Maharashtra is greater than the average level of India. The number of the school-going children per thousand in Maharashtra is 213 while the average for India is 179.

The literary tradition of the Maharashtrians goes back to the saint-poets, among whom Tukaram is considered the greatest. The saint-poets coming from various castes produced a vast amount of devotional literature in the verse form. Their writings are still vastly popular throughout Maharashtra. Along with these saint-poets, Pundits wrote conventional metrical compositions drawing heavily for their subjects on ancient epic and mythological literature. Mention must also be made of the folk literature which was popular among the masses. With the introduction of the western education under the British rule, a generation of new writers produced modern forms of literature: essays, novels, drama, short stories and lyrical poetry. Since Independence, Marathi writers have followed world trends like realism, surrealism, and existentialism. In recent times, writers from the depressed classes are giving vent to their life-experiences and creating what is commonly called the literature of revolt. Journalism also started with the British rule and played its part very effectively in the social and political awakening of the Marathi people. More or less ideologically oriented during the British rule, it has become rather professional and commercial in the post-independence period.

Maharashtrians are known for their love of classical music and drama. They played a major role in popularizing classical music in the Indian Subcontinent. Marathi drama has a rich tradition of 150 years.

Maharashtrians have not been far behind in adapting to the global revolution in science and technology of the 1990s. They have attained some distinction especially in computer software. A large number of highly educated men and women from Maharashtra have settled abroad, mainly in the United States, some of them holding high positions in teaching institutions and business concerns.

ROHINI LELE

Further Reading

Census of India 1991, *State Profile 1991*, Delhi: Registrar General and Census Commissioner, 1998

Kolenda, Pauline, *Regional Differences in Family Structure in India*, Jaipur: Rawat Publications, 1987

Maharashtra Rajya, *Marathi Vishwakosh, Khand Barava,* Mumbai: Maharashtra Rajya Marathi Vishwakosh Nirmiti Mandal, 1985 (The State of Maharashtra, *Marathi Encyclopaedia, Vol.12,* Mumbai: Maharashtra State Marathi Encyclopaedia Publication Committee, 1985)

Maharashtra State Gazetteer, *Maharashtra: Land and Its People*, Mumbai: Government of Maharashtra, 1968

Majumdar, R.C., and V.G. Dighe, editors, *The Maratha Supremacy, Bharatiya Vidya Bhavan's History and Culture of the Indian People, Vol. 8*, Bombay: Bharatiya Vidya Bhavan, 1977

Omvedt, Gail, *Cultural Revolt in a Colonial Society: The Non-Brahman Movement in Western India: 1873 to 1930*, Bombay: Scientific Socialist Education Trust, 1976

Malawi

Capsule Summary

Country Name: Republic of Malawi
Location: Southern Africa
Total Population: 11,651,239 (July 2003)
Ethnic Divisions: major African peoples are Chewa, Lomwe, Tonga, Tumbuka, and Yao. Minorities include Indians, Europeans, and white South Africans
Languages: English (official), Chichewa (official), and other important regional languages
Religion: Protestant (55%), Roman Catholic (20%), Muslim (20%), indigenous beliefs (3%), other (2%)

Malawi lies in south-eastern Africa and has a population of 9.95 million; its government is a presidential-parliamentary democracy. The ethnonyms of the African peoples of Malawi correspond to their languages: Chewa (Nyanja), Lambya, Lomwe, Mpoto, Ngoni (Zulu), Nyakyusa, Sena, Tonga, Tumbuka, and Yao. Non-African groups include Indians (Kachchi-speaking), English, and Afrikaans native speakers. Christians form 75 percent of the population while Muslims form 20 percent. The GDP per capita was US$600 in 2002.

The time of the arrival of the first Bantu peoples in today's Malawi cannot be determined. Apparently these Bantu immigrants came in contact with a pre-existing population of hunters and gatherers, whom they either annihilated or assimilated. Between the fourteenth and sixteenth centuries CE another Bantu-speaking group, the "Maravi" (supposedly from the Congo), invaded the southern part of Malawi. The Maravi chiefdoms flourished in the sixteenth and seventeenth centuries within the territory of the Chewa (Nyanja) people and are therefore often ethnically identified with the Chewa. The Maravi states later collapsed one after the other, mainly due to destabilization by the Portuguese in the seventeenth century, but also owing to nineteenth century events such as intrusions of Yao and Ngoni and the slave trade. In 1891 the territories west and south of Lake Malawi were declared a protectorate by the British, the traditional chiefdoms not being unified at that time and not being able to provide any effective resistance. British missionaries exercised an intensive influence in the protectorate with the result that most of the Malawians are Christians today, and they created the written forms of Chichewa and Chitumbuka, while colonial administrators established them as lingua francas (governmental and trade languages). Another legacy of the colonial era is the high visibility of the Tumbuka, Chewa, and Yao, and therefore their reputation to be the "predominant people" of modern Malawi, even though, for example, Lomwe speakers outnumber the Yao and Tumbuka. This resulted from Tumbuka and Yao intellectuals being trained by missionary schools, while indirect rule was exercised during colonial times designating relations of domination and subordination among Africans along ethnic lines, mainly in favor of Tumbuka, Yao, and Ngoni, with communities and regions being structurally based on the colonial economy.

In 1964 the opposition against the British led to the proclamation of independent Malawi, autocratically ruled by Hastings Kamuzu Banda and his Malawi Congress Party (MCP).

During Banda's reign the "Chewa-ization" of Malawi was promoted; he himself was a Chewa, and the Chewa represent the largest ethnic group of Malawi. The claims of ethnicity could, if properly cultivated, have provided him with a very large compliant constituency among the common folk who would not challenge his autocratic rule. He may have also been persuaded by ethnic stereotypes of the time: the Chewa were popularly said to be unambitious, somewhat backward, and easily controlled, while Tumbuka, Ngoni, and Yao were said to be proud, warlike, and born to rule. Therefore he chose his loyal cadres among the Chewa; members of all other ethnic groups were considered potential opponents.

Banda took several measures to create his rural Chewa constituency: first he invested capital into the central region which was mainly inhabited by Chewa in order to develop its economy; secondly he Chewa-ized Malawian national identity through language policy and by the invention of a pre-colonial history dominated by Chewa tradition. Thirdly, Banda decided in 1968 that ChiNyanja, renamed ChiChewa, would be the only official African language in Malawi, mainly at the cost of ChiTumbuka, the dominant language in the north, which was banned from the civil service and media. However, Banda's main weapon for the supremacy of Chewa culture was simply repression; he frequently harassed and prosecuted Tumbuka intellectuals and civil servants by accusing them of tribalism, and he removed Tumbuka teachers from their jobs. In addition to that, the north was forced to stagnate economically. The Yao-dominated south did not suffer as much as the north from presidential paranoia since it was the center of the nation's commercial economy. Underneath the façade of national unity the rift between Chewa and non-Chewa became ever wider.

At the beginning of the 1990s, Malawi was hit by an economic crisis. Massive protests against Banda led to a referendum approving multiparty rule in 1993 and to free elections in 1994. Bakili Muluzi, a Yao Muslim and leader of the southern-based United Democratic Front (UDF), was elected to the Presidency, beating his main rivals Banda and Chihana, the candidate of the Tumbuka-based Alliance for Democracy (AFORD). In these elections, the domination of the Chewa emerged as an important variable for UDF and AFORD: non-Chewa districts consistently voted in opposition to the MCP (Banda's former party) even though this meant supporting candidates who were not of the voter's own ethnicity, non-Chewa Malawians often identifying with an opposition candidate simply because the candidate was not a Chewa.

After the elections of 1994, Muluzi's policy was to present himself as a figure of broad national unity. He supported the north by reinstating ChiTumbuka in the media and promised to improve the region's infrastructure. Muluzi won the 1999 elections against an MCP-AFORD coalition, but opposition leaders claimed fraud, violence erupting mainly in opposition strongholds of northern Malawi. Angry MCP supporters razed ten mosques and mobs targeted Muslims in protest

against Muluzi. During this turmoil, deep-seated prejudices against the Muslim minority came to light which apparently lay in the identification of Muslims with ruthless commercial practices, in particular the slave trade in the nineteenth century.

The Indians of Malawi, an economically important minority, are burdened with similar prejudices. After 1910, when Indian immigration was prohibited in the South African Union, the number of Indians, especially those from Gujarat, increased substantially in Malawi. They mostly came as merchants, and soon an Indian stereotype was created by the African majority which persists today: "the Indian" is a trader who does not invest in the country but sends his profits abroad, is a member of a secluded, purely "Indian" social and economic network which torpedoes African—and therefore "orderly"—commerce. However, the prejudice against the Indian minority has not yet lead to major violence.

REINHARD KLEIN ARENDT

See also **Gujaratis; Muslims in Africa; Slavery; Yao**

Further Reading

Forster, Peter G., "Culture, Nationalism, and the Invention of Tradition in Malawi," *The Journal of Modern African Studies*, 32, no.3 (1994)

Kalinga, Owen J.M., "The Production of History in Malawi in the 1960s: The Legacy of Sir Harry Johnston, the Influence of the Society of Malawi and the Role of Dr Kamuzu Banda and his Malawi Congress Party," *African Affairs*, 97 (1998)

Kaspin, Deborah, "The Politics of Ethnicity in Malawi's Democratic Transition," *The Journal of Modern African Studies*, 33, no.4 (1995)

Lienau, Cay, *Malawi. Geographie eines unterentwickelten Landes*, Darmstadt: Wissenschaftliche Buchgesellschaft, 1981

Power, Joey, "Race, Class, Ethnicity, and Anglo-Indian Trade Rivalry in Colonial Malawi, 1910–1945," *The International Journal of African Historical Studies*, 26, no.3 (1993)

Malays

Capsule Summary

Location: The Malay Peninsula, and littoral parts of the archipelago
Total Population: Tens of millions
Language: Bahasa Melayu
Religion: Islam

"The Malays" is a broad category of people who are to be found in Malaysia and other littoral parts of the archipelago. The history of the Malays in Malaysia has its roots in the migration of Minangkabau (and later other Indonesian) settlers to the peninsula of Malaysia beginning in pre-Islamic times. The Minangkabau have a long established practice of *rantau* whereby a young man leaves the family village and goes in search of experience in the wider economic world. In pre-Islamic, times a number of adventurous Minangkabau moved to Malacca and other coastal places of the archipelago. Over the centuries, other settlers from coastal Sumatra also moved to the Peninsula. Because of the presence of strong linking family threads between Sumatra and the Malay Peninsula, the Malay world is seen by most social scientists to extend beyond the Malays of Malaysia. Today the Malay world may be said to include the Malays of Malaysia, Islamic coastal Sumatran and Javanese communities, coastal groups within Sarawak, Sabah, Kalimantan and Sulawesi, and inhabitants of Brunei, southern Thailand, and southern Philippines. However, boundaries of the Malay world are by no means definite, and wax and wane depending on the context.

Language

The language, bahasa Melayu, was used for trading purposes and also used in religious writings in the pre-colonial and colonial era. This meant that places like Aceh and Riau in Sumatra were as much an integral part of the Malay world as were the principalities of Malacca, Johore, Kedah, Kelantan, and Trengganu. Bahasa Melayu was used extensively throughout the archipelago as the language that formed a bridge between cultures and local language groups. With the advent of the colonial era, but particularly during the nineteenth and twentieth centuries

bahasa Melayu gradually bifurcated as inhabitants in the Dutch sphere of influence adopted Dutch words for newly introduced items, such as *speda* for bicycle, and those in the English sphere of influence adopted English words such as *baisekel* for bicycle. Many other subtle differences of usage also occurred.

As independence movements began, assertion of a national language became important for the indigenous participants in what was to become Malaysia and Indonesia. Over the last fifty years of the twentieth century the languages have become more nationally distinctive. Malaysia and Indonesia have each set up their own national language development centers. Spelling has been standardized in each country and new words, particularly those with technical meanings, have been officially incorporated into the languages. The languages are now quite distinct, but are mutually intelligible.

The category "Malays" has thus tended to be leached from Indonesian society because the political category, "Indonesians" covers all the citizens of "Indonesia." Nonetheless the history of the archipelago attests to a broadly existing Malay world.

History

The history of the Malays consists of a series of stories, for there were a number of Malay polities. There was no ruler who united them all, but a number of rulers or *rajas* who sometimes vied with each other for power, who sometimes cooperated against a common enemy, and who used marriage between members of ruling families as a means of consolidating partnerships. These kingdoms were known as *kerajaan*. After their conversion to Islam, they were also known as sultanates, with the ruler also being known as the Sultan.

These stories tell of the Srivijaya empire that existed prior to the thirteenth century with its center in Sumatra and control extending to most of the Malay Peninsula; of the Acehnese sultanate of the sixteenth and seventeenth century where control extended down the west coast of Sumatra and across into parts of the Malay Peninsula; of the vicissitudes within Srivijaya and of movement of the center to Malacca at the beginning of the fifteenth century; and of the rise of Johor in the seventeenth century. Brunei in North Borneo was an independent kingdom with numbers of warlords acting as subservient rulers. This was the situation that the English adventurer, Rajah Brooke encountered when he arrived in Sarawak (western Borneo) in the nineteenth century. And on the east coast of the Peninsula, according to the historian, Paul Wheatley, Patani (in Southern Thailand) was considered to be the center of the former kingdom of Langkasuka, a kingdom that exercised power in the centers of Kelantan and Trengganu. For over a thousand years, Langkasuka flourished as a center of Malay culture, coming under Thai domination only in the early nineteenth century. It was able to maintain a degree of autonomy from the power of Srivijaya because of the overland trading route across the isthmus—between Langkasuka on the east and Kedah on the west.

There was frequent trade between China and these *kerajaan* during the centuries of flourishing Malay culture. Precious local items such as rhinoceros horn, ivory from elephant tusks, spices, and the woods of ebony and sandalwood were exchanged for porcelain, gold and silver items, lacquerware, silk, and umbrellas. When these commodities were imported into the Malay kingdoms they were used, displayed, and valued by the members of the ruling hierarchy, the most important of whom were looked upon as god-kings.

The history of the rise and fall of these kingdoms is the history of the Malay world. Throughout that history, the notion of the leader (raja) as god-king was one that had its roots in Hindu-Buddhist culture. With the coming of Islam to the region and, over time, the conversion of the leaders of these *kerajaan* to Islam, the maintenance of a court culture with a wealthy god-like ruler was retained. Trade remained the source of wealth. As well as barter, coins were used and money-changing dealers were part of the market place. Each of the sultanates had their own coinage, and local museums display these locally produced coins. The court was set up with an extensive palace or dwelling for the ruler and compound of dwellings for his retainers, a mosque—often with a center of learning attached, and a market or trading center. Dwellings outside were often arranged in quarters for traders from particular parts of the trading world—Arabs, Indians, Chinese, later-Europeans, Javanese, Buginese (from Sulawesi) and others. Local traders came from the hinterland bringing valuable forest products, spices and—depending on the region—gold, silver, and other precious

metals. This pattern was as much true for Java as for Sumatra where the kingdoms of Majapahit and Banten are examples of similar centers of power. The common people lived along the riverbanks and outside the court complex in wooden or *atap* dwellings.

Rivalry for power and dominance between individual trading centers of the region was rife. Control of resources and access to sea and land routes was crucial. One such example is the movement of power from Palembang (Sumatra) to Malacca (Malay Peninsula) at the beginning of the fifteenth century. At this time, the center of power in the region had shifted from Srivijaya to Malacca (Melaka) and this port assumed Srivijaya's rich cultural legacy in conjunction with an assertive, aggressive economic control over all traffic using the Strait: It was the Palembang [Srivijaya] tradition which was Malacca's heritage. To quote from the *Sejarah Melayu*: "From below the wind to above the wind Melaka became famous as a very great city, the raja of which was sprung from the line of Sultan Iskandar Zul-karnain [Alexander the Great]; so much so that princes from all countries came to present themselves before [the ruler]." One can add that, costumes (including textiles of silk and gold), weaponry, jewelry, house decoration, and items for ritual and religious practice were made for use by the Sultan and the wealthy traders (*orang besar* or *orang kaya*) of this port-city.

Islam, through the court mosque, buttressed the ruler. Historical epics (hikayat) were written by official scribes within the mosque to enhance the ruler's position. Numbers of these hikayat give us an insight into the historical period in which they were writing. Many give long genealogies establishing the credentials of the ruler or tell of wars and battles in which the victors are proudly depicted. Examples are Hikayat Ketoeroenan Radja Deli (Medan), Hikayat Radja-Radja Pasai (North Aceh), Bustan as-Salatin (Aceh), Hikayat Perang Sabil (Aceh), Hikayat Pahang (Pahang), Hikayat Johor serta Pahang (Johore and Pahang) and Terombo asal oesoel ketoeroenan Radja negeri Kota Pinang (Penang). The region of the Sultanate is in brackets.

Malay Society

Malay culture has historically been one of great hierarchies. Language that connotes subservience, along with manners and dress that depict recognition of status and gender differences, were all adhered to meticulously. Up until the middle of the twentieth century, Malay society was very much bifurcated into court culture and the culture of the commoners who lived in wooden huts outside the court complex. The court culture was lavish and ostentatious.

Examples of the extravagant court culture are to be found in all the sultanates. These elaborate court cultures included the presence of skilled craftspeople who undertook metalworking, spinning, weaving, and woodcarving on behalf of the Sultan and his entourage. The arts of music, dancing, and drama were highly developed. For such a florescence of culture to occur, stability and patronage were essential. A Chinese source gives the following description of the people of Langkasuka: '[The] people wear their hair loose and [have] sleeveless cotton garments. The king as usual, rides upon an elephant under a canopy, preceded by drums and flags and surrounded by a fierce-looking body-guard.' A description of any of the sultanates would add: Those of the raja's family wore silk. Sometimes it was woven with gold threads in a supplementary weft. Jewelry was of gold and involved intricate filigree work. Weaponry was elaborate and consisted of a kris or rencong with a highly bejewelled hilt and an ivory or sandalwood scabbard. Such traditions have continued on until the twenty-first century with weddings of elite Malays displaying many of the characteristics of their ancient forebears.

The common person lived simply and relied on subsistence agriculture. Rice was the staple diet. It was grown on cultivated plots using the wet rice method, although in the highlands, which tended to be peripheral to the ruler and his kingdom, dry rice was grown on the steep hillsides. The people were Muslim and adhered to the precincts of Islam. Earlier animist beliefs of magic and the spirit world infused their thinking also. Rites of passage—births, weddings, circumcisions and deaths plus the building of a new house or the return of a family member from a long voyage—were occasions for a feast of either celebration or mourning, involving whole communities. Prayers were said, certain practices were adhered to, men and women were usually in separate groups and a strong feeling of communal association was engendered.

Rivers were the principal means of transport. They allowed the easy transport of goods from the hinterland that were so valuable as trading items. In order for a settlement to be established, the currents of the sea and the ease of access by the large sailing ships to a port were crucial, as ships were the principal means of bringing imports to these kingdoms. Access to fresh water was crucial for the settlement. A strategic loca-

tion that allowed visual access to enemy incursions was also important. These Malay kingdoms were therefore located up river—not too far from the sea, but in a tactical position where hinterland resources were rich and there was access to a suitable docking facilities for the trading vessels that plied the seas.

Independence

There has been no broad-based move for independence involving all those who are seen to be part of the Malay world. Independence movements have taken place separately within either the British or the Dutch spheres. The exception was within the island of Borneo, where a land border was shared with the British and the Dutch and where moves for greater Malay cooperation were initiated in the immediate post-war period but not allowed to bloom.

Within Indonesia at the end of the twentieth century, there has been a strong independence movement among the Acehnese for independence from Jakarta; there have also been smaller movements for independence in Riau and in Kalimantan. These movements all hark back to what are seen in retrospect as the "golden" days of the kingdoms or sultanates that existed in their regions.

Within the Malay and Borneo States the situation was different from Indonesia in that an armed uprising by Malays against the colonial ruler did not take place on the same scale. The Malay sultans within what became Malaysia had a long history of cooperation with the British for their mutual financial benefit. However it was the British who retained the upper hand. The noted Malaysian historian Khoo Kay Kim wrote

> The British undermined the powerful position of the *orang besar* [wealthy men who were close to the Sultan]. They introduced Western practices in land administration and Western laws to tighten political control over the Malay states. The system of revenue collection was overhauled in order to provide the necessary infrastructure for economic development.

In effect, the British ruled the Malays through their Sultan.

Large numbers of Chinese who were involved in both the lucrative tin-mining trade and in the growing of pepper and gambier in the south meant that the political configuration was different from that which existed within Sumatra and other parts of the archipelago. For example in 1884, the historian Skinner estimated that the population of the State of Johor had a larger number of Chinese than Malays.

The change within the Malay community was the result of two factors: the movement of Malays to the urban centers where Chinese and Indians dominated the economic activities, and Malays saw themselves as left behind and wished to change that situation. The second factor was the involvement of Malays in education where an attitude gradually developed that it was important to take control of their own destiny. In fact it was the British who encouraged education for the Malays in the Federated states (those states primarily on the west coast), whilst in Kelantan and Trengganu, it was the Muslim community that provided education. Malay students went to Britain and to the Middle East and there developed a broad-based mood for change.

By the 1930s, Malays were involved in a number of associations for the protection and advancement of the Malay interests. These were taken up by a number of Malay language publications throughout the Peninsula. This growing awareness led to the transformation of many passive and submissive commoners into questioning, critical citizens. When the Japanese arrived in 1942, they dislocated the political control that the British had established. Radical Malays now existed in each of the Malay states. Many of them had received military training from the Japanese. These Malays set up many groups that aimed to demand greater involvement for Malays in the political scene. Intellectuals and radicals from Indonesia influenced a number of the groups. These groups were a direct challenge to UMNO (United Malay National Organization) with whom the British were working closely (and with whom they eventually worked out an arrangement for the new nation of Malaysia). Indeed it can be said that the growing presence of these Malay-left groups was a manifestation of democracy beginning to occur within the Malay community.

Within Malaysia, the Malays are not a homogenous ethnic group of people. The political exigencies of the last fifty years of the twentieth century within Malaysia have meant that Malays can be seen as a socially constructed group with certain unifying and clearly identifiable practices.

The observance of Islam, the use of the Malay language as mother tongue, and adoption of certain cultural practices in their rites of passage have been as much defining characteristics of being Malay as blood. "The Malays" are a category that is in the making within Malaysia. An Iban, Bidayuh, or Melanau living in Sarawak who converts to Islam is considered to have "masuk Melayu"—become Malay. A Muslim Minangkabau immigrant from West Sumatra will be regarded as Malay, as will a Muslim Mandailing Batak from North Sumatra, or an immigrant from Mindanao (Philippines) who comes to Sabah. A Batak Christian from North Sumatra will be regarded as an anomaly and will probably retain the nomenclature *Indonesian*. A baby of a Malay father and a Chinese mother will also be regarded as Malay, with the wife having to formally convert to Islam. However the offspring of a non-Moslem Chinese father and a Malay mother would be likely to have great social problems, as the mother would have transgressed cultural boundaries. Conversion from Islam to another religion such as Catholicism or Buddhism is not sanctioned.

Malaysians must be identified by race according to their law. There is therefore an ongoing need to include and exclude people from the Malay category. Politically, the government is eager to increase the number of Malays within the society, for up until 1998 it was assumed that Malays would primarily vote for the United Malay National Organization (UMNO). UMNO is part of an umbrella of parties within the ruling Barisan Nasional (BN). With the jailing of the then Deputy Prime Minister, the Malay vote has become much more dispersed. Economically and educationally, there are potential privileges in Malaysia for those who fall within the category Malay.

The presence of the Malay left (*kiri*) and the Malay right (*kanan*) can be seen in Malaysian politics at the beginning of the twenty-first century. With independence movements also occurring within parts of the Malay world in Indonesia, national boundaries can be seen to be rather more contingent than they were in the latter quarter of the twentieth century.

BARBARA LEIGH

See also **Malaysia**

Further Reading

Andaya, Barbara Watson, and Leonard Y. Andaya, *A History of Malaysia*, London: Macmillan Asian Histories Series, 1982

Kahn, Joel, and Francis Loh Kok Wah, *Fragmented Vision: Culture and Politics in Contemporary Malaysia*, Sydney: Allen and Unwin, 1992

Khoo Kay Kim, *Malay Society: Transformation and Democratisation*, Kuala Lumpur: Pelanduk, 1991; reprinted, 1995

Leigh, Barbara, *The Changing Face of Malaysian Crafts: Identity, Industry and Ingenuity*, Kuala Lumpur: Oxford University Press, 2000

Milner, A.C., *Kerajaan: Malay Political Culture on the Eve of Colonial Rule*, Tuscon: The University of Arizona Press, 1982

Wheatley, Paul, *The Golden Khersonese*, Kuala Lumpur: University of Malaya Press, 1966

Malaysia

Capsule Summary

Location: Southeast Asia, between one and seven degrees north of the equator

Total Population: 23,092,940 (July 2003)

Languages: Bahasa Melayu (official), English, Chinese dialects, Tamil, Telugu, Malayalam, Panjabi, and several indigenous languages including Iban and Kadazan

Religions: Islam (official), Buddhism, Daoism, Hinduism, Christianity, Sikhism, and Shamanism in East Malaysia

Malaysia comprises the peninsula (West Malaysia) and East Malaysia (Sabah and Sarawak). Altogether there are 13 states and two Federal Territories of Kuala Lumpur (the country's capital) and the island of Labuan. Each one of the states in the peninsula has a king called Sultan. The country's constitutional monarch called Yang Di Pertuan Agong is elected from the nine Sultans once every five years. The government is elected once every five years under parliamentary democracy and is headed by the Prime Minister. Malaysia is now governed by the coalition government called National Front (formerly the Alliance) led by the Malay party called United Malays National Organization (UMNO), with the Chinese party Malaysian Chinese Association (MCA) and the Indian party Malaysian Indian Congress (MIC) as the other major partners. Most of Malaysia's export trade is with Japan and the United States; its per capita GDP was US$8,800 in 2002.

History

Malaya (now Peninsular Malaysia) lies at a strategic meeting point for sea travels from the west and east through the Straits of Malacca. Indeed the significance of the Malay kingdom of the fifteenth century owed much to this strategic location. It was then that Islam began to take root here. Previously the local peoples, who had their own indigenous religions, were under the influence of Hinduism and Buddhism, especially during the period of the Malay Srivijaya Empire. The Portuguese took Malacca in 1511 and destroyed the sultanate. The British came towards the end of the eighteenth century, marking the beginning of direct and indirect British rule until 1957 when Malaya gained independence. During the colonial period, many immigrants from China, India, and the rest of the Malay

Archipelago came to Malaya in response to the expanding colonial economy. This turned Malaya into a very plural society, which worried the indigenous Malay elite. After the Second World War, Malay nationalism grew in strength, and by 1946, the Malays of different states became quite united as a nation. Sabah and Sarawak were also under the British influence; the former was a British Protectorate under the British North Borneo Chartered Company, while the latter was ruled by the Brooke family, the White Rajah (White King). In 1963, Sabah, Sarawak and Singapore joined Malaya to form the Federation of Malaysia, but in 1965, Singapore became an independent country.

Society and Ethnicity

The population of Malaysia is 22 million, about 50 percent of which are Malays, who comprise ethnic Malays and people whose forebear came from different Indonesian islands, such as the Javanese and Banjar, as well as descendants of other Muslim immigrants such as Arabs. There are also the Jawi Peranakans in Penang, who are offspring of union between South Indian Muslims and Malay women. The descendants of these Muslim immigrants are now assimilated into the mainstream Malay society although some of them still maintain their original identity as a sub-identity. For example, some Javanese communities identify themselves as both Malays and Javanese. The Malays are Muslims, and defined to be so in the Constitution. Malay is the national language and Islam is the official religion. But Malaysia is not an Islamic state and all citizens are guaranteed by the Constitution to have the freedom to practice their religions and cultures. Indeed each ethnic group continues to speak its own language among themselves, while English is an important language in the private sector, along with Malay and Chinese languages.

At the time of independence, Malays were economically weak compared to the Chinese, and special privileges were included in the Constitution to help them. Since the 1970s, the Malay-dominated coalition government has pushed the affirmative action policy aggressively to help the *bumiputera* (sons of the soil), mainly Malays, in all fields. As a result there is now

779

a growing Malay middle class and a class of Malay capitalists. But the policy has also led to polarization of ethnic groups, with non-Malays complaining of discrimination in the government sector, statutory bodies, and universities.

The Chinese, comprising 28 percent of the population, are the second largest category. In relation to the Malays and other ethnic groups, the Chinese form an ethnic group, although internally they are differentiated into different speech groups. Most of them are Hokkiens (Minnan people), followed by the Hakka (Kheh), Cantonese, Teochiu (Teochews), Hainanese, Hockchiu, Kwongsai, Henghua, Hockchia, and other smaller groups. Despite the constraints of Malay political dominance, the Chinese have their own government recognized Chinese-medium primary schools as well as 60 independent Chinese secondary schools. Thus many Chinese Malaysians are literate in Chinese. Like other Malaysians, the younger generations are also literate in Malay, the national language. Most Chinese Malaysians are Buddhists and followers of Chinese religion, and there are Christians, Muslims and followers of other faiths as well as atheists.

Next in number are the Indians, at about 8 percent, but this category is broad as it covers all peoples of South Asia origin like the Tamils (majority), Malayalis, Punjabis, Telegus, and Sinhalese. In the nineteenth century many Indians were brought in as estate laborers, and many continue to be marginalized waged laborers. The economically better class comprises merchants and professional peoples like lawyers and teachers. English and Malay are the lingua franca among the Indians while most speak their own mother tongues. Hindusim is the major religion, with Deepavali and Thaipusam as the major festivals. Other religions include Sikhism, Islam, and Christianity.

Apart from these three main ethnic groups, there are a number of small minority groups in the peninsula. In the northern states of Kelantan, Perlis and Kedah, there are ethnic Thais, locally called the Siamese. A majority of them are Theravada Buddhists (Thai tradition). In Kedah and Perlis there are also Thai-speaking Muslim communities called "Sam-Sam." Many of the Thais have close interaction with ethnic Chinese, and in Kelantan, many of the localized Chinese can speak the local Thai dialect, too. There are many Thai temples in these regions, most of which are also sponsored by the local Chinese.

The colonial experiences had produced some Eurasian communities in the country. One such community of Portuguese Malaysians is found in Ujong Pasir, Malacca. Some of them still speak the creolized Portuguese language called Cristao (pronounced Christang), besides English and Malay. Seen as the poorer Eurasians, many of them are fishermen. They are Catholics, and their annual celebration of Fiesta San Pedro attracts many tourists. Another Eurasian community is the Penang Eurasians who are of British origin from Penang. They have a tradition of marrying Chinese. Malacca is also home to a creolized South Indian community called Chitty. They identify themselves as Indian (specifically Chitty) but speak Malay as their home language and women wear Malay-styled clothes. Their settlement in Gajah Berang has many Hindu temples. In Malacca, too, are found the Babas, the creolized Chinese who also self-identify as "Peranakan Cina," Chinese Peranakans. They identify as Chinese but Malay is their mother tongue, while many also speak English. Like the Chitty and the Portuguese Malaysians, their women's ethnic attire is of Malay/ Indonesian style, generally sarong and *kebaya* top. The women are called *nyonya*, and the delicious spicy *nyonya* food (Baba food) which has both Chinese and localized features, is well known in Malaysia and Singapore.

The aboriginal people, most of whom are descendants of the earliest settlers in the Malay Peninsula, are today known in Malay as Orang Asli, meaning "original people." Totaling about 90,000 people, they are usually divided into three broad categories, namely Semang comprising Kensiu, Kintaq, Jahai, Lanoh, Mendriq and Batek; Senio comprising Semai, Temiar, Jah Hut, Chewong, and Ma' Betise' (Mah Meri); and Aboriginal Malays comprising Temuan, Semelai, Temoq, Semaq Beri, Jakun, Orang Kanak, Orang Kuala, and Orang Selatar. The largest groups are the Semai and Temiar. Most of the Orang Asli are Austroasiatic Mon-Khmer speakers, while the Proto-Malay groups such as the Jakun are Austronesian speakers, as are Malays. Even the Jakun who are looked down by the mainstream Malay society are distinct people with their own Malay dialect. Historically the Orang Asli were swidden cultivators while the Semang groups like the Batek were hunters and gatherers (and some of them still are). Today most of them are marginalized farmers and poorly paid workers. Officially administered by the Malay-controlled Department of Orang Asli Affairs, the Orang Asli are losing their ancestral lands to rural and infrastructure development such as the building of roads and dams, and most live in government settlements. They also encounter government effort to assimilate them into the Malay society, including conversion to Islam. Some educated Orang Asli now try to articulate their causes through the Malaysian Orang Asli Association, while the non-governmental organization Center for Orang Asli Concerns has been vocal in advocating Orang Asli interests.

Minorities in East Malaysia

While Malays, Chinese and Indians are distributed all over Malaysia, the indigenous peoples in East Malaysia are quite different from those in Peninsular Malaysia. The largest category in Sabah is Kadazan/Dusun (about 25 percent of the state's 1.4 million people). But in the context of Malaysia as a whole they are a minority group. The other populations in Sabah (including Labuan), according to the 1991 census, are Chinese (15.6 percent), Bajau (about 15.2 percent), Malays (8.9 percent), Murut (3.9 percent), followed by other indigenous peoples (19.3 percent), and others (12.7 percent). Other indigenous minorities include Rungus, Lun Dayeh, Bisaya, Kedayan, Illanun, Suluk, Ida'an, Orang Sungai, Tidong, and others. About 54 percent of the population in Sabah are Muslims and the rest are Christians, Buddhists, followers of Chinese religion, or other indigenous religions. Bajaus and Malays are Muslims, while most of the Kadazan/Dusun as well as Rungus are Christians. There are many immigrants from Indonesia and the Philippines, especially from the Sulu region. These immigrants add to the Muslim population in the state. In party politics, the major players are Malays, Chinese, Kadazan/Dusun, and Bajau.

In Sarawak, the largely non-Muslim indigenous peoples are loosely referred to as Dayak, although the label is more associated with the Iban and the Bidayuh, in the past called Sea Dayak and Land Dayak respectively. Most Ibans and Bidayuhs observe their traditional religious rites, although they are many Christians, too. The label Orang Ulu (literally Upriver People) refers to the interior groups comprising Kayan, Kenyah, Lun Bawang, Kelabit, Bisaya, Berawan, Kejaman, Sekapan, Lahanan, Punan Ba, Sian, Bhuket, Penan and other smaller groups. Of these the Penans are until recently nomads, and many still lead semi-nomadic life. Most of the Orang Ulu people are now Christians belonging to the Borneo Evangelical Mission, locally called SIB or Sidang Injil Borneo. A declining number still observe traditional indigenous religions, and there are some Muslims, too. The major Muslim groups, other than ethnic Malays,

include Kedayan and Jatti Meirek who also identify as Malays politically, while many of the Melanau are Muslims with the rest being Christians and followers of traditional religion. In fact Muslim Melanau identify themselves as both Malays and Melanau. In terms of population size of the state's 1.7 million people (1991 census), the Iban (29.8 percent) are followed by Chinese (28 percent), Malays (21.2 percent), Bidayuh (8.3 percent), Melanau (5.7 percent), other indigenous peoples (6.1 percent) and others (0.9 percent). An interesting feature of Sarawak's indigenous minorities is the formation of communal associations, ethnic associations that serve to articulate the respective groups' ethnic interest. This is partly encouraged by competition for state and national resources along ethnic line as well as by logging activities since the 1970s. Logging has affected the livelihood of the indigenous minorities in the interior, many of whom still practice swidden agriculture (also called shifting cultivation) as well as hunting and gathering jungle products. The construction of the Bakum Dam in the Belaga District in interior Sarawak, which began in the late 1990s, had resulted in the resettlement of 15 longhouse settlements of more than eight thousand people belonging to Kayan, Kenyah, Lahanan, Penan Talun and Bhuket groups. Resettled in Sungai Koyan with electricity and water supplies, they are given relatively little land.

In a sense Malaysia is a land of minorities. While the Malays are numerically and politically dominant, they have minority complex in a land where almost the other half of the population is non-Malays and non-Muslims. This majority with minority complex is reflected in the affirmative action policy for them. Politics in Malaysia remains ethnically polarized, and the major political parties are communal parties that are based on ethnic lines. The ideology of *bumiputera* polarizes Malays and non-Malays. Nevertheless since Independence, Malaysia has remained a relatively stable and prosperous state, except for the racial riot in 1969. The fragile democracy, generally efficient civil service and judiciary, as well the relatively professional security forces, have all helped to preserve a relatively harmonious multiethnic nation.

TAN CHEE-BENG

See also **Malaysia; Orang Asli**

Further Reading

Andaya, Barbara Watson, and Leonard Y. Andaya, *A History of Malaysia*, London: Macmillan Education, 1982

Dentan, Robert Knox, et. al., *Malaysia and the Original People: A Case Study of the Impact of Development on Indigenous Peoples*, Boston: Allyn and Bacon,1997

Husin Ali, Syed, *The Malays: Their Problems and Future*, Kuala Lumpur: Heinemann Asia, 1981

King, Julie K., and John Wayne King, editors, *Languages of Sabah: A Survey Report*. Pacific Linguistics Series C, No. 78, Canberra: Department of Linguistics, Research School of Pacific Studies, The Australian National University, 1984

Lee, Kam Hing, and Tan Chee-Beng, editors, *The Chinese in Malaysia*. Kuala Lumpur: Oxford University Press.

Tan, Chee-Beng, "Ethnic Identities and National Identities: Some Examples from Malaysia," *Identities* 6(4): 441–480

Malcolm X (African-American)

Malcolm X, Muslim name El-Hajj Malik El-Shabazz, was an African-American civil rights leader in the 1950s and early 1960s who articulated concepts of race pride and black nationalism. He was known for his outspokenness and articulation of the anger felt and injustices suffered by many African-Americans during the modern African-American Civil Rights Movement and as a prominent member of the Nation of Islam from 1952 until 1964. Malcolm X was assassinated in February 1965 by members of the Nation of Islam.

Born Malcolm Little on 19 May 1925 in Omaha, Nebraska, Malcolm was one of eight children of Louise Norton Little, homemaker, and Earl Little, an outspoken Baptist minister who supported black nationalism as articulated by Marcus Garvey. Growing up in Lansing, Michigan, Malcolm saw his house burned down (1929) and his father killed (1931) by a local white supremacist group The Black Legion. His mother was placed in a mental institution and he then spent a number of years in detention homes. In his early teens, he moved to Boston to live with his sister where he was eventually arrested and imprisoned for 8 to 10 years for armed robbery in 1946. While in prison Malcolm was converted to the Nation of Islam, a black Muslim group that professed the superiority of black people and the inherent evil of white people. In 1952, he was released from prison and went to Nation of Islam headquarters in Chicago, met the Nation's leader, Elijah Muhammad, and embraced its doctrine. Following in the tradition of the Nation, he changed his last name to "X," a custom among Nation of Islam followers who considered their family names to have originated with white slaveholders. Malcolm became an Assistant Minister in the Nation in 1953 at Detroit Temple No. 1. The next year he was appointed Minister at the first Nation of Islam temple in Boston. He also became a national spokesman for the Nation of Islam and was charged by Elijah Muhammad with establishing new mosques in cities such as Detroit, Michigan and Harlem, New York. Malcolm used newspapers, radio, and television to communicate the Nation of Islam's message across the United States. As a result of his drive, conviction, and extremely effective oratory skills, the Nation of Islam grew in numbers from 500 in 1952 to 30,000 in 1963.

As racial tensions ran increasingly high during the early 1960s, Malcolm's outspokenness and colorful personality captured the U.S. government's attention. The Federal Bureau of Investigation agents infiltrated the Nation of Islam and covertly monitored the group's activities. In 1963, Malcolm learned that Elijah Muhammad was secretly having relations with as many as six women in the Nation of Islam, some of which had resulted in children. Malcolm refused Muhammad's request to keep the matter quiet despite his loyalty to the organization. In addition, Malcolm received severe criticism after making disparaging comments after the assassination of President John F. Kennedy and was soon silenced for 90 days by Muhammad. Later that year, he founded the Organization of Afro-American Unity, a civil rights organization with a platform that called for a bloodless revolution to solve the race problem in America, that stated that not all whites were inherently evil and that white individuals, not all whites collectively, were responsible for race problems, that believed all blacks from all religions should come together to help solve the race problem, and that did not endorse strict racial separation as the Nation of Islam had.

In March 1964, Malcolm X terminated his relationship with the Nation of Islam and founded the Muslim Mosque, Inc. In that same year, he went on a pilgrimage to Mecca, Saudi Arabia. The trip greatly affected his Muslim believes and his assessment of the relationship between the races, as he ate, drank, slept, and worshipped with Caucasian Muslims. He returned to the United States with a new message for all races, one of cooperation to fix the race problem in America. His separation from the Nation of Islam and his public criticism of Elijah Muhammad placed Malcolm in physical danger. There were numerous attempts on his life. For example, on February 14, 1965, his home in East Elmhurst, New York where his family lived was firebombed. On February 21, 1965, at a speaking engagement in the Audubon Ballroom in New York City, three gunmen assassinated the 39-year-old Malcolm X. Fifteen hundred people attended his funeral in Harlem on February 27, 1965 at the Faith Temple Church of God in Christ, now Child's Memorial Temple Church of God in Christ. The assassins were members of the Nation of Islam and were convicted of first-degree murder in March 1966. Malcolm X is buried at the Ferncliff Cemetery in Hartsdale, New York.

Capsule Biography

Malcolm X. Born Malcolm Little May 19, 1925 in Omaha Nebraska; family moved to Milwaukee, Wisconsin, 1926; Family moved to East Lansing, Michigan, 1929; attended public schools in East Lansing and Mason, Michigan; arrested and sent to prison, 1946–1952; became a minister in the Nation of Islam in Detroit, 1953; married Betty X, 1958; Minister, Nation of Islam, 1953–1963; Founder, Organization of Afro-American Unity, 1963; Assassinated, 21 February 1965, New York City, New York.

Selected Works

Malcolm X, As Told to Alex Haley, *The Autobiography of Malcolm X*, Ballantine Books, Inc., 1992.

RICHARD VERRONE

See also **African-American Nationalism and Separatism**

Further Reading

Baldwin, Lewis V., et al., *Between Cross and Crescent: Christian and Muslim Perspectives on Malcolm and Martin*, Gainesville: University Press of Florida, 2002
Breitman, George, editor, *Malcolm X Speaks: Selected Speeches and Statements*, New York: Grove/Atlantic, 1990
DeCaro, Louis A., *Malcolm and the Cross: The Nation of Islam, Malcolm X, and Christianity*, New York: New York University Press, 1998
Jenkins, Robert L., and Mfanya Donald Tryman, *The Malcolm X Encyclopedia*, Colorado: Greenwood Publishing Group, 2002
Myers, Walter Dean, *Malcolm X: By Any Means Necessary*, New York: Scholastic, 1994
Rickford, John R.,, *Betty Shabazz—A Biography: Her Life with Malcolm X and Fight to Preserve His Legacy*, Napierville, IL: Sourcebooks, 2000
Rickford, Russell J., *Betty Shabazz: A Life Before and After Malcolm X*, Naperville, IL: Sourcebooks, 2003.

Maldives

Capsule Summary

Country Name: *Dhivehi Raajjeyge Jumhooriyyaa*, Republic of Maldives (formerly Maldive Islands)
Location: Southern Asia, southwest of the southern tip of India in the northern Indian Ocean
Total Population: 329,684 (2003)
Languages: Divehi (an Indo-European tongue related to Sinhalese), English.
Religion: Sunni Islam

The Maldives are located in southern Asia, southwest of the southern tip of India and about 674 kilometers (420 miles) west of Sri Lanka, in the northern Indian Ocean. The country has a total land area of about 298 square kilometers (115 square miles) and is made up of a chain of 1,190 small coral islands that are grouped around the Malé island. It is one of the smallest states in southern Asia.

The population of the Maldives is estimated at 329,684 (2003, CIA), up from about 213,200 in 1990 (1990, census). It is predominantly rural with around 70 percent of the people living in villages and farms. The country's capital city, Malé, is home to about 66,000 people (2003), or about 20 percent of the population. The Maldives has a high population growth rate of 2.91 percent (2003, CIA), and it is estimated that under the current growth rate the population could double by 2030. The country has one of the highest population densities in the world, standing at around 1,100 people per square kilometer (2,860 people per square mile).

The Republic of Maldives is a unitary republic, and its form of government is presidential democracy. The country declared independence from the Great Britain on July 26,1965. It became a republic in November 1968 following the national referendum of March 1968. In 1968 the country adopted its first Constitution. A new revised Constitution was ratified in 1997, and it came into effect in 1998. The *Majlis* (Parliament) is a unicameral 50-member national legislative body. The president is the head of state. He is selected by the *Majlis* members and elected by popular vote for a five-year term. The president nominates the cabinet. There are no political parties in Maldives as of 2003.

The Maldives is a heterogeneous country. The majority of the population is of Sinhalese (related to the Sinhalese of Sri Lanka) and Dravidian origin, although there are significant elements of the Arab, African and Indian influence. The majority of the population is Sunni Muslims.

However, religion does not play an important role in the political life, although there was an increase in religious practice and the influence of the Islamic solidarity after beginning of the U.S.-led war in Afghanistan and Iraq. The current ethnic and religious structure was mainly formed fifteenth and seventeenth centuries, and did not change significantly during the colonial era.

The GDP per capita in the Maldives is among highest among southern Asian countries (in purchasing power parity) at around US$3,900 (2002, CIA). Most of the population is engaged in agriculture (including fishing), industry (including mining, manufacturing and construction) and services (including tourism). In 2002 the UNDP's Human Development Index (HDI) put Maldives in 84th place (out of 173), behind Georgia, Peru, and Grenada, but ahead of Turkey, Jamaica, and Turkmenistan.

RAFIS ABAZOV

Further Reading

Cain, Bruce D., and James W. Gair, *Dhivehi (Maldivian)*, München: Lincom Europa, 2000

Forbes, Andrew, *Maldives: Kingdom of a Thousand Isles*, Hong Kong: Odyssey Publications, 1st edition, 2004

Johari, J.C., et al., *Governments and Politics of South Asia*, New Delhi: Sterling Publishers, 1991

Lamberti, Stefania, *Maldives*, London: New Holland, 1997

Maldives: Country Economic Memorandum: Policies for Sustaining Economic Growth, Washington, DC: The World Bank, 1999

Maldives Ministry of Planning and Development, *Vulnerability and Poverty Assessment, 1998*, Malé: Ministry of Planning and National Development in cooperation with the United Nations Development Program, 1999

Maldives President's Office Home Page. <http://www.presidencymaldives.gov.mv/>

Maldives, 25 Years of Independence, Bangkok, Thailand: Media Transasia, 1990

Ministry of Women's Affairs & Social Security Site Home Page. <http://www.urcmaldives.gov.mv/>

Mali

Capsule Summary

Country Name: Republic of Mali

Location: West Africa; bordered by Senegal, Mauritania, Algeria, Niger, Burkina Faso, Côte d'Ivoire and Guinea

Total Population: 11,626,219 (July 2003)

Languages: French (official), Bambara (80%), Peul and Songhai widely spoken

Religions: Muslims (90%), African traditional religions (9%), Christians (1%)

The Republic of Mali, with an area of about 1,240,192 sq. km (478,841 sq. miles), is a landlocked country in West Africa bordered by seven countries: Senegal to the west, Mauritania to the northwest, Algeria to the northeast, Niger to the east, Burkina Faso to the southeast, Côte d'Ivoire to the south, and the Republic of Guinea to the southwest. With about 60 percent of its land area desert and savannah, Mali is among the poorest countries in the world, according to the UN Human Development Report (2003). The country's main export, cotton, over the years has been vulnerable to fluctuations in world prices. Mali has largely depended on foreign aid to finance its economic development. In 1997, for example, the International Monetary Fund

(IMF) recommended its structural adjustment program to the Malian government, which has continued its implementation to help stimulate and diversify the country's economy and attract foreign investment. A mid-2002 United Nations estimate put Mali's population at 12.6 million. With a GDP per capita of $900 (2002), Mali continues to be ranked among countries with the lowest living standard in the world. The country has over twenty ethnic groups among which the Mande (Bambara, Malinke, and Sarakole) comprise 50 percent of the population, Peul or Fulani 17 percent, Voltaic 12 percent, Songhai 6 percent, Tuareg and Moors 10 percent, and others 5 percent. An even larger number of languages and dialects are spoken throughout Mali. French is the official language, although 80 percent of the population speaks Bambara. Fulani, Songhai, and Tamasheq (Tuareg Berber) are also widely spoken. Muslims in Mali comprise 90 percent of the population, while those that practice indigenous African religions make up 9 percent. A tiny Christian minority of 1 percent is mostly concentrated in Bamako, the capital. A constitution approved by a popular referendum in January 1992 established Mali as a multiparty republic after about three decades of single-party rule since independence on September 22, 1960. The president is elected directly to a five-year term, and he in turn appoints a prime minister. After the 2002 presidential election, Amadou Toumani Touré was inaugurated as Mali's president on June 8. He appointed Mohamed Ag Hamani as Prime Minister and Minister of African Integration, the first Tuareg to become prime minister in Mali.

History

The Republic of Mali derives its name from the ancient Kingdom of Mali (circa 800–1550s CE) which prospered by controlling the lucrative trans-Saharan trade in gold, salt, slaves, and kola nuts. During the fourteenth century when the kingdom reached its peak under Mansa Musa (reigned 1307–1337), extended from the Atlantic Ocean on the west to Gao on the middle Niger in the east. By the mid-sixteenth century, the empire had all but crumbled as successive succession disputes after the mid-fourteenth century not only eroded the power of the empire's leadership but also hampered its ability to collect revenue from the rich trade caravans traversing its territory.

During the late nineteenth century French military expansion into what would become Mali culminated in the capture of Bamako in 1883, Segou in 1890, and Timbuktu in 1894. Fighting however continued in the northern desert strongholds of the Tuareg until 1916 when the French claimed victory. During the period of French colonial rule, marked political and socioeconomic changes took place in Mali, at the time Soudan Français. On the administrative level, for instance, the French imposed a centralized system in which the *commandants de cercles*, representing the governor of French West Africa, and traditional chiefs, mostly chosen for their allegiance to the French, became the agents of French colonial rule. With the introduction of a system of forced labor through the *Office du Niger* and taxation, which required payment initially in kind and later in money, most peasants and others who had previously practiced subsistence farming were forced into the cash crop economy based on the cultivation of cotton, peanuts, and gum Arabic for export.

Resistance to French rule continued during the colonial period. Muslim leaders were opposed to domination by an "infidel" French regime. Sheikh Mohammad al-Tishiti Hamalla, founder of the Hamallist Movement, was the most famous of the Muslim leaders. He led a series of revolts against the colonial administration between 1922 and 1946. Similarly, the nomadic Tuareg in the northern part of Mali resisted French attempts to force them into a sedentary lifestyle.

When Soudan Français obtained internal autonomy within the French community in 1958, it became the République Soudanaise. Mali merged with Senegal in April 1959 to form the Federation of Mali, which gained independence from France on June 20, 1960. However, after only two months, Senegal seceded from the federation and the Republic of Mali was proclaimed on September 22. Modibo Keita became the country's first president.

Politics, Economy, and Ethnic Tensions

A major outcome of French colonial policy was Mali's dependence on cash crops, especially cotton and peanuts, for export income. Fluctuations in the world price of these commodities meant a drop in export earnings for Mali. In addition, as the price of imports, including petroleum, increased during the 1970s and 1980s, Mali fell short of paying for its imports. Stated-led development programs in the first two decades after independence and International Monetary Funds (IMF) austerity measures during the 1980s failed to alleviate Mali's chronic economic problems.

Beginning in the late 1980s the government of President Moussa Traoré had to deal with rebellion among the northern Taureg who accused the government of neglecting them during two periods of drought in the 1970s and 1980s. Many Tauregs died because of the droughts and thousands migrated to neighboring countries. The government's failure to alleviate the economic hardship facing the country led to protests for a multiparty democracy and free elections. Despite a government ban on mass gatherings, protesters organized pro-democracy rallies that attracted massive turnouts, especially in the major cities. Violent retaliation from the government against protesters led to the death of 106 people and the injury of more than 700 in 1991. However, the political situation in Mali has stabilized in recent years, as evidenced by the 2002 presidential election, which most international observers conceded was better organized and more transparent than previous elections.

TAMBA E. M'BAYO

Further Reading

Bingen, R. James, David Robinson, and John M. Staatz, *Democracy and Development in Mali*, East Lansing: Michigan State University, 2000

Condrad, David C., *A State of Intrigue: The Epic of Bamana Segu According to Tayiru Banbera*, Oxford: Oxford University Press, 1990

Coquery-Vidrovitch, Catherine, and Odile Goerg, editors, *L'Afrique occidentale au temps des Français: Colonisateurs et colonisés (circa 1860–1960)*, Paris: La Découverte, 1992

Diarrah, Oumar, *Le Mali de Modibo Keita*, Paris: Editions l'Harmattan, 1986

Imperato, Pascal James, *Historical Dictionary of Mali*, Lanham, Maryland: Scarecrow Press, 1996

Malta

Capsule Summary

Country Name: Republic of Malta

Location: Southern Europe, islands in the Mediterranean Sea, south of Sicily (Italy)

Total Population: 400,420 (July 2003)

Ethnic Group Populations: Maltese (descendants of ancient Carthaginians and Phoenicians, with strong elements of Italian and other Mediterranean ethnicity)

Languages: Maltese (official), English (official)

Religion: Roman Catholic (98%)

The Republic of Malta is an archipelago located in the central Mediterranean Sea south of the island of Sicily made up of the islands of Malta, Gozo, and Comino. Founded some 7,000 years ago, Malta has been a home, stronghold, trading post, and refuge to many as it lies at the crossroads of Mediterranean maritime routes. There have been three main eras in Maltese history that have shaped its history: the Arab Occupation from 870 to 1090 provided the basis of the Maltese language; the Order of St. John, which occupied the Islands from 1530 to 1798, shaped the Islands artistically, soci-ally and culturally; and the British Period, from 1801 to 1964, which introduced the concept of British justice with a unified code of laws, democracy and administration. During this period, the British also helped launch the Islands into the modern industrial age and helped link Malta with the worldwide community.

The islands make up a total of 316 square kilometers (31.25 percent arable land), have 196.8 kilometers of coastline, and have a population of just over 400,000. The capital is Valletta, located on the main island of Malta. Malta obtained its independence from the United Kingdom on September 21, 1964 and has a republican government with a Chief of State, a Prime Minister, and a unicameral House of Representatives, and operates under a Constitutional legal system based on English common law and Roman civil law. Malta's main natural resources are limestone, salt, and arable land, its main exports are machinery, transport equipment, and manufactures (to Singapore 17.3 percent, United States 11.4 percent, Germany 9 percent, and to France 7.2 percent), and its major imports are machinery and transport equipment, manufactured and semi-manufactured goods; food, drink, and tobacco (from Italy 18.3 percent, France 12.1 percent, South Korea 11.3 percent, UK 7.5 percent). The economy is dependent on foreign trade, manufacturing, and tourism, and in 2002 per capita GDP was US$17,200. Malta is privatizing state-controlled firms and liberalizing markets in order to prepare for membership in the European Union to which it has applied for membership. The island remains divided politically, however, over the question of joining the EU.

RICHARD BURKS VERRONE

Further Reading

Borg, Victor Paul, *The Rough Guide to Malta and Gozo*, London: Rough Guides, 2001

Craig, Phil, and Tim Clayton, *The End of the Beginning: From the Siege of Malta to the Allied Victory at El Alamein*, New York: Simon & Schuster, 2003

Gregory, Desmond, *Malta, Britain, and the European Powers, 1793–1815*, Fairleigh Dickinson University Press, 1995

Luttrell, Anthony, *Making of Christian Malta: From the Early Middle Ages to 1530*, Ashgate Publishing, 2002

Sire, H.J.A., *Knights of Malta*, Yale University Press, 1996

Wilson, Neil, *Malta*, Lonely Planet Publications, 2000

Manchu

Capsule Summary

Location: More than 50% of Manchu live in the Northeast of China, the rest of Manchu are scattered over all of China
Total Population: 9,821,180
Languages: Manchu and Chinese Mandarin
Religion: Shamanism

The Manchu is the most recent of 55 ethnic minorities officially recognized by the People's Republic of China (PRC) and is the third largest ethnic group, apart from the Han and Zhuang people in China. The total population of the Manchu based on the 1990' national census is 9,821,180, which represents 0.86 percent of China's population. The Manchu originally are from the northeast of China, in Liaoning, Jilin and Heilongjiang provinces. At present, 46.2 percent of Manchu live in Liaoling, 10 percent live in Jilin and 12 percent live in the Heilongjiang. The rest are now scattered over China, mainly in Beijing, Hebei and Inner Mongolia. The Manchu language belongs to the Tungus subfamily of the Altaic language group. For the last 300 to 400 years most Manchu have adopted the Chinese language as their daily communication, but since 1980s, there has been some strong language revival activities initiated by the Manchu. The traditional costumes of the Manchu are the long gowns. Male Manchu wear a narrow cuffed short jacket over a long gown with a belt at the waist. Females wear silk, satin or cotton long gowns and embroidered shoes. Women coiled their hair on top of their heads.

Men grew the back of their hair long and wore a long plait or queue. That men wear a long queue became a political symbol of the Qing dynasty. Historically the Manchus believed in Shamanism. During the Qing dynasty Shamans were employed to chant scriptures and perform religious dances when imperial services were held. Shamanism remains popular among the Manchus in the areas of Ningguta and Aihu County in the Northeast China.

History

The ancestry of the Manchu is believed to be the Sushen tribe which, 2000 years ago, lived along the reaches of the Heilong and Wusuli rivers north of the Changbai Mountains in the northeast of China. The Sushens later used the name Yilou, Huji (Wuji) Mohe. In the tenth century Jurchen people inherited the cultural traditions of the Mohe and also absorbed other tribes in the northeast. Using new tactics of mounted warfare the Jurchen conquered much of China establishing the Jin Dynasty (1115–1234) dynasty. During this period Jurchen groups were widely dispersed through Manchuria and northern China. This Dynasty collapsed in 1234 and the Jurchen withdrew to the north. From the mid-sixteenth century repeated internecine wars broke out among the Jurchens. Nurhachi, a leader of Jianzhou Jurchens united the different groups and established the "Eight Banner" military system, in order to establish political and military control. In 1616, Nurhachi proclaimed himself "Sagacious Khan" and established the State of Late Jin. In 1635 Nurhachi's son, Hung Taiji chose the name of Manchu. In 1644 the Manchu marched south of Shanhaiguan Pass and conquered China and established the Qing Dynasty.

The Manchu ruled China for nearly 300 years until 1911. As an imperial group in China, Manchus enjoyed great privilege during the Qing Dynasty. The Manchu language was referred to as the national language, however was rarely used even in the imperial court. Manchu status was closely linked with the "eight banner system." Those who belonged to the eight banners could enjoy special privileges and live a comfortable life. They were eligible to earn their living by stipends and rents as banner men.

Manchus after the Fall of the Qing Dynasty

The revolution led by Dr. Sun Yat-Sen overthrew the last Qing dynasty and ended the Manchu imperial rule in 1911 by establishing The Republic of China (ROC). For the sake of political stability and maintenance of the territory that the Manchu Qing government had annexed, Manchu and another four nationalities were recognized by the provisional president of the ROC, Sun Yat Sen; the Manchu, Han, Mongol, Tibetan and Muslim Turks (Hui). The original flag of the Republic of China had five colors symbolizing these five races. Despite their political and military influence Manchus still suffered great political prejudice and economical loss after the 1911 revolution. Most Manchus returned to their homeplace in the northeast. Those who stayed in Beijing and other centers took lower grades of work such as Rickshaw men and laborers. Most Manchus in the northeast engaged in agriculture. Their main crops include soybean, corn, millet, tobacco and apples. People live in remote mountainous areas where gathering ginseng, mushroom and fungus make an important sideline. Traditionally the Manchus are excellent in archery and horsemanship.

In 1931 the Japanese, after establishing military control of the Manchuria established Manchukuo as their puppet state. The last Manchu Emperor of the Qing Dynasty Aisin Giro Puyi was then made to be the puppet head of the state. Manchukuo collapsed when the Japanese surrendered in 1945.

Manchu Identity Reconstruction

After 1949, Manchus were initially not recognized as an independent nationality because they speak the same language and share the same cultural customs of the Han. It was not until 1955, after strong petitions of from the Manchu that their status as one of the 56 ethnic groups in the PRC was established

Following strong lobbying from Manchu groups during the early 80s the Government has taken step to promote and revive Manchu customs, languages and culture. Thirteen Manchu nationality autonomous counties were established between 1985 and 1990. In these counties in Liaolin province (8), Hebei province (4) and Jilin province (1) and places such as Beijing Manchu language instruction has been revived. Also historical sites have been identified, preserved and promoted. Such major historical sites as the Eastern and northern mausoleums (Nurhachi and Huang Taiji's mausoleum), Qing Dynasty Street and the Shengyang Imperial Palace in Shengyang, the home of the Manchu are well preserved.

LINDA TSUNG

Further Reading

Crossley, P.K., *Orphan Warriors: Three Manchu Generations and the End of the Qing World*, Princeton, New Jersey: Princeton University Press, 1990

Crossley, P.K., *The Manchus*, Cambridge, Massachusetts: Blackwell Publishers, 1997

Rigger, S., "Voices of Manchu Identity, 1635–1935," in *Cultural Encounters on China's Ethnic Frontiers*, edited by S. Harrell, Hong Kong University Press, Hong Kong, 1994

Mande

Capsule Summary

Location: West Africa
Population: 20 million
Major groups: Bambara, Diola, Malinke, Mende, Soninke
Major Languages: Bambara, Diola, Malinke
Religion: Islam, Animism, and combinations of the two. No numerical data by ethnic group are available

Group of peoples in West Africa who speak Mande languages and have a common cultural heritage. There are now about 20 million Mande speakers divided into numerous subgroups, speaking twenty-six varieties of Mande languages and dialects. The largest number of Mande—Bambara, Malinke, and Soninke subgroups—live in Mali, where 80 percent of the population speak Bambara as a first or second language. The Malinke represent also one third of the total population of Guinea and almost half that of The Gambia. One fifth of the population of Senegal is Mande, Malinke and Diola; these also constitute a large segment of the population of the Ivory Coast, where Diola is the most widely spoken African Language. A different subgroup, the Mende, resides mainly in Sierra Leone.

Linguists often subdivide Mande speaking populations into two groups: the Mande-tan, or "nuclear Mande," inhabiting the plateau of western Sudan, who created the Malian empires of the past: Ghana and Mali, and the Mande-fu, or "peripheral Mande," who live further south, as far as the Guinean coast, who were mostly traders.

Religious beliefs of the Mande go from strict observance of Islamic law to persistence of the purest animist beliefs, and syncretic situations in between. Most Mande share cultural features. Descent and inheritance are patrilineal, marriages polygynous. The societies of the mostly Muslim Mande-Tan are strictly hierarchical, those of the mostly animist Mande-Fu are decentralized and egalitarian.

Rural Mande have been and are now mainly agriculturalists. Occupations of present-day urban Mande differ in accordance with where they reside. The Diola, traditionally caravan traders, are now settled in towns of the Ivory Coast, Burkina Faso, Mali, and Ghana and engage in commerce. Today's Soninke have one of the highest rates of labor migration in West Africa, and can also be found working in France.

History

The original Mande territory was the eastern part of the plateau, south of the Sahara between the Senegal and Niger rivers. Early inhabitants were Soninke and Bambara farmers believed to have reached the region before the Common Era and to have formed the kingdom of Ghana by the fourth century CE. By the eighth century, Ghana ruled a vast area, including gold-producing lands to its south and south-Saharan trade centers to its north. The kingdom's wealth came from tribute from conquered groups and taxes on trade. This trade, developed by the Diola, was the mainstay of the Ghana Empire and fostered the spread of Islam, introduced by northern merchants.

In the late eleventh century, when Saharan Berber Almoravids conducted a jihad to convert its inhabitants, Ghana declined. The Almoravids' domination was brief, but the war disrupted trade and the pastoralists' herds turned the fragile soil into desert. Groups broke away from the Empire. Southerly Malinke, the who had formed satellite kingdoms of the Ghana empire, now fought each other for supremacy. In 1235, under king Sundiata, hero of the best known epics of West African oral literature, the Keita kings of Mali prevailed and incorporated the remnants of ancient Ghana into their own empire.

Sundiata expanded his territory and reestablished peace, enabling agriculture and trade to recover. His authority was widely accepted. As a Muslim he was trusted by Muslim merchants, and, willing to meet the expectations of the predominantly animist inhabitants, he earned their loyalty by performing traditional rites expected by them from kings. He created a system that survived the dangers inherent in ill-defined rules of succession.

For fifty years after his death (1255) his heirs governed successfully, strengthened bonds with the Muslim world with their pilgrimages to Mecca, making the glories of their empire known beyond its borders, and developed new trade routes to the East via Jenne, Timbuktu, and Gao. Malian gold and copper reached Europe. At its apex (early fourteenth century) the Mande empire extended from Cape Verde to Agades (present-day Niger), from southern Mauretania to the forest. This was the time of the reign of Mansa Mousa, (1307–32) who, upon his return from Mecca (1324), emulated the luxury he had seen in eastern cities: a sumptuous court, great mosques, libraries, and the development of sciences, arts, and letters. Timbuktu became a major Muslim teaching center with a prestigious university.

The population of the empire, however, was too diverse to remain cohesive. Mossi and Wolof rebelled. The Tuareg seized Timbuktu. The creation of Portuguese trading posts on the Guinean coast altered the orientation of trade and attracted Mende and Dan, towards the coast. By the late sixteenth century Mali the area was dominated by the Songhai, and then invaded by Moroccans (1591).

A number of smaller Mande kingdoms survived in Mali and Ghana and tried to regain trade supremacy. In the seventeenth and eighteenth centuries Mande political power was limited to the Bambara states of Segu and Kaarta. In the nineteenth century the Mande found themselves enmeshed in Sudanic jihads, either as Muslim Diola traders, or as animist Bambara whose conversion the jihadists sought. Then came the Mande empire of Malinke Samori Touré (1830–98). based on the commercial expansion of the Diola.

Samori proclaimed himself a religious leader and established a powerful chiefdom in the Kankan region of Guinea. A capable tactician and administrator, he expanded his rule from there. He sold captured booty and slaves and used the proceeds to equip his armies for further conquests. Controlling the gold resources of Bouré and eager to extend his reign to the Niger, Samori might have succeeded in creating a new Mande empire, had he not been stopped by the French, who had much greater resources. Early encounters with them were indecisive and led to a treaty defining a common boundary (1894). Samori felt safe and resumed his conquests. From the French point of view, however, the treaty was an expedient to buy time while they were engaged elsewhere. The truce ended in 1897. French forces defeated Samori decisively in 1898.

The era of colonialism had set in. When independence came to the region in 1960 the Mande groups found themselves split, and citizens of the different states colonial powers had created.

L. NATALIE SANDOMIRSKY

See also **Côte d'Ivoire; Guinea; Mali; Senegal; Sierra Leone; Sudan**

Further Reading

Djata, Sundiata A., *The Bamana Empire by the Niger: Kingdom, Jihad, and Colonization, 1720–1920,* Princeton: Marks Wiener, 1997

Little, K., *The Mende of Sierra Leone,* London: Routledge & Kegan Paul, 1970

Ly-Tall, Madina, *Contribution à l'histoire de l'Empire du Mali (XIII–XVIe siècles)* [Contribution to the history of the Mali Empire (thirteenth–sixteenth centuries)], Dakar: Nouvelles Editions Africaines, 1977

Mann, Kenny, *Ghana, Mali, Songhay: The Western Sudan,* Parsippany, New Jersey: Dillon Press, 1996

McIntosh, Roderick J., *The Peoples of the Middle Nige, the Island of Gold,* Malden: Blackwell, 1998

Niane, Djibril Tamsir, *Histoire des Mandingues de l'Ouest: Le royaume dy Gabou* [History of the Western Mandingo: The Kingdom of Gabou], Paris: Khartalka, 1989

Person, Yves, and Françoise Ligier, *Samori: La renaissance de l'empire mandingue* [Samori: The rebirth of the Mandingo Empire], Paris, Dakar: Editions ABC, 2000

Pollet, Eric, and Grace Winter, *La société Soninké* [Soninke Society], Bruxelles: Editions de l'Institut de Sociologie, Université libre de Bruxelles, 1972

Mandela, Nelson (South African)

Nelson Rolihlahla Mandela (1918–) is a leading figure in the struggle against apartheid, emerged from twenty-seven years in prison without bitterness and within five years had become president of South Africa. After serving as president for five years, he handed over the reigns of power but remained a hugely respected international statesman.

He was born on July 18 1918, in the small village of Mvezo in the Transkei region of what is now the Eastern Cape province of South Africa, and grew up in nearby Qunu. His clan name was Madiba, and he was a member of the aristocracy among the Xhosa-speaking Thembu people, but like most Xhosa boys he spent much time in the fields looking after the animals. When his father died, he moved into the residence of the acting Thembu regent, who became his mentor. He was educated at a village school, then at the Methodist missionary school of Healdtown near Fort Beaufort, in the old Eastern Cape heartland. He then studied at the nearby University of Fort Hare, until he left over an act of resistance. Moving to Johannesburg in the Transvaal, he worked as a clerk in a law firm while completing his first degree through the University of South Africa. Under the influence of Walter Sisulu, he joined the African National Congress (ANC) and in 1944 was one of the founding members of the ANC Youth League, which helped radicalize the organization. He supported the Youth League's Africanist position, which rejected working with non-Africans, but when he studied law at the University of the Witwatersrand, he met white and Indian communists, and his ideas began to change. From 1947 he was a member of the executive of the Transvaal ANC. In 1951 he opened a law office with Oliver Tambo in Johannesburg, but his political work dominated his life.

He was 'volunteer in chief' in the Defiance Campaign of 1952, and the M-Plan, drawn up in case the organization had to go underground, was named after him. He was restricted ('banned'), then arrested in December 1956 and charged with treason. For years he had to travel to Pretoria to attend the trial, and he was detained in the 1960 state of emergency. After he was acquitted of treason in 1961, he went underground. He helped organize a three-day stayaway from work in 1961, and its relative failure helped persuade him that it was necessary to adopt the armed struggle. He helped establish and organize Umkhonto we Sizwe (MK), the armed wing of the ANC/Communist Party, and was named its commander-in-chief at its launch on 16 December 1961. Known as 'the Black Pimpernel', he traveled abroad and underwent military training in Algeria. Soon after his return, he was arrested in August 1962 near Howick, Natal, and sentenced to five years in jail. He was then summoned in 1963 to join the other MK leaders who had been arrested at Rivonia in the dock in Pretoria. After making a magnificent speech, ending 'I am prepared to die for what I believe', he was among those sentenced to life imprisonment and sent to Robben Island prison, off Cape Town, in 1964.

On the Island, through sheer force of personality and moral authority, he was able to do much to improve conditions for the prisoners, and he exerted major influence over political prisoners who arrived over the years. He rejected an offer by the Minister of Police in 1976 to settle in, and recognize, the Transkei Bantustan. Instead, he became the main international symbol of apartheid repression, though Amnesty International refused to recognize him as a prisoner of conscience. Probably because of his renown, he was moved to Pollsmoor prison on the mainland outside Cape Town in 1982. After the township revolt broke out in late 1984, the State President offered to release him if he renounced violence, but he rejected this with defiance. By mid-1985 he was working to bring about a negotiated settlement between the government and the ANC, though it was difficult for him to keep Tambo, President of the ANC, fully informed of what he was up to. He met the Minister of Justice, when he had to go into hospital in Cape Town in November 1985, and the Commonwealth Eminent Persons Group in Pollsmoor in early 1986, and from May 1988 he was engaged in regular talks with senior government officials. In December 1988, after treatment for tuberculosis, he was transferred to a house at Victor Verster prison near Paarl, and from there he was taken to have tea with State President Botha in July 1989. In December that year, he met Botha's successor, F.W. de Klerk. On February 11, 1990 he walked to freedom, after 10,000 days of imprisonment, at the age of 71, showing no bitterness for all the lost years.

He soon revealed himself to the public as a remarkable human being. His old-worldly dignity and courtesy, which he extended to the most lowly, was combined with a firm, fearless and sometimes imperious leadership. He enjoyed wearing colorful shirts, after decades of prison garb. The ANC soon elected him Deputy President, and then in July 1991 President. At a number of points in the multi-party negotiations that took place between December 1991 and November 1993 his leadership was decisive in moving the process forward. On numerous visits to foreign countries, he was hailed as a moral leader second to none. In 1993 he and De Klerk were jointly awarded the Nobel Peace Prize. He led the ANC's election campaign in early 1994, and in the election itself he himself voted for the first time, at Inanda in KwaZulu-Natal. After the ANC's victory, he was on May 10, 1994 sworn in as the country's first democratically elected president at the Union buildings, Pretoria. Later that year, he told his amazing life-story in his autobiography, Long Walk to Freedom.

Though he never stopped emphasizing that he was only a loyal servant of the ANC, as president he worked for national reconciliation within the country, and to promote South Africa abroad. He soon became a widely revered leader, among whites as well as blacks, because of his obvious desire to bring about reconciliation in the deeply divided country. He wore the rugby jersey of the all-white team, and took tea with the widow of the main architect of apartheid. Some said that he spent too much time outside the country, and were critical of him for, say, devoting so much energy to securing an international deal over Libya's refusal to hand over suspects in the Lockerbie bombing affair. He seemed unable to rid himself of incompetent ministers, out of a deep sense of loyalty to those who had stood by him in the years of struggle. Other critics said that he did not do enough to bring about social and economic transformation.

He had announced early on in his presidency that he would not stand again as President in the 1999 general election, and in December 1997 he handed over the leadership of the ANC to Thabo Mbeki, who was already, as deputy president, running the day-to-day affairs of the country.

After June 1999, Mandela continued to be very active, despite his age, and continued to win widespread international admiration. No-one else on the international stage had greater moral authority and credibility in negotiating in conflict situations. He now spent much time on the conflict in Burundi in particular, but in early 2001 he spoke out to denounce the extent of corruption in the new government in South Africa, and of the need for a new spirit of hope in the nation.

Capsule Biography

Born July 18,1918 in Transkei; Educated at Healdtown school and the universities of Fort Hare, South Africa and the Witwatersrand, graduated with a law degree; Set up law practice in Johannesburg and worked for the African National Congress. Leading member, Defiance Campaign; Arrested in 1956 and charged with treason; Helped found Umkhonto we Size; Arrested and brought before the courts with the other ANC leaders caught at Rivonia; Sentenced to life imprisonment at Robben Island, where he remained from 1964 until he was moved to Pollsmoor prison on the mainland in 1982; Released from jail on February 11, 1990; Deputy president, then president, ANC. Awarded the Nobel Peace Prize with F.W. de Klerk in 1993. Won the democratic election, April 1994; Sworn in as president, May 10, 1994; Retired as ANC president in 1997, and as president of the country in June 1999; Separated from second wife Winnie (b. September 26,1936), April 1992; Married Graca Machel, widow of the former President of Mozambique, on his eightieth birthday.

Selected Works

No Easy Walk to Freedom, 1965
The Struggle is My Life, 1978
Nelson Mandela Speaks 1993
Long Walk to Freedom: the Autobiography of Nelson Mandela, rev. ed., 1995

CHRISTOPHER SAUNDERS

Further Reading

L.Callinicos, *The World that made Mandela* Johannesburg: STE Publishers, 2000

S. Johns and R.H. Davis, editors, *Mandela, Tambo and the African National Congress,* New York: Oxford University Press,1991

F. Meer, *Higher than Hope: The Authorized Biography of Nelson Mandela,* London: Harper Collins, 1990

M. Meredith, *Nelson Mandela. A Biography,* London: St. Martin's Press, 1997

D. Ottaway, *Chained Together: Mandela, de Klerk and the Struggle to Remark South Africa,* New York: Random House1993

A. Sampson, *Mandela. The Authorised Biography,* London: Harper Collins, 1999

A. Sparks, *Tomorrow is Another Country,* Sandton: University of Chicago Press, 1994

Marcos, Subcomandante (Amerindian)

Subcomandante Insurgente Marcos emerged as an international figure on New Year's Day, 1994, when the Zapatista Liberation Army (EZLN) took over five towns and over 500 ranches in Chiapas, Mexico in a non-violent indigenous people protest. Seizing a government radio transmitter in San Cristobal de las Casas, the administrative and commercial center of Chiapas, Subcomandante Marcos called the Mexican government to a dialog with native minorities. Protesting against neoliberal global forces, specifically the North American Free Trade Agreement (NAFTA), which went into effect on January 1, 1994, and the lack of free elections in the country, Marcos called for the transformation of Mexican politics. As a spokesperson for the EZLN and the "voice for voices that had not been heard," Marco demanded that the Mexican government guarantee the liberty and justice of indigenous minorities through greater democratic participation. In an attempt to revolutionize the media as well as Mexican politics, Marco and the EZLN continue to bombard the international media in a war of words from the Lancandon Jungle; their ballistic support—the Internet.

Indigenous unrest in Chiapas in 1994 reflected the neo-liberal modernization of the Mexican economy, including hydroelectric dams that produced 55–60 percent of Mexico's electricity, wells that produced 21 percent of its oil and 47 percent of its natural gas, and plantations producing more than half of the coffee crop (Russell 1995, 12). The EZLN argued that Mexican government promotion of the development of coffee plantations, dams, and roads did not benefit peasant farming economic opportunities. They argued that NAFTA brought cheap food imports that threatened to erode the Mayan corn market (Russell 1995, 17). To avoid the loss of culture and further economic distress, the EZLN sought Indian participation in the development and production of natural resources in the Chiapas region (Russell 1995, 105). Marcos called for investment in Chiapas that would benefit Indians and not just create a greater demand for cheap labor.

The Marcos presented to the world by both mainstream and alternative media sources since January 1994 is that of a mysterious revolutionary guerrilla. He wears a black ski mask, dark olive fatigues, rubber boots, a black poncho, and red-tipped bandaleros crisscrossing his chest. He smokes a pipe, carries a short-barreled shotgun, and frequently rides a horse. Fueled by media representations of a revolutionary symbol that combines the legends of El Zorro and Che Guevara, "Marcos mania" quickly swept through Mexico, Latin America, and the North American vanguard left after the EZLN spokesperson's 1994 New Year's Day debut. The romantic rebel was nicknamed "the Sup" by an adoring popular youth mass.

Subcomandante Insurgente Marcos, the curious world learned, is a mestizo, 5'8" tall, about 160 pounds, with amber eyes ad a graying beard. Marcos is described as quiet, kind, serene, calm, but he claims not to be religious (Ross 1995, 298). He is playful and has a talent for talking with children (298). The international press finds Marcos extremely charming and intelligent and is eager to report his many communiqués transmitted from the Lancandon Jungle. His message reveals a quick wit. He speaks softly, but with intensity, and has the poise of a celebrity in front of the media or in the presence of government agents. Bold, strategic, articulate, flirtatious, defiant, sarcastic, poetic, and often militant, Marcos presents a charismatic and legendary figure to his national and international audience.

Marcos reports to journalists that his reason for wearing a mask is not to mask his "true" identity, but to develop an identity as one of the many leaders within the Indigenous Clandestine Revolutionary Committee of the General Command of the Zapatista Army of National Liberation (Ross 1995). In support of "the Sup's" statement that no one leader dominates the EZLN, a large number of General Command leaders tell reporters that they are all "Marcos" (Ross 1995, 297). Subcomandante Marcos refers to the other Zapatistas as his "elders," defining himself as a Ladino who came to the jungle to learn, working himself up to the ranks of Subcomandante and the role of press spokesperson because of his ability to speak four languages.

Rafael Sebastian Guillen Vincente, as the Mexican government asserts is the Subcomandante's "true" identity, is a middle-class, non-Indian, former university professor, who came to the Lancandon Jungle of Chiapas with a brigade of twelve volunteer health workers for a human rights organization in 1984. The brigade members shared medical knowledge and skills with the Indians, and in return, the Indians taught them how to live in the mountains and how to walk and think like Indians (Ross 1995, 279). Marcos says the volunteers worked to build self-defense squads, alliances, and logistical support bases, and also to earn the respect of the peasant indigenous organizations in the jungle (280). The Subcomandante told Irish journalist Michael McCaughan in March 1994 that his commitment to minority justice was a gradual process of becoming aware of the injustices and making choices to act on his beliefs. "It meant starting over again, being another person, someone who is authentic" (http://home.san.rr.com/revolution.marcos.htm). Subcomandante Insurgente Marcos is married to an indigenous woman and lives in a traditional Maya village in the mountains of the Lancandon Jungle of Chiapas.

The Mexican government "unmasked" Subcomandante Marcos as a non-native, but they have not been able to discredit him as an authentic spokesperson of the Tzotzil, Tzeltal, Choi, Tojoalabal, Man, and Zogue native speakers of Chiapas. The voice that speaks for over six million Mexican Indians with 56 distinct cultures and a hundred language dialects continues to symbolize and represent the suffering oppressed of Mexico. In 1995, government attempts to capture Marcos resulted in a demonstration of 100,000 people wearing masks and shouting, "We are all Marcos." Marcos vows to wear the mask until the "true identities" of all the indigenous people are known.

As an effective media manipulator, Marcos' terse communiqués are worded carefully, politely, and often poetically. Employing folk tales, riddles, political polemics, and philosophical musings, the literary genius Marcos reflects on the state of the world from the perspective of illiterate indigenous peoples. In his demands that the Mexican government include indigenous peoples in its democratic process, Marcos builds a bridge for minorities who have been present, but ignored in the development of dominant structures. Through the use of the Internet, Marcos brings the indigenous of Chiapas out of cultural isolation into a conversation with the powerful of Mexico and the world. His statement to the world on January 1, 1994 is from "all minorities who are untolerated, oppressed, resisting, exploding, and saying 'Enough!'"

Subcomandante Marcos also writes from the perspective of his personal identity, as one who reflects on the struggles of an individual who must make sense of a rapidly changing world in order to participate in it in a more humane fashion. Marcos speaks to reporters, writers, poets, playwrights, priests, professors, and anyone who would further the minority message to the world, hoping to capture their creative imaginations.

He represents the EZLN in public dialogs to further the revolutionary goals of work, land, shelter, bread, health, education, democracy, liberty, peace, independence, and justice for all minorities. The attention of the international media and human rights organizations guarantees the safety of Marcos and the EZLN. You may contact "the Sup" at www.ezln.org.

Capsule Biography

Subcomandante Insurgente Marcos (Rafael Sebastian Guillen Vicente). Born in 1957 in Tampico, Jalisco, Mexico, son of a middle-class furniture chain owner. Attended school in Tampico, Guadalajara, and Monterrey; studied in the department of philosophy and letters at the National University in Mexico City. Awarded a student national medal of excellence in 1981; awarded an honorary degree from the National Autonomous University in 1995. Part-time humanities professor at a left-wing activist center for working class students in the early 1980s until 1984; joined a human rights volunteer organization as a health worker assigned to Mayan peasants in the mountains of Chiapas in 1984; spokesperson for the Zapatista Liberation Army (1994-present). Member of the Revolutionary Indigenous Clandestine Committee of the General Command (CCRI-CG) of the Zapatista Liberation Army (EZLN).

Selected Works

The Fourth World War, translated by irlandesa, on line at http://www.inmotionmagazine.com/auto/fourth.html

The Story of Colors: A Bilingual Folktale from the Jungles of Chiapas, 1999

Shadows of tender fury: the letters and communiqués of Subcomandante Marcos and the Zapatista Army of National Liberation, 1999

Zapatista Encuentro: Documents from the Encounter for Humanity and Against Neoliberalism, La Realidad, Mexico, 1998

Our Word is Our Weapon: Selected Writings of Subcomandante Insurgente Marcos, 2002

Questions & Swords: Folktales of the Zapatista Revolution, 2001

BARBARA DILLY

Further Reading

Boremanse, Didier, *Hach Winik: The Lancandon Maya of Chiapas, Southern Mexico,* [Institute for Mesoamerican Studies, Monograph 11], Albany: The University of Albany, State University of New York, 1998

Cancian, Frank, and Peter Brown, "Who is Rebelling in Chiapas?" in *Crossing Currents: Continuity and Change in Latin America,* edited by Michael B. Whiteford and Scott Whiteford, Upper Saddle River, New Jersey: Prentice Hall, 1998

Collier, George A., "Restructuring Ethnicity in Chiapas and the World," in *Contemporary Cultures and Societies of Latin America,* edited by Dwight B. Heath, Prospect Heights, Illinois: Waveland Press

Kicza, John, "The Indian in Latin America," in *Crossing Currents: Continuity and Change in Latin America,* edited by Michael B. Whiteford and Scott Whiteford, Upper Saddle River, New Jersey: Prentice Hall, 1998

Marcos, Subcomandante, *Our Word is Our Weapon: Selected Writings of Subcomandante Insurgente Marcos,* New York: Seven Stories Press, 2000

Marcos, Subcomandante Insurgente, "Communiqué to Vicente Fox, December 2, 2000, *Multinational Monitor* (March 2001)

Ritchie, Mark, "Free Trade versus Sustainable Agriculture: The Implications of NAFTA," in *Crossing Currents: Continuity and Change in Latin America,* edited by Michael B. Whiteford and Scott Whiteford, Upper Saddle River, New Jersey: Prentice Hall, 1998

Ross, John, *Rebellion from the Roots: Indian Uprising in Chiapas,* Monroe, Maine: Common Courage Press, 1995

Russell, Phillip L., *The Chiapas Rebellion,* Austin: Mexico Resource Center, 1995

Stavenhagen, Rudolfo, "Indigenous Organizations: Rising Actors in Latin America" in *Contemporary Cultures and Societies of Latin America,* edited by Dwight B. Heath, Prospect Heights, Illinois: Waveland Press, Inc., 2001

A Storm from the Mountain: The Zapatistas Take Mexico, film, Cambridge, Massachusetts: Big Noise Films, 2001

Wild, Nettie, *A Place Called Chiapas: Eight Months inside the Zapatista Uprising,* film, Canada: Zeitgeist Films Ltd, 1998

Zapatista, film, Cambridge, Massachusetts: Big Noise Films, 1998

Mari

Capsule Summary

Location: Mari El, Bashkortostan, Tatarstan, Udmurtia, Kazakhstan, Kirov, Sverdlovsk and Perm in Russia, the Russian Federation

Total Population: about 670,000

Languages: western (*kuryk mary*) and meadow-eastern Mari (*olyk-erwel marij*)

Religions: folk religion, orthodoxy and non-religion

The Mari belong to the Volga branch of the Finno-Ugrian peoples. They have been earlier called Cheremis, which is an ethnonym used by outsiders. Their own ethnonym, Mari, which literally means "human being" or "man," has officially been used since the 1920s. There are 670,000 Mari, and half of them live in the Mari El, which is an autonomous republic in the Russian Federation. Mari form there a minority (43 percent) while the Russians (47.5 percent) are the largest ethnic group. Other minorities are, for example, the Tatars (6 percent). Over 60 percent of the population of Mari El are urban, but the Mari (69 percent) live in small rural villages.

The Mari can be divided into four sub-ethnic groups based on their linguistical, cultural-ecological and historical distinctions. Almost half of the total number of 670,000 live outside the titular republic of Mari El. The western group is mountain Mari (*kuryk mary*), who live on the hilly right-bank of the Volga River and in the south-western corner of the Mari El. They are closely related to the Mari who live in the Vetluga River basin on the other side of the Volga. Meadow Mari (*olyk marij*) live on the flat lands on the left-bank of the Volga between Vetluga and Viatka Rivers. The third is small group of south-western Mari, who live in the south-west outside Mari El. They have not an own standard language

and are largely assimilated to Russian. The fourth group, eastern Mari (*erwel marij*), who live in diaspora to the east of the Viatka in the Kama River basin and along its tributaries flowing down out of the Ural Mountains. The largest group live in Bashkortostan (106,000). Mari are found as ethnic minorities also in Udmurtia (9,500), Tatarstan (19,000), Kazakhstan (12,000) and in the provinces of Kirov (45,000), Perm (6,000) and Sverdlovsk (31,000).

The traditional culture of the Mari was based on farming, cattle keeping and beekeeping, which also today form the basic economy of rural Mari. The main industries today are machinery, machine tool manufacture and paper manufacturing.

History

During the Middle Ages the Mari were in close contact with Volga Bulgars and Kazan's Tatars. The majority of early Mari remained loyal to the Tatars in the sixteenth century, when the Russian conquest of the Volga Basin began. After the fall of Kazan's Khanate, the Muscovite state began to subjugate the Mari. A period of "Cheremis Wars" (1553–1580) extended into the second half of the sixteenth century. The violent time with pressure from colonization, heavy taxation and forced Christianization led that many Mari migrated to the east. Now they are known as Eastern Mari.

The October Revolution in 1917 had deep changes in the life of the Mari. The Mari Autonomous Province was created in 1921 and in 1936 it was elevated in status to the Mari Autonomous Soviet Socialist Republic (ASSR). This meant a period of collectivization and industrialization. In the post-Soviet era, in 1992, the ASSR was re-named as the Republic of Mari El.

At the end of the Tsarist Empire, there were signs of ethnic awakening among the Mari people. In 1917 *Marii Ushem* (The Union of Mari) was founded. However, it was forcibly disbanded and its leaders were repressed during the Stalinist period of terror in the 1930s. Many Mari intellectuals as priests, researches and authors were accused for nationalism and persecuted.

After the break of the Soviet Union in 1991, *Marii Ushem* was reborn and was joined by scores of other ethnic and cultural Mari organizations. In 1993 a Mari parliament was elected. The general economic crisis in Russia is delaying the revival of Mari culture and identity.

Language and Culture

The Mari belongs to the Finno-Ugric languages. The amount of Mari speakers is today estimated as 542,000. Mari is divided into four main dialects: mountain Mari, south-western Mari, meadow Mari and eastern Mari.

There are two literary languages, because the differences between these two different written forms are regarded as so big that it is hard to understand each other. The meadow and eastern Mari form the basis of eastern written language, which is called meadow-eastern Mari (*olyk-erwel marij*). The western Mari (*kuryk mary*) is based on the dialect spoken by meadow Mari.

Earlier Mari language was subjected to the strongest and most prolonged exposure to neighboring Tatar and Chuvash languages while the influence of Russian is a relatively new phenomenon. The dominance of Russian threatens the position of Mari. Especially in the towns Russian is used at home and the Mari children are studying in Russian classes. In the countryside there are Mari classes, but the further education is given in Russian. There is also a shortage of schoolbooks in Mari. In the Mari State University in Yoshkar-Ola it is possible to study Mari and Finno-Ugric languages, literature and folkloristics on Mari. Besides, also a Mari research institute (MarNii) is an important institute for promoting Mari culture and language.

The official status of Mari language in the Mari El has been under changes. According to the language law, Mari has the same status as Russian. In practice it has been estimated that 90 percent of all official information is given in Russian. Many Mari are today bilingual.

In spite of the financial and political difficulties (the Mari have only few members of Mari Parliament), a number of newspapers and 7–8 books a year are published in Mari. In Yoshkar-Ola, there is a Mari publishing house, a Mari theatre, and a TV-channel. These institutions play an important role in maintaining and reconstructing Mari identity. Important national symbols—a flag and a national anthem of Mari—were created during the 1990s.

Religion

Since coming under Russian control in the sixteenth century, the Mari, especially the mountain Mari, converted to Russian Orthodoxy. The current group of eastern Mari escaped the wars, heavy taxation, and forced conversion. The eastern and the meadow Mari have preserved their own folk religion, which is based on a deep reverence for nature. Religious rituals and animal sacrifices are performed in sacred groves by a *kart*, a priest. During the Soviet era, the folk religion was forbidden and had to be practised in secret. In the 1930s, priests were persecuted. During the 1990s, the position of folk religion has changed and it is coming to be a part of the public Mari identity.

HELENA RUOTSALA

Further Reading:

Lallukka, Seppo, *From Fugitive Peasant to Diaspora: The Eastern Mari in Tsarist and Federal Russia*, Helsinki: The Finnish Academy of Science and Letters, 2003

Popov, N.S, editor, *Ètniceskaâ kul'ura marijcev: Tradicii i sovremennost*. Yoshkar-Ola: MarNII, 2002

Saarinen, Sirkka, "Die Dialekte des Tscheremissischen: Einteilung und Klassifizierungskriterien," in *Dialectologia Uralica. Veröffentlichungen der Societas Uralo-Altaica, Band 20*. Wiesbaden: der Societas Uralo-Altaica, 1985

Saarinen, Sirkka, "Myth of a Finno-Ugrian Community," *National Papers,* 29, no. 1 (2000) Sepeev, G.A, editor, *Ètnografiâ marijskogo naroda: Ucebnoe posobie dlâ starsih klassov,* Yoshkar-Ola: Marijskoe kniznoe izd-vo, 2001

Taagepera, Rein, *The Finno-Ugric Republics and the Soviet State*, London: Hurst, 1999

Marley, Bob (Jamaican)

Bob (Robert Nesta) Marley was a pioneer of reggae, a Jamaican-born form of popular music, and the first popular musician from a developing country to become a success on an international scale. Marley was also a spokesperson, activist, and symbol for the Rastafarian religion, Black independence, and peace in Jamaica and beyond. Marley left musical, political, and spiritual legacies whose influences are still felt today.

Born in the country but raised in Trenchtown, a shantytown slum of Kingston named for its sewer, Marley grew up in a Jamaica that, until 1962, was under British colonial rule, beginning with the British takeover from the Spanish in 1670. British rule (and even the earlier Spanish tenure) had been harsh; the plantation system in Jamaica was among the worst in the Caribbean, and economic and social repression under the crown continued until independence (and after, under neocolonial rule). As the product of the short marriage of a teenager and a middle-aged officer in the West Indian arm of the British Army, he could be said to embody his country's colonial inheritance. Alongside the history of colonial oppression, however, Jamaica also had a long history of resistance. Rebellions in the seventeenth, eighteenth, and nineteenth centuries, such as the nearly eighty year long resistance by a group of ex-slaves called the Maroons, helped force the end of slavery in the British colonies and brought a measure of reform to the white-planter dominated economy. The Pan-Africanist movements of the Jamaican-born Marcus Garvey and the Rastafarians fought for rights and freedom for the poor of Jamaica.

Marley's music comes out of these two strands of Jamaican history. When M. first emerged from Trenchtown in the early '60s, the music he played with his first band (with Bunny Livingston and Peter Tosh, and later known as the Wailing Wailers) was an early form of reggae called ska, a music that resulted from the combination of local musical styles and American rhythm and blues (mostly picked up from New Orleans radio stations). While some of their early recordings were pop, dance music, their first minor hit, 1963's "Simmer Down," was about local toughs, and betrayed a nascent interest in turning popular music to political subjects. Under greater influence from American music, particularly bebop and then soul and rock, and from local folk traditions, the music evolved into rocksteady and then reggae proper, without the horns and slower beat of ska, and with scratching rhythm guitar, foregrounded bass guitar, one-drop drumming, and rougher vocals. Under the influence of Rastafarianism, to which M. converted from Christianity in 1967, M. became the preeminent artist of this "roots reggae." Rastafarian beliefs—in the spiritual powers of marijuana, in the presence on earth of God in the form of Haile Selassie, King of Ethiopia, and in a Pan-Africanist, Black Power political philosophy—influenced reggae immeasurably. The spirituality of reggae, sometimes good-times, sometimes mystical, and sometimes militant, made for music that celebrated good feeling and godliness and condemned injustice. Marley's music, developing all of these aspects of reggae, eventually received the notice of the music world outside of Jamaica.

During the early and mid '70s the Wailers ventured out into what Rastafarians call "Babylon," which denotes the corrupt material world but also refers to the White, Western world (as in the title of their live album recorded in Paris, 1978's *Babylon by Bus*). They received European and American airplay, followed by record sales, tours with major American acts, and even a cover version of "I Shot the Sheriff" by English rock guitarist Eric Clapton. On the heels of this success, after their first big American hit (1975's "No Woman No Cry"), Tosh and Livingston left the band, and Marley's music and behavior as a public figure grew more political. The Jamaican ruling class was already alarmed upon the 1974 release of *Burnin'*, as much at the liner and cover pictures of Marley and others, hair in dreadlocks, smoking marijuana, as at the Black Power message of songs such as "Get Up, Stand Up," "Burnin' and Lootin'" and of course "I Shot the Sheriff". The recognition awarded Marley made him the face of Jamaica, and they did not want that particular dreadlocked image representing them. Things got worse when Marley became involved in national politics, particularly in the divisive and violent 1976 election campaign between Prime Minister Michael

Manley and Edward Seaga. His ties to Manley led to an assassination attempt in December of that year.

Marley's prominence also led to his being asked to perform, upon his return to Jamaica after a long exile and convalescence, in the "One Love Peace Concert" of 1978. The concert, ostensibly organized to raise money for charity, was meant to keep the country's recently violent internal tensions from erupting into conflict on a massive scale. It ended with Marley persuading Manley and Seaga to join hands with him on stage as his band played. Police and military abuses continued, and opposition remained, but there was no coup and no civil war.

Marley died in 1981, from a cancer that his Rastafarian beliefs would not allow him to treat, and was mourned by Jamaica and the world. Just prior to his death, he was awarded the Jamaican Order of Merit, and upon his death was given a state funeral. His legacies to the developing world—his calls for equality and justice, his condemnations of greed and oppression—are matched by those he left to the whole world. Jamaican reggae has undergone a series of rejections and embraces of Marley's musical legacy, turning to dance-hall rapping or toasting and to DJs, while its influence on European and American music, such as the embrace of reggae by punk bands like the Clash, has waxed and waned. But Marley's larger international influences—the messages of love that are an inextricable part of his politics, the expressed hope for unity of the formerly colonized and formerly colonizing—have endured.

SAMUEL COHEN

Capsule Biography

Born in Rhoden Hall, Jamaica, February 6, 1945. Studied at Stepney School, St. Ann's, Jamaica; Model Private School, Kingston, Jamaica. Apprenticed as a welder; owned music publishing, recording, and licensing companies. Awarded Jamaican Order of Merit, April 1981. Died in Miami, Florida, May 11, 1981,

Selected Works

Catch a Fire, 1972
Burnin', 1973
Natty Dread, 1975
Live, 1975
Rastaman Vibrations, 1976
Exodus, 1977
Babylon by Bus, 1978
Kaya, 1978
Uprising, 1980

Further Reading

Davis, Stephen, *Bob Marley,* second edition, Rochester, VT: Schenkman, 1990.
Dolan, Sean, *Bob Marley.* New York: Chelsea, 1997
Stephens, Gregory, *On Racial Frontiers: The New Culture of Frederick Douglass, Ralph Ellison, and Bob Marley,* Cambridge, New York: Cambridge UP, 1999.
Timothy White, *Catch a Fire: The Life of Bob Marley,* revised Edition, New York: Holt, 1996

Maroons (Bush Negroes)

Capsule Summary

Location: Africa, Caribbean Islands; Central America, North America; South America
Languages: Native and African Dialects
Religions: Variety, but mostly African in origin

The Maroons are also called *Bush Negroes,* bands of runaway slaves who entrenched themselves in mountains and forests to escape slavery. The term "Maroon" derives from Spanish *cimarrón*—originally bestowed upon domestic cattle that took to the hills in the island of Hispaniola. It was later applied to bands of American Indians who had escaped Spanish slavery. It was used in the 1530s to describe outlaw bands of African-American runaway slaves who preyed on white plantations. They were known variously as *palenques, quilombos, mocambos, cumbes, mambise,s* or *ladeiras.* Maroon societies ranged from tiny bands to large communities encompassing thousands of members such as the Palmares, which covered an area in Brazil of more than 1,000 square miles.

For more than four centuries, Maroon communities proliferated from the Guianese rainforest to the mountains of the Jamaican interior, including the British North American colonies, and later the United States. In Brazil, Peru, the United States, and the Caribbean

Islands, Maroon communities flourished in the hard-to-reach backwaters and wherever inaccessible terrain existed dotting the fringes of plantation America. The impenetrable jungles and mountainous terrains provided Maroons a safe haven. From these hideouts, they harried white owned plantations to secure provisions.

The first Maroon community in the Americas was established in the early sixteenth century by Africans on the island of Samaná, off the coast of Hispaniola (Price 1979, 419). Several of such communities emerged throughout the Americas over the next three and half centuries as slaves sought to free themselves from slavery and establish their independence. The Maroons of Jamaica date back to 1655, when the British captured that island. When the British conquered Jamaica, many of the Spanish inhabitants fled to neighboring Cuba, leaving behind their slaves. With the departure of their Spanish masters, about 1500 slaves decided to seek refuge on the north and east sides of the mountains rather than to submit to the conquerors.

The Maroons of the Costa Chica in Mexico began escaping in the late sixteenth century from Spanish cattle ranches and estates and remained independent until the abolition of slavery in Mexico in 1829. The Palenqueros Maroons of Colombia emerged during the seventeenth century. The Spanish failed attempts to eradicate them, forcing the colonial government and the ancestors of the Palenqueros came to terms between 1713 and 1717. In the eighteenth century, the powerful Maroon community that settled in the mountains of Jamaica carved out a significant area of influence. From their mountain hideouts, they resisted slavery and carried out frequent raids which threatened the prosperous British sugar plantation industry. The threat to the plantation system forced the planters to sign a treaty with the Maroons of Trelawney Town in March, 1738. Under the terms of the treaty, the Maroons were given 1500 acres of crown land to ensure their independence and to avoid future conflicts.

Treaties between Maroons and white planters were frequent. Such treaties between the planters and Maroons where know of in Brazil, Colombia, Cuba, Ecuador, Hispaniola, Mexico and Suriname because Maroonage on a large scale threatened the foundations of the plantation system. This forced many planters to offer Maroon communities their freedom, recognized their territorial integrity, and made some provision for meeting their economic needs. In return, the treaties required Maroons to end all hostilities toward the plantations, to return or aid in hunting them down all future runaways. But many Maroon societies were also

unsuccessful. Many were crushed by massive force of arms. However, Maroonage continued to pose a nagging problem for many planters up to the emancipation.

The actions of Maroon communities in the Atlantic world dispel the myth of the docile slave. The violent resistance to enslavement which began in the West African interior and mutinies during the Middle Passage continued in organized rebellions in the New World plantations as they strove for independence. Successful resistance from these communities had long-term impacts of the political, social and economic development of the region as well as European encounters with the other parts of the world. In the French colony of Saint-Domingue, Maroons helped to launch the Haitian Revolution, resulting in one of the first independent republics in the Americas in 1804. Their leadership and actions helped shape the history of the Western Hemisphere.

The initial Maroons in the New World colonies came from a wide range of ethnic and linguistic backgrounds in West and Central Africa. Over time, those born in the New World became important part of the population. From their diverse background, they developed a unique sense of collective identity and created new communities and institutions that integrated cultural elements drawn from their African background. The African background is also reflected in the political system of the great seventeenth century Brazilian Maroon community of Palmares, the development of the kinship system of the Ndjuka Maroons of Suriname and the influence of the matrilineal Akan. Their heritage, creativity and resistance became part of the post-Columbian American landscape. African continuities are also reflected in religions like Brazilian *candomblé* and Haitian *vaudou*.

The unique ability of Maroons to forge new cultures and identities, and develop solidarity out of diversity was important for their survival as individuals and as communities. The African cultural traits reflected the often heterogeneous communities from which they emerged but Maroons also borrowed from their environments. Their social and geographical isolation is reflected in the distinct languages, which comprise large components of African lexicon, phonology and grammar. The music, dance, verbal arts and spiritual traditions of contemporary Maroon peoples are predominantly African in origin.

The political organization of early Maroon communities was largely shaped by military considerations and subsistence. Strong military and leadership skills were important for the survival of Maroon communities who were often under siege. Bayano of Panama, Yanga of Mexico, Ganga Zumba of Brazil, Benkos Bioho of Colombia, Nanny and Kojo of Jamaica, Boni of Suriname and John Horse or Juan Caballo of the southern United States and Mexico were among the early Maroon leaders who achieved fame for their exceptional military and organizational skills.

Descendant of Maroon communities still form semi-independent enclaves in several parts of the Western Hemisphere. They include the Kwinti of Suriname, the Aluku of French Guiana, the Windward and Leeward Maroons of Jamaica, the Palenqueros of Colombia and Belize, the Garífuna of the Atlantic coast of Central America, the Maroons of the Costa Chica region in Mexico, and the Seminole Maroons of Texas, Oklahoma, Mexico and the Bahamas. Their unique history and African heritage is still evident in cultural traditions that were forged during the earliest days of their American experience.

CHIMA J. KORIEH

Further Readings

Campbell, Mavis C., *The Maroons of Jamaica 1655–1796: A History of Resistance, Collaboration and Betrayal,* Granby, Massachusetts: Bergin and Garvey, 1988

Herskovits, Melville J., and Frances S. Herskovits, *Rebel Destiny: Among the Bush Negroes of Dutch Guiana,* New York: McGraw Hill, 1934

Kopytoff, Barbara, "The Development of Jamaican Maroon Ethnicity," *Caribbean Quarterly,* 22, no. 2/3 1976

Lenoir, J.D., "Surinam National Development and Maroon Cultural Autonomy," *Social and Economic Studies,* 24 (1975)

Price, Richard, *Maroon Societies: Rebel Slave Communities in the Americas,* Baltimore: Johns Hopkins University Press, 1979

Marshall Islands

Capsule Summary

Country Name: Republic of the Marshall Islands
Location: North Pacific Ocean, Oceania, a group of atolls and reefs, about one-half of the way from Hawaii to Australia
Total Population: 56,429 (July 2003)
Ethnic Group Populations: Micronesian
Languages: English; two major Marshallese dialects from the Malayo-Polynesian family; Japanese
Religions: Christian (mostly Protestant); native spiritual traditions

The Republic of the Marshall Islands (RMI) is a nation consisting of twenty-none coral atolls and five small low-lying islands in the north Pacific Ocean, mid-way between Hawaii and Australia, with a population of just over 50,000. The islands were first inhabited around 2000 BCE by Micronesian navigators who called the Marshalls *Aelon Kein Ad,* or "our islands." Micronesia, including the Marshall Islands, came under Spanish rule in 1494 (via the Treaty of Tordesillas) and Europeans first came to the islands in 1529. They remained under Spanish authority until 1885 when they were ceded to Germany which formed a protectorate over the islands in 1886. The area was given its name by British Naval Captain William Marshall, who sailed through the area while transporting convicts for New South Wales. In 1914, Japan captured the Marshalls from Germany, and in 1944, were liberated by the Allied Forces in World War II. After the war, the United States administered the Marshalls as the easternmost part of the UN Trust Territory of the Pacific Islands until 1986 when the Marshall Islands attained independence under a Compact of Free Association. Compensation claims by the Marshallese continue as a result of U.S. nuclear testing on some of the atolls between 1947 and 1962. In fact, in 1954 on Bikini Atoll, the United States nuclear testing program detonated the most powerful hydrogen bomb ever tested by the United States The Marshall Islands have been home to the United States Army Base Kwajalein (USAKA) since 1964.

The RMI encompasses 181.3 square kilometers (16.67 percent arable land) with 370.4 km of coastline. Its natural resources include coconut products, marine products, and deep seabed minerals. The RMI's economy is greatly assisted by financial assistance from the United States. Per capita GDP was US$1,600 in 2001. Under the terms of the Compact of Free Association, the United States has provided more than US$1 billion in aid since 1986. The RMI's exports are copra cake, coconut oil, handicrafts, and fish (to the United States,

Japan, Australia, and China), and its major imports, which far outweigh exports, are foodstuffs, machinery and equipment, fuels, beverages, and tobacco (from the United States, Japan, Australia, New Zealand, Singapore, Fiji, China, and the Philippines). The Marshalls are governed by a constitutional government based in the capital of Majuro on Majuro Atoll, which is made up of a chief of state, a unicameral Parliament elected by popular vote and which elects the executive from its members, and a legal system based on adapted Trust Territory laws, acts of the legislature, municipal, common, and customary laws. The RMI is a member of the international community, having joined the United Nations in 1991.

RICHARD BURKS VERRONE

Further Reading

Dibblin, Jane, *Day of Two Suns: US Nuclear Testing and the Pacific Islanders*, New Amsterdam Books, 2000

Hart, Kevin, *Sung for Anidreb: A Brief History of the Marshall Islands*, Equatorial Pub, 1998

Hezel, Francis, *The First Taint of Civilization: A History of the Caroline and Marshall Islands in Pre-Colonial Days, 1521–1885*, University of Hawaii Press, 1983

Kelin, Daniel, *Marshall Island Legends and Stories*, The Bess Press, 2003

Niedenthal, Jack, *For the Good of Mankind: A History of the People of Bikini and Their Islands*, Micronitor/Bravo Publishers, 2001

Weisgall, Jonathan, *Operation Crossroads: The Atomic Tests at Bikini Atoll*, United States Naval Institute Press, 1994

Mauritania

Capsule Summary

Official Name: *Al Jumhuriyah al Islamiyah al Muritaniyah*, Islamic Republic of Mauritania

Location: Northwestern Africa, between Senegal, Mali and Algeria

Total Population: 2,912,584 (2003)

Languages: Hassaniya Arabic (official), Pulaar, Soninke, Wolof (official), French

Religion: Islam

Mauritania is located in the northwestern Africa, bordering Senegal in the south, Mali in the east and southeast, Algeria in the northeast, and Western Sahara in the north. The country has a land area of 1,030,700 square kilometers (393,000 square miles) and it is slightly smaller than the state of South Carolina in the United States.

According to the CIA estimates (2004), the population of Mauritania is estimated at 2,912,584, up from 1,864,236 (1988 census). It is predominantly rural with around 40 to 45 percent of the people living in cities and towns, as there was a large inflow of people from the rural areas during the series of devastating droughts in the 1990s. The country's capital city, Nouakchott, is home to about 700,000 people (2004), or 35 percent of the population. The Mauritania has a high population growth rate of 2.91 percent, and it is estimated that the population could double by 2030. Mauritania has a relatively low population density, standing at around 3 people per square kilometer (7.5 people per square mile).

Mauritania is a unitary state, and its form of the government is a presidential democracy. It was a French colony, and it obtained independence on November 28, 1958, under the constitution of the Fifth French Republic. The country declared its full independence on November 28, 1960.

The president is elected by the popular vote for a six-year term; he appoints the prime minister with the Parliament approval. The bicameral legislature consists of the 56-seat *Majlis al-Shuyukh* (Senate), its members are elected by municipal leaders for six-year terms; and the 81-seat *Majlis al-Watani* (National Assembly); its members elected by a popular vote to for the five-year terms.

Mauritania is a multiethnic country. The representatives of primarily Arab-Berber (Maure) descent, who are ethnically and linguistically close to the Arabs of northern Africa, make up about 70 percent of the country's population. There are five major black African ethnic groups in Mauritania, including the Toucouleur (an offshoot of the Fulbe), the Fulbe (the second largest black African group), the Soninké, Wolof, and Bambara. Small groups of other ethnic Africans also live in the southern Mauritania. The representatives of black African descent make up around 30 percent of the population. These figures are contested and some local groups claim that the numbers do not reflect a reality. It is very difficult to verify these claims and counter-claims, as it is very hard to obtain reliable statistical and demographic data from many regions of the country. The Mauritanian society is very complex and highly stratified, and it has a number of social, cultural and other barriers between various groups of the society. In the 1970s the country was involved in the war in Western Sahara, which destabilized stability and political environment not only in Mauritania, but also in the whole region. In the 1980s Mauritania also experienced tensions with neighboring Senegal, which resulted in the repatriation of Mauritanian nationals from Senegal and the repatriation or expulsion of Senegalese nationals from Mauritania. In summer 2003 there was a military coup attempt, which seriously undermined political situation in the country.

The Arab and Wolof languages are official languages of the country. However, many communities preserve their own native languages at the family and community levels. French language is used in the business community and among the elite in the main metropolitan area. The government attempted to reform educational system in the country in the 1990s in order to lift the literacy rate and to provide quality education for all country's citizens. Islamic education establishments were an important part of life for a long time; however, they could not provide modern skills necessary to develop modern industries and technologies and to manage complex issues of globalization era. There is an attempt to develop a modern education system in the country, including higher education institutions. For this purpose the University of Nouakchott, the National College of Administration and the National College of Sciences were established in the early 1980s.

Islam is the official religion of the country and the majority of the Mauritania's population is of Muslim background. Islam plays an important role in the country's politics and social life. Militant Islamic groups did not play a prominent role in the country before and after September 2001 terrorist attacks on the United States and beginning of the U.S.-led was in Afghanistan and Iraq, although some radical Islamic groups were very vocal in the local political and religious debates and in the mass media.

Mauritania's GDP per capita is among lowest in the western Africa (in purchasing power parity), at around US$1,700 (2003, CIA). Traditionally the country largely relied on export of primary natural resources and agricultural production, but in the 1990s and early 2000s it attempted to diversify its economy and developed new sectors. Mauritania possesses several newly discovered oil fields and if they would be successfully developed for export to the international market, the country might substantially improve its living standards. In February 2000, Mauritania qualified for debt relief under the Heavily Indebted Poor Countries (HIPC). In 2003 the UNDP's Human Development Index (HDI) put the Mauritania in 154th place, behind Gambia, Nigeria and Djibouti, but ahead of Eritrea, Senegal and Guinea.

RAFIS ABAZOV

Further Reading

Freedom House, "Mauritania," in *Freedom in the World 2003*, Washington, DC: Freedom House, 2003

Fleischman, Janet, *Mauritania's Campaign of Terror: State-Sponsored Repression of Black Africans*, New York: Human Rights Watch, 1994

Mauritania Government Official Web Site. <http://www.mauritania.mr/>

Office National de la Statistique Home Page. <http://www.ons.mr/>

Pazzanita, Anthony G., and Alfred G. Gerteiny, *Historical Dictionary of Mauritania*, 2nd Edition, Lanham, Maryland: Rowman and Littlefield, 1996

Robinson, David, *Paths of Accommodation: Muslim Societies and French Colonial Authorities in Senegal and Mauritania, 1880–1920 (Western African Studies)*, Ohio: Ohio University Press, 2000

Ruf, Urs Peter, *Ending Slavery: Hierarchy, Dependency and Gender in Central Mauritania*, Transcript Verlag, 2001

Mauritius

Capsule Summary

Country Name: Republic of Mauritius

Location: Southern Africa, island in the Indian Ocean, east of Madagascar

Total Population: 1,210,447 (July 2003)

Languages: English (official), Creole, French (official), Hindi, Urdu, Hakka, Bhojpuri

Religions: Hindu (52%), Christian (28.3% [Roman Catholic 26%, Protestant 2.3%]), Muslim (16.6%), other (3.1%)

Per Capita GDP: US$3500

Mauritius, an island in the south west Indian Ocean, was not permanently settled until 1722. As a result the population of 1.2 million is of recent immigrant origin. It is generally broken down into three main groups—Indo-Mauritians (both Hindu and Moslem), Sino-Mauritians and General PopulationÑand several sub-groups, which may be defined on the basis of linguistic, ethnic, social, religious or racial characteristics.

Although inter-group violence has occasionally marked the country (most notably prior to independence in 1968), such episodes are rare and the various communities live together peaceably. However, there is limited social interaction between groups, and even a degree of physical segregation, with certain areas or towns being identified with specific groups. There is also a strong symbolic assertion of identity, particularly through the use of language. More than 20 languages are spoken on a regular basis throughout the island, although few as a first language. Language also serves as a unifying force: Kreol, a language with French lexical basis and Bantu syntax, is spoken as a first language by more than half the population and is a strong marker of Mauritian identity.

Mauritians descended from immigrants from the Indian subcontinent—imported in the nineteenth and early twentieth centuries to replace the liberated slaves on the sugar plantations—form a numerical majority, but the internal subdivisions of the group are sufficiently clear for it to be acceptably divided into at least three separate categories. Two of these categories are Hindu, who, together, account for approximately 52 percent of the total population. Hindus are divided into Tamils and others. Tamil is spoken as a mother tongue by four

percent of Mauritians, thus ranking it fifth among languages, and it provides a strong symbol of group identity for Tamils, reinforcing that based on religion: more than half of Mauritius's Hindu temples are Tamil. A further 25 percent of temples are Telugu, and Telugus are the other major southern Indian ethnic group represented in Mauritius.

Other Hindus trace their origins to northern India, particularly from the poorer areas of Bihar and Orissa, but also from Maharashtra. Although the caste system as found in India does not exist in Mauritius, a basic form nevertheless operates and provides for some discrimination against those perceived as being of low caste. It is particularly relevant in establishing marriage preferences. The two principal north Indian Hindu sects are the Sanata (orthodox) and the Arya Samaj (reformist).

Moslems, originally from the western part of the Indian subcontinent and specifically Gujerat, account for 17 percent of the population. Many speak Gujerati; there was a resurgence of interest in Urdu when Pakistan gained independence, and a number of Moslems now also speak Urdu, although rarely as a mother tongue. The majority of Moslems follow the Hanafite rite of Sunni Islam, but there are Shafi'i Sunni, Shi'ite (principally Isma'ili but also Ithna Ashari) and Ahmadi minorities.

A small minority of Indo-Mauritians (about 20,000) profess the Christian faith and may be described as "creolized" Indians.

The principal language of Indo-Mauritians is Bhojpuri (Bihari), spoken by 30 percent of the population. In addition to the languages already mentioned, Hindi, Marathi, and Arabic are also spoken, although the latter rarely as a first language. Hindus generally live in rural areas whereas Moslems are concentrated in Port Louis, the capital, and other urban areas in the center of the island.

Sino-Mauritians are the smallest of the three primary groups. Accounting for three percent of the population, the majority are Christian although a significant minority are Buddhist. They have established an economic niche as traders and although there are Chinese-run groceries in villages throughout the island most live in Port Louis, where there is a distinct Chinese quarter. The community is almost entirely of Hakka origin, but few of the young speak Hakka, preferring Kreol.

The General Population is the most heterogeneous of the three principal categories and includes all those who do not fall into one of the two preceding groups. Internal divisions are established on a social basis, since the origins of the group (principally African and European) provide a cultural continuum rather than a basis for classification; all are Christian: Catholic and Protestant sects are present, others are not numerically significant.

The Franco-Mauritians, numbering about 15,000, are the descendants of British and French immigrants. They are economically dominant, owning most of the island's sugar estates and other large businesses, and are distinguished by informal endogamous marriage practices. In social contexts they rarely mix with other groups, although their economic importance accords them significant informal influence in government.

The remainder of the General Population, slightly less than 30 percent of the total, are informally classified on the basis of skin color (and thus their presumed ancestry as European or African), into Colored (or Mulatto) and Creole groups. The darker-skinned Creoles are the descendants of slaves brought to the island in the eighteenth and early nineteenth centuries from Madagascar and East Africa, while the Colored population are the descendants of unions between Europeans and Africans. Most of the General Population speak Kreol as a mother tongue (no African languages are spoken in the country) and thus perceived differences in skin color have become an important factor in determining relationships between different members of the group.

The Republic of Mauritius also includes some outlying islands. Rodrigues has a Christian population of Afro-Malagasy origin who have a culture similar to that of their Creole counterparts in Mauritius. The central (Indo-Mauritian dominated) government has often been accused of colonialism and discrimination against both Rodrigues and the Rodrigans, and there have long been tensions between the two islands which were visibly manifested at independence when Rodrigans refused to raise the new Mauritian flag.

Agalega, a Mauritian dependency close to Seychelles, has a small population who are culturally similar to the Seychellois, while the Chagos Archipelago was detached from Mauritius by Britain at independence for military purposes and its inhabitants expelled. Known as Ilois, and with a distinct cultural identity, for many years most lived in conditions of squalid poverty and suffered discrimination in Mauritius. Mental illness and suicides claimed many victims early on, while drugs and prostitution were often the only recourse for those who survived. A British High Court decision in late 2000 recognized the illegality of the British government's actions and confirmed the Ilois' right to return to their islands.

Since gaining its independence in 1968, Mauritius has moved from a low-income, agricultural economy to a middle-income industrialized economy with growing financial and tourist sectors. In 2002 the estimated per capita GDP was US$10,100.

IAIN WALKER

Further Reading

Arno, Toni, *Ile Maurice, une societe multiraciale*, Paris: L'Harmattan, 1986

Benedict, Burton, *Indians in a Plural Society: A Report on Mauritius*, London: HMSO, 1961

Benoit, Gaetan, *The Afro-Mauritians: An Essay*, Moka, Mauritius: Mahatma Gandhi Institute, 1985

Bissoondoyal, Uttam, editor, *Indians Overseas, the Mauritian Experience*, Moka, Mauritius: Mahatma Gandhi Institute, 1984

Bowman, Larry W., *Mauritius: Democracy and Development in the Indian Ocean*, Boulder: Westview Press, and London: Dartmouth, 1991

Durand, J. and J-P.L. Durand, *"Le Maurice et Ses Populations*, Bruxelles: Editions Complexe, 1978

Eriksen, Thomas Hylland, *Common Denominators: Ethnicity, Nation-Building, and Compromise in Mauritius*, Oxford and New York: Berg, 1998

Lau Thi Keng, Jean-Claude, *Inter-ethnicite et Politique l'Ile Maurice*, Paris: L'Harmattan, 1991

Madeley, John, *Diego Garcia: A Contrast to the Falklands*, London: Minority Rights Group, 1985

Mazandarani

Capsule Summary

Location: Northern Islamic Republic of Iran, near Caspian Sea.
Total Population: Approximately 3–5 million
Language: Mazandarani
Religion: Shi'a Muslim

Mazandarani language belongs to the Caspian group of the Northwestern branch of the Iranian family, and is deeply related to the Gilaki, Rashti, and Shahmirzani languages. The Mazandarani language (also named *Tabri*) remains unwritten. Mazandarani people live in northern Iran's province of Mazandaran, a clearly differentiated region from the historic, ethnic, and linguistic points of view. It is there that early Iranian civilization flourished.

Mazandarani represents the conglomeration of different ethnic groups that arrived in this area through a complicated history. In this ethnic mix there were Turkic tribes (especially from Azerbaidjani ancestry), Persians, and Armenians. Other smaller Mazandarani groups include the Qadikolahi and the Palavi.

History

In 652, during the caliphate of Osman, Saad-Ebn-Aas, the governor of kufah, conquered the coasts of the Mazandaran region, Roomian, and Damavand. At the end of the Sasanid empire (690), the remaining members of the Sasanian court each tried to establish their power in different corners of the country. This struggle generally resulted in founding of petty states in the former Sasanian territories, especially in the stretch of land between Alborz Mountains and the Caspian Sea, that is to say, in modern Mazandarani territory. The people of this area were famous for their bravery and fighting qualities. They refused to surrender to the Arab occupiers, and they kept the Zoroastrian faith and their loyalty to the Sasanians.

During the caliphate of Abou Jafar Mansour (758–780), the second Abbasi caliph, the Mazandarani revolted against him. Some Mazandarani groups still mainly of Zoroastrian religion until the last quarter of the ninthcentury, when the Abbasid rulers finally Islamized the northern Irani region. Afterwards, in 1048,

Sultan Mahmoud Ghaznavi entered in Mazandarani territory through Gorgan and badly damaged people. Sultan Mohamad Kharazmshah conquered Mazandaran in 1228. Tgen Mongols governed the region and finally Taymourian overthrew them. Vandad Homroz established an independent dynasty in Mazandaran in 1403. After the death of Amir Taymour, Sadat Marashi (1429–1472) returned to the region and ruled over there. Mazandaran' country was incorporated into the Persian empire by Shah Abbas I in 1596. The feudal government continued till 1628.

Starting in the eighteenth century, Iran found itself involved in the "Great Game" (to use Kipling's phrase), in which the great powers of the time, Britain and Russia, were engaged in a struggle for influence. At stake for the former was a retention of its authority over the Indian subcontinent, and for the latter, countering British influence and securing access to the warm seas. At that time, the rulers of Iran tried desperately to preserve their country's independence by opposing Russia and Britain. In 1723, the Mazandarani were conquered by the Russian empire until 1732, when Nadir Shah Afshar managed to drive the Russians out of the occupied territories

Cultural, Economic and Political Trends

Mazandaran country was a plural region with several communities of Hebrew and, especially, Armenian ancestry. A probably legendary tradition remarked that Shah Abbas I founded the city of Farahabad as an essentially Jewish town. By the other hand, the same Shah Abbas installed more than 7,000 Armenians in Ashraf (nowadays Behshahr), and around 30,000 in Farahabad. But these communities fled afterwards from Mazandaran region or disappeared into the Mazandarani cultural system. Nowadays, there are not Armenians nor Jews in this area.

Agriculture dominates the economy of the Mazandarani. Most of them are settled farmers who grow crops such as rice, wheat, barley, tea, fruits, and cotton. They also raise some cattle in the humid mountains of the region, beneficed by the wet winds coming through the Caspian Sea. In addition to farming, the Mazandarani are famous for breeding Arabian horses.

The decade of the 1970s saw a number of important agricultural reforms in the Mazandaran province. This processes affected the traditional Mazandaran culture, highly connected with its subsistence patterns constructed throughout hundreds of years. This ancient economic structures disappeared in a few years, even months. Farming economy became a large-scale business operation that included the production, processing, and distribution of agricultural products, as well as the manufacturing of farm machinery, equipment, and supplies. But the Mazandarani society resist these attends to acculturate them: for example, although many of the Mazandarani farmers are settled, some maintain the nomadic lifestyle of their ancestors. These nomads use the higher, cultivated regions for grazing their animals. Their herds include a certain breed of humped cattle, as well as Asian buffalo, which are used as beasts of burden. This nomadic lifestyle guaranteed, in the ancient times, in spite of a lot of invasions and aggressions by different overpowering empires and states, the survival of the Mazandarani ethnic core.

The Irani's interest toward the Mazandarani resources increased through the 1970s since the economic value of the zone was centered in oil exploitation. For example: in Mazandaran Province 9.9 billion Iranian rials (US$1 = 70 Rials) has been spent constructing 8.5 km of barriers along the coasts of Bandar Turkmen, Nowshahr, Ramsar, and Tonekabon. This accelerated and enormous modernization process, centered in the exploitation of the zone but without visible benefits for the local population, highly affected the Mazandarani lifestyle, and marginalize them as a first step to their final disparition as a differentiated ethnic community. Moreover, the traditional landscape and ecological environment of the area suffered an important process that erode its ancient main features.

Nowadays, Mazandarani people still without any possibility to create a written language, and this situation in the modern Iran society implies an increasingly politics of Persianization. This acculturation process is not only important in a linguistic sense, but also in a social and cultural sense. Due to the lack of support from the state institutions, Mazandarani's minority is not able to increase its cultural and linguistical heritage, nor to stop its process of dissolution into the mainstream Persian melting pot.

JOAN MANUEL CABEZAS LÓPEZ

Further Reading

Coppiters, Bruno, editor, *Contested Borders in the Caucasus*, Brussels: Vrije Universitet, 1996

Kazemi, Farhad, *Poverty and Revolution in Iran: The Migrant Poor, Urban Marginality, and Politics,* New York: New York University Press, 1980

Vaziri, Mostafa, *Iran as Imagined Nation: The Construction of National Identity*, New York: Paragon House, 1994

Melanesians

Capsule Summary

Location: Southwest Pacific Ocean
Total Population: approximately 6 million
Languages: A great variety of Papuan and Austronesian languages
Religions: Christianity and indigenous religions

In 1832 the French explorer Dumont d'Urville described the island South Pacific as the home of three regional racial groups: the Melanesians, Polynesians and Micronesians. D'Urville used the term Melanesians (black islanders) to refer to the dark-skinned inhabitants of the area of the southwest Pacific that now contains New Guinea, the Solomon Islands, Vanuatu, Fiji, New Caledonia, and adjacent islands. In contrast to the "hospitable" lighter-skinned Polynesians, the Melanesians were characterized as "bellicose" and "savage." Anthropologists reject the idea that there is such a thing as a Melanesian race, along with the associated racist stereotypes, although the term continues to be used to refer to the people of this region. It is important to emphasize that "Melanesians" constitutes a label, applied by outsiders, that greatly simplifies an immense amount of human diversity.

Background

Melanesians speak more languages than people in any other comparable region of the world. The languages form two large and very distinct families. The Austronesian group is related to Polynesian and Indo-Malay languages, while the non-Austronesian (or Papuan) languages are both very diverse and unique to the area.

Melanesia has been inhabited at least since the Ice Ages of 50,000 years ago. At that time the build-up of ice at higher latitudes lowered sea levels substantially, and present-day New Guinea, Australia and other nearby islands formed the landmass biogeographers call Sahul. The initial settlers of Sahul came from Sunda, another landmass to the west, located where the Indonesian archipelago stands today. Linguists and archaeologists conclude that they were the ancestors of speakers of the Papuan languages now found mostly in the interior of the large islands. The descendants of these ancient migrants produced an array of tribal societies and cultures in the course of their long adaptation to an extremely varied and changing environment.

About 4,000 years ago, a set of migrants from the area around Taiwan, thought to include the ancestors of contemporary Polynesians, began to establish themselves along the coasts and small islands of Melanesia. They are associated with a distinctive type of pottery called "lapita," and were speakers of Austronesian languages. They mixed with the established Papuans, contributing to the enormous variety of languages, societies and cultures that are located in Melanesia.

Although Britain, France, Germany and Holland colonized the area, the European powers (with the exception of France) never attracted substantial numbers of settlers to their Melanesian colonies. The unsavory reputation of the region, its tropical diseases, and the availability of land for settlement in near-by Australia and New Zealand, kept most Europeans away. As a result, Papua New Guinea, the Solomon Islands, Vanuatu and Fiji achieved independence with indigenous majorities. Melanesians became members of minority groups in Australia, West Papua and New Caledonia.

Melanesian Minorities

Two distinct Melanesian minority populations existed in the northern part of Queensland during the late 1800s. One was made up of immigrant laborers, mostly from the Solomon Islands and Vanuatu. Over 60,000 individuals were imported to work on sugar plantations between 1863 and 1904. Most of these workers were gone by the early 1900s, sent home by an act of the Australian Parliament designed to protect that government's white Australia policy. The few who remained faced discrimination, poor job prospects, low education and bad housing. Some chose to move to the Torres Straits Islands in the Arafura Sea, which were annexed by Queensland in 1879.

The people of the northern part of the Torres Straits are closely related to the inhabitants of nearby Papua New Guinea. Those in the southern islands have tended to be associated with Australian Aborigines. Torres Straits Islanders (21,000 people, 15,000 of whom now reside on the Australian mainland) are recognized as indigenous inhabitants of Australia. They have faced, along with Aborigines, substantial difficulties in Australian society. One recent hopeful development for them was the outcome of a claim initiated in 1982 by Eddie Mabo. In 1992 the Australian High Court finally upheld his case for recognition of native title to land on Murray Island. This ruling effectively dismantled the Australian doctrine of terra nullius, the ideology that the continent was uninhabited prior to British colonization. Australia's indigenous people can now re-negotiate their land claims and possibly attain a more secure existence in the "lucky country."

The western half of the island of New Guinea became a province of Indonesia in 1963. Known as West Papua or West Irian, this territory of 162,000 square miles is rich in copper, oil and gold. Seeking to assimilate West Papua (population 1.5 million) into Indonesia, the Indonesian government has moved in people from other parts of the country and encourages multinational corporations to exploit its natural resources. The indigenous Papuans, members of small tribal horticultural societies, have become marginalized by the Indonesianization of the province. It is difficult for them to establish businesses or compete with migrants from other areas for jobs, and they suffer when land is alienated for development and mining projects. A small, poorly supplied guerrilla movement, O.P.M, has resisted the Indonesians since the 1960s, engaging in sporadic kidnappings, sabotage and ambushes of troops. The brutality of the occupation of West Papua, especially during the Suharto era, had the effect of encouraging local support for the guerrillas.

Another area of Melanesia that has been colonized by outsiders is New Caledonia. In the 1850s the French administration alienated all land not under cultivation by native people, for distribution to settlers. They also established a convict settlement on the main island and pushed the indigenes onto reserves. Indigenous resistance was unsuccessful. Now the local people, or "Kanaks," are either subsistence farmers or work in the nickel mines (New Caledonia contains 20 percent of the world's nickel) and on settler holdings. They make up 44 percent of a population of 200,000.

Violence against the French regime re-surfaced in the 1980s, resulting in the promise of a referendum to determine the future of the territory. The referendum, held in 1998, which Kanak nationalists expected to be a vote on independence, turned into a platform for gradual devolution. Over the next 15–20 years the people of New Caledonia will be granted more power to run their own affairs. They may then be able to decide whether they want a continued association with France or full independence. In the meantime, like the Melanesians in Australia and West Papua, the Kanaks have yet to attain equality in the society outsiders have constructed on their land.

HAL B. LEVINE

Further Reading

Brookfield, Harold, and D Hart, *Melanesia*, London: Methuen, 1971

Chowning, Ann, *An Introduction to the Peoples and Cultures of Melanesia*, Menlo Park: Cummings, 1977

Denoon, Donald, editor, *The Cambridge History of the Pacific Islanders*, Cambridge: Cambridge University Press, 1997

Kirch, Patrick, *On the Road of the Winds: An Archaeological History of the Pacific Islands before European Contact,* Los Angeles: University of California Press, 2000

Langness, Lewis, and J.C.F. Weschler, *Melanesia: Readings on a Culture Area*, Scranton: Chandler, 1971

Sillitoe, Paul, *An Introduction to the Anthropology of Melanesia Culture and Tradition,* Cambridge: Cambridge University Press, 1998

Melting Pot Vs. Ethnic Stew

The term *melting pot* refers to the idea that societies formed by immigrant cultures, religions, end ethnic groups, will produce new hybrid social and cultural forms. The notion comes from the pot in which metals are melted at great heat, melding together into new compound, with great strength and other combined advantages. In comparison with assimilation, it implies the ability of new or subordinate groups to affect the values of the dominant group. Sometimes it is referred to as amalgamation, in opposition to both assimilation and pluralism.

The concept of *ethnic stew* is similar to that of melting pot, though the degree of cultural distinctiveness is higher in the former without reaching the level of the "salad bowl" thesis which claims rhat different groups keep their differences, while maintaining relations among each other.

Although the term "melting pot" may be applied to many countries in the world, such as Brazil, Bangladesh, or even France, mostly referring to increased level of mixed race and culture, it is predominantly used with reference to the United States and the creation of the American nation as a distinct "new breed of people" amalgamated from many various groups of immigrants.

As such it is closely linked to the process of Americanization. The theory of melting pot has been criticised both as unrealistic and racist because it focused on the Western heritage and excluded non-European immigrants. Also, despite its proclaimed "melting" character its results have been assimilationist.

The history of the melting pot theory can be traced back to 1782 when J. Hector de Crevecoeur, a French settler in New York, envisioned the United States not only as land of opportunity but as a society where individuals of all nations are melted into a new race of men, whose labours and posterity will one day cause changes in the world (Parrillo 1997). The new nation welcomed virtually all immigrants from Europe in the belief that the United States would become, at least for whites, the "melting pot" of the world. This idea was adopted by the historian Frederick Jackson Turner (1893) who updated it with the frontier thesis. Turner believed that the challenge of frontier life was the country´s most crucial force, allowing Europeans to be "Americanised" by the wilderness (Takaki 1993). A major influx of immigrants occurred mainly after the 1830s, when large numbers of British, Irish, and Germans began entering, to be joined after the Civil

War by streams of Scandinavians and then groups from eastern and southern Europe as well as small numbers from the Middle East, China, and Japan. Before the outbreak of World War I in 1914, the American public generally took it for granted that the constant flow of newcomers from abroad, mainly Europe, brought strength and prosperity to the country. The metaphor of the "melting pot" symbolized the mystical potency of the great democracy, whereby people from every corner of the earth were fused into a harmonious and admirable blend. A decline in immigration from northwestern Europe and concerns over the problems of assimilating so many people from other areas prompted the passage in the 1920s of legislation restricting immigration, one of the measures reflecting official racism.

One of the early critiques of the melting pot idea was Louis Adamic, novelist and journalist who wrote about the experience of American immigrants in the early 1900s and about what he called the failure of the American melting pot in *Laughing in the Jungle* (1932). Both the frontier thesis and the melting pot concept have been criticized as idealistic and racist as they completely excluded non-European immigrants, often also East and South Europeans. The melting pot reality was limited only to intermixing between Europeans with a strong emphasis on the Anglo-Saxon culture while the input of minority cultures was only minor. Some theorists developed a theory of the triple melting pot arguing that intermarriage was occurring between various nationalities but only within the three major religious groupings: Protestant, Catholic, and Jewish. Milton Gordon and Henry Pratt Fairchild proposed the assimilation theory as an alternative to the melting pot one (Parrillo 1997).

Many current proponents of the melting pot are inspired by the "English only" movement with exclusive emphasis on Western heritage and argument against pluralism and accommodation and related policies, such as bilingual education.

Ideally the concept of melting pot should also entail mixing of various "races," not only "cultures." While promoting the mixing of cultures the ultimate result of the American variant of melting pot happened to be the culture of white Anglo Saxon men with minimum impact of other minority cultures. Moreover, the assumption that culture is a fixed construct is flawed. Culture should be defined more broadly as the way one approaches life and makes sense of it. Group's beliefs are determined by conditions and so culture is a continuous process of change and its boundaries are always porous. In a racist discourse, however the culture needs to be seen as a predetermined and rigid phenomenon that would be appropriate for replacing the no longer acceptable concept of race in order to perpetuate inequalities. Many multicultural initiatives aiming at integration/ inclusion of minorities, while following the melting pot ideal, often result in assimilationist and racist outcomes. Melting pot would assume learning about other cultures in order to enhance understanding, mixing, and mutual enrichment; in practice it often tends to ignore similarities of different "races" as it does not include them.

The shortages of the melting pot and salad bowl paradigms can be expressed in the following summarising parables: In the case of the melting pot the aim is that all cultures become reflected in one common culture, however this is generally the culture of the dominant group—*I thought this was mixed vegetable soup but I can only taste tomato.* In the case of the salad bowl, cultural groups should exist separately and maintain their practices and institutions, however, *Where is the dressing to cover it all?* The solution may be offered by the concept of the ethnic stew where all the ingredients are mixed in a sort of pan-Hungarian *goulash where the pieces of different kinds of meat still keep their solid structure.*

LAURA LAUBEOVA

See also **Assimilation; Globalization and Minority Cultures; Integration**

Further Reading

Gazer, Nathan, and Daniel Patrick Moynihan, *Beyond the Melting Pot*, 2nd edition, Cambridge: The MIT Press, 1970

Gordon, Milton M., *Assimilation in American Life*, New York: Oxford University Press, 1964

Parrilo, Vincent, *Diversity in America*, Thousand Oaks, California: Pine Forge Press/A Sage Publications Company, 1996

Parekh, Bhikhu, *Rethinking Multiculturalism. Cultural Diversity and Political Theory*, London: Macmillan Press, 2000

Parrilo, Vincent, *Strangers to These Shores. Race and Ethnic Relations in the United States,* Boston, London: Allyn and Bacon, 1997

Takaki, Ronald, *A Different Mirror. A History of Multicultural America,* Boston, Toronto, London: Little, Brown and Company, 1993

Willet, Cynthia, editor, *Theorizing Multiculturalism: A Guide to Current Debate*, London: Basil Blackwell Press, 1998

Yankelowich, Daniel, *New Rules*, New York: Random House, 1981

Menchu, Rigoberta (Amerindian)

Rigoberta Menchu Tum, an Amerindian social activist and a UNESCO Goodwill Ambassador, was awarded the Nobel Peace Prize in 1992 and forced into exile from her native Guatemala in 1981. Her work has included participation with the United Nations for a declaration of the rights of indigenous people. She was born to Vincente and Juana Menchu in a Guatemalan highland, Quiche Mayan peasant community. The Quiche are one of twenty-two Mayan Indian groups in Guatemala. The Menchu family owned enough land to avoid having to pick coffee beans and cotton as migrant workers on large plantations or fincas on the south coast of Guatemala, as was the case for many of the subsistence farmers in their community (Stoll 1999, 24–25). Rigoberta's father and mother were respected in their village and the region as traditional Quiche leaders and as Catholic Action catechists. Menchu's father was also a member of the CUC (Campesino Committee for Unity), organized to protect the property rights of indigenous and poor farmers.

The large-scale, non Mayan landowners who influenced local politics and military activities associated the work of Catholic Action catechists with guerilla organization. For their identification as leaders of grass roots political activities, the Menchus were labeled as Communists. In 1979, Menchu's older brother Petrocinio, also a catechist, was kidnapped, tortured, and murdered by the military. A year later, in 1980, while attending a CUC protest at the Spanish Embassy in Guatemala City, her father, along with other peasants, students, and trade union workers, were killed in a Guatemalan army grenade attack. Shortly after, in 1980, Menchu's mother was kidnapped, raped, tortured, murdered, and her body desecrated.

Conflicting details of what happened next present Menchu in two different scenarios between 1980 and 1981. In the version anthropologist David Stoll carefully researches, the deaths of her parents occurred while she was away at a Catholic boarding school in Chiantla. In Stoll's version of Menchu's story, she is smuggled out of the country instead of returning to her village to face a similar violent end (Stoll 199, 165). In the version represented in her autobiography, translated by anthropologist Elisabeth Burgos-Debray,

Menchu never attended school. In her version of the story, she idealizes her father as a revolutionary leader and hero who died a martyr's death and herself as a finca laborer and solidarity organizer in the CUC. According to her testimony, Menchu helped lead peasant labor union strikes on the southern coast.

Whether Menchu returned to her village after her parent's death or not, it is clear that, in fear of reprisals by the Guatemalan army, she obtained political asylum from the Guatemalan Church in Exile, a liberal Roman Catholic diocese in Chiapas, Mexico. There is no disputing, that while in Mexico, she recruited catechists into peasant resistance movements and helped co-found the United Representation of the Guatemalan Opposition (RUOG). In 1982, Menchu traveled to Europe to solicit international support for her work. In Paris, leftist anthropologist Elisabeth Burgos-Debray recorded Menchu's testimonial and published it in Spanish as her autobiography in 1983. It was published in English in 1984 and since into 12 additional languages. The text drew significant international attention and human rights support to the plight of the oppressed in Guatemala. It also ascended within the multicultural and women's studies canons in American higher education.

In 1987, Menchu returned to Guatemala from exile in Mexico to help found the National Committee for Reconciliation and to participate in the negotiation of peace talks between the Guatemalan National Revolutionary Union and the Guatemalan government. As a result of her work for indigenous social justice and reconciliation between ethnic and cultural groups, Menchu was honored with the Nobel Peace Price in 1992. She was the youngest recipient ever.

An internationally recognized political strategist, ideological visionary and literary genius, Menchu's life and work reflect the political, ideological, and literary controversies of her age. Caught in the crossfire of socialist, feminist, and multi-cultural antagonisms, her life and work are scrutinized for authenticity. Critics charge that she deliberately identifies with ideological banners as they convenience her agenda, and then abandons them when they become unpopular to her causes. Rigorous investigation into the details of Menchu's autobiography reveals that many first person accounts were actually culturally authentic representations of the collective history of the Mayan people, not her personal life (Stoll 1999). She responds to attacks on her credibility as a minority representative by asserting that her critics have over-simplified her life and experiences. The autobiography reflects a Latin American revolutionary political tra-dition of the 1970s and 1980s in which the facts of oppression and repression are communicated to the international community through literary "testimo-nies" in attempts to arouse moral, political, and eco-nomic support (Lancaster 1999).

The controversy over Menchu's history centers on whether she can legitimately represent the illiterate oppressed Mayan minority when she herself experi-enced a middle-class life and education. There is no doubt, however, that members of her family were tor-tured and murdered, even if the details of her personal history are not all depicted accurately in her autobiog-raphy. Nor does anyone doubt that her knowledge of traditional Quiche culture and command of Quiche, Mam, Cakchiquel, and Tzutuhil Mayan Indian dia-lects. Nor is it disputed that her awareness of the extent of the suffering of indigenous and other poor peoples in Guatemala, was obtained while living among Mayan peasants.

Another debate regarding the text's authenticity is whether or not she should have earned the Nobel Prize if she actually aligned herself with guerrillas and their revolutionary tactics as her autobiography suggests. Since receiving the Nobel Prize in 1992, Menchu has distanced herself from her connections with revolu-tionary grass roots organizations and focused more of her attention on serving as a mediator among diverse interests. The Rigoberta Menchu Tum Foundation, funded with her Nobel Prize cash award of $1.2 million, continues to influence international awareness of polit-ical and economic conditions of the indigenous of Guatemala. Menchu also works to negotiate peaceful and culturally appropriate solutions by reconciling cul-tural differences between native and non-native peo-ples. Foundation offices in Guatemala City, New York City, and Berkeley, California establish programs to improve education, health care, housing, and emp-loyment training and development opportunities in Guatemala. The Foundation also protects refugees, defends political prisoners, and facilitates the return of indigenous Guatemalans who fled to Mexico.

Menchu successfully draws international and national attention to minority issues in Latin America. In support of the Zapatista demands for indigenous rights in January, 1994, Menchu led an "Indigenous Peace Initia-tive" of delegates from Chile, Nicaragua, Guatemala, Canada, Mexico, New Zealand, and Lapland in Chiapas Mexico. As a direct result Mayan peoples of Guatemala participated in constitutional reforms in 1996 that recog-nized their human rights and cultural identities.

Historically juxtaposed as a symbol of women's liberation, the noble naïve savage of human rights' activists, an icon for the international left, a model of multi-cultural discourse for intellectuals, a subversive Latin American guerilla in opposition to global neolib-eralism, and a cynical politician, Rigoberta Menchu emerges as a personality much more coherent and authentic to the twenty-first century than to the twen-tieth century.

Capsule Biography

Rigoberta Menchu Tum. Born January 9, 1959, in the village of Chimel, near San Miguel de Uspantan, the capital of El Quiche (a northwestern province), Guatemala. Attended Cath-olic boarding schools in Chichicastenango for a year and a half at age six or seven, another in San Miguel Uspantan from the ages of 12 to 14; studied for two years at the Colegio Belga in Guatemala City. Domestic worker while at Catholic boarding schools; catechist for the Catholic Action, a Jesuit directed program in the highlands of Guatemala and Chiapas; founder and director of the Vicente Menchu Foundation in 1992, renamed the Rigoberta Menchu Tum Foundation in 1995. Received the Nobel Peace Prize in 1992; the French Legion of Honor; 14 honorary doctorate degrees, Served as the Goodwill Ambassador for the United Nations declared Year of Indigenous Peoples (1993); member of the United Nations International Indian Treaty Council; presides over the Indigenous Initiative for Peace at the UN; appointed the United Nations Educational, Scientific, and Cultural Organization (UNESCO) Goodwill Ambassador the years 2000–2010; served on an advisory board for the Council of Foreign Relations in New York: associated with many grass-roots organizations, including the Guatemalan Campesino Community for Unity (CUC) and member of its National Coordinating Committee, the United Representation of the Guatemalan Opposition (RUOG), the Committee of Peas-ant Unity, American Continent's Five Hundred Years of Resis-tance Campaign, the National Committee for Reconciliation, the Guerilla Army of the Poor (EGP), and the 31st of January Popular Front that protested the 500 year anniversary of Columbus' invasion of the Americas.

Selected Works

I, Rigoberta Menchu: an Indian Woman in Guatemala, 1983; translation from Spanish, 1984; Eighteenth reprint 1995
Trenzando el Futuro: Luchas Campesinas en las Historia Reciente de Guatemala, (Future Involvement: Peasant Struggles in Recent Guatemalan History), 1992

"The Quincentennial—A Gift of Life: A Message from the Indigenous People of Guatemala," *Social Justice,* 19, no. 2 (1992)
Rigoberta: La nieta de los Mayas, (Rigoberta: A Little Mayan Girl), with Dante Liano and Gianni Mina, in *Crossing Borders,* 1998

BARBARA J. DILLY

See also **Guatemala; Latin Americans**

Further Reading

Lancaster, Roger N., "Rigoberta's testimonio: Controversies over 'I Rigoberta Menchu,'" *North American Congress on Latin America (NACLA) Report on the Americas,* 32, no. 4 (1999)
Montejo, Victor, *Testimony: Death of a Guatemalan Village,* Willimantic, Connecticut: Curbstone Press, 1987
Perera, Victor, *The Bird Who Cleans the World and Other Mayan Fables,* translated by Wallace Kaufman, Williamantic, Connecticut: Curbstone Press, 1992
Perera, Victor, *Unfinished Conquest: The Guatemalan Tragedy,* Berkeley: University of California Press, 1993
Smith, Carol A., and Marilyn M. Moors, editors, *Guatemalan Indians and the State, 1540 to 1988,* Austin: University of Texas Press, 1990
Smith, Christian, "The Spirit and Democracy: Base Communities, Protestantism, and Democratization in Latin America," in *Crossing Currents: Continuity and Change in Latin America,* edited by Michael B. Whiteford and Scott Whiteford, Upper Saddle River, New Jersey: Prentice Hall, 1998
Stavenhagen, Rudolfo, "Indigenous Organizations: Rising Actors in Latin America," in *Contemporary Cultures and Societies of Latin America,* edited by Dwight B. Heath, Prospect Heights, Illinois: Waveland Press, 2002
Stoll, David, *Rigoberta Menchu and the Story of All Poor Guatemalans,* Boulder, Colorado: Westview Press, 1999
Warren, Kay B., *Indigenous Movements and Their Critics: Pan-Indian Activism in Guatemala,* Princeton, New York: Princeton University Press, 1998
Wearne, Phillip, forward by Rigoberta Menchu, *Return of the Indian: Conquest and Revival in the Americas,* Philadelphia: Temple University Press, 1996

Mexican-Americans

Capsule Summary

Location: United States, majority in Southwest
Total Population: Estimated 22.5 million in the United States
Languages: Spanish, English
Religion: Predominantly Christian (Roman Catholic)

Mexican American is a term used to describe people who immigrated to the United States or whose ancestors were born in Mexico. Mexican Americans are the largest of all U.S. Hispanic groups, representing 58 percent of the nation's 38.8 million Latinos. The majority of Mexican Americans reside in the west and southwestern states (California, Colorado Arizona, New Mexico, and Texas). Other large concentrations of Mexicans can be found in metropolitan cities in Illinois, Florida and New York. Currently, the United States is home to more Spanish-speaking residents than any other country in the world, with the exception of Mexico. It is difficult to find statistics related only to Mexican Americans due to the tendency to group all people of Spanish-speaking ancestry into one cluster. Due to the rise in the Hispanic population more efforts are being made to keep track of sub-groups within the Hispanic community.

Historically, Mexican Americans have been among the most economically deprived of ethnic groups. Educational attainment for Mexican Americans is lower compared to their Anglo and other Hispanic and ethnic counterparts. While there have been improvement over the years, Mexican Americans still lag in several socioeconomic areas. According to the U.S. Census Bureau, in 2002, 51 percent of Mexican Americans aged 25 years or older had a high school degree. In comparison, the graduation rate of White non-Hispanics is about 90 percent. In addition, Mexican Americans are less likely than other groups to work in a managerial or professional occupations, less likely to go to college, and for those that make it to college, less likely to graduate. Male dominance, gender expectations and a strong family orientation that exists in the Mexican heritage make it even more difficult for female Mexican Americans to complete their education.

History

Spanish explorer, Juan Ponce de Leon, landed on the coast of Florida in 1513 and began the Hispanic tradition in the United States. He was followed by many other Spanish explorers who established settlements throughout the southwest. Spanish conquerors intermarried with Mexican and Indigenous Indians, thus many Mexican Americans today have a mixed heritage of Spanish, Mexican and Indian ancestry. Conflicts between the United States and Mexico date back to the 1800s, as migration into Mexican, then Spanish, territory proceeded and acquisition followed. Mexico declared its independence from Spain in 1821 after eleven years of fighting for independence. The war left Mexico economically devastated and prompted the opening of trade with the United States. In 1821, the Santa Fe Trail was opened which served as a delivery route for traders. The trail, which spanned 900 miles from the Great Plains to Mexico, increased Mexico's economic dependence on the United States.

The Mexican-American War began April 25, 1846 and lasted two years. The Treaty of Guadalupe Hidalgo ended the war on February 2, 1848. The war was fought to defend the rights of the citizens of the Republic of Texas to choose their destiny. At the time, there was a movement to annex Texas to the United States. Mexico did not recognize Texas's independence and made plans to recapture Texas. The Treaty of Guadalupe Hidalgo ended the war. In effect, the treaty ceded to the United States the territory that today includes the states of California, Arizona, New Mexico, Nevada, Utah, and parts of Colorado and Wyoming. In addition the treaty fixed the Rio Grande as the boundary of Texas. The United States assumed the claims of its citizens against Mexico (estimated at $3.25 million) and paid Mexico an additional $15 million for the land and economic recovery. Although the treaty guaranteed Mexicans and their descendants land rights, the estimated 70,000 to 100,000 Mexicans who lived in the annexed areas found themselves in turmoil as they lost their land and faced discrimination.

Due to poor economic conditions and an unstable government, Mexican immigrants were attracted to the United States Consequently migration to the United States increased significantly after 1850. In contrast to the Mexican economy, the United States economy was booming. The U.S. Southwest needed cheap, unskilled and semi-skilled labor to work in agriculture, mining, and the railroad industry. In 1890 there were over 75,000 Mexican immigrants in the United States. By 1900 the number surged to between 380,000 and 560,000. In the years following 1900 the immigration pattern saw several surges as Mexicans sought work and the United States economy grew. There were several efforts over the years to reduce immigration such

as the Good Neighbor Policy of 1934, a repatriation program, which returned half a million people to Mexico. Some left voluntarily while others were forced out. Many of those that returned to Mexico were American-born. During World War II, the United States found a need for seasonal workers and in conjunction with the Mexican government instituted the Bracero Program.

The Bracero Program

In the late 1930s employment in Mexico was scarce and the crop fields were not producing enough for families to earn a decent living. The Mexican agricultural worker was forced to find other means of survival. At the same time the United States was experiencing a labor shortage due to World War II. As a result of these situations, on August 14, 1942, the governments of Mexico and the United States instituted the Bracero Program. Bracero is a Spanish term meaning "strong-armed ones" and is used in reference to temporary/seasonal workers or farm workers. The Bracero Program, also referred to as the Mexican Farm Labor Supply Program and the Mexican Labor Agreement, was sanctioned by Congress through Public Law 45 of 1943. Over the 22 years that the program was in effect, an estimated four million Mexican farm laborers came to the United States to work in the agricultural fields on a temporary basis.

Because braceros were experienced farm laborers, they helped convert the United States agricultural system into one of the world's most prosperous. Lured by the promise of high earnings and a desire to improve their situation, many impoverished Mexicans abandoned their homes to join the United States labor force. The arrival of the braceros altered the social environment and economy of the United States.

Under the Bracero Program, farm employers requesting braceros had to first make reasonable efforts to obtain domestic workers. Although braceros could not understand English, they would sign employment contracts without fully understanding the conditions. Much of the braceros' freedoms were limited. The only way they could return to Mexico is if their contract expired or in the case of an emergency. Over the years of the program the braceros suffered from oppression and harassment at the hands of abusive foreman and exploitive farm owners. In addition to agricultural work, many braceros worked on the railroads. Many deaths occurred due to accidents, exhaustion and sunstroke. In 1961, a report from the California Senate Fact Finding Committee on Labor and Welfare reported that many unethical farm owners lied about efforts to employ domestic laborers because it was much cheaper to hire braceros. Many believe that the Bracero Program oppressed agricultural workers and adversely affected the wages of domestic workers.

Due to technological improvements, an excess of illegal immigrants, and declining public acceptance, the Bracero Program lost its attractiveness. In May 1963, Congress voted against further extension of the program and the program officially expired on Dec 31 1964. Lee G. Williams, The U.S. Department of Labor officer in charge of the program, described the program as a form of legalized slavery. Although the Bracero Program officially ended, the migration patterns it established continued as many illegal immigrants crossed the border to work on United States farms.

The uneducated braceros experienced human rights violations that did not go unnoticed. American labor leader, third generation Mexican American, César Chávez successfully educated the country on the civil rights abuses endured by braceros. He founded the United Farm Workers of America and improved the lives of tens of thousands of Mexican migrant workers and Chicanos in the United States Dolores Huerta, another influential leader in the civil rights movement, worked with Chavez to organize farmworkers. Efforts to initiate another bracero-like program in the late 1990s faced much debate and resistance due to the negative connotation the term has for many Mexican Americans. Consequently, the Agricultural Job Opportunity Benefits and Security Act of 1999 failed to gain the needed support for passage.

The Zoot Suit Riots

An early event that influenced the Chicano Movement was the Zoot Suit Riots. During World War II, there was ethnic and racial paranoia. In California and along much of the West Coast, Japanese Americans had been sent to "internment camps." With no Japanese citizens around, many Americans turned to the "zoot suiters" as the scapegoats for all that was wrong in Los Angeles. Wide-brimmed hats, broad-shouldered long coats, high-waisted peg-legged trousers and long chains became the fad for young Mexican Americans. Called pachucos, these young Mexican Americans ventured outside of the barrios and became a perceived threat by the local community. Even though there were a disproportionate number of Mexican Americans serving in the military, military men became resentful because the zoot suiters were not wearing military uniforms. Local newspapers portrayed zoot suiters as gangsters and fueled fears of a "Mexican crime wave." In 1942 racial tension between the Anglo military men and young Hispanics exploded after a young Mexican American was killed at a party. The Los Angeles Police Department arrested 600 men of Hispanic descent as suspects.

On June 3, 1943, a number of sailors claimed to have been beaten and robbed by pachucos. The following night 200 sailors hired a fleet of cabs and drove into East Los Angeles. They beat up and stripped the clothing off any Mexican American they could find. Young black and Filipino males were also assaulted. As Mexican Americans fought back, the resulting battle became one of the worse race riots in Los Angeles history. On June 8, the riots stopped when the city was declared off limits to military men. The local press praised the military rioters for confronting the "Mexican crime wave." On June 9, the Los Angeles City Council issued an ordinance banning zoot suits from being worn. Nationwide condemnation of the military rioters and civil authorities followed.

The Chicano Movement

In response to a renewed sense of pride in their cultural roots, Mexican Americans began to organize in a quest for social justice. The actions collectively became known as The Chicano Movement. This movement gained momentum during the 1960s and lasted into the 1970s as civil rights gained importance in the psyche of the Chicano people. The goal of the Chicano Movement was to improve the social, educational, economic and political lives of Mexican Americans in the United States

In the 1960s, life for Mexican Americans left much to be desired. One third of Mexican American families lived below the federal poverty line; unemployment among Mexican Americans was twice the rate of that for non-Hispanic Whites; 80 percent of Mexican Americans were employed in unskilled or semi-skilled jobs; and the high school drop out rate was among the highest of all ethnic groups. These conditions provided the basis for the Chicano Movement. The term Chicano, derived from the Spanish word meaning "the poorest of the poor," was adopted to express the fight to improve the life of Mexican Americans.

Hundreds of organizations got involved to improve the system. Participants ranged from moderate to radical in thought and action. Organizations included the

Community Service Organization, United Farm Worker's Union, The National Chicano Moratorium, the Mexican American Youth Organization (MAYO), The Crusade for Justice, CASA – Hermandad General de Trabajodores, La Raza Unida Party, La Alianza de Pueblos Libres, The Brown Berets, and many more. Over time the Movement raised the ethnic pride felt by Chicanos. Many Chicanos support the notion that the Chicano Movement continues today. During the height of activism to improve the plight of Mexican immigrants and Mexican Americans, the term "Chicano" had associations with radicalism. Today the term has been diluted and is used by many mainstream Mexican Americans to indicate acceptance of their heritage.

DENISE T. OGDEN

See also **Mexico**

Further Reading

Acuña, Rodolfo, *Occupied America*, New York: Harper Collins, 1988

Aranda, José F., Jr., "When We Arrive—A New Literary History of Mexican America," Tuscson: The University of Arizona Press, 2003

Camarillo, Albert, *Chicanos in a Changing Society: From Mexican Pueblos to American Barrios in Santa Barbara and Southern California, 1848–1930*, Cambridge: Harvard University Press, 1979

Campa, Arthur, *Hispanic Culture in the Southwest*, Norman: University of Oklahoma Press, 1979

Cardoso, Lawrence, *Mexican Emigration to the United States, 1897–1931*, Tucson: University of Arizona Press, 1980

Carroll, Patrick J., *Felix Longoria's Wake—Bereavement, Racism, and the Rise of Mexican American Activism*, Austin: University of Texas Press, 2003

Chávez, John R., *The Lost Land: The Chicano Image of the Southwest*, Albuquerque: University of New Mexico Press, 1984

Gómez-Quiñones, Juan, *Chicano Politics: Reality and Promise, 1940–1990*, Albuquerque: University of New Mexico Press, 1990

Gonzalez, Gilbert G., and Raul A. Fernandez, *A Century of Chicano History*, New York: Routledge, 2003

Gutiérrez, David G., *Walls and Mirrors: Mexican Americans, Mexican Immigrants and the Politics of Ethnicity*, Berkeley: University of California Press, 1995

Márquez, Benjamin, *LULAC: The Evolution of a Mexican American Political Organization*, Austin: University of Texas Press, 1993

Reisler, Mark, *By the Sweat of Their Brow: Mexican Immigrant Labor in the United States: 1900–1940*, Westport, Connecticut: Greenwood Press, 1976

Rendon, Armando B., *Chicano Manifesto*, New York: Macmillan, 1971

Rosales, Francisco A., *Chicano!: The History of the Mexican American Civil Rights Movement*, Houston: Arte Publico Press, 1996

Sánchez, George, *Becoming Mexican American: Ethnicity, Culture and Identity in Chicano Los Angeles, 1900–1945*, New York: Oxford University Press, 1993

Skerry, Peter, *Mexican Americans: The Ambivalent Minority*, New York: The Free Press, 1993

The Politics of Chicano Liberation, 1st edition, New York: Pathfinder Press, 1977

Weber, David J., *Foreigners in Their Native Land: Historical Roots of the Mexican Americans*, Albuquerque: University of New Mexico Press, 1973

Mexico

Capsule Summary

Country Name: *Estados Unidos Mexicanos* or United Mexican States

Location: North America

Total Population: 104,907,991 (July 2003)

Ethnic Populations: Mestizo (Amerindian-Spanish) [60%], Amerindian or predominantly Amerindian (30%), white (9%), other (1%)

Languages: Spanish (official) and 50 regional indigenous languages

Religions: nominally Roman Catholic (89%), Protestant (6%), other (5%)

Estados Unidos Mexicanos (United Mexican States), conventionally called Mexico, is located in southern North America between the Gulf of Mexico and Caribbean Sea to the east and the North Pacific Ocean to the west, and is bordered on the north by the United States of America, and on the south by the nation states of Belize and Guatemala. A representative, democratic, federal republic, Mexico has 31 states (*estados*) and a federal district (Distrito Federal, the seat of government at Mexico City). Because of its geographic location, topography, geology, and climates, Mexico has diverse ecology. As the location of advanced New World cultures (Olmec, Teotihuacan, Maya, Toltec, Zapotec, Tarascan, and Aztec, among others), physical geography has played a significant role in isolating indigenous cultures from one another in pre-Hispanic times and from European incursions beginning in 1519.

The current population is 104,907,991 (July 2003), with 32.3 percent at or below the age of 14, and a birth rate of 21.92 births/1,000 indicative of future major demographic increases. The per capita GDP was US$8,900 in 2002. Mexico has the largest indigenous population of any Latin American country, with 56 indigenous peoples speaking at least 50 native languages and includes about 30 million persons. The government officially recognizes 49 "ethnic groups" (ethnic peoples). The *mestizo* population (mixed Amerindian and Spanish heritage) accounts for about 60 percent of the population.

Native populations declined markedly because of epidemic diseases and exploitation during the period 1519 to 1600, so that only about 1.5 million indigenous persons remained out of an estimated 15 million. Slaves from the Caribbean and Africa were imported for labor and immigration was encouraged, attracting diverse ethnic groups from Europe and East Asia. Miscegenation was widespread so that ideal ethnic "types" were defined: *mestizos* (mixtures of Europeans, particularly Spanish, and Amerindians), mulattos (Europeans and Africans), *zambos* (Africans and Amerindians), and *chinos* (Asians of various mixtures). Caucasians ("whites") were divided into peninsular (those born in Iberia) and *criollo* (those born in the New World) and never numbered more than 15,000. Over time, ethnicity became redefined socioculturally and economically rather than racially or genetically in Latin America, hence the term *mestizo* refers to a person who has adopted Mexican Hispanic culture or anyone "culturally Mexican," while *ladino* is used in many Latin American countries to identify individuals who are culturally Hispanic. The acculturation process for natives living in remote villages has taken centuries.

Today the major linguistic groups are: Nahuatl (1,400,000 speakers) concentrated in Veracruz, Hidalgo, Oaxaca, Puebla, Morelos and México (state); Maya (750,000) mainly in Quintana Roo, Campeche, and Yucatán); Mixtec (400,000) in Oaxaca and Guerrero; Zapotec (400,000) in Oaxaca; Otomi (300,000) in Hidalgo; Tzotzil (235,000) in Chiapas; Totonac (220,000) in Puebla and Veracruz; Mazateco (175,000)

in Oaxaca; and Tzetal (170,000) in Chiapas. Natives (Amerindians exclusively or predominantly) account for about 30 percent of the population, persons of European origin 9 percent, and others including African-American Mexicans, about 1 percent.

Although inhabiting every state and the federal district, indigenous peoples are concentrated in 10 states in southern and southeast Mexico (demographically rank ordered): Oaxaca, Veracruz, Chiapas, Yucátan, Puebla, México (state), Hidalgo, Guerrero, Distrito Federal, San Luis Potosí, and Michoacán. The ethnic Nahua peoples (1,197,328 1990 Census) account for 22.67 percent of the native population of Mexico and are concentrated in the Huasteca, northern and southern Sierra de Puebla, Morelos, and Guerrero (431,805), in the state of Mexico (26,927), and Sierra de Puebla (100,000).

The following tabulation includes demographic estimates and geographic location by state of other geopolitical unit for 38 other ethnic groups: *Cahita* (including the Haqui, Mayo, Tehueco, and Yaqui; 50,000) in southern Sonora and northern Sinaloa; *Chatino* (30,000) along the Pacific coast of Oaxaca; *Chinantec* (70,000) situated in the Papaloapan River Basin and northern Oaxaca; *Chocho* (ethnonyms: Chochol, Chocholteca, Chochoteco, Chono, and Hochón; 1,200) concentrated in the Mixteca Alta region of northern Oaxaca; *Ch'ol* (ethnonym: Chol; 100,000) in Chiapas; *Chontal* (ethnonyms: Chontales and Chontol Maya; 31,000) in Tabasco; *Cora* (ethnonyms: Nayaritas and Nayares; 11,500 persons in 10 communities) in Nayarit; *Cuicatec* (12,000) located in northwestern Oaxaca; *Guarihío* (ethnonyms: Guarijio, Huarijio, Varohíros, and Warijíro; 1,000) concentrated in Alto Rio Mayo, Sonora; *Huichol* (ethnonyms; Huichole, Tevi, and Wizarika; 20,000) living in the Sierra Madre Occidental in the states of Jalisco, Nayarit, Zacatecas, and Durango; *Lacandon* (ethnonyms: Lakandon and Lacandone; 300) in Chiapas; *Mam* (ethnonym: Mam Maya) 500,000 in western Guatemala with 3,000 in southeastern Chiapas; *Mazahua* (ethnonym: Mazahuas; 128,000) inhabiting Michoacan and northern portions of the state of Mexico; *Mazatec* (170,000) in northern Oaxaca and southern Veracruz; *Mixe* (ethnonym: Mije; 80,000) in Oaxaca; *Mixtec* (ethnonym: Ñuu Savi; 330,000) in Oaxaca, Guerrero, and Puebla; *Otomí*, two branches: Highland and Sierra Otomí (ethnonym: Otomí of the Sierra: 40,000) with the former located north of the Basin of Mexico and Sierra Otomí in eastern Hidalgo and parts of Veracruz and Puebla; *Otomí* of the Mezquital Valley (ethnonym: Otomí;

118,000) in Hidalgo; *Pame* (4,700) in San Luis Potosí; *Popoloca* (26,000) in southern Puebla; *Popoluca* (29,000) in southern Veracruz; *Seri* (ethnonyms: Ceri, Comacaac,. Heri, Sadi, Sori, Tepoca, Tiburone, and Upanguayma; 700) living in two villages on the Sonoran coast; *Tarahumara* (ethnonyms: Salámuli, Rarámuri, Tarahumar, Tarahumari, and Taraumar; 65,000) in western Chihuahua; *Tarascans* (ethnonyms: Michuguaca, Phurhépecha, Puerecha, and Tarascos; 175,000) in Michoacan; *Tepehua* (8,800) in Hildago and Veracruz; *Tepehuan* of Chihuahua (ethnonyms: Northern Tepehuca, and Òdami; 10,000) in Chihuahua; *Tepehuan* of Durango (16,000) primarily in Durango with some in adjacent Nayarit and Zacatecas; *Totonac* (ethnonyms: Totonaca and Totonaco; 210,000) in Puebla and Veracruz; *Tzeltal* (50,000) in Chiapas; *Tzotzil* of Pantelhó (ethnonyms: Catarineros, Santa Catarina Pantelhó, and Tzotzil Maya; 14,000) in Chiapas; *Tzotzil* of Chamula (ethnonyms: Batz'i Krisamoetike, and Chamula; 100,000) in central Chiapas; *Tzotzil* of San Andrés Larraínzar (ethnonyms: Anresero and Batz'i vinik; 15,500) in highland Chiapas; *Tzotzil* of San Bartolomé de los Llanos (ethnonyms: San Barteleños, Totiketik, and Tzotziles; 10,000) Chiapas; *Tzotzil* of Zinacantan (ethnonyms: Sotz'leb, Zinacantecos and Zinacantecs; 24,000) in central highland Chiapas; *Yaqui* (ethnonyms: Cahita, Yoeme, and Yoreme; 10,000) in southeastern Sonora; *Yukateko* (ethnonyms: Máasehual, Maya, and Mayero; 500,000) in Yucatán, Quintana Roo, Campeche, and Tabasco; *Zapotec* (ethnonyms: Ben 'Zaa, Bimii Gula'sa', Tsapotecatl, Za, and Zapateco; 380,000) in Oaxaca and the Isthmus of Tehuantepec; and *Zoque* (ethnonyms: Soques, Tsoque. Tzoques, and Zoc; 45,000) in the Gulf Coast plain of Tabasco, eastern Oaxaca, and southwestern Chiapas.

African Mexican populations in Mexico date to 1528 and the census of 1810 found that blacks comprised 10.1 percent of the population, the majority of whom came as slaves, often from the Caribbean Islands rather than directly from the African continent, during nearly 300 years of Spanish conquest and administration. Conservative estimates are that 3 percent of all Mexicans have some African heritage although other calculations range up to 75 percent. Today 16 towns in the Pacific Costa Chica region are overwhelmingly African Mexican as are several communities in Veracruz. Chinese and Philippine emigrants, "Chinos de Manila," were established in Mexico City by 1635, with large-scale immigration of Chinese in 1876, and Japanese and a few East Indians (mostly bound for the British West Indies) dur-

ing the mid-nineteenth century. Oriental merchants clustered in Sonora so that by 1919 the Chinese numbered 6,078 but only 3,571 in 1930 as they were expelled and their businesses nationalized. Some moved back to China, others entered the United States, and new enclaves were established in Mexico City, Chihuahua, and Baja California Norte.

The Irish Potato Famine (1845–49) caused an influx of Irish males to come to America and join the U.S. Army, and some of these Catholic Irish troops defected to the Mexican side during the Mexican War (1846–48) and became known as "San Patristas." French immigrants came to Mexico City during the period of French intervention in Mexico (1862–67) and remained afterwards. Following the American Civil War (1861–65) an unknown number of American families from the former Confederate States (primarily Texas, Louisiana, and Alabama) migrated to Mexico after 1865 and relocated in northern and central Mexico. Since 1871 Italians migrated to Mexico and 30,000 Italian Mexicans now reside in communities in the Distrito Federal and states of Puebla, Veracruz, and San Luis Potosí. In the early decades of the twentieth century, cosmopolitan Mexico City attracted diverse upper class Americans, Europeans, and Latin Americans. During the period 1920 to 1945, number of Ashkenazi Jews and German Catholics immigrated to the state of Mexico, Veracruz, and the Distrito Federal. Republican refugees from the Spanish Civil War (1936–39) migrated since 1938, and German, Austrian, and East Europeans came after World War II.

Because of civil strife in Guatemala since the 1980s, many Mayan-speaking Mam refugees fled into rural and urban centers in Chiapas. Of the estimated 150,000 refugees at least 50,000 have remained illegally in Mexico. For nearly a decade, the Zapatista National Liberation Army in Chiapas and National Indigenous Congress opposed the federal government's repressive policies against native peoples. Recognizing that the indigenous populations have faced discrimination, the Mexican government approved an Indian Rights bill in April 2001 that is to be a constitutional amendment if approved by a majority of state legislatures. It remains to be seen if this conflict will be defused by the new Mexican administration led by Vicente Fox.

Since the 1950s, Mexico has been a conduit for illegal immigrants coming into the United States from Central and South American countries, notably Guatemala, Nicaragua, Costa Rica, El Salvador, Ecuador, and Peru. Economic, civil, and religious conflicts also led to numbers of illegal aliens from countries in Southeast and

Southwest Asia (Vietnam, Cambodia, Turkey, and Afghanistan) venturing to Mexico in hopes of immigrating to the United States. Many, however, have settled in Mexico, hence, Mexico is a heterogeneous nation of minorities, many of whom are transient. The central Mexican state of Zacatecas has a population of 1,351,207 (2000), but demographers estimate that because of drought and a lack of industrial employment, almost the same number of Zactecans live in the United States. Nonetheless, the ethnic and linguistic diversity of Mexico has been used politically to strengthen the nation economically through cultural tourism.

CHARLES C. KOLB

See also **Mexican-Americans**

Further Reading

Cimet, Adina, *Ashkenazi Jews in Mexico: Ideologies in the Structuring of a Community*, Albany: State University of New York, 1997

Dow, James W., editor, *Encyclopedia of World Cultures, Volume VIII: Middle America and the Caribbean*, Boston: G.K. Hall & Co., 1995

Ember, Melvin, and Carol Ember, editors, *Countries and Their Cultures*, New York: Macmillan Reference, (under the auspices of the Human Relations Area Files at Yale University), 2001

Jackson, Robert H., *Race, Caste and Status: Indians in Colonial Spanish America*, Albuquerque: University of New Mexico Press, 1999

Kramer, Ignacio, and Jeffrey Lesser, editors, *Arab and Jewish Immigrants in Latin America: Images and Realities*, London: Cass, 1998

Menchaca, Martha, *Recovering History, Constructing Race: The Indian, Black, and White Roots of Mexican Americans*, Austin: University of Texas Press, 2002

Minority Rights Group, *No Longer Invisible: Afro-Latin Americans Today*, London: Minority Rights Group, 1995

Musacchio, Humberto, *Milenios de México*, 3 vols., Mexico, DF: Hoja Casa Editorial, 2000

Vogt, Evon Z., editor, *Handbook of Middle American Indians, Volume 7: Ethnology*, Austin: University of Texas Press, 1969

Werner, Michael, editor, *Encyclopedia of Mexico: History, Society, and Culture*, Chicago and London: Fitzroy Dearborn, 1997

Whetten, Nathan L., *Rural Mexico*, Chicago and London: University of Chicago Press, 1948

Miao

Capsule Summary

Location: Guizhou, Yunnan, Hunan, Sichuan and Guangxi provinces in China
Total Population: 7,398,035
Languages: Three main languages with numerous dialects of varying degrees of closeness
Religion: Various, including Christian

The Miao have been officially recognized as one of 55 ethnic minorities by the People's Republic of China (PRC) government. The total population of the Miao based on the 1990' national census is 7,398,035, which represents 0.65 percent of China's population. The Miao live across many areas in the southwest of China mainly in Guizhou, Yunnan, Hunan, Sichuan and Guangxi. They can also be found in Hainan Island in Guangdong and southwest Hubei province. Because of their huge geographical spread it is impossible to generalize about the nature of the areas in which they live. Miao are generally regarded to be hill people

conducting slash and burn agriculture of hardy dryland crops ranging from upland rice to cold weather crops such as buckwheat, oats corn and potatoes. However other groups of Miao such as those near Guiying are valley dwellers whose main crop is rice grown in paddy fields. The Miao also live in Thailand and Laos where they are referred to as the "Hmong" or "Meo."

Linguist generally agree that there are three separate languages spoken by the Miao in different regions. The Xiangxi language of Yunnan with some 800,000 speakers divide into two major dialects of which the larger has been provided with Pinyin Romanization for school texts and other publications; the Qiandong languages found in central and eastern Guizhou break into three subdivisions or dialects the largest of which, with over 1 million speakers has its own Pinyin system and; the Chuan Quian Dian language with over 2 million speakers in Sichuan, Yunnan and Guizhou has seven sub divisions which are then broken down into up to four dialects for each sub division. Not all dialects are mutually intelligible. Only two have their own Pinyin system.

The typical Miao family is small and monogamous. Parents usually arrange marriages but unmarried young men and women have the freedom to court. Mass courting occasions sometime take place in holiday periods, when young women from a host village sing antiphonal love songs to young men from neighboring villages. If couples are attracted they exchange love tokens. But they must win the approval of their parents before marrying.

Because timber resources are plentiful in most Miao areas, houses are usually built of wood and roofed with fir bark or tiles or are thatched. In central and western Guizhou, houses are roofed with stone slabs. Houses vary greatly in style. In mountainous areas they are usually built on slopes and raised on stilts. Animals are kept under the stilted floors. In the Zhaotong area in Yunnan and on Hainan Island, most Miao live in thatched huts or "branch houses" made of woven branches and twigs or bamboo strips plastered with mud.

History

The term Miao originally was applied around the third century BCE to the many indigenous peoples of the southwestern frontier of China. The term was used interchangeably with "Man" or "Yi" which means barbarian. In the third century CE, the ancestors of the Miao went west to present day northwest Guizhou and south Sichuan along the Wujian River. In the fifth century some Miao groups moved to east Sichuan and west Guizhou. In the ninth century some were taken to Yunnan as captives. In the sixteenth century some Miao settled on Hainan Island. As a result of these large-scale migrations over many centuries the Miao became widely dispersed.

The Miao had no written script until the early 1900s. Attempts to spread Christianity motivated western missionaries to create a Romanized phonetic alphabet for the Miao oral languages. One of these script was created by a British missionary Samuel Pollard who set up Miao schools in Shimenken (stone threshold), located on the Wumeng mountains between Yunnan, Guizhou and Sichuan. Thousands of Miao people were converted as Christians, at the same time receiving a form of education. Shimenken became known as the most prestigious Miao cultural region in the southwest of China.

Since 1949

After 1949 Miao were defined as a single entity. Visible differences were attributed to historical drift within small populations, to separation and dispersion of the original core population, to influence from neighboring peoples, and to the characteristics of particular localities (e.g., altitude and climate) but it was assumed that there was great unity underlying superficial differences.

This method of definition had much to do with the many difficulties the State had in identifying the non-Han population. These difficulties included a lack of linguists, sociologists and anthropologists. Initially over 400 minority groups, a large number of which were in the Yunnan and Sichuan regions, asked to be recognized. Inevitably many separate ethnic groups have therefore been embraced as Miao.

The Miao were also classified as pre-literate despite widespread use of the missionary-introduced writing system among the Hua Miao, its adoption by some of the Chuan Miao, and attendance at Chinese schools by individuals from virtually all groups.

Generally speaking, despite official recognition as a minority and possibly because of their scattered and diverse nature the Miao have not progressed economically during 40 years of socialist reconstruction. According to the 1982 census, only 1,436 were enrolled in post-secondary schooling, a figure well below the national average. As of 1985, in all of Zhaoting prefecture, with its heavy concentration of Hua Miao, there had been only one Hua Miao College graduate since 1949. In some areas, the Miao are the poorest of the ethnic groups, for reasons beyond their control. They continue to be regarded as backward and ignorant by Han villagers and cadres. Their response is to hold on even more tightly to their traditions and to a glorified, romanticized image of their past.

LINDA TSUNG

See also **Hmong**

Further Reading

Diamond, N., "Defining the Miao, Ming, Qing and Contemporary Views," in *Cultural Encounters on China's Ethnic Frontiers*, edited by S. Harrell, Hong Kong: Hong Kong University Press, 1994

Ma, Y., *China's Minority Nationalities*, Beijing: Foreign Language Press, 1989

Schein, L., *Minority Rules, The Miao and the Feminine in China's Cultural Politics*, Durham and London: Duke University Press, 2000

Micronesia

Capsule Summary

Country Name: Federated States of Micronesia
Location: Oceania, island group in the North Pacific Ocean, about three-quarters of the way from Hawaii to Indonesia
Total Population: 108,143 (July 2003)
Languages: English (official), Trukese (Chuukese), Pohnpeian, Yapese, Kosrean, Ulithian, Woleaian, Nukuoro, Kapingamarangi
Religion: Christianity (97%)

Formed on May 10 1979, the Federated States of Micronesia were formally part of the United States Territory of the Pacific Islands. Micronesia is comprised of four constituent states: Kosrae, Pohnpei, Chuuk and Yap which are part of the Caroline Islands group. Kosrae, Pohnpei, Chuuk and Yap consist of more than 957 islands and atolls totaling 461 square miles that extend across 3 million square miles of the west central Pacific Ocean. Its economy is primarily based on farming and fishing; per capita GDP was US$2000 in 2002.

Originally visited by Spanish explorers in the sixteenth century, it wasn't until the mid-eighteenth century that Europeans began to arrive in large numbers when Germany purchased Caroline Islands group from the Spanish. Driven by commercial interests, Germany set out to colonize the Caroline Islands, establishing a colony on October 12, 1899 calling it *Die Kolonie*. Germans then set up administrative centers on Pohnpei, Yap, Saipan and Jaluit to exploit the lucrative Copra trade. In 1910, Pohnpeians' rose up against the German colonial rule in the Sokehs rebellion of 1910–11. Following the Sokehs rebellion the Germans confiscated all native owned land in *Die Kolonie* with the exception of Protestant and Catholic missions.

German rule lasted until 1914 when the Japanese took control of Micronesia before the onset of World War I when the Japanese Navy took control of the Caroline Islands. Following World War I, the Japanese were formally granted control of Micronesia via the League of Nations mandate on December 20, 1920. Once Japan established colonial rule of Micronesia, they set about developing extensive economic undertakings on Yap, Chuuk and Pohnpei to feed the growing needs of Japanese colonial expansion. During their rule the Japanese excluded islanders from participating in their political and economic affairs. In 1935, the Japanese began to develop Chuuk as military base. Chuuk would later play a key role in Japanese war strategies in the South Pacific.

Following World War II, much of Micronesia's economy and infrastructure had been destroyed. Politically, Micronesia was set up as a Trust Territory with the United States given administrative responsibility over Kosrae, Pohnpei, Chuuk and Yap. In the decade following, the United States set up a series of military bases.

In 1965, the United States agreed to let Micronesia establish their own government – setting up a house of representatives and a senate. A commission was established in 1967 to investigate options for self-government and independence. Initial attempts at negotiations throughout the 1970s failed but in July 1978, Chuuk, Kosrae, Pohnpei and Yap voted to share a constitution, and on May 10, 1979, they became the Federated States of Micronesia (FSM). Under a 15-year compact signed with the United States in 1982, Micronesia agreed to let the United States control its relations with other countries and maintain its exclusive military access to the islands. In turn, the United States guaranteed annual funding.

KEITH A. LEITICH

See also **Pacific Islanders**

Further Reading

Hanlon, David L., *Remaking Micronesia: Discourses over Development in a Pacific Territory, 1944–1982*, Honolulu: University of Hawaii, 1998
Heine, Carl, *Micronesia at the Crossroads: A Reappraisal of the Micronesian Political Dilemma*, Honolulu: University of Hawaii, 1974
Poyer, Lin, *The Ngatik Massacre: History and Identity on a Micronesian Atoll*, Washington, DC: Smithsonian Institution Press, 1997
Storie, Monique Corriveau, *Micronesia*, Oxford and Santa Barbara, California: Clio Press, 1999
Zezel, Francis X., *The New Shape of Old Island Cultures: A Half Century of Social Change in Micronesia*, Honolulu: University of Hawaii, 2001

Migrations

At the beginning of the twenty-first century, many countries exhibited high levels of immigration. In the last forty years, the number of those who live outside their country of birth has doubled from 75 to 150 million. More than half of these migrants live in countries of the South. In the Western world, the immigrants' share has doubled during the same period from 3 to 6 percent. Nevertheless, not more than 2.5 percent of the entire world population live actually outside their country of birth, and can be designated as migrants.

History of Migrations

When one considers migration from an historical perspective, population shifts such as transhumance and nomadism in early human history become apparent. The great empires—for instance Aztec and Egypt—used subordinated people coming from distant regions to construct their cities and monuments. The mercantile and colonialist period witnessed the shipment of millions of slaves from Africa to the Americas. Large groups of descendants from these Africans today live in the South of the United States and in Brazil. After the abolition of slavery among colonial European powers, substantial numbers of indentured labor arrived from India, China and Japan and worked on European colonial plantations in the Caribbean, India and the Pacific Ocean. European development realized large colonies of European settlers in the Americas. Involuntary and state-induced migration included servants, convicts, and members of religious minorities. British settlers, for instance, went to Canada, New Zealand, Australia, the United States, and Southern Africa. French settlers went to Canada, North and Western Africa, and Indochina. Dutch settlers went to South Africa, and Indonesia.

During the colonial period from the seventeenth to the nineteenth centuries, groups of laborers were needed to construct communication networks, to work in the mines, and on rubber plantations. The colonial powers recruited free or forced laborers for these tasks. The labor market was internationalized by the migration of thirty-five million Europeans to the United States during this time. Poles in Germany, and Irish in Britain accompanied industrialization. France, Italy and Japan supplied the necessary work force by migrants from rural areas. The end of the First World War and the peace treaties which supported the idea of "one state=one nation" were followed in Europe by large mass movements.

Post-1945

In the post-1945 period, several forms of migration predominated. State formations following on nationalist movements resulted in mass migration. Current examples include the former Union of Soviet Socialist Republics (USSR), and the former Yugoslavia. Mass displacements accompanied the two World Wars, localized wars, natural disasters, economic and political crises. Immediately after 1945, masses of people from Eastern Europe fled to Western Europe. Indeed, one of every six migrants in the world is a refugee concerned with the United Nations High Commissioner for Refugees.

Since the 1970s, unskilled labor migration has been pursued in spite of rules limiting access to European countries and North America. Before 1970, the prosperous economies of Western Europe asked for migrants from Southern Europe and Northern Africa. In fact, these flows concern often illegal, undocumented laborers who may—in countries such as France, sometimes and years later—be partially regularized. At other times, population flows look for new destinations, such as the Near East.

Actual Migration Phenomena

There is another phenomenon which concerns highly qualified people, such as scientists, engineers, and medical staff who use the global economy to their advantage and cross international frontiers. A last phenomenon concerns asylum-seekers, people who often look for legal recognition as refugees in European countries or in North America. Constitutional provisions in France and Germany attract these migrants who are not rarely exposed to hostile reactions in host-countries.

Today, 90 percent of migration movements take place in the poorer countries of the world. Only

5 percent of the migrants attain Western Europe, and another 5 percent attain other prosperous regions, such as North America or Australia. In front of an opening and liberalization of markets, of mass mobility, of global mediascapes and networks, it becomes increasingly difficult to control migration on a national and regional basis. History shows that migration can only slowed down by diminished differences of wealth or by military interventions. The classical immigration countries react actually with stricter immigration controls, and the population with xenophobic emotions. Beside economic and welfare state arguments against immigration, another argument underlines that native values and local cultures are in a dangerous position. Moreover, failure of integration, assimilation, acculturation, and multiculturalism is proclaimed, by referring to the thesis of S. Huntington about the "clash of civilizations." Actually, there is another migration tendency: increasing demands for immigrants in Western European countries, because of the aging of its population which, in some years time, will no longer be able to furnish enough laborers in relation to a growing share of pensioners.

Actual research topics in migration studies are network migration and transnational communities. Recent studies show that migrant communities, after their establishment in one country, try to act as bridgeheads for other migrants, such as neighbors or relatives. In most of the former migration theories, migration was considered as the decision of individual actors evaluating their arguments to move elsewhere to work, or as a result of social and economic disparities between countries. The role that the presence of relatives or friends played, was underestimated. In Europe, the results of network migration began to be seen in the seventies, when labor recruitment had stopped, but the immigration of spouses and children continued. Migrants who had often arrived as single people, were now entitled to bring in members of their family. In the past, network migration already occurred, but it was restricted to some communities, such as Greeks, Lebanese, or people coming from India and China. Once family reunion had occurred, the probability of returning decreased. The temporary migration from the beginning had turned into a settlement migration.

Today, network migration is facilitated by means of transport and communication. Migrants go back on holidays to their home countries, they can watch videos from home, calling home and the internet became inexpensive. These tendencies—as researchers found—do not necessarily reinforce the migrants' orientations towards the host society: migrants may prefer contacts with their own family at home.

ULRIKE SCHUERKENS

See also **Colonialism; Diaspora; Integration; Multiculturalism; Population Shifts; Refugees**

Further Reading

Faist, Thomas, *The Volume and Dynamics of International Migration and Transnational Social Spaces*, Oxford: Clarendon, 2000
Gosh, Bimal, *Huddled Masses and Uncertain Shores: Insights into Irregular Migration*, The Hague: M. Nijhoff, 1998
Joppke, Christian, editor, *Challenge to the Nation-State: Immigration in Western Europe and the United States*, Oxford: Oxford University Press, 1998
SOPEMI, *Trends in International Migration: Annual Report 1999 Edition*, Paris: OECD, 1999
Stalker, Peter, *Workers without Frontiers: The Impact of Globalization on Migration,* Boulder: Lynne Riener, 2000
Taylor, Edward J., et al., *Worlds in Motion: Understanding International Migration at the End of the Millennium*, Oxford: Clarendon Press, 1998

Minangkabau

Capsule Summary

Location: western central Sumatra; Jakarta and other Indonesian cities
Total Population: approximately 7 or 8 million
Languages: Minangkabau; Indonesian
Religion: Islam

The Minangkabau are an ethnic group originating in the mountains of central western Sumatra, an island in Indonesia. About four million Minangkabau people live in the province of West Sumatra, where they make up the large majority of the population. Almost as many Minangkabau people now live outside of West

Sumatra, mostly in the Indonesian capital of Jakarta on the island of Java, and in other Indonesian cities. Minangkabau people make up between three and four percent of the total population of Indonesia. Malay communities in the Malaysian state of Negeri Sembilan acknowledge Minangkabau ancestry, but do not consider themselves to be Minangkabau.

The Minangkabau are closely linked to Malays, and their language is closely related to Malay and to the Indonesian national language, in which most Minangkabau are fluent. Minangkabau people are Muslims. They are sometimes considered unusual in the Islamic world because they follow a matrilineal system, in which a person's clan identity is inherited from his or her mother.

Minangkabau clans are divided into lineages, with each lineage group holding collective rights over property such as rice fields and houses. Use-rights for this property are divided among the women of the lineage and passed down from mother to daughter. Men may inherit lineage leadership titles from their mothers' brothers, giving them authority in lineage and *nagari* (village) affairs. Although social roles are divided by gender, both men and women influence family and community decisions.

Every *nagari* follows its own version of *adat*, or traditions and customs. All versions of *adat* are relatively egalitarian, and decision-making by consensus is an important philosophical element of Minangkabau culture. In traditional village life, several generations of women from the same lineage lived together in a large house. Minangkabau boys slept in the *surau* (prayer house), where they studied religion, self-defense, and other subjects. Today, it is still the norm for men to move into their wives' homes upon marriage. However, many Minangkabau homes now revolve around nuclear families, and children mostly study in state schools and sleep at home.

There is a long history of Minangkabau men seeking wealth and experience away from their villages before marriage. Today, many Minangkabau people continue to migrate, but often nuclear families move permanently away from West Sumatra, where the opportunities for employment are limited. Minangkabau people have spread throughout Indonesia. They have gained a reputation as particularly skilled traders. Some migrants retain close ties to Minangkabau society; others largely assimilate into Indonesian urban society.

According to legend, Minangkabau society originated when a son of Alexander the Great founded the Minangkabau kingdom. Historically, the kingdom can be traced back to Adityawarman, who ruled over an Indic–influenced kingdom in the fourteenth century. Minangkabau royalty came to control the trade of gold that linked Sumatra to Asian, Middle-Eastern, and European societies. By the seventeenth century, the Dutch had begun an effort to monopolize trade in Minangkabau products.

In the sixteenth century, Islam began to spread through Minangkabau society, but it remained somewhat peripheral until the early nineteenth century, when the Padri movement called for the strict application of Islamic values in Minangkabau society. Many previously marginalized villages that were now the focus of the exploding international trade in coffee embraced the movement. Villages that resisted were subject to violent raids, and most of the royal family was killed. Dutch military action helped to halt the Padri movement, clearing the way for the Dutch colonists to control the trade in coffee. Nevertheless, the Padri movement cemented the central role of Islam in Minangkabau life. Today, Islam is integral to Minangkabau identity, and to be considered ethnically Minangkabau, a person must be Muslim.

Minangkabau people developed a reputation throughout the Dutch East Indies as dynamic and modern intellectual and religious thinkers. Out of myriad minority groups in the region, Minangkabau people played by far the largest role in Indonesia's nationalist movement. Only natives of Java, which dwarfs Minangkabau in terms of population, matched their influence. Among the most prominent Minangkabau figures of this period were Mohammad Hatta, Indonesia's first vice president, and Sutan Sjahrir, Indonesia's first prime minister. Hatta, along with Sukarno, officially declared Indonesia's independence on August 17, 1945. Later, he also served as prime minister.

In 1958, Minangkabau leaders in West Sumatra rebelled against the central Indonesian government in Jakarta, refusing to recognize its authority until it adopted reforms. This reflected widespread dissatisfaction in Minangkabau society with a central government that they found corrupt, overly influenced by communists, unresponsive to Islamic concerns, and unjust in its exploitation of the region's resources. The autocratic character of the central government seemed to be at odds with the more democratic inclinations of Minangkabau political culture. Minangkabau people sometimes contrast this culture with what they feel are the more hierarchical tendencies of the Javanese political culture that came to dominate Indonesia.

The rebellion ended in 1961, crushed by military forces brought in from Java. After this, Minangkabau society found itself governed mostly by figures brought in from Java, as they were thought to be more loyal to the government in Jakarta. Eventually, Minangkabau people moved back into leadership positions, but they continue to play a smaller, less visible role in national leadership than they once enjoyed.

Under President Suharto's "New Order" government, from the late 1960s until the late 1990s, Minangkabau society came under increasingly tight control from the central government. For example, a 1979 law created a uniform system of local government across Indonesia, based largely on a Javanese model, and stripped the traditional *nagari* leadership of most of its relevance.

Since Suharto's fall in 1998, during Indonesia's *reformasi* (reform) period, local governments have gained a greater measure of autonomy. A movement has grown in West Sumatra to reestablish the traditional functions of the *nagari* and the *surau* in Minangkabau life. These efforts are still in their early stages. During the *reformasi* period, the Minangkabau community has managed to largely avoid the interethnic, interreligious, and separatist conflicts that have plagued many communities in Indonesia.

GREGORY M. SIMON

See also **Indonesia**

Further Reading

Abdullah, Taufik, *Schools and Politics: The Kaum Muda Movement in West Sumatra*, Ithaca, New York: Cornell Modern Indonesia Project Monograph Series, 1971

Benda-Beckmann, Franz von, *Property in Social Continuity: Continuity and Change in the Maintenance of Property Relations through Time in Minangkabau, West Sumatra*, The Hague: Martinus Nijhoff, 1979

Benda-Beckmann, Keebet von, *The Broken Stairways to Consensus: Village Justice and State Courts in Minangkabau*, Cinnaminson, New Jersey: Foris Publications, 1984

Blackwood, Evelyn, *Webs of Power: Women, Kin, and Community in a Sumatran Village*, Oxford and Lanham, Maryland: Rowman & Littlefield Publishers, 2000

Dobbin, Christine, *Islamic Revivalism in a Changing Peasant Economy: Central Sumatra, 1784–1847*, London and Malmö: Curzon Press, 1983

Drakard, Jane, *A Kingdom of Words: Language and Power in Sumatra*, Oxford and New York: Oxford University Press, 1999

Errington, Frederick, *Manners and Meaning in West Sumatra: The Social Context of Consciousness*, New Haven: Yale University Press, 1984

Josselin de Jong, P.E. de, *Minangkabau and Negri Sembilan: Socio-Political Structure in Indonesia*, The Hague: Martinus Nijhoff, 1980

Kahin, Audrey, *Rebellion to Integration: West Sumatra and the Indonesian Polity, 1926–1998*, Amsterdam: Amsterdam University Press, 1999

Kahn, Joel, *Constituting the Minangkabau: Peasants, Culture, and Modernity in Colonial Indonesia*, Oxford and Providence, Rhode Island: Berg Publishers, 1993

Kato, Tsuyoshi, *Matriliny and Migration: Evolving Minangkabau Traditions in Indonesia*, London and Ithaca, New York: Cornell University Press, 1982

Minorities and Language

Language is for many minorities one of the most important cultural core values. It is one of the basic criteria in boundary-marking of communities, along with religion and culture. In many cases the reference to the existence of a minority refers to a "linguistic," "religious" or "cultural" minority, each not necessarily being exclusive and often overlapping.

There tend to be two diametrically opposed views as to how the nature of the relationship between language and minorities should be seen. Instrumentalists see language as a tool, as acquired and manipulable. Individuals learn languages, and they are therefore relatively free to adopt any other language they may desire. Language in itself has little intrinsic value beyond being a tool for communication, an instrument that can be discarded for another, more effective instrument if need be. Primordialists see language as having a much different position for minorities and other groups. Language is not something one chooses to learn: individuals inherit their language almost at birth as a "mother-tongue." Language for can from an even more radical primordialist point of view to epitomize a minority's very soul, even to the point of a language being seen as having a life of its own.

Without taking a primordialist or instrumentalist position, what remains undeniable is that the question of language is often a sensitive one for many minorities. Language is central to feelings of community and culture, of tradition and "belonging," since it is an obvious marker of membership. In addition, language can play a major role in terms of economic opportunity and success for members of a minority, since the dominance of one language in a State will be advantageous in terms of access to and distribution of public resources to individuals who have greater fluency of the official or majority tongue. Linguistic minorities will often be seriously disadvantaged in economic and employment opportunities if their language is not used by the State in some of its official functions.

Because of the high visibility of language membership, language sometimes serves as a red flag for intolerance and discrimination: members of a minority may be seen as "outsiders" since their language is not that of the State or ethnic majority. This phenomenon is by no mean a uniquely modern one. The Old Testament contains a passage in Judges on the people of Gilead seeking out and massacring members of the Ephraimites. These "others" were identified by their accent in pronouncing the initial sound in the word "shibboleth." The passage is one of the earliest written accounts of "ethnic cleansing" aimed at a minority distinguishable by their language.

With the ever strengthening intrusion of the Nation-State after the eighteenth century came an increasing focus on language matters which deeply affected minorities in Europe and other parts of the world. Nation-building from this period onwards sought to unite various minorities into a more centralized form of society where government would play an increasingly active role in many aspects of life which previously had been beyond the pale of State intervention. This process found language diversity to be if not clearly an obstacle, then most certainly a nuisance. The need to create amongst the whole population a sense of belonging to the Nation as represented by the State meant also the need to create symbols for this new national ideal, and in many countries, France, Indonesia and Turkey being prime examples, one of the strongest of symbols became the language and culture of the new Nation, usually the language of the majority.

Simultaneously with these increasing attempts at forging national consciousness and unity through a common language, conforming to the aspirations of the controlling majority in many States worldwide, came resistance from many linguistic minorities. Many of the ethnic conflicts still underway today have their origins during this period of "State-building" and involve linguistic minorities (Sri Lanka, Sudan, Corsica, Basque Country, etc.), though at the same time some of these groups may also be ethnic or religious minorities.

This prominence of language must be seen in light of the essential function that language plays in society. Humans, *homo sapiens*, are by definition "language animals," and as such language provides the essential medium for the existence, development and dignity of social communities such as linguistic minorities. Language serves as a marker in that everyone can be identified through language as belonging to at least one linguistic community. It also serves as the basis of culture, imprinting an individual's culture and worldview and the means to perpetuate these to other members of a community, including linguistic minorities.

Language is thus intimately connected to an individual's persona, but also to his or her links to and place within a community and society at large. Furthermore, language can have great symbolic importance. Linguistic differences are highly visible. This means, especially in the case of minorities who may have grievances against the State, that language differences can be co-opted for nationalist goals. Language can serve as a mobilizing factor in situations where power and resources are unevenly distributed along minority and majority ethnic lines.

Language therefore creates unique problems in terms of a State's policies towards its use which have serious consequences for minorities. While it is possible, desirable and even common for a State to remain "neutral" in terms of race or religion, such a line of conduct is usually impractical when dealing with language. A State must necessarily restrict itself to conduct its affairs in, at most, a limited number of languages. No government can afford to provide services and documents in every language spoken on its territory.

Most States tend to use one or two languages over all others, usually under the designation of an official or national language (Israel, Sri Lanka, Canada, Finland, Sudan, Indonesia, France, El Salvador, etc.). Some countries have in theory no official language, but in practice they still tend to restrict their activities to one single language (Australia, Japan, United States) and prohibit more or less formally the actual use of other languages by officials of the State.

While necessity would seem to lend support to a State's linguistic preference for one or a limited number of languages, the matter may involve dire consequences for minorities. By choosing one or a few languages over all others, a State is signalling the dominance of those for whom the official language is their mother tongue. Their language is dominant, minority languages are ignored, even banned. The majority is therefore privileged in that it does not have to worry about learning another language, be it to have access to government employment or services. The majority is free to use its language at home, in business, in schools, and in their community without considering whether it is a handicap not to sufficiently master any other language. Minorities do not enjoy the same benefits or advantages. Members of numerically large minorities can interpret such a linguistic preference for the language of the majority as evidence of intolerance and an attack against one of their fundamental identity-related qualities, as well as an unjustified interference in and lack of respect for their identity.

In this sense, the choice of an essentially exclusive official language may lead to tensions in a State where a high percentage of the population are members of a linguistic minority. In simple terms, there would appear to be little reason to deny any of the advantages associated with the use of their language when a minority represents, for example, the majority of inhabitants in large parts of the country, or if it represents 20, 30, or even 40 percent of the population.

This understanding of the potency of language demands of minorities tends to be supported in a number of studies dealing with conflicts around the world. There appears to be an unmistakable correlation. Conflicts involving minorities and language friction appear where the language of a minority has been suppressed or ignored. Rather than language diversity or the presence of large numbers of minority groups within a State being in themselves causes of conflict, conflicts tend to appear where there has been a denial of the language rights of a substantial minority, rather than any inherent undesirable consequence to a State with a diverse linguistic mosaic.

This has led to a number of developments. Many international organizations, including the United Nations, the Organisation for Cooperation and Security in Europe (OSCE), the Council of Europe, have developed policies, recommendations, declarations, resolutions and even treaties which emphasize the requirement for policies which acknowledge the centrality role of language for many minorities. There has been was a definite trend in the closing decades of the last century towards agreement on the desirability of adopting constructive measures for the use of minority languages.

Among the more noteworthy of these documents are the United Nations' Declaration on the Rights of Persons belonging to National or Ethnic, Religious and Linguistic Minorities; two Council of Europe treaties, the Framework Convention on the Protection of National Minorities and the European Charter for Regional or Minority languages; and a series of expert recommendations prepared for the OSCE High Commissioner on National Minorities, including the Oslo Recommendations on the Linguistic Rights of National Minorities and the Hague Recommendations on the Educational Rights of National Minorities.

They all recognize the importance of language for minorities, the need to maintain social peace and cohesion, as well as of finding a proper balance between the requirements of nation-building and the reality of the presence, within the boundaries of many countries, of large groups of individuals speaking a non-official or non-dominant language.

Among the growing consensus is that the principle that democratic States must respect cultural diversity. This means more than just tolerance and respect of the language of minorities, but also its promotion as far as is reasonably possible. As explained in the European Charter on Regional or Minority languages, linguistic diversity is one of the most precious elements of the European cultural heritage.

Minority and human rights documents also emphasize pluralism and respect for individuals. This suggests an increasing acceptance that linguistic preferences ought to be acknowledged and accommodated, rather than ignored or even suppressed. The increasingly prevailing view is therefore that governments should treat diversity and the languages of minorities as assets, and ought to encourage linguistic minorities to conserve their own language while at the same time providing ample opportunities for them to learn the official or national language.

FERNAND DE VARENNES

See also **Equal Opportunity; Languages, Disappearing; League of Nations and Minorities; OSCE High Commissioner for National Minorities; United Nations and Minorities**

Further Reading

Calvet, Louis-Jean, *La guerre des langues et les politiques linguistiques*, Paris: Payot, 1987
de Varennes, Fernand, *Language, Minorities and Human Rights*, Dordrecht: Martinus Nijhoff, 1996

Fishman, Joshua A., *Language and Ethnicity in Minority Socio-linguistic Perspective*, Clevedon: Multilingual Matters, 1989

Haarmann, Harald, "Language in Ethnicity," in *A View of Basic Ecological Relations*, Berlin: Mouton de Gruyter, 1986

Laponce, Jean, *Langue et territoire*, Québec: Presses de l'Université Laval, 1988

McRae, Kenneth, *Conflict and Compromise in Multilingual Societies*, Waterloo: Wilfrid Laurier University Press, 1983

Milian i Massana, Antoni, *Derechos linguisticos y derecho fundamental a la educacion: Un estudio comparado*, Barcelona: Generalitat de Catalunya, 1994

Packer, John, and Kristian Myntti, editors, *The Protection of Ethnic and Linguistic Minorities in Europe*, Åbo: Åbo Akademi University, 1993

Skutnabb-Kangas, Tove, and Robert Phillipson, editors, *Linguistic Human Rights: Overcoming Linguistic Discrimination*, Berlin: Mouton de Gruyter, 1994

Minority Rights Group International

Minority Rights Group International (MRG) is a rights-based international non-governmental organization that works to secure justice for minorities and indigenous peoples and to promote intercommunity cooperation. Its activities include research and publishing, public education, partnership projects, advocacy, capacity building and training. This entry describes MRG's origins, development and current work and assesses its impact.

Origins and Development

MRG was established in 1965 as an educational charity (nonprofit organization) in London, UK, with the aim of protecting 'the rights of minorities to coexist with majorities by objective study and consistent international exposure of violations' (founding statement). Its original sponsors were George Cadbury, Milovan Djilas, Dr. Robert Gardiner, Dr. Dharam Ghai, Lord Arnold Goodman, Lord (Joe) Grimond, David Kessler, Dr. Joseph Needham and Lady Butler Spence. Professor Roland Oliver of London University's School of Oriental and African Studies was MRG's first council chair, and in 1969 Laurence Gandar, a South African campaigning editor, became its first director. MRG began to commission and publish reports on minorities facing hardship and discrimination, beginning with *Religious Minorities in the Soviet Union* (1970) and *The Two Irelands* (1971).

Ben Whitaker, a former UK MP, became director in 1971, and MRG's reports continued with publications on the Kurds, Palestinians, Sri Lankan Tamils and other minorities, as well as on thematic topics such as the roots of prejudice. In 1974 MRG gained consultative status with the United Nations (UN) Economic and Social Council and began to regularly give evidence at UN sessions. In 1975 Ben Whitaker also became UK Expert to the UN Sub-Commission on the Prevention of Discrimination and Protection of Minorities (since 1999 the UN Sub-Commission on the Promotion and Protection of Human Rights). MRG launched projects on education, Gypsy/Traveler rights and minority arts in the 1970s, established affiliate groups in France, Italy, Switzerland, Belgium and the United States, and published a three-volume 'World Minorities' book series. By 1988 it had sold almost half a million copies of its reports worldwide, informing and influencing key audiences on minority rights.

Alan Phillips succeeded Ben Whitaker as director at the end of 1988, and MRG moved to new offices in Brixton, south London, one of the UK's most culturally mixed boroughs. MRG representations at the UN increased in frequency, especially regarding minority rights in Central and Eastern Europe and the Former Soviet Union. Participating at the 1990 Conference on Security and Cooperation in Europe (CSCE; predecessor to the Organization for Security and Cooperation in Europe, OSCE), MRG significantly influenced the *Document of the Copenhagen Meeting of the Conference on the Human Dimension of the CSCE* (1990), with its key provisions for minorities. Also in 1990 MRG joined the UN Working Group on the Declaration on the Rights of Minorities and sponsored a conference in Copenhagen, Denmark, on minorities in Eastern Europe, followed a year later by a major meeting in Leningrad, Russia, on minority rights in the Former Soviet Union.

Increasingly involved in developing and promoting international standards and mechanisms for minority protection, MRG played a leading role in advancing the UN Declaration of the Rights of Persons belonging to National or Ethnic, Religious and Linguistic Minorities in 1992 and in the establishment of the UN Working Group on Minorities in 1995. MRG was also instrumental in achieving the Council of Europe's (CoE) Framework Convention for the Protection of National Minorities of 1994, which came into force in 1998 with Alan Phillips as UK expert to, and subsequently vice-president of, the convention's monitoring body. MRG's advocacy helped ensure that the 1993 World Conference on Human Rights, held in Vienna, Austria, resulted in a declaration and programe of action that included significant wording on minority and indigenous peoples' rights.

MRG published its *World Directory of Minorities* first in 1990 and then, in an expanded edition, in 1997. In the early 1990s Sir John Thomson, a former UK Ambassador to the UN, had become its chair of council, and he was succeeded in 1999 by Dr. Neelan Tiruchelvam, a highly respected international jurist, human rights practitioner and Sri Lankan Tamil MP. Dr. Tiruchelvam was killed later the same year by a suicide bomb attack in Colombo, Sri Lanka, that shocked the global human rights community. In 2000 MRG renamed its annual advocacy training program held in Geneva, Switzerland, the Neelan Tiruchelvam Training in International Minority Rights, and in 2001 instituted the first Neelan Tiruchelvam Memorial Lecture. Professor Patrick Thornberry took up the duties of council chair in late 1999, and at the end of 2000 Alan Phillips left MRG, to be succeeded as director by Mark Lattimer.

Current Activities

Although a relatively small organization (approximately 27 staff and an income of US$2.25 million [UK£1.5 million] in 2000), MRG's range of work is wide. It has published over 100 reports and books on minority communities and indigenous peoples and their rights, as well as educational materials, training guides, workshop reports and occasional papers. Besides exposing violations, MRG seeks to promote international standards, good practice and intercommunity cooperation and to support the growth of strong and healthy civil societies. Since the early 1990s it has undertaken programmatic work in collaboration with partners, first in Central and Eastern Europe, and subsequently in Southeast Europe, the Horn and Central Africa, South and Southeast Asia, the Middle East, Latin America and the Caribbean, Cen-

tral Asia and the Pacific. Its European and Asian regional programes are now supported by project officers based in Budapest, Hungary, and Mumbai (Bombay), India, respectively. Maintaining its international advocacy profile, MRG participates at the UN Human Rights Commission and its Sub-Commission, the UN Working Group on Minorities, the UN Working Group on Indigenous Populations, OSCE Human Dimension meetings, the Council of Europe, the Stability Pact for Southeast Europe, and in the World Conference Against Racism process. MRG's work now explicitly embraces economic, social and cultural as well as civil and political rights, and in 1999 this was signaled by the launch of a program under the name Minority Rights and Development.

MRG's current programs include work with indigenous and tribal peoples in South and Southeast Asia, religious minorities in South Asia, pastoralist communities in the Horn and East Africa, the Batwa Pygmies of the Great Lakes of Africa, minorities in Central, Eastern and Southeast Europe, Roma in Southeast Europe, and Afro-descended communities in Latin America. Activities include research reports, translations, workshops, consultancy, capacity-building, training, and mentoring. As far as possible, MRG seeks to support members of minorities and indigenous peoples in advocating for their own rights.

Concluding Assessment

International human rights non-governmental organizations will remain necessary while states and inter-governmental bodies fail to ensure the full and universal enjoyment of human rights. MRG therefore clearly continues to have a role. While its approach has at times been criticized as tending to promote divisions and to reify ethnic differences, MRG has always recognized the right of communities to self-identify (or not) as minorities and/or indigenous peoples, and has acknowledged that identities can be fluid and multiple and that minorities are often far from homogeneous. MRG has undoubtedly contributed to international recognition that minority and indigenous peoples' rights are at the core of many key contemporary human rights, security and sustainable development issues.

MILES LITVINOFF

See also **United Nations Working Group on Minorities; United Nations Working Group on Indigenous Populations; OSCE High Commissioner for National Minorities; Tiruchelvam, Neelan (Tamil-Sri Lanka)**

Further Reading

MRG, "The MRG Story: 1969–1990," pamphlet, London: MRG, 1990

MRG, editors, *World Directory of Minorities*, London: Longman, and Chicago: St James Press, 1990

MRG, editors, *World Directory of Minorities*, London: MRG, 1997

MRG Web site. <www.minoirityright.org>

Phillips, Alan, and Allan Rosas, editors, *The UN Minority Rights Declaration*, Turku, Finland: Åbo Akademi University Institute for Human Rights, and London: MRG, 1993

Phillips, Alan, and Allan Rosas, editors, *Universal Minority Rights*, Turku, Finland: Åbo Akademi University Institute for Human Rights, and London: MRG, 1995

Whitaker, Ben, editor, *Minorities: A Question of Human Rights?* Oxford, New York: Pergamon Press, 1984

Miscegenation

For as long as humans have populated the earth, inter-group mating and marriages have been commonplace. As such, it is argued that there are no discrete or pure biological races. Of one species, human populations are capable of inter-breeding across generations and reproduce offspring who can in turn inter-breed. In the eighteenth and nineteenth century, now discredited evolutionary theories emerged which maintained that distinct races existed, that could be differentially ranked on the bases of heredity, physical characteristics and intelligence. The architects of this racial hierarchy positioned White Europeans at the top and Black Africans at the bottom. Any inter-breeding across racial borders was said to threaten the assumed purity and supremacy of the White race.

Amalgamation was the initial term used to describe sexual reproduction-within or outside the context of marriage-involving individuals who were presumed to belong to distinct races, especially those sociologically and biologically designated as Black or White. With the publication of his pamphlet *Miscegenation: The Theory of the Blending of the Races Applied to the American White and Negro,* in 1864, David Goodman Croly introduced the word miscegenation, which he thought sounded more scientific than amalgamation. He combined two Latin words *miscere* (to mix) and *genus* (race) to create miscegenation. Along with hybridization, miscegenation and amalgamation are terms used interchangeably. Black-White miscegenation dates back to the sixteenth century and the beginning of the transatlantic slave trade, wherein West Africans were forcibly removed from their homelands and sold as chattel slaves to work on plantations in the Southern United States, the Caribbean and Brazil. In societies, whose economies were originally dependent on the exploitation of non-White slaves, miscegenation between slave women and their slave masters contributed to the viability of the labor force. The different laws and rules instituted to manage mixed race offspring born during and after the abolition of slavery would form the bases of contemporary racial politics and conflicts.

Historical Origins of Miscegenation

The biological distinction between varieties and species was the intellectual precursor to the major scientific debate of the nineteenth century over whether human races were of one species, monogenesis, or separate species, polygenesis. The potential fertility of mulattoes, the term used to describe the offspring of sexual unions between Black slaves and White Europeans or Americans, was used to defend both monogenesis and polygenesis. Biologist Carolus Linnaeus suggested that successful reproduction of fertile mulatto offspring was proof positive in support of same species status. American physician and natural historian, Samuel Morton, introduced the concept of biological hybridity to the separate origins discussion. He accepted that mulattoes were fertile, but provided evidence which he claimed proved that mulatta women had difficulty bearing children. He speculated that if mulattoes reproduced exclusively with each other, over generations, their offspring's fertility would diminish to the extent that they would all die out. This he concluded proved that Whites and Blacks were not varieties of a single race but an entirely separate species. One of Morton's opponents was John

Bachman, who maintained that it was virtually impossible for hybrids to be "relatively sterile" as Morton claimed. Morton insisted that not only were mulattoes as fertile as so called pure races, but that he could provide evidence of successful intermarriage and procreation among mulattoes across five generations. He also opposed the idea put forward by Morton and his colleague Agassiz that there was a natural and moral repugnance between so-called races which functioned as a social barrier. Having awarded Black Africans same species status, Bachman justified ownership of slaves on the contested grounds that they were an inferior variety of the species.

Josiah Nott and George Gliddon, who were both students of Morton, asserted that individuals without at least one White ancestor were uncivilized and lacked the alleged superior mental capacity of their White European and American counterparts. The theory of unilateral hybridity put forward by French anthropologist French Paul Broca endorsed sexual relations between White men and Black women on the grounds that such a union would produce not only fertile offspring but children who would more closely approximate their White father's supposed racial superiority. Sexual unions between Black men and White women were thought to produce sterile children. What can be described as racial enhancement was practiced by White slave masters in the form of sexual exploitation of Black and mulatta slave women in the antebellum American South, pre-emancipation Brazil and South Africa as well as the Caribbean. Contradictory social relationships between masters and slaves were formed based on the regulation and control of domestic arrangements. Gender and race specific sexual restrictions were imposed, which meant that White men had unlimited sexual access to White, Black, and mulatta women. As White women were considered symbols of virtue and morality, sexual liaisons between Black men and White women were forbidden. During and after slavery in the United States, Black men could be punished violently just for looking in the direction of a White woman.

Legal and social categories were constructed which determined hierarchies and maintained racial boundaries between Whites and Blacks, citizens and subjects, illegitimate children and heirs. The links among race, gender, sexuality and power were particularly strong in the plantation Southern United States. The one drop rule was instituted in order to keep the offspring of White male plantation owners born to enslaved Black women under their control for sexual and economic exploitation. The one drop rule of social hypodescent dictated that one known African ancestor made a person Black. The system ensured that mixed race children of White male slave owners were automatically disinherited and became Black slave laborers.

Racial Degeneracy, the Rise of Eugenics, and Anti-Miscegenation Legislation

With his theory of evolution by natural selection, Charles Darwin, author of *The Origin of Species: The Preservation of Favored Races in the Struggle for Life*, published in 1859, had been instrumental in silencing proponents of polygenesis. Evolution by natural selection was based on change. Random variations within populations provided the basis for adaptation to changing environmental circumstances. Social Darwinism, the application of Darwinian theory to society, assumed that races were fixed and distinct. Social Darwinists also differed from Darwin in their understanding of the concept of fitness. For Darwin, the fitness of a population was measured by the number of offspring produced. Social Darwinists believed that there was a natural hierarchy of races, which was maintained by the distribution of races according to fitness.

These ideas gained prominence during the late nineteenth century and altered inter-racial relations throughout the British Empire, in the United States, and in Brazil. In the early twentieth century, Darwin's cousin Francis Galton coined the phrase Eugenics. The scientific mission of the Eugenics movement was the eradication of inferior and unfit races and the elevation of superior races, based on the belief that intelligence, criminality, and other social traits were in and of themselves determined exclusively by heredity. The foundation of Eugenics was the idea of racial degeneracy, which was belief in the deterioration of an allegedly superior race via miscegenation. Racial degeneracy was thought to be prevented by four means: selective breeding of the fit races with each other, social segregation of the fit and unfit races and legal sanctions against miscegenation, or sterilization and in certain instances physical extermination of those deemed unfit.

In the inter-war period, the campaign of selective breeding to ensure racial hygiene and purity culminated in the Nazi Experiment and Hitler's Final Solution. In addition to ordering the extermination of those considered unfit, such as Jews, Gypsies, homosexuals, and the mentally disabled, Hitler demanded forced sterilizations of German women who gave birth to non-Aryan children including Afro-Germans, who were themselves involuntarily sterilized. In studies of miscegenation in inter-war Britain, White women who were married to Black men and or had children with them were described as "immoral and of below average intelligence." In Liverpool and Cardiff, two British cities with large mixed race communities, associations were established for the "Welfare of Half-Caste Children," who were perceived as a moral problem and as a threat to the presumed racial purity of the nation. Although an informal color bar and racial conflict persist in certain British cities, statutory laws were never enforced to segregate races nor to prohibit inter-racial marriages and sexual relationships.

This was not the case in either apartheid South Africa or the Jim Crow Southern United States. The belief was that increased contact would lead to increased mixing which would in turn lead to the social and moral degeneracy of the allegedly pure White races. In South Africa of the 1950s through to the early 1990s, the Immorality Act, which was " to prohibit illicit carnal intercourse between Europeans and non-Europeans," the Mixed Marriages Act, the Group Areas Act, and the Population Registration Act were enforced to "protect the health and safety of the pure White Volk," from the allegedly "impure" Black and Colored majority. In the Southern United States of the 1890s through to the 1960s, separate but unequal Black and White social institutions existed. Jim Crow was a post-slavery caricature of a Black man as happy and humble, which then became the label for the form of government sanctioned racism known as Jim Crow segregation. By 1915, the one drop rule had become firmly entrenched in the collective American conscience. On a state by state basis, laws maintaining the White/Black power imbalance were implemented for virtually every social institution: housing, property ownership, inheritance, voting rights and privileges, education, health, and marriage. Anti-miscegenation laws were put in place to make inter-racial marriage and sexual relations criminal offenses. On June 12, 1967, with Loving vs. Virginia Supreme Court, the Supreme Court deemed anti-miscegenation laws unconstitutional. Federal law superseded state laws. It took individual states longer to remove these statutes from their books. In 1883, Alabama introduced anti-miscegenation law, but did not overturn this until March 1999, which indicates the ways in which earlier views on miscegenation still manifest themselves in contemporary attitudes towards race, sexuality and gender. In fact, Black Americans were given civil and voting rights before they were given the right to marry across the color line.

Rules of Miscegenation

There are social, cultural and political variations in the rules determining the social status of the offspring of miscegenation. In his book *Who is Black?*, James Davis refers to different rules or statuses, which determine the social position not just of mulattoes but of other mixed race offspring. In the first status position, the individual occupies a lower status than either of her or his parents, such as Anglo-Indians in India. In the second status position, the individual achieves a higher status than either parent, such as the *mestizos* of Mexico. In the third status position, the individual is a member of an intermediate group which acts as a buffer between the White minority and the Black majority, as is the case with Coloreds in South Africa. The fourth status position is not fixed, but rather is said to be negotiated on the basis of social class and color, such as in Brazil. The fifth status position also known as the one drop rule dictates that the individual occupies the same position as the lower status parent, such as in the United States. In the past ten years, many of these designations have shifted. A Black Power Movement in Brazil has inspired more mulattoes to identify as Black. In the United States, a Mixed Race Movement has emerged, wherein mixed race children, many born after the legalization of inter-racial marriages in 1967, are asserting a distinct multiracial identity separate from one drop rule Black. In post-apartheid South Africa, there is tension between Coloreds who wish to retain this buffer identity and those who are claiming African or Black identifications. These dynamic geographical and cultural groupings represent diverse outcomes to a common heritage of slavery, colonialism, miscegenation, and racial discrimination. The concepts of miscegenation and mixed race highlight the contested nature of race as a scientific idea which attaches hierarchical meanings to physical differences. These create, explain, justify, and maintain social inequalities and injustices, and perpetuate differential access to privilege, prestige and power.

JAYNE IFEKWUNIGWE

Further Reading

Brah, Avtar, and Annie Coombes, editors, *Hybridity and its Discontents: Politics, Science and Culture*, London: Routledge, 2000

Davis, James, *Who is Black?* University Park, Pennsylvania: Pennsylvania State University, 1991

Malik, Kenan, *The Meaning of Race*, London: Macmillan, 1996

Parker, David, and Miri Song, editors, *Rethinking Mixed Race*, London and Sterling, Virginia: Pluto Press, 2001

Root, Maria, editor, *The Multiracial Experience*, London and Thousand Oaks, California: Sage, 1996

Williamson, Joel, *New People: Miscegenation and Mulattoes in the United States*, London and Baton Rouge: Louisiana State University Press, 1995

Young, Robert, *Colonial Desire: Hybridity in Theory, Culture and Race*, London: Routledge, 1995

Zack, Naomi, *Race and Mixed Race*, Philadelphia: Temple University Press, 1993

Model Minority

The concept "model minority" was first introduced in 1965 and used in reference to Japanese Americans. By 1982, Newsweek used the term to include all Asian-Americans. Since then, it was further popularized by the journalist William Peterson in an article for the New York Times Magazine. It was aided in its popularization by President Ronald Regan, among others, Now, its use has been expanded out to be a catch-all phrase to describe Asian-Americans as a hard-working, well-educated, and successful minority community. Considering the historical context it is not surprising the idea took hold very quickly.

There were two prominent forcefields impinging on American society after the Second World War. The first was the negative stereotype leveled at the Asian-Americans in general and Chinese-Americans in particular, who, since the turn of the century had been cast as lazy, stupid, and inscrutable–one prototype being the movie character Charlie Chan. Asians, especially Chinese, were coolies who laid railroad tracks across the North American continent, ran laundries for the white population, and operated opium dens. Asian Indians were termed rag heads because of the distinctive turban worn by the Sikhs. They provided cheap labor for harvesting California's abundant agricultural produce. The Japanese were quiet and insular; consequently they were regarded with suspicion—suspicion that the public considered justified due to the deceptive attack on Pearl Harbor and such atrocious incidents as the Bataan Death March

The second force had to do with the repercussions and aftermath of the Civil Rights Movement. The Movement had stirred the conscience of a nation which began looking for ways to cut ugly racism from its society. Besides, the United States had become a world leader and felt it had to live up to the rhetoric of equality and justice that they had advocated. As a result, the country looked for other areas where injustice was being practiced and found a ready but redeemable situation in immigration laws and policies—they had favored Europeans, especially Western Europeans, while discriminating against Asians, especially the Chinese, who were our ally in the Second World War—another example of the United States not living up to its own moral standards.

Throughout United States history, immigration laws had opened doors to the people of Western Europe and inhibited Asians. John F. Kennedy fulfilled a campaign promise by initiating legislation to make immigration laws more equitable. President Lyndon Johnson signed the bill into law in 1965, and it took effect in 1968. The new legislation eliminated the national origins criteria that had dominated United States immigration laws since their inception and changed the criteria to favor needed skills and education. Countries like India had invested heavily in education and had a large unemployed and under employed population who were qualified to enter the United States under the new laws, much to the surprise of the original framers on the legislation–they had expected European domination of the immigration stream to continue. The "new immigrants," a term coined by Charles Keely, immediately entered the middle and upper economic brackets of American society, and their successes were noted. Thus, at the time of Peterson's article in the New York Times Magazine, the model minority label struck a responsive cord in American culture. It was interpreted as showing that America was the land of opportunity for all who are willing to work, regardless of race, color, or creed. People envisioned the categorization as signaling that the end of racism and discrimination was near. The model minority concept sent a message to all minorities in the United States that if you work hard enough, you can have the "American dream" and pull yourselves out of the lower class. It hid the real problem of racial discrimination by claiming that Asian-Americans were no longer discriminated against.

To explain what happened, it is necessary to realize that the pre-1965 Asian population was very small and was composed of families that had been in the States but occupying low socioeconomic positions. The post-1965 immigrants were highly educated and trained individuals who immediately stepped into middle- and higher-income vacancies in both industry and self-employment. Thus the post-1968 statistics show a rapid rise in income and position among the Asian-American population. Average family income rose as the statistics showed a tremendous jump in Asian immigration. The income of the wealthy overshadowed and hid the plight of the poor Asians. Starting around 980, the highly educated and innovative element was being countered by a second wave of less talented immigrants who were sponsored by relatives under the family reunification clause of the immigration laws. That tremendous statistical rise caused by the first wave, however, was due to the influx of the highly qualified and able foreign-trained immigrants who were educated in their home societies, which also saved the United States a tremendous amount of money in education costs. In other words, their success was not necessarily due to opportunities or lack of discrimination in the United States. Their success was due to the elite status of the recently arrived who, after arrival in the States, quickly filed for permanent residency so they would soon be able to sponsor parents, siblings and children. Taken from any perspective, the United States was receiving the highest educated, best paid talent the world had to offer.

Initially the categorization of "model minority" was well received by the Asian-American community because it symbolized to Asian-Americans that they were accepted and successful in America. However, it was not long before problems with the label began to arise in many and diverse areas. One of the first had to do with the relationships between minority groups, especially Asians and African-Americans. The implication of the label was quickly interpreted to mean that if the Asian-Americans can do so well in America, especially recent immigrants, the African-Americans and other disadvantaged minorities should also be able to do as well, especially those that were born in this country. The African-American community immedi-

ately felt the judgment and sense of superiority attributed to Asian-Americans. It caused animosity and a rift between minority communities when they should have been united to fight discrimination and racism. Whether intended or not, the situation smacked of the "divide and rule" policies of the British colonial administrators who promoted animosity between Hindus and Muslims in India so they would not unite against their colonial masters. This was done by giving benefits, praise, or favored treatment to one over the other. The ramifications quickly became clear in New York City and Log Angeles. When violence broke out in these areas, the rift generally included an Asian vs. black component, other times it was a more specific conflict such as developed between the Koreans and the Black community in Los Angeles. Or the Asian Indians and white youth gangs in New Jersey who called themselves "Dot Busters" of New Jersey, "dot" refereeing to the bindi worn on the forehead of Indian women. Thus, the minority communities, especially the Asian-Americans, perceived the "model minority" label to be a means by which racists were bringing about divisions within the minority communities so they would not be united and exert their numerical strength.

Before going on, one must ask, Is the concept "model minority" a valid one? Are the criteria used to label a group "model minority" valid? First of all, justification for using the concept or label "model minority" is based on the statistical evaluation of a community. Are statistics a valid criteria? For example, Asian-Americans have the highest family income, yet their families are generally larger than white families, consequently family average income may be higher, but per capita income is lower for Asians as opposed to whites. Also, if the Hispanic communities would not have been included in the white category, Asian-Americans would not have outranked the whites. Why are Asians considered a model minority based on average family income? Shouldn't whites be rated higher because their average per capita income is higher? Also, 26 percent of Asian-Americans have a bachelor's degree while only 17 percent of Americans as a whole have the degree, yet Asian-Americans are twice as likely to be poor as non-Hispanic whites. Is it right to lump all Asians or all whites into one category? Isn't there sufficient variation in the various sub-groups to prohibit such generalizations? The fact of the matter is that there is sufficient variation that lumping is generally misleading. For example in 1980, American-born Filipinos earned 58 percent of what white males earned. Those born in the Philippines, however, earned 38 percent of white male salaries.

Other criticisms of the model minority concept are possible. For example, more than half of the Asian Pacific community live in only five metropolitan areas, namely, Washington, DC, Honolulu, San Francisco, Los Angeles and New York. In fact, over 90 percent of the Asian-American community are in these cities. These are high income and high cost-of-living-areas; in other words, Asian-Americans live in places where one has to earn more and spend more. Yet, in these high-density areas, the percentage of Asian-Americans in low income occupations, such as service workers, laborers, farm laborers, and private household workers, is considerably higher than among whites, Even in 1970, 25 percent of all gainfully employed Chinese men in the United Statues were cooks, waiters, busboys, dishwashers, and janitors.

A detailed study of the San Francisco area revealed that Asian-American professionals were clustered in accounting, dentistry, health technology and engineering. They were under represented in law, teaching, administration, social services and the higher levels of medical professions. Managers were more likely to be self-employed rather than members of large firms. Sales persons were primarily retail clerks, and seldom brokers or insurance agents. Clerical workers were primarily file clerks, typists, or office machine operators, not secretaries or receptionists. Few Asians had jobs in heavy-machine, electrical, paper, chemical, or construction industries. Most female operators were garment workers. In summary, Asian-Americans were concentrated in occupations that did not pay as well as other jobs in the same industries.

The low unemployment rate among Asian-Americans used to depict their economic successes merely camouflages their high underemployment. Asians generally prefer low-paying, seasonal or part-time jobs over welfare or public assistance.

The "model minority" label also has the effect of placing a stigma on those Asian-Americans who, as individuals or as a group, were not as successful as their counterparts both in or out of their native community. The statement is very common, "If he (she he or they) can do it, we can do it also." When the individual or group did not measure up to the: model minority" norm they were despised. Nothing had to be said, it was just understood. However, groups cast in the lower spectrum causes feelings of isolation and depression. Also, Asian Indian women have the highest suicide mortality rate among all women ages 15–24 and boys in grades 5–12 are twice as likely to suffer physical abuse over white male children.

The high participation of Asian women in the labor force is because of the low wages of the male members of the family. Asian-American women earn a higher median income than white females but they generally have superior educational qualifications and live in locations with higher wages. Also, a larger percentage work full time which drives up their median income. In general, Asian-American men and women do not receive the returns commensurate with their education as high as those of the white community. A California study, found that, on the average, whites earned $522 more per year of education as opposed to $438 for Japanese, $320 for Chinese, $340 for Mexicans, and $284 for blacks.

Last, the model minority label was a major cause for the elimination of some programs that helped minorities, especially Asians, to survive or get established–an unjust price some had to pay for being labeled with an unjust stereotype.

ARTHUR HELWEG

See also **Japanese-Americans**

Further Reading

Chan, Sucheng, *Asian Americans: As Interpretive History,* Detroit: The Gale Group, 1991
Daniels, Roger, *Guarding the Golden Door,* New York: Hill and Wang, 2004
Kitano, Harry H.L., and Sue Stanley, "The Model Minorities," *Journal of Social Issues,* 29, no. 1–9 (1973)
Petersen, William, "Success Story: Japanese American Style," *New York Times Magazine* (Jan 6, 1996)
———, *Japanese Americans: Oppression and Success,* New York: Random House, 1992

Mohajirs

Capsule Summary

Location: Pakistan's Punjab and Sindh provinces, especially the latter
Total Population: 30 million
Language: Urdu
Religion: Islam

In 1947, Mohajirs flooded into both East and West Pakistan following the creation of that state as a homeland for the Muslims of the Indian subcontinent. Although as early as 1825 some Indian Muslims had begun to think of India as a *dar-ul-harb* (land unsuited to Muslims) and to consider migrating to a suitable *dar-ul-Islam*, it was Mohammed Ali Jinnah's Two-Nation Theory, realized by the birth of Pakistan, that made such migration practical. It was the two-way exchange of populations in the resulting partition of India—Muslims to Pakistan; Hindus and Sikhs to India—when no fewer than 30 million people moved from one state to the other that caused the presence of Mohajir immigrants (and later their descendants) to become a social problem in Pakistan.

The followers who accompanied the Prophet of Islam in his flight to Medina in 622 CE to escape persecution in Mecca were called Mohajirs. In 1947 and in the years immediately following, immigrants from India usually were referred to in Pakistan as refugees, but as they came to be identified as a separate ethnic group the apt term *Mohajirs* gained currency, first among the migrants themselves and then by those native to the region. Even though born in Pakistan, the offspring of such immigrants continue to be regarded as Mohajirs, the term having become shorthand for native Urdu speakers. The 1979 Soviet invasion of Afghanistan brought two million Afghan refugees to Pakistan, but these Pashto-speaking Muslims have never been regarded as Mohajirs.

In the subcontinent, geographical propinquity played a critical role in the pattern of migration which took place following the 1947 Partition. Immigration to East Pakistan was more gradual than that to West Pakistan; the bulk of these migrants came from West Bengal in India and were Bengali-speaking Muslims who readily assimilated. As late as the 1961 census they amounted only to 1.7 percent of the population of that wing. A sizable contingent, however, came from Urdu-speaking areas farther west in India, including Bihar. After the 1971 war these "Biharis" were persecuted in newly independent Bangladesh, and only a few of them succeeded in resettling in the former west wing.

In contrast, the 1947 refugees in West Pakistan arrived as a flood of people, principally from the north of India but also from Hyderabad (Deccan) and other princely states. Those from India's East Punjab, who mostly settled in Pakistan's adjoining Punjab province, were linguistically and culturally similar to their new neighbors, whose only complaint arose from the suspicion that some refugees were afforded greater compensation by the government than they deserved. The others, Urdu speakers all, turned south toward the province of Sindh, especially its urban centers, where they soon overshadowed natives of the city Hyderabad and to dominate Karachi, the country's only port, its capital, and its banking and commercial center. As early as 1951 roughly half the urban population in Sindh province reported themselves to be Urdu speakers, a proportion that reached about 80 percent in Karachi. Native Sindhis, at first hospitable to the newcomers, later came to feel overwhelmed by them.

In Punjab, where the Mohajirs were more dispersed than in Sindh, they also were more readily assimilated because neither their culture nor their language was as alien as in Sindh. In Sindh most leadership positions—whether in business, public administration, education, or the professions—had been occupied by Hindus, who fled to India at the time of Partition, leaving a vacuum which the educated Mohajirs quickly filled. By the second decade of the country's existence, the Mohajirs and the Punjabi elites had arrogated to themselves most of the important positions in the federal government. Though the English language was continued as a convenience for the conduct of administration and higher education, Urdu, with its highly developed literary history, was promoted in the misguided belief that it would encourage national integration amongst the millions whose mother tongues were as diverse and mutually unintelligible as Pashto and Sindhi.

Probably no leader did more to diminish the prominence of the Mohajirs than Ayub Khan, who came to power in 1958 as administrator of the martial law declared by Pakistan's president in an attempt to dampen ethnic rivalry and regional dissension. Unlike the earlier rulers of Pakistan, who themselves had been Mohajirs, General Mohammed Ayub Khan came from a village in Hazara, and he adopted a policy of replacing high-ranking Mohajir officers in both civil and military positions with other qualified persons—though few of them from East Pakistan. Most significantly, he moved the capital away from that Mohajir stronghold Karachi to a new site on the Potwar Plateau, not far from his own native place, and named the new city Islamabad.

It was during a later period of military rule, that of General Mohammed Ziaul-Haq (1977–88), himself a Mohajir, that the Mohajirs became a political force as well as a social problem. Numerous riots had broken out—first in Karachi between Mohajirs and Pathans and later between Mohajirs and Sindhis in Hyderabad—leading to the creation in 1986 of the Mohajir Quami Movement (MQM) under the charismatic leadership of Altaf Hussain. As a political party the MQM participated in the coalition government of Benazir Bhutto (1988–90), though the federal government was then no more capable of stemming ethnic violence than it had been under Zia. Meanwhile, bombings, kidnappings, and massacres continued, with property damage in Karachi alone amounting to more than $50 million. It was estimated that more than 3,600 people in Karachi were killed by political violence between 1996 and 1998. In that city and its sprawling suburbs different factions established "no-go zones" where members of opposing groups risked death if they dared to enter.

Finally, after the intervention of the army and the paramilitary Rangers, ethnic violence was significantly dampened. Meanwhile, the MQM itself had undergone a transformation, one branch becoming known as the Muttahida Qaumi Mahaz (United National Movement), while a splinter group continued as the Haqiqi (true) faction of the MQM. Under whatever name, the MQM phenomenon did bring to a focus some legitimate grievances of the Mohajirs and it gave them a public voice to be reckoned with. Carrying Jinnah's Two-Nation concept a step further, one of their spokesmen has argued that the Mohajirs themselves now constitute a separate "nation" within Pakistan.

CHARLES BOEWE

See also **Bangladesh; Bihari; Exchange of Population; Jinnah, Muhammad Ali (Pakistan); Punjabi; Refugees**

Further Reading

Ahmed, Akbar S., "Tribes, Regional Pressures, and Nationhood," in *Old Roads, New Highways: Fifty Years of Pakistan*, edited by Victoria Schofield, Karachi and New York: Oxford University Press, 1997

Alavi, Hamza, "Nationhood and the Nationalities in Pakistan," in *Economy and Culture in Pakistan: Migrants and Cities in a Muslim Society*, edited by Donnan Hastings and Pnina Werbner, Basingstoke, England: Macmillan, 1990; New York: St. Martin's Press, 1991

Chitkara, M.G., *Mohajir's Pakistan*, New Delhi: APH Publishing, 1996

Gankovskii, IUrii Vladimirovich, *The Peoples of Pakistan: An Ethnic History*, Moscow: Nauka Publishing House, and Lahore: People's Publishing House, 1971

Harrison, Selig S., Paul H. Kreisberg, and Dennis Kux, editors, *India and Pakistan, The First Fifty Years*, Washington, DC: Woodrow Wilson Center Press and Cambridge: Cambridge University Press, 1999

Haydar, Afak, "The Mohajirs in Sindh: A Critical Essay," in *Contemporary Problems of Pakistan*, edited by J. Henry Korson, Boulder, Colorado: Westview Press, 1993

Rashid, Abbas, and Farida Shaheed, *Pakistan: Ethno-Politics and Contending Elites*, Geneva, Switzerland: United Nations Research Institute for Social Development, 1993

Sayeed, Khalid bin, *Pakistan: The Formative Phase, 1857–1948*, 2nd edition, Karachi and New York: Oxford University Press, 1992

Moldova

Capsule Summary

Official Name: *Republica Moldova* (Republic of Moldova)
Location: Southeastern Europe, between Romania and Ukraine
Total Population: 4,439,502 (July 2003)
Languages: Moldovan (official, very close to the Romanian language) Russian, Gagauz (a Turkish dialect)
Religions: Eastern Orthodox Christians, Roman Catholics, Jewish, Baptist

Moldova (also known as Bessarabia and conventionally called "Moldavia" from 1940 until 1991) is located in southeastern Europe, bordering with the Ukraine in the east and Romania in the west. The country has a total area of 33,843 square kilometers (13,000 square miles)—slightly larger than Maryland—and it is the second smallest republic in the former Soviet Union, after Armenia.

The population of Moldova was estimated at 4,439,502 in July 2003. It is one of the least urbanized countries among the western republics in the former Soviet Union with just around 54 percent of the population living in the cities and towns. The country's capital, Chisinau (formerly Kishinev), is home to about 14 percent of the population. Moldova has a population growth rate close to zero due to low birth rate (14.31 births/1,000 population (2003)) and sizeable permanent and temporary emigration. Moldova has one of the highest population densities in the former Soviet Union standing at 130 people per square kilometer (340 per square mile) with most of the population concentrating in the northeastern and central parts of the country.

Moldova is a presidential democracy. The country, which was part of Romania from 1918 until 1940 and part of the Union of Soviet Socialist Republics (USSR) since 1940 (as Moldavian Soviet Socialist Republic), declared its independence from the Soviet Union in 1991. According to the new Constitution ratified in 1994, the president is the head of the state with strong executive authority and is elected by popular vote for a four-year term. The *Parliamentul,* the Parliament, is a unicameral 104-member national legislative body. The president nominates the prime minister and the cabinet (with the recommendation from the prime min-

ister). However, the *Parliamentul* must approve the prime minister and the cabinet. The president has constitutional power to dissolve the parliament. Since the independence all political parties, including opposition organizations and radical nationalist parties, have been allowed to function freely in the country, although the Communist Party was briefly banned after an coup attempt in August 1991. The voters' preferences are often divided according to the ethnic base. Tensions between ethnic Moldavans and ethnic minorities, who are predominantly of Ukrainian and Russian origin, led to an outbreak of the civil war in 1992. In 1992 the Trans-Dniester region, which is in the east of Moldova and is predominantly populated by the ethnic Russians and the Ukrainians, declared independence from Moldova (not recognized by any state). In 1997 there was an attempt made to reach a compromise between the Moldovan government and the separatists, however, some disputed issues still need to be settled.

Moldova is a multiethnic country with a very diverse population. Ethnic Moldovians, who are culturally and linguistically close to Romanians, make up 62.0 percent of the country's population. Ethnic Ukrainians make up the largest minority group of around 13.8 percent of the population, ethnic Russians make up 13.0, Gagauz make up 3.5 percent, Jewish make up 1.5 percent, Bulgarian make up 2 percent, and other groups make up 1.7 percent (1989). The current ethnic structure was largely formed after the Second World War when the Soviet government encouraged migration of skilled workers from various parts of Russia and the Ukraine. However, the newcomers had rarely studied local language and culture, since the Soviet government encouraged the use of the Russian language and promoted the so-called Soviet internationalist culture. This policy led to increase of the minorities' share in the Moldova's population during the Soviet era (1944–1991), although after 1991 around 70,000 residents, mainly the representatives of the ethnic minorities, chose to emigrate to Russia, the Ukraine, and the developed countries. Ethnic division of the society is profound, and it affected the political development in Moldova throughout the 1990s.

The Moldovan language, which is distinctive from Russian or any Slavic languages and is very close to Romanian, was made an official language of the country in 1989. The Law on Languages also replaced the Cyrillic script which had been introduced by the Soviet government in 1938 with the Latin alphabet. The Moldovan language, which some nationalist groups call a Romanian language, is increasingly replacing the Russian language in the state institutions and in primary, secondary, and tertiary education. The language policy and historical heritage are in the center of the political debates and disagreements between the Moldovan government and the ethnic minorities and even within Moldovan nationalist groups. The so-called Romanian camp insists that Moldovan culture and language cannot be separated from Romanian culture and language and that Moldova has to become a part of Romania, while the "Independentalist" camp insists that Moldovians formed their own distinct culture and language and that the independence is a political reality. The 1994 Moldovan Constitution provides the Gagauz with a certain degree of cultural autonomy and allows the use of Gagauz language, which is close to Turkic languages, among the Gagauz population. Meanwhile, the Russian and Ukrainian are widely spoken in urban areas of the republic.

Moldovan government abolished restrictions on religious practice after achieving independence in 1991 and all ethnic groups experienced growing interest in religion. Majority of population (97 percent) in Moldova belongs to the Eastern Orthodox Church, including Turkic-speaking Gagauzs. There are also other religious communities (Catholic, Jew and others), who are allowed to practice their belief without restrictions.

The breakdown of the Soviet Union in 1991, the civil war and political instability of the early 1990s largely contributed to steep economic decline in Moldova. Despite all difficulties, the Moldova's government was decisive in implementing radical economic reforms, privatizing most of the industrial enterprises, dismantling collective farms and introducing its own currency, the *Lei*. Agriculture, services and manufacturing are the main pillars of the Moldova's economy, contributing 31.0, 34.0 and 35.0 percent to the GDP respectively (1999). The per capita GDP in 2002 was US$2,600. Moldovan politicians keep a high hope that they will be able to join the European Union in near future. However, despite radical economic changes and achieving economic stabilization, Moldova remains one of the poorest countries of the former Soviet Union with 75 percent of population living below the poverty line (1999) and a sizeable number of people leaving for other countries in search of jobs and a better standard of living. In 1998, the UNDP's Human Development Index (HDI) put Moldova in 102nd place, behind China, Turkmenistan, and Tunisia but ahead of South Africa and Tunisia.

RAFIS ABAZOV

Further Reading

Bruchis, Michael, *Nations, Nationalities, People: A Study of the Nationalities Policy of the Communist Party in Soviet Moldavia*, Boulder: East European Monographs; New York: Distributed by Columbia University Press, 1984

Chinn, Jeff, and Robert Kaiser, *Russians as the New Minority: Ethnicity and Nationalism in the Soviet Successor States*, Westview Press, 1996

Dawisha, Karen, and Bruce Parrott, editors, *Democratic Changes and Authoritarian Reactions in Russia, Ukraine, Belarus and Moldova*, Cambridge University Press, 1997

Donald, Dyer L., editor, *Studies in Moldavian History: The History, Culture, Language and Comparative Politics of People of Moldova*, Boulder: East European Monographs; New York: Distributed by Columbia University Press, 1996

King, Charles, *The Moldovans: Romania, Russia, and the Politics of Culture*, Stanford, California: Hoover Institution Press, 2000

Moldova Home Page. <http://www.ournet.md>

Moldovan Parliament Home Page. <http://www.parliament.md>

Monégasque

Capsule Summary

Location: enclave in the southern coast of France
Total Population: 5,000
Language: Monégasque
Religion: Roman Catholic

Monégasques are a numerically small people, formed in Southern Europe, adjacent to many-million French and Italian nations.

Man has lived on the territory of Monaco since very long time. Not far from Monaco City, fossils of *Homo sapiens sapiens* with some Negroid features age 40,000 years were found; it was called Grimaldi man. In the tenth through the ninth centuries BCE Phoenicians settled there, but in the fifth century BCE they were moved out by the Phoenecaeans—an ethnic group of the Greek origin famous for their great navigational skills. The Greeks were removed then by Carthaginians. In the second century, Romans came to Monaco, and in the period when it was a part of the Roman Empire, Roman soldiers and traders brought the Christian faith (100 CE). In the fifth century the Goths and in the seventh century Lombards invaded into Monaco's territory. From the eighth to the tenth century the territory of Monaco belonged to Arabs, and later for some time the lands of Monaco were under the authority of the County of Provence and the Bishopric of Nice. But then Frederick I, emperor of the Holy Roman Empire, passed the territory as a County of Vintimille to one of the Genoese navigators. Another Genoese—François Grimaldi who was expelled from Genoa as result of internecine wars—realized an intricate plan and captured Monaco. But only in 1489 Monaco managed to get completely rid of the dependence on the Genoese Republic.

The position of the small and weak state was not easy. In order to maintain its independence it had to maneuver between two powerful states—France and Spain, who claimed influence in the region. At first, Monaco's ruler was oriented toward France, then in 1524 he got into the alliance with Spain, but in 1641 went back to the alliance with France after the latter helped him to oust the Spanish garrison.

When in 1713 the male line of the house of Grimaldi was interrupted, the name of the dead prince Grimaldi was taken by his son in law—Count Thorigny. In 1792, during the French Revolution, the ruling prince was overthrown, and a year later the territory of Monaco was incorporated into France. However, after Napoleon's downfall Grimaldi retur-ned and re-headed the principality. In 1814 it was put under protection of France, but already a year later, under the decision of the Congress of Vienna it was passed to the protection of the Kingdom of Sardinia. In 1848, during new French revolutionary upheavals, revolt broke out in Monaco but was suppressed by Sardinian troops. In 1861, in accordance with the treaty between France and Sardinia, French protection over Monaco was restored.

The railway between these countries, constructed in 1868, strengthened the ties between Monaco and France. In 1918, after World War I, Monaco signed a treaty with France which guaranteed the independence of the principality, alhough there was an article in the treaty stated that in case of the extinction of the dynasty of Grimaldi, Monaco should become an autonomous state under France's protection.

Monaco was an absolute monarchy until 1911 when the Constitution of Monaco was adopted and the principality became a constitutional monarchy. The power is shared between the prince and the elected National Council. Admittedly, in 1959 Prince Rainier III suspended part of the Constitution and dissolved the National Council. But by 1962 the rights of the National Council were restored, and a new, more liberal Constitution was granted to the principality.

This brief historical survey shows how difficult the history of this small state has been, and which ethnic and cultural components influenced the contemporary appearance of Monégasques. It should be noted that at present Monégasques number only five thousand and comprise just 16 percent of the total population of the principality which was 32,000 people in 2000. In spite of their small number, Monégasques are undoubtedly a separate people with a specific language and strong ethnic self-consciousness. They profess Roman Catholicism.

The Monégasque (Munegasc) or Ventimigliese language is, along with Genoese, one of the dialects of the Ligurian language. The latter, though mainly spread on the territory of Italy—in Liguria—is more distinct from Standard Italian than from French. The Monégasquee language was nearly extinct in the 1970s, but the introduction of this language in school syllabi as a compulsory subject changed the situation. In addition to their native language Monégasques know French.

The French language is native for the majority of French people settled in Monaco; French residents of Monaco numbered 15,000, or 47 percent of the total population, in 2000. Admittedly, for one third of these French people, Provencal, not French is a native language. They are descendants of the French cities Nice and Cannes and speak the Niçard (Niçois) dialect of Provençal. In addition to Monégasques and French, a significant group of Italians also permanently live in Monaco. Many of them speak the Genoese dialect of the Ligurian language which is close to Monégasque. There are also groups of Americans, British, Belgians, Spaniards, Swiss, Russians, Greeks, Dutch, Germans, Jews, and others in the principality.

Monégasques do not make a majority of population in their principality. Though they enjoy some privileges in comparison with other residents of Monaco. Only Monégasques have suffrage, they do not have to pay taxes. It is also necessary to note that the living standard is high in Monaco and gross domestic product per capita is considerably higher there than in neighboring France and Italy. At the same time Monaco subjects are restricted in one right: they are forbidden to gamble in famous Monaco's casino. By the way, the casino brings huge incomes to Monaco's authorities controlling this business. However, even larger income is brought with the taxes from international banks located there, as well as from tourism. Not only roulette but also picturesque nature attracts prosperous people there.

PAVEL PUCHKOV

Further Reading

Grimes, Barbara F., *Ethnologue: Languages of the World,* 13th edition, Dallas, Texas: Summer Institute of Linguistics, 1996

Johnstone, Patrick, *Operation World,* 5th edition, Grand Rapids, Michigan: Zondervan Publishing House, 1993

Tur, Jean-Jacques L., "Les micro-etats euroṕens: Monaco–Saint-Marin–Liechtenstein," *Notes et ́utudes documentaires,* 4210 (1975)

Mongolia

Capsule Summary

Country: Mongolia (Mongol Uls)
Location: Eastern Inner Asian steppes, landlocked between Siberia (Russian Federation) to the North, and China to the South
Population: 2,712,315 (July 2003)
Minorities: Kazakh, Tuva, miscellaneous Mongolian minorities
Languages: Halh Mongol (official), Kasakh, Tuva, miscellaneous Mongolian dialects, Turkic, and Russian
Religions: Tibetan Buddhist Lamaism (96%); Muslim (primarily in the southwest), Shamanism, and Christian (4%) [1998]

Mongolia is a sparsely populated country whose major claim to fame is its tradition of nomadic pastoralism. This particular way of life, common to the major ethnical groups of Mongolia, is still the backbone of its national economy. The country has been independent since 1911 when two centuries of Sino-Manchu domination ended, but was a satellite state of the Union of Soviet Socialist Republics (USSR) from 1924 to 1990. It has since been noted for its willingness to reform its political and economic structures. In recent years, however, climatic and economical crises have threatened its development, and Mongolia remains dependant on massive international subsidies. Per capita GDP was US$1,900 in 2002.

The country is dominated by the Halh Mongol ethnic group which constitutes about 80 percent of the total population. The rapidly growing Mongolian nationalism is above all a Halh nationalism which defines ideal Mongol identity through Halh ethnicity. The official language is Halh Mongolian. Most Mongolian ethnic groups in Mongolia can be roughly organized within three categories: "Central" Mongols, Oirat (Western Mongols), and Buryat (Northern Mongols). The Darhat, a cohesive and conservative minority having cultural ties with Turkish and Tungus Siberian peoples, lie outside of these three groups.

Apart from Halh, Central Mongols comprise Dariganga, Hotgoïd, Uzemchin, Harchin, Tsahar, Horchin.

Oirat Mongols cover a complex ethnic mosaic including Durbet, Bayat, Zahchin, Torgut, Oöld, Hoton, Myangat. The Buryat, linguistically akin to Central Mongols, but culturally quite distinct, are the Buryat proper and the Barga Buryat.

These Mongolian ethnic groups add up to roughly 97 percent of the total population. Mongolian dialects are mutually understandable, and as Halh is the dialect used at school, Mongolian minorities tend to lose their linguistic specificities. The remaining 3 percent comprise Kazakh and various non-Muslim Turkish groups related to the people of Tuvan Republic of the Russian Federation. A few Russian and Chinese families have also settled in Mongolia, some for many generations.

Religious divisions globally correlate ethnic and linguistic divisions. Most Mongolian groups and "Tuvans" are Buddhists, with a strong shamanistic tendency amongst the Buryat and Darhat. Kazakh are Muslims.

Mongolia as a state finds its historical and ideological legitimacy in the widely known Empire of Chinggis Haan (Genghis Khan), whose birth place was in the territory of the actual Republic of Mongolia. His descendants reigned over China until 1370, when the newly funded Ming dynasty pushed them back into the steppes, over the Great Wall. Political disunity between the Mongols became the rule. Oirat and Buryat were beyond the reach of these later emperors' power who rarely managed actual control of even the Central Mongols. Emperor Dayan Khan (1480–1517) was the last to achieve this. Afterwards, his empire was shared between his sons and the youngest one, according to the Mongolian rule of inheritance, received the heartland of the Chinggisid empire, which was to become Halh Mongolia. The split between Outer Mongolia, the actual Republic of Mongolia, and Inner Mongolia, currently a Chinese autonomous region, was achieved. Halh Mongolia joins the Manchu empire in 1691, 55 years after Inner Mongolia and becomes a military reserve and a buffer between the Chinese empire proper and expanding Russia. Halhisation of the various Outer Mongolian groups progresses thereafter except for a few groups under special administration. Two such groups are the Dariganga, set apart by their status of imperial horse breeders, and the Darhat, personal serfs of the highest Buddhist dignitary. The progressive conquest of the Oirat by the Manchu empire extends Outer Mongolia to the West. These new territories under military administration, were less exposed to Halh influence and remain to this day an ethnic mosaic. The fall of the Sino-Manchu empire in 1911 enables Outer Mongolia to claim its independence. The Pan-Mongolian ideology of the first decades of the century failed largely due to Outer Mongolian government's lack of interest. Buryatia (North of Mongolia, next to the Baïkal lake), remains a part of Russian Siberia, and Inner Mongolia is proclaimed an "Autonomous Region" within China in 1947. The political changes in China lead fractions of Inner Mongolia groups (Barga, Uzemchin...) to migrate to Outer Mongolia.

Kazakh, distinct from the Halh both in language and religion, are the most visible minority in Mongolia. They benefited from a favorable treatment during the communist period and still are the only minority with a special educational system. In Bayan Olgii province, where they constitute the local majority, they benefit from courses in their own language. A political Kazakh movement promotes regional autonomy but the emigration of a good third of the Mongolian Kazakh to Kazakhstan in 1992–93 has undercut its impact. Nowadays there are officially two full national status within Mongolian citizenship: Mongol and Kazakh.

"Tuvan" do not actually constitute a unified minority but a constellation of isolated groups whose histories widely diverge. While some of these groups are clearly Tuvan in origin and culture, others are barely distinguishable from the surrounding Mongols and do not recognize themselves as belonging to any "Tuvinian" group. During the communist era, when "nationalities" (as defined by Stalinist doctrine) were officially attributed, the debate on the very existence of such a group caused changes in official categories as late as the 1980s. Since the collapse of the communist government, agreements between the Mongolian and Tuvinian governments enable Tuvinians of Mongolia to pursue their studies in Tuvinian universities. Some courses in Tuvinian as a second language have been set up in areas of dense Tuvinian population. Tsaatan, a numerically very small minority belonging to the "Tuvinian" group, is well known in the Western countries. Contrarily to the other "Tuvinian" of Mongolia, they are reindeer herders, which make them exotic both to the Mongolian and the Western eyes. The touristic exploitation of this dying-out minority is all the more deplorable as they are actually a mere group of the more numerous reindeer herders of the Republic of Tuva. They have had the historical misfortune of finding themselves on the wrong side of the international border, in numbers too small to maintain their culture successfully.

Darhat, as hunters and shamanists, are represented by the dominant Halh as embodying the archaic Mongolian, for better or for worse. This tends also to be true of the Buryat, but is in their case compensated by their reputation as modern intellectuals.

Mongolian Chinese have heavily suffered from the uneasy memories of the colonization of Mongolia. Their numbers have been greatly reduced by purges in the 1980s.

YVES DORÉMIEUX

See also **Buriats; Kazaks; Mongols, Tuvans**

Further Reading

Bulag, Uradyn Erden, *Nationalism and Hybridity*, Oxford: Clarendon Press, 1996

Kotkin, Stephen, and Bruce Elleman, editors, *Mongolia in the 20th Century: Landlocked Cosmopolitan*, New York: M.E. Sharpe, 1999

Szynkiewicz, Slawoj, "Ethnic Boundaries In Western Mongolia: A case study of a Somon in the Mongol Altai Region," *Journal of the Anglo-Mongolian Society*, 10, no.1 (1987)

Mongols

Capsule Summary

Location: East of the Inner Asian steppe in Russian Siberia, Mongolia and China mainly
Total Population: About 7,800,000
Language: Mongolian Languages (Russian or Chinese for some groups)
Religion: Mainly lamaïst (Gelugspa) Buddhism and folk religion including shamanism; some Muslims and Christians

The Mongolian supra-ethnic group comprises populations living mainly in the Republic of Mongolia (2.4 million), in China (4.8 million) and in the Russian Federation (500,000). In China they reside in the Inner Mongolia Autonomous Region (3.4 million), in Xinjiang Uygur Autonomous Region (140,000), Qinghai (70,000), Heilongjiang (140,000), Liaoning (590,000), Jilin (160,000), Hebei (140,000), Henan (65,000) and in small numbers in other regions. In the Russian Federation, they inhabit the Kalmyk Autonomous Republic (150,000), and the Buryat Autonomous Republic, Chita Oblast and surrounding regions (350,000). Small Mongolian diasporic communities may be found in Korea, Taiwan, France, Germany, and the United States. There are a few groups claiming Mongolian ancestry in Yunnan (China) or Afghanistan, for example, but they are culturally integrated with the surrounding populations. The classification as Mongolian of a Yunnan group by the Chinese State comes mainly from local political reasons.

Their culture is associated with Inner Asian nomadic pastoralism but quite a few groups are agriculturists or hunters. Most of them follow Gelugspa Buddhism and have common folk religious practices.

Mongolian languages belong to the Altaïc family (with Turkish and Tungus). Most of them are mutually understandable except for such small groups as Dagur and Monguor. Main branches are Eastern (in Inner Mongolia and North-Eastern China), Western (in Kalmykia, Xinjiang, Inner Mongolia and West of the Mongolian Republic), Central (in Mongolian Republic, Inner Mongolia), Northern (in Buryatia, North-Eastern China, Northern Mongolia Republic).

While most Mongols are minority subjects of the Russian and Chinese multiethnic States, one third of the Mongols live in their own independent country, landlocked between Russia and China. Any claim of Mongolian identity necessarily implies its definition towards this independent state, be it from the minorities' members' or the governing states' points of view.

The origin of the Mongolian groups is the establishment of the Mongol Empire of Chinggis Han (Genghis Khan) in 1206. He federated various proto-Mongol and Turkish tribes under the name of "Mongols" and conquered China, Russia, and parts of the Middle East. During the following generations, the Empire split, but the reference to Mongolian identity as a source of political legitimacy endured in the whole of Inner Asia and beyond. In the Western regions of Inner Asia, the Mongolian identity proper was however submerged by various Turkish identities.

The groups nowadays known as Mongols are heterogeneous in their relation to this political foundation. Buryat and Dagur, Siberian peoples, stayed largely outside the scope of the Empire as neighbors, more than members. Their reference to a supra-ethnic Mongolian identity appears to be the product of the

Pan-Mongolist ideology of the beginning of the twentieth century. Western Mongols (Oirad) warred with the inheritors of the imperial tradition (Eastern and Central Mongols) from the sixteenth to the eighteenth century, and actually pushed them in the arms of the Sino-Manchu Empire. Garrisons stationed in far away regions of the Chinggisid Empire founded the "Mongols" of Yunnan and the Khazara of Afghanistan, groups of Mongolian ancestry but culturally indistinguishable from their neighbors.

Apart from those, the only Mongolian group outside of the Eastern Inner Asia are the Kalmyk of the Volga. They are a Western Mongolian division who left the Altaï region during the seventeenth century to settle there. A number of them left Russia with the White armies in the twenties, and established communities mainly in France and the United States. Kalmyk were one of the Punished Peoples after the Second World War, like the Chechens and other peoples of the Northern Caucasian region.

Eastern and Central Mongols were conquered by the Manchu Empire during the seventeenth century. The southern regions, which were to become Inner Mongolia, were integrated into the Chinese Empire proper in 1636, while the northern, who went over to Manchu sovereignty in 1691, were kept under a special administrative statute which deliberately isolated them from Chinese influence. The destinies of Inner and Outer Mongolia diverged and the Pan-Mongolian temptations of the beginning of the twentieth century failed to reunify them. Outer Mongolia became a satellite of the USSR in 1924, but political strife kept on in Inner Mongolian region until 1947. The Pan-Mongolist ideology was unable to find widespread popular support and was mainly advocated by the Inner Mongolian princes and various Mongol intellectuals, including some Dagur and Buryat ones. The Japanese attempt to cash in on this ideology to gain allies against both the Chinese and the Russians caused the pro-Russian Outer Mongolian government to repress it harshly and provoked its final failure. In 1947, Inner Mongolia turned back to China for good.

Chinese and Mongols have a long history of deliberate lack of mutual understanding. The perplexity of the Chinggisid generals, wondering whether to put the Chinese peasants to the sword in order to establish pasture lands on their fields, echoes with the traditional Chinese view of those pastures as a barbaric wilderness to be settled and cultivated. Under the influence of the Inner Mongolian communist leader Ulanhu, however, the Mongols managed to attain a privileged position in China as the exemplary minority. Ulanhu, a politician of national import, obtained the recognition of a large territory as constituting the Inner Mongolian Autonomous Region, and bargained for legal minority rights. In exchange, the Inner Mongolian communist brought the region to the communist Chinese two years before the very founding of the Popular Republic of China. Ideologically, this Mongolian support enabled the Chinese communists to demonstrate their anti-imperialist orthodoxy. These partial concessions have since been severely eroded. The state-supported Chinese settlement in Inner Mongolia has further reduced the demographic import of the Mongols in their own Autonomous Region and, while education in Mongolian is widely available, the heavy preeminence of Chinese language encourages Sinization of the elites and urban population. Nonetheless, Secessionism stays low, not merely amongst the Mongols of Inner Mongolia, but also in the less favored groups of the other regions. Xinjiang's Mongols do not seem to be taking any part in the local separatist movements. This is probably linked in their case to the Buddhist/Muslim differentiation with the Turkish peoples (Uighur, Kazakh). While Mongols of China and elsewhere share the Gelugspa Buddhism with the Tibetans, they have shown no desire to ally themselves with their separatist movements and, because of Chinese pressure, the Dalai Lama is not so welcome anymore in the Republic of Mongolia.

ALEXANDRA MAROIS AND YVES DORÉMIEUX

See also **Kalmyk; Buriats; China; Siberian Indigenous Peoples**

Further Reading

Bulag, Uradyn E., *Mongols at China's Edge: Nation, Ethnopolitics, State*, Lanham, Boulder: Rowman & Littlefield, Forthcoming Humphrey, Caroline, and David Sneath, editors, *Culture and Environment no. 1 and 2; The End of Nomadism?*, Cambridge: The White Horse Press, 1996; 1999

Humphrey, Caroline, and Uradyn E. Bulag, editors, "Special Issue on Mongolia," *Central Asian Survey*, 17, no. 1 (1998)

Hurelbaatar, A., "A Survey of the Mongols in Present-Day China: Perspectives on Demography and Culture Change," in *Mongolia in the Twentieth Century: Landlocked Cosmopolitan*, edited by Stephen Kotkin and Bruce Elleman, New York: M.E. Sharpe, 1999

Jagchid, Sechin, and Paul Hyer, *Mongolia's Culture and Society*, Boulder, Colorado: Perseus, 1979

Montagnards

Location: Central Vietnam
Total Population: approx. 1,178,000 (1.84 percent of total population)
Languages: various Austronesian and Austroasiatic families
Religions: Indigenous and Christian (Protestant & Catholic)

The generic name *Montagnard* is a French word, meaning "mountaineer." The name is applied to non-Kinh (Viêt), indigenous, upland groups of Central and, to some extent Northern, Vietnam. It has no derogatory connotation, contrary to the word *moï* which was widely used by Vietnamese and French alike, meaning "barbarian" or "savage," and having a strong derogatory meaning. The name *Montagnard* gained wider acceptance during the Vietnam War when American Special Forces enlisted upland peoples in their war effort and shortened the name to "Yard." Therefore in American English the name *Montagnard*—with its shortened form "*Yard*"— has a very strong political connotation and is viewed negatively by the present Vietnamese administration. The phrase "Central Highlanders," or "Upland Indigenous Peoples of Central Vietnam" is an apt and more neutral description.

Ethnic Subdivisions

These are subdivided into 15 ethno-linguistic groups: the Jarai (240,000), Ede or Rhade (195,000), Bahnar (136,000), Koho (100,000), Sedang (97,000), Hre (95,000), Raglai (70,000), Mnong (67,300), Stieng (50,000), Ko Tu (37,000), Jeh Trieng (27,000), Ma (26,000), Co (23,000), Cho Ru or Churu (15,000), Rmam (250), Brau (250). Major ethno-linguistic groups, like the Ede, Jarai, Bahnar, and others are divided into sub-groups like the Ede Kpâ, the Bahnar Ala-Công, the Mnong Gar, etc. Austronesian (Malayo-Polynesian) speakers are the Jarai, Ede, Raglai, and Cho Ru, while all the other are Austroasiatic (Mon-Khmer) speakers.

Location & Geography

The *Montagnards* of Central Vietnam inhabit the provinces of Gia Lai-Kontum, Dac Lac, Lam Dong, and Khanh Hoa, and they overlap in neighboring provinces and countries (Laos and Cambodia). Their habitat is the Central and Southeastern Highlands, *Tay Nguyen* or *Hauts-Plateaux,* of Vietnam, roughly from Hue to Saigon (Ho Chi Minh City), at an elevation varying from 100m to 2000m. This area used to be heavily forested, and contained a rich fauna and flora. But in the past 20 years the forest cover has diminished drastically due to the influx of lowland Viêt settlers attracted by the prospect of land suitable to growing coffee and other plantations and whose number is today more than 60 percent of the local population. It has to be noted also that other ethnic groups from Northern Vietnam have been relocated in the Central Highlands.

Ethnography

In spite of the linguistic divide between Austronesian speakers and Austroasiatic speakers, many common cultural traits, like longhouses, matrilineal descent, or beliefs in a host of spirits called *yang,* were found among groups belonging to either linguistic family. They were all upland shifting agriculturists who relied on forest products, hunting, and fishing to supplement their diet. Their society was characterized by a strong sense of solidarity at the village level, no overall political organization at the regional level, and some degree of stratification together with forms of slavery or debt bondage. Feasts of prestige entailing the sacrifice of large animals like pigs and water buffaloes, the consumption of rice wine, and the playing of gongs were ritual elements found throughout the area.

The Jarai and Rhade (or Ede) had large villages containing up to 60 longhouses occupied by members of the same matrilineal descent group. Their society was based on exogamous matrilineal clans, and the village organization rested on a headman and a council of elders and wealthy villagers. Although social organization was basically egalitarian, ranking by wealth and prestige played an important role. The traditional religious beliefs included an extensive pantheon of spirits, *yang,* and among the Jarai, the existence of politico-religious functionaries called *sadet* whose power was acknowledged by the neighbouring Bahnar. Death was associated with elaborate rituals entailing a belief in the rebirth of the soul of the deceased.

The Raglai, another Austronesian group, lived on the Eastern Slopes of the Hauts Plateaux and in the coastal hills neighbouring the China Sea. Their settlement pattern was more scattered, and they share common traits with the lowland Chams. The Cho Ru likewise are closely related to the Chams.

The Austroasiatic Bahnar, east of Kontum, as well as the Sedang, lived in villages characterized by a centrally located communal or men's house. Descent was patrilineal. Several villages, governed by a council of elders and a village headman, were traditionally regrouped in an administrative entity called *toring*. Social stratification was marked with ranking by wealth. The Sedang had a bilateral kinship system and lived in longhouses, forming tightly organized communities with some degree of stratification.

All or most *Montagnards* had and still keep a rich folklore including long, chanted poems or epics describing the feats of supernatural heroes.

History

Prior to the French presence, the upland communities had a long history of contact with lowlanders, especially the Cham, the Khmers and the Lao. The occupation of the Hauts Plateaux started with the foundation of the Catholic mission in Kontum in 1850. In 1899, the Darlac Province was created. From 1913 to 1926, a French administrator, L. Sabatier, ruled over the Montagnards and promoted policy based on the Montagnard customary law and the development of a Montagnard, mostly Rhade, elite. It would form the core of what came to be known as the FULRO, an acronym meaning the United Front for the Liberation of Oppressed Races. The FULRO played an important role from 1958 spearheading a Montagnard ethnonationalist movement.

In 1946 the Admiral T. d'Argenlieu creates the Commissariat for the PMSI (Montagnard People of Southern Indochina). In the meantime the Viet Minh made contact with the upland peoples, and Ho Chi Minh asserted the multinational character of the Vietnamese State during the Pleiku conference in 1946.

In 1955, Diem abolished the autonomous Montagnard Province and a movement to oppose his policy of forced integration is created. Called the BAJARAKA, an acronym based on the names of major ethnic groups (Bahnar, Jarai, Rhade, Koho), it was eventually replaced by the FULRO. The FULRO conducted a struggle for independence, allying itself with the Viet Minh temporarily after the fall of Ban Me Thuot, and then conducting an armed opposition to the Socialist Administration of Hanoi until 1992.

From 1967 onward, the Montagnards have suffered from the occupation, deportation, and bombardments inflicted by the Southern Vietnamese, American, and Northern Vietnamese troops. It is estimated than in 1975, 85 percent of all upland villages had been destroyed by bombing. More than 200,000 Montagnard people lost their lives between 1965 and 1975.

After 1975, the Vietnamese Socialist Government imposed a very tight control over all populations living on the Hauts Plateaux under a policy dubbed as "one field-one house" in order to stop shifting cultivation and all form of nomadism, as well as traditional customs such as life in longhouses. Some of the Montagnard groups associated with the Americans, like the Jarai and the Churu, suffered from deportation and the imprisonment of their leaders. Today, spontaneous movements of rebellion have reappeared in the Ban Me Thuot and Pleiku areas, in response to land shortages created by the influx of Viêt settlers, absence of religious freedom, and unequal treatment by the administration.

CHARLES MACDONALD

See also **Vietnam**

Further Reading

Condominas, G., *We Have Eaten the Forest: The Story of a Montagnard Village in the Central Highlands of Vietnam*, New York: Hill and Wang, 1977

Evans, G., "Central Highlanders of Vietnam," in *Indigenous Peoples of Asia*, edited by R. H. Barnes, A. Gray, and B. Kingsbury, Ann Arbor, Michigan: Association for Asian Studies, Monograph and Occasional Paper Series No. 48, 1995

Hickey, G. K., *Free in the Forest: Ethnohistory of the Vietnamese Central Highlands 1954–1976*, New Haven: Yale University Press, 1982

Hickey, G.K., *Sons of the Mountains: Ethnohistory of the Vietnamese Central Highlands to 1954*, New Haven: Yale University Press, 1982

Hickey, G. K., *Shattered World*, Philadelphia: University of Pennsylvania Press, 1993

Salemink, O., "Primitive Partisans: French Strategy and the Construction of a Montagnard Ethnic Identity in Indochina," in *Imperial Policy and Southeast Asian Nationalism 1930–1957*, edited by Antlöv and Tonneson, London: Curzon Press/NIAS, 1995

Montenegrins

Capsule Summary

Location: Serbia-Montenegro (formerly the Yugoslav Republics of Serbia and Montenegro)
Total Population: approximately 650,000, one-third of whom live in Serbia
Language: Serbo-Croatian
Religion: Eastern Orthodox Christian

According to the 1991 census, Montenegrins constitute 62 percent of the population of the Republic of Montenegro. Of the remainder, 9 percent are Serbs, and 29 percent are Muslim Slavs, Albanians, and a small minority of Croats, Gypsies (Rom), and others. However, it should be noted that the distinction between Montenegrins and Serbs is very problematic.

The Montenegrins are linguistically and historically related to the other South Slavic peoples of the Balkans: Slovenes, Croats, Bosnian Muslims, Serbs, Macedonians, and Bulgarians. The ancestors of the contemporary Montenegrins entered the Balkans with other Slavic-speaking tribes during the sixth and seventh centuries CE, migrating from an area beyond the Carpathians. Evidence suggests that their original homeland lies somewhere in Russia or Ukraine. The Montenegrins have particularly close ties to the Serbs. Montenegro is one of the two constituent republics which remained in Yugoslavia following the secession of Slovenia, Croatia, Bosnia, and Macedonia in 1991. With the demise of Yugoslavia in 2003, Montenegro formed a loose union with Serbia, reflecting a desire by many Montenegrins for eventual total independence.

History

Montenegro was the smallest republic in the former Yugoslavia with an area of 13,038 square kilometers. Its history is closely tied to its geography. Like other areas of the western Balkans, it is largely mountainous. Much of the western region consists of *karst*, rugged expanses of deforested, infertile limestone highlands lacking navigable rivers or other natural routes of communication. Further to the interior are found lofty, forested mountains, rising in places to over 8,000 feet. Here alpine pastures and plateaus have traditionally supported a peasant economy based on the herding of sheep, goats, and cattle. Only the coastline which stretches for 188 kilometers along the Adriatic Sea offers an easily accessible door to the outside world.

The Montenegrins take great pride in their centuries of virtual independence. The first Montenegrin state, known as Zeta, emerged thirty years before the Battle of Kosovo in 1389 when the Serbs were defeated by the Ottoman Turks. While most of the Balkans soon fell under five centuries of Turkish rule, during most of this period, the Montenegrins remained largely free in their mountain strongholds.

The first Montenegrin state was founded by the BalSic clan who ruled until 1422 when a new dynasty was established by Stevan Crnojevic. Cut off by the Turks and Venetians from the coast and the fertile plains around the present capital of Podgorica, Stevan's successor, Ivan, withdrew into the mountains where he founded his capital at the small town of Cetinje from where for over 400 years a constant struggle was waged against the Turks. With the end of Crnojevic rule in 1516, Montenegro, which like Serbia had accepted Orthodox Christianity from Byzantium, became a theocratic state ruled by prince-bishops called *vladike* (sing.*vladika)*. These were elected by local tribal assemblies, and then consecrated by the Serbian Patriarch. While the threat of Islam had endowed the Church with great influence, the fragmented tribal nature of the society limited the scope of central authority. Thus, a difficult and vital task of the rulers was to maintain the ephemeral unity of their unruly highland subjects. The period through the end of the mid-nineteenth century was characterized by periodic battles between the Montenegrins and the Turks and their Islamized Slav and Albanian allies, with territory frequently changing hands. The most famous and last of the ecclesiastical rulers was Petar Petrovic Njegos who ascended to power in 18 O. He has been immortalized by his epic poem, *The Mountain Wreath,* which celebrates the heroic struggle of the Montenegrins against Islam. Following his death in 1851, he was succeeded by Danilo

Petrovic II who, wishing to marry, declared himself "Prince of Montenegro." Henceforth, civil and religious authority were to remain separate. Under his rule, central government and the military were strengthened, and much of the former autonomy of the tribes was greatly diminished. When Danilo was assassinated in 1860, sovereignty passed to his nephew, Nikola I, who eventually took the title of "King."

The period of Nikola's rule was one of Europeanization and modernization, one which saw the establishment of a national bank, the expansion of the educational system, the opening of post offices, the construction of roads and a railway, the revision of the legal code, and the introduction of a parliamentary system. Nikola also enhanced Montenegro's place in European society by marrying his daughters into the German, Russian, Italian, and Serbian royal families. By the end of his rule, Montenegrin territory had expanded to approximately its present boundaries except for a section of the Adriatic coast which remained under Austrian sovereignty until the end of World War I.

In 1912, Montenegro joined Serbia, Bulgaria and Greece in the First Balkan War against Turkey. With the alliance's victory over the Ottomans, Montenegro obtained territory which gave it a common border with Serbia. There was at this time a strong sentiment for unity with Serbia, and King Nikola, who was feuding with the Serbian King, was forced into exile in Italy.

During World War I, Montenegro joined Serbia in the fight against Austria, and with the defeat of Germany and Austria, it became part of the newly formed Kingdom of the Serbs, Croats, and Slovenes (subsequently renamed Yugoslavia). However, the loss of independence was never accepted by a large minority who remained loyal to King Nikola. During the interwar period, separatists were severely repressed by the royalist Yugoslav regime. Thus, up to the present time, Montenegrins have remained divided over the issues of independence and ethnic identity. Moreover, in many cases, this conflict has reflected traditional tribal antagonisms.

Following Yugoslavia's defeat by the Axis powers in 1941, Montenegro was occupied by Italy. During World War II, Montenegrins played prominent roles in both the Communist Partisan and Royalist Chetnik resistance movements. With the victory of the Partisans and the establishment of Tito's Marxist state, Montenegro became one of the six constituent republics of the "New Yugoslavia." Today, it remains united in a tenuous relationship with Serbia.

Society and Culture

Centuries of isolation and a history of determined resistance to Turkish and Islamic domination have shaped the Montenegrin national character. This has been expressed in an heroic ethos constructed from frequently embellished accounts of the violent struggle for freedom, a struggle immortalized in the folk epic poetry with which almost every Montenegrin is familiar. Reflecting this value system is an archaic, patriarchal tribal form of social organization which survived almost intact well into the nineteenth century, and remnants of which even today characterize the Montenegrin mentality.

Traditionally Montenegrins were organized into a system of patriclans known as "brotherhoods" whose membership was determined by common descent through the male line from a real or fictive founding ancestor. Clans were exogamous with strong prohibitions against intermarriage with any patrilateral kin. Among other obligations, clan membership entailed the participation of adult male "clan brothers" in the conduct of the blood feuds which were common in Montenegrin society well into the twentieth century. The clans in turn were organized into a number of semi-autonomous tribes organized on the basis of territorial proximity. The principal function of the tribes was to mobilize fighters in times of warfare and to resolve disputes and feuds among their constituent clans. In contemporary Montenegro, although the blood feud has for the most part disappeared and the tribes have largely lost their political significance, clan and tribal loyalties, as well as the values associate with them, still persist. Moreover, it is these characteristics and affinities which most distinguish the Montenegrins from the Serbs to whom they are otherwise culturally and ethnically closely related. This close relationship is reflected by the fact that the highest rate of interethnic marriage in former Yugoslavia was between Serbs and Montenegrins. However, even though the Serbs and Montenegrins share dialects of the same language, write in the same Cyrillic alphabet, and have the same religious and historical roots, the question remains unanswered as to exactly how pervasive the sense of a separate Montenegrin ethnicity may be and how this will affect the future of the newly formed state of Serbia-Montenegro.

ANDREI SIMIC

Further Reading

Boehm, Christopher, *Blood Revenge: The Anthropology of Feuding in Montenegro and Other Tribal Societies*, Lawrence: University Press of Kansas, 1984

Djilas, Milovan, *Land without Justice*, New York: Harcourt Brace, 1958

Hammel, Eugene A., *Alternative Social Structures and Ritual Relations in the Balkans*, Englewood Cliffs, New Jersey: Prentice-Hall, 1968

Saltzman, Alice, "Montenegro in Historical Perspective," in *Montenegrin Social Organization and Values: Political Ethnography of a Refuge Area Tribal Adaptation*, edited by Christopher Boehm, New York: MMS Press, 1983

Simie, Andrei, "Montenegro: Beyond the Myth," in *Crises in the Balkans*, edited by Constantine P. Danopoulos and Kostas G. Messas, Boulder, Colorado: Westview Press, 1997

Mordovans

Capsule Summary

Location: Republic of Mordovia (Russian Federation) and different regions scattered throughout Russia and Siberia
Total Population: nearly 1.8 million
Language: Moksha and Erzya
Religion: Christian Orthodox Church; Sunni Muslims

The Republic of Mordovia is located at the Volga-Oka river basin where only 27.2 percent of the Mordovans live. Its capital city is Saransk. Most of the Mordovans dwell in compact groups in the provinces of Samara, Penza, Orenburg, Ulianovsk and Nizhni-Novgorod, partly also in Central Asia and Siberia.

In addition to several smaller tribes (Tengushev, the Teryukhan and the Karatay), Mordovans are subdivided in two main groups: Erzya and Moksha, who were closely related to each other until the fifteenth century when they settled within their traditional territories bounded by the Volga, Oka and Sura rivers. The Tengushev are ethnically Erzya, but speak Moksha. The Mishars are a group of Mordovans that have adopted the Tatar language and converted to Sunni Islam; they are counted as Tatars. The Erzya Mordovan subgroup inhabit the eastern area of the Mordovia's Republic, adjacent areas from Nizh-Novgorod region, Chuvasia republic, northern Orenburg zone and the frontiers of Bashkotorstan and Tatarstan. The Erzyan language is also spoken in Azerbaijan, Kazakhstan, Kyrgyzstan, Turkmenistan, Ukraine, Uzbekistan, and in sparse areas of Southern Siberia. On the other hand, the Moksha Mordovans are centered in the western areas in the regions of Ryazan, Penza, Samara and Tambov.

Christian Mordovans retained several traditional beliefs from the ancient shamanistic background. For example, the use of the birth placenta for curing sterility is an old Mordovan tradition, and, earlier people were afraid that a person assisting the birth or a sterile woman might steal it. There are also many rituals and customs related to death that are deeply connected with the ancient animistic beliefs.

During the first millennium CE, patriarchal kin relations were characteristic of Mordvinian tribes. According to current research data, every Mordovan tribe consisted of several patriarchal kin groups, which, in their turn, included several patriarchal families, whose head was usually *kudatya* (from *kudo-atya*, "old man"). A kin group or several kin groups formed a village (*vele*). The chief of a tribe was the *tyushtya* (*tyoksh*, "highest," *atya*, "old man"), who was elected by the elders.

Until the beginning of the twentieth century, the traditional institution shaping the ethnic type of thinking and behavior of the Mordovans was the village community. It regulated the economic, social and cultural everyday life of the Mordovan peasantry. Village community was, in its turn, divided into family groups who all originated from different ancestors. Village communities were conducted by elders *pryavt*s (*prya*, "head"), who were elected at the general meeting of the representatives of farms *velen' promks* (from the words *vele*, "village," *promks*, "body, meeting"). The village assembly also kept an account of the number of farms in the village and the number of inhabitants and live stock in every family, and also of the size and return of taxes.

Mordovans are mentioned for the first time by the Gothic historian Jordanes in the sixth century, when Mongols and Tatars were ruling over them. Proto-Mordovins began to separate into present day Erzas and Mokshas around the first century. The separation was complete by the seventh century, and by the twelfth century they were quite distinguishable.

In the eighth century, the Mordovans (presumably the Erzya tribes) were tributaries of the Bulgars who settled in the Volga region (Volga *Bolghari*). The Erzya and Moksha were mentioned in a tenth century diplomatic message by the Khazar Khagan Joseph. Fortified towns are built (Arzamas, Nizhni-Novgorod, Ryazan).

In 1172, the Russian principalities of Suzdal, Ryazan and Murom joined forces to conquer the Mordvin capital at Nizhniy Novgorod. Russian expansionism continued, with Muscovy joining in the land grab. Russian peasants were resettled in the region and the colonized territory then annexed by the Russian principalities. The Hungarian monk traveler Julianius (Rubrook) traveled through Mordvinia in 1236 CE, taking note of the "Morduans" who were still very warlike and took human heads as trophies.

In the mid-thirteenth Century, the Mordvin suffered the Mongol conquest as it passed enroute from the Volga Bulgars to Russia, and thereafter fell under the rule of the Golden Horde. Eventually, they allied themselves with the Russian resistance. When the last Kazan Khanate fell in 1552 CE, the Mordovans were annexed to the newly emerging Russian state. The Russian supremacy forced the Mordovans to move eastwards. The subdued Mordovan people were converted to the orthodox faith. Several uprisings were led by Mordovans leaders, like S. Razin (1671) and Nesmeyan Vasilyev (1743–45). Another revolt, in 1804, put an end to the active resistance of the Mordovans. Some of the Mordovans left their ancestral land. In the eighteenth and nineteenth Centuries Mordovans emigrated en masse from the pressure of Russian colonization. In 1928, the district of Mordovia is created in the Central Volga, but areas settled by Mordovans are brought under different administrative territories. In the 1950s, continued industrialization and colonization encourage assimilation of the Mordovan ethnicity.

In contemporary times, both Moksha and Erzya peoples of the Mordovan nation are largely endangered, and a major language shift has increased since the 1990s: 46 percent of rural and 84 percent of urban Mordovans preferred to educate their children in Russian schools. Nowadays, collective aims are trying to reinforce the language and the culture of the Mordovans, basing efforts in the success of a new democratic atmosphere which may guarantee their survival.

JOAN MANUEL CABEZAS LÓPEZ

See also **Russia**

Further Reading

Lallukka, Seppo, "Changing Age-Sex Composition as an Indication of Ethnic Reidentification: The Mordvins," *Nordic Journal of Soviet and East European Studies*, 4, no. 4 (1987)

Mikkor, Marika, "On the Customs Related to Death in the Erza Villages of Sabajevo and Povodimovo," *Folklore*, no. 14, Institut of Estonian Languages (2000)

Werth, Paul W., "Armed Defiance and Biblical Appropriation: Assimilation and the Transformation of Mordvin Resistance, 1740–1810," *Nationalities Papers*, 27, no. 2 (1999)

Moro

Capsule Summary

Location: Philippines, Southern Palawan, Southwestern Mindanao, Sulu Archipelago
Total Population: 5 million
Languages: Malayo-Polynesian (Austronesian), Philippine
Religion: Islam

In the last half century the fight for an independent Muslim state in the Southern Philippines has displaced several hundred thousand Muslims, known as Moros, from their home lands, and many have taken refuge on other Philippine islands or in nearby Malaysia. Over120,000 people have been killed as government troops and various Islamic rebel groups have fought to control the region, resulting in economic disaster and extreme poverty. There is evidence of linkages between Moro liberation organizations and radical Islamic terrorists in recent years. The Moros are members of Philippine ethnic groups, such as the Maguindano, Maranao, and the Kalagan on Mindanao; Tausug, Samal, Badjao (Sea Gypsies) in the Sulu archipelago; Yakan on Basilan island; Sangil on Balut Isalnd; Jama Mapun on Cagayan de Sulu, and the Malebugnon (Molbog) on Balabac and Palawan islands.

In the thirteenth century Arab tradesman and Islamic missionaries brought Islam to the Philippines so that when Spain began its colonization in the sixteenth century, Islam was established among coastal communities and ethnic groups in Southern Palawan, Southwestern Mindanao, and the Sulu Archipelago. The Spanish called these peoples Moros because their Muslim beliefs and fierce fighting were reminiscent of the Moors (Latin *Mauros*) who invaded Spain in the eighth century. The principal points of conflict with the Spanish were the attempts to Christianize the Muslim population, and stop the brisk slave trade by Moros who raided coastal populations throughout the southern islands. The Moros were never brought under control during 300 years of Spanish rule although military steamships, heavy armament, and a series of forts established Spain's presence in the area toward the end of the nineteenth Century. Efforts to entice immigration of Christianized Filipinos into Moro lands with government incentives failed; however, prisoners from all over the islands were dispatched to a large penal colony on Palawan.

The Spanish-American War and the Treaty of Paris (1898) made the Philippines an American colony. American soldiers encountered fierce Moro fighters and their famed swords: the *kris* (10–12-inch double edge wave blade developing into straight end); the *barung* (12–18-inch single edged leaf shaped cleaver like blade); and, the *kampilan* (35–40-inch bifurcated handle single edged blade wider at the end leading to an upward curving prong). The U.S. forces discovered that the standard issue Colt 38 double action revolver did not have the stopping power to push back the frenzied charges of Moro warriors and in 1901 a shipment of 500 mothballed, refurbished single action Colt 45s, the favorite revolver of gunfighters on the Western frontier, was effectively used in Mindanao skirmishes. This led eventually to the design of the automatic Colt 45.

The United States recognized that the Moros constituted a unique and separate population and entered into agreements with area leaders (sultans) and local officials (datus) of the various ethnic groups to maintain the peace throughout the region. Government policies during this period (1898–1946) aimed at subduing the fighters, containing the Muslims to their lands, and exerting socio-political control through anti-slavery laws, taxation, compulsory education, and mandatory military service. When the Philippines became an independent nation after World War II, forty years of vigorous resettlement programs in the colonial period had tipped the balance so that Christianized settlers on the Mindanao frontier now outnumbered the Moros.

Twice at the changing of the colonial guard—Spain giving way to America, and America stepping aside for Philippine independence—Moro peoples petitioned for the formation of an independent state. The concept of a single centralized government maintaining unity and peace for all the Philippine islands and ethnic groups always prevailed. It has never extinguished the fires of separatist sentiment. The new Philippine nation continued the resettlement programs and hundreds of thousands of non-Muslim Filipinos flooded into Mindanao provinces legally claiming title to lands, purchasing it from local residents, or some cases, simply taking the land. Land disputes, religious and cultural differences, and extreme poverty spawned violent behavior on all sides. The government maintained garrisons in outbreak areas and armed immigrant settlers for their own protection.

Gangs emerged among the settlers such as the Ilagas, ("rats") and the Muslims (Blackshirts, and Barracudas) and they engaged in bloody gang warfare. Fanatical, syncretistic, revitalistic cults with names like Rock Christ, and the Philippine Benevolent Missionary Association were composed primarily of immigrants. They became para-military units who supported President Ferdinand Marcos' 1972 martial law and kidnapped or murdered thousands of suspected rebels and their sympathizers. Local politicians and ethnic leaders also hired their own soldiers adding more gun totters to this volatile area. In some places in Moro land, the Maoist backed New People's Army (NPA) sought to gain ground and entered into conflict with government troops. By the mid 1970s, Muslim Mindanao was the scene of prolonged gun battles, and violent human rights abuses, perpetrated by calloused murderers like the Tadtad ("chop") gang who killed people slowly by chopping them into small pieces.

The Moros are bound together by a common religious thread; however, age old ethnic rivalries, differences of opinion regarding autonomy within the Philippine nation or an independent state, and competition among leaders have fragmented attempts to organize a single representative organization. In the decade following World War II, the Muslim Association of the Philippines (MAP) sought to advance the social welfare of its constituency and eventually voiced a desire to use Pakistan as a model for a separatist government. The former governor of a Mindanao province, Utog Matalam, put together a coalition in the 1960s, the Muslim

Independent Movement, which later became the Mindanao Independence Movement (MIM), and advocated for Bangsamoro ("Moro nation") independence. The 1968 killing, the Jabidah Massacre, of Muslim Philippine Army soldiers by government troops, apparently over a pay protest while they were being trained for a secret mission to Sabah, began to turn the more peaceful Muslim demands into widespread, militant armed conflict.

The Moro National Liberation Front (MNFL) entered this scene as a tripartite coalition headed by a former University of the Philippines professor, Nur Misuari, who brought in the Tausogs and Samals. He was joined by a second in command, Hashim Salamat of the Maguindanaos, and Rashid Lucman, a Maranao, from the Bangsa Moro Liberation Front (BMLF). Using its strong ties with Libya, and the Organization of the Islamic Conference (OIC), the group was able to exert enough influence to force President Marcos to come to the bargaining table and sign a 1976 peace agreement in Tripoli. Massive military forces withdrew from Mindanao and former soldiers and rebels went into business, petty corruption, and crime. These factors along with disagreements over the planned autonomy sparked more revolts, and the return of government troops.

The MNLF split several times. Hashim Salamat started the Moro Independent Liberation Front (MILF) and the BMLF broke away to eventually become the Moro National Liberation Front Reformist Movement. The MNLF signed several more agreements with the Philippine government: the 1987 Jeddiah Accord, a statement to continue discussions about full autonomy to various islands and provinces subject to the democratic process; and, a 1996 peace pact in which the MNLF accepted autonomy instead of independence. Only the MILF survived into the twenty-first century as a powerful Muslim armed force and socio-political voice promoting an independent state; however, it did so by shifting goals and leadership several times. The various agreements, cease fires, and central government legislative actions of the last ten years have fractured the movements for an independent Moro land. For example, some Muslim areas have opted for limited autonomy under Republic Act 6734 or the Organic Act for the Creation of the Autonomous Region for Muslim Mindanao (ARMM), while others continue to bear arms or peacefully unite against anything short of independence. Some rebel leaders and their communities have laid down their arms and are participating in U.S. AID and Philippine government funded programs aimed at community development and job training.

Moro connections with outside terrorist individuals and groups are well known by the Philippine and Western intelligence communities. Some MNFL and MIFL members received training or encouragement in Libya with Muslim friends, in Sabah with Malaysian Islamic militants, in Pakistan with radical elements, or in Afghanistan with the Taliban, and perhaps, even with the al-Qaeda, or their members in other countries. Malaysian and Indonesian members of the al-Qaeda linked terrorist group responsible for the October 2002 Bali bombings, the Jemaah Islamiah (JI), have been sighted in MIFL camps, leading some observers to speculate that a JI cell exists on Mindanao. However, these external groups did not create the Philippine Muslim uprisings, nor do they control the local groups, and it is unlikely that they are the major source of the arms that fuel the friction.

A young Moro militant Abdurajak Janjalani met Osama bin Laden's brother-in-law, Mohammed al-Khalifa, in 1990 and returned to Basilan and Jolo islands to organize a separatist group, the Abu Sayyaf. They began as a letter writing group advocating independence but quickly turned into a kidnapping and bombing terrorist unit responsible for the 1993 kidnapping of 70 Christians and the bombing of a Philippine Airlines 747. When Janjalani died his brother assumed control and the Abu Sayyaf political agenda took a back seat to the greed of snatching people for profit. While the MNFL was trying to hold to a peace agreement, the Abu Sayyaf went on a rampage. In fourteen months in 2000–2001, the group successfully kidnapped three sets of hostages: 51 from Basilan, 30 from a Malaysian resort, and several Filipinos and two American missionaries from a Palawan vacation spot. In the first two instances, they exchanged captives for huge ransom amounts, topped by the Libyan government's payment of $25 million. New Tribes Mission has a no ransom policy and the two missionaries were held for over a year during which several captives, including an American citizen, were beheaded. Some were released, or left behind when they were wounded in gun battles, and the Abu Sayyaf continued to add local hostages to the group. This case is one of the reasons American advisors were sent to the Philippines to train government troops to become more efficient in expeditions against Muslim rebels. Eventually Philippine troops overran the Abu Sayyaf unit holding the captives, and missionary Gracia Burnham emerged as the only survivor.

F. Douglas Pennoyer

See also **Moro National Liberation Front**

Further Reading

Burnham, Gracia, and Dean Merrill, *In the Presence of My Enemies*, Carol Stream, Illinois: Tyndale House Publishers, 2003

Kiefer, Thomas M. *The Tausug: Violence and Law in a Philippine Moslem Society*, New York: Holt, Rinehart and Winston, 1990

McKenna, Thomas, *Muslim Rulers and Rebels: Everyday Politics and Armed Separatism in the Southern Philippines*, Berkeley: University of California Press, 1998

Rogers, Steven, "Beyond the Abu Sayyaf," *Foreign Affairs*, 83, no. 1 (Jan–Feb 2004)

Moro National Liberation Front (Mnlf)

Capsule Summary

Location: Southern Philippines
Total Population: 12 million
Language: 10 subgroups (see main entry)
Religion: Muslim

The "Moroland" (or Southern Philippines) is composed of Mindanao island (the second largest island of the Philippine islands), the Sulu archipelago, Palawan, Basilan and the neighboring islands. It has the area of 116, 895 square kilometers (more than one third of the whole Philippine islands), with the population of more than twenty million of which 12 million are Muslims (or about 5 percent of the Philippine population). They can be classified linguistically into 10 subgroups: the Maguindanao of North Cotabato, Sultan Kudarat, and Maguindanao provinces; the Maranao of Lanao del Norte and Lanao del Sur provinces; the Tausug, mostly of Jolo Island; the Samal, mostly in the Sulu Archipelago; the Bajau, mostly in the Sulu Archipelago; the Yakan of Zamboanga del Sur province; the Ilanon of southern Mindanao; the Sangir of southern Mindanao; the Melabugnan of southern Palawan; and the Jama Mapun of the Cagayan Islands.

The Moro are not racially different from other Filipinos but—with a separate Islamic faith (introduced from Borneo and Malaya in the fourteenth century) and local cultures—have remained outside the mainstream of Philippine life and have been the object of popular prejudice and national neglect. Moro conflict with ruling powers has a centuries-long history: from the sixteenth to the nineteenth century they resisted Roman Catholic Spanish colonialists, who tried to extirpate their "heresy"; in the first decade of the twentieth century they battled against U.S. occupation troops in a futile hope of establishing a separate sovereignty; and, finally, they spawned insurgencies against the independent Philippine government, especially from the late 1960s onwards.

Historically, Moros have never constituted a collective entity. The various groups or tribes have often been fiercely independent, have clashed with one another at times, and have independently grafted Islamic tenets and practices onto their distinct local cultures. Nevertheless, internal differences have been outweighed by the common grievances that the Moro have experienced vis-à-vis non-Muslims in the Philippines. After World War II, their traditional grievances as religious and economic outcasts were exacerbated by the great migration of northern Christian Filipinos into the southern provinces, where they bought up land and tried to Christianize the schools and other institutions.

The main resistance group espousing Moro separatism—the Moro National Liberation Front (MNLF), founded in 1968—instituted a terrorist insurgency that left 100,000 dead, drew in about half of the Philippine armed forces, and drove some 50,000 Muslim refugees to Sabah, East Malaysia, before a cease-fire was arranged in late 1976. The government in Manila could not win militarily against the MNLF for two reasons. First, the MNLF were fighting a "jihad" (holy war) for the establishment of an Islamic state. Second, the MNLF had a safe haven in Sabah. The then chief minister in Sabah, Mustapha Harun, gave the MNLF land to set up training bases and helped channeled Arab money to buy arms and supplies. Mustapha himself was a Moro and harbored dreams of creating a

Sulu nation with himself as Sultan. Some elements in the Muslim-dominated Malaysian federal government purposely looked the other way because of an ongoing territorial dispute with Manila. Manila had an outstanding claim on Sabah citing the historical control over Sabah by the Sulu Sultanate. However, due to Malaysia and Philippine's membership of the Association of Southeast Asian Nations (ASEAN) the claims were never actively pursued or discussed by both countries.

The Organization of Islamic Conference (OIC) tried to serve as a peacemaker between the two sides but were only partly successful. The Philippine government was suspicious of OIC's sincerely given that many of its members, such as Libya, were strong supports of the MNLF's claim for an independent Islamic state. Under diplomatic pressure from the OIC, the threat of an oil embargo by Islamic oil producing countries, and an unsatisfactory military situation, the Ferdinand Marcos regime entered into negotiations with the MNLF. The talks between the two belligerents were conducted in Jeddah, Saudi Arabia during January 1975. They failed to reach an accord and were broken off. A second round of talks held in December 1976 in Tripoli, Libya produced the "Tripoli Agreement." The MNLF agreed to political autonomy within the Philippine state—not independence—for a Moroland much reduced in territorial size. The new borders comprised 13 provinces, instead of 22, or only 60 percent of the historic homeland of the Moros. But four months later in 1977 the MNLF president, Nur Misuari, renewed a demand for total independence and Tripoli accord was dead.

The guerilla war carried on for most of the late 1970s and 1980s, while various talks, some held under the auspicious of the OIC others direct, were held without much success. When Marcos was finally overthrown in 1986, the new administration of Corozon Aquino again offered autonomy to the Moro region. In January 1987, the MNLF signed an agreement with Manila relinquishing its goal of independence for Muslim regions and accepting the government's offer of autonomy. The Moro Islamic Liberation Front (MILF), the next largest faction formed by ex-MNLF fighters, refused to accept the accord and initiated a guerilla war that lasts until the present day. The MILF—which did not recognize the autonomous region—showed no sign of surrendering, and it promised to remain a potent military and political force in the southern Philippines.

The Philippine government, meanwhile, pressed ahead with plans for Muslim autonomy. Article 10 of the 1987 Philippine constitution mandates that the new congress establish an Autonomous Region in Muslim Mindanao. In the November 1989 plebiscite, only two Mindanao provinces—Maguindanao and Lanao del Sur—and two in the Sulu Archipelago—Sulu and Tawitawi—opted to accept the government's autonomy measure. The fragmented four-province Autonomous Region for Muslim Mindanao, with its own governor and unicameral legislature, was officially inaugurated on November 6, 1990.

No further progress was made in the peace arena until Fidel Ramos, a former armed forces of the Philippines (AFP) chief, became president in 1992. Another peace agreement between the Philippine government and the MNLF was signed on September 2, 1996. The agreement was signed by the government chief negotiator Manuel Yan, MNLF's long term leader Nur Misuari, Indonesian Foreign Minister Ali Alatas, and Secretary General Hamid Algabid of OIC. Later, Misuari ran for and won the governorship of the Autonomous Region for Muslim Mindanao in the September 9, 1996, elections, a post he still holds.

This peace agreement was signed without the support of the MILF, who argued that anything less than an independent Islamic Moro state was unacceptable. Armed activity by the MILF and smaller MNLF splinter-groups such as the Abu Sayaff continued at a relatively low level through the late 1980s until today, with sporadic clashes between government and Muslim forces. Most of the endemic violence in Muslim areas are directed at rival clans, not at the military's peacekeeping forces. Many are also criminal in nature, with kidnapping gangs masquerading as Islamic fighters. The Moro movement remained divided along tribal lines in two major factions-. Misuari's MNLF based in the Sulu Archipelago, and the Mindanao-based MILF.

Most scholars estimated 125,000 lives were lost directly in the 25-year revolt.

JAMES CHIN

See also **Moro; Philippines**

Further Reading

McKenna, Thomas M., *Muslim Rulers and Rebels: Everyday Politics and Armed Separatism in the Southern Philippines*, Berkeley and Los Angeles: University of California Press, 1988

Bauzon, Kenneth E., *Liberalism and the Quest for Islamic Identity in the Philippines*, Quezon City: Ateneo de Manila University Press, 1991

The MNLF-GRP Peace Process: Mindanao in Transition, General Santos City, Philippines: Research and Development Center, Mindanao State University, 1999

Rodil, B.R., *The Lumad and Moro of Mindanao*, London: Minority Rights Group, 1993

Vitug, Marites Dañguilan, and Glenda M. Gloria, *Under the Crescent Moon: Rebellion in Mindanao*, Quezon City, Philippines: Ateneo Center for Social Policy & Public Affairs, Institute for Popular Democracy, 2000

Morrison, Toni (African-American)

In 1993, Toni Morrison was the first African-American woman writer to win the Nobel Prize for Literature. Morrison's career exemplifies the tremendous shifts that have occurred in literature, literary production, and cultural criticism since the 1960s. Morrison attended Howard University where she majored in classics and received her Masters degree from Cornell University where she completed a thesis on William Faulkner and Virginia Woolf. She then taught at Texas Southern University and Howard University. While teaching, Morrison's interests shifted from classics to African-American literature and culture. After her divorce from her husband in 1964, Morrison moved to New York City and became an editor at Random House. In retrospect, this move proved significant for not only Morrison's own career as an editor and writer but for African-American women writers in general. While working as an editor at Random House, Morrison edited books by Toni Cade Bambara, Angela Davis, and Gayl Jones. At Random House, Morrison fostered the resurgence of African-American women writers and began her own career as a novelist.

Morrison's writing has examined the multiple layers of discrimination and oppression faced by African-Americans. Morrison's writing, especially her historical fiction, explores how race infects American culture and shapes African-American identity and community. Morrison has specialized in reconstructing the past for African-Americans and recovering the community's lost history. Morrison's efforts constitute a particularly post-Civil Rights era response to the lingering effects of race and racism in the United States after the dismantling of formal racial barriers.

The Bluest Eye (1970), Morrison's first novel, begins with the phrase "Quiet as it's kept." These opening words of the novel are illustrative of the types of themes that she will explore throughout her career. *The Bluest Eye* addressed the problem of incest and child abuse within an African-American family as metaphors for the ways in which racism gets turned inward against the very things that people love or should love most dearly. The novel is set in the narrator's past, prior to the major successes of the Civil Rights movement. It is precisely in retelling past events that healing can occur. *The Bluest Eye*, like all of Morrison's work, seeks to demonstrate the psychological and social wounds left by the United States's culture of racism and to offer the possibility of racial healing.

Morrison next published *Sula* (1973), a historical novel set primarily in the 1920s and 1930s that examines the relationship between two African-American women. *Sula* depicts the difficulty of developing solidarity among African-American women because of ways that racism and gender roles shape African-American women's lives. Morrison next published *Song of Solomon* (1977), which consolidated her reputation as a novelist. In *Song of Solomon*, Morrison responded to some of her critics by writing about how the history of slavery and segregation affected African-American men. *Song of Solomon* narrates the journey of a young midwestern African-American man's self-discovery.

After completing *Song of Solomon*, Morrison began experimenting with her themes and style. Setting the majority of the story in the Carribean on the hacienda of a rich white American, she examines the relationship between black and white cultures in the Americas in *Tar Baby* (1981). This novel furthers Morrison's critique of white cultural domination by telling the story of a black model, who falls in love with the wrong kind of black man. By depicting this failed romance between two black people, Morrison shows how white values haunt black people and limit their ability for romantic or communal union. *Tar Baby* is fairly unique among Morrison's novels as it includes major characters who are white.

In 1984, Morrison resigned from her position at Random House and continued her experimentation. Morrison wrote a play entitled "Dreaming Emmett" (1986). This play updated the story of Emmett Till's 1956 murder and examined how the nature of the struggle for civil rights has changed due to the War on Drugs in the early 1980s. *Tar Baby* and "Dreaming Emmett" demonstrate Morrison's attempt to deal more directly with contemporary issues and suggests that Morrison's historical fictions cannot be read as simply criticizing past events.

Morrison then published *Beloved* (1987), which has generally been considered her finest novel. Morrison developed the novel from the story of Margaret Garner, an enslaved women who escapes with her children but tries to kills them when she is about to be captured and returned into slavery. Morrison learned of Garner's story in the early 1970s when editing *The Black Book* (1974) for Random House. Morrison fictionalizes Garner's story in *Beloved* in order to narrate the voices and inner lives of African-Americans whose point of views have been elided from the telling of history. Told in a series of flashbacks, Morrison describes the events that could make Garner's decision to try to kill her children seem reasonable while showing the effects of this act on Garner's family and the African-American community as a whole.

After receiving considerable critical and popular acclaim for *Beloved*, Morrison used this fame to produce cultural criticism as well as writing novels. In her essay "Unspeakable Things Unspoken" (1989) and her book *Playing in the Dark: Whiteness and the Literary Imagination* (1992), Morrison describes how the traditional study of literature privileges whiteness. She also examines how African-American cultural practices and African-American characters have served as a necessary foil to much of what has been considered great in American literature. Morrison next published *Jazz* (1992) a historical novel that describes what the Harlem Renaissance and the Jazz Age meant for ordinary African-Americans who migrated to Harlem from the South. This novel examines the difficulty of formerly colonized peoples in establishing romantic relationships. Simultaneous with the publication of *Jazz*, Morrison edited a collection of essays on the Clarence Thomas confirmation hearings entitled *Race-ing Justice, En-Gendering Power: Essays on Anita Hill, Clarence Thomas, and the Construction of Social Reality* (1992). This book collected essays by leading scholars in law, cultural studies, literature, women's studies, and African-American studies that explained how race and gender effected the hearings.

In 1993, Toni Morrison won the Nobel Prize for Literature. Since then, Morrison has edited another collection of essays on the relationship between law and American culture. This second collection, *Birth of Nationhood: Gaze, Script, and Spectacle in the O.J. Simpson Case* (1997), examined the case, the media coverage of it, and the racially-divided public reaction to it. Most recently Morrison has published *Paradise* (1998), another historical novel. This novel is set in the late 1960s and the early 1970s. Morrison creates a fictional all-black town that had chosen to isolate itself by settling in a remote part of Oklahoma and depicts this town's response to the National Association for the Advancement of Colored People's (NAACP) litigation strategy that focused on integrating America, the growth of the Black Power movement, and the rise of feminism and African-American feminism. Morrison has also recently edited collections based on the writings of James Baldwin, Huey Newton, and Toni Cade Bambara.

Toni Morrison currently resides in New Jersey and teaches at Princeton University.

Capsule Biography

Chloe Anthony Wofford. Born February 18,1931 in Lorain, Ohio. Studied in public schools in Lorain; Howard University, Washington DC, B.A., 1953; Cornell University, Ithaca, New York, M.A., 1955. Taught at Texas Southern University, Houston, Texas, 1955–1957; Howard University, Washington DC, 1957–1964; State University of New York at Purchase, 1971– 1972; Yale University, New Haven, Connecticut, 1975–1977; State University of New York at Albany, 1984–1989; Bard College, Avondale-on-Hudson, New York, 1986–1988; University of Californa, Berkeley, 1987; Princeton University, Princeton, New Jersey, 1989-Present. Editor, Random House, New York, New York, 1965–1967: Senior Editor, Random House, New York, New York, 1967–1984. *Sula* wins Ohoana Book Award and is nominated for the National Book Award, 1974; *Song of Solomon* wins Fiction Award of the National Book Critics' Circle and an award from the American Academy and Institute of Arts and Letters, 1977; *Beloved* wins Pulitzer Prize for Fiction, 1988; Appointed to National Council on Arts, 1977; Elected to American Academy and Institute of Arts and Letters, 1981; Schweitzer Professor of the Humanities, 1984–1989; Robert F. Goheen Professor of the Humanities, 1989-Present. Awards: Melcher Award, 1988; Before Columbus Foundation, 1988; Elizabeth Cady Stanton Award from the National Organization of Women, 1988; America's

Commonwealth Award from the Modern Language Association, 1989; Chianti Ruffino Antico Fattore International Literary Prize, 1990; Nobel Prize for Literature, 1993; Jefferson Lecturer in the Humanities by the National Endowment for the Humanities, 1996: and National Arts Club's Gold Medal, 1999

Selected Works

The Bluest Eye, 1970

Sula, 1973

The Black Book, compiled by Middleton Harris, edited by Toni Morrison 1974

Song of Solomon, 1977

Tar Baby, 1981

"Dreaming Emmett," 1986

Beloved, 1987

"Site of Memory," *Inventing the Truth: The Art and Craft of Memoir*, edited by William Zissner, Boston: Houghton Mifflin, 1987.

"Unspeakable Things Unspoken: The Afro-American Presence in American Literature," *Michigan Quarterly Review*, 28, Winter (1989).

Jazz, 1992

Race-ing Justice, En-Gendering Power: Essays on Anita Hill, Clarence Thomas, and the Construction of Social Reality, edited by Toni Morrison, 1992

Playing in the Dark: Whiteness and the Literary Imagination, 1992

Birth of Nationhood: Gaze, Script, and Spectacle in the O.J. Simpson Case, edited by Toni Morrison and Claudia Brodsky Lacour, 1997

Paradise, 1998

RICHARD SCHUR

See also **National Association for the Advancement of Colored People (NAACP)**

Further Reading

Andrews, William, and Nellie McKay, editors, *Toni Morrison's "Beloved": A Casebook*, New York: Oxford University Press, 1999

Conner, Marc, editor, *The Aesthetics of Toni Morrison*, Jackson: University of Mississippi Press, 2000

Gates, Henry Louis, and K.A. Appiah, editors, *Toni Morrison: Critical Perspectives Past and Present*, New York: Amistad Press, 1993

Grewal, Gurleen, *Circles of Sorrow, Lines of Struggle: The Novels of Toni Morrison*, Baton Rouge: Louisiana State University Press, 1998

Heinze, Denise, *The Dilemma of Double-Consciousness: Toni Morrison's Novels*, Athens: University of Georgia Press, 1993

Peterson, Nancy, editor, *Toni Morrison: Critical and Theoretical Approaches*, Baltimore: Johns Hopkins University Press, 1997

Sumana, K., *The Novels of Toni Morrison: A Study in Race, Gender, and Class*, London: Sangman Books, 1998

Taylor-Guthrie, Danille, editor, *Conversations with Toni Morrison*, Jackson University Press of Mississippi, 1994

Mossi, *See* Burkina Faso

Mozambique

Capsule Summary

Country Name: Republic of Mozambique

Location: Southeast Africa; bordered on east by Mozambique Channel that separates it from island of Madagascar in Indian Ocean

Total Population: 17,479,266 (July 2003)

Minority Populations: Makonde, Makua-Lomwe (or Alolo), Yao (or Ajaua), Swahili, Chicunda, Chuabo, Sena, Maravi, Chopi, Shona (or Caranga), Tonga, western Europeans (mainly Portuguese), southern Asians (mainly Indians), *mestiços*, and *assimilados*

Languages: Chopi, Chwabo, Koti, Kunda, Lomwe, Makhuwa-Maca, Makhuwa-Makhuwana, Makhuwa-Metto, Makhuwa-Shirima, Makonde, Makwe, Manyika, Marendje, Mazaro, Mwani, Ndau, Ngoni, Nsenga, Nyanja, Nyungwe, Podzo, Portuguese (official), Ronga, Sakaji, Sena, Shona, Swahili, Swati, Tonga, Tsonga, Tswa, Yao, Zulu

Religions: Native-spiritist, Christianity, Islam, syncretism of native-spiritist and Christianity

Mozambique is located in Southeastern Africa, bordering the Mozambique Channel, between South

Africa and Tanzania. Mountains and plateaus dominate northern Mozambique, descending to highlands in the central region. Northern people include the Makonde, Makua-Lomwe or Alolo (at five million, the largest minority group), and Yao or Ajaua. The farthest southern advance of Islam in Africa penetrated the upper part of Mozambique, and Arabs raided along the coast and into the uplands. Curving through the central portion of the country is the Zambezi River, the fourth largest in Africa. The people of its valley include the Chicunda, Chuabo, and Sena. Above the Zambezi, possibly having emigrated from the Congo, are the Maravi. The southern part of the country consists of rolling lowlands. Its inhabitants include the Chopi, Shona or Caranga, and Tonga (from Zulu people). Minute numbers of Europeans, Euro-Africans, and Indians appear in the country, especially the south and cities. The native minorities of Mozambique divide into numerous sub-groups, differing extensively in their historic economic pursuits, social structures, and sizes and roles relative to each other.

In the far south lies the national capital, Maputo. The Portuguese were the colonial overlords of the region since the sixteenth century, developing trade in slaves and other commodities up the coastal region and Zambezi valley. The south has been the traditional economic and administrative center of the country. Trade with South Africa increased with the late-nineteenth century development there of rich mineral resources. White southerners and their allies controlled the commerce. Hundreds of miles of rail lines were laid in the first part of the twentieth century to the south and west into Zimbabwe, formerly Rhodesia.

Until independence in 1975, the dominant elite in Mozambique was a tiny minority of white Portuguese. Supporting them were further small minorities of mixed-race *mestiços* and natives assimilated (*assimilados*) to European ways. Portuguese influence in the country diminished as one moved into the interior. Portugal attempted systematic settlement in the interior toward the end of the nineteenth century as other European nations enlarged their interests in Africa.

Mozambicans have tended to divide between northerners and southerners. A complex of antagonisms has grown around differences between colonized and colonizer, debtor and creditor, governed and governor, rural and urban, black and white, victim and combatant, non-Christian and Christian, upland and lowland, and native and foreign.

Various degrees of poverty are common to all the country, but what sparse wealth does exist concentrates in the south and mostly in the capital and a few other cities.

The poverty of Mozambicans results from the very unbalanced development that occurred under Portugal, one of the poorest countries of Europe. Promises of riches, nonetheless, have always been part of Mozambique's history.

Independence from Portugal occurred on July 25, 1975. Most Portuguese administrators, businessmen, and professionals fled the country. Civil war broke out between two rival groups trying to dominate the new national government.

In 1964 the Marxist-Leninist Frente de Libertação de Moçambique (FRELIMO – Mozambique Liberation Front) began armed struggle for independence. It assumed the national government in 1975. However, Mozambique's powerful capitalist, white-dominated neighbors, Rhodesia and South Africa, formed and financially-backed an anti-Communist movement, the Resistênica Nacional Moçambicana (RENAMO – Mozambican National Resistance). It was strongly backed by United States President Gerald Ford and Secretary of State Henry Kissinger. FRELIMO received support from the Soviet Union. Events unraveled in a manner similar to those occurring at the same time in Portugal's other major African colony, Angola.

RENAMO maneuvered against FRELIMO throughout the country, attacking in the south and occupying strongholds in the highlands. FRELIMO held the capital in the south, and RENAMO raided around there and in the north. The conflict assumed a north-south character; and everywhere it left hundreds of thousands dead, wounded, or displaced. Only the end of apartheid in South Africa and of the cold war between East and West brought reconciliation between FRELIMO and RENAMO. It was a peace of exhaustion.

At independence in 1975, Mozambique was one of the world's poorest countries, and its economy continued to suffer as a result of civil war. Governmental economic reforms began in 1987. Mozambique reconstituted itself in 1990 as a multi-party state, established regular elections, and allowed private investment. In the latter part of the nineties, Mozambique began to offer some possibility of fulfilling its economic promise. In 2002 it achieved an annual rate of economic growth of 7.7 percent, reaching a per capita income with purchasing power of US$1,100. Nonetheless, Mozambique remains dependent upon foreign assistance, and the majority of the population remains below the poverty line (approximately 70 percent in 2001).

In 2000 epic floods ravaged the land and people, who mostly reside in the rural interior. A cholera epidemic broke out in the wake of the floods. Health-related problems have produced considerable minorities in Mozambique. It has one of the highest rates in Africa of people infected with HIV or suffering from AIDS. Parents who have died from this disease have left many orphans. War produced a sizable minority of handicapped soldiers and civilians, refugees, displaced persons, and further orphans.

While the country has an exceptional birth rate of nearly 3.8 percent, its rate of population growth is just under 0.8 percent. Only three percent of the population is over 65, and nearly two thirds of this group is female. Life expectancy is less than 32 years for both sexes. Two thirds of the population is under 21. Both adults, and even more so, older people are minorities. Males are 1.5 percent less than females, a surprising balance given the years of warfare. However, the number also reflects how war along with disease has equally devastated soldiers and civilians.

Mozambique has used education, particularly emphasis on literacy, as a basis for social, economic and cultural improvement. Such an effort may offer some long term opportunity for a common, beneficial development among the country's varied peoples.

EDWARD A. RIEDINGER

Further Reading

Azevedo, Mario Joaquim, *Historical Dictionary of Mozambique*, Metuchen, New Jersey: Scarecrow, 1991

Cabrita, João M., *Mozambique: The Tortuous Road to Democracy*, New York: Palgrave, 2000

Christie, Frances, and Joseph Hanlon, *Mozambique and the Great Flood of 2000*, Bloomington: Indiana University Press, 2001

Darch, Colin, *Mozambique*, World Bibliographical Series, vol. 78, Oxford, England, and Santa Barbara, California: ABC-Clio Press, 1987

Hall, Margaret, *Confronting Leviathan: Mozambique since Independence*, Athens: Ohio University Press, 1997

Muhammad, Elijah (African-American)

Elijah Poole (Muhammad), born in Sandersville, Georgia, was the founder and leader of the Nation of Islam. He claimed to have received the word of Allah (God) in 1931 and this teaching became the basis of the Nation's politically radical theology.

Poole attended school until the third grade, when he quit school to work in fields as a sharecropper. The realities of southern racism and poverty forced Poole to work to put food on his family's table. His parents Marie and Wali Poole, sharecroppers and former slaves, worked on a small cotton farm and raised thirteen children. Muhammad remembered his parents as subjects of cruel oppression by the white ruling class of post-Civil War Georgia. He continually spoke about the brutality he witnessed and its affects on his childhood. At the age of sixteen, Poole left home, finding random work and a wife, in Clara Evans. They would have eight children, Emmanuel, Ethel, Lottie, Nathaniel, Herbert, Elijah, Jr., Wallace and Akbar.

In 1923, as part of the wave of blacks moving into the North, Muhammad, Clara, and their two children, moved to Detroit, where he worked for the Cherokee Brick Company and the Southern Railroad Company. As with many African-Americans who joined this exodus as part of the Great Migration, Muhammad was in search of a better life. The economic opportunity and large black population (250,000) drew Poole to this presumably Northern promise land.

It was there, while working on a Chevrolet assembly line, that Muhammad met his mentor, Wallace Fard Muhammad, a silk peddler and founder of the Nation of Islam and Temple No. 1 in Detroit. Learning about a man from the East, and understanding that he was causing a stir, Muhammad attended a meeting at the Temple of Islam.

Shortly thereafter, in 1931, Poole, overwhelmed by the message and power of Fard, accepted his teachings. Poole acknowledged Fard as Allah, not as the creator, but the latest God that appears as man. He told Poole that he was sent, to waken the "spiritually dead," the so-called Negro in America. Before long, Poole had invited and convinced his entire family to accept the teachings of Fard. Fard embraced Poole as a student of sorts, renaming him "Karriem" and designating him as minister. Later he was promoted to "supreme minister" with the name of Elijah Muhammad, anointing him as the "last messenger."

Before vanishing, three and half years after their initial meeting, Fard taught Muhammad the essential teachings of the Nation of Islam: (1) black civilization dominated earth for trillions of years; (2) blacks were destined for slavery and were taken to Africa as part of a toughening up process; (3) Yacob's story, a history that chronicles the creation of the white race; and (4) that the domination of whites was coming to an end. In the meantime, Muhammad oversaw the development of independent black (Muslim) businesses, Islamic religious centers, schools, and the creation of The Final Call to Islam in 1934.

Muhammad soon became W.D. Fard's favorite student, working as an assistant minister of the Nation of Islam until 1934, when Fard mysteriously disappeared, leaving Muhammad in control of the burgeoning Nation of Islam.

While in Washington, DC, to conduct research and develop a Mosque, Muhammad was arrested on May 8, 1942 for allegedly evading the draft. He claimed however, that he refused rather than evaded the law on the grounds that he was first and foremost a Muslim who would not participate in a war he believed was fraught with "infidels" (Muhammed 1965).

Upon his release, Muhammed returned to New York to reinvigorate the Nation. He enhanced recruitment efforts, focusing on the most disempowered members of the black community. Under his post-War leadership, the organization grew into a leading force within the black community. He specifically called upon blacks to develop their own economic enterprises to become less dependent on the "white man." As such, the Nation slowly developed a number of businesses, ranging from agriculture, shipping and banking, to publishing and commerce. Under Muhammad's guidance, the Nation additionally built schools, a paramilitary defense wing (Fruit of Islam), attracting many new "converts" and establishing temples throughout the country. What linked all of their activities together, and the preachings of Muhammad were the goals of separating from whites, while creating a powerful black community based in Islam, all in preparation for the end of the white race.

Malcolm X was introduced to the Nation of Islam in 1948, while serving a prison term in Massachusetts. After his release in 1952, he met Elijah Muhammad and, the following year, moved into Muhammad's home. After serving as minister of temples in Boston and Philadelphia, Malcolm X became minister of New York's Temple 7 in 1954 and was soon recognized as the leading spokesman for the Nation of Islam. After several years of growing tension within the organization, Muhammad suspended Malcolm in 1963 for making controversial comments following President Kennedy's assassination.

Elijah Muhammad's vision of black liberation was in stark opposition to that of Martin Luther King, Jr. and the mainstream civil rights movement. While King and others sought integration through nonviolent protest (direct action), lobbying, voting and other means to demonstrate the moral depravity of racism, Muhammad advocated permanent separation of African-Americans and whites. He continually reminded the followers of the Nation that Allah would free African-Americans through an inevitable race war. As such, Muhammad barred its members from political participation, as in the directive to ignore the 1963 March on Washington. Disobeying such orders were grounds for expulsion from the Nation of Islam.

Muhammad died of congestive heart failure at the age of 77. Shortly after his death, Muhammad's followers split into two groups. One group, led by Elijah Muhammad's seventh son, Wallace Muhammad, eventually abandoned many of Elijah Muhammad's teachings and merged with traditional Islam. The other group, led by Minister Louis Farrakhan, continues to build the Nation of Islam according to Elijah Muhammad's teachings.

Capsule Biography:

Elijah Muhammad. Born Elijah Poole on October 7, 1897 in Sanderville, Georgia. Studied up until third grade in segregated Sanderville public schools. Assistant Minister of Temple No. 1, Detroit, 1931–34; Supreme Minister/Last Messenger of Allah, 1934–1975. Instrumental in growth of Nation of Islam, the procurement of black freedom and advancement of the principles of Black Nationalism. Died in Chicago, February 25, 1975.

DAVID LEONARD

See also **African-American Nationalism and Separatism; Farrakhan, Louis (African-American); King, Martin Luther, Jr. (African-American); Malcolm X (African-American)**

Selected Works

Message to the Blackman in America, Chicago: Muhammad Mosque of Islam No. 2, 1965

Further Reading

Evanzz, Karl, *The Messenger: The Rise and Fall of Elijah Muhammad*, New York: Vintage Books, 2001

Gardell, Mattias, *In the Name of Elijah Muhammad: Louis Farrakhan and the Nation of Islam*, Durham: Duke University Press, 1996

Lincoln, C. Eric, *The Black Muslims in America*, 3rd edition, Trenton: Africa World Press, 1994

Mulattos (South African Coloreds)

Capsule Summary

Location: Southern tip of the African continent, mostly in the Western Cape province of South Africa
Total Population: approximately 3.5 million
Languages: Afrikaans (majority) and English
Religions: Christian (majority) and Muslim

South African Coloreds are a people of mixed European, indigenous African and slave ancestry living in the southern tip of the African continent, mostly in the Western Cape province of South Africa. There are approximately 3.5 million Coloreds. Their first language is Afrikaans, a variant of the Dutch spoken by the seventeenth century colonists, which also borrowed grammar and vocabulary from Malay and other African and European languages. Most Coloreds are Christians (Dutch Reformed, Anglican, Congregational, Methodist, or Roman Catholic). Those who are Muslim are also known as Cape Malays. Coloreds are not nor have they ever been a homogeneous group. Their varied experiences reflect the complex histories and composition of South African society which was and is socially divided not only on the bases of religion but also region, social class, ethnicity, race, and gender. Over a 350 year period, South Africa has evolved from Dutch settlement, to British colony, to apartheid state, and finally in 1994, to a multiracial democracy. For most Coloreds, their history begins and continues in the Western Cape province in general and the city of Cape Town also known as "The Mother City" in particular.

History of the Social and Political Formation of Coloreds

South Africa is the most highly industrialized country in Africa. Before April 27,1994, when Nelson Mandela became the first democratically elected Black president, South Africa was the last nation in continental Africa ruled by a white minority. For over 40 years, the white-controlled National Party enforced a legislated system of racial segregation known as apartheid, which divided the land and its people based on four main racial groupings: black, white, Asian, and Colored. Coloreds are the mixed race descendants of the first Dutch settlers and the indigenous African population (Khoikhoi and San) or slaves who were brought to the Cape in the eighteenth century from other parts of Africa (Mozambique, Madagascar, Angola and Guinea) as well as the Dutch East Indies and parts of South and South East Asia (Indonesia, Sri Lanka, India, and Malaysia).

The term Colored dates back to the emancipation of slaves in 1834. Both the 1865 and the 1875 Census recorded Coloreds as all nonwhites including Africans (the remaining Khoikhoi and San also known as the derogatory term Hottentots as well as those known as Bantu-speaking people or the more problematic label Kaffirs, who migrated from East and West Africa to South Africa in 500 BCE and had settled in the North and East). By the turn of the century, both the colonial administration and the subordinate group of mixed race descendants of inter-racial marriages and sexual liaisons between indigenous Africans, Europeans and slaves redefined Colored as a separate and intermediate category, which excluded Africans. Precipitated by a banking crisis in 1866, it is argued that dramatic shifts in the ethnic composition of the work force in the Western Cape in part contributed to the redefinition of the Colored category. Before 1904, Bantu-speaking Africans comprised a small percentage of the working class. By 1904, over 45 percent of unskilled laborers were Bantu-speaking. In the latter part of the nineteenth century, the British had also imported Social Darwinism, whose proponents put forward the false notion that Europeans were superior to Africans on the evolutionary scale. When popularized, such thinking fueled European hostility towards Africans including racial stereotyping.

According to this racial hierarchy, mixed race Coloreds were allegedly inferior to their European but superior to their African ancestors. It was believed that mixed race people's European lineage was evidence of their superiority. Enforcing this divide and rule ideology was a strategy to ensure that mixed race Coloreds did not form alliances with other non-Europeans. At a time when, discrimination against all nonwhites was rising, the Colored elite began to assert their autonomous social and political position and in so doing distanced themselves from Africans. Influenced by the political advancements of parallel Colored organizations, the 1904 Census recognized them as a separate group distinct from whites and Africans. With the Population Registration Act of 1950, which socially engineered Coloreds as a discrete population group, apartheid legislation completed this consolidation process. The system afforded Coloreds and Asians (Indian and Chinese) fewer advantages than their white European counterparts (Dutch, German, French Huguenots, British, Portuguese, Jewish, Greek, Italian) but more privileges (education, employment, voting and property rights) than black Africans (Zulu, Xhosa, Swazi, Ndebele, South Sotho-Tswana, Venda, Tsonga).

Since 1994, there have been ongoing debates regarding the fate of Colored communities in a democratic South Africa. Are they black (a badge of resistance to apartheid and a symbol of political solidarity with other oppressed blacks), Colored (an assertion of their historical roots and an artifact of apartheid), or *bruin mense* (brown people and as such a legitimate minority group)? Not discounting the genealogical fact of racial mixing during colonialism and slavery, this debate is complicated by the fact that the concept of mixed race itself has been contested. The term mixed race suggests the existence of pure races and, some would argue, reinforces false ideologies of racial purity and pollution that were at the heart of apartheid institutions.

Contemporary Coloreds in South Africa descend from the offspring of sexual unions between Dutch settlers and either imported slaves or indigenous Africans (San and Khoikhoi). With the exception of a subgroup of practicing Muslim Coloreds called Cape Malays, Colored cultural practices including language and religion were almost identical to that of the Dutch now known as Afrikaners. This unbreakable bond between whites and Coloreds was forged during slavery and is evident in surnames carried by contemporary Coloreds.

In 1828, the government, under British control since 1806, made English the only official language of the colony and abolished slavery in 1834. After official emancipation on December 1, 1834, Cape Coloreds reaped few benefits. Under the apprenticeship system which lasted from 1834 to 1838, slaves were to continue working as laborers for their former owners. The Masters and Servants Ordinance of 1841 dictated that though they were no longer slaves, they were still servants. In 1853 the parliamentary franchise was established, which independent of race entitled anyone over twenty one, male and a property owner or with appropriate income to stand for parliament. In 1893, when the Colored community began gaining political ground, the then prime minister Cecil Rhodes found loopholes in the legislation which impeded their progress. Colored children attended inferior mission schools, while their white counterparts attended government schools which provided education comparable to that available in Europe. On average, Coloreds received lower wages than whites.

By the time of the Boer War in 1899, parallel Colored organizations demonstrated their strength by calling for the formation of a Colored Corps to fight against the Boers. After the war, in 1902, the African Political Organisation (APO) was established "to promote unity between colored races"-based on the nineteenth century notion of Colored as nonwhite. In time the APO became a platform for "Colored People's social, political and civil rights-such as education and franchise." The Cape Malay medical doctor Abdullah Abdurahman is most closely associated with the APO, which was instrumental in the establishment of Colored trade unions such as the APO Federation of Labour founded in 1919. This was at a time when Colored labor preference policies were being implemented and applied.

White supremacy was institutionalized in the form of discriminatory legislation. These laws were also set in motion to ensure that Coloreds and Africans did not form strategic political alliances. Devised by the South African Natives Commission, the 1913 and 1926 Native Land Acts enforced territorial segregation by which the country was divided into black and white areas. Eighty-seven percent of the land was allocated to whites and 13 percent of the land was set aside as Native Reserves. During the period from 1904 to 1948,

Coloreds suffered certain setbacks, such as the introduction of the Civilised Labour Policy which favored White workers or the creation of the Colored Affairs Department (CAD) in 1943. Colored exemption from influx control among other preferential policies ensured that antagonism between Coloreds and Africans persisted, and solidarity between Colored political parties such as the APO, the Afrikaner National Bond (ANB), the National Liberation League (NLL) and other political bodies such as the Industrial and Commercial Worker's Union (ICU), the African National Congress (ANC), the All African Convention (AAC) could not be sustained.

The foundation of the entire apartheid structure was the Population Registration Act of 1950, which dictated that all South Africans must be classified as members of a particular group, which were then subdivided. Members of these statutory racial groups were either afforded or denied differential privileges. There were two main groups, whites and nonwhites. Of the whites, there were Afrikaans speaking, English speaking and immigrants (Italians, Greeks, etc.). Of the nonwhites, there were Coloreds, Asians, and those designated Bantu (African). Within the nonwhite group, Coloreds were subdivided into seven categories: Cape Colored, Malay, Griqua, Chinese, Indian, other Asiatic, other Colored. According to this act, Asians were included as Coloreds. In practice, a distinction was generally made between Asians and Coloreds. Bantus or Africans were subdivided into eight groups, North-Sotho, South-Sotho, Swazi, Tsonga, Tswana, Venda, Xhosa, Zulu.

The four generic racial classifications Colored, black, Asian and white were imposed by the apartheid state and in no way reflected the diverse histories within and among groups. The social formation of the Colored group emerged in four ways. There were the Christian Cape Coloreds, offspring of sexual unions between settler Europeans and African slaves from Mozambique, Madagascar, Angola and Guinea. There were the Muslim Cape Malay who were the descendants of liaisons between European settlers and Asian slaves from what are now known as Indonesia, Sri Lanka, India, and Malaysia. There were also offspring from the intermixing of African and Asian slaves with the indigenous San and Khoikhoi. Until their gradual decimation by the Europeans as a result of small pox, sexually transmitted diseases, and fire power, the San and the Khoikhoi are the original inhabitants, who were said to have populated Southern Africa from about 10,000 BCE. The Khoikhoi are said to have migrated from what is now Botswana and are also thought to be the by-products of earlier intermarriage between Bantu and San. They were located most predominantly on the Cape Coast. There was also intermixing between Asian and African slaves and other Africans such as Xhosas, who are located in the Eastern Cape. The offspring of sexual unions between indigenous Khoikhoi and primarily Boers were known as Basters and could be found in the Northwestern Cape. With the exodus of Boers from the Cape Colony as a result of British reoccupation, the number of these children increased.

Apartheid dictated that the boundaries between white and African were clearly demarcated as were those between Asian and African and white and Asian. Who was classified as Colored as opposed to African or white was never a straightforward matter and was based on subjective criteria such as physical appearance and social mannerisms. Racial classification determined an individual's residence, education and potential for economic mobility. Africans were still subject to influx control, but now had to carry pass books for the purposes of working outside their designated locations or townships. Europeans, Coloreds and Asians were issued identity documents, which did not restrict their movements. In 1955, the Colored Labour Preference Policy improved the relative position of Coloreds and widened the social divide between Africans and Coloreds. Unequal apartheid policies provided incentives for Africans to attempt classification as Coloreds and for Coloreds to try to "pass for white."

There was and is a tension between the ways in which racial categories organized South African society during apartheid and resistance to this legislated imposition. During the Black Consciousness movement in the 1960s and 1970s, many Africans, Asians, and Coloreds adopted the collective political identification black. Under the leadership of the South African Students' Movement, which was the black consciousness organization working in secondary education, an uprising took place in the African township of Soweto. On June 16, 1976, 15,000 African youths took to the streets in protest against the decree that certain subjects must now be taught in Afrikaans. Many were injured and two were killed including twelve-year-old Hector Petersen who became the defining symbol of the brutality of apartheid. Within days, the protest spread to other townships and galvanized many Coloreds in the Western and Eastern Cape, who had been inspired by the Black Consciousness movement to join forces with Africans. Steve Biko was one of the main proponents of this movement. His activism contributed to his death in custody in 1977.

The Black Consciousness movement had been preceded in the 1950s by extra-parliamentary campaigns of non-violent mass action organized by the ANC, the Pan-African Congress (PAC), and the Communist Party of South Africa (CPSA). Two radical Colored organizations were also active at this time: the South African Colored People's Organisation (SACPO) and the Non-European Unity Movement (NEUM). Evidence of political unity across non-European groups was the National Day of Protest on the June 26, 1950, which was supported by leaders of the ANC, the APO, and the South African Indian Congress (SAIC) and was spearheaded by Nelson Mandela. To coincide with the 300-year celebration of Dutch settlement, on June 26, 1952, the Defiance Campaign against Unjust Laws was launched, wherein protesters deliberately broke apartheid laws. In July 1952, 20 leaders were charged under the Suppression of Communism Act, which prohibited any form of opposition to the White minority government. In 1954, this was amended to ban anyone for "furthering the aims of communism."

Non-violent protests of the 1960s were met with government violence and retribution. Up to and throughout the 1980s, state violence and political protest persisted. The South African economy continued to suffer from international sanctions which were imposed as a result of the government's racial policies. In 1984, the government introduced a new constitution that transformed the office of the President from a figurehead, which it became with the formation of the Republic of South Africa in 1961, to the position of monarch. The Colored Voters Act had disenfranchised Coloreds. Through the formation of a tricameral (white, Colored, Asian but not African) parliament, the new Constitution would provide Coloreds and Asians with official representation in government. Opposition to the new constitution led to the formation of the United Democratic Front (UDF), which represented the banned ANC and acted as a multiracial umbrella for 575 affiliated organizations. In 1988, the UDF and 16 other organizations were officially banned.

By the time F.W. De Klerk was elected President in 1989, the wheels of transition were already in motion. After the elections, he released many of the Rivonia Eight. When Parliament reconvened in 1990, De Klerk announced that he would be lifting the bans on the ANC, the SACP, the PAC and all affiliated organizations. He also intended to begin negotiations, which would lead South Africa towards a new political structure. As he would play a crucial role in this process of transition, after 27 years in prison, on February 11, 1990, Nelson Mandela was released from prison. Following Mandela's release, in 1991, key apartheid acts were overturned, including The Population Registration Act, the Group Areas and Natives Land Acts. The Abolition of Racially Based Measures Act, which abolished 60 pieces of apartheid legislation, was also passed. In 1993, the tricameral parliament agreed an interim constitution. This paved the way for the first democratic elections on April 27, 1994, wherein every South African adult was entitled to vote. On May 2, 1994, Nelson Mandela was sworn in as the new president of South Africa.

It is argued by some that the affirmative action policies and post-apartheid land redistribution programs favor Africans over Coloreds. Two phrases which sum up this Colored resentment are: "we were not white enough under apartheid, now we are not black enough post-apartheid" and "this is apartheid in reverse . . . Blacks have forgotten that some of us were part of the struggle also." This discontent has led to a new form of Brown Nationalism wherein Colored activists, such as Peter Marais, have been campaigning for a program of economic and political empowerment for Coloreds. This Colored demand for priority treatment is in part based on reclamation of their Khoikhoi and San ancestry (The United Nations recently granted the Khoikhoi and San First Nation status).

Lingering concerns suggest that the precise social and political roles for Coloreds in the ongoing projects of transformation, reconstruction and development are unclear. If whites, Africans, Coloreds and Asians continue to cling to the same ethnic and racial categories that were officially abolished in 1991, one could argue that the future is uncertain for all South Africans. The challenges facing first Mandela's and now Thabo Mbeki's administration are how to create equal opportunities for all South Africans when the playing field has not always been level.

JAYNE IFEKWUNIGWE

See also **Apartheid; Mandela, Nelson; South Africa**

Further Reading

Bickford-Smith, Vivian, *Ethnic Pride and Racial Prejudice in Victorian Cape Town*, Cambridge: Cambridge University Press, 1995

February, Vernon, *Mind Your Colour: The 'Coloured' Stereotype in South African Literature*, London: Kegan Paul, 1981

Field, Sean, "Ambiguous Belongings: Negotiating Hybridity in Cape Town," *Kronos: Journal of Cape History*, no.25 (1998/1999)

Goldin, Ian, *Making Race: The Politics and Economics of Coloured Identity in South Africa*, Cape Town: Maskew Miller Longman, 1987

James, Wilmot, Daria Caliguire, and Kerry Cullinan, editors, *Now That We Are Free: Coloured Communities in a Democratic South Africa*, Cape Town: IDASA (Institute for Democracy in South Africa), 1996

Keegan, Timothy, *Colonial South Africa and the Origins of the Racial Order*, London: Leicester University Press, 1996

Maharaj, Gitanjali, editor, *Between Unity and Diversity: Essays on Nation-Building in Post-Apartheid South Africa*, Cape Town: IDASA and David Philip Publishers, 1999

Marx, Anthony, *Making Race and Nation: A Comparison of the United States, South Africa, and Brazil*, Cambridge: Cambridge University Press, 1998

Nuttall, Sarah, and Carli Coetzee, editors, *Negotiating the Past: The Making of Memory in South Africa*, Oxford: Oxford University Press, 1998

Shell, Robert C.H., *Children of Bondage: A Social History of the Slave Society at the Cape of Good Hope, 1652–1838*, Wesleyan, Connecticut: Wesleyan University Press, 1994

Spencer, Jon Michael, *The New Colored People*, New York and London: New York University Press, 1997

Western, John, *Outcast Cape Town*, Minneapolis: University of Minnesota Press, 1981

Multiculturalism

In the last decades of the twentieth century, international migrations, the emergence of new states, the end of the Cold War, economic and cultural globalization have contributed to significant changes in the ethnic composition of societies. The numbers of persons involved are much larger than in previous migration waves. *De facto*, these movements of population (refugee movements, asylum seekers, permanent immigration, contract labor) have led to the creation of multicultural societies, even if the states concerned did not apply multiculturalism as a policy strategy, as is the case in Australia and Canada.

International migrations imply the admission in individual states of great numbers of individuals belonging to different ethnic groups. Former colonial states such as some Arab, Asian or African states sent migrants who had traditionally occupied low-status positions in relation to international standards, and desired to better their situations. International migrations include the problematic sphere of integration into the social, economic, and cultural systems of the host society. To admit and to integrate are closely related concepts. Politics of admission are linked to disparate integration policies, such as the German guest-worker (*Gastarbeiter*) model, the British pluralist model, and the French assimilationist model.

The topic of multiculturalism indicates still another dimension: that of the individual actor. Migrants construct personal identities often by melding elements of their country of origin to those of the receiving country. This "double belonging," in which an individual belongs to two different cultural or ethnic groups at once, shapes the actions of individuals and groups. It influences attitudes and norms insofar as the international migrant of the first generation links two social worlds. The problem raised by a multicultural society is how to situate these migrants within their own culture and the culture of the host society. In Europe and the United States especially and in differing ways, political decisions influence the outcome of these integration processes. In the United States, multiculturalism as a policy commits immigrants to interact with their own communities. Conflicting ethnic situations such as those in Rwanda (the 1994 genocide) and Bosnia and Herzegovina (Serbian-Croat war in 1992–95) challenge the need to cope with ethnic and cultural diversity through policies that favor minority groups' rights in modern societies. Multiculturalism is a democratic policy response to such ethnic diversities. As a systematic response to such challenges, a few countries including Australia, Canada, and Sweden have adopted multiculturalism as policy.

Social theorists such as Emile Durkheim, Max Weber and Karl Marx argued the loss of saliency of ethnic groups in modern-industrialized societies in favor of class as one of the principal elements structuring social life. Yet, the conflicts of the last quarter of the twentieth century witnessed a rediscovery of ethnicity accompanied by the development of international policies that ought to contribute to improved relations among ethnic groups.

Problems of Contemporary Multi-Ethnic Societies

The rapid adoption of the notion of multiculturalism in the last decades was linked to an increasing awareness of the limits of existing policies related to interethnic relations. The Australian scholar Christine Inglis (1996) distinguished three interrelated referents of multiculturalism which are nevertheless distinctive: the demographic-descriptive, the ideological-normative and the programmatic-political. According to Inglis, the *demographic-descriptive* occurs where multicultural is used to describe ethnically or racially diverse segments in the population of a society or State. Existing differences are seen as socially significant, but may vary over time and space. I*deological-normative* multiculturalism suggests a model for political action based on sociological, ethical, and philosophical considerations surrounding ethnic diversity within contemporary society. Here rights of individuals and social groups and their equitable access to fundamental societal institutions are emphasized with an impetus on reducing social conflicts based on inequality. *Programmatic-political* multiculturalism refers to specific types of programs and polities designed to respond to and manage ethnic diversity. This notion of multiculturalism was first used by a Canadian Commission which in 1965 recommended that multiculturalism replace the bicultural (French and British) policy in Canadian society.

Only a few states in the world can be described as ethnically homogenous. Most of the societies in the present-day world are characterized by multiethnic social identities. Ethnic relations in those countries which have recently gained independence are often violent as a result of the collapse of states or end of colonialism. New relationships must be established between native-born ethnic groups and immigrants in such cases. The difference in legal status is often accompanied by social divisions between migrants and dominant ethnic groups. The range of variations of ethnic relations is most marked in Western European countries. Until the 1970s, Germany, Switzerland and other European countries accepted guest-workers. In the 1980s, family reunification contributed to a stabilization of these migrant communities in host countries. In the 1990s, renewed needs for labor allowed Germany to introduce some 200,000 workers from Central and Eastern Europe. In Switzerland, 72,000 people were admitted. France, Belgium and the United Kingdom received large contingents of migrants from their former colonial territories. Since January 1992, the free circulation of members of the European Union served as another important source of international migrations. European countries have furthermore large population groups of students, businesspeople, and refugees with different rights to residence. For countries such as Australia, Canada, and the United States, which have long histories of settler immigration, new regions of origin of migrants meant changes in the composition of ethnic minorities. These countries differ from others in their acceptance of permanent settlement and immigration. In Australia, for example, the access to citizenship is quite simple with a basic requirement of two years of permanent residence.

Policy-issues in multiethnic societies include topics such as social and welfare services, housing, health, education, employment, political decision-making and access to citizenship. Persons concerned are not only migrants and their spouses, but often locally born children. Further policy issues include the maintenance of distinctive elements of ethnic cultures, such as language and religion. The avoidance of racism and discrimination is another issue. The involvement of the minority in national identity constitutes an important symbolic factor. The significance of these elements varies according to the group and over time.

Policy Models of Multi-Ethnic States

On one side are policies based on an assimilationist model (such as that observed in France) that ask individuals to abandon their particular linguistic, cultural and social characteristics and accept those of the dominant group. Assimilation (forced or voluntary) does not emphasize the maintenance of cultural, linguistic or social practices. It is argued that due to the complete absorption in the host society, ethnic conflicts disappear. In this model, the individual is forced to change rather than the legal, educational or health institutions of the state. On the other side are policies emphasizing a differentialist model which avoids conflicts by minimizing contacts with ethnic minorities. An extreme version of this model is the expulsion of ethnic minorities.

More common are politics that limit the participation of minority members in society (in Germany for example.). The third approach is multiculturalism (as seen in Canada) which aims at integrating individuals and groups into society without losing their unique characteristics. Participation is often cited as the reason for the absence of ethnic conflict.

Multiculturalism in Practice

Canada was the first country to adopt an official policy of multiculturalism in 1971. The initial policy focus was on the right to preserve one's own culture as a part of Canadian national identity. Later on, issues such as equality, social participation and national unity were evoked. Legislation supported this policy: discrimination on the basis of race or ethnic origin was forbidden; ethnic cultures and languages should be protected. Like Canada, Australia is an immigrant nation that adopted a multicultural model in order to deal with a nascent awareness of the deficiencies of the assimilation model. The disadvantages which faced many non-English speaking background immigrants led to the emergence of an ethnic rights movement. In 1978, Australia adopted multiculturalism as official policy. The aim was first to serve newly arrived immigrants with culturally and linguistically adequate settlement services. Second, it was admitted that cultural maintenance should be supported. In a later phase, the emphasis lay on issues of social inequity and racism. The Australian policy on multiculturalism was formulated in the 1989 National Agenda for a Multicultural Australia, which was applicable to all Australians, including the Aboriginal population. The National Agenda identified several issue including the rights to cultural identity and social justice, and the need for effective use of the skills of all Australians.

Sweden's national identity was not based on an immigrant ideology. However, after the Second World War, the country received large numbers of refugees and Finnish workers originating from the free movement in the Nordic labor market after 1954. Furthermore, workers from the former Yugoslavia contributed to the expanding economy. In the 1990s, asylum seekers from Asia, Africa and other non-European regions contributed to Swedish cultural diversity. In 1975, the earlier policy of assimilation was changed by emphasizing three principles: equality, freedom of choice, and partnership. Equality was designed to give immigrants the same standards of living as the autochthonous population. Freedom of choice signified the right to choose between one's own cultural identity and that of Sweden. Partnership implied that the different groups (minority groups and the native population) benefited from common activities. The Swedish policy is often referred to as integration. Recent policy measures included issues such as the role of minorities in the labor market, and in housing.

A common feature of Canada, Australia, and Sweden is the focus on language and educational issues. All three countries have concentrated on the need for migrants to be fluent in the national language. To assure this, their governments have instituted programs to language instruction. However, critics have noted that that neither special language instruction or other types of educational programs are sufficient alone to ensure equality in participation and access. Emphasis, it has been argued, must be on the needs of individuals, and not only on the functions of systems. In these countries, issues of discrimination in employment and other areas received therefore a particular anti-discrimination legislation. These measures prove the necessity of complementary initiatives to achieve multicultural policy aims.

Currently, there is evidence that the assimilationist model is being questioned because assimilation is not taking place as intended. The growing level of international mobility and the existence of networks among migrants across nations evince culturally based distinctiveness such as migrants who prefer contacts with their own families staying in their home countries by frequent traveling or inexpensive internet or phone communication. Nevertheless, the existence of large immigrant minority groups in multiethnic societies suggest multiculturalism as an alternative policy model to other models. In its first phases, it requires a much larger role of the state than other models. This active engagement is compatible with political traditions in many European and Asian states, and other regions of the world. Yet, the adoption of multiculturalism over other national models of integration seems difficult. Its emphasis on a participatory and consultative process represents nevertheless an advance in democratic processes in multiethnic societies. Even if some states consider that the support of a multicultural model encounters difficulties, programs and objectives compatible with a multicultural model may be implemented. As such, they may be valuable in some societies, even if other integration models are favored. The popularity of the notion of multiculturalism results among others and not at least from its emphasis on the fact that diversity is considered as a benefit for majority and minority ethnic groups.

Many states favor models that can be characterized as assimilationist or differentialist. In situations characterized by violent ethnic conflicts where a tradition of inter-ethnic hostility exists, the role of multiculturalism as a policy model is complex at the very least. The positive message of multiculturalism to minorities may here be represented as a resistance to integration. Multiculturalism as a policy model permits the address of democratically societal issues of inequality and exclusion, and contradicts the idea that the majority is opposed to the rights of minority groups.

ULRIKE SCHUERKENS

See also **Assimilation; Australia; Bosnia and Herzegovina; Canada; Colonialism; Diaspora; Integration; Population Shifts; Refugees; Rwanda**

Further Reading

Bennett, David, editor, *Multicultural States: Rethinking Difference and Identity*, London: Routledge, 1998

Inglis, Christine, *Multiculturalism: New Policy Responses to Diversity*, MOST Policy Paper 4, Paris: UNESCO, 1996

Modood, Tariq, and Pnina Werbner, editors, *The Politics of Multiculturalism in the New Europe: Racism, Identity and Community*, London: Zed Books, 1997

Rex, John, "Multikulturalismus in Europa und Nordamerika," *Berliner Journal für Soziologie*, 2, 1996

Schuerkens, Ulrike, editor, "International Migrations and the Issue of Multiculturalism," Special Issue of the *International Review of Sociology*, 10, no.3 (2000)

Wieviorka, Michel, *Une société fragmentée? Le multiculturalisme en débat*, Paris: Ed. de la Découverte, 1996

Multiethnic State

A multiethnic state is a twentieth-century term for an old reality: a state that rules several ethnic and/or religious minorities within its borders. In the past two centuries, the leaders of such states have tried various means of governing their diverse populations, with fateful consequences for the world. A review of several prominent multiethnic entities is useful for determining key elements in their success or failure.

The Ottoman Empire ruled many ethnic groups in its lifetime. When they appeared in Europe in the fourteenth century, the Ottomans sought to extend the reach of Islam and conquered much of the Middle East and southeastern Europe by the seventeenth century. The Ottoman rulers organized the conquered peoples, among which were Arabs, Greeks, Armenians, Serbs, Bulgarians, and Romanians into *millets*—communities based on their religion. In the first centuries of Ottoman rule, this arrangement worked well enough. The non-Muslims did not enjoy the same rights as Muslims—they paid more taxes, they were not equal under the law and faced sundry other restrictions. By comparison with states like Inquisition-era Spain, however, life in the Ottoman state was satisfactory, because the non-Muslim populations could live quietly and practice their religion as they wished.

This changed with the onset of imperial decline in the eighteenth century. The Ottoman empire was most effective in the fifteenth through seventeenth centuries, when it enjoyed a series of gifted leaders and conquest came easily. After Ottoman warriors were stopped outside Vienna in 1683, a combination of corruption in the leadership and a breakdown of central authority led to lawlessness and violence against non-Muslims. The Greeks and Serbs responded by rebelling against Ottoman rule during the first decades of the nineteenth century. The Romanians began to break away in the 1850s, and Bosnians and Bulgarians revolted in the eastern crisis of 1875–1878. Even the Armenian community, known for centuries as the most loyal *millet*, eventually became disillusioned. They did not revolt, preferring to lobby quietly with the great powers for provisions guaranteeing their security in the 1878 Treaty of Berlin. However, this move turned the increasingly besieged Ottoman leadership against them. Sultan Abdulhamid II saw the Armenians' solicitation of great power patronage as treasonous and helped incite pogroms against Armenian areas in 1894–95 and 1909 in which thousands were killed.

In 1908, the reform-minded Young Turk regime deposed Abdulhamid and declared its commitment to secularization and reform. Some hoped they would decentralize the state and enfranchise its Armenian and other non-Muslim subjects. However, faced with major territorial losses in war and continuing demands from Armenians for autonomy, they chose instead to attempt to rid the empire of what they regarded as a treacherous minority. They accomplished this in apparently coordinated attacks on Armenian areas in 1915 under the cover of World War I, in the course of which hundreds of thousands of Armenians died. Just three years prior to its demise, the multiethnic Ottoman state committed the first act of ethnic mass murder in the twentieth century.

Following World War I, it was believed that large multiethnic states that suppressed the aspirations of ethnic minorities had caused the war. The Versailles peacemakers accordingly tried to create compact national states from the ruins of the Ottoman, Russian and German empires. However, they found it impossible to reconcile geopolitical reality with the desire to punish the losers and reward the victors. Consequently, some new states looked like small versions of the dead empires. The new Czechoslovak state was the brainchild of T.G. Masaryk, a philosophy professor at Prague University. Early in World War I, he began campaigning for an independent Czech and Slovak state. He lobbied the British and French governments, rallied support in American émigré communities and mustered a Czech legion to fight alongside the Allies. At the Versailles peace conference, Masaryk's efforts were crowned with success in the creation of a new "Czechoslovak" state. But Masaryk wanted more than Czech and Slovak majority lands. He believed that the Hungarian lands near the Danube to the south would be important natural frontiers, and that the coal-rich Sudetenland, with its large German population, would be essential to the new state's viability. The peacemakers gave him what he wanted. The Sudeten Germans were outraged. Their representatives declared before the peace conference that they wanted to live in Germany, not Czechoslovakia. Their protest was unavailing because the peacemakers wished to reward their ally, Masaryk, and keep the new Germany small and impotent.

The Germans' unhappiness notwithstanding, Czechoslovakia functioned well at first. In fact, German citizens escaped the onerous reparations levied on their relatives in Germany and enjoyed full rights in a functioning democracy. However, the worldwide financial crisis of the early 1930s and the rise of a frankly revisionist Nazi Germany after 1933 combined to poison relations between the Czechs and Germans. The financial crisis hit the industrial Sudetenland harder than

other areas, causing increased resentment, and the Nazi party immediately began to agitate among the Sudeten Germans. As time went on, the Germans became increasingly aggressive with the Czech leadership, demanding by April 1938 a Nazi German autonomous entity within Czechoslovakia. Czech leaders correctly interpreted these moves as dangerous and rejected them, until Adolf Hitler demanded the outright transfer of the Sudeten Germans at the Munich conference of 1938. Hungarian representatives then demanded the return of the majority Hungarian lands, after which Slovak leaders declared they wanted a separate arrangement. In March 1939, when the Germans attacked what remained of Czechoslovakia, yet another multiethnic state lay in ruins.

The aftermath of World War II simultaneously witnessed the resurrection of the Czech state and the emphatic rejection of its multiethnic character. The new government dealt harshly with its remaining Germans, whom it deemed responsible for Czech suffering in the war. Czech officials and their counterparts in Poland stood by as millions of Germans were forcibly evicted from their homes and turned out into the bitter cold winter of 1945–46.

On the other hand, the multiethnic idea found new life in postwar Yugoslavia. Cobbled together by the same peacemakers who had made the Czechoslovak state, the first Yugoslavia joined Serbs, Croats, Slovenes, Bosnians, Macedonians and Albanians in one administrative unit. Serb-Croat animosity over control of the state and Italian irredentist activities helped weaken the state before Axis intervention and partition in 1941. A bloody struggle against the occupiers ensued, within which a civil war between rival resistance groups raged. Out of this cauldron emerged J.B. Tito and the Communist-affiliated Partisan movement. They had fought successfully against the invaders while winning the allegiance of much of the former Yugoslavia with promises of a better future under the Partisan banner, "Brotherhood and Unity."

The state began auspiciously. It included six republics—Slovenia, Croatia, Serbia, Macedonia, Bosnia, Montenegro—each of which had guarantees of political and economic and linguistic equality. After a dramatic 1948 separation from J.V. Stalin and the rest of the Communist world, Yugoslavia became the darling of the western world, for its apparent resolution of the south Slav question and innovative economic experiments. Throughout the 1950s and 60s, Yugoslavia presented itself as a harmonious, multiethnic state nominally associated with the socialist camp, yet open to the west.

The undisputed key to Yugoslavia's success was its founder, J.B. Tito He enjoyed universal respect, thanks to his leadership in the war, and had a gift for balancing the wishes—and resentments—of all the constituent groups. For example, he regularly took disproportionate amounts of revenue from the wealthier republics, such as Croatia and Slovenia, and distributed them in the poorer areas, so that those citizens would enjoy a semblance of economic equality. When the wealthier republics protested, Tito would resurrect the ghosts of the country's fratricidal conflict, reminding them of their good fortune. He could and did use his absolute authority to punish overt displays of nationalist sentiment or pointed criticism, imprisoning even former comrades such as Milovan Djilas.

Unfortunately, Tito proved to be mortal. His 1980 death, which coincided with a severe economic crisis, robbed the country of its lone unifying principle. Slovenes and Croats promptly renewed their complaints of economic exploitation by the federal government, while Serbs decried years of second-class treatment in the Tito years. Meanwhile, a serious crisis between Serbs and Albanians in the Kosovo region was brewing. An opportunistic Serbian politician, Slobodan Milosevic, championed the Serbs there in 1987 and used his sudden fame to wage a ruthless campaign for the national leadership. Alarmed by what they perceived as Milosevic's intent to impose Serb domination on Yugoslavia, Slovenes and Croats declared their independence. This led directly to bloody Serb-Croat conflict over Bosnia, in which both sides claimed territory and attempted to expel by violence Bosnian Muslim residents That conflict destroyed the much-touted multiethnic paradise of Yugoslavia less than a decade after an acclaimed Winter Olympic games in the Bosnian capital, Sarajevo.

The United States represents a continuing, if imperfect, model of multiethnic success. For most of its existence, it has welcomed immigrants from troubled areas worldwide. Newcomers typically settle in large cities such as New York or Los Angeles, where they can draw strength from other immigrants as they find employment and learn the common language, English. After acquiring citizenship, they can vote in annual local and national elections, where they often find they have inordinate influence because they can represent the margin of victory for ambitious candidates. They absorb the unspoken understanding that old world conflicts do not belong in the new country, and they enjoy freedom of conscience in the absence of an official religion. To be sure, many United States residents of longer standing regard newcomers with skepticism. Some have established political action committees dedicated to restricting immigration and/or establishing English as the mandatory language of administration. In the main, however, there has been remarkably little conflict in the twentieth century between ethnic minorities and the United States government, which continues to absorb millions more each year.

Based on the previous examples, it appears that a successful multiethnic state will have certain fundamental criteria. It will ideally be a secular entity. The Ottoman Empire was an avowed theocracy, which regarded non-Muslims as second-class citizens. This had many implications over time, not the least of which was that non-Muslims could not count on the courts to protect them from lawlessness when order inevitably broke down in the eighteenth and nineteenth centuries. Their only recourse was violent revolt or appeals to the Great Powers, both of which were regarded and punished as treason even by reform-minded Ottoman governments. A second necessity for a modern multiethnic state is voluntary association and consensus. The Sudeten Germans enjoyed full rights in a functioning Czechoslovak democracy, but they were forced into that arrangement and never really reconciled to life there. When conditions worsened for all nationalities, they quickly embraced Nazi agitators, who promised them what they had always wanted: union with Germany. Finally, successful multiethnic states have strong and well-established national institutions that transcend the influence of any one individual. Emerging from three decades of ethnic conflict, beleaguered Yugoslav citizens undoubtedly benefited from Tito's strong leadership, a combination of cunning, common experience and absolute authority. He was the chief executive, judge and legislator in Yugoslavia. Yet he failed to create institutions that would maintain unity among the constituent groups after his passing. Milosevic lacked the ability and the inclination to be a force for unity. But he was able to demagogue his way to the national leadership and rerun the old nightmare of ethnic warfare, based on Tito's example of one-man rule. The Balkans are much the poorer for that.

Multiethnic states have caused an inordinate amount of trouble in the twentieth century. Yet they will likely continue to be a feature of the geopolitical landscape in the 21st, because of the prohibitive costs of independent existence for smaller peoples. Secularism, consensus, respect for the rule of law and a spirit of inclusiveness appear to be the most reliable foundation for such states and their diverse populations.

BRIGIT FARLEY

Further Reading

Gross, Feliks, *The Civic and the Tribal State. The State, Ethnicity and the Multiethnic State*, Westport: Greenwood Press, 1998

Jelavich, Barbara, *History of the Balkans*, 2 vols., Cambridge: Cambridge University Press, 1983

Macartney, C.A., *National States and National Minorities*, New York: Russell and Russell, 1968

Naimark, Norman, *Fires of Hatred: Ethnic Cleansing in 20th Century Europe*, Cambridge: Harvard University Press, 2001

Rothschild, Joseph, *East Central Europe between the Two World Wars*, Seattle: University of Washington Press, 1974

Muslims in Africa

Capsule Summary

Location: Africa; largest concentrations in North and West Africa
Total Population: approximately 195 million
Religion: Islam

Muslims are people who practice Islam, the religion preached by Muhammad in the early 600s CE. Islam means submission to the will of God (*Allah*). Islam is the second largest of the world's religions, and Muslim majorities exist in more than forty-eight countries and form a significant minority in many others. Out of Africa's population of about 450,000,000, Muslims account for nearly 44 percent, approximately 15 percent of the world's total Muslim population. Muslim populations in Africa are unevenly distributed, with heavy concentrations in North and West Africa. The East African coast has pockets of Muslims from Somalia to Mozambique. Algeria, Djibouti, Libya, Mauritania, Morocco, and Somalia have nearly 100 percent Muslim populations. In Egypt, Gambia, Guinea, Niger, Senegal, and Tunisia, Muslims are 80 to 90 percent of the population. Muslim majorities of 60 to 75 percent are found in Chad, Mali, and Sudan. Nigeria, Africa's most populous country, has a Muslim population of about 45 percent. Muslims also form large minorities in Cameroon, Ethiopia, Guinea-Bissau, Ivory Coast, Liberia, Sierra Leone, and Tanzania. Smaller Muslim minorities live in South Africa, the Democratic Republic of the Congo (Zaire), the Central African Republic, and other countries.

History

From the Arabian Peninsula Islam penetrated Africa through North and East Africa by conquest, trade, migration, and missionary activities. In North Africa, most conquered peoples embraced Islam through the gradual transmission of the religion (islamization) and the Arabic language (arabization). In East Africa, Islam probably arrived on the coast as early as the seventh century when a few Muslims, persecuted in Mecca, crossed the Red Sea to seek refuge in Abyssinia (Ethiopia).

Islam spread along the Red Sea coast to the eastern coastal regions, up the Nile valley into the Sudan, and westward across the desert into the Magrib. By the eigth and nineth centuries North African merchants plying the trans-Saharan trade routes were among the first Muslims to reach the Western Sudan. Berber-speaking nomads familiar with the southern Sahara were also active agents in this process. By the eleventh century Manding-speaking traders had established "commercial diasporas" farther south, even though they did not engage in active Islamic proselytizing. This was the preserve of Muslim clerics who interacted mostly with local rulers. During the eighteenth and nineteenth centuries Muslim *jihads* (holy war) were waged in many parts of West Africa. Despite these *jihads* most Africans became Muslims by choice and not coercion.

A few Muslim leaders attempted to resist European colonialism, but failed. Most chose to accommodate the colonial powers by serving in formal and informal capacities within the colonial administration. Some were co-opted to serve as intermediaries for the colonial authorities. Although some Muslim brotherhoods like the Qadiriyya and the Tijaniyya resisted French colonialism defeat forced them to abandon their militancy. To a certain degree, the expansion of Islam was facilitated by the opening up of routes and railways in the interior of the continent during the colonial period. Many Muslim trading posts became administrative centers.

Education, Society, and Politics

Although most African Muslims do not speak Arabic, they endeavor to learn the *Qur'an* in Arabic. *Qur'anic* schools run by learned African Muslim teachers have developed a tradition of pedagogy which begins with learning the *Qur'an* by rote. Children born of Muslim parents go to secular schools, but they usually spend a few years in *Qur'anic* schools.

An increasing number of African Muslims continue to make the pilgrimage to Mecca (*hajj*) even with the increasing costs of air travel. At the same time, it is not uncommon to see African Muslims combining Islam and traditional African religious practices. Thus African beliefs in good and bad spirits is often associated with Muslim beliefs in *jinns* (spirits).

Africa is home of three principal religious traditions—indigenous, Islamic, and Christian—which African historian Ali Mazrui has aptly called its triple heritage. While it is true that the capacity to accommodate other faiths has been a hallmark of the historical Islamic tradition, indigenous tolerance in Africa has also often ameliorated Muslim-Christian rivalry. Leopold Senghor, a Christian, presided over Senegal's predominantly Muslim population for two decades after independence, working with leaders of the Muslim brotherhoods such as the Mourides and Tijaniyya.

Minority Muslims in East and Central Africa play significant roles in politics. In Tanzania, Julius Nyerere, a Roman Catholic ruled the nation from 1961 to 1985 without any evident challenge to his religious credentials. Although he insisted that Tanzania's politics knew no religion, Muslim traders were very active in the nationalist party of TANU. When Nyerere died his successor, Ali Hassan Mwinyi, was a Muslim from the tiny island of Zanzibar. In Kenya the Muslim minority has often been regarded as a threat by the government. In 1992, the government banned the formation of a Muslim party, fearing that it might become too powerful. In Malawi, with a smaller Muslim minority, a Muslim became president in 1994. The government in post-colonial Mozambique, on the other hand, banned some Muslim organizations. But in South Africa, where the apartheid climate (1948–1994) led to the radicalization of Islam, Nelson Mandela appointed a Muslim minister of justice when he became president in 1994.

In most countries in Africa where Islam is predominant Muslim identity is often taken for granted and is rarely articulated in relation to other creeds. Though Islam prescribes special relations between Muslims, Christians, and Jews, religious conflicts have been ignited in many parts of Africa because of the implementation of *Sharia* or Islamic law. In Nigeria, clashes between Muslims and Christians have led to many deaths and the expulsion of Christians from states that insist on the strict observance of *Sharia*. In the southern Sudan, rebel forces fighting against the Muslim- and Arab-dominated Sudanese government define themselves as Christian and animist minorities fighting against northern Muslim domination and Islamic fundamentalism. In Egypt, Christians such as the Coptic minority exist in significant numbers, about 10 percent of the population. In the recent past the Coptic Church and its leaders have experienced persecution and repression. Copts have been targeted by militant Islamic activists in spite the Egyptian government's condemnation of Islamic extremism. In Algeria, Muslim fundamentalists fighting for control of the government have fomented a reign of terror that has resulted in the brutal murder of thousands of Algerians.

Islamic missionary activities with local missionaries playing more active roles are on the rise in many parts of Africa. Also, a wider variety of Islamic groups including Sunnis of the Shafi'i legal school, Shi'is, and Pakistani Ahmadis have in recent years won more converts in Africa.

TAMBA M'BAYO

Further Reading

Brenner, Louis, editor, *Muslim Identity and Social Change in Sub-Saharan Africa*, London: Hurst & Co, 1993

Levtzion, Nehemia, and Randall L. Pouwel, editors, *The History of Islam in Africa*, Athens, Ohio: Ohio University Press, Oxford, England: James Curry, and Cape Town, South Africa: David Philip

Nanji, Azim, editor, *The Muslim Almanac: A Reference Work on the History, Faith, Culture, and Peoples of Islam*, New York, London, Bonn: Gale Research, 1996

Trimingham, John, *Islam in West Africa*, Oxford, England: Clarendon Press, 1959

———, *Islam in East Africa*, Oxford, England: Clarendon Press, 1964

———, *The Influence of Islam upon Africa*, London and New York: Longman, and Beirut, Lebanon: Librairie du Liban, 1980

Willis, John Ralph, editor, *Studies in West African Islamic History I: The Cultivators of Islam*, London: Frank Cass, 1979

Muslims in Europe

Of the 23 million Muslims living in Europe today, at least thirteen million are estimated to be living in Western Europe. The vast majority practice Sunni Islam. In Western Europe, five million Muslims live in France, 3.5 million in Germany, two million in Great Britain, 700,000 in Italy, 695,000 in the Netherlands, 500,000 in Spain, 300,000 in Switzerland, and 250,000 in Sweden. Although in some places such as the Netherlands, Muslims' countries of origin are varied, in others immigration is drawn from particular regions. In France and Spain, most Muslims come from North Africa, in Germany Muslims tend to be of Turkish origin, and in Great Britain, Muslim immigrants from the Indian subcontinent and East Africa comprise the majority of the Muslim population. In Eastern Europe, significant Muslim populations date back to the Ottoman occupation in the fifteenth century.

Muslims in Europe have a long history. In 711, Muslim general Tariq Ibn Ziyad conquered Spain, although the advance of the Muslims was stopped in 732 near Tours, France. For the next seven centuries, Muslims ruled Spain, called al-Andalus, until the fall of Granada in 1492. During this period, considered a golden age of Islamic civilization, religious tolerance, philosophy, science and culture experienced a flourishing. Muslim influence can still be found in the architecture throughout Spain, in the language, and in place names, such as Gibraltar (derived from the Arabic for Mountain of Tariq).

After Spanish Catholics expelled the Muslims from Europe, the European powers increasingly began to explore Muslim lands for profit and colonization. In 1798, Napoleon Bonaparte occupied Egypt, marking the beginning of the end of the Ottoman Empire's domination of the Middle East. After World War I, the Ottoman Empire collapsed, and by then the British, French, and Italians had fully colonized the Middle East and North Africa.

Since the Ottoman conquest of the Balkans in the fifteenth century, there have been significant Muslim minority populations across Eastern Europe, including indigenous converts. Communist rule in Eastern Europe and the Balkans in the twentieth century suppressed ethnic and religious differences between Muslims and Orthodox Christians. These tensions resurfaced in the 1990s and resulted in the genocide of thousands of Muslims in Bosnia-Herzegovina, formerly a part of Yugoslavia.

Since 1945, Western Europe has experienced several waves of Muslim immigration. As former European colonies in Muslim lands fell to independence struggles, many Muslims immigrated to Europe to seek employment, usually menial, from the former colonizers. The first waves of Muslim immigration were comprised of North Africans, Muslims from the Indian subcontinent, and Turkish migrants. More recent waves have included Muslim refugees fleeing wars and repression in the former Yugoslavia, Iraq or Afghanistan. Since the end of the Cold War, Muslims from the former Soviet Union and Eastern European countries have increasingly begun to immigrate to Western Europe.

Throughout Western Europe over the past three decades, there has also been an increase in the number of Islamic converts, many of whom are attracted to Sufism, a form of mystical Islam. Yusuf Islam, the pop singer formerly known as Cat Stevens, is perhaps the most famous European convert to Islam. France boasts about 50,000 converts, and Spain has an estimated 6,000. Spanish converts believe that Islam represents a return to an authentic Spanish identity, located in the period of Muslim rule over Spain.

The relationships of Muslim immigrants to their host countries vary in the degree of the host country's tolerance of religious and cultural traditions and efforts at integration. In Germany, for example, Turkish workers have historically been referred to as "Gastarbeiter," or "guest workers," the term implying that these workers were guests who would someday go home. Throughout Europe, Muslims have been victims of racism and misunderstanding. Controversies over the integration of Muslims into the local population include recent debates in France over the permissibility of the headscarf in public settings, particularly schools. The headscarf issue challenges French ideas about *laïcite* or secularism and reflects animosities toward a growing Muslim population. European perceptions of Islam have been influenced by events such as the 1979

Iranian revolution, the Salman Rushdie affair, the Arab/Israeli crisis and the war in former Yugoslavia. Turkey's repeated requests for membership in the European Union also drew attention to the presence of Muslims in Europe. Since the terrorist attacks in the United States on September 11, 2001, there has been an increased interest in the situation of Muslim minorities in Europe, and at times outright hostility and acts of violence toward Muslims.

Some have argued that despite allowing Muslims to practice their religion freely, Western European governments have made little effort to integrate Muslim immigrant populations, resulting in social marginalization, poverty, and the relegation of immigrants to poor housing projects that are hotbeds of crime, violence, and religious fundamentalism. Muslims in Europe have not been unified politically, resulting not only from differences in religious belief and national origin but also from the poor socioeconomic condition of many immigrants.

As places of worship, mosques have not provided a source of unity to Muslim populations in Western Europe because they tend to be financed and controlled by special interests outside the country. The Saudi government, for example, finances mosques throughout Europe but also demands that teachings in the mosques be restricted to the strict Saudi brand of *Wahabbism*, which frequently does not resonate with most Muslim populations.

Although Muslims in Europe have not yet formed political organizations capable of addressing their concerns as a religious minority, this appears to be changing by country. In Great Britain and the Netherlands, there are Muslim representatives in national government, and in other countries, Muslim organizations have begun to use democratic legal channels to appeal for greater tolerance and recognition of the Muslim presence. In many countries, second and third generations of Muslim immigrants born on European soil have begun to search for an identity that attempts to merge their parents' culture and traditions with their own efforts at integration into European society.

RACHEL NEWCOMB

Further Reading

Allievi, Stefano, and Jorgen Nielsen, editors, "Muslim Networks and Transnational Communities in and across Europe," in *Muslim Minorities Vol. 1,* Brill, 2003

Haddad, Yvonne Yazbeck, and Jane Smith, editors, *Muslim Minorities in the West*, Rowman & Littlefield, 2002

Metcalf, Barbara Daly, editor, *Making Muslim Space in North America and Europe*, Berkeley: University of California Press, 1996

Nielsen, Jorgen, *Muslims in Western Europe*, Edinburgh: Edinburgh University Press, 1995

Nonneman, Gerb, Tim Niblock, and Bogdan Szajkowski, editors, *Muslim Communities in the New Europe*, United Kingdom: Ithaca, 1998

Muslims in South Asia

Capsule Summary

Location: Indian subcontinent or South Asia

Total Population: approximately 120 million in India (Pakistan and Bangladesh are Muslim majority countries of equal size, making them, along with Indonesia, by far the largest Muslim populations in the world.)

Languages: Urdu, Bengali and regional dialects

Religion: Islam

Muslims are a religiously defined ethnic group, part of a worldwide religion which numbers about one billion adherents. Although they are a majority of the population in Pakistan and Bangladesh, they constitute the largest minority group in the Republic of India, a significant minority in Sri Lanka (formerly Ceylon) and a small minority in the Kingdom of Nepal. The most important fact about South Asian Muslims, at least in North India as well as Pakistan, is that Muslims ruled this area for six hundred years from the twelfth to the nineteenth centuries CE. They are therefore a "former ruling elite minority" who had the now dominant Hindus as their subjects. Their principal problems in India stem from adjustment to minority status as they are now among the poorest groups in a very poor country. The other source of their sense of oppression is that since 1947 when the British Indian Empire was partitioned between India and Pakistan according to which religion had a majority in each province, the two independent successor states have been enemies, which have fought four wars over possession of the border state of Kashmir. That state has a two-thirds Muslim majority but its Hindu ruler acceded to India which has doggedly retained the area by force with the help of some local collaborators, on the ground that India is a secular state which does not recognize the "two nation theory." This is the belief, upon which Pakistan is founded: namely that Hindus and Muslims are totally different and antithetical nations, each of which must have its own sovereign state. These conflicting bases of nationhood, religion and secularity, render the position of the huge Muslim minority left in India by partition suspect in the eyes of many Hindus especially those who want India to be a Hindu state. The mutual slaughter during the mass migrations of 1947, Hindus and Sikhs from Pakistan and Muslims from adjacent parts of North India, worsened the antipathies for at least a generation.

History

Islam came to the subcontinent within a century of its founding in Arabia in the seventh century CE. There were two paths of entry: to South Asia by sea by Arab merchants to the Southwest, Southeast coasts and Ceylon, areas which they never ruled and in which they enjoyed generally amicable relations with the dominant Hindu and Buddhist populations, respectively.

The other route was through the passes of the Northwest Frontier and Baluchistan to the fertile provinces of Sind and the Punjab. This route was characterized by military invasion by recent converts to Islam who, except in Sind (711 CE), were not Arabs but Turks, Persians, Afghans, and Mongols. The invaders settled permanently and established feudal, aristocratic empires which spread in waves southward until they eventually (seventeenth century CE) conquered almost the entire peninsula which now constitute Pakistan, India and Bangladesh.

In the northwest and northeast, the areas which now consist of Pakistan and Bangladesh, a majority of the population were converted to Islam, largely by the efforts of Muslim mystics (sufis). In the plains of North India and the Deccan plateau of the south on the other hand, where Hinduism was strongest, only a minority and they of the lower castes of Hindus, were converted.

This was the situation when the British East India Company gradually, between 1757 and 1857 CE, annexed the Muslim, Hindu and Sikh kingdoms which had formed on the ruins of the last Muslim Mongol (Mughal) empire. When European conceptions of nationalism were brought back to India from Great Britain by Indian students educated there, such as M.K. (Mahatma) Gandhi, Jawaharlal Nehru and Mohammedali Jinnah, the Indian National Movement broke into two parties, the Indian National Congress (founded 1885) which included some Muslim leaders like Maulana Abul Kalam Azad, and the Muslim League (founded 1906) which, inspired by the poet Iqbal and led by Jinnah, a former Congress member, demanded a separate country for Muslims in those areas where they had a majority. Thus it was that South Asian Muslims emerged from colonial subjection in two (and after the secession of Bangladesh from Pakistan in 1971) into three roughly equal populations, majorities in Pakistan and Bangladesh and a huge minority of about 12 percent of the population of India. Ceylon was a separate colony of Great Britain, so the Muslims or Moors there became a peaceable minority in the new country of Sri Lanka, although in recent years they have been caught in the middle of the civil war between separatist Tamil Hindus and the Buddhist majority. All Muslims, whether in a minority or majority, look to the center of their religion and object of pilgrimage in Saudi Arabia, outside of South Asia. This leads, as in the case of Zionist Jews regarding Israel, to problems of split loyalties.

Society

All Muslims are, unlike Hindus, equal in the eyes of their religion, regardless of social class or nationality. Naturally, proponents of the "Two Nations Theory" wish to emphasize the homogeneity of the Muslim community. But three centuries of contact with Hindus, from whose religion most of them were converted, has left them with some of the attributes of hereditary caste: occupations, residence, religious role and sub-group in-marriage or endogamy. While South Asian Muslims deny this, in practice they tend to act like Hindu sub-castes or jatis except in the most modern urban environments. They are quite diverse in other ways too: language, ritual, and sect (Sunni, Shia, Ismaili). There even developed an informal kind of sub-group hierarchy, comparable to the Hindu castes or varnas: the descendants of the Prophet Mohammed, called Sayyids, are at the top in prestige; other Arab-descended people, called *Shaikh*, are second; and descendants of later converts from outside the subcontinent: Persians, Turks, Mongols and Afghans are third. These three are collectively known as nobles or *Ashraf*, somewhat akin to the three "twiceborn" castes among Hindus. The rest of the Muslim population, by far the largest percent, who have no claim to foreign origin, are the commoners. They are in turn organized into brotherhoods or *biradaris* by traditional occupation. Like Hindu *jatis*, they tend to reside together and marry within the group. In coastal south and west India, there are small but economically important and tightly organized Muslim business communities like the Khojas, Memons, Daudi Bohras, Navayats and Marakayars as well as the fiercely Muslim peasants of Northern Kerala state, called Moplahs, all of whom have mother tongues different from Urdu, the language of North Indian and Pakistani Muslims.

Leadership has normally been in the hands of the *Ashraf*, although, as among Hindus, the lower status groups, called "Other Backward Castes," are now producing their own politicians. These, to gain acceptance, still press the same upper class demands which are of little benefit to the poor, for instance, preservation of the Muslim character of Aligarh Muslim University. A path to social mobility among Muslims, lacking theologically to Hindu lower castes, is through religious education and attainment of religious roles such as *mulla* (in charge of a mosque or place of worship), *moulana* or *moulvi* (a religious scholar), *mufti* (religious judge) and *sajjada nashin* (head of a *sufi* shrine centered on the tomb or *dargah*). Since most of the *ashraf* abandoned religious education in the twentieth century to obtain modern education in English in order to take on modern jobs such as civil servant (or in Pakistan and Bangladesh, army officer), and the modern professions, lower middle class but religiously educated Muslims have taken over these religious positions and assumed leadership roles in politics. This is especially true in North India because some of them, such as the Ali brothers and Maulana Abul Kalam Azad, played a prominent part in the Nationalist Movement against the British and because so much of the modern Muslim upper and middle class in North India and Hyderabad state, emigrated to Pakistan after 1947.

This latter group of emigrants called *Muhajirin*, played a disproportionately big role in the bureaucracy, army, business and politics of Pakistan for a generation. Even there, the men of religious learning, *ulema*, have been increasingly prominent in politics with the spread of Islamization throughout the Muslim world in the 1980s. The successful revolt of East Pakistan against West Pakistan in 1971 led in the former (now Bangladesh) to a sudden status reversal for the Urdu-speaking "Biharis" (from their origin in the Indian state of Bihar) who suddenly became a depressed and suspect minority. In West Pakistan (now just Pakistan), the *Muhajirin* have lost power more gradually to the indigenous provincial groups: Punjabis, Sindhis and Pathans. By 1985, some of the poorer sections of the *Muhajir* students in Karachi, their principal base as they are half of its population, felt their job prospects so diminished by special quotas for Sindhis that they organized a separate political party, the *Muhajir Qaum Mahaz* (M.Q.M.), which has had a tumultuous and violent history as successive Pakistani regimes, both civilian and military, broke electoral agreements with it and failed to incorporate it into civil society. In this sense, the *Muhajirin* have become a Muslim minority within a Muslim majority state. So too have the *Ahmadiyya*, an heretical sect of Muslims who, like the Mormons in the United States, believe in a latter day revelation.

It should be evident from much of the foregoing discussion that South Asian Muslims are severely divided internally. Not only are there divisions of sect, language and social class, but they are ideologically divided according to their reactions to the challenge of the West and modernity in the past two centuries into the orthodox (led by the traditional *ulema*), revivalists (the often castigated "fundamentalists" of the Western media) who wish to purify Islam by going back to the fundamentals of the original Islam of the seventh century CE, the modernists who wish to adapt Islam to the demands of modern life, and the secularists who reject the whole of the beliefs and rituals of the religion, but remain culturally Muslim and are often ideologically Marxist. The orthodox are organized in all three countries (India, Pakistan and Bangladesh) by the *Jamiat-ul-Ulema* (Association of Religious Scholars); the revivalists by the *Jama'at-i-Islami* (Community of Islam) and the modernists to some extent by the Muslim League in both India and Pakistan. The secularists are, by definition, not organized as Muslims but are to be found as individuals scattered throughout the political spectrum including the Congress Party and particularly in the parties of the Left. There are even a few token Muslims in the parties of "*Hindutva*" (those who want India to be a Hindu state culturally) such as the B.J.P. (Indian People's Party). Muslims have some representation in central and state cabinets, legislatures and judiciary, although this has been declining in the past two decades with the rise to power of the B.J.P. and various regional and caste parties. It is still far more representation than the tiny Hindu and Sikh minorities in Pakistan and Bangladesh get.

Occupationally, most Muslims in North and interior India are stuck in declining artisan trades, peasantry and manual labor. In coastal west and south India however, not only are the Muslim business sects and communities flourishing, but many poor and uneducated Muslims from these regions (especially Kerala) as well as from Pakistan have benefited from employment in the Arabian Gulf during the oil boom, from which they have sent home large remittances to buy land and build homes. In Bombay, Muslims because of the courtly tradition of music and dance in Lucknow, have enjoyed a niche in the movie industry ("Bollywood") as actors, singers, directors much like American Jews in Hollywood. Less creditably, they have been disproportionately involved in criminal gangs comparable to the Mafia. Because of their military tradition since the Muslim invasions, Muslims do well in sports such as cricket and soccer football like African-Americans, but also like them tend not to invest their incomes wisely.

A number of Islamic traditional practices, even if not specifically required by the Holy Book (the Quran), put Muslims in conflict with both Hindu and modern society. These include polygamy, female seclusion (purdah), proselytization and easy divorce. Plural marriage is charged, incorrectly, by Hindu militants to be the cause of the higher Muslim birthrate. Actually all the religious minorities such as Christians and Sikhs (except Parsis or Zoroastrians) have higher birthrates than Hindus. Purdah (the veil) makes Muslim lower middle class women conspicuous and keeps them disproportionately illiterate or undereducated and marrying young, thus increasing their lifetime fertility. Easy and unilateral (male initiated) divorce called triple talaq, and absence of maintenance for divorced Muslim women render them vulnerable to male dominance and penury if divorced. The Indian Supreme Court attempted to rectify this in a famous decision in 1986 awarding alimony to Shah Bano Begum. This was taken by orthodox Muslims to be a state invasion of the Muslim Personal Law or Shariat and led to a huge demonstration which compelled the then Prime Minister, Rajiv Gandhi, to back down and exempt Muslim men from paying alimony. In the British-style Indian parliamentary system, the legislature can overrule the judiciary. Feminists worldwide were outraged.

Islam, like Christianity and Buddhism and unlike Hinduism and Judaism, encourages conversion from other faiths. Many Hindus believe that this is accomplished by force, deception or inducements and at the expense of the Hindu majority. In 1981, several villages of Hindu untouchables, led by their recently educated young men, converted to Islam in South India which caused a public uproar and revival of the Vishwa Hindu Parishad (World Hindu Council) in order to reconvert the lost sheep by a ritual called Shuddhi (or cleansing.). Although Hindus of all kinds constitute four fifths of the population of India, politicized Hindu militants fear that their majority in India will be lost in the "ethnic numbers game" through conversion, lower birthrates and illegal immigration of Muslim Bangladeshis into eastern India and as far away as Mumbai and Delhi.

Official language policy is a grievance of North Indian Muslims despite the fact that Hindi, the constitutional link language spoken by 40 percent of the population, is closely related in grammar and vocabulary to Urdu which has become, since Partition, practically the mother tongue only of North Indian Muslims and the Muhajrin of Karachi. The main differences between the two languages are that Urdu is written in Arabic script while Hindi has its own script (devanagari) and official Hindi has increasingly substituted words from Sanskrit, the ritual language of Hinduism, for the many Persian and Arabic words in Urdu. The Three Language Formula whereby children were to be educated in their mother tongue plus Hindi (in non-Hindi speaking areas) and English has been violated in much of North India by substituting Sanskrit, a dead language, for Urdu, a living one.

Another issue which deeply affects Muslims of all classes and ideologies is the frequent occurrence of "communal," that is Hindu-Muslim, riots which have been increasing since the death of Nehru, the first Prime Minister of India, in 1964. The casualties have been largely Muslim and the Government of India seems to be incapable of stopping, let alone preventing them. The violence culminated in December 1992 with the countrywide riots following the destruction of the Babri Masjid (the Mogul Emperor Baber's mosque in Ayodhya). Hindu militants, allied to the B.J.P. conspired to destroy the mosque after a well organized campaign, on the ground that it had displaced a Hindu temple in honor of the birthplace of the legendary Hindu God-king, Rama. Indignant Muslims rioted and Hindu fanatics retaliated by killing thousands of

Muslims. This naturally has caused a great sense of insecurity, even fear of genocide among the minority which inhibits them from seizing opportunities in the new Indian economy of privatization, globalization and information technology. It has also bolstered the power of the *ulema*.

Prospects

Lest the above analysis seem to predict too gloomy a future for Indian Muslims, a number of more hopeful points need to be made. First, *Hindutva*, unlike Nazism for the German Jews, does not prescribe expulsion or extermination of the minority. To the contrary, it demands assimilation of Muslims into the mainstream of Indian life and culture. On the face of it, this is no more than the United States and many other western countries expected of their minorities until 1965 when multiculturalism displaced the "melting pot" as the goal of policy towards European immigrants. Muslims in North America and Europe are still compelled to conform to a common set of laws which, for instance, forbid polygamy and triple *talaq* divorce. For practical purposes of employment, they must learn the dominant language be it English, French or German despite multilingual education. But they are protected, at least in the United States by the separation of church and state. The Indian sense of secularism is one of equal treatment of all religions, rather than separation and this has not been well implemented. The proponents of *Hindutva* demand respect for the majority religion, not reconversion to it, but even the alternative national anthem, *Bande Mataram*, creates friction by referring to India (*Bharat*) as a goddess which is forbidden polytheism (*shirq*) to orthodox Muslims.

There have actually been fewer communal riots during the recent period of B.J.P rule than under the preceding Congress Party although this may be partly because the B.J.P. lacks a majority in Parliament and has to rule in coalition with other regional and secular parties.

Secondly, as the memory of the bloodbath of 1992 recedes, it is possible that a new generation of Muslims or at least the educated segment of that generation, will outwardly conform to the mainstream which, after all, may mean conformity to a modern Western culture, equally alien to the Hindu and Muslim traditions in food, speech and customs and make their way as individuals, albeit in the face of considerable Hindu prejudice and discrimination as long as India and Pakistan remain at enmity.

THEODORE WRIGHT

See also **Bangladesh; India; Indonesia; Pakistan**

Further Reading

Ahmad, Imtiaz, editor, *Caste among the Muslims*, New Delhi: Manohar, 1973

Ahmad, Mumtaz, *State Politics and Islam*, Indianapolis: American Trust Publications, 1986

Ahmed, Akbar, *Discovering Islam: Making Sense of Muslim History and Society*, London: Routledge & Kegan Paul, 1988

Eaton, Richard M., *Essays on Islam and Indian History*, New Delhi: Oxford University Press, 2000

Engineer, Asghar Ali, *Islam and Muslims: A Critical Reassessment*, Jaipur: Printwell Publishers, 1985

Ewing, Katherine P., editor, *Shariat and Ambiguity in South Asian Islam*, Berkeley: University of California Press, 1988

Ghosh, Partha, "Ideology and Contention," in *BJP and the Evolution of Hindu Nationalism*, New Delhi: Manohar, 1999

Hardy, Peter, *The Muslims of British India*, Cambridge: Cambridge University Press, 1972

Khalidi, Omar, *Indian Muslims since Independence*, New Delhi: Vikas, 1995

Krishna, Gopal, "Indian Muslims in the Nation-Formation Process," in *Contributions to South Asian Studies 2*, edited by Gopal Krishna,, Delhi: Oxford University Press, 1982

Madan, T.N.,editor, *Muslim Communities of South Asia*, 2nd edition, New Delhi: Manohar, 1995

Metcalf, Barbara D., editor, *Moral Conduct and Authority: The Place of Adab in South Asian Islam*, Berkeley: University of California Press, 1984

Shahabuddin, Syed, and Theodore P. Wright, Jr., "India: Muslim Minority Politics and Society," in *Islam in Asia: Religion Politics & Society*, edited by John L. Esposito, New York: Oxford University Press, 1987

Wright, Theodore P., Jr., "The Indian State and its Muslim Minority: From Dependency to Self-Reliance?" in *India: Fifty Years of Democracy and Development,"* edited by Yogendra K. Malik and Ashok Kapur, New Delhi: APH Publishing, 1998

Muslims in the Americas

Muslims have been in the Americas since the time of Christopher Columbus, who sailed to the New World in 1492 with a crew of Moorish Muslim sailors. Today, there are approximately four million Muslims throughout Latin America, 650,000 Muslims in Canada, and an estimated six million Muslims in the United States. The majority are Sunni, with a small Shi'ite minority population. In the United States, only 25 percent of the Muslim population is of Arab origin. 30 percent are from the Indian subcontinent, one-third are African-American, and the remainder are either converts or immigrants from Eastern Europe, Turkey, or Iran. The largest Muslim communities in the United States are located in urban areas such as Boston, New York, Detroit, Dearborn, Toledo, Chicago, and Los Angeles.

Beginning with the slave trade in the seventeenth century, at least one out of every ten African slaves brought to the Americas was Muslim. Religious practices disappeared, however, as most slave owners forced slaves to convert to Christianity. The first wave of voluntary Muslim migration to the United States came from Greater Syria between 1875 and 1912. The second wave followed the First World War. Muslim immigrants came to escape political turmoil in the Middle East after the collapse of the Ottoman Empire and subsequent colonization of the region by European powers. The first American mosque was built in Detroit in 1922, and in Edmonton, Alberta in 1938. Since WWII, Muslims have also arrived from the former Soviet Union and the Indian subcontinent. This final wave of immigration has been characterized by more professionals, skilled laborers, and businesspeople than earlier waves, which were comprised mostly of blue-collar workers.

African-American Muslims account for at least one-third of the population of Muslims in the United States today. In 1913 in Newark, New Jersey, Drew Noble founded the Moorish Science Temple, which advocated a return to Islam as a way of recovering the true African-American heritage. In 1930, Wallace Fard founded the Lost-Found Nation of Islam, a black nationalist group that did little to promote the teachings of Islam, although asserting that Islam was the true religion of Africans. From 1934, Elijah Muhammad led the Nation of Islam, encouraging blacks to adopt Islam and reject oppression by whites. His most notable convert was civil rights leader Malcolm X, who later rejected the racially charged teachings of the Nation of Islam for the broader doctrines of Sunni Islam. Most African-American Muslims have followed suit, and the Nation of Islam today has only about 20,000 members.

Although African Muslim slaves were also brought to Latin America, there was no significant Muslim presence in Latin America until the first wave of immigration in the 1850s and 1860s, when Arab Muslims and Christians from Syria and Lebanon settled in countries like Argentina, Brazil, Venezuela and Colombia. Further groups from the Indian subcontinent came to Paraguay and the Caribbean. The number of Muslims in Latin America today is estimated to be around 1.5 million.

Most Americans received their first exposure to Islam during the 1960s, when the Nation of Islam attracted attention in the struggle to end discrimination against blacks. During the past two decades, however, the media has increasingly begun to associate Islam with international turmoil. Political unrest in the Middle East and the Iranian revolution in 1979 have led to a portrayal of Islam as a religion that threatens Western civilization. Terrorist attacks, most significantly on the World Trade Center and the Pentagon on September 11, 2001 by the extremist group Al-Qaeda, have contributed to the tendency to draw sweeping generalizations about Muslims. The number of hate crimes and instances of discrimination against Muslims has increased dramatically over the past few years. Government anti-terrorist legislation has singled out Muslims and Muslim immigrants. The Patriot Act, passed in October 2001, gave authorities the right to search without warrants and detain terrorism suspects without providing due process, legal counsel, or public evidence. Thousands of Muslims have been arrested since September 11, 2001 and detained indefinitely without public evidence. In 2002, the government initiated the National Security Entry/Exit Registration System (NSEERS), for which all non-immigrant visitors from a specific list of Muslim countries were required to register their presence in the United States. During the one year the laws were operative, 13,000 Muslims were deported.

Despite negative stereotypes, the religion continues to attract converts, especially among black and Hispanic communities as well as in Latin America. Converts have been attracted to Islam's democratic message as a response to oppression or social disenfranchisement. Latin American converts to Islam reject Catholicism as a religion forced upon the region's indigenous inhabitants, and cite the fact that Spain was a Muslim country from the seventh to the fifteenth century.

Although the Nation of Islam was a formidable political organization in the 1960s, for the most part Muslims in the Americas have not formed organizations or linked their identity to the religion until recently. In the United States, early waves of Muslim immigrants assimilated with the general population and identified themselves as Arab, rather than as Muslim or Christian. Since the 1970s Muslim immigrants have begun to form organizations to promote solidarity and proper religious observances. Notable among these are the Islamic Society of North America and the Council on American-Islamic Relations (CAIR). ISNA has sought to facilitate the practice of Islam in a predominantly Christian culture by encouraging development of mosques, community centers, and Islamic schools. Established in 1994, the Council on American-Islamic Relations (CAIR) protects the rights of Muslims and responds to attacks on civil liberties, hate crimes, or anti-Muslim rhetoric. The response to Muslims in the Americas since September 11 reveals that Islam is widely stereotyped as a monolithic, violent religion that oppresses women and promotes terrorism. In the face of legal discrimination and cultural misunderstandings, it is uncertain whether Muslim minorities will follow the example of earlier immigrants by becoming assimilated, or pursue other strategies for wider acceptance.

RACHEL NEWCOMB

See also **Malcolm X (African-American)**

Further Reading

Haddad, Yvonne Yazbeck, editor, *The Muslims of America,* Oxford: Oxford University Press, 1993
Marsh, Clifton, *The Lost-Found Nation of Islam*, Sparrow Press, 2000
Metcalf, Barbara Daly, editor, *Making Muslim Space in North America and Europe*, Berkeley: University of California Press, 1996
Smith, Jane Idleman, and Yvonne Haddad, editors, *Muslim Communities in North America*, State University of New York Press, 1994

Muslims: Shi'a in Sunni Countries

Capsule Summary

Location: Worldwide, with concentrations in Iran, Iraq, India, Pakistan, Middle East
Population: Worldwide, Shi'as constitute 10–15% of the overall Muslim population; India (106,742,110), Iran (58,492,720), Iraq (17,093,700), Pakistan (22,968,720), Afghanistan (1,505,340), Saudi Arabia (1,136,750), Kuwait (805,600), Turkey (10,979,550), Lebanon (1, 312,800), Bahrain (416,100)
Language: Varies
Religion: Shi'a Islam

Shi'i Muslims represent around 10 to 15 percent of the world's Muslim population and are spread throughout Iran, Iraq, India, Pakistan, Afghanistan, Lebanon, Azerbaijan, Saudi Arabia and elsewhere in the Middle East. They comprise a majority, 88 percent, of Muslims in Iran, 65 percent in Iraq, 66 percent in Azerbaijan, 57 percent in Bahrain, 40 percent in Kuwait, 30 percent in Lebanon, 15 percent in Turkey, 15 percent in Pakistan, 10 percent in India, 6 percent in Afghanistan, and 5 percent in Saudi Arabia.

The word *shi'i* comes from the Arabic meaning the "partisans" of 'Ali, the cousin and son-in-law of the Prophet Muhammed. The Shi'a (or Shi'ites) believe that Mohammed designated 'Ali as his successor to lead the Muslims, but that political differences among the community of believers resulted in the unjust selection of the first three caliphs, Abu Bakr, Umar, and

Uthman, before 'Ali took his rightful place as leader of the Muslim people.

Although both Sunni and Shi'i Muslims believe in the Qur'an and the five pillars of Islam (prayer, fasting, tithing, pilgrimage and charity), there are significant doctrinal differences resulting from this early communal split. Shi'a are reliant on the authority of an entrenched clergy, and legal differences include the Shi'i practice of temporary marriage (mut'a), in which marriages can be contracted for a fixed period of time. Reverence for the twelve Shi'i imams, and mourning celebrations of their death and martyrdom, characterize the popular religious observances of Shi'i communities. The tombs of the imams, located throughout Iraq, Saudi Arabia, and Iran, are the focus of intense devotional observances.

History

After the Prophet's death in 632 CE, the first four "rightly-guided" (rashidun) caliphs codified many Islamic practices. The Shi'a, who advocate a strict adherence to Islamic law (shari'a), believe that the first three caliphs instituted customs that diverged from the teachings of the Prophet. They consider the first three caliphs to be illegitimate, and assert that only 'Ali, the fourth caliph, had the divine right to rule over the Muslim people. 'Ali, who married Muhammed's daughter Fatima, was caliph from 656–661 CE until he was assassinated in the city of Kufa.

Shi'a consider designated descendents of 'Ali and Fatima to be imams, religious and political leaders who are without sin and have the divine right to interpret the shari'a. The Twelvers (also called Imami or Ithna Ashariyya), who comprise the majority of Shi'a in Iran, Iraq, Lebanon, and Bahrain, believe that there were twelve imams and that the last one, the mahdi, who disappeared in 874 CE, will return at the end of time. The Seveners, also known as Isma'ilis, regard the seventh, Isma'il (d.760), as the last imam, and believe that Isma'il or his son will return as the mahdi. By contrast, the Twelvers believe that Isma'il was succeeded by his brother.

Of particular importance to all Shi'a is the third imam, Husayn, the son of 'Ali who was killed in 680 at Karbala fighting the Umayyad caliphate that had taken over after his father's death. Today, the celebration of 'ashura serves as a reminder to Shi'a of Husayn's martyrdom, a time after which the world abandoned the path of righteousness.

The Shi'a did not hold significant political power until the tenth century, when the Fatimids (909–1171), an Isma'ili dynasty, controlled much of Syria and North Africa, in direct competition with the Umayyad dynasty of Baghdad. In the sixteenth century, the Shi'i Safavid dynasty (1501–1732) rose to power in Iraq. Their rule was marked with conflicts with the Ottoman Empire over control of Iraq. Although Shi'a continued to represent the majority Islam in Iran, the westernizing procedures instituted by the Pahlavi regime (1925) angered religious Shi'a, who fomented the Iranian revolution in 1979, after which Islamic law was established in Iran.

Since the eighth century there have been numerous schisms within Shi'i Islam, resulting in localized versions of Shi'ism such as the Zaydis, still present in Yemen, and the 'Alawites (or Nusayri), an offshoot of Twelvers who are today a minority population in Turkey and Syria, although in Syria the ruling Assad family is Alawite. In the eleventh century, the Fatimid Isma'ilis split into two factions, Nizariya and Mustaliya, the former establishing itself in Iran and the latter spreading into India, China, Russia, and Southeast Asia.

Another splinter group originating in Isma'ili Shi'ism are the Druze, who live primarily in Israel, Syria, and Lebanon. In the eleventh century an Isma'ili missionary who ultimately rejected Ismai'ili doctrine, al-Darazi, spread the teachings of Hamza ibn 'Ali, who preached the divinity of the sixth Fatimid caliph, al-Hakim (985–1021). The Druze, whose holy book is entitled The Epistles, do not accept Islamic shari'a and believe that Hamza and al-Hakim will eventually return. Druze populations have experienced occasional waves of persecution, continuing into the past century, when the large Druze population in Syria was deprived of its rights. Currently the most stable community of Druze resides in Israel.

Current Status of Shi'i Minorities

The history of Shi'i minorities has been one of marginalization and persecution by Sunnis, who consider Shi'i beliefs to be heretical. In many countries, Shi'i minorities have been poor, undereducated, largely rural, and late to receive the benefits of government-sponsored modernization projects. Today, Twelver Shi'a are minorities in Kuwait, Saudi Arabia, and Oman. In Iraq, the Shi'a represent 60 percent of the population, although during the regime of Saddam Hussein (1979–2003), they were victims of oppression and genocide.

Throughout the 1980s and 1990s, an estimated 200,000 Shi'a fled to Iran, and they are now a significant voice in the struggle to form a new Iraq. In Afghanistan during the 1990s, the 20 percent minority Shi'a population further experienced repression, exile, and genocide by the Taliban, the Islamist movement that ruled most of Afghanistan from 1996 to 2001.

The Shi'a themselves are by no means a monolithic group, and internal conflicts result from differences in ethnic identity (Arab and Persian, for example), degree of religiosity, or the national politics of the countries in which Shi'a reside. Since the 1950s, motivated by a sense of injustice experienced at the hands of both the West and autocratic Sunni regimes, Shi'a have formed political movements, some of them espousing violence, throughout the Middle East. While a sense of Shi'a identity was already present in Arab countries prior to the 1979 Iranian revolution, the revolution nonetheless strengthened the political consciousness of Shi'i populations.

RACHEL NEWCOMB

See also **Afghanistan; Druze; Genocide; Ismailis; Iran; Iraq; Muslims: Sunni in Shi'a Countries; Oman; Saudi Arabia**

Further Reading

Cole, Juan R., and Nicki R. Keddie, *Shi'ism and Social Protest*, New Haven: Yale University Press, 1986

Daftary, Farhad, *The Isma'ilis: Their History and Doctrines*, Cambridge: CambridgeUniversity Press, 1990

Haeri, Shahla, *Law of Desire: Temporary Marriage in Shi'i Iran,* Syracuse: Syracuse University Press, 1989

Hourani, Albert, *A History of the Arab Peoples*, Cambridge, Massachusetts: Harvard University Press, 1991

Pinault, David, *The Shiites: Ritual and Popular Piety in a Muslim*, London: I.B. Taurus and Co., 1992

Muslims: Sunni in Shi'a Countries

Capsule Summary

Location: Worldwide including Egypt, Turkey, Saudi Arabia, Afghanistan, Iran, Iraq, Bahrain, Lebanon, and other parts of the Middle East and Africa
Populations: Egypt (54,000,000); Ethiopia (8,400,000), Jordan (4,100,000), Iran (3,305,000), Iraq (7,968,350), Bahrain (154,086), Kuwait (825,421)
Language: Varies
Religion: Sunni Islam

The word *Sunni* is derived from the Arabic word *sunnah*, meaning "custom" or "example," and refers to the behavior of the Prophet Muhammed, whose life Sunni Muslims attempt to emulate. Sunni Muslims represent the majority in most Muslim countries, including Egypt (90 percent), Turkey (99 percent), Saudi Arabia (100 percent), and Afghanistan (84 percent). Sunni are minorities in Iran (5 percent), Iraq (41 percent), Bahrain (25 percent), and Lebanon (18 percent). However, despite their minority status in Iraq, Bahrain and Lebanon, Sunni Muslims are frequently part of the ruling class.

Beliefs and Practices

Shi'i and Sunni Islam have taken divergent paths since the Prophet Muhammed's son-in-law Ali (the first *imam* of the Shi'a tradition) was bypassed in the election of caliph after the death of the Prophet. Unlike the Shi'a, Sunnis believe that individuals should have direct contact with God, unmediated by a clergy. This is in direct contrast to the Shi'a doctrine of the intercession of an *imamate*. Sunnis regard the Qur'an and the sayings *(hadiths)* of the Prophet Muhammed as the basic source for Islamic principles. *Hadiths* were handed down orally until they were compiled by Bukhari and Muslim in written form during the ninth century, with *hadiths* categorized as reliable if the chain of transmission leading back to the Prophet could be determined.

With regard to legal matters, Sunni Islam is divided into four schools (*madhabs*) of jurisprudence, all codified in the eighth century. Named for their founders, the four schools include Hanafi, Maliki, Shafi'i and Hanbali, and each derives guidance on legal matters from Qur'an and the *hadiths*, as well as from analog-ical reasoning (*qiyas*) and consensus (*'ijma*). The first school, the Hanafi, established the principle of consen-sus and placed the highest emphasis on analogy in forming laws. Hanafi *madhab* became widespread dur-ing the Ottoman Empire and remains prominent in those countries formerly under Ottoman control, as well as in India and Central Asia. Preferring the method of consensus in determining law, the Maliki school is today followed throughout North and West Africa and Sudan. For the Shafi'i *madhab*, the Qur'an and *Sunnah* of the Prophet are considered more impor-tant than the reasoning of experts, and Muslims in Bahrain, Egypt, Southeast Asia, and East Africa are Shafi'i adherents. The final school, Hanbali, places Qur'an and *hadith* above all other sources, and is today represented by Wahabbi Muslims of Saudi Arabia. Muslim countries vary in the degree to which their laws are derived from these sources, however. Saudi Arabia applies Islamic law to all matters while other countries follow a specific school of jurisprudence only with regard to family matters such as marriage and inheritance.

In response to challenges from sects considered unorthodox, the Sunnis also developed theological schools. In the seventh century the Kharijites, who felt that good deeds were as important as the profession of faith, and in the eighth century the Mu'tazilites, who argued that the freedom of God was limited, presented significant challenges to orthodox Islam. The Ash'ariyya and the Maturdiyya theological doctrines arose within Sunni Islam to refute these tendencies, asserting that the understanding of the essence of God lay beyond the human ability to reason.

Representing 85 percent of the Muslim world, Sunni Islam often incorporates local practices derived from indigenous customs, such as pilgrimages to saints' tombs. For centuries Sufism, a type of mystical Islam, has been a strong and varied tradition charac-terized by the quest of the individual to overcome the weaknesses of the ego (*nafs*) and unite with God. Many Sunnis regard such practices as heretical innovations. Wahabbism, followed in Saudi Arabia, arose in the eighteenth century in response to these "innovations" and demanded a return to the orthodox, purified teach-ings of Islam.

Sunni Minorities in the World

Sunni Muslims are the majority population in most Muslim countries, with a few exceptions. In Iran, Shi'i Persians are the largest religious and ethnic group (51 percent), but the country has a significant number of ethnic minorities, and 10 percent of the population (Turkmen, Baluchi, and Kurd) are also Sunni Muslims. Despite the constitutional guarantee of protection for religious minorities, Sunni minorities in Iran experi-ence discrimination. Sunni mosques have been closed or demolished, and Sunnis have no parliamentary rep-resentation, in contrast to other religious minorities, such as Jews, Zoroastrians, and Armenians. This policy was undoubtedly devised to keep the Sunnis from forming leadership that would challenge the authority of the Shi'i government.

In Iraq, Sunnis are demographically a minority since 60 percent of the population are Shi'a, al-though leadership of the country has historically been in the hands of Sunni Muslims. During the Ottoman Empire, elite Sunni Muslims enjoyed priv-ileges from the ruling Ottomans while simulta-neously many tribes in southern Iraq converted to Shi'a Islam. British indirect rule in the 1920s placed a Sunni monarch, King Faisal, in control of the government, and Sunni authority in the political sphere has continued until recently. Saddam Hussein's Sunni-dominated Ba'ath party, in power from 1968 until 2004, further repressed Shi'a politi-cal ambitions, resulting in some instances in outright genocide.

Sunnis are the minority population in Bahrain, but the ruling family of Bahrain is also Sunni. Similarly, although in Lebanon the Shi'a comprise the majority of the 70 percent Muslim population, the minority Sunnis share governing powers with the Maronite Christians. Other Muslim sects in Lebanon include Isma'ili, Druze, and Alawites.

Within Sunni countries, minority groups that fol-low schools of Sunni jurisprudence different from the official state version have experienced some repres-sion. In Saudi Arabia, followers of the Shafi'i and Maliki schools have seen a gradual diminishment of their rights by the majority Hanbali school. Serious conflicts have arisen as a result of religious tensions among Sunnis, such as the Algerian civil war of the 1990s. However, in most countries Sunni Muslims do not differ over strictly religious matters, and as minorities they often enjoy political power dispropor-tionate to their numbers. The schism that has divided Islam into Sunni and Shi'a since the formation of the religion has tended in most instances to favor the Sunni.

RACHEL NEWCOMB

See also **Armenians; Bahrain; Druze; Iran; Iraq; Ismailis; Muslims: Shi'a in Sunni Countries; Zoroastrians**

Further Readings

Al-Azmeh, Aziz, editor, *Islamic Law: Social and Historical Contexts*, London: Routledge, 1988

Enayat, Hamid, *Modern Islamic Political Thought: The Response of the Shi'i and Sunni Muslims to the Twentieth Century*, New York: Macmillan, 1982

Hourani, Albert, *A History of the Arab Peoples*, Cambridge, Massachusetts: Harvard University Press, 1991

Schimmel, Annemarie, *Mystical Dimensions of Islam*, Chapel Hill: University of North Carolina Press, 1975

Myanmar (Burma)

Capsule Summary

Location: Southeast Asia, bordering Bangladesh, India, China, Laos and Thailand.

Total Population: 42,510,537 (July 2003)

Languages: primarily BaMaLo (Burmese), though indigenous tongues are spoken by 35% of the population

Religions: Buddhist (89%), Christian (4% [Baptist 3%, Roman Catholic 1%]), Muslim (4%), animist (1%), other (2%)

Myanmar (Burma) has an indisputable ethnic and religious plural society. A central plain (with some forested regions, *yoma*) dominated by the Ayeyarwady (Irrawady), Sittang and Salween rivers, is the homeland of the majority BaMa (Burman) peoples. This innermost core is surrounded by hills and mountains, and a complex sociology of ethnic minorities. About one half of the country is composed of territory traditionally occupied by these minorities, some still very isolated in rough hill country around Burma's permeable national borders with Bangladesh, India, China, Laos and Thailand. Myanmar's population is settled in seven divisions, populated largely by Burmese (in colonial times called Ministerial Burma) and seven states (identified with ethnic or tribal groups, Frontier Burma). The latter terms *ministerial* and *frontier* have not been used since the 1947 Constitution, but they indicate something of the demographic arrangement nonetheless. About two-thirds of the population is BaMa, and ethnic minorities comprise the rest. But because Myanmar has experienced a great deal of inter-ethnic mingling over a period of centuries, only in the remote hills could one expect to find an example of an aboriginal people untouched by migration and intermarriage.

To simplify this complex topic, a 1931 census identified eight major ethnic groups and 135 so-called national or principal races, and was the last official attempt to make a comprehensive ethnic enumeration. The ethnic groups are BaMa, Rakhine, Shan, Mon, Chin, Kayin, Kayah or Karenni and Kachin. Although the demographic percentages may appear dated, analysts extrapolate from these figures to arrive at approximate community sizes today (e.g., BaMa 65 percent; Karen 9 percent; Shan 7 percent; Chin 2 percent; smaller groups like the Mon, Kachin and Wa at 1 percent each; Indian 7 percent, though many of the latter have subsequently left the country).

Another hypothesis focuses on language categories, based on several waves of early migrations from central Asia, Tibet, China and the Indian subcontinent into Myanmar. Four language categories are foremost: the Tibeto-Burman, Austro-Thai, Karennic and Mon-Khmer. Dozens of what might loosely be called ethnic groups and sub-sects are associated with these categories. The Tibeto-Burman peoples may have been associated with the earliest identifiable civilization, the Pyu, in Sri Ksetra (Pyay/Prome), dating from the fifth century CE. But the most significant Tibeto-Burman constituency was the arrival of the BaMa (Burmese) in the north about the eighth century CE. Burmese political power quickly accelerated, with expansion to the south from their great capital at Pagan (1044–1287 CE). Although the Burmese absorbed many religio-cultural features from subjugated kingdoms like the Mon, it was the BaMa language that eventually dominated the country identified today as Myanmar. The Rakhine represent a very old sub-sect of the Tibeto-Burman family in western Myanmar (Arakan), speaking an archaic BaMa dialect. This region also experienced the influence of neighboring India's religio-cultural traditions. A Hindu-Buddhist polity (Dinnyawaddy) was established as early as the second century, followed by the remarkable Buddhist kingdom of Mrauk U with its stunning capital, 80 kilometers (50 miles) up the Kaladan River from the Bay of Bengal (defeated by the BaMa in 1784). Numerous hill tribes are also related to the Tibeto-Burman peoples. North of the Rakhine, the Chin are in turn divided into about forty subgroups and, numbering as many as 1.5 million, are largely along the Myanmar/India (Mizoram) border, where many are still engaged in *taungya* or slash-and-burn agriculture. The Naga in north east Myanmar (Patkai Range, near the Chindwin River) are an Indo-Mongoloid people of about 100,000 whose language is related to the Tibeto-Burmese family, and with a distinct aboriginal culture, until fairly recently based in part on head-hunting. The Lahu and the Akha, ethnic minorities with populations of about 150,000 each, are found largely in western Myanmar (Kentung).

Like other hill peoples, each community has a distinct dress for men and women, including ornaments and jewelry. Elsewhere, the Kachins form an important category of the Tibeto-Burman language family. Various sub-sects include the Jinghpaw from the headwaters of the Chindwin and Ayeyarwady Rivers, and the Azi, Maru, Lashi, Hkahku, Nung and Rawang (mostly in the Putao region of the far north). The Yao and the Hmong (Miao), of Sino-Tibetan heritage, are also widely dispersed in other parts of mainland Southeast Asia. Lisu people are related to the Kachin, residing mostly in remote villages in the Myitkyina area near the Chinese border. A final Tibeto-Burman group are the Intha from Inle Lake, well-known for a curious one-legged rowing technique and, like most of the smaller minorities, a community about 150,000.

Also on the eastern side in Myanmar, but associated with the Austro-Thai family of languages, are the Shan, of Yunnan origin, and closely related to the Thais (Shan is derived from the same root as Siam, "free"). For two centuries after the collapse of the BaMa kingdom of Pagan, the Shan ruled large parts of historic Burma from their own splendid capital at nearby Ava. Later, under the British *raj* (1885–1948), the Shan essentially governed themselves through their princes (*sawbwas*), a system only given up in 1959.

Neighboring Karen in present-day Kayah and Kayin states were among the earliest peoples to come from China, though their Karennic language has a different word order from Tibeto-Burman tongues.

Major Karen subgroups are the Kayah, Karenni (Red Karens), Pwo and Sgaw, the latter living largely among the BaMa as wet-rice cultivators in the great Ayeyarwady delta. Some isolated Karen-related minorities are the Lahta (Zayein) and Yinbaw in Kayah state, and the Pa-O in the Taunggyi –Inle Lake-Kalaw area of the Shan state. Other smaller Karen-related ethnic groups are the Bre (Kayaw), an isolated community which has suffered greatly from the ravages of anti-government conflict in the area, and the Padaung (possibly as many as 50,000), celebrated for the brass neck rings traditionally associated with their "giraffe-necked" women. At the turn of the millennium, an estimated 200,000 Karens remain displaced within Myanmar, and 150,000 seek refuge in border camps within Thailand. A fourth linguistic cluster is the Mon-Khmer. The Mon are still a substantial (four million) ethnic minority in the southeast. Their forebears are among the earliest settlers of the fertile Ayeyarwady delta, with a sophisticated culture dating back to the fifth century CE, and with substantial capitals at Thaton, Martaban, and Pegu. Attacked by the Burmese king Anawrahta in the eleventh century, the Mon lost final control of the south in 1757. Possible Mon refugees from this period settled in Heho and Kalaw, ancestors of the Taungyo. The Palaung of the northern Shan state are another community whose predecessors were among the earliest inhabitants of Myanmar, and, like so many ethnic groups, are further divided into sub-sects (e.g., Silver and Gold Palaung). They are related to the Wa, traditionally associated with the Shan state, and head-hunter animists until the mid-twentieth century. In 1968 the Wa came under the control of the Communist Party of Burma. Twenty years later, they abandoned the Communists and were among the first of twenty ethnic militias to sign a ceasefire in 1989 with the Myanmar State Law and Order Restoration Council (a precursor of the present military junta, the State Peace and Development Council). The terms permitted the United Wa State Army control over much of the lucrative but dangerous and corrupting Thai border narcotics industry, providing them a maverick but enviable autonomy they will not willingly surrender. Other ethnic minority groups more specifically related to a Chinese heritage are the Panthay (Chinese Muslims, with possible Central Asian roots) and the Kokang. The latter entered Myanmar in the seventeenth century and, even under the British, enjoyed effective self-rule until 1948, when they became a constituent part of the Shan state. This is by no means a comprehensive list.

Hundreds of dialects and languages, many locked into a small geographic zone, perhaps a ravine or hill tract, have long been noted by anthropologists. These, and the peoples they represent, are not likely to retain aboriginal isolation or perhaps in some cases even identity for much longer.

Added to these essentially tribal divisions is the matter of religious diversity. Although the Theravada Buddhism of the BaMa majority is shared by the Rakhine and most Shans and Karens, Myanmar has large communities of Christians, Hindus and Muslims. Christianity is more often than not identified with tribal minorities, such as Chin, Kachin and Karen. It thus carries with it the stigmata of colonialism and close identity with the ethnic minorities. But Christians (by far the biggest and most important denomination is that of the Baptists, composed of a million or more adherents) do not suffer the same kind of discrimination that the Muslims suffer, associated as they are with Indian heritage. Composing up to 13 percent of the population (the state claims only 3 percent), Muslims are found in several groups. The largest group (one million) are the Rakhine Muslims (their unofficial name, Rohingya, is derived from the word Rakhine). Few have Myanmar citizenship and, although common, refugee sanctuary in neighboring Bangladesh is uncertain and problematic. Another cluster are Muslims who are the offspring of mixed marriages between an Indian Muslim and a Burmese (usually the mother), sometimes called Zerbadees (now an impolite term).

On the other hand, Hinduism is embraced largely by offspring of previous generations who came directly from India during the British *raj*. The Hindu faith is seen by the BaMa majority to be close to Buddhism, but notwithstanding the recognition that the two faiths are branches of the same tree, racial discrimination, subtle and not so subtle, is prevalent. Indians, whether Hindu or Muslim, are still regarded by many as *kala*, or "foreign," even if Myanmar born, and are distinct ethnic minorities. It should be noted that although there are Muslim and Hindu areas in the cities and countryside, for the most part they are not ghettoized communities, and live and work among the BaMa.

Modern History

The perspective of Myanmar's history from the homelands of the minorities in the hills must be different from that of the majority Burmese. Any account of Myanmar's traumatic experiences leading up to the present will inevitably involve differences of interpretation associated in part with ethnicity. After World War II, there was not much time to work out what a nation and nationalism might best mean in Burma's circumstance. The architect of Burma's sovereignty, Bogyoke Aung San, inherited a powerful tradition of Buddhist and BaMa political activism. Intent on building a framework for a new union of Burma, he sidestepped the religious and collateral BaMa ethno-national claims to superiority, and met with key Shan, Chin, Kayah and Kachin leaders in Panglong, a small town in Shan State. On February 12, 1947, the Panglong Agreement was signed, described as a general agreement providing for Frontier Area representation in the government's Executive Council, and an agreement in principle for the autonomy of the Frontier Areas in internal administration. A further guarantee of the right to withdraw from this quasi-federal arrangement after ten years eased its acceptance with unsavory signatories. A central weakness of the Agreement, however, was the conspicuous absence of the Karen, Karenni, Rakhine (Arakanese) and Mon. But whatever might be said about the deficiencies of Panglong, it remains an historic triumph of sorts, not yet to be duplicated. Assassinated in 1947, Aung San's successor, U Nu, lacked the vision to carry the ethnic accord and infant federalism forward. Instead, in a well-meaning but disastrous step backward, in 1960 he proposed a Union based in part on Buddhism as the state religion. U Nu's Parliamentary period was short-lived, and in 1962 General Ne Win took over the country with a regime that has, with a few name changes, remained in place ever since. The Ne Win *khit* (era) is marked by several unsavory features pertinent to the ethnic and religious minorities. Among these were the 1963 exodus of approximately 300,000 Indians and 100,000 Chinese, most with more or less just the clothes on their backs. Resistance came from a National Democratic Front of ten ethnic organizations struggling not so much for independence as for the hint of federalism promised by Aung San. A new Constitution in 1974 referred to the "national races," but there was no provision for federalism, and the huge Muslim Rohingya was not even mentioned. Myanmar experienced a major anti-government uprising in 1988, which, combined with Daw Aung San Suu Kyi's electoral victory in 1990, suggested that a democratic opposition was at least a possibility. However, so striking and immediate were the political problems confronting the majority Burmese in the heartland of the nation that regional and ethnic issues became sidelined. Once again, at a critical hour, important ethnic constituencies, needs, and ambitions went unrepresented. A phenomenon of great importance during the 1990s was the remarkable success of government initiatives to enter into informal cease-fires with twenty ethnic rebel factions, including, in 2004, the last major force of the Karen National Union. Except for one or two minor fringe groups (e.g., the Arakan Independence Alliance), Myanmar's minorities are not agitating to break away from the state. There is some hope that a renewed National Convention aimed at formulating a fresh Constitution will fully involve ethnic minorities and bring Myanmar closer to fulfilling the national destiny Aung San had in mind when the modern state was born over half a century ago.

In 1989, the Burmese military authorities promoted the name Myanmar as the country's conventional name. This decision, however, was not approved by Burmese legislation, and the United States does not formally recognize the name.

Myanmar is a country rich in natural resources but that suffers great poverty. In 2002 the per capita GDP was US$ $1,700. The economic sector is dominated by agriculture (60 percent), followed by services (31 percent), and industry (9 percent, 2002).

BRUCE MATTHEWS

See also **India; Hindus; Khmer; Thailand**

Further Reading

Diran, Richard K., *The Vanishing Tribes of Burma*, London: Weidenfeld & Nicolson, 1997
Enriquez, C.M., *Races of Burma*, Delhi: Government of India, 1933
Furnivall, J.S., *The Governance of Modern Burma*, New York: Institute of Pacific Relations, 1958
Lintner, Bertil, *Burma/Myanmar: Strong Regime, Weak State?* edited by Morten Pedersen, et al. Adelaide: Crawford House, 2000
Naing, U. Min, *National Ethnic Groups of Myanmar*, translated by Hpone Thant, Yangon: Thein Myint Win Press, 2000
Smith, Martin, *Burma: Insurgency and the Politics of Ethnicity*, London: Zed Books, 1999
Taylor, R.H., *The State in Burma*, Honolulu: University of Hawaii Press, 1987
Yegar, Moshe, *The Muslims of Burma*, Wiesbaden: Otto Harrasowitz, 1972

N

Namibia

Capsule Summary

Country Name: Namibia
Location: Southern Africa, on the coast of the Atlantic Ocean
Total Population: 1,927,447 (July 2003)
Ethnic populations: Sān (or Bushmen) (!Kung [incl. !Xu and Ju|'hoansi], Kxoe [or Mbarakwengo] and Nharo); Hai‖om; Nama; Damara; Ovaherero (and Ovahimba, Tjimba-Herero); Okavango (Kwangari, Mbunza, Shambyu, Gciriku); Mbukushu; Rehoboth Basters; Tswana; Fwe (incl. Yeyi, Totela, and Lozi); Subia. About 50 percent of the population belong to the Ovambo tribe and 9 percent to the Kavangos tribe; Herero (7%), Damara (7%), Nama (5%), Caprivian (4%), Bushmen (3%), Baster (2%), Tswana (0.5%)
Languages: English 7% (official), Afrikaans common language of most of the population and about 60% of the white population, German 32%, indigenous languages: oshiWambo; Sān; Khoekhoegowab (spoken in different forms and dialects by Nama, Damara, and Hai‖om); otjiHerero; ruKavango (ruKwangari, shiShambyu, ruGciriku); thiMbukushu; siFwe (and siYeyi, siTotela, siLozi); siSubia
Religions: Christian 80% to 90% (Lutheran 50% at least), indigenous beliefs 10% to 20%

Namibia is a predominantly semi-arid country located in southwestern Africa. Indeed, as a former German colony and then British Protectorate and South African mandated territory, the country was known as Südwestafrika and South West Africa.

If recent estimates of the population growth rate are correct, the present national population is around 1.9 million. The impact on population growth of the country's estimated HIV-positive population of 11.1 percent, however, is as yet unknown. What is certain is that this disease is having devastating effects in terms of disproportionately affecting women between the ages of 15 and 24 years, increasing numbers of orphans, and becoming a primary cause of mortality among children below the age of five years.

Namibia's majority are the Owambo people who mainly inhabit north-central Namibia and make up some 50 percent of the total population. This makes all other ethnic or language groups numerical minorities within the country. Approximately 72 percent of Namibia's population was classified in the 1991 census as rural dwellers, although rural-urban linkages, for trade and employment purposes, are important for many households.

Historical records indicate that the Namibia of European contact, in the 1700s and 1800s, was inhabited by a diversity of peoples experiencing and making the most of new influences on the territory. These included the intrusion of European mercantile capital from the South African Cape, which tended to distort exchange-based relationships existing at the time, and the raiding of livestock by well-armed commando units, also from the Cape.

Missionary activities in southern and central Namibia, orchestrated primarily by the German Rhenish Mission in the nineteenth century, anticipated German colonial rule through the establishment of protective alliances. By exploiting and exacerbating local rivalries, African Namibians were encouraged to accept German rule and protection in return for rights over land and respect for traditional leadership. Such concessions over land provided the model for land acquisition by German business interests anxious to secure access to resources with potential financial value, especially the country's diamonds and livestock pastures. This process eventually made possible the annexation and establishment of a German colonial government over the territory in 1884. The reduced areas of land and numbers of livestock to which African Namibians retained access, the enforcing of colonial laws forbidding the hunting of animal wildlife and the collection of resources from "the wild," and the rinderpest epidemic of 1897 in which an estimated 90 percent of the country's livestock perished led to devastating impoverishment among surviving African Namibians at the turn of the century.

Despite bitter resistance, including a war fought mainly by the Herero and Nama against German rule from 1904–1907, huge tracts of land in southern and central Namibia were alienated from Namibians and enclosed for use as commercial livestock ranches by the time of German defeat in World War I. The remote northwest of the country, together with the populous Owamboland and northeast of the country, remained relatively unpoliced by colonial authorities. That split in the territory was later marked by the veterinary cordon fence (or Red Line), restricting movement of livestock and other agricultural produce from north to south. This prevented Namibians in the north from capitalizing on the emerging formal economy south of the Red Line. In the south, African Namibians were restricted to Native Reserves, tiny areas of land compared to their original territories. This erosion of the basis for indigenous livelihoods, combined with the imposition of a system of taxes, forced Namibians, particularly men, into a migrant labor system that supplied the labor needs of the formal white economy.

After Germany's defeat in 1918, the territory became a League of Nations mandate administered by South Africa. Policies mirrored those of apartheid South Africa and included enforced migrant labor for mining and farming, restrictions on movement by Africans, and the establishment of an expanded system of Reserves or "homelands" for African habitation. Given these exclusionary and racist policies, the League of Nations mandate was revoked by the United Nations (UN) in the late 1960s. This remained unenforced by the international community, however, and Namibia only became independent of South Africa in

1990 after years of armed resistance to the South African administration.

Today Namibia's government is dominated by the Marxist South West African People's Organization (SWAPO), which has been voted in with a two-thirds majority in all national elections since independence. Other major political parties include the breakaway Congress of Democrats (CoD), the United Democratic Front (UDF), which has strong Damara support, and the conservative Democratic Turnhalle Alliance (DTA), which has strong Herero support.

Throughout history access to land and natural resources has been the crucial factor enabling self determination and economic sufficiency. As a first step towards dismantling the apartheid legacy of managing and allocating land along racial lines, the new government has reformed the administrative system and delineated new administrative boundaries. Land held under freehold title by settler (i.e., European) families, and land held communally by indigenous Africans, now occurs within the same administrative region. Unfortunately, however, this has had little effect on the distribution of land between a settler minority and Namibia's African majority. The latter have access to a relatively small proportion of the country's least productive land (in central and southern Namibia) and rarely have inalienable title to land. More than ten years after independence, Namibia's current Land Reform Bill has yet to be approved and it remains unclear as to how progressive this will be in terms of redistributing land. The removal of people from ancestral lands was also associated with the creation of conservation areas: thus, Hai‖om were evicted from Etosha National Park, Khomani Damara from Daan Viljoen Game Park, and Damara and Sān (and later, Ovaherero) from Waterberg Plateau Park.

There are other factors that impinge on particular ethnic groups. For example, the Constitution of 1990 allowed all Namibian citizens to move to wherever they wish on communal land, albeit with the unmonitored *proviso* that they respect the rights of people already inhabiting an area. This seems to be particularly problematic for populations of Sān (in the Okakarara District, Otjozondjupa Region) and Damara (in the Khorixas District, Kunene Region) where frequently wealthier Herero cattle herders are claiming pasture and water and influencing decisions regarding donor-funded environment and development initiatives. Finally, even as the southern Africa's Working Group for Indigenous Minorities (WIMSA) has accomplished a great deal on behalf of Namibians identified as Sān or Bushmen, other groups who cannot claim a Sān identity, but who share similar experiences of marginalization, have been unable to access the benefits that such institutional representation can provide.

The Namibian economy is highly dependent upon mineral extraction and processing, namely diamond, lead, zinc, tin, silver, tungsten, uranium, and copper. Mining comprises 20 percent of the GDP. The mining sector employs only about 3 percent of the population, whereas approximately 50 percent of the population depends on subsistence agriculture for livelihood. Although the per capita GDP income in 2002 was a relatively high $6,900, it belies the great inequality of income distribution; approximately one-third of Namibians earned annual incomes of less than $1,400 in 1994. The economy is closely linked to that of South Africa, with the Namibian dollar (NAD) linked to the South African rand (ZAR).

SIAN SULLIVAN

See also **Damara; Sān (Bushman); South Africa**

Further Reading

Adams, Fiona, and Wolfgang Werner, *The Land Issue in Namibia: An Inquiry*, Windhoek: Namibian Institute for Social and Economic Research, University of Namibia, 1990

Bley, Helmut, *Namibia under German Rule*, Hamburg: Lit Verlag, 1996

Dreschsler, Horst, *"Let Us Die Fighting": The Struggle of the Herero and Nama against German Imperialism*, Berlin: Academie Verlag, 1966

Gordon, Robert J., "The Stat(u)s of Namibian Anthropology: A Review," *Cimbebasia*, 16 (2000)

Hartmann, Wolfram, Jeremy Silvester, and Patricia Hayes, editors, *The Colonising Camera: Photographs in the Making of Namibian History*, Cape Town: University of Cape Town Press, Windhoek: Out of Africa, and Athens: Ohio University Press, 1998

Hayes, Patricia, Jeremy Silvester, Marion Wallace, and Wolfram Hartmann, editors, *Namibia under South African Rule: Mobility and Containment 1915–46*, Oxford: James Currey, Windhoek: Out of Africa, and Athens: Ohio University Press, 1998

IDAF, *Namibia: The Facts*, London: IDAF Publications Ltd.

Katjavivi, Peter H., *A History of Resistance in Namibia*, Paris: Unied Nations Eduational,Scientific an Cultural Organization, London: James Curry, and Addis Ababa: Organization of African Unity, 1988

Kinahan, John, *Pastoral Nomads of the Central Namib Desert: The People History Forgot*, Windhoek, Namibian Archaeological Trust and New Namibian Books, 1991

Lau, Brigitte, *Southern and Central Namibia in Jonker Afrikaner's Time*, Windhoek: Windhoek Archives Publication Series No. 8, 1987

Malan, J.S., *Peoples of Namibia*, Pretoria: Rhino Publishers, 1995

Nasser, Gamal Abdel (Egyptian)

Nasser, Gamal Abd-Al (gamalu c abdu n-nâsir) was the first president of Egypt from 1954 to 1970. His domestic and foreign policies and Arab Nationalism earned him great respect and popularity in the Middle East and catapulted the Arab world into the forefront of international affairs. Nasser took part in the 1948 war against Israel in which Egypt was humiliated because its army was in poor shape and the Israeli forces were far superior. He also served in Sudan where he met like-minded officers, who in 1949 created the revolutionary secret Free Officers organization, *El-Dhobatt El-Ahrar*. Their goal was to end the British occupation of Egypt that began in 1882 when

General Gordon was killed during an uprising, and remove corrupt King Farouk, who had gained the throne through Western support and the landowning elite who profited from the poor minority.

On July 23, 1952, the Free Officers led a coup d'etat, the 1952 Revolution that overthrew Farouk, who went into exile. General Mohammed Neguib, whose high ranking legitimized the coup became the first Egyptian to rule the country in over 2,000 years. However, he was only a titular leader; few people realized that 34-year-old Nasser held the real power. The last king, Ahmad Fouad, was removed in 1953 and Egypt was declared a Republic. General Naguib was removed and Nasser became prime minister in 1954 and president in 1956 when he established a new Constitution. Nasser enjoyed conspiring, trusted no one, and abhorred criticism. Yet he was charismatic, warm-hearted, and a born leader.

Nasser's rise surprised the West; France, Britain, and Israel were taken aback by this bold Arab nationalist whom they feared would unify the Arabs. Egypt became the centre of an international crisis when Nasser nationalized the Suez Canal after the West withdrew its offer to finance the Aswan Dam. Nasser insisted on the withdrawal of British troops, and the Israelis sent a sabotage team to derail the talks. The team was captured by the Egyptians. This is known as the Lavon affair. On October 19, 1954, The Anglo-Egyptian Suez agreement was concluded and the British withdrew their 80,000 troops. Nasser was deemed a hero.

Nasser was thought by the French to be aiding Algeria, which wanted independence from France. Britain and France deemed Nasser to be an enemy of the West. The French secretly sent weapons to Israel. The consequence of these events was the 1956 Suez Crisis, a misguided, collective attempt by France, Israel, and Britain to remove Nasser from power. The attack failed because they did not have international support. The United Nations (UN) forced them to withdraw. This became a watershed in the history of the Middle East. Nasser had confronted the West and he was quickly idolized.

Victory against the hated British, French, and Israelis made Nasser a celebrated figure in Egypt and the Arab world. With this victory, Nasser began the Pan-Arab unity movement. Its expansion began with Syria and Egypt joining together to become the United Arab Republic. However, this only lasted until 1961 when Syria seceded because the programs of the two countries were never unified. Nasser's criticisms of the West cost him the financing of the Aswan Dam, a project that would deliver Egypt out of its poverty and industrialize the country. He then turned to the Soviet Union for aid. This was important because during the Cold War, the two superpowers, the United States and the Soviet Union, vied for support and hoped to influence countries. Nasser had become the leading Arab statesman. In 1958, Arab nationalists removed the monarchy in Iraq, and in 1962 Algeria gained independence.

Nasser exacerbated his estrangement from the West because of his financial and military support of the leftist guerrillas in the Yemeni civil war who wished to overthrow the monarchy. He began to rely on the Soviet Union for military and technical assistance in order to fight U.S.-backed Israel. He also helped support the creation of the Palestine Liberation Organization (PLO). Nasser provoked Israel into the Six Days' War in June 1967. He weathered Egypt's crushing defeat because his people considered him a hero. He offered his resignation, but huge spontaneous crowds in Cairo supported the extraordinarily popular Nasser, who remained in power.

Nasser became an important figure in the developing world. He saw the benefits of nonalignment with either superpower, so he joined India's Jawaharlal Nehru and Indonesia's Ahmed Sukarno to create the Non-Aligned Movement.

Domestically Nasser's land reforms broke up the feudal estates. Using the ideals of Arab socialism, he appropriated 243,000 hectares (2,430 square kilometers) of farmland from the rich landowners and redistributed it to the fellaheen, the poor underclass of serfs. He had never forgotten what it was like to be poor. He nationalized banks and industries. Completion of the Aswan Dam increased the arable land around the Nile River by 15 percent. A new industrial base was to be generated by the Aswan Dam's electricity. Universal education programs were established.

On the negative side, Egypt was a police state under Nasser where mail and telephone calls were censored. The educated classes and the elite of the prerevolutionary era were removed from influence, leading to an undereducated and inept bureaucracy. The economy stagnated and the agricultural reforms and industrial improvements were so inefficient that no progress was made.

Biography

Nasser was born on January 15, 1918 in a suburb of Alexandria, Egypt. His father was the local postmaster. He grew up in a British-controlled village and later moved to Cairo. Although he began his postsecondary education by studying law, he graduated from the Royal Military Academy in July 1938 as second lieutenant and became a career army officer. The man who had raised the Arab consciousness was felled by a heart attack. Nasser's unexpected death on September 28, 1970, at the age of 52, plunged the Egyptians into a grief they had not previously encountered.

Selected Works

The Philosophy of the Revolution, 1959

ANNETTE RICHARDSON

See also **Egypt**

Further Reading

Heikal, Mohamed, *Nasser: The Cairo Documents,* London, New English Library, 1973

Love, Kennett, *Suez: The Twice-Fought War*, New York: McGraw-Hill Book Company, 1969

Neff, Donald, *Warriors at Suez: Eisenhower Takes America into the Middle East*, New York: Linden Press/Simon & Schuster, 1981

Nutting, Anthony, *Nasser*, London, Constable, 1972

Stephens, Robert, *Nasser: A Political Biography*, London: Allen Lane/The Penguin Press, 1971

National Association for the Advancement of Colored People (Naacp)

The National Association for the Advancement of Colored People (NAACP) is the oldest and most celebrated civil rights organization in the United States. Since its formation in 1909, the group has been at the forefront of numerous struggles for equality in America, calling on the nation as a whole to abide by the fourteenth and fifteenth amendments to the Constitution and to end all racial violence and discrimination—social, political, and economic. Though the organization gained its greatest victories during the modern civil rights movement, the group's presence is still felt and needed, as *de facto* discrimination is prevalent in America at the dawn of the twenty-first century.

Before the creation of the NAACP, there were other groups that constructed platforms that the interracial organization would build upon. For example, the Afro-American League, which was assembled in 1890 and would later become the Afro-American Council, created a strategy to challenge discrimination in America that was similar to that of the NAACP. Around the turn of the century, a group of radicals, led by W.E.B. Du Bois and William Monroe Trotter, began to challenge what they perceived as the Council's conservative leadership and the influence of Booker T. Washington within the organization. By 1905, the two created their own group, the Niagara Movement, which was dedicated to persistent agitation for civil rights, equal education, and general human rights. Both these organizations would continue their struggles up to the development of the NAACP.

The creation of the NAACP was precipitated by an article by William English Walling, in which he graphically described the two days of racial violence that took place in Springfield, Illinois in August 1908 and lamented that there was no "large and powerful body of citizens" prepared to respond and come to the aid of the black population. Mary White Ovington wrote to Walling asking him to meet her and a few others in New York to discuss the "Negro Problem." During January 1909, Ovington, Walling, Dr. Henry Moskowitz, Oswald Garrison Villard, Charles E. Russell, Bishop Alexander Walters, and Rev. William Henry Brooks met, discussed the race question, and decided to call a larger conference to address the issue. In February, the group presented a call written by Villard and signed by 60 prominent black and white Americans, including W.E.B. Du Bois, Ida B. Wells-Barnett, Mary Church Terrell, and Jane Addams. The call reflected the platforms of the Afro-American Council and the Niagara Movement, emphasizing the protection of black rights guaranteed by the fourteenth and fifteenth amendments.

In response to the call, the National Negro Conference, held May 30–June 1, 1909, created the Committee of Forty, whose mission was to develop plans for the creation of an effective organization tentatively called the "Committee for the Advancement of the Negro Race." The committee's plans were implemented the following year at a second annual conference where the organization's permanent name was adopted and the group's first officers were selected.

They included Moorfield Storey as president; William E. Walling as executive committee chairman; John E. Milholland as treasurer; Oswald Garrison Villard as disbursing treasurer; Frances Blascoer as executive secretary; and W.E.B. Du Bois, the only black officer, as director of publicity and research.

Once the organization was created, the group immediately began what has been nearly a century of militant protest and litigation against the denial of constitutional rights of African Americans. Within the first year, the group began agitating for better job opportunities for blacks and greater protection from racial violence in the South. The group also established its first local branch in Chicago and, under the guidance of Du Bois, launched *The Crisis*, a magazine that quickly became the leading voice in the black struggle. Du Bois published political articles and literary works aimed at educating the readership, white and black, about black culture, history, and American racism. He hoped to instill pride in the African-American community and stir the audience of both races to action. The magazine grew from its initial publication of 1,000 copies in 1910 to a circulation of 16,000 the following year and 100,000 by 1918.

By the end of the fifth year, the association had 24 branches and had initiated numerous crusades against discrimination. Among other things, the group had begun campaigning against the exclusion of black lawyers from the American Bar Association, laid the ground work for a legal attack on residential segregation, protested a number of anti-intermarriage bills, and objected to President Woodrow Wilson's policy of segregating African-American government employees. In the next few years the group continued to battle against racial injustice, campaigning, for example, against the racist film, *The Birth of a Nation*. The organization also called for the African American population to "close the ranks" in support of the war effort and the association's president argued the Louisville residential segregation case before the Supreme Court.

As World War I came to a close, black America experienced a series of race riots in numerous cities throughout the nation, the most horrendous occurring in East St. Louis in 1917 and Chicago in 1919. The NAACP responded in 1917 with a silent parade of 15,000 in Harlem. In 1919, the group called for the creation of a Legal Defense Fund to employ lawyers to increase the association's attempts to end such lynching and mob violence and bring the culprits to justice. In that same year, the organization also published its famous study on lynching, *Thirty Years of Lynching in the United States, 1889–1918*.

Much of the period's violence was precipitated by white soldiers returning home to find a large black population in their northern neighborhoods and job markets. This migration, due in large part to wartime prosperity, aided the NAACP as more African Americans joined the organization. In fact, black membership grew so quickly that by 1920 their membership fees were supplying most of the association's income. More importantly, during this period African Americans began to play a role in the organization's leadership. In 1916, James Weldon Johnson was hired as field secretary and in 1918 Walter White became assistant executive secretary.

In the 1920s, in addition to its continued propaganda campaign against lynching and other forms of racial violence, the NAACP stepped up its use of the courts to challenge racial injustices. The organization utilized two criteria when deciding upon a case: first, whether it involved injustice or discrimination in relation to race; second, whether it would establish a precedent for protecting black rights as a whole. (These criteria were on the national level; the local branches continued to accept nearly any case of injustice.) During the 1920s The association took on numerous cases including the Arkansas riot case, Dr. Ossian Sweet's murder case, and the beginning of the challenge of the Texas "white primary" system. What would have the greatest impact on the organization, however, was its decision toward the end of the decade to begin its challenge against segregated southern schools in its effort to overturn *Plessy v. Ferguson*.

This new legal initiative was launched by the recently formed NAACP legal committee, which by 1935 decided to develop its own legal staff. Before this time, the association had worked with numerous, mainly white, lawyers who worked on a pro bono basis or for a nominal fee. For a number of reasons, however, by mid-1935 the group decided to employ Charles H. Houston, the Dean of Howard Law School, as its full-time special counsel. Houston put together a legal team, with a considerable black presence, which included his former student, Thurgood Marshall.

The NAACP's new legal staff created a two-pronged strategy to fight southern educational discrimination. It directly attacked the exclusion of blacks from professional and graduate programs at southern state schools and indirectly contested segregation and discrimination at the primary and secondary levels in issues such as salaries, facilities, and length of school terms. The group sought to force the South either to strengthen African American institutions or to desegregate them on the basis that it was too costly to keep them open. During this period, it is also important to note that Du Bois left the organization due to arguments over the policies of the association, the autonomy of *The Crisis*, and personality conflicts.

The first step in the new legal strategy was to win victories on the local and state levels to create a precedent that the association could build upon to dismantle *Plessy*. Before Houston left the NAACP's legal committee, Marshall would replace him as special counsel. He successfully tested his strategy in the Maryland Supreme Court case *Murray v. Maryland*. In 1938, the association also won a case on behalf of William Gibbs in an attempt to equalize teachers' salaries. The victory set a precedent for similar cases throughout the country. In the same year William Hastie succeeded Arthur Spingarn as chairman of the Legal Committee and soon after the Committee became the NAACP Legal Defense and Educational Fund, Inc. (LDF).

In addition to the educational fight, the organization continued to challenge and gain victories in cases involving other racial injustices. During World War II, the association pursued the integration of the armed forces and the opening of federally funded defense contracts. In the 1940s, the group also gained favorable decisions from the Supreme Court in a few key cases. These victories included the last of the three cases argued against the all white Texas primary, *Smith v. Allwright* (1944); a challenge against segregation in interstate travel, *Morgan v. Virginia* (1946); and against restrictive housing covenants, *Shelley v. Kraemer* and *McGhee v. Sipes* (1948).

In 1947 members of the NAACP, working with President Harry S. Truman's Committee on Civil Rights, released a report entitled *To Secure These Rights* which recommended the elimination of "segregation based on race, color, creed, or national origin, from American life." The following year President Truman issued executive order 9981, which barred segregation in the military, and the LDF undertook a series of suits aimed at directly challenging the *Plessy* doctrine. In 1950, the Supreme Court took decisive steps in two LDF cases, *Sweatt v. Painter* and *McLaurin v. Oklahoma*. In the former, the court ruled that the separate law school created in Texas to accommodate Herman Sweatt was not and could not

be equal to that of the state university for white law students. In the latter, the court decided that the University of Oklahoma graduate school could not segregate G.W. McLaurin.

These victories seriously weakened the South's segregation policies in higher education and the following year the LDF launched its offensive on a second front with their "Equality under Law" campaign. This aimed at segregation on the primary and secondary educational levels by filing suits against school districts in Georgia, South Carolina, Kansas, and Delaware. On May 17, 1954, the Supreme Court ruled on these cases, plus a fifth in connection with the school system in the District of Columbia, in the case known as *Brown v. Board of Education*. The court affirmed the NAACP's argument that separate educational facilities were inherently unequal and that in the field of education, the doctrine of "separate but equal" had no place. Thus the ruling set a precedent that would allow the LDF to strive to completely overturn the *Plessy* decision.

The court's decision in *Brown* and the success of the Montgomery Bus Boycott are often seen as the origins of the modern civil rights movement. In the history of the movement the NAACP is often overshadowed by Martin Luther King, Jr. and the activists of the newer civil rights organizations, but the association continued to contribute and was often in the forefront of the struggle for civil rights. As Roy Wilkins, the executive director, declared in the mid-1960s, "NAACP branches put up the money and others get the credit." The association struggled to see that *Brown* was enforced and pushed for the passage of Fair Employment Practices Committee (FEPC) laws, equal housing legislation, and other civil rights laws. With the organization's membership continuing to grow to over 400,000 in 1963, it lobbied for the passage of the Civil Rights Act of 1964 and the Voting Rights Act of 1965.

Since the end of the civil rights movement and the success of the NAACP's initial goals, the end of de jure segregation, and the enforcement of the fourteenth and fifteenth amendments, the organization has been groping to create effective programs to meet new challenges. Throughout the years, however, the NAACP has continued to be at the forefront of the struggle to protect African Americans against racial injustice, fighting to ensure all citizens the full protection of the civil rights legislation that the group fought from its inception to create.

SHAWN LEIGH ALEXANDER

See also **Du Bois, W.E.B.; Education Rights**

Further Reading

Factor, Robert L., *The Black Response to America: Men, Ideals, and Organization, From Frederick Douglass to the NAACP,* Reading, Massachussets: Addison-Wesley Publishing, 1970

Hughes, Langston, *Fight for Freedom: The Story of the NAACP,* New York: Norton, 1962

Kellogg, Charles Flint, *NAACP: A History of the National Association for the Advancement of Colored People, Vol. 1, 1909–1920,* Baltimore: John's Hopkins University Press, 1967

Kluger, Richard, *Simple Justice: The History of Brown V. Board of Education and Black America's Struggle for Equality,* New York: Knopf, 1976

Meier, August, *Negro Thought in America, 1880–1915: Racial Ideologies in the Age of Booker T. Washington,* Ann Arbor: University of Michigan Press, 1963

Meier, August, and John H. Bracey, "The NAACP as a Reform Movement, 1909–1965: To Reach the Conscience of America," *The Journal of Southern History* 59, no. 1 (1993)

Ross, B. Joyce, *J.E. Spingarn and the Rise of the NAACP,* New York: Atheneum, 1972

Tushnet, Mark V., *The NAACP's Legal Strategy against Segregated Education, 1925–1950,* Chapel Hill: University of North Carolina Press, 1987

Wedin, Carolyn, *Inheritors of the Spirit: Mary White Ovington and the Founding of the NAACP,* New York: Wiley, 1998

Wilson, Sondra Kathryn, editor, *In Search of Democracy: The NAACP Writings of James Weldon Johnson, Walter White, and Roy Wilkins (1920–1977),* New York: Oxford University Press, 1999

Zangrando, Robert L., *The NAACP Crusade against Lynching, 1909–1950,* Philadelphia: Temple University Press, 1980

Nationalism

Nationalism has had a profound effect on the situation of the world's minorities. Most often, minorities have found themselves within the boundaries of nation-states that pursed policies of cultural homogenization. This has led to bitter disputes between majority and minority groups. The status of the minorities is closely connected to the type of nationalism within a particular state. In nation-states where civic nationalism prevails, minorities have been accommodated within the existing state; in nation-states where ethnic nationalism prevails, minorities have been the targets of aggressive acculturation campaigns. Over the post–World War II period, the establishment of the international human rights regime has added important constraints on state sovereignty. Consequently, international protection of minorities has increased.

The Origins and Evolution of Nationalism

Nationalism is a political movement that advocates unity of the nation and the state. States have existed prior to nationalism, but, with the coming of nationalism, states were transformed into *nation-states*. That is, they are no longer content with claiming sovereignty over a territory, but they also claim to be the national homeland of a specific nation.

Nationalism is inconceivable without the idea of the nation, but the nation is a term that cannot be objectively defined. From its initial connotation of corporate bodies in medieval universities, this term evolved in the course of the last five centuries to mean a political community of citizens and later on, an ethnic community that shares bonds of social solidarity. Despite attempts to pinpoint the origins of nations in ethnic, racial, or other forms of primordial solidarity, the nation has never been successfully defined according to such objective criteria, although common definitions include a community that shares a common language, religion, culture, and perceived history.

Consequently, the majority of contemporary research on this topic has adopted the view that the nation is a form of community that is *socially constructed.* This means that the nation is a man-made construct, the product of deliberate human action and imagination. What sets the nation apart from similar human groups (like tribes or ethnic groups) is that the nation is a *secular cultural community* unique to the modern world. Key ingredients for nation-building include communications and transportation technologies (such as printing and railroads), which have made it possible for people to conceive of bonds with other citizens who live in other parts of the same state. In his book,

Imagined Communities (1991), Benedict Anderson made this point abundantly clear by developing a persuasive and influential argument that the nation is "an imagined community," that is, a community born out of the collective imagination of the people. Anderson points out that while the nation is imagined, it is by no means imaginary. On the contrary, it has an important effect on social life.

The scholarly production on nationalism and its connections to the nation-state is voluminous. Moreover, during the last 30 years there has been an explosion of research that largely outdated the pre-1970 literature. While nationalism was initially a topic for historians, during the last 20 years the social scientific community has produced an extensive and novel body of work. Most scholars agree that nationalism began as a European and North American phenomenon and it is closely connected to the modernization of these societies.

During the post–World War II period, Ernest Gellner developed a highly influential sociological theory on the origins and nature of nationalism. According to Gellner, the nation is a contemporary community that is a corollary of the process of industrialization and modernization. In sharp contrast to the nationalists' own proclamation, Gellner argues that nationalism makes the nation a reality. In particular, mass literacy provides a key ingredient for nation-building because it enables a mass of people to receive standardized education. Gellner's theory continues to be the object of debate among the scholarly community.

A major alternative view has been developed by sociologist Anthony D. Smith, who suggests that modern nations are born out of a premodern *ethnies*, or ethnic community. Smith disagrees with Gellner's contention that nationalism invents nations through cultural mobilization and the construction of a print-based national culture. For Smith, nations have their roots in premodern sentiments of social solidarity. Although the history of nations is sometimes traced back to several centuries, the overwhelming majority of scholars of nationalism today are in agreement with each other over the relatively recent nature of this social transformation. Depending on the researcher and the specific case in question, the origins of nationalism can be traced to sometime between the sixteenth and nineteenth centuries.

Nation-Building and Citizenship

The most intensive period of nation-building occurred during the last two centuries via the establishment of compulsory education, permanent armies based on universal conscription, the writing of national history, rituals of identity, literature, and the rise of communications technologies that made possible for people living far away from each other to imagine that they are members of the same nation.

These nation-building strategies carried with them the growing necessity for popular participation in government. Indeed, nationalism was initially connected to the rights of the people to rule over the nation. In principle, this is not problematic. But the extension of citizenship rights over a state's population carried with it an important problem: Who were the "people" that made up the nation? Were they going to be defined in terms of their living within the boundaries of the state? Were they going to be defined in terms of their belonging to a specific ethnic group?

An affirmative answer to the first question gave birth to the civic nationalism of England and other British postcolonial societies (including the United States). An affirmative answer to the second question gave birth to the ethnic nationalism of Eastern Europe and many Third World countries. Numerous scholars of nationalism have also commented or elaborated on this distinction. Some of them have rejected the one or the other type of nationalism, but most of them would agree that there are at least these two types of nationalism.

Nationalism and Minorities

Not surprisingly, minorities are facing a different situation depending upon the type of nationalism that prevails within the specific state they live in. In states oriented toward civic nationalism, the incorporation and accommodation of minorities has become a major issue of domestic politics over the last century.

Although prejudice and discrimination exist in Western Europe and North America, the state and its various administrative and legal agencies usually have sought to affirm the principle of equality before the law, thereby opening up avenues for constructing multicultural societies. This was a slow and contested process and it was only in the post-1960 period that Western democracies granted full civic rights to their minority population.

In states oriented toward ethnic nationalism, the situation was worse. There the incorporation of minorities was conceived as forceful acculturation into the culture of the dominant ethnic group. Not surprisingly, bitter disputes over minorities erupted in the newly constructed states of Eastern Europe and the postcolonial

Third World countries. During the first half of the twentieth century, the most bitter minority disputes took place in Eastern Europe, where many states were crafted out of the remnants of the Habsburg and Ottoman empires. The ethnic intermixing of peoples made it very difficult to agree on mutually accepted boundaries, and the minorities left outside the boundaries of specific nation-states were the objects of acculturation policies by rival nation-states. Extensive population exchanges were carried out in a futile attempt to construct ethnically homogeneous nation-states. It is important to remember that during the first half of the twentieth century, the homogeneous nation-state was considered to be the prevailing form of state worldwide. Minorities were viewed as anomalies within presumably homogeneous nation-states.

In the Soviet Union (and later in post–World War II Yugoslavia), the Communist Party attempted to solve this infamous "national question" by constructing "states" that were formally independent yet under firm Communist control. This strategy was effective for a considerable period—although, obviously it did not solve the problem completely. Under Communist rule, national identity was formally affirmed and protected, whereas more extreme nationalists were jailed. This strategy of containment and accommodation broke down in the 1980s, because of the Communists' loss of legitimacy and the opening of many Eastern European societies to Western democratic ideals. The result was the swift return of many preexisting disputes about minorities, leading eventually to the well-publicized collapse of Yugoslavia in the 1990s as well as a host of similar disputes in the former Soviet Union.

Nation-States and Minorities

In the course of the twentieth century, the changing norms of the international community seriously affected the situation of minorities and their legal status vis-à-vis their states. Until World War II, the international community recognized the primacy of state sovereignty on minority issues. Furthermore, the post–World War I regime of international minorities was skewed against the losers of World War I, thereby leading to resentment and revisionism.

In the aftermath of World War II, the new institutional arrangement expressed in the United Nations (UN), and the subsequent treaties signed during the 1948–89 period, led to a significant shift in international standards. First, the post–World War II period witnessed a shift from collective rights to individual rights. The shift was inspired by a strong desire to avoid the bitter disputes about national minorities that were so pervasive in the interwar period.

Second, the various treaties signed in the second half of the twentieth century instituted a de facto curtailment of state sovereignty by institutionalizing and formalizing the state's responsibility to treat all citizens according to the same legal standards. During the post-1989 period, the North Atlantic Treaty Organization (NATO) and the United States have individually expressed their desire to see a further codification of these principles as well as their eventual transformation to binding legal guides. Such codification would mean that military intervention could be expected in cases in which these principles were not upheld. The 1999 NATO-led war against Yugoslavia was carried out on these premises. Despite the success of the NATO intervention in this particular instance, there is still no solid agreement about the use of such a strategy, because the member states of the European Union wish to adopt a much more flexible approach.

However, as the preceding discussion illustrates, the current reconfiguration of state sovereignty has meant that minorities are enjoying considerable protection under international law, and they have the legal status and--thanks to the information revolution—the technological ability to bypass their state and appeal directly to an increasingly global audience. The persecution of minorities by nationalist majorities, however, still continues in some countries (e.g., Myanmar, Indonesia, and Sudan).

VICTOR ROUDOMETOF

See also **Colonialism; Exchange of Population**

Further Reading

Alter, Peter, *Nationalismus,* Frankfurt: Suhrkamp, 1983, translated by Stuart McKinnon-Evans as *Nationalism,* London and New York: Arnold, 1989

Anderson, Benedict R.O'G., *Imagined Communities: Reflections on the Origin and Spread of Nationalism,* London: Verso, 1983; revised and expanded edition, New York: Verso, 1991

Breuilly, John, *Nationalism and the State,* New York: St. Martin's Press, and Manchester: Manchester University Press, 1982; 2nd edition, Chicago: University of Chicago Press, 1994

Brubaker, Rogers, *Nationalism Reframed: Nationhood and the National Question in the New Europe,* Cambridge and New York: Cambridge University Press, 1996

Featherstone, Mike, editor, *Global Culture: Nationalism, Globalization, and Modernity,* London and Newbury Park, California: Sage, 1990

Gellner, Ernest, *Nations and Nationalism,* Ithaca, New York: Cornell University Press, and Oxford: Blackwell, 1983

Greenfeld, Liah, *Nationalism: Five Roads to Modernity,* Cambridge, Massachusetts: Harvard University Press, 1992

Hobsbawm, Eric J., *Nations and Nationalism since 1780: Programme, Myth, Reality,* Cambridge and New York: Cambridge University Press, 1990

Kedourie, Elie, *Nationalism,* London: Hutchinson, 1960; 2nd edition, New York: Praeger, 1961

Musgrave, Thomas D., *Self-Determination and National Minorities,* Oxford: Clarendon Press, and New York: Oxford University Press, 1997

Nations and Nationalism: The Official Journal of the Association for the Study of Ethnicity and Nationalism. <http://www.nationalismproject.org>

Smith, Anthony D., *The Ethnic Origins of Nations,* Oxford: Blackwell, 1986; New York: Blackwell, 1987

Ndebele

Capsule Summary

Country Name: Ndebele
Location: southwestern Zimbabwe (especially the 30–50 miles surrounding the city of Bulawayo), northwestern Botswana, and the Central ancient Transvaal region (Northeastern South Africa)
Total Population: 2.5 million
Language: IsiNdebele (Nguni group of the Southern Bantu family)
Religions: Predominantly Christian (Catholic, Protestant, and especially linked to independent African churches); traditional religion (animistic).

The people of Ndebele, also called *Ndebele*, are known by a variety of alternative names. Many neighboring African tribes refer to them as Manguni or Madzwiti. According to their own usage, the correct term for the group is *AmaNdebele*. The most usual singular form is *IliNdebele*. English speakers normally refer to them as Matabele, and the Western part of Zimbabwe is known as Matabeleland. There is considerable doubt as to how the Ndebele first acquired their name. According to some theories, it is a Sotho word meaning "those of the long shields," but all theories agree that it was a name first given by the Sotho-Tswana peoples, whom the Ndebele passed before reaching Zimbabwe, and that the original form was the Sotho *Matabele*. Since the Ndebele at that time lacked a convenient generic term for themselves, they adopted this title in its Nguni form of *AmaNdebele*. The balance of the evidence suggests that this term was in use to describe peoples of Nguni stock living in predominantly Sotho or Tswana areas long before the founders of the present-day Zimbabwe's Ndebele had left their original home in Zululand.

The Ndebele are in many ways elusive. It is partly due to the fact that the original group consisted of a conquering people who continually absorbed alien elements. In short, the Ndebele had all the characteristics of a political and social entity that welds its heterogeneous elements into a more homogeneous whole. We may say that the word *Ndebele* refers to people who have one or more of the following characteristics: refer to themselves as Ndebele; were themselves, or had ancestors who were part of the Ndebele state and subjects of the Ndebele King; order their lives according to a pattern they call "the Ndebele way" (*umtetu wamandebele*); and speak Ndebele in their homes.

The Nguni language, brought from Zululand by the original Ndebele conquerors, was one of the cultural traits that distinguished them most clearly from neighboring peoples. For instance, when a young *Holi* (a man of non-Nguni origin) was allowed to join a regiment and become a warrior, it is said by the Ndebele that he was trained "to grow clever" (*uhuhlakanipa*). The Ndebele are the only one of the many Nguni conquest states in Southern Central Africa where the Nguni language has survived.

The IsiNdebele (the Ndebele language), moreover, was influenced by the surrounding idioms, which resulted in two main Ndebele linguistic groups: Northern (in Botswana and Zimbabwe) and Southern (in South Africa). Zulu is probably the Nguni language closest to Ndebele and, in fact, most adult Ndebele men have a considerable knowledge of Zulu. But a great many Ndebele forms which are closer to Xhosa (another Nguni idiom) are also found. Twelve thousand Ndebele live in Botswana, and nearly 1 million in the Transvaal region of South Africa. The Ndebele of Southern Africa are divided into four subtribes, of which two, the Manala and the Ndzundza, live mainly in the Pretoria and Mpumalanga areas of South Africa. The Northern Ndebele of Botswana and Zimbabwe are highly influenced by the Sotho culture.

Ndebele History

In the beginning of the nineteenth century, the Zulu king Shaka, in what is now Kwazulu-Natal region of South Africa, conquered a group of people who were under the rule of chief Matshobana of the Kumalo clan. Matshobana's son, Mzilikazi (born in 1790), was captured and enrolled in Shaka's army, where he rose to the position of *induna* (Zulu name for a state official appointed by the king, or by a local chief), and was placed in command of a military *kraal* (family homestead) at Gibixegu. In 1822, after a raid, he failed to hand over all the cattle he had captured, an act of treason punishable by death, of which King Shaka came to hear. Mzilikazi decided that discretion was the better part of valor, and set out with his followers for the high lands across the Drakensberg. However, before leaving Natal, they were attacked by an expedition sent by King Shaka, in which many of Mzilikazi's followers were killed. Evading further punitive expeditions, they trekked over the Transvaal and the Orange Free State, raiding for cattle and food, capturing young men who were incorporated into Mzilikazi's army, and attacked the Southern Sotho king Mosheh, but were defeated. They then trekked northward, and in 1825, settled on the upper Apies River. Cattle raids by the Griquas led to a move westward again in 1832, and Mzilikazi built his royal kraal at Mosega in the Marico valley. In 1836, Mzilikazi sent a mission to the Governor of the Cape, and concluded a treaty with the British Crown by which he pledged himself to be a faithful friend and ally of the Colony and to admit missionaries to his dominions.

Under the pressure of both the Zulu and Boers (peasants of Dutch stock), who made several successful attacks on them in 1836 and 1837, the Ndebele left the Marico valley. During the march north, the Ndebele divided into two sections, one under the command of the king himself, the other under the *induna* Gundwane. The king's section marched farther west, whereas that of Gundwane's entered the country of Kalanga, and finally reached the country close to Bulawayo, near the hill *Intaba YezInduna* ("the mountain of the state official"). The year of their arrival, generally assumed to be 1838, is normally considered the founding date of the Ndebele nation. The country

in which they settled was part of the Rozwi empire, and in a great many cases, the autochthonous people accepted the newcomers without fighting.

Mzilikazi then established Ndebele overlordship in the areas where he and his followers had settled, building many military kraals in various parts of the country under "regimental" or "town" chiefs (*Izinduna zamabuto*). His first permanent capital was at Inyati, in the flat country, some 40 miles to the north of Bulawayo, but he later moved to Mhlahlandlela; this capital was also moved as a unit several times. The Kalanga who remained in the area were brought under the Ndebele rule. They included the Nanzwa, the Nyai, the Tonga, and the Ila. Within 20 years of their arrival, the Ndebele had firmly established their supremacy in an area now known as Matabeleland, and their power was virtually unopposed over an even wider area.

When Mzilikazi died in 1868, Uncombate, the Chief Counsellor, assumed the regency until Lobengula was installed as king. As late as 1888 and 1893, the Ndebele were raiding into Tonga and Ila countries across the Zambezi River. The Pioneer Column sent by C. Rhodes and the British South Africa Company (BSA) entered Mashonaland in 1890 and clashed with the Ndebele forces in Bulawayo (1893). After this war, the Ndebele came under the direct rule of the BSA; the Ndebele appeared to accept the new colonial regime, but in 1896, there was a rebellion and an attempt to drive the Europeans out of the country. This was the last occasion on which the Ndebele nation acted as, or was treated as, a single political unit. Apart from these political changes, the Ndebele way of life was profoundly affected by various other developments that followed the establishment of the BSA rule. Land was alienated for European use and settled by white farmers. A large modern industrial town began to grow at Bulawayo, in the heart of the old Ndebele kingdom. Missionaries and traders came in increasing numbers. The resultant culture was nonetheless Ndebele, and in their own areas the Ndebele still have a specific way of life, with a complex system of law, customs, and morals, and they feel strongly about actions that offend it.

Ndebele Internal Subdivisions and Social Structure

The Ndebele adopted a number of alien customs, while the absorbed peoples adopted those of the original Nguni core or retained their own in varying degrees. Finally, the different relationships to the Ndebele king of the many conquered and raided tribes meant that the Ndebele kingdom and "the Ndebele" as an ethnic unit did not comprise the same peoples. For the years between 1840 and 1893, the important features that were common to all Ndebele were that they were subjects of the Ndebele king, had served or were liable to serve in his regiments, and had adopted the Ndebele way of life and language, even though some of the older people of other stocks may have retained part of their parent cultures.

The Ndebele recognized the tribal intermixture in their nation and formalized it by means of a social structure that can perhaps be best described as a caste system, for lack of a specific term for it in Ndebele. The whole nation was divided into three categories: the *Zanzi*, the *Enhla*, and the *Holi*. The Zansi, the "people for down country" (the coastal lowlands of present-day Eastern South Africa), were Mzilikazi's adherents, who had fled with him from King Shaka, and his descendants. The Holi, who came to form the majority of the nation, were the people of Shona, Kalanga, and other origins.

Ndebele People in Contemporary Times

In South Africa, a nominally autonomous Ndebele "state" (a "Homeland" or "bantustan"), KwaNdebele was established in a small contiguous territory in central Transvaal (present-day Northwestern Mpumalanga) in 1977. This later became nominally independent in 1981. Like the other "bantu territorial authorities," KwaNdebele was an instrument of the racist government of Pretoria for exclusion and oppression of non-white South Africans. Theoretically ruled by the members of the AmaDzundza dynasty, James Mahlangu was the last Chief Minister of the Homeland of KwaNdebele (1990–1994).

During Zimbabwe's fight for independence (obtained in January 1980), the Ndebele supported the Zimbabwe African Peoples Union (ZAPU), of Joshua Nkomo. In November 1980, the conflict between the ZAPU (a Ndebele-based party) and the ZANU (mainly Shona-based) resulted in more than 60 deaths. In February 1981, a Ndebele uprising took place against Zimbabwe's government. The revolt was centered in the capital of Matabeland, Bulawayo, which resulted in the death of 1,350 people. One year later, 2,000 soldiers arrived in Matabeleland to reinforce the 5,000 military forces. It is believed that during the 1980s, some 20,000 Ndebele people were killed in Matabeleland because of their suspected opposition to the Shona-based ruling party.

In 1999, during the late Vice President Joshua Nkomo's burial, President Robert Mugabe admitted wrongdoing, describing the massacres as an "act of madness" which would not be repeated again. Since April 2003, the president is under pressure to release reports of the alleged massacre of thousands of Ndebele by government security forces during the mid-1980s. The Zimbabwe Lawyers for Human Rights and Legal Resources Foundation is needling President Mugabe to publish the reports and initiate a national reconciliation process after ducking the issue for years. The attorneys are seeking a Supreme Court order compelling him to release the findings of two government-appointed commissions of inquiry into the alleged purges between 1982 and 1987.

JOAN MANUEL CABEZAS LÓPEZ

See also **Botswana; South Africa; Zimbabwe**

Further Reading

Chanaiwa, D., "African Humanism in South Africa," in *Independence Without Freedom*, edited by A. Mugomba and M. Nyaggah, Oxford: ABC-Clio Press, 1980

De Kiewiet, W., *The Imperial Factor in South Africa. A Study in Politics and Economics*, London: Frank Cass, 1965

Gann, L.H., and T.H. Henriksen, *The Struggle for Zimbabwe: Battle in the Bush*, New York: Praeger, 1981

Gluckman, M., "The Kingdom of the Zulu of South Africa," in *African Political Systems*, edited by D. Fortes, E.E. Evans-Pritchard, Oxford: Oxford University Press, 1940

Hughes, A.J.B., and J. Van Velsen, *The Ndebele of Southern Rhodesia*, London: International African Institute, 1954

Kriger, N., *Zimbabwe's Guerrilla War: Peasant Voices*, Cambridge: Cambridge University Press, 1992

MacMillan, W.M., *Bantu, Boer and Briton*, Oxford: Clarendon Press, 1963

Moffat, R.U., *John Moffat. C.M.G., Missionary*, New York: Negro Universities Press, 1969

Pakenham, T., *The Scramble for Africa*, London: Avon Books, 1992

Palley, C., *The Constitutional History and Law in Southern Rhodesia, 1888–1965*, Oxford: Clarendon Press, 1966

Samkange, S., *On Trial for My Country*, London: Heinemann, 1969

Troup, F., *South Africa: An Historical Introduction*, Middlesex: Penguin Books, 1975

Negritos

Capsule Summary

Location: Mainland Southeast Asia, Thailand, Malaysia, and the Philippines
Total population: 40,000
Languages: Austroasiatic, Austronesian, and Andamanese
Religions: Animistic beliefs, some conversion to Christianity (in Philippines) and Islam (in Malaysia)

Negritos are peoples distinguished by small stature, dark skin, and curly or kinky black hair, existing in pockets in Mainland and Island Southeast Asia. Genetic studies have not yet established a connection to the pygmy populations in Africa and Papua New Guinea. Negritos have become marginal, often culturally isolated, minorities who suffer intense pressure from more technologically advanced societies. Immigrant peoples looking for land crowd into their traditional territories upsetting the ecological balance and diminishing their land base. They face persecution and racial discrimination, enslavement and land theft, kidnappings and even murder. Their numbers are dwindling as they come in contact with new diseases; face severe diet changes due to the disappearance of their plant and animal food sources; adopt new habits such as consuming alcohol and foodstuffs that lack nutrients and are high in sugar content.

Andaman Islands

There are four Negrito groups in the Andaman Islands, in the Indian Ocean: the Great Andamanese, the Onge, the Jarawa, and the Sentinelese. The Andamanese Negritos studied so far exhibit the small size characteristic of Negrito people elsewhere. For women, the average height is 54 inches (137 cm) and the average weight is 95.5 pounds (43.4 kg). The men average 58.5 inches (148.5 cm) in height, and 87 pounds (39.5 kg) in weight. They all show the tragic effects of contact with the outside world through their dramatic depopulation in the last 150 years. The Great Andamanese were relocated to Strait Island and today, there are fewer than 50 people. Once comprising ten tribes and two major subdivisions (north and south), their population decreased from nearly 4,000 to just over 600 by the turn of the twentieth century. This was due to a series of diseases like syphilis, measles, smallpox, and bronchitis that spread from escaped British convicts and naval personnel. Recent population figures show that the number of Andamanese has increased from 19 (1961) to 37 (1996). The Onge on Little Andaman Island are surrounded by coral reefs. The resources of the sea and the well-established island forest system once provided them a stable subsistence base of wild animals, gathered root crops, fish, and mussels. However, starting with a population of 700 in 1860s, they dropped to 150 in 1951 and now are down to just under 100. After India's independence, they were victimized by the influx of immigrants, most notably in the 1960s, and the forests became poor-soil agricultural plots. The Onge are in two settlements where they receive food and medical attention from government officials. The outlook for their continued survival is not promising as they struggle with diseases like tuberculosis. Unless the problems of high sterility and infant mortality rates are solved, this group is in grave danger of extinction.

The fierce Jarawa, numbering around 250, inhabit the west coast of the South Andaman and Middle Andaman Islands. They represent an aggressive stance by a Negrito group to stop infringement into their territory. Forests on the two islands were declared the Jarawa Reserve Forests by the Indian government. The tribe is engaged in a type of warfare as they resist the infringement of settlers with occasional forays into the settlers' homes to take away weapons. They resisted the building of a Great Andaman Trunk Road through the Reserve with roadblocks; they killed elephants, dogs, cattle, and even strangers in an effort to halt the influx of timber buyers, building contractors, and settlers who ventured into the forest. Officials have proposed a number of solutions, including relocation, but continue to use police force to keep the Jarawa and the settlers apart.

The Sentinelese, the only inhabitants of North Sentinel Island, a small 28 square-mile (72 square-kilometer) island off the west coast of South Andaman island, are a hunting-gathering society who depend on resources of the sea. Their bellicose nature and a barrier reef have kept them isolated from the contact problems suffered by other Negritos. They have steadily resisted attempts at contact over the years and have vanished into the forest when landing parties arrive with gifts. More than one shipwrecked sailor has died from a Sentinelese arrow. In recent times, a solitary male that shot arrows from the shore wounded a photographer who attempted to land in a boat. However, at various times, people have handed gifts to the Sentinelese. Population estimates range from 100 to 400, but they are based on sightings from helicopters. Over the years people have seen a few items of Sentinelese culture including bow, arrows, spears, baskets, wooden buckets, fishing nets, and lean-tos. Official government policy at this time is to prevent intrusion by outsiders into the waters around North Sentinel Island; stop physical contact with the Sentinelese to avoid introduction of diseases; and, to restrict exploitation of the natural resources to only the native population. They remain the least understood tribal group in the world, and the Sentinelese are an example of the rare circumstances that converge to make it possible for a Negrito group to survive in the twenty-first century.

Thailand

Several hundred Manik Negritos, also know as Manne or Mani, and called *Sakai* by the Thai, inhabit the highlands at the southern end of the Khao Bantat range in Southern Thailand. This area is now protected by Thai law as a Wildlife Sanctuary, along with the area to the north, the Khao Chong National Park, which is also patrolled and protected. To prevent illegal logging, cultivation, and other intrusive activity, officials conduct surveillance by helicopter and ground patrols. The Manik survive by harvesting forest fruits, gathering root crops, and hunting animals. They move in small groups exploiting the resources in an area and move on to other places upon exhausting the immediate harvest. Expert herbalists, the Manik maintain their traditional knowledge of herbs and medicinal plants.

Friends of People Close to Nature, a non-profit organization, has uncovered the problems facing the Manik including a decline in population by 50 percent during a recent 14-year period; poaching by Thai people throughout the Wild Sanctuary in response to the demand by restaurants for wild meat; illegal logging even after a ban on logging; and, the expansion of rubber tree plantations into protected areas. Moving to nearby Malaysia is not a viable option for the Manik. The policy of placing them in special villages and restricting their movement in the forest is untenable for these nomadic hunter-gatherers. In addition to day-by-day hunger brought about by dwindling forest resources, the Manik face the serious problem of a shrinking gene pool.

Central Peninsular Malaysia

Negrito people (Batek, Semang) who live in peninsular Malaysia and speak Austroasiatic languages number around 4,000. The Batek in Kelantan, Terengganu, and Pahang, call themselves *batek hep* "people of the forest," and now support themselves in a variety of ways. They constantly change activities and rotate between hunting and gathering, gathering and the sale of forest products, crafts produced for tourists, occasional hired labor, and forest guides. Several extended families move together in camps, staying in one for a few months, then disbanding and moving to form another group. They are concerned that the forest resources are fast diminishing as vast areas of the forest are logged, and rubber plantations begin to dominate the landscape. Although their lifestyle is simple, their belief system is an elaborate web of gods and spirits, tied together in an oral epistemology passed down through generations with deliberate care. As animists, they rely on their shamans to call on the spirits to intervene when faced with problems. Some Batek have converted to Islam and are in the process of becoming sedentary cash crop farmers.

Philippines

The bulk of the Negrito population (29 Austronesian Negrito language groups, totaling about 31,000 speakers), is located in the Philippines. These groups include the Batak on Palawan, the Mamanua on Mindanao, the Ati on Panay, the Agta groups in Eastern Luzon, and the Ayta groups in Northwestern Luzon. According to a current theory, their ancestors moved to the Philippines perhaps in the late Pleistocene, travelling across the Sundaland bridges, created by low sea levels. Austronesian immigrants moved down from Taiwan around 2,500 BCE or possibly earlier. Thus the agriculturalists with their grain and domesticated animals met the hunter-gatherers, who lost their original languages. Lawrence Reid believes that a pidgin language developed and evolved into the modern Philippine Negrito languages all of which show a relationship to the other Austronesian languages of the Philippines. He found traces of the non-Austronesian language in words shared only by Negrito groups.

Over half a century of stellar work by the Summer Institute of Linguistics has resulted in a wealth of data on the Negrito groups, including word lists, grammar, dictionaries, and cultural studies. Thomas Headland's long-term study of The San Ildefonso Agta, and the publication of a quantitative database of demographic variables over a 44-year period, is a unique contribution not only to Negrito studies, but also to the fields of hunting and gathering. He and other anthropologists have also documented the continuing plight of the Agta as they face the loss of their lands and resources in the largest tropical forest on Luzon. Elsewhere on Luzon, the Pinatubo Negritos were displaced by the eruption of their mountain in 1991 and were transferred to lowland resettlements. Their forestlands, long since decimated by loggers in the 1950s, were dealt a deathblow by a natural, cataclysmic event. Some are now returning to attempt cultivation in a drastically changed environment.

The Nagpana Ati of Barotac Viejo, Panay island, provide an example of ways in which governments and a free enterprise market system often interact with Negritos. The Negritos were given reserved lands on a nearby mountain by the municipal government in the 1950s where they practiced slash and burn agriculture, and cultivated upland rice and root crops as their main staples. The Ati gathered orchids and forest herbal medicine plants and hunted wild pig, deer, and monitor lizards. They traded these items to lowlanders for food, clothing, and cash. However, in the 1960s, loggers harvested the forest trees. The forest gave way to grasslands, and lowlanders began to pasture their cattle on the mountain. This led to fencing of the land, and the outsiders began planting upland gardens, which they eventually claimed as their land. The deer and lizards vanished, and the orchids, as well a number of herbal medicine plants, all part of a balanced forest ecosystem, disappeared. In the 1980s, the Philippine government tried a reforestation project and hired the Ati to help plant seedlings and care for the growing trees. The Ati, however, desperate for cash and food, waited until the trees grew into young saplingsand harvested the trees illegally at night. They burned the wood in pits and sold the charcoal to eager lowland buyers. This resulted in failure of the reforestation project. Because the land could no longer sustain the Negrito population, the men went to work on sugar plantations on other islands.

F. Douglas Pennoyer

See also **Malaysia; Philippines; Thailand**

Further Reading

Bellwood, Peter, *Prehistory of the Indo-Malaysian Archipelago*, Sydney: Academic Press, 1985; revised edition, Honolulu: University of Hawaii Press, 1997

Early, John D., and Thomas N. Headland, *Population Dynamics of a Philippine Rain Forest People: The San Ildefonso Agta*, Gainesville, Florida: University Press of Florida, 1998

Endicott, Kirk, *Batek Negrito Religion: The World-view and Rituals of a Hunting and Gathering People of Peninsular Malaysia*, Oxford: Clarendon Press, 1979

Fox, Robert, "The Pinatubo Negritos: Their Useful Plants and Material Culture," *Philippine Journal of Science*, 81, no. 3–4 (1952)

Pennoyer, F. Douglas, "Inati: The Hidden Negrito Language of Panay, Philippines," *Philippine Journal of Linguistics*, 17, 18, nos. 2, 1 (1986, 87)

Rambo, A.T., *Primitive Polluters: Semang Impact on the Malaysian Tropical Rain Forest Ecosystem*, Ann Arbor, Michigan: University of Michigan Press, 1985

Reid, Lawrence A., "Possible Non-Austronesian Lexical Elements in Philippine Negrito Languages," *Oceanic Linguistics*, 33, (1994)

Winzeler, Robert L., editor, *Indigenous Peoples and the State: Politics, Land, and Ethnicity in the Malaysian Peninsula and Borneo*, New Haven: Yale University Southeast Asia Studies, 1997

Nepal

Capsule Summary

Country Name: Kingdom of Nepal
Location: Land-locked Himalayan Kingdom in South Asia located between India and China
Population: 26,469,569 (July 2003)

Languages: Nepali (official; spoken by 90% of the population), about a dozen other languages and 30 major dialects; English is spoken in many government offices and businesses (1995)
Religions: Hinduism (86.2%), Buddhism (7.8%), Islam (3.8%), other (2.2%)

The Kingdom of Nepal, the only Hindu state in the world today, is located in Southern Asia, between China and India. Its capital city, Kathmandu, had a population of 701,962 in 2001. King Prithvi Narayan Shah unified the kingdom in 1769, after two centuries of rule by an absolute monarchy. Nepal's journey toward genuine representative government started in 1959 when the center-left Nepali Congress won the first general elections, but the parliament was dissolved the following year. In 1990, widespread unrest and pro-democracy demonstrations, however, resulted in the country transforming into a constitutional monarchy with executive power vested in the prime minister and the cabinet. After three decades of party-less *panchayat* (village council) system, multi-party elections were held in 1991, which saw the Nepali Congress form the government. However, a Maoist (communist) insurgency, launched in 1996, gained momentum and has continually threatened democracy.

The emergence of the Communist Party of Nepal (United Marxist-Leninist) as a major force witnessed the growth of radical elements in the past decade. The fighting between security forces and the Maoist rebels led to the killing of hundreds of civilians, rebels, and security personnel.

In June 2001, King Birendra Bir Bikram Shah Dev died in a bloody shooting at the royal palace that also claimed the lives of most of the royal family; his son, Crown Prince Dipendra, was believed to have been responsible for the killings, and then shot himself. While still clinging to life, Dipendra was crowned king; he died three days later and was succeeded by his uncle, the current chief of state (a hereditary monarch), King Gyanendra Bir Bikram Shah. In October 2002, the king dismissed the prime minister and his cabinet after they dissolved the parliament and were subsequently unable to hold elections because of the Maoist insurgency. The country has presently negotiated a cease-fire with the insurgents although conflicts persist at the border with India.

The Hindu upper castes dominate the political arena and bureaucracy. Nepal's actual demographic composition is difficult to ascertain. The country is home to about 20,000 Tibetan refugees as well as 95,000 Bhutanese refugees of Nepali origin. Numbering around 2 million, the Buddhists constitute nearly 8 percent of the population. There are about 630,000 Muslims (3.8 percent). In 1990, the Christian population was estimated at 50,000. The Muslim presence in Nepal predates the founding of the Hindu kingdom and can be traced to the Delhi Sultanate and the Mughal Empire that ruled the plains. Christianity, too, entered Nepal before the establishment of the kingdom in the eighteenth century.

The period between 1768 and 1990 witnessed a ban on religious preaching and conversions and also expulsion of the converts, permanently in the case of Christians and temporarily in the case of Muslims. However, after the Kingdom became a constitutional monarchy, preaching and conversion, though banned legally, were tolerated. At that time demands emerged to declare Nepal a secular state, but these were rejected. The policy on religious minorities remains the same as enunciated by the 1962 Constitution. In practice, Nepal now follows a more liberal policy toward Muslims and Christians.

Wars over borders with China, Tibet, and British India during the eighteenth and nineteenth century resulted in the country's present-day boundaries. Nepal historically maintained a position of neutrality in foreign affairs as it balanced its relationships with China, the Soviet Union, the United States, and India. India's proximity, cultural influence, and substantial economic aid have made it the most influential foreign power in Nepal, but its military and political interference in the Nepal's affairs has become a source of conflict for the government.

The immigration of Nepalese into southern Bhutan, which began following the Sinchula Treaty of 1865 between the British India and Bhutan, led to ethnic tensions in Bhutan. Though the Nepali immigration was formally banned in 1958, there remain apprehensions in Bhutan of Nepali domination. There are also fears that the Nepali speakers in Bhutan might demand a "separate Nepali state" as part of greater Nepalese ambitions. The promulgation of the new Citizenship Act in 1985 restricted Nepali immigrants from acquiring Bhutanese citizenship and in 1991, the Nepali language was banned in schools in Bhutan. Following the ethnic conflicts in early 1990s, a large number of refugees left Bhutan for Nepal. In addition to straining relations between Bhutan and Nepal, the ethnic conflict in Bhutan and the presence of Bhutanese refugees in Nepal have created socio-economic as well as political problems for the government of Nepal.

The national mosaic comprises linguistic, religious, ethnic, caste, and regional groups. Ethnic groups include Brahman, Chetri, Newar, Gurung, Magar, Tamang, Rai, Limbu, Sherpa, Tharu, and others (1995). Traditionally, Nepal has been dominated by Brahmins and Chetris.

Although Nepali, which is related to Sanskrit and Hindi, is the official language, over 20 other languages are spoken. The Constitution of 1990 states that any languagespoken as the mother tongue should be treated as a national language. However, to encourage Nepali, the government banned the use of ethnic minority languages in official transactions in 1999. Nepal is among the poorest and least developed nations in the world, with a per capita GDP income of $1,400 (2002). Agriculture including rice, corn, wheat, sugarcane, and root crops provides livelihood for 80 percent of the country's population and accounts for 40 percent of the GDP. Industries such as tourism and textile production suffered during the 1990s as a result of communist insurgencies and more recently due to the September 11, 2001 bombings in the United States. Although the government has installed economic reforms, Nepal's diminishing foreign trade, landlocked geography, and technical insufficiency hamper economic growth tremendously.

P.R. KUMARASWAMY AND D. SHYAM BABU

See also **Bhutan; Christians: Overview; Hindus; Muslims; Nepalese**

Further Reading

Ansari, Hamid, "Muslims in Nepal," *Journal, Institute of Muslim Minority Affairs*, 3, no.1 (1981)

Ansari, Tahir Ali, "Muslim Minorities in Nepal," *Journal, Institute of Muslim Minority Affairs*, 9, no.1 (1988)

Gaborieau, Marg, "Varying Identities of Nepalese Muslims," in *Islam, Communities and Nation: Muslim Identities in South Asia and Beyond,* edited by Mushirul Hasan, New Delhi: Manohar, 1998

Hutt, M., editor, *Nepal in the Nineties: Versions of the Past, Visions of the Future*, London: Oxford University Press, 1994

Skar, H., "Nepal Indigenous Issues and Civil Rights: The Plight of the Rana Tharu," in *Indigenous Peoples of Asia*, edited by R. Barnes, A. Gray, and B. Kingsbury, Ann Arbor, Michigan: Association for Asian Studies

Upreti, B.C., "The Nepali Immigration in Bhutan: Growing Conflict between National and Ethnic Identities," in *Bhutan: Society and Polity*, edited by Ramakant and R.C. Mishra, New Delhi: Indus, 1996

Nepalese

Capsule Summary

Location: Mostly in the Himalayan Kingdom of Nepal but also found in significant numbers in Bhutan and Northern as well as Northeastern India
Total Population: About 60 percent of Nepal's population or 12.6 million (1995); about 35 percent of Bhutan's population, or 600,000
Language: Nepali
Religion: Predominantly Hinduism

Nepalese are the inhabitants of Nepal, the only Hindu kingdom in the world today located on the northeast border of India and bounded by Tibet, China, and India. Specifically, *Nepalese* refers to an ethno-linguistic group who speak Nepali language and practice Hinduism. They are present not only in Nepal but in significant numbers in Bhutan and the Indian states of Sikkim, West Bengal, and the Northeast. Nepalese (including Lhotsampas—one of several Nepalese ethnic groups) numbered 748,842 in Bhutan (2003); 16,454 in Bangladesh (2001); 11,054,148 in Nepal (2001); and 2,811 in the United States.

Nepali, the official language of Nepal and an Indo-Iranian language, is spoken by 90 percent of the population, although Nepalese speak a dozen other languages and about 30 major dialects. Nepali is commonly written in the Devanagari script. The Constitution of 1990 stated that all languages spoken as mother tongue are to be treated as national languages. However, to encourage the Nepali language, the government banned the use of ethnic minority languages in official transactions in 1999.

Although Nepal's history has ancient roots—by fourth century BCE, the Newars of the central Kathmandu valley had apparently developed a flourishing Hindu-Buddhist culture in the region—it has been an independent state only since 1769. That year, the Gurkha King Prithvi Narayan Shah conquered and unified the various Nepalese principalities and established his kingdom. From 1846 to 1950, the Rana rulers, beginning with Jung Bahadur Rana as the prime minister, controlled the government rendering the Shah Kings figureheads. The office of the prime minister was also made hereditary. Ongoing border struggles with Tibet, China, and British India occurred throughout the eighteenth and nineteenth centuries and culminated in 1923 with the recognition of Nepalese sovereignty by Great Britain.

The Nepalese represent a centuries-long mixing of Mongolians (who came from the north) and peoples who migrated from the Ganges plain in the south. Ethnically, the northern region is occupied by groups belonging to Bhote (or Bhotias), the Himalayan Highlanders or Tibeto-Mongolians. The central region, including the capital city of Kathmandu, is populated mainly by Pahari, the people of Indian origin as well as by Newars, one of the earliest indigenous people to come under Hindu influence for over a millennium. The tropical plains of southern Nepal, known as Terai, are populated by people who settled from India, with most of them belonging to Tharu, the low-caste Hindus. There is also a significant Muslim population in Terai. The Hindu caste system, a kind of social and class-based system that is rooted in the *Vedas,* the ancient texts, is prevalent in the central and southern regions. Ethnic and caste identities often intricately overlap and ethnic groups are further subdivided into occupation-based divisions.

The Hindu upper castes dominate the political arena and bureaucracy of Nepal. Tribal and caste distinctions remain significant among the Nepalese; the Brahmins for example (the Hindu priest class) retain great political influence overall. The national mosaic comprises of linguistic, religious, ethnic, caste, and regional groups. Ethnic groups include the Brahman, Chetri, Newar, Gurung, Magar, Tamang, Rai, Limbu, Sherpa, Tharu, and others. Historically Nepal has been dominated by Brahmins and Chetris with the language and culture of the Hindu population.

The hill people who speak Tibeto-Burman languages are under-represented in the government. The same is true of Hindi speaking Hindus of Terai, some of whom migrated from India. The ethnic diversity is compounded by the presence of various linguistic communities including Gurung, Magar, Tamang, Rai, Limbu, Thakali, Sherpa, Tharu, and Raute. The linguistic minorities who inhabit the hills face concerns such as landlessness, deforestation, and bonded labor brought about by the influx of upper caste Hindus.

The period between 1768 and 1990 witnessed a ban on religious preaching, conversions, and expulsion of the converts, permanently in the case of Christians and temporarily in the case of Muslims. However, after the Kingdom of Nepal became a constitutional monarchy, preaching and conversion, though banned legally, have been tolerated. In fact, at that time there were demands to declare Nepal a secular state that were subsequently rejected. The policy on religious minorities remains the same as enunciated by the 1962 Constitution. In practice, Nepal now follows a more liberal policy toward Muslims and Christians.

During the twentieth century, however, ongoing political and ethnic conflicts have plagued Nepal and the Nepalese people. The Communist Party of Nepal was established in 1949 amid the predemocratic movement against the autocratic Rana regime. Maoist insurgency in Nepal took over much of the western countryside, and communist agitators infiltrated the tribal regions. In the hills of Sikkim and Darjeeling, meanwhile, ethnic Nepalese called for a separate homeland called Gorkhaland. In 1986, a separatist movement erupted near Nepal in Darjeeling (West Bengal), under the banner of Gorkha National Liberation Front (GNLF). Nepalese represented the majority of rebels who sustained the movement until the Central and State governments agreed to create an autonomous Darjeeling Gorkha Hill Council. Although the 1988 agreement ruled out the principle demand for a separate Gorkhaland, it appeased the agitators.

In the eastern region, refugees from Bhutan live in villages and resettlement camps. The immigration of Nepalese into southern Bhutan, which began following the Sinchula Treaty of 1865 between the British India and Bhutan, has since led to ethnic tensions in Bhutan. Though Nepali immigration was formally banned in 1958, there are apprehensions in Bhutan of Nepali domination. There are also fears that the Nepali speakers in Bhutan might demand a "separate Nepali state" as part of Greater Nepalese ambitions. Moreover, the gradual influx of Nepalese into Sikkim was one of the principle factors, as Bhutanese interpret, facilitating Sikkim's "integration" into India in 1975.

As a result, Bhutan has been trying to restrict the influence of Nepalese in Bhutan, known as Lhotsampas, and the resultant policies have exacerbated the animosity between the Bhutanese and the Nepalese. The promulgation of the new Citizenship Act in 1985 restricted Nepali immigrants from acquiring Bhutanese citizenship and in 1991, the Nepali language was banned in schools in Bhutan. Following the ethnic conflicts in early 1990s, a large number of refugees left Bhutan for Nepal. In addition to straining relations between Bhutan and Nepal, the ethnic conflict in Bhutan and the presence of Bhutanese refugees in Nepal have created socioeconomic and political problems for the government of Nepal.

P.R. KUMARASWAMY AND D. SHYAM BABU

See also **Bhutan; Hindus; India; Nepal**

Further Reading

Ansari, Hamid, "Muslims in Nepal," *Journal, Institute of Muslim Minority Affairs*, 3, no.1, (1981)

Ansari, Tahir Ali, "Muslim Minorities in Nepal," *Journal, Institute of Muslim Minority Affairs*, 9, no.1, (1988)

Baral, Lok Raj, "Bhutanese Refugees in Nepal: Insecurity for Whom?" in *Refugees and Regional Security in South Asia*, edited by S.D. Muni and Lok Raj Baral, New Delhi: Konarak, 1996

Gaborieau, Marg, "Varying Identities of Nepalese Muslims," *Islam, Communities and Nation: Muslim Identities in South Asia and Beyond*, edited by Mushirul Hasan, New Delhi: Manohar, 1998

Hutt, M., editor, *Nepal in the Nineties: Versions of the Past, Visions of the Future*, London: Oxford University Press, 1994

Levine, Nancy E., "Caste, State and Ethnic Boundaries in Nepal," *Journal of Asian Studies*, 46, no.1 (1987)

Skar, H., "Nepal Indigenous Issues and Civil Rights: The Plight of the Rana Tharu," in *Indigenous Peoples of Asia*, edited by R. Barnes, A, Gray, and B. Kingsbury, Ann Arbor, Michigan: Association for Asian Studies

Upreti, B.C., "The Nepali Immigration in Bhutan: Growing Conflict between National and Ethnic Identities," in *Bhutan: Society and Polity*, edited by Ramakant and R.C. Mishra, New Delhi: Indus, 1996

Netherlands

Capsule Summary

Country Name: Kingdom of the Netherlands, commonly known as the Netherlands ("low countries") or simply Holland (a name derived from *Houtland*, "wooded land").
Location: Northwestern Europe, on the North Sea, between Belgium and Germany.
Total Population: 16,150,511 (July 2003)
Ethnic Populations: Frisians, Turks, Moroccans, Southern Europeans, Antilleans, Surinamese, Moluccans, Indonesians, Ghanians
Languages: Dutch, Frisian (both official)
Religion: Roman Catholic (31%); Protestant (21%); Muslim (4.4%); other (3.6%); unaffiliated (40%), (as of 1998)

The Kingdom of the Netherlands is a northwestern European country bordered by the North Sea, Belgium, and Germany. Its total area is 41,526 square kilometers (16,195 square miles), slightly less than twice the size of New Jersey. The marine climate is temperate, with cool summers and mild winters. The terrain is mostly coastal lowland and reclaimed land (polders); there are some hills in the southeastern province of Limburg. A large part of the Netherlands is below the sea level. The capital is Amsterdam, and The Hague is the seat of government. The Dutch government is a constitutional monarchy. Its executive branch consists of the chief of state (Queen Beatrix since April 30, 1980).

There are 12 provinces and 2 non-European dependent areas: Aruba and Netherlands Antilles. The two chief ethnic groups in the Netherlands are Dutch and Frisians, descended from the Franks, Frisians, and Saxons. Dutch and Frisian are the two official languages (Frisian is spoken in the province of Friesland in the Netherlands and is the Germanic language most closely resembling modern English. While constituting a numerical minority, Frisians do not experience ethnic discrimination in the Netherlands by the Dutch, nor are they denied any rights other citizens enjoy).

History

In the first century BCE, Julius Caesar conquered most of the present-day area of the Netherlands, then inhabited by Frisians. The region was incorporated into the Roman economic and political spheres. Romans influenced the local culture, built bridges (in Maastricht), and established large farms.

The decline of the Roman Empire allowed the Saxons to invade the eastern part of the region, whereas the Franks moved into the west and south. By 800 CE, the entire territory of the Netherlands was part of the realm of Charlemagne. During the ninth and tenth centuries Norsemen frequently invaded the coastal areas. The gradual development of powerful towns was a notable feature of Dutch history during the twelfth, thirteenth, and fourteenth centuries, and the area—with a strategic location at the mouths of three major European rivers (Rhine, Maas or Meuse, and Schelde)—became an important trading center. At that time the Dutch nation did not exist, but gradually over the following centuries the region developed common culture and came to be called the Netherlands.

In the sixteenth century most of the Netherlands was ruled by Spain. In 1579, an anti-Spanish alliance of all northern and some southern territories, known as the Union of Utrecht, was formed. This alliance was the final stage in separating the northern part of the Low Countries, which later became the Netherlands, from the southern part, which became Belgium. The region united by the Union of Utrecht became the nucleus of the present Dutch nation. In 1581, the Dutch provinces within the Union of Utrecht proclaimed their independence from Spain.

The seventeenth century was the golden age of Dutch culture in which arts and commerce flourished. By the mid-seventeenth century, the Netherlands was the foremost commercial and maritime power of Europe, and Amsterdam, the financial center of the continent. About 1600 CE the first Dutch merchant vessels sailed from Amsterdam to Java, initiating Dutch explorations around the world, which resulted in the establishment of many trading posts in Africa, Southeast Asia, and the Americas. A significant colonial power, the Netherlands maintained possessions in South Africa, South and Southeast Asia, North America, and the Caribbean.

This golden age of Dutch history ended in the early eighteenth century, a time of wars against England and France. The economic and political power of the Netherlands declined as it lost colonies to Great Britain. By the end of the eighteenth century, the republic of the seven United Provinces was replaced by the Batavian republic, modeled on the French republic. The Batavian republic survived until 1806, when Emperor Napoleon transformed the country into the kingdom of Holland; in 1810 he incorporated it into the French empire. In 1815, the Congress of Vienna restored the independence of the Netherlands. The second half of the nineteenth century was marked by liberalization of the Dutch government under the impact of the revolutions in the 1840s. The new constitution of 1848 became the foundation of the present Dutch democracy.

The years from 1880 to 1914 were a period of economic expansion, but this ended during World War I, when the Netherlands suffered economic hardship. An intensive effort to rebuild the country and to restore its trade and industry characterized the period after World War II. In 1945, the Netherlands became a member of the United Nations (UN). The country was a founding member of the North Atlantic Treaty Organization (NATO) and the European Community (EC, later the European Union, [EU]), and participated in the introduction of the Economic and Monetary Union (EMU) in 1999.

Society and Ethnicity

Ethnic groups by population in the Netherlands are the Dutch 83 percent, other 17 percent (of which 9 percent are of non-western origin, mainly Turks, Moroccans, Antilleans, Surinamese, and Indonesians [1999]). As of 2001, the minority populations numbered: Turks (320,000); Moroccans (273,000); Southern Europeans (162,000); Surinamese (309,000); Antilleans (117,000); Moluccans (40,000); Ghanians (16,000); and refugees from the former Yugoslavia (179,000) (Figures from Smeets e.o. Jaarboek Minderheden 2003).

The republic has a lengthy history of immigration, originally from other European countries and later after World War II, from its former colonies: Dutch-Indonesians and Moluccans, Antillese and Surinamese, and *gastarbeiders* (guest workers) from the Mediterranean countries, principally Turkey and Morocco. More recently large numbers of asylum-seekers, especially from Africa, have immigrated to Holland. These guest workers initially had limited rights as they were considered temporary residents; since the 1980s, however, it has become apparent that many are staying in the Netherlands permanently, and the government has initiated policies to protect these minorities and ensure them extended rights (such as family reunification and the right to stay with families as legal residents). The policies of Netherlands have largely supported the distinct cultural identities of minorities while also encouraging assimilation. On the other hand, even though the government has installed liberal measures to minimize discrimination and racism toward peoples "other than" the Dutch, the socioeconomic position of many minority groups remains below that of the indigenous population. For example, whereas immigrants constitute nearly 9 percent of the total potential labor force, their rate of unemployment is 23 percent compared to 8 percent among the Dutch population.

Roman Catholics constitute about 34 percent of the Dutch population, Protestants 27 percent, and Muslims 4 percent; the country also has a small Jewish community. About 34 percent or more of the population claims no religious persuasion. The Roman Catholics are concentrated in the southern part of the country; Protestants are divided among several denominations, the largest being the Dutch Reformed church. The Netherlands has no official religion, but the Reformed Church has had a close association with the state since the founding of the Dutch republic. All the country's monarchs have been members of the Reformed church.

The Netherlands is one of Europe's most comprehensive welfare states. Much of national income is spent on education, health, employment stimulation, and social welfare. The Netherlands has long been recognized for its liberal approach to social policy. Prostitution has been legalized, and possession of small amounts of marijuana and cannabis-related substances has been decriminalized. In 2000, the Netherlands became the first country to allow homosexual couples to marry and adopt children, and in 2001, the Dutch parliament enacted legislation legalizing euthanasia and assisted suicide.

The Netherlands has a strong economy heavily dependent on foreign trade. Per capita GDP is $27,200 (2002). The labor force includes services, 73 percent; industry, 23 percent; and agriculture, 4 percent (1998). Industrial activity is predominantly in food processing, chemicals, petroleum refining, construction, microelectronics, fishing, and electrical machinery. The Netherlands is also a large exporter of agricultural products such as grains, potatoes, sugar beets, fruits, vegetables, and livestock. In 2001 the euro replaced the guilder as the Dutch currency.

LUDOMIR LOZNY

See also **Frisians; Indonesia; Indonesians; Turks**

Further Reading

Esner, Rachel, *The Netherlands*, 7th edition, London: A&C Black, 2002

Frank, E.H., *The Modern Netherlands*, New York: Praeger, 1971

King, Peter, and Michael Wintle, *The Netherlands*, Cambridge: Clio Press 1988

"The Netherlands," in *World Factbook*, Washington D.C., 2003

Ozmańczyk, J., and Anthony Mango, *Encyclopedia of the United Nations and International Agreements*, edited by Jan Ozmańczyk and Anthony Mango, volume 3, 3rd edition, New York and London: Routledge, 2003

Schuchart, Max, *The Netherlands*, New York: Walker, 1972

Smit, Pamela, *The Netherlands, 57 B.C. to 1971*, Dobbs Ferry, New York: Oceana Publications, 1973

New Zealand

Capsule Summary

Country Name: New Zealand
Location: Southwest Pacific Ocean. New Zealand consists of two main islands along with a number of smaller islands. The land area of the country is 270,534 square kilometers (105,508 square miles).
Total Population: 3,951,307 (July 2003).
Languages: English, Maori.
Religions: Christian (60%); no religion (20%); other religions (20%)

New Zealand, like the United States, Canada, and Australia, was once a British colony. Although it is politically, economically, and culturally similar to these other English-speaking countries, New Zealand has a smaller population (3.9 million), which is less ethnically diverse, with a relatively high number of indigenous people (15 percent). Its per capita GDP is $20,100 (2002). Relations between the descendants of the British colonizers (known locally as pakeha) and the Maori people have generally overshadowed issues of other minority groups in the country.

The ancestors of the Maori came from the Cook Islands, Tahiti, or the Marquesas roughly 1,000 years ago. The settling of an empty land, so large and cool in comparison to the rest of Polynesia, resulted in the creation of a unique people and culture. The first Europeans to visit local waters sailed under the command of the Dutch explorer Abel Tasman in 1642. They left promptly after four crewmembers were killed in an incident with local people who came out to meet the ships in canoes. Although Tasman never actually set foot on land, his voyage gave the country its western name, New Zealand. It remained unvisited by other Europeans for the next 127 years.

Captain James Cook landed on the North Island in 1769 during a British scientific expedition on its way back from Tahiti. By living there for 6 months, and making further journeys in 1773 and 1777, Cook gathered an impressive corpus of information about New Zealand and its people. Although he claimed parts of the country for the Crown, the British Empire only took steps to extend its sovereignty after a significant number of British subjects began to reside in New Zealand. The sealers and whalers from the Australian colonies, along with escaped convicts, traders and missionaries, introduced potatoes, pigs, new diseases, Christianity, and the musket as they established themselves along the coast. The muskets and communicable diseases had a severe impact on the Maori population. The British Colonial Office took steps to incorporate New Zealand into the Empire in 1840 prompted by the missionaries to protect the natives, and by the fact that the New Zealand Company was purchasing vast tracts of land for settlers. On February 6, that year, over 500 chiefs signed the Treaty of Waitangi. The Treaty gave the Crown the right to govern while guaranteeing the chiefs, control of their resources. Despite this apparent mutual consent, the colonization of New Zealand soon became contentious and violent.

The Maori population declined further as the pace of colonization and the power of the settlers grew. By 1858 Europeans outnumbered Maori 59,000 to 56,000. The Maori became more and more reluctant to sell their remaining land. Skirmishes increased and in 1860, war broke out in Taranaki. In the aftermath, the government confiscated large blocks of territory and set conditions to make it easier for Maori to sell more of their land. In the early 1870s, the indigenous population became a marginalized, declining "fourth world" group outnumbered five to one by the settlers.

Growth in settlement was stimulated by the discovery of gold in the South Island. Chinese laborers began to arrive in the country in the late 1800s to work and rework areas of the gold fields. They were the targets of numerous official and unofficial acts of discrimination despite the fact that by 1881, they numbered only 5,000. The Chinese population decreased subsequently as Chinese women were prevented from entering the country. At this stage, with Maori numbers declining, New Zealand had little ethnic diversity: the non-indigenous population remained over 95 percent British, and only 0.5 percent Asian, until the end of World War II.

After the war, a need for labor developed as a result of policies to stimulate the economy. The government wanted the country to produce much of what was being imported. As new factories opened, Maori began to migrate to the cities and became a substantially urbanized group by the late 1970s. Unskilled workers from the Pacific Islands also moved to New Zealand's towns from the 1950s. People from the Cook Islands, Niue, and Tokelau had unrestricted entry as citizens of New Zealand's territories. Western Samoans and Tongans were admitted by quota for specified periods.

Resentment against these migrants grew, especially as the economy began to cool down in the mid-1970s. The existence of a pool of unskilled workers concentrated in crowded suburbs gave New Zealand cities a patina of the social problems found in the ghettos of North America. Although the Pacific Islanders made up a minority of illegal migrants, the media and politicians portrayed them as undesirable people who overstayed. Economic policy changed in the 1980s, abandoning import substitution in favor of export expansion, which resulted in a shift in labor market requirements from unskilled to skilled and professional workers. The downsizing that followed had a severe impact on Maori and Pacific workers. They were among the first to lose their jobs during a period when the state began to drastically cut welfare benefits. Despite these difficulties, people from the aforementioned islands succeeded in establishing a strong presence in New Zealand. They make up 6 percent of the total population and their numbers are expected to double in the next 50 years. Sports people and entertainers from the Pacific, and more upwardly mobile second and third generations, have achieved a measure of acceptance in the country that contrasts greatly with the xenophobia of the 1970s.

The emphasis on attracting skilled workers and entrepreneurs from areas with potential for trade growth led to an influx of people from Taiwan, Hong Kong, and Korea in the 1990s. In 1996, the country experienced a net gain of 29,000 migrants. The concentration of Asians in particular suburbs of Auckland led to calls for controls on their numbers. These were instituted in 1997 with a consequent diminution of immigrant arrivals.

New Zealand faces the new millennium with a substantially more diverse population than at any other time in its history. Despite this fact, ethnic and minority politics continue to revolve around Maori-pakeha relations. With a growing, urbanized, politically active population, Maori aspirations have led to an emphasis on partnership and a bicultural relationship between New Zealand's indigenous people and the government. The major aim of biculturalism is to revive and implement the principles of the Treaty of Waitangi, return a measure of sovereignty to indigenous groups, and close the remaining socio-economic gaps between the country's Maori and non-Maori citizens.

HAL LEVINE

See also **Maori**

Further Reading

Fleras, Augie, and Paul Spoonley, *Recalling Aotearoa, Indigenous Politics and Ethnic Relations in New Zealand,* Auckland: Oxford University Press, 1999

Levine, Hal B., *Constructing Collective Identity, A Comparative Analysis of New Zealand Jews, Maori and Urban Papua New Guineans,* Franfurt Am Main: Peter Lang, 1997

Pearson, David, *A Dream Deferred: The Origins of Ethnic Conflict in New Zealand,* London: Allen and Unwin, 1990

Sinclair, Keith, editor, *The Oxford Illustrated History of New Zealand,* Auckland: Oxford University Press, 1990

Spoonley, Paul, Cluny Macpherson, and David Pearson, editors, *Nga Patai: Racism and Ethnic Relations in Aotearoa/New Zealand,* Palmerston North: The Dunmore Press, 1996

Ngugi Wa Thiong'o (Kenyan)

Ngugi wa Thiong'o is one of Africa's best-known novelists, a prolific writer of fiction, nonfiction, and criticism, and a foremost postcolonial voice. His development as an artist and intellectual has paralleled and played a large part in the development of the writing and thinking of the post and neocolonial world away from the constraining influence of Western culture and toward the recovery, expression, and in some ways creation of native cultures.

Ngugi wa Thiong'o's life and career has in many ways followed the pattern of the lives of many intellectuals who have emerged from the postcolonial situation. Educated primarily under the British system, with some exposure to independent Kikuyu schools, which were closed or taken over by the British, he excelled within a curriculum that taught the texts of another land in a foreign language. His youth was marked by the Mau Mau Rebellion, a violent uprising by the Kikuyu people against British control; the state of emergency under which the people of his country lived from 1952 to 1960, led to the destruction of his boyhood home, the deaths of relatives and friends, and a lifelong concern for the effects of colonialism and the struggle for independence. Educated at universities in Africa and England, he absorbed the traditions of the West and was also able, outside of that formal education, to gain exposure to the contemporary literature of Africa and to enter the ongoing conversation about postcolonial culture. Returning to his native land and studying Marxist writers and the work of liberationist thinkers such as Frantz Fanon, he confronted the problems faced by newly independent nations and struggled for the establishment of national culture and against the continuing legacy of postcolonial compromise and corruption. These efforts included the abolishment of the Department of English at the University of Nairobi and the establishment of a Department of Literature devoted to studying the literature of native and diasporic Africa and the Third World. They also included the dropping of his Christian first name in recognition of the Church's implication in colonialism. Writing explicitly in his own work about conditions in Kenya after independence led to his year-long detention, during which he made the decision to write fiction only in his native language, Kikuyu, rather than in English, and began doing so on a roll of toilet paper hidden from his guards. Forced to remain in England in 1982 upon learning he would be arrested on his return to Kenya, he began his exile, and soon his American academic career, which continues today.

As is true of Léopold Sédar Senghor and many other writers and social thinkers from African nations that gained independence, Ngugi wa Thiong'o's life is shaped in many ways by the conflict between colonial and native cultures. His life story is one of continuing attempts to escape the legacy of colonialism and to reshape his national culture. As have many of these

NGUGI WA THIONG'O (KENYAN)

writers, he has drawn the subjects of his work largely from this situation, and has struggled with the problem of writing about them in the language and forms of the colonizing culture. He is perhaps best known for his midcareer decision to pursue no longer his creative work in English. The short history of contemporary African fiction began with Amos Tutuola's *Palm Wine Drinkard* and Chinua Achebe's *Things Fall Apart,* books written in English. As Achebe sought to correct Western literature's picture of Africa, embodied most prominently in Joseph Conrad's *Heart of Darkness*, by telling the story of the Igbo people of Nigeria from their own point of view, Ngugi wa Thiong'o has sought to correct the errors of a literature that tries to tell its own story in the language of another. As he explained in his 1986 essay collection *Decolonising the Mind,* writing in a language other than that of one's own people means not only restricting one's audience to an English-reading elite, but it also means not taking full advantage of a rich source of oral and folk traditions specific to one's native culture, thereby risking the loss of that specific culture and all that it provides. As he explains, "Language carries culture, and culture carries, particularly through orature and literature, the entire body of values by which we perceive ourselves and our place in the world."

Among Ngugi wa Thiong'o's most celebrated and influential works are his novels written in English, *Weep Not, Child* (1964), *The River Between* (1965), *A Grain of Wheat* (1967), and the last, *Petals of Blood* (1977). *Weep Not, Child,* written while he was in school in England, tells the story of a young Kenyan receiving a Western education at the same time that his village is destroyed during the rebellion. *The River Between* explores the long-lasting destructive effects of Christian missionary activity in Africa. *A Grain of Wheat,* perhaps his best-known novel, tells the story of the Emergency of the 1950s through the life of a village, focusing not just on the ravages of the time on individual lives and on the still-surviving community, but also on the divisions that surface within the community under the pressures of neocolonialism. *Petals of Blood,* along with a number of theater pieces, landed Ngugi wa Thiong'o in jail because of their harsh criticisms of post-independence rule. Other works in English include his memoir of that time, *Detained* (1981), his essays, collected in *Homecoming* (1972), and the plays *The Black Hermit* (1968) and *The Trial of Dedan Kimathi* (with Micere Mugo, 1976)). Since turning to Kikuyu, Ngugi has written the play *I Will*

Marry When I Want (1977, with Ngugi wa Mirii) and the novels *Devil on the Cross* (1980) and *Matagari* (1989). The last, one of his most important recent works, is a novel based on a Kikuyu folktale, which tells the story of a rebel fighter in newly independent Kenya who finds that nothing has really changed and decides to continue to fight for true liberation. That an arrest warrant is rumored to have been issued for this fictional character is testament to the success of this novel and to Kenyan authorities' continued fear of his influence.

SAMUEL COHEN

Biography

Born James Thiong'o Ngugi, January 5, 1938, in Kamiriithu, Kenya. Studied at Makerere University in Kampala, Uganda, B.A., 1963; University of Leeds, England, B.A., 1964. Was chair of the Department of Literature at the University of Nairobi, 1972–1977. Left Kenya in 1982 and taught at various universities in the United States before becoming professor of comparative literature and performance studies at New York University in 1992.

Selected Works

Weep Not, Child, 1964
The River Between, 1965,)
A Grain of Wheat, 1967
The Black Hermit, 1968,)
Homecoming: Essays on African and Caribbean Literature, Culture, and Politics, 1972
The Trial of Dedan Kimathi, 1976
Petals of Blood, 1977
Ngaahika Ndeenda, 1977; [I Will Marry When I Want, 1982]
Caitaani Mutharaba-ini [Devil on the Cross],1980
Detained: A Writer's Prison Diary, 1981
Writers in Politics, 1981
Maitu njugira [*Mother, Sing for Me*], 1981
Decolonising the Mind, 1983
Matigari, 1989
Moving the Centre, 1993
Penpoints, Gunpoints, and Dreams: Towards a Critical Theory of the Arts and the State of Africa, 1998

SAMUEL COHEN

See also **Kenya**

Further Reading

Cantalupo, Charles, editor, *Ngugi Wa Thiong'o: Texts and Contexts*, Trenton: Africa World Press, 1995
Cook, David, and Michael Okenimkpe, *Ngugi Wa Thiong'o: An Exploration of His Writings*, London: Heinemann, 1983
Killam, G.D., *An Introduction to the Writings of Ngugi*, London: Heinemann, 1980

Killam, editor, *Critical Perspectives on Ngugi wa*

Lovesy, Oliver, *Ngugi Wa Thiong'o*, New York: Twayne, 2000

Ogude, James, *Ngugi's Novels and African History,* London: Pluto, 1999

Robson, Clifford, *Ngugi Wa Thiong'o*, London: Macmillan, 1979

Sicherman, Carol, editor, *Ngugi Wa Thiong'o: The Making of a Rebel: A Source Book in Kenyan Literature and Resistance*, London: Zell, 1990

Williams, Patrick, *Ngugi Wa Thiong'o*, Manchester: Manchester University Press, 1999

Nicaragua

Capsule Summary

Country Name: Nicaragua
Location: Central America
Total Population: 5,128,517 (July 2003)
Languages: Spanish, English, Amerindian dialects
Religions: Roman Catholic, Protestant

The Republic of Nicaragua (República de Nicaragua) is the largest of the Central American republics, with an area of 50,446 square miles (130,688 square kilometers), or slightly larger than New York State. It is bounded by Honduras on the north, the Caribbean Sea on the east, Costa Rica on the south, and the Pacific Ocean on the west. The country is divided into three distinct regions: Pacific Coastal Lowlands, Central Highlands (forested and mountainous), and the Caribbean Region (an extensive, flat Atlantic coastal plain rising to central interior mountains). The narrow Pacific coastal plain is interrupted by volcanoes. The climate in the lowlands is tropical with distinct cooler, wet and dry seasons in the highlands. Today, the agricultural Pacific lowlands with their cotton-producing farms are home to about 60 percent of the population, while the Central Highlands with coffee plantations and Caribbean coastal plain are less populous. Nicaragua is characterized by its agricultural economy, a history of autocratic governments, and an imbalance in regional development. The majority of the settlements and economic and industrial activities are concentrated in the western half of the country. Per capita GDP is $2,200 (2002). Politically, there are 16 departments.

In the sixteenth century, before the Spanish Conquest, Nicaragua was inhabited by only a few aboriginal cultures. Chief among these were the Nicarao Indians, whose name derives from their paramount ruler and from whom Nicaragua derived its name. The Miskito (Muskito or Mosquito) Indians of the Caribbean coast were the second most significant tribe. Nicaragua was initially seen by Christopher Columbus in 1502, but an overland Spanish expedition from Panama under Hernandez de Cordoba arrived there in 1522. Nicaragua became a Spanish colony but achieved its independence from Spain in 1821 and from the Central American Federation in 1839. Nearly 31,000 Nicaraguans were killed during the Contra-Sandinista war and hundreds of thousands more became refugees in other Central American countries and Mexico, and the United States. Nonetheless, Nicaragua's population dramatically increased from 2.5 million to nearly 4 million during Sandinista rule (1979–1990). There was a massive population displacement characterized by an internal migration of people from rural areas and the areas of conflict, a rapid demographic expansion in Nicaragua's cities, and both legal and illegal migration to the United States where an estimated 700,000 Nicaraguans reside.

Nicaragua's population numbers 5,128,517 (July 2003); about 69 percent are mestizo (of mixed Indian and Spanish descent) also called *ladino*, a term more commonly used in Central America. *Ladino* defines individuals who are Spanish-speakers and follow Spanish-American lifeways in terms of clothing, housing, and food consumption. In addition, the term covers those Indians who have adopted Spanish-American culture. Hence the term is indicative of cultural rather than biological traits since indigenous peoples are often categorized as ladino for social or political reasons. Approximately 17 percent of the population is of European origin and additional 9 percent African-American (mostly through Jamaica and other Caribbean islands) and 5 percent

Amerindian. The annual demographic growth rate is 3 percent.

The Pacific coast is home to a small number of Monimbó and Subtiava Indians (fewer than 2,000). Although ladinos constitute the largest single group on the Caribbean coast, the population of that region also includes Miskito, Sumo, and Rama Indians as well as Garinagu (formerly known as Black Carib until 1980) who are the descendants of African slaves and Carib Indians, and Creoles (English-speaking blacks). The Garunagu are also incorrectly known as Garífuna (the language they speak).

Nearly all Nicaraguans speak Spanish; it is the sole official language in all but the east coast regions where, under the 1987 Nicaraguan constitution and the Atlantic Coast Autonomy Law of 1987, Miskito, Sumo, Rama, and Creole English have equal status with Spanish. On the Pacific coast, the aboriginal languages have disappeared, although place-names and many nouns in Nicaraguan Spanish reflect this heritage.

Because Nicaraguans have both European and Amerindian ancestry, Nicaragua's culture reflects a mixture of Ibero-European and Indian heritage. The Indians of the eastern half of the country remain ethnically distinct and retain tribal customs and languages. A large black minority of Jamaican origin is concentrated on the Caribbean coast. In the mid-1980s, the central government divided the eastern half of the country (the former department of Zelaya) into two autonomous regions and granted the inhabitants limited self-rule. The 1995 constitutional reform guaranteed the integrity of the unique cultures of the region and gave them a say in the use of the natural resources of the area.

Today Nicaragua is 54 percent urban. The capital is Managua, the nation's largest city with 575,000 inhabitants with nearly 1 million people in the metropolitan area. Seven other cities have populations greater that 20,000 that include Chinandega, Léon, Granada, Jinotega, Masaya, and Matagalpa. The urban centers generally have substantial ladino and European populations, whereas Amerindian peoples reside in the rural areas. Approximately 400 Arabs from the Middle East and 7,000 Chinese also reside mainly in the urban areas.

The official language is Spanish, but English and indigenous languages are spoken on the Caribbean coast. Although there is no official religion in Nicaragua, Roman Catholicism is predominant (about 85 percent), but there are rapidly growing numbers of evangelical Protestants, and significant Anglican and Moravian communities on the Caribbean coast. Conservative Protestant fundamentalism grew considerably during the 1980s. There are also very small Jewish communities in the larger cities.

CHARLES C. KOLB

See also **Amerindians: South and Central America**

Further Reading

CIDCA (Centro de Investigaciones y Documentación de la Costa Atlántica), *Ethnic Groups and the Nation State: The Case of the Atlantic Coast in Nicaragua*, Stockholm: Stockholms universitet, Socialantropologiska institutionen, 1987

Dow, James W., editor, *Encyclopedia of World Cultures, Volume VIII: Middle America and the Caribbean*, Boston: G.K. Hall & Company, 1995

Ember, Melvin, and Carol Ember, editors, *Countries and Their Cultures*, New York: Macmillan Reference, Human Relations Area Files, Yale University, 2001

Hale, Charles R., *Resistance and Contradiction: Miskitu Indians and the Nicaraguan State*, Stanford: Stanford University Press, 1994

Jackson, Robert H., *Race, Caste and Status: Indians in Colonial Spanish America*, Albuquerque: University of New Mexico Press, 1999

Minority Rights Group, *No Longer Invisible: Afro-Latin Americans Today*, London: Minority Rights Group, 1995

"Nicaragua," in *The CIA World Factbook 2002, 2002* <http://www.odci.gov/cia/publications/factbook.af.html>

Rudolph, James D., editor, *Area Handbook for Nicaragua*, Washington, DC: U.S. Government Printing Office, 1982

Sanchez, Consuelo, *La conformación étnico-nacional en Nicaragua*, México: Instituto Nacional de Antropología e Historia, 1994

Téfel, Reinaldo Antonio, *Nicaragua antes sus desafíos*, Managua: Foro Democrático, 2000

Nigeria

Capsule Summary

Country Name: Federal Republic of Nigeria
Location: West Africa, bordering Gulf of Guinea, between Benin and Cameroon
Total Population: 133,881,703 (July 2003)
Ethnic Populations: Hausa and Fulani, Yoruba, Igbo (Ibo), Ijaw, Kenuri, Ibibio, Tiv
Languages: English (official), Hausa, Yoruba, Igbo (Ibo), Fulani
Religions: Muslim (50%), Christian (40%), indigenous beliefs (10%)

The Federal Republic of Nigeria is located on the West African coast. Its 356,669 square miles (923,768 square kilometers) borders the Atlantic Ocean, Benin, Cameroon and Chad. Nigeria is the most populous country in Africa. The population of 130 million people consists of a pluralistic society that encompasses 250 ethnic groups who speak more than 120 languages with 400 different dialects. Lagos, once the capital, is its largest city; in 1991, Abuja was made the capital city. Nigeria has been making a transition from military to civilian rule. According to 2003 estimates, 50 percent of the Nigerian population is Muslim, and Islam is the dominant religion in the northern part of the country. Forty percent of Nigerians are Christians and various forms of Christianity predominate in the south. Catholicism is found most frequently among the Igbo, and Protestantism is practiced by the Yoruba. Each faith is a minority in the other's region. In addition, 10 percent of Nigerians practice indigenous beliefs.

History

Present-day Nigeria is much smaller than its original boundaries due to historical developments and territorial fluctuations of empires. People have lived in the area since prehistoric times, and a variety of cultures prospered in successive and sometimes simultaneous stages. The Nok culture thrived from 500 BCE to 200 CE. The Fulani established their empire around 600 CE. The Igbo Ukwu date their culture from 900 CE as did the Kanem, who intermarried with the Benin whose kingdom flourished from 1400 to the 1600s. The Hausa culture emerged around 1000 CE and eventually merged with the Fulani. Ife culture predominated from the eleventh to the fifteenth centuries. The Songhai had a huge trading empire that lasted from 1400 to 1592. The Aro were prominent in the eighteenth century. The Oyo city state became powerful but collapsed in the nineteenth century. Portuguese encroachment in the late fifteenth century, and subsequent British control in the late eighteenth century brought significant cultural changes to Nigeria. The slave trade, supported by local chiefs, who sold Yorubas to the British, ultimately proved deleterious. In the early nineteenth century, the Fulani leader Usman dan Fodio brought much of the northern area under the loose control of an Islamic empire centered in Sokoto. The city of Lagos was the first land acquired by Great Britain in 1861. By the early nineteenth century, the British attempted to stop the slave trade. Their ships would intercept the slave vessels, emancipate those onboard, and take them to Sierra Leone from where many would migrate back to Nigeria.

In 1886, the British consolidated their power by forming the Royal Niger Company, which later came under the control of the British Government. In 1901, Nigeria became a British protectorate and was divided into the northern and southern provinces, and Lagos on the southwest coast. The Fulani emirs (rulers) were deposed and defeated in battle, whereas others collaborated with British rule. The capital of the Sultanate, Sokoto, collapsed shortly after. By 1903, the conquest of the emirates was complete.

Western education and the development of a modern economy proceeded more rapidly in the south than in the north, where, for example Muslims dominated.

The British command met with various forms of resistance throughout the country; they waged wars with the indigenous groups in the south including the Yoruba of Ijebu, the Aro of Eastern Igboland, and the Aniocha of Western Igboland. In the north many Muslims resorted to migration as a form of resistance (*hijra*).

Nigeria achieved independence on October 1, 1960, as a federation of three geographic regions (northern, western, and eastern); its constitution provided for a parliamentary form of government. Today the country's legal system is based on a combination of English common law, Islamic *Shariah* law (only in some northern states), and traditional law. Since independence Nigeria has slipped into a pattern of coup, counter coup, assassinations, corruption, and ethnic rivalry.

Ethnicity and Society

The indigenous Nigerians are considered Black Africans. Three dominant ethnic groups make up about 70 percent of the population. In descending population size they are the Hausa-Fulani in the north, the Yoruba in the southwest, and the Igbo in the southeast.

The following are the most populous and politically influential groups: the Hausa and Fulani, Yoruba, Igbo (Ibo), Ijaw, Kanuri, Ibibio, and Tiv. These three minorities together account for 68 percent, more than two-thirds, of Nigeria's 133 million people. Of the remaining 32 percent, groups of notable size include Ijaw (the fourth largest ethnic group), 10 percent; Kanuri, 4 percent; Ibibio, 3.5 percent; and Tiv, 2.5 percent. All others, spread among hundreds of ethnicities, represent 12 percent (1.6 million people). The Hausa-Fulani constitute 29 percent of the Nigerian population. The Hausa have lived in the area for more than a thousand years. They represent a fusion of the northern Hausa with their early nineteenth-century conquerors, the Fulani. Fulani rule lasted for about 100 years, from the early 1800s to the early 1900s, until British colonization. The Fulani were responsible in large part for the spread of Islam throughout Western Africa, realized through a series of holy wars (*jihad*). Largely nomadic and herders, the Fulani's political and economic power had the effect of linking numerous, previously isolated, groups in the region. Whereas the majority of Fulani have assimilated with the Hausa, there is a minority that do not speak Hausa nor intermarry. Today the majority of Hausa-Fulani are Muslims. The Yoruba, who dwell in southwestern areas of Nigeria, are the second-largest ethnic group, accounting for approximately 20 percent of the population. Yoruba regard the city of Ile-Ife as their ancestral home. Their original kingdom of Oyo (circa 1400) had been one of the largest states in West Africa before the invasions of the Fulani and the spread of European contact, and especially British colonization. Several Yoruba cities, including Lagos, were founded hundreds of years ago; many of Nigeria's present-day urban areas (including Lagos, Ibadan, and Abeokuta) are located in Yorubaland. The majority of Yorubans are Christians, with large numbers in the Church of Nigeria (Anglican); Catholic; Pentecostal; and Methodist, and some are Muslim. The Igbo (Ibo) are found in the southeastern area of Nigeria. They represent 18 percent of Nigeria's people and originally settled in numerous autonomous villages. They received Christianity and missionary education under the influence of the British rule in the 1900s, despite their history of maintaining cultural and political unity. Many Igbo accepted Western education and ways and, as a result, held important positions in business and government during colonial rule, later playing a major role in securing Nigerian independence from Britain in 1960. Igbo presently live in small, decentralized, democratic settlements, although a smaller proportion live in large towns and are culturally much closer to the Edo of neighboring Benin City (in Edo state) than to the Igbo east of the lower Niger valley. Igbo today are predominantly Protestant and a combination of syncretized religions.

The population of the middle belt of Nigeria comprises nearly 200 ethnic groups. The Nupe, the Tiv, the Bura, and the Pabir are the largest of these groups. Attempts to assimilate these groups have been unsuccessful.

Although English is the official language, it is not the most widely spoken. English is used from primary school through university years; its use is the result of British colonial rule in the nineteenth century. The official use of English has bridged the barriers created by the many languages extant in this diverse nation. Many Nigerians are trilingual: English; a pidgin or local vernacular; and a more widely used lingua franca such as Hausa. Nigerian Muslims also use Arabic while participating in religious rites. The multilingualism developed over many years of trading across areas of this vast nation and with other nations. This eased communication among the many ethnic groups of Nigeria. Linguistics provides the greatest differences among the ethnic groups. After independence, English was retained as Nigeria's official language. It is taught at all educational levels and is used to communicate across the country. Non educated people use pidgin as their common language. In addition, there are three broad linguistic groups: Niger-Congo, Nilo-Saharan, and Afro-Asiatic. Each of these groups has numerous language subgroups. The ancient languages of Bade and Margi are also spoken as is Arabic, especially in the north. No clear language boundaries exist so confusion is readily apparent. Some groups can communicate but others can only communicate with subgroups. Most Nigerians are multilingual, speaking English and several other languages or dialects.

Religion is another ethnic indication. Islam was introduced in the ninth century CE and dominates in northern Nigeria. In the nineteenth century a Fulani leader was dissatisfied with the growing combination of Islam with traditional religions. He called for the Sokoto *jihad*, holy war, to bring the Hausa Muslims back into the fold; they had practiced a less traditional style of Islam. The result was the creation of the Sokoto caliphate that conquered Hausaland. Protestant Christianity and a local variation of Christianity are predominant in the Yoruban territories, whereas the Igbo and surrounding areas largely follow the Roman Catholic faith. Traditional African faiths are merged with elements of Christianity in the evangelical Aladura Church that strongly focuses on individuals. Islam is a minority faith in the south, whereas Christianity is a minority faith in the north.

Postindependence

Since independence, the Nigerian people have experienced significant political upheavals; a political coup is followed by a countercoup, military dictatorships, suspension of the constitution, manipulated elections, assassinations, and civil discontent. Although the majority of the troubles in Nigeria evolve from the unequal distribution of wealth, ethnic tensions are intertwined because ethnic groups believe that their economic well-being is threatened. For example, in January 1966, a group largely consisting of Igbo army officers initiated a coup in which Prime Minister Balewa was killed. The commander was General Johnson Aguisi-Ironsi who quickly controlled the entire country. Six months later he was killed and Yakubi Gowon took over with a military regime. He was strongly opposed by Colonel Odumegwu Ojukwu who rejected Gowon's restructuring of Nigeria. In May 1967, Ojukwu declared the Eastern Region independent from Nigeria and named it Biafra. Thousands of people suffered excruciating atrocities and destruction of property was unprecedented. The Biafrans lost the civil war and finally surrendered in 1970. Gowon was overthrown in 1975. A coup d'etat failed in 1976.

Nigeria elected a constituent assembly in 1977 that drafted a new constitution, published in September 1978, and in effect lifted the ban on political activity, allowing for the formation of political parties, and creating a second republic. Military rule thus ended in 1979. However, in December 1983, the military overthrew the civilian government as major general Muhammadu Buhari emerged as the leader of Nigeria's new ruling body, the Supreme Miltary Council (SMC), followed by another SMC general Ibrahim Babangida, who overthrew the Buhari government in 1985. Nigeria entered modern times when the public demanded an end to the succession of military regimes that followed throughout the 1980s and 1990s. As a first step to return the country to civilian rule, an American-style presidential constitution replaced the British parliamentary model. The transitional governments, however, continued to be corrupt, especially that of General Sani Abacha who ruled from 1993 to 1998, dissolved all democratic institutions, and was accused of numerous civil and human rights violations. These governments used violence against their critics, killed protesters, and suspended union movements.

In June 1998, upon Abacha's sudden death, General Abdulsalam Abubakar came to power. He freed political prisoners, ended harassment of political opponents, and set a timeline for transition to civilian rule. Three viable political parties emerged: the People's Democratic Party (PDP), the Alliance for Democracy, and the All People's Party. Elections were held in 1999 for local, state, and federal positions. The presidential election was monitored by an international team of observers, including former U.S. President James Carter. Former military head of state, Olusegun Obasanjo, a freed political prisoner, ran as a civilian candidate and won the election. The emergence in 1999 of a democratic Nigeria put an end to 16 years of military rule. Nigerians finally held a legal election that year, and a civilian government was elected. Many leaders of the various regimes viewed their position of power as an avenue to offer coveted positions to their ethnic compatriots. Nigerians welcomed the change, although Obasanjo's challenge has been to quell the country's ongoing ethnic tensions and fighting. He was re-elected in 2003.

Each ethnic group is protective of its territory due to historical habitation and inheritance. People living in a specific area, no matter how long, are perpetually considered outsiders. Despite the improved political situation, ethnic tensions escalating into violence have emerged in Nigeria. In 1999, the Ijaws and the Urhobos fought the Itsekiris over socioeconomic factors. The destruction of homes, businesses, and schools has left unspeakable scars and created an economically stagnant area. Tensions between the Ijaws and the Ilajes in the Ondo State and similar conflicts in the Anambra State as well as tensions between the Sagamu, Jukon/Tivs, the Ife/Modakeke and others are based on underdevelopment which causes extreme poverty. These people have all traditionally coexisted peacefully. Nigeria's peoples have suffered through religious wars, civil discontent, military dictatorships, and independence. However, they all share a sense of community and deem their difficulties temporary.

Nigeria's abundant natural resources include large deposits of petroleum and natural gas; its oil-rich economy was hampered by years of military rule; however, oil still represents 20 percent of the GDP. Other industries include coal, tin, columbite, palm oil, peanuts, cotton, rubber, wood, hides, and skins. Agriculture (including cocoa, peanuts, palm oil, corn, and rice) traditionally comprises a large portion of the economic sector, although in recent years it has failed to keep pace with population growth. The GDP per capita income was $900 in 2002. Although many Nigerians became city dwellers in the last decade of the twentieth century, most people still live in rural areas.

ANNETTE RICHARDSON

See also **Benin; Fulani; Hausa; Yoruba**

Further Reading

Arnold, Guy, *Modern Nigeria*, London: Longman, 1977

Coleman, James S., *Nigeria: Background to Nationalism*, Berkeley: University of California Press, 1958

Falola, Toyin, *The History of Nigeria,* Westport, Connecticut: Greenwood Press, 1999

Hargreaves, John D., *Decolonization in Africa*, London: Longman, 1988

Harmon, Daniel E., *Nigeria 1880 to the Present: The Struggle, the Tragedy, the Promise*, Philadelphia: Chelsea House Publishers, 2001

Isichei, Elizabeth Allo, *A History of Nigeria,* London: Longman, 1983

Kao, Alhajia Aminu, *Politics and Administration in Post Military Era*, Lagos: Nigerian Institute of International Affairs, 1976

Rosenberg, Anne, *Nigeria: The Land,* New York: Crabtree Publishing Company, 2001

Northern Ireland

Capsule Summary

Country Name: Northern Ireland
Location: Northeast corner of the island of Ireland, Western Europe
Total Population: 1.6 million
Languages: English, Irish
Religion: Protestant (56%), Catholic (44%)

According to historian Richard Rose, "Many talk about a solution to Ulster's political problem but few are prepared to say what the problem is. The problem is there is no solution" (1971). Rose's grim analysis of Northern Ireland during the 1970s reflects the general pessimism that has dominated coverage of the Northern Ireland imbroglio.

The perception that the conflict in Northern Ireland is intractable is influenced by its longevity. England first involved itself in Irish affairs in 1169, and during subsequent centuries the extent of its rule ebbed and flowed depending on the strength of Irish resistance and the domestic priorities of the British state. The nature of British rule was fundamentally altered in the sixteenth century when England became a Protestant state while Ireland remained Catholic. Whereas in the past, English settlers had been assimilated into Irish society to an extent which endangered British rule, henceforth, colonizers could be distinguished from the colonized by religion. England's conversion to Protestantism coincided with its growth as an imperial power, and Irish Gaelic Chieftains were finally defeated in 1603 and many left *en masse* 4 years later leaving Ireland leaderless and defenseless. Britain embarked on an intensive policy of plantation, particularly in the North of the country, which had been the center of Gaelic resistance. These settlers, mainly English Anglicans and Scottish Presbyterians, are the descendants of present-day unionist population. The country remained predominantly Catholic, however, and almost every generation witnessed a major nationalist rebellion against British rule. The slow democratization of the British polity allowed an Irish nationalist parliamentary movement to develop while the physical force tradition continued to attract a substantial minority of adherents. When the separatist Sinn Fein party gained a majority of Irish seats in 1918, they declared

917

the country independent and established a parliament in Dublin. To complement these political endeavors, a war for independence was fought by the Irish Republican Army (IRA) against British forces. In deference to unionist resistance and British strategic objectives, Ireland was partitioned in 1920 by a unilateral act of the British Parliament. Two new states were created, the Irish Free State (now the Republic of Ireland), which was almost homogeneously nationalist, and Northern Ireland, which had a 2–1 unionist majority. The advantage of partition from the perspective of the British Government was that it enabled Westminster to distance itself from what it saw as the Irish abyss, which had dominated British politics throughout the late nineteenth and early twentieth centuries and dispatched many leaders to an early political grave. Interest and knowledge of Irish affairs progressively waned after 1920, and after a brief resurgence during World War II and its immediate aftermath, declined rapidly so that by the 1960s Northern Ireland did not merit the full time attention of one single official. Contrary to popular opinion in Ireland, such matters rated very low in British priorities and were rarely discussed in cabinet. Experience, they believed, had demonstrated that since partition, Northern Irish problems were sporadic, short-lived and generally faded away, sorting themselves out without recourse to British involvement.

With an inbuilt majority, Northern Ireland possessed the formal features of a parliamentary democracy but in reality was a one-party state. Anti-Catholic discrimination was enshrined as official policy within the unionist state and a pervasive and heavily structured apparatus of economic hegemony was devised, which proved remarkably effective in regulating and stunting the natural evolution of the nationalist minority. The inequality and exclusion cascaded downward from generation to generation with disproportionate levels of emigration and unemployment, and the systematic exclusion of Catholics from every level of political, social, and economic power. Complementing this system of economic apartheid, the state invoked an impressive series of repressive laws enforced by paramilitary police, which was almost entirely Protestant in composition. A combination of social and political forces during the 1960s brought about the establishment of a nonviolent campaign with the objective of attaining basic civil rights within a state, which could not accommodate such a demand as its very *raison d'être* was the maintenance of Protestant union-

ist supremacy in perpetuity. The violent response of state security forces and civilian irregulars to the civil rights campaign would precipitate a social conflagration and an armed nationalist insurgency, which would propel an entire society downward into a spiral of violence.

The "Troubles"

The present "Troubles" (euphemism favored by the Irish when describing the war) began on August 12, 1969. Embittered and disillusioned by the failure of the Northern Ireland Government to deliver reforms, nationalists were further incensed by the provocative unionist march through the city of Derry. Rioting ensued, and when the Bogside and the Creggan areas were attacked by unionist civilians, aided by the Northern Ireland security forces, barricades were thrown up to protect the nationalist ghettos. British troops arrived on August 15 and were initially welcomed by nationalists who believed that the troops might protect them from the worst excesses of the unionist regime. It was anticipated that British soldiers would be needed only for a couple of months, but after three decades of conflict, there are still thousands of troops in Northern Ireland.

A number of key events in the early 1970s contributed to the development of a full-scale conflagration. In July 1970, British troops imposed a curfew on the Falls area of Belfast, a nationalist stronghold, while on August 9, 1971, internment without trial was introduced. Internment rejuvenated the civil rights movement, which held a series of marches to oppose the law. At one of these marches, on January 30, 1972, British troops opened fire on protesters killing 14 civilians and injuring over a hundred. Quickly dubbed "Bloody Sunday," the massacre escalated hostilities further and in March 1972, the British administration abolished the Northern Ireland Government and imposed direct rule from London. By this stage, the war had escalated to alarming proportions. In 1970, 13 people were killed; in 1972 there were 467 deaths and over 10,000 recorded shooting incidents. Direct rule was never considered anything but a stopgap solution until a durable form of devolved government could be established.

Several initiatives were tried: talks with the IRA (1972, 1975); a constitutional convention (1974–75); limited devolved power (1982–86); and the Anglo-Irish Agreement (1985). The most promising initiative, perhaps, was the Sunningdale Agreement, which came into effect on January 1, 1974. Under the terms of the agreement, power was to be shared between Catholics and Protestants in a new Northern Ireland executive, whereas a Council of Ireland would provide a legislative link between the Irish Government in Dublin and the new cabinet in Belfast. The executive, however, provided a unifying focus for dissent enabling politicians, paramilitaries, and proletarians to form a potent, if transient, alliance, which would halt the erosion of Protestant privilege. The electricity supply—which was under militant Protestant control—was cut, and aided by British Government inertia and widespread intimidation, the Executive collapsed after only 5 months. Twenty-five years would pass before a similar power-sharing executive could be established again.

Separate Lives

In Northern Ireland, society is segregated almost entirely along sectarian lines. There are Catholic villages and Protestant villages, and within larger urban areas, there are Catholic estates and Protestant estates. Whereas segregation is a symptom of conflict, it also contributes to the continuation of conflict because there is often an absence of social acquaintances from the other side. This in turn leads to stereotyping and reinforces mutual suspicion. The two communities live separately, read nationalist and unionist newspapers, and even play different sports. Moreover, the two communities are highly endogamous with intermarriage sometimes viewed in similar terms to that which existed in the American South. While both nationalists and unionists speak English, the Irish language is considered as a badge of resistance by many nationalists and has enjoyed a huge revival in recent years.

The biggest fallacy and source of confusion is the belief that religion is the root cause of Northern Ireland conflict. Like all popular errors, it has a basis somewhere in truth. Almost all Protestants are unionists and a similar proportion of Catholics are nationalist. However, the fundamental issue is not theological. If it were so, it would be impossible to understand how Catholics and Protestants are able to live peaceably in Southern Ireland, in Britain, or in any other part of the world. Indeed, the trend in Europe since the end of World War II has been for Catholics and Protestants to merge politically into Christian Democratic Parties. The conflict centers on the issue of power. Protestant unionists have exercised it for 400 years, and Catholics want their share and are often willing to fight for it. Indeed, pro-

tagonists pride themselves on their unwillingness to compromise on fundamental principles. The two most common unionist slogans are "No Surrender" and "Not an Inch" (of territory). When the IRA was asked to decommission its explosives and weapons, graffiti appeared on Belfast walls declaring "Not an ounce, not a bullet." Such intransigence has made brokering agreements difficult, as protagonists have tended to view political developments in zero-sum terms.

Unionism

Unionism is, at heart, a defensive ideology. It seeks to defend the political union between Great Britain and Northern Ireland. As a defender of the constitutional status quo, unionism is also a conservative ideology. Unionists believe that there are two distinct peoples in Ireland, unionist and nationalist (or Protestant and Catholic). The inability of nationalists, North and South, to recognize the democratic legitimacy of the Northern Ireland state was the cause of instability in Northern Ireland. While unionists view themselves as a unique people, they have acknowledged similarities with the Israelis and white South Africans. Destiny brought them to Ireland to fulfil a special civilizing mission, and their survival and prosperity is due to their fidelity to God. This view is best expressed by unionism's most popular politician, the Reverend Ian Paisley: "The Almighty does not make mistakes; He alone is infallible. Our presence in Ulster is no accident of history . . . We have an historic and Divine Commission. We are the defenders of Truth in this Province and in this island . . . Ulster is the last bastion of Evangelical Protestantism in Western Europe; we must not let drop the torch of Truth of the eternal conflict between Truth and Evil . . . We are a special people, not of ourselves, but of Divine mission. Ulster arise and acknowledge you God."

For those who adhere to such a worldview, the problem in Northern Ireland can be said to be truly religious. Despite this apparent certainty, however, the unionist sense of identity is often difficult to pin down. Depending on circumstances, an individual unionist might describe himself as British, Irish, Northern Irish, or an Ulsterman. In recent years, "British" has been the most popular description but "British" is not a nationality, it is a political allegiance. Moreover, in many ways the Protestant community is more fragmented than its Catholic counterpart, a fact which only exacerbates feelings of insecurity.

Nationalism

The nationalist conception of past and present is radically at variance from that of the unionist community. From the nationalist perspective, the Irish nation was subjected to 800 years of colonization, a process that debased their culture and stifled economic and political progress. When the Crown could no longer hold the entire island, it carved out the maximum area within which its unionist allies could safely hold a majority. This policy of partition, according to the nationalist view, is the root cause of troubles in Northern Ireland. Nationalists contend that the people of Ireland form one nation and have been artificially divided to further British interests. Responsibility for the conflict is assigned to the British Government, which imposed partition, and it is maintained that the Northern Ireland state could not exist without Britain's political, economic, and military support. Like their Protestant counterparts, Northern Ireland Catholics are among the most devout in the world, and have the highest rate of church attendance and lowest divorce rate in the western world.

The Path to Peace

Since 1969, academics and politicians have offered a plethora of solutions which might offer a middle way between the unionist wish to remain within the United Kingdom and the nationalist desire for a united Ireland. But a solution which was not negotiated between all the major players and which was imposed at a time of war had little chance of success. This all changed when, on August 31, 1994, the IRA announced a "complete cessation of hostilities." The British Army and the IRA had reached a stalemate; neither had defeated the other and neither could attain outright military victory. After several false starts, a peace accord, popularly known as the Good Friday Agreement, was negotiated on April 10, 1998, by the all parties except that of Reverend Ian Paisley. The "solution" which is presently being implemented is power-sharing. Northern Ireland remains within the United Kingdom though the British Government made it clear that, should a majority wish to become part of a united Ireland, it will legislate for the same. In the meantime there is a weak Irish Dimension with Dublin playing a consultative and supervisory role. Though the Good Friday Agreement is remarkably similar to that negotiated at Sunningdale a quarter century before, its chances for success are greater as the new dispensation has the support of both the IRA and the unionist paramilitaries who brought down the previous power-sharing institutions. Peace, however, is not merely the absence of war. The decommissioning of weapons is a process that has taken years to negotiate; the dismantling of sectarian mind-set will take much longer.

DONNACHA Ó BEACHÁIN

See also **Catholics in Northern Ireland; Ireland; Irish Republican Army; Sinn Fein**

Further Reading

Brewer, John D., and Garreth I. Higgins, *Anti-Catholicism in Northern Ireland,* London: Macmillan, 1998

Conroy, John, *Belfast Diary: War as a Way of Life,* Boston: Beacon Press, 1995

Coogan, Tim Pat, *The Troubles,* London: Arrow, 1996

Murray, Raymond, *The SAS in Ireland,* Cork and Dublin: Mercier Press, 1997

O'Leary, Brendan, and John McGarry, *Explaining Northern Ireland,* London: Blackwell, 1995

O'Malley, Padraig, *The Uncivil Wars: Ireland Today,* Boston: Beacon Press, 1999

Rose, Richard, *Governing without Consensus: An Irish Perspective*, Boston: Beacon Press, 1971

Whyte, John, *Interpreting Northern Ireland,* Oxford: Clarendon Press, 1990

Norway

Capsule Summary

Country Name: Kingdom of Norway
Location: Scandinavia, Northern Europe
Form of government: Constitutional monarchy, democracy
Total Population: 4,546,123 (July 2003)
GDP per capita: $33,000 (2002)
Languages: Norwegian (bokmål and nynorsk), Saami
Ethnic languages: Kveni, Finnish, Romani, Romanes, Hebrew, Yiddish
Religion: Lutheran
Indigenous people: Saami
National minorities: Kvens, Skogfinns, Gypsies, Romani/Travellers, Jews

Ethnic composition by citizenship (2000): Norwegian (96%), Swedish (0.56%), Danish (0.43%), Bosnia-Herzegovinian (0.27%), British (0.25%), Yugoslavian (0.23%), American (0.19%), Pakistani (0.16%), German (0.15%)

Norway is a kingdom in Northern Europe. Early signs of statehood are found in the Viking Age (700–1100 CE), when Norwegians raided large parts of Europe. In 1380, Norway and Denmark became unified under a double-monarchy. In 1814, Norway became part of the Swedish-Norwegian Union, and in 1905, it gained independence and established monarchy. Norway was neutral during World War I (1914–18). German forces occupied Norway from 1940 to 1945 during World War II. It became a founding member of the Nordic Council (1952), the Nordic Council of Ministers (1971), and the North Atlantic Treaty Organization (NATO) (1949).

The dominant population is Norwegian (93.7–94.9 percent); the national minorities constitute approximately 1.1–2.3 percent of the total population. The Saami are recognized as an indigenous people, but satisfy the criteria for recognition as a national minority as well. Their language is Saami, which exists in a number of dialects. Their number is estimated to be between 35,000 and 80,000 (0.8–1.8 percent of the population), mostly living in Northern Norway, and in the capital of Oslo. National minorities are the Kvens (10,000–15,000; 0.22–0.33 percent), living North of the Polar Circle; Skogfinns, or Forest Finns, (several thousand; 0.02–0.08 percent) in Southern-Central Norway bordering Sweden; Gypsies (300–400; 0.009 percent) mostly living in Oslo; Romani or Travellers (some 1,000; 0.4 percent); and Jews (1,100; 0.02 percent). The language spoken by Kvens is Kven Finnish, although many Kvens only speak Norwegian due to assimilation. The Skogfinns originally spoke Finnish, but are assimilated, and now speak Norse with some Finnish elements. Neither considers Finland their homeland/kin-state. The language spoken by Gypsies is Romanes, whereas the Romani speak Romani. The Jews are predominantly Norwegian speaking, but a few hundred also speak Hebrew, and some elderly members of the community even understand Yiddish. Besides these national minorities, a number of immigrant communities live in Norway.

History

All national minorities in Norway have a long tradition, going several hundred years back in history. The Kvens, Skogfinns, and Romani appear as distinct groups back in the 1500s and 1600s. Kvens were mentioned in the Viking Age (700–1100 CE), but a true immigration probably began in the 1700s. In the 1500s, the Skogfinns (or Forest Finns) arrived in present-day Norway, eventually settling in the woodlands bordering Sweden. This area was named Finnskogen—Finnish Forests. Initially, the Kvens and Skogfinns were welcome as settlers, adding population to low-density areas. The Kvens were important as peasants in Northern Norway. However, in the 1800s, that perception changed. Norway feared a Russian and later a Finnish "danger," and this was the legitimation for strict assimilation policies, enforced during Norse nation-building after Norway's independence from Sweden in 1905. The policy of "fornorskning" (Norwegianization) was pursued openly until the 1960s. All minorities were affected by this policy. The identity of the Saami, Skogfinns, and Kvens in Norway was weakened because assimilation was supported by cultural policies and, for instance, requirements for fluency in Norwegian as a precondition for landownership (land law of 1902).

The Jewish, Gypsy, and Romani communities were also subject to persecution, deportation, and hardship that constitute forced assimilation. In the case of the Romani group, this included sterilization, compulsory institutionalization, and ordered foster care for children, all of which were sanctioned and supported by the authorities. Only in February 1998 did the Norwegian government apologize to the Romani, regretting the discrimination and persecution.

Jews were banned from immigration to Norway during the Danish-Norwegian reign, which began in the 1600s. The constitution of 1814 granted the rights of worship and religion to all citizens, but continued to ban Jews from entering Norway. Only in 1851 was the constitution altered, and in the following years small groups of Jews settled in Norway, especially those from Germany, Austria-Hungary, and Denmark. More followed after 1880 because of nationalism and anti-Semitism in Central and Eastern Europe, and by 1920 some 1,500 Jews were living in Norway. However, during the Nazi occupation of Norway from 1940 to 1945, 767 Jews were deported to German concentration camps where nearly 750 Jews were killed and 230 families annihilated. Another 1,300 sought refuge in Sweden. By 1946, only 559 Jews remained in Norway; in 2001 the number of Jews was the same as that in 1940.

Gypsies seemed to have arrived in Scandinavia around 1500. For centuries, it was difficult to make a distinction between Gypsies (Roma) and Romani/ Travellers. Linguistically, both groups are close, but it is still disputed if the language indicates common roots, or has to be explained by cultural encounters. In the 1800s, the Romani were called *fante,* and the Norwegian authorities started to define a policy approach, enabling them to gain control over this travelling community. Around 1900, offensive instruments were adopted. A special Norse Mission among homeless was established, and this Mission placed probably a total of 1,500 Romani children in foster care. In 1934, Norway adopted a law on sterilization, which, according to theories of eugenics, was used and enforced against the Romani group. By 1977, a total of 128 Romani were sterilized by the authorities; 17 others were sterilized without the consent of the individuals.

The Saami can be traced back several thousand years, living in all of Northern Scandinavia and the Kola Peninsula. In Northern Norway, Saami lived in the areas of Finnmarken and Troms. Until the 1600s, Denmark-Norway, Sweden, and Russia taxed the Saami, because no state borders were determined. In 1613, the coastal area came under sovereign control of the Danish-Norwegian king. In 1751, a border treaty was signed by

Sweden and Denmark-Norway, but nomadic Saami kept the right to cross the border until Finland was incorporated into Russia in 1809. In 1852, the boundary was enforced, and the Saami lost the right to cross the border to Finland. The Saami were subjected to the Norwegian assimilation policies in the 1800s. Only after 1945, the authorities decided to abandon assimilation and gradually promoted the Saami language and culture. Saami education was granted in 1967, and a joint Nordic Saami institute was established in 1973. A conflict over the Alta dam eventually led to the creation of a committee on Saami rights and on cultural issues (*Samerettsudvalget*) in 1980. In 1987, Norway adopted a Saami Law, and a special parliament, the *Sametinget*, convened in 1989. The same year, a Saami university was established for students from all Scandinavian Saami communities. In 1990, the Saami Law was revised, stating that Saami and Norwegian are equal languages. In 1999, the Norwegian king Harald apologized to the Sameting for the Norwegian policies against the Saami. Currently, a special action plan and social policy aimed at the Saami are being developed.

Society

In the late 1980s and 1990s, considerable changes took place in Norway's minority policy, aimed at inclusion and integration with acceptance of cultural diversity and distinct identities. First, the approach toward the Saami was revised. In 1988, the constitution was amended with the §110a, obligating the authorities to ensure that the Saami community can secure and develop its language, culture, and society. The International Labor Organization (ILO) Convention 169 on the rights of indigenous people was ratified in 1989. In 1992, Norway's parliament, *Storting*, ratified the Council of Europe's Charter on Regional or Minority Languages (1992), recognizing Saami as a protected language. Norway was the first country to ratify the Charter. In March 1999, Norway ratified the Council of Europe's Framework Convention on the Protection of National Minorities (1995). Norway decided not to specify the groups included in its declaration; however, the Framework Convention applies to Kvens, Skogfinns, Romani, Gypsies, and Jews. Whereas the Kvens, Skogfinns, Gypsies, and Jews had no reservations to recognition as national minorities, some of the Romani groups objected out of fear for negative consequences such as stigmatization, discrimination, or persecution. However, this group was also included. The Saami did not want to be included, because their rights were guaranteed better through the ILO Convention 169.

Norway adopted new standards for its minority policy, aiming at inclusion, equal rights, compensation, and support for ethnic revival. It declared that it intends to fulfill the objectives and ideals included in both international legal instruments adopted by the Council of Europe. Currently, Norway is defining political standards for this inclusive policy. In December 2000, the government issued a report concerning the national minorities, emphasizing the new approach, and committing itself to the fact that Norway is home to cultural diversity. On January 1, 2001, a new office for Saami, Minority and Immigrant affairs was established within the Ministry for Local and Regional Affairs. Its task, among others, is to coordinate the Saami policy, and to develop and coordinate the policy toward other minorities. The Norse, Kvens, and Saami traditionally have been living in the same geographical region leading to close contacts and intermarriages. Therefore, the people living north of the Polar Circle sometimes hold multiple identities, including Kveni, Finnish, Norwegian, and Saami elements.

Thus, Norway is currently undertaking efforts to promote the situation of the national minorities, compensating for previous discrimination, persecution, hardship, and assimilation prevalent until the latter part of the 1900s. Unfortunately, minorities continue to experience discrimination. Only in 1997, Finnish was granted status as a second language to be taught in districts with a Kven population. In 1999, Norway started compensating Jewish victims of the Holocaust. In mid-2000, a compensation of 131,4 mio. NOK was paid to 1,000 persons; in addition, 150 mio. NOK were paid to Jewish communities in Norway. The infringements against the Romani will be subject to the work of a new center, which was scheduled to be built in 2002 in Elverum, for documentation and dissemination of the Romani's culture and history. The cultural heritage of the minorities is now claimed to be an integral part of Norway's cultural heritage, obligating the government to pay special attention to the culture and traditions of the minorities. Funding for cultural activities and language training for the minorities is now made available at a larger scale.

JØRGEN KÜHL

See also **Diaspora: Jewish; Indigenous Peoples; Roma (Gypsies); Saami**

Further Reading

CBSS Working Group on Assistance to Democratic Institutions. Round Table on "The Rights of Minorities in the Baltic Sea Region" (Moscow, 30–31 March 2000). Compilation of National Presentations, Stockholm: Council of the Baltic Sea States, 2000

Sami—the Indigenous People of Norway, The Norwegian Ministry of Local Government and Labour, Oslo: Department of Sami Affairs, 1995

Stortingsmelding nr. 41 (1996–97). Om norsk samepolitikk. Tilråding fra Kommunal-og arbeidsdepartementet av 18. April 1997, godkjent i statsråd samme dag, Oslo, 1997

Stortingsmelding nr. 15 (2000–2001). Nasjonale minoritetar i Noreg—Om politikk overfor jøder, rom, romanifolket og skogfinnar. Tilråding frå Kommunal- og regionaldepartementet av 8. desember (2000) godkjend i statsråd same dagen, Oslo, 2000

Tägil, Sven, editor, *Ethnicity and Nation Building in the Nordic World*, London: Hurst, 1995

Ocalan, Abdullah (Kurd)

Abdullah Ocalan, known to his followers as "Apo," has since the 1980s been seen by many Kurds within both Turkey and the Diaspora as the embodiment of the Kurds of Turkey, due to his role as founder and leader of the Kurdistan Workers Party (PKK).

Ocalan comes from a poor peasant family from the Gaziantep region of Turkey. Educated in Turkish at school, his first language was Turkish not Kurdish, and in his younger days he was deeply religious. His main aim as a student was initially to join the Turkish army, but, having failed the exams, he entered the Political Science Faculty of Ankara University, discovered Socialist literature, and, like many other radical Kurdish students, became part of the fragmented Turkish left wing of the 1970s. However, he came to view the Turkish Left as chauvinist on the Kurdish issue. Seeing the need for a specifically "Kurdish National Liberation Movement," he severed relations with other Turkish left-wing groups.

Ocalan moved from Ankara back to the southeast in 1975. In 1977 he and his associates drew up a "Party program draft" and formed the PKK in November 1978 in a village near Diyarbakir. Following the 1980 military coup, Ocalan left Turkey for Syria and parts of Lebanon controlled by Syria. Armed operations against the Turkish state commenced in 1984. Since then, over 30,000 people have died in the ensuing conflict, with the authorities destroying or forcibly evacuating thousands of Kurdish villages.

The 1977 document clearly spelt out the later PKK program and presaged the vicious PKK war against all perceived agents of the Turkish state, including school-teachers as well as Village Guards (local villagers armed by the state as a paramilitary force). Armed activity was to be a crucial PKK weapon in both gaining support and undermining state control. Of special interest in this program is the "minimum objective" to establish a Kurdish state, and whether it was foreseen by Ocalan to include the parts of "Kurdistan" in neighboring countries. While the PKK is always referred to by the Turkish establishment as a separatist organization, Ocalan, despite the 1977 program, has been ambivalent on this crucial point, and has been careful to deny that the PKK's overriding aim is an independent Kurdistan. On the question of relations with Kurds in neighboring countries, Ocalan again has shown ambivalence, at times siding with different Kurdish factions in Iraq.

The PKK has a tight professional organizational structure made up of a political nucleus, the party; its full-time fighting force, the Kurdistan National Liberation Army (ARGK set up in 1986); and a widespread popular front, the National Liberation Front of Kurdistan (ERNK set up in 1985). Despite being characterized as "bandits" by the authorities, the PKK grew into a formidable force. In this it was greatly aided by the government's repressive measures and continuing military methods. These, combined with the continued use of legislation that has outlawed all moderate Kurdish political voices, have resulted in the PKK being seen almost by default as the main Kurdish organization within Turkey.

Ocalan was adept at changing policy to suit conditions. In 1989, Islamic messages and quotes from the Koran became widespread in PKK propaganda. However, for the inner core of the party and the ARGK, religious practices were forbidden, and the cadres had to accept unquestionably Ocalan's interpretations of Marxist-Leninism. Ocalan kept a rigid internal control over the PKK with frequent bloody purges.

In January 1995, a major meeting at which Ocalan abandoned much of the PKK's hitherto Marxist trappings and denounced Soviet communism coincided with major diplomatic moves on part of Turkish Kurds. Efforts to set up a Kurdish Parliament in Exile were finalized. Immediately before, in an attempt to upgrade its international standing the PKK issued a "Declaration of Intention" to abide by humanitarian laws and rules specified by the Geneva Convention.

Ocalan left the comparative safety of Syria in October 1998 after military threats from Turkey compelled Syria to change its policy towards harboring him. He then attempted to find another secure base from which to continue his operations. However, this proved difficult. He was arrested in Rome in November 1998 but Italy refused to extradite him to Turkey as Italy does not return people who may face the death penalty. This caused a storm of anti-Italian feeling among Turks in Turkey. Countries like Germany where the PKK had been implicated in a number of crimes also did not seek extradition, perhaps fearing a reaction from its large Kurdish population. He was then refused access by a number of European countries and eventually flew to Kenya on February 2, 1999 where on February 15 he was kidnapped, drugged, and transported back to Turkey by a special Turkish military force. He was detained and tried in a special military prison on the island of Imral in the Sea of Marmara and sentenced to death on June 29, 1999.

Although Turkey retains the death penalty, nobody has been legally executed since 1984. Ocalan raises strong conflicting emotions. Kurds in many countries see him as a father figure and vigorously protested his arrest, while for many Turks he is a hated figure. His defense counsel has applied to the European Court in protest at the handling of the trial, during which three of his lawyers who were not allowed private access were sentenced to jail terms. Although a government coalition partner had campaigned on a promise to see him hang, it is unlikely that the sentence will be carried out.

With the arrest of Ocalan, the scale of armed conflict dropped significantly. During his trial Ocalan reportedly pleaded for his life and stated he was willing to serve the Turkish state, and even apologized for past actions. In August 1999 he declared through his lawyers that the PKK's armed struggle was over. In the same statement, he ordered his fighters to withdraw from Turkey by September 1, and said his rebels would disarm if Turkey offered an amnesty. However, the authorities only offered amnesty to those not involved in armed activity.

In October 2003, Ocalan's death penalty was commuted to life in prison, with no possibility for parole. In 2004, the European Court of Human Rights ruled that Ocalan had not received a fair trial, and the government of Turkey had thus violated his human rights. The Turkish government objected to the ruling, arguing that the European Court had not thoroughly considered all aspects of the case. Although the ruling by the European Court of Human Rights is not binding, Turkey is expected to come under significant international pressure to hold a retrial if the European Court's Grand Chamber upholds the verdict after the Turkish government's appeal.

Capsule Biography

Abdullah Ocalan. Born 1948 in Omerli village near Urfa, Turkey. Primary and secondary education in Gaziantep; studied at Political Science Faculty of Ankara University. Formed PKK in 1978. Arrested in Nairobi, Kenya in February 1999, tried and sentenced to death in Turkey in June 1999. Currently detained in Imral prison.

HUGH POULTON

Further Reading

Bohler, Britta, *De Zwerftocht van een Leider: Achter de Schermen van de zaak Ocalan*, Amsterdam: Associated Press, 2000

Chaliand, Gerard, *The Kurdish Tragedy*, London and New Jersey: Zed Books, 1994

McDowall, David, *The Kurds: A Nation Denied*, London: Minority Rights Group, 1992

Poulton, Hugh, *Top Hat, Grey Wolf and Crescent: Turkish Nationalism and the Turkish Republic*, London: Hurst, and New York: New York University Press, 1997

Occitans

Capsule Summary

Location: Southern half of France and Monaco, but also some small portions in Italy (Alpine Valleys in Piemont region) and Spain (Aran Valley); about 190,000 sq. km (74,100 sq. miles)
Total population: 13 million
Language: Occitan (non-official in France, official in Italian and Spain). Almost all speakers are biligual in French, Italian, Spanish or Catalan
Religion: Roman Catholic

Occitans were never politically unified. In southern France, where Occitan culture is centered, seven historical Occitan regions can be defined acording to linguistic varieties and historical evolution: Languedoc Gascogne, Guyenne, Limousin, Auvergne, Dauphiné, and Provence. Although initiated in the thirteenth century, French control over the area was not completely achieved until the nineteenth century. Today, the area roughly comprises the French administrative regions of Aquitaine, Limousin, Auvergne, Rhône-Alpes, Provence-Alpes-Côte d'Azur, Midi-Pyrinées and Languedoc-Roussillon, in addition to small portions in Italy and Spain. About 13 million people live in the area, of which 2.5 milion speak the Occitan language and between 4 and 5 million can understand it. However, Article 2 of the French Constitution states that French is the only official language for the whole country. France has not signed the European Charter for Minority Languages, issued by the Council of Europe.

Celts, Iberians, and Greeks settled in the current Occitan area prior to the Roman conquest starting in the second century BCE. Southern Gallia, which corresponds to today's Occitan area, experienced a more intense Romanization and earlier Christianization compared to the northern part. In the eighth century, Charlemagne's empire entirely embraced today's Occitan territory, but the area was split up as Charlemagne's lands were divided among his sons.

During the medieval period, the Occitan language, resulting from evolution of Latin, became an international language used by poets and troubaadours throughout Europe. Politically, the region was divided into a plethora of states that in general were nominal subjects of the French Capet dynasty but were inde-

pendent in practice, although Aquitaine remained attached to the English Plantagenet dynasty for three centuries after Eleanor of Aquitaine married Henry II in 1154. At the beginning of the thirteenth century, the Pope called for a crusade against the Cathar heresy, which was widespread in the Occitan region. The French heeded the call and invaded the Occitan principalities. Peter I of Aragon crossed the Pyrennes trying to mantain clout in the area but was defeated and killed in the battlefield of Muret in 1213.

This marked the begining of French political domination, accompanied with cultural repression in the following centuries. In 1539, the French language was made compulsory in the Occitan area. During the modern era, some segments of Occitan society favored a noncentralized state in France, but they faced an increasing centralization policy carried out from Paris by the Valois and Bourbon dynasties. Despite the federalist ideals of the Bourdeaux-centered Girondins (one of the most influential political groupings in late-eighteenth century France), the coming of the French Revolution did not reverse centralization but deepened it.

The Occitan language was rediscovered in the nineteenth century under the influence of Romanticism. The Nobel prize-winning poet and linguist Frédéric Mistral played a major role in reviving Occitan language and culture: *Mireio,* his most successful work, was published in 1958 and obtained great acclaim in France and abroad. The Occitan revival was mirrored in the Catalan culture renaissance taking place on the other side of the Pyrenees: In 1935, Loïs Alibèrt published in Barcelona an Occitan grammar that laid the foundations of a standard language.

Today, the Occitan language is not commonly studied or used in France. Approximately 40 schools (the so-called *Calendretas*) have been set up through private inititive (mainly parents' associations). These provide schooling in Occitan to some 2,000 children. Only recently, the French government began giving some financial assistance to these schools under certain conditions (*i.e.,* schools have to function for more than five years before they can receive state funds).

Language remains the most important basis for Occitan identity. Spoken Occitan is not unified but manifests itself in several dialects. Languedocien is the variety found inthe Languedoc Province from Montpellier to Toulouse, Bordeaux, and Albi. Mostly spoken in rural communities, fluent speakers comprise 10 percent of the population in the region, and about 20 percent more have some knowledge of the language.

The Provençal variety is spoken from the Nimes area in southeastern France to the Italian Alpine Valleys. There are 250,000 fluent speakers and 800,000 with some knowledge in France. As of 1990, there were 100,000 speakers of the Transalpin dialect in Italy, and 4,500 in Monaco as of 1988.

Auvergnat, the variety found in central France, is in a highly fragmented situation, with limited intelligibility between northern and southern varieties. The Gascon language is spoken in the southeastern province of Gascogne, especially in the Bearn region, where more than half of the population speak it and 70 percent understand it. Bearn was one of the last parts of the Occitan area to be united with France: it remained independent until its last suzerain, Henry of Bourbon, who had also become king of France as Henry IV, died in 1620.

In Spain, a dialect of the Gascon language is spoken in the Aran Valley, near the headwaters of the Garona River in the northwest corner of the autonomous region of Catalonia. This linguistic variety, known as Aranese, has 3,814 speakers, plus 1,283 who understand it out of 5,922 in the valley (1991 census). It has had an official status in the area since the 1980s, together with Catalan and Spanish. Public institutions are compelled by law to protect and promote its use at school, in publications, and other areas.

In Italy, Occitan is spoken in 12 valleys (known as *Valadas Occitanas*), comprising 120 municipalities and 180,000 people. The Italian goverment has recently recognized minority rights to the communities defining themselves as Occitan.

MARTÍ GRAU

Further Reading

Armengaud, André, and Robert Lafont, editors, *Histoire d'Occitanie*, Paris: Hachette littérature, 1979

Bourrilly, V.L., *Histoire de la Provence*, Paris: Presses Universitaires de France, 5th edition, 1972

Camproux, Ch., *Histoire de la littérature occitane*, Paris: Payot, 1953

Duvernoy, Jean, *Le Catharisme: La Historie des Cathares*, Privat, Toulouse, 1979

Mussot-Goulard, Renée, *Les Occitans: Un mythe?* Paris: A. Michel, 1978

Okinawans

Capsule Summary

Location: Okinawa, Japan
Total Population: 1.3 million (residents in Okinawa alone, as of March 2001)
Language: Officially Japanese, but Ryukyu dialect exists
Religion: Buddhism, Shintoism, and Christianity

Most Okinawans live in Okinawa, Japan's southernmost and westernmost prefecture, although some have moved to other regions in Japan for reasons of marriage, work, or schooling. Okinawa is located in the Nansei Islands, also called the Ryukyu Islands, which have been part of the Japanese territory since the beginning of the seventeenth century. The prefecture is composed of 160 islands and islets varying in size and abundant in natural resources and beauty. It stretches out from, but is well offshore from, Kyushu in southern Japan.

Okinawans have maintained their own culture distinct from mainstream Japanese culture. Okinawa's geographical and natural characteristics and history have contributed to its distinctiveness. Okinawan culture is particularly known for dyeing and weaving, lacquer ware, pottery, and public entertainment, which suggests the influence of trading with China and Southeast Asian countries during the fourteenth to sixteenth centuries. Today the Japanese government formerly recognizes the cultural treasures in Okinawa, and thirteen items are registered as *Japan*'s—not only Okinawa's—traditional arts and crafts. This official recognition gives Okinawa status as the second cultural prefecture after Kyoto.

Okinawans had lived in a relatively peaceful society until they came into contact with the Japanese, who set themselves up as rulers over Okinawa in the seventeenth century. With a large portion of their land still occupied by the American military, the Okinawan struggle with historical legacy continues today.

It is believed that the original ancestors of today's Okinawans were Yamashita cave dwellers and Minatogawa people. The former date back 32,000 years. Their remains have been excavated in Naha, today the capital of Okinawa. The Minatogawa date back 17,000 years and have been discovered in Gushikami Village. It appears that they gradually moved from Kyushu and the Amami Islands to the Nansei Islands, although the reason for this migration is unknown.

Approximately 7,000 years ago, Ryukyuans, who practiced hunting and gathering, had already made contact with Kyushu. It is recorded that Ryukyu had its first contact with China around 605–607 CE. China was the first county that invaded Ryukyu and, in the fourteenth century, established a supremacy that lasted for five centuries. The word "Okinawa" appears in Japan's official documentation for the first time in 753 CE, although the islands were mainly called "Ryukyu" until much later.

A period from the twelfth century to 1609 is named "Ko-Ryukyu," meaning "Old Ryukyu." In the twelfth century, an agriculture-based society was formed, and with its development, local warlords called *aji* (or *anji*) appeared to rule their community. They built castles and fortresses and fought against one another to enlarge their territory. Thus, agricultural communities turned into territories won and lost by war, and eventually developed into kingdoms.

By the fourteenth century, three kingdoms existed: *Hokuzan* (Northern), *Chuzan* (Central), and *Nanzan* (Southern). This period is called the *Sanzan Jidai* (Three-Mountain Period). In 1429, Sho Hashi (reigned 1422–1439) from *Nanzan* finally unified the islands for the first time in Okinawa's history and founded the Ryukyu Kingdom, which lasted for about 450 years.

Around this time monks from Japan brought Buddhism into Ryukyu along with Japanese art and cultural practices. Ryukyuans believed in three gods and that numerous other lesser gods co-existed with those three gods. These lesser gods were responsible for human life, and manifested themselves as village protectors or gods of kitchens, ponds, wells, trees, and rocks. Buddhism gradually merged and overlapped with these indigenous beliefs over centuries, creating a unique belief system and style of worship.

The Ryukyu Kingdom successfully built a strong trade relationship in East and Southeast Asia, which greatly reinforced Ryukyu's extensive economic as well as cultural development. From 1477 to 1526, during the reign of Sho Shin, the Ryukyu kingdom experienced a golden age. In addition to achieving economic and cultural prosperity, Sho Sin stabilized the political and social order by centralizing the political system.

In 1609, Ryukyu was conquered by the Satsuma-han, Japan's local government in southern Kyushu. The Satsuma-han wished to absorb Ryukyu into their territory in order to ease their own financial difficulties. Although the central Edo government initially attempted to persuade the Satsuma-han to negotiate with the Ryukyuans peacefully, the Edo eventually permitted them to militarily invade Ryukyu.

The Edo government and the Satsuma-han imposed a series of obligations upon the Ryukyuans while treating them as foreigners. Dealing with social chaos, Ryukyuan leaders such as Haneji Choshu and Saion sought to improve their circumstances by more willingly accepting the customs and developments of modern Japan. Thus, Ryukyu entered the modern era already aligning itself with Japan.

In 1853, United States Commodore Matthew C. Perry visited Naha. His main business in Naha included signing a treaty that guaranteed various rights to American citizens and other foreigners in Ryukyu. The intention behind this event was that the United States, knowing that the islands were now under Japanese rule, planned to occupy the territory if it failed in its negotiation with the Edo government to establish a diplomatic relationship.

In 1868, the Meiji Restoration concluded the rule by the Edo government (1603–1868) and authority was returned to the emperor. In 1876, a nationwide language unification program was initiated, which meant that Ryukyuans were expected to learn the dialect of the region around Tokyo, Japan's official common language. In 1879, the name Ryukyu was replaced with Okinawa. The last Ryukyuan king, Sho Tai (1949–1879), was dethroned, and the Ryukyu Kingdom was ended. All lands and people now came under the jurisdiction of the Meiji government.

Okinawans experienced difficulties assimilating to Japanese culture during the early years of the Meiji Period. There was also a strong sense of repulsion among the former Ryukyuan ruling class. The Meiji Government therefore put off reforms such as land and infrastructure management and taxation systems to allow Okinawans time for adjustment. Despite this attempt to evade distrust among Okinawans, delayed reforms merely created a larger social and economic gap between Okinawa and other prefectures.

In 1885, a conscription system was applied in Okinawa. Immediately after the Sino-Japanese War of 1894–95, Okinawans began to receive imperial education and were sent to fight as Japanese soldiers in the Russo-Japanese War of 1904–05. While the militaristic government imposed assimilation upon them for its national interest, mainlanders often treated Okinawan soldiers with some level of social discrimination, calling them *Ryukyu-jin* (Ryukyuans).

In 1942, the Japanese government built a naval base in Okinawa as a shield against its enemies, after suffering serious losses in the Midway Sea Battle. In 1944, the government quickly decided upon an evacuation plan to send 100,000 Okinawans to the mainland. However, people's anxiety about relocation and fear of American submarines hindered the process. One of the greatest tragedies was that of the *Tsushima-maru*, which was sunk by a U.S. submarine on August 22, 1944. Of the 1,700 Okinawans on board, 1,500 perished. In October 1944, an American B29 aircraft bombed Naha for several hours, destroying 90 percent of the city. Finally, on March 26, 1945, American troops landed on Okinawa, initiating the only battle of the war conducted on Japanese soil. Okinawans were either directly or indirectly instructed by the Japanese army to take their own lives and preserve their honor. Those Okinawans who survived lacked shelter and food. Many turned to suicide in desperation.

With the defeat of Japan in World War II, the United States occupied Okinawa, using it as a base from which to resist communist China and Russia. While postwar recovery in other parts of Japan progressed, Okinawans continued to face difficulties and inconveniences under American control. For example, they had no currency until 1946, and bartering was the only method available to them to obtain daily necessities. Earning a living was made difficult by the fact that the main jobs available were military-related and offered low wages.

After the troubling decades under American occupation, Okinawa was finally returned to Japan on May 15, 1972. Nonetheless, even after the end of Cold War, 85 percent of Okinawa's land remains American territory today. Okinawa occupies only one percent of the entire Japanese territory, yet it is home to 75 percent of the U.S. military bases in Japan. Approximately 26,000 out of 48,000 American servicemen stationed in Japan are in Okinawa. This number equals more than one-quarter of the total U.S. military presence in the Asia-Pacific region.

AI HATTORI

Further Reading

De Vos, George A., and William O. Wetherall, *Japan's Minorities: Burakumin, Koreans, Ainu and Okinawans*, London: Minority Rights Group, 1983

Haring, Douglas G., *Okinawan Customs: Yesterday and Today*, Rutland, Vermont: Charles E. Tuttle Company, 1969

Kerr, George H., *Okinawa: The History of an Island People*, Rutland, Vermont: Charles E. Tuttle Company, 1968

Lebra, William P., *Okinawan Religion: Belief, Ritual, and Social Structure*, Honolulu: University of Hawaii Press, 1985

Smith, Gregory, *Visions of Ryukyu: Identity and Ideology in Early-Modern Thought and Politics*, Honolulu: University of Hawaii Press, 1999

Oman

Capsule Summary

Official Name: *Saltanat Uman* (Sultanate of Oman)
Location: Middle East
Total 2003 Estimated Population: 2,807,125 (includes 577,293 non-nationals)

Language: Arabic (official), also English, Baluchi, Urdu, Indian dialects
Religions: Muslim (Ibadhi Muslim 75 percent), Sunni Muslim, Shi'a Muslim, Hindu

The Sultanate of Oman is located on the Arabian Peninsula in the Middle East, bordering Yemen in the southwest, Saudi Arabia in the west, and the United Arab Emirates in the northwest. Iran is across the Gulf of Oman in the north. The country has a land area of 309,500 square kilometers (119,500 square miles) making it slightly smaller than the state of New Mexico in the United States.

The population of the Sultanate of Oman is estimated at 2,807,125 (2003, CIA), up from 1,305,000 in 1990. Some other estimates put the figure at about 3,000,000 if all undocumented workers and expatriates are included. It is predominantly urban with around 80 percent of the people living in cities and towns. The country's capital city, Masqat (also Muscat), is home to about 685,000 people (2001 est.) or about 26 percent of the total population. The Sultanate of Oman has a population growth rate of 3.38 percent, one of the highest in the Arabian Peninsular. It is estimated that the population could double by 2025 if the current birth rate (37.47 births per 1,000 population) and immigration remain at the same level. Due to the extremely harsh climate in the deserts, which cover more than 60 percent of the country's territory, Oman overall has a low population density of around 9 people per square kilometer (23 people per square mile). However, it has a very high population density in the coastal areas.

The Sultanate of Oman is an absolute hereditary monarchy. In this political system the ruler appoints the cabinet of ministers. The bicameral parliament that consists of *Majlis al-Dawla* and *Majlis al-Shura* has a very limited advisory power. The modern political system represents the legacy of Oman's history. Oman traces its beginning to the Imamate that was established in the eighth century by the Ibadi Muslims, a branch of Kharijites sect in Islam. The country's importance grew with the rise of the maritime trade, as it is strategically located on the Gulf of Oman. The Gulf is used by the rulers of Oman to control trade in the region. The Portuguese seized Masqat City in the sixteenth century and retained their control until the mid-seventeenth century. In the early nineteenth century, Great Britain negotiated a series of security treaties with Oman. In the twentieth century, however, Oman experienced a major political turmoil as some groups in the central and western areas of Oman rebelled against the central authorities. The discovery of oil did not contribute to improving the lives of the majority of the population, and popular rebellions continued between the 1950s

and 1970s. Sultan Qaboos, who came to power in 1970, managed to stabilize the country through a series of political reforms and an energetic push of economic changes.

Oman is a multi-ethnic country. Representatives of several local Arab tribes make up about 75 percent of the country's population, according to 2003 estimates. Minorities from South Asia, Iran, and some other Arab countries account for about 20 percent of the total population. Various other groups, including Europeans and Americans, together make up the remaining 5 percent of the population. The current ethnic structure was formed in the twentieth century, as migrants from various Asian countries arrived in Oman as traders or low-skill workers. Most of these immigrants are not citizens and have no political rights. There have been some tensions in Oman between the local native population and minorities, mainly due to economic turmoil and an "Omanization" program introduced in 1988 that aims to replace most of the foreigners by local workers.

Arabic is the official language of the country. English is widely spoken in the major metropolitan areas but not in the rural regions. Many communities preserve their own native languages and their members speak Hindi, Urdu, and other languages at the family and community levels.

In the late 1990s and early 2000s, Oman, like neighboring Iran and Saudi Arabia, saw a growing radicalization of various Islamic groups. Islam is the official religion of the country and the majority of the population, approximately 97 percent, is of Muslim background. There is a very small expatriate community of Christians whose religious practices are generally tolerated. Oman's GDP per capita, in purchasing power parity, is around $8,300, according to 2002 estimates. The unemployment rate of 5 percent is relatively low according to regional standards, but it is expected to rise during the next 5–10 years as a significant proportion of young people enter the workforce. The country largely relies on the exporting of its petroleum and petrochemical production; nonetheless, agriculture, mining, and services remain important sectors of the national economy and provide employment for about 80 percent of the population. In the 1990s, the government of Oman initiated a series of economic reforms, including liberalization of the economy and the introduction of a privatization program, but Oman's economy is still vulnerable to the volatility of the oil prices in the international market. In 2003, the UNDP's Human Development

Index (HDI) put Oman in seventy-ninth place, behind Kazakhstan, Suriname, and Jamaica, but ahead of Fiji, Peru, and Lebanon.

RAFIS ABAZOV

Further Reading

Clements, Frank A., *Oman*, Oxford, England; Santa Barbara, California: Clio Press, 1994

Cordesman, Anthony H., *Bahrain, Oman, Qatar, and the UAE: Challenges of Security*, Boulder, Colorado: Westview Press, 1997

Kechichian, Joseph A., *Oman and the World: The Emergence of an Independent Foreign Policy*, Santa Monica: Rand, 1995

Lienhardt, Peter, *Shaikhdoms of Eastern Arabia*, New York: Palgrave, 2001

Looney, Robert E., *Industrial Development and Diversification of the Arabian Gulf Economie*, Greenwich, Connecticut: JAI Press, 1994

Mansur, Ahsan, and Volker Treichel, editors, *Oman Beyond the Oil Horizon: Policies toward Sustainable Growth*, Occasional papers of the International Monetary Fund; no. 185, Washington, D.C.: International Monetary Fund, 1999

Riphenburg, Carol J., *Oman: Political Development in a Changing World*, Westport, Connecticut: Praeger, 1998

Orang Asli

Capsule Summary

Location: Interior and particularly northern part of Peninsular Malaysia, small groups in Southern Thailand
Total population: approximately 93,000 (1994)
Language: Several languages and dialects referred to as "Aslian", part of Austroasiatic Mon-Khmer language family; many also speak Malay, some Thai
Religion: Indigenous animist, many Muslim converts in Malaysia

Orang Asli is a term commonly applied to small minority groups found in Malaysia and far South Thailand. *Orang* means "people" and *Asli* means "original," and the term is commonly translated as "aboriginal people." Malays apply the term to other minority ethnic groups such as those in Sarawak, but this entry is confined to the mainland peoples. In spite of research by ethnologists, linguists, anthropologists, and others, little is known of the pre-modern history of the Aslian peoples. Their status as indigenous is sometimes queried with suggestions that they migrated from elsewhere in quite recent times, but archaeological and linguistic studies suggest this is untenable and that the Aslian peoples are descendants of the earliest population of the region. Many scholars now believe that much of ancient Southeast Asia was occupied by Aslian-type peoples who were forced into interiors and jungle habitats as the great waves of Austronesian migration and the downward pressure of Tai-speaking peoples from southern China displaced them. The relationship between Aslian peoples, the Andaman Islanders, the Negrito peoples of the Philippines, and the Eastern Indonesians remains to be established, with systematic studies of mitochondrial DNA offering the best possibility of resolving this issue.

In Malaysia, the Orang Asli are divided into three main classifications: Semang, Senoi, and Proto-Malay. Semang are small-statured, dark-skinned hunters and foragers, with tightly curled "Negroid" hair, who use a largely bamboo-based culture including the blowpipe for hunting. Senoi are taller, lighter, with wavy hair, and generally undertake a mixed horticultural economy, which includes some hunting and foraging but generally relies on dry rice-swidden agriculture. Today these economies have been significantly affected by state policies, which have tried to enforce settlement on the nomadic Semang and cultural assimilation on the Senoi. Some Senoi live on the coast and are fishermen, others have rubber, oil, or cocoa plantations. The "Proto-Malay" speak mostly Austronesian dialects and are thought to be descendants of a wave of early migration prior to the arrival of the present Malay peoples. Today they are culturally and religiously little differentiated from their Malay neighbors.

The Semang, classified as *Negritos* in Malay-government terms, are by far the most distinctive of the Aslian groups. They include the Kintak Bong, Kensiu, Batek, Lanoh, Mendrik, and Jahai, and are located mostly in interior mountain jungles. Traditionally their range included Southern Thailand, and there are around 300 people still living there, some in semi-settlement and others mostly in the jungle. Altogether, these groups now number only around 3,000 people.

Aslian peoples are sometimes known in the region as "Sakai." This is a pejorative term meaning "slave," and its usage reflects the fact that for unknown generations the Orang Asli were expected to act as subordinates to the local Malay elites. Slave raids were common in the eighteenth and nineteenth centuries, the raiders being mostly Malays who considered Orang Asli to be non-human savages. Raiders would swoop on a village, kill the adult, men and take away the women and children, giving them to local rulers or chieftains. The slave trade continued into the twentieth century. Today the attitude towards the Aslian peoples by both the Thai and Malay dominant groups retains elements of the same attitude: while Aslians are considered quaint and interesting, even a tourist-attraction, they are still commonly described as a lower form of being.

The animist religion practiced by Aslian peoples is similar to that found among most hunter-gatherer groups. The close relationship with an untransformed natural world provides the grounds for an identification between humans and nature, based on an ethic of respect, and the need for harmonious relations with plants and animals. Belief in ghosts and spirits and the practice of rituals to maintain the well-being of the forest and its spaces form central aspects of their religion, while an ancestral deity spirit is widely recognized. During the period of British colonial domination in Malaysia, Catholic and Protestant missionaries began working among the Orang Asli, but by far the greatest impact has been the almost relentless pressure by the Malay government and its agents to enforce conversion to Islam. While Aslian peoples in the more remote hinterlands have been able to resist these pressures, many in close contact with Malay neighbors have yielded, thus splitting families and communities. Converts frequently leave their home groups and often seek wage labor in towns and cities, where they assimilate to everyday Malay society. This process must have been going on for generations, although slavery, and later the Malayan Emergency, have had much greater impact on the survival of the Aslian peoples.

After Japan was defeated in World War II, the thousands of Chinese Communists who had been fighting underground against the Japanese did not surrender their arms but instead took to the jungle and continued to fight against the British, who had returned as colonial masters to Malaysia. In 1948, a State of Emergency was declared in order to defeat them. Until then most of the Aslian peoples had remained isolated in largely inaccessible parts of the country. These events, however, intruded dramatically on their lives with such traumatic effect that they could no longer remain isolated from national events. Particularly those groups living in the deep jungle became involved in an armed conflict that really had nothing to do with them. However, the Communists needed their jungle skills to provide them with food, lead them through the hidden jungle pathways, and help them to hide out in the many networks of caverns in this limestone region. The British and their allies realized they had to prevent this and began a program of forced resettlement and recruitment of Orang Asli into military units. Many remote areas were bombed or strafed by helicopter gunships on the assumption that the Communists were sheltering among the Orang Asli.

The Aslian peoples, especially those in the northern interior jungles, saw their lives completely disrupted by these events and were never fully able to return to their previous condition. The resettlement process was a disaster, with many deaths of older community figures and of young men in the violence. Since that time, development pressures as a result of the modernizing policies of the Malay state have added a further dimension of struggle. The Orang Asli today remain an identifiable element of the modern Malay state, but their way of life has been irremediably altered. Shortage of game, contamination of water sources, and above all the effects of deforestation, together with waves of epidemic diseases, create a series of conditions, which people have no ability to counter. The fact that some groups and communities continue to survive at all is remarkable.

ANNETTE HAMILTON

See also **Malays; Malaysia; Thailand**

Further Reading

Cary, Iskandar, *Orang Asli: The Aboriginal Tribes of Peninsular Malaysia*, Kuala Lumpur: Oxford University Press, 1976

Dentan, Robert Knox, *The Semai: A Non-Violent People of Malaya*, New York: Holt, Rinehart and Winston, 1968

Endicott, K., "The Effects of Slave Raiding on the Aborigines of the Malay Peninsula," in *Slavery, Bondage and Dependency in South East Asia*, edited by Anthony Reid, St. Lucia: University of Queensland Press, 1983

Endicott, K., *Batek Negrito Religion*, Oxford: Clarendon Press, 1979

Evans, Ivor H.N., *The Negritos of Malaya*, Cambridge: Cambridge University Press, 1937

Leary, John D., *Violence and the Dream People*, Ohio: Center for International Studies, 1995

Rashid, Razha, *Indigenous Minorities of Peninsular Malaysia: Selected Issues and Ethnographies*, Kuala Lumpur: Intersociaetal and Scientific, 1995

Winzeler, Robert L., editor, *Indigenous Peoples and the State; Politics, Land and Ethnicity in the Malayan Peninsular and Borneo*, Yale University Southeast Asia Studies, 1997

Osce High Commission on National Minorities

The Organization for Security and Co-operation in Europe's (OSCE) High Commission on National Minorities (HCNM) is an independent institution in the framework of OSCE . The High Commissioner has been active since 1993 in conflict-prevention through early action and early warning mechanisms. While not possessing tools for enforcement, the HCNM has acted in de-escalating interethnic tensions, and it alerts the OSCE in case of an escalation of tensions beyond the capacities of the Commissioner. The main areas of activity for the High Commissioner have focused on the Russian minority in the Baltic States and the Albanian minority in Macedonia, as well as the status of national minorities in other Central and Eastern European countries and in the Central Asian Republics of the former Soviet Union. In addition, the HCNM has engaged in a study of Roma. Despite the multiple limitations of this institution, it has been a significant factor in reducing tensions between minorities and majorities in a number of cases.

The office of the High Commissioner on National Minorities was created in 1992 by the CSCE (later OSCE) in an attempt to address the apparent increase in interethnic tensions in Europe, especially in post-communist countries. The office of the High Commissioner is based in The Hague, Netherlands. In addition, the non-governmental Foundation on Inter-Ethnic Relations was established to facilitate the work of the HCNM.

While the mandate of the High Commissioner is limited to national minorities, there is no universally accepted definition of what constitutes a national minority, within either the OSCE or elsewhere. This institution has consequently adopted a pragmatic approach in identifying national minorities by focusing on the self-ascription by members of groups who share distinct characteristics (e.g., language, culture, and ethnicity). In the light of the absence of both a universal definition of national minorities and general standards of minority rights, the HCNM repeatedly has charged its experts with refining the existing standards and recommendations on the protection of minority rights.

As an instrument of conflict prevention, the High Commissioner is not tasked with protecting national minorities or advocating the interests of a particular minority. His work is rather based on preventive diplomacy in cases of minority-majority conflicts. The High Commissioner has a mandate that encompasses two separate types of activities. The Commissioner is charged with preventing conflict by engaging government and national minorities in a dialogue to resolve differences. The institution is responsible for warning the OSCE of conflicts before they reach a violent level.

Although there are a number of countries that have national minorities with a possibility of conflict, the High Commissioner is constrained by his resources from acting in all cases. The High Commission can become involved in prevention of any conflict, when the Commissioner considers the situation of a national minority within a country as being prone to conflict. The Commissioner has the discretion to select potential conflicts on the basis of his ability to contribute in managing or resolving the particular conflict.

The High Commissioner is charged with gathering information on the issue and talking with parties involved in the potential conflict—both government and minority representatives, as well as other international organizations active in the country, the kin-state of the minority, and outside experts. The High Commissioner has the power to visit any OSCE member country for investigation without the consent of the government. His most important limitation is the prohibition from including terrorists, or any groups that advocate the use of force, in his discussions. On the basis of his information gathering and visits, the High Commissioner issues reports and makes recommendations on how to address the potential conflict. Usually the HCNM also drafts recommendations directed specifically at the government of the country in question. These recommendations, as well as the other instruments of the High Commission are non-binding for both the respective country and the OSCE. The most important functions thus consist of encouraging a dialogue between the minority and the government aimed at resolving the potential conflict. If the government fails to engage in a dialogue or it ignores the recommendations of the HCNM, his power derives from the ability to disclose the non-compliance of a government to the OSCE.

In terms of formal competences, the High Commissioner can issue an "early warning" to the Senior Council of the OSCE in which he outlines the reason why there is a danger of conflict in a particular country. Furthermore, he can request authorization to engage in "early action." The Senior Council can subsequently charge him with continued and intensified work on a particular case. In practice, however, "early action" does not differ substantially from the regular work of the High Commission.

The first High Commissioner was the former Dutch Minister for Foreign Affairs Max van der Stoel. During his appointment, which was renewed three times in 1995, 1998, and 1999, he was pivotal in shaping the work of this new institution. In November 2000, the Ministerial Council of the OSCE appointed the Swedish diplomat Rolf Ekius as High Commissioner for three years, effective from July 1, 2001.

The HCNM has been involved in potential conflicts in over ten countries since 1993. Its activities have focused exclusively on the formerly Communist countries of Central and Eastern Europe and Central Asia. In addition, in 1993 the Commissioner issued an extensive report on the status of the Roma across a number of countries. The most extensive involvement of the High Commissioner took place in Estonia, Latvia, and Macedonia.

The High Commission worked intensively on the conflict between the Russian minority in Latvia and Estonia and the respective governments over citizenship laws in both countries. The integration of the mostly Russian population not only constituted a significant domestic challenge with Russians numbering over 40 percent of the population in both countries,

but also had regional security implications involving Russia as the kin-state of the minorities in these recently independent countries. The HCNM made a number of visits to both countries and issued numerous recommendations to the respective governments. These addressed predominantly the stringent language-knowledge requirements for obtaining Estonian and Latvian citizenship and the laws governing the status of non-citizens in the two countries. In the course of the High Commissioner's nearly ten-year involvement, both countries adopted a number of the recommendations made by HCNM.

In Macedonia, the High Commissioner acted in an attempt to diffuse the tensions between the Macedonian government and the large Albanian minority, which numbers between a quarter and a third of the population. Besides facilitating an overall dialogue between Macedonians and Albanians on improving interethnic relations and issuing recommendations on stronger local self-government and strengthening co-operative institutions of the national communities, the work of the HCNM focused on promoting a new population census and on Albanian-language education. The promotion of a census was an effort to clearly establish the number of Albanians living in Macedonia. The Yugoslav-wide census of 1991 underreported the number of Albanians in Macedonia. As numerical strength can translate to the degree of political representation, the share of the Albanian population in Macedonia emerged as a controversial topic in the early 1990s. After one of his first missions in the country in 1993, van der Stoel recommended an internationally organized census. Although this census was held in 1994 under the supervision of the Council of Europe, the number of Albanians in Macedonia has remained under dispute.

More significantly, the HCNM recommended the establishment of a training facility for teachers in Albanian. Throughout the 1990s, van der Stoel sought to mediate between the demands of the Albanian minority for an Albanian-language university in Macedonia and the position of the Macedonia government, which offered instruction in Albanian only in a limited number of fields within the existing framework of the existing university in Skopje. The tensions in Macedonia increased with the creation of an unofficial Albanian-language university in Tetovo. In 2000, the mediation of the HCNM resulted in the creation of a internationally funded, private Southeast European University in Tetovo, with instruction in Albanian, English, and Macedonian, in the fields of law, business administration, public administration, communication and computer studies, and teacher training. The establishment of the University can be considered one of the major successes of Commissioner van der Stoel, who also became the Chairman of the International Board of the University.

In addition to these prominent missions, the High Commissioner has acted upon tensions between governments and national minorities in a number of other countries. Largely, the work of the HCNM has focused on making specific policy recommendations to governments. Such work is aimed at identifying key issues of contention instead of addressing the overall state of interethnic relations. HCNM proposals take not only the demands of the minority into account but weigh them with the legitimate interests of the majority. In addition, the Commissioner's proposals consistently seek to address problem within the existing state structure.

The work of the High Commissioner is an example of low-key diplomacy, aimed at discretion and confidence-building between the government, the minority, and the High Commissioner himself. In some countries, the conflictual nature of the interethnic relations addressed by the HCNM did create some reserved and occasionally even hostile reactions by political representatives and the media of the majority. Nevertheless, the work of the High Commissioner has been respected by most governments and a number of governments themselves have called upon him to become active in their country (e.g., Moldova, Ukraine). While not all recommendations made by the High Commissioner have been implemented, the rate of success has been significant despite the absence of enforcement mechanisms.

The relative success of the High Commission is to a large degree connected with the use of the office by the first High Commissioner Max van der Stoel. As the mandate of the Commission was relatively vague, practice had to shape the influence and significance of this new institution. Van der Stoel largely used the independence of the institution and its unique ability to engage in domestic non-violent conflicts to act as a mediator between governments and minorities. The report issued by the HCNM on the status of Roma in 1993 at the request of the Chairman-in-Office of the OSCE demonstrates that the work of the institution goes beyond the narrow scope of addressing minority issues exclusively as a function of regional stability.

The High Commissioner on National Minorities is a unique institution among international organizations. It can be distinguished from other organizations and institutions by its exclusive emphasis on preventive diplomacy with the aim of conflict prevention. Furthermore, the ability of the HCNM to work on countries and national minorities without the consent of the respective government offers the institution the possibility of becoming active in cases of potential conflict where other international organizations are restrained by the principle of non-interference. As a relatively small institution with limited structural and logistical resources, the success of the HCNM is largely dependent on the credibility of the High Commissioner as an individual among governments and national minorities. While the creation of the HCNM was in recognition of the signifi-cance of internal interethnic conflict as a major source of instability in Europe, the limited resources and powers given to this institution have restrained the influence of the High Commissioner to a small number of the non-violent interethnic conflicts in Europe.

FLORIAN BIEBER

Further Reading

Foundation on Inter-Ethnic Relations, *The Role of the High Commissioner on National Minorities in OSCE Conflict Prevention. An Introduction*, The Hague: Foundation on Inter-Ethnic Relations, 1997

Packer, John, "The Role of the OSCE High Commissioner on National Minorities in the Former Yugoslavia," *Cambridge Review of International Affairs*, 12, no. 2, (Spring/Summer) 1999

Stoel, Max van der, "The Role of the OSCE High Commissioner on National Minorities in Conflict Prevention", in *Herding Cats: Multiparty Mediation in a Complex World*, edited by Chester A. Crocker, Fen Osler Hampson, and Pamela All, Washington D.C.: United States Institute for Peace, 1999

Touval, Saadia, "Does the High Commissioner Mediate?" *New York University Journal of International Law and Politics*, 32, no. 3, (2000)

Vassilev, Stefan, "The HCNM Approach to Conflict Prevention," *Helsinki Monitor*, 10, no. 3, (1999)

Zaagman, Rob, and H. Zaal, "The CSCE High Commissioner on National Minorities: Prehistory and Negotiations," in *The Challenges of Change: The Helsinki Summit of the CSCE and its Aftermath*, edited by Arie Bloed, Dodrecht: Martinus Nijhoff Publishers, 1994

Zaagman, Rob, *Conflict Prevention in the Baltic States: The OSCE High Commissioner on National Minorities in Estonia, Latvia and Lithuania*, Flensburg: European Centre for Minority Issues, 1999

Zellner, Wolfgang, and Falk Lange, editors, *Peace and Stability through Human and Minority Rights: Speeches by the OSCE High Commissioner on National Minorities*, Baden-Baden: Nomos, 1999

Ovambo

Capsule Summary

Location: Southwestern Africa, mostly in the northern territory of Namibia
Total Population: approximately 700,000
Language: Each community has its own dialect, but a language called *Oshivambo* is used by major media to communicate to Ovambo citizens
Religion: During the colonial era, most Ovambo converted to the Lutheran faith

Ovambo is a term generally used to refer to a collection of people in southwestern Africa who belong to any of several matrilineal political communities in northern Namibia, including the Kwanyama, Ndonga, Kwambi, Ngandjera, Kwaluudhi, Nkolonkadhi, Eunda, Mbalantu, Mbandja, Evale, Kafima, and Ehanda. Following the 1884 Berlin Conference which divided Africa into several dozen colonies, the latter four groups found themselves under the colonial rule of the Portuguese while the others, comprising the larger populations of Ovambos, fell under the territorial authority of the Germans. Today the term "Ovambo" usually refers to those political communities, identified above, that fall within the boundaries of the Republic of Namibia and who represent approximately half the population of that country of 1.4 million. Current distributions of the Ovambo are: Kwanyama (36 percent), Ndonga (29 percent), Kwambi (12 percent), Ngandjera (8 percent), Mbalantu (7 percent), Kwaluudhi (5 percent), Eunda and Nkolonkadhi (3 percent). Most of the leadership of Namibia, including President Sam Nujoma, are members of the Ovambo.

Prior to German colonial rule, the political structure of Ovambo communities was built around the hereditary rule of a king called the *omukwaniilwa*. These kings rarely ruled their communities alone; rather, they negotiated with their counselors (*omalenga*) concerning most matters. Ovambo kings engaged in regional trade beyond the area of Ovamboland. Ovambo trading caravans made regular visits into central Namibia where they traded iron and copper goods for ostrich egg shells and cattle possessed by the Herero. Ovambo trade routes also extended north into Angola and east into areas populated by Bushmen.

The basic unit of economic production was the male-led family homestead or *egumbo*. The household purchased the right to cultivate its land from the king or through his counselors, typically for one to four head of cattle. It was the king who decided when to till and when to harvest. The family could be forced to give up its fields if someone else offered the king higher payment for the land or if the family fell into disfavor with the king or the district headman.

Once Namibia was claimed as a colony, German authorities concentrated on confiscating land in central Namibia from Herero and Nama communities and left the Ovambo alone. When resistance campaigns by the Herero and Nama were met with genocidal responses from the Germans, various Ovambo communities offered refuge to the survivors of these central Namibian groups. Colonial efforts to ignore the Ovambo ended in 1908 when diamonds were discovered in southern Namibia along the border with South Africa. Needing a reliable labor supply, Germans began looking to the Ovambo to provide migrant labor. The expansive influence of European powers in Ovamboland met with consternation from many inside northern Namibia, especially from King Mandume Ndemufayo of the Kwanyama, the largest Ovambo community. However, before the Germans could institutionalize a migrant labor system for the diamond industry, World War I broke out. On July 9, 1915, German forces in Namibia surrendered to South African troops.

Shortly after Germany's surrender, South African officials met with various leaders of Ovambo communities to secure their cooperation in recruiting laborers for the diamond fields in southern Namibia. King Mandume expressed apprehension about diverting his Kwanyama men to the diamond fields and away from defending Kwanyama sovereignty against Portuguese incursions from northern bases in Angola. This decision only added to the growing concerns of South African officials that Mandume was not a reliable collaborator for colonial objectives in Namibia. On February 6, 1917, South African troops, aided by the leadership of the Ondonga and Ukuambi communities, assassinated the thirty-year-old king near his residence at Ehole. South African officials never allowed the Kwanyama to have a king again; rather, a Council of Headmen governed this community for decades to come.

In general, Ovambo leaders were willing to collaborate with South African efforts to exploit the territory's diamond resources, which constituted the primary source of revenue generated in Namibia. This was especially the case with Chief Martin Ga Kazikua of the Ondonga, the second largest community among the Ovambo and the closest geographically to white settlements to the south. South African authorities often relied on Chief Martin for information about the internal politics of other Ovambo communities. Martin also established close relations with leaders of the Finnish Missionary Society, which established a mission station within Ondonga territory.

In 1932 South Africa again confronted a rebellious Ovambo leader, this time Chief Iipumbu of the Ukuambi. South Africa brought in its Air Force and bombed the chief's residence. Iipumbu surrendered and was flown to Kwanyama territory where he was forced into exile. Colonial officials again appointed a Council of Headmen to rule the Ukuambi. Never again would an Ovambo chief pose a threat to South Africa's occupation of Namibia.

After World War II, the contract labor system resumed extensive recruitment of Ovambos for the diamond industry. As labor abuses heightened, protests and labor actions ensued, and many Ovambos fled Namibia to seek alternative employment in South Africa and elsewhere. In the late 1950s, Ovambo workers and students residing in Cape Town formed the Ovamboland Peoples Congress (OPC), and later the Ovamboland Peoples Organization (OPO), under the leadership of Andimba Toivo ya Toivo. On April 19, 1960, the OPO was transformed into the South West African Peoples Organization (SWAPO) with another Ovambo, Sam Nujoma, serving as President. In 1966, SWAPO initiated an armed struggle to secure self-determination from the white minority government in Pretoria. For twenty-three years, SWAPO and South African troops fought a low-scale war of attrition, with Ovamboland suffering the brunt of warfare and martial law. SWAPO often targeted Ovambo chiefs who continued to collaborate with South African officials. Finally, in 1989, the United Nations supervised national elections inside Namibia that resulted in SWAPO winning a landslide election. Namibia achieved formal independence on March 21, 1990 with Sam Nujoma elected as the first President. Ovambos continue to dominate key positions in the Namibian government and economy.

ALLAN D. COOPER

See also **Africa: A Continent of Minorities?; Namibia**

Further Reading

Eirola, Martti, *The Ovambogehahr: The Ovamboland Reservation in the Making*, Jyvaskyla: Historical Association of Finland, 1992

Siiskonen, Harri, *Trade and Socioeconomic Change in Ovamboland, 1850–1906*, Helsinki: SHS, 1990

Tonjes, Hermann, *Ovamboland*, Windhoek: Namibia Scientific Society, 1996

Williams, Frieda-Nela, *Precolonial Communities of Southwestern Africa: A History of Owambo Kingdoms 1600–1920*, Windhoek: National Archives of Namibia, 1991

3